PATROLOGY

VOL. IV

THE GOLDEN AGE OF LATIN PATRISTIC LITERATURE
FROM THE COUNCIL OF NICEA
TO THE COUNCIL OF CHALCEDON

Contributors:
Angelo Di Berardino (Ch.V)
Professor at the Augustinianum
Jean Griboment (Ch. IV)
Professor at the Pontifical University Urbaniana and at the Augustinianum
Vittorino Grossi (Ch. VII)
Professor at the Augustinianum
Adalbert Hamman (Ch. I, VIII)
Professor at the Augustinianum
Maria Grazia Mara (Ch. III)
Professor at the University of Rome and at the Augustinianum
Manlio Simonetti (Ch. II)
Professor at the University of Rome and at the Augustinianum
Basil Studer (Ch. IX)
Professor at the Anselmianum and the Augustinianum
Agostino Trapé (Ch. VI)
Professor at the Pontifical Lateran University and at the Augustinianum

AUGUSTINIAN PATRISTIC INSTITUTE - ROME

PATROLOGY

Edited by
ANGELO DI BERARDINO

with an introduction by
JOHANNES QUASTEN

VOLUME IV

The Golden Age of Latin Patristic Literature
From the Council of Nicea
to the Council of Chalcedon

Translated into English by
REV. PLACID SOLARI, O.S.B.

CHRISTIAN CLASSICS, INC.
WESTMINSTER, MARYLAND
1986

The present work is a translation from the Italian edition of *Patrologia*, Vol. III, published by Marietti, Turin, Italy, 1978.

© 1986 by Christian Classics, Inc., Westminster, MD

Cloth Edition ISBN: 0-87061-126-7
Paperback Edition ISBN: 0-87061-127-5
Library of Congress Catalog Card Number: 83-72018
All Rights Reserved
Printed in the United States of America

INTRODUCTION

The present volume is intended as the continuation of my *Patrology*, volumes I and II in the Italian edition and volumes I, II, and III in the English edition.

The golden age of Latin Christian Literature is so broad that a single author is not adequate to treat all of it. The bibliography of St. Augustine alone, for example, fills entire volumes. Furthermore, my prolonged illness has prevented me from completing the work.

I am therefore extremely grateful to this team of eight scholars of the Patristic Institute, the Augustinianum, in Rome, for having taken it upon themselves to compile this work, which is the completion of the Latin section of my volume, *The Golden Age of Greek Patristic Literature*.

Johannes Quasten

PREFACE

The present volume is connected ideally with the well-known work of Professor Johannes Quasten, of which it is intended to be the continuation.

The period treated extends from the Council of Nicea to the Council of Chalcedon, so this volume is therefore a counterpart to Volume III of *Patrologia* in the Italian edition.

This is the age of the turningpoint under Constantine and his successors; of figures such as Hilary, Ambrose, Jerome, Augustine, Leo the Great; of the Arian crisis, the Christological heresies, Pelagianism; of the progressive political and cultural separation of East and West.

While following in its general outlines the methodological criteria of Quasten, the work attempts to see the Fathers in their political and social context and to give more space to the problematics of contemporary patristic research.

The contributors enjoyed a certain freedom of approach and development in the treatment of the individual Fathers. This diversity, which expresses the originality of each contribution, should not jeopardize the essential points of the exposition.

The Editors

LIST OF ABBREVIATIONS

AAB	Abhandlungen. Academy of Berlin.
AAM	Abhandlungen. Academy of Munich.
AAWW	Anzeiger der Österreichischen Akademie der Wissenschaften. Vienna.
AB	Analecta Bollandiana. Brussels.
AC	Antike und Christentum, ed. F. J. Dölger. Münster.
ACL	Antiquité classique. Louvain.
ACO	Acta conciliorum oecumenicorum, ed. E. Schwartz. Berlin.
ACW	Ancient Christian Writers, ed. J. Quasten and J. C. Plumpe. Westminster (Md.), and London
AER	American Ecclesiastical Review, Washington, D.C.
AGP	Archiv für Geschichte der Philosophie. Berlin.
AGWG	Abhandlungen der Gesellschaft der Wissenschaften. Göttingen.
AHD	Archives d'histoire doctrinale et littéraire. Paris.
AIPh	Annuaire de l'Institut de philologie et d'histoire orientales et slaves. Paris and Brussels.
AJA	American Journal of Archaeology. Princeton.
AJPh	American Journal of Philology. Baltimore.
AKK	Archiv für katholisches Kirchenrecht. Mainz.
AL	Acta Linguistica. Copenhagen.
ALG	Sankt Augustinus — Der Lehrer der Gnade. Würzburg, 1955– (German translation of the anti-Pelagian works of Augustine).
ALMA	Archivum Latinitatis Medii Aevi (Bulletin du Cange). Paris and Brussels.
ALW	Archiv für Liturgiewissenschaft. Regensburg.
ANF	Ante-Nicene Fathers. Buffalo and New York.
Ang	Angelicum. Rome.
ANL	Ante-Nicene Library. Edinburgh.
Ant	Antonianum. Rome.
AnThA	Année théologique augustinienne. Paris.
APF	Archiv für Papyrusforschung. Leipzig.
APh	Archives de philosophie. Paris.
AR	Archivum Romanicum. Florence.
ARW	Archiv für Religionswissenschaft. Berlin and Leipzig.
ASS	Acta Sanctorum, ed. the Bollandists. Brussels.
AST	Analecta Sacra Tarraconensia. Barcelona.
AT	Année théologique. Paris.
ATG	Archivo teológico granadino. Granada.
AThR	Anglican Theological Review. New York.
Aug	Augustinianum. Rome.
AugL	Augustiniana. Louvain.
AugMag	Augustinus Magister. Congrès international augustinien, Paris, Sept. 21–24, 1954. Vols. I and II: Communications; vol. III: Acts.
AugStudies	Augustinian Studies. Villanova.
AurAug	Aurelius Augustinus. Die Festschrift der Görres-Gesellschaft zum 1500 Todestage des hl. Augustinus, Cologne, 1930.
BAB	Bulletin de la classe des lettres de l'Académie Royale de Belgique. Brussels.
BAC	Biblioteca de Autores Cristianos. Madrid.
BAGB	Bulletin de l'Association G. Budé. Paris.
BALAC	Bulletin d'Ancienne Littérature et d'Archéologie Chrétienne. Paris.
BAPC	Bulletin of the Polish Academy. Krakow.
BA	Bibliothèque Augustinienne, Oeuvres de Saint Augustin. Paris.
BBR	Bulletin de l'Institut Historique Belge de Rome.

BEHE Bibliothèque de l'École des Hautes Etudes. Paris.
Bess Bessarione. Rome.
BFC Bollettino di filologia classica. Turin.
BGTh Beiträge zur Förderung der Theologie. Gütersloh.
BHL Bibliotheca Hagiographica Latina Antiquae et Mediae Aetatis, ed. the Bollandists. Brussels.
BHTh Beiträge zur historischen Theologie. Tübingen.
Bibl Biblica. Rome.
BICS Bulletin of the Institute of Classical Studies of the University of London.
BiNJ Bijdragen van de Philosophische en Theologische Faculteiten der Nederlandsche Jezuïeten. Roermond, Netherlands, and Maastricht, Belgium.
BiZ Biblische Zeitschrift. Paderborn and Freiburg.
BJ Bursians Jahresbericht über die Fortschritte der klassischen Altertumswissenschaft. Leipzig.
BJR Bulletin of the John Rylands Library. Manchester.
BKV Bibliothek der Kirchenväter, ed. F. X. Reithmayr and V. Thalhofer. Kempten.
BKV^2 Bibliothek der Kirchenväter, ed. O. Bardenhewer, Th. Schermann, and C. Weyman. Kempten and Munich.
BKV^3 Bibliothek der Kirchenväter. Zweite Reihe, ed. O. Bardenhewer, J. Zellinger, and J. Martin. Munich.
BLE Bulletin de littérature ecclésiastique. Toulouse.
BM Benediktinische Monatschrift. Beuron.
BNJ Byzantinisch-Neugriechische Jahrbücher. Athens.
BoZ Bonner Zeitschrift für Theologie und Seelsorge. Düsseldorf.
BTAM Bulletin de théologie ancienne et médiévale. Louvain.
BVM Bologolovskij Vestnik. Moscow.
Byz Byzantion. Brussels.
BZ Byzantinische Zeitschrift. Leipzig and Munich.

CBQ Catholic Biblical Quarterly. Washington.
CC Civiltà Cattolica. Rome.
CCL Corpus Christianorum, Series Latina. Turnhout and Paris.
CD La ciudad de Dios. Madrid.
CE The Catholic Encyclopedia. New York.
Ch Das Konzil von Chalcedon. Geschichte und Gegenwart, ed. A. Grillmeier and H. Bacht, 2 vols. Würzburg, 1953-54.
CH Church History. Chicago.
ChQ The Church Quarterly Review. London.
CHR The Catholic Historical Review. Washington, D.C.
CIL Corpus Inscriptionum Latinarum. Berlin.
CJ Classical Journal. Chicago.
Clavis Clavis Patrum Latinorum (SE 3), ed. E. Dekkers and A. Gaar.
CPh Classical Philology. Chicago.
CPG Clavis Patrum Graecorum, ed. M. Geerard, vols. I-IV. Turnhout.
CPL Clavis *(supra)*.
CPS Corona Patrum Salesiana. Turin.
CPT Cambridge Patristic Texts.
CQ Classical Quarterly. London and Oxford.
CR The Classical Review. London and Oxford.
CRI Comptes-rendus de l'Académie des Inscriptions et Belles Lettres. Paris.
CSCO Corpus Scriptorum Christianorum Orientalium. Louvain.
CSEL Corpus Scriptorum Ecclesiasticorum Latinorum. Vienna.

CSHB	Corpus Scriptorum Historiae Byzantinae. Bonn.
CT	Codex Theodosianus.
CTh	Collectanea Theologica. Lvov.
DA	Dissertation Abstracts. Ann Arbor, Michigan.
DAC	Dictionary of the Apostolic Church, ed. J. Hastings. Edinburgh.
DAL	Dictionnaire d'archéologie chrétienne et de liturgie, ed. F. Cabrol, H. Leclercq. Paris.
DAp	Dictionnaire d'apologétique, ed. A. d'Alès. Paris.
DB	Dictionnaire de la Bible, ed. F. Vigouroux. Paris.
DCA	Dictionary of Christian Antiquities, ed. W. Smith and S. Cheetham, 2 vols. London.
DCB	Dictionary of Christian Biography, Literature, Sects, and Doctrines, ed. W. Smith and H. Wace, 4 vols. London.
DDC	Dictionnaire de droit canonique, ed. V. Villien, E. Magnin, and R. Naz. Paris.
DHC	Documents Illustrative of the History of the Church, ed. B. J. Kidd, 2 vols. London.
DHG	Dictionnaire d'histoire et de géographie ecclésiastique, ed. A. Baudrillart. Paris.
Did	Didaskaleion. Turin.
DLZ	Deutsche Literaturzeitung. Leipzig.
DOP	Dumbarton Oaks Papers. Cambridge, Mass.
DR	Downside Review. Stratt-on-the-Foss, Bath.
DS	H. J. Denzinger and A. Schönmetzer, ed., Enchiridion Symbolorum. Barcelona.
DSp	Dictionnaire de la spiritualité, ed. M. Viller. Paris.
DSt	Dominican Studies. Oxford.
DT	Divus Thomas. Freiburg (S).
DTC	Dictionnaire de théologie catholique, ed. A. Vacant, E. Mangenot, and E. Amann. Paris.
DTP	Divus Thomas. Piacenza.
EA	Enchiridion Asceticum, ed. M. J. Rouët de Journel and J. Dutilleul, 4th ed. Barcelona.
EB	Estudios bíblicos. Madrid.
EBrit	Encyclopaedia Britannica, 14th ed. Chicago-London-Toronto.
EC	Enciclopedia cattolica. Rome
ECl	Estudios clássicos. Madrid.
ECQ	Eastern Churches Quarterly. Ramsgate.
EE	Estudios eclesiásticos. Madrid.
EH	Enchiridion Fontium Historiae Ecclesiasticae Antiquae, ed. Ueding-Kirch, 6th ed. Barcelona.
EHPR	Etudes d'histoire et de philosophie religieuse.
EHR	English Historical Review. London.
EL	Ephemerides Liturgicae. Rome.
EM	Estudios Marianos. Madrid.
EO	Échos d'orient. Paris.
Eos	Eos. Commentarii Societatis Philologicae Polonorum. Lvov.
EP	Enchiridion Patristicum, ed. M. J. Rouët de Journel, 25th ed. Barcelona.
EPhM	Ephemerides Mariologicae. Madrid.
ES	Enchiridion Symbolorum, ed. Denzinger-Umberg, 30th ed. Barcelona.
Et	Études. Paris.
EtByz	Études byzantines. Paris.
EtC	Études classiques. Namur.

ETL	Ephemerides Theologicae Lovanienses. Louvain.
ExpT	The Expository Times. Edinburgh.
FC	The Fathers of the Church. New York.
FF	Forschungen und Fortschritte. Berlin.
FKDG	Forschungen zur Kirchen - und Dogmengeschichte. Göttingen.
FLDG	Forschungen zur christliche Literatur - und Dogmengeschichte. Paderborn.
Folia	Folia: Studies in the Christian Perpetuation of the Classics. New York.
FP	Florilegium Patristicum. Bonn.
FRL	Forschungen zur Religion und Literatur des Alten und Neuen Testamentes. Göttingen.
FS	Franciscan Studies. St. Bonaventure, N.Y.
FThSt	Freiburger theologische Studien. Freiburg i.B.
GAb	Abhandlungen der Gesellschaft der Wissenschaften zu Göttingen.
GCS	Die griechischen christlichen Schriftsteller. Leipzig.
GGA	Göttingische gelehrte Anzeigen. Göttingen.
Gno	Gnomon. Berlin.
Greg	Gregorianum. Rome.
GTT	Gereformeerd Theologisch Tijdschrift. Aalten, Netherlands.
HAPhG	Heidelberger Abhandlungen zur Philosophie und ihrer Geschichte. Heidelberg.
Hermathena	Hermathena. A Series of Papers on Literature, Science, and Philosophy. Dublin and London.
Hermes	Hermes. Zeitschrift für klassische Philologie. Berlin.
HispS	Hispania Sacra. Madrid and Barcelona.
HJ	The Hibbert Journal. London.
HJG	Historisches Jahrbuch der Görresgesellschaft. Cologne.
HS	Harvard Studies and Notes in Philology and Literature. Cambridge, Mass.
HSCP	Harvard Studies in Classical Philology. Cambridge, Mass.
HThR	Harvard Theological Review. Cambridge, Mass.
HTS	Harvard Theological Studies. Cambridge, Mass.
HVS	Historische Vierteljahrsschrift. Leipzig.
HZ	Historische Zeitschrift. Munich and Berlin.
IER	The Irish Ecclesiastical Record. Dublin.
IKZ	Internationale kirchliche Zeitschrift. Bern.
ILCV	Inscriptiones Latinae Christianae Veteres, ed. E. Diehl. Berlin.
ILS	Inscriptiones Latinae Selectae, ed. H. Dessau. Berlin.
Isis	Isis. Quarterly Organ of the History of Science Society. Bruges, Belgium, and Cambridge, Mass.
ITQ	The Irish Theological Quarterly. Dublin.
JAC	Jahrbuch für Antike und Christentum. Münster.
JBL	Journal of Biblical Literature. New Haven.
Jdai	Jahrbuch des Deutschen Archäologischen Instituts. Berlin.
JEH	The Journal of Ecclesiastical History. London.
JHS	Journal of Hellenic Studies. London.
JL	Jahrbuch für Liturgiewissenschaft. Münster.
JLH	Jahrbuch für Liturgie und Hymnologie. Kassel.
JQR	Jewish Quarterly Review. Philadelphia.
JR	Journal of Religion. Chicago.
JRS	Journal of Roman Studies. London.

JS	Journal des Savants. Paris.
JSOR	Journal of the Society of Oriental Research. Chicago.
JThSt	Journal of Theological Studies. Oxford.
KA	Kyrkohistorisk Arskrift. Stockholm.
KGA	Kirchengeschichtliche Abhandlungen, ed. M. Sdralek. Breslau.
KT	Kleine Texte für Vorlesungen und Übungen, ed. H. Lietzmann. Berlin.
Latomus	Latomus. Revue des études latines. Brussels.
LCC	Library of Christian Classics, ed. J. Baillie, J. T. McNeill, and H. P. van Dusen. London and Philadelphia.
LCL	Loeb Classical Library. London, England, and Cambridge, Mass.
LF	Liturgiegeschichtliche Forschungen. Münster.
LFC	Library of the Fathers of the Holy Catholic Church, eds. E. B. Pusey, J. Keble, and J. H. Newman. Oxford.
LJ	Liturgisches Jahrbuch. Münster.
LNPF	A Select Library of Nicene and Post-Nicene Fathers of the Christian Church, ed. P. Schaff and H. Wace. Buffalo and New York.
LQ	Liturgiegeschichtliche Quellen. Münster.
LQF	Liturgiegeschichtliche Quellen und Forschungen. Münster.
LThK	Lexikon für Theologie und Kirche. Freiburg i.B.
LThK[2]	*idem,* 2d ed. Freiburg.
LThPh	Laval théologique et philosophique. Quebec.
LZ	Liturgische Zeitschrift.
LZB	Literarisches Zentralblatt. Leipzig.
M	First Edition of the Maurists of the Works of St. Augustine. Paris.
MAH	Mélanges d'archéologie et d'histoire. Rome and Paris.
Mansi	J. D. Mansi, Sacrorum conciliorum nova et amplissima collectio. Florence, 1759-1798. Reprint and continuation: Paris and Leipzig, 1901-1927.
MBTh	Münsterische Beiträge zur Theologie. Münster.
MD	La Maison-Dieu. Paris.
MDAI	Mitteilungen des deutschen archäoligischen Instituts. Römische Abteilung. Heidelberg.
MGH	Monumenta germaniae historica. Hanover and Berlin.
MGWJ	Monatsschrift für Geschichte und Wissenschaft des Judentums. Breslau.
MM	Münchener Museum.
Mnem	Mnemosyne. Leyden.
MS	Mediaeval Studies. Toronto.
MSCA	Miscellanea agostiniana. Rome, 1931.
MSCI	Miscellanea isidoriana. Rome.
MSLC	Miscellanea di studi di letteratura cristiana antica. Catania.
MSR	Mélanges de science religieuse. Lille.
MStHTh	Münchener Studien zur historischen Theologie. Munich.
MTS	Münchener theologische Studien. Munich.
MTZ	Münchener theologische Zeitschrift. Munich.
Mus	Le Muséon. Louvain.
NA	Neues Archiv der Gesellschaft für ältere deutsche Geschichtskunde. Hanover.
NADG	Neues Archiv der Gesellschaft für ältere deutsche Geschichtskunde. Hanover.
NBA	Nuova Biblioteca Agostiniana. Rome.
NC	La nouvelle Clio. Brussels.
ND	Nuovo Didaskaleion. Catania.
N.F.	Neue Folge.

NGWG Nachrichten der Gesellschaft der Wissenschaften zu Göttingen.
NJKA Neue Jahrbücher für das klassische Altertum. Leipzig.
NKZ Neue kirchliche Zeitschrift. Erlangen and Leipzig.
NRTh Nouvelle revue théologique. Tournai.
N.S. New Series, Nouvelle Série, Nuova Serie.
NSch New Scholasticism. Washington, D.C.
NTA Neutestamentliche Abhandlungen. Münster.
NTT Nieuw Theologisch Tijdschrift. Haarlem.

OC Oriens Christianus. Leipzig.
OCh Orientalia Christiana. Rome.
OCP Orientalia Christiana Periodica. Rome.
ODC The Oxford Dictionary of the Christian Church, ed. F. L. Cross. London.
OLZ Orientalistische Literaturzeitung. Leipzig.
Or Orientalia. Commentarii Periodici Pontifical Institute Biblici. Rome.
Orph Orpheus. Rivista di umanità classica e cristiana. Catania.
OrSyr L'Orient Syrien. Paris.
OstkSt Ostkirchliche Studien. Würzburg.

PB Pastor Bonus. Trier.
PC Paraula Cristiana. Barcelona.
PG Migne, Patrologia, series graeca.
Phil Philologus. Leipzig.
PhJ Philosophisches Jahrbuch der Görresgesellschaft. Fulda.
PhW Philologische Wochenschrift. Leipzig.
PL Migne, Patrologia, series latina.
PLS Migne, Patrologia, series latina. Supplementum ed. A. Hamman.
PO Patrologia Orientalis. Paris.
PS Patrologia Syriaca, ed. R. Graffin. Paris.
PSt Patristic Studies, ed. R. J. Deferrari. Washington, D.C.
PThR Princeton Theological Review. Princeton.
PWK Pauly-Wissowa-Kroll, Realencyklopädie der klassischen Altertumswissenschaft. Stuttgart.

QLP Questions liturgiques et paroissiales. Louvain.

RABM Revista de archivos, biblioteca y museos. Madrid.
RAC Rivista de archeologia Cristiana. Rome.
RACh Reallexikon für Antike und Christentum, ed. T. Klauser. Leipzig.
RAL Rendiconti della Reale Accademia Nazionale dei Lincei, Classe di Scienze, Morale, Stòria e Filologia. Rome.
RAM Revue d'ascétique et de mystique. Paris.
RAp Revue pratique d'apologétique. Paris.
RB Revue Bénédictine. Maredsous.
RAug Recherches Augustiniennes. Paris.
RBibl Revue biblique. Paris.
RBPh Revue belge de philologie et d'histoire. Brussels.
RC Revue critique d'histoire et de littérature. Paris.
RCC Revue des Cours et conférences. Paris.
RCCM Rivista di cultura classica e medievale. Rome.
RDC Revue de droit canonique. Strasbourg.
RE Realencyklopädie für protestantische Theologie und Kirche, founded by J. J. Herzog, 3d ed. A. Hauck. Leipzig.
REA Revue des études arméniennes. Paris.
REAN Revue des études anciennes. Bordeaux.

REAug	Revue des études Augustiniennes. Paris.
REB	Revue des études byzantines. Paris.
REG	Revue des études grecques. Paris.
RELA	Revue des études latines. Paris.
ReIC	Religión y cultura. Madrid.
Religio	Religio, ed. E. Buonaiuti. Rome.
RET	Revista española de teología. Madrid.
RevR	Review of Religion. New York.
RevSR	Revue des sciences religieuses. Strasbourg.
RF	Razón y Fe. Madrid.
RFE	Revista de filología española. Madrid.
RFIC	Rivista di filogia e Istruzione Classica. Turin.
RFN	Rivista di filosofia neoscolastica. Milan.
RGG	Religion in Geschichte und Gegenwart, ed. Gunkel-Zscharnack. Tübingen.
RH	Revue historique. Paris.
RHE	Revue d'histoire ecclésiastique. Louvain.
RHEF	Revue d'histoire de l'Église de France. Paris.
RHL	Revue d'histoire et de littérature religieuse. Paris.
RhM	Rheinisches Museum für Philologie. Frankfurt M.
RHPR	Revue d'histoire et de philosophie religieuse. Strasbourg.
RHR	Revue d'histoire des religions. Paris.
RIL	Rencidonti del R. Istituto Lombardo di Scienze e Lettere. Milan.
RLM	Revue liturgique et monastique. Maredsous.
ROC	Revue de l'Orient chrétien. Paris.
ROL	Revue de l'Orient Latin. Paris.
RPh	Revue de philologie. Paris.
RQ	Römische Quartalschrift. Freiburg i.B.
RQH	Revue des questions historiques. Paris.
RR	Ricerche religiose. Rome.
RSCI	Rivista di storia della chiesa in Italia. Rome.
RSFR	Rivista di Studi Filosofici e Religiosi. Rome.
RSH	Revue de synthèse historique. Paris.
RSLR	Rivista de storia e letteratura religiosa. Florence.
RSO	Rivista degli studi Orientali. Rome.
RSPT	Revue des sciences philosophiques et théologiques. Paris.
RSR	Recherches de science religieuse. Paris.
RStR	Ricerche di storia religiosa. Rome.
RT	Revue Thomiste. Paris.
RTAM	Recherches de théologie ancienne et médiévale. Louvain.
RTP	Revue de théologie et philosophie. Lausanne.
RTr	Rivista trimestrale di studi filosofici e religiosi. Perugia.
RUO	Revue de l'Université d'Ottowa.
SA	Studia Anselmiana. Rome.
SAB	Sitzungsberichte. Academy of Berlin.
SAH	Sitzungsberichte. Academy of Heidelberg.
SAM	Sitzungsberichte. Academy of Munich.
SAPF	Swiety Augustin. Pisna Filozoficzne. Warsaw.
SAW	Sitzungsberichte. Academy of Vienna.
SC	La Scuola Cattolica. Milan.
SCA	Studies in Christian Antiquity, ed. J. Quasten, Washington, D.C.
SCh	Sources chrétiennes, ed. H. de Lubac and J. Daniélou. Paris.
Schol	Scholastik. Freiburg, West Germany, and Eupen, Belgium.

SD	Studies and Documents, ed. K. Lake and S. Lake. London and Philadelphia.
SE	Sacris Erudiri. Jaarboek voor Godsdienstwetenschappen. Bruges.
SIF	Studi italiani di filologia classica. Florence.
SJMS	Speculum. Journal of Medieval Studies. Cambridge, Mass.
SKGG	Schriften der Königsverger Gelehrtengesellschaft. Berlin.
SM	Studien und Mitteilungen zur Geschichte des Benediktinerorderns und sener Zweige. Munich.
SO	Symbolae Osloenses. Oslo.
So	Sophia. Milan.
SP	Studia Patristica. Acts of the International Conventions of Oxford (TU). Berlin.
SPCK	Society for Promoting Christian Knowledge. London.
SPM	Stromata Patristica et Mediaevalia, ed. C. Mohrmann and J. Quasten. Utrecht.
SPMed	Studia Patristica Mediolanensia. Milan.
SQ	Sammlung ausgewählter Quellenschriften zur Kirchen- und Dogmengeschichte. Tübingen.
SSL	Spicilegium Sacrum Lovaniense. Louvain.
SSR	Studi storico-religiosi. Rome.
ST	Studi e Testi. Rome.
StBN	Studi bizantini e neoellenici. Rome.
StC	Studia Catholica. Nijmegen.
StGKA	Studien zur Geschichte und Kultur des Altertums. Paderborn.
STh	Studia Theologica. Lund.
StP	Studia Patavina. Padua.
ThBl	Theologische Blätter. Leipzig.
ThGl	Theologie und Glaube. Paderborn.
ThJ	Theologische Jahrbücher. Leipzig.
ThLB	Theologisches Literaturblatt. Leipzig.
ThLZ	Theologische Literaturzeitung. Leipzig.
ThQ	Theologische Quartalschrift. Tübingen.
ThR	Theologische Revue. Münster.
ThStKr	Theologische Studien und Kritiken. Gotha.
ThZ	Theologische Zeitschrift. Basel.
TJHC	Theology. Journal of Historic Christianity. London.
TP	Transactions and Proceedings of the American Philological Association. Lancaster, Pa.
TS	Theological Studies. Baltimore.
TSt	Texts and Studies, ed. J. A. Robinson. Cambridge.
TThZ	Trierer theologische Zeitschrift. Trier.
TU	Texte und Untersuchungen. Leipzig.
TZ	Theologische Zeitschrift. Basel.
UTQ	University of Toronto Quarterly. Toronto.
VC	Vigiliae Christianae. Amsterdam.
VD	Verbum Domini. Rome.
VetChr	Vetera Christianorum. Bari.
VS	La Vie spirituelle. Paris.
VT	Verzeichnis der Sigel für Kirchenschriftsteller, ed. Bonifatius Fischer. Freiburg, 1963[2].
VV	Vizantijskij Vremennik. Petersburg. New Series, Moscow.
WJB	Würzburger Jahrbücher für klassische Altertumswissenschaft.

WS	Woodbrooke Studies. Manchester.
WSt	Weiner Studien. Zeitschrift für klassische Philologie. Vienna.
WZKM	Wiener Zeitschrift für die Kunde des Morgenlandes. Vienna.
ZAM	Zeitschrift für Askese und Mystik. Innsbruck and Munich.
ZAW	Zeitschrift für die alttestamentliche Wissenschaft (Giessen). Berlin.
ZBW	Zentralblatt für Bibliothekswesen. Leipzig.
ZDADL	Zeitschrift für deutsches Altertum und deutsche Literatur. Wiesbaden.
ZDMG	Zeitschrift der deutschen morgenländischen Gesellschaft. Leipzig.
ZDP	Zeitschrift des deutschen Palästinavereins. Leipzig.
ZKG	Zeitschrift für Kirchengeschichte (Gotha). Stuttgart.
ZkTh	Zeitschrift für katholische Theologie. Innsbruck.
ZMR	Zeitschrift für Missions- und Religionswissenschaft. Münster.
ZMW	Zeitschrift für Missionswissenschaft. Münster.
ZNW	Zeitschrift für die neutestamentliche Wissenschaft und die Kunde der älteren Kirche. Giessen; Berlin.
ZST	Zeitschrift für systematische Theologie. Gütersloh.
ZTK	Zeitschrift für Theologie und Kirche. Tübingen.

TABLE OF CONTENTS

III. AMBROSE OF MILAN, AMBROSIASTER AND NICETAS
by Maria Grazia Mara

IV. THE TRANSLATIONS. JEROME AND RUFINUS
by Jean Griboment

V. CHRISTIAN POETRY
by Angelo DiBerardino

VI. SAINT AUGUSTINE
by Agostino Trapè

VIII. WRITERS OF GAUL

by Adalbert Hamman

IX. ITALIAN WRITERS UNTIL POPE LEO THE GREAT
by Basil Studer

CHAPTER I

THE TURNABOUT OF THE FOURTH CENTURY

A Political, Geographical, Social, Ecclesiastical, and Doctrinal Framework of the Century

by Adalbert Hamman

THE CHRISTIAN WEST

Christianity, born in the East, developed above all within the confines of the Roman Empire, the frontiers of which it scarcely crossed. The Gospel message, having gone out from Jerusalem, advanced behind the conquests of the legions and put down roots at Rome in order to send forth the Good News from there into the West and to the entire world.

At first the church was treated as something foreign and thus was persecuted. The fourth century opened with the Persecution of Diocletian, one of the bloodiest, but closed with the legislation of Theodosius, which substituted Christianity for the Roman religion. The reconciliation and the resultant alliance between the two powers dominates the history of the fourth and fifth centuries, as they involve themselves in a common destiny, even more readily recognizable in the West.

From 325 until 451 political events weave a background for the development of the Church, which little by little officially established itself. Constantine's victory at the Milvian Bridge made him master of the West. Twelve years later in 324, with the Battle of Chrysopolis, his dominion extended over both East and West. The foundation of Constantinople, bridge and hinge between the two worlds, symbolized and solemnized the unity.

Since it was an artificial and transient unity, it was already broken at the death of Constantine by the division of the Empire among his three sons, reestablished by Constantius and, afterward, by Julian the Apostate. The former, a protector of Arianism, menaced the unity of the Church; the latter sought, in a desperate attempt, to reestablish a declining paganism. Some years later, Theodosius authorized the Christian religion as the religion of the state "transmitted to the Romans by the Apostle Peter," and declared paganism to be illegal.

From the abdication of Diocletian until the death of Theodosius (395), the Roman Empire was united under the authority of a single person for only 22 years and some months. Under the sons of Theodosius the two *partes* of the Empire drew apart and set themselves against one another. Unity was restored only in a provisional manner for four months in 423.

The common destiny of East and West was frail and precarious. It camouflaged antagonisms too deep to allow it to endure. It had previously served the expansion of the church and its penetration into the West. The separation of the two halves of the Christian world in the fourth century, and especially in the fifth, profoundly affected the *Unam sanctam.* East and West developed along different and diverse lines, and it is this fact which justifies a distinct study of Greek and Latin authors in two different volumes of the *Patrology.*

In general, the Latin Fathers are more sensitive than the Greek to the symbiosis of church and state. To the eyes of Jerome and Augustine, the fall of Rome assumes apocalyptic dimensions. But Jerome and Augustine are far from representing the whole church. The misfortunes of Rome bring the Bishop of Hippo to realize how much the Two Cities, for as much as they are intermingled, are fundamentally independent.

The peace reestablished by Constantine allowed the church not only to emerge from its clandestine existence, but also to set up its organization and hierarchy, to dedicate itself to the education of a Christian population ever more numerous and diverse, to formulate and arrive at a deeper understanding of the elements of the faith, to establish monastic life under diverse forms, to provide the West with a more faithful version of the Bible, and to take cognizance of its own existence and autonomy.

All these advantages carried with them the risk of deception. The emperor was not always disinterested in his favors. His generosity carried the risk of turning Christ into an *imperator;* privileges and exemptions compromised the church with a totalitarian state, isolating it from the flock oppressed by taxation. As an opposite party to the state, the spiritual power saw itself obliged to adapt itself to Roman legislation and to bend its discipline to the benefit of the state.

The leaders of the church themselves, Silvester, Hosius, Athanasius, and Donatus, rather than being attentive to the autonomy of the two powers, solicited and tolerated imperial interventions. The appeals of someone such as Firmicus Maternus to the secular arm embarrass us because of their intolerance. The victims of secular interventions did not cast doubt on the principle of intervention by the state. A lamentable confusion, of which the two powers suffered the consequences, was the result. The church began to experience a trial more terrible than persecution: the often burdensome protection of the state. Both the Donatist Crisis and the history of Arianism permit a verification of the accuracy of such an affirmation. The Donatists, overwhelmed by their multitudes, resorted to the Roman authorities for security or for arbitration between two candidates. Interventions by the secular authorities succeeded one another for as long as the African schism endured.

In 405 the Emperor Honorius promulgated edicts which proscribed the Donatist sect, inflicted fines on the recalcitrant and threatened exile. Augustine, previously a partisan of tolerance, resigned himself to the use of compulsion on the part of the state, which was indisputable from the point of view of efficacy, if somewhat less so from that of principle.

Arianism penetrated into the West only by means of the favor of the emperor. Without the intervention of Constantius there is a strong probability that the conflict would have been limited to the East. Hilary, who was so intimately involved in the crisis, confessed never to have heard of the faith of Nicea before his exile (*De syn.* 91). In a pamphlet, the intrepid defender of orthodoxy did not limit himself to castigating the crimes of the Arians and the complicity of the emperor, but he also underlined the inadmissible interference of the state in the affairs of the church.

"You distribute the episcopal sees to your partisans and substitute good bishops with bad ones. You put priests in prison, use your armies to terrorize the church, convoke councils and compel the Western bishops assembled at Rimini to impiety after having terrorized them with threats, weakened them with famine, annihilated them by the cold and led them astray by lies" (*C. Const.* 7; PL 10, 584).

It is indeed true that the Council of Serdica (343), under the influence of Hosius of Cordova, had already formulated the principle of non-intervention by the emperor in ecclesiastical affairs. The strong personality of Ambrose, on the morrow of the defeat of Arianism, imposed on the emperor a respect for the principle thus expressed: *"Imperator intra Ecclesiam non supra Ecclesiam est"* (*Ep.* 21, 36; PL 16, 1061).

According to the report of Theodoret, when Theodosius arrived in Milan, the bishop excluded him from the choir and placed him in the nave with the faithful. Whether authentic or legendary, this anecdote allows one to judge how the West kept its distance on the political plane in comparison with the Byzantine tradition and decreed its emancipation with regard to the latter. The efforts of Ambrose were aimed at protecting the church against all rash interference on the part of the state and obliging the civil authority to respect the moral law. At the same time, however, they sealed a close collaboration between the two powers. *Ratione peccati,* the *princeps* was obliged to observe Christian morality; *ratione peccati,* Ambrose imposed public penance on the emperor after the massacre at Thessalonica.

Augustine, who had not hesitated to have recourse to the secular arm, affirmed more distinctly than the other Fathers the distinction between the Two Cities. He dreamed of a Christian state where the true faith might reign in the tranquility of order as a pledge of the well-being of all. The facts showed him that this dream transcended earthly cities and realms.

In the course of the fourth and fifth centuries the church strengthened its expansion and progress in the West. Its cultural arena expanded, deepened, and diversified. The contrast between the third century and those following is astonishing.

North Africa, Latin in its Christian expression since 180, released all its splendor in the incomparable Bishop of Hippo. The Vandal invasion provoked a retreat of the Christians to Europe. The monk Donatus came to Arcavica (Cuenca) with his monks and his library. The exiled African bishops found refuge in Sardinia and Naples and saved the archives of their churches and the manuscripts of Augustine.

The Roman Church became more latinized in the course of the fourth century. Italy asserted itself not only with Ambrose, but also with Eusebius of Vercelli, Lucifer of Cagliari, Zeno of Verona, Philastrius of Brescia, Rufinus of Aquileia, Julian of Eclanum; and, in the following generation, Maximus of Turin and Peter Chrysologus of Ravenna.

Gaul made its entry into Christian literature. Thanks to its bishop, Hilary, the obscure city of Poitiers exercised a role of prime importance in the Arian controversy. In the fifth century, Christian Gaul displayed the most creative literary activity among the ancient provinces, producing works in the areas of theology and scriptural commentary, homiletics, liturgy and hagiography, poetry, and history with such distinguished writers as Prosper, John Cassian, Salvian, and Vincent of Lérins. Among the wealth of poets can be named Paulinus, who took up residence at Nola, Ausonius, Claudius Marius Victorius, Paulinus of Pella, and Orientius. This flowering of literature extended beyond the Council of Chalcedon with Faustus of Riez, Paulinus of Périgueux, Sidonius Apollinaris, and Elpidius Rusticus.

Provence became a center of great vitality with its monastic foundations, with its metropolis, Arles, its councils, and its men of prime importance, such as John Cassian and Hilary of Arles. An outpost was also established in *Helvetia* under Salonius, bishop of Geneva.

The church emerged and organized itself in the Iberian Peninsula. Episcopal sees increased in number and councils were held. The famous Council of Elvira took place at the beginning of the fourth century. The number of writers likewise increased: Hosius of Cordova, Potamius of Lisbon, Gregory of Elvira, Pacian of Barcelona, and Orosius and Avitus of Braga, as well as the austere layman Priscillian, who became a dissident, and two genuine poets, Iuvencus and Prudentius.

Jerome was by origin a Dalmatian, as were his disciple Philip and the bishop, Lawrence the Mellifluous; and Nicetas of Remesiana was from Mediterranean Dacia. The two well-known champions of Arianism, Ursacius and Valens, from the Danubian provinces, the hinge between East and West and a favorite breeding ground of heterodox Christian communities. In the frontier regions, which were in fact Arian, there were the Goths, evangelized by prisoners from Cappadocia. Wulfila was, after a certain fashion, primate of *Gothia* and was responsible for its evangelization. At ease in his knowledge of both Greek and Latin, this bishop translated the Bible into the language of his countrymen, inventing the letters and the alphabet. This translation was of great prophetic and missionary importance, for it removed Christianity from its dependence on Graeco-Latin culture. To the preceding must be added what remains of the works of the two Arian bishops, Palladius of Ratiara in Dacia, and Maximus, opponent of Augustine (PLS I, 691-728). There is, however, no comparison between the evangelization within the Empire and that beyond its frontiers (Armenia, Persia, Ethiopia).

"UNITAS" AND "ROMANITAS"

In the course of the first centuries, Christianity had put down roots and developed within the political, economic, and cultural unity of the Empire. Christianity had found in Greek language and culture a means of expression, of unity, and of expansion. The principal Western theologians, Hilary, Ambrose, and Jerome, formed part of a spiritual elite which moved at ease in Greek culture. Ambrose, having been unexpectedly named bishop, made his theological apprenticeship with the Greek masters Origen and Didymus the blind. Jerome and Rufinus opened the West to Greek exegesis and theology.

This was, however, a one-way street, for there was not to be found in the East the same curiosity with regard to the West, even the Christian West. The imperial court established at Constantinople, instead of introducing Latin, was itself Hellenized. Only official documents and works of hagiography came to be translated into Greek. Augustine himself was little known in the East.

At Rome, Greek remained the language of liturgy and of letters until the fourth century. It was the language of the philosophers and the cultured classes, as well as of the merchants and of the slaves coming from the East. But there was a rupture between the third and fourth centuries at the moment when Latin began to assert itself in pastoral and liturgical life. While the epitaphs of the Roman bishops continued to be in Greek until Gaius (†296), the two languages were able to co-exist side by side. Pope Julius still addressed two letters in Greek to Anastasius (Jaffé 341 and 343). The use of Latin in the liturgy seems to have been an accomplished fact at the time of Pope Damasus, although not without opposition, as is attested by Ambrosiaster.

The East remained not only the cradle but also the womb from which proceeded the thought and spirituality that fecundated the West. Jerome took up residence in the East to carry out his exegetical labor, without, however, being able to facilitate any exchange. Rufinus translated Origen there. Aetheria, like many others, went there in pilgrimage to draw from the sources and John Cassian received there his monastic formation. The *Vita Antonii* became the vade mecum of spiritual life in the West and played a role in the conversion of Augustine.

The latinization of the Roman Church rendered relations with the East more difficult. It was not easy to understand one another when there was no longer the basis of a common language. Basil already complained of the inopportune interventions of Roman authority and of the scant attention given by the pope to his inquiries (*Ep.* 238 and 214). Damasus was ill informed of events in Syria and Asia Minor. At the end of the fourth century this obstacle was not insurmountable, but conditions grew worse in the following century.

Celestine I, responding to Nestorius in 430, explained his delay on account of the time necessary to find a cleric capable of translating the Greek text (Jaffé 374). This abrupt decadence was caused by the barbarian invasions, but also by the more modest origins of the clergy. Eastern and Western bishops meeting in councils no longer understood one another, a state of affairs which did not facilitate the resolution of theological controversies. The Latin terminology formulated in the Trinitarian and Christological controversies did not always correspond to the Greek. All these factors hindered the West from following the theological currents of the East, and thus Augustinian doctrines tended to monopolize the field. At the same time, this latinizing accentuated the importance of the Oriental patriarchal sees.

The chasm between East and West was created by political events, by language and vocabulary, and by intellectual and theological traditions. Except for the intervention of the imperial authorities, the Latins risked ignoring Arianism, and the same holds true for the Origenist polemic and the Trinitarian and Christological controversies. East and West, in the fourth century and especially in the fifth, had different centers of interest, and each developed its own crises and heresies in relation to its own particular preoccupations. Priscillianism, Donatism, and Pelagianism were typically Western concerns for which the Easterners never developed any interest. Even though he was at Bethlehem, Jerome never succeeded in mobilizing the Orientals to take a position against Celestius and Julian of Eclanum. The bishop of Jerusalem was content to refer them to the Roman Patriarch.

Whereas Hilary and Ambrose developed an exegesis and a theology nourished by Greek sources, close to that of Origen, Athanasius, and the Cappadocians, the same was not true for Augustine, who was not at ease with Greek. A comparison of the *De Spiritu Sancto* of Ambrose with the *De Trinitate* of Augustine is sufficient to perceive how the Doctor of Hippo develops at last a strictly Occidental Trinitarian theology, distinct from the Greek tradition. The West is summarized and reaches its acme in and through the great Augustine in such a way as to subsequently produce only imitators and copiers. The Doctor of Hippo came so to dominate the Western scene as to eclipse Tertullian and Hilary of Poitiers.

Divided from the East, the West began its own history at the end of the fourth century and above all in the fifth, which developed parallel to that of the East and split the *Unam Sanctam.* The two great branches of the ancient world began to live in different intellectual climates with different theological preoccupations which gradually estranged them from one another. Whereas Ambrose had corresponded with Basil, there is no Eastern correspondent among the letters of Augustine. There was no longer an exchange between Eastern theologians and their Western counterparts in the fifth century. The Greeks had little interest in Latin thinkers. Photius knew only one work of Augustine, translated into Greek. On the other hand, the Latins knew Greek texts only in translation.

THE CHURCH AND THE EMPIRE IN THE WEST

The separation was rendered more severe by the great Germanic, Asiatic and Slavic invasions. Illyria, that bulwark of Roman culture where the councils of the fourth century had flourished, was dismembered. This point of contact between the two worlds foundered under the blows of the invaders in 380. While the East remained relatively unscathed, the West, because of the decadence of its institutions, was more vulnerable and lay more at the mercy of the invaders. The army was Roman in name only, with the bulk of the troops formed from barbarian contingents who defended the Empire against other barbarians. Corruption and graft extended to all levels of administration. The decline in the birth rate was tragic and impoverishment was rampant.

The political and economic scene shows to what extent the Empire was worn out, poorly defended and open to all the waves of the barbarian invasions. Throughout the entire course of the fifth century these waves broke one after another over the West: Vandals, Visigoths, Franks, Alamanni, Burgundi. "All of Gaul burns like a torch," wrote one contemporary observer (Orientus, *Comm.* 2, 184).

In 410, the Visigoths sacked Rome. What appeared to be *the* end of the world was only the end of *a* world and of *a* conquest. Augustine meditated on the incident in *The City of God.* The Vandals crossed the Iberian Peninsula, settled in *Africa proconsularis* and were besieging Hippo as Augustine lay dying. The last emperor in the West, Romulus Augustulus, was deposed in 476.

Although the majority of the Visigoth and Vandal invaders were Arian, no one asked the reason why. After a momentary disorientation, taken aback by the Goths of Wulfila, the Western church, bound to Roman civilization and given rather to action than to speculation, found in the task of evangelization a new mission and a new opportunity of expansion.

In the West, the greater part of the Christian authors of the age believed in the perpetuity of the Eternal City and honored *Romania,* a word which appeared in Orosius at that moment in which Roman civilization as it then existed felt itself to be menaced from every side. Provincials, such as Jerome and Augustine, or Orosius in Spain, and *a fortiori* the Roman Ambrose were dazzled by the prestige of Rome. The Bishop of Milan admired and exalted the Empire, which had put an end to wars, joined peoples together and fostered evangelization. The providential role of Rome in the spread of the Gospel was a leitmotiv of every apology of the fourth century and would appear again in Leo the Great.

Ambrose never even imagined the fall of Rome, although the storm was already brewing on the horizon. His identification of the Goths with Gog was the sign of a certain myopia; a factor which did not facilitate the return of the Arians to the *oikumene.* Prudentius made things worse and protested against the pessimism of Symmachus. It was a difficult matter for all to dissociate the destiny of the Church from that of the Empire.

The victory of Alaric in 410 assumed apocalyptic contours. *Quid salvum est si Roma perit?* Rome, the mother of the entire civilized world, the creator of law and mistress of peoples had been wounded and profaned. All those enamoured of the *Urbs* lived in a state of mind like unto the end of the world.

At the fall of Rome, Jerome halted his commentary on Ezechiel. "My voice is faint, the sobs smother my words. She has been conquered, this city which has conquered the universe."

For Jerome, the misfortune was not the mere downfall of the

Roman world, but the victory of the barbarians who were dominant from that point on.

Christians and pagans alike questioned and accused one another. Augustine recounted the gossip circulating in Africa as to what good it did the city to preserve the body of Paul, the body of Lawrence, the remains of so many martyrs. Where were the *memoriae apostolorum* (*Serm.* 296, 6; PL 38, 1355)? The incident, however, gave rise to one of the most celebrated of Augustine's works, which posterity would copy with the greatest zeal and would not cease to commentate, especially in times of tragedy.

Even more serious than the narrow political outlook of Prudentius, who sang of "the world led back to unity by the Roman peace," was the disdain which he felt for the barbarians. "There is a greater difference," he said, "between them and the Romans than between quadrupeds and bipeds." Orosius, himself an admirer of *Romania,* was less severe toward the barbarians, whom he considered capable of improvement. Indeed, he considered the occasion propitious for their evangelization.

A century later, Sidonius Apollinaris, bishop of Clermont-Ferrand at a time when the province had been ceded to the Visigoths, incapable himself of reading the signs of the times, still sang the praises of *Roma eterna* and remained allergic to the Burgundi, whom he reproached for their stench of garlic. For all these nostalgics, "the stench which emanates from the barbarians is the very stench of hell."

Not all Christian writers were of the same opinion. The Sibylline Oracles and Tertullian had already manifested a certain reserve. Arnobius the Younger, a witness of the invasions, did not believe in the perpetuity of Rome. Salvian of Marseilles, virulent and lucid, kept his distance from the Empire and considered the purification to be necessary. He realized that Rome enjoyed no monopoly on God's solicitude and that the arrival of the barbarians was providential for salvation history.

In the course of the fifth century there began a new turn of events. The course of affairs prepared the church to dissociate itself from *Romania,* to break its solidarity with an empire adrift and to discover new horizons opened by the invasions for its mission of evangelization.

The economic and social situation was to a great extent bound to the political history of the Roman Empire. The state, worn out by its conquests and its vastness, was demographically and economically impoverished. The economic regression, already begun in the second and third centuries, grew worse in the fourth and fifth and sorely oppressed the working classes both in the cities and in the rural areas. Instead of providing remedies, the political authorities developed a program of heavy taxation which weighed most heavily on the weakest. The works of Salvian of Marseilles and the letters and sermons of the Latin Fathers and the Cappadocians allow one to appraise the depth of the economic and social crisis. The descriptions of Ambrose are strangely similar to those of Basil and of John Chrysostom. At Antioch as at Milan, the same causes produced the same effects. Nevertheless, there is a need for careful distinctions, since conditions were not the same, for example, in Africa and Gaul. The Fathers were moralists and made no pretenses of carrying out analyses of political economics.

Immense landed fortunes were amassed. Such a factor is connected with the circumcellions in Africa. The *clarissimi* lived on their *latifundia* to escape costly responsibilities. They constructed *villae* for themselves in which reigned an extravagance which was insulting and offensive to the misery of the poor. The mosaics of the rich dwellings of the Iberian Peninsula, Sicily, Africa and Aquitaine offer an eloquent witness of this down to the present day. Ambrose and John Chrysostom never tired of denouncing and criticizing the unjust distribution of the goods given by the Creator to all.

According to Salvian, the taxes were fixed arbitrarily. The high functionaries — the large property holders with all the more reason — took advantage of their position to corrupt the agents of the treasury and escape from taxation. The poor were the ones obliged to pay. If the *curiales* and the senators obtained tax reductions from the emperor, if the rich divided them up among themselves and forgot the poor (*De gub.* V, 34) — nothing new under the sun!

If only the great landowners had given some proof of *humanitas* to alleviate the inequities of the situation! But on the contrary, they were often rapacious and inhuman. They arrogated to themselves the right to judge, punish and cast into prison the tenants who were unable to pay their rents.

The government made use of groups banded together in *collegia:* workers in the service of the state, agents of the treasury, miners and workers at the mints. Every worker, marked by birth, was simply fixed hereditarily in his profession. The common man, poorly paid and housed, was crushed by taxes. The civil servant at least had the possibility of recovering his losses through his administrative functions and of taking advantage of the *sportula.*

The landed proprietor also used tenant-farmers who were bound indissolubly by heredity to the land, from which they could not free themselves. It was not allowed to sell the land without the tenants nor the tenants without the land. The tenant-farmer occupied an intermediate position between liberty and slavery and was not allowed to take on public offices.

Salvian distinguished between two types of tenant-farmers. Some had lost all of their property to pay back taxes. Without resources and evicted from their homes, they took refuge with the neighboring landowner, who leased them some land in return for services rendered. They thus became sharecroppers of the rich. From that point on they were bound to that land and were not allowed to leave it. They had given up their freedom.

Others found themselves in less desperate situations. In order to avoid an eventual forced expropriation, they put themselves under the protection of the *maiores.* They lost the ownership of their property, of which they preserved the usufruct. They no longer paid property taxes, but paid a rent to the proprietor and the poll tax to the state (*De gub.* V, 38-39). From either case there issued the same result: the absorption of the smaller landholdings by the larger. As a result of this, the sons of these tenants became servants, subject to the *corvée* (ibid., 45). The foundation was thus laid for the Middle Ages and the feudal system. The *chrysargyron,* a tax imposed by Constantine and payable every five years, was a veritable Sword of Damocles. In order to pay it, the *tenuiores* had recourse to a moneylender. All of the writers of the age, Christian or pagan, were unanimous in condemning usury as a cancer of society. Interest rates were unbelievable and the moneylenders brazenly exploited the years of bad harvest and the scarcity of consumer goods.

Last of all, the slaves whose lot was declining, were considered things, *res.* They had no rights. Their situation varied over a wide spectrum, depending on their talents, their origins or their masters. They were able to put aside a *peculium* toward purchasing their freedom. Instead of condemning the institution of slavery in itself, the church contributed rather to improving the conditions of slaves, to promoting their manumission, especially in the fifth century, and to obtaining the recognition of their human dignity. The Fathers were too much men of their times to be able to condemn an institution which, in that age, was universally accepted.

Toward the end of the fourth century, there arose the phenomenon of workers and farmers who took refuge in the forests or went into exile in order to escape from their lot and from the agents of the treasury. The exploited looked to the barbarians, and some of those condemned *ad metalla* joined up with the invaders. The same phenomenon holds true in the case of the *Bagaudae.* They had nothing to lose. Some members of the lower classes attempted to escape from their condition by entering into ecclesiastical orders. Valentinian I forbade this to bakers in 365 (CT 14, 3, 11), and in 446, Valentinian III forced all workers who were not yet deacons to leave the clerical state.

In North Africa, rebels against society, slaves, and seasonal laborers maintained the Donatist Schism. It would be difficult not to admit that the enduring success of this sect was due in part to the utilization of social unrest and to recruitment among the indigenous peoples, who remained barbarian, in the face of a local church too closely bound to a *Romanitas* which it would not survive. The social condition of the Empire, in addition to provoking the revolt of the indigenous Africans and Gauls, favored the reawakening of "nationalism" and the revolt against Roman domination.

The Gospel of the Beatitudes moved wealthy proprietors to divest themselves of their own possessions and give them to the poor. Paulinus, who owned an entire province, provided an example all the more remarkable because more exceptional. Ausonius himself, less sensitive to the ideal of the Gospel, did not understand him. The minor nobleman Prudentius lived from the income of his fields and did not hesitate to dirty his hands to cultivate the earth.

In their homilies and their writings, the Latin Fathers as well as their Eastern counterparts criticized above all the unjust distribution of goods arising from the greed of men. According to Ambrose, poverty was an insult to the munificence of the Creator. Even though it was legitimate to own property, it was bound to the sinful condition of man. The treatise *De Nabuthe* manifests a rare courage. The labor of man is worth more than landed wealth, often ill-acquired. All the Fathers condemned luxury and usury, avarice and attachment to material goods. That which is superfluous must be used to procure that which is necessary for those who are in need.

The Church exerted itself to bring remedies to the social conditions of the age. To high-sounding statements, it preferred action and the education of consciences to put an end to the intolerable situations. Slaves already had been chosen as bishops of Rome, and ministers were being recruited more and more from the humbler classes, with care being taken not to accept those who were seeking only to escape from their social status. The communities disposed of revenues which were not all of the same class. The benefits from the state consisted above all of spectacular constructions and of exemptions, which carried the danger of compromising the clergy and separating them from the laity. The church received inheritances from the faithful, who would have done better to have spent their fortunes on behalf of the needy while still alive.

Fathers and councils repeated that the offerings made to the church, except what was necessary for its ministers, belonged to the poor. *"Non sunt illa nostra sed pauperum,"* wrote Augustine (*Ep.* 185, 35; PL 33, 809). It happened that these material goods, which tended to mount up, aroused criticism from pagans, such as Ammianus

Marcellinus, as well as from bishops, such as Lucifer of Cagliari, or from priests, such as Faustinus and Marcellinus, who proposed a return to poverty (*Coll. Avellana* 3).

In reality the social responsibility of the Christian community lay in the hands of the bishop, for whom it was a wearying task. Augustine complained of having to concern himself with the management of farms (*In Ioh.* 6, 25). The patrimony of the church tended to grow and needs multiplied and diversified. In the face of the failures of the civil authority, the bishop was obliged to concern himself with the city, defend the interests of the citizens, intervene in the secular courts, soften the rigors of the laws, ameliorate the condition of prisoners, and obtain a reduction or a postponement of taxes. This activity as *moderator,* comparable to the Swedish *ombudsman,* was mentioned by all of the Fathers. Their *tuitio* was not limited to Christians only. This type of position in society would continue to grow at the time of the invasions. In the face of differing, discordant and contradictory forces, the hierarchy with its structures presented itself as endowed with order, continuity and the right to speak in the name of God.

The economic crisis, the social conditions of the West and the various waves of invasions forced the bishops to organize relief, distribute grain, receive refugees, watch over the city like a sentinel, meet with the invaders and, at times, even to organize the defense. The bishop had to remain as "the father of the people" in the midst of his flock, like the Bishop of Hippo during the siege of the city, or to ransom his countrymen, like Severinus, the Apostle of Noricum, who was taken prisoner by the Rugi and the Alamanni. In 449, Leo I refused to go to the Council of Ephesus, which opened on August 1, because Rome was in danger (Jaffé 425).

CLASSICAL CULTURE AND CHRISTIAN CULTURE

The classical format of education was still maintained in the fourth century. Christians followed the lectures of pagan professors and entrusted their sons to the *grammaticus,* who continued to follow the classical model of instruction. The rhetors who became Christians adapted themselves to a diversified public as, for example, Ausonius, whose works have raised doubts at times regarding his Christian faith.

It is certain that mythology and the humanistic ideal of the pagan works began to constitute a problem and to run afoul of Christian sensibilities. Was not such a type of classical education harmful, and a corruptive influence? Was it possible to separate the culture from the paganism with which it was so intimately connected? How was it possible to admire the beauty of the ideas without paying respect to the pagan religion, without reviving its sentiments?

"Why," wrote Magnus, "tarnish the splendor of the church with pagan iniquities?" These objections were raised not only by the *simpliciores* but also by the intellectuals converted to Christianity. Even a council, albeit a local one, of Carthage (398) at the time of Saint Augustine came to the point of formally prohibiting the reading of pagan books by the faithful as well as by bishops. Even though the prohibition had little effect, it came to be included in the *Decretum Gratiani*. This attitude, carried to the extreme, threatened to imperil the literary heritage and to destory classical works, as the crusaders would do to the Greek temples. The majority would give evidence of moderation. Nevertheless, the Latin Fathers displayed a greater reserve compared with the Cappadocians. No one held to the radicalism of Origen or of Cyprian.

Gregory Nazianzus, who was on good terms with numerous rhetors, praised classical culture and eloquence. Basil requested the young to take the honey and leave the gall. Hilary emerged from a background in philosophy and remained faithful to it. Ambrose and Jerome, having been formed by pagan masters, experienced the seductions of profane culture. The *De officiis* of the Bishop of Milan betrays even in the title the influence of Cicero. Jerome was so impregnated by the Latin authors that Magnus was able to reproach him for the abundance of profane citations (*Ep.* 70). Augustine and Paulinus showed themselves to be more reserved.

The Fathers introduced a fundamental distinction as a line of demarcation. The intellectual disciplines, i.e., grammar, rhetoric and dialectics, refined the spirit, facilitated the study of Scripture and were of use for the expression of the faith. But the same did not hold for the themes and concepts which included a morality and a polytheism censured by the Gospel. There thus arose a problem of adaptation and discrimination. How was it to be resolved? In what kind of school was such a formation to be sought? Schools did not exist in the West for those who wanted to deepen their understanding of the faith. The church itself had not organized anything for the clerics who were preparing to serve it. The West showed a serious delay in comparison with the East. Some Latins passing through Constantinople at that time were amazed to hear that at Nisibis there were "regularly instituted schools where the Sacred Scripture was the object of an organized course of instruction as existed in the territory of the Roman Empire for secular studies such as grammar and rhetoric." The West only gradually became aware of its delay.

The Latin clerics learned their profession by practicing it with the reading of the sacred text, the singing of the hymns and the songs, and the practical initiation into the liturgy under the direction of a bishop or an experienced priest. How fortunate the clergy of Hippo!

Ambrose learned the essentials with the priest, Simplicianus. As for the remainder, he had to "teach before having learned" (*De off.* I 1, 4).

Whoever wished to learn exegesis or theology, whether cleric or layman, was obliged to apply himself at his own risk and peril, taking advantage of whatever opportunities were available. Neither school nor instructor were to be found. Jerome acquired his own formation by listening to the lessons of masters in the East. Hilary did not have this opportunity.

The formation of the Latin Fathers took place outside of schools and ecclesiastical directives; a fact which, thanks to their solid classical formation, favored their liberty of thought and expression. But not all the bishops were a Hilary, an Ambrose or an Augustine. At the time when the episcopal sees multiplied and the incumbents came from a more modest origin, the low cultural level made itself felt. Augustine deplored this situation, which he was able to notice in the African synods, in *De catechizandis rudibus*.

From the fourth century and above all in the fifth, the church began to organize communities for the formation of future ministers, at Vercelli, perhaps at Tours, and certainly at Hippo, where Augustine established a *monasterium clericorum* and advised the African episcopate to follow his example. Other Fathers followed suit: Hilary at Arles, Proclus at Marseilles and Peter Chrysologus at Ravenna.

An event external to the life of the church accelerated the transformation. On 17 June 362, Julian prohibited all Christians by edict from teaching pagan literature. The emperor did not want anyone "to teach that in which he does not believe." This first assault on the liberty of education struck profoundly the pagans themselves, such as Ammianus Marcellinus. The measures of Julian, for as much as they were of brief duration, made a lasting impact. They provoked an awareness of the moral significance of the pagan works and caused the idea to be born in the latter part of the fourth century of a distinctively Christian education and culture.

The historian Socrates relates how, as a consequence of the edict of Julian, the two Apollinari, father and son, the one a grammarian and the other bishop of Laodicea, composed, the former a grammar "in harmony with the Christian faith," the latter "the gospels and doctrines of the Apostles" in the form of Platonic dialogues. Following their example, the Latin poets produced paraphrases of the Old and New Testament, without, however, equaling the divine lyricism of the symbolic poetry of the Bible.

The works of Iuvencus and the *Heptateucus* of Cyprian show evidence of effort rather than of inspiration. Neither faith nor poetry had anything to gain from these laborious attempts. They are works more of apologetics than of lyricism. Christian poetry affirmed its originality in the liturgical hymn and, in its minor form, in the epitaphs of Damasus. No one is able to challenge the genuine inspiration of Prudentius. His work aspired to blend the two cultures, and in this he almost succeeded.

For the majority of the Latin Fathers, writing was much more an obligation than an entertainment, a mission rather than a literary competition. It was their soul rather than their artistry which was expressed; it was their faith that spoke. Their task was to convince rather than to charm, and their work was an extension of their preaching. It formed part of the mission of the bishop.

It is necessary to realize that this cost Augustine not only the sacrifice of his *otium,* but also the refinement of word and expression and the technical brilliance of the rhetor which carried with it the danger of going over the heads of his people at Hippo. It is true that he made up for this when he spoke at Carthage where he polished his form with careful attention to the refined taste of his audience.

All the Fathers gave evidence of their classical culture and knew how to put it to use. Hilary came to the faith through philosophy. When he had become a Christian, he always used the rhetoric of Quintilian to defend the Christian religion. It was normal for him to make use of his store of secular literature to instruct the people. Ambrose did not write in the same manner in which he spoke, which undoubtedly explains the discrepancy between the *De sacramentis* and the *De mysteriis.* In the *De officiis ministrorum,* the Bishop of Milan, faithful to the tradition of the first Christian centuries, assimilates all that is valid in Stoic morality without sacrificing in any way the originality of Christianity.

The same influence was operative in the Christian literature of the golden age of patristics: in exegesis, theology, art, apologetics and poetry. There was everywhere present a continuity with the ancient civilization which helped to forge Christian culture. Christianity had great vitality and the men of the church possessed a sufficiently clear and robust faith to follow the counsel of Basil: make off with the honey and leave the gall.

Further distinctions are necessary, however. None of the Latin Fathers presents the primal innocence of a Gregory Nazianzus. No evidence remains of a profound conflict in Hilary or in Ambrose. But the same is not true of Jerome and Augustine inasmuch as both betray a difficulty which calls for analysis.

The problem of culture for the Fathers, for Paulinus, Jerome, Augustine, was inextricably linked with their spiritual adventure. The greatest of the Fathers, both Latin and Greek, were converts. For Hilary, Jerome and Augustine conversion signified a choice and a break. They had received from the church the book — the Bible — which transmitted to them the word of God.

Conversion of the spirit and of the heart was also a conversion to the truth, to the cult and culture of the Bible which revealed to them that which neither Vergil nor Cicero had been able to offer them: another dimension, a new vision of the world. Every conversion also signified the discovery of the Bible.

For Hilary, faith arose from the study of the Scripture, which became the book of his life. In the Thebaid, Chromatius introduced the young Jerome to biblical studies. The preaching of Ambrose gave Augustine a taste for the Bible, the point of anchorage for his conversion.

The cultivated Latins, nourished on Cicero and Vergil, at first felt repugnance in the face of the literary poverty and coarseness of style of the Scriptures. This was the experience for Arnobius and Lactantius, for Jerome and Augustine. This effect is rendered more comprehensible by the fact that the Latin versions of the Bible before Jerome, which had originated among the common people, were the work of translators of mediocre ability. A similar repugnance was evidence during the Renaissance at a time when classical culture was again in the ascendant.

The correspondence invented in the fourth century between Seneca and Saint Paul was intended, in its own way, to offer an example and to show that the pagan philosopher had known how to grasp what was essential, questions of form aside. It was a tribute rendered to Christian literature by a representative of pagan culture.

Paulinus made a choice between the Bible and Cicero, and found in the Scripture an indispensable nourishment. Jerome was more stubborn. The Bible did violence to his spirit even though it filled his heart. He was torn between the cultivation of style and the coarse word of the living God. He himself presents the drama that tormented him yet another time, even though he had retired into the desert. A voice demanded of him who he was. He responded that he was a Christian. "No," the voice replied. "You are a Ciceronian." And the incorrigible champion of the *hebraica veritas* remained faithful to the end to the masters of Rome who had formed him. Even Ambrose, especially in his Christian ethics, is an heir of Cicero. For the educated Christian of the age, Christian culture consisted in mastering the Bible in the same way that the man of letters mastered his Homer or his Vergil. Their biblical erudition is one of the more salient traits of nearly all the Latin authors. They knew by heart an innumerable quantity of verses and passages which came spontaneously to mind whether they were speaking or writing.

Through reading and memorizing the sacred texts, the Fathers acquired an extraordinary virtuosity in playing with the citations and threading them like pearls on a necklace to such an extent that certain texts of Jerome, Paulinus and Augustine appear to be a medley of scriptural citations. The integration is so skillfully done that it is almost impossible to recognize the variation from text to citation. At Hippo as at Antioch, the people themselves completed a citation begun by an orator, having been caught up in the act by their very training.

It is thus with good reason that many of the laity began to take an interest in exegesis and theology in the fourth and fifth centuries. It is sufficient to name Lactantius, Firmicus Maternus and Victorinus, as well as Tyconius, Marius Mercator and Prosper of Aquitaine. It was to them as well as to clerics that Augustine addressed his *De doctrina christiana,* in which he unfolded a program which was an expression of his personal experience.

For the Christian, all knowledge and culture rested on the Bible. The Bible formed the proper object of this culture, a concept which would continue into the Middle Ages when Abelard would again present his theological work as an "introduction to the Sacred Scripture."

Augustine, ordained a priest, had in mind a knowledge of the Bible attained by assiduous reading from Genesis to the Apocalypse when he requested some months' time *ad cognoscendas divinas scripturas.* Biblical citations, scarce up until then in his works, began to multiply and to integrate themselves in perfect harmony with the text. The codex Lagarde 34 of the University of Göttingen, as H. J. Vogels had noted, contains 13,276 citations from the Old Testament and 29,450 from the New among the works of Augustine (cf. *Aur. Aug.*, p. 413).

For Hilary of Poitiers, it was the duty of faith to point out God's pedagogy in the story of humanity. Only a long familiarity with the books of both Testaments enabled one to discover the laws of this pedagogy according to which the stages of salvation were organized. God's interventions were revealed in events and in persons.

The Old Testament preserved all of its value and served as a support both for typology and for allegory. The New Testament was studied in relation to the Old. The selection of readings for the liturgy facilitated this parallelism, although this procedure presented the risk of restricting somewhat the laws of progression and of neglecting the phases of development. The Fathers had a feeling for history even though they did not always have an historical sense. That explains their somewhat atemporal perception of the Word of God, which does not always harmonize with the historical perspective. Abraham is not Moses. That which they lost in *lectio humana* they gained in *lectio divina.*

Christ is the keystone of the entire Scripture and the link between the two Testaments. This Christocentrism governs the method of the Fathers: Christ is the hinge of the entire Scripture whose material is arranged in reference to Him. The diverse parts find their cohesion in the unique revelation of the incarnate Word, and thus they come to be somewhat limited with regard to their temporal value. "Read the books of the prophets," says Augustine, "and if you do not find Christ there, there is nothing more insipid and more senseless. If you do find Christ, the word not only becomes savory but it even inebriates" (*In Ioh.* 9, 3). The following expression of Augustine would become famous: *"In vetere novus latet et in novo vetus patet"* (*Quaest. in Hept.* 2, 73).

The universal importance of salvation for Jews and Gentiles is based, for Hilary of Poitiers, on the physical reality of Christ which, on the one hand, excludes any attempt at a Platonic interpretation and, on the other, requires the inclusion of all humanity in the humanity of Christ. It is Christ who makes it possible to go beyond the shell and reach the kernel, to read the Spirit in the letter, where it lies hidden but whence it emerges by faith.

This is particularly true for the Psalter, which Hilary, Ambrose, Augustine and Jerome all commentated. Even Christ made reference to this book while speaking with the disciples of Emmaus. It is the book of his prayer, of his mission and of his oblation, and the People of God are able to find Christ and the church therein.

Typology, which may seem strange to us, was a method common to all the Fathers, Latin and Greek, including Jerome himself. According to H. Smith, it seemed to them to be the only truly scientific method. Numerous studies in recent years have allowed us to better understand it. Nevertheless, typology itself does not explain everything and the history of patristic exegesis remains to be written.

In any case, the Latin and Greek Fathers proceeded by an opposite path from modern scholars. They proceeded from the perception of faith, for which they at times prescinded from the literal and semantic sense and minimized the exegetical endeavor. Scripture for them was not a dead book but a living reality and the testimony of a lived history. The text breathes, according to the expression of Claudel. The work of God, "the living and efficacious word, does not realize its true fulfillment and its full significance except by the transformation which it brings about in him who receives it."

It is necessary, furthermore, to distinguish the position proper to each of the Fathers. Augustine was not Jerome. Even among the Latins there was a tension between exegesis and theology. Jerome, at first an admirer of Origen, had recourse to the original Greek and Hebrew text and was truly a pioneer. It is possible to contrast him with the mysterious author called Ambrosiaster.

Once he had satisfied the exigencies of the literal sense or, as

Augustine called it, the historical sense, the Bishop of Hippo threw himself with all his might into the allegorical or mystical interpretation of the text in which he was unequaled, seeking out a mystery in places where the text was clearly corrupt or poorly translated. The exegesis of the Fathers has its limits and does not correspond to our own criteria. It is necessary, therefore, not to judge the Fathers by certain allegorical extravagances or inconsistent accommodations. That would be to confuse the embellishment with the substance and to throw out the baby with the bathwater. The interpretation of the Latin Fathers, following closely Origen and the Alexandrian school, confesses that the Spirit dwells in the word as in the church. The progress of exegesis brings the cup to our lips, and the faith of the Fathers leads us to know the *sobria ebrietas.*

THE LIFE OF THE CHRISTIAN COMMUNITY

The religious peace allowed the Western church to perfect its organization, to multiply the number of dioceses and parishes, and to expand and build itself up while preserving its unity. "If the faith is one," says a Roman council held under Pope Damasus, "there must exist only one tradition. If the tradition is one, the discipline of the church must be one" (Canon 5).

The Council of Nicea had established that one bishop was to be named for each *civitas.* The dioceses multiplied in Spain and Gaul in the fourth century, and the number of episcopal sees in Gaul doubled, although they did not always coincide with the *civitates.* In Africa at the time of Augustine there were some four hundred sees (the number he gives for the Donatists). They were sufficiently numerous in Gaul at the end of the century to be grouped into ecclesiastical provinces. Hilary of Arles dedicated himself to this development and exercised the role of leader of the Gallic episcopate.

Constantine and Theodosius made efforts to harmonize the structure of the church with that of the state. But unfortunately, the model from which the church might have drawn inspiration was unstable. The *provincia,* which was the most stable structure, when transferred into the ecclesiastical organization formed the territory of a metropolitan see. The presence of the papacy hindered the development of great sees in the West in the manner of the East. Carthage alone formed an exception and enjoyed an undisputed prestige.

It is necessary to take into account the importance which the councils in Africa, Spain and Gaul assumed from the fourth century on. The bishops came together, came to agreement among themselves, enacted legislation and established norms for discipline and liturgical life. Such an organization served as a bulwark for the church in the face of the barbarian invasions and was an essential element of ecclesiastical life in the fourth and fifth century.

The fourth and fifth centuries marked an important date and a progress in the history of the papacy. The Roman See strengthened its authority and superiority in relation to the councils, confirmed its prerogatives in regard to Constantinople and the East and, for a certain time, preserved the unity of the church.

Rome, unrivaled in the West, affirmed its authority in the Donatist and Pelagian disputes and, by multiplying its interventions, strengthened its disciplinary jurisdiction in spite of African resistance. From the fifth century on it took over direction of missionary activity. Celestine I sent Germanus of Auxerre to England to combat Pelagianism, and two years later gave Ireland its first bishop.

The Fathers, who in general were leaders of communities, above all were pastors. As men responsible for a portion of the People of God, they had to keep watch over the faith, discipline, progress and orthodoxy of their churches. This was the essential activity in the lives of men such as Ambrose and Augustine.

The church and the churches are communities of faith founded on the risen Christ — the People of God which offers Him worship in spirit and in truth. The life of the church is organized around the Eucharist. If the church, and above all the bishop, unite together to celebrate the Eucharist, the Eucharist in turn unites the church. "How can we exist," exclaimed the African martyrs, "without coming together for the eucharistic synaxis?" To the *domus ecclesiae* there succeeded the spacious basilicas.

The word "church" (i.e., assembly) came to be used also to indicate the place of meeting. In the West as in the East "vast churches are seen rising from the ground" (Eusebius, HE, VII, 1, 5). The largest church in Africa, Damous el Kerita, at Carthage, measured 65 meters in length. The dimensions of the structures depended on the number of the faithful. The Constantinian churches continued to use the style of the Hellenistic basilica for the needs of the Christian cult. The bishop presided at the throne in the apse, from which he addressed the assembly.

Architecture employed its dimensions, forms and symbolism for baptistries and for the *martyria* which, since they were either built over the tombs or housed the relics of the martyrs, were already attracting crowds. In order to delight the eyes and to educate the faithful, frescoes and mosaics displayed a Bible in images, a catechism in pictures.

The triumph of orthodoxy manifested itself in turn in an iconography which tended to express a theological language. The progress of Christianity was evident in the aesthetic creations and triumphant art which exalted the *Pantocrator*.

At the moment when the West freed itself from Greek tutelage it had to find its own liturgical forms which differed among themselves within the Latin linguistic unity from Africa north to Rome, and from Milan to Gaul. It is difficult to establish in the West classifications similar to those in the East. At most, a distinction can be made between the Roman rite, an expression of the importance of the Apostolic See, and non-Roman rites. Among the latter, some were already established, such as the Gallic and Visigothic, while others were still in an embryonic stage, such as that of Milan and those of the north of Italy.

The fourth and fifth centuries were the golden age not only of patristics but also of the liturgy. The Fathers were the liturgists of their time who enriched the liturgies of the West with their genius. Patristics and liturgy are based on the same texts and the same writers and are complementary disciplines.

Rules and texts replaced the liberty of improvisation and composition with the intent of putting an end to the age of "chatterers and incompetents," according to a saying of Augustine. To the dossier of liturgical books could also be added the biblical manuscripts intended for use in the liturgy and which from this point on contained indices for liturgical use. From the end of the fourth or the beginning of the fifth century there existed in North Africa the *libelli missarum.*

Elsewhere, Gennadius asserts that Voconius of Castellum, Musaeus of Marseilles, Claudianus Mamertus at Vienne, Priscillian and Paulinus of Nola all composed liturgical texts. He also mentions the existence of *libelli missarum, Sacramentorum liber,* homilaries and lectionaries of which we have lost all trace. From all this literature there remains only the Roman Canon of the Mass preserved for us in the *De sacramentis* and the Visigothic *Liber ordinum* in use in Spain from the fifth century.

In the West as well as the East, the fourth and fifth centuries were also the golden age of the baptismal and mystagogical catecheses. Each of the Fathers made his own contribution to this literature; Ambrose, Augustine, Peter Chrysologus and Leo the Great, as well as lesser-known figures such as Chromatius, Zeno, Gaudentius, Nicetas and Maximus of Turin.

Later liturgical collections, the homilaries, have saved or restored a great number of sermons, have enriched the dossier of Augustine and have preserved homilies of unknown authors. It is from these homilaries that there emerged one of the most sensational finds in recent decades: the commentary on Saint Matthew by Chromatius of Aquileia which was broken up in passages of patristic readings in liturgical collections.

Preaching is an integral part of the liturgy and figures among the essential duties of the bishop. Ambrose preached at Milan every

Sunday and feastday and on the days of Lent; and the same took place in Carthage and Hippo. At Rome, on the other hand, it seems that the bishops neglected the ministry of the word to a certain extent. With the exception of Pope Liberius, Leo the Great is the first to furnish us with a *corpus* of sermons for feasts and liturgical seasons.

This homiletic literature is essentially biblical and is tied to the passages selected for the liturgy. The Latin Fathers give the impression of having commented to a lesser extent than the Greek on the Old Testament, except for Genesis and the Psalms. This last book was held in high esteem by all and served as the manual of prayer for the church and the itinerary back to God. Ambrose left sketches of characters from the Old Testament which he delivered as homilies before committing them to writing.

Some 3000 homilies have been preserved from the years 325-451, half of them belonging to John Chrysostum and Augustine. Many Fathers are known to us only through a sermon or through homilies, not to mention those who remain anonymous. This patrimony, mainly African in origin, gathered in collections, embellished and enlarged, enjoyed considerable success thanks to two centers of diffusion: Naples and Arles. Augustine took the lion's share.

This preaching, which began with a passage listened to by the assembly gathered together, was generally improvised and, whether at Milan or Hippo, was taken down by stenographers as it was delivered. It commented on the events of the day and made allusion to pagan feasts, to scandals or the barbarian threat or, at Hippo, to the schismatic Donatist movement.

The rhetorical procedures encountered with the Latins — to a lesser extent than with the Greeks — were part of classical culture. The majority of the Fathers were more concerned with authentic eloquence at the service of the People of God, closer to the common people and their language, than with the refinements of men of letters. But the simplification in form in no way signified a decline in the quality of instruction. Augustine expounded on the generation of the Word and the Trinitarian processions to his people, composed of dock workers, and in the *Enarrationes in Psalmos* and the commentary on Saint John introduced them into the enclosed garden of his spiritual experience.

After the heroic period of the persecutions this preaching was intended to bestir a society which had remained pagan and to lay bare the tacit connivances of the Christians with a past that was not totally laid to rest. Above all, Augustine attacked the spectacles, along with the games of the circus and the theater, "the final liturgy which draws crowds," the violence and immorality of which were a permanent provocation. The African councils prohibited them, but in vain.

The church made efforts to substitute Christian feasts for pagan ones. Sunday, the day of the Resurrection, was already a feastday and day of rest since the time of Constantine. The *sanctum triduum* prepared for the feast of Easter, which was a day of festival and was prolonged for a period of fifteen days during which time the courts were in recess.

A period of forty days served as a preparation for baptism, as a time of reconciliation for brave penitents and as an occasion of spiritual exercises for all. The final three days were the most solemn. In the night between Saturday and Sunday, the entire city was illuminated and candles brightened the streets as the faithful, bearing torches in their hands, went to the liturgical assemblies. The Christians listened with serious attention to the majestic pages of the Bible and the catechumens heard for the final time the great stages of the history of salvation, the history of the People of God which had become their own history. Toward the end of the vigil, the bishop, surrounded by his ministers, preached the homily. How many times did Ambrose and Augustine stir the emotions with one of those discourses which we still have the joy to read! Like John Chrysostom at Antioch, Augustine remembered that Easter night in which he had received the sacrament of new life at Milan.

Easter was truly the feast of the Christian faith. In other instances, the West gave proof of adaptation and flexibility, and rather than fighting against the pagan feasts, sought to Christianize them. Thus it was that the *Natalis solis invicti,* which Rome had borrowed from the East in 274 and which was celebrated with great display throughout the Empire in the fourth century, became for Christians the feast of Christmas. The Fathers delighted in presenting Christ as the true light of the world, the *sol iustitiae.*

Now that peace was established, the Christian people, inclined toward a concrete religion which spoke to the heart, developed the cult of the martyrs, and the clandestine celebrations became solemn public functions which attracted multitudes. Anniversaries, inventions, translations: all were occasions for a festival, for preaching by the pastor — an aspect in which Ambrose and especially Augustine joined — and for a *refrigerium,* a meal with libations and dancing for the people, in such a manner that the atmosphere of the pagan festivals seemed to flourish again. Paganism was the noxious weed which continually cropped up whenever the church relaxed its guard even for a moment.

The cult of the martyrs grew out of the cult of the dead but also out of the memory of Christ the Martyr. Like the pagans, the Christians visited the tombs and partook of a meal there, the *refrigerium,* which all too easily degenerated into pagan superstition. The church, especially at Rome, sought to give it a charitable purpose in the feeding of the poor, and the generosity of Pammachius would become famous in this regard. Ambrose prohibited the *refrigerium* at Milan, which was taken as an affront by Augustine's mother, Monica. Africa remained more tolerant, but, since the abuses were tending to multiply, the church was constrained to prohibit the practice at the synod of Hippo, although Augustine encountered resistance when he attempted to enforce the synodal decision. During the fifth and sixth centuries, councils in Gaul at various times prohibited the meal for the dead, which shows how deeply rooted the custom was in popular practice.

In the fourth century another form of piety developed, often bound to the cult of the martyrs and then to that of the saint — the pilgrimage. In addition to the holy places already mentioned, Rome and the tombs of Peter and Paul attracted pilgrims and, subsequently, crowds. The abundance of relics conferred on it the status of a holy city, and gradually it began to equip itself to receive the pilgrims. Ambrose described the celebration in the *Basilica Apostolorum* constructed over an ancient *memoria* on the Appian Way by Constantine or Constantius: "Crowded masses pass through the streets of so great a city . . . One could believe that the whole world was coming forward."

Rome was not a unique example. Nola attracted those devoted to the martyr Felix. Carthage celebrated with pride the memorial of Saint Cyprian, as Saragossa did that of the deacon, Vincent. Saint Martin who, though not a martyr, was one of the most popular saints in the history of Gaul, was venerated at Tours. The discovery of the remains of the martyrs Gervasius and Protasius at Milan in 385 gave rise to great celebration. Paulinus and Augustine applied their genius to extolling the saints and the martyrs.

The liturgy inspired the composition of hymns, one of the truly original creations of the age. Hilary, fascinated by his experience in the East, composed liturgical poems which made of him "an authentic poet." Ambrose introduced into the liturgy the antiphonal singing of the psalms and of hymns, some of which he composed himself and which enjoyed a rapid diffusion throughout the West. The poetical works of Prudentius of Calahorra entered into use in the assembly and enriched the Latin liturgy.

WESTERN MONASTICISM

Monastic life in the West, less spectacular and more sporadic than in the East, played a predominant role in the religious life of the fourth and fifth centuries and would soon render exceptional services to the cultural life as well. Eastern influence and inspiration were undeniable and even attracted Westerners to Jerusalem and Bethlehem. Nevertheless, in Rome, North Africa, Gaul, Spain and Britain there developed an indigenous style of cenobitic life devoted to prayer, *lectio divina,* work and ascesis.

The first monks to be seen in the West were the companions of Saint Athanasius during his exile. According to Jerome, their presence at Rome was the starting point "of those numerous monasteries of virgins and innumerable throng of monks" which were to be seen in the *Urbs* and its surroundings (*Ep.* 127, 8). The monastery of Saint Agnes traced its origins back to perhaps the middle of the fourth century. Sixtus III founded a community of men at San Sebastiano, *ad catacumbas.*

At Milan, at the city gates, there was a convent of men directed by Ambrose himself. At the same period, Chromatius was the director of a community at Aquileia, and there was a monastery of nuns at Bologna and another at Verona.

Monasteries multiplied in North Africa during the course of the fourth century and became a training ground of bishops. Augustine, for his part, established a community of clerics who lived a life of poverty together. His directives for them are found in the sermons 355 and 356 and in the *De opere monachorum.* The African monasteries served as places of refuge during the Vandal invasions.

In Gaul in the fourth century, the ascetics at first pursued perfection while living in the world, without fixed rules. Each one went on his way toward God according to his own temperament and in an isolated manner. There were ascetics of both sexes, virgins, and widows, principally at Rouen and Tours. They practiced a regimen of moderate solitude with a diet adapted to the climate. The accent was placed on prayer more than on work and on apostolic activity more than on service to the community and the sick. Saint Martin was the model of this type of monasticism. John Cassian, the last of the Latin Fathers to be at ease with Greek language and culture, because of his origin, his formation, and his prolonged sojourns at Jerusalem and among the Desert Fathers in Egypt, served as a link between East and West and brought to Gaul the benefits of the experience of Eastern monasticism.

In the fifth century, Marseilles and Lérins were centers of monastic life and served as seminaries of great bishops. Honoratus, Vincent, Eucherius and Hilary were neither ignorant or nor did they fight against the classical culture which had formed them, but rather they maintained and developed it. They undoubtedly had a rich library at their disposal and their influence radiated throughout Provence and through the whole of Gaul.

Monastic life was known in the Iberian Peninsula already in the fourth century, as is witnessed by the Council of Saragossa (380) and a letter of Pope Siricius to Hymerius. At more or less the same period, Bachiarius became the forerunner of the itinerant monks.

While the rich aspired to a sober and plain life, the poor endeavored to escape from the fiscal and economic *munera,* for which reasons both were accused of being deserters. In order for slaves to become monks, it was necessary to obtain the permission of their masters. It happened, nevertheless, that fugitive slaves and *originarii* (tenant farmers) were received in the monasteries and became monks.

It is difficult to underestimate the importance and the position of virgins and of widows (who refused a second marriage in order to consecrate themselves to the spiritual life) who lived a life of seclusion. All the Fathers took an interest in them and writings, letters, and tracts intended for them occupy an important place in the literature of the period. Ambrose was their undisputed teacher. To him is attributed a letter *ad virginem lapsam* which is almost certainly a work of Nicetas (PLS III, 199).

Some rich or well-to-do Christians such as Ausonius, Paulinus and Prudentius, while not embracing such radical forms of ascetic life, led a life of semi-seclusion on their estates. This *otium rusticum,* similar to traditional values, adapted itself to a comfortable life without great renunciation. Paulinus subsequently disposed of his property in Aquitaine. What remained allowed him to support his servants and disciples at Nola, construct a sumptuous basilica and provide generous alms until the end of his life.

The church of the Late Empire intensified and extended the work of evangelization. The progress was apparent in two areas: deeper penetration among the elite and missionary activity in rural areas. The senatorial nobility and those people bound to the land had offered the most enduring resistance to the Gospel.

The Roman aristocracy had remained a bulwark of tradition and of paganism. The conversion of men such as Marius Victorinus from the intellectual sphere and Ambrose and his family from among the Roman patricians gave evidence of a change which the austere Jerome then fostered among the aristocracy. Prudentius, supplying the names of the Roman families who had become Christians, wrote, "Look at the assembly of the venerable Catos taking the white garments of the catechumens and putting aside the insignia of the pontificate." There was a rhetorical flourish in this Christian poet, at least inasmuch as Rome was concerned. The movement of conversion in the aristocratic society centered around Saint Martin became more pronounced in Gaul during the course of the fourth century. It is sufficient to call to mind Paulinus from Aquitaine, Eucherius, and Honoratus and Salvian of Marseilles.

For a long time, Christianity in the West appeared as an urban religion. There had been little contact with rural areas, grouped together in *vici* and *villae,* until the fourth century. The inhabitants of the countryside, however, were little inclined to change their customs and ceremonies. Some movements of resistance were able to be mingled with the activities of the socially discontent, especially in Africa. The relations between masters, who also were Christians, and their dependents rarely had a spiritual character.

From the fourth century on, a missionary effort began to take shape. Regional centers for the evangelization of the countryside were established by Ambrose around Milan and by Augustine in the environs of Hippo. The Bishop of Hippo soon realized that these activities demanded priests who could speak Punic. Saint Martin was the first missionary in the countryside of Gaul, and Gregory of Tours mentions five parishes which he established. Through Paulinus of Nola we know the names of a certain number of parishes in rural Gaul at that time when *diocesis* and *parrochia* were still synonymous. At the same time, a like effort was being developed in Italy and in North Africa.

A missionary task which imposed itself in the course of the fifth century was the evangelization of the Goths and the barbarians. A certain Theophilus, bishop of *Gothia,* took part in the Council of Nicea. Christianity had penetrated that region through the efforts of prisoners taken in Cappadocia in the third century. Wulfila was a descendent of these on his mother's side. Under pressure from the Emperor Constantius, these Goths passed over to Arianism, and the emigration of this barbarian world caused the Arian flood of the Danubian provinces to pour out over the West. Through the Visigoths, Arianism passed over to the Ostrogoths, the Gepidae and the Vandals, then to the Rugi, Alamanni and Lombards. Disconcerted at first in the face of this invasion, the church outlined a timid counteroffensive.

Orosius saw a promise of evangelization in the barbarian invasions and Severinus began a mission in Noricum and Dacia. The efforts of John Chrysostom, of Theotimus of Tomi, of Nicetas of Remesiana and of their unknown emulators "have not proved useless among the invaders of the Danubian provinces." Nevertheless, this effort was paralyzed by the antibarbarian animosity of the last Romans and of all of *Romania.* It was necessary to await the sixth century to see a coordinated movement for leading the Goths back to Catholic unity.

From within, the church was menaced by schism and heresy. The West knew neither the theological ferment nor the great Trinitarian and Christological controversies of the East. Even Arianism, which allowed Hilary to display his genius, remained a foreign product. The difficulties which Ambrose experienced with the Arians at Milan were more of a political than of a doctrinal nature. Priscillian, a Spanish ascetic, gave the name to the first Western controversy, which was localized in Spain.

The name of Augustine has remained bound to the great doctrinal conflicts of the West: Donatism and Pelagianism. While the former was a specifically African affair, this was not the case with the latter. It is symptomatic that the question of liberty and of grace and not the Trinitarian mystery (as in the East) would be at the heart of the first great theological debate in the West. Although limited to the Latin world, Pelagianism struck deep roots at the beginning of the fifth century. The Bishop of Hippo encountered adversaries far more fearful than Faustus of Milevi or Cresconius. Pelagius and Julian, consummate dialecticians, caused him no end of trouble and forced him to give greater precision to his thought and nuance to his arguments. Augustine emerged from these polemics as the great doctor of grace.

The controversy was not limited to a discussion among clerics. As had happened in the East, laymen among the Latins also became impassioned over the arguments. Marius Mercator, Prosper of Aquitaine, Hilary of Marseilles and the count, Valerian, from the court at Ravenna discussed the question and carried on an exchange of letters with Augustine.

At the same time, this first specifically Latin controversy testified to the autonomy which the West was beginning to exercise in relation to the East, as a result of which it began to develop its own particular theology which henceforth would dominate and obsess the Latin mind.

Theology must not, however, be restricted to controversy. That is only one side of the coin. For the Fathers, theology was usually expressed in exegesis. *Theologia* — as Thomassin would say in regards to the Fathers — *hoc est Scripturarum meditatio.* Revelation was the proper object of theology. To engage oneself with theology meant to apply oneself to listening to the Word of God, received in the faith of the church and lived in communion with her. Saint Augustine said, *"Intellige ut credas verbum meum, crede ut intelligas Verbum Dei"* (*Serm.* 43; PL 38, 358). A more concise definition of the science and wisdom which constitute the mission of the theologian does not exist.

The times of crisis gave rise to polemical works. "Wretched heretics," cried Saint Hilary, "who oblige us to lay hands on the Ark of the Covenant." Once the storm had passed, it was possible to work out conclusions in peace and there began to be elaborated such monumental works as the two treatises *De Trinitate* and *De civitate Dei.* In the moment the Fathers withdrew from the controversy to work out a theology — a new and exceptional event — their construction consisted of a full utilization of the Bible.

History shows that polemical works age rapidly and in a lamentable fashion both with regard to their argumentation and at times with regard to their importance. It is sufficient to consider the manuscript tradition to realize this: 6 manuscripts of the *Contra Adimantum* in comparison with 233 of the *De Trinitate,* 368 of the *Enarrationes* and 394 of the *De civitate Dei.* When the heart thrills, the pen flies.

In the course of its history, the church has without fail returned to the Fathers because of their existential significance. In them, theology, rather than being reduced to a *disputatio,* is a living reality, an existential acquisition. The understanding of the faith responds to the universal problem of man, who is therein engaged in his totality. Augustine opposed Pelagius in the name of his spiritual experience. His theology of grace was the story of his life.

Endeavor and effort reach their full development only in the wisdom which has God as its beginning and its object and which is the expression of experience: *orando, et quaerendo et bene vivendo,* as Augustine says. It is significant, though in no way surprising, that the commentaries on the Psalms of Hilary, Ambrose, Jerome and Augustine reveal traces of their steps on the way toward God; while the treatises of the *De Trinitate* of Hilary and of Augustine finish with a contemplative prayer.

SUMMARY BIBLIOGRAPHY

For a general bibliography, see the works of H. Jedin, F. Lot, R. Remondon and S. D'Elia listed below.

For the East, cf. J. Quasten, *Patrology.* vol. III. Utrecht, 1960.

H. Jedin, ed., *Handbuch der Kirchengeschichte.* Vol. I: K. Baus, *Von der Urgemeinde zur frühchristlichen Grosskirche.* Freiburg im Br., 1972; Vol. II: K. Baus, et al., *Die Reichskirche nach Konstantin dem Grossen.* Freiburg im Br., 1975. (Eng. transl. Vol. I: *From the Apostolic Community to Constantine.* London - New York, 1980; Vol. II: *The Imperial Church from Constantine to the Early Middle Ages.* London - New York, 1980).

A. Fliche and V. Martin, *Histoire de l'église* I - IV. Paris, 1935-38 (Eng. transl. *A History of the Catholic Church,* 2 vols. London - St. Louis, 1956[2]).

J. Daniélou and H. Marrou, *Des origines à Grégoire le Grand.* vol. I of *Nouvelle Histoire de l'Eglise.* Paris, 1963 (Eng. transl. *The First Six Hundred Years.* London - New York, 1964).

O. Seek, *Geschichte des Untergangs der antiken Welt.* 6 vols. Berlin, 1895-1921; reprint 1966 (remains a classic).

I. Seipel, *Die wirtschaftethischen Lehren der Kirchenväter.* Vienna, 1907 (dated).

R. Thouvenot, *Salvien et la ruine de l'Empire romain: MAH* 38 (1920) 145-163.

F. Lot, *La fin du monde antique et les débuts du Moyen Age.* Paris, 1927, 1968[3] (biased; broad select bibliography care of M. Rouche).

H. Delahaye, *Les origines du culte des martyrs.* Brussels, 1933[2].

A. Solari, *La crisi dell' impero romano.* 5 vols. Milan, 1933-1937.

E. Peterson, *Der Monotheismus als politisches Problem.* Leipzig, 1935.

M. Viller - K. Rahner, *Askese und Mystik.* Freiburg, 1939.

H. Berkhof, *Kirche und Kaiser.* Zürich, 1947.
R. Latouche, *Les grandes invasions et la crise de l'Occident au Ve siècle.* Paris, 1946.
A. Piganiol, *L'Empire chrétien* (325-395). Paris, 1947, 1972² (contains often peremptory personal judgments).
K. Farner, *Christentum und Eigentum.* Bern, 1947 (radical critique).
G. Bardy, *La question des langues dans l'Eglise ancienne.* Paris, 1948.
P. Courcelle, *Les lettres grecques en Occident.* Paris, 1948.
P. Courcelle, *Histoire littéraire des grandes invasions germaniques.* Paris, 1948, 1964² (noteworthy contribution).
K. F. Stroheker, *Der senatorische Adel im spätantiken Gallien.* Tübingen, 1948 (bibliography of important personages).
B. Kötting, *Peregrinatio religiosa.* Münster, 1950.
S. Mazzarino, *Aspetti sociali del quarto secolo.* Rome, 1951 (stimulating).
W. Ensslin, *Die Religionspolitik des Kaisers Theodosius der Grosse.* Southern Bavaria, 1953.
B. Biondi, *Il diritto romano cristiano.* 3 vols. Milan, 1952-1954.
Ch. Courtois, *Les Vandals et l'Afrique.* Paris, 1955.
H. A. Wolfson, *The Philosophy of the Church Fathers.* Cambridge (Mass.), 1956, 1976² (biased).
O. Chadwick, *Western Asceticism.* London, 1958.
J. Gaudemet, *L'Eglise dans l'Empire romain.* Paris, 1958.
Ch. Mohrmann, *Etudes sur le latin des chrétiens.* 4 vols. (*Storia e letteratura* 65, 87, 103, 143) Rome, 1958-1965, 1977.
E. Stein, *Geschichte des spätrömischen Reiches* I. Vienna, 1928 (French transl. *Histoire du Bas-Empire.* 2 vols. Paris and Brugges, 1949; reprint Amsterdam, 1968).
H. Hagendahl, *Latin Fathers and the Classics.* Göteborg, 1958 (primarily studies Jerome).
S. Mazzarino, *La fine del mondo antico.* Milan, 1959 (transl. German, Munich 1961; English, London 1966; French, Paris 1973).
G. Ladner, *The Idea of Reform: Its Impact on Christian Thought and Action in the Age of the Fathers.* New York, 1959, 1967².
E. Auerback, *Lingua letteraria e pubblico nella tarda antichità latina e nel Medioevo.* Milan, 1960.
A. G. Martimort, *L'Eglise en prière. Introduction à la liturgie.* Paris, 1961 (Italian transl. Rome, 1963).
Théologie de la vie monastique. Etudes sur la tradition patristique. Paris, 1961.
G. Barbero, *Il pensiero politico cristiano dai Vangeli a Pelagio.* Turin, 1962.
Il passagio dall'antichità al Medioevo in Occidente. Spoleto, 1962.
A. Momigliano, *The Conflict between Paganism and Christianity in the Fourth Century.* London, 1963 (Italian transl. Turin, 1968; collection of articles).
H. J. Diesner, *Untergang der römischen Herrschaft in Nordafrika.* Weimar, 1964.
A. H. M. Jones, *The Later Roman Empire* (284-602). 3 vols. plus maps. Oxford, 1964 (primarily concerned with economic questions).
P. R. Coleman-Norton, *Roman State and Christian Church.* 3 vols. London, 1966 (collection of texts).
A. Grabar, *Le premier art chrétien.* Paris, 1966.
S. D'Elia, *Il Basso Impero nella cultura moderna.* Naples, 1967.
F. Paschoud, *Roma Aeterna. Etude sur le patriotisme romain dans l'Occident latin à l'époque des grandes invasions.* Neuchâtel, 1967.
A. Hamman, *Vie liturgique et vie sociale.* Paris, 1968 (Italian transl. Milan, 1973; social implications of the liturgy).
R. Remondon, *La crise de l'empire romain, de Marc-Aurèle à Anastase.* Paris, 1970² (Italian transl. Milan, 1975; schematic presentation with current bibliography).
La storiographia altomedievale. Spoleto, 1970.
A. H. M. Jones - J. R. Martindale - J. Morris, *The Prosopography of the Later Roman Empire.* vol. I A.D. 260-395, vol. II A.D. 395-527. Cambridge, 1971, 1980.

P. Brown, *Religion and Society in the Fourth Century.* London, 1972. (Italian transl. Milan, 1976).
S. D'Elia, *Introduzione alla civiltà del Basso Impero.* Naples, 1972.
S. Mazzarino, *Antico, Tardo Antico ed età constantiniana,* 2 vols. Bari, 1974, 1980 (important collection of articles).
G. Colombas, *El monacato primitivo.* Madrid, 1974 (Italian transl. *Il monachesimo delle origini.* Milan, 1984).
J. Holland Smith, *The Death of Classical Paganism.* London and Dublin, 1975.
Ch. Pietri, *Roma Christiana,* 2 vols. Rome, 1976.

CHAPTER II

HILARY OF POITIERS AND THE ARIAN CRISIS IN THE WEST

Polemicists and Heretics

by Manlio Simonetti
Bibliography by Sever Voicu and Angelo di Berardino

Hilary of Poitiers and the Arian Crisis in the West

INTRODUCTION

Only after the death of Constantine (337) did the West begin to concern itself seriously with the Arian crisis. The division of the Empire between Constans (West) and Constantius (East) assured Julius, bishop of Rome, and the Western bishops of sufficient security and freedom of movement to take up the cause of the Eastern defenders of the Nicene creed who were variously persecuted and harassed by their adversaries under the leadership of Eusebius of Nicomedia, the protector of Arius, who was openly favored by the Emperor Constantius.

In order to understand the situation in the East, there must be taken into account the reaction of a vast part of the Eastern episcopate against the profession of faith defined at Nicea in 325 which, while anti-Arian in its inspiration, was formulated in such a way as to present traces of Monarchian elements. It thus left dissatisfied and perplexed many spokesmen of the Eastern episcopate who, though certainly not Arian, were even less inclined toward Monarchian positions. Eusebius of Caesarea and Eusebius of Nicomedia had taken advantage of these sentiments to set in motion a campaign intended to isolate and leave in straits the more active Eastern supporters of the Nicene faith and to create a vast swell of opinion, a right and proper anti-Nicene front. This front united elements of widely disparate doctrinal tendencies, from moderate Arians to orthodox believers of the Alexandrian tradition who considered the Nicene formula to be too open to the danger of Monarchianism. The principal supporters of the Nicene formula, including Eustathius of Antioch, Asclepas of Gaza, Marcellus of Ancyra and Athanasius of Alexandria, having been accused on various charges, were deposed and sent into exile. Although they were authorized to return to their sees after the death of Constantine, they were immediately constrained to flee again and a good number of them, among whom were Athanasius and Marcellus, sought refuge at Rome.

Under the leadership of Julius of Rome, the West immediately took the side of these exiles, considering their adversaries to be pure and simple Arians. The Westerners were moved to take such a position both because of the active presence of the exiles, who presented the complicated terms of the Eastern disagreements on the basis of too simplistic an identification between anti-Nicenes and true and proper Arians, as well as because of the far lower sensitivity in the West to Monarchian doctrines, as a result of which the Monarchian positions of someone like Marcellus did not arouse that scandal which instead they provoked in the East. The strife soon escalated in a series of encounters until at Serdica (343) it culminated in the failure of the ecumenical council convoked by the emperors and the splitting of Christianity into two mutually hostile branches. The accord concluded in 346, by which Athanasius was authorized to return to Alexandria, left the terms of the conflict unresolved on both the political and the doctrinal plane.

After the violent death of Constans (350), when Constantius took charge also of the West after a difficult war and became sole emperor, the religious situation changed profoundly. The emperor acted swiftly to also reunite in the religious sphere the two parts of the empire which were already united politically, and in this action he obviously favored the anti-Nicenes who were dominant in the East. The Western episcopate was initially subjected to various pressures, culminating in the Councils of Arles (353) and Milan (355) in order that they might adhere to the condemnation imposed by the already remote Council of Tyre (355) against Athanasius. While the Bishop of Alexandria was once again expelled from his see and found refuge among the monks of the Egyptian desert, the Western bishops, with a few exceptions, submitted and signed the condemnation. The few recalcitrant bishops were deposed and exiled in the East (Eusebius of Vercelli, Lucifer of Cagliari, Hilary of Poitiers and a few others). Thereupon, a small council of notably philo-Arian bishops meeting at Sirmium in 357, although they did not repeat the Arian doctrine in its radical form, published a profession of faith distinctly anti-Nicene in tone (prohibition of the use of the term *homoousios* = consubstantial, the distinctive term of the Nicene creed) and very much open to moderate Arian positions. The publication of the formula provoked reactions in the West as well as in the East. In the East, an ample concentration of bishops, mainly Asiatic, who were hostile to Arianism as well as to the Nicene faith, gave rise to a reaction intended to impose the formula according to which the Son was not *homoousios* but *homoiousios* with respect to the Father; that is, not of the same substance (an expression which in a Monarchian sense was able to identify the Son with the Father in the mode of one single person), but of like substance. The anti-Arian opposition in the East aligned itself along this formula for years.

There followed an agitated succession of actions and reactions. At first, Basil of Ancyra, leader of the homoiousians (as the partisans of the *homoiousios* were called in the West) obtained the support of Constantius and caused his own ideas to prevail at the Council of Sirmium in 358. His adversaries, however, reorganized immediately and proposed the formula according to which the Son was defined as generically like to the Father according to the Scriptures (*homoios,* on account of which the supporters of this formula were called homoeans). This wording, as defined in the compromise formula of Sirmium signed on May 22, 359, was made to prevail at the Council of Rimini in 359 and was confirmed by the Council of Constantinople in 360. The majority of the 400 Western bishops assembled at Rimini were distinctly anti-Arian, but the minority of Arian sympathizers, strengthened by the open support of Constantius, succeeded in imposing the will of the emperor.

The death of Constantius (361) and the accession to power of Julian the Apostate, who was studiously neutral with regard to the conflict, allowed the anti-Arian majority, homoousian in the West and homoiousian in the East, to reorganize. In the East, the strife continued and became further complicated for doctrinal and personal reasons. The confused situation which resulted permitted the moderate Arian minority to come to the fore, especially with the support of the emperor Valens (364-378), at the expense both of the radical Arians, again active in these years, as well as of the anti-Arian majority, who had witnessed the difficult rapprochement of the homoiousians and the homoousians. However, with the advent of Theodosius (379), a zealous supporter of the Nicene faith, the fortunes of both the moderate and the radical Arians declined rapidly. Their final defeat was ratified at the Council of Constantinople in 381, which also marked the triumph of the doctrinal position of the Cappadocians (Basil of Caesarea, Gregory Nazianzus and Gregory of Nyssa).

In the West, on the other hand, the much more united homoousian majority rapidly imposed itself under the leadership first of Hilary, then of Ambrose, and with the diligent efforts of the Roman bishops, Liberius and Damasus. Arianism remained alive in a few isolated sees, among which was Milan, and above all in Illyria and Pannonia, where it had achieved a position of a certain importance. Here, a few small communities put up a tenacious resistance, directly and indirectly aided by the large number of auxiliaries in the army of Gothic extraction, who had become Christians of the Arian faith as a result of the missionary activity of the Arian Goth, Wulfilas. These Arian groups in the West assured the heresy of a continuity until the moment in which the great invasions of the Germanic tribes, who in large part had become Arian Christians, reestablished Arianism on a far different basis in many regions of the West.

It was in this context that there arose the collection of anti-Arian and Arian literature. In general, it is sufficient to note here that it was only after 350, at the time when Constantius sought to impose a form of disguised Arianism also in the West that the theological terms of the controversy seriously began to develop with greater depth, especially in Gaul and Spain. Between 356 and 360, there developed an authentic flowering of doctrinal literature with the great figures of Hilary and Marius Victorinus, who were in turn surrounded by lesser but by no means irrelevant personages such as Phebadius of Agen, Potamius of Lisbon and Gregory of Elvira. Ambrose began his activity around 380, and Faustinus must also be mentioned. A flowering of Arian literature took place at a still later date on the part of authors of uncertain origin, who, Latin or Goth, were undoubtedly under the direct or indirect influence of Wulfilas.

HILARY

All that we know of Hilary, bishop of Poitiers, is connected with the Arian controversy and is drawn for the most part from his own works. It was from these sources, including writings of Hilary no longer extant, that Jerome derived the information supplied in *De vir. inl.* 100. It is only by way of conjecture that his birth is dated around the beginning of the fourth century and his election as bishop of Poitiers around 350. From hints given in his works, especially in the prologue to the *De Trinitate,* it has been inferred that Hilary came from a pagan family and was converted to Christianity because he was disgusted both by the prospect of a life dedicated to pleasures and by the contradictions of the philosophers, and because he had been enlightened through contact with the Sacred Scriptures. However, these are *loci communes* and thus possess no precise autobiographical value.

Hilary is encountered for the first time at the council which met in 356 at Béziers, shortly after the Council of Milan in 355 which had witnessed the Western bishops submit to the condemnation of Athanasius under pressure from Constantius and the leaders of Arianism in the West. Hilary had broken off communion with such leaders, among whom in Gaul was the influential Saturninus of Arles. On account of this, he was indicted at Béziers together with Rodanius of Toulouse and, because he persisted in his anti-Arian attitude, was deposed and exiled to Phrygia. The years of exile in the East represented a decisive moment for Hilary's cultural and doctrinal formation. It was here, in fact, that he came into contact with the works of the Greek Christian writers, especially those of Origen, which influenced him profoundly, eliminating the materialistic remnants deriving from the influence of Tertullian and converting him to Platonic spiritualism. As regards his theological formation, Hilary, by his own admission, hardly possessed a profound comprehension of the complex terms of the Arian controversy before he departed for exile. In Phrygia, however, he came into contact with the homoiousians who were largely predominant in Asia Minor. Thanks to these contacts, he developed substantially his understanding of the Arian controversy and, in particular, became convinced of two things: 1) that a correct formulation of the problem in an orthodox sense required that one keep one's distance not only from Arianism but also from the opposing danger represented by Sabellian Monarchianism, toward which danger the West was scarcely sensitive; 2) that the Nicene theology, based on the *homoousion,* did not represent the sole valid alternative which the orthodox could oppose to the Arians, given the suspicion of Sabellianism which surrounded that term in the East, but that in the same sense the homoiousian solution also appeared on the whole to be acceptable. These fundamental principles, practically brand new for Westerners, governed the works Hilary wrote during his exile, the *De Trinitate* and the *De synodis.*

Hilary took part in the Council of Seleucia among the ranks of the homoiousians (September 359). His presence there is surprising inasmuch as he had been deposed and exiled. According to Sulpicius Severus (*Chron.* II 42), the officials in charge of summoning the bishops of Asia, in the absence of any specific provision regarding Hilary, allowed him to reenter into the general convocation. In any case, we know for certain — the fact is corroborated by other sources — that Hilary enjoyed a freedom of movement during his exile which was otherwise denied to other Westerners who found themselves in the same situation, such as Eusebius of Vercelli and Lucifer of Cagliari. When the council ended, representatives of the homoiousians and the Arians went to Constantius at Constantinople to present to him the results. Hilary also went to Constantinople, and it was here toward the end of the year that he received the news that the Western bishops meeting at Rimini had given in to imperial pressure and had signed the so-called Creed of Rimini, which could only be described as philo-Arian. Shaken by such unexpected and catastrophic news, Hilary presented Constantius with a request for permission to hold a public debate with Saturninus of Arles, who had himself arrived in the capital from Rimini. It does not appear that his request was granted. Instead, he was soon authorized to return home without having been asked to subscribe to the philo-Arian profession of faith. Sulpicius Severus explains the measure (*Chron.* II 45) by noting that Hilary was considered to be a disseminator of discord and a mischief-maker in the East, and he points out that Hilary's return home did not imply a reinstatement in his episcopal see.

When Hilary returned to Gaul, that region had passed under the control of Julian, whose neutrality with regard to the Arian controversy favored the recovery of the anti-Arians, who were the decisive majority in that area. Hilary received a triumphant welcome and was the moving spirit of the council which met at Paris in 351, where he caused a moderate attitude to prevail with regard to both doctrine and discipline. A dogmatic position was proposed which was compatible with both the homoousian and the homoiousian formulation, and it was decided to condemn only the leaders of the Arian party in the West, and to reserve indulgence and understanding for the many bishops who at Rimini and elsewhere had yielded to heresy only under coercion. Thus Gaul was quickly freed from the remnants of Arianism and bishops of other regions were given an example of equilibrium and moderation which was rapidly taken up on all sides.

Hilary appears again at Milan in 364, involved together with Eusebius of Vercelli in an attempt to dislodge from that see the Arian bishop, Auxentius, who had been in residence since 355. The attempt failed, and Hilary was forced to return to his own country. Nothing more is heard of him. Jerome gives 367 as the date of his death (*Chron.* s.a.).

Hilary carried on his literary activity not only in the doctrinal field in support of his political actions, but also in the area of exegesis. Nor did he scorn poetry. A good part of his literary composition has come down to us.

Editions: CPL 427-472. — PL 9-10; PLS 1, 241-286. — A. Zingerle, CSEL 22 (1891). — A. L. Feder, CSEL 65 (1916).

Studies of language and style: M. F. Buttell, The Rhetoric of St. Hilary of Poitiers (PSt 38). Washington, 1933. — M. V. Brown, The Syntax of the Prepositions in the Works of Saint Hilary (PSt 41). Washington, 1934. — R. Kinnavey, The Vocabulary of St. Hilary of Poitiers (PSt 47). Washington, 1935. — M. E. Mann, The Clausulae of St. Hilary of Poitiers (PSt 48). Washington, 1936. — T. Gimborn, The Syntax of the Simple Cases in St. Hilary of Poitiers (PSt 54). Washington, 1939. — R. B. Sherlock, The Syntax of the Nominal Forms of the Verb, exclusive of the Participle, in St. Hilary (PSt 76). Washington, 1947.

Studies: Ch. Kannengiesser: DSp 7(1969)466-499 (494ff bibliography). — A. L. Feder, Studien zu Hilarius von Poitiers I-III. Vienna, 1910-12. — R. Favre, La communication des idiomes d'après Saint Hilaire de Poitiers: Greg 18(1937)318-336. — J. E. Emmenegger, The Functions of Faith and Reason in the Theology of Saint Hilary of Poitiers. Washington, 1947. — G. Giamberardini, De incarnatione Verbi secundum S. Hilarium Pictaviensem. Piacenza, 1948; *idem,* S. Ilario de Poitiers e la sua attività apostolica e letteraria. Cairo, 1956. — L. Malunowicz, De voce "sacramenti" apud S.

Hilarium Pictaviensem. Lublin, 1956. — M. Meslin, Hilaire de Poitiers. Paris, 1959. — I. F. McHugh, The Exaltation of Christ in the Arian Controversy. The Teaching of St. Hilary. Shrewsbury, 1959. — P. Galtier, La *Forma Dei* et la *Forma servi* selon saint Hilaire de Poitiers: RSR 48(1960)101-118; *idem,* Saint Hilaire de Poitiers, le premier docteur de l'église latine. Paris, 1960. — E. Boularand, La conversion de saint Hilaire de Poitiers: BLE 62(1961)81-104. — A. Fierro, Sobre la gloria en San Hilario. Una síntesis doctrinal sobre la noción biblica de "doxa." Rome, 1964. — J. Doignon, Une compilation de textes d'Hilaire de Poitiers présentée par le pape Célestin Ier à un concile romain en 430: Oikumene. Catania, 1964, 477-497. — A. Charlier, L'Église corps du Christ chez saint Hilaire de Poitiers: ETL 41(1965)451-477. — A. Martínez Sierra, La prueba escriturística de los arrianos según S. Hilario de Poitiers. Santander, 1965. — M. J. Rondeau, Remarques sur l'anthropologie de saint Hilaire: SP 6(TU81) (1962)197-210. — C. F. A. Borchardt, Hilary of Poitiers' Role in the Arian Struggle. The Hague, 1966. — G. Blasich, La risurrezione dei corpi nell'opera esegetica di S. Ilario di Poitiers: DTP 69(1966)72-90. — R. L. Foley, The Ecclesiology of Hilary of Poitiers: Diss., Harvard 1968 (cf. HThR 61[1968]639). — E. Goffinet, Lucrèce et les conceptions cosmologiques de saint Hilaire de Poitiers: Antidorum W. Peremans, Louvain 1968, 61-67. — Hilaire de Poitiers. Évêque et docteur. Cinq conférences données à l'occasion du XVIe centenaire de sa mort. Paris 1968, 61-68. — A. D. Jacobs, Hilary of Poitiers and the Homoeousians. A Study of the Eastern Roots of his Ecumenical Trinitarism: Diss., Emory Univ. 1968. — Ch. Kannengiesser, L'héritage d'Hilaire de Poitiers, I. Dans l'ancienne Église d'Occident et dans les bibliothèques médiévales: RSR 56(1968)435-456; *idem,* Hilarie et son temps. Actes du Colloque de Poitiers. Paris, 1969. — Y. M. Duval, Vrais et faux problèmes concernant le retour e'exil d'Hilaire de Poitiers et son action en Italie en 360-363: *Athenaeum* 48(1970)251-275. — J. Doignon, Hilaire de Poitiers avant l'exil. Paris, 1971. — A. Peñamaría de Llano, Fides en Hilario de Poitiers: *Miscelánea Comillas* 29(1971)5-102; *idem,* La salvación por la fe en Hilario de Poitiers. Palencia, 1972-73. — J. M. McDermott, Hilary of Poitiers: the Infinite Nature of God: VC 27(1973)172-202. — I. Opelt, Hilarius von Poitiers als Polemiker: VC 27(1973)203-217. — A. Peñamaría de Llano, Libertad, mérito y gracia en la soteriología de Hilario de Poitiers. Precursor de Pelagio o Agustín: REAug 20(1974)234-250. — J. W. Jacobs, The Western Roots of the Christology of St. Hilary of Poitiers: A Heritage of Textual Interpretation: SP 13 (TU116) (1975)198-203. — A. Peñamaría de Llano, Hilario de Poitiers: una fe episcopal en el siglo IV: EE 51(1976)223-240. — L. Cignelli, L'esegesi di Giovanni 14, 28 nella Gallia del secolo IV: Studii biblici Franciscani liber annuus 24(1974)329-358. — J. Doignon, Ordre du monde, connaissance de Dieu et ignorance de soi chez Hilaire de Poitiers: RSPT 60(1976)565-578; *idem,* Christ ou oint? Un voacable biblique appliqué par Hilaire de Poitiers à l'évêque Rhodanius de Toulouse: RHE 72(1977)317-326; *idem,* Une addition ephémère au texte de l'Oraison dominicale chez plusiers Pères latins: BLE 78(1977)161-180. — B. de Gaffier, Saint Hilaire, patron du royaume des Francs: AB 95(1977)24. — G. Pelland, Le thème biblique du règne chez saint Hilaire de Poitiers: Greg 60(1979)639-674. — M. Pellegrino, Martiti e martirio nel pensiero di S. Hilario de Poitiers: SSR 4(1980)45-58. — A. Peñamaría de Llano, La salvación por la fe. La noción fides en Hilario de Poitiers. Burgos, 1981.

DOCTRINAL WORKS

1. *De Trinitate*

Hilary's chief doctrinal work is the *De Trinitate,* in twelve books. We do not know if this title, which is attested only from the time of Casiodorus (*Inst.* I 16) and Venantius Fortunatus (*Vita Hil.* 14) and only in the more recent manuscripts, is the original one. Jerome (*De *vir. inl.* 100) gives it the title *Adversus Arianos libri* and others know it as *De fide*. The most ancient manuscripts transmit it without a title. The work was written during the years of exile, as can be ascertained from a precise allusion in X 4. Because of the breadth of the work and in light of Hilary's intense activity in the East, some consider the work to have been begun in the West before his exile. However, at the very beginning Hilary clarifies his position as being equidistant from the opposed heresies of Arianism and Sabellianism, and such a clarification could not have been suggested to him by any Western source, but could have come only from his contact with the homoiousians during his enforced sojourn in Phrygia. That the work was terminated before his return to Gaul can be ascertained from the final chapters (55-56) of book XII, which form a type of appendix added to that book with no connection to the preceding material and which have as their object the refutation of errors concerning the Holy Spirit. In this sense, these chapters bear witness to the first skirmishes in the controversy concerning the Holy Spirit which arose in the East precisely around 360. Only in the East could Hilary have had any knowledge of this new question of which the West would take cognizance only after a delay of many years.

Book I is exclusively introductory in character. After a prologue in which the author treats in a general way of the incomprehensibility of the divine nature and makes mention of his own *itinerarium ad Deum,* there follows an ordered and detailed summary of the work, book by book. The actual treatise itself, comprising books II-XII, is divided into three parts. The first part, which includes books II-III, presents a general exposition of the matter which was at that time the object of the controversy, namely the question of the relation between the Father and the Son and of the divine nature of the Son. In book II, Hilary defines the Catholic position in respect to the various heresies and affirms the reality and eternity of the divine generation of the Son, with a certain overture of a specifically Trinitarian character, i.e., also including the Holy Spirit. Book III, then, is dedicated particularly to the refutation of the arguments advanced by the Arians regarding the inferior status of the Son in relation to the Father, and closes with a lengthy peroration on the insufficiency and presumption of human wisdom.

The second part includes the books IV-VII, and its connection with the first part of the work is merely external and superficial. With the affirmations of the Arians having been presented, Hilary relates in a Latin translation the entire text of the profession of faith which Arius in his day had sent to Alexander of Alexandria, and which represented a fundamental document of the Arians. He then begins a refutation of the text, beginning with its first sentence. The refutation of the second sentence starts only at the beginning of book V. In reality, however, Hilary is only making use of the external prop of the Arian text in order to unfold an ample argumentation of his own, developed in four points. In the first point (book IV), Hilary demonstrates with abundant illustrations drawn chiefly from Genesis (theophanies) and the Prophets that the Old Testament already knew of the presence of the Son as God alongside the Father. In the second point (book V), having examined the same Old Testament passages from a somewhat different angle, Hilary shows that the Son is not only God, but true God as is the Father, although He does not constitute a second God. The third point (book VI, from ch. 23 on) presents the same question, examined this time with the guide of New Testament passages, and concludes that Christ in in truth the Son of God. Finally, in the fourth point (book VII), Hilary concludes the demonstration by affirming, always with the guide of passages from the New Testament, that Christ is true God like the Father, together with whom He constitutes one only God.

Within this well-articulated complex, chapters 1-23 of book VI represent a type of *excursus*. Hilary relates for a second time the entire text sent by Arius to Alexander and follows it with a concise and complete refutation. Hilary does not mention the motives which induced him to repeat the text of Arius for a second time, and thus to introduce a considerable element of disorder and disturbance into the ordered structure of books IV-VII.

The third part of the *De Trinitate* comprises the remaining books VIII-XII. The argument is put forward at the beginning of book VIII: having declared in books IV-VII *quae pia sunt,* i.e., the Catholic teaching, Hilary intends to refute *quae impia sunt,* i.e., the chief arguments put forward by the Arians. Thus, book VIII, by taking up again the material treated at the end of book VII, namely the unity of the Father and the Son, refutes by means of this argument the Arian doctrine which considered that union to be merely a moral one. Books IX, X and XI are dedicated to the systematic refutation of the arguments proposed by the Arians to demonstrate the inferiority of the Son with respect to the Father. In book IX, Hilary discusses some Gospel passages in which Christ speaks — or seems to speak — of himself as inferior to the Father and explains them in view of the *oeconomia* of the Incarnation. Book X treats of the passion and death of Christ, which the Arians presented as proof of the imperfect character of his divinity. Hilary, however, explains them by distinguishing the impassible divinity from the assumed humanity. Analogously, book XI explains the *subiectio* of the Risen Christ to the Father (1 Cor. 15:26). Finally, book XII is dedicated to the interpretation of Prov. 8:22, a key passage for Arian doctrine, whose explanation is inserted by Hilary into long reflections on time and eternity. This book concludes with the appendix formed by chapters 55-56 on the Holy Spirit, as mentioned above.

From this summary exposition, it is clear that the structure of the *De Trinitate* presents more than one problem. To this must be added the fact that the closing of book III has the aspect of concluding an entire work rather than just a single book. Above all, it is noteworthy that at books V 3 and VI 4 authoritative manuscripts make reference to books IV and V respectively as though they were books I and II. From this we effectively conclude that books II and III of the *De Trinitate* were composed by Hilary during the first period of his exile in the East as an independent work in themselves, and that the actual books IV and V were written as the beginning of a new and different work. On a subsequent occasion, Hilary fused the two works. Since he makes a precise allusion in book IX 10 to an argument expounded in book I, we are able to conclude that this fusion took place at some unidentifiable moment between the composition of book VI and of book X. With the work completed in a uniform fashion, Hilary furnished the ample summary forming the final part of book I, which he then added to the original prologue (I 1-19).

To compose his vast work, Hilary made use of various sources. Novatian is present in many of the arguments advanced in books IV and V on the Old Testament theophanies, as well as elsewhere. It is also clear that Hilary was well acquainted with the *Adversus Praxean* of Tertullian. The influence which the homoiousians exercised on Hilary has already been mentioned above. It is visible not only in the anti-Sabellian concern which pervades the work from start to finish, but also in various individual arguments which find their exact match in the surviving documents of the homoiousian party, such as the evident tendency to avoid the use of images, even traditional ones, in speaking of the divinity. It must be noted, however, that Hilary exercised considerable liberty in his use of sources. Some of them, Novatian for example, have often been radically reworked. As far as the homoiousians are concerned, Hilary, deeply rooted in the theological patrimony of the West, stored up their suggestions with the purpose of elaborating a complete doctrine of the relation of Father and Son which would be much more balanced and articulate than was theirs. On the other hand, it does not appear that Hilary made direct use of Athanasius, from whose conception of the Trinity he is considerably removed. For its genius and completeness, as well as for the simple material dimensions of the work, the *De Trinitate* represents a new element in Latin theological literature. It consequently exercised a strong influence on anti-Arian writers both of the contemporary and immediately succeeding generation as well as on posterity, as is witnessed by the great number of manuscripts which have transmitted the work.

Editions: PL 10, 9-472. — P. Smulders, CCL 62, 62A (1979, 1980).

Translations: English: W. Sanday, LNPF, 2d series, IX (1898, reprint 1973). — S. McKenna, FC 25(1954). *French:* A. Blaise, De Trinitate et ouvrages exégétiques. Namur, 1964 (selections). — A. Martin, La Trinité, 3 vols. Paris, 1981. *German:* A. Antweiler, Zwölf Bücher über die Dreieinigkeit. Munich, 1933-34. *Italian:* G. Tezzo, La Trinità. Turin, 1971.

Studies: A. Beck, Die Trinitätslehre des Heiligen Hilarius von Poitiers. Mainz, 1903. — P. Smulders, La doctrine trinitaire de s. Hilaire de Poitiers. Rome, 1944; *idem,* Remarks on the Manuscript Tradition of the *De Trinitate* of Saint Hilary of Poitiers: SP 3 (TU 78) (1961)129-138. — L. J. Daly, A Fourth-century Textbook on the Trinity: AER 142(1960)10-21. — J. Doignon, Lactance contre Salluste dans le prologue du De Trinitate de Saint Hilaire?: RELA 38(1960)116-121. — P. Löffler, Die Trinitätslehre des Bischofs Hilarius zwischen Ost und West: Diss., Bonn, 1958. — M. Simonetti, Ilario e Novaziano: Studi . . . A. Schiaffini (= RCCM 7, 1965)1034-47; idem, Note sulla struttura e la cronologia del *De Trinitate* di Ilario di Poitiers: Studi Urbinati 39(1965)274-300. — J. Moingt, La théologie trinitaire de Saint Hilaire: Hilaire et son temps. Paris, 1969, 159-173. — P. Smulders, Eusèbe d'Émèse comme source du De Trinitate d'Hilaire de Poitiers: ibid., 175-212. — W. G. Rusch, Some Observations on Hilary of Poitiers' Christological Language in the *De Trinitate:* SP 12 (TU 115) (1975)261-264.

2. *De synodis*

During the early months of 359, when preparations were well advanced for the coming Councils of Rimini and Seleucia, on whose outcome the various parties in the dispute placed a value of decisive importance, Hilary, although he was already engaged in the composition of the *De Trinitate,* wrote the *De synodis.* He had by that time come to the conviction that the attitude of the Westerners, who without a doubt regarded as Arians all the Easterners who did not accept the Nicene *homoousion,* was too simplistic and scarcely suited for inspiring a truly efficacious anti-Arian policy. His contact with the homoiousians had shown him that many of the Eastern bishops were at the same time anti-Arian and anti-Nicene, inasmuch as they saw in the *homoousion* the danger of Sabellianism. To be sure, the difference between the affirmation that Christ is of the same substance of the Father *(homoousios)* and the assertion that he is like to the Father in substance *(homiousios)* did not escape Hilary. Beyond these divergences, however, he also perceived fundamental convergences between the two groups in rejecting the fundamental Arian propositions. Furthermore, Hilary was convinced that only an agreement between the anti-Arians in the East and West would be able to bring the struggle against the Arians to a favorable conclusion. Thus, with the idea of contributing to the rapprochement of the two parties in light of the coming councils, Hilary wrote the *De synodis,* addressing it to the bishops of Gaul and neighboring regions, but directing it in the final part especially to the bishops of the East.

The work is divided into two parts. In the first part (ch. 1-65), Hilary takes the Creed of Sirmium of 357 as his starting point and examines the various formulations of faith published by the Easterners between 341 and 357, which the Westerners considered as a whole to be declarations of Arian faith. As such, however, Hilary rejects only the most extreme, the *blasphemia Sirmiensis* of 357. To the others he gives a quite favorable interpretation and, by exploiting their deliberate vagueness on crucial points of the controversy and their oft-confirmed condemnation of the propositions of radical Arianism, seeks to show their orthodoxy also in relation to the theological premises dominant in the West. In the second part (ch. 66-92) he compares the *homoousios* and the *homoiousios* and interprets the concept *like in substance* as equivalent to *equal in substance*. He was well aware of the criticisms directed against both terms by the various parties. Nevertheless, he skillfully shows how either the one or the other is able to be interpreted respectively in an orthodox and in a heterodox fashion so that in the end, the one term is equivalent to the other, provided they are correctly interpreted. It did not make sense for there to be a separation based only on the distinction between the two words.

It is too easy to point out the arbitrary decisions and forced meanings especially in the first part of Hilary's work, where he seeks to align the Trinitarian formulation underlying the various Eastern formulae, centered above all on the distinction of the divine hypostases (= persons), with the formulation dominant in the West, intended especially to emphasize the unity of the divine substance. It must be kept in mind, however, that the *De synodis* was written to foster the union of the anti-Arians of East and West at a point beyond the differences which divided them. Thus it is more than understandable that Hilary emphasized everything which could bring the two sides together and sought to minimize the points of disagreement. The *De synodis,* a work of rare intelligence and penetration, reveals for the first time in a Western theologian a full awareness of the complex religious reality of the East. It was an example destined to remain unique. A work of such a nature was not able to succeed in pleasing the extremists, especially in the West, among whom was Lucifer of Cagliari, who did not hesitate to criticize the work of his colleague. As it has come down to us, the *De synodis* is accompanied by a brief appendix in which Hilary defends himself precisely against the accusations of Lucifer. Writing by this time after the unfortunate epilogue of the Council of Rimini, he makes some concession to his interrogator and admits to having defended the *homoiousion* above all for tactical reasons. Still, he continues to propose his own solution in which *homoiousion* equals *homoousion.*

Editions: PL 10, 471-546.

Translations: English: W. Sunday, LNPF 2d series IX (1898, reprint 1973)4-29.

Studies: P. Courcelle, Fragments non identifiés de Fleury-sur-Loire: RELA 32(1954)92-97 (including fragments of the *De synodis*). — P. Galtier, Saint Hilaire trait d'union entre l'Occident et l'Orient: Greg 40(1959)609-623.

HISTORICAL WORKS

1. *Liber ad Constantium*

Under the name *Liber* I *ad Constantium* there has been designated for a long time a complex of two writings which in all probability belong to the collection known as *Fragmenta historica* (see below). The first text is a letter sent by the Western bishops meeting at the Council of Serdica (343) to the Emperor Constantius, requesting him to put an end to the persecutions directed against the supporters of the creed of Nicea. The second part of the *liber* is a narrative text of Hilary's in which he records the irregular procedure by which the Council of Milan (355) proceeded against Athanasius and Eusebius of Vercelli. Hilary wrote this text in 356, immediately after the occurrence of these events and before he went into exile.

2. *Liber* II *ad Constantium*
3. *Liber contra Constantium*

The so-called *Liber* II *ad Constantium* dates to the year 359. Hilary, who had gone to Constantinople after the Council of Seleucia, addresses a petition to Constantius, asking him to authorize a debate between Hilary and Saturninus of Arles, who had been responsible for Hilary's unjust condemnation at Béziers and who was himself in the capital at that time. The request is accompanied by an invitation to not follow the new definition of faith published at Rimini but instead to return to the baptismal faith which was consecrated by the Council of Nicea.

Obviously, Hilary's petition brought no result. Completely convinced by then of the *fides ariana* of the emperor and embittered by the events of Rimini (359) and Constantinople (360), Hilary wrote down clearly and in a detailed manner exactly what he thought of Constantius in a book entitled *Liber contra Constantium.* In terms of the most violent invective, the emperor is compared with the most nefarious of the persecutors, Nero, Decius and Maximian. Indeed, he is worse, because unlike they, who were openly hostile, he rather is treacherous and outwardly gentle with the intent of enslaving rather than openly punishing. The usual accusations against the Arians are documented with important details relative to the Council of Seleucia in which Hilary took part. Jerome (*De vir. inl.* 100) says that Hilary wrote the pamphlet after the death of Constantius. It is clear from the text itself, however, that the author was still in exile when he was writing. Since Hilary returned to Gaul while Constantius was still alive, it is possible that the diffusion of the work only took place in a subsequent period. Nevertheless, the possibility cannot be excluded that Hilary made the work known while still in the East. In relation to such a possibility the parallel episode presented by the pamphlet of Lucifer against Constantius can be considered.

4. *Contra Auxentium*

The *Contra Auxentium* comes from the year 364. Hilary wrote it after his fruitless attempt together with Eusebius of Vercelli to expel from the important episcopal see of Milan the Arian, Auxentius, who had occupied that see since 355. The brief document, which is addressed in the style of a circular letter to Catholic bishops and their faithful, recalls rapidly the events at Milan, where a group of some ten bishops had met and had presented the emperor with an accusation against Auxentius. The latter, in the presence of the magistrate, had proposed a declaration of faith which was substantially Catholic, and had signed it. But then, in a separate instance, he had written to the Emperor Valentinian and had presented his own version of the facts along with a new profession of faith which repeated the formula of Rimini. Since the emperor had established a policy of neutrality with regard to the religious controversies, he did not recognize in the charges brought against Auxentius a valid motive for intervention and thus he had the Catholic bishops leave Milan. Hilary dwells precisely on the duplicity of Auxentius and to this end adduces copies of the letter of Auxentius to Valentinian.

5. *Fragmenta historica*

In 1598, on the basis of a Parisian manuscript, N. LeFevre published two series of documents dealing with the Arian controversy in the West which were completed at several points with more or less ample reflections in the nature of a commentary. He did not preserve the order of the two series intact, and further alterations in the order of the documents were introduced by P. Coustant, who made a new edition of this material in 1693 (= PL 9) and published it under the title of *Fragmenta* belonging to a historical work of Hilary on the Council of Rimini. From that time on, the work was normally referred to as the *Fragmenta historica*. All of the material was reexamined at the beginning of this century by A. L. Feder, who subsequently published a new edition on the basis of more manuscripts. He considered it opportune to return to an arrangement of the documents which was closer to the manuscript tradition (and thus different from that of Coustant) and preferred to give the work the innocuous title of *Collectanea antiariana Parisina*.

Hilary's authorship of the entire collection, attested for the second series by the manuscript tradition, has never been seriously questioned, although the fact must not be overlooked that extraneous documents easily find their way into a collection of this nature. As to the origin of the collection, there are two possibilities: either it is material collected and partially commented by Hilary in view of a work which was never written, or it is a collection of documents extracted from a larger work of Hilary's. After having reexamined and completed various hypotheses, especially of Wilmart, Feder was decisively inclined toward the second of the two possible solutions.

Feder distinguished three sections within the material. The first comprises, in addition to the preface, various documents relating to the Council of Serdica (343) and the years immediately following accompanied by an ample commentary from Hilary (*frag.* B I-II; A IV). This section, which also includes the so-called *Liber I ad Constantium* (see above), was prepared by Hilary in 356 in the interval between the Council of Béziers and his departure for exile. The second section includes documents and related observations in the form of a commentary connected with the Countil of Rimini, to which are added various letters of Pope Liberius (*frag.* B III, VII, VIII; A VI, VII, VIII, IX). The third section is composed of letters and documents subsequent to 359, some regarding the decisions to be made in the case of bishops who had signed the formula of Rimini, others regarding conflicts between Germinius, Valens and Ursacius (*frag.* B IV, V, VI; A I, II, III). By comparing this material with the *liber adversum Valentem et Ursacium, historiam Ariminensis et Seleuciensis synodi continens,* which Jerome mentions (*De vir. inl.* 100), Feder has advanced the hypothesis that Hilary on various occasions wrote three books against the two Arian bishops, from which the respective documents of the first, second and third sections were extracted by an unknown figure active, with anti-Arian intentions, before 403. The *Chronicon* of Sulpicius Severus composed around this date in fact makes use of this collection.

The reconstruction of Feder has found broad acceptance among scholars up to the present day, even if there is some hesitation with regard to certain points. Above all, it must be kept in mind that not all of the material which has been passed down to us could have been collected by Hilary. The *frag.* A II, a letter of Eusebius of Vercelli to Gregory of Elvira, is with all probability a falsification of the Luciferians (cf. Infra. Eusebius; Lucifer and the Luciferians). The documents relating to Germinius, Valens and Ursacius (*frag.* A III; B V, VI), are from the final months of 366, and it is difficult to believe that Hilary, if he died in 367, could have known of them, given the distance between Gaul and Illyria. However the matter stands, the extremely great importance of this collection for an acquaintance with the Arian controversy must be emphasized. Through it, we have the knowledge of precious documents otherwise unknown, such as those relating to Germinius and his companions, or the letters in which the exiled Liberius agrees to sign the condemnation of Athanasius, whose authenticity, long contested, is now no longer doubted by anyone. In a more general way, the *Fragmenta historica* are for us the fundamental documentation for the knowledge of the Arian controversy in the West between 343 and 366.

Editions: PL 10, 553-572 (Liber II ad Const.), 571-606 (Liber I ad Const.), 606-618 (C. Aux.), 627-724 (Frag. hist.); cf. PLS I, 281-285. — A. L. Feder, CSEL 65(1916)195-205 (Liber II ad Const.), 39-193 (Frag. hist.).

Studies: A. Wilmart, L'Ad Constantium liber primus de saint Hilaire de Poitiers et les fragments historiques: RB 24(1907)149-179, 291-317. — A. Feder, Studien zu Hilarius von Poitiers. Die sogenannten Fragmenta Historica und der sogenannte Liber I ad Constantium: SAW 162, 4, Vienna, 1910. — Y. M. Duval, Une traduction latine inédite du Symbole de Nicée et une condamnation d'Arius à Rimini. Nouveau fragment historique d'Hilaire ou pièces des actes du Concile?: RB 82(1972)7-25. — J. Doignon, L'Elogium d'Athanase dans les fragments de l'*Opus historicum* d'Hilaire de Poitiers antérieurs à l'exil: Politique et théologie chez Athanase d'Alexandrie. Paris, 1974, 337-348. — H. Crouzel, Un "resistant" toulousain à la politique proarienne di l'empereur Constance II: l'évêque Rhodanius: BLE 77(1976)173-190. — R. Klein, Constantius II und die christlich Kirche. Darmstadt, 1977. — W. Tietze, Lucifer von Calaris und die Kirchenpolitik des Constantius II. Zum Konflikt zwischen Kaiser Constantius II und der nikäisch-orthodoxen Opposition: Diss., Tübingen, 1976. — P. Smulders, Two Passages of Hilary's *Apologetica responsa* rediscovered: *Bijdragen Tijdschr. v. Filos.* 39(1978)234-243.

EXEGETICAL WORKS

We possess three works from Hilary of an exegetical nature: the *Commentary on Matthew*, the *Commentary on the Psalms* and the treatise *De mysteriis*. Because of the archaic nature of certain of the principles and the traces of materialism in its anthropology, the *Commentary on Matthew* betrays that it was certainly composed before Hilary's exile (356). The other two works, however, which show profound traces of contact with Origen, especially the *Commentary on the Psalms,* were composed after his return from exile. It is not possible to be more precise.

Studies: M. Simonetti, L'esegesi ilariana di Col. I:15a: VetChr 2(1965)165-182. — G. T. Armstrong, The Genesis Theophanies of Hilary of Poitiers: SP 10 (TU 107) (1970)203-207. — Ch. Kannengiesser, L'exégèse d'Hilaire: Hilaire et son temps. Paris, 1969, 127-142. — A. Peñamaría de Llamo, Exégesis alegórica y significado de fides en san Hilario de Poitiers: *Miscelánea Comillas* 30(1972)65-91. — J. Doignon, Les implications théologiques d'une variante du texte latin de I Corinthiens 15:25 chez Hilaire de Poitiers: Aug 19(1979)245-257.

1. *Commentary on Matthew*

The *Commentary on Matthew* is a rather brief work in which the principal events reported in the Gospel of Matthew are recounted, sometimes with brief comments, sometimes with a more prolix commentary. Like the two other exegetical works of Hilary, this one appears to be an *opus continuum,* which was conceived by its author as a unit and which does not show any evidence of having been derived directly from a collection of homilies. Since Hilary, inasmuch as he was a bishop, was certainly engaged in preaching, it is possible to presume a connection between this preaching and his exegetical works. Nevertheless, even if Hilary did take his point of departure from his preaching, he has radically reworked the material in a manner quite different from the superficial revision which Ambrose gave to his homilies for the purpose of publication.

Hilary prefers a type of interpretation which goes beyond the literal sense to perceive a more profound meaning by way of allegory: *typica ratio, interior significantia,* etc. The two senses are superimposed one on the other on the basis of a relationship of similarity in such a way that the literal significance, without being forced, draws attention to the spiritual significance, which in its turn imposes itself on the literal without doing it violence. Even though there is no lack of instances of a mere literal interpretation of the text (the tribute to Caesar, a good part of the Passion, etc.), Hilary's commentary is inspired above all by the need to draw out precisely the spiritual significance of the Gospel. To this end, he makes use of generally conventional procedures, such as assigning an allegorical significance to numbers and animals, but without insisting, in the Alexandrian fashion, on the etymology of Hebrew names. Among the symbols of a more conventional type can be mentioned the boat, always a symbol of the church (8, 1; 13, 1), and the desert, which symbolizes the lack of divine grace (2, 2; 11, 4).

But beyond these typical procedures, Hilary tends to gather together the spiritual significance of the Gospel of Matthew in a rather more organic and homogenous manner and interprets the deeds and words of the life of Jesus in the light of the consequences which derive from them. He thus perceives in them the prefiguration of the hostility of the Jews toward the church, the abolition of the old economy and the preaching of the Gospel to the pagans. Although these motives are indeed already present in the Gospel, Hilary systematically gives prominence to them even when the Gospel text contains something quite different: e.g., the hostility of the Jews toward Christ and the church is symbolized by Herod, who orders the murder of the Innocents (1, 6), while the lamp under the bushel (Mt. 5:15) prefigures the exclusivism of the Synagogue (4, 13) and the episode of the mother and *fratres* of Jesus (Mt. 12:46ff) represents the inability of the people to draw near to Christ (12, 24). On the contrary, the episodes of the healing of some sick person are readily interpreted as prefigurations of the call of the gentiles: the *puer* of the *tribunus* (7, 3-4 about Mt. 8:5ff), the paralytic (8, 5 about Mt. 9:2) and the daughter of the Canaanite woman (15, 12 about Mt. 15:22ff).

Editions: PL 9, 917-1076 (ed. Coustant and Maffei). — A. L. Feder, CSEL 65(1916)232 (fragments). — J. Doignon, SCh 254, 258 (1978-79).

Studies: M. Simonetti, Note sul commento a Matteo di Ilario di Poitiers: VetChr 1(1964)35-64. — W. Wille, Studien zum Matthäuskommentar des Hilarius von Poitiers. Hamburg, 1968. — J. Doignon, L'argumentation d'Hilaire de Poitiers dans l'exemplum de la tentation de Jésus (In Matthaeum 3, 1-5): VC 29(1975)296-308; *idem,* Citations singulières et leçons rares du texte latin de l'Évangile de Matthieu dans l'"In Matthaeum" d'Hilaire de Poitiers: BLE 76(1975)187-196. — P. C. Burns, The Christology of Hilary of Poitiers' Commentary on Matthew (*Stud. Ephem. Augustinianum* 16). Rome, 1981. — J. Driscoll, The Transfiguration in Hilary of Poitiers' Commentary on Matthew: Aug 29(1984)395-420.

2. *Commentary on the Psalms*

Jerome, in *De vir. inl.* 100, writes that Hilary *scripsit et in Psalmos Commentarios, primum videlicet et secundum, et a LI usque ad LXII et a CXVIII usque ad extremum, in quo opere imitatus est Origenem, nonnulla etiam de suo addidit.* The work which has come down to us is even more ample than Jerome states and includes the commentary also to Psalms 9, 13, 14, 63 to 69, and 91. Internal references indicate that the work was originally even more extensive. The great extension of the work evidently did not favor its preservation intact, but rather fostered the division into various parts.

As far as the derivation of the *Commentary on the Psalms* from Origen is concerned, an assessment based on a systematic comparison of the two works is not possible since Origen's work exists only in fragments which are at times of dubious authenticity. It is possible to make only a partial comparison involving above all the prologue and the commentary on the first two psalms since a fairly good amount of Origen's work containing this section has survived. The comparison confirms the statement of Jerome. Hilary has taken over much from Origen, showing at times a literal dependence but more often showing a dependency with regard to the meaning: Scriptural citations, paraphrases, choice of images, and examples and objections brought forth for the purpose of a complete catechesis. From Origen, Hilary has derived all the arguments of a general and introductory nature expounded in the prologue: the Old Testament canon, the explanation of the formula *in finem,* the division of the psalms into five books, the determination of the author of the psalm on the basis of the name in the *inscriptio* and the attribution to the same author of the anonymous psalms immediately following, and the notice according to which Esdras was the first to collect the psalms into one book. The hermeneutical principles are obviously derived from Origen: the obscurity of the sacred text which is removed by recourse to allegorical interpretation, thus allowing the psalms to be interpreted as prefigurations of Christ's life on earth from birth to resurrection to exaltation. From Origen, too, comes the image which concludes the prologue: the Book of Psalms is similar to a great and beautiful city in which there are many houses. Each house is opened with a different key and all the keys are piled up and mixed together. With greater or lesser effort according to the capacity of the individual interpreter, it is necessary to seek the key which fits each individual house, i.e., the fundamental theme, differing from psalm to psalm, which permits the proper interpretation of each one.

Jerome says that Hilary added something of his own to that which he derived from Origen. Many of these original contributions are easily identified, such as the discussions on the Latin translation of the texts of the psalms or the statements of a Trinitarian character which show signs of the results of the Arian controversy. For reasons mentioned above, however, it is impossible to come to a comprehensive evaluation. The general impression which arises from a continuous reading of the entire work is that of finding oneself in a typically Origenist atmosphere, which is a good indication that on the whole Hilary followed his model closely.

Editions: Cf. CPL 438. — PL 9, 221-908; PLS I, 241-246. — A. Zingerle, CSEL 22(1891). — A. Wilmart, Le dernier Tractatus de S. Hilaire sur les psaumes: RB 43(1931)277-283.

Translations: English: W. Sunday, LNPF 2d series IX (1898, reprint 1973)236-248 (only psalms 1, 54 and 130).

Studies: A. Casamassa, Appunti per lo studio del Tractatus super psalmos di S. Ilario: Miscell. Miller, Rome 1951, 231-238. — A. Gariglio, Il commento al psalmo 118 in S. Ambrogio e S. Ilario: Atti Acc. Sc. Torino 91(1956-57)356-370. — E. Goffinet, Kritisch-filologisch element in de Psalmencommentaar van de H. Hilarius van Poitiers: RBPh 38(1960)30-44; *idem,* L'utilisation d'Origène dans le commentaire des Psaumes de saint Hilaire de Poitiers. Louvain, 1965. — N. J. Gastaldi, Hilario de Poitiers, exegeta del Salterio. Un estudio de su exégesis en los comentarios sobre los salmos. Paris, 1969. — F. X. Murphy, An Approach to the Moral Theology of St. Hilary of Poitiers: SP 8 (TU 93) (1966)436-441. — G. Lutz, Das Psalmenverständnis des Hilarius von Poitiers. Diss., Trier, 1969. — L. F. Ladaria, Juan 7, 38 en Hilario de Poitiers. Un análisis de Tr. Ps. 64, 13-16: EE 52(1977)123-128.

3. *De mysteriis*

The *De mysteriis,* included in the list of works given by Jerome in *De vir. inl.* 100, was published only in 1887 by G. B. Gamurrini who discovered the work in a manuscript from Arezzo. In the prologue, which is partially mutilated, Hilary states that all of Scripture declares the Incarnation of Christ whether in deeds or in words. Such a hermeneutical criterion must be directed to the interpretation of the Old Testament. Christ is prefigured in the sleep of Adam, the flood of Noah, the blessing of Melchizedek, the justification of Abraham, the birth of Isaac and the servitude of Jacob. The events recounted are real ones, but God works through man so that the human actions are imitations of the divine plan, in the sense that those events were especially willed by God to prefigure and symbolize the future reality of the Incarnation (ch. 32).

There follow some Old Testament episodes with the relevant Christological interpretations, selected on the basis of this hermeneutical criterion: Adam and Eve symbolize Christ and the church, Cain and Abel symbolize the passion of Christ and so on up to Joshua, who is a figure of Christ as Rahab is a figure of the church. A good part of these typologies displayed by Hilary in the *De mysteriis* are highly traditional ones, but there is no lack of apparently original traits, such as the interpretation of Eve as a prefiguration of the resurrection of the flesh, thanks to the connection between the bone of Adam from which Eve is fashioned and the field of bones in Ezech. 37:4 (ch. 5). The procedure which draws the allegory from a connection between the scriptural passage under examination and another one which it superficially resembles on the basis of some detail (in this case the bones) is typically Origenist. The influence of Origen is also apparent in other hermeneutical procedures, such as that which bases the allegorical interpretation on the etymology of Hebrew names.

Editions: CPL 427. — PLS I, 246-270. — A. L. Feder, CSEL 65(1916)1-38. — J. P. Brisson, SCh 19bis(1967[2]).

Translations: French: Brisson, op. cit.

Studies: P. J. G. Gussen, Hilaire de Poitiers, Tractatus Mysteriorum I, 15-19: VC 10(1956)14-24. — K. Gamber, Der Liber mysteriorum des Hilarius von Poitiers: SP 5 (TU 80)(1962)40-49. — M. G. Bonanno Degani, A proposito di un passo di S. Ilario (Tract. myst. I, 5 = p. 84, 4 Brisson): RSLR 1(1965)258-259.

HYMNS

Hilary is the first Western writer whose activity as a writer of hymns is certified. Jerome (*De vir. inl.* 100) attributed a *liber hymnorum* to him and the Fourth Council of Toledo approved the singing of hymns of the same type as those of Hilary and Ambrose. From the *liber,* three hymns, largely incomplete, have come down to us, transmitted by the Arezzo codex containing the *De mysteriis.* The first, *Ante saecula qui manes,* is an alphabetical hymn of which the first nineteen stanzas have survived in a tetrameter of two lines in glyconic verse alternating with two in a minor asclepiadean with various prosodic and metrical liberties. The content of the hymn develops Trinitarian themes, especially that of the relation of Christ to the Father. The second hymn is also alphabetical in stanzas of two iambic senary with a certain prosodic liberty. Since the first stanzas are missing, the hymn begins for us with the letter "F": *Fefellit saevam.* A female entity is speaking, most probably the soul born into the Christian life by baptism, who exalts the victory of Christ over death and expresses the hope of being able to rise to eternal life. The third hymn, *Adae carnis,* which is not alphabetical, is composed of tristichs of trochaic septenary, these also showing some prosodic license. The first ten stanzas are extant (the tenth is mutilated). The hymn is about the temptations of Jesus, which the tenth verse begins to discuss after the poet describes the demon's dominion over the world.

An entirely different manuscript tradition attributes to Hilary the *Hymnum dicat,* a long hymn of trochaic septenary arranged in distichs, which sings of the redemptive work of Christ, especially the passion. Different opinions have been advanced concerning the probability of Hilary's authorship, which seems to be excluded by well-founded considerations regarding the style and meter.

Even Hilary's writing of hymns is to be inserted into the context of the Arian controversy, for it was during his exile in the East that Hilary became acquainted with the hymns which the heretics and the orthodox circulated to publicize their own propositions and combat those of their adversaries. Once back in the West, where only hymns of Scriptural derivation were in use, Hilary thought to use such a means of propaganda himself. Thus the decidedly doctrinal tone of the three surviving hymns, especially of the first, is not accidental. The form is extremely developed even to the point of intricacy and obscurity, in deference to the particular tendencies of the pagan poetry of the period; a characteristic which is all the more evident by contrast with the studied simplicity of the Ambrosian hymns. It is not surprising, therefore, that Hilary's initiative did not enjoy a particularly happy conclusion. Jerome in fact notes (PL 26, 380) that *Hilarius in hymnorum carmine Gallos indociles vocat.*

Editions: PLS I, 271-281. — A. L. Feder, CSEL 65(1916)207-223. — V. Buzna, De hymnis sancti Hilarii episcopi Pictaviensis. Coloczae, 1911. — N. Myers, The Hymns of Saint Hilary of Poitiers in the Codex Aretinus. Philadelphia, 1928. — A. S. Walpole, Early Latin Hymns. Cambridge, 1922 (reprint: Hildesheim, 1966)5-15.

Translations: English: Myers, op. cit.

Studies: M. Pellegrino, La poesía de Sant' Ilario de Poitiers: VC 1(1947)201-226. — M. Simonetti, Studi sull'innologia popolare cristiana dei primi secoli: Mem. Accad. Lincei, Atti cl. sc. mor. st. fil. s. 8, 4(1952)341-485. — J. W. Halporn, Metrical Problems in the First Arezzo Hymn of Hilary of Poitiers: *Traditio* 19(1963)460-466. — G. del Ton, Sanctus Hilarius primus ex Latinis christianis scriptoribus hymnographus: *Latinitas*

16(1968)86-95. — M. J. Rondeau, L'arrière-plan scripturaire d'Hilaire, Hymne II, 13-14: RSR 57(1969)438-450. — K. Smolak, Unentdeckte Lukrezspuren: WSt n.s. 7(1973)216-239. — J. Fontaine, L'apport de la tradition poétique romaine à la formation de l'hymnodie latine chrétienne: RELA 52(1974)318-355.

LOST WORKS AND *SPURIA*

Two of Hilary's works mentioned by Jerome (*De vir. inl.* 100) have been lost: the *Liber ad praefectum Sallustium sive contra Dioscorum* and an exegetical work derived from Origen's commentary on Job, the *Tractatus in Iob,* of which only a very few fragments passed down by other authors remain. On the other hand, it is certain that a letter *ad Abram filiam* and two hymns transmitted under his name do not in fact belong to Hilary.

Editions: PL 10, 549-552 (*ad Abram filiam*), 879-884 (*de dedic. eccl.*); PLS I, 285-286. — A. L. Feder, CSEL 65(1916)227-251. — F. Blatt, Un nouveau texte d'une apologie anonyme chrétienne: in Dragma M. P. Nilsson. Lund, 1939, 67-95.

Studies: J. Doignon, Une compilation de textes d'Hilaire de Poitiers présentée par le pape Célestin Ier à un concile romain en 430: in *Oikoumene.* Catania, 1964, 447-497; *idem,* Hypothèse sur le contenu du Contra Dioscorum d'Hilaire de Poitiers: SP 7 (TU 92)(1966)170-177. — Y. –M. Duval, La "manoeuvre frauduleuse" de Rimini. A la recherche du "Liber adversus Ursacium et Valentem" d'Hilaire: Hilaire et son temps. Paris, 1969, 51-103. — G. Folliet, Le fragment d'Hilaire "Quas Iob litteras." Son interprétation d'apres Hilaire, Pélage et Augustin: Hilaire et son temps. Paris, 1969, 149-158.

HILARY'S THEOLOGY

As a contemporary of Athanasius and Marius Victorinus and having in common with them an allegiance to the Nicene party, Hilary developed a Trinitarian theology that was completely original in respect to both of these men. The essential parameters of the work are established by the total adherence to Scriptural data in comparison to the scant consideration attached to the implications of a philosophical nature, the traditional formulation based on the tension *natura (substantia)/persona* taken over from Tertullian and Novatian, and the acute anti-Sabellian sensitivity derived from his contact with the homoiousians which was in no way inferior to his anti-Arian sentiment.

Hilary obviously makes use of the traditional themes of Christ the Logos, the Wisdom and the Power of God (*Trin.* VII 11.27; IX 12, etc.), taking care to emphasize clearly in an anti-Monarchian sense the subsistance of the divine Word (II 15; VII 11; *Syn.* 46). The theme of the image is also clearly emphasized. Christ is the true and living Image of God (VII 37), unlimited, incorporeal, invisible (VIII 48, 49), inasmuch as he is the Firstborn of all creation (Col. 1:15), that is, he reveals the Father carrying out the creation (VIII 49-51). On the other hand, the theme Christ-light, fundamental for Athanasius, is rare (VII 27). Furthermore, Hilary often manifests his mistrust of the use of sensible images to represent in some way the mystery of the divine life (IV 2; VI 9; VII 28). He considers the traditional images of the root and the plant, of the source and the stream, and of the fire and the heat to be insufficient for expressing the relationship of unity/ distinction between the Father and the Son, because they could give the idea of an *extensio* of the Father in the Son (= Photinus): (IX 37).

Hilary insists in particular, as do the homoiousians, on the names of "Father" and "Son," and reduces the names of Logos, Wisdom, Image, etc. to that of Son (VII 11, 37; III 23). He is convinced, as were many in his time, that the name of an object indicates its nature (VI 44; VII 9). Thus the names Father and Son are sufficient in themselves to indicate the nature of the divine persons, on the basis of the baptismal formula and the solemn revelation of Mt. 3:17: *Hic est filius meus* (II 3, 5, 8; VI 23).

Hilary's Trinitarian discourse is founded on a Scriptural base of unusual breadth. In his polemic with the Arian affirmation that only the Father is true God, he develops in *Trin.* IV-V a complex demonstration founded on numerous passages from the Old Testament and insisting on the tension between unity *(natura)* and distinction *(persona)*. Thus in the biblical episodes of the creation of the world and of man, Hilary sees the Logos at work in the sense of putting into effect the will of the Father. The alternation "God said"/ "God made" in the course of the biblical account assured both the distinction of the Son (the God who makes) with respect to the Father (the God who says) and his divine nature and power. The plurals *faciamus, nostram* of Gen. 1:26 exclude the possibility that God can be considered *solitarius,* i.e., unipersonal, after the manner of Sabellius, while the fact that the image of the Father and the Son is one only *(imaginem,* not *imagines)* indicates the *proprietas unius naturae in utroque* (IV 16-18; V 5). When he takes up the question of the apparitions of God to the patriarchs (theophanies), Hilary confirms on the one hand the authentically divine, and not angelic, character of the Logos who revealed Himself to Abraham, Jacob, etc., and on the other maintains the distinction between the Father and the Son (IV 23, 24, 25; V 11, 20). Even if the discussion of the theophanies still preserves a subordinationist tint in the concept of the Logos as the God who reveals Himself to men, Hilary firmly establishes by appeal to various texts of the prophets those fundamental concepts which lend themselves to expressing the distinction between God the Father and God the Son, such as Bar. 3:36; Is. 45:14; 43:10; Hos. 1:7 (IV 35-40; V 39).

In books VI and VII, Hilary develops the discussion of the unity/ distinction of the Father and the Son on the basis of numerous *testmonia* from the New Testament. It is here that Hilary thoroughly treats the fundamental theme of the generation of the Son, who did not come from nothing or from preexistent matter, as though his origin derived from some creative act (VI 13; VII 14; XII 36ff), nor from any nature other than the very nature of the Father Himself (VII 27, 31, 39). It is an ineffable generation, and thus is devoid of any analogy with physical generation; without passion, emission, splitting or division (VI 35; VII 14, 27, 28, 36; V 37; VIII 56). The Father has given all of Himself to the Son without losing anything of His own being, because there was neither *protensio* nor *transfusio*, given the unity of nature *in utroque: a vivente vivus, a vero verus, a perfecto perfectus* (VII 41, 39; II 20; IX 31). It is more than obvious that Hilary distinguishes perfectly well between us, children of God by adoption, and the unique and only Son by nature (III 11, 22; IV 33; XII 13).

Hilary is also quite explicit in the affirmation that the fact of being generated does not imply a chronological posteriority of the Son with respect to the Father. The Son is eternal, always the Son, because he is born of an atemporal generation which is incomprehensible to us (III 3; X 7; XII 15). We, in fact, who are immersed in time, have no possibility of conceiving and defining that which is atemporal and eternal except in categories which are necessarily temporal (XII 26, 27, 37, 38). The Son is *natus* not *coeptus,* i.e., generated *ab aeterno,* so that it is not possible to say of him either that he was existing or that he did not exist before he was born (VII 14; XII 31). In order to demonstrate the coeternity of the Son with the Father, Hilary brings forward the traditional arguments of the reciprocity of the concepts father/son (XII 21, 23), of the incomprehensibility of God without His Logos (VII 11) and of the contrast between *erat* of John 1:1 and *fecit* of Gen. 1:1 (II 13-15). Above all, he is convinced that the eternity of God does not admit of a before and an after in relation to the Son (XII 25).

The divine nature of the Son *non degenerat per nativitatem* (VII 22). Thus, he has all the perfections of the Father and possesses divinity *corporaliter* (Col. 2:9), *non ex parte sed tota, neque portio est sed plenitudo* (VIII 56, 54), because *dedit pater omnia et accepit filius omnia* (IX 31; VI 26 on John 16:15 and Mt. 11:27), *res potestas virtus nomen* (V 24). Inasmuch as he is *forma et imago* of the Father he contains the Father wholly in himself (XII 24) and is equal to Him in *operatio virtus honor potestas gloria vita* (VII 20; VIII 12; IX 23; IV 6; V 7; IX 39; II 11).

Consequently, Hilary is most attentive in opposing the arguments which the Arians were proposing to demonstrate the inferiority of the Son with respect to the Father, and the last four books of the *De Trinitate* are dedicated precisely to this refutation. The Gospel passages on the inferiority and passibility of Christ over which the

Arians made a great deal are referred to his humanity, although in a less general and superficial way than with Athanasius. Jesus' lack of knowledge (Mt. 24:36) is explained *per dispensationem,* as an adaptation of the Son to the limitations of the human nature he assumed (IX 63, 66, 75). His passibility is referred, indeed, to his humanity, but with the clear specification that Christ suffered not only with his body but also with his soul (X 14, 15, 19). The *subiectio* (1 Cor. 15:24-28) is related to the *exinanitio* of the Son in the assumption of the *forma servi* (Phil. 2:7) in strict connection with his glorification and eternal reign *qua homo* and as representative of all of humanity; this latter point intended in polemic not only with Arius but also with Marcellus of Ancyra (XI 21ff). In this context, Hilary proposes the idea of the human body of Christ as a real body but a celestial one, devoid of imperfections and capable of feeling the violence of the passion but not the pain; an idea that is not without a slight hint of docetism (X 18, 23).

The tension of unity/distinction of the Father and the Son is expressed by Hilary above all with the opposition nature/person. The unity of nature is based, as we have seen above, on the identity of the name *deus* attributed by the Scripture to the Father and to the Son (V 8, 20; VII 13). Hilary speaks variously of *natura indifferens, indiscreta* (VII 8; VIII 51), *indissimilis* (*Syn.* 42); of *aequalitas naturae, unitas naturalis, natura non dividua* (IX 53; VII 5; IX 69). He speaks also of *una, indifferens substantia, unitas substantiae* (IV 42; VI 10; *Syn.* 69), of *indifferens genus* (VII 27), and of one *essentia* (*Syn.* 42, 69). The four terms are proposed as essentially identical in *Syn.* 12. As regards the semantic correspondence *hypostasis-substantia* which so confused the Latins, Hilary understood that the Easterners used *hypostasis* in the sense that the Westerners attached not to substance but to person (*Syn.* 32).

Hilary, following Tertullian and Novatian, does not perceive in *persona* the insufficiency which instead Marius Victorinus noticed for the purpose of characterizing the distinction Father/Son within the limits of the unity of nature. He speaks of the *discretio personarum* and contrasts it precisely to the unity of nature (IV 24, 42; V 10; VII 40 etc.). He considers it opportune as well to state precisely against the Arians that the distinction of persons does not imply a separation between the Father and the Son (III 14; V 11; VIII 38). The foundation is perceived in the diverse manner in which the two participate in the same work, the efficient cause being the Father and the instrumental cause the Son (IV 16), and in the *missio* which distinguishes the Father who sends from the Son who is sent (III 14; V 11). But within the articulation of the divinity itself, the distinction is perceived only with regard to origin, in that one generates and one is generated; a point made also by Athanasius (VII 20; *Syn.* 47). The relationship of generation which at once unites and distinguishes between the Father and Son has precisely the function of indicating the unity of the divine nature and the distinction of the two persons (VI 19; VII 21, 27, 31; IX 27, 36, 57).

In refuting the Arian interpretation of John 10:30, *ego et pater unum sumus,* according to which the union of the Son with the Father is one of volition and not of nature and contrasting to this unity of nature our own voluntary unity in Christ (VIII 7-12), Hilary is careful not to leave his flank open to the danger of Sabellianism. In this sense, he takes up again the interpretation given to the Johannine passage by Tertullian and Novatian: the Father and the Son are *unum* (= one nature) and not *unus* (= one person) by virtue of birth and generation, because *"sumus" non patitur singularem* (i.e., a single person) and *"unum" naturam non discernit in genere,* so that *neque unum diversitatis est* (against the Arians) *neque sumus unius est* (against the Sabellians) (VII 5, 31; VIII 4). In virtue of his unity with the Father, the Son, *verus deus,* is neither a second god nor does he destroy the divine monarchy (II 11; III 4; IV 15, 33). There is one single God because there is one single divine principle, while the Son has derived his divinity from the Father in virtue of the unity of *natura,* though distinct in *persona; pater et filius non persona sed natura unus et verus deus* (V 10; VII 32; *Syn.* 69).

In order to make a synthesis of the mystery of the unity/distinction in God, Hilary, like Marius Victorinus, multiplies the formulae: *ex deo deus; unus ex uno; ex uno in unum; alter ab altero et uterque unum* (III 4; V 37; VII 32; VIII 52); *unus deus uterque* (IV 33; V 10). At VIII 36, Hilary specifies that God is *unus,* not *solus.* The latter expression is the term he uses to indicate the unipersonal God of Sabellius, just as with the same end in mind he speaks of God as *solitarius, in solitudine* (III 1; IV 17, 18, 20; VIII 36; IX 36). Another of Hilary's favorite ways of expressing himself to distinguish his concept of divine unity from the heresy of Sabellius is the contrast *unitas/unio,* where *unio* indicates precisely the indistinct personal unity of Father and Son (*haeresis unionis, Syn.* 26) (VII 8; VIII 38). God is one alone not *per unionem* (V 2); the divine unity is *unitas substantiae* not *unio personae* (IV 42); the unity of nature is antithetical to the *solitudo unionis* (VIII 28); the generation distinguishes the *unitas* from *unio* (VII 5, 21). The *aequalitas* between Father and Son, which presupposes the distinction, cannot exist where there is an *unio,* and it does not admit *nec solitudinem* (against Sabellius) *nec diversitatem* (against Arius) (VII 15). God is *unus uterque* in the *proprietas* of the persons, not in the *unio,* in a rapport of perfect reciprocity.

From as much as has been expounded up to this point, the evident homoousian formulation of Hilary's theology, based on the theme of the unity of nature of the Father and the Son (= unity of substance), is clear. On the other hand, it is also clear that unlike Athanasius, Marius Victorinus and Gregory of Elvira, Hilary displays little sympathy for the term *homoousios,* which he almost does not introduce at all into the *De Trinitate.* His overture to the homoiousians and his acute anti-Sabellian sensitivity placed him on his guard against the equivocal interpretations to which the *homoousion* loaned itself. He was acquainted with the criticisms brought against the term from numerous quarters (IV 4; *Syn.* 68) and in the *De synodis* he clarifies its meaning and its limits in such a way as to exclude the Sabellian interpretation (ch. 69, 71). However, his defense is less rigid than that of Athanasius and Marius Victorinus, because he is aware that the term is not scriptural, effectively lends itself to misunderstanding and needs to be carefully clarified to be acceptable (ch. 67, 69, 71). Hilary's attitude in the *De synodis* toward the *homoiousion* is about the same. He is well informed on the criticism directed against this term by the anomoeans as well as by the homoousians regarding the impossibility of admitting in God a relationship of likeness, i.e., accidental in nature, but he does not make much of it as he insists on the non-scriptural origin likewise of this term (ch. 67, 81). He is instead much more attentive to the misunderstanding that can result from a relationship of likeness: sheep's milk is similar to cow's milk but is not identical. True likeness, however, can only derive from the equality of nature (not of person); only gold can be like unto gold (ch. 67, 71, 72ff, 76, 89).

The concept of *homoousion,* which *per se* is a generic term (all beings of one and the same species share the same substance), takes on its full significance in Hilary as in Athanasius only in light of the relationship of complete interpenetration between themselves within the bounds of the distinction of persons of the Father and the Son on the basis of John 10:30; 14:9-10. Since they are spiritual beings, they are able to coexist the one in the other *per naturae unitatem, per virtutis potestatem, per honoris aequalitatem, per nativitatis generationem* (IX 51; V 39, 57). In God, *nihil differt esse et inesse,* so that the being of the Son consists precisely of being-in-the-Father, and vice versa (VII 41; III 23).

Hilary has the opportunity to speak of the Holy Spirit on several occasions but never inserts the Holy Spirit into the question of the inter-Trinitarian relations and conforms himself to the terms of the polemic which at that time involved only the relationship between the first two divine persons. He distinguishes carefully between spirit, intended as the generic divine substance, and the Holy Spirit, whom he defines as *usus, donum, munus* of God to man in virtue of his sanctification. The Holy Spirit *in Christo est* and *omne omnibus patet unum,* having been given *ad agnitionem eius quae indulta est veritatis* (II 1, 29, 31, 32, 35; VIII 34; X 5). In his lengthy presentation of the Holy Spirit in VIII 21ff as gift, the active *virtus* of God and of Christ together in order to emphasize in this way their unity, Hilary further distinguishes the Holy Spirit as the *res* of the nature of the Father and the Son, the *virtus una* active in God and in Christ (VIII 23, 25, 26, 31, 39). In this context, commenting on John 16:15 (the Holy Spirit receives from Christ) and John 15:26 (the Holy Spirit proceeds from the Father), Hilary seems to identify the *accipere* and *procedere,* the origin of the Holy Spirit and his mission in the world at the behest of the Son, and has the Holy Spirit derive his origin from the unique nature of the Father and the Son. In this way, he anticipates the Augustinian doctrine of the dual procession of the Holy Spirit. It must be taken into account, however, that Hilary conceived of the Holy Spirit, who *procedit* and *accipit,* not as a divine *persona,* but only as gift, as *res* of the divine nature. Tertullian had already defined the Holy Spirit as a person, so that Hilary's silence in this regard is significant.

At the end of the work (XII 55-56), Hilary returns to speak briefly of this problem in an appendix inspired by the necessity to take some sort of position in relation to the statements which were beginning to circulate in the East around 360 concerning the nature of the Holy Spirit. Not even in this context in which he affirms that the Holy Spirit is to be considered neither as generated from the Father like the Son, nor created like the creatures, does Hilary ever define the Spirit as *persona,* but still as the *res* of the Father who derives from the Father through the Son. Since not even Phoebadius, following Tertullian, had experienced any difficulty in considering the Holy Spirit to be a *persona* like the Father and the Son, Hilary's silence on this point cannot be considered accidental. It is possible that he had connected the concept of divine person with that of generation, which he employed as an element not only of union but also of distinction between the Father and the Son, so that he was not able to speak of person also in reference to the Holy Spirit. Hilary's Trinitarian definitions, e.g., that of II 1 which would be cited by Augustine (*De Trin.* VI.10.11), *infinitas in aeterno, species in imagine, usus in munere,* must be understood in the light of this imperfect alignment of the Holy Spirit with the Father and the Son in the articulation of the divine reality.

These few difficulties notwithstanding, Hilary's Trinitarian synthesis was recognized by his contemporaries and successors in the West as a tour de force never before attempted even in the East; i.e., the effort to deal in a comprehensive manner with the entire discussion of the topic in conformity with the data of Scripture and tradition while keeping in mind all the Arian arguments without exception. Hilary is never afraid to confront even the most delicate issues of the controversy, even those with respect to which the Catholic position was weakest, and to provide them with an explanation consistent with the fundamental principles which inspired his work. Precisely for this reason, Hilary's contemporaries and successors among the Latin anti-Arian polemicists had frequent recourse to his work as to a fundamental and complete text from which they were able to draw according to the circumstances this or that element useful for the polemic with their adversaries, who tended habitually to split into factions on many particular questions.

Anti-Arian Writers

HOSIUS

Hosius, born around 256, was already bishop of Cordova around 300 at which time he confessed to the faith during the Persecution of Diocletian. As a friend of Constantine, he was entrusted by the emperor with the task (ca. 324) of bringing about peace in the Arian controversy, and in this official capacity he exercised a considerable influence on the development of the Council of Nicea (325) and the decisions adopted there. After the death of Constantine, Hosius played a role of primary importance in the Council of Serdica (343), when the Western Church drew up in defense of the Nicene doctrine and its supporters in the East against the Eastern churches dominated by the Eusebians (moderate Arians). At the time when the Emperor Constantius, who supported the moderate Arians, was sole emperor and the churches of the West had given in to the will of the emperor, Hosius refused to sign the condemnation of Athanasius in 356. The following year, however, by then more than a centenarian, he was forced to sign the second formula of Sirmium, which was openly sympathetic to the Arian cause. He died shortly thereafter. This yielding of Hosius, obviously due to the weakness brought on by advanced age, was not dramatized by Athanasius, but did provoke the most violent reactions among the anti-Arians in the West: Hilary, Phoebadius and especially the Luciferians in Spain.

Less prominent than his political role was Hosius' literary activity. Nothing of his preaching seems to have been committed to writing, and two works recorded by Isidore of Seville (*De vir. ill.* 5), the *De laude virginitatis* and the *De interpretatione vestium sacerdotalium,* have been lost. In substance, there remain from Hosius some canons approved at the Council of Serdica in 343 (edited in Turner, *Ecclesiae Occidentalis monumenta iuris antiquissima* I 2), and two letters. The first letter was written by Hosius and Protogenes of Serdica to inform

Bishop Julius of Rome regarding certain decisions made at the Council of Serdica. The second and far more important one, related by Athanasius (*Hist. Arian.* 44), was written in 356 by Hosius to the Emperor Constantius, who was insisting that the bishop sign the condemnation of Athanasius. In this letter, for the first time since the beginning of the policy of collaboration between the empire and the church inaugurated by Constantine in 313, a spokesman of the ecclesiastical hierarchy proposes that it is appropriate for the emperor to abstain from interfering in the internal affairs of the church, such as was the Arian controversy. On the basis of Mt. 22:21, Hosius affirms the separation of the two powers. For such reasons, this letter is a very important document in the history of the church.

Editions: Cf. CPL 537-540. — PL 8, 1317-1328; 10, 557-564; 632-648; 56, 839-848; PLS I, 184-196. — A. Feder, CSEL 65(1916)103-126, 181-184. — C. H. Turner, Ecclesiae Occidentalis monumenta uirus antiquissima I, II, 3. Oxford, 1930, 452-544, 644-653.

Studies: F. Loofs, Hosius (oder Osius) von Corduba: RE 8(1900)376-382. — C. H. Turner, Ossius (Hosius) of Corduba: JThSt 12(1910)275-277. — S. Cunill, Osius, bisbe de Cordoba: AST 2(1925)285-289. — S. Sureda Blanes, La cuestión de Osio de Córdoba y de Liberio, obispo de Roma. Madrid, 1928. — U. Moricca, Storia della letterature latina cristiana, II/1, 158(bibliog.) and 192-201. — R. Serratosa, Osio de Córdoba y Tajón de Zaragoza precursores de la Escolástica: *Estudios* 7(1951)85-95; *idem,* Algo más sobre Osio de Córdoba: *Estudios* 13(1957)65-84. — V. C. de Clercq, Ossius of Cordoba. A Contribution to the History of the Constantinian Period. Washington, 1954. — H. Kraft, 'Ομοούσιος: ZKG 61(1954-1955)1-24 (History of the term in Hosius and others); *idem,* Ossius of Cordoba and the origins of Priscillianism: SP I (TU 63)(1957)601-606; *idem,* Prosopography of Ossius (Hosius) of Cordoba: Folia 11(1957)251-264 (= J. M. F. Marique, Leaders of Iberean Christianity 50-650 A.D. Jamaica Plain, Mass., 1962, 127-140.) — U. Domínguez del Val, La bibliografía de los últimos tiempos sobre Osio de Córdoba: CD 171(1958)485-489; *idem,* Osio de Córdoba: RET 18(1958)141-165, 261-281. — H. Chadwick, Ossius of Cordoba and the Presidency of the Council of Antioch: JThSt 9(1958)292-304. — B. Llorca, El problema de la caída de Osio de Córdoba: EE 33(1959)39-56. — M. Aubinau, La vie grecque de "saint" Ossius de Cordue: AB 78(1960)356-361. — V. C. de Clercq, LThK2 7(1962)1269-1270. — G. Langgärtner, Das Aufkommen de ökumenischen Konzilsgedanken. Ossius von Cordoba als Ratgeber Constantins: MTZ 14(1965)11-26. — G. S. M. Walker, Ossius and the Nicene Faith: SP 9 (TU 94)(1966)316-320. — K. M. Girardet, Kaiser Konstantius II als "episcopus episcoporum" und das Herrscherbild des kirchlichen Widerstandes (Ossius von Corduba und Lucifer von Calaris): *Historia* 26(1977)95-128.

EUSEBIUS OF VERCELLI

Eusebius, Sardinian by birth, became a lector of the Church of Rome and first bishop of Vercelli, and played a considerable role in the Arian controversy between 355 and 364. Since he was unwilling to subscribe to the condemnation of Athanasius, he was deposed by the Council of Milan in 355 and exiled first to Scythopolis in Palestine, then to the Thebaid in Egypt. After he was set free in 362 at the accession of Julian to the throne, he participated in the Council of

Alexandria in 362 and went immediately afterward to Antioch, where he disapproved of the conduct of his friend, Lucifer of Cagliari, which was intended to exacerbate the conflicts among the anti-Arians in that city. On his way home, he held a conference at Sirmium (Pannonia) with Germinius, an important spokesman of moderate Arianism. He appears again in 364 at Milan, engaged together with Hilary in an unsuccessful attempt to expel the local bishop, Auxentius, who was an Arian. His death is fixed around 370.

Eusebius' political activity seems to have been much more extensive and important than his literary activity. Since his translation of Eusebius of Caesarea's commentary on the Psalms, which Jerome mentions (*De vir. inl.* 96), has been lost, there remain under his name three letters: two transmitted in an ancient *Vita* of dubious reliability and the third in Hilary's *Fragmenta historica* (11, 5 = A II 1-2 ed. Feder). He is considered by some to be the author of the famous *Codex Vercellensis,* a pre-Jerome Latin translation of the gospels. The first letter, of undoubted authenticity, is drawn from a correspondence among several parties regarding the Council of Milan. Eusebius, who did not wish to attend — he obviously foresaw the pressure the emperor would bring to bear on the counciliar fathers — responds positively to the explicit invitation of the emperor and announces his arrival. The second letter was written and sent secretly to his faithful at Vercelli from Scythopolis, where he was being virtually held prisoner by Patrophilus, the Arian sympathizer who was bishop of that city. In this letter, Eusebius recounts the maltreatment to which he had been subjected along with the priests and deacons who had followed him into exile. There is also reproduced here the text of a brief communication which Eusebius had written to Patrophilus in which he stated his firm intention to begin a hunger strike if he were further impeded in his contact with the faithful who came to visit him. This letter to the people of Vercelli also is certainly authentic. The same, however, cannot be affirmed of the third letter, which is transmitted in the *Fragmenta historica.* In this letter, Eusebius congratulates Gregory of Elvira who had resisted pressure from Hosius and refused to enter into communion with bishops sympathetic to the Arian cause. Because it shows signs of the capricious accusations directed against Hosius by the Luciferians in the *Libellus precum,* the letter is considered to be a falsification produced precisely by the Luciferians (cf. Lucifer and the Luciferians).

Recently, the tiny literary heritage of Eusebius has been substantially enlarged, thanks to the attribution to him of books I-VIII of the collection of pseudo-Athanasian writings which goes under the name of *De Trinitate* (cf. Quasten, *Patrology,* vol II, p. 33). We will attempt to complete the data of Quasten here, keeping in mind that the attribution of the pseudo-Athanasian work to Eusebius of Vercelli, which was proposed many decades ago by Dom Morin on the basis of an isolated witness in a Vatican manuscript of little authority, and which was subsequently retracted by the same Dom Morin, has been recently taken up again by V. Bulhart, who has published the critical edition of the collection under the name of Eusebius in CCL 9, and who, following Schepens, has proposed for it a dating of 345-347. If the attribution and especially the dating proposed by Bulhart are accepted, the panorama of doctrinal literature relating to the Arian crisis is profoundly changed. The pseudo-Athanasian *De Trinitate*, in fact, presents a much more evolved Trinitarian doctrine than that heretofore known around the middle of the fourth century, even in comparison to Hilary and Athanasius. It is a Trinitarian doctrine which would anticipate the decisive results of Cappadocian theology and the solutions proposed as a result of the questions concerning the Son and the Holy Spirit around 360-370 in the East and later in the West by Ambrose and others. But precisely because the work reflects without a shadow of a doubt the theological situation characteristic of the years between 380 and the beginning of the fifth century, it cannot be carried back to the years proposed by Bulhart nor even attributed to Eusebius; all the less so as the foundation in the manuscripts for such an attribution is more than precarious. The most recent studies confirm the hypothesis, already variously advanced with varying success, according to which the work is to be located in Spain precisely around the years 380-400. It is to be attributed with good probability to Luciferian circles.

Editions: Cf. CPL 105. — PL 12, 959-968; 62, 237-286; PLS I, 305-307, 1741-1742. — V. Bulhart, CCL 9(1957)1-205, 451-479 (cf. B. Fischer, VT p. 260).

Studies: A. E. Burn, On Eusebius of Vercelli: JThSt 1(1899)592-599. — C. H. Turner, On Eusebius of Vercelli: JThSt 1(1899)126-128. — A. Jülicher, Eusebios, Bischof von Vercellae: PWK 6(1907)1441-1443. — P. Godet, DTC 5(1913)1553-1554. — P. Schepens, Pour l'histoire du Symbole "Quicumque": RHE 32(1936)548-569; *idem,* L'Ambrosiaster et S. Eusèbe de Verceil: RSR 37(1950)295-299. — V. C. de Clercq: DHG 15(1963)1477-1483. — E. Crovella, *Bibliotheca Sanctorum* 5(1964)263-270. — M. Simonetti, A proposito di una recente edizione dei 11. X-XII del De Trinitate dello pseudo Atanasio: RCCM 3(1961)108-113; *idem,* Qualche osservazione sul De Trinitate attribuito a Eusebio di Vercelli: RCCM 5(1963)386-393. — M. Capellino, Storia di S. Eusebio di Vercelli e spiritualità del suo cenobio nella Chiesa del IV secolo. Rome, 1971. — L. Dattrino, Il De Trinitate pseudoatanasiano. Rome, 1976. — J. T. Lienhard, Patristic Sermons on Eusebius of Vercelli and their Relation to his Monasticism: RB 87(1977)163-172.

LUCIFER AND THE LUCIFERIANS

Concerning Lucifer, bishop of Cagliari, we know only the events connected with the Arian controversy. The hypothesis proposed in modern times that he was of African origin has no documentary support. Lucifer appears as the representative of Liberius, bishop of Rome, at the Council of Milan in 355, called to reexamine the case of Athanasius, who was persecuted by the Arians with the support of the Emperor Constantius. We have from Lucifer a letter written on this occasion to Eusebius of Vercelli, asking him to participate in the work of the council. At Milan, Lucifer was one of the few who were not willing to bend to the will of the emperor, and he refused to sign the condemnation of Athanasius. As a result, he was deposed and sent into exile, first at Germanicia in Syria, then at Eleutheropolis in Palestine and finally at the Thebaid in Egypt. It was there that he received in 362 the edict of Julian allowing all the exiles of Constantius to return to their sees. While Eusebius, his companion in exile, went to Alexandria to participate in the council convoked by Athanasius, Lucifer preferred to travel to Antioch, where the anti-Arian community was divided into two hostile factions. Instead of bringing peace, Lucifer energetically supported the smaller of the two factions, composed of intransigent partisans of the Nicene creed, against the majority which supported Meletius, a more moderate anti-Arian. The result of this was to aggravate that Schism of Antioch which would subsequently prove to be a great stumbling block for attempts to unite the anti-Arians of East and West in one block. Vexed because Eusebius, who had arrived at Antioch, did not approve of his conduct and considering too mild the provisions made by the Council of Alexandria with regard to bishops compromised by Arianism who wished to return to the Nicene faith, Lucifer returned to the West. According to the *Libellus precum,* he passed through Naples and Rome, but other than that we have no further information of him. Jerome (*De vir. inl.* 95) places his death during the reign of Valentinian (364-375).

During his years of exile (355-361), Lucifer addressed five very violent pamphlets to the Emperor Constantius. In the *De non conveniendo cum haereticis* he combats the statement by which the emperor had accused those who did not want to subscribe to the condemnation of Athanasius of being enemies of Christian unity and he energetically affirms that it is not possible for a Catholic to have contact with a heretic, who in any case is equated with a pagan idolater. It is as such that he considers, *apertis verbis,* the Emperor Constantius, who supports the Arians. The *De regibus apostaticis* is dedicated to refuting the statement of Constantius by which he had proposed the prosperity of his reign as evidence of the justice of his favorable policy to the Arians, which evidently met with God's favor. Lucifer retorts that God always gives the sinner the time and the opportunity to redeem himself and thus the punishment of the evil monarch is able to be much delayed in time. In the two books *Pro sancto Athanasio,* the longest and most compelling of his writings, Lucifer attacks the emperor in reference to the irregular conduct which had taken place at the Council of Milan, where Athanasius had been condemned without having been heard in person. In this text, Lucifer furnishes some details about the procedures of that council.

From a brief exchange of letters between Lucifer and Florentius, *magister officiorum* of the imperial court, we learn that Lucifer had taken care to have forwarded to the emperor a codex containing his writings against him. The emperor, astonished at the violence of the accusations directed against him, wanted to know if Lucifer had actually sent those writings, which Lucifer confirmed. When he learned that the emperor had complained of having been insulted, he aggravated the matter in the *De non parcendo in Deum delinquentibus* in which he sustains that his offensive attitude is precisely the one which must be maintained toward those who favor heresy. Finally, in the *Moriendum esse pro Dei Filio,* Lucifer, perhaps disappointed that Constantius, far more patient than he had ever supposed, was not taking any measures against him, confirms his unshakable decision to be ready to face even death in defense of the Nicene faith, bulwark against the Arian heresy.

All five pamphlets of Lucifer are developed on the basis of the same simple cliché, i.e., on the basis of a constant and systematic appeal to Sacred Scripture as the only element which can demonstrate and prove the theses upheld in the single works. Thus, in the *De non conveniendo cum haereticis,* he begins by producing the punitive measures decreed by Moses on various occasions for the Israelites who had established contacts with the neighboring peoples. He then proceeds in an orderly fashion to the books of Joshua, Kings and the Psalms to extract material of a similar nature, and finally concludes with some passages from the New Testament. In the *De regibus apostaticis,* following the same criteria, the examples of Saul, Solomon and Rohoboam are adduced, among others, to demonstrate that God does not always punish sinful kings without delay. These two treatises are far shorter than the other three, where the same method is applied with greater diligence and thus greater extension. In the *Pro sancto Athanasio* and the *De non parcendum in Deum delinquentibus,* the documentation and proofs are taken first from the Old Testament then from the New. In the *Moriendum esse pro Dei Filio,* however, which is less exasperated in tone than the preceding works, the documentation is drawn only from the New Testament.

The recourse to Sacred Scripture for demonstrating the truth of his propositions is for Lucifer not merely a means of carrying on his polemic. In reality, there is apparent in his vehement and heated pages the total identification between the historical situation experienced by the author and that narrated in the sacred books. In his threats and invective, Lucifer feels himself to be truly inspired on a par with Moses and Elijah, just as for him Rohoboam, Ahab and so many other wicked monarchs of the Old Testament are reincarnate in Constantius. It is possible to request from such an easily excitable character even the greatest sacrifices for the defense of the Nicene faith, but not possible to expect a calm and considered evaluation of the complicated terms of the Arian controversy. Even when he was sent into exile in the East, Lucifer, in contrast to Hilary, did not take advantage of his proximity to the principal centers of the conflict to deepen his understanding of the question, but embittered his attitude even more and identified as a radical Arian every adversary of the Nicene mold of orthodoxy. He even found a way to violently criticize the practical and far-seeing attitude of Hilary, who in the *De synodis* was seeking to minimize the conflicts between the anti-Arians in the East (non-Nicenes) and in the West (Nicenes) for the purpose of establishing a common front against the Arians (cf. "Hilary"). The conduct of Lucifer at Antioch in 362 has been treated above. On the whole, it is clear that his actions brought more harm than good to the cause of Nicene orthodoxy.

Just as he did not concern himself with obtaining a better understanding of the political conditions of the conflict, Lucifer also neglected the doctrinal aspect. Here and there in his writings are found expressions of strict adherence to the Nicene creed and to the faith in the divinity of the Trinity. But it is a matter of stereotyped expressions which are often repeated but never reflected upon in a personal manner. The pages of Lucifer are of interest to the linguist for the numerous vulgarisms scattered about and to the biblical scholar for the numerous citations of scriptural passages in a pre-Jerome Latin translation, but the student of the history of theology finds nothing truly of interest there.

It is known from the *Libellus precum* (cf. "Faustus"), that the name "Luciferians" was used to designate certain zealous partisans of Nicene orthodoxy at Rome around 380. They had never approved of the mild measures taken by the Council of Alexandria in 362 and subsequently confirmed in various ways by other councils with regard to the bishops who wished to return to the observance of the Nicene faith after having signed the pro-Arian formula of Rimini (359). For this reason, these Luciferians refused to enter into communion with the bishop of Rome, Damasus, who thus harassed them in every way. Similar communities had been formed in various cities of Spain, Italy, Germany and in the East and sought to form a common front among themselves. These events have been placed together by modern scholars under the general term of the Luciferian Schism. Given the present status of our understanding, it is not possible to ascertain whether Lucifer of Cagliari was actually the initiator of this schismatic movement or whether he was just the prototype on which the schismatics intended to model themselves because of his well-known intransigence.

For our purposes, the schism is of interest only because some of its adherents carried on a certain literary activity. The more important of these, Gregory of Elvira and Faustinus, will be treated in a separate section. It is sufficient here to recall that some Luciferian circles, probably in Spain, were responsible for the forgery of certain documents. Aside from the letter of Eusebius of Vercelli to Gregory of Elvira, which was treated above under Eusebius, there must also be taken into consideration two letters of Athanasius to Lucifer, known only in a Latin text, in which Athanasius praises highly the anti-Arian attitude of the bishop of Cagliari. With all probability the books X-XI of the collection known as the pseudo-Athanasian *De Trinitate* are to be considered a product of the Luciferians, and it is possible that this same circle is responsible for the homogenous unit formed by books I-VIII of that same collection (cf. "Eusebius of Vercelli").

Editions: Cf. CPL 112-118. — PL 13, 767-1049; PLS I, 351-352. — W. Hartel, CSEL 14(1886). — G. F. Diercks, CCL 8(1978). — G. Cerretti, Lucifero vescovo de Cagliari e il suo "Moriendum esse pro Dei Filio." Pisa, 1940 — A. Saba, Fides sancti Luciferi episcopi in un codice antichissimo della Biblioteca Ambrosiana: Studi . . . P. Ubaldi, Milano 1937, 109-116. — V. Ugenti, De regibus apostaticis et "Moriendum esse pro Dei Filio." Lecce, 1980. — J. Avilés, El tratado "De regibus apostaticis" de Lucifer de Cagliari. Barcelona, 1979.

Studies: E. Amann: DTC 9/1(1926)1032-1044. — M. M. Todde: *Bibliotheca Sanctorum* 8(1967)272-274. — G. Krüger, Lucifer, Bischof von Calaris und das Schisma der Luciferianer. Leipzig 1886 (reprint: Hildescheim, 1969). — L. Saltet, Fraudes littéraires des schismatiques Lucifériens aux IVe et Ve siècles: BLE 7(1906)300-326. — A. Merk, Lucifer von Calaris und seine Vorlagen in des Schrift "Moriendum esse pro Dei Filio": TQ 94(1912)1-32. — F. Piva, Lucifero di Cagliari contro l'imperatore Costanzo. Trent, 1928. — G. P. Thörnell, Studia Luciferiana. Uppsala, 1934. — P. M. Marcello, La posizione di Lucifero di Cagliari nelle lotte antiariane del IV secolo. Nuoro, 1940. — B. Fischer, Zur textüberlieferung des Lucifer von Cagliari: Festgabe G. Leyh, Leipzig 1950, 49-50. — A. Allgeier, Der Text einiger kleiner Propheten bei Lucifer von Calaris: Miscellanea . . . A. Miller, Rome 1951, 286-300. — C. Zedda, La dottrina trinitaria di Lucifero de Cagliari. Rome, 1950 (= DTP 52(1949)276-329). — S. Pilia, Il valore del Codice Genovefiano 1351 nella tradizione manoscritta delle opere di Lucifero da Cagaliari: Annali della Facoltà de Lettere . . . di Cagliari 28(1960)475-498. — P. Juvanon du Vachat, Recherches sur le schisme de Lucifer de Cagliari. Diss., Paris, 1961. — F. Flammini, Osservazioni critiche sul De non conveniendo cum haereticis di Lucifero di Gacliari: RCCM 4(1962)304-334. — M. Simonetti, Appunti per una storia dello scisma Luciferiano: Atti del convegno de Studi religiosi sardi, Padua 1963, 67-81. — M. M. Todde, Peccato e prassi penitenziale secondo Lucifero de Cagliari. Vicenza, 1965. — G. Castelli, Lucifero da Cagliari e il suo atteggiamento di fronte alla cultura classica: *Rivista degli Studi Classici* 16(1968)219-223. — Y. M. Duval, S. Jérome devant le baptême des hérétiques: d'autres sources de l'"Altercatio luciferiani et orthodoxi": REAug 14(1968)145-180. — G. Castelli, Studio sulla lingua e lo stile di Lucifero da

Cagliari: *Atti Accad. Scienze Torino,* cl. sc. Morali 105(1971)123-247. — S. Longosz, The Invective of Lucifer of Calaris: *Roczniki teol. - Kanonicze* 19, 4(1972)181-194. — I. Opelt, Formen der Polemik bei Lucifer von Calaris: VC 26(1972)200-226. — A. Figus, L'enigma di Lucifero di Cagliari. A ricordo del XVI centenario della morte. Cagliari, 1973. — G. F. Diercks, Les formes verbales périphrastiques dans les oeuvres de Lucifer de Cagliari: Corona gratiarum . . . E. Dekkers I, Brugges 1975, 139-150. — J. Liébaert, Lucifer de Cagliari: *Catholicisme* 7(1975)1250-1251. — W. Tietze, Lucifer von Calaris und die Kirchenpolitik des Constantius II. Diss. Hamburg, 1976. — K. M. Girardet, Kaiser Konstantius II als "episcopus episcoporum" und das Herrscherbild des kirchlichen Widerstandes: *Historia* 26(1977)95-128. — G. F. Diercks, Les contaminations syntactiques et les anacoluthes dans les oeuvres de Lucifer de Cagliari: VC 34(1980)130-144.

MARIUS VICTORINUS

The notices on Marius Victorinus given by Jerome (*De vir. inl.* 101) and Augustine (*Conf.* VII 2, 3-4) are concerned above all with the final part of his life. Because his conversion to Christianity, which is dated around 355, took place *in extrema senectute,* the date of his birth is to be placed around 280/285. An African by birth, he was an instructor of rhetoric and came to Rome to teach around 350. He achieved such a reputation that a statue was erected in his honor in the Forum (Jerome, *Chron.* s.a. 354). Unexpectedly, however, this rhetor, already advanced in age, who had practiced and defended the pagan religion and participated in the cults of the mysteries, converted to Christianity. There is no information regarding the motives which brought on this event. Augustine refers to the account of Simplicianus, who had been a friend of Marius Victorinus and who testified that while still a pagan, the rhetor was in the habit of reading the Sacred Scriptures. Nevertheless, we do not know to what end he did this, whether it was to combat them or indeed out of personal interest. Marius Victorinus was well versed in Neoplatonic philosophy, and this cultural attitude was able to foster an approach to Christian literature. In any case it is certain that his conversion, given his reputation, caused quite a stir.

As soon as he had converted, Marius Victorinus involved himself in the struggle against Arianism with a series of works which, however, do not seem to have carried any real weight in the controversy. In 362 Julian issued the famous edict which, although in an indirect manner, forbade Christian teachers to give instruction. Indignant, Marius Victorinus gave up his instructor's chair, and from that moment, all trace of him is lost. It is known from Augustine that in 386 he had already been dead for some time.

The copious literary production of Marius Victorinus divides itself neatly into two parts. The first part consists of a series of treatises of a grammatical and philosophical nature, including commentaries on writings of Cicero and Aristotle and translations of works of Aristotle,

Porphyry and perhaps of Plotinus. It concerns his literary production prior to his conversion to Christianity, and thus will not be considered in the present context.

The second part of his production includes the works composed when he was already a Christian, which are immersed in this new reality. These works in turn divide into two sections, the one containing works of a doctrinal nature, the other of an exegetical nature.

Editions: Cf. CPL 94-100. — PL 8, 993-1310. — A. Lochner, Teubner 245-246. Leipzig, 1972-76.

Studies: E. Benz, Marius Victorinus und die Entwicklung der abendländischen Metaphysik. Stuttgart, 1932. — D. Rosato, La dottrina trinitaria di Mario Vittorino africano. Naples, 1942. — M. Simonetti, La processione dello Spirito Santo nei padri latini: *Maia* 7(1955)308-324. — P. Hadot, Un vocabulaire raisonné de Marius Victorinus Afer: SP 1 (TU 630)(1957)195-208. — J. Vergara, La teología del Espíritu Santo en Mario Victorino. Mexico, 1959 (= *Ecclesiastica Xaveriana* 6[1956]35-125). — W. M. Hagan, The Incarnation according to Marius Victorinus. Woodstock, 1960. — A. Vaccari, Le citazioni del Vecchio Testamento presso Mario Vittorino: Bibl 42(1961)459-464. — A. Dempf, Der Platonismus des Eusebius, Victorinus und Pseudo-Dionysius. Munich, 1962. — J. Châtillon, Théologie er philosophie dans l'oeuvre de Marius Victorinus: Saint Thomas d'Aquin aujourd'hui, Bruges-Paris 1963, 241-248. — M. T. Clark, The Earliest Philosophy of the Living God. Marius Victorinus: *Proceedings of the American Catholic Philosophical Society* 41(1967)87-94. — P. Hadot, Porphyre et Victorinus. Paris, 1968. — Ch. Kannengiesser - G. Madec, A propos de la thèse de Pierre Hadot sur Porphyre et Victorinus: REAug 16(1970)159-178. — P. Hadot, Marius Victorinus. Recherches sur sa vie et ses oeuvres. Paris, 1971. — J. A. Jungmann, Marius Viktorinus in der karolingischen Gebetsliteratur und im römischen Dreifaltigkeitsoffizium: *Kyriakon* . . . J. Quasten 2, Münster 1970, 691-697. — M. T. Clark, The Neoplatonism of Marius Victorinus: SP 11 (TU 108)(1972)13-19. — A. Ziegenaus, Die trinitarische Ausprägung der göttlichen Seinsfülle nach Marius Viktorinus. Munich, 1972. — M. Simonetti, All'origine della formula teologica una essenza-tre ipostasi: Aug 14(1974)173-175. — M. T. Clark, The psychology of Marius Victorinus: Aug. Studies 5(1974)149-166. — P. Courcelle, Grégoire le Grand devant les conversions de Marius Victorinus, Augustin et Paulin de Nole: Latomus 36(1977)942-950. — E. Thomassen, The Structure of the Transcendent World in the Tripartite Tractate: VC 34(1980)358-375. — M. T. Clark, The Neoplatonism of Marius Victorinus the Christian: Essays in honor of A. H. Armstrong, London 1981, 153-159.

THEOLOGICAL WORKS

The first group comprises a series of works, anti-Arian in content, whose chronological and logical order gives rise to some difficulties because of a certain disorder in the manuscript tradition of the texts. They are listed here according to the recent studies of P. Hadot, in the most probably chronological order, which is also able to be perceived on the basis of the author's citations of his own writings in the course of the various works.

1) *Candidi Arriani ad Marium Victorinum rhetorem de generatione divina.*
2) *Marii Victorini rhetoris ad Candidum Arrianum.*

3) *Candidi Arriani epistola ad Marium Victorinum rhetorem.*
4) *Adversus Arrium liber primus (pars prima: c.* 1-47). *Liber primus de Trinitate.*
5) *Adversus Arrium liber primus (pars altera: c.* 48-64). *Quod Trinitas homoousios sit.*
6) *Adversus Arrium liber secundus. Et graece et latine de homoousio contra haereticos.*
7) *Adversus Arrium liber tertius. De homoousio.*
8) *Adversus Arrium liber quartus. De homoousio.*
9) *De homoousio recipiendo.*
10) *Hymnus primus.*
11) *Hymnus secundus.*
12) *Hymnus tertius.*

To understand the significance of this succession of works, it is necessary to consider that n. 1-4 form a kind of dossier of letters between the Arian, Candidus, and Victorinus. In n. 1, the Arian gives a presentation of the Arian heresy in a markedly philosophical form, making use especially of the themes and methods of Neoplatonic philosophy. In n. 2, Victorinus responds to him, giving a refutation on the basis of an identical philosophical approach. In order to combat the Catholic affirmation of Victorinus according to which Christ has been begotten by God and not created, Candidus, in n. 3, lets the ringleaders of Arianism have the floor and gives the Latin translation of two fundamental documents from the first years of the Arian conflict, the letter of Arius to Eusebius of Nicomedia and the letter of Eusebius of Nicomedia to Paulinus of Tyre, two texts which present Arianism in its most radical form. The response of Marius Victorinus (n. 4) takes this presentation of Arian doctrine into account, but is also attentive to the new politico-religious situation which was taking shape in 358. That was the hour of the ephemeral victory of Basil of Ancyra, the leader of the homoiousian party, who imposed the homoiousian doctrine on the Council of Sirmium in 358. Victorinus probably received word of this when the bishop of Rome, Liberius, returned to Rome from Sirmium. He did not accept the philosophical formulation, which applied an accidental quality, that of "like," to God, and he gave a detailed refutation of it.

The neat break on the external plane between the two parts of book I *Adversus Arrium* denotes a second phase in the anti-Arian activity of Marius Victorinus completely clear of the connection with Candidus. In this regard, the opinion is becoming ever more widespread among scholars that this phantom Arian friend of Victorinus, about whom nothing else is known and who expresses himself exactly like Victorinus with regard to concepts and form, is nothing else than a literary fiction invented by the rhetor himself. Since he was accustomed from his scholastic experience to discussions *in utramque partem,* he imagined a fictitious Arian correspondent in order to be able to present both Arianism and the Catholic Trinitarian doctrine on the basis of the same Neoplatonic philosophical approach and to illustrate on this basis the superiority of the latter doctrine over the former. But the continual novelties which followed one another on the political and doctrinal planes of the controversy during the confused years from 357 to 359, with first the Arians, then the homoiousians and finally the homoeans (moderate Arians) prevailing, convinced Victorinus to abandon his literary fiction in order to follow more closely the ever-changing reality of the movement.

In this sense, the second part of book I *Adversus Arrium* (n. 5) continues to be conditioned by the question posed by the homoiousians, by the defense of the *homoousios* against them and by the demonstration that the formulae *deum de deo, lumen de lumine* present in the pro-Arian formula of Sirmium of 357 necessarily imply the *homoousios.* The events of 359, the compromise formula drawn up at Sirmium on May 22, 359, and the formula of Rimini from the end of the same year qualify the composition of book II *Adversus Arrium* (n. 6), in which the defense of the Nicene *homoousios* is accompanied by a more balanced statement of his position in relation to Basil of Ancyra, whom the events of that year had relegated to second place behind the emergence of the homoeans. The books III and IV *Adversus Arrium* (n. 7-8) propose again the theme of the *homoousios* with a series of ever-more profound variations but still without a more precise connection to the situation, which had effectively stagnated after 359. The brief little treatise known by the name of *De homoousio recipiendo* brings forward in an abbreviated form themes which were already treated in the book II *Adversus Arrium.* The connection of Marius Victorinus' argument with the events of 358-359 permits the chronological order of numbers 1-9 to be approximately fixed in the following manner: n. 1-4 from the years 358-359; n. 5 from 360; n. 6-9 from the years 361-363.

The three hymns, which in the manuscript tradition follow the prose treatises but which are possibly to be dated around 358-359, are also doctrinal in content and present in a synthesized form the major themes developed in the treatises. They have a rough rhythmical structure which shows here and there, especially at the end of the verse, a cretic and iambic meter. However, it is not possible to give an overall interpretation of the three poems according to the norms of traditional meter. The first hymn, *Adesto,* composed of 78 verses which cannot be grouped together in homogenous stanzas, presents in a dense and concise form the theme of the great mystery of the relation between the Father and the Son. The second hymn contains 62 verses which are divided into stanzas of three verses separated by the refrain, *Miserere Domine, miserere Christe,* which is also the opening verse. In respect to the preceding hymn, this second one has a less doctrinal and more personal tone, and expresses the desire of the composer to be liberated from the world in order to be joined to Christ. The third hymn, *Deus, Dominus,* which is considerably longer than the others (285 verses), is divided into stanzas by the repetition of the refrain, *O beata Trinitas.* The stanzas, however, which are initially composed of three verses of a single word each indicating respectively the Father, the Son and the Holy Spirit, gradually increase in form and lose at times their perfect symmetry. Nevertheless, they preserve their initial character of presenting the Trinitarian mystery in terse and concise forms which express the character of the three divine persons and their mutual relations. It is superfluous to repeat that the hymn presents in such a concise form the same doctrinal attitude and markedly Neoplatonic character as the treatises; see e.g., the terse definition of the three persons in verses 71-73: *Status, Progressio, Regressus.* Nevertheless, in spite of this pronounced doctrinal and philosophical *facies,* the hymn presents solemn and hieratic cadences and at times a rhythm so finely scanned that it finally speaks not only to the reader's intelligence but also to his aesthetic sensitivity.

Editions: PL 8, 999-1146. — P. Henry-P. Hadot, SCh 68-69(1960); *idem,* CSEL 83(1971). — A. Locher, Teubner 246. Leipzig, 1976.

Translations: English: M. T. Clark, FC 69(1981). *French:* Henry-Hadot, SCh 68-69. *German:* P. Hadot-U. Brenke, Christlicher Platonismus. Die theologischen Schriften des Marius Victorinus. Zurich, 1967.

Studies: P. Frassinetti, Le confessioni agostiniane e un inno di Mario Vittorino: *Giornale Italiano di Filologia* 2(1949)50-59. — P. Hadot, De lectis non lecta componere (M. Victor. adv. Ar. II, 7): SP 1 (TU 63)(1957)209-220; *idem,* Les hymnes de Victorinus et les hymnes "Adesto" et "Miserere" d'Alcuin: AHD 35(1960)7-16. — M. Simonetti, Nota sull'ariano Candido: Orph 10(1963)151-157 (= *Oikoumene,* Catania 1964, 39-45). — P. Nautin, Candidus l'arien: L'homme devant Dieu . . . H. de Lubac 1, Paris 1964, 309-320.

EXEGETICAL WORKS

In the years following 362, Marius Victorinus turned his attention to exegesis with a series of commentaries on the Pauline epistles, of which three, on Ephesians, Galatians and Philippians are extant, although with some *lacunae.* From indications given in these three commentaries, it is probable that Marius Victorinus also wrote commentaries on Romans and on 1 and 2 Corinthians. He was the first Christian writer to have written commentaries in Latin on the letters of Paul. He did not consider it convenient to make use of

Greek commentaries, such as the many writings of Origen, but produced a work of his own. For this reason, it can be observed in a general fashion that Marius Victorinus does not betray an appreciable knowledge of antecedent Christian literature, whether Latin or, especially, Greek. The impression gained from his Christian writings is that he had only a summary knowledge even of the Old Testament. It is certain that once he became a Christian, Marius Victorinus brought to his new condition of life all the cultural baggage, both philosophical and grammatical, which he had acquired as a pagan, and this cultural formation formed the foundation of his literary activity in the Christian camp.

In the commentaries on the Pauline letters, it is above all the grammarian who is in evidence, the master who is accustomed to explaining Cicero and Vergil to his pupils, though the Neoplatonic philosophical attitude is recognizable on several occasions. Each commentary is preceded by a brief introduction in which Marius Victorinus declares the reasons why Paul wrote the particular letter, of which he gives a brief summary. (We do not possess the preface to the commentary on Philippians because the initial part of the text is mutilated.) There follows a systematic commentary based on an attentive critical reading of the text, for which Victorinus makes use of more than one Latin copy with occasional references to the Greek original, and conducted according to a strictly literal method. In instances where Paul himself makes use of allegory, e.g., Gal. 4:22ff, the exegete expounds briefly on the allegory but does not take from it the cue for those amplifications so dear to interpreters of the Alexandrian tradition. It is precisely this literalism which indicates the most characteristic aspect of the Pauline commentaries of Marius Victorinus and which clearly distinguishes him from the Greek exegetical tradition, which up to that time was dominated by the Alexandrian school and thus by a strongly allegorizing type of interpretation. However, such isolation in respect to tradition can also be interpreted as a conscious detachment from a manner of interpretation which could appear arbitrary and exaggerated to someone who for so many years had expounded the pagan classics according to the usual norms of interpretation of a predominantly literal type. In a more general manner, the attitude of Marius Victorinus can be connected with a movement of reaction against Alexandrian exegesis which began to take shape on several fronts toward the end of the fourth and the beginning of the fifth centuries. To remain in Latin circles, Ambrosiaster and Pelagius also interpreted Paul in a literal fashion.

The scholastic experience of Marius Victorinus is also evident in his method of exposition, which is simple and plain in comparison to the intricate and obscure form of the doctrinal treatises, where the philosophical component is prevalent. Precisely in order to facilitate an appreciation of the entire sense of the passages under examination, Victorinus is careful to give them in anticipation a general sense which is then made more precise and more profound in the explanation of the details. In instances where the Pauline text offers him precise support, he does not hesitate to make an overture of a doctrinal character which is perfectly in line with the original theological formulation of the treatises: see, e.g., the commentary on Phil. 2:6ff (PL 8, 1207ff).

In such a manner, Marius Victorinus succeeds in grasping well, on the basis of the summary exposition in the prefaces, the development of Paul's thought in the individual letters. Nevertheless, the commentary on Galatians is formulated on the polemic of Paul against Jewish observances of a legal character with such a sharpness in tone that at times it extends to affirmations which are untenable in the light of Christian tradition. The fact is that Marius Victorinus, who as a pagan must not have had any sympathy for the Jewish religion, did not believe it to be suitable to modify such an attitude once he became a Christian. His insufficient knowledge of the Old Testament, which forms the Jewish background to the Christian religion, was mentioned above. It is thus to be explained how he was able to arrive at the affirmation that God, the Father of Christ, *longe separatus est a deo Iudaeorum* (PL 8, 1247d), which statement, gnostic in tone, is unacceptable to every orthodox Christian. Furthermore, there are those who would see in the introductions to the commentaries of Marius Victorinus influences from the Marcionite prologues to the letters of Saint Paul.

Always in adherence to the Pauline text, Marius Victorinus insists much on the theme of justification by faith, which is seen as a gift of divine grace. The devaluation of good works, the remembrance of which can deceive us regarding nonexistent merits of our own, is to be seen in the light of a Platonizing interpretation of the Pauline opposition between faith and works visualized as an opposition between intellectual, contemplative activity and practical activity. For Marius Victorinus, the knowledge of the mystery which Paul speaks of especially in Ephesians is essential for salvation. Such a mystery, which for Paul represented the salvific plan of God for the world through the redemptive work of Christ, becomes for Victorinus, ever immersed in the context of the Arian controversy, above all the mystery of the generation of the Son by the Father and of the creation of the world by Christ (PL 8, 1265ff).

Editions: PL 8, 1145-1294. — A. Locher, Teubner 245. Leipzig, 1972. — F. Gori, CPS 8(1981).

Studies: A. Souter, The Earliest Latin Commentaries on the Epistles of St. Paul. Oxford, 1927, 8-38. — A. Lochner, Formen der Textbehandlung im Kommentar des Marius miktorinus zum Galaterbrief: Silvae . . . E. Zinn, Tübingen 1970, 137-143. — K. T. Schäfer, Marius Victorinus und die antimarchionitischen Prologe zu den Paulusbriefen: RB 80(1970)7-16. — W. K. Wischmeyer, Bemerkungen zu den Paulusbriefkommentaren des C. Marius Victorinus: ZNW 63(1972)108-120. — P. Hadot, A propos d'une récente édition des commentaires de Marius Victorinus sur les Épîtres de saint Paul: Latomus 35(1976)133-142. — F. Gori, Per il testo dei Commentari in Apostolum di Mario Vittorino: RFIC 104(1976)149-162; *idem,* Altre note al testo dei Commentarie in Apostolum di Mario Vittorino: SSR 1(1977)377-385. — B. Lohse, Beobachtungen zum Paulus-Kommentar des Marius Victorinus und zur Wiederentdeckung des Paulus in der lateinischen Theologie des vierten Jahrhunderts: *Kerygma und Logos,* Festsch. Andresen, 1979, 351-366. — W. Erdt, Marius Victorinus Afer, der erste lateinische Pauluskommentator. Frankfurt, 1980.

THEOLOGICAL REFLECTION

If in the commentaries on Paul Marius Victorinus appears above all as the grammarian, it is in the theological treatises that he is recognized as the Platonic philosopher. From the second century, and especially with Origen and his school, the influence of Platonic philosophy in the elaboration of Christian Trinitarian doctrine had steadily increased, developing in an organic manner in a rather continuous line. Marius Victorinus, on the other hand, inserts himself in a very personal way into this line. His immediate attachment is to the texts of Porphyry and other Platonizing literature (*Oracula Chaldaica,* etc.) rather than to the Platonism of the Alexandrian Christian tradition. From this there developed a doctrinal synthesis closely attached to these pagan sources and quite original in Christian circles. On the other hand, the necessity of inserting these Platonic threads into the fabric presented by the statements of the creed of Nicea imposed a radical work of adaptation and reinterpretation of these threads which makes for the profound originality of this thinker, who was destined to remain an isolated example in Christian tradition, but who, because of this, is no less worthy of consideration.

From Platonic tradition both pagan and Christian, Marius Victorinus received the point of departure for his Trinitarian reflections: the concept of the absolute transcendence of God. God is one, anterior to any qualification and every category, even that of being (substance); He is one, but not a numerical entity (*Ad. Ar.* I 49; III 1; IV 19). Seen from this point of view, the relation between the Father and the Son is seen as a self-definition of the infinite Father. The Son is the Father who limits Himself, the self-definition of the Father; he is the capacity of thinking which is externalized and is defined as thought (*Ad. Ar.* I 31; IV 37). On the other hand, the Father is not an abstract entity, because all things are derived from Him. He is non-being not through privation but through transcendence (*Ad. Ar.* IV

23). He transcends being but is not without being because of this; He is *substantia ante substantiam* (*Ad. Ar.* II 1). Seen under this new aspect, the relation between the Father and the Son is defined as determination and qualification of the divine substance. Father/Son = being in potency/being in act; the Father is *esse,* the Son is *sic esse* (*Ad. Ar.* I 29).

Marius Victorinus inserts himself into the traditional scheme which saw in the Son the active, creative word of the Father and presented the relation between Father and Son as *esse/moveri, agere, operari;* as *substantia/operatio, actio, motus* (*Ad. Ar.* I 4, 42; III 3). The Son is the being in action of the Father, who is being directed into Himself (*Ad. Ar.* I 19; III 7). In such a relation, Marius Victorinus sees in a Platonic fashion a remainder of subordinationism, not only because the Father is *causa* of the Son, but also because the condition of repose is *sine molestia,* while in motion there is *molestia,* in *agere* there is *passio* (*Ad. Ar.* I 3, 13; IV 31, 32). On the other hand, the presentation of the Son as a creative act of God directed downwards, toward the exterior, allows the author to unite creation and redemption in a wonderful way as the two moments in which Christ communicates life to the world, first creating it and then redeeming it.

The act with which the Father passes from rest into movement is the act of generation. The Son is true Son, real, distinct both from the sons by adoption as well as, in his intelligible nature, from the sons of a material nature (*Ad. Ar.* I 14, 15). Inasmuch as he is *voluntas Patris,* the Son is *alter* in respect to the Father (*Ad. Ar.* I 31). On the other hand, since the generation is the act with which God passes from rest (Father) to motion (Son), it is in effect self-generation, it is the will which generates itself but without splitting, so that the Son, though *prodiens* from the Father, always remains in the Father (*Ad. Ar.* III 17; I 31, 2, 5, 26). The passage from rest to motion must be understood as a purely logical, not chronological, succession (*Ad. Ar.* I 31), inasmuch as being is endowed with an interior movement (*Ad. Ar.* IV 8).

In this manner Marius Victorinus is able to apply every definition and qualification equally to the Father and to the Son, always with the fundamental difference that everything that is said of the Father is intended as referred to God directed inward on Himself, while that which is said of the Son is intended as referred to God directed outward in view of creation: interior motion and exterior motion, hidden life and revealed life, thought in repose and thought in action (*Ad. Ar.* I 31, 32, 42, 52). From this articulate reasoning, the author derives, against the Arians, the absolute equality of the Father and the Son (*Ad. Ar.* IV 29), confirmed by the heavy use of the *homoousion;* one substance, one potency, one divinity (*Ad. Ar.* I 7-9, 11). They have every attribute and qualification in common in a relationship of compenetration and reciprocity, *uterque in utroque* (*Ad. Ar.* I 15, 32). In such a complete identity, the distinction, the otherness of the Father and the Son, is revealed on the basis of the concept of predominance, current in the Platonism of the period, according to which the various individualities in the intelligible world which are contained the one in the other are differentiated among themselves by the predominance of one aspect, by the particular manner according to which one *is* the other (Hadot). Thus, given the fact that both the Father and the Son are *esse* and *motus, potentia* and *actio, substantia* and *vita,* the Father is more *(magis) esse, potentia, substantia;* the Son is more *motus, actio, vita* (*Ad. Ar.* I 20, 33; II 3; III 11). There derives from this, against the accusations of Sabellianism directed at the *homoousion,* the fact that the Father and the Son are *idem* not *ipse,* inasmuch as the identity does not exclude otherness (*Ad. Ar.* I 54; IV 30).

Among the theologians of his time, Marius Victorinus is the only one who, even before the outbreak of the controversy regarding the Holy Spirit, perfectly inserted the third person into the articulation of the divine life and being in a strictly Trinitarian concept of God. This originated from the articulation which he gave, still under the influence of Platonic images, to the concept of *motus.* Given the tension Father/Son = *esse/motus,* the *motus* in its turn is articulated in two dimensions: Christ = *vivere, vita;* the Holy Spirit = *intellegere, sapientia* (*Ad. Ar.* I 12, 32; III 8, 9). Developing in the manner of a line from a point in the work of creation and illumination of the universe, the *motus* (Son) is at first life, when he creates and gives life to the world, then is understanding and wisdom when he illuminates it and leads it back to God (*Ad. Ar.* I 26; IV 7). The action of the life (Christ) is made manifest in the Incarnation, but the wisdom (Holy Spirit) works in the interior of the heart. Thus, Marius Victorinus speaks of *Christus in aperto, manifestus,* and of *spiritus occultus* (*Ad. Ar.* I 13; III 14). The Son *(motus)* unfolds himself as the Holy Spirit only after Christ has terminated his work with the Ascension. Therefore, while Christ derives from the Father, the Holy Spirit derives from Christ by an analogous relationship (*Ad. Ar.* I 13): *ingenitus, unigenitus, genito genitus* (Hymn I 75). That is, in the movement which has generated the Son, there has also been implicitly generated the Holy Spirit, who is one of the two components of this movement. Given the relationship of reciprocity and compenetration, there exists between them the same tension of identity/otherness as we have noted between the Father and the Son: *alter alter* = *idem* (*Ad. Ar.* IV 17, 18, 33).

The separation of the *motus* into *vita* and *intellegentia* is seen by Marius Victorinus in terms of a separation from the Father for the creating of the world and a return to the Father together with the world, that is, as a process of descent and ascent *(descensio vita, ascensio sapientia: Ad. Ar.* I 51; *status, progressio, regressio: Hymn* III 71-73) in which the Holy Spirit has the function of reuniting the Son with the Father: *patris et filii copula* (*Hymn* I 4). It is interesting to note that by making use of a category of a Pythagorean type which was essential in Gnosticism, Victorinus sees the movement of descent *(vita),* to the extent that it is a fertile act by which God disseminates Himself outside of Himself, as the female dimension, and the movement of ascent, to the extent that it is a turning back of God to Himself, as the masculine dimension of a Logos conceived of androgynously (*Ad. Ar.* I 51).

Thus, the Trinity of Marius Victorinus has the characteristic of resolving itself into a double dyad; the first is composed of the Father and the Son, and the Son then separates into the dyad Christ/Holy Spirit. The unity, which is strongly emphasized at both levels, summarizes the entire Trinity *in unum* (*Ad. Ar.* III 4, 8; IV 21). To safeguard the internal distinction of the Trinity, Victorinus rejects with an anti-Sabellian intention the term *persona* as a term insufficiently individualizing (*Ad. Ar.* I 11, 41), and prefers instead the more generic *potentia.* God is *tripotens* (*Ad. Ar.* I 50, 52; III 17; IV 21).

The ambiguity of the term Son (= Christ and = Christ + the Holy Spirit) leads Marius Victorinus to deal with the problem of the unity of God both in reference to the Father and the Son as well as in more specifically Trinitarian terms. In this way, he is the first theologian who considered the Holy Spirit to be *homoousios* with the Father and the Son. This term is intended in the sense of real and true identity in regard to the Trinity as well as in regard to the relationship of the Father and Son, in such a way that the three names are synonymous (*Ad. Ar.* I 54). In such an identity each one of the three has *potentiam suam* (personality, individuality) through which he is other in respect to the others on the strength of the specific action inherent in the *potentia* (concept of predominance). All three are *vox,* but the Father is *vox in silentio,* the Son is *vox* and the Holy Spirit is *vox vocis* (*Ad. Ar.* I 13, 59).

Up to this point we have sketched the principal lines of the Trinitarian discourse of Marius Victorinus, presenting them in light of their internal dynamic which is profoundly conditioned by Platonic parameters. However, this must not lead to the concept of an abstract discourse in fundamental opposition to the Arians. In reality, Marius Victorinus was aware, as has already been indicated, of the complexity of the situation in the years 357-359, and in light of this he developed a treatise which was always firmly anchored in the data of Scripture, in spite of his insufficient knowledge of the Old Testament. He defends the *homoousion* against all adversaries and combats the Sabellian interpretation of the terms by means of the distinction between unity of substance and plurality of *existentiae* (persons) which proceeds from the diverse *operationes* (*Ad. Ar.* I 18, 41). In spite of his polemical stance, he is prepared to enter into discussion with the homoeans and the homoiousians because they consider Christ to be begotten of the Father. On the contrary, he excludes any overture toward those who would give a beginning to Christ, among whose number he reckons, together with the real and true Arians, also Marcellus and Photinus (*Ad. Ar.* II 2). The refutation of the Arian theses is developed by Marius Victorinus not with the precision of Athanasius and Hilary, but in a rather more universal manner which does not give much emphasis to individual arguments of a Scriptural nature. In like fashion, even the Scriptural data which support his own proofs are often times taken over by him in a broader and more comprehensive fashion; a good part of book I *Adversum Arrium* (ch. 3-28) appears as a continuous reading of John, the Synoptics and Paul in an anti-Arian sense. His preference for John is quite clear and at times takes the form of extensive citations. In the pages of Victorinus it is more obvious than ever to what extent the Fourth Gospel was the foundation of anti-Arian Trinitarian theology.

The position of Marius Victorinus in the context of the anti-Arian polemic appears to be that of an isolated individual who is little bound to preceding tradition. Nor does he seem to have exercised any influence in the years immediately following his work. It is necessary to wait until Augustine for an intelligent if marginal utilization of Victorinus' Trinitarian reflections. (In spite of the unimpressive fortunes of Marius Victorinus, the manuscripts which contain his exegetical treatises also attribute to him three works which are certainly not his but which are difficult to locate with regard to date and place: the *De verbis scripturae: factum est vespere et mane dies unus,* the *Liber ad Iustinum Manichaeum* and the *De physicis*). As explanation for the scant fortunes of Marius Victorinus' theological reflections there can be advanced the difficulty of understanding his anti-Arian works, which were written in an excessively technical and rather involved style with a copious use of Greek terms (Jerome calls them *valde obscuros: De vir. inl.* 101). To this can be added the novelty of the doctrinal presentation in contrast with the explanations more firmly rooted in tradition, such as those of Ambrose and Hilary.

POTAMIUS

According to the testimony of Phoebadius (*C. Ar.* 5), Hilary (*Syn.* 3, 11) and others, Potamius, bishop of Lisbon around 350, passed noisily over to the ranks of the Arians in 357, *praemio fundi fiscalis* to use the words of a clearly hostile source (*Lib. prec.* 32; CCL 69, 368). He played a notable role in supporting the Formula of Sirmium of 357 and took part in the Council of Rimini in 359 among the ranks of the bishops who were partisans of a moderate Arianism. After this date there is no further reliable report of him.

There exists no precise information on the character and extent of Potamius' literary production. Four writings of his are extant: the *De Lazaro* and the *De martyrio Esaiae prophetae,* which are homiletic in nature; and the *Epistula ad Athanasium* and the *Epistula de substantia,* which are doctrinal in character. Although doubts were raised in the past regarding the authenticity and integrity of the letter to Athanasius, internal criteria, above all the stylistic character, guarantee the authenticity of the four works. To these must be added a fragment of a letter transmitted by Phoebadius (*C. Ar.* 5). Furthermore, Alcuin (PL 101, 113) reports a passage from a letter in which Athanasius accuses Potamius of considering the Son a creature according to the doctrine of Arius.

This passage from Athanasius and the fragment transmitted in Phoebadius, which is Arian in tone, are to be situated in the years between 357 and 359, during which time Potamius was a member of the Arian faction. On the contrary, it is not easy to establish the chronology of the *Epistula ad Athanasium* and the *Epistula de substantia,* which are explicitly anti-Arian in content. Some scholars have decided for the more obvious chronology in view of the change of sides of 357 and have located the two texts in question in the years immediately preceding that date, thus considering them to be a witness to the doctrinal activity of Potamius before his passage into the ranks of the Arians. The *inscriptio* of the letter to Athanasius, however, refers explicitly to the Council of Rimini (359) and certain themes developed here and in the *Epistula de substantia* seem clearly intended to refute the Formula of Sirmium of 357, which we know was approved and signed by Potamius. In the light of these elements, it seems that Potamius at first allied himself (357) with the Arians who were openly favored by the Emperor Constantius, but that on a subsequent occasion, when the anti-Arian reaction began in the West after 360. he preferred to return to orthodoxy, as did nearly all the bishops who in one way or another had been compromised by Arianism in the West. The two texts would therefore have been composed precisely to ratify this new change of side by the brash bishop of Lisbon. The *De Lazaro* and the *De martyrio Esaiae prophetae,* the chronology of which it is impossible to establish, are two brief compositions of a homiletic nature which are dedicated to the illustration of the well-known episode from the Gospel and of the supposed martyrdom of the prophet Isaiah. The interest of the author does not lie strictly in the interpretation of the two passages in either a literal or an allegorical manner, but exclusively in their description, intended to present the two episodes in the most effective way possible for his listeners. The two works are characterized by the tendency to force the tone as much as possible, far beyond the limits of good taste, and to dwell with particular pleasure on the most macabre and repelling details (the stench which arose from the body of Lazarus, the quartering of Isaiah's body with the saw), always with a preference for strong colors (the wailing of the sisters of Lazarus, the tears of Jesus, etc.). It is a heavy style, a "Spanish baroque" *ante litteram,* which appears as a truly characteristic trait of the author.

Although the context is quite different, the same style of writing, directed more to an external effect, appears in the two doctrinal letters which, as noted above, are anti-Arian in tone in contrast to the pro-Arian fragment transmitted by Phoebadius. The *Epistula ad Athanasium* takes a stand on certain points of the Trinitarian question which were debated during the years 357-359 as it praises the indefatigable fidelity of Athanasius to the Nicene faith. The same themes are treated to a much greater extent in the *Epistula de substantia,* which represents a noteworthy attempt to clarify the significance of substance in relation to the Godhead. Since by "substance" (ch. 3) he means that by which a thing is what it is, he outlines the substantial unity of the Trinity in a general way as a substrate common to all three persons, just as everything which is made with wheat or with wool has respectively the same substance. But going beyond this too general concept of likeness, Potamius arrives, especially when he outlines the unity of action in the Trinity, at a statement of the absolute identity between the persons of the Father and the Son and of their reciprocal and total compenetration (ch. 18, 19).

The most characteristic part of this work is the final section, from ch. 22 on. Departing from Gen. 1:26 where man is said to have been made in God's image, Potamius strives to discover the image of the one and triune God not in the interior man, as Augustine will subsequently do, but precisely in the exterior features of the face. A very discreet allusion in this direction is also to be found in the contemporary anti-Arian works of Marius Victorinus. By contrast, Potamius, with his typical poor taste, dwells on a series of highly original variations designed to detect in the eyes, the ears, the cheeks and the arms of man the tension between plurality and unity. The discussion centers above all on the relation between Father and Son, which was the principal theme of the discussions around 355-360 (there are two eyes but only one visual capacity). However, the discussion tends to extend in a certain way also to the Holy Spirit in a universal vision of the Trinity which is characteristic of Western thought during these years, in contrast to the East which was polarized rather on the distinction of the divine persons.

Editions: Cf. CPL 541-545. — PL 8, 1409-1418 (cf. 11, 251-254); PLS I, 202-216. — A. Wilmart, La letter de Potamius à saint Athanase: RB 30(1913)257-285; *idem,* Le "De Lazaro" de Potamius: JThSt 19(1918)289-304. — A. C. Vega, Opuscula omnia Potamii episcopi Olisiponensis. El Escorial, 1934.

Studies: U. Domínguez del Val: Repertorio de historia de las ciencias eclesiásticas en España I, Salamance, 1967, 5-6. — E. Hennecke: Potamius: RE 15(1904)579-580. — J. A. Ferreira, Aqueda de Pótamio primeiro Bispo documentalmente conhecido de Lisboa (357-359), na heresia ariana: *Memorias Acad. Cien. de Lisboa, Classe Letras III,* 1938(1940)117-127. — J. Madoz, Potamio di Lisboa: RET 7(1947)79-109. — A. De J. Da Costa, Subsídios bibliográficos para una Patrologia portuguesa: *Theologica* (Braga) 1(1954)67-85,211-240. — U. Domínguez del Val, Potamio de Lisboa. Su ortodoxia y doctrina sobre la consustancialidad del Hijo: CD 172(1959)237-259. — A. Montes Moreira, Potâmio e as origens do Cristianismo en Lisboa: *Itinerarium* 10(1964)378-381; *idem,* O "De Lazaro" de Potâmio de Lisboa: *Itinerarium* 11(1965)19-53; *idem,* Dois textos mariológicos de Potâmio de Lisboa: *Itinerarium* 13(1967)457-464 [= Textus mariologici Potamii Olisiponensis: De primordiis cultus Mariani 3, Rome 1970, 205-211]; *idem,* Potamius de Lisbonne et la controverse arienne. Louvain, 1969; *idem,* Le retour de Potamius de Lisbonne à l'orthodoxie nicéenne: *Didaskalia* 5(1975)303-354. — M. Simonetti, La crisi ariano e l'inizio della riflessione teologica in Spagna: Hispania Romana, Acc. Lincei, Rome 1974, 127-147.

PHOEBADIUS

Phoebadius, bishop of Agen in Gaul, was, along with Servatius of Tongres, one of the most representative members of the large delegation of Gallic bishops at the Council of Rimini (359). This group was distinguished by an insuperable hostility toward the Arians, and Phoebadius was the last of the bishops gathered at Rimini to capitulate in the face of the pressure of the imperial delegates. He signed the pro-Arian Formula of Rimini only after certain clarifications had been placed in writing which, in his opinion, attenuated its Arianizing tone. After these events we have no further information about Phoebadius, except that Jerome (*De vir. inl.* 108) says that he was very old in 392. It can easily be supposed that he participated in the anti-Arian activity promoted by Hilary in Gaul from 361 on.

Jerome (ibid.) speaks of other brief writings of Phoebadius which he admits never to have read, and he specifically names only the *Contra Arrianos,* the one work of Phoebadius extant today. This is a brief treatise in which Phoebadius refutes in a rather systematic fashion the pro-Arian Formula of Sirmium of 357, and thus the treatise is to be dated between the end of 357 and the beginning of 358. The influence of Tertullian's *Adversus Praxean,* which is often reproduced *ad litteram,* is obvious. In connection with this it must be noted, however, that Tertullian in his treatise had opposed the Monarchian teaching of Praxeas, which was poles apart from the radical subordinationism of the Arians. Nevertheless, since his ignorance of Greek did not allow him to make use of the anti-Arian writings of Athanasius and the other Eastern writers, Phoebadius was forced to have recourse to the writings of Tertullian in order to find material on the Trinitarian question. In order to use this material, though, he had to radically modify its basic formulations so as to turn the anti-Monarchian polemic to an anti-Arian purpose. All of this demonstrates in Phoebadius a notable mastery of the terms of the complex controversy and a capacity to rethink them, if not in an original way, at least in a manner in keeping with the necessities of the moment.

The brief work of Phoebadius is a precise witness of how the anti-Arian Trinitarian doctrine was developing in support of the Nicene Symbol around the years 355-360. Phoebadius knows and uses the terminology of Tertullian in the same way as Potamius; *substantia* indicates the common divine nature, and *persona* indicates the individuality of the Father and the Son, to whom he occasionally joins the Holy Spirit. As is usual in the West, the weight of the argument is in defense of the unity of the divine substance shared by the three persons, although the distinction of persons also receives a certain emphasis in an anti-Sabellian sense which, even if it is not confirmed to the same extent as in Hilary, is nevertheless unusual in the West at this time.

Particular mention is owed to the position of Phoebadius in relation to the formula of 357 which, although basically pro-Arian, was intended as a compromise formula acceptable in part to all. As far as Phoebadius was concerned, it was merely a lie which sought to stealthily introduce real and true Arianism in its radical form. According to Phoebadius, the prohibition contained in the formula of using the term *homoousios* (consubstantial), the distinctive term of Nicene theology, is directed to this end. Therefore, although he avoids the specific use of the disputed term, he insists in a special way on the concept of divine substance *(ousia);* the only adequate concept, according to him, for designating the Son's belonging to the reality of the Father and thus to His full divinity; a fact denied by his adversaries.

Editions and Studies: Cf. CPL 473. — PL 20, 11-30; PLS I, 785. — V. C. de Clerq: DHG 16(1967)785-790. — A. Wilmart, La tradition des opuscules dogmatiques de Foebadius, Gregorius Illiberitanus, Faustinus: SAW 159, 1. Vienna, 1908. — J. Dräseke, Die Schrift des Bischofs Phöbadius von Agennum "Gegen die Arianer" eingeleitet und übersetzt. Wandsbeck, 1910. — A. Durengues, Le livre de S. Fébade contre les Ariens. Agen, 1927. — P. P. Gläser, Phoebadius von Agen. Augsburg, 1979.

GREGORY OF ELVIRA

At the time between 357 and 359 when the Arian question reached its greatest intensity in Spain, Gregory had just become bishop of Elvira in Hispania Baetica. Jerome, in his *Chronicon* (s.a. 387), mentions that Gregory never yielded *Arrianae pravitati,* and modern scholars tend to interpret this information in the sense that Gregory did not yield to sign the Arian formula at the Council of Rimini. From other sources, however, we know that all of the more than four hundred Western bishops gathered at Rimini in 359 were forced by every possible means to sign. It is therefore preferable to believe that Gregory did not take part in the council and that he subsequently refused to sign the formula. In any case, it does not appear that he suffered any reprisals for his intransigent attitude. He later appears around 380-385 in the capacity of leader in the West of the so-called Luciferian Schism (cf. "Lucifer and the Luciferians"). Jerome (*De vir. inl.* 105) describes him as being very old in 392 and there are reasons to believe that he was still alive in the first years of the fifth century.

At the beginning of the present century all that was known of Gregory's literary activity was contained in the scanty references of Jerome (ibid.), *viz.* that he had composed some *tractatus* (i.e., homilies) *mediocri sermone et de fide elegantem librum.* However, a series of successful attributions, especially on the part of Dom Morin and Dom Wilmart, completed by the discovery of manuscripts in Spanish libraries due to the work of A. C. Vega, have permitted a complex of works to be attributed with absolute certainty to Gregory and have made him the most important and best-known Spanish author prior to Isidore of Seville.

The *Tractatus de libris sanctarum scripturarum,* published for the first time in 1900, were initially attributed to Origen under the name of *Tractatus Origenis* on the basis of an indication in one of the manuscripts. This attribution later proved to be untenable and the attribution of Gregory was proposed on the basis of comparisons in language and style with the *De fide* and the *Tractatus in Cantica canticorum* which at that time also were beginning to be attributed to Gregory. The attribution was later confirmed by a medieval testimony published by Vega. The *Tractatus de libris sanctarum scripturarum* consists of twenty fairly extensive homilies all dealing with a scriptural topic. The first nineteen are dedicated to the allegorical illustration of passages and episodes from the Old Testament arranged in order from Genesis to Zechariah. The last homily, based on Acts 2:1-2, is dedicated to an illustration of the activity of the Holy Spirit. The *Tract.* 3 in many instances coincides word for word with Rufinus' translation of Origen's *Hom. Gen.* 7, 2-3, and the comparison between the two texts leads to the belief that Gregory borrowed from Rufinus. The translation of Rufinus was made around the year 403, so if Gregory's dependence on Rufinus is accepted the composition of the *Tractatus* must be placed shortly after that date, at a time when Gregory was more than 75 years of age.

The *Tractatus de arca Noe,* which was also transmitted under

Origen's name, illustrates the episode of the ark for the space of several pages, interpreting the ark in an allegorical manner as a figure of the church and Noah as a figure of Christ. The *Tractatus in Cantica canticorum* presents the interpretation of the Canticle of Canticle up to Cant. 3:4 in five short books according to the traditional interpretation which sees in the two royal spouses who are the protagonists of the work the figures of Christ and the Church. Other exegetical texts can be noted of more modest dimensions but always characterized by allegorical interpretation, such as the *Expositio de psalmo XCI* and the *Fragmenta tractus in Gen.* 3:22 *et* 15:9-11.

The *De fide,* to the contrary, is of a doctrinal rather than an exegetical nature. Gregory wrote a first edition of this work anonymously in 360 to refute the pro-Arian formula approved by the Council of Rimini and to confirm the validity of the Nicene theology centered on the term *homoousios* for indicating the consubstantiality of the Son with the Father and thus his perfect divinity. The work enjoyed a certain success in Catholic circles but also provoked unfavorable reactions because some points gave the impression of proposing Monarchian (Sabellian) affirmations. Gregory therefore published a second edition of the same work a few years later (ca. 363-364), this time not in an anonymous form since the pro-Arian Emperor Constantius was dead. This second edition was furnished with a long preface in which the author defends himself from the accusations brought against him, and which permits us to know the entire story. Gregory did not fail to take advantage of this opportunity to modify numerous points of the first edition which could appear doctrinally ambiguous. Both editions of the work have been preserved, though by different channels; the first under the name of Ambrose, the second under the name of Gregory Nazienzus. In modern times, from the seventeenth century on, the two works began to be published fused into one, and since the incorrectness of the attribution to Ambrose and Gregory Nazienzus was recognized, others were proposed as the author, including Phoebadius and Gregory of Elvira. The attribution to Phoebadius dominated the field until the beginnings of the present century, at which time Gregory's name was again proposed simultaneously with the publication of his other works, mentioned above. The attribution to Gregory has won decisive acceptance and can be considered as absolutely certain.

To these works, which are published as authentic in the recent edition of CCL 69, there are added some others under the heading of *Dubia et spuria.* Of these, the long fragments *De Salomone,* containing an allegorical interpretation of Prov. 30:19 and transmitted under the name of Ambrose, and two brief *Fragmenta expositionis in Ecclesiasten* (Eccl. 3:2 and 3:6) can certainly be considered authentic on the basis of clear correspondences in language with the other works. On the contrary, the attribution to Gregory of the *De diversis generibus leprarum,* an allegorical interpretation of various passages of Genesis which speak of the impurity contracted with leprosy, remains much more uncertain. Most recently, Gregory's name has been suggested for a profession of faith extant in various editions under various titles: *libellus fidei, fides catholica, fides Romanorum.* The points of contact between this text and the authentic works of Gregory are too general for the attribution to be able to be considered convincing. In any case, it should be noted that the conception of the Holy Spirit which appears in the so-called *fides catholica* is much more advanced than that presented in the *De fide,* while the *fides Romanorum* shows an interest for the real and not apparent corporeal nature of the humanity of Christ which shows traces of the polemic with the Priscillianists. Therefore, if this text is to be attributed to Gregory, it must be situated many years after the *De fide,* i.e., not before 380.

As much as we know of Gregory of Elvira, confirmed by Jerome's data, reveals this author's preeminent interests of an exegetical nature, which were directed above all to the interpretation of the Old Testament. The attention of other contemporary bishops (e.g., Zeno of Verona) also was concentrated chiefly on the Old Testament. This evidence, disconcerting at first, can be explained by the necessity of bringing about a better understanding of this part of Sacred Scripture, the ignorance of which must have been deeply rooted in the common people if even men of letters such as Lactantius and Marius Victorinus display a less than superficial understanding of the topic. To this there can be added the obligation of the anti-Manichaean polemic with the scope of defending the canonicity of those parts of the Scripture which the Manichaeans called into question. In this sense, Gregory's lines of interpretation are those ones already traditional, developed at the time of the polemic against the Gnostics, which was similar in so many respects to the anti-Manichaean polemic. Gregory, in fact, interprets the Old Testament in a predominantly allegorical fashion with typological interpretations intended to perceive in figures and episodes of the Old Testament the anticipations and prefigurations of figures and events of the New Testament.

Gregory, however, knows how to insert himself into the fabric of this traditional interpretation in a personal way which gives evidence of long study and meditation on the subject. He knows how to distinguish in the Old Testament a *triplicem significantiam* (*Tract. script.* 5, 1), *id est prophetiae, historiae et figurae,* where the prophecy lies *in praescientia futurorum,* the *historia* (i.e., literal interpretation) *in relatione gestorum,* and the *figura* (i.e., typological interpretation) *in similitudine rerum,* to prescind from those passages which are of value only for exhortation or edification. On occasion, Gregory considers the literal interpretation to be sufficient, as in the case of the field of bones of Ez. 37:1-4. Usually, however, he prefers typological allegory in order to bring out the Christological sense of the Old Testament, which perceives the figure of Christ in Joseph, in the vision of Abraham at Mamre, in the *vas fictile* of 2 Kgs. 2:20-22 and in a thousand other places. This allows him, with the aid of the same Spirit who inspired the sacred writer, to discover the spiritual sense of Scripture which is hidden under the veil of the letter and often escapes the *simpliciores* (*Tract.* 8,1; 11, 2; 16, 8-9; 17, 3; 19, 12). All of this along with other hints of a methodological character (cf. the *defectus litterae* in *Tract.* 3, 20) point to Origen's criteria of interpretation, which Gregory, already advanced in age, could have learned from the translations of Jerome and Rufinus. Traces of an Origenist flavor are also to be found in the commentary on the Canticle, although they are placed alongside of quite notable divergences from the interpretation of the Alexandrian; e.g., the skins of Solomon and the tents of Kedar in Cant. 1:5 are interpreted in a negative sense with regard to the color black, which Origen on the contrary had assumed in a nobly positive sense. In general, it can be said that for the Canticle Gregory prefers the traditional typology of bridegroom = Christ and bride = church, and does not refer to the supplementary interpretation, typically Origenist, of the bride = the soul. In short, diverse influences can be noted in Gregory's exegesis, Alexandrian alongside Asiatic, the latter visible in hints that hearken back to Irenaeus (*Tract.* 9, 12). Both, however, are assimilated in a personal manner.

Gregory's doctrinal interests are concentrated above all in the *De fide,* with some scattered traces in the exegetical works. In the *De fide,* written to refute the Formula of Rimini of 359 but attentive also to the Formula of Sirmium of 357 and to the results of discussions carried on with pro-Arian elements, Gregory centers his attention on the defense of the term *homoousios,* and shares with Phoebadius the conviction that if this word is eliminated, the way lies open to Arianism. His defense presents traditional characteristics, based on the utilization of Tertullian, Novatian, Phoebadius and pre-exile Hilary. He is aware (ch. 7) of the danger of Sabellian Monarchianism, the antithesis of Arianism, but his prevailing interest is undoubtedly against Arianism. Therefore, Gregory takes pains more to demonstrate the substantial unity of the Son with the Father and his full divinity rather than to distinguish him from the Father, although he does make use of Tertullian's term *persona* in the manner of Phoebadius and Lucifer. This formulation along with traces of an archaic flavor provoked the criticisms of the first edition of the writing, mentioned above, and forced the author to revise his work. With respect to the first edition, the second is more balanced in the tension between unity of nature and distinction of person in the Father and the Son, more precise in terminology and more open to Trinitarian formulae, that is, broadened to include also the Holy Spirit within the divine reality, a factor missing in the first edition.

Gregory is a good witness both of the necessity to bring doctrinal notions in the Trinitarian question up to date, which necessity was recognized as a result of the Arian crisis even in such a peripheral area as Spain, as well as of the difficulty encountered in this process of updating by theologians scarcely familiar with Greek and distant from the more vital centers of Christian culture.

Editions: Cf. CPL 545-557. — PL 17, 549-568 (= 20, 31-50 and 62, 449-463); PLS I, 352-527 (cf. 1743-1746). — A. C. Vega, España Sagrada 55. Madrid, 1957. — V. Bulhart, J. Fraipont, CCL 69(1967)1-283. — M. Simonetti, Gregorio di Elvira, La fede. Turin, 1975.

Translations: Italian: Simonetti, op. cit.

Studies: J. Collantes Lozano: DSp 6(1967)923-927 (bibliog.). — P. Batiffol - A. Wilmart, Tractatus Origenis de libris Ss. Scripturarum. Paris, 1900. — G. Morin, Autour des Tractatus Origenis: RB 19(1902)225-245. — J. Haussleiter, Novatians Predigt über die Kundschafter in direkter Überlieferung und in einer Bearbeitung des Cäsarius von Arles: NKZ 13(1902)119-143. — A. Wilmart, Les "Tractatus" sur le Cantique attribués à Grégoire d'Elvire: BLE 7(1906)233-299; *idem,* La tradition des opuscules dogmatiques de Foebadius, Gregorius Illiberitanus, Faustinus, SAW 159, 1. Vienna, 1908; *idem,* Arca Noe: RB 26(1909)1-12; *idem,* Un manuscrit du Tractatus du Faux Origène sur le psaume XCI dans une collection espagnole: RB 29(1912)274-293. — H. Koch, Zu Gregors von Elvira Schrifttum und Quellen: ZKG 51(1932)238-272. — F. Regina, Il "De Fide" di Gregorio di Elvira. Naples, 1942. — A. C. Vega, Una gran figura literaria del siglo IV: Gregorio di Elvira: CD 156(1944)205-258; *idem,* Dos nuevos tratados de Gregorio de Elvira: CD 156(1944)515-553. — J. Collantes Lozano, San Gregorio de Elvira. Estudio sobre su eclesiologia. Granada, 1954. — T. Ayuso Marazuela, El salterio de Gregorio de Elvira y la Vetus Latina Hispana: Bibl 40(1959)135-159. — L. Galmés, La fe según Gregorio de Elvira: Teologia espiritual 3(1959)275-283. — M. Simonetti, Alcune osservazioni a proposito di una professione di fede attribuita a Gregorio di Elvira: RCCM 2(1960)307-325. — V. Bulhart, Die Konjunktionen que und qui in den Tractatus Origenis: SE 11(1960)5-11; *idem,* Ignis sapiens: SE 13(1962)60-61 (Tract. 17, 32 and Minucius Felix). — F. J. Buckley, Christ and Church according to Gregory of Elvira. Rome, 1964. — E. Mazorra, Correcciones inéditas de Adolf Jülicher a la edición príncipe de los Tractatus Origenis: EE 41(1966)219-232; *idem,* La carta de Eusebio de Vercelli a Gregorio de Elvira y los cronicones: EE 42(1967)241-250; *idem,* El patrimonio literario de Gregorio de Elvira: EE 42(1967)387-397. — C. Vona, Gregorio de Elvira. I Tractatus de libris sacrarum scripturarum. Fonti e sopravvivenza medievale. Rome, 1970. — U. Domínguez del Val, Herencia literaria de Gregorio de Elvira: *Helmantica* 24(1973)281-357. — M. Simonetti, La doppia redazione del De Fide di Gregorio di Elvira: Forma Futuri, Studi M. Pellegrino, Turin 1975, 1022-1040. — M. Didone, Gregorio di Elvira e la paternitá del De Salomone e dell 'Explanatio beati Hieronymi: *Divinitas* 24(1980)178-210. — D. Gianotti, Gregorio di Elvira interprete del Cantico dei Cantici: Aug 24(1984)421-439.

FAUSTINUS

What little is known of Faustinus is taken from his writings, which are likewise the source of the information in Gennadius (*De vir. inl.* 16). Around 380 he was a priest at Rome of the schismatic sect of the Luciferians and had some contact with Flaccilla, wife of the Emperor Theodosius. Precisely at the request of Flaccilla, and thus before 386, the year in which the empress died, Faustinus wrote his *De Trinitate,* which is extant along with two other of his works. After unfolding a synthesis of the Arian doctrine, Faustinus follows it first with a comprehensive presentation of the Catholic teaching, then with some particular discussions intended to illustrate particular key points of the controversy (the Son is not a creature but is true Son and true God; the immutability of the Son, especially in relation to the Incarnation) and with scriptural passages much discussed by the opposing sides (Jn. 14:28; Acts 2:36; Prov. 8:22). The work concludes with a brief but exhaustive treatise on the Holy Spirit.

The work does not present marks of originality. Faustinus draws his inspiration from Gregory of Elvira, at that time the recognized leader of all Luciferians in the West, and from Hilary. Ambrose and other authors appear to have been used to a much lesser extent. Within the limits of these sources, Faustinus moves with competence and without difficulty, notwithstanding the rigid technicality of the treatment, which is a characteristic of the minor literature, both Arian and anti-Arian, and which confirms the notably high average level attained by both parties. In comparison to the *De fide* of Gregory and the *De Trinitate* of Hilary, the work of Faustinus, written some twenty years later, displays a greater theological knowledge in those arguments which were subsequently developed in the latter phase of the controversy, especially with regard to the theology of the Holy Spirit.

Attached to this work, which is Faustinus' most involved doctrinal composition, there is a very brief profession of faith which he sent to Theodosius. It is evident from this that the adversaries of the Luciferians were accusing Faustinus of harboring Sabellian and Apollinarian ideas. On the basis of the extant data the second accusation cannot be substantiated, because the *De Trinitate* is precise in its affirmation (ch. 33) that the Incarnate Logos took to himself a complete man composed of body and soul. The accusation of Sabellianism leveled against the Luciferians derives from their refusal to accept the Catholic doctrine of the Eastern theologians formulated by Basil on the tension between one divine *ousia* (substance) and three hypostases, inasmuch as it escaped them that hypostasis in this instance was to be assigned the same meaning as the Latin *persona.*

Together with a Luciferian priest by the name of Marcellinus, otherwise unknown, Faustinus also addressed to Theodosius in 384 an extensive petition *De confessione verae fidei et ostentatione sacrae communionis et persecutione adversantium veritati,* commonly referred to as the *Libellus precum.* The aim of the petition was to obtain from the emperor the cessation of the persecutions directed against the Luciferians by their Catholic adversaries in various parts of the Empire both East and West, and it is a text of fundamental importance for a knowledge of the Luciferian Schism. It gives reports, albeit in disordered form, on the Luciferian communities in the East, especially in Egypt and Palestine, as well as on those in the West, especially in Italy and Spain as well as in Germany. The text does not lack fictitious elements, especially when treating of events which by that time lay twenty years or more in the past, such as when it ruthlessly attacks the aged Hosius of Cordova for yielding in 357 or when it makes claims of personal contacts between Lucifer of Cagliari and Gregory of Elvira. When it gives information regarding the current state of the schismatics, however, the *libellus* seems to be completely reliable. It bears witness to the rigid intransigence of these schismatics, who had not desired to have any contact with bishops who in one way or another had compromised with Arianism, even if they had subsequently returned to Nicene orthodoxy. A rescript of Theodosius is joined to the petition granting freedom of worship to all those who in the West are in communion with Gregory of Elvira and in the East with Heraclides of Osrhoene and prescribing that they not be subjected to any difficulties by their opponents.

Editions: Cf. CPL 119-120, 1571. — PL 13, 37-108 (cf. PLS I, 307-308). — K. Künstle, Eine Bibliothek der Symbole. Mainz, 1900, 148-149. — A. Hahn, Bibliothek der Symbole und Glaubensregeln der alten Kirche. Breslau, 1897 (reprint: Hildescheim, 1962) n. 202, 277f. — O. Günther, CSEL 35, 1(1895)LVIII-LX, 5-44. — M. Simonetti, CCL 69(1967)287-392, 410-437.

Studies: G. Bareille: DTC 5/2 (1913)2105-2107 (cf. DHG 16, 738). — A. Wilmart, La tradition des opuscules dogmatiques de Foebadius, Gregorius Illiberitanus, Faustinus, SAW 159, 1. Vienna, 1908. — M. Simonetti, Note su Faustino: SE 14(1963)50-98.

ALTERCATION BETWEEN HERACLIANUS AND GERMINIUS, BISHOP OF SIRMIUM

This brief text, discovered and published by C. Caspari in 1883, is one of the most characteristic documents in our possession regarding the Arian controversy. It consists of the account of a public debate held at Sirmium on January 13, 366, between Germinius, the local bishop and authoritative spokesman of the moderate Arians, and Heraclianus, an otherwise unknown layman held captive along with other of his companions as propagandists of the Nicene faith. After some initial blows in which Heraclianus stands up to Germinius and which end with an act of violence at his expense, the bishop agrees to *altercare.*

The debate is divided into four parts. In the first, Heraclianus and Germinius debate the divinity of the Holy Spirit and the equality of the Father and Son, which Germinius denies but without being able to prevail over Heraclianus. In the second part, the priest Theodorus seeks in vain to confound Heraclianus by bringing forward the well-known Gospel passage on the ignorance of the Son (Mk. 13:32; Mt. 24:36). In the third section, Heraclianus combats a no better qualified Agrippinus again on the question of the inferiority of the Son and the creatureliness of the Holy Spirit. Finally Germinius takes the floor and again denies the divinity of the Holy Spirit, but Heraclianus refutes him and supports his affirmation of the unity of the three divine persons with a profession of faith which reproduces almost *ad litteram* a passage of Tertullian's *Apologeticum* (21, 12-14). At this point the debate becomes animated. Germinius accuses Heraclianus of being a heretic and the crowd, which is hostile for the most part, calls for Heraclianus and his companions to be brought before the *consularis* and put to death, inasmuch as they *seditionem fecerunt et de uno populo duos fecerunt.* Germinius, however, wisely refuses to go to such extremes. The prisoners are forced to humble themselves *sub manibus* of Germinius and are released.

This is a text of great importance because it presents a live account of an episode of the Arian controversy and bears witness to the passions aroused by the various parties in the struggle. The general impression which is drawn from a reading of the text is that it has been somewhat reworked by Catholic hands, which have presented Germinius as more of an Arian than he really ever was and have magnified the figure of Heraclianus in the face of inept and violent adversaries. In spite of the revisions, however, the text abounds in precious details which are absolutely trustworthy, such as the conclusion which reveals the wise moderation of the pro-Arian bishop. The arguments proposed are in substance those which can be found in the works of the theologians of both parties, although presented here in a rapid and rough form. The recourse to the text of Tertullian, the content of which was already outdated for the purposes of the dispute, bears witness to the persistence of elements tending toward archaisms in circles of Latin-speaking Christians of a low cultural level.

Editions: Cf. CPL 687. — PLS I, 327, 345-350. — C. Caspari, Kirchenhistorische Anekdota I. Christiania, 1883, 133-147.

Studies: M. Simonetti, Osservazioni sull'Altercatio Heracliani cum Germinio: VC 21(1967)39-58.

Arian Literature

Arianism struggled to gain a foothold in the West. With the exception of the two Illyrian bishops, Valens of Mursa and Ursacius of Singidunum (Belgrade), who already appear as partisans of Arius in 335 at the Council of Tyre which condemned Athanasius, it is necessary to wait until the years following 350 to perceive more durable traces of Arianism. Once Constantius, who was clearly of a pro-Arian tendency, had become sole emperor following the death of Constans, the propaganda in this direction enjoyed some measure of success in the West, especially in Illyricum, but also in Gaul, Spain and elsewhere. Very little is known of the literary activity of these Western Arians prior to 380. A certain amount has surely been lost, but the distinct impression is that this primary phase of Arian activity in the West did not give rise to any appreciable literary output. Mention can be made here of some synodal documents and a few letters.

The oldest Arian document in the Latin language extant today is the diffuse formula of faith published at Sirmium in 357 as a result of the efforts of Valens, Ursacius and Germinius; the latter being the bishop of Sirmium elected in place of the deposed Photinus in 351 and who was a faithful collaborator of the other two Illyrian bishops. Although it avoids the terms of radical Arianism which the Arians themselves had repudiated by then, this formula opens wide the door to real and true Arianism on account of the clear subordinationist formulation with which it outlines the relationship between Christ and the Father. The prohibition of the use of the term *homoousios,* the badge of the Nicene creed, defines the scope of this formula which was intended to be the real liquidation of the Nicene formula of 325. Much shorter is the profession of faith of Rimini (359), which the minority of pro-Arian bishops led by the three above-named Illyrians and vigorously supported by the Emperor Constantius imposed on the anti-Arian and pro-Nicene majority of the Western bishops, who were too little organized to be able to resist the emperor's pressure. The formula is more moderate than that of 357, and the tone is purposely general enough to allow each individual, and thus even the Arians, to interpret it according to his own convictions. The Son is defined here only as similar to the Father according to the Scriptures.

In 364, as has been mentioned already, Hilary of Poitiers and Eusebius of Vercelli traveled to Milan to attempt to depose from that important see the Arian bishop Auxentius, elected in 355 to replace Dionysius, who had been deposed and exiled for his attachment to Athanasius and the Nicene faith. At that time, the emperor Valentinian I, who ruled the West, had inaugurated a policy of non-intervention in religious questions and concerned himself with them only when they disturbed the public order. Auxentius, therefore, appealed to the emperor in a letter which was added as an appendix to Hilary's *Contra Auxentium.* In this letter, the Arian bishop complains of Hilary's activities against him and reaffirms his attachment to the Formula of Rimini, which the Arians always considered as the official formula of faith.

The *Fragmenta historica* of Hilary (*frag.* 13-15 = A 3; B 5-6 ed. Feder) have transmitted three documents probably composed around 365-366. The first of these is a profession of faith of Germinius in which this bishop, whose debate with the layman Heraclianus has been treated above (cf. p. 91), distances himself from the neutral vagueness of the Formula of Rimini in order to take up again certain expressions from the compromise formula of May 22, 359, which defined the Son as being like to the Father in everything. This text was certainly not able to indicate Germinius' adherence to the Catholic Nicene party, but it did represent in any case a definite estrangement from the Arian positions which were firmly entrenched around the Formula of Rimini. Because of this, Valens, Ursacius and other Illyrian bishops who were alarmed by the change of sides of their influential colleague summoned a small council at Singidunum and sent Germinius an official letter, dated December 18, 366, inviting him to clarify that he intended the "like according to the Scriptures" of Rimini without further specifications *(absolute),* and not in the sense of like in everything or like according to substance. It is not known whether or how Germinius may have responded to this invitation. Instead, there exists an extensive declaration of his addressed to Palladius of Ratiaria, another Arian spokesman of that region, and to seven other bishops. Here, Germinius clarifies his doctrinal position in an unambiguously anti-Arian sense. In fact, he interprets the likeness of Christ to the Father as a complete likeness, *excepta innativitate,* i.e., he distinguishes Christ only because he is generated while the Father is ingenerate. He also clarifies that he intends the divine generation as a real generation by which the Son comes to possess all the prerogatives of the Father. The text avoids defining the Son as *homoousios* with respect to the Father, but its content is perfectly orthodox. The progressive estrangement of Germinius from the formula of 357, in the composition of which he had himself participated, is completed here. Whether this was a question of a sincere conviction or merely a political move in view of the progressive deterioration of the Arian fortunes in both East and West is not able to be determined.

This uncertainty is to a certain extent characteristic of the entire evaluation that can be given to these Arian documents. It was mentioned above that not even the formula of 357 can be defined as an expression of radical Arianism, i.e., of that Arianism proposed by Arius at the beginning of his activity and taken up again from around 355 by Aetius and Eunomius, the ringleaders of Arianism in the East. More moderate still is the Formula of Rimini, which defines a real and true central position between the extremes of the homoousian and homoiousian doctrines on the one hand and radical Arianism on the other. The question can therefore be raised as to whether these formulae, especially the extensive and elaborated one of 357, effectively represented the convictions of Valens, Ursacius and their other collaborators, or whether they were merely the convenient screen for an Arianism of a more radical stripe, such as that of Aetius and Eunomius.

We do not possess the necessary elements to render a judgment in response to this question, all the less so as the above-mentioned Arian bishops give the impression of having been politicians above all, who do not seem to have worked out the doctrinal terms of the conflict in a personal manner. Hilary reports (*Frag. hist.* 10, 2-3 = B 8, 2, 1-2 ed. Feder) that when he arrived at Constantinople toward the end of 359 the commission responsible for reporting the definitive results of the Council of Rimini to Constantius was circulating a *Liber* of Valens and Ursacius which contained definite Arian statements but which the two refused to recognize as their own. Nothing more is known of this text, and thus the uncertainty mentioned above remains.

Editions: (Germinius) A. Fder, Hilarii opera, CSEL 65(1916)47-48, 160-164. — Cf. CPL 685-686. — (General) R. Gryson, Scolies ariennes sur le concile d'Aquilée. SCh 267(1980); *idem,* Scripta Ariana latina I: Collectio Veronensis. CCL 87(1982); *idem,* Littérature arienne latine I: Débats de Maximinus avec Augustin. Scolies ariennes sur le concile d'Aquilée. Louvain, 1982.

For further bibliography, consult the individual works as well as the sections regarding Arianism in the East in: J. Quasten, *Patrology,* vol. II. Utrecht, 1960, ch. I, III and IV. Some of the more important recent works are listed here.

Studies: A. Martínez Sierra, La prueba escriturística de los arrianos según Hilario de Poitiers: *Miscellanea Comillas* 41(1964)293-377. — M. Simonetti, Studi sull'arianesimo. Rome, 1965; *idem,* Arianesimo latino: *Studi Medievali* s. 3, 8(1967)663-774. — M. Meslin, Les Ariens d'Occident. Paris, 1967. — Y.–M. Duval, Sur l'arianism de Ariens d'Occident: MSR 26(1969)145-153. — P. Nautin, RHR 177(1970)70-89. — L. J. van der Lof, Traditio im arianischen Streit: *Nederl. Theol. Tijdschrift* 24(1970)421-429. — M. Simonetti, La tradizione nella controversia arians: Aug 12(1972)37-50. — E. Boularand, L'hérésie d'Arius et la foi de Nicée 1-2. Paris, 1972. — H. Silvestre, A propos d'une récente édition de la Damnatio Arii de Rimini: RHE 68(1973)102-104. — M. Simonetti, La cattedra di Pietro durante la controversia ariana: *ArcheolClas* 25-26(1973-74)676-687); *idem,* La crisi ariana nel IV secolo. Rome, 1975.

WULFILA AND ARIANISM IN ILLYRIA

In the West toward 380 Arianism had been reduced to a few small enclaves, concentrated above all in Illyria, which led a wretched existence, surrounded by hostility from the then-triumphant Catholics and persecuted by diverse imperial edicts. Already doomed to extinction, these groups found unexpected aid in the Gothic soldiers who at that time were serving in ever-increasing numbers within the ranks of the Roman army. Indeed, these soldiers were often Christians who had been converted from the traditional paganism of their people thanks to the tenacious and courageous efforts of Wulfila, a Goth who had become a Christian at an early age — if in fact he was not already a Christian from birth — and who was the descendant of a Cappadocian family whom the Goths had carried off during a raid. Having been elected bishop through the efforts of Eusebius of Nicomedia in 341 when he was only age 30, Wulfila was an Arian Christian and remained tenaciously faithful to this confession. He began to convert his compatriots to Arianism with ever-increasing success, in spite of every kind of difficulty.

Supported by these Gothic soldiers, who because of their privileged condition had nothing to fear from the anti-Arian measures of Theodosius and the other Roman emperors, the Arian groups in the West assured the continuity of Arianism up to the moment of the great invasions. In spite of their poor consistency, these were pugnacious groups who did not fear to profess their faith in the most open way possible and even sought to actively propagate it. Between the end of the fourth and the beginnings of the fifth centuries, they gave rise to a flourishing literary activity of which, in spite of its clear heretical stamp, not a little has survived until the present through various channels. These works are quite different among themselves with regard to form, but they all betray a strongly organic and unitary doctrinal formulation down to the details, so that it is easy to suppose a common matrix for them all. The identification of the authors, however, meets with considerable difficulty since, with few exceptions, these works have been transmitted either anonymously or under a false name.

On the other hand, we are acquainted with some of the leaders of this late Western Arianism: Palladius of Ratiaria, who was condemned at the Council of Aquileia in 381 together with Secundianus of Singidunum; Auxentius of Dorostorum, a pupil of Wulfila, who is not to be confused with the Arian bishop of Milan of the same name who flourished a generation earlier; and Maximinus, who would contend with both Ambrose and Augustine. Only in the case of the latter is it possible to reconstruct his literary personality by means of a series of works of which some are certainly his while others can be attributed to him with a great degree of probability. Various other works, however, remain without an author, which explains the attempts of modern scholars to attribute them to one or the other of the persons mentioned above, but always with extremely precarious results. M. Meslin has recently taken up this attempt again on a vast scale. On the one hand, he has attributed to Maximinus more works than those which by nearly unanimous consent are to be attributed to him. On the other, he has proposed, indeed reproposed, the attribution to Palladius of Ratiaria of two fundamental works which will be treated below. Summing up these attributions of his, Meslin has made Maximinus the disciple of Palladius, and has made the latter, of whom are known only a few pages included in a work of Maximinus, the real theorist of Western Arianism. In this way, he has relegated Wulfila, who previously had usually been recognized as the founder of this Western Arianism, to a position of insignificance. The thesis of Meslin has been variously refuted and is unacceptable. Wulfila can be considered as the master and motivating figure in a more or less direct manner of all the Arian writers active on the doctrinal plane whose works are extant today.

From Wulfila himself, who was able to express himself in Latin, nothing remains in this language other than a brief profession of faith which he is supposed to have pronounced at the moment of his death. However, the so-called *Epistula de fide, vita et obitu Ulfilae,* which will be treated below, reports in a trustworthy manner on his doctrinal attitude, and it is precisely on this basis that the uncertainty evident among modern scholars regarding the exact position of this personage in the complex panorama of Arian doctrines is to be resolved. The fact that in 360 at Constantinople he signed a formula of faith corresponding for the East to that signed by the Western bishops at Rimini has caused some to place him among the ranks of the moderate Arians. Yet others have considered him to be a radical Arian, and others still to be an Arian *sui generis* who is unable to be placed in a particular group. Nevertheless, the examination of the doctrinal data, both that which can be traced back to Wulfila himself as well as that witnessed in the works of his pupils, gives prominence to a strongly homogeneous doctrine, as mentioned above, which clearly leans in the direction of radical Arianism. In fact, all the distinctive points of this doctrine can be verified precisely in Eunomius. These Arians disassociated their name from that of the repeatedly condemned heresiarch only for reasons of practical expediency.

For the sake of convenience, this Arian literature will be examined by dividing it into three parts: 1) the works of Maximinus; 2) exegetical works; 3) doctrinal works.

Editions: Cf. CPL 689 and 692. — PLS I, 691-728. — Fr. Kauffman, Aus der Schule des Wulfila. Auxenti Dorostorensis Epistula de fide vita et obitu Wulfilae. Strassburg, 1899.

Studies: A. Lippold: PWK 17(196172)512-531. — J. Zeiller, Les origines chrétiennes dans les provinces danubiennes de l'Empire romain. Paris, 1918. — M. Simonetti, L'arianesimo di Ulfila: Romanobarbarica 1(1976)297-323.

MAXIMINUS

Maximinus is the sole Arian writer in the Latin language some of whose works are known and to whom others can be attributed with good probability. On the other hand, little is known about his life, and what information there is derives from his writings. Since he had already composed the *Dissertatio contra Ambrosium* in 397 and was, by his own admission, a few years younger than Augustine, his birth can be placed around 360-365. His close relationship with the Arian bishops Palladius and Secundianus who were condemned at Aquileia in 381 suggests that he was Illyrian, and it was perhaps in Illyria that he found the Arian community of which he was the head, as is certainly clear from his *Homilies.* He appears in 427 together with the barbarian troops in the service of Rome who had been sent to Africa to quell the rebellion of Bonifacius and who were under the command of the *comes* Sigiswulf. This detail points toward a Gothic background, but Augustine and Possidius, who relate the fact, do not define him as such, and the disdain with which he speaks of the barbarians in his writings has led Meslin to suggest that he was Roman by birth. The only specific detail of his life of which we are informed was the public debate held at Hippo with Augustine in 427 or 428 on the topic of Trinitarian doctrine. After this date there is no further notice of him, and it is only with difficulty that he can be identified with an Arian leader of the same name active in Sicily in 440 (Hydatius, *Chron.* 120).

As for his works, the *Dissertatio Maximini contra Ambrosium* (= DM) is the title given to a work composed of various parts which is contained in the codex Parisinus 8907. First there are related the acts of the Council of Aquileia of 381, annotated in several points with polemical considerations of Maximinus who, among other things, cites texts of Cyprian. In the second part, diverse witnesses are brought forth from the Arian side: the so-called *Epistula de fide, vita et obitu Ulfilae,* treated below, and a long exposition of Palladius of Ratiaria which is strongly polemical in tone with regard to the Council of Aquileia, which had condemned him, and especially with regard to Ambrose, who had been the implacable accusor of the Arian bishop at that council. These pages of Palladius are of great importance from a doctrinal point of view. The work concludes with the notice of an appeal by Wulfila, Palladius and Secundianus to Theodosius against the deliberations of the council, the results of which were negative. This final part appears to have been added to the text at a later date, but the pages of Palladius against Ambrose must have been written only a short time after the proceedings of the council, about 382. Maximinus' work of compilation appears to be prior to 397 and was probably done around 395.

It has been noted that in 427 or 428 Maximinus held a public debate at Hippo with Augustine on themes relating to the Arian controversy; the so-called *Collatio Augustini cum Maximino Arrianorum episcopo* (=CM). The debate, which has been preserved in the trustworthy account of the *notarii,* can be divided into three parts. In the first part, Augustine moves against Maximinus with great energy, seeking to catch him in a contradiction (ch. 1-10); in the second part, Maximinus succeeds in freeing himself from these straits by asking for clarifications which allow Augustine to display a series of traditional anti-Arian arguments (ch. 11-14); and the third part consists of a long soliloquy of Maximinus who, while expounding in detail the Arian doctrine, intentionally prolongs his discourse so as to leave only a minimal margin of time for the reply of Augustine (ch. 15-26). The latter has a verbal declaration inserted in the account in which he promises to reply in writing to the arguments presented by his rival, and Maximinus in his turn promises to respond in writing to this reply of Augustine. (The reply of Augustine is represented by the two books *Contra Maximinum* together with which the *Collatio* has been handed on. It does not appear that Maximinus responded to Augustine.) This work is of great importance from the historical view because of the directness and drama with which it presents the conflict, and from the doctrinal view because we have in the words of Maximinus a detailed exposition of Arian doctrine. The work presents here and there some confusion in the sequence of questions and responses, is often disorderly and does not follow a clear design. Some observations of Maximinus perhaps betray the necessity of coming up on the spur of the moment with arguments to oppose an adversary very much accustomed to debating. But on the whole the exposition fits with what can be found in other sources and, thanks to its extent, offers valuable clarifications on many points.

The *corpus* of Maximinus' works has been considerably enlarged since Dom Capelle attributed to him nearly all of the works contained in the ancient codex Veronensis LI, which previously had been attributed to Maximus of Turin. These consist of a thick collection of texts of a homiletic character and of varied argument and tone, of which a good number show obvious traces, at time very obvious, of Arianism. Dom Capelle proposed the attribution to Maximinus in 1929 on the basis of numerous similarities with the *Dissertatio* and the *Collatio.* This attribution was confirmed by a note of Scipione Maffei who had catalogued this manuscript under the name of Maximinus in 1742. He evidently read this name in the codex, which it is no longer possible to do today. A brief description of the text follows.

Three *tractatus* of some length are dedicated, respectively, *contra haereticos, contra Iudaeos, contra paganos.* The first considers the Catholics to be the heretics and combats their doctrine of the equality of the divine persons with traditional Arian arguments. The other two *tractatus* are homilies of an apologetic nature which resume polemical arguments, largely those used in earlier times, against the Jews and the pagans; the former are criticized on account of their ritual prescriptions and refusal to recognize the messianic character and divinity of Christ, while the latter are reproached for their astral fatalism and polytheistic conception of the deity, which is useless because of their ignorance of the true God. A characteristic element of both of these homilies is the great abundance of citations introduced from earlier Christian literature. The preferred writers are Cyprian, of whom passages are cited both from works which are authentic as well as from works already erroneously attributed to him, and the pseudo-Clementine *Recognitiones,* used in the Latin translation of Rufinus. Since this translation of Rufinus dates from 406, that date constitutes the *terminus post quem* for the composition of the homilies.

A second, very homogeneous group of texts is composed of fifteen homilies preached by Maximinus either on important feasts (Epiphany, Easter, Ascension) or on the memorials of certain famous martyrs. It is significant that the commemoration of Cyprian also is included alongside those of Peter and Paul and of Stephen. It is a collection of texts which are, for the most part, brief and which accompany the commemoration of the festival with an overture of a moral and hortative character. Arian features can be found in this group of texts, but they are rather rare and are treated in passing and never introduced with a clearly polemical intent.

The third group of texts is composed of twenty-four brief *Expositiones de capitulis Evangeliorum,* to which Bruni, the first editor of the collection (1784), added a fragment entitled *De nominibus apostolorum.* These are explanations of Gospel passages, at times brief, at times developed to the extent of forming a short homily, which follow one another without a definite order. It is a small collection, drawn from a larger compilation of texts intended for liturgical use. In expounding the Gospel passages, Maximinus does not neglect allegorical interpretation, which is always of a highly traditional kind (the two brothers of Lk. 15:12 represent the Jews and the gentiles; the foal of Mt. 21:7 symbolized the gentiles), but he makes sparing use of it, and prefers to take from the reading of the Gospel passage teachings above all of a moral character, which are drawn from the literal sense.

Recently, Meslin has proposed to considerably enlarge once again the literary heritage of Maximinus by attributing to him the two large anonymous Arian exegetical works, the *Opus imperfectum in Matthaeum* and a *Commentarium in Iob,* to which would be added the ancient Latin translation and abridgement of Origen's *Commentary on Matthew,* the style of which has much in common with the prose of the *Opus imperfectum in Matthaeum.* However, it is extremely difficult, not to say impossible, to attribute to one and the same author two such different exegetical works. Serious elements favoring an attribution to Maximinus are lacking in both works.

Editions: Cf. CPL 692-701, 705. — PL 57, 781-806, 829-832; PLS I, 691-763 (cf. 1751-52). — Fr. Kauffman, Aus der Schule des Wulfila. Strassburg, 1899. — A. Spagnolo, C. H. Turner, An Arian Sermon from a Ms. in the Chapter Library of Verona: JThSt 13(1912)19-28; *idem,* An Ancient Homiliary I-III: JThSt 16(1915)161-176, 314-322; 17(1916)225-235. — C. H. Turner, On Ms. Veron. LI (49) of the Work of Maxim[in]us: JThSt 24(1923)71-79. — B. Capelle, La liste des apôtres dans un sermon de Maximin: RB 38(1926)5-15; *idem,* Les homélies "de lectionibus evangeliorum" de Maximin l'Arien: RB 40(1928)49-86. — R. Gryson, Débat de Maximinus avec Augustin. Scolies ariennes sur le concile d'Aquilée. Louvain, 1980.

Studies: L. Saltet, Un texte nouveau. La dissertatio Maximini contra Ambrosium: BLE 2(1900)118-129. — J. Zeiller, Les origines chrétiennes dans les provinces danubiennes de l'Empire romain. Paris, 1918. — É. Amann: DTC 10/1(1928)466-472. — B. Capelle, Un homéliaire de l'évêque arien Maximin: RB 34(1922)81-108, 224-233. — J. M. Hanssens, Massimino il Visigoto: SC 102(1974)475-514. — R. Gryson, Les citations scripturaires des oeuvres attribuées à l'évêque arien Maximinus: RB 88(1978)45-80.

EXEGETICAL LITERATURE

Included under this heading are three definitely Arian works of an exegetical character for which it is not possible to determine an author: the *Opus imperfectum in Matthaeum* and the *Commentarius in Iob,* whose proposed attribution to Maximinus was mentioned above, and the *Tractatus in Lucam.*

The *Opus imperfectum in Matthaeum* is the most extensive existing commentary on Matthew in Latin from antiquity. The work in its present state is incomplete, as it stops at chapter 25 of Matthew, and has *lacunae* here and there. There is an involved manuscript tradition since no codex transmits the work in its entirety and certain parts of it are witnessed only in rather recent manuscripts (*saec.* XIV and XV). This evidence and the fact that passages of Jerome, Chromatius and Leo the Great have been found among the material transmitted as part of the *Opus* have suggested the hypothesis that all the completions introduced into the text by the more recent manuscripts are to be considered as later additions drawn from various sources in order to provide in some manner a conclusion to the work which had been passed down in an incomplete form. However, even if it is beyond doubt that passages from other works have crept into the manuscript tradition, it is nevertheless true that the work in its entirety presents itself as a homogeneous unit, both because of certain themes which run from one chapter to another (e.g., the theme of persecution), as well as because even the more recent parts reveal the Arian inspiration which characterizes the remainder of the work.

With regard to such passages, it must be kept in mind that the *Opus* was for a long time attributed to John Chrysostom, and it was under this name that it was enthusiastically read and admired in the Middle Ages. Given this diffusion, the Arian elements, few in number but very important, were singled out and corrected in some fashion both in the later manuscripts as well as in the early printed editions. For this reason, the best edition available, that of Montfaucon which was reprinted in PG 56, is practically useless in those places where the text displays an Arian content. There is also uncertainty regarding the original language of the work. The presence of many Greek elements led to the theory of a translation from Greek, but the discovery that the author had used passages of Jerome's *Commentary on Matthew* destroyed that hypothesis, since it is difficult to imagine that a Greek writer would have made use of a Latin text. The evidence that these passages are most probably to be considered as subsequent interpolations has removed that difficulty, however, and a Greek origin for the work has recently been proposed again by P. Nautin, who has suggested as author the Arian priest Timothy, who was active as Constantinople in the first decades of the fifth century. The recent discovery of a brief fragment of the *Opus* in Greek seems to decisively strengthen this hypothesis. However, given the extremely confused state of the manuscript tradition, it is advisable to await the critical edition of the work, which has been in preparation for some time, before finally deciding on this and the other question mentioned above. In the meanwhile, mention can be made of the recent publication by R. Etaix of six previously unknown fragments of the work which, on the whole, are fairly extensive.

The work itself concerns a vast commentary on Matthew of a prevailingly allegorical character carried out according to criteria closely reminiscent of those of Origen: symbolic interpretation of numbers, animals and plants; the importance connected for the purpose of allegory to the real or presumed etymology of Hebrew names; the contrast between letter and allegory compared to that between flesh and spirit. This shrewd method of interpretation is placed at the service of an understanding rich in suggestive themes and motifs which sometimes opens into a doctrinal element but more often prefers themes of a strongly existential coloring: man seen in the struggle between good and evil, between the devil, who has enslaved his flesh, and God, who with His grace aids the soul, which is free in its decision, but unstable and unable to realize its salvation without divine help.

The work is particularly interesting on the ecclesiological level. It was written by the leader of a small Arian community which was under unceasing pressure from the then-dominant Catholics and which was witnessing its already emaciated ranks grow thinner by the day. Through the example of the Gospel, the author attempts above all to encourage and confirm his little flock in the Arian faith, and thus there is a continual insistence on the themes of temptation and persecution which represent the great sieve which will separate out the best. In such an atmosphere there is a natural emphasis on the theme of the last judgment, which will witness the final defeat of the persecuting powers and the triumph of the oppressed. There enters here the motif of the anti-Christ, whose army is represented precisely by the Catholic church. The start of the final age is made to begin with Constantine and Theodosius, the two emperors who persecuted the Arians.

The title *Anonymus in Iob* is used to indicate a commentary on Job in three books which interprets that text from the beginning to Job 3:19. It was written in Latin and handed down erroneously under the name of Origen, and thus is not to be confused with another commentary on Job, still partially unedited, which is extant in the original Greek also under a false attribution to Origen. The Arian character of this commentary is revealed by a few elements of a doctrinal nature, some of which are blatant (the three marauding bands in Job 1:7 symbolize the consubstantial Trinity of the Catholics: 428). The *Anonymus* makes sparing use of allegory, and the basic one is that which sees Job as a symbol of Christ in his suffering and passion. It prefers instead the literal interpretation which leads into sometimes extensive and elaborate explanations of a moral character; e.g., on faith, on harmony and on marriage. Examples are drawn by preference from other passages of the Old Testament. The tone of the work is always grave and often exaggerated in keeping with the prevailing interests of a moral and didactic character.

The very fact that the anonymous author takes the suffering Job as a symbol of the passion of Christ reveals the optomistic formulation which is given to the interpretation of the person of Job and extended to his children. The emphasis, however, is not on Job who recognizes himself to be a sinner, but rather on Job seen in a rather Stoic light as the prototype of the wise man, as the innocent man tried by temptation. The dramatic problem posed by this biblical text, i.e., the suffering inflicted by God on the just man, has escaped the author, who places the responsibility for the calamities which afflict Job on the devil alone.

A palimpsest originally from Bobbio and now preserved in the Biblioteca Ambrosiana (C 73) contains fragments of a commentary on the Gospel of Luke, the so-called *Tractatus in Lucae Evangelium,* which was first published by A. Mai in 1828. They are fragments, at times fairly extensive, of a commentary on some forty verses from chapter 1, 4, 5 and 6 of the Gospel of Luke. There are only a few marginal elements of a doctrinal nature, but they are sufficient to identify the author as an Arian. Nothing is known of the author, and the only chronological datum, which is a general one, is obtained from the citation of a passage of the Latin translation of Flavius Josephus' *De bello Iudaico,* which was made around 370. This work too can be dated for the most part to that period which witnessed the flowering of Arian literature in the Latin language, namely, between the end of the fourth and the beginning of the fifth century.

Since only a small part of this Arian work is extant, for the most part in a fragmentary state, it is not easy to form any precise idea from what remains of the exegetical criteria which guided the author in his interpretation of the Lucan text. It is clear that he knows the allegorical method well and makes use of it in a highly traditional fashion (e.g., the two boats of Lk. 5:2 taken as a symbol of the churches: 337). However, the use of allegory is anything but prevalent in the surviving fragments, which are dominated by a type of exegesis directed above all to a didactic and moralizing attempt. It is a marvel, in a writer who appears rather well endowed culturally, that the etymology of Gennesareth (337) is derived not from the Hebrew, according to the normal practice, but by means of a connection with the Greek *gennao.* The work has been carefully composed with regard to its form, and the author makes frequent use of comparisons (330, 336, 341, 342), which is not a usual procedure in exegetical works. This detail recalls a similar tendency which is noticeable in the *Opus imperfectum in Matthaeum,* and it is possible to establish also other points of contact between the two works, although the *Opus* seems more inclined to allegory and is theologically richer. In any case the comparison between the two works could be pressed more deeply.

Many scholars still insist on detecting at the roots of the doctrine of Arius the tendency to interpret the Sacred Scripture in a literal rather than an allegorical manner. It is a question of a hypothesis devoid of valid foundations. For as much as pertains to Arian exegetical literature in Latin, it has been noted how the diverse works do not present uniform exegetical criteria. To a decidedly allegorizing work such as the *Opus imperfectum in Matthaeum* there can be contrasted the meager tendency toward allegory of the *Anonymus in Iob.* As far as Maximinus is concerned, he has been seen to make use of allegory as well as of a type of literal interpretation according to the exigencies of the situation. It would not be methodologically correct to attempt to draw elements from this late Arian literature for making a judgment in regard to the very origins of the movement. It is sufficient to point out here that the surviving Arian Latin texts do not present a homogeneous criterion for the interpretation of Sacred Scripture, but rather demonstrate the same variety of criteria which is evident in contemporary Catholic literature.

Opus imperfectum in Matthaeum: Editions: Cf. CPG 4569 and CPL 707. — PG 56, 611-948. — R. Étaix, Fragments inédits de l'"Opus imperfectum in Matthaeum": RB 84(1974)271-300.

Studies: H. J. Sieben: DSp 8(1972)362-369. — F. Kaufmann, Zur Textgeschichte des "Opus imperfectum in Matthaeum." Kiel, 1909. — G. Morin, Quelques aperçus noveaux sur l'Opus imperfectum in Matthaeum: RB 37(1925)239-262. — J. P. Bouhot, Remarques sur l'histoire du texte de l'Opus imperfectum in Matthaeum: VC 24(1970)197-209. — M. Simonetti, Note sull'opus imperfectum in Matthaeum: A. Giuseppe Ermini 1(1970)117-200 (= Studi Medievali 10[1969]1-84); *idem,* Per una retta valutazione dell'Opus imperfectum in Matthaeum: VetChr 8(1971)87-97. — P. Nautin, L'Opus imperfectum in Matthaeum et les Ariens de Constantinople: RHE 67(1972)381-408, 745-766. — A. Stuiber, Ein griechischer Textzeuge für das Opus imperfectum in Matthaeum: VC 27(1973)146-147. — M. Simonetti, Su due passi dell' "Opus imperfectum in Matthaeum" pubblicati di recente: Aug 15 (1975)423-428. — R. Girod, La traduction latine anonyme du Commentaire sur Matthieu: Origeniana, Bari 1975, 125-138.

Anonymus in Iob: Editions: PG 17, 371-522.

Tractatus in Lucam: Editions: A. Mai, Scriptorum veterum nova collectio 3, 2. Rome, 1828, 191-207. — PLS I, 327-344. — Cf. CPL 704.

Studies: M. Meslin, Les Ariens d'Occident. Paris, 1967. Cf. Simonetti, RSLR 4(1968)563-571. — P. Nautin, RHR 177(1970)70-89.

DOCTRINAL LITERATURE

This section includes three very important Arian texts:

1) the so-called *Epistula de fide, vita et obitu Ulfilae* (= U). This is a text of considerable length which Maximinus has related in its entirety in his *Dissertatio contra Ambrosium.* In one passage (PLS I, 705), the author claims to have been a disciple of Wulfila and to have learned the *sacras litteras* from him. This disciple is commonly identified with Auxentius of Durostorum, but this name which appears at the beginning of the letter was completed by Kaufmann, the first editor of the text, from a rather corrupt passage of the Parisian manuscript. In spite of this uncertainty with regard to the author, the text is nevertheless of immense importance for the documentation it gives in its first part about the doctrine of Wulfila and in its second part about his activity among the Christianized Goths. It has to have been written only a few years after the death of Wulfila (383). The text concludes with a brief profession of faith which Wulfila dictated at the time of his death as a spiritual testament. This last document is a text which, although brief, proposes a radical interpretation of the Arian doctrine both in clearly subordinating the Son to the Father as well as in considering the Holy Spirit to be a creature. The most developed doctrinal exposition of the *epistula* agrees with this profession of faith

and thus makes known the actual theological attitude of the great leader of Western Arianism.

2) *Sermo Arrianorum* (=SA). Around 418 Augustine had at hand this text of an unknown author which had been sent to him in order that he might refute it and against which he immediately composed the *Contra sermonem Arrianorum.* Fortunately, some manuscripts which contain this work of Augustine have the Arian text presented first. It consists of a brief work which can be imagined to have circulated among the Goths who had descended into Italy with Alaric and Ataulphus. It does not have the appearance of a real sermon, but rather of a complete exposition of Arian doctrine in a schematic and compact form which gives the text the character of a genuine catechism. Its importance lies precisely in the completeness and organic manner in which the subjects are presented. The *Sermo* constitutes, in fact, the pole around which are gathered the particular elements which are found in the other more prolix but also more disordered Arian sources.

3) *Fragmenta Arriana* (=FA). In 1828, A. Mai published 21 fragments contained in a palimpsest originally from Bobbio which was preserved in part in the Vatican Library and in part in the Biblioteca Ambrosiana. The final two fragments belong to the apocryphal *Ascension of Isaiah,* while the first 19 are all definitely of Arian tone and inspiration. Although they are so strongly similar in tone and style as to be able to be attributed to the same author, they, nevertheless, seem to be drawn from various works of a homiletic, dogmatic or polemical nature. *Frag.* 17 contains an extensive profession of faith, and elsewhere there are related passages from some of the very first Arians, such as Athanasius of Anazarba and Theognis of Nicea, and of some of the anti-Arians such as Hilary, Phoebadius and Ambrose; the former obviously presented in a positive light, the latter as having been refuted by them. The author is often involved in polemics against the Macedonians as well, one of the leaders of whom *frag.* 9 names as Soziphanes (according to Mai; the text is no longer legible), otherwise unknown. (The identification proposed by Meslin with Sophronius of Pompeiopolis, one of the leaders of the homoiousians at the Council of Seleucia in 359 is not convincing.) The author of these fragments likewise remains anonymous. The names of Wulfila, Auxentius, Palladius and Maximinus have been proposed but without solid supporting arguments. The same must be said regarding the attribution to Palladius, recently repeated by Meslin, who, again without a well-founded reason, considers the *Sermo Arrianorum* to be an extract from the works of Palladius. It can only be stated that the author presents himself as an Arian bishop of a community where

Arianism is losing ground also because of the hostility of the civil authorities. This suggests a date around the end of the fourth century or the beginning of the fifth. The close connection with Wulfila and his school points, as far as the location is concerned, to the regions around the Danube.

Editions: Epistula . . . Ulfilae: Cf. sopra p. 90. Sermo Arrianorum: Cf. CPL 701. — PL 42, 677-684. Fragmenta Ariana: CPL 705. — A. Mai, Scriptorum veterum nova collectio 3, 2. Rome 1828, 208-237. — PL 13, 593-628.

Studies: B. Capelle, Un homéliare de l'évêque arien Maximin: RB 34(1922)108. — M. Meslin, Les Ariens d'Occident. Paris, 1967 (cf. Simonetti: RSLR 4[1968]563-571). — P. Nautin: RHR 177(1970)70-89.

On the basis of these texts, to which can be added the *Dissertatio contra Ambrosium* and the *Collatio* with Augustine of Maximinus as well as various elements present in the exegetical works, especially the *Opus imperfectum in Matthaeum,* it is possible to form a complete exposition of the Arian doctrine professed in the Western circles out of which these documents arose.

Underlying the doctrine of Wulfila and his school, in the footsteps of Arius and Eunomius, is the concept of God the Father as absolutely transcendent, not only with respect to the world of creation but also in regard to the other divine persons which tradition placed alongside Him in the profession of faith. The Father is the only true God, He is God and Father of all inasmuch as He is *omnium auctor* (FA 4, 604; 15; U 707), and He is God of the Son (SA 25). As a result, the Catholic affirmation that considered the Father, Son and Holy Spirit to be *unus Deus* must be rejected (CM 13; DM 697). The uniqueness of the Father derives from His being the sole Ingenerate One, *sine principio* and *ante principium,* where *principium* is intended in both a chronological (the Father is eternal, without beginning or end) and an ontological sense; He is *causa sui* and the cause of all that is, including the Son; He is the *unus auctor* (CM 5; FA 4, 604).

The absolute transcendence and uniqueness of the Father is normally emphasized by placing *solus* before his attributes; He is *solus sapiens, solus invisibilis,* etc., not in the sense that no one else, even the Son, is wise, good, etc., but in the sense that not even the Son is wise and good to the same degree as the Father, because all these perfections subsist in the Father without chronological or ontological beginning, whereas all other beings possess them as derived to a greater or lesser extent from Him (CM 15, 13, 14, 23). Because of His transcendence, the Father is not able to enter into direct contact with creation; He does not descend *ad humana contagia* (FA 4, 603; CM 13), but always acts through the mediation of the Son.

Because of this, the later Arians had no difficulty in calling the Son, as their predecessors had already done, *genitus* and *unigenitus* in order to emphasize his uniqueness with regard to creation. He is the *unus unigenitus apud ingenitum* (Maximin. *Serm.* 2, 737), his relationship to the Father is that of generation (CM 15, 8), and his transcendence with respect to the world of creatures is highlighted (U 707). His generation is clearly distinct from creation (OIM 803a) as a voluntary generation which caused no modification or diminution in the Paternal substance (SA 2; U 703).

However, to this series of highly traditional statements the Arians added another which distinguishes and defines the Son with respect to the Father not only by his very person, but also by substance and nature. The Father and the Son are each *singularis* and *incomparabilis* precisely because each of them is an unique and singular reality in substance, nature and kind (OIM 829b; SA 31; FA 1, 569bc, 598b; 4, 602). In order to deny the derivation of the Son from the substance of the Father, which the Catholics affirmed, the Arians imagined this according to a carnal and animal type which was thus unworthy to be applied to the divine sphere (OIM 889b). This care to distinguish between the Father and the Son even with regard to substance and nature raises doubts as to whether they really conceived of the divine generation of which they speak as a real generation. In fact, they also speak of the Son as *constitutus, creatus, factus* (SA 2; U 703; FA 4, 604). Following the exegesis of Arius, they interpret Prov. 8:22-25, in which the divine wisdom (the Son) is said to be *creata* and then also *generata* by God, in the sense that in God generate is synonymous with create (U 703; FA 15; 17, 623). In this way, the Father is also defined as *creator, factor* of the Son (U 704). On the other hand, the process of creation by which the Son takes his origin from the Father is singular and different from that by which all other beings take their origin from God. In fact, only the Son is created directly from the will of God, while all the other beings are created directly by the Son according to the will of the Father (U 704). For this reason, the Son is both *primogenitus* and *unigenitus* (SA 1), and his uniqueness and singularity is preserved with regard to the rest of creation. He is the *unus ab uno* (CM 15, 13).

But if the Son did not derive from the substance of the Father, from whence did the Father create him? As is known, Arius had at first spoken openly of creation out of nothing, but immediately thereafter had declined to express his thought on this point in order to avoid the scandal of a statement so far removed from tradition. Thus, all subsequent Arians, including Wulfila and his disciples, prefer to remain silent on this point, except (CM 15, 13) to refer sporadically to the will and the power of God as though to a source (material) from which the Son would have drawn his origin. But though they find themselves in difficulty on this point, they are nevertheless categorical in their denial of the coeternity of the Son in relation to the Father. They affirm that the Father generated/created the Son *ante saecula* and before every other creature (CM 15, 5; FA 17, 623), but this merely signifies generation/creation before time, i.e., before the world. For them, the Son is not *sine initio,* although he is *sine fine* (FA 4, 604; OIM 856a). Thus he cannot be called *consempiternus* and *coeternus* in relation to the Father (DM 711).

The Arians based the radical subordinationism which characterized their doctrine on the premise that the Father was the chronological and ontological *principium* of the Son. Following the Fourth Gospel above all, they emphasized that the Son has drawn being, life, knowledge, power, in short everything he is or has, from the Father (FA 1, 598ab; 6, 609; 4, 602-604; DM 702). They understand those Johannine passages (Jn. 5:19, 30) which express the perfect conformity of Christ to the will of the Father not in terms of a harmony of will and action, but rather in the sense of an impossibility, an incapacity of the Son to work unless following the order and will of the Father. They preserve the language of John but totally falsify the spirit (SA 4.20; FA 3.4, 603). Thus the omnipotence of the Son is relative (DM 724), and he is totally *subditus, subiectus* with respect to the Father, whose *minister* he is (FA 1, 596c, 598a; U 707; SA 15.17).

The Arians bring forward even the Incarnation of the Son as proof of his radical inferiority, inasmuch as it admitted of visibility, passibility and mortality (DM 718; FA 4, 603). They distinguish in Christ a human nature and a divine nature and clearly affirm that it was not in the divine nature that he was made visible and suffered. However, the very fact that he became incarnate and entered into contact with the world is an indication of inferiority with respect to the Father, who is absolutely transcendent (CM 13; 15, 26; FA 13, SA 7). Even if indirectly, the divine Logos *passus est . . . iniuriam* because of the passible and moral flesh (SA 13).

On the basis of all these arguments the Arians outline the subordination of Christ in respect to the Father in a manner quite radically different than had the theologians of the second and third centuries. They sharply reject the doctrine of the equality of the divine persons proposed by the Catholics and definitely separate the Son from the reality of the Father and bring him closer to the world of creation, although without having him coincide with it (SA 32; FA 4, 602).

Having been separated and irremediably removed from the Father on the plane of nature and substance, the Son remained joined to Him only on the moral plane. The Arians of the school of Wulfila had no difficulty in accepting the Formula of Rimini, which stated that the Son is like the Father according to the Scriptures (CM 15, 15), but they intended this likeness in an external manner as likeness in will and action (SA 32; DM 711). The scarcity of allusions to the subject shows how little they had considered this concept, which was fundamental for the Catholics.

The accentedly inferior status to which the Arians relegated Christ did not hinder them from continuing to define him not only as Son, as has been seen, but also as God. However, such a definition was proposed in such a way as to emphasize the inferiority with respect to the Father and thus was preferably accompanied by some qualification such as *Deus Verbum, Deus unigenitus* etc. (SA 1; FA 4, 605a; CM 15, 8). He was God, but was *magnus quidem Deus, non tamen primus* (OIM 874), he was *secundus Deus* (U 703).

The Son functioned primarily as a mediator; thanks to him the Father was in touch with the world of creation. Such activity began with creation, and the Son was generated/created by the Father precisely in order to bring about the creation of the world (SA 3; FA 15, 620a). It was the very fact that Christ is creator which assured his divinity; he was God inasmuch as he was *creator,* and was the only creature to share this prerogative with the Father (FA 3). Once the world had been created, the Son governed it, and from this derives his complete dominion over all creation, of which he is *rex* and *dominus* FA 1, 598a; U 707) in a dominion which would have no end and which was destined to reach its perfection at the end of the world (SA 34). In force of such prerogatives, the Son is the object of adoration on the part of creatures (SA 27; CM 15, 2), and in the triple dignity of *rex, propheta* and *sacerdos* (OIM 613a, 629b) he is the only channel through which man, and indeed all creation, can enter into contact with God (SA 33; FA 5; CM 12; 15, 4, 19).

As for the Catholics so also for the Arians, the culmination of the activity of Christ in the world was represented by the Incarnation. Distinguishing here for the sake of convenience between the purpose of the Incarnation and the manner in which it came about, it is possible to affirm that, with regard to the first point, the position of the Arians coincided fundamentally with that of their adversaries: Christ descended to earth to redeem sinful man, whom the sin of Adam had subjected to the power of the devil and of death. He submitted himself as man to sin and death in order to make man the son of God (Maximinus, *Serm.* 3, 758; 15, 761; FA 10, 614). In any case, it must be noted that in keeping with the fundamental tendency of their thought, the redemptive work of Christ was also seen in a clearly subordinationist light (SA 8, 612ff).

With regard to the manner of the Incarnation, the Latin Arians had no doubts concerning the miraculous birth of Christ from the Virgin, and they place in sharp relief the unique character of his generation both human and divine: *Deus sine matre, homo sine patre* (Maximinus, *Serm.* 1, 732). The union with the man did not imply any alteration in the divine nature of the Logos, but, while coexisting in one single person with the humanity (OIM 635a), the divinity remained immune to death (FA 13) even if it indirectly experienced the humiliation of the cross (DM 718; SA 7. 13). To fully understand this last affirmation, it is necessary to recall that from the very beginning the Arians had assumed a Christological conception of the type *logos/sarx,* already apparent in the East in the second half of the third century, according to which the Logos had assumed a human body deprived of a soul, the functions of which were exercised by the Logos himself. This question had been only of marginal interest in the first phase of the conflict. Subsequently, however, this Christological formulation had been employed to great advantage by Apollinarius of Laodicea, and from here arose another polemic which in the East variously interfered in the Arian crisis.

The rather late texts in question here reflect this new phase of the debate, and it is possible to find some explicit statements according to which Christ did not possess a soul along with his human body (FA 13, 617; OIM 853c. 859c). This point of the controversy is clearly evident especially in the *Opus imperfectum in Matthaeum,* in full agreement with the doctrine of Apollinarius, who had maintained that if one admitted the assumption on the part of the Son of a humanity which included also a soul and thus completely self-sufficient, then the union of this humanity with the divine nature would have taken place only on an external level. Thus, the divinity would have remained completely estranged from the suffering of the humanity on the cross to such an extent that God would have participated only in a very indirect manner in the redemption. To the contrary, the union of the divine Logos with a human body which was incapable of acting on its own assured an intrinsic union between the humanity and the divinity and thus a direct participation of the divinity in the work of redemption. This is precisely the sense of the various statements of the OIM (653b, 777b, 889c) in which the Catholics, who uphold the assumption of a complete man on the part of the Son, are accused of believing that the redemption had taken place only through the work of a *purus homo* without the participation of the divinity; something which for the author of the OIM, in keeping with the entire tradition, was impossible to admit.

With regard to the Holy Spirit, the Latin Arians were perfectly in line with Eunomius. Since they affirmed on the basis of New Testament passages that everything had been created by the Father through the means of the Son (Jn. 1:3; 1 Cor. 8:6), they considered the Holy Spirit to be the first and the greatest of the creatures created by the Son according to the will of the Father (U 704; SA 10.26). It has been seen that Christ, for the Arians, was also a creature, but was endowed with the dual prerogative of having been created directly by the Father and of being, in his turn, creator according to the will of the Father. Neither the one nor the other of these prerogatives were attributed to the Holy Spirit. Since he was created by the Son as were the other creatures, the Holy Spirit neither performed any creative activity nor exercised any governance over creation (U 705; FA 14; 15, 620ff). It followed that the Holy Spirit, in distinction to the Son, was not considered either *Deus* or *dominus,* nor could he be the object of adoration (FA 3; 14; U 707).

From this it is clear that for the Arians the Holy Spirit did not enter into the divine sphere, but formed part of the created sphere, which was understood as a complex of beings created by the Son according to the will of the Father. On the other hand, tradition systematically placed the Holy Spirit alongside the Father and the Son in the baptismal formula and the profession of faith. Therefore, in deference to tradition, the Arians systematically treated the Holy Spirit in correlation with the other divine persons, but only to enhance his radical inferiority with respect to the Father and the Son (SA 31; U 704; FA 14). Just as the Son is the *minister* by means of whom the Father acts in the world, so is the Holy Spirit the *minister* whom the Son uses to carry out the will of the Father (SA 13, 14, 18, 20, 22; FA 2; 14; 15). His activity, however, is not as extensive as that of Christ. The Holy Spirit is not *ubique diffusus* but acts only within the confines of the church as an illuminating and sanctifying *virtus* (CM 15, 22; FA 3, 601). In his more restricted limits, he acts as a second mediator after Christ and with Christ, while the latter intercedes with the Father (FA 14, 619b).

With regard to the Trinity considered on the whole, that is with regard to the complex of relations which connect and characterize the divine persons one with respect to the other, the Arians were more inclined to combat the doctrine of the Catholics than to affirm their own. The fundamental accusation which they leveled against their adversaries was that of confusing the three divine persons by considering them equal in nature and honor and thus professing the heresy of Sabellius. The distinction of persons which the Catholics introduced into the Trinity was for the Arians insufficient and fictitious, because it was not accompanied by a distinction of nature, substance and dignity (DM 702, 713, 716, 724; U 704; OIM 807b). On the other hand, from the Catholic doctrine of the perfect equality of the divine persons the Arians also occasionally deduced the charge of tri-theism, perfectly antithetical to that of Sabellianism (DM 724).

On their part, the Arians made rather sparing use of the term *trinitas* (FA 2), as Eunomius also had done. In fact, their insistence on the distinction into three substances as well as into three persons (SA 27) and their denial of the equality of the persons in order to arrange them in a precise hierarchical order led to the result that they proposed a Trinity which was not ordered horizontally like the equal one proposed by the Catholics, but rather vertically, based on the inferiority of the third person with respect to the second and of the second with respect to the first.

A conception of this kind was able to find points of reference in tradition, e.g., in Tertullian and in Origen, but in these authors, the full divinity of the three persons was beyond discussion as was their distinct separation from the created sphere. By contrast, the Arians professed a Trinity which was not only graded but which was heterogeneous in its three members, who were in fact separated from one another not only in dignity but also in substance and nature. If the Son, although on a radically viscerated basis, participated in some way in the divinity of the Father, such a prerogative was denied to the Holy Spirit, who participated instead in the created sphere. It follows that the Arians were not able to speak of the Trinity as God, which, in fact, they never did. For them, the Trinity was only a concept inherited from tradition but devoid of any real content. For these reasons, they spoke of it almost exclusively in a polemical context to deny the doctrine proposed by their adversaries.

GOTHIC LITERATURE

The few documents of Gothic literature which are still extant are connected in a more or less immediate manner with the missionary and literary activity of Wulfila. They consist mainly of a few manuscripts containing a partial translation of the New Testament (the Gospels and the Pauline corpus with the exception of Hebrews). Other texts are extremely few in number, and include some glosses and some documents of a predominantly linguistic interest as well as the remains of a commentary on John and the beginning of a calendar (S.J.V.).

Editions: E. Dietrich, Die Bruchstücke der Skeireins. Strassburg, 1903. — E. A. Kock, Die Skeireins. Text nebst Übersetzung. Lund, 1913. — W. Streitberg, Die gotische Bibel I. Heidelberg, 1919[2].

Translations: German: Kock, op. cit.

Studies: A. Wilmart, les évangiles gothiques: RBib 36(1927)46-61. — E. A. Thompson, Early Visigothic Christianity: Latomus 21(1962)505-519; *idem,* The Visigoths in the Time of Ulfila. Oxford, 1966. — F. Haffner, Fragment der Ulfilas-Bibel in Speyer: Pfälzer Heimat (März 1971)1-5. — P. Scardigli, Die Goten. Sprache und Kultur. Münich, 1973. — E. A. E. Ebbinghaus, The First Entry of the Gothic Calendar: JThSt 27(1976)140-145.

Heretical and Anti-Heretical Writers of the Fourth Century

The Arian controversy polarized for the most part the interests of the Latin Christian writers for the second half of the fourth century. Nevertheless, there was no lack of other heretical and schismatic movements which gave life to a literature more or less polemical in tone. The following chapter is dedicated to this literature. It must be noted, however, that the authors dealt with here are different with regard to interests and character, and that some of them are treated in this chapter only for the sake of convenience.

DONATIST LITERATURE

The Donatist schism had its origins in the polemics which followed the persecution of Diocletian and Galerius in Africa. In this persecution, as in preceding ones, the heroism, at times fanatic, of a few had contrasted with the timid attitude of many who either gave way before the violence of the persecutors or in some way compromised with them. Many members of the hierarchy were among this latter group, because in obedience to the first decree against the Christians they had handed over the sacred books and other sacred vessels, hence the name *traditores.* Mensurius, the bishop of Carthage, although himself not guilty of such practices, certainly did not approve of the fanatical attitude of certain intransigent Christians during the persecution which could so easily irritate the Roman authorities. Difficulties thus arose for him at Carthage, while other conflicts set him in opposition to part of the Numidian episcopate. When Mensurius died in 311, three bishops hastily consecrated the deacon Caecilianus, who was also of a moderate tendency, as his successor. This election, however, was not pleasing to the extremists, who were determined to oppose Caecilianus, and who were further instigated in this by Lucilla, a rich matron whom the deacon had criticized on account of certain superstitious practices. It was objected against the validity of Caecilianus' election that the Numidian bishops, traditionally invited to the election of the bishop of Carthage, had not taken part in it, and that Felix of Aptungi, a *traditor,* had been among the consecrating bishops. Therefore, a group of 70 Numidian bishops met in Carthage, nullified the election of Caecilianus and in 312 elected in his place Majorinus, a favorite of Lucilla, who distributed a large sum of money among the electors on this occasion. When Majorinus died after a short time, a successor was found in Donatus, who proved to be a skillful organizer of his party.

Since the African Church was divided into two factions, the Donatists took the initiative of appealing to Constantine in 313 and asked the mediation of the bishops of Gaul in resolving the split.

Constantine agreed, and in October of 313 three bishops from Gaul and some Italian bishops met in Rome under the presidency of Miltiades, the bishop of Rome. Since their decision was favorable to Caecilianus, the Donatists then appealed to the authority of a council which met at Arles in 314. Meanwhile, an investigation conducted in Africa proved the innocence of Felix in regard to the accusation of *traditio.* The Council of Arles also decreed in favor of Caecilianus, but the Donatists did not submit even this time. Only in 316 did Constantine decide to bring force to bear against them and sent their leaders into exile. However, the partisans of Donatus continued the schism in spite of the violence of the soldiers, so that the emperor recalled the exiles with an edict of tolerance in 321.

The tenacity of the Donatists in defending their cause must be explained not only by the fanaticism of certain Christian circles in Africa, especially among the common people, and the organizing capability of Donatus, who immediately assumed the role of charismatic leader, but it must also be taken into account that a decisive factor in firing the Donatist zeal was played by the anti-Roman sentiment which was widespread among the poorer classes, who were oppressed by the excessive fiscal measures of the imperial administration and reduced to the darkest misery. In their eyes, the Roman Empire appeared as an instrument of the devil and an uncompromisingly anti-Christian force, and thus many in Africa had not approved of the new course which Constantine had given to the relations between the empire and the church. The conflicts which arose between Caecilianus and Majorinus provided the spark which caused this anti-Roman sentiment to burst into flame. In opposition to the church of Caecilianus which collaborated with the hated oppressor, the Donatists considered themselves as constituting the real church, the perfect church of the poor and the martyrs, and from this attitude arose their intransigence and the violence of their actions against the members of the Catholic church.

For a long time the Donatists had a free hand in Africa and Numidia, and Donatus knew how to take advantage of this situation to organize his church and put pressure on the Catholics, who were incapable of mounting an effective opposition to the schismatics. Only in 347 did Constans intervene by sending two high officials, Macarius and Paulus, with the mission of resolving the conflict. Donatus and his followers, however, openly refused to collaborate with the Roman authorities and did not accept their interference in the affairs of the church. Macarius then had recourse to force, and amidst all types of violence the Donatist churches were dispersed and their leaders, including Donatus, sent into exile. But when Julian authorized the exiles to return home in 362, the Donatists immediately reorganized under the able leadership of Parmenian, the successor of Donatus. Once again the Catholic church saw itself reduced to a bad state and an anxious defense in spite of the various schisms which afflicted their opponents.

Only at the end of the century with Aurelian of Carthage and Augustine were the Catholics able to react in a certain measure and with some success, although even then they were able to triumph over their adversaries only with the aid of imperial power. As a result of a council held by the Catholics at Carthage in 404, Honorius published an edict against the schismatics the following year. In 411 a great conference was held at Carthage in which the leaders of both parties took part, and which resulted in the defeat of the Donatists. Another, more drastic decree of Honorius followed in 412 which led to the destruction of the Donatists as an organized and functioning force, but the anti-Roman *animus* which had nourished the Donatists' fanatic zeal subsequently grew sharper. A few years hence, the Vandal invasion would place the African churches before new and more pressing problems.

The Donatists wrote much to defend and propagate their ideas regarding the true and perfect church, although without a great variety of themes or richness of doctrine. All of this literature, with the exception almost exclusively of some hagiographical texts, did not survive the destruction of the sect. Nevertheless, something is able to be known of this literature, especially of the refutations by the Catholics, above all by Augustine and Optatus, to which can be added the information of Jerome with regard to Donatus (*De vir. inl.* 93) and of Gennadius with regard to Vitellius and Macrobius (*De vir. inl.* 4 and 5). The information is most abundant in reference to some works of Donatus, Parmenian, Petilian and Cresconius.

Around 336, Donatus wrote an *Epistula de baptismo* in which he maintained the thesis that the members of the Catholic church, inasmuch as they were deprived of divine grace, could not be considered Christians, and, as a result, baptism administered by them had no value. Therefore, the Catholic who went over to the Donatists had to be rebaptized. This thesis would become the fundamental point of Donatist doctrine and practice. Donatus also wrote a work on the Trinity which was entitled *De Spiritu Sancto* according to Jerome, and *De Trinitate* according to Augustine. According to the latter, Donatus proposed here a subordinationist concept of the Trinity which approached the Arian doctrine. Furthermore, it is known that on the occasion of the Council of Serdica (343), there were attempts to reach an agreement between Arians and Donatists which remained without concrete results.

Parmenian, who was a native of Spain or Gaul, was the leader of the

Donatists from 362. Skillful and moderate, he ruled the Donatist church with effectiveness until his death around 391. In addition to the *Psalms* which he composed for liturgical use as a means of propaganda, he also wrote a treatise in five books against the Catholics (ca. 362), the content of which is known in summary form from the refutation by Optatus. In the first book, Parmenian expounded the Donatist doctrine on baptism; in the second he established the characteristics of the true church and sought to overcome the difficulty deriving from the fact that the Donatists were limited only to Africa by alleging the presence of a small Donatist community at Rome; in the third book he accused the Catholics of responsibility for the schism and for the intervention of political power; in the fourth book he presented the sufferings of the Donatists and the persecutions to which they were subject; and in the fifth book he interpreted the anathemas of the Old Testament *de oleo et sacrificio peccatoris* in a manner hostile to the sacraments administered in the Catholic church. Parmenian also wrote a letter (ca. 378) to Tyconius, a dissident Donatist who will be treated below (cf. p. 119), the content of which can be obtained from the refutation of Augustine *(Contra epistulam Parmeniani)*. In this letter Parmenian accuses Tyconius of inconsistency, because he rejected fundamental points of the Donatist creed yet did not wish to become a member of the Catholic church. Against the argument of Tyconius regarding universality as the distinctive characteristic of the true church, Parmenian maintained that the only true church was the Donatist by force of the persecutions of which it was made the object by the political power (church of the martyrs). The letter also contained an exposition of the theory of baptism, mentioned above.

Petilian of Constantina was in the forefront of the Donatist ranks at the turn of the fourth and fifth centuries, and played a leading role at the conference at Carthage in 411. His *Epistula ad presbyteros et diaconos* (ca. 401) reviewed all the questions which were the object of dispute between Catholics and Donatists, while his *De unico baptismo* (ca. 410) was dedicated specifically to baptism. The *Epistula* was refuted in a detailed fashion by Augustine in books I and II *Contra litteras Petiliani.* When Petilian reacted with an *Epistula ad Augustinum,* this was refuted in book III *Contra litteras Petiliani.* The defense of Petilian was then taken up by a certain Cresconius, to whom Augustine replied with the four books *Contra Cresconium.* In his work, Cresconius also dealt with baptism, the responsibility for the schism and the persecutions. These arguments were again treated in letter form by a certain Fulgentius, who is known from the reply in the *Contra Fulgentium* of pseudo-Augustine.

Since they extolled their martyrs, the Donatists also took an interest in hagiography. There can be mentioned the *Acta* of Saturninus, Dativus, Felix and companions, who were martyred during the persecution of Diocletian for not having handed over the sacred books, as well as the *Acta* of Marculus and the *Acta* of Maximianus and Isaac, who were victims of the anti-Donatist repression at the time of Constans. The visions which comfort the prisoners recall the *passio* of Cyprian in the version of Pontius and the *Passo Perpetuae,* while the amplifications of a rhetorical character and the overall tone of the narration recall the so-called epic passions rather than the simplicity of the historical *Acta.* The *Acta* of Saturninus are accompanied by an appendix which recalls in a polemical fashion the attitude of Mensurius and Caecilianus, who were both hostile to the *confessores* during the persecution of Diocletian.

Editions: K. Ziwsa: CSEL 26(1893)(Optatus). — Cf. PLS I, 183-190. — Conlatio anni 411, ed. S. Lancel, CCL 149A(1974); *idem,* SCh 104-105(1972).

Studies: J. Ferron, Donato: DHG 14(1960)649-650. — T. Sagi-Bunič, Controversia de Baptismate inter Parmenianum et S. Optatum Milevitanum: Laurentianum 3(1962)167-209. — E. Dinkler, Parmenianus: PWK 36, 3(1949)1549-1553; *idem,* Petilianus: PWK 37(1937)1132-1136. — J. M. del Estal, Testimonio positivo de Petiliano sobre la inexistencia de monacato en Africa antes de San Agustín: *Studia Monastica* 3(1961)123-136. — B. Quinot, C. Litteras Petiliani III 40, 48 et le monachisme en Afrique: REAug 13(1967)15-24. — See also the bibliography provided under Optatus and Augustine.

Hagiography. Editions: Cf. CPL 719-721, 2055. — PL 8, 689-715. — P. Franchi de' Cavalieri, Note hagiografiche 8(ST 65). Rome, 1935, 3-71. — *Saturninus and Dativus*: Cf. BHL 7492. — PL 8, 760-766. — *Marculus*: Cf. BHL 5271. — PL 8, 767-774. — *Isaac and Maximinus*: Cf. BHL 4473-4474. — PL 8, 767-774. — *Donatus and Advocatus*: BHL 2303b.

Studies on Donatism: Cf. "Optatus" and "Augustine," *infra.* P. Monceaux, Histoire littéraire de l'Afrique chrétienne IV-VII. Paris, 1912-1923. — G. Bareille: DThC 4(1939)1701-1728 (cf. DHG 14(1960)654-655). — J. P. Brisson, Autonomisme et christianisme dans l'Afrique romaine de Septime Sévère à l'invasion vandale. Paris, 1958. — B. Baldwin, Peasant Revolt in Africa in the Late Roman Empire: *Notthingham Medieval Studies* 6(1961)3-11. — E. L. Grasmück, Coercitio. Staat und Kirche im Donatistenstreit. Bonn, 1964. — E. Tengström, Donatisten und Katholiken. Soziale, wirtschaftliche und politische Aspekte einer nord-afrikanischen Kirchenspaltung. Stockholm, 1964. — S. Lancel, Originalité de la province ecclésiastique de Byzacène aux IVe et Ve siècles: *Cahiers de Tunisie* 12(1964)139-154. — W. H. C. Frend, Martyrdom and Persecution in the Early Church. Oxford, 1965. — S. Lancel, Aux origines du Donatisme et du mouvement des circoncellions: *Cahiers de Tunisie* 15(1967)183-188. — S. Gherro, Stato e Chiesa di fronte alla controversia donatista nei primi anni dell'età costantiniana: *Studia et documenta historiae et iuris* 36(1970)359-409. — W. H. C. Frend, The Donatist Church. Oxford, 1952[1], 1971[2]. — R. B. Eno, Some Nuances in the Ecclesiology of the Donatists: REAug 18(1972)46-50. — M. Overbeck, Augustin und die Circumcellionen seiner Zeit: *Chiron* 3(1973)457-463. — W. H. C. Frend, Heresy and Schism as Social and National Movements, in D. Baker, ed. Schism, Heresy and Religious Protest. Cambridge, 1972, 37-56. — D. Raynal, Culte des martyrs et propagande donatiste à Uppena: *Cahiers de Tunisie* 21(1973)33-72. — K. M. Girardet, Kaisergericht und Bischofsgericht. Bonn, 1975. — J. S. Alexander, A Note on the

Identity of the "Man of God" of 1 Kings XIII, in Gesta Coll. Carthag. 3.358: JThSt 28(1977)109-112. W. H. C. Frend, K. Clancy, When did the Donatist Schism Begin?: JThSt 28(1977)104-109.

TYCONIUS

Tyconius, mentioned above as the object of an attack by Parmenian, occupied an important position in the ranks of the Donatists because of the breadth of his learning, especially in the Scriptures, and because of his moderation and independence of judgment which were so foreign to the characteristic fanaticism of the schismatics that he ended up in conflict with them as well. Active between 370 and 390, he knew how to cleverly single out the weak points of the ecclesiology and the baptismal doctrine of the Donatists, and he did not hesitate to point them out in his writings. Precisely for that reason he was the object of the refutation of Parmenian, and around 380 was condemned by a Donatist council. But not even then did Tyconius wish to join the Catholic church, which he considered a church of *traditores,* so he went his own way and attended to his beloved studies. Augustine had a great esteem for this singular personality, and it is from him that many pieces of information are drawn concerning Tyconius, as well as from Gennadius (*De vir. inl.* 18).

His *De bello intestino* and *Expositiones diversarum causarum,* two works written between 370 and 375 which caused the falling out between Tyconius and the Donatists, are no longer extant. They were two related works, the first dedicated to the exposition of the author's ideas and the second to their defense. It was here that Tyconius asserted that universality was the constitutive characteristic of the true church and contested the pretense of the Donatists of forming the church of the perfect by showing among other things, that there were good and bad to be found in the midst of the schismatics themselves. Continuing his polemic with the Donatists, Tyconius maintained in the same manner as Optatus that the efficacy of baptism could not depend on the moral condition of the priest who administered it.

The entire text is preserved of Tyconius' *Liber regularum* or *Liber de septem regulis.* Composed around 392, it is, as far as is known, the most ancient manual of biblical hermeneutics written in the West. Augustine esteemed it to such an extent as to give detailed notice of its contents in the final chapters of book III of *De doctrina christiana.* The work does not consist of an organic and systematic exposition of the interpretative principles of Sacred Scripture, but rather contains certain rules, the application of which allows the interpretation in an allegorical sense of difficult or ambiguous scriptural passages so that the reader can draw instruction and edification even from these. Each of the seven rules is stated and explained by means of a crowded network of scriptural citations which are not always clear. Furthermore, there is no lack of digressions, which render the development of the exposition even more obscure. The basic points are as follows:

The first rule, *De Domino et corpore eius,* explains that the Scripture, whenever it refers to Christ, does not make a distinction between him and his body, i.e., the church, but passes indiscriminately from one to the other. The stone hewn from the mountain which destroys the kingdoms of the world in Dan. 2:34 is a figure of Christ, but when the stone becomes a mountain which fills the whole earth it is no longer properly speaking a figure of Christ but of his church. The second rule, *De Domini corpore bipartito,* explains with a clear anti-Donatist intent that the Scripture refers to Christ as to a body formed of two parts, composed respectively of good and bad. For this reason, the bride of Cant. 1:4 says, "I am black but beautiful," and Paul in Rom. 11:28 speaks at the same time of *inimici* and *dilecti.* The third rule, *De promissis et lege,* is intended to clarify above all the Pauline passages in Romans and Galatians in which the Mosaic Law is presented sometimes in a positive sometimes in a negative light. Tyconius explains the apparent contradiction on the grounds of the progress from the old economy, founded on the Law, to the new, founded on faith, and calls attention to the propaedeutic function of the Law (Gal. 3:24). In an anti-Gnostic and anti-Manichaean context, the author insists on the value of the free will, which together with the gift of grace, determines the salvation of each individual, and he draws attention once more, against the Donatists, to the conception of the church as composed of good and evil (e.g., Esau and Jacob who struggle in their mother's womb). The fourth rule, *De specie et genere,* on the basis of passages mainly from the prophets, explains that at times Scripture passes from the particular to the general, that is, from the part to the whole, and vice versa. In this point, too, Tyconius displays a special interest for the church, in an anti-Donatist sense. In this manner he states that the various cities and peoples named in the Old Testament are figures of the church, at times of the entire church (the whole), at times only of a good or a bad part of it (the part). By means of this alternation from the general to the specific and vice versa he interprets, among other things, the passage in Jonah (ch. 3) relating to Nineveh. The fifth rule, *De temporibus,* proposes to resolve by means of synecdoche (the part for the whole and vice versa) certain apparent contradictions present in the chronological computations in the Scriptures. By taking into account that the Scripture can indicate in these computations at times the part for the whole and the whole for the part, it is possible to resolve, for example, the contradiction between Gen. 15:13 (the Hebrews will be oppressed in Egypt for 400 years) and Ex. 12:40 (the Hebrews dwell in Egypt for 400 years) on the basis that the Hebrews were not oppressed for all of the 400 years spent in Egypt, but only from the time of Joseph's death. The sixth rule, *De recapitulatione,* explains why Scripture sometimes reduces to one significant moment a concept which chronologically is much more comprehensive. The eschatological warnings of Mt. 24:15-18 and Lk. 17:30ff are valid not only for the Parousia but must be observed always. The seventh rule, *De diabolo et corpore eius,* corresponds exactly to the first. When the Scripture refers to the devil, it includes indiscriminately his body also, i.e., those who belong to him. For example, when Isaiah speaks of the fall of Lucifer from heaven (Is. 19:12ff), the mention of all the kings and all the peoples can be referred to the body of the devil.

Prior to the *Liber regularum* Tyconius had written a commentary on the Apocalypse which has been lost in its entirety, but of which a manuscript at Turin, originally from Bobbio, has preserved copious fragments relating to the commentary on chapters 2, 3, 7, 8, 9, 10, 11, and 12. This work of Tyconius enjoyed a great popularity between the fifth and the seventh centuries and was much used by other commentators. Careful comparisons among the commentaries on the Apocalypse of Primasius, Bede and especially Beatus of Liebana (seventh century) are able to impart a much broader knowledge of the text of Tyconius. In any case, the fragments from the Turin manuscript are sufficient to furnish a rather precise idea of the general characteristics of the work.

The interpretation is of a predominantly allegorical nature, and Tyconius made use of his rules (e.g., for the alternation between general/specific cf. 2, 21-23; 12, 1). The interpretation tends to consider certain particulars of the Johannine text in a spiritual way, such as the idols and the fornication of Apoc. 2:20 and the cataclysms and catastrophies of Apoc. 11:6, 13; 12:4. At times, particular eschatological elements are realized in the life of the church, e.g., Apoc. 7:17. The predominant interest of Tyconius is the relationship between Christ and the church. The latter in particular, in keeping with the basic line of Tyconius' thought, is represented under the most varied forms: the angels of Apoc. 2:19; 8:2, 6; 10:10; 11:18; the new Jerusalem of Apoc. 3:12; the altar of Apoc. 8:3; the elders of Apoc. 9:7; the candelabra of Apoc. 11:4; the woman clothed with the sun of Apoc. 12:1 (Christ is the sun, the Apostles the crown of twelve stars, the heretics are the moon under the woman's feet and the Incarnate Christ is her son). Tyconius polemizes in this work as well against the particularism of the Donatists *qui angustam nituntur facere ecclesiam dei,* which instead is spread throughout the entire world (3, 9.

10. 12). Two peoples are contained in it, namely the good and the bad, *pars dei quae luci est comparata, et pars diaboli tenebrarum obscuritatibus circumsepta* (8, 12).

Editions: Cf. CPL 709-710. — PL 18, 15-66. — F. C. Burkitt, The Rules of Tyconius. Cambridge, 1894. — F. Lo Bue and G. C. Willis, The Turin Fragments of Tyconius' Commentary on Revelation. Cambridge, 1963.

Studies: E. Dinkler, PWK 6, 1(1936[2])849-856. — T. Hahn, Tyconius-Studien. Ein Beitrag zur Kirchen und Dogmengeschichte des 4. Jahrhunderts. Leipzig, 1900 (reprint: Aalen, 1970). — H. A. Sanders, Beati in Apocalypsim libri XII. Rome, 1930. — K. Forster, Die ekklesiologische Bedeuting der Corpus-Begriffes im Liber Regularum des Tyconius: MTZ 7(1956)173-183. — J. Ratzinger, Beobachtungen zum Kirchenbegriff des Tyconius im "Liber regularum": REAug 2(1956)173-187. — L. J. van der Lof, Warum wurde Tyconius nicht katholisch: ZNW 57(1966)260-283. — A. Pincherle, Nuovi frammenti di Ticonio: RSLR 5(1969)756-757. — G. Bonner, Towards a Text of Tyconius: SP 10(TU 107, 1970)9-13. — P. Cazier, Le *Livre des règles* de Tyconius. Sa transmission du *De doctrina christiana* aux *Sentences* d'Isidore de Séville: REAug 19(1973)241-261. — E. Romero Pose, Ticonio y el sermón "in natali sanctorum innocentium": Greg 60(1979)513-544; *idem,* Et caelum ecclesia et terra ecclesia. Exegesis ticoniana de Apocalipsis 4, 1: Aug 19(1979)469-486. — A. Pincherle, Alla ricerca de Ticonio: SSR 2(1978)357-365. — K. B. Steinhauser, The Structure of Tyconius' Apocalypse Commentary. A Correction: VC 35(1981)354-357.

OPTATUS

The Catholic church in Africa and Numidia, deprived of an effective leader prior to Augustine and Aurelius, sought with difficulty and small success to withstand the pressure of the Donatists who, together with their efficacious proselytizing, were flooding over every field. In the literary camp, prior to the stream of Augustine's anti-Donatist works, we, like the ancients, know of only one other writing from the Catholic side against the Donatists, that of Optatus of Milevi. Nothing is known of this author except that he was bishop of Milevi in Numidia, and even Jerome knew only of the books written *adversus Donatianae partis calumniam* at the time of Valentinian and Valens (*De vir. inl.* 110). Jerome evidently does not give the precise title of the work nor do the manuscripts, which have only *liber* I, II etc. of Optatus of Milevi. The title *adversus Parmenianum Donatistam* which is to be found in some modern editions is therefore not to be considered as the original title and possesses only an indicative value, inasmuch as in his work Optatus does in fact refute the anti-Catholic work of the Donatist bishop.

This work of Optatus, as it has been transmitted in the manuscripts, is divided into seven books and is furnished with an appendix containing documents relating to the Donatist controversy. Jerome, however, speaks only of six books (loc. cit.), and Optatus himself, when he describes the plan of his work at I 7 lists six points which correspond exactly to the content of the first six books. There has thus been no lack of those who consider book VII to be an inauthentic addition by another hand. In reality, it is also the work of Optatus and, as is clear from its beginning, was added to the work on a subsequent occasion to further define his position against the schismatics. From indications drawn from some manuscripts, it appears that on this occasion Optatus also revised the first six books here and there, making some modifications and additions, such as part of ch. 8 of book III. It is likely that the appendix was also added on this occasion, and the doubts advanced by some concerning the authenticity of some of the documents contained here are unfounded. On the basis of Jerome's information and of certain internal indications, the first draft of the work can be dated around 370-374. The mention of Siricius as the current bishop of Rome can be considered as a specification added at the time of the second edition, since Siricius was elected bishop of Rome in 385. Thus, this second edition can be dated around 385-390.

It has been noted that the work of Optatus was conceived as a systematic refutation of the pro-Donatist writing of Parmenian. To begin with, Optatus calls attention rapidly to the five basic points in which the writing of Parmenian was developed and the six into which his own response was divided. But before passing to the orderly and systematic treatment of his six arguments, Optatus criticizes the statement of Parmenian, who, when he was extolling baptism, had even spoken of the purification of the *sordes* of the flesh of Christ in his baptism in the Jordan. He then makes reference to the condemnation which Parmenian had confirmed against past heretics (Marcion, Praxeas, Sabellius, Velentinus, etc.) and introduces a fundamental point of his treatise, namely, the distinction between heretics and schismatics; the latter are guilty only on the level of ecclesiastical discipline, while the former are guilty on the level of doctrine and for that reason are rightly rebaptized. When he has finished his preface, Optatus treats the first point of his refutation which concerns the *traditores,* who had provided the spark which ignited the Donatist crisis. Against Parmeniun, who had maintained the invalidity of Caecilianus' episcopal election, Optatus relates the entire history of the beginnings of the schism up until the Roman council presided over by Miltiades and places the guilt of the Donatists clearly in relief. He points above all to the fact, which had been brought to light by the deacon, Nundiniarius, that some of the very Numidian bishops who had accused Felix of Aptungi of being a *traditor* had themselves been *traditores,* as is clear from the first of the documents contained in the appendix.

The second book discusses Parmenian's statement that only the Donatist church represents the one, catholic church because it alone is endowed with the suitable prerogatives. The pharisaical presumption of the Donatists is refuted by Optatus on the basis of the fundamental proof that the Donatist church is circumscribed in a tiny part of the world, while the Catholic church in Africa is in communion with all the other churches. At this point Optatus greatly extols the unity of the church and the primacy of the Church of Rome, a list of whose bishops he provides (ch. 2-3), and views with irony the attempt of the Donatists to establish a community of their own at Rome. Parmenian's affirmation that no one can consider himself to be part of the church who feeds on blood (of the Donatists) provokes a response of Optatus, who treats in great detail the violent acts of which the Donatists themselves were guilty against Catholic clergy and laity. In the third book, Optatus deals with the accusation leveled against the Catholics of having requested the intervention of Roman military force against the Donatists. He seeks to minimize this intervention, the licitness of which he nevertheless defends, although in an indirect manner, in chapter 7 on the basis of Old Testament episodes. He points out again the acts of violence committed by the Donatists and condemns their fanatic attachment to Donatus. He disputes that the Donatist victims of the Roman repression can be considered as martyrs, because it is possible to speak of martyrs only when there has been persecution by the pagans. The Donatists, on the other hand, *quicquid potuerunt pati, si occidi malum est, mali sui ipsi sunt causa* (ch. 6). It is in such a context that Optatus takes up the consideration of the chief point of the Donatist controversy, which was the attitude of the Donatists and of the Catholics in relation to the Roman Empire. Nevertheless, he does this in a tone which tends to suggest that, in spite of the differences, the two opposing camps share substantially the same faith (ch. 9). Optatus is a complete and convinced loyalist. Since the emperors have become Christians, the identification of Christianity with the Empire is for him an accomplished fact (*non enim respublica est in ecclesia sed ecclesia in respublica* is said in ch. 3), so that the hostility of Donatus for Constantine, the *catholicus imperator,* becomes for him inexcusable. Given this mentality, Optatus was the least suited for penetrating that complex of socio-economic motives which lay at the base of the Donatists' repudiation of the Empire and the policy of cooperation between it and the church, and for this reason the more profound significance of these facts escaped him.

In book four, the shortest, Optatus dwells on the Donatist refusal to accept as valid the anointing and the eucharist presided over by Catholic priests, whom the schismatics considered as sinners. He relentlessly insists on the radicalism of the Donatists who wish to exasperate an argument which does not touch on the fundamental points of the profession of faith, and he points out the presumption of those who judge the Catholics as sinners and confutes the rather general Scriptural passages which the Donatists advanced in support of their refusal of the sacraments administered by Catholic priests. The same theme of book four is taken up again and developed in book five in relation to the doctrinally more important point over which the Donatists and Catholics were divided; the refusal of the Donatists to recognize as valid the baptism administered by Catholic priests whom they regarded as sinners, and their resulting practice of rebaptizing Catholics who passed over to the ranks of the schismatics. In support of such practices the Donatists invoked the authority of Cyprian, who had not considered baptism administered by heretics as valid. Optatus observes that the baptism administered by real heretics, who alter the formula of faith, cannot be considered valid. But between Catholics and Donatists, *una est ecclesiastica conversatio* (ch. 1), for which reason the baptism administered either by the one group or the other is to be considered valid. There are in fact three components *(species)* of baptism: *prima in Trinitate, secunda in credente, tertia in operate.* However, only the first two of these, the exactness of the baptismal formula intended as a summary of the rule of faith and the faith of the candidate, are indispensable elements, not the sanctity of the minister: *operarii mutari possunt, sacramenta mutari non possunt* (ch. 4). In fact, if the validity of baptism were to depend on the sanctity of the minister, it would be tantamount to admitting that the will of man could present an impediment to the saving will of God, which takes on concrete form precisely in the gift of baptism. It is not the minister who infuses the divine spirit into the one baptized, but rather God Himself. There is contained here in more than outline form the Augustinian doctrine according to which a sacrament is effective *ex opere operato* and not *ex opere operantis.*

The sixth book is dedicated to the illustration of the excesses of the Donatists, who precisely to emphasize their conviction of the invalidity of the Catholic sacraments and ordinations to the greatest extent had even gone to the extent of destroying the altars and chalices of the Catholic churches, washing and sprinkling with salt the churches themselves in order to purify them, and forcing the consecrated virgins to change their woolen garments. In book seven, which, as has been noted, was added to the others after an interval of several years, Optatus returns to point out again the excesses of the Donatists and to defend the conduct of Macarius, the emissary of Constans, who had used military force against the Donatists. In this book, which is more conciliatory in tone than the preceding six, Optatus contrasts the Donatist thesis, according to which the church harbors only the perfect in her bosom, with the idea of the church which is one throughout the entire (Roman) world and is like the cultivated field of the parable in Mt. 13:24ff: *et in uno agro nascuntur diversa semina, sicut in ecclesia non est similis turba animarum* (ch. 2). The separation between the grain and the weeds will take place only on the day of judgment with the decisive intervention of God.

The moderate tone and irenic tendency of Optatus' polemic have been often emphasized, and this is a characteristic which distinguishes his work from others of the same literary genre, which are usually much more aggressive and violent. This is due to the fact that Optatus tends to minimize the points of contrast between the Catholics and the Donatists so as to present the latter as radical extremists who exaggerate that contrast by fanaticism. In this way, he gladly emphasized the pharisaism, at once ingenuous and proud, of those who pretended to constitute the church of the perfect, while it was not difficult for him to demolish, at times with a stroke of good-natured irony, the inconsistent doctrinal arguments which propped up that illusion. The fact is that Donatism fed above all on religious fanaticism and anti-Roman hatred, with respect to which the doctrinal baggage counted for little. Precisely for this reason, it can be questioned what type of real validity and efficacy this work of Optatus enjoyed among the Donatists, in spite of the fact that it is so well measured and articulate. Its significance can be seen in the need especially from the Catholic side to reply to the work of Parmenian, in order to demonstrate to the undecided and the indifferent of both camps just how weak were the pro-Donatist arguments proposed in it.

The ancients did not know of any work of Optatus other than the anti-Donatist one treated here. Some sermons in the great mass of pseudo-Augustinian sermons, one on Easter and another on Epiphany, have recently been attributed to him, but such an attribution is anything but certain. The authorship of Optatus seemed more certain for a sermon which mentions the slaying of the Holy Innocents, since one of the manuscripts which transmits the work attributes it to Optatus of Milevi. However, certain features of the text (the reality of persecution, detachment from the world) seem more likely to have arisen out of a Donatist matrix. Therefore, the name of Optatus of Thamugadi, one of the Donatist leaders, has been proposed for it.

Editions: Cf. CPL 244-249. — PL 11, 883-1104; PLS I, 287-302. — C. Ziwsa: CSEL 26(1893). — A. Wilmart, Un sermon de saint Optat pour la fête de Noël: RevSR 2(1922)271-302.

Studies: B. Capelle, Optat et Maximin: RB 35(1923)24-26. — A. Pincherle, Due postille sul donatismo: RR 18(1947)160-164. — T. Sagi-Bunič, Controversia de Baptismate inter Parmenianum et S. Optatum Milevitanum: *Laurentianum* 3(1962)167-209. — Y. M. Duval, Quelques emprunts de saint Léon à saint Augustin: MSR 15(1958)85-94. — S. Blomgren, Eine Echtheitsfrage bei Optatus von Mileve. Stockholm, 1959; *idem,* Spicilegium Optatianum. *Eranos* 58(1960)132-141. — A. C. de Veer, À propos de l'authenticité du livre VII d'Optat de Milève: REAug 7(1961)389-391. — H. J. Diesner, Volk und Volksaufstände bei Optatus von Mileve. In *Kirche und Staat im spätrömischen Reich.* Berlin, 1963. — H. Silvestre, Trois sermons à retirer définitivement de l'héritage d'Optat de Milève: *Proceedings of the African Classical Association* 7(1964)61-62. — V. Saxer, Un sermon médiéval sur la Madeleine. Reprise d'une homélie antique pour Pâques attribuable à Optat de Milève († 392): RB 80(1970)17-50. — A. Goda, Les mots "fides" et "fidelis" chez Optat de Milève: *Rocznik teol.-kanoniczne* 19(1972)172-180 (in Polish with résumé in French). — L. Malunowiczówna, Signification du mot "sacramentum" chez Optat de Milève: ibid., 163-170, *idem.* — R. B. Eno, The Work of Optatus as a Turning Point in the African Ecclesiology: *The Thomist* 37(1973)668-685. — E. Nash, Convenerunt in domum Faustae in Laterano. S. Optati Milevitani I 23: RQ 71(1976)1-21. — E. Romero Pose, Ticonio Y el sermón In natali sanctorum innocentium: Greg 50(1979)513-544.

ZENO

In a letter written around 380 (I 5, 1), Ambrose mentions Zeno as the recently deceased bishop of Verona, whom local tradition ranks in eighth place in the list of bishops of that city. Jerome and the other ancient biographers are silent in his regard, but some manuscripts have transmitted around 90 homilies under his name, which through internal indications can be recognized as the work of a single author who was active after 360, inasmuch as he made use of Hilary's *Commentary on the Psalms.* There is no valid reason to disregard the attribution of the manuscripts so that by now no one doubts that the homilies actually are to be attributed to Zeno, bishop of Verona.

The collection of homilies in its present state is divided into two books of unequal length, the first containing 62 texts and the second containing only 30. Of these homilies, only about thirty appear to be complete or at least organically developed to some extent, and the others are either outlines, summaries or fragments which are sometimes repetitious. It therefore seems evident that the edition of the collection was not made by Zeno but by others who put together what material they had at their disposal. It is thus likely that the collection was made after the death of the bishop. From indications drawn from the manuscripts, it can be ascertained that the collection was made at Verona itself for needs of a liturgical nature. The silence of every other source regarding the literary work of Zeno can be easily explained by the fact that this was an exclusively local diffusion of the homilies and probably took place at a time somewhat removed from the death of the bishop. In any case, the obvious care evidence by some of the longer homilies, including the formal aspect, suggests that at least these texts were revised by the author after they had been pronounced.

The reminiscences of such African authors as Tertullian and Lactantius which occur in the pages of Zeno, and the inclusion in the collection of homilies of a text in honor of Saint Arcadius, an obscure

Mauretanian martyr, have led to the common opinion among scholars that Zeno was of African origin. However, the first argument is inconsistent, while the second, although more significant, does not appear decisive for determining the native land of Zeno.

Various themes are treated in this collection of homilies. As is to be expected, the majority of them are of an exegetical nature, while some treat of baptismal and Easter themes and still others are concerned with topics of a moral character, such as *de continentia, de avaritia, de pudicitia, de timore, de patientia,* etc. In these latter texts there is a clear tendency to illustrate and vary the exposition by means of examples which are almost always drawn from the Old Testament; Joseph and Susannah are examples of modesty (I 1), while Daniel, Jonah and Peter are examples of fear of the Lord (II 2). As can be seen from the complete texts of the collection, the tone of the exposition is grave, the language is cultivated and there is evidence of a certain use of rhythmical clauses. In short, there is not noticeable in Zeno any need or occasion to adjust the tone of the discourse to the capacities of an audience of a low level.

The greatest part of the homilies of an exegetical nature have as their object passages of the Old Testament (cf. Gregory of Elvira), including events (the dream of Jacob I 37) and personalities (Job I 15, Abraham I 43, Jonah I 34). The particular preference for this part of Sacred Scripture, mentioned above, is also evident in other contexts: only Peter represents the New Testament as an example of faith in I 36, 7-8 while the Old Testament is represented by Enoch, Noah, Abraham, Isaac, Jacob, Joseph, Moses, Joshua, etc. Zeno shows an even more exact preference for the Book of Daniel, especially for the episode of Susannah and of the three young men. A recurring anti-Jewish vein (I 18, 51, 61, etc.) which is developed especially in the context of Easter corresponds to this preference for the Old Testament. The only one of the complete or nearly complete homilies which is dedicated to a passage of the New Testament is II 5 on 1 Cor. 15:24, which deals with a passage employed in the Arian controversy and displays a development of a completely doctrinal character.

The evident preference of Zeno for themes and figures from the Old Testament is to be explained in the line of tradition which interpreted the Old Testament in a prevailingly, if not exclusively, Christological key. The exegesis of the more complete homilies is developed along these lines, where the various Old Testament personalities are assumed as prefigurations of Christ. For the most part it is a question of traditional motifs, such as in the case of Jonah (I 34), of Jacob (I 37), of the patriarch Judah in the episode with Thamar (I 13), and of the parable of the Good Samaritan which is interpreted in reference to Adam (the man beaten and robbed) and

Christ (the Samaritan). The figure of Job (I 15) is also interpreted in this sense, which is an unusual extension of this exegetical criterion. If the interpretation in the homilies is by and large traditional, the same does not seem to be the case in a quantity of particular details, which reveal an exegete who is alert to understand even the subtle shades of meaning in the scriptural passage which he is interpreting. An exegetical theme with important doctrinal implications, such as Gen. 1:26-27 (the creation of man in the image of God), often engaged the attention of Zeno (I 28; II 4, 30) with results tending toward a dualistic anthropology which sees the image of God in the spiritual element in man.

Among the existing complete homilies, few of them treat of doctrinal themes in a formal manner (I 2 on the Resurrection; II 5 on 1 Cor. 15:24 in an anti-Arian sense). However, indications of this nature, spread throughout the entire length of the *corpus,* are frequent enough to reveal a bishop who, in spite of some traces of millenarianism in I 2, was fairly well abreast of the most controverted questions of his time, i.e., the Trinitarian question and the Christological question. With regard to the former, Zeno is very precise in polemics with the Arians in affirming the equality and coeternity of the persons in the articulation of the divine nature, and he applies the scriptural passages which suggest the inferiority of Christ to the human element without involving that divine nature by which the Son is equal to the Father (II 5). The attention is directed above all to the relationship between the Father and Son, but there is no lack of Trinitarian formulae which include also the Holy Spirit within the divine reality (I 7, 17, 45; II 5). Attention can be directed to the final image of I 7 in which the Father and the Son are likened to two seas, distinct between themselves *sui proprietate, locis vocabulisque* (divine persons), but where the same water (one single divine nature) passes from one to the other to signify the compenetration between the two persons.

On the Christological plane, Zeno does not seem to have been sensitized to the Apollinarian question, which did not have great repercussions in the West. Instead, his attention is directed to the danger represented by the Photinians, whose center of activity, Pannonia, was not far from Northern Italy. The repeated affirmation in various fragments of the homily on the Nativity of Christ (I 54; II 8, 12) of the double birth of Christ, from the Father *qua Deus* and from Mary *qua homo,* is directed against these heretics. The rare theme according to which Christ entered into Mary through her ear, that is, through the word of the angel at the Annunciation, is related in I 3, 19.

Homily I 39, dedicated to the martyr Arcadius, constitutes a completely isolated part of the collection, which makes no mention of other martyrs. It is an important part because the exceedingly legendary tone in which it describes the suffering of the martyr bears witness that already around 360 the genuine tradition relating to the martyrs was being distorted by the admission of those exaggerated accents of a legendary rather than historical nature which are characteristic of so many of the Acts of the martyrs extant today.

Editions: Cf. CPL 208. — PL 11, 253-528. — B. Löfstedt, CCL 22(1971).

Translations: German: A. Bigelmair, Des hl. Bischofs Zeno von Verona Traktate (BKV² 10). Munich, 1934. — Th. Michels, Des hl. Zeno von Verona Österliche Ansprachen. Berlin, 1927. *Italian:* G. Ederle, San Zeno. Sermones I-IV. Verona, 1955-1960. With regard to the translations cf. B. Löfstedt, CCL 22, 55*-59*.

Studies: J. B. C. Giullari, S. Zenonis episcopi Ver. Sermones. Verona, 1900² (text with commentary and notes). — A. Bigelmair, Zeno von Verona. Münster, 1904. — H. Januel, Commentationes philologicae in Zenonem Veronensem. Regensburg, 1905-1906. — F. C. Arnold, Zeno, Bischof von Verona: RE 21(1908)657-663. — K. Ziwsa, Zur stilistischen Würdigung des Zeno Veronensis. In *Festgabe zum 100 jähr. Jubiläum des Schottengymnasiums.* Vienna, 1907, 372ff. — E. Löfstedt, Patristische Beiträge: *Eranos* 10(1910)6-29. — M. Stepanich, The Christology of Zeno of Verona. Washington, 1948. — R. Rosini, Il primato di Cristo secondo S. Zeno, vescovo di Verona: StP 10(1963)3-36. — O. Perler, Die Taufsymbolik der vier Jahreszeiten im Baptisterium bei Kelibia. In Mullus. Festschrift Th. Klauser. Münster, 1964, 282-290. — F. E. Vokes, Zeno of Verona, Apuleius and Africa: SP 8(TU 93, 1966)130-134. — Y. –M. Duval, Les sources grecques de l'exégèse de Jonas chez Zénon de Vérone: VC 20(1966)98-115. — G. de Apoli, L'iniziazione cristiana nei "Sermoni" di S. Zeno di Verona: *Rivista liturgica* 54(1967)407-417. — J. Doignon, Refrigerium et catéchèse à Vérone. In Hommages à M. Renard, III. Brussels, 1969, 220-239. — B. Löfstedt, Zur Sprache des Zeno Veronensis: *Acta classica* 12(1969)87-102. — G. B. Pighi, Sancti Zenonis Veronensis ep. historica popularisque persona: *Latinitas* 20(1972)121-134. — L. Palanca, The Prose Rhythm and Gorgianci Figures in the Sermons of St. Zeno of Verona, Diss. Catholic Univ., Washington, D.C., 1970. — W. Wistrand, Textkritisches zu Zeno Veronensis. In *Classica et Mediaevalia* F. Blatt. Copenhagen, 1973, 223-238. — K. Wegenast, Zenon: PWK II-19(1972)147-149. — W. Hübner, Das Horoskop der Christen (Zeno 1, 38L.): VC 19(1975)120-137. — G. P. Marchi, A. Orlandi, M. Brenzoni, Il culto di san Zeno nel Veronese. Verona, 1972. — G. Philippart, La fête de S. Zénon de Vérone le 8 décembre: AB 92(1974)347-348. — B. Löfstedt, D. W. Packard, A Concordance to the "Sermons" of Bishop Zeno von Verona. New York, 1975. — Studi Zenoniani in occasione del XVI centenario della morte di san Zeno. Verona, 1976. — C. Truzzi, La liturgia de Verona al tempo di San Zeno: StP 27(1980)539-564.

PHILASTER

The fourth century witnessed the flowering of a multitude of heresies: Arianism in its various forms, Apollinariansm, Priscillianism and others. Thus it is necessary to arrange all these sects in some kind of order and to review them and the others which preceded them. Just as between the second half of the second century and the beginning of the third, an age which also witnessed a great flowering of heresies, there arose the anti-heretical writings of Justin, Irenaeus,

Hippolytus and pseudo-Tertullian, so at this time appear Epiphanius, Augustine and Philaster.

Jerome does not treat of Philaster in his *De viris inlustribus,* and we have only some very general information concerning him which can be gathered from a sermon in his honor given by Gaudentius, his successor as bishop of Brescia. According to Gaudentius, he was an itinerant preacher and controversialist active in the second half of the fourth century, who, at Rome and elsewhere, was ready to enter into debate with pagans, Jews and heretics. He sought to oppose the Arian bishop, Auxentius, at Milan, but was unsuccessful and as a consequence suffered a beating. As bishop of Brescia, he was among the signatories of the decisions of the Council of Aquileia in 381, which deposed the Arian bishops Palladius of Ratiaria and Secundianus of Singidunum. We are familiar with his *Diversarum haereseon liber.* Augustine describes this work briefly in *Ep.* 222, where he compares the 156 heresies described by Philaster with the 80 described by Epiphanius and from the comparison obtains the not inconsiderable information supplied by Epiphanius as well as the diverse concept of heresy professed by the two authors; a concept which in reality is difficult to determine. Between the two works, Augustine definitely prefers that of Epiphanius, and it is clear that the work of Philaster did not enjoy much esteem.

In describing the composition of Philaster, Augustine distinguishes 28 heresies which appeared among the Jews prior to the Incarnation of Christ, and 128 which are proper to the Christian era. The division into two parts is confirmed by the manuscript tradition, in fact, a manuscript at Leningrad which contains the work has only the 128 heresies of the second group. As to the sources utilized by Philaster, Lipsius proposed to include the *Syntagma* of Hippolytus among others, but the prevailing opinion is that Philaster drew only from Epiphanius, for the most part, and from Irenaeus. Philaster's work was composed subsequently to that of Epiphanius (376-377) and must be dated between 380 and 390. On the basis of the numerical calculations made by Philaster in chapters 106 and 112, Marx advanced the hypothesis of a second edition of the work made in 430, but it is preferable to assume that Philaster simply erred in his calculations.

In the brief preface, Philaster states that he wishes to treat of the heresies and various errors which have sprung up since the beginning of the world, first under the Jews then in the Christian era. In considering Christian doctrine as an absolute measure of the truth in a non-historical and atemporal manner, Philaster follows Epiphanius and Hippolytus. Unlike these two, however, he does not consider the different Greek philosophical schools as heresies, although his judgment on pagan culture and literature in general is completely negative. He limits himself to the Jewish world. With regard to this, the conspicuous increase in the number of heresies described has already been noted. It must be pointed out that all the ancient heresiologists tend to inflate in a more or less artificial manner the number of heresies, evidently to better develop the details and to emphasize to a greater extent the danger to the faith which arises from this quarter. This latter point becomes an obsession in Epiphanius. Philaster goes even further, and his delight in piling up heresy on top of heresy seems to point to an excessive display of erudition. This augmentation is achieved in an absolutely arbitrary manner by raising the protagonists of this or that episode of the Old Testament to the rank of heretics with precise titles *(Musuritae, Troglodytae, Puteoritae)*. From about the eighteenth heresy listed, all the rest are nothing more than propositions of a doctrinal or disciplinary nature which Philaster considers erroneous but which do not appear to have given rise to actual heretical or schismatic movements. In this regard it must be emphasized that Philaster completely ignores the distinction between heresy and schism which even his contemporary Optatus, for example, knew well. The level of Philaster's investigations is certainly modest. He draws on Irenaeus and especially Epiphanius in a superficial manner and summarizes the information from these sources usually in extremely brief notices which give only a general presentation of the various heresies. Even in those instances where Philaster describes contemporary heresies and thus was able to take advantage of an ample documentation in primary sources, the level of the presentation does not improve. Obviously, there is no lack of errors and misunderstandings; e.g., in heresy XC, Melitius is said to have been a follower of Arius, whereas to the contrary Arius had been at first a follower of Melitius. Also, the presentation of the Arian heresy (LXVI) attributes to Arius concepts which had not been current at the beginnings of the Arian conflict but which arose only around 360. Given the anti-Arian activity of Philaster, this lack of information can only be surprising and bears little favorable witness to the doctrinal and heresiological preparation of this author. In short, the modern reader cannot help but share the hardly flattering judgment which Augustine made concerning Philaster.

Editions: Cf. CPL 121-121a. — PL 12, 1111-1302. — B. Marx, CSEL 38(1898). — F. Heylen, CCL 9(1957)207-324, 481-584 (indices).

Studies: P. C. Jurent, Étude grammaticale sur le latin de S. Filastrius. Erlangen, 1904 (*Romanische Forschungen* 19[1906]130-320). — F. Marx, Über die Trierer Handschrift des Filastrius zur Ergänzung der Wiener Ausgabe: Berichte über die Verhandlungen d. k. säch. Gesel, d. Wiss. z. Leipzig Phil. hist. Kl. 56(1904)43-105. — R. Schmid, Philaster: RE 15(1904)294-295. — A. Engelbrecht, Studein über den Lukas-kommentar, mit einem Anhang über eine bisher verschollene Handschrift des Filastrius: SAW 146, 8(1903)46-54. — G. Ficker, Philastrius: RGG 4(1913)1492-1493. — J. Wittig, Filastrius, Gaudentius u. Ambrosiaster. In *Ambrosiaster-Studien.* Breslau, 1909, 3-56. — F. Ceccopieri, L'uso di "quod, quia, quoniam" in Filastrio: BFC 30(1923)48-51. — Th. Stangl, Zu Filastrius c.109, 2: PhW 32(1915)862-863. — H. Koch, Philastrius: PWK 38(1938)2125-2131. — G. Bardy, Le "De haeresibus" (de Saint Augustin) et ses sources: MSCA II(1931)397-416. — M. J. Rondeau, Les polémiques d'Hippolyte de Rome et de Filastre de Brescia concernant le psautier: RHR 171(1967)1-51.

GAUDENTIUS

The little information known of Gaudentius is drawn from his own writings (*Serm.* 16 and 21). When Philaster, the bishop of Brescia, died sometime after 390, Gaudentius, who had been his pupil, was in the East and it was there that he received the notice of his designation to succeed his teacher. Gaudentius claims to have declined the office at first and to have accepted only under pressure from Ambrose and other bishops. In 405, together with two other Italian bishops, he traveled at the behest of Honorius to Constantinople to request from Arcadius a reexamination of the case of John Chrysostom, who had been deposed and exiled. Together with the other two bishops, Gaudentius was poorly received and in fact was imprisoned and sent back to the West in a boat which was on the point of sinking. In 410, Rufinus dedicated the Latin translation of the pseudo-Clementine *Recognitiones* to him.

Gaudentius enjoyed a good reputation as a preacher, but it is only by chance that some of his homilies have survived. As can be derived from the preface which precedes the homilies, a high official of Valentinian II, Benevolus by name, had been unable because of illness to hear a series of homilies which Gaudentius had delivered during Easter Week, and requested them from the bishop. Gaudentius sent him copies of these homilies and added another five, also on scriptural topics. Modern scholars have added another six sermons to this homogeneous block on the basis of solid internal criteria.

Almost all the ten Easter homilies are concerned with the passages of Exodus which were read during the liturgy, although homilies 8 and 9 deal with the Johannine passage on the Wedding of Cana. In perfect harmony with the liturgical celebration in which they were delivered, the homilies on Exodus present the traditional typological reading of that book of the Bible, which from the beginnings of Christian exegesis had been interpreted as the prefiguration of the paschal mystery and of those rites connected with it. Thus the departure of the Hebrews from Egypt and the passage through the desert symbolize the liberation of the Christians, who through the sacrifice of Christ have escaped from the hands of Pharaoh (the devil) and from the slavery of Egypt (death). In this typological and sacramental context, Christ is the paschal lamb who frees from sin and with his body mystically nourishes the Christians, who rise in him through baptism. The first-born of the Egyptians who are destroyed by the angel symbolize the demons defeated by Christ, and the unleavened bread signifies innocence, intended above all in a doctrinal sense as the rejection of heresy. There is no lack in these homilies on Exodus of elements of this type, which are directed in particular against the Marcionites and Manichaeans who denied the Old Testament and did not consider it to be inspired by the Supreme God. The two homilies on the Wedding Feast at Cana defend marriage against the Manichaeans and exalt the virginity of Mary. Gaudentius takes a notable stand here against parents who consecrate their still-young children to a life of virginity. Although this life represents the ideal of perfection, it cannot be imposed.

The five homilies added by Gaudentius to the series of Easter homilies include four sermons on Gospel passages and one in honor of the Maccabees. These homilies, which demonstrate a good mastery of the material, treat of diverse themes, such as the Maccabees as examples of fortitude and faith for Christians. While speaking on Jn. 14:26 (*Serm.* 14), Gaudentius presents his listeners with a brief treatise *de Spiritu Sancto,* which is obviously in perfect line with the Catholic theology of the time and affirms the full divinity of the third person of the trinity. *Serm.* 13, on Christmas, engages the preacher in behalf of the poor against the avarice of the rich.

The six homilies which have been attributed to Gaudentius by modern scholars are of varied content. *Serm.* 16 *de ordinatione sui* presents autobiographical elements mentioned above; *Serm.* 17 deals with the dedication of a basilica; and *Serm.* 18 *ad Serminium* interprets the difficult Gospel passage of the dishonest steward (Lk. 16), and sees in this personage a symbol of the devil who seeks to harm the Christians even after the coming of Christ. *Serm.* 19 *ad Paulum diaconum* treats of Jn. 14:28, "the Father is greater than I," a *locus classicus* in the Arian controversy which Gaudentius explains in the sense that Christ is inferior to the Father only *qua homo,* an explanation which was current especially in the West. *Serm.* 20 is a brief panegyric of Peter and Paul, and *Serm.* 21, *de vita et obitu beati Filastrii* contains the little information known about this personality as well as some information about Gaudentius himself. The authenticity of this last homily was contested by Marx, the editor of Philaster, but without a sound motive.

Although he does not display originality in any field, Gaudentius shows himself always at ease whether in exegesis, in the enunciation of Trinitarian doctrine in polemic with the Arians, or in overtures of a disciplinary or hortatory nature. His simple, clear and precise form testifies to the author's good scholastic preparation. On the whole, Gaudentius presents all the characteristics which were then required of a bishop who was zealous in keeping abreast of his responsibilities, which were no longer only of a pastoral nature, but included political and civic duties as well. He gives evidence of scholastic preparation, of a more than superficial competence in the fields of exegesis and doctrine, and of the capacity to engage the faithful on the disciplinary and moral plane.

Editions: Cf. CPL 139-143. — PL 20, 827-1006. — A. Glück, CSEL 68(1936).

Translations: Italian: G. M. Mariotti, Le opere di S. Gaudenzio vescovo di Brescia, tradotte in esatta, se non elegante, versione italiana. Breno, 1913.

Studies: J. Wittig, Filastrius, Gaudentius und Ambrosiaster. In *Ambrosiaster-Studien.* Breslau, 1909, 1-56. — K. Chr. Knappe, Ist die 21. Rede des hl. Gaudentius (Oratio B. Gaudentii ep. de vita et obitu B. Filastrii) echt? Zugleich ein Beitrag zur Latinität des Gaudentius. Progr., Osnabruck, 1908. — A. Jülicher, Gaudentius: PWK 7, 1(1910)859-861. — A. L'Huillier, Che cosa sappiamo noi della liturgia di Brescia al tempo di S. Gaudenzio: *Brixia sacra* 2(1911)291-294. — G. Gaggia, Sulle opere e sulla dottrina di S. Gaudenzio: *Brixia sacra* 2(1911)282-290. — C. R. Norock, St. Gaudentius of Brescia and the Tome of St. Leo: JThSt 15(1913)593-596 (= S. Gaudenzio di Brescia e il tomo di S. Leone Magno: *Brixia sacra* 6[1914]91.) — H. A. Birch, A Comparison of the Styles of Gaudentius of Brescia, the "De sacramentis" (ascribed to St. Ambrose) and the "Didascalia Apostolotum" or "Fragmenta veronensia." Risca (Monmouth) 1924. — P. Nautin, Hippolyte, Contre les hérésies. Paris, 1949, 208-213 (influence of Hippolytus); Cf. Une homélie inspirée du traité su la Pâque d'Hippolyte. SCh 27(1950) index. — F. Trisoglio, Gaudenzio da Brescia scrittore. Turin, 1960. — A. Brontesi, Ricerche su Gaudenzio da Brescia: *Memorie storiche della diocesi di Brescia* 29(1962)99-198; *idem, Bibliotheca Sanctorum* 6(1965)47-54. — L. Boehrer, Gaudentius of Brescia. Sermons and Letters, Diss., Catholic Univ. of America. Washington, D.C., 1965. — P. Viard: DSp 6(1967)139-143. — G. M. Bruni, Teologia della storia secondo Gaudenzio da Brescia. Vicenza, 1967. — M. Bettelli Bergamaschi, Brescia e Milano alla fine del IV secolo. In Ambrosius Episcopus II. Milan, 1976, 243-283. — F. Trisoglio, Appunti per una ricerca delle fonti di S. Gaudenzio da Brescia: *Rivista de Studi Classici* 24(1976)50-125.

PACIAN

The few pieces of information extant regarding Pacian come from Jerome (*De vir. inl.* 106) who was a friend of Pacian's son, Exter, the Praetorian Prefect. Pacian was bishop of Barcelona and died at an advanced age during the reign of Theodosius, at least a few years before 392, when Jerome wrote his *De viris inlustribus.*

According to Jerome, Pacian wrote various *opuscula,* including the *Cervus et contra Novatianos.* It is known that Pacian wrote the *Cervus* (or *Cervulus*), which has been lost, in order to dissuade the faithful from participating in the pagan festivities which celebrated the new year. As Pacian himself admits at the beginning of his *Paraenesis,* his description of these festivities was so vivid and effective that it had the result rather of moving his readers to participate in them than of dissuading them from taking part. Some of Pacian's works are extant which, although they are of various types, are all homogeneous since they all deal with the question of penance.

Three letters addressed by Pacian to a Novatian by the name of Simpronianus are of particular importance. In the first, he contrasts the plurality of heresies, which take their names from their founders (Apollinarists, Marcionites, Novatians, etc.), to the unity of the Catholic church. It is here that Pacian writes the well-known phrase: *Christianus mihi nomen est, catholicus vero cognomen,* and explains the meaning of catholic: *catholicus ubi unum, vel, ut doctores putant, oboedientia omnium nuncupatur, mandatorum scilicet Dei.* This allusion to the different names of the heretics which accompanies the various observations concerning the excessive rigorism of the Novatians was not appreciated by Simpronianus. This much can be deduced from Pacian's second letter, in which he states that he is accusing the Novatians not for their name but for their doctrine. A particular significance attaches to the third letter, which is a proper anti-Novatian tract in which Pacian relates and refutes one by one certain fundamental affirmations of the Novatians which were contained in a text sent to him by his friend.

From the ensemble of all these precise references there emerges an exhaustive description of this heretical doctrine, which was based on the fundamental concept that the church, inasmuch as it is the Body of Christ, must be absolutely free of every stain and wrinkle and thus cannot accept sinners into her bosom. Thus the only form of penance allowed is that which accompanies baptism, and every form of post-baptismal penance is prohibited. If God had permitted men to do penance several times, it would be as though He had given permission to sin. Pacian also relates some of the New Testament texts on which the Novatians based their rigid doctrine: Mt. 18:15; Jn. 15:1; 1 Cor. 5:3-5.

Pacian's refutation is detailed and touches on arguments of various kinds. He refers to the beginnings of the schism, making use of information drawn from the epistles of Cyprian, and draws attention to the fact that Novatian, before he separated himself from the Catholic church, had approved the pardon of the *lapsi,* which he instead began to deny after the schism. In particular, he emphasizes the irregularity of Novatian's episcopal ordination. However, the weight of Pacian's argument is brought to bear above all on the innumerable New Testament passages which, in opposition to the few advanced by his adversaries, assure the pardon of the sinner, not whose death, but whose conversion and life is desired. The Apostles themselves, with their weaknesses which were pardoned them, bear witness to the breadth of the church's view on the matter from the very beginning. To the merciless rigidity of the Novatians, Pacian opposes a more comprehensive and balanced conception of man, whose weakness easily gives in to sin, but precisely to whom penance assures purification and the return to the church.

In a church whose members were becoming ever more numerous and ever more liable to fall into sin, the penitential practice was becoming of essential importance in the life of the community. From this need arose the *Paraenesis ad paenitentiam,* which Pacian dedicated to the treatment of three questions: the various ways of sinning; sinners who, without public penance, continue to participate in a sacrilegious manner in the life of the community, *in conspectu hominum timidissimi, ante deum vero impudentissimi;* and sinners who admitted their sin but refused penance. This work of Pacian brings into sharp focus the fundamental difficulty which constituted the obstacle to the practice of post-baptismal penance: many Christians did not feel capable of facing public penance because of the sacrifices it involved and because of the notoriety it conferred on the public sinner. From this comes the exhortation to overcome timidity and human pride, especially since *apud inferos exomologesis non est.*

Pacian's sermon on baptism recalls the human condition following the sin of Adam and the sacrifice of Christ which has liberated man from slavery to the devil and has given him birth to a new life. The baptismal washing and its accompanying anointing, because they cleanse from sin and confer the gift of the Spirit, are the means which assure man of his participation in the redemption brought by Christ. These are customary concepts which Pacian knows how to express in an especially effective manner, thanks to his excellent scholastic formation.

Dom Morin attributed the *Liber ad Iustinum Manichaeum,* transmitted as a work of Marius Victorinus but definitely not belonging to him, to Pacian as well as the *De similitudine carnis peccati,* which Morin published in 1913. These attributions, which were made on the basis of observations of language and style, have not met with the unanimous consent of scholars. The *De similitudine* has most recently been applied to Eutropius.

Editions: Cf. CPL 561-563. — PL 13, 1051-1094. — L. Rubio Fernández, San Paciano. Obras. Barcelona, 1958.

Translations: Spanish: L. Rubio Fernández, op. cit.

Studies: A. Grüber, Studien zu Pacianus von Barcelona. Munich, 1901. — R. Kauer, Studien zu Pacianus. Vienna, 1902. — J. M. Dalmau, La doctrina del pecat original en Sant Pacia: AST 4(1928)203-210. — J. Villar, Les citationes bibliques de Sant Pacia: *Estudis Universitaris Catalans* 17(1932)1-49. — C. McAuliffe, The Mind of Saint Pacianus on the Efficacy of the Episcopal Absolution in the Early Church: TS 6(1945)51-61. — S. González, La penitencia en la primitiva Iglesia española. Salamanca, 1950, 73-79. — M. Martínez, S. Paciano, obispo de Barcelona: *Helmantica* 3(1952)221-238. — P. A.

Sullivan, St. Pacian, Bishop of Barcelona: Folia 4(1950)43-44. — L. Rubio, El texto de san Paciano: *Emerita* 25(1957)327-368. — U. Domínguez del Val, Doctrina eclesiológica de San Paciano de Barcelona: HJ 77(1958)83-90; *idem,* La teología de San Paciano de Barcelona: CD 171(1958)5-28. — F. Di Capua, Ritmo e paronomasia nel trattato "De similitudine carnis peccati" attribuito a Paciano di Barcellona: *Scriti minori* 1. Rome, 1959, 419-430. — U. Domínguez del Val, Paciano de Barcelona. Escritor, teólogo y exégeta: *Salmanticensis* 9(1962)53-85. — A. Anglada, "Christiano mihi nomen est, catholico vero cognomen" a la luz de la doctrina gramatical: *Emerita* 32(1964)253-266; *idem,* La fuente del catálogo heresiológico de Paciano: *Emerita* 33(1965)321-346; *idem,* La tradición manuscrita de Paciano de Barcelona: *Emerita* 35(1967)137-161. — A. Martínez Sierra, Teología penitencial de S. Paciano de Barcelona: *Miscelánea Comillas* 47-48(1967)75-94; *idem,* San Paciano, teólogo del pecado original: *Miscelánea Comillas* 49(1968)279-284. — A. Anglada, Le corruttele del membro Aquarum in penitis ignibus fuerit alla luce della metafora della febbre (Paciano "Paen." 11, 5): VetChr 14(1977)253-272. — S. Constanza, La polemica di Paciano e Simproniano sull'uso di citare i poeti classici: VetChr 15(1978)45-50. — A. Anglada, Unas notas críticas al texto de Paciano de Barcelona: *Emerita* 47(1979)11-34.

PRISCILLIAN AND THE PRISCILLIANISTS

In light of the lack of precise information, the birth of the Spaniard, Priscillian, is generally placed toward the middle of the fourth century and the beginning of his activity around 370-375. Sulpicius Severus, whose *Chron.* II 46-51 is the principal source for the tragic developments of Priscillian's life, describes him as being cultivated and of noble birth, uncommonly eloquent, frugal and detached, but blames him for having introduced the Gnostic heresy into Spain and for having indulged in the practice of magic. It is certain that he preached a particularly rigid asceticism. His preaching met instantly with great success, beginning, so it seems, in Southern Spain. Sulpicius observes that he enjoyed particular popularity among women, but adds that two bishops, Instantius and Salvianus, also attached themselves to Priscillian, who was a layman. He was immediately opposed and persecuted with implacable tenacity by Idacius of Merida and Ithacius of Ossonuba. A council held at Zaragoza toward the end of 380 condemned the ideas propagated by Priscillian and his followers, but made no definite provisions regarding the persons themselves. It then happened that Instantius and Salvianus consecrated Priscillian as bishop of Avila, in order to support his work and lend him more authority. However, Idacius and Ithacius obtained from the Emperor Gratian a decree which sentenced the Manichaeans to exile in terms comprehensive enough so as to be able to include Priscillian and his followers as well. These latter went first to Aquitaine, where they were joined by Euchrozia, a lady of noble birth, and then to Italy in an unsuccessful attempt to obtain the support of Damasus and Ambrose. The Priscillianists had more success with certain high officials, who obtained the annulment of Gratian's decree and thus permitted Priscillian and Instantius to return home. Salvianus had died in Italy.

Ithacius, however, did not let up. After various fruitless attempts, he accused Priscillian and his followers before Maximus, the usurper who had established himself at Trier following the murder of Gratian. Maximus, who was attempting to shore up his precarious position by any means, considered that an intervention in the affair would be able to increase his influence with the Catholic hierarchy, and thus he handed Priscillian and Instantius over to a council which met at Bordeaux in 384. Instantius was deposed from his episcopal dignity, but Priscillian did not wish to appear before the council and appealed directly to the emperor. Idacius and Ithacius then journeyed to Trier and made use of every means at their disposal to obtain the condemnation of Priscillian and his followers. Only at a subsequent time, when the clear possibility of a death sentence arose, did they draw back and leave the prefect, Evodius, to sustain the charge. From the Catholic side, pressure was brought to bear to avoid the capital sentence, especially by Martin of Tours, who for this reason traveled to Trier. When Martin departed from the city, however, the party of Priscillian's most intransigent enemies prevailed with Maximus against him, and together with some of his followers he was condemned for immorality and magic. Priscillian was beheaded along with Euchrozia and others, while Instantius and still others were sent into exile. This was the first time that any Christian had been condemned to death for heresy. Great consternation ensued in the Catholic camp, for which Ambrose, among others, made himself the spokesman, although at an earlier time he had refused to meet with Priscillian. The reaction struck also at the accusers of Priscillian. Ithacius was deposed and Idacius avoided the same fate only by voluntarily resigning. Sulpicius Severus observes that the condemnation was to no avail in putting an end to the movement, which for many years remained active in Spain and southern Gaul.

Jerome (*De vir. inl.* 121) does not seem much convinced of the charges of Gnosticism brought against Priscillian, whom he describes as having written *multa opuscula, de quibus ad nos aliqua pervenerunt.* At the end of the last century, however, nothing was known of Priscillianist literature other than the Pauline canons, which will be treated below, so that the attempt to define the particulars of Priscillian's doctrine had to be based only on the accounts, for the most part confused and vague, of the anti-Priscillianist writers and of the accusations brought against the heretics by the hierarchy (Council of Toledo in 400). From these documents it was derived that the Priscillianists were accused of Gnostic doctrines and encratism (distinction between the God of the Old Testament and the God of the New Testament, the divine nature of the soul, the only apparent reality of the humanity of Christ, the condemnation of matrimony and all material things in a broad sense, magical practices and astrology). They were also accused of Monarchianism, i.e., of identifying the divine persons of the Trinity among themselves. However, Döllinger had already proposed the name of Priscillian as the author of eleven anonymous unedited texts contained in a manuscript at Würzburg. Döllinger's suggestion was taken up by Schepps, who published the texts in 1889. Whoever was expecting a decisive witness to the nature of the Priscillianist heresy had to be disappointed by this publication, since the content of the treatises, with the exception of some details, is strictly orthodox. It is precisely on this basis that Ch. Babut advanced the thesis of the fundamental orthodoxy of Priscillian, whose ascetic rigorism, nourished by a liberal dose of prophetic fervor, attracted to himself the hatred and persecution of the bishops, who by that time were completely worldly.

The thesis of Babut is too radical and superficial to be convincing. It is, in fact, clear that the dossier of Priscillianist writings is predominantly defensive in character in relation to the charges which had been leveled against Priscillian and his followers, so that it purposely avoids treating the arguments and themes characteristic of the movement. The *Liber apologeticus* which opens the collection can be considered to be a document produced by the Priscillianists at the Council of Bordeaux, and from this we know that Priscillian did not attend the council but that Instantius acted as spokesman instead. Dom Morin considered the latter to be the author of the *Liber* as well as of the other treatises. The thesis of Morin has not gained unanimous acceptance and it seems difficult to completely eliminate from the collection the name of Priscillian, who is known to have been for a long time the most representative figure of the movement. On the other hand, the eleven treatises appear rather homogeneous from the point of view of their form (e.g., the frequent recurrence of expressions of Hilary), so that they appear to be the work of one and the same author. Recently, Chadwick has supported the attribution of many of the works in the collection to Priscillian.

The *Liber apologeticus* appears to be a kind of profession of faith presented to a council (that of Bordeaux) in which the author dwells in particular on the condemnation of heretical sects. After the condemnation, already customary, directed against the Arians, who are curiously designated as *Binionitae* (i.e., they believe in a binity, not the Trinity), there follows condemnation directed against the Monarchians, Adoptionists, Docetists, Novatians, Manichaeans and Gnostics of various types (Nicolaitans, Ophites, etc.). The central part of the text dwells especially on the description and condemnation of astrological doctrines. It is clear that the text takes aim at heresies which preach doctrines of the type that were attributed precisely to the Priscillianists by their adversaries. The condemnation directed against the same heresies, although in a much shorter form, also appears in the second treatise, the *Liber ad Damasum episcopum,* which includes a description of the anti-Priscillianist activity of Idacius. It has already been mentioned that this appeal to Damasus brought no results.

At the end of the first treatise, the anonymous author expresses his conviction to speak prophetically through the inspiration of the divine Spirit. With this theme is connected the third treatise, the *Liber de fide et apocryphis,* which is doctrinally the most important work of the collection and which confirms the twelfth anathema of the Council of Toledo I in 400 against those who accept scriptures other than those recognized by the Catholic church. In this treatise, the author maintains with ingenious and revolutionary arguments that not all the inspired writings have been included in the canon, so that not all of the apocryphal writings can be condemned *en masse* just because the heretics have introduced some interpolations into them. Indeed, even these books are inspired by the prophetic Spirit and can be read, keeping in mind the necessary caution in consideration of the heretical interpolations. The fundamental conviction on which the entire discourse rests is clearly expressed at the end: the divine Spirit is not limited to the canonical books alone. "Where Christ is, there is liberty" (2 Cor. 3:17); "I, too, have the Spirit of the Lord."

The other eight treatises, except for the last, which is a lengthy benediction, are homilies or passages from homilies, and all of them other than the fourth, which deals with Easter, are concerned with scriptural questions. The homilies are all on passages or episodes from the Old Testament and were evidently introduced into the apologetic dossier to counteract the charge of dividing the God of the Old Testament from the God of the New Testament in the Gnostic manner and thus of rejecting the Old Testament. The texts, which often have a hortatory coloring, are based on the traditional typological interpretation which perceives in the events of the Old Testament the *typus* of the new economy, a concept which is clearly expressed more than once. A *triformis intellectus* of the Scripture is presented in *Tract.* VI (Schepss, p. 70) in relation to the tripartite division of man into flesh, soul and spirit. Scripture either destroys the works of flesh in us, or builds up the soul or makes present in us the redemptive work of Christ.

The *Canones epistularum Paul apostoli* are also extant, and are furnished with an introduction in which a bishop by the name of Peregrinus states that the canons are those of Priscillian and not of Jerome and adds that he has arranged them *iuxta sensum fidei catholicae* after having eliminated *quae pravo sensu posita fuerant.* It is a question of 90 propositions summarizing Paul's entire doctrine, which are listed one after another and are at times accompanied by the Pauline passages to which the canons make explicit reference.

Nothing remains from the Priscillianist writers Tiberianus, Latronianus and Asarbus mentioned by Jerome (*De vir. inl.* 122, 123) and others. In 1913, Dom Morin published an anonymous *De trinitate fidei catholicae* which can be assigned with all probability to Priscillianist circles and perhaps to Priscillian himself. It confirms the genuineness of the accusation of Monarchianism brought against Priscillian by his contemporaries and which had found only an extremely vague confirmation in the texts published by Schepss (p. 75 and 103). However, the major interest of this otherwise intricate and obscure text lies rather in its having formulated the treatment of the Trinity on the correlation Father/Son = *sensus (nous)/verbum* explained in patterns which distantly resemble Tertullian. In short, it is a treatment which is archaic in tone and which is quite consistent with certain expressions of a binitarian character. Considering that mid-fourth century Spain had shown itself with Potamius and Gregory of Elvira to be aligned with more doctrinally advanced positions than the Arian camp, this Priscillianist *De Trinitate* represents a contact with circles which had remained rather behind in regard to this question. The Monarchian elements of which Priscillian is said to have been accused can be interpreted in the same sense. It can be supposed that his prevailing ascetic interests were responsible for his neglect of advancement in the Trinitarian question. With regard to the basic themes of his preaching, it is not possible to be more precise than to say that it centered around a rigorous encratism nourished, as always, by a distinctly negative conception of the material world, with possible influence from astrology.

Editions: Cf. CPL 785-796b. — PL 31, 1213-1222 (= 42, 667-678); 56, 582. — G. Schepss, CSEL 18(1889). — G. Morin, Etudes, textes, découverts. Maredsous, 1913, 151-205. — D. De Bruyne, Epistula Titi de dispositione sanctimonii: RB 37(1925)48-72. — K. Künstle, Antipriscilliana. Freiburg, 1905. — PLS 2, 1389-1542.

Studies: I. Dierich, Die Quellen zur Geschichte Priscillians. Breslau, 1897. — G. I. Mercati, I due Trattati al popolo di Priscilliano. In *Note di Letteratura cristiana antica* (ST 5). Rome, 1901, 127-136. — E. Edling, Priscillianus och den äldre Priscillianismen, I, Adademisk Afhandling. Uppsala, 1902. — K. Künstle, Das Comma Johanneum. Auf seine Herkunft untersucht. Freiburg i. B., 1905. — F. Lezius: RE 16(1905)59-65. — H. Leclercq, L'Espagne chrétienne. Paris, 1906[2], 151-212. — E. Herzog, Priscillian: Kirchliche Zeitschrift (1897)223-237; *idem,* Priscillianisches: *Revue Int. Theol.* 14(1906)220-229. — C. H. Turner, Priscillian and the Acts of Judas Thomas: JThSt 7(1906)603-605. — J. Chapman, Priscillian, The Author of the Monarchian Prologues to the Vulgate Gospels: RB 24(1907)318-335. — E. Ch. Babut, Priscillien et le priscillianisme. Paris, 1909; *idem,* Paulin de Nole et Priscillien: RHL 15(1910)97-130; 252-275. — E. Buonaiuti, Priscilliano e Priscillianismo. *Rivista storico-critica Scienze Teologiche* 5(1909)775-779. — G. Morin, Un traité priscillianiste inédit sur la Trinité: RB 26(1909)255-280. — L. Talmont, La cause de Priscillien: *Revue Augustinienne Louvain* 15(1909)455-459. — M. Hartberger, Priscillians Verhältnes zur hl. Schrift: BiZ

8(1910)113-129. — P. Monceaux, La question du priscillianisme: JS 9(1911)70-76. — A. E. Burn, Priscillian and Priscillianism: ChQ 74(1912)142-156. — A. Puech, Les origines du priscillianisme et l'orthodoxie de Priscillien: BALAC 2(1912)81-95, 161-213. — G. Morin, Pro Instantio. Contre l'attribution à Priscillien des opuscules des manuscrits de Würzburg: RB 30(1913)153-172. — M. Hartberger, Instantius oder Priscillian: ThQ 55(1913)401-429. — E. Buonaiuti, Instanzio o Priscilliano?: *Rivista scienza delle Religioni* (1916)41-53. — E. Suys, La sentence portée contre Priscillien: RHE 21(1925)530-538. — J. Svennung, Adnotationes criticae ad Tractatus Priscillianeos. In Festschrift Per Persson. Uppsala, 1922, 137-143. — J. Martin, Priscillianus oder Instantius: HJG 47(1927)237-251. — Z. García Villada, La vida de Santa Helia. Un tratado priscilianista contra el matrimonio?: EE 2(1923)270-279; *idem,* Historia eclésiastica de España, I, 2. Madrid, 1929, 93-145; *idem,* La causa de la muerte de Prisciliano y sus compañeros: *Razón y Fe* 86(1929)500-508. — J. A. Davids, De Orosio et S. Augustino priscillianistarum adversariis. Commentatio philologica. The Hague, 1930. — Macías García, Una página de la historia de la antigua Astúrica. Los obispos Santo Toribio y Santo Dictinio y el priscilianismo y los bárbaros en Galicia. Orense, 1931; *idem,* El priscilianismo y los Godos en Galicia, a mediados del siglo V. Orense, 1931. — P. Perdret Casado, Xesús ante o Priscilianismo: *Logos* 28/29(1933)58-68. — S. D'Alès, Priscillien: RSR 23(1933)5-49; *idem,* Priscillien et l'Espagne chrétienne à la fin du IVe siècle. Paris, 1936. — J. Pérez de Urbel, La teología trinitaria en la contienda priscilianista: RET 6(1946)589-606. — T. Ayuso Marazuelo, Nuevo estudio sobre el Comma Joanneum: Bibl 28(1947)83-112, 216-235; 29(1948)52-76. — J. M. Ramos y Loscertales, Prisciliano. Gesta rerum. *Acta Salmanticensia,* Salamanca, 1952. — C. Torres Rodríguez, Prisciliano doctor itinerante, brillante superficialidad: Cuadernos Est. Gallegos 27(1954)75-79. — J. Madoz, Arianismo y priscilianismo en Galicia: *Braca Augusta* 8(1957)68-87. — B. Fischer, Algunas observaciones sobre el "codex goticus" de la Colegiata de S. Isidro de Léon y la tradición española de la Vulgata: *Archivos Leonenes* 15(1961)5-47. — A. Barbero de Aguilara, El priscilianismo, herejía o movimiento social?: *Cuadernos Hist. España* (1963)5-41. — A. de Santos Otero, Der apokryphe Titusbrief: ZKG 74(1963)1-14. — P. Sáinz Rodríguez, Estado actual de la cuestión priscilianista: *Anuario de Estudios Medievales* 1. Barcelona, 1964, 653-657. — B. Vollman, Studien zum Priszillianismus. Die Forschung, die Quellen, der fünfzehnte Brief Papst Leos des Grossen. St. Ottilien, 1965. — R. López Caneda, Prisciliano: su ideología y su significado en la historia cultural de la Galicia: Revista e la Universidad de Madrid 13(1964)629-631; *idem,* Prisciliano, su pensamiento y su problema historico. S. go de Compostela, 1966. — A. Orbe, Doctrina trinitaria del anónimo priscilianista De Trinitate fidei catholicae: Greg 49(1968)510-562. — J. L. Orella, La penitencia en Prisciliano (340-385); *Hispania Sacra* 21(1968)21-56. — H. Chadwick, Priscillian of Avila. Oxford, 1976. — B. de Gaiffier, Priscillien mentionné dans le martyrologe hiéronimien: AB 94(1976)234; *idem,* Priscillien: AB 94(1976)396-398. — A. B. J. M. Goosen, Achtergronden van Priscillianus' christelijke Ascese. Nijmegen, 1976. — J. M. Blázquez, Prisciliano, introductor del ascetismo en Hispania. Las fuentes: 1° Concilio Caesar-augustano. Zaragoza, 1980, 65-121. — A. Orbe, Heterodoxia del Tractatus Genesis: HispS 33(1981)285-311.

CHAPTER III

AMBROSE OF MILAN
AMBROSIASTER AND NICETAS

by Maria Grazia Mara

AMBROSE OF MILAN

LIFE

Ambrose was born at Trier while his father, also named Ambrose, was administering the Prefecture of Gaul (cf. *Vita Ambrosii* 3, 1). The date assigned by scholars for his tenure of this office fluctuates between 334 and 337 for the beginning and 340 as the end. The exact year of Ambrose's birth is uncertain. Some scholars favor 339 and others 337, since they assign different dates to the "movements of the barbarians" to which Ambrose alludes in his *Ep.* 59, 4 and which coincided with his fifty-third year. (For the date of Ambrose's birth, cf. A. Paredi, *S. Ambrogio e la sua età.* Milan, 1960², pp. 17ff).

The fact that Ambrose belonged to the *gens Aurelia,* a fact witnessed by the metrical inscription dedicated to St. Nazarius (*Aur. Ambrosius,* E. Diehl, ILCV n. 1800), was denied by Amati and Campenhausen and maintained by Delehaye, and appears to find confirmation in Ambrose's own expression, "the noble Symmachus, your relative" (*De exc. fratris* 32). Ambrose was born into an aristocratic and Christian family, as is suggested by a reference to the virgin Sotheris, his relative, who suffered martyrdom during the persecution of Diocletian (*Exh. virg.* 12, 82; *De virg.* 3, 7, 38ff).

After the premature death of his father, Ambrose arrived together with his mother and two brothers at Rome, where he was certainly in residence prior to Christmas of 353 when his sister, Marcellina, was veiled as a virgin by Pope Liberius in the Basilica of St. Peter. No particular information is available regarding the adolescence of Ambrose. It is known that he studied rhetoric and was advanced to the position of a lawyer, in which capacity he was employed in 368 in the Prefecture of Sirmium (cf. *Vita Ambrosii* 5, 1 and 2). Toward 370 he was nominated *consularis Liguriae et Aemiliae* with his residence at Milan. The most explicit testimony to the impartial wisdom of his administration is provided by the events following the death of the Arian bishop, Auxentius. Vigorous conflicts had arisen between the Catholics and the Arians regarding the election of a successor, and when Ambrose intervened to exercise his responsibility as *consularis* and restore the peace, he was acclaimed as bishop as much by the Catholics as by the Arians, although he was only a catechumen at the time. He was baptized and a week later was consecrated bishop. Faller in 1948 (*Ambrosiana,* 97-112) and Paredi in 1960 (*Sant 'Ambrogio e la sua età,* 2d ed., 175) both proposed December 7, 374 as the date of the episcopal consecration, differing in this from the proposals of Campenhausen (*Ambrosius von Mailand,* 26), Delehaye (*Analecta Bollandiana* 48[1930]192) and Dudden (*The Life and Times of Saint Ambrose,* Oxford, 1935, 68), who preferred the date of December 1, 373. In these circumstances, "He bestowed all the gold and silver he possessed on the church for the poor. He even gave the church the landholdings he owned, reserving their usufruct to his sister, and left nothing here below which he could call his own" (*Vita Ambrosii* 38).

In order to live up to his new responsibilities, Ambrose devoted himself, under the direction of Simplicianus, to acquiring a profound knowledge of Sacred Scripture, of the Greek Fathers and of Jewish and pagan writers such as Philo and Plotinus. Augustine testifies to the intense and assiduous study of Ambrose (*Conf.* VI 3, 3). This study, complemented by extended prayer on the Word of God, was to become the source of Ambrose's pastoral activity and preaching. Against this background can be placed the historical, political and social events which Ambrose experienced as a protagonist along with the repercussions which these had on his theological, moral and ascetical thought.

At the beginning of his episcopate, relations with Valentinian I, who had approved his election (cf. *Ep.* 21, 7), were carried on in a climate of respect and peace, as Ambrose himself said to Valentinian II (*Ep.* 21, 5), reminding him of his father's conduct in all that concerned the autonomy of the church in relation to the Empire.

If on the one hand his prudence led Ambrose to avoid any radical substitutions among his clergy (cf. M. Simonetti, *La crisi ariana nel IV secolo.* Rome, 1975, p. 438; and M. Meslin, *Les ariens d'Occident.* Paris, 1967, p. 45), on the other his opposition to Arianism was clear from the beginning. One witness was his request for the remains of Dionysius, the Catholic bishop of Milan who had died in Armenia where he had been forced into exile by the persecution of Constantius. From a probable correspondence between Ambrose and Basil of Caesarea, perhaps initiated by the request for the relics of Dionysius, there remains only the *Ep.* 197 of Basil (PG 32, 709-713).

The year 375 was marked by two particularly significant events: the death of his brother Satyrus and the death of Valentinian I. In the funeral oration, given in January-February 375 (cf. J. R. Palanque, append. III, n. 4) and in the second oration given eight days later, are to be found various theological and pastoral themes: the humanity and divinity of Christ, the position occupied by the Son in the Trinity, and a reproach against the Luciferians who had gone into schism for having pushed the Nicene formula to the extreme.

Valentinian I died on November 17, 375, during the campaign

along the Danube. In addition to *Ep.* 21, mentioned above, Ambrose also makes mention of the emperor in *Ep.* 17, 16 *bis,* to describe, perhaps with more imagination than with exact regard for the facts, the words of Valentinian with reference to the return of the Altar of Victory into the Senate. The memory of Valentinian I is also present in the funeral oration in honor of Valentinian II, where Ambrose praises the faith of the father for resisting the pressure from Julian to apostasize (*De obit. Valent.* 55).

The presence of Ambrose is not evident in the first years of the government of Gratian. Under the influence of the poet Ausonius, Gratian assumed a liberal and indulgent attitude as is witnessed by his behavior toward the Senate, where until 382 he permitted the presence of the Altar of Victory, which had been removed from the Senate hall by Constantius II in 357 but immediately returned there under Julian. During the years 376-377 Ambrose was engaged in calming the agitation stirred up by the Arian priest Julianus Valens, who had been expelled from Pettau by the Catholic population of the place (*Ep.* 11, 3; Cf. Simonetti, op. cit., p. 438). The Arian problem was always a constant preoccupation for Ambrose. One instance of his concrete intervention in this question outside of Milan took place at Sirmium in 376, where Ambrose, in spite of the activity of the empress mother Justina (for the pro-Arian attitude of Justina, cf. Ruf. HE II 15; Socr. HE V 11; Sozom., HE VII 13; Philos., HE X 7; Simonetti, op. cit., p. 438), obtained the election of the bishop Anemius, who was of solid Nicene faith. (For details, in a clearly hagiographical style, relative to a riot organized by Justina against Ambrose, cf. *Vita Ambrosii* 11). Also at Sirmium, around 378, is to be located the meeting between Ambrose and Gratian, who had requested to be instructed in the faith against the Arian heresy (cf. *De fide* IV 1). The attribution of some documents relating to the Council of Sirmium (cf. Teod. HE IV 8-9), especially the passage regarding the doctrine of the three hypostases, to the sphere of Ambrose's anti-Arian politics has not met with agreement among scholars: Zeiller (p. 323) and von Campenhausen (p. 35) are favorable while Simonetti (p. 441 n. 19) is opposed.

The relations between Ambrose and Gratian marked an increase in the anti-heretical politics of the Empire. Perhaps to extol Gratian, who had to face the destruction of the West under the chastisement of God, Ambrose wrote the *De Noe,* in which he likened the emperor to the figure of the patriarch. Gratian's policy appeared ever more closely bound to the Catholic positions, especially after his meeting with Ambrose which took place at Milan in the summer of 379. Ambrose obtained the restitution of a basilica which the Arians had succeeded in taking by accusing the bishop of selling the sacred vessels to ransom prisoners (*Ep.* 2, 28; *De off.* II 70, 136. Ambrose speaks of the restitution in *De Spir. S.* I 19-21). Various scholars have assigned to Ambrose the responsibility for Gratian's edict of April 22, 380 (*Cod. Theod.* XVI 5, 5. 4), which stiffened sanctions against the heretics. In the summer of the same year the three books on the Holy Spirit were presented to Gratian in order to complete the instruction he had received in the *De fide*.

A new intervention of Ambrose with Gratian regarding anti-Arian policy took place in 381 on the occasion of the Council of Aquileia (cf. Simonetti, *op. cit.* 527-528, 542-548; for the intervention of Ambrose cf. *Ep.* 9 to the bishops of Gaul, *Epp.* 10, 11 and 12 to the Emperors Gratian, Valentinian II and Theodosius). The *Epp.* 12 and 14, addressed to Theodosius, can be placed in the context of the anti-Arian polemic and in close connection with the Council of Rome of 382.

Ambrose's attention was not directed solely toward the Arian problem, but was also occupied with the anti-Catholic opposition which arose from other quarters (cf. L. Cracco Ruggini). In 382, Gratian again had the Altar of Victory removed from the Senate. On more than one occasion the Senate sought to have it returned, but without success. Meanwhile, the imperial ordinances against the pagans followed one upon the other (*Cod. Theod.* XVI 7, 1 and 2; *Cod. Iust.* I 7, 2). The murder of Gratian in 383 and the seizure of his territory by the usurper Maximus marked a measure of rest in the crescendo of the anti-pagan policy inspired by Ambrose. In 384 (for the date cf. J. R. Palanque, append. III n. 22), Symmachus addressed a petition to Valentinian II for the return of the Altar of Victory and the restoration of the privileges suppressed by Gratian, but he was refused (cf. *Relatio* III of Symmachus and *Epp.* 17 and 18; *Vita Ambrosii* 26; Prud. *C. Symm.*). Ambrose's success in this affair was undoubtedly due in part to the service the Bishop of Milan had rendered to Valentinian II and Justina in pleading their case before Maximus, who had conquered all of Gaul. However, the Arian problem was destined to regain its primary position among the pastoral concerns of Ambrose. At Easter 386, Auxentius, the Arian bishop of Durostorum, who had been at Milan at the court of Justina for some time, requested that a basilica be assigned him for the services (cf. *Ep.* 20 to his sister, Marcellina and 21 to Valentinian II; *C. Auxentium; Vita Ambrosii* 13). Ambrose underlined his refusal by occupying the Basilica Porciana together with a multitude of the faithful. It was in these circumstances that the Ambrosian chant had its origins (cf. Aug. *Conf.* IX 7).

The discovery of the bodies of the martyrs Gervasius and Protasius and the accompanying liturgical celebrations provided an occasion of spiritual joy and a momentary distraction from the claims of the Arians. For an evaluation of the historical significance of this event, the diverse opinions of O. Seeck (V, 207), von Campenhausen (p. 215f) and the acute observations of Meslin (*Les ariens d'Occident*. Paris, 1967, p. 53ff) can be consulted. Ambrose relates the event to his sister, Marcellina in *Ep*. 22.1. In the context of the tension which had arisen between Ambrose and Valentinian II over the question of the basilica, the position of Valentinian II was weakened as a result of the manifest disapproval of Maximus for the pro-Arian policy of the young emperor (cf. *Nisi clementiae,* Coll. Avell. XXXIX, summarized by Theod. HE V 14). Some scholars, contrary to the opinion of the majority, place the second mission of Ambrose to Maximus on behalf of Valentinian II in 386. Ambrose himself furnishes a report of his mission to Trier in *Ep*. 24. From Paulinus (*Vita Ambrosii* 19), on the other hand, comes the news of the excommunication inflicted on Maximus for having sentenced Priscillian to death. On his return to Milan, Ambrose underlined his break with Maximus in the *Enerratio psalmi* LXI.

Ambrose, whose relations were strained with both Valentinian II and Maximus at that time, dedicated himself intensely to his pastoral activity until the summer of 387.

The invasion of Maximus, the flight of the court from Milan in the summer of 387, the return of Valentinian II in the company of Theodosius in the summer of 388, and the defeat and death of Maximus signaled the beginning of a new stage in the pastoral activity of Ambrose, who by that time was reconciled with Valentinian II.

The reception of the victor, Theodosius, by Ambrose had been prepared in advance, for the law of June 14, 388 (*Cod. Theod.* XVI 5, 15), by which Theodosius struck against the heretics had inclined Ambrose favorably toward the emperor. Nevertheless, both the bishop and the emperor were aware of the need to define the limits of their mutual spheres of influence. Ambrose intervened immediately in behalf of the defeated followers of Maximus, and Theodosius acceded to his wishes (*Ep*. 40, 25). At the end of 388, however, there occurred the well-known affair of the synagogue and of the sanctuary of the Valentinians at Callinicum. Theodosius' reaction and the position taken by Ambrose are documented in the *Epp*. 40 and 41, the first addressed to Theodosius and the second to his sister, Marcellina. The victory of Ambrose, who blocked the reconstruction of the synagogue, was won at a price. Toward the end of 389, the Senate, noticing a change in Theodosius' attitude with regard to the pagan world, renewed its request for the abrogation of the decrees of Gratian. The new intervention of Ambrose with Theodosius marked another victory for the Bishop of Milan. Theodosius, however, emphasized the independence of his decision from the intervention of Ambrose by means of a decision directed against the bishop when he forbade the members of the court to speak with outsiders concerning matters of imperial policy (*Ep.* 51, 2). Other provisions, little favorable to the church, followed (*Cod. Theod.* XII 1, 121; XVI 2, 27).

The tension between Theodosius and Ambrose had not been resolved when the massacre at Thessalonica occurred in the summer of 390. In his *Ep.* 51, sent to Theodosius after the massacre, Ambrose alludes to the various interventions on his part for avoiding the massacre. Paulinus refers to the same interventions (*Vita Ambrosii* 24), although without better documentation. Ambrose invited Theodosius to perform public penance before again entering church and receiving the sacraments. The reconciliation after the public penance took place at Christmas of 390. Different interpretations have been given for the motives leading up to the massacre at Thessalonica (cf. J. R. Palanque, op. cit., p. 288ff and S. Mazzarino, *L'impero romano* III, p. 379ff). For Mazzarino, the intervention of Ambrose goes back to his constant anti-Arian preoccupation.

In 392, Ambrose's interventions were directed in particular toward a solution of the Schism of Antioch. To this end, councils were convened first at Capua then at Alexandria, but they were unable to bring about the abdication of Flavian in favor of Evagrius. To the contrary, a council meeting at Caesarea in Palestine in 393 recognized the legitimacy of Flavian's position. Ambrose enjoyed greater success with another problem posed at the Council of Capua, that of the heresy of Bonosus, who was condemned, although the question of sanctions against him was deferred to another council. At the Council of Milan of 393, convened by Ambrose, Jovinian was condemned together with his teachings and his followers.

Ambrose's concerns for the internal life of the church alternated with those for peace in the civil and political world. While he was on his way to Gaul, where he had been sent by Valentinian in order to restore peace between the emperor and the general Arbogast, he received the notice of the death of Valentinian, who was assassinated in May, 392 (*De ob. Valentin.; Ep.* 53). Ambrose's relations with Valentinian's successor, the Catholic, Eugenius, were neither simple nor clear. Ambrose sent him the *Ep.* 57 in which he recognized his title of *clementissime imperator,* but he abandoned Milan when he knew Eugenius was about to enter the city. He retired first to Bologna, where he discovered the bodies of the martyrs Vitalis and Agricola (*Vita Ambrosii* 27), then to Florence, where he consecrated a basilica (*Exhortatio virginitatis;* according to some scholars, his meeting with Paulinus of Nola took place on this occasion). He returned to Milan in

August of 394 (*Ep.* 61, 1) when Eugenius had left the city to confront the troops of Theodosius. In the purely political camp, it was Theodosius who determined Ambrose's conduct, and the difficulties in the relations between Theodosius and Eugenius influenced the relations between Ambrose and Eugenius. Ambrose justified before Theodosius the recognition he gave to Eugenius and explained the motives for his departure from Milan (*Ep.* 61 to Theodosius). Once he had recovered the confidence of Theodosius, Ambrose solicited his clemency toward his defeated enemies (*Ep.* 62). A perfect concord then reigned in the relations between Ambrose and Theodosius until the death of the latter on January 17, 395. Forty days later, Ambrose preached the funeral oration in his honor in the presence of Honorius *(De obitu Theodosii).*

Ambrose's relations with the general Stilicho, to whom the young Honorius had been entrusted, were nuanced in such a way as to reveal the decline of his influence in the purely political field. On the other hand, his spiritual activity became more intense and revealed itself in events such as the discovery of the relics of the martyrs Nazarius and Celsus, embellished with suitable miracles in the hagiographical literature (*Vita Ambrosii* 32-33), the entrance of Paulinus into Nola, and the creation of new episcopal sees in northern Italy and the naming of the respective bishops. The *Ep.* 63, the longest of his letters, addressed to the Church of Vercelli which was split into rival factions, is considered as a veritable treatise on the election of bishops.

While returning from Pavia in February of 397, on one of his trips necessitated by his attendance at an episcopal election, Ambrose fell ill. He died at Milan on April 4, 397.

Editions: Vita Ambrosii (of prime importance, written by Paulinus around 422 at the request of Augustine): PL 14, 27-46 and 51-72 (Greek); M. S. Kaniecka, (PSt 16). Washington, 1928 (with English translation, intro. and commentary); M. Pelligrino (Verba Seniorum 1). Rome, 1961 (with Italian translation); A. A. R. Bastiaensen, L. Canali, C. Carena, Vita di Cipriano, Vita di Ambrogio, Vita di Agostino. Milan, 1975 (with crit. text, Italian translation and commentary).

Translations: English: J. A. Lacy, FC 15. Washington, 1952. *Italian:* M. Pellegrino. Rome, 1961. M. Simonetti. Rome, 1977.

Studies: G. Grutzmacher, Die Lebensbeschreibung des Ambrosius von seinem Sekretäre Paulinus: In *Geschichtliche Studien A. Hauck.* Leipzig 1916, 77-84. — J. R. Palanque, La vita Ambrosii de Paulin. Étude critique. RSR 4(1924)26-42, 401-420. — L. Alfonsi, La struttura della vita Beati Ambrosii di Paolino di Milano: RIL 103(1969)784-798. — R. Klein, Die Kaiserbriefe des Ambrosius: *Athenaeum* 48(1970)335-371. — C. Riggi, Lineamenti della personalità di S. Ambrogio nel ricordo agostiniano: *Salesianum* 37(1975)3-37.

Sources for Ambrose's Bibliography: Rufinus HE II 11; 15-16; 18(PL 21, 521-525, crit. ed. T. Mommsen, Eusebius Werke II. Leipzig 1903, II, 1-2). — Socrates HE IV 30; V 11

(PG 67, 544, 593-596, Eng. transl. Zenos, LNPF sect. 2, II [1890]1-178 [reprint 1952]). — Sozomen, HE VI 24; VII 13, 25 (PG 67, 1353-56, 1448-49, 1493-97, Eng. transl. Hartranft, LNPF sect. 2 II [1890]). — Theodoret of Cyrrhus HE IV 6; V 13; 17 (PG 82, 1132-33, 1225-28, 1232-37, crit. ed. L. Palmentier. Leipzig, 1911).

Biographical and historical studies: P. Beatrice, et al., *Cento anni bibliografia ambrosiana* (1874-1974) (SPMed 11). Milan, 1981. — A. Baunard, Histoire de St. Ambroise. Paris, 1871. — A. De Broglie, Saint Ambroise. Paris, 1899. — P. De Labriolle, Saint Ambroise. Paris, 1908. — A. Largent: DTC 1(1909)942-951. — U. Moricca, Sant'Ambrogio. Turin, 1928. — E. K. Rand, Founders of the Middle Ages. Cambridge, Mass. 1928, 69-101. — H. von Campenhausen, Ambrosius von Mailand als Kirchenpolitiker. Berlin-Leipzig, 1929. — J. R. Palanque, Saint Ambroise et l'Empire Romain, Contribution à l'histoire des rapports de l'Église et del'État à la fin du quatrième siècle. Paris, 1933. — F. H. Dudden, The Life and Times of St. Ambrose, 2 vol. Oxford, 1935. — J. Wytzes, Der Streit um den altar der Viktoria. Amsterdam-Paris, 1936. — E. Buonaiuti, Sant'Ambrogio. Rome, 1923. — R. Wirtz, Der heilige Ambrosius und seine Zeit. Trier, 1924. — F. J. Dolger, Die erste Schreibunterricht in Trier nach einer Jugenderinnerung des Bischofs Ambrosius von Mailand: AC 3(1932)62-67. — A. Wilmart, Saint Ambroise et la legende dorée: EL 50(1936)169-206. — L. Malunowicz, De ara Victoriae in Curia Romana quomodo certatum sit. Wilno, 1937. — J. H. van Haringen, De Valentiniano II et Ambrosio, Illustrantur et digeruntur res anno 386 gestae: Mnem 5(1937)28-33, 152-158, 229-240. — A. Queirolo, Ambrogio de Milano, console di Dio. Rome, 1939. — I. Schuster, Sant'Ambrogio vescovo di Milano. Milan, 1940; *idem,* Sant'Ambrogio e le piú antiche basiliche milanesi. Milan, 1940. — L. Castano, Sant'Ambrogio. Turin, 1940. — A. Grazioli, La giurisdizione metropolitana di Milano a Verona all'epoca di sant'Ambrogio: SC 69(1940)373ff. — B. Biondi, L'influsso di Sant'Ambrogio su la legislazione religiosa del suo tempo, in Sant'Ambrogio nel XIV centenario della nascita, Milan 1940, 387-420. — L. Saba, L'opera politica di Sant'Ambrogio, ibid., 533-569. — R. Paribeni, La romanità di sant'Ambrogio, ibid., 17-29. — A. Paredi, Sant'Ambrogio. Milan, 1960². — W. Wilbrand, Heidentum und Heidenmission bei Ambrosius von Mailand: *Missionswissenschaft und Religionswissenschaft* 1(1938)193-202. — G. J. Cordiglia, La malattia e la morte di sant'Ambrogio: SC 69(1941)148-154. — A. Zavaglio, S. Ambrogio e Crema: *Bollettino storico Cremonese* 6(1941)141-146. — I. Schuster, La più antico rappresentazione di S. Ambrogio. In Miscellanea G. Mercati V. (ST 125). Vatican City 1946, 48-60. — O. Faller, La data della consacrazione vescovile di sant'Ambrogio. In *Ambrosiana.* Milan 1942, 97-112. — P. Gorla, Vita di sant'Ambrogio dottore delia Chiesa. Milan, 1944. — U. Pestalozza, La religione di Ambrogio. Milan, 1949. — A. Calderini, Appunti sulla prima ambasceria di sant'Ambrogio a Treviri. In Misc. Galbiati III. Milan 1955, 111-116. — V. Grumel, La deuxième mission de saint Ambroise auprès de Maxime: REB 4(1951)154-160. — A. Alfoldi, A conflict of Ideas in the Late Roman Empire. Oxford, 1952. — M. Journon, Ambroise de Milan. Paris, 1956. — J. Doignon, Perspectives ambrosiennes: SS. Gervais et Protais, génies de Milan: REAug 2(1956)313-334. — E. Moneta Caglio, Dettagli cronologici su s. Ambrogio: *Ambrosius* 32(1956)275-290. — N. Casini, Discussioni sull'ara della Vittoria: *Studi Romani* 5(1957)501-517. — H. Glaesener, L'empereur Gratien et Saint Ambroise: RHE 52(1957)466-488. — G. B. Montini, L'eredità di sant'Ambrogio: *Ambrosius* 33(1957)33ff. — G. Handler, Wulfila und Ambrosius. Stuttgart, 1961. — G. D. Gordini, B. Parodi D' Arenzano: *Bibliotheca Sanctorum* I. Rome 1961, 945-989. — G. Lazzati, ed., Ambrosius Episcopus (SPMed VI and VII). Milan, 1976. — Ambrogio nel XVI centenario della sua elezione popolare a vescovo di Milano. Milan, 1975.

General Studies: R. Morgan, Light in the theology of Saint Ambrose. Diss., Pont. Univ. Greg., Rome, 1963. — P. Segalla, La conversione eucaristica in S. Ambrogio. Padua,

1967. — S. Pasquetto, Morte di Adamo e novità di vita in Cristo nella dottrina di S. Ambrogio. Venice, 1967. — J. J. Marcelic, Ecclesia Sponsa apud S. Ambrosium. Rome, 1967. — B. Maes, La loi naturelle selon Ambroise de Milan. *Analecta Gregoriana* 162. Rome, 1967. — R. Johanny, L'Eucharistie centre de l'Histoire du Salut chez Saint Ambroise de Milan. Paris, 1968. — G. Matt, Jesus Christus fons vitae. Ein Verständnis der Vermittlung des Lebens in der Theologie des hl. Ambrosius. Rome, 1968. — F. Szabo, Le Christ Createur chez Saint Ambroise. Rome, 1968. — R. Gryson, Le prêtre selon saint Ambroise. Louvain, 1968. — P. Courcelle, Recherches sur les Confessions de saint Augustin, App. IV: Aspects variés du platonisme Ambrosien. Paris, 1968; *idem,* Polemiche anticristiane e platonismo cristiano: da Arnobio a s. Ambrogio. In *The Conflict between Paganism and Christianity in the Fourth Century.* Oxford 1963, 151-192. — C. Morino, Church and State in the Teaching of St. Ambrose. Washington, 1969. — L. Beato, Teologia della malattia in s. Ambrogio. Turin, 1968. — F. Canfora, Simmaco e Ambrogio o di una antica controversia sulla tolleranza e l'intolleranza. Bari, 1970. — C. Calcaterra, La catechesi pasquale di Ambrogio di Milano. Rome, 1972. — E. Aletti, Il ritratto di s. Ambrogio. Rome, 1974. — Allegretti, La vita di s. Ambrogio nell'edizione milanese del 1492. Milan, 1974. — G. Piccolo, Saggio di Bibliografia Ambrosiana. Ambiente, fonti e spiritualità (1930-1970): SC 98(1970)187-207. — M. Oberti-Sobrero, L'etica sociale in s. Ambrogio di Milano. Turin, 1970. — J. A. Mara, The Notion of Solidarity in St. Ambrose's Teaching on Creation, Sin and Redemption. Rome, 1970. — M. S. Ducci, Senso della tipologia mariana in s. Ambrogio e suo rapporto con lo sviluppo storico e dottrinale. Bogotà, 1971; *idem,* Sviluppo storico e dottrinale del tema Maria-Chiesa e suo rapporto col pensiero teologico mariano di s. Ambrogio: *Ephemerides Mariologicae* 23(1973)363-404. — G. Giavini and C. Terraneo. Per una lettura biblica ambrosiana: *Ambrosius* 49(1973)322-325. — V. Monachino, S. Ambrogio e la cura pastorale a Milano nel sec. IV. Milan, 1973. — G. Gottlieb, Ambrosius von Mailand und Kaiser Gratian. Göttingen, 1973. — P. Courcelle, Recherches sur saint Ambroise. Paris, 1973. — G. Madec, Saint Ambroise et la Philosophie. Paris, 1974. — D. Tettamanzi, Valori cristiani del matrimonio nel pensiero di S. Ambrogio: SC 102(1974)451-474. — T. G. Ring, Auctoritas bei Tertullian, Cyprian und Ambrosius. Würzburg, 1975. — G. Toscani, Teologia della Chiesa in s. Ambrogio (SPMed 3). Milan, 1974. — L. F. Pizzolato, Rassegna di studi ambrosiani: *Ambrosius* 50(1974)381-383. — A. Brambilla, S. Pietro in Gessate, Milano: la cappella Grifo e l'iconografia de s. Ambrogio. Milan, 1974. — L. Cracco Ruggini, Ambrogio e le opposizioni anticattoliche fra il 383 e il 390: Aug 14(1974)409-449. — H. Crouzel, Fonti prenicene della dottrina de s. Ambrogio sulla risurrezione dei morti: SC 102(1974)373-388. — E. Cattaneo, La religione a Milano nell'età di s. Ambrogio nel Quattrocento milanese. Milan, 1974. — J. M. Soto Rábanos, El matrimonio "in fieri" en la doctrina de San Ambrosio y San Juan Crisóstomo. Rome, 1976. — J. Schmitz, Gottesdienst im altchristlichen Mailand. Bonn, 1975. — C. Corbellini, Ambrogio e i Barbari, giudizio o pregiudizio?: RSCI 31(1977)343-353. — H. Savon, S. Ambroise et la Philosophie: RHR 191(1977)173-196. — M. P. McHugh, The Demonology of Saint Ambrose in the Light of Tradition: WSt 12(1978)205-231. — R. Gryson, Melchisédech, type du Christ, selon saint Ambroise: RThL 10(1979)176-195. — R. Cantalamessa, La concezione teologica della Pasqua in sant'Ambrogio. In *Studi G. Lazzati* (SPMed 10). Milan 1980, 362-375. — E. Lamirande, Quelques visages de séductrices. Pour une théologie de la condition féminine selon Saint Ambroise: *Science et Esprit* 31(1979)173-189. — A. L. Fenger, Aspekte der Soteriologie und Ekklesiologie bei Ambrosius von Mailand. Bern, 1981.

WRITINGS

The intense pastoral, social and political activity of Ambrose also found expression in his writings. It is difficult even today to establish a precise date for many of these works, just as it is at times difficult to determine whether the work was originally intended as a homily or as a treatise.

Since it is not possible to follow a chronological order of composition, the exegetical works will be presented here in the order in which they appear in the PL (14-15), which is the same order as the books of the Bible.

The other works of Ambrose are customarily classified as moral and ascetical writings, dogmatic works, and miscellaneous compositions (sermons, letters and hymns). The pseudo-Ambrosian writings also merit a brief treatment.

Studies: E. Dassmann, Die Frömmigkeit des Kirchenvaters Ambrosius von Mailand. Münster, 1965. — H. Savon, Quelques remarques sur la chronologie des œuvres de Saint Ambroise: SP 10(TU 107). Berlin 1970, 156-160. — G. Billanovich, M. Ferrari, La tradizione milanese delle opere di Sant' Ambrogio. In *Ambrosius Episcopus* (SPMed 6-7). Milan 1976, 5-102. — J. Fontaine, Prose et poésie: l'interférence des genres et des styles dans la création littéraire d'Ambroise de Milan, ibid., 124-170. — H. Savon, Maniérisme et allégorie dans l'œuvre d'Ambroise de Milan: RELA 55(1977)203-221. — O. Faller, L. Krestan, Wortindex zu den Schriften des hl. Ambrosius (CSEL 4 suppl.). Vienna, 1979. — G. Bartelink, Sprachliche und stilistische Bemerkungen in Ambrosius' Schriften: WS 13(1979)175-202.

EXEGETICAL WORKS

Following Philo and Origen, Ambrose accepts the triple sense of Scripture: literal, moral and allegorical-mystical. In reality, an allegorical exegesis of a typological and moral character prevails in his works.

The major portion of these works originated as homilies which were then revised and completed by Ambrose himself.

The topics selected for his preaching (homilies) and teaching (treatises) are drawn from the Old Testament, with the exception of the systematic commentary on the Gospel of Luke.

Studies: P. DeLabriolle, Saint Ambroise et l'exégèse allégorique: Annales phil. chrét. 155(1907-1908)591-603. — G. Lazzati, Esegesi e poesia in Sant' Ambrogio: *Annuario Università cattolica Sacro Cuore* (1957-58, 1958-59). Milan 1959, 75-91; *idem,* Il valore letterario dell'esegesi ambrosiana. Milan, 1960. — A. Vecchi, Appunti sulla terminologia esegetica di s. Ambrogio: SMSR 24(1967)655-664. — L. F. Pizzolato, La Sacra Scrittura fondamento del metodo esegetico di sant'Ambrogio (SPMed 6). Milan 1976, 393-426. — H. Savon, Saint Ambroise devant l'exégèse de Philon le Juif. 2 vol. Paris, 1977. — E. Lucchesi, L'usage de Philon dans l'œuvre exégètique de saint Ambroise. Leiden, 1977. — L. F. Pizzolato, La dottrina esegetica di s. Ambrogio (SPMed 9). Milan, 1978.

1. *Hexaemeron*

As the title indicates, this work is a commentary on the narrative of Gen. 1:1-26 relating to the six days of creation and is composed of nine homilies collected in six books. The homilies were given during the six days of Holy Week in a year which scholars locate between 386 and 390.

Books 1, 3, and 5 each contain two homilies and thus indicate that on the first, third, and fifth days Ambrose must have preached once in the morning and again in the evening.

The popularity of this work of Ambrose is indicated by the numerous manuscripts containing it, the classification of which was made by Schenkl (CSEL 32, 1, p. xxxiii-lii). Codes 192 of Orléans (sec. VIII), from the seventh century, is of particular interest. Although it contains only a fragment from I 29 to II 3, it nevertheless appears to go back to the lost archetype.

Ambrose made use of the similarly titled work of Basil of Caesarea and, according to Jerome (*Ep.* 84, 7), also of the lost works of Origen and Hippolytus of Rome. This fact has at times conditioned the reading of the work and made scholars more attentive to noticing the contributions from other authors (e.g., Cicero, Philo, Vergil) than to recognizing the originality of the work itself.

Editions: PL 14, 133-288. — C. Schenkl, CSEL 32, 1(1897)3-261. *Manuscripts:* B. Kraft, Die Handschriften der Bischöflichen Ordinariatsbibliothek in Augsburg. Augsburg 1934, 61ff. — F. Blatt, Studia Hibernica: *Classica et Mediaevalia* 14(1953)230. — K. Forstner, Schriftfragmente des 8. und früheren 9. Jahrhunderts in Salzburger Bibliotheken: *Scriptorium* 14(1960)236-237.

Translations: English: J. J. Savage, FC 42. New York 1961, 1-283. *German:* E. J. Niederhuber, BKV2. Kempten-Munich, 1914. *Italian:* L. Asioli. Milan, 1930. — E. Pasteris (CPS 4). Turin, 1937. G. Coppa. Turin 1969, 111-387. — G. Banterle (S. Ambrosii Opera 1). Milan-Rome, 1979. *Polish:* T. O. Wladyslaw Szoldrski, etc., Hexaemeron. Warsaw, 1969.

Studies: M. Klein, Meletelemata Ambrosiana. Königsberg 1927, 45-81. — M. Cesaro, Natura e cristianesimo negli Exaemeron di san Basilio e di sant'Ambrogio: Did. Ns. 7(1929)53-123. — P. Courcelle, Nouveaux fragments du Platonisme chez saint Ambroise: RELA 34(1956)220-239. — J. M. Duval, Sur une page de Cyprien chez S. Ambroise, Hexaemeron 6, 8, 47 et De habitu virginum 15-17: REAug 16(1970)25-34. — J. Pepin, Théologie cosmique et théologie chrétienne. Ambroise, Hexaem. I, 1, 1-4. Paris, 1964; *idem,* Textes et doctrines de la fin de l'antiquité. Idées grecques sur l'homme et sur Dieu. Paris, 1971; *idem,* Exégèse de "in Principio" et théorie des principes dans l'Exaemeron (I, 4, 12-16) (SPMed 6). Milan 1976, 427-482; *idem,* Echos de théories gnostiques de la matière au début de l'Exaemeron de saint Ambroise: *Studiea J. H. Waszink.* Amsterdam 1973, 259-273. — V. Nazzaro, Esordio e chiusura delle omelie di Ambrogio: Aug 14(1974)559-590. — P. Siniscalco, Poesia e religiosità nel IV Discorso de Ambrogio sulla creazione (Hex. III 1, 1ff): SSR 1(1977)83-103.

2. *De Paradiso*

From *Ep.* 41, 1 addressed to the bishop Sabinus, it is known that this work is to be assigned to the beginning of Ambrose's episcopate. Scholars date it variously between 374 (von Campenhausen) and 383 (Schenkl), with the period between 375-378 meeting with the most consent (Rauschen, Bardenhewer, Schanz, Palanque). The most recent critical edition was that done by Schenkl, and is based fundamentally on two manuscripts (sec. XI) from the eleventh century (CSEL 32, 1, p. lii-lviii).

Ambrose comments on the text of Genesis relating to the earthly paradise and the first sin, following closely the commentary of Philo (for the sources cf. Schenkl, op. cit., p. xxi-xxii).

The pastoral intent of the work, which is possibly a redaction of previous homilies, does not hesitate to find expression in polemical tones against the Gnostics, Manichaeans (op. cit., p. 286, 23; 287, 23; 289, 8; 292, 5; 294, 4; 296, 19; 298, 1), Sabellians, Photinians and Arians (op. cit., p. 317-318).

Editions: PL 14, 291-332. — Schenkl, CSEL 32, 1(1897)265-336.

Translations: English: J. J. Savage, FC 42. New York 1961, 287-356. *Italian:* P. Siniscalco, Opere di S. Ambrogio II, 1. Milan-Rome, 1984.

3. *De Cain et Abel*

According to Palanque, the work consists of two books (others consider the division to be a later development) and was conceived as a written work.

To the contrary, Kellner, Foerster, Bardenhewer, and Schanz judge the work to be a collection of sermons because of its dominant oratorical and hortatory tone.

Palanque considers the work to be connected to the *De Paradiso,* to which it refers at the beginning and the theme of which it continues by commenting on Genesis 4 in succession to the commentary on Gen. 2:8-3:19 in the *De Paradiso.*

Ambrose shows the influence of Philo in his extensive commentary on the difference between the sacrifices of Cain and Abel, which were respectively refused and accepted by God.

For the manuscript tradition, consult Schenkl.

Editions: PL 14, 333-380. — Schenkl, op. cit., 339-409.

Translations: English: J. J. Savage, FC 42. New York 1961, 357-437. *Italian:* P. Siniscalco. Opere di S. Ambrogio II, 1. Milan-Rome, 1984.

Studies: P. Siniscalco, Immagini del bene e del male in Ambrogio (De Cain et Abel 1, 4f; Exp. Ev. s. Luc. 4, 7ff). In *Paradoxos Politeia, Studi G. Lazzati.* Milan 1979, 458-474.

4. *De Noe*

Although this too is a commentary on Genesis, it is not a continuation of the preceding work but begins rather with Genesis 6. Kellner, Foerster, and Bardenhewer, who maintain a homiletic origin for the work against Palanque, who considers it to have been a written work from the beginning, think it forms part of a series of treatises on the patriarchs which follows the succession of patriarchs from Noah to Abraham.

The dating of the work is uncertain, although the years 378-379 or 383-384 are given as the most likely.

The exegesis of Ambrose, again influenced by Philo, dwells

particularly on the interpretation of the ark as a figure of the human body, on the description of the flood, on the piety of Noah and the impiety of Ham. There are several references to unspecified calamities which are making life difficult and are explicitly affecting the church.

Schenkl dates the work to around 384. He considers the title *De Noe* as reported by the oldest manuscripts to be the original, and holds the title *De Noe et archa* of the more recent manuscripts to be a subsequent addition (CSEL 32, 1, p. xxiii-xxvi).

Editions: PL 14, 381-438. Schenkl, op. cit., 413-497.

5. *De Abraham (libri duo)*

The two books must be considered separately. The first book, according to some scholars, was not originally a written work in spite of the initial phrase: *Abraham libri huius titulus est.* Palanque considers the passages I 24, I 25, I 59, and I 89 of the first book as testimony to the homiletic origin of the work which, considering its length, comprises several homilies.

The content of the first book, which is directed to the catechumens, covers the entire story of Abraham from his voacation until his death, as it is presented in Genesis 12-25.

The second book, on the other hand, is a written treatise. Because of its erudite character, which is so different from the moral exposition of the first book, Schenkl and Bardenhewer consider that Ambrose was addressing the baptized and no longer catechumens. Palanque differs from that opinion, and notes above all the difficulty of Ambrose's speech, which is rich with untranslated Greek quotations. The commentary, which is of an allegorical nature following the exegesis of Philo, is concerned with the life of Abraham up to the account of the covenant in Gen. 17:21.

Various hypotheses have been advanced concerning the date of composition. Palanque proposes the years 382-383, while the Maurists, Tillemont, Schenkl, Bardenhewer, and Schanz place it around 387, Ihm after 387, and Rauschen after 388. For the sources and manuscript tradition cf. Schenkl, CSEL 32, 1, p. xxvi-xxviii, lxi-lxiii, lxvii-lxxiii.

Editions: PL 14, 441-524. — Schenkl, op. cit., 501-638. — A. Vaccari, Locus Ambrosii de Abrahamo 2, 11 emendatus: *Biblica* 3(1922)449-450.

Studies: A. De Vivo, Nota ad Ambrogio, De Abraham I 2, 4 (SPMed 7). Milan 1976, 233-242.

6. *De Isaac et anima*

The *De Isaac et anima* is a written treatise in spite of the opinions of Kellner and Bardenhewer to the contrary. There are various opinions concerning the dating of the work. Palanque proposes a date of 391 while Willbrand considers that the work has to be placed after the *Exp. Lc.* 10, 154ff, and sees in *De Isaac* 17 a development of Ambrose's statements in *Exp. Ps.* CXVIII 2, 33ff. The Maurists believed the work to date to Easter of 387; Schenkl, to around 388.

The exegesis of the Canticle of Canticles 1-8, which is interpreted by some as referring to the coming of Christ and to the church, is placed here by Ambrose in the context of the marriage of Isaac and Rebecca and thus seems to be intended rather as an allegory of the union of Christ with the soul. On the other hand, given the scarcity of the references to Isaac, the work seems more properly to be a treatise on the soul, which explains the title *De anima* given in some manuscripts.

With regard to the sources, especially the presence of Origen's commentary on the Canticle of Canticles, consult Schenkl CSEL 32, 1, p. lxxvi-lxxviii.

Editions: PL 14, 527-560. — Schenkl, op. cit., 641-700.

Translations: English: M. P. McHugh, FC 65. Washington, 1965, 10-65. *French:* D. Gorce, Saint Ambroise, Traités sur l'Ancien Testament. Namur, 1967 (incomplete).

Studies: P. Courcelle, Recherches sur les Confessions de s. Augustin. Paris, 1968², p. 115 n. 3 (correction of 8, 78); *idem,* Plotin et saint Ambroise: RPh 76(1950)29-56. — P. Hadot, Platon et Plotin dans trois sermons de s. Ambroise: RELA 34(1956)202-220. — G. Piccolo, Per lo studio della spiritualità ambrosiana: I sermoni "De Isaac vel anima": SC 98(1970)32-74.

7. *De bono mortis*

There is nearly unanimous consent regarding the homiletic origin of this work. According to Palanque, it consists of two homilies with complementary themes contained, respectively, in ch. 1-29 and 30-57.

Palanque proposes a date of 390, in which case Ambrose edited the work after the *Hexaemeron,* the *Exp. Evang.,* and after the *De Isaac,* with which it is explicitly linked.

After presenting the three types of death — spiritual death (through sin), mystical death (through identification with Christ), and physical death (through the separation of body and soul) — the work demonstrates by means of continuous scriptural citations that death is an inestimable good. A catechesis on the day of judgment in the presence of the glorious Christ, which takes its point of departure from Book IV of Esdras, is joined to the moral teaching.

For the sources and the manuscript tradition, cf. Schenkl, CSEL 32, 1, p. xxxii-xxxiii and lxxvi-lxxvii.

Editions: PL 14, 567-596. — Schenkl, op. cit., 703-753. — W. T. Wiesner, De bono mortis (PSt 100). Washington, 1970 (text., intro., commentary).

Translations: English: W. T. Wiesner, op. cit. — M. P. McHugh, FC 65. Washington 1972,

70-113. *Italian:* F. Portalupi, De Bono mortis, Turin, 1961. *German:* J. Huhn, Des hl. Kirchenvaters Ambrosius Schrift der Tod, ein Gut. Fulda, 1949. *Polish:* P. Sgoldrski. Warsaw, 1970. *French:* M. H. Stébe, P. Cras, Le chrétien devant la mort. Paris, 1980.

Studies: V. Ussani, Per un codice ignoto del de bono mortis di S. Ambrogio: *Rivista storico-critica scienze teol.* 5(1909)934-943. — P. Courcelle, Plotin et Saint Ambroise: RPh 76(1950)29-56. — P. Hadot, Platon et Plotin dans trois sermons de S. Ambroise: RELA 34(1956)202-220.

8. *De fuga saeculi*

Scholars seem to be in accord concerning the homiletic origin of this work. The Maurists and Tillemont dated it to around 387, while Palanque places it in 394 and connects it with the political situation which prevailed after the death of Theodosius. Schenkl and Bardenhewer tend toward a date shortly after 391. Ambrose presents a moral and exegetical discourse on the vanity of the world and the necessity for the Christian to hold himself aloof from it. He develops this theme by using the idea of the cities of refuge described in Num. 35:11ff, together with other passages of the Old and New Testaments as well as the *Legum allegoriae* and especially the *De fuga et inventione* of Philo.

For the manuscript tradition, cf. Schenkl, CSEL 32, 2, p. xxviii-xxviiii.

Editions: PL 14, 597-624. — Schenkl, op. cit., 163-207.

Translations: English: M. P. McHugh, FC 65. Washington 1972, 281-323. *Italian:* F. Portalupi, S. Ambrogio De fuga saeculo. Turin, 1959. *Polish:* P. Sgoldrski. Warsaw, 1970.

Studies: H. Savon, op. cit.

9. *De Iacob et vita beata*

This work in two books, which Palanque dates to 386; the Maurists, Tillemont, Schenkl, Bardenhewer, and Schanz to 387; and Rauschen to 388, makes use of 2 Maccabees to show the difference between true happiness and earthly happiness. The martyrdom of the elderly Eleazar and of the seven brothers is inserted by Ambrose into a context which appears to allude to a revival of the Arian positions and the resulting difficulties for the bishop and those faithful to him. The references to Jacob (II 3-42) are not sufficient to justify the title of the work, which has for its central theme the happiness of the wise man. In some manuscripts the work has the title *De vita beata.*

For the question of the dependence on pseudo-Josephus and for the sources in general, consult Schenkl, CSEL 32, 2, p. xiv-xv.

Editions: PL 14, 627-670. — Schenkl, op. cit., 3-70.

Translations: English: M. P. McHugh, FC 65. Washington 1972, 119-184. *French:* D. Gorce, Saint Ambroise, Traités sur l'ancien Testament. Namur, 1967 (incomplete).

Studies: A. Solignac, Nouveaux parallèles entre saint Ambroise et Plotin. Le "De Jacob et vita beata" et le περὶ εὐδαιμονίας (Enn. I, 4): APh NS 19(1956)148-156.

10. *De Ioseph*

The date assigned to this sermon fluctuates between 387 (the Maurists, Tillemont, Schanz), 388 (Ihm, Rauschen, Palanque) and 389-390 (Schenkl, Bardenhewer). Palanque prefers to date 388 because of an allusion to the eunuch, Calligonus, of whom Ambrose also speaks in a letter to Marcellina (*Ep.* 20), and because of the mention of a scarcity of grain owing to unwise administration which could point to the famine which occurred precisely in 388. Schenkl considers the work to be a late reminiscence of that famine. This homily, which forms part of the series of the biographies of the patriarchs, begins from Gen. 37:6ff and, with ample citations from the Old and New Testaments, presents Joseph not only as the example of a chaste man, but under a more significant and original aspect as the example also of universality of salvation in Christ (ch. 41ff). With regard to the sources, cf. Schenkl, who has particularly emphasized the presence in the work of material from Vergil (CSEL 32, 2, p. xvii). In producing the critical edition, Schenkl gave preference to the seventh-century text found in the library at Boulogne-sur-Mer (ibid., p. xxi-xxviii).

Editions: PL 14, 673-704. — Schenkl, op. cit., 73-122.

Translations: English: M. P. McHugh, FC 65. Washington 1972, 189-237.

11. *De Patriarchis*

Scholars are divided in their opinion as to whether this work was originally intended as a homily or a treatise. In the manuscripts, it follows the *De Ioseph,* the commentary of which it continues concerning the Book of Genesis, especially chapter 49.

Palanque places the redaction of the work after 390. The influence of Philo is obvious in the *De Patriarchis,* as is the allegorical exegesis of Genesis 48 from Hippolytus' *Commentary on the Blessings of Jacob.*

For the manuscript tradition of this work, Schenkl attributes primary importance here, as in the case of the *De Ioseph,* to the seventh-century text from the library of Boulogne-sur-Mer.

Editions: PL 14, 707-728. — Schenkl, op. cit., 125-160.

Translations: English: M. P. McHugh, FC 65. Washington 1972, 243-275.

Studies: H. Moretus, Les Bénédictions des patriarches dans la littérature du IVe au VIIIe siècle: BLE 11(1909)398-411; 12(1910)28-40, 83-100. — M. Simonetti, Note su antichi commenti alle Benedizioni dei Patriarchi: *Annali Facoltà Lettere Cagliari* 28(1960)1-71.

12. *De Helia et Ieiunio*

Scholars are in agreement regarding the homiletic origin of this work, and there remains only a divergence of opinion as to whether it is a question of one single Lenten homily, as Palanque, Bardenhewer, and Schanz maintain, or of several homilies, as Schenkl proposes.

The work is dependent on three homilies of Basil (I on fasting, XIV on drunkenness, and XIII on the exhortation to baptism) not only for its content but also for the formal division of the three homilies.

The work is dated between the years 377, proposed by Tillemont, and 390, proposed by the Maurists.

Ambrose's polemic against the style of life of the rich is expressed by means of citations from the Old and the New Testaments.

The critical edition of Schenkl (for the evaluation of the manuscripts cf. CSEL 32, 2, p. xxxviii-xxxx) is considered to be substantially valid by M. J. Buck.

Editions: PL 14, 731-764. — Schenkl, op. cit., 411-465. — M. J. A. Buck, Pst 19. Washington, 1929.

Translations: English: M. J. A. Buck. op. cit.

Studies: C. Weyman, Zu Ambrosius: RhM 64(1909)328-329. — S. Zincone, Alcune osservazioni sul testo "De Helia et ieiunio" di Ambrogio: Aug 16(1976)337-351.

13. *De Nabuthae historia*

This composition is based on the story narrated in 3 Kgs. 21, and interprets the entire scriptural narrative by means of a detailed spiritual exegesis. The oppression of the poor Naboth by King Ahab is inserted by Ambrose into the particular social, political, and religious situation of which he is himself one of the protagonists.

The critical edition of Schenkl, substantially accepted by McGuire, has been recently revised by the critical edition of M. G. Mara, which reduces the importance given by Schenkl to the codex *Paris.* 1732 (*saec.* VIII) in favor of the codex *Vat.* 5760 (*saec.* X-XI), which is particularly important for the restoration of some readings when it coincides with the two groups of manuscripts.

The years between 386 and 395 have been proposed for the dating of the work, and various scholars are in agreement on the years 389-390 as the more likely time of composition.

Although the influence of Basil had been clearly emphasized, McGuire presented in addition a precise picture of the classical sources of the work. Only recently has M. G. Mara reemphasized the originality of *De Nabuthae,* which in any case follows the customary themes of the diatribe.

Editions: PL 14, 765-792. — Schenkl, op. cit., 469-516. — M. McGuire, PSt 15. Washington, 1927 (with English transl. and commentary). — M. G. Mara, Ambrogio.

La storia di Naboth. Introduzione, commento, edizione critica, traduzione. L'Aquila, 1975.

Translations: English: M. McGuire, op. cit. *French:* F. Quéré-Jaulmes, A. Hamman, Riches et pauvres dans l'Eglise ancienne (Lettres chrétiennes 6). Paris 1962, 219-268. — A. Hamman, Ambroise de Milan. Richesse et pauvreté ou Naboth le pauvre (Les Pères dans la foi 5). Paris, 1978. *German:* J. Huhn, De Nabuthae. Freiburg, 1950. *Italian:* L. Dalle Molle, S. Ambrogio De Nabuthae. Brescia, 1952. — M. G. Mara, op. cit.

Studies: H. Dressler, A Note on the Nabuthae of St. Ambrose: *Traditio* 5(1947)311-312. — L. Rosadoni, Clemente di Alessandria, Basilio di Cesarea, Giovanni Crisostomo, Ambrogio di Milano: il buon uso del denaro. Turin, 1971. — A. Portolano, La dimensione spirituale della proprietà nel "De Nabuthae Jezraelita" di Ambrogio. Naples, 1973. — V. R. Vasey, The Social Ideas in the Works of St. Ambrose, especially in the De Nabuthe. Diss., Rome, 1974.

14. *De Tobia*

This writing, which begins with a brief reference to the first chapters of the Book of Tobit, is an invective against the rich and particularly against the plagues of usury and avarice. Citations from the Old and the New Testament are used in support of Ambrose's arguments.

Definite sources for the work are Vergil, from the classics, and a homily of pseudo-Basil (*Homelia in Ps.* XIV 2) from Greek patristics.

Scholars are for the most part in agreement concerning the homiletic origins of the work, although they differ greatly concerning the dating. Von Campenhausen proposes a date of around 376, Bardenhewer before 380, and Palanque 389, while Wilbrand locates it between the years 387 and 390, since this was the period when the influence of the Basilian or pseudo-Basilian homilies was prevalent in the writings of Ambrose (cf. W. Wilbrand, *"Zur Chronologie einiger Schriften des hl. Ambrosius":* HJG 41[1921]19).

The evaluation of the manuscripts by Schenkl (CSEL 32, 2, p. xxxxiii-xxxxv) and his subsequent critical edition have been substantially accepted by Zucher.

Editions: PL 14, 797-832. — Schenkl, op. cit., 519-573. — L. M. Zucher, De Tobia: PSt 25. Washington, 1933. — M. Giacchero, De Tobia. Saggio introduttivo. Genoa, 1965 (text with transl.).

Translations: English: L. M. Zucher, op. cit. *Italian:* Anon., Tobia. Libro unico. Milan, 1898. — M. Giacchero, op. cit.

15. *De interpellatione Iob et David*

The narration of the misfortunes of Job, taken from that book of the Bible, and of those of David, presented by means of citations of the Psalms, underlines on the one hand the fragility of the human condition (with reference to Pss. 38 and 41), and on the other the happiness and well-being of the wicked (with reference to Ps. 72).

Certain elements seem to allude to a particular historical situation. Some scholars see a reference to the fall of Gratian and the weakness of Valentinian II in the discourse on the fragility of the human condition and of human power, as well as an allusion to the prosperity of the usurper Maximus. The passages IV 15, IV 23-25, and IV 29 contain clear references to the anti-Arian polemic.

The dating of the work is controversial. Palanque proposes a date of 387 on the sole basis of a resemblance to the *De apologia David.* The Maurists, Tillemont, and Schanz place the work in 383, while Schenkl locates it in 394.

The critical edition of Schenkl, which is based on the codex *Paris.* 1732 (*saec.* VIII), presents a text composed of four homilies in the following order, which is not completely secure:

I. *De interpellatione Iob et de hominis infirmitate;*
II-III. *De interpellatione sancti Iob;*
III-IV. *De interpellatione David.*

Editions: PL 14, 835-890. — Schenkl, op. cit. 211–296.

Studies: J. R. Baskin, Job as moral exemplar in Ambrose: VC 35(1981)222-231.

16. *De apologia prophetae David.*

In this work, which recounts the sins of King David and his repentence, Ambrose seems to focus on how great is the capacity of rulers for misdeeds when their passions rage, and at the same time how great is God's forgiveness when they repent.

A political interpretation has been advanced for the subject of the treatise. In King David, guilty of adultery, Ambrose was indicating Valentinian II, who was guilty of the spiritual adultery which had led him to support Justina in her pro-Arian sympathies, and Maximus, who was responsible for the deaths of Gratian and Priscillian and who was a twofold usurper; first of the territory of Gratian and then that of Valentinian II.

Those who consider Ambrose's reference to be limited to the deaths of Gratian and Priscillian place the work around 394, while those who see also the possibility of including the usurpation of the territory of Valentinian II date it to 387. Schenkl dates the work between 383 and 386, while Palanque prefers 387.

A problem is raised by the dedication *ad Theodosium Augustum* which is present in only two manuscripts, one of which, however, is the codex *Paris.* 1732 indicated by Schenkl as the most reliable. The proposed solutions vary between considering the work to have been dedicated to Theodosius from the beginning to considering the dedication *ad Theodosium Augustum* to be a subsequent addition on the part of Ambrose.

The *Apologia David altera,* which follows the *De apologia prophetae*

David in various manuscripts subsequent to the eleventh century, is regarded by different authors as a pseudo-Ambrosian work, although its authenticity has been defended by R. H. Connolly ("Some Disputed Works of St. Ambrose": DR 65[1947]7-20, 121-130).

Editions: PL 14, 891-960. — Schenkl, op. cit., 299-355. — P. Hadot, M. Cordier, SCh 239(1977).

Studies: F. Claus, La datation de l'Apologia Prophetae David et l'Apologia David altera. Deux œuvres authentiques de saint Ambroise (SPMed 7). Milan 1976, 168-193.

17. *Enarrationes in XII Psalmos Davidicos*

Ambrose dedicated a total of twelve homilies to the commentary of Psalms 1, 35-40, 45, 47, 48, 61. The commentary to Psalm 43 remained incomplete at his death. The homilies were given on diverse occasions and are not always easy to date, in spite of the attempts made in this direction (cf. J. R. Palanque, op. cit., Table *chronologique* p. 518-519, 550-553, 555). For the most part, they must be assigned to the last part of Ambrose's life.

The exegesis of the psalms, although in itself an attempt to understand the messianic sense, is nevertheless concerned at the same time to give a moral interpretation concretely bound to the current ecclesiastical and political situation.

The work, which was edited after the death of Ambrose, echoes in some homilies (cf. Psalm 1) its Basilian and Origenist models. The study done by Nohe is of particular interest for the reconstruction of the text of the Psalms used by Ambrose.

Editions: PL 14, 963-1238. — M. Petschenig, CSEL 64(1919). — L. F. Pizzolato. Milan, 1980 (with Italian transl.).

Studies: A. Nohe, Der Mailänder Psalter. Seine Grundlage und Entwicklung (FThSt 61). Freiburg Br, 1936. — Richesses et déficiences des anciennes psautiers latins (*Collectanea biblica latina* 13). Rome, 1959. — H. Leeb, Die Psalmodie bei Ambrosius. Vienna, 1967. — L. F. Pizzolato, La "Explanatio Psalmorum XII." Studio letterario sull'esegesi di sant'Ambrogio (*Archivo Ambrosiano* 17). Milan, 1965. — H. Maur, Das Psalmenverständnis des Ambrosius von Mailand. Leiden, 1977.

18. *Expositio Psalmi CXVIII*

In this work, which is a collection of twenty-two homilies commenting on the twenty-two stanzas with which Paslm 118 sings the praises of the Law, Ambrose presents to the faithful the means useful for obtaining perfection.

The homilies are assigned a date between 386 and 390. The exegesis, which is of a moral type, is concerned with the conversion of the soul. Images of a military, athletic, judicial, and medical nature follow one upon the other throughout this protreptic on the *sequela Christi.* A typological exegesis applied to the church is also to be found.

The critical edition of Petschenig remains unsurpassed.

Editions: PL 15, 1261-1604. — M. Petschenig, CSEL 62(1913).

Translations: French: D. Gorce, Exposé sur le psaume cent-dix-huit. Namur, 1963 (incomplete).

Studies: C. Weyman: PhW(1914)181-187. — L. Castiglioni, Spigolature ambrosiane. In *Ambrosiana.* Milan 1942, 121ff. — C. Charlier, Un œuvre inconnue de Florus de Lyon: La collection de Fide et Montpellier: *Traditio* 8(1952)100. — F. Blatt, Studia Hibernica: *Classica et Medievalia* 14(1953)229ff. — A. Gariglio, Il commento al salmo 118 in s. Ambrogio e in s. Ilario: *Atti Acc. Scienze Torino* 90(1955-56)356-370.

19. *Expositio Evangelii secundam Lucam*

The chronological problem presented by this work is among the most complex of all the Ambrosian writings. Some scholars consider the homilies on which the work is based to have been given in the years 377-378, while others favor the years between 385 and 389, and still others propose a longer span of time, from 377 to 389, which embraces the better part of Ambrose's episcopate. There are also various hypotheses concerning the publication of the work. Ambrose could have chosen from various homilies on the same Lucan passage the one he considered most appropriate, or within one and the same homily he could have added, deleted or substituted different parts, or he could even have collected fragments of various homilies and given them a certain continuity. As it exists now, the work is the result of a careful revision on the part of Ambrose, who published it before 389.

This is the only extant New Testament commentary of Ambrose, and is one of the few works in which the exegesis is careful to follow the development of the scriptural passage.

Nine of the ten books of the Amerbach edition are definitely based on homilies. It does not appear that the same affirmation can be made for book III, which originated as a written work with a strong dependence on the Περὶ διαφωνίας ἐυαϑϑλίων of Eusebius of Caesarea. Vergil occupies a privileged place among the classical sources, and from the Fathers, in addition to the retouched work of Eusebius, the homilies of Origen are present in the first two books and references to Hilary's commentary on Matthew are scattered throughout the work. Ambrose's utilization of these sources has been carefully studied by Dom Tissot, whose work can be consulted for further information.

Clear attention is given in the exegesis to the triple sense of Scripture. Ambrose not only seeks to explain various passages of the Scripture by reference to other texts of Scripture, but he passes continuously from a historical and literal interpretation (on which he dwells to a very limited extent) to the moral, mystical, and allegorical exegesis which he uses more frequently.

The pastoral concern to avoid errors in the Trinitarian and Christological field is present there, where Ambrose takes aim at the Arians and the Sabellians or Patripassionists, especially in the person of Photinus of Sirmium. Christ, God and man, is placed at the center of a *devotio* which will be taken up again centuries later. The study of Mohrmann emphasizes the importance of this work in the literary field. The interpretation of the judgments rendered by Jerome, Augustine, Cassiodorus, and Bede has been carefully determined by Dom Tissot.

The critical text of K. and H. Schenkl, which was recognized as substantially valid by Dom Tissot, has been revised in the edition of M. Adriaen.

Editions: PL 15, 1607-1944. — C. & H. Schenkl, CSEL 32, 4(1902). — M. Adriaen, CCL 14(1957). — G. Tissot, SCh 45 and 52(1955-1958).

Translations: French: G. Tissot, op. cit. *German:* J. Niederhuber, BKV² 21(1915) (books I-VIII). *Italian:* R. Minuti, Rome, 1966. — G. Coppa (S. Ambrosii Opera 11, 1-2). Rome-Milan, 1978. *Spanish:* M. Garrido Bonaño, (BAC). Madrid, 1966.

Manuscript studies: C. Charlier, Un œuvre inconnu de Florus de Lyon: *Traditio* 8(1952)94-102. — E. Dekkers, Un fragment du VIIe-VIIIe s. du Com. de s. Luc par s. Ambroise: SE 9(1957)114-115. — H. Silvestre, Notes de lecture ad Corpus Christ. XIV et XCIV: *Scriptorium* 13(1959)260. — *On the biblical text used by Ambrose:* D. de Bruyne, Sommaires, divisions et rubriques de la Bible latine. Namur 1914, 288-330. — *Emendations:* A. Orbe: Greg 39(1958)784-785 (review of the edition of M. Adriaen); ibid, Nondum receperat typum (Exp. Ev. sec. Lucam X 166): Greg 42(1961)107-112.

General studies: A. Engelbrecht, Studien über den Lukaskommentar des Ambrosius (SAW 146, 8). Vienna, 1903. — G. M. Rolando, Recostruzione teologico-critica del testo latino del Vangelo di san Luca usato da Ambrogio: Bibl 26(1945)238-276, 27(1946)3-17. — P. Rollero, L'influsso dell'Expositio in Lucam di Ambrogio nell'esegesi agostiniana. In *Augustinus Magister* II. Paris 1954, 211-220; *idem,* La Expositio Evangelii secundum Lucam di Ambrogio come fonte dell'esegesi agostiniana. Turin, 1958. — H. C. Puech, P. Hadot, L'entretien d'Origène avec Héraclide et le Commentaire de Saint Ambroise sur l'Evangile de Saint Luc: VC 13(1959)204-234. — H. Silvestre, Notes de lecture: Latomus 20(1961)132ff. — D. Ramos-Lisson, La doctrina de la "Salus" en la "Expositio Evangelii secundum Lucam" de s. Ambrosio: *Scripta Teologica* 5(1973)629-666. — A. Pincherle, Note sulla tradizione indiretta della "Expositio secundum Lucam" di S. Ambrogio. In *Forma Futuri* (Mesc. Pellegrino). Turin 1975, 1097-1114.

20. *Expositio Isaiae prophetae*

Of this lost work there remain only some fragments which Ballerini has collected from citations in the following works of St. Augustine: *De gratia Christi* 49, 54; *De peccato originali* 41, 47; *De nuptiis et concupiscentia* I 34, 40; *Contra Iulianum* II 8, 22; and *Contra duas epistulas pelagianorum* IV 11, 29-31. The critical edition of Ballerini has made use of the critical edition of Augustine's works by C. F. Urba and J. Zycha in CSEL 42, 164, 205, 251, and CSEL 60, 559-567.

Editions: P. A. Ballerini, CCL 14(1957)403-408.

MORAL AND ASCETICAL WORKS

1. *De Officiis ministrorum*

The dating of this work poses notable difficulties and embraces a span of time extending from 377, according to Baronius, until 391, according to the Maurists and Bardenhewer. The attempt of Palanque to assign the work to the second half of 389 is not convincing. A number of scholars are in agreement concerning the homiletic origin of the work (Ihm, Bardenhewer, Schmidt, Palanque), but they have abandoned the attempt to establish the number and extent of the homilies.

Ambrose has followed his Ciceronian model in the title, the division into three books, and in the formal content of the work: I. on that which is virtuous, II. on that which is practical, III. on the opposition between that which is virtuous and that which is practical.

This composition, which is dedicated especially to the clergy but perhaps also to all the faithful, diverges substantially from its exemplar by demonstrating the radical difference between Stoic morality, which has its point of reference in man, and Christian morality, which has its point of reference in God. This difference is explained by Ambrose not so much by means of examples drawn from the Bible in place of the pagan Greek and Roman examples used by Cicero as by means of the eschatological orientation which dominates the entire work. There is as yet no critical edition.

Editions: PL 16, 25-194. — G. Tamietti. Turin, 1906[4]. — A. Cavasin (CPS ser. lat. 15). Turin, 1938. — Cf. E. Buergi, Prolegomena quaedam ad S. Ambrosii libros De officiis tres. In *Jahre Stella Matutina* I 75(1931)43-68. — G. Banterle (S. Ambrosii Opera 13). Rome-Milan, 1977.

Translations: English: H. de Romestin, LNPF 2nd ser. 10(1896, reprint 1969)1-89. *Italian:* A. Cavasin, op. cit. — G. Banterle, op. cit. *German:* J. Niederhuber, BKV[2](1917).

Studies: R. Thamin, Saint Ambroise et la morale chrétienne au IVe siècle. Etude comparée des traités "Des devoirs" de Cicéron et de saint Ambroise. Paris, 1985. — L. Visconti, Il primo trattato di filosofia morale cristiana (il De officiis di s. Ambrogio e di Cicerone): *Atti R. Acc. Arch. Lett. Arti Napoli* 24(1906)41-61. — P. Cannata, De s. Ambrosii libris qui inscribuntur "De officiis ministrorum" quaestiones. Modica, 1909. — P. de Labriolle, Le "De officiis ministrorum" de saint Ambroise et le "De officiis" de Cicéron: *Rev. cours de conférences* 16, 2(1907-08)176-186. — G. Novari, Del preteso stoicismo ciceroniano nei libri De officiis di s. Ambrogio. Parma, 1911. — P. Cannata, De syntaxi ambrosiana in libris qui inscribuntur De officiis ministrorum. Modica, 1911 — Probst, Les éléments cicéroniens dans le De officiis de s. Ambroise. Paris, 1936. — J. T. Muckle, The De officiis ministrorum of St. Ambrose (MS 1). New York, 1939. — T. Deman, Le De officiis de saint Ambroise dans l'histoire de la théologie morale: RSPT 37(1953)409-424. — B. Citterio, Spiritualità sacerdotale nel "De officiis" di sant'Ambrogio: *Ambrosius* 32(1956)157-165. — L. Orabona, L'"usurpatio" in un passo di sant'Ambrogio (De off. I 28) parallelo a Cicerone (De off. I 7) su "ius commune" e "ius privatum": *Aevum* 33(1959)495-504. — O. Hiltbruenner, Die Schrift "De officiis ministrorum" des hl. Ambrosius und ihr ciceronisches Vorbild: *Gymnasium*

71(1964)174-189. — E. Boularand, L'amitié d'après saint Ambroise dans le De officiis ministrorum: BLE 73(1972)103-123. — M. Testard, Observation sur le thème de la "conscientia" dans le "De officiis ministrorum" de saint Ambroise: RELA 51(1973)219-261. — L. F. Pizzolato, L'amicizia nel "De officiis" di s. Ambrogio e il "Laelius" de Cicerone: *Archivo Ambrosiano* 27(1974)53-67. — M. Testard, Etude sur la composition dans le "De officiis ministrorum" de saint Ambroise. In *Ambroise de Milan. XVIe Centénaire de son élection épiscopal.* Paris 1974, 155-197. — K. Zelzer, Zur Beurteilung der Cicero-Imitation bei Ambrosius, "De officiis": WS 11(1977)168-191. — L. J. Swift, Iustitia and ius privatum; Ambrose on private property: AJPh 100(1979)176-187. — W. Steidle, Beobachtungen zu des Ambrosius Schrift De officiis: VC 38(1984)18-66).

2. *De virginibus*

Ambrose composed this work for his sister, Marcellina, in the form of a letter. However, the prevailing thesis — admittedly not unanimous — tends toward a homiletic origin. It was definitely completed by December 377.

Considered to be among the first of his writings, this composition presents the customary elements of a spoken discourse presented with a rhetorical perfection which manifests Ambrose's erudition.

The Bishop of Milan draws abundantly on Origen's mystical exegesis of the Canticle of Canticles. Generous use is made of scriptural citations and there is no lack of references to pagan works.

To the models of Agnes (I 2, 5-9), Mary (II 2, 6 - 3, 19) and John the Baptist (III 5, 25 - 6, 31), which as *exempla* dominate each book, other figures are also joined.

This composition, which is held to be the first organic treatise of spirituality and theology on the theme of virginity in Latin, maintains a balanced and positive judgment on matrimony.

The great number of manuscripts permitted O. Faller to make an accurate critical reconstruction of the text, which was substantially confirmed by I. Cazzaniga.

Editions: PL 16, 197-244. — O. Faller, Ambrosii De Virginibus: FP 31(1933). — I. Cazzaniga, Corpus Script. Lat. Paravianum. Turin, 1948. — M. Salvati, CPS ser. lat. 6(1955)15-163.

Translations: English: H. De Romestin, op. cit., 363-387. *German:* J. Niederhuber, BKV2(1917). *Italian:* R. Cristofoli. Milan, 1930. — M. I. Bianco. Alba, 1941, 19542. — M. Salvati, op. cit. — G. Coppa. Turin, 1969. *Spanish:* Conca. Madrid, 1914. — F. Medina Perea. Madrid, 1914. — F. De B. Vizmanos. BAC 45(1949)669-720.

Studies: E. Franceschini, Verginità e problema demografico in sant'Ambrogio. In *Sant'Ambrogio nel XVI centenario della nascita.* Milan 1940, 209-233. — L. Cazzaniga, Note ambrosiane. Appunti intorno allo stile delle Omelie verginali. Varese, 1948. — L. Dossi, Sant'Ambrogio e Sant'Atanasio nel "De virginibus": *Acme* 4(1951)241-262. — G. Cremaschi, Il De virginibus de s. Ambrogio in un codice ignoto del sec. XII: *Atti Ist. Veneto* 110(1951-52)44-45. — J. Doignon, La première exposition ambrosienne de l'exemplum de Judith (De virg. II 4, 24). In *Ambroise de Milan.* Paris 1974, 219-228. — M. L. Danieli, S. Ambrogio: La verginità, le vergini, le vedove. Pagine sclete sulla verginità. Rome, 1974. — M. L. Ricci, Precisazioni intorno alla fonte di Sant'Ambrogio,

"De virg." 18, 115: VetChr 14(1977)291-299. — C. Riggi, La verginità nel pensiero di S. Ambrogio: *Salesianum* 42(1980)789-806.

3. *De viduis*

Considered by some to be a reworked homily and by others to be a treatise, this work was published shortly after the *De virginibus* and is to be dated between 377 and 378. In its treatment of widowhood, the work never condemns second marriages.

Editions: PL 16, 247-276.

Translations: English: H. De Romestin, op. cit., 391-407.

Studies: M. L. Danieli, La verginità, le vergini, le vedove. Pagine scelte sulla verginità. Rome, 1974.

4. *De virginitate*

Ambrose published this work around 378, making use of one or more of his homilies to defend what he had written in the *De virginibus* and to reaffirm the value of virginity. Paragraphs 14-23 are regarded as interpolations (cf. PLS I, 576).

Editions: PL 16, 279-316. — I. Cazzaniga, Corpus Script. Lat. Paravianum. Turin, 1954. — M. Salvati, op. cit., 169-297.

Translations: Italian: R. Cristofoli. Milan, 1930. — M. I. Bianco. Alba, 1941, 1954[2]. — M. Salvati, op. cit. *Spanish:* S. Andrés. Madrid, 1943.

Studies: R. D'Izarny, La verginité selon saint Ambroise. Lyons, 1952 (cf. review of Botte: BTAM 6[1950-53] n. 1657). — P. Courcelle, Nouveaux aspects du Platonisme chez saint Ambroise: RELA 34(1956)220-239.

5. *De institutione virginis*

This composition, which was probably a homily given for the *velatio* of the young Ambrosia, is preceded by a letter addressed to the grandfather of the young girl, Eusebius, who was a friend of Ambrose and perhaps the bishop of Bologna. It is to be dated between 391 and 392.

This protreptic to virginity, which presents Mary, the mother of Jesus, as a model, refutes the error of Bonosus of Sardica concerning the *post partum* virginity of Mary.

Editions: PL 16, 319-348. — M. Salvati, op. cit., 303-397.

Translations: Italian: R. Cristofoli. Milan, 1930. — M. I. Bianco. Alba, 1941, 1954[2]. — M. Salvati, op. cit. *Spanish:* F. De Vizmanos, BAC 45(1949)721-754.

Studies: J. A. De Aldama, La carta ambrosiana "De Bonoso": *Marianum* 25(1963)1-22.

6. *Exhortatio virginitatis*

This homily was delivered by Ambrose at Florence in 393 (some scholars propose 394-395) on the occasion of the dedication of a basilica constructed through the munificence of the widow, Juliana. It is the last of the five works in which virginity is the dominant theme.

Editions: PL 16, 351-380. — M. Salvati, op. cit., 403-499.

Translations: Italian: R. Cristofoli. Milan, 1930. — M. I. Bianco. Alba, 1941, 1954[2]. — M. Salvati, op. cit.

Studies: I. Cazzaniga, Note Ambrosiane. Appunti intorno allo stile delle omelie verginali. Varese, 1948.

DOGMATIC WORKS

1. *De fide ad Gratianum*

This treatise of five books forms the response to the request of Gratian to be instructed in the faith against the Arian heresy. There is no doubt concerning the written origin of the first two books, but numerous scholars affirm a homiletic origin for the last two, which lack signs of a definite unity. The origin of the third book is disputed. The first two books are assigned to the period between the end of 377 and the summer of 378. Books III-V, which resulted from a new request by Gratian, were already published by the end of 380.

For the numerous historical and political references, consult the edition of O. Faller (*Prolegomena* II).

Ambrose dedicates considerable space to the refutation, without real innovations, of six Arian denials (*De fide* I 34-40) and states:

the Son is not unlike the Father;
the Son did not have a beginning;
the Son was not created;
the Son is good;
the Son is true God;
the Son does not have a divinity other than that of the Father.

The explanation of the inferiority of Christ in relation to the Father occupies, for the most part, books III-V.

Among the sources for the work are Athanasius, Basil, Didymus and Hilary (cf. ed. Faller, *Prolegomena* III). The critical edition of O. Faller offers the best reconstruction of the text up to the present.

Editions: PL 16, 549-726. — G. Vizzini, De fide ad Gratianum Augustum. Liber primus. Rome, 1905. — O. Faller, CSEL 78(1962).

Translations: English: H. De Romestin, op. cit., 201-314.

Studies: L. Herrmann, Ambrosius von Mailand als Trinitätstheologe: ZKG 69(1958)197-218. — A. Campana, Il codice ravennate di s. Ambrogio: *Italia Medioevale e Umanistica* 1(1958)15-68. — A. Pertusi, Le antiche traduzioni greche delle opere di s. Ambrogio: *Aevum* (1944)184-207.

2. *De Spiritu Sancto*

This treatise, which was completed by Ambrose in 381 and

dedicated to Gratian, continues the instruction begun in the *De fide*. The demonstration of the divinity of the Holy Spirit and his place in the Trinity is supported by scriptural citations. Ambrose follows closely the similarly titled work of Didymus of Alexandria, and keeps also in mind the Περὶ ἰοῦ ἁγίου πνεύμαῖος and the *Adversus Eunomium Liber* III of Basil and the *Epistulae ad Serapionem* I and IV of Athanasius.

For a more detailed reference to the sources, an accurate analysis of the manuscripts and the question of the manuscript tradition, consult the critical edition of O. Faller (*Prolegomena* IV and V).

Editions: PL 16, 731-850. — G. Vizzini, Biblitheca Sanctorum Patrum. Rome, 1905-06. — O. Faller, CSEL 79(1964)15-222. — C. Moreschini. Milan 1979, 7-355.

Translations: English: H. De Romestin, op. cit., 93-158. — R. J. Deferrari, FC 44(1963)35-213. *Italian:* C. Moreschini, op. cit.

Studies: Th. Schermann, Die griechischen Quellen des hl. Ambrosius in ll. de Spiritu Sancto. Munich, 1902. — M. Simonetti, Sul "De Spiritus Sancti potentia" di Niceta di R. e nelle fonti del "De Spiritu sancto" di S. Ambrogio: *Maia* 4(1951)1-10. — A. Campana, Il codice ravennate di S. Ambrogio: *Italia Medioevale e Umanistica* 1(1958)15-68.

3. *De incarnationis dominicae sacramento*

Edited at the beginning of 382, the work is composed of two parts: the first (par. 1-78) relates the text of a homily given by Ambrose in the Basilica Porciana, and the second (par. 79-116) is the written response to a question proposed by Gratian: *quomodo possunt ingenitus et genitus esse unius naturae atque substantiae?*

The homily, which makes use of Scripture to respond to the questions of two Arian chamberlains, begins by condemning every schism and dwells on the perfection of the two natures in the one divine person of Christ in refutation of the Apollinarian heresy.

Ambrose makes use of the *Epistula ad Epictetum* of Athanasius in the first part, while the *Adversus Eunomium* I and II of Basil provide the principal source for the second part, which deals with the Arian problem.

For the sources and manuscript tradition, consult the edition of O. Faller (*Prolegomena* IX-XI).

Editions: PL 16, 853-884. — O. Faller, CSEL 79(1964)223-281.

Translations: English: R. J. Deferrari, FC 44(1963). *Italian:* E. Bellini. Milan, 1974. — E. Belline, C. Moreschini. Rome, 1979.

Studies: A. Campana, op. cit. — E. Bellini, Per una lettura globale del "De Incarnationis Dominicae sacramento": SC 102(1974)389-402.

4. *Explanatio symboli ad initiandos*

This homily, whose authenticity had long been disputed, has

recently been confirmed as a genuine work of Ambrose by Connolly, Faller, and Botte.

Editions: CPL 153. — PL 17, 1193-1196. — R. H. Connolly, The Explanatio Symboli ad initiandos, a work of St. Ambrose (TSt 10). Cambridge, 1952. — O. Faller, CSEL 73(1955)1-12. — B. Botte, SCh 25 bis(1961)46-59.

Translations: English: R. H. Connolly, op. cit. *French:* Botte, op. cit., 47-59.

Studies: G. Morin, Pour l'authenticité du "De sacramentis" et l'"Explanatio symboli" de saint Ambroise: JL 8(1928)86-106. — R. H. Connolly, St. Ambrose and the Explanatio Symboli: JThSt 47(1946)185-196. — F. R. M. Hitchcock, The Explanatio Symboli ad initiandos compared with Rufinus and Maximus of Turin: JThSt 47(1946)46-59.

5. *Expositio fidei*

Theodoret of Cyr in his Eranistes (PG 83, 181-188) reproduces a Christological hymn whose attribution to Ambrose is still the subject of discussion (PL 16, 847-850).

Studies: A. Pertusi, Le antiche traduzioni greche delle opere di sant' Ambrogio e l'Expositio Fidei a lui falsamente attribuita: *Aevum* 18(1944)184-207. — G. Bardy, L'Expositio fidei attribuée à S. Ambroise. In *Misc. Mercati* I (ST 121). Vatican City 1947, 199-218. — M. Richard, Notes sur les florilèges dogmatiques du Ve et VIe siècle. In *Actes VI Congrès International Et. Byz. I.* Paris 1950, 314-316. — A. Lumpe, Moderamen zur Entstehung von Ps. Ambr. Epist. de fide: *Museum Helveticum* 13(1956)176-177.

6. *De mysteriis*

The *De mysteriis* is a careful selection and reworking of earlier homilies published around 390 (Dom Botte considers it to be a treatise which merely has the literary form of a homily). Ambrose addresses the neophytes concerning the rites of Baptism and the Eucharist and explains their symbolism by means of the Scripture. The Ambrosian authorship of the work has been reconfirmed by O. Faller and Dom Botte. For the manuscript tradition, consult the edition of Faller (*Prolegomena* 6*-125*; 51*-59*), keeping in mind the variants provided by the edition of Botte.

Editions: PL 16, 405-426. — G. Rauschen, FP 9(1914)73-91. — O. Faller, CSEL 73(1955)13-116. — B. Botte, SCh 25 bis(1961)156-192.

Translations: English: H. De Romestin, op. cit., 317-325. — T. Thompson. London, 1919, reed. by J. H. Srawley, London, 1950. *French:* B. Botte, op. cit., 157-193. — A. Hamman, L'initiation chrétienne (Lettres chrétiennes 7). Paris 1963, 61-85. *Dutch:* F. Vromen. Twee verhandelingen over geheimen. Bruges, 1964. *German:* J. Niederhuber, BKV2 32(1917).

Studies: J. Quasten, Baptismal Creed and Baptismal Act in St. Ambrose's De mysteriis and the De sacramentis. In Mélanges J. de Ghellinck I. Gembloux 1951, 223-234. — E. J. Yarnold, The Ceremonies of Initiation in the "De Sacramentis" and the "De Mysteriis" of St. Ambrose: SP 10 (TU 107). Berlin 1970, 453-463. — C. Mohrmann, Observations sur "De Sacramentis" et "De Mysteriis" de Saint Ambroise (SPMed 6). Milan 1976, 103-123. — G. Pozzi, Riflessioni intorno allo stemma dei codici del De mysteriis e del De Sacramentis di S. Ambrogio. *Italia Medioevale e Umanistica* 2(1959)57-72 (on the manuscript tradition).

7. *De sacramentis*

The *De sacramentis,* which seems to be a contemporary work with the *De mysteriis,* consists of six homilies on Christian initiation through Baptism, Confirmation and Eucharist. The work's lack of cohesion, the frequent repetitions, and the careless style, characteristics so different from the other works of Ambrose, gave rise to doubts concerning its authenticity. However, these doubts have been laid to rest through the work of Faller, Botte, and Chadwick, who have established that the *De sacramentis* is the stenographic record of homilies given to the neophytes. If the theme is essentially the same in both the *De mysteriis* and the *De sacramentis,* there is nevertheless no lack of differences between the works, such as the presence in the latter of instructions on prayer, a commentary on the petitions of the Our Father, and long citations taken from the Canon of the Mass. Consult the edition of O. Faller for questions regarding the manuscript tradition.

Editions: PL 16, 435-482. — G. Rauschen, FP 9(1914)92-131. — O. Faller, CSEL 73(1955)13-116. — H. Chadwick. On the Sacraments. London, 1960. — B. Botte, SCh 25 bis(1961).

Translations: Dutch: F. Vromen. Bruges, 1964. *English:* Th. Thompson, op. cit. — R. J. Deferrari, op. cit., 269-328. *French:* B. Botte, op. cit. *Italian:* G. Coppa. Opere di S. Ambrogio. Turin, 1969.

Studies: Th. Schermann, Die pseudoambrosianische Schrift "De sacramentis." Ihre überlieferung und Quellen: RQ 17(1903)237-255. — C. Atchley, The Date of De Sacramentis: JThSt 30(1929)281-286. — G. Morin, Pour l'authenticité du "De Sacramentis" et de l'"Explanatio symboli" de saint Ambroise: JL 8(1928)86-106. — O. Faller, Was sagen die Handschriften zur Echtheit der sechs Predigten s. Ambrosii de Sacramentis?: ZkTh 53(1929)41-65; *idem,* Ambrosius der Verfasser von De sacramentis. Die inneren Echtheitsgründe. Leipzig, 1940. — R. H. Connolly, The De Sacramentis a Work of St. Ambrose. Downside Abbey, 1943. — J. Quasten, Sobria ebrietas in Ambrosius De sacramentis. Ein Beitrag zur Echtheitsfrage. In *Misc. Liturgica L. C. Mohlberg I.* Rome 1948-49, 117-125. — O. Perler, L'inscription du baptistère de sainte–Thècle à Milan et le De sacramentis de saint-Ambroise: RAC 27(1951)145-166. — J. Quasten, Baptismal Creed and Baptismal Act in St. Ambrose's De mysteriis and De sacramentis. In Mélanges J. de Ghellinck I. Gembloux 1951, 223-234. — C. Mohrmann, Le style oral du De Sacramentis de Saint Ambroise: VC 6(1952)168-177. — G. Lazzati, L'autenticità del "De sacramentis" e la valutazione letteraria delle opere di s. Ambrogio: *Aevum* 29(1955)17-48. — B. Botte, review of O. Faller: RTAM 23(1956)341-343. — F. Petit, Sur les catéchèses postbaptismales de saint Ambroise. A propos de De Sacramentis IV 29: RB 68(1958)256-265. — K. Gamber, Die Autorschaft von "De Sacramentis": RQ 61(1966)94-104; *idem,* Nochmals zur Frage der Autorschaft von De Sacramentis: ZkTh 91(1969)586-589; *idem,* Nachwort, ibid., 589. — E. J. Yarnold, The Ceremonies of Initiation in the "De Sacramentis" and "De Mysteriis" of St. Ambrose: SP 10 (TU 107). Berlin 1970, 453-463; *idem,* Ideo et Romae fideles dicuntur qui baptizati sunt. A note on De Sacramentis I 1: JThSt 24(1973)202-205. — H. M. Riley, Christian Initiation. A comparative study of the interpretation of the baptismal liturgy in Ambrose of Milan (*Studies in Christian antiquity* 17). Washington, 1974. — C. Mohrmann, Observations sur "De sacramentis" et "De mysteriis" de saint Ambroise (SPMed 6). Milan 1976, 103-123. — D. Ramos-Lisson, La tipologia de Jn. 9:6-7 en el De Sacramentis (SPMed 6). Milan 1976, 336-344. — R. Iacoangeli, La catechesi escatologica di S. Ambrogio: *Salesianum* 41(1979)403-417. — A. G. Martimort, Attualità della catechesi sacramentale di Sant' Ambrogio: VetChr 18(1981)81-103.

8. *De paenitentia*

This work, which is to be situated within the span of years between 384 and 394, originated as a written treatise. It is composed of two books in which Ambrose combats the statements of the Novatians concerning the power of the church to remit sins. In the course of his argument, Ambrose reveals elements of particular interest concerning the penitential discipline at Milan in the fourth century.

For the sources, especially Tertullian and Cyprian, as well as for the manuscript tradition, consult the edition of Faller (*Prolegomena* 61*-80*).

Editions: PL 16, 485-546. — O. Faller, CSEL 73(1955)117-206. — R. Gryson, SCh 179(1971).

Translations: English: H. De Romestin, op. cit., 329-359. *French:* R. Gryson, op. cit. *Italian:* G. Coppa. Turin 1969, 623-706. — E. Marotta. Rome, 1976. *Polish:* P. Szoldrski. Warsaw, 1970.

Studies: H. Frank, Ambrosius und die Büsseraussöhnung in Mailand. Münster, 1938. — G. Odoardi, La dottrina della penitenza in sant'Ambrogio. Rome, 1941. — J. Romer, Die theologie der Sünde und der Busse beim hl. Ambrosius. St. Gallen, 1968. — R. Marchioro, La prassi penitenziale nel IV secolo a Milano secondo s. Ambrogio. Rome, 1975.

9. *De sacramento regenerationis sive de philosophia*

This work is no longer extant. Fragments found in Augustine (and Claudianus Mamertus?) are noted in CSEL 11, 131, ed. A. Engelbrecht. The oldest edition is that of P. A. Ballerini, *S. Ambrosii opera omnia* IV. Milan 1879, 905-908.

Studies: M. Ihm, Studia Ambrosiana: *Jahrbuch f. Klass. Philol. Supp.* 17, 1(1889)76. — G. Mace, S. Ambroise et la philosophie. Paris 1974, 247-337.

MISCELLANEOUS WORKS: SERMONS, LETTERS, HYMNS

These works have already been cited in part in the biography of Ambrose, because they form an integral part of the political and historical fabric against which the figure of the Bishop of Milan receives its full prominence. The following indications are intended to emphasize certain aspects of these works within a general view of the literary genre to which they belong.

1. Sermons

a) *De excessu fratris*

This work, dating from the year 378, is composed of two books which are the redactions of two homilies given respectively during the funeral of Satyrus and at the commemoration *in die septimo*. It is the result of a careful reworking and manifests in the customary consolatory style Ambrose's rhetorical and classical culture, the richness of his warm humanity and the Christian reality of death lived and presented in its pastoral dimension.

For the manuscript tradition consult the critical edition of Faller (*Prolegomena* 80*-101*), which corrects that of Albers.

Editions: PL 16, 1345-1414. — P. B. Albers, FP 15(1921). — O. Faller, CSEL 73, 7(1955)207-325.

Translations: English: H. De Romestin, op. cit., 161-197. — J. J. McGuire, FC 22(1953, 1968²)161-259. *German:* R. Loebe. In *Mancherlei Gaben und ein Geist* 50(1910) Heft 1-4 (only book I). *Italian:* G. Coppa, op cit., 771-810.

Studies: F. Savio, L'anno della morte di S. Satiro: CC 53/4(1902)529-540. — B. Albers, Über die erste Trauerrede des hl. Ambrosius zum Tode seines Bruders Satyrus. In *Festgabe Ehrhard.* Bonn 1921, 24-52. — M. L. Ricci, Definizione della "Prudenza" in sant'Ambrogio. A proposito di De excessu fratris 44-48: SIF 41(1969)247-262. — J. Doignon, Lactance intermédiaire entre Ambroise de Milan et la Consolation de Ciceron?: RELA 51(1973)208-219. — A. Palestra, Note al libro I del "De excessu fratris" di S. Ambrogio: *Archivo Ambrosiano* 27(1974)25-52. — H. Savon, La première oraison funèbre de saint Ambroise (De excessu fratris I) et les deux sources de la consolation chrétienne: RELA 58(1980)370-402.

b) *De obitu Valentiniani*

When the remains of Valentinian II were returned to Milan in 392, Ambrose delivered a funeral oration in his honor in which he recalled significant moments in the relations between the bishop and the emperor. He condemned the assassins of the young Valentinian, whose gifts of spirit and government he recalled with affection. From the edition published by Ambrose, there was formed an ancient archetype on which depend the manuscript *Paris. lat.* 1920 (*saec.* XIV), and the manuscripts of Milan and Heiligenkreuz, which are considered to be the best. In some instances it has been possible to restore a most reliable text with the help of a group of older manuscripts which are generally considered less trustworthy. The critical edition of Faller contains an ample chapter on the manuscript tradition (*Prolegomena* 101*-113*).

The funeral oration, which is rich in scriptural citations, displays a preference for the Canticle of Canticles, and shows the influence of Origen's commentaries on the Canticle and on Exodus.

Editions: PL 16, 1417-1444. — T. A. Kelly, PSt 58(1940). — O. Faller, CSEL 73(1955)327-367.

Translations: English: T. A. Kelly, op. cit. — R. J. Deferrari, FC 22(1953, 1968[2])265-299. *Italian:* G. Coppa, op. cit., 813-850.

c) *De obitu Theodosii*

In the funeral oration delivered forty days after the death of Theodosius (February 25, 395) in the presence of Honorius, Ambrose does not restrict himself to presenting the figure of an emperor firmly anchored in the Catholic faith, but also underlines his capacity for government. There is an obvious attempt in the oration to strengthen the position of Honorius and invite him to continue the same political and social line, and the reference to the law promulgated in favor of the rural population by Honorius on March 24, 395, confirming his father's provisions from 393, was intended to arouse an immediate approbation. The influence of Origen is frequently manifested in the oration, and particular attention is merited by chapters 40-50 which are intended, through the figure of the Empress Helen, to recall the finding of the cross. The exaltation of the harmony in the relations between the church and empire achieved under Theodosius is the purpose of these chapters, which some scholars consider to be subsequent written additions. In reality, however, it is more likely that they belong to the integral body of the oration. For a judgment on this question as well as for the manuscript tradition, consult the edition of Faller (*Prolegomena* 114*-125*).

Editions: PL 16, 1447-1488. — M. D. Mannix, PSt 9(1925). — O. Faller, CSEL 73(1955)369-401.

Translations: English: M. D. Mannix, op. cit. — R. J. Defarrari, op. cit., 307-332. *German:* J. Niederhuber, BKV[2] 32(1917). *Italian:* G. Coppa, op. cit., 853-883.

Studies: G. Bonamente, Fideicommissum e transmissione del potere nel "De obitu Theodosii" di Ambrogio: VetChr 14(1977)273-280. — W. Steidle, Die Leichenrede des Ambrosius für Kaiser Theodosius und die Helene-Legende: VC 32(1978)94-112.

d) *Sermo contra Auxentium de Basilicis trandendis*

This discourse, given on Palm Sunday 386, is one of the texts from the anti-Arian polemic of Ambrose's episcopate. The basic reasons for Ambrose's refusal of Valentinian II's request to assign a church in which the Arians might celebrate their Easter liturgy is explained by the bishop to the faithful assembled in the basilica.

*Editions:*PL 16, 1049-1053.

Translations: English: H. De Romestin, op. cit., 430-436.

2. Letters

The collection of Ambrose's letters forms one of the most important sources of documentation for a knowledge of their author and of the religious and political situation of his time. There are 91 extant letters, keeping in mind that *Ep.* 23 is not considered authentic. Some of these letters have already been mentioned in the section dedicated to Ambrose's life: e.g., *Ep.* 59 to Severus of Naples, used to cast some light on the date of his birth; and *Ep.* 21 to Valentinian II in which Ambrose recalls his relations with Valentinian I, takes a more tenacious stance against the Arian, Auxentius, and reaffirms the autonomy of the church. Equally concerned with the problem of relations between the church and the empire are *Ep.* 1 to Gratian, *Ep.* 57 to Eugenius, and *Ep.* 51 to Theodosius on the occasion of the massacre at Thessalonica.

The letters dealing with the Arian problem are, among others, *Ep.* 2 to the bishop Constantius of Clotema; *Ep.* 10, 11, and 12 to the Emperors Gratian, Valentinian II, and Theodosius from the Council of Aquileia; *Ep.* 13 and 14 to Theodosius in the name of the Italian bishops; *Ep.* 21 to his sister, Marcellina, keeping her abreast of the continuous engagements with the Arians; and *Ep.* 21 to Valentinian II concerning the same topic.

Ep. 17 and 18 are historical documents concerning Ambrose's anti-pagan attitude and containing the text of Symmachus' *Exposito* addressed to Valentinian II with reference to the Altar of Victory.

Some light is cast on the anti-Jewish policy of Ambrose by *Ep.* 40 to Theodosius, insisting that the synagogue at Callinicum not be reconstructed, and *Ep.* 41 to Marcellina, in which Ambrose relates the homily given in the presence of the emperor on the difference between the Church and the Synagogue.

The Bishop of Milan's preoccupation with the life of the church is always and everywhere obvious: *Ep.* 15 and 16 to the bishops of Macedonia on the death of the bishop of Thessalonica; *Ep.* 19 to Vigilius of Trent on the danger of mixed marriages with pagans or Gothic "heretics"; *Ep.* 22, the second letter to Marcellina, treating of the discovery of the bodies of Gervasius and Protasius and containing the transcripts of the homilies given on that occasion; *Ep.* 23 to the bishops of Emilia establishing the date of Easter; *Ep.* 37 and 38 to Simplicianus; *Ep.* 42 and 46 bis, the former against Jovinian and the latter against Bonosus; *Ep.* 54 and 55 to Eusebius of Bologna; *Ep.* 58 to Paulinus of Nola; *Ep.* 63 to the Church of Vercelli; *Ep.* 81 to the clergy of Milan.

According to Klein, the division of the collection of letters into ten books is the work of Ambrose himself, although Book X was published only after his death. For the manuscript tradition, consult the work of Faller, whose critical edition was halted by his death. The edition of the remaining books has been entrusted to Michaela Zelzer, who has collated other manuscripts considered more important.

Editions: PL 16, 913-1342. — M. Lavarenne, Prudence, Psychomachie, Contre Symmaque. Paris, 1948 (contains the edition of *Ep.* 17 and 18 and of the *Relatio Symmachi*). — O. Faller, CSEL 82(1968)(Epistularum libri I-VI).

Translations: Dutch: J. Wytzes, Brieven (Klassieken der Kerk I, 2). Amsterdam, 1950 (Letters 17, 18, 20, 21, 40, 41, 51, 57). *English:* H. De Romestin, op. cit. (letters 17, 18, 20, 21, 22, 40, 41, 51, 57, 61, 62, 63). — M. M. Beyenka, FC 26(1954) 1968[2]) (letters 1-91). — S. Greenslade, Early Latin Theology. Selections from Tertullian, Cyprian, Ambrose and Jerome. London, 1956 (letters 10, 17, 18, 20, 21, 22, 40, 41, 51, 57, 63). *Italian:* G. Coppa, op. cit. (letters 17, 18, 20, 21, 22, 40, 41, 51, Relatio).

Studies: W. Willebrand, S. Ambrosius quos auctores quaeque exemplaria in epistolis componendis secutus sit. Commentatio philologica. Münster, 1909. — G. Mamone, Le epistole di sant'Ambrogio: Did. N.S. 1(1924)3-143; *idem,* La forma delle lettere di sant'Ambrogio, *idem,* 145-164. — G. Lazzati, Il valore letterario della esegesi ambrosiana. Milan, 1960. — R. Klein, Die Kaiserbriefe des Ambrosius. Zur Problematik ihrer Veröffentlichung: *Athenaeum* 48(1970)335-371. — B. Semplicio, Mistero pasquale e spiritualità del sacerdote nelle lettere di S. Ambrogio. Piacenza, 1972. — R. Klein, Der Streit um den Victoria altar, die dritte Relatio des Symmachus und die Briefe 17, 18 und 57 des Mailänder Bischofs Ambrosius. Darmstadt, 1972. — G. L. Rapisarda, La personalità di Ambrogio nelle Epistole XVII e XVIII: Orph 20(1973)5-143. — J. P. Mazieres, Les lettres d'Ambroise de Milan à Orontien. Remarques sur leur chronologie et leur destinataire: *Pallas* 20(1973)49-57. — M. Zelzer, Die Briefbücher des hl. Ambrosius und die Briefe extra collectionem: AAWW 112(1975)7-23. — M. Forlin Paturcco and R. Roda, Le lettere di Simmaco ad Ambrogio. Vent'anni di rapporti amichevoli (SPMed 7). Milan 1976, 284-297. — E. Lucchesi, Utrum Ambrosius Mediolanensis in quibusdam epistulis Philonis Alexandrini opusculum quod inscribitur "Quis rerum divinarum heres sit" usurpaverit an non quaeritur: Mus 90(1977)347-354. — M. Zelzer, Zu Aufbau und Absicht des zehnten Briefbuches des Ambrosius. In *Latinität und alte Kirch,* Festschrift R. Hanslik. Vienna 1977, 251-362; *Eadem,* Probleme der Texterstellung im zehnten Briefbuch des hl. Ambrosius und in den Briefen extra collectionem: AAWW 115(1978)415-439.

3. Hymns

The conflict at Milan between 385 and 386 concerning the Arians' request for a basilica provided the precise historical context out of which arose the Ambrosian hymnody. To the recitation of a psalm there alternated the singing of a hymn which drew its content not from the Scriptures, but rather from the religious festival being commemorated, from the exaltation of the Apostles and martyrs, the praise of God during the hours of the day, or from doctrinal truths. By 396, the singing of hymns alternating with the antiphonal chanting of the psalms was already a patrimony of the Church of Milan, from whence it spread abroad, and Ambrose is recognized as the founder of the liturgical hymnody of the Western Church. He drew his models from pagan religious poetry and from popular Christian religious songs. The themes proposed by Ambrose are easily comprehended and speak to the heart rather than to the intellect by means of vivid images which are easily impressed in the memory. The melodies, composed by Ambrose himself, are applied to iambic dimeters grouped in quatrains, which facilitate learning and memorization.

In the *Sermo contra Auxentium* 34, Ambrose recalls the facility with which the faithful were composing hymns according to the model he had created, which may explain the quantity of these compositions attributed to him.

In reality, scholars, supported by the testimony of St. Augustine, are in agreement on the attribution of only four hymns to Ambrose: the *Aeterne rerum conditor* (Augustine, *Retract.* 1, 21); *Deus creator omnium* (*Conf.* 9, 12); *Iam surgit hora tertia* (*De nat. gr.* 63); and *Intende qui regis Israel* (*Serm.* 372).

Dreves, the same as Biraghi before him, considers another fourteen hymns to be authentic: *Illuminans Altissimus, Hic est dies verus Dei, Agnes beatae virginis, Victor Nabor Felix pii, Grates tibi Jesu novas, Apostolorum passio, Apostolorum supparem, Amore Christi nobilis, Aeterna Christi munera, Splendor paternae gloriae, Nunc Sanctae nobis Spiritus, Rector potens verax Deus, Rerum Deus tenax vigor,* and *Iesu corona virginum.*

The best critical edition of the hymns mentioned here is that of Steier. Not all scholars share the opinion of Biraghi, Dreves, and Steier. Walpole tends toward the authenticity of eighteen hymns, while Simonetti considers that, to the four definitely authentic hymns, only four more can be added: *Grates tibi Iesu novas, Splendor paternae gloriae, Aeterna Christi munera,* and *Hic est dies verus Dei;* although he is inclined to recognize Ambrosian authorship for two others: *Victor Nabor Felix pii* and *Agnes beatae virginis.* Hymn V, whose authenticity has been denied by Simonetti, has been the object of study by Mohrmann, who considers it Ambrosian.

Three inscriptions in distichs also form part of Ambrose's poetical compositions: one for the tomb of his brother, Satyrus; one for the baptistry of Saint Thecla, and one in honor of Saint Nazarius. The question is still open regarding the authenticity of the twenty-one *tituli* which are placed as captions for scenes from the Old and the New Testaments.

Editions: L. Biraghi, Inni sinceri e carmi di sant'Ambrogio. Milan, 1862. — A. Steier, Untersuchungen über die Echtheit der Hymnen des Ambrosius (*Jahrbücher für kl. Philologie, Suppl.* 28). Munich 1903, 549-662 (text: 651-660). — Kl. Blume, G. M. Dreves, Analecta hymnica medii aevi, vol. 50. Leipzig 1907, 10-21. — A. S. Walpole, Early Latin Hymns. Cambridge 1922 (reprint: Hildescheim 1966), 16-114. — G. Del Ton, Gli inni di S. Ambrogio. Como, 1940. — W. Bulst, Hymni Latini antiquissimi LXXV, psalmi III. Heidelberg, 1956. — M. Simonetti, Innologia ambrosiana. Alba, 1956. — E. Bolisani, l'innologia cristiana antica. Sant'Ambrogio e i suoi imitatori. Padua, 1963. — L. Sollazzo, Inni di Sant'Ambrogio. Parma, 1964.

Epigrams: F. Bücheler, A. Riese, Anthologia latina II, 2. Leipzig 1887, n. 906-907, 1421. — E. Diehl, ICLV I. Berlin 1925, n. 1800, 1801, 1841, 2165. — PLS I, 585-587.

Tituli: S. Merkle, Die ambrosianische Tituli: RQ 10(1896)185-222. — PLS I, 587-589.

Studies: G. M. Dreves, Der Hymnus des hl. Ambrosius "Agnes beatae virginis": ZkTh 25(1901)356-365. — G. Mercati, Paralipomena Ambrosiana (ST 12). Rome, 1904. — H. Vogels, Hymnus "Splendor paternae gloriae." In Festschr. A. Knöpfler. Munich 1907, 314-316. — J. B. van Bebbern, Der Brevierhymnus: en clara vox redarguit, eine hymnologische Studie: ThQ 89(1907)373-384. — A. S. Walpole, Notes on the Text of the Hymns of St. Ambrose: JThSt 9(1908)428-436. — Kl. Blume, Ursprung des ambrosianischen Lobgesanges: *Stimmen aus Maria Lach* (1911)274-287, 401-414, 487-503. — P. P. Trompeo, Intorno alla composizione degli innin di Ambrogio: *Atene e Roma* 16(1903)35-40. — H. Fuchs, Latina III: Hermes 58(1933)348-349. — F. J. Dölger, Die Inschrift des hl. Ambrosius im Baptisterium der Theklakirche von Mailand: AC 4(1934)155-156. — A. Silvagni, Studio critico sulle due sillogi medievali di iscrizioni cristiane milanesi: RAC 15(1938)107-122. — G. Ghedini, L'opera di Biraghi e l'innologia ambrosiana: SC 68(1940)160-170, 275-285. — G. P. Pighi, Commentariolus electorum: *Aevum* 18(1944)14-51 (on two Ambrosian epigrams). — P. Courcelle, Quelques symboles funéraires du néoplatonisme latin et le vol de Dédale. Ulysse et les Sirènes: REAN 46(1944)66. — Ch. Mohrmann, La langue et le style de la poésie chrétienne: RELA 25(1947)280-297 (= Études sur le Lat. des chrétiens I. Rome 1958, 151-168). — O. Perler, L'inscription du baptistère de Sainte-Thècle à Milan et le De Sacramentis de saint Ambroise: RAC 27(1951)145-166. — M. Simonetti, Studi sull'innologia popolare cristiana dei primi secoli: *Atti Acc. Naz. Lincei. Memorie sez.* 8, 4(1952)339-485. — D. Norberg, L'hymne ambrosien. In *Au seuil du moyen âge. Etudes linguistiques, métriques et littéraires.* Padua 1974, 135-149; *idem,* Le début de l'hymnologie latine en l'honneur des saints, ibid., 150-162. — M. P. Cunningham, The Place of the Hymns of St. Ambrose in the Latin Poetic Tradition: *Studies in Philology* 52(1955)509-514. — M. Simonetti, Osservazioni cirtiche sul testo di alcuni inni ambrosiani: ND (1953-55)45-48. — M. M. Beyenka, St. Augustine and the Hymns of St. Ambrose: *The American Benedictine Review* 8(1957)121-132. — N. Corneanu, Aspecte din lirica ambroziană: *Studii teologice* 11(1959)443-452. — F. Dell'Oro, Testi liturgici per la festa dei martiri Nabore e Felice: *Archivio Ambrosiano* 27(1974)235-245. — G. Angeloni, S. Ambrogio maestro e caposcuola della innografia cristiana: *Ambrosius* 50(1974)401-434. — J. Fontaine, L'apport de la tradition poétique romaine à la formation de l'hymnodie latine chrétienne: RELA 52(1974)318-355. — L. Szelestei-Nagy, Zeitmass und Wortbetonung in den frühchristlichen Hymnen in lateinischer Sprache: *Annales Universitatis Budapestinensis* 2(1974)75-89.

The following works are falsely attributed to Ambrose:

1. *Hegesippus sive de bello iudaico,* a work published toward the end of the fourth century giving a Latin translation of Flavius Josephus' history of the Jewish War. In the prologue of the work are mentioned the *Res gestae Machabaeorum,* which were studied by Morin (cf. RB 31[1914]83; PLS I, 576, CPL 169).

2. *Lex Dei sive mosaicarum et romanarum legum collatio,* a work dated to the end of the fourth century, which is of great interest for the history of law (cf. PLS I, 589; CPL 168; J. Baviera, *Fontes Juris Romani antejustiniani* 2. Florence 1968^2, p. 544; C. Hohenlohe, *Ursprung und Zweck der "Collatio legum."* Vienna, 1935).

3. *De lapsu virginis,* attributed to Nicetas of Remasiana q.v.

4. *Te Deum,* attributed by some scholars to Nicetas of Remasiana q.v.

AMBROSIASTER

Ambrosiaster (pseudo-Ambrose) is the name commonly given to the author of the commentaries on the Pauline epistles written presumably at Rome in the second half of the fourth century. The work is attributed in most manuscripts to Ambrose, although in some it is attributed to a certain Hilary, and in others is presented as anonymous. It must in fact have been anonymous from the beginning; a fact which is variously explained by W. Mundle, A. Souter, and A. Stuiber.

The identity of the author has been much discussed, although without reaching as yet any definite and reliable conclusions. Numerous hypotheses have been advanced, and on the basis of the most varied elements (mostly linguistic, but also epigraphical, biographical, etc.), the following have all been proposed at one time or another as the author of the anonymous commentaries: The Luciferian deacon named Hilary; Tyconius the Donatist; the Roman priest Faustinus; the Jewish convert Isaac, who was an opponent of Pope Damasus and later returned to Judaism; the Roman prefect Decimius Hilarianus Hilarius; Hilary, bishop of Pavia; Evagrius, bishop of Antioch; the imperial minister Claudius Callixtus Hilarius; the son of Pacian of Barcelona by the name of Emilianus Dexter; and, finally, Nicetas of Remesiana. Morin was especially interested in the question and between 1899 and 1928 proposed all of five different hypotheses.

One of the controverted questions relating to the identity of Ambrosiaster concerns whether he was of Jewish or pagan background. He has a notable knowledge and interest for Jewish institutions, although some of his statements seem to indicate instead that he was a convert from paganism.

There is also a question as to whether Ambrosiaster was Greek or Latin by birth, and thus whether the linguistic difficulties present in his writings are to be attributed to the non-Latin origin of the author or merely to his stated aversion to the Greek manuscripts and his adherence to the Latin translations.

The generally accepted dating of Ambrosiaster's works comprises a span of time from 363 to 384, i.e., following the death of the Emperor Julian and during the pontificate of Pope Damasus (366-384). Rome is generally indicated as the place of composition, although it appears that the author had some contact with Northern Italy and Spain.

To this same author, Souter definitely attributes the *Quaestiones Veteris et Novi Testamenti,* transmitted under the name of Augustine, as well as an anonymous commentary to chapter 24 of the Gospel of Matthew. There is a lack of agreement concerning the attribution to Ambrosiaster of other writings, such as the fragments *De Petro Apostolo* and *Incipit de tribus mensuris*, the *Lex Dei sive Mosaicarum et Romanarum legum collatio* and the *De bello iudaico*.

Many questions thus remain open. In addition to the unresolved question of the identity of the so-called Ambrosiaster, it is also necessary to examine closely the significance of certain of his expressions of a theological character which could lead to a better understanding of the problem of his sources, which has not been sufficiently considered. There has been much discussion and argument concerning this author's influence on Pelagius and Augustine, but it has not yet been possible to distinguish clearly the genesis of his thought. Is he strictly bound to the Latin theological tradition, or has he been influenced in some manner by the Greek Fathers, even though he probably did not know that language? Did he have any contacts with the Eastern or Syriac world? If his travels were numerous, as Bardy affirms, did they give him merely a knowledge of the customs and manners of the peoples he visited, or did they foster an understanding of theological traditions other than his own?

Finally, it is necessary to better understand how much influence a certain juridic mentality exercised on Ambrosiaster's thought and his interpretation of the faith, and to what extent the tendency to moralizing and rationalism can be actually attributed to the author himself.

Studies: R. Simon, Histoire Critique des principaux Commentateurs du Nouveau Testament. Rotterdam 1693, 133-147. — J. B. Morel, Dissertation sur le véritable Auteur des commentaires sur les épîtres de S. Paul faussement attribués à S. Ambroise et sur l'Auteur de deux autres Ouvrages qui sont dans l'Appendice du troisième tome de S. Augustin. Paris, 1762. — J. Langen, De commentariorum in epistolas paulinas, qui Ambrosii, et questionum biblicarum, quae Augustini nomine feruntur scriptore dissertatio. Bonn, 1880; *idem,* Geschichte der römischen Kirche bis zum Pontificate Leo's I. Bonn 1881, 599-610. — C. Marold, Der Ambrosiaster nach Inhalt und Ursprung: ZWTh 27(1884)415-470. — A. Jülicher, Ambrosiaster: PWK I(1894)1811-1812. — A. von Harnack, Der pseudoaugustinische Traktat contra Novatianum, in Abhandlungen Alexander v. Öttingen gewidmet. Munich 1898, 54-93. — G. Morin, L'Ambrosiaster et le juif converti Isaac, contemporain du pape Damase: RHL 4(1899)97-121. — Th. Zahn, Der "Ambrosiaster" und der Proselyt Isaak: ThLB 20(1899)313-317. — A. E. Burn, The Ambrosiaster and Isaac the Converted Jew: ExpT5 (1899)368-375. — H. Zimmer, Pelagius in Irland. Berlin 1901, 117-121. — J. Wittig, Papst Damasus I. Rome, 1902. — J. Mercati, Il commentario latino di un ignoto chiliasta su s. Matteo: ST 11(1903)3-49. — G. Morin, Le fragment "Contra Arrianos" de l'Hilaire papyrus de Vienne: SAW 146(1903)18-21; *idem,* Hilarius l'Ambrosiaster: RB 20(1903)113-121, Appendix: Deux fragments d'un Traité contre les Ariens attribué parfois à saint Hilaire, 125-131. — A. Souter, A New View About "Ambrosiaster": ExpT 7(1903)442-445. — F. Cumont, La polémique de l'Ambrosiaster contre les païens: RHL 8(1903)417-436, Appendix: L'Ambrosiaster et el droit romain, 437-440. — C. H. Turner, An Exegetical Fragment of the Third Century: JThSt 5(1903-04)218-

241. — A. Souter, Reasons for Regarding Hilarius (Ambrosiaster) as the Author of the Mercati-Turner Anecdoton: JThSt 5(1903-04)608-621; *idem,* A Study of Ambrosiaster (TSt 7, 4). Cambridge, 1905. — T. Zahn, Ein alter Kommentar zu Matthäus: NKt 16(1905)419-427. — C. H. Turner, Ambrosiaster and Damasus: JThSt 7(1905-06)281-284; *idem,* Niceta and Ambrosiaster: JThSt 7(1906)355-372. — J. Wittig, Der Ambrosiaster-Hilarius. Ein Beitrag zur Geschichte des Papstes Damasus I: KGA 4(1906)4-66; *idem,* Filastrius, Gaudentius und Ambrosiaster. Eine literarhistorische Studie: KGA 8(1909)1-56. — W. Schwierholz, Hilarii in epistola ad Romanos librum I. Ein Beitrag zur Ambrosiasterfrage: KGA 8(1909)57-96. — H. Zeuschner, Studien zur Fides Isaatis. Ein Beitrag zur Ambrosiasterfrage: KGA 8(1909)97-148. — H. Brewer, War der Ambrosiaster der bekehrte Jude Isaak?: ZKTh 37(1913)214-216. — G. Morin, Anonyme du IVe siècle: le Contra Arrianos du Papyrus de Vienne: *Anecdota Maredsolana* 2, 1(1913)8-9; *idem,* Qui est l'Ambrosiaster? Solution nouvelle: RB 31(1914)1-34. — A. Souter, The Identity of the "Ambrosiaster": A Fresh Suggestion: ExpT 7(1914)224-232. — G. Morin, Una nuova possibilità a proposito dell'Ambrosiastro: *Athenaeum* 6(1918)62-71. — W. Mundle, Die Exegese der paulinischen Briefe in Kommentar des Ambrosiaster. Marburg, 1919. — J. H. Baxter, Ambrosiaster cited as "Ambrose" in 405: JThSt 24(1922-23)187. — G. Bareille, E. Mangenot, Isaac: DTC 8(1924)1-8. — H. Koch, Cyprian in dem Quaestiones Veteris et Novi Testamenti und beim Ambrosiaster. Ein Beitrag zur Ambrosiasterfrage: ZKG 45(1926)516-551. — A. Souter, The Earliest Latin Commentaries on the Epistles of Paul. Oxford 1927, 39-95. — G. Bardy, Ambrosiaster: DBS 1(1928)225-241. — H. Koch, Der Ambrosiaster und zeitgenössische Schriftsteller: ZKG 47(1928)1-10. — G. Morin, La critique dans une impasse: à propos du cas de l'Ambrosiaster: RB 40(1928)251-255. — A. D'Alès, L'Ambrosiaster et Zénon de Vérone: Greg 10(1929)404-409. — C. Martini, Quattuor fragmenta Pelagio restituenda: Ant 13(1938)293-334. — A. Pincherle, Ambrosiastro: Enc. It. 2(1929)806-807. — C. Martini, Ambrosiaster. De auctore, operibus, theologia. Rome, 1944. — E. Dekkers, VC 3(1949)62-63. — M. Michalski, Problem autorstwa tak swanego "Ambroziastra" w swietle jego nauke christologicznej. Krakow, 1950. — P. Schepens, L'Ambrosiastre et saint Eusèbe de Verceil: RSR 37(1950)295-299. — H. J. Vogels, Ambrosiaster und Hieronimus: RB 66(1956)14-19. — P. Photiadès, Les diatribes cyniques du Papyrus Genève 271, leurs traductions et élaborations successives: *Museum Helveticum* 16(1959)116-139. — H. J. Vogels, Die Überlieferung des Ambrosiasterkommentars zu den Paulinischen Briefen: NGWG (1959)107-142. — K. Gamber, Fragen zu Person und Werk des Bischofs Niceta von Remesiana: RQ 62(1967)222-231. — R. Hoven, Notes sur Érasme et les auteurs anciens: ACL 38(1969)169-174. — A. Stuiber, Ambrosiaster: JAC 13(1970)119-123. — M. Zelzer, Zur Sprache des Ambrosiaster: WSt NF 4(1970)196-213. — L. Wallach, Ambrosiaster und die Libri Carolini: *Deutsches Archiv f. Erforschung des Mittelalters* 29(1973)197-205. — R. E. Reynolds, Isidore's Texts on the Clerical Grades in an Early Medieval Roman Manuscript: *Classical Folia* 29(1975)95-101. — R. Riedinger, Zur antimarkionitischen Polemik des Klemens von Alexandria: VC 29(1975)15-32. — A. Pollastri, Ambrosiaster. commento all lettera ai Romani: aspetti cristologici. L'Aquila, 1977.

WRITINGS

1. Commentary on the Pauline Epistles

Ambrosiaster composed a systematic commentary on the thirteen epistles of Paul. The *Commentary on Romans* exists in three different versions, all the work of Ambrosiaster, of which the third appears to be the final and definitive edition. The *Commentary on the two Letters to the Corinthians* is extant in two versions and, according to Vogels, the commentaries to the other letters would also have existed in a dual version.

The interpretation of each letter is preceded by a prologue in which the author presents the community to which Paul's letter was addressed and explains the Apostle's purpose for writing. By means of a careful exegesis which omits nothing of the Pauline text, the following commentary examines phrases of the Apostle varying in length from two or three words to groups of different verses joined together. For this reason, Ambrosiaster's commentaries are of particular importance for establishing the transmission of the Latin text of the Pauline letters in a form spread throughout Italy in the second half of the fourth century before the revision brought about by the Vulgate.

The exegesis is of a historical and literal type, without further investigations by means of allegory or research into symbols, and is intended to present the theological motivation behind the Pauline expressions. It is rich in scriptural citations and animated by polemics against pagans, heretics and Judeo-Christians. In this manner, the author is close to the exegetical tradition of the Antiochene School, although he does not explicitly reject the Alexandrian method, which he does not seem to know in the elaborate form presented by Origen. He makes use, in any case, of typological interpretation.

Editions: PL 17, 47-536. — A. Amelli, *Spicilegium Casinense* 3, 2(1901)1-383. — H. J. Vogels, CSEL 81, 1-3(1966-69).

Studies: A. Souter, "Emmaus" Mistaken for a Person: ExpT 13(1901-02)429-430; *idem,* The Genuine Prologue to Ambrosiaster on II Corinthians: JThSt 4(1902-03)89-92; *idem,* A Study of Ambrosiaster (TSt 7, 4). Cambridge, 1905. — D. de Bruyne, Prologues bibliques d'origine Marcionite: RB 24(1907)1-16. — P. Corssen, Zur überlieferungesgeschichte des Römerbriefes: ZNW 10(1909)36-45, 97-102. — W. Schwierholz, Hilarii in epistola ad Romanos librum I. Ein Beitrag zur Ambrosiaster-frage: KGA 8(1909)57-96. — W. Mundle, Die Exegesi der paulinischen Briefe in Kommentar des Ambrosiaster. Marburg, 1919. — H. J. Vogels, Untersuchungen zur Geschichte der lateinischen Apokalypse-Übersetzung. Düsseldorf, 1920. — W. Mundle, Die Herkunft der "marcionitischen" Prologe zu den paulinischen Briefen: ZNW 24(1925)56-77. — A. von Harnack, Der marcionitische Ursprung der ältesten vulgata-Prologe zu den Paulusbriefen: ZNW 24(1925)204-218. — M. J. Lagrange, Les prologues prétendus Marcionites: RBibl 35(1926)161-173. — A. Souter, The Earliest Latin Commentaries on the Epistles of St. Paul. Oxford 1927, 39-95. — G. Bardy, Ambrosiaster: DBS 1(1928)238-240. — C. Martini, Ambrosiaster. De auctore, operibus, theologia. Rome, 1944. — B. Leeming, The Mysterious Ambrosiaster: DR 73(1955)263-275. — H. J. Vogels, Untersuchungen zum Text paulinischer Briefe bei Rufin und Ambrosiaster. Bonn, 1955; *idem,* Ambrosiaster und Hieronymus: RB 66(1956)14-19; *idem,* "Librarii dormitantes." Aus der Überlieferung des Ambrosiaster-Kommentars zu den paulinischen Briefen: SE 8(1956)5-13; *idem,* Das Corpus Paulinum des Ambrosiaster. Bonn, 1957; *idem,* Die Überlieferung des Ambrosiaster-Kommentars zu den Paulinischen Briefen: NGWG(1959)107-142. — F. H. Tinnefeld, Untersuchungen zur altlateinischen Überlieferung des I Timotheusbriefes. Wiesbaden 1963, 63-70. — H. J. Frede, Altlateinische Paulus-Handschriften. Freiburg, 1964; *idem,* Ein neuer Paulustext und

Kommentar, 2 vols. Freiburg, 1973-74. — A. Pollastri, Il prologo del commento alla Lettera ai Romani dell'Ambrosiaster: SSR 2(1978)93-127; *idem,* Sul rapporto tra cristiani e giudei secondo il commento dell'Ambrosiaster ad alcuni passi paolini: SSR 4(1980)313-327.

2. *Quaestiones Veteris et Novi Testamenti*

The *Quaestiones Veteris et Novi Testamenti,* which have been handed down under the name of Augustine, are extant in three collections, each containing a variable number of treatises: 127 in the collection considered by Souter as a second edition, 150 in another collection, and 115 in the third and most recent collection (composed between the eighth and the twelfth centuries). Souter considers both of the first collections to be the work of Ambrosiaster, who first composed the collection of 150 *Quaestiones* and then subsequently revised and corrected it, eliminating the shorter and less important questions to form the collection of 127 *Quaestiones.* More recently, C. Martini has proposed that neither of these two collections was assembled and arranged by the author, but are the work of a later compiler who indiscriminately placed together *Quaestiones* from both the first and second editions of the same work originally made by Ambrosiaster.

The questions are of varying length and treat of different questions. The majority are of an exegetical nature while others are dogmatic in character with a speculative scope and still others are polemical or apologetic in tone (cf. *Quaestiones* 44, 91, 97, 102, 114, 125). Finally, others which criticize abuses or witness to contemporary customs are of a particular historical interest (cf. *Quaestiones* 101, 109, 115).

Editions: PL 35, 2215-2422. — A. Souter, CSEL 50(1908), emendations to the edition of Souter in E. Löfstedt, Vermischte Beiträge zur lateinischen Sprachkunde: *Eranos* 8(1908)112-113.

Studies: A. Souter, An Interpolation in Ambrosiaster: ExpT 13(1901-02)380; *idem,* De codicibus manuscriptis Augustini quae feruntur quaestionum Veteris et Novi Testamenti CXXVII: SAW 149(1904)1-25; *idem,* An Unknown Fragment on the pseudo-Augustinian "Quaestiones Veteris et Novi Testamenti": JThSt 6(1904-05)61-66; *idem,* A Study of Ambrosiaster (TSt 7, 4). Cambridge, 1905. — G. Bardy, Ambrosiaster: DBS 1(1928)240-241; *idem,* La littérature patristique des "Quaestiones et Responsiones" sur l'Écriture sainte. L'Ambrosiaster: RBibl 41(1932)343-356. — C. Martini, Ambrosiaster. De auctore, operibus, theologia. Rome, 1944; *idem,* De ordinatione duarum Collectionum, quibus Ambrosiastri "Quaestiones" traduntur: Ant 21(1947)23-48. — G. C. Martini, Le recensioni delle "Quaestiones Veteris et Novi Testamenti" dell'Ambrosiaster: RStR 1(1954)40-62.

DUBIOUS WORKS

1. Commentary on Matthew 24

Mercati and Turner have published fragments from the manuscript *Ambrosiano* I 101 sup. (*saec.* VIII) containing an anonymous commentary on certain verses from the eschatological chapter of Matthew's Gospel (Mt. 24:20-24, 27-30, 32-35). These fragments, which show the author's moderate millenarianism and witness to a time of persecution for the church, were attributed by Mercati to an anonymous chiliast and by Turner to Victorinus of Pettau, whom he considered partly as the original author and partly as the translator of a Greek source (perhaps Hippolytus). Souter, to the contrary, maintained the possibility of Ambrosiaster's authorship and was followed in this by Martini, who has demonstrated the validity of such a thesis from both the philological and the theological point of view.

Editions: G. Mercati, Anonymi chiliastae in Matthaeum XXIV fragmenta, in Varia sacra (ST 11). Rome 1911, 1-49. — C. H. Turner, An Exegetical Fragment of the Third Century: JThSt 5(1904)218-241. — PLS I, 655-668.

Studies: A. Souter, Reasons for Regarding Hilarius (Ambrosiaster) as the Author of the Mercati-Turner Anecdoton: JThSt 5(1903-04)608-621. — Th. Zahn, Ein alter Kommentar zu Matthäus: NKZ 16(1905)419-427. — C. Martini, Ambrosiaster. De auctore, operibus, theologia. Rome, 1944. — H. J. Vogels, Ambrosiaster und Hieronymus: RB 66(1956)15.

2. *De tribus mensuris* and *De Petro apostolo*

The fragments *Incipit de tribus mensuris* and *De Petro apostolo* are also contained in the same manuscript, *Ambrosiano* I 101 sup. (*saec.* VIII), as the anonymous commentary on Matthew 24, and were published together with this latter work by Mercati.

The second of these works, the *De Petro apostolo,* in addition to treating Peter's denial, explains how the Lord, who had ordered his disciples to prepare themselves and to carry a sword (Lk. 22:36-38) subsequently forbade Peter to make use of the same at Gethsemane (Lk. 22:49-51; Mt. 26:52). The work was attributed to Ambrosiaster by Zahn, who noted a parallel with *Quaestio* 104. Martini confirmed the attribution and pointed out the affinity of the fragment with other passages from the works of Ambrosiaster.

The fragment *Incipit de tribus mensuris,* which explains the significance of the three measures of flour into which the woman in the parable (Mt. 13:33 and Lk. 13:21) has placed the yeast, has been compared with the works of Ambrosiaster by Martini, who attributed it to him on the basis of linguistic and doctrinal elements.

Editions: G. Mercati, op. cit., 46-49.

Studies: A. Souter, Reasons for regarding Hilarius (Ambrosiaster) as the Author of the Mercati-Turner Anecdoton: JThSt 5(1903-04)608-621. — Th. Zahn, Ein alter Kommentar zu Matthäus: NKZ 16(1905)419-427. — C. Martini, Ambrosiaster. De auctore, operibus, theologia. Rome, 1944. — A. Pollastri, Nota all'interpretazione de Matteo 13, 33/Luca 13, 21 nel frammento Incipit de tribus mensuris: SSR 3(1979)61-78.

3. *Lex Dei sive Mosaicarum et Romanarum legum collatio, De bello iudaico* and Other Fragments

Another group of writings has been attributed to Ambrosiaster, above all on the basis of his identification with Isaac. Such is the case, for example, with the *Lex Dei sive Mosaicarum et Romanarum legum collatio,* a work in which Mosaic and Roman laws are collected and compared in order to demonstrate the priority of the Old Testament tradition over Roman jurisprudence. The attribution to Ambrosiaster was proposed by Wittig, followed by Schanz. In 1935, Hohenlohe proposed the attribution of the work to Ambrose or one of his followers. The question of authorship remains open.

The *De bello iudaico* (or *De excidio urbis Hierosolymitanae*), which is a free translation of Flavius Josephus' work of the same title, was composed toward the end of the fourth century and has been handed down under the name of Hegesippus. This too was proposed as a work of Ambrosiaster by Wittig, but such an attribution has not met with the consent of scholars.

Finally, two fragments, the *Contra Arianos* of pseudo-Hilary and the *Sermo* 246 of pseudo-Augustine, which Martini claimed for Pelagius, have been attributed to Ambrosiaster by Wittig along with numerous other works, all on the basis of an identification of Ambrosiaster with Isaac.

Editions: Lex Dei: Th. Mommsen, Collectio librorum iuris anteiustiniani III. Berlin 1890, 136-198. — G. Baviera, Fontes iuris Romani anteiustiniani II. Florence 1968², 544-589. *De bello iudaico:* PL 15, 2061-2310. — V. Ussani, CSEL 66, 1(1932). *C. Arianos* and *Serm.* 246: PL 39, 2198-2200. — H. S. Seldmayer, Der "Traktatus contra Arrianos" in der Wiener Hilarius-Handschrift: SAW 146, 2(1903)1-18. — C. Martini, Quattuor fragmenta Pelagio restituenda: Ant 13(1938)293-334; *idem,* Ambrosiaster. Rome 1944, 189-197. — G. Morin, Hilarius l'Ambrosiaster. Appendice: Deux fragments d'un traité contre les Ariens attribués parfois à saint Hilaire: RB 20(1903)113-131.

Studies: J. Mercati, Un foglio dell'Ilario papiraceo di Vienna (ST 5). Rome 1901, 99-112. — G. Morin, Le fragment "Contra Arianos" de l'Hilaire papyrus de Vienne: SAW 146, 2(1903)18-21. — J. Wittig, Der Ambrosiaster-Hilarius. Ein Beitrag zur Geschichte des Papstes Damasus I: KGA 4(1906)4-66. — O. Scholz, Die Hegesippus-Ambrosius-Frage. Eine literarhistorische Besprechung: KGA 8(1909)149-165. — G. Morin, La Question de l'Ambrosiaster: *Anecdota Maredsolana* 2, 1(1913)8-9, *idem,* L'opuscule perdu du soi-disant Hégésippe sur les Machabées: RB 31(1914)83-91. — C. Hohenlohe, Ursprung und Zweck der "Collatio legum." Vienna, 1935. — C. Martini, Quattuor fragmenta Pelagio restituenda: Ant 13(1938)293-334; *idem,* Ambrosiaster, De auctore, operibus, theologia. Rome 1944, 161-197.

THEOLOGY

1. Trinitarian Theology

One of the basic themes present in the writings of Ambrosiaster is the affirmation of the Trinitarian faith, which constitutes the nucleus of the Christian confession. Against the Arians, the author explicitly states the consubstantiality between the ingenerate Father, the Son, generated in view of creation, and the Holy Spirit, although he also distinguishes the specific tasks of each of the persons, especially of the Father, the Creator from whom all things proceed, and of the Son, the Redeemer. Against Sabellius, on the other hand, Ambrosiaster insists on the distinction of the three divine persons and states that God is one, although not *"singularis,"* i.e., not one person only.

2. Christology

Ambrosiaster frequently maintains and defends the full divinity and humanity of Christ, in opposition to both Photinus and Marcion. The person and work of Christ, generally indicated by the titles "Savior" and "Lord" and identified with the "power" and "wisdom" of God, are in fact at the center of his theological construction. In summary, the following basic affirmations can be obtained from his thought: Christ is God and has the same prerogatives as the Father; he is also true man, composed of body and soul, having become incarnate to destroy the work of the devil and manifest himself fully to creation; in this way he fulfilled the prophecies which announced his Incarnation and redemptive work; he has exercised and continues to exercise the mediation between the Father and mankind; his divinity was in no way reduced by his Incarnation or his death; by his death and resurrection he has liberated mankind from the power of the demon and with his resurrection he has offered them the supreme manifestation of the Son of God.

3. The World, Mankind, Sin, and Redemption

God created matter and from it, by means of Christ, he made the world. He formed man from the earth in order to destroy the pride of the devil, who had aspired to become god. Man, placed in the world, was in fact to have displayed the sovereignty of the one and only God, since he contained in himself the divine image; which image was explained by Ambrosiaster in the sense that, "One single man has been created by one single God" (*Quaestio* II 3).

However, Adam preferred the devil to God, committed a sin like unto idolatry and lost the gift of immortality which God had granted him by putting at his disposal the fruit of the tree of life. The sin of the first man was reflected on the entire human race as an inheritance.

The practical consequences of the solidarity of mankind with Adam are: 1) death, both physical (applicable to all) and spiritual (bound to personal sin) and the detention of all souls in the nether world until the Redemption; 2) the corruption of the flesh, by means of which the sin of Adam is transmitted from parents to children; 3) the entrance of sin (which Ambrosiaster often identifies with the devil) into the world and its dominion over mankind, in whose members it institutes the "law of sin," taking advantage of the weakness of their fallen flesh and, consequently, of their inability to resist the suggestions of the demon. Man has sold himself to sin — the devil, who by right exercises dominion over him.

The right which Satan had acquired over sinful man was nullified by the Redemption of Christ. Ambrosiaster explains the Redemption in the following way: Christ was sent by the Father to preach to mankind a true knowledge of God and the remission of sins. The demon, afraid of losing his own power over souls, brought about the death of Christ. But since Christ was without sin and did not merit death, the devil was guilty of a sin of murder and by that very fact lost his dominion over the souls detained in the netherworld. Mankind, which used to belong to Satan, now belongs to the risen Christ who has conquered sin and death. Redeemed mankind has received justification and divine sonship through the gift of the Holy Spirit. and, furthermore, has received life and glory with the promise of the eschatological resurrection.

With the Redemption, Christ has abolished or has overcome by means of new gifts the negative consequences of Adam's sin. Nevertheless, man has not simply returned to the state of his first parent, but has acquired a far better status by receiving, for example, the Holy Spirit, which had not been given to Adam. Thus man, who now possesses body, soul, and the Holy Spirit, has grown in his own likeness to the creative Trinity, the mystery of which has been made manifest by the coming of Christ, and which is the object of the faith of the redeemed.

4. Justification and Salvation

The problem of justification is fundamental for Ambrosiaster. Leaving aside the law, justification is obtained solely by means of faith in Christ: *sola fide, sine operibus legis.* By such an expression, Ambrosiaster intends only the ritual practices of the Law (the Sabbath, circumcision, new moons, dietary laws, etc.), for only the ritual aspect of the Law has been superceded by the coming of Christ. The other part of the Law, that regarding God and morality, retains all of its value also in Christianity. The Pauline concept of justification by faith, prescinding from the Law, is therefore explained in Ambrosiaster by means of a distinction between the diverse parts or aspects of the Mosaic Law.

Furthermore, for Ambrosiaster, faith, not the Law, constitutes merit in the sight of God and brings about the claim to an eternal reward. Ambrosiaster assigns a considerable value to man's self-determination and his free will, and makes him the author of his own destiny. God aids the efforts of man and calls to salvation those whom He knows by His foreknowledge will obey and be saved.

5. Paganism and Judaism

Ambrosiaster's position in regard to paganism and Judaism is also interesting. He attributes to pagans, as to every creature, the possibility of recognizing and honoring on the basis of a natural judgment one God and Creator. The *Quaestiones* 114 and 115, entitled "Adversus paganos" and "De fato" are dedicated in particular to a discussion with pagan religion. The former of these questions, which is of a polemical and apologetic character, aims especially at criticizing the Oriental cults flourishing at Rome in the fourth century, while the latter is directed principally against astrology. For the discussion with paganism, Ambrosiaster must have made use of some writings containing philosophical objections against Christianity. It could be a question of the anti-Christian polemic of the Emperor Julian, as Cumont suggests, or of Porphyry's *Against the Christians,* as Courcelle maintains.

Ambrosiaster manifests a particular interest in and a considerable knowledge of Jewish religion, rites and customs. He takes an interest in the name "Jews" and recognizes their prerogatives, although he insists clearly on the necessity of faith for their justification. He makes note of the attitude of the Jews in regard to Christ and his Apostles (especially Paul, whose struggle with the Judaizing Christians is particularly emphasized by Ambrosiaster), and sees in the lack of faith in the Christ promised by the Law the reason for the Jewish estrangement from the Law and the Promise. He seeks the reason why the Mosaic Law was given by God (to teach man that sins are also punished by divine justice and to give him moral guidance), and explains how the Law, which brought life, was able to become the "law of death." Ambrosiaster divides the Mosaic Law into three principal parts: the divine, the natural or moral, and the ritual or law of works, to which he adds the law of vindictive justice promulgated in Leviticus 24:17-22. Of these parts, he maintains that only the natural or moral law has continued to maintain its validity with the coming of Christ, while the first and the fourth were fulfilled by Christ and the law of works was abolished. The New Law promulgated by Christ represents the epitome and at the same time the perfection of the Old.

Studies: E. Buonaiuti, La genesi della dottrina agostiniana intorno al peccato originale. Rome, 1916. — A. J. Smith, The Latin Sources of the Commentary of Pelagius on the Epistle of St. Paul to the Romans: JThSt 19(1918)162-230. — A. Casamassa, Il pensiero di s. Agostino nel 396-397, i "tractatores divinorum eloquiorum" di Retract. 1 23, 1 e l'Ambrosiaster. Rome, 1919. — A. Souter, Pelagius' Expositions of Thirteen Epistles of St. Paul (TSt 9, 1). Cambridge 1922, 176-183. — M. Zappalà, A proposito dell'Ambrosiaster: RTr 3(1922)460-467. — G. Arendt, La tradizione cattolica in favore del privilegio paolino nel coniuge infedele battezzato in una setta acattolica: Greg 4(1923)329-332. — E. Buonaiuti, Agostino e la colpa ereditaria: RR 2(1926)401-427; *idem,* Pelagio e l'Ambrosiaster: RR 4(1928)1-17. — B. Leeming, Augustine, Ambrosiaster and the "massa perditionis": Greg 11(1930)58-91. — J. Rivière, Le dogme de la Rédemption après saint Augustin. Paris 1930, 194-196; *idem,* Le "droit" du démon sur les pécheurs: RTAM 3(1931)126-130; *idem,* La "justice" envers le démon avant saint Augustin: RTAM 4(1932)308-316. — A. Gaudel, Péché originel: DTC 12(1933)367-371. — J. Jäntsch, Führt der Ambrosiaster zu Augustin oder Pelagius?: *Scholastik* 15(1934)92-99. — G. Bardy, Formules liturgiques grecques à Rome au IVe siècle: RSR 30(1940)109-112. — M. L. W. Laistner, The Western Church and Astrology during the Early Middle Ages: HThR 34(1941)251-275. — Th. Klauser, Der Übergang der römischen Kirche von der griechischen zur lateinischen Liturgiesprache, in *Miscellanea G. Mercati I* (ST 121). Vatican City 1946, 467-482. — R. Balducelli, Il concetto teologico di carita attraverso le maggiori interpretazioni patristiche e medioevali di I Cor. 13. Rome 1951, 55-72. — M. Maccarone, Vicarius Christi: *Lateranum* N.S. 18(1952)36-40. — K. H. Schelkle, Paulus, Lehrer der Väter. Düsseldorf, 1956. — O. Heggelbacher, Vom Rechtsdenken der nachkonstantinischen Zeit. Eine Studie zu sog. Ambrosiaster, Festschrift A. Ehrhard. Munich 1957; *idem,* "Vom römischen zum christlichen Recht." Juristische Elemente in den Schriften des sog. Ambrosiaster. Freibourg, 1959. — W. Dürig, Der theologische Ausgangspunkt der mittelalterlichen liturgischen Auffassung des Herrschers als Vicarius Dei: HJ 77(1958)174-187. — P. Courcelle, Critiques exégétiques et arguments antichrétiens rapportés par Ambrosiaster: VC 13(1959)133-169. — R. Aroud, Quid non est ex fide peccatum est. Quelques interprétations patristiques, in *L'homme devant Dieu.* Mélanges P. H. de Lubac I. Paris 1964, 127-145. — A. Valeschi, Lettera e spirito nella legge nuova: linee di teologia patristica: SC 92(1964)497-500. — Alessandro da Ripabottini, La dottrina dell'Ambrosiastro sul privilegio paolino: *Laurentianum* 5(1964)429-447. — L. Vökl, Von römischen zum christlichen Recht. Stellungnahme zu Heggelbachers gleichnamigem Werk in Sinn eines Beitrages zur Ambrosiaster–forschung: RQ 60(1965)120-130. — H. Crouzel, Séparation ou remariage selon les Pères anciens: Greg 47(1966)488f. — R. Cantalamessa, "Ratio paschae." La controversia sul significato della pasqua nell'Ambrosiaster, in Girolamo e in Agostino: *Aevum* 44(1970)219-241. — P. Grelot, La traduction et l'interprétation de Ph. 2,6-7. Quelques éléments d'enquête patristique: NRTh 93(1971)1009-1026.

NICETAS OF REMESIANA

There is little definite information concerning the life and activity of Nicetas, whose identity, until the end of the last century, remained shrouded in uncertainty because of confusion with Nicetas of Aquileia (454-485) and Nicetius of Trier (527-566). The figure of Nicetas was brought clearly to light as a result of the studies of Morin and Burn. Remesiana (the modern Bela Palanka in Serbia) was located in Mediterranean Dacia, which was politically joined to the East by Theodosius in 379, but remained ecclesiastically dependent on the Roman patriarchate. It is known for certain that Nicetas was twice in Italy, in 398 and 402, as the guest of Paulinus of Nola, who dedicated to him the *Propempticon* (*Carm.* 17: PL 61, 483ff), written on the occasion of Nicetas' return to Dacia. Paulinus mentions Nicetas at other places in his works (*Carm.* 27, 150ff, 651; *Ep.* 29, 14, 321). From the way he speaks, it seems that Nicetas also exercised his pastoral ministry outside the confines of the diocesan boundaries of Remesiana, and it should be kept in mind that the invasions had brought numerous pagans into the Danubian regions at that time. Nevertheless, there is no certain evidence that Nicetas preached the Gospel north of the Danube in present-day Romania.

Nicetas is also named in a letter (around 409) of Innocent I (*Ep.* 17: ibid., 527) which can be dated with certainty to 414. On the other hand, it does not seem possible to maintain the identification of Nicetas with a certain *Nicha,* who was among the addressees of a letter sent by Germinius of Sirmium to the bishops of the region (PL 13, 573; cf. also Hilary, *Fragm. hist.* 15: PL 10, 719). The year 414 remains the last chronological point of reference relative to the biography of Nicetas, thus his death must be placed after that date.

Editions: CPL 646-652. — PL 52, 837-876. — PLS III, 189-202. — A. E. Burn, Niceta of Remesiana. His Life and Works. Cambridge, 1905 (contains a general introduction). — K. Gamber, Textus patristici et liturgici 1, 2, 5, 7. Regensburg, 1964-69.

Translations: English: G. C. Walsh, FC 7(1949) (De div. Apell., De rat. fidei, De Sp. sanct. pot., De symb., De vig. serv. Dei, De util. hymn.).

Studies: W. A. Patin, Niceta, Bischof von Remesiana als Schriftsteller und Theologe. Munich, 1909. — E. Amann, DTC 11(1930)477-479. — J. Zeiller, Un ancien évêque d'Illyricum, peut-être auteur du "Te Deum," Saint Niceta de Remesiana: CRI (1942)356-369. — D. M. Pippidi, Niceta di Remesiana e le origini del cristianesimo daco-romano: *Revue historique du Sud-Est Européen* 23(1946)99-117. — I. Coman, Il campo missionario di s. Niceta di Remesiana (in Romenian): *Biserica Ortodoxa Romîna* 66(1948)337-356. S. C. Alexe, The utility of ecclesiastical chant in the community according to St. Nicetas of Remesiana (in Romenian): ibid., 75(1957)153-182. — I. Coman, L'opera letteraria di s. Niceta di Remesiana (in Romenian): *Studii teologice* 9(1957)200-232. — K. Gamber, Ist Niceta von Remesiana der Verfasser von De Sacramentis?: *Ostkirchliche Studien* 7(1958)153-172; *idem,* Ist Niceta von Remesiana der Verfasser des pseudoambrosianischen Sermo De Spiritu Sancto?: ibid., 11(1962)204-206; *idem,* Fragen zu Person und Werk des Bischof Niceta von Remesiana: RQ 62(1967)222-231. — S. C. Alexe, St. Nicetas of Remesiana and Patristic Ecumenism from the 4th to the 5th Century (in Romenian): *Studii teologice* 21(1969)453-587. — D. B. Saddington, The Educational Effect of Catechetical Instruction in the Fourth Century A.D.: *Euphrosyne* 5(1972)249-271.

WRITINGS

1. *Instructio ad competentes*

This principal work of Nicetas, which is divided into six books and is addressed to the candidates for Baptism, is extant in a fragmentary state. Gennadius (*De vir. ill.* 22: PL 58, 1073-74) states that it was written *simplici et nitido sermone* and provides information concerning the content of the individual *libelli.* From book I, *Qualiter se debeant habere competentes,* and book II, *De gentilitatis erroribus,* there remain only a few fragments. Book III was formed by two treatises which have been preserved separately: the *De ratione fidei,* which affirms the divinity and consubstantiality of the Son against the Arians, and the *De Spiritus Sancti potentia,* on the divinity of the Holy Spirit against the Macedonians. Book IV, *Adversus genealogiam* or *genethlologiam,* against the use of a horoscope, has been lost, while book V, the *Explanatio symboli,* has been preserved in its entirety and provides one of the most ancient and interesting expositions on the symbol of faith. There is a certain affinity between this work and the *Catecheses* of Cyril of Jerusalem, and it must be kept in mind that Nicetas knew Greek, even though he was Western and Latin in mentality and culture. It is important to note, too, that in this commentary on the creed there appears for the first time in Western circles the formula "communion of saints." Finally, the identification of book VI, *De Agni paschalis victima,* with the *De ratione Paschae,* variously attributed to Athanasius (PG 28, 1605) or Martin of Braga (PL 72, 49), is much discussed and remains uncertain. Cassiodorus (*Instit.* 16: PL 70, 1132) renders an interesting judgment on these baptismal catecheses when he invites those who desire to obtain a synthesis of the knowledge of the Trinity without wearying themselves by much reading to consult the book of Nicetas on the faith. In effect, this work, like the other works of Nicetas, is the fruit more of a pastoral than of a theoretical concern, in keeping with the figure of a missionary bishop.

Editions: PL 52, 847-876. — A. E. Burns. Cambridge, 1905. — K. Gamber, Textus patristici et liturgici 1, 2, 5. Regensburg, 1964-66; *idem,* Der Sermo "Homo ille." Probleme des Textes und Frage der Autorschaft: RB 80(1970)293-300 (critical edition of the sermon, preserved in three liturgical manuscripts, which is an excerpt from the *Instructio ad competentes*).

Translation: English: G. G. Walsh, FC 7(1949)13-53.

Studies: M. Simonetti, Sul "De Spiritu Sancti potentia" di Niceta de Remesiana e sulle fonti del "De Spiritu Sancto" di S. Ambrogio: *Maia* 4(1951)239-248. — K. Gamber, Die sechs Bücher "Ad competentes" des Niceta von Remesiana: *Ostkirchliche Studies* 9(1960)123-173; *idem,* Nochmals zur Schrift Ad competentes des Niceta von Remesiana: ibid., 13(1964)192-202. — G. A. Nicolae, The Teaching on the Holy Spirit in the Treatise "De Spiritus Sancti potentia" of St. Nicetas of Remesiana (in Romenian): *Ortodoxia* 16(1964)240-248. — J. Mühlsteiger, Sanctorum communio: ZkTh 92(1970)113-132. (For an important fragment of the *Instructio ad competentes* in the *cod. Vidobonensis* 515, cf. Scriptorium 26[1972]243-244).

2. *De diversis appellationibus*

This brief writing, perhaps from the period of Nicetas' youth, illustrates the various titles attributed to Christ, such as word, wisdom, light, way, truth, life, etc. Nicetas displays his pastoral concern for aiding the spiritual life of the faithful in his exposition.

Editions: PL 52, 863-866. — A. E. Burn. Cambridge, 1905. — K. Gamber, Textus patristici et liturgici 1. Regensburg 1964, 37-39 (presented as *sermo* 2 of book II of the *Instructio*).

Translation: English: G. G. Walsh, op. cit., 9-12.

3. *De vigiliis servorum Dei*

Nicetas composed this work in defense of the custom of nocturnal vigils dedicated to prayer and meditation. He illustrates the antiquity and utility of the practice with examples drawn from the Old and New Testament.

Editions: PL 30, 240-246 (among the apocryphal letters of Jerome). — PL 68, 365-372 (under the name of Nicetius of Trier). — A. E. Burn. Cambridge, 1905. — C. H. Turner, JThSt 22(1921)305-320. — K. Gamber, Textus patristici et liturgici 1. Regensburg 1964, 55-91 (presented as *sermo* 3 of book IV of the *Instructio*).

Translation. English: G. G. Walsh, op. cit., 55-64.

4. *De psalmodiae bono (De utilitate hymnorum)*

This sermon advocates, on the basis of the Scripture, the singing of hymns and psalms. It is noteworthy that Nicetas attributes the *Magnificat* to Elizabeth as well as to Mary in conformity with certain Latin biblical manuscripts.

Editions: PL 68, 371-376 (under the name of Nicetius of Trier). — PLS III, 191-198. — A. E. Burn. Cambridge 1905, 67-82. — C. H. Turner, JThSt 24(1923)225-252. — K. Gamber, Textus patristici et liturgici 1. Regensburg 1964, 93-100 (presented as *sermo* 4 of book IV of the *Instructio*).

5. *De lapsu virginis*

Attempts have been made to identify the *libellum ad lapsam virginem,* attributed by Gennadius (*De vir. ill.* 22) to Nicetas, with the pseudo-Ambrosian *De lapsu virginis* (or *De lapsu Susannae*), which is extant in two versions, one an amplification of the other. The work is addressed to a consecrated virgin by the name of Susanna, and urges her to acknowledge the fault of which she was guilty and do penance. In his edition of the text, K. Gamber has recently defended the attribution of the shorter edition to Nicetas.

Editions and Studies: PL 16, 383-400 (with the works of Ambrose). — A. E. Burn. Cambridge 1905, 112-131. — I. Cazzaniga, Corpus Scriptorum Latinorum Paravianum. Turin, 1948; *idem,* La tradizione manoscritta del "De lapsu Susannae." Turin, 1950. — K. Gamber, Textus patristici et liturgici 7. Regensburg, 1967. — G. Morin identified the *Ad lapsam virginem* mentioned by Gennadius with an *Epistula ad virginem lapsam* in RB 14(1897)198-202 (cf. A. E. Burns, op. cit., 131-136; PLS III, 199-202), but subsequently changed his opinion in: Études, textes découvertes. Maredsous 1913, 16.

6. The *"Te Deum"*

A separate treatment is merited by this hymn of thanksgiving and praise to the Trinity which formed part of the Office of Matins already in the sixth century and has been handed down in three slightly different versions. Its attribution to Nicetas, which is still under discussion and remains uncertain, is possibly due to the report of Paulinus of Nola that Nicetas composed hymns and liturgical chants (*Carm.* 17, 90ff: PL 61, 485), as well as to the fact that Nicetas wrote a sermon on liturgical chant (*De psalmodiae bono*). The *Te Deum* is composed in rhythmic prose, which is fairly unusual in Latin hymnody. Its original scheme was perhaps of Greek origin.

Editions: PL 86, 944. — A. E. Burn. Cambridge 1905, 83-91. — M. Frost, JThSt 34(1933)250-257, 39(1938)388-391, 42(1941)195-198, 43(1942)59-68, 192-194.

Translation: English: G. G. Walsh, op. cit., 65-76.

Studies: G. Morin, L'auteur du Te Deum: RB 7(1890)151-159; *idem,* Nouvelles recherches sur l'auteur du Te Deum: RB 11(1894)49-77, 337-339; *idem,* Le Te Deum, type anonyme d'anaphore latine préhistorique?: RB 24(1907)180-223. — P. Cagin, Te Deum ou Illatio? (*Scriptorium Solesmense* I, 1). Solesmes, 1906. — A. E. Burn, The Hymn Te Deum and its Author. London, 1926. — J. A. Jungmann, Quos pretioso sanguine redemisti: ZkTh 61(1937)105-107. — A. Baunstark, "Te Deum" und eine Gruppe griechischen Abendhymnen: OC 34(1937)1-26. — J. Brinktrine. Eine aufallende Lesart in der mozarabischen Rezension des Te Deum: EL 64(1950)349-351. — M. Simonetti, Studi sull'innologia popolare cristiana dei primi secoli: *Atti Acc. Naz. Lincei, Memorie Ser.* 8, 4(1952)478-481. — E. Kaehler, Studien zum Te Deum. Göttingen, 1958. — K. Gamber, Das "Te Deum" und sein Autor: RB 74(1964)318-321.

CHAPTER IV

THE TRANSLATIONS JEROME AND RUFINUS

by Jean Gribomont

THE TRANSLATIONS

From the dawn of history in Latium and Etruria, urban civilization grew up along the lines of Eastern models, and the weapons, jewelry, and vessels hidden in the tombs are either imports or copies of imported models. The appearance of writing in the seventh century B.C. was a promising sign deriving from this innovation. With the growth of Rome and the expansion of her conquests, classical art and literature came to be established on the same principle: Greek was the language not only of the manual laborer and the merchant, but was studied by the sons of the aristocracy in preference to Latin.

From the end of the first century A.D. there was a decline in Greek in the West until it disappeared in the fourth century, and though Rome continued to draw on her Greek heritage until the time of Charlemagne and beyond, she did so in an ever-decreasing amount. Possible causes of this development were the end of the importation of Eastern slaves, the orientation of commerce toward more flourishing centers such as Constantinople or a closed economy in the West. In any case, the political and administrative division of the empire functioned at the same time both as cause and effect.

During the classical period, thoroughly Hellenized souls harbored a suspicion against *latine loqui,* and a true humanism liberated Roman culture. As Greek gradually declined, there was an increase of literal, even slavish, translations, especially in Christian circles. There was an awareness of a gulf opening between earlier times, and the patrimony of the coming Middle Ages was being rapidly amassed. No longer was there a capacity for transposing, adapting, and assimilating Eastern models with any profundity, and the times were past when Eastern rhetoricians and philosophers flocked to the court of Rome for exhibitions and panegyrics.

At the end of the fourth century there remained grouped around the Senate, in the Neoplatonic circle of Macrobius, a small *élite* who were capable of commenting on Vergil and the *Somnium Scipionis* with the aid of Greek Platonic literature, as P. Courcelle has shown.

The situation was different in the church, where there was an exchange of personnel: Athanasius at Rome, Trier, Aquileia; Hilary in Asia Minor. It is evident, too, that Ambrose or Marius Victorinus, in cultural centers such as Milan and Rome, were able to make superb use of Greek literature.

To study the translations and adaptations of the fourth century, it is necessary to return to the origins of Christian Latin literature. Outside of the Christian religious tradition, there is no example known of such great importance being attached to the scrupulously faithful transmission of a sacred book across linguistic barriers. This phenomenon was tied to groups of humble culture who were incapable of direct access to the canonical texts from a world so distant in space and time, yet the content of which they ardently desired to communicate to the Western world.

There is little chronological or geographical information available concerning these ancient translations. The most complete list is that compiled by A. Siegmund, whose systematic presentation is based on the point of destination and diffusion of the ancient manuscripts. Information regarding the point of origin and the translator is as a rule inaccessible, so that Siegmund made no attempt at a classification based on a history of the translations. The general impression is that the fourth century must have been a more favorable period for this activity than an earlier age, the production of which has not been well preserved; or than a later age, when knowledge of Greek was declining. Nevertheless, it can be presumed that there were numerous exceptions to this general observation.

At Rome, the last popes for whom a Greek epitaph is preserved are Eytychian and Gaius (283, 296), while the first Latin epitaph is that of Cornelius (253). K. Wessel has collected 178 Greek Christian inscriptions in the West, of which many are without a date or are visibly later than the period under consideration. The origin of the deceased is indicated on 107 of these inscriptions, and it is almost always a question of natives of Asia Minor, Phoenicia, Egypt or Southern Italy. Half of those referred to in the inscriptions are Romans (often coming from the cemetery of the colony of merchants at St. Paul's), but 27 are from Syracuse, 10 from Salona, 7 from Aquileia, 5 from Trier, 3 from Carthage, 3 from Constantia (Romania), 2 from Rimini, 2 from Verona, 2 from Reggio Calabria and 2 from Vienne. This dispersion gives some idea of the geographical area that must be taken into consideration when dealing with the question of these translations. Around 360, Marius Victorinus (*Adv. Ar.* II 8, 35; SCh 68, 416: cf. SCh 69, 915), writing in Latin, cites a Greek *oratio oblationis* (of an Eastern "parish" at Rome?), but it is probable that many communities were already making use of a Latin liturgy; a change which in any case took place no later than the episcopate of Ambrose and Damasus. G. Bardy (op. cit., p. 157-160) has examined papal letters sent to the East in an attempt to see whether the Greek text is that of the Roman original or represents a subsequent translation.

On the basis of an *argumentum e silentio,* Bardy exaggerated the decadence of Greek in the West. Nevertheless, the fact remains that the two best specialists in translations, Jerome and Rufinus, were ignorant of the Greek language and literature up to the time of their monastic conversion. *Ante enim quam converteretur, mecum pariter et litteras graecas et linguam penitus ignorabat* (Rufinus, *Apol. contr. Hier.* II 9, 20-22: CCL 20, 91). Both of them in fact remained strangers to profane Greek culture, in spite of their sojourn in the East and Jerome's desire to display a stunning erudition. Nevertheless, their literary merits bear witness to the quality of the Roman schools around 350, while the literary career of the young Augustine, at Milan rather than Rome, and the exceptional maturity of Ambrose testify that the transfer of the capital had given Milan a new importance on the cultural as well as the political plane. Such cultural circumstances could obviously evolve from one year to another. The vicissitudes of the Arian crisis, for example, demonstrate that the West held a different ecclesiastical and intellectual position according to whether the empire was divided between two brothers (with opposing interests) or whether it was united under Constantius and Valens. The little world of the translators abounded in animosities and conflicts. Even among the supporters of the Nicene faith there can be noted that customary aggressiveness of the cultivated classes, such as in the polemical bent of Jerome which tears at Ambrose and vanquishes Rufinus. Within the treasure of Greek culture, the Arian publicists obviously chose different works than the friends of Athanasius, and it most assuredly was not Damasus who wished for the dissemination of the *Constitutiones Apostolicae.* Origen the philosopher, close to Philo and Plotinus, who was of interest to Ambrose, was not the erudite Origen passed along by Eusebius of Caesarea who interested Jerome, nor the spiritual Origen read by Rufinus and so dear to John of Jerusalem, Melania and Evagrius. Ambrose loved Basil, whom along with Gregory Nazienzus, Rufinus likewise imitated. The Pelagians, for their part, turned to Theodore of Mopsuestia and John Chrysostom. Monasticism inspired other choices and other contrasts. Just as today, for example, among modern publishing houses printing translations of German theology, one takes an interest in critical editions of texts, another in Lutheran theology, and another in Marxist, Freudian or existentialist points of view, so the Latin translators in their time followed different policies, especially from the time that Damasus succeeded in taking the initiative in hand.

Studies: K. Wessel, Inscriptiones graecae christianae veteres Occidentis. Diss., Halle, 1936. — F. Blatt, Remarques sur l'histoire des traductions latines: *Classica et Mediaevalia* 1(1938)217-242. — P. Courcelle, Les lettres grecques en Occident. De Macrobe à Cassiodore. Paris, 1943^2, 1948 (English trans. Cambridge, Mass., 1969). — G. Bardy, La question des langues dans l'Église ancienne I. Paris, 1948. — A. Siegmund, Die

Überlieferung der griechischen christlichen Literatur in der lat. Kirche bis zum XII Jahrh. Munich-Pasing, 1949. — P. Boyancé, La connaissance du grec à Rome: RELA 34(1956)111-131. — B. Altaner, Kleine patristiche Schriften (TU 83). Berlin, 1967 (survey of the translations available as sources for Augustine). — W. Berschin, Griechisch-lateinisches Mittelalter. Von Hieronymus zu Nikolaus von Kues. Bern, 1980. — F. Winkelmann, Spätantike lat. Übersetzungen der christlichen griechischen Literatur: ThLZ 95(1967)229-240. — E. Dekkers, Les traductions grecques des écrits patristiques latins: SE 5(1953)193-233.

1. The Versions of the Bible

The Bible served as the model for the Christian translations, and its story is by far the best documented and the most complex. There are innumerable manuscripts of the Vulgate containing traces of earlier translations, just as there are also numerous manuscripts containing the books of the Bible from the *Vetus Latina.* There are infinite citations, at times lengthy as in the *Florilegia* or the liturgical lectionaires, which contain precious elements for locating the editions in time and place. A whole new science has been created which is no longer a simple section of the textual criticism of the Greek Bible. With the edition of the *Vetus Latina* of Beuron, this science has reached such a level as to be able to serve as a model for the work of textual criticism in all languages. Nevertheless, those who would be able to make use of it all too often hesitate to take the necessary instruments in hand for fear of not succeeding in benefitting from them.

The documentation available in the biblical field bears witness to a prolonged and obscure process which probably affected other types of translations as well. The result was a transformation of the whole mentality of the Christian people; their vocabulary, syntax (Semiticisms), images and hopes. All the other translations and all of Christian Latin literature, especially the exegetical works, are centered around the Bible, as will be seen below (section 3, *infra*).

The first citations, those of Tertullian (ca. 200), still have a very personal character and can be integrated only with difficulty into the scheme of subsequent evolution. On the other hand, the abundant citations of the *Testimonia* and the complete collection of Cyprian's writings represent a Bible which, though the work of several translators, is fairly uniform and which is generally designated *Africana,* since it is witnessed primarily at Carthage. This designation, however, in no way indicates that its latinity connects it with any one definite province, nor is it intended to indicate the place of origin or restrict the area of dissemination. This Bible *Africana* is prior to Cyprian, who already notes some corrections. The same text occurs in a slightly more evolved form in the hands of the Donatists in the fourth century, as well as in Lactantius and in the works of Zeno of

Verona and even in the Books of Wisdom and Sirach in the Vulgate. The Greek exemplar of the *Africana* is the "Western" text, i.e., a popular form enriched with glosses and influenced by harmonizing tendencies which also survives in the ancient Syriac version *(Vetus Syra)* but which was destined to almost totally disappear in Greek under pressure from more accurate editions produced in such centers as Alexandria and Antioch.

The greater part of the Latin documentation from the succeeding period is already obviously "European." This term covers a great variety of phenomena, but fundamentally supposes the reference to a less vulgar Greek exemplar and a more modern latinity which reflects a new and more elevated social status than that of earlier times. This linguistic evolution is not without coherence, for there was no attempt to violate that spirit which required that the same Latin equivalent always had to correspond in a uniform manner to each Greek word. A judicious use of the statistics can often explain how the process developed. According to Augustine and other contemporary witnesses, the "European" editions of the Bible appeared so different one from another as to be judged the work of different translators. On the basis of their testimony, some historians defend, even today, the existence of a plurality of Latin translations. However, the most competent scholar in the field today, Bonifatius Fischer, founder of the Vetus Latina Institut of Beuron, perceives traces of the original African background in all of the European texts down to the very end of their evolution. The evolution of the text took place more rapidly in those books or chapters that were exposed to a more frequent usage, such as those employed frequently in the liturgy. It is licit to describe this same phenomenon in terms of new versions of the text, provided that recognition is given to the profound influence exercised on the versions, consciously or otherwise, by the prior translations of Jerome.

In order to appreciate clearly the strictness with which the Greek and Latin texts were compared, it is sufficient to consider the bilingual manuscripts in use since the fourth century: the *Codex Bezae* (D) of the Gospels, the *Laudianus* of Acts (E), the Claromontanus of Paul (D), the Veronensis of the Psalter (R) and others more recent. In these manuscripts the Latin text presents an earlier version corrected to bring it into conformity with the Greek text, which in these cases is still the "Western" type. Even if these bilingual texts are on the margins of the main stream of evolution of the Latin Bible, the scrupulosity with which these corrections have been made is by no means an aberrant phenomenon, as it can also be observed in a good number of revisions in instances where the Greek text was not recopied together with the Latin.

Every extant manuscript merits an individual study. Nevertheless, the relations which connect the thousands of successive waves in which the process of editing occurred also demand a comparative study to illuminate those elements which are distinctive and those which are communal in each witness. The usual procedure of the critical editions in which a normative text is established from which the variants depend is no longer sufficient, except in the case of the Vulgate, where there exists a clearly identified edition over and above the variants. Following the example of A. Jülicher, B. Fischer has conceived the idea of a multilinear edition where the variants are introduced between the lines, with an apparatus which consists of producing the necessary documentation word by word. Instead of a fixed text there is rather a movement, within which it is possible to distinguish, in the continuous lines of the text, the more significant tendencies of an evolution dominated by a certain number of types corresponding to ecclesiastical centers, literary personalities, or linguistic circles. Not even the better known centers permit the development of a rigid *stemma codicum,* inasmuch as the details of the text appear too complex and the contaminations too diversified. It is possible to reach only certain statistics, which are open to exceptions. Many ingenious theories proposed by distinguished scientists have crumbled under the careful examination of the problem in its entirety, and thus it is necessary to guard against putting too much trust in out-of-date generalities.

Within a very general frame of reference, every book of the Bible from Genesis to the Apocalypse has its own history. The first collection of relevant material was that made by P. Sabatier, whose three volumes *in folio* remain unsurpassed, in spite of their limits and the care required in their use. The Vulgate will be considered here under Jerome, along with the books translated by others. After a series of varied studies on the individual biblical books, the Institut at Beuron has begun to publish a monumental edition of the *Vetus Latina.* The volumes already published are accompanied by prolegomena which completely renew the whole question.

Editions: P. Sabatier, Bibliorum sacrorum latinae versiones antiquae seu Vetus Latina. Rheims, 1743-1749 (reprint, Turnhout 1976). — Vetus Latina. Die Reste der altlat. Bibel nach Petrus Sabatier neu gesammelt und herausg. von der Erzabtei Beuron. Freiburg: I. Verzeichnis der Sigel für Handschriften und Kirchenschriftsteller, ed. B. Fischer 1949; I, 1. Verzeichnis der Sigel für Kirchenschriftsteller, 1963[2] (with 5 supplements to 1970); II. Genesis, ed. B. Fischer 1951-1954; XI, 1. Sapientia Salomonis, ed. W. Thiele 1977ff (in process of publication); XXIV Epist. ad Ephesios, ad Philippenses et ad Colossenses, ed. H. J. Frede 1962-1971; XXV Epist. ad Thessalonicenses ad Hebraeos, ed. H. J. Frede 1975ff (in process of publication); XXV, 1. Epist. Catholicae, ed. W. Thiele 1956-1969; (vol. VII, 1. Judith has been announced). — Itala. Das Neue Testament in altlateinischer Überlieferung nach den

Handschriften hsg. A. Jülicher, W. Matzkow, K. Aland, I-IV (Gospels). Berlin, 1938-1963 (Mt.-Lk.[2] 1970-1976). — T. Ayuso Marazuela, La Vetus Latina Hispana. Madrid, 1953-1962 (Psalter; it does not appear the work will be continued). — *General collections of texts:* Old Latin Biblical Texts, 7 vols. Oxford, 1883-1923. — E. S. Buchanan, ed. Sacred Latin Texts, 4 vols. London, 1912-1916. — Collectanea Biblica Latina, 14 vols. Rome, 1912-1914. — Aus der Geschichte der lat. Bibel, 8 vols. Freiburg, 1957-1974. — A. Dold, ed. Texte und Arbeiten, 54 + 4 vols. Beuron, 1917-1964 (publications mainly of palimpsests). *Principal partial editions:* U. Robert, Pentateuchi versio latina antiquissima e cod. Lugdunensi. Paris, 1881; *idem,* Heptateuchi partis posterioris versio latina antiquissima e codice Lugdunensi. Lyons, 1900. — M. Haupt, Veteris antehieronymianae versionis libri II Regum . . . fragmenta Vindobonensia. Vienna, 1877. — R. Weber, Les anciennes versions latines du deuxième livre des Paralipomènes. Rome, 1945. — F. Vattioni, Tobia nello Speculum e nella prima Bibbia di Alcalà: Aug 15(1975)169-200. — P. M. Bogaert, La version latine du livre de Judith dans la première Bible d'Alcalà: RB 78(1968)7-32, 181-212; *idem,* Recensions de la vieille version lat. de Judith: RB 85(1975)7-37, 241-265; 86(1976)7-37, 181-217. R. Weber, Le Psautier romain et les autres anciens psautiers latins. Rome, 1953. — P. Capelle, Le texte du psautier latin en Afrique. Rome, 1913. — A. Nohe, Der Mailänder Psalter. Freiburg, 1936. — T. Ayuso Marazuela, Psalterium visigotico-mozarabicum. Madrid, 1957. — G. Hoberg, Die älteste lat. Übersetzung des Buches Baruch. Freiburg, 1902. — L. Mattei-Cerasoli, Liber Baruch. Cava, 1935. — D. de Bruyne, Les anciennes traductions latines des Machabées. Maredsous, 1932. — (Each manuscript of the Gospels has been edited separately in the above-mentioned collections, but all the oldest Latin texts are presented in Jülicher, op. cit.) — J. Belscheim, Die Apostelgeschichte und die Offenbarung Iohannis in einer alten lat. Übersetzung. Christiania, 1879; *idem,* Acta Apostolorum ante Hieronymum latine translata. Christiania, 1893. — D. de Bruyne, Les Fragments de Freising. Rome, 1921. — C. Tischendorf, Codex Claromontanus. Leipzig, 1852. — H. J. Frede, Pelagius der irische Paulustext, Sedulius Scottus. Freiburg, 1962; *idem,* Ein neuer Paulustext und Kommentar. Freiburg, 1973-74.

Studies: A bulletin on the Latin Bible, compiled by P. M. Bogaert, has been published in the RB since 1964 as a continuation of the bulletin of ancient Christian literature published in the RB since 1921. It offers a brief critical comment on numerous titles.

General Studies: E. Stummer, Einführung in die lat. Bibel. Paderborn, 1928. — B. Botte, Latines (versions): DB Suppl., fasc. 25(1952)334-347. — The Cambridge History of the Bible, vol. I. ed. P. R. Ackroyd, C. F. Evans; vol. II. ed. G. W. Lampe. Cambridge, 1969-70. — *The Itala:* H. Rönsch, Itala und Vulgata: Das Sprachidiom. Marburg, 1875. — E. Vineis, Studio sulla lingua dell'Itala. Pisa, 1974. — *Other books of the Old and New Testament:* U. Rapallo, Per una definizione diacronica e tipologica del calchi ebraici nelle antiche versioni del Levitico: RIL 103(1969)369-437. — A. V. Billen, The Old Latin Texts of the Heptateuch. Cambridge, 1927. — Richesses et déficiences des anciens psautiers latins. Rome, 1959. — J. Schildenberger, Die altlat. Proverbien. Beuron, 1941. — H. von Soden, Das lat. Neue Testament in Afrika. Leipzig, 1909. — H. J. Vogels, Evangelium Colbertinum. Bonn, 1952-53; *idem,* Untersuchungen zum Text paulinischer Briefe bei Rufin und Ambrosiaster. Bonn, 1955; *idem,* Das Corpus paulinum des Ambrosiaster. Bonn, 1957. — H. Zimmermann, Untersuchungen zur Geschichte der altlat. Überlieferung des II Korintherbriefes. Bonn, 1960. — E. Nellessen, Untersuchungen zur altlat. Überlieferung des I Thessalonicherbriefes. Bonn, 1965. W. Thiele, Wortschatzuntersuchungen zu den lat. Texten der Johannesbriefe. Freiburg, 1958. — H. J. Vogels, Untersuchungen zur Geschichte der lat. Apokalypse-Übersetzung. Düsseldorf, 1920. — (Cf. especially the *indices verborum* of Billen (Hexateuch), Capelle and Weber (Psalter), Schildenberger (Proverbs), von Soden (N.T.) and Thiele (John).)

2. Apocrypha

Since it is not possible to classify the translations from a chronological point of view, the attempt has been made to arrange them according to a structure which would reflect cultural criteria and which would extend from the more or less popular texts close to the biblical versions up to the adaptations of Neoplatonic speculation such as are found in Ambrose or in Marius Victorinus and which receive their crown in the original work of Augustine.

Obviously, not all the biblical apocrypha emerge from the same popular circles, and some were for a time accepted by the church while others are impregnated with encratism or Priscillianism. However, the *Decretum Gelasianum* (ch. 5), a sixth-century unofficial work composed possibly in southern Gaul, contains, in no apparent order, a list of 60 works noted as "apocrypha," i.e., condemned books. Not all are translations from Greek. The list in fact begins with the Acts of the Arian Synod of Rimini and contains works of Tertullian, Tyconius, Lactantius, Commodian, and Cassian. Nevertheless, it contains mainly the apocryphal Gospels, Acts, and Apocalypses, as well as Old Testament apocrypha. The rigor of censorship to which each of these works was subjected is not known. J. Daniélou did not hesitate to date some of these translations prior to Tertullian and to ascribe them to perfectly legitimate circles. These writings were often transmitted under very poor conditions, which makes it difficult to trace the eventual adaptations introduced into the primitive traditions in the fourth century at the time the new biblical translations were being revised.

Since the complete list of the editions and publications for each of these apocryphal works would be too long, the following is intended merely as a reference to the bibliographies and some of the more recent studies.

Editions: H. Dörrie, Passio SS. Machbaeorum (IV Mac.). Göttingen, 1938. — A. Siegmund, Die Überlieferung der griechischen christl. Literatur in der lat. Kirche bis zum XII Jahr. Munich-Pasing 1959, 33-48. — W. Schneemelcher, Neutestamentliche Apocryphen. Tübingen, 1959-64 *(passim)*. — B. Bischoff, Mittelalterliche Studien I. Stuttgart 1966, 150-171. — H. Kim, The Gospel of Nicodemus. Toronto, 1973. — Oratio Manassa, III-IV Esdras, Ps. 151, Epist. ad Laodicenses. In R. Weber, *Biblia Sacra,* II. Stuttgart 1975[2], 1907-1976. — Ps. Philon, Les antiquités bibliques, ed. D. J. Harrington. SCh (1976)229-230.

Studies: F. Stegmüller, Repertorium Biblicum Medii Aevi. I. Initia biblica, Apocrypha, Prologi. Madrid, 1949. — A. Kurfess, Alte lat. Sibyllenverse: ThQ 133(1953)80-96. — A. Wenger, L'assomption de la T. S. Vierge. Paris, 1955. — E. De Strycker, La forme la plus ancienne du Protévangile de Jacques. Brussels, 1961; *idem,* Une ancienne version latine du Protévangile de Jacques: AB 83(1965)365-410. — O. Mazal, Die Überlieferung des Evangelium Ps. — Matthaei in der Admonter Riesenbibel: *Novum Testamentum* 9(1967)61-68. — M. Meslin, Les Ariens d'Occident. Paris 1967, 235-244 (on the apocrypha). — J. Daniélou, La littérature latine avant Tertullien: RELA

48(1970)357-375. — M. Zelzer, Zu den lat. Fassung der Thomas-Akten: WSt 84(1971)161-179. — A. M. Denys, Concordance latine du Liber Jubilaeorum sive Parva Genesis. Louvain, 1973.

3. Exegesis

Before leaving the Bible, it is necessary to consider the exegetical works which necessarily accompanied the introduction to the Old and the New Testament in the Latin world. These works are distributed throughout an entire cultural span. The apocryphal legends constitute one form, and the pastoral homilies of a moralizing tone another. The translations of Origen or Theodore of Mopsuestia and the adaptation of rabbinical works present further forms which will be treated subsequently under Jerome and the Pelagians.

Along with the ancient translations of the Bible, treated in the preceding section, there must also be mentioned the translations and adaptations of Flavius Josephus, among which are counted the *Histories of Hegesippus* (end of the fourth century), attributed falsely but significantly to Ambrose, and for whom the authorship of Isaac the Hebrew has also been proposed. There is thus evidence of a tendency to begin biblical history from a Jewish perspective.

Latin exegesis grew out of the homilies and biblical commentaries composed for the purpose of edification and which have been treated in the sections dedicated to the various authors: Hilary, Fortunatianus, Chromatius, Zeno, Gaudentius, Maximus, Peter Chrysologus, Gregory of Elvira, the Africans, Nicetas and the anonymous writers. Except perhaps in Africa, it is possible to recognize with the passage of time, and even in the works of a single preacher, a gradual increase of Greek influence, especially of an Origenist tendency. This is especially true in Hilary and Ambrose.

These exegetical-homiletic compositions were transmitted under unfavorable circumstances. The level of culture by the end of the fourth century contributed to the loss of earlier compositions, and it was not least of all the new Trinitarian orthodoxy which counseled the advisability of letting them disappear completely. Half of the fourth century thus has the aspect of a literary desert in which it is difficult to follow the traces of Greek influence. At the very end of this period — provided P. Nautin is correct in his identification of the author of the *Opus imperfectum in Matthaeum* with the Arian priest, Timothy of Constantinople — an Arian Latin, who occasionally drew inspiration from Jerome, translated this work along with Origen's commentary on Matthew (*Vetus interpretatio* as *Commentariorum series:* CCS 10 and 11), and perhaps also the fragments on Luke (PLS I, 327-344).

Other works are of a more technical nature. The later Latin Bibles are provided with *Capitula,* summaries to aid in finding a desired text, to which prefaces are sometimes added. Such instruments go back in part to this period and represent a serious attempt at an introduction to the sacred books. The *Onomastica* containing the explanations of Hebrew (proper) names are numerous, and not a few were translated before the time of Ambrose. The *Quaestiones* on the Old and New Testament of Ambrosiaster, as well as his Pauline commentaries and those of Marius Victorinus, which are treated in the sections devoted to the works of these two authors, have a true scientific value and display a sound knowledge of contemporary Greek exegesis, which they do not hesitate to oppose on occasion. H. J. Frede has recently discovered another commentary to the Pauline epistles which is prior to that of Pelagius, with which it displays points of contact at least with regard to its Antiochene tendency, to prescind from its theology of grace. Finally, mention must be made of the commentary on Job (PG 17, 371-522), which Nautin holds to be a possible translation from Greek in opposition to M. Meslin.

Editions: V. Ussani, Hegesippi qui dicitur Historiae libri V: CSEL 66 and 66, 2 (1932-1960). — C. Boysen, Flavii Iosephi Opera ex versione latina antiqua: CSEL 37(1898). — F. Blatt, The Latin Josephus. I. Copenhagen, 1958. — (The *Capitula* are edited with the various books of the Vulgate in the major critical editions.) — F. Wutz, Onomastica sacra. Leipzig, 1914-1915. — P. Salmon, Les Tituli Psalmorum des manuscrits latins. Rome, 1959. — J. Regul, Die antimarcionitischen Evangelienprologe. Freiburg, 1969. — H. J. Frede, Ein neuer Paulustext und -kommentar. Freiburg, 1973-74.

*Studies:*B. Altaner, Kleine patristiche Schriften (TU 83). Berlin 1967, 437-447. — M. Meslin, Les Ariens d'Occident. Paris, 1967. — The Cambridge History of the Bible. I and II. Cambridge, 1970, 1969. — P. Nautin, Review of Meslin, op. cit.: RHR 177(1970)70-89; *idem,* L'opus imperfectum in Matthaeum et les Ariens de Constantinople: RHE 67(1972)381-408, 745-766. — R. Girod, La traduction latine anonyme du Commentaire sur s. Matthieu, in *Origeniana.* Bari 1975, 125-138.

4. Hagiography

The hagiographical legends are in general addressed to the same audience as the biblical apocrypha, and some of them have in fact been inserted in the Gelasian Decree. The *Acts of Peter* and those of Paul and Thecla combine the two literary genres and were altered on several occasions during the fourth century precisely as versions of Scripture. The intent of this section is to give a general view of the evolution of this literature and of the role played by the various translations. However it is far from possible to be able to compose a synthesis which distinguishes by region and chronological period the various nuances according to which the cult of the martyrs developed among the Greeks and the Latins. The information in this section will be limited to this cult, while the following section will treat of monastic literature.

In bilingual regions, it is perhaps necessary to regard two editions of one and the same text (Greek and Latin) as twins rather than as original and translation. The problem arises already at the beginning of the third century with the passion of Perpetua and Felicity (BHL 6633-34) and that of the martyrs of Scillium (BHL 7527-28). At this point, Latin Christian literature was still in its beginning stages, which may explain the presence of the Greek version. An analogous problem is presented by some of the treatises of Tertullian. Two martyrs under Diocletian, Euplus of Catania (BHL 2728-31) and Irenaeus of Sirmium (BHL 4466) were both from bilingual regions, and if the Latin texts of their martyrdom are truly ancient, it is possible that they are contemporary with the Greek versions. The question has been raised whether Egypt may be considered in some way among the bilingual regions with the *passiones* of Dioscorus (BHL 2203ff) and Philea of Thmuis (BHL 6799), as the *passio* of the latter of these in Latin is known already by Rufinus. Both of these are valuable documents whose translation at an early date can be easily understood. Unfortunately, these attempts were not followed by others. The region around Adrianople, where Philip, bishop of Heraclea, was martyred under Diocletian (BHL 6834) is perhaps also to be considered as bilingual in this period. There are reasons for supposing that the Latin text of his *passio* is a free adaptation of a lost Greek original.

Other texts also come from Asia Minor, such as the ancient version of the martyrdom of Polycarp (BHL 6870), the *passio* of Pionius, who died under Decian (BHL 6852) and that of Carpus, Papilus, and Agathonike of Pergamum. Since Eusebius associates Pionius and Carpus with the memory of Polycarp, in spite of the chronological and geographical differences, there is a possible connection between all these texts, which could have come from Smyrna. The Latin versions of these texts are all free adaptations. The *Acta disputationis Acacii* (BHL 25), of uncertain origin, also can be added to this list. The Greek text has been lost, but it must have been of good quality, and seems to have been the exemplar for the Latin copy.

It should be noted that none of these versions comes from Rome. Their geographical diversity suggests that it is a matter of texts which arose in the outlying areas of the empire.

The *inventio* of St. Stephen (BHL 7850) constitutes an unusual case. It was composed by Avitus of Braga around 415 and is presented as the translation of a lost Greek original. It can be questioned, however, whether this is not merely a contrivance to lend greater credibility to the text.

Editions and Studies: Cf. the works of the Bollandists or the various articles of the Bibliotheca Sanctorum. Rome, 1961-70. — A. Siegmund, Die Überlieferung der griechischen christlichen Literatur in der lat. Kirche bis zum XII. Jahrhdt. Munich-Pasing 1949, 214-225 (very general treatment). — B. Fischer, Vetus Latina I, 1.

Freiburg 1963[2], 23-57 (provides a list of the *vitae* of the saints with information concerning period, Latin text and the possible existence of a Greek exemplar). — J. Griboment, Panorama des influences orientales sur l'hagiographie latine: Aug 24(1984)7-20.

5. Monastic Literature

For obvious reasons, no monastic literature was translated before the second half of the fourth century, and in the majority of cases it is a question of translations which are later than the period under examination here. In a certain sense, monastic literature represents the same popular phenomenon as the biblical writings, the apocrypha and hagiography, as monasticism arose out of humble surroundings from which no literature would ever have proceeded had not that extraordinary spiritual revolution intervened and thrust the monastic movement into the center of attention. Nevertheless, a revolution often produces leaders of great ability, and Athanasius, Basil, and Evagrius, whose ascetical works were rapidly disseminated in the West, did not belong to the inferior levels of the cultural world. It happens every now and then that intellectuals who have broken with their own class become in fact the most active transmitters of the subversive germ which has infected them back across the cultural barrier. The Latin translators who occupied themselves with monastic literature were often of a superior cultural formation, which nevertheless did not hinder them from preaching the counter-culture of the Copts, much to the scandal of the pagan traditionalists who were locked in their sterile imitation of the classics.

Athanasius sought and obtained the support of the monastic movement in his long struggle against Arianizing imperial policy. The *Vita Antonii,* which is a panegyric of the hero of this popular movement, offered Athanasius an unexpected opportunity to seal this alliance by sketching the profile of the thaumaturge faithfully bound to the cause of the bishop and the Catholic faith. Although written in Greek (357?), the *Vita* was directed in particular to the Westerners (Prologue, PG 26, 837A) and was immediately translated, twice in fact, into Latin. Evagrius of Antioch, an Easterner of noble birth and a convinced Nicene, who had lived in Italy for many years (the same Evagrius who brought Jerome to the East and who became bishop of the intransigent Nicene minority at Antioch), made an elegant Latin translation around 370 which enjoyed enormous success and exercised a decisive influence on the formation of monastic latinity. Another translation, an anonymous one, which has been preserved in only one manuscript, seems to be an incomplete effort which is full of trial attempts preserved under the form of duplicate translations. H. W. Oppenbrouwers has even suggested that it was a translation begun for passing pilgrims in Egypt at the "outer mountain," the guest quarters of Anthony's monastery, and he makes note of a curious Origenism. Whatever the story of this text, it would be a mistake to search therein for an echo of a monastic Latin, which did not yet exist. Thus, it is all the more valuable an aid for demonstrating how a Latin could attempt to interpret the monastic phenomenon which was still alien to his tradition.

Except for the work of Jerome and Rufinus, the monastic translations are probably later than the period under consideration here. Two versions of the *Senteniae* of Evagrius to monks and virgins are extant, one a translation by Rufinus and the other anonymous (Gennadius?). There are also two versions of the *Historia lausiaca,* one incomplete and both leaving much to be desired. The ancient translations of two ascetic discourses of pseudo-Basil have been published, one found among the works of Chrysostom and the other discovered by Wilmart. The works of Ephrem in Latin present a complete mystery. It is certain that after the deaths of Augustine and Cassian, the Western world showed a greater interest for this type of work than for the speculations of Greek theology.

Some monastic traditions arrived in the West by means of oral transmission. Martin of Tours was evidently acquainted with some of these, as is witnessed by Sulpicius Severus. John Cassian presents the typical example in his dialogues with famous persons, filled with references to Evagrius or to Origen.

The Eastern narratives of the monastic world inspired medieval literature down to Boccaccio.

Editions: Vita Antonii, version of Evagrius: PG 26, 837-976 (bottom of the page). *Anonymous version:* G. Garitte. Brussels-Rome, 1939. — H. Oppenbrouwers. Nijmegen, 1960. — G. J. M. Bartelink, Milan, 1974. *Evagrius, Sententiae:* PL 20, 1181-1188 = PG 40, 1277-1286. *Alternate version:* A. Wilmart: RB 28(1911)143-153 and J. Leclercq: *Scriptorium* 5(1951)195-213 (Cf. CPG 2888 and 2890).

Studies: T. T. Lorie, Spiritual Terminology in the Latin Translation of the Vita Antonii. Utrecht-Nijmegen, 1955. — H. W. Oppenbrouwers, La technique de la traduction dans l'antiquité d'après la première version latine de la Vita Antonii, in Mélanges Ch. Mohrmann. *Nouveau Recueil.* Utrecht-Antwerp 1973, 80-95.

6. Canonical and Ecclesiastical Documents

These are the translations of the official declarations and proceedings of synods which are easily dated, at least with regard to the *terminus post quem.* The number of these documents multiplies after 430, but already from 256 there is preserved in the collection of Cyprian's letters a letter (*Ep.* 75) of Firmilian of Caesarea in Cappadocia which was probably translated at Carthage. The translation of the creed and the canons of Nicea probably took place after the double synod of Serdica (343) and shortly before that of Rimini-Seleucia (359), both of which occasions forced the Eastern and

Western episcopates to compare their respective positions. At Rome, in order to "improve" the Nicene canons in favor of the Apostolic See, the Western canons of Serdica were added to them without distinction; a procedure which in 419 provoked the most vigorous protests from the African Church as well as the significant phenomenon of requests to Alexandria, Antioch and Constantinople for new and more exact translations. The first Latin text of the Nicene creed appeared at Rimini, while Hilary translated other Eastern formulas of faith in his *De synodis*. For their part, the Arians circulated a Latin version of other canonical authorities: the *Canons of the Apostles*, the *Didascalia* and the *Apostolic Tradition*.

Editions: C. H. Turner, Ecclesiae Occidentalis Monumenta Iuris Antiquissima. Oxford, 1899-1939. — E. Tidner, Didascaliae Apostolotum, Canonum ecclesiasticorum, Traditionis apostolicae versiones latinae. Berlin, 1963.

Studies: E. Schwartz, Die Kanonessammlungen der alten Reichskirche. In *Gesammelte Schriften*. IV. Berlin 1960, 203-270 and *passim*. — G. L. Dossetti, Il Simbolo di Nicea e di Costantinopoli. Rome, 1967. — Y. M. Duval, Une traduction latine inédite du symbole de Nicée et une condamnation d'Arius à Romini: RB 82(1972)7-25.

7. Pastoral Works

Following a somewhat artificial scheme, an attempt will be made here to divide the authentically patristic works into two categories by taking into account the cultural level with which they are concerned: pastoral works on the one hand and philosophical-religious compositions on the other.

The most ancient translations, which possibly go back to the second century, were connected with the books of the Bible and were the object of subsequent revisions. These included the *Didaché* (or rather one of its sources, the *Duae viae*), the letter of Clement, Barnabas, and Hermas. (The translation of Ignatius goes back only to the Middle Ages.)

The *Adversus haereses* of Irenaeus presents a work of considerable length which was probably translated only in the fourth century with an antiheretical intent. The technique of the translation is particularly important, above all when it concerns a passage for which the original Greek has been lost.

The supposed Roman background of Hippolytus was not sufficient to have him translated into Latin, except for his *Chronicle (Liber generationis)* and, in the area of canonical literature, the *Apostolic Tradition* (cf. section 6, *supra*). In spite of this fact, Gregory of Elvira, Ambrose, and Gaudentius of Brescia drew inspiration from his exegesis. It is possible that the relatively aristocratic character of his culture was responsible for the scarce dissemination of his works, as had been the case with the Apologists, unless there was some censure applied against them.

In the case of Tertullian, it is perhaps the author himself who was responsible for the translations, if the Greek text (lost) of the *De spectaculis*, the *De baptismo* and the *De virginibus velandis* was prior to the Latin edition. In the case of these texts as with the *Passiones* of the African martyrs (cf. section 4, *supra*) it is a question of the origins of Latin Christian literature.

From the semi-Arian, Eusebius of Emesa, there exists a fine collection of homilies in Latin which was possibly already known to Ambrosiaster. The cathechetical homilies of Cyril of Jerusalem were not translated, although they inspired Ambrose and Nicetas of Remesiana. The rites described by Cyril were perhaps too different from those in use in the West.

It is strange that, except for the *Vita Antonii*, the works of Athanasius were not translated in the fourth century, in spite of the authority which he enjoyed in the West. In fact, his polemical works lagged somewhat behind the actual events as a result of his exile and his difficulties in precisely understanding his adversaries. It is possible that this lack of contemporaneity did not go unnoticed.

A homily has preserved an extract from a lost work of Didymus, but it is difficult to tell whether the translation dates back to this period. Only one book of Didymus, the *De Spiritu Sancto*, was translated, which will be treated in the section on Jerome.

The dedicatory letter of the translator of the dialogue against the Jews, the *Disputatio Iasonis cum Papisco*, of Aristo of Pella, has been preserved, and the anti-Manichaean *Acta Archelai* of Hegemonius were translated around 400, perhaps in Africa. Finally, the *Anacephalaiosis* attributed to Epiphanius of Salamis was known to Augustine around 423 in either Greek or Latin, as was the *De mensuris et ponderibus* of the same author.

Editions: For details concerning works and authors, cf. A. Siegmund, Die Überlieferung der griechischen christlichen Literatur in der lat. Kirche bis zum XII Jahrhdt. Munich-Pasing, 1949 and also the CPG. — E. Buytaert, Eusèbe d'Emèse. Discours conservés en latin. Louvain, 1953-57. — P. M. Bogaert, Fragment inédit de Didyme l'Aveugle en traduction latine ancienne: RB 73(1963)9-16.

Studies: S. Lundström, Neue Studien zur lat. Irenäusübersetzung. Lund, 1948; *idem*, Übersetzungstechnische Untersuchungen auf dem Gebiete der christlichen Latinität. Lund, 1955.

8. Platonism and Erudition

It was especially the pastoral and homiletic aspect of Origen's works which found a resonance in the Latin world. As has been noted in connection with exegesis, many preachers found a rich nourishment in Origen up to the time when Jerome and Rufinus undertook the systematic exploitation of his work. Nevertheless, P. Courcelle and P. Hadot have recently demonstrated that the Origenism of Ambrose is bound to an erudite Neoplatonism which also includes the use of Philo and Bail, and of which Marius Victorinus was an exponent before his conversion.

It would be interesting to know the atmosphere in which the Archdeacon Calcidius received his formation, who translated and commented the *Timaeus* of Plato, making use of Porphyry, but following Numenius more closely than Plotinus. Obviously, mention must also be made of the work of the Platonizing circles which played a role in the conversion of Augustine.

Basil and Gregory Nazienzus, in effect, went beyond Origenism. Rufinus is the great advocate of this Origenism, but Basil also knows of other routes, which he follows above all in his homilies on the *Hexaemeron*. These were subsequently used by Ambrose and were translated in their entirety around 400 by Eustathius in Italy. The translation of the *Physiologus*, made about the same time, also can be attributed to these same circles.

How the work of the Cappadocians, and of Gregory of Nyssa in particular, remained outside the mainstream of Western thought in regard to its more significant manifestations remains unclear. Its exceptional importance was immediately recognized, but there seem to have been factors which held it in check. One possible explanation is offered by the antipathy of Rome toward the ecclesiastical policy of Basil or towards the Council of Constantinople of 381. Another explanation could be an anti-Origenist opposition arising from a sort of inferiority complex, or simply the inability to rise to that cultural level, which was equally as demanding as the most important works of Origen or the apologetical works of Eusebius. Rufinus conceived an interest for this work, but was paralyzed by the opposition of his enemies.

It must also be questioned whether the connection of the Pelagians with the school of Antioch is merely the result of the vicissitudes of history. Chrysostom's homilies on Paul, Matthew, and *ad neophytos* were translated by Anianus of Celeda (415-419) for both theological and exegetical purposes, and Theodore of Mopsuestia was subsequently translated or adapted by Julian of Eclanum. In spite of its somewhat marginal character, this current of thought was not without influence on medieval exegesis.

Augustine himself, in his *Contra Iulianum,* cites passages of Chrysostom on several occasions. Three of these passages (and two passages cited later by Leo the Great) reappear in a collection of 38 homilies, some translated from Greek, others authentically Latin, which circulated under Chrysostom's name. The translation of the Greek homilies has been attributed to Anianus of Celeda and was the result of an attempt to find authoritative support for the Pelagian party;

which criterion could have guided the selection of texts. However, the unity of the Greek section is problematic. In at least one instance the existence of a revision of the primitive Latin text has been demonstrated. In any case, of the texts attributed by Augustine to Chrysostom, one is from Potamius of Lisbon, and another, which does not belong to the collection of 38 homilies, comes from the *Homilia exhortatoria ad sanctum baptisma* of Basil of Caesarea, of which no Latin version is known.

Editions: Cf. n. 7 *supra.* — E. Amand de Mendieta, S. Y. Rudberg, Eustathius, Ancienne version latine des homélies sur l'Hexaéméron de Basile de Césarée. Berlin, 1958. — J. H. Waszink, Timaeus a Calcidio translatus (Plato latinus 4). London-Leiden, 1962; *idem,* Calcidius: JAC 15(1972)236-244. — L. De Coninck, Iuliani Aeclanensis. Opera: CCL 88; *idem,* Theodori Mopsuesteni Expositio in Psalmos: CCL 88A. — H. B. Swete, Theodori episcopi Mopsuesteni in epistolas B. Pauli Commentarii. Cambridge, 1880-1882.

Studies: M. Huglo, Les anciennes versions latines des homélies de s. Basile: RB 64(1954)129-132. — A. Wilmart, La collection des 38 homélies de saint Jean Chrysostome: JThSt 19(1918)305-327 (cf. J. A. de Aldama, Repertorium pseudochrysostomicum. Paris 1965, 222-223). — J. P. Bouhot, Version inédite du sermon "Ad neophytos" de S. Jean Chrysostome, utilisée par S. Augustin: REAug 17(1971)27-41. — B. Altaner, Augustinus und Basilius der Grosse: RB 60(1950)17-24 (= Kleine patristiche Schriften) (TU 83). Berlin 1967, 269-276; *idem,* Augustinus und die griechische Patristik: RB 62(1952)201-215 (= *loc. cit.,* 316-331).

9. General Summary

The systematic work of Jerome and Rufinus comes at the end of a long trajectory of Greek thought in the West, in which all social classes played some part. Although the historians of philosophy tend to give a privileged place to the importance of Neoplatonism, the Bible and its exegesis nevertheless remain the true center of interest, both from the point of view of the quantity of versions and revisions as well as from that of the scope and profundity of its influence on the Christian people. It is no accident that the police of Diocletian vented their fury explicitly on the "drug" represented by the sacred books, while the martyrs, their minds and hearts steeped in the Scriptures, boasted of possessing them in their hearts, out of reach of all destruction. Even if the hierarchy preserved its role of safeguarding the canon, it was the entire people who tested the fidelity of the translations and interpretations.

With regard to this slow assimilation, we have particular information on points of detail, but the only overall view is that offered by the monumental *Vetus Latina* of Beuron, with its successive lines of emendation. It is a question of a relative, not an absolute, chronology in an anonymity lifted to some extent by the initials invented by scholars. As for geography, the epigraphical and hagiographical texts focus attention on the peripheral zones. However, the well-known examples of Hilary, Evagrius of Antioch, Jerome, Rufinus, and Cassian serve as a good reminder not to forget the role of the travelers alongside the established institutions. Rome does not seem to have exercised such a central role as might have been expected. Then as today, it was the work of other centers of learning which was followed and disseminated at Rome.

It is difficult to know just how to measure the importance of this phenomenon in Western culture. The linguistic consequences of this operation can be clarified if the role of the Bible and of hagiography in providing linguistic models is recalled. It is possible to speak of a "Christian Latin," the expression of a cultural revolution, which is conditioned in its vocabulary and syntax by the Bible. The problem is a broader one, however, since this Christian Latin fits into the context of the evolution of popular and late Latin, in the company of Trimalchio and the *Mulomedicina.* The graffiti of Pompeii show that the atmosphere in which the new faith spread was not one which always respected the rules, orthographic and otherwise, of the classical style, but that much in the way of popular Greek or, indirectly, Hebrew, it had at its disposal basic expressions which arose from the nature of the language. The authority which these imitations enjoyed facilitated the renewal of the written language and constituted a phenomenon of immense historical importance. Refined men of letters such as Jerome recognized the validity of this new literature.

Studies: C. Mohrmann, Études dur le latin des chrétiens I-IV. Rome, 1958-77. — E. Löfstedt, Late Latin. Oslo, 1959. — O. Hiltbrunner, Latina Graeca. Semasiologische Studien über lat. Wörter im Hinblick auf ihre Verhältnis zu griech. Vorbildern. Bern, 1958. — S. Elkund, The Periphrastic, Completive and Finite Use of the Present Participle in Latin with Special Regard to Translations of Christian Texts in Greek up to 600 A.D. Uppsala, 1970. — F. Abel, L'adjectif démonstratif dans la langue de la Bible latine. Tübingen, 1971.

JEROME

Eusebius Hieronymus, who holds pride of place among the translators, was born at the edge of the Latin world in the tiny fortified city of Stridonia on the border between Dalmatia and Pannonia. The region, ravaged by the Goths during the lifetime of the saint (ca. 376), seems to have been closely attached to Latin culture. In the neighboring cities of Aquileia, *Altinum,* Concordia, and *Haemona* (Lubiana), Jerome made his life-long friends and enemies. The date of his birth is disputed, since in his later years Jerome complained so of the burden of his age that Augustine, who never saw him, affirmed that he died "old and decrepit." The chronicle of Prosper places his death in his ninety-first year, and makes 331 the year of his birth. F. Cavallera, however, has brought together multiple indications which point to 347 as the *terminus post quem,* and it seems better to accept this date, even though there is no lack of those who would gladly sacrifice something for the sake of tradition.

His brother, Paulinian, and his younger sister followed Jerome into monastic life, which suggests that his father, Eusebius, was a pious Christian. He possessed property, *villulae* (*Ep.* 66, 14), the sale of which in 398 necessitated a trip on the part of Paulinian, who at that time was residing in Bethlehem. Eusebius provided an education for his son, but since he remained a provincial without great renown, Jerome was obliged to continually seek out benefactors and benefactresses; something which exercised an influence on his character, alternatingly adulatory and irritable to an extreme degree.

Toward 360-367, while still very young, he undertook an excellent course of studies in grammar and then rhetoric at Rome. Aelius Donatus was the master toward whom he showed the most gratitude, but all of his works display a familiarity with the classics, especially Cicero and Vergil, and an exceptional stylistic vigor, which was further honed by polemic. Even if he learned the rudiments of Greek, it was only in the East that he acquired a fluency in this tongue, and he always remained ignorant of classical Greek literature, in spite of his efforts to pretend the contrary. In his youth he transcribed a veritable library of secular works which subsequently proved to be of great value. It is possible that during this time when he was attempting to learn the basics of philosophy, which was never his specialty, he allowed himself some experience of the "*dolce vita,*" since he was not as yet baptized. He did not break his ties with his compatriots, Bonosus, Rufinus, and Heliodirus, with whom it was his custom "to visit on Sundays the tombs of the Apostles and martyrs. We penetrated into the subterranean crypts where the bodies of the departed were buried to the right and the left. It was so dark that it seemed as though the verse of the psalm was being fulfilled and we were descending alive into the netherworld. Here and there a ray of light eased the dreadful darkness." There then follows a verse from the *Aeneid* (2, 755) to balance the citation of Ps. 54:16, illustrating the delicate sensitivity of the author (*In Hiez.* 12, 244-254).

Although he was proud of having been baptized in Rome, Jerome does not speak of the circumstances in which he took that step. He then left Rome to seek his fortunes in the imperial city of Trier, and it was there that he was seduced by the Eastern ideal of monasticism, then in vogue. It is known, too, that he occupied his spare time in copying the works of Hilary. He returned to his homeland together with Bonosus around 370 and for some years lived with Rufinus, Chromatius, and Heliodorus as a "choir of the blessed" grouped around Valerian, bishop of Aquileia (Jerome, *Chronicle,* year 374).

This beatitude ended in quarrels, due among other things to the sharp tongue of the young ascetic (*Ep.* 7, 11 and 12). For Jerome and Rufinus, these disagreements turned into an opportunity for a pilgrimage to the monastic world of the East. In 373, Evagrius of Antioch, the nobleman and friend of Jerome who translated Athanasius, returned home, and Jerome either followed him or perhaps went with him since, like Evagrius, he too passed through Cappadocia. The first of Jerome's letters which have been preserved date from this period — a happy consequence of his being away from home. These letters are still seasoned with Vergil, but their author had by this time begun to come into serious contact with Greek. During a period of asceticism in the so-called Desert of Chalcis (south of Aleppo), he took advantage of the presence of a converted Jew to undertake an exercise in intellectual asceticism: his initiation into Hebrew.

In spite of the ardent praises with which he invited his friends to come to the desert, this eremitical novitiate lasted less than two years (375-377), and was agitated by disputes with the monks of the place, whose orthodoxy Jerome, strong in his Roman faith, did not even attempt to understand. Since the Antiochene Schism was at its height, Evagrius attached himself to the small ultra-Nicene minority guided by Paulinus. It was in these circumstances, after his experience in the Chalcis, that Jerome received ordination to the priesthood, albeit without any pastoral responsibilities. Paulinus was seeking followers and thus Jerome did not have a community to serve. The experience of the desert had in any case been exceptionally fruitful both for Jerome's linguistic skills as well as for his spiritual life, and he saw therein a claim to glory in his own eyes as well as in those of the West. In the meanwhile, Rufinus had remained in Egypt and Bonosus had become a hermit on an island off the coast of Illyria.

It was at Chalcis that his famous "vision" took place, in which Jerome saw himself flogged before the tribunal of Christ for having remained more a Ciceronian than a Christian. His vivid account of this nightmare to the young Eustochium (*Ep.* 22, 30), encouraging her to study the Bible, exposes a genuine psychological crisis, which, however, never forced him to take seriously the literary oath he swore on that occasion. In any case, no interruption can be noticed in his custom of citing the classics, and in later years in the course of their quarrels, Rufinus took great pleasure in reminding Jerome of this oath.

The schism of the Antiochene Church was not an obstacle to the progress of exegesis in both factions. Diodore, a coadjutor of Meletius and future bishop of Tarsus, began an approach to the Scriptures based on a certain rationalism which is known as the Antiochene

School of exegesis. At that time, Jerome, who belonged to the opposing faction, displayed a taste for other things. He was acquainted with the exegete, Apollinarius of Laodicea, an old friend of Paulinus. Although his doctrine on the Incarnation was tending to become more than suspect, relations had not yet arrived at a final break, and Jerome followed his lessons, at least as far as exegesis was concerned.

Around 380, it was necessary for Paulinus to travel to Constantinople to seek the recognition of his episcopal authority from the new emperor, Theodosius. His rival, Meletius, was growing old and some peaceful souls, such as Gregory Nazienzus, who at that time was bishop of the capital, would have liked to have taken advantage of the death of one of the two competitors to reach an accommodation. However, the Council of Constantinople came to decisions of another sort; Gregory resigned his office and returned to his poems, while Paulinus along with his protector, Epiphanius of Cyprus, and his secretary, Jerome, set off for Rome to seek the aid of Pope Damasus. The encounter with Gregory had confirmed Jerome in his nascent enthusiasm for Origen, whom he began to translate. (According to P. Nautin, the translation of the homilies of Origen had begun already at Antioch.)

At Rome, the influence of his Eastern patrons and the prestige of his learning and ascesis opened many doors to Jerome. Damasus, who by this time was a peacemaker of nearly eighty, took him as his secretary and confidant "in chartis ecclesiasticis" (*Ep.* 123, 9). This work did not prevent him from extending his apostolate into the salons of aristocratic women, in the houses of the widows Marcella and Paula (the mother of Eustochium). The demands of these biblical circles constrained him to improve his Hebrew with the help of a rabbi, who gave him books and lessons. He even taught the rudiments of the sacred language to his noble benefactresses, who probably already had a formation in Greek. Rome was at that time overwhelmed by a tide of ascetic propaganda whose currents were at times contradictory and led inevitably to mutual criticisms. Pious and erudite letters, brilliant disputations and satires of the clergy all came together in this debut which presaged an exceptional career. Jerome believed himself to already be the designated successor of Damasus.

With the election of Pope Siricius in December 384, the atmosphere changed and the following summer, Jerome shook the dust from his sandals on the hostile city and the "Senate of the Pharisees" who had dared to malign his friendship with the noble ladies. Nautin shrewdly notes (*L'excommunication,* p. 8) that Paula and Eustochium departed ostensibly after Jerome but joined him at Reggio Calabria and continued with him to Cyprus, where they were greeted by their friend, Epiphanius, and then to Antioch, where they were received by Evagrius. In the East, these allies of the deceased Damasus were a slight bit embarrassing. An expedition organized by Paulinus undertook a systematic pilgrimage to the holy places, perhaps with a piety less candid than Egeria would show some years later, but with the scientific interests which already characterized the thought of Jerome, for whom allegories were no longer sufficient and who did not hesitate to make recourse to erudite Jews (prologue to the Hexapla translation of Paralipomenon). Paula carried her alms into Egypt, where it was necessary to go to become acquainted with the paradise of the monks. Jerome took advantage of this opportunity to school himself in the Origenist gnosis of Didymus the Blind.

In the summer of 386 the dual ascetic community took up residence in Bethlehem, some distance from the noise of Jerusalem and also from Rufinus and his benefactress Melania, who were installed on the Mount of Olives, and who showed themselves more closely bound to Egyptian Origenism without those reservations which grew up between bishop John and Jerome, the priest of Paulinus of Antioch. The monastery at Bethlehem, which remained a Latin community, included three classes of religious divided according to social rank, as well as guest quarters. The exceptional library of Caesarea, founded by Origen and enriched by Eusebius, was within easy reach, and presented ideal conditions for a biblical school. There were lacking only the excavations, which in any case were not all that necessary at a time when antiquity was still alive and Judaism was flourishing at the very gate of this polyglot chaplain of a multi-millionairess.

The foundation at Bethlehem was thus accompanied by an intense literary activity: meticulous biblical translations, adaptations of exegetical treasures, and, for diversion, a few novels of monastic hagiography. The style is less affected than that of previous years and is more pleasing to modern tastes. The Old Testament took precedence over the New, and Hebrew over Greek. Ecclesiastical history attracted Jerome for a certain time, but he limited himself to writing the *De viris inlustribus*. The contemporary scene was never lost from view, however, as Jerome never gave up a taunting polemic.

The Origenist crisis, in fact, soon poisoned relations with Jerusalem. The opportunity was provided by Epiphanius of Salamis, who was intent on imposing his own brand of orthodoxy. Epiphanius, who was a native of Palestine, disputed John of Jerusalem's moral authority for the region, while Gelasius of Caesarea, the metropolitan, seemed to have little to do with the affair. In 393, a mysterious visitor by the name of Atarbius made a circuit of the monasteries demanding signatures against Origen; Jerome signed, Rufinus refused. The difference in choice is explained by the presence of Epiphanius behind the scenes. On the feast of the dedication of the Basilica of the Holy Sepulchre, Epiphanius initiated a homiletic dual with John on the question of anthropomorphisms. Tension reached a climax when the Cypriot bishop ordained Jerome's brother, Paulinianus, in the spring of 394 in disregard of the rights of the ordinary. The rupture took the form of Jerome's excommunication. Theophilus of Alexandria intervened and at first wrote openly in favor of the local ordinary, but John's enemies succeeded in shifting the conflict to the terrain of Origenism. The Praetorian Prefect, Rufinus of Constantinople, was threatening Jerome with expulsion when his assassination on November 27, 395 modified the situation. After he had given indications of repentence and exchanged the sign of peace with Rufinus, Jerome was reconciled at Easter 397. These ceremonies did not impede Jerome from conducting an intense literary propaganda campaign at Rome in order to assure his victory in public opinion, and perhaps precisely with the intent of anticipating Rufinus' return to Rome, which took place in this same period.

Rufinus intended to continue the work, well begun by Jerome but then abandoned in favor of his Hebrew exegesis, of translating Origen and at the same time of purging his works of the errors for which he could be blamed and which, according to Rufinus, were the result of heretical interpolations. The polemics which accompanied this attempt and lasted until the death of Rufinus (410) will be treated below. Jerome thus associated himself with the campaign of Theophilus. Evagrius Ponticus, the "Tall Brothers," who were brutally expelled from Scete, and finally John Chrysostom, all the enemies of the Pharaoh, became victims of his pen, as Rufinus and Melania already had been.

Among the correspondence of Jerome for that same year, 397, a young African bishop by the name of Augustine makes his appearance, who paid his respect to the authority of the translator and exegete of Bethlehem, though not without some reservations owing to a spirit which moved along other paths. Jerome did not immediately understand the importance of his correspondent and waited to be called upon a second time in 402 before he gave a conceited reply to what he detected as criticism. Augustine's humility had the better part, however, and the two ended by uniting their genius in an alliance against a common enemy: Pelagius.

Jerome, Pelagius, and Rufinus all enjoyed close relations with a small ascetic circle of noble Roman families. The death of Pope Siricius and the election of Anastasius (December 399) rendered Jerome once again acceptable. One of his disciples, also named Rufinus but called the Syrian, perhaps because of his long sojourn in

Palestine, returned to Rome in the spring of 399 and became one of Pelagius' most active friends. There is a tendency to attribute to him the completion of the revision of the New Testament according to Jerome's principles, inasmuch as Jerome himself had not proceeded beyond a revision of the gospels during his stay in Rome.

Paula's death in 404 was a hard blow for Jerome. He found consolation in the translation of monastic works of little literary merit but of great interest for cenobitic life, such as the Rule of Pachomius and his letters, as well as other treasures from Pachomian Coptic circles. He finished his translation of the Hebrew Bible in 405 and began a series of long commentaries on the prophets.

The barbarians devastated the empire like an apocalyptic menace which urged the adoption of asceticism and the rejection of worldly things. The fall of Rome on August 24, 410, was another hard blow for a man whose strength was beginning to fail and whose friends were preceding him in death.

The origins of Pelagianism will be treated elsewhere (cf. ch. VII). After he left Africa, Pelagius took refuge in Jerusalem, where he was well received by bishop John. In 414, Jerome took a stand against him in the conviction of finding in this danger the one he had already fought against in the past. A group of Pelagian terrorists took revenge in 416 and burned Jerome's monasteries, but the council meeting at Antioch (417) concluded with the expulsion of the heretic.

After the death of John of Jerusalem and that of Eustochium, Jerome passed away on September 30, 419, without having been able to finish the *Commentary on Jeremiah,* which concluded the cycle of the prophets.

Studies: For bibliography prior to 1959 cf. P. Antin, CCL 72. The following list includes only titles subsequent to that date, with some exceptions.

Biography: F. Cavallera, S. Jérôme. Sa vie et son œuvre I, 1-2. Louvain, 1922 (Fundamental work; vol. II was never published). — J. N. D. Kelly, Jerome, His Life, Writings, and Controversies. London, 1975. — Ch. Piétri, Roma christiana, 2 vols. Rome, 1976 *passim.*

Writings: G. Grützmacher, Hieronymus, I-III. Leipzig, 1901-08. — J. Steinmann, S. Jérôme. Paris, 1958 (*German transl.* Hieronymus, Ausleger der Bibel. Cologne, 1961. *English transl.* S. Jerome and His Times. Notre Dame, 1960). — C. Favez, S. Jérôme peint par lui-même. Brussels, 1959. — Y. Chaffin. S. Jérôme. Paris, 1961. — C. C. Mierow, St. Jerome, the Sage of Bethlehem. Milwaukee, 1959. — R. and M. Pernoud, S. Jérôme. Paris, 1961 (*English transl.* St. Jerome, New York, 1962). — P. Antin, Recueil sur s. Jérôme. Brussels, 1968; *idem,* Jérôme, antique et chrétien: REAug 16(1970)35-46 (will appear in German in RACh). — M. Testard, S. Jérôme, l'Apôtre savant et pauvre du patriciat romain. Paris, 1969. — D. Groce, S. Jérôme et son environnement artistique et liturgique: Coll. Cisterc. 36(1974)150-178.

Date of birth: P. Hamblenne, La longévité de Jérôme. Prosper avait-il raison?: Latomus 28(1969)1081-1119. — P. Jay, Sur la date de naissance de s. Jérôme: RELA 51(1973)262-280. — A. D. Booth, The Date of Jerome's Birth: Phoenix 33(1971)346-

352. — P. Antin, La vieillesse chez s. Jérôme: REAug 17(1971)43-54. — C. Gnilka, Altersklage und Jenseitssehnsucht: JAC 14(1971)5-23.

Place of birth: G. Del Ton, S. Girolamo di Stridone. Trieste, 1962.

Chronology: P. Nautin, Études de chronologie hiéronymienne: REAug 18(1972)209-218, 19(1973)69-86, 20(1974)251-284; *idem,* La date du De viris inlustribus de Jérôme, de la mort de Cyrille di Jérusalem et de celle de Grégoire de Nazianze: RHE 56(1961)33-35; *idem,* La date de la mort de Pauline, de l'épître 66 de Jérôme et de l'épître 13 de Paulin de Nole: Aug 18(1978)547-550. J. J. Thierry, The Date of the Dream of Jerome: VC 17(1963)28-40.

Relations with his contemporaries: J. Matthews, Western Aristocrasies and Imperial Court A.D. 364-425. Oxford, 1976. — P. Brown, The Patrons of Pelagius. The Roman Aristocracy between East and West: JThSt 21(1970)56-72. — P. Jay, Jérôme auditeur d'Apollinaire de Laodicée à Antioche: REAug 20(1974)36-41. — M. Turcan, S. Jérôme et les femmes: BAGB I(1968)259-272. — S. Jannacone, Roma 384. Struttura sociale e spirituale del gruppo geronimiano: GIF 19(1966)32-48. — A. Lippold, Paula: RE Suppl. 10(1965)508-509. — A. Paredi, S. Girolamo e s. Ambrogio, in Mélanges E. Tisserant 5 (ST 235). Vatican City 1964, 184-198. — P. Nautin, La lettre de Théophile d'Alexandrie à Jean de Jérusalem et la réponse de l'Église de Jérusalem: RHE 69(1974)365-394. — Y. M. Duval, Sur le insinuations de Jérôme contre Jean de Jérusalem: de l'arianisme à l'origénisme: RHE 67(1970)353-374. — E. Bihain, Les sources d'un texte de Socrate relatif à Cyrille de Jérusalem: *Byzantion* 32(1962)81-91. — O. Tescari. De beato Hieronymo quem Rufinus adversarius pro viro mendaci habuit: *Studi Romani* 9(1961)19ff. — K. Romaniuk, Une controverse entre s. Jérôme et Rufin d'Aquilée à propos de l'ép. aux Ephésiens: *Aegyptus* 43(1963)84-106. — P. Nautin, L'excommunication de s. Jérôme: *Annuaire de l'Ecole pratique des Hautes Etudes,* Ve section 80/81(1971/73)7-37. — E. D. Hunt, St. Silvia of Aquitania: JThSt 23(1972)351-373. — G. Sanders, Egérie. S. Jérôme et la Bible, in *Corona Gratiarum,* Misc. E. Dekkers I. Bruges 1975, 181-199. — H. Crouzel, S. Jérôme et ses amis toulousains: BLE 73(1972)125-146. — Y. M. Duval, S. Augustin et le commentaire sur Jonas de s. Jérôme: REAug 12(1966)9-40. — A. M. La Bonnardière, Jérôme informateur d'Augustin au sujet d'Origène: REAug 20(1974)42-54. — R. F. Evans, Pelagius: Inquiries and Reappraisals. New York, 1968. — J. Coleiro, The Decay of the Empire and the Fall of Rome in St. Jerome's Letters and Lives of the Hermits: *Journal of the Fac. of Arts,* Univ. of Malta 1(1957)49-57. — F. Paschoud, Roma aeterna. Etudes sur le patriotisme romain dans l'Occident latin à l'époque des invasions. Rome, 1967. — M. Pavan, I cristiani e il mondo ebraico nell'età di Teodosio il Grande: *Ann. Fac. Lettere e Fil.,* Univ. di Perugia 3(1965-66)367-530. — E. D. Hunt, From Dalmatia to the Holy Land. Jerome and the World of Late Antiquity: JRS 67(1977)166-171. — K. Sugano, Das Rombild des Hieronymus. Bern, 1983. — A. D. Booth, The Chronology of Jerome's Early Years: *Phoenix* 25(1981)237-259.

WRITINGS

Jerome played an important role in the transmission of biblical and patristic texts in the West, and his own works give evidence of contact with a Greek documentation of exceptional richness in exegesis, history and spirituality. In addition to this he had received an excellent formation in Latin which renders him full of sentiment and humanity whether in the passion of polemics or in his letters.

Jerome took a great interest in the dissemination of his own works.

After having copied so many books in his youth to form a library, he was able to obtain, thanks to the generosity of Paula, a team of copyists and to organize a chain of dissemination through his Roman friends and their correspondents. The consequences provoked by his polemical treatises can be considered as publicity moves for his writings, and they may well have been purposely exaggerated. His correspondence was published under his own supervision, and A. Chastagnol believes that the first 45 letters were already used in 392 by the editor of the *Historia Augusta.* Often, Jerome's Bible is conceived of as an official edition, promulgated by Damasus and adopted by the Roman Church, or in fact by the entire Catholic West. This is an anachronism, however, since the Vulgate was born book by book, dedicated each time to a different friend. The name of Damasus figures effectively at the beginning of the revision of the Gospels, the initiative for which is generously attributed to him. In reality, his influence at most should be limited to having approved the project of his young friend, or perhaps having expressed the desire for the production of a better version, in which case this profession of humility before a person of rank in the attribution to Damasus would be nothing more than a commonplace literary device.

B. Lambert has dedicated almost 300 pages to the inventory of the manuscripts, conducted by means of the catalogues, but the history of the manuscript tradition of Jerome's works remains to be written. Even the critical editions are by necessity very discreet with regard to the history of the text.

Editions: The complete editions are: Sweynheyn and Pannarz. Rome, 1468. — Erasmus I-IX. Basel, 1516-1520. — M. Victorius I-IX. Rome, 1565-1572. — J. Martianay, A. Pouget I-IV. Paris, 1693-1706. — D. Vallarsi I-IX. Verona, 1734-1742, 1766-1772[2] (less correct). Among the reeditions mention must be made of the PL 22-30. Paris, 1845-1846, 1864-1865[2] (modifies the pagination) which prints the second edition of Vallarsi. A new edition is in preparation in the CCL, and almost all the biblical works have appeared. They are as follows: CCL 72(1959) P. Antin, ed., Bibliographia selecta (to be consulted for prior bibliography); Hebraicae Quaestiones in libro Geneseos (according to the ed. of P. De Lagarde), Leipzig 1869; Liber interpretationis hebraicorum nominum (by the same editor), Onomastica sacra, Göttingen 1887[2]; Commentarioli in Psalmos (according to the edition of G. Morin), Anecdota Maredsolana III, 1. Maredsous 1895; Commentarius in Ecclesiasten, ed. M. Adriaen (on the basis of the excellent manuscript of Würzburg Mp th. q. 2, saec. V, with attention also to the Paris. lat. 13349, saec. VIII). — CCL 73 and 73A(1963): In Isaiam, ed. M. Adriaen. The text is that of Vallarsi since it is difficult to establish a critical text given the number of the manuscripts. The editor gives in the apparatus the readings of the oldest manuscripts. If used wisely, the appartus provides the basis for a solid text. In Isaia parvula Adbreviatio, ed. G. Morin, according to the Anecdota Maredsolana III, 3. Maredsous 1903. — CCL 74(1960) In Hieremiam, ed. S. Reiter. A very satisfactory critical edition which uses the text but not the valuable index of CSEL 59(1913). — CCL 75(1974), In Hiezechielem, ed. F. Glorie. The text is substantially that of Vallarsi compared with some ancient manuscripts. The editor did not exercise the reserve of Adriaen in vol. 73 and has at time corrected Vallarsi in a manner which makes it difficult for the reader to recognize the good readings of the manuscripts. — CCL 75A(1964) In Danielem, ed. F. Glorie. Cf. remarks re. vol. 75. — CCL 76 and 76A(1969-1970) In Prophetas minores, ed. M. Adriaen. Cf. remarks re. vol. 73. — CCL 77(1969) In Mattheum, ed. D. Hurst, M. Adriaen. Edition made on the basis of ancient manuscripts. CCL 78(1958) Opera homiletica = Treatises on the Psalms, on Mark and various homilies. Improvement of the edition of G. Morin, Anecdota Maredsolana III, 2-3. Maredsous 1897-1903. — F. Nuvolone, Notulae manuscriptae II-IV: *Freib. Z. Phil. Theol.* 26(1979)525-572. — Cf. the respective works *infra* for the translations of the Bible, of the Greek Fathers, for the letters (CSEL) and the editions of individual works.

Studies: E. Arns, La technique du livre d'après s. Jérôme. Paris, 1953. — G. Kloeters, Buch und Schrift bei Hieronymus. Diss., Münster, 1957. — B. Lambert, Bibliotheca Hieronymi Manuscripta I-IV (in seven vols). Steenbrugge, 1969-1972 (with careful examination of the *Spuria* and indices of titles, incipit and explicit). — H. Hagendahl, Die Bedeutung der Stenographie für die spätlat. christlichen Literatur: JAC 14(1971)24-38. — A. Chastagnol, Le supplice inventé par Avidius Cassius. Remarques sur l'Histoire Auguste et la lettre 1 de s. Jérôme: *Bonner Historia-Augusta Colloquium* 1970. Bonn 1970, 95-107.

Translations: English: J. H. Hritzen, St. Jerome. Dogmatic and Polemical Works. Washington, 1965. *French:* A. Dumas, Jérôme. Textes choisis et présentés. Namur, 1960. — C. Olivier, Jérôme. Textes choisis et introduits. Paris, 1963. *German:* C. Olivier, Hieronymus. Stuttgart, 1965. *Italian:* E. Casimasi, Girolamo, opere scelte. Turin, 1971. — L. F. Pizzolato, A'amicizia cristiana. Testi di s. Girolamo ecc. Turin, 1973.

THE BIBLICAL TRANSLATIONS

In the eyes of Western culture and in the life of the church, Jerome's principal reputation is that of a translator of the Bible. However, it should not be imagined that he translated all of the Scriptures nor that his work of translation followed a uniform plan or method. The reality remains more subtly nuanced, even within the limits of a single book.

Editions: The *editio princeps* is that of Gutenberg (the 42-line Bible), Mainz 1452 (q.v.), which is itself a monument of human history. This reproduced a late text disseminated by the University of Paris. Reprint in facsimile: Johann Gutenberg, Die zweiundvierzigzeilige Bibel. Zürich, 1978. — R. Estienne, Paris 1528, 1532[2], 1540[4]. — The edition *sistina* (Rome 1590) was destroyed immediately after the death of Sixtus V. — The *Clementina* (published by authority of Clement VIII) Rome 1592, 1593[2], 1598[3] was for a long time the official text, *ne varietur,* for Catholics. — Biblia Sacra iuxta latinam vulgatam versionem ad codicum fidem I-XVI. Vatican City, 1926-1981 (Genesis-Daniel; critical edition). — H. de Sainte-Marie, S. Hieronymi Psalterium iuxta Hebraeos. Rome, 1954. — Biblia sacra iuxta vulgatum versionem . . . recensuit R. Weber. Stuttgart, 1969, 1983[3]. Manual of the text scrupulously revised which is normally better than the preceding critical editions.

Reference works: F. P. Dutripon, Vulgatae editionis . . . Concordantiae. Paris, 1880[8]. — Peultier, Concordantiarum . . . Thesaurus. Paris, 1897. — G. De Zamora, Sacrorum Bibliorum Concordantiae. Rome, 1627. — B. Fischer, Novae Concordantiae Bibliorum Sacrorum iuxta vulgatam versionem cirtice editam, 5 vols. Stuttgart, 1976 (according to the edition of Weber and taking into account the principal variants). — W. E. Plater, H. I. White, A Grammar of the Vulgate. Oxford, 1926. — J. Griboment, L'Eglise et les versions bibliques: *La Maison-Dieu* 62(1960)41-68.

1. The Gospels.

The preface *Novum opus* attributes the initiative for this revision to Damasus († 384), although it has been explained above in what sense this is to be understood. Jerome complains that he has been forced to respect the linguistic tastes of the public and promises not to make corrections where it is not demanded by the Greek text. It is nevertheless the work of a beginner and though it is of an overall good quality, it contains enough irregularities and shows scarce consideration for the above-mentioned principles of revision. In order to evaluate the revision, it is necessary to make reference to the edition of Stuttgart (Weber) which was able to make use, among other things, of the fragments from Sankt Gall which are contemporary with Jerome and in which alternative readings are already found in the margins. In his New Testament, Weber corrects the Oxford (Wordsworth-White) edition 772 times, and rejects the hypothesis according to which the basic text selected by Jerome practically coincided with the *Codex Brixianus* (f), which approximates the Vulgate exclusively for reasons of contamination. Jerome systematically rejects contaminated readings from parallel passages and from the "Western" Greek text, but that is not sufficient to affirm that he follows a Greek exemplar closely related to the *Vaticanus*. Fischer is in favor rather of a proto-Antiochene text and shows how Vogels has exaggerated considerably the novelty of Jerome's edition.

2. The Remainder of the New Testament.

Jerome's prefaces dedicating the work to one of his friends have not been preserved for Acts, the Epistles, or the Apocalypse. The technique of the reviser is analogous to that of Jerome, but presents a markedly more systematic character, and the resulting text is quite different from that which is found in Jerome's citations. Pelagius is the first author to make use of the Vulgate, especially in his commentary on Paul, although his marked preference for some readings of the *Vetus Latina* must be noted. D. De Bruyne did not hesitate to propose Pelagius as the reviser of the Vulgate, but B. Fischer presents good reasons for preferring Rufinus the Syrian, who was a disciple of Jerome and friend of Pelagius.

Editions: I. Wordsworth, H. I. White, H. F. D. Sparks, Novum Testamentum . . . secundum editionem s. Hieronymi I-III. Oxford, 1889-1954. — H. I. White, Novum Testamentum latine. Editio minor. Oxford, 1911. — R. Weber, ed., Biblia Sacra. Stuttgart, 1975.

Studies: J. Vogels, Vulgatastudien. Die Evangelien der Vulgata. Münster, 1928; *idem,* Handbuch der Textkritik des Neuen Testamentes. Bonn, 1955[2]. — B. Fischer, Das Neue Testament in lateinischer Sprache = K. Aland, Die alten Übersetzungen des Neuen Testaments. Berlin 1972, 1-92 (excellent). — A. A. Bell, Jerome's Role in the Translation of the Vulgate New Testament: NTS 23 (1977)230-233.

3. The First Revision of the Psalter.

In his preface to the "Gallican" Psalter, Jerome mentions a rapid revision of the psalter done at Rome together with the revision of the Gospels mentioned above. The Greek text followed at that time did not have the value of the edition of Origen's *Hexapla* (cf. *infra*) nor of the original Hebrew. The conjecture has been advanced that the Roman psalter, which has been used up to the present in St. Peter's Basilica, and which in the Middle Ages was the normal liturgical text in Italy, was identical with this first revision of Jerome, but there are no proofs in this regard. The Roman psalter, without a preface and without traces of a revision, seems more likely to be identified with the text Jerome wanted to correct. This first revision of St. Jerome, a work of his youth which he later repudiated, did not have an opportunity to be disseminated since it was confined between the old traditional text and subsequent revisions of a better quality, and it disappeared. The same fate would probably have happened in the case of the Gospels, had not Jerome undertaken a second revision in the East on the basis of a better Greek exemplar.

It must be noted, however, that these Roman revisions of the Gospels and the Psalter, whose level is still modest and in which Jerome is in training, deal with the most frequently read books of the Scripture for which the need of a better edition was obviously urgent. If the initiative for this revision can truly be attributed to Damasus, it would then be necessary to recognize in this pope an authentic pastoral concern.

Studies: D. De Bruyne, Le problème du psautier romain: RB 41(1929)297-324.

4. The Gallican Psalter and the Revision from the *Hexapla*.

In the library of Caesarea, Jerome had the opportunity of consulting the monumental critical work completed for the Greek text in Origen's *Hexapla*. The different versions were contained in parallel columns, and the text of the Septuagint was adapted to the Hebrew text by adding those elements, distinguished by an asterisk, which were present in the version of Theodotion and in Hebrew but were lacking in the traditional Greek text, and by marking with oboli certain Greek passages which were lacking in the Hebrew. During a period of some years, from 387 to 392, Jerome considered transmitting this work to the Latin world, as Paul of Tella would do around 615, translating it faithfully into Syriac. Important portions of the Wisdom books have been preserved from the *Hexapla*: Job, the three books of Solomon, and the Psalter. Only the preface to Chronicles is extant, which, in the Bible of Theodulf is added to the preface of the version from the Hebrew of the same books. This version of the Wisdom books from the *Hexapla* enjoyed great popularity in the fifth century and for a short while became the Vulgate text itself. St. Augustine prized it highly and desired that Jerome finish the same work for the entire Bible (Jerome, *Ep.* 56, 2 and 104, 3 = Augustine, *Ep.* 28 and 71). However, the erudite hermit of Bethlehem had changed objectives and did not accept the invitation. He claimed to have finished this task in the past but to have lost the text "through the dishonesty of some unknown person" (*Ep.* 134, 2). The *Hexapla* psalter is relatively close to the old traditional text. It was adopted in the Irish liturgy and then, toward the end of the eighth century, in Carolingian Gaul, in which circumstances it received the name of the Gallican Psalter. It consolidated and extended its influence to the point of penetrating into the Bibles of the universities, the Clementine Vulgate, and almost everywhere in the Latin liturgy. It was only under Pius XII that permission was obtained to substitute it by a new version.

Editions: Job: C. P. Caspari, Das Buch Job. *Christiana,* 1893. *Wisdom books:* A. Vaccari, L'uso liturgico di un lavoro critico di S. Girolamo: *Riv. Biblica* 4(1956)357-373; *idem,* Recupero d'un lavoro critico di s. Girolamo: *Scritti di erudizione e di filologia* II. Rome 1958, 83-146; *idem,* Cantici Canticorum Vetus latina translatio a S. Hieronymo ad graecum textum hexaplarem emendata. Rome, 1959. *Gallican Psalter:* Biblia sacra . . . ad codicum fidem X. Vatican City, 1953. — Biblia Sacra. Stuttgart, 1983.

Studies: A. Thibaut, La revision hexaplaire de s Jérôme: Richesses et déficiences des anciens psautiers latins. Rome 1959, 107-149. — J. H. Gailey, Jerome's Latin Version of Job from the Greek. Chapters 1-26. Its Text, Character and Provenance. Diss., Princeton, 1945. — C. Estin, Les Psautiers de Jérôme à la lumière des traductions juives antérieures. Rome, 1984.

5. The New Version Based on the Hebrew.

Jerome has possessed a familiarity with Hebrew for some time, but without the aid of the versions of Aquila and Symmachus he would certainly not have been capable of facing his difficulties on his own. To the extent that he was rereading the *Hexapla* version of the Septuagint, he was forced to examine the original more closely. His travels had given him a knowledge of the topography of Palestine, and the translations of the *Onomasticon* of Eusebius and the *Liber locorum* had presented him with specific problems. Before turning his hand to the *Hexapla* version of Genesis, he wished to clarify his ideas and thus undertook the edition of a work of a purely technical character, the *Quaestiones hebraicae,* in which he compared the ancient versions and attempted to establish the sense of the text. In spite of his original intention these *Quaestiones* did not continue beyond Genesis and Jerome changed his original plan, considering it necessary to translate directly from the Hebrew (or rather, from the versions of Aquila and Symmachus, which complemented one another). This decision coincided with his abandonment in 392 of his projected translations of Origen and his refusal to continue his commentaries on St. Paul. It is not known with which book Jerome began, whether with Kings, which were relatively easy and in a certain sense similar to Chronicles which had just been revised; or with the Prophets, who had not yet been attacked in the revision from the *Hexapla*; or with Job and Psalms, which had already been revised though perhaps in an unsatisfactory fashion. Some information emerges from the recent critical edition of Ezechiel and its prologue, from which it is apparent that this particular book was completed shortly after Jerome had read the *Apology for Origen* of Pamphilus in the translation of Rufinus. It is thus to be dated around the beginning of 398. Esdras can be dated to 394, Chronicles to 396 and the books of Solomon to the summer of 398. The Octateuch was only begun later and was finished in 404 after the death of Paula. Esther was finished in 405. The order is not easily explained.

From as much as can be inferred from the prefaces to the individual books (unless this is just a form of literary propaganda), Jerome's initiative was more criticized than admired. His friends encouraged him, but Rufinus and his group, Augustine, and others feared the loss of the Bible of the church and a fall into a Jewish perspective. Jerome responded by adducing the example of the New Testament, which does not cite exactly the Septuagint. This was a weak argument, since it was almost never a question in the New Testament of a recourse to the Hebrew text, and, in any case, the great majority of the citations of the apostolic writings were drawn precisely from the Septuagint. The literary quality of the new translations and the divisions among the defenders of the old Latin translations turned the tide in favor of Jerome. His translations of the Prophets succeeded in imposing themselves without resistance, and the Wisdom Books ended up supplanting the versions based on the *Hexapla*; even the old translations of the Historical Books gave way, although there are still a good number of manuscripts. The version of the Psalter based on the Hebrew was taken over into many erudite versions of the Bible, but it never gained any foothold in the liturgy.

The difference between the Hebrew and the Greek text varied greatly from book to book, and thus the difference between the Vulgate and the old Latin translations varied in like manner. On the whole, the Wisdom Books differed less than the Prophets, although Ezechiel remained close to the old text while Jeremiah differed greatly. In a book such as Genesis, Jerome showed greater respect for the oracles, prayers, and formulas which were more firmly rooted in the devotion of the church in his day, whereas in the narratives he gave free play to his inspiration. The paradoxes of Ecclesiastes stimulated him, while Tobias invited him to embellish the stories. It seems that the inspiration of these books did not impress him in the same manner as the Pentateuch. On the other hand, the obscure texts of the prophets were treated with a respect which would make the much less scrupulous modern translators blush.

Jerome had a Hebrew text at his disposal which was extremely close to our Masoretic text, but to interpret it he used the ancient versions of the *Hexapla,* which are poorly known today. He also had direct recourse to rabbis, although the frequency of this should not be exaggerated after the contacts of the first years. His apologetic concerns are apparent every now and then. He is certainly very proud when his own knowledge is of use, and he emphasizes this in his commentaries.

"We have the pleasure of possessing in the Vulgate a translation of the sacred books which is a poetic monument; which I would not hesitate personally to consider a masterpiece of the Latin language. If it is not inspired in the theological sense, it is certainly 'inspired' in the literary sense" (P. Claudel, *J'aime la Bible,* p. 55; as cited by J. Steinmann, *S. Jérôme,* p. 212). Bound by the popular tradition of the old versions, Jerome manifests a much surer taste than in the affectation of his letters or the animation of his polemics. On the one hand, the greatness of the inspired author can be felt through Jerome's translation, while on the other, fifteen centuries of prayer and reading have conferred on the text a certain patina like unto a venerable paleochristian basilica; it has enjoyed an authority over the arts and languages throughout the West. The very fact that the text has lived through so many ages is not one of the least elements of its beauty. The agility of the pen, though always mindful to the fidelity due to obscure oracles, nevertheless assured that the majesty of the subject did not dampen the liveliness and spontaneity of the text; and if the translator was constrained to have recourse to bold Hebraisms, the Middle Ages have rendered the expressions sacred and familiar. To remain untouched by this language it would be necessary to be saturated with a rigid classicism, as was sometimes the case in the Renaissance, though not with such men of culture as Erasmus.

Studies: P. Jay, La datation des premières traductions de l'Ancien Testament sur l'hébreu par s. Jérôme: REAug 28(1982)208-212.

6. The Deuterocanonical Books.

"The Book of Jesus, son of Sirach, the Wisdom of Solomon, Judith, Esther, Tobias and Maccabees are read for edification, but do not enjoy canonical authority" (Preface to Proverbs); "III and IV Esdras are nothing but foolish fancies" (Preface to Esdras). As can be seen, Jerome did not deign to take an interest in the deuterocanonical books, but made a free translation of Tobias and Judith, "*magis sensum e sensu quam ex verbo verbum transferens*" (Preface to Judith). He did not decide, however, to omit the chapters added in the Greek text to Daniel and Esther.

Those who first made a collection of the good biblical translations that would form the Vulgate—without doubt in a library rather than in one large volume—seem also to have included the majority of the deuterocanonical works which the church did not wish to do without. In any case they only appear in the manuscripts at a later date subsequent to a definite revision. Wisdom and Sirach make their appearance in a late and interpolated text which is unworthy to be associated with the work of Jerome, while Maccabees are a revision from the Greek text. Baruch is missing in almost all the manuscripts, and the version that ended up in the Bible of the University of Paris and in the printed Vulgate was introduced later, around 800, by Theodulf of Orléans.

Studies: J. Griboment, L'édition vaticane de la vulgate et la Sagesse de Salomon dans sa recension italienne: RSLR 4(1968)472-476.

TRANSLATIONS AND REFERENCE WORKS

At the beginning of his career, Jerome displayed an acute sense of priorities, and turned his attention to serious works which were indispensable for scientific work.

1. The *Chronicle* of Eusebius.

Before taking up his *Ecclesiastical History,* and perhaps much earlier than the conventional date of 303, Eusebius edited a comparative table of the different chronicles of his day. Such a chronicle undoubtedly belongs to a minor literary genre, but it introduces into the sequence of events a mathematical scale, perhaps only approximate, which can serve as the indispensible framework for arranging the psychological, sociological, philosophical, or theological observations of which history proposes to provide a comprehensive view. Because of the work's excessive erudition and the difficulty of translation, the Greek text has been lost. Jerome discovered the work at Constantinople in 380 while he was still very young, understood its value and carefully copied it, continuing it down to 378.

Editions and studies: Cf. J. Quasten, Patrology III. Utrecht-Antwerp 1975, 311-314. — A. A. Mosshammer, Two Fragments of Jerome's Chronicle: RhM 124(1981) 66-80. — R. Helm, Eusebius' Werke VII. Die Chronik des Hieronymus, GCS 23. Berlin, 1956. — D. S. Wallace-Hadrill, The Eusebian Chronicle: The Extent and Date of Composition of its Early Editions: JThST 6(1955)248-253 (The concordance between Jerome and the Ecclesiastical History against the Armenian version of the Chronicle is the result of a revision by Eusebius. Cannot such a revision be attributed to Jerome?). — A. Grisart, La Chronique de s. Jérôme. Le lieu e la date de sa composition: *Hélikon* 2(1962)248-258 (at Trier in 368-371?).

2. The *Onomastica: Liber locorum, Liber nominum.*

Around 390, precisely when he was working on the *Quaestiones hebraicae,* Jerome compiled a list of Hebrew names which the Septuagint had transcribed without translating (on the relationship between these three works, cf. Klostermann, p. xxvi, n. 4). Eusebius had compiled a list of geographical names arranged according to the initial letter and, under each letter, according to the order of the books of the Bible. For each entry, he added the translations from the *Hexapla,* then an identification in the terminology of the fourth century along with some information regarding the locality (the distances were indicated in Roman miles). Jerome completed this list and on the basis of his own knowledge he at times changed the order (it should be noted that Klostermann, editing Jerome against Eusebius, had to rectify the modifications introduced by the former; for the primitive order, cf. earlier editions, Lagarde or PL 25) but at other times remained faithful to his exemplar and merely noted his disagreement.

The etymological significance of these mysterious names constituted a philological problem on to which was grafted a spiritual interpretation. Some lists of Greek translations were circulating under the names of Philo and Origen. Jerome, who considered himself capable of discerning the value of a good number of etymologies, composed a general work classified according to the Greek alphabet, all of which offers sufficient proof that he translated rather than composed himself.

Editions and studies: Cf. J. Quasten, Patrology III. Utrecht-Antwerp 1975, 336-337. — E. Klostermann, Eusebius' Werke III, 1. Das Onomastikon der biblischen Ortsnamen, GCS 11, 1. Leipzig, 1904 (imposes Eusebius' order on Jerome). — P. De Lagarde, Onomastica Sacra. Göttingen, 1870, 1872[2] (Greek text and Jerome's Latin version of the two Onomastica). — CCL 72, 57-161 (reprints only the edition of the *Liber nominum*). — T. D. Barnes, The Composition of Eusebius' *Onomasticon:* JThSt 26(1975)412-415. — J. Wilkinson, L'apport de s. Jérôme à la topographie: RBibl 81(1874)245-251. — F. Wutz, Onomastica sacra. Untersuchungen zum Liber interpretationis nominum hebraicorum des hl. Hieronymus. Leipzig, 1914-15.

3. *De viris inlustribus.*

This catalogue of Christian writers which dates to 393 and contains a list of Jerome's own works up to that date could pass for an original composition. In reality, in spite of the new scheme inspired by Suetonius, the substance of the work is drawn from the *Ecclesiastical History* of Eusebius, with some additions for the Latin world. Jerome would like to create the impression that he is familiar with the works he is describing, but it is not difficult to point out his errors of interpretation which betray his ignorance. However, the very idea of composing a handbook of patrology bears witness to his intellectual curiosity, which intended to establish the basis for a history of exegesis.

Editions: E. C. Richardson, Hieronymus, Liber de viris inlustribus. Leipzig, 1896.

Translations: English: E. Richardson, LNPF3, ser. 2(1892) 359-384 (reprint: 1969). *Italian:* G. Gottardi, S. Girolamo, Uomini illustri. Siena, 1969.

Studies: G. Brugnoli, Il titolo de viris inlustribus: *Annali fac. Lettere e Filos.* Bari 28(1960)363-380. — P. Nautin, La date du De viris inlustribus: RHE 56(1961) 33-35. — A. Ceresa-Gastaldo, La tecnica biografica del De viris illustribus di Girolamo: *Renovatio* 14(1979)221-236. — S. Pricoco, Motivi polemici e prospettive classicistiche nel De viris inlustribus de Girolamo: SicGym 32 (1979)69-98. — I. Opelt, Hieronymus' Leistung als Literarhistoriker: Orph. I (1980)52-75.

TRANSLATIONS OF ORIGEN AND DIDYMUS

1. Origen's Homilies on the Prophets and on the Canticle.

From 381, owing to the influence of Gregory Nazienzus (or already at Antioch, according to Nautin), Jerome became enamored of the writings of Origen. His interest was not as of yet directed toward the learned treatises, but rather toward the homilies, which transmitted the admirable interior life of the erudite scholar (cf. Jerome's preface to the homilies on the Canticle). At Constantinople, a friend of Jerome, the priest Vincent, assumed the expenses for the secretarial staff necessary for such an undertaking of translation.

Jerome's choice fell at first on the 14 homilies on Jeremiah (12 are preserved in the original Greek) and then on those on Ezechiel. The order of the homilies in the editions of Jerome's works (PL 25) is different from that of Origen's works (GCS), which offers a better text but omits Jerome's prologues. Two years later, at Rome, Jerome offered Damasus the two homilies on the Canticle, which he regarded as the masterpiece of the Alexandrian. After 392, he translated another 9 homilies on Isaiah (Baehrens regards homily 9 as spurious because it contradicts homily 6). Although these homilies are not accompanied by Jerome's customary preface, Rufinus testifies to their authenticity since he cites them as an example of how Jerome had once corrected Origen with the same orthodox glosses which he was denouncing in Rufinus' translation of the *De principiis.*

Editions: CF. J. Quasten, Patrology II. Utrecht-Antwerp 1953, 46-48. — W. A. Baehrens, Origines' Werke VIII, GCS 33. Leipzig, 1925. — P. Husson, P. Nautin, Origène. Homélies sur Jérémie I: SCh 232 and 238. Paris 1976-77. —

Translations: English: R. P. Lawson, Origen. The Song of Songs. Commentary and Homilies (ACW 26). London-Westminster, 1957. *French:* O. Rousseau, Origène. Homélies sur le Cantique des Cantiques. Sch 37(1953). — P. Husson, P. Nautin, op. cit.

Studies: V. Peri, Solomon oppure Solon? Su una lezione dell'Om. Ez. V 3 di Origene in latino: *Aevum* 33(1959)526-528; *idem,* I passi sulla Trinità nelle omelie origeniane tradotte in latino da s. Girolamo (SP 6). Berlin 1962, 155-180. — G. Lomiento, Note sulla traduzione geronimiana delle Omelie su Geremia di Origene: VetChr 10(1973)243-262.

2. Origen's Homilies on Luke.

Vincent, Rufinus, and Augustine greatly valued Jerome's translations of Origen and invited him to continue. However, as he gradually grew accustomed to the work, Jerome preferred to sign the commentaries with his own name, although he continued to make use of the work of Eastern exegetes. He subsequently made translations of Origen and Didymus only with the perverse intention of exposing the borrowings and weaknesses of other translators. Such is the case with the 39 homilies of Origen on Luke which he translated in 390 with the intent of tearing to pieces the commentary of Ambrose on the same Gospel, "a jay adorned with peacock feathers" (Jerome's preface to the translation). Work on the *Quaestiones hebraicae* was suspended momentarily in order that he might show Paula and Eustochium the *modus operandi* of the Bishop of Milan.

Editions: Cf. J. Quasten, Patrology II. Utrecht-Antwerp 1953, 46-48. — M. Rauer, Origenes' Werke IX (GCS 35). Leipzig, 1941.

Translations: French: H. Crouzel, SCh 87(1962).

3. The *De principiis*.

Rufinus translated the four books of the *De principiis* in 398, presenting them as the continuation of Jerome's work and adapting the text to the sensibilities of the time. Jerome responded from Bethlehem in 399 with a translation intended to emphasize the heresies contained in the work. By an irony of fate, regretted by modern scholars, the copyists placed Jerome's version on the index and preserved the edifying adaptation of the text of Rufinus.

Editions: P. Kotschau, Origenes' Werke V (GCS 22). Leipzig, 1913. H. Crouzel, M. Simonetti, SCh 252, 253, 268, 269, 312(1978-1983).

Translations and Studies: Cf. J. Quasten, Patrology II. Utrecht-Antwerp 1953, 61-62.

4. The Treatise of Didymus on the Holy Spirit.

Following the line of the translations of Origen, the translation of Didymus' treatise on the Holy Spirit, which dates to the years 387-390, has been left until now. Jerome was moved to this new undertaking by the urge to show up the treatise of Ambrose on the same subject and show how the Bishop of Milan was plundering the riches of Greek theology. The translation is especially valuable since the Greek text has been lost.

Editions and Studies: PG 39, 1033-1086 = PL 23, 103-154. — Cf. J. Quasten, Patrology III. Utrecht-Antwerp 1975, 95-97. — L. Doutreleau, Etude d'une tradition manuscrite: le De Spiritu Sancto de Didyme, in Kyriakon, Festschrift J. Quasten I. Münster 1970, 352-389.

TRANSLATIONS OF POLEMICAL TEXTS

Among the letters of Jerome there can be found documents of Theophilus of Alexandria, the proceedings of a synod in Jerusalem and other Eastern texts which were translated and disseminated in the West with a polemical intent. Among these documents the following can be mentioned: *Ep.* 51, of Epiphanius to John of Jerusalem (394); *Ep.* 87 and 89 of Theophilus to Jerome (399-400); *Ep.* 90 of Theophilus to Epiphanius and *Ep.* 91 of Epiphanius to Jerome (400); *Ep.* 92 and 93, the synodal letter of Theophilus and the response of Dionysius of Lydda (400); *Ep.* 96, 98 and 100, which are festal letters of Theophilus (translated in 403 and 404); and *Ep.* 113 of Theophilus to Jerome (405). Jerome used the opportunity to add a bit of spice to the text of the letters in order to use them to the best advantage, and did not hesitate to justify such a procedure in *Ep.* 57, *De optimo genere interpretandi,* in which he appealed to his broad experience as a translator to justify the liberties he took at the expense of John of Jerusalem.

To this dossier there can be added the translation of a small treatise against Origen (composed under the influence of Theophilus?). It is not completely certain that the translation is actually that of Jerome. (The piece is published by G. Morin, *Anecdota Maredsolana* III, 3. Maredsous 1903, 103-122. Cf. L. Chavoutier, Qùerelle origéniste et controverses trinitaires à propos du traité Contra Originem de visione Isaiae: VC 14[1960] 9-14.)

PACHOMIANA

A translation of a collection of Coptic Pachomian documents (in the broad sense of the term) which had already been translated into Greek was requested of Jerome after the death of Paula (404). The Latin translation preserves the simple character of the work. Ample Coptic and Greek fragments have been discovered which give some idea of the difficulties Jerome encountered in understanding a world so different from his own.

Editions: A. Boon, Pachomiana latina. Louvain, 1932 (= Praecepta, Praecepta et Instituta, Praecepta atque Iudicia, Praecepta ac leges; Eipstulae S. Pachomii, Epistula Theodori, Liber Orsiesii). The Monita Pachomii are not the work of Jerome and form another recension of Ep. 3. Coptic fragments are included in an appendix in Boon; cf. also L. T. Lefort, Oeuvres de S. Pachôme et de ses disciples (OCSO 159-160). Louvain, 1964. — H. Quecke, Die Briefe Pachoms. Regensburg, 1975. — E. Krischker, Zur Sprache der Regula Pachomii in der lateinischen version des Hieronymus. Diss., Vienna, 1966.

BIBLICAL COMMENTARIES

After the study of the translations, no change of subject is involved in considering the commentaries of Jerome, as they are to a great extent adaptations of the literary treasures of the library at Caesarea.

It is necessary to begin by enumerating the letters which constitute treatises or in which are inserted erudite or mystical discourses: *Ep.* 18A and 18B to Damasus on Isaiah 6; *Ep.* 28 also to Damasus on *Hosanna; Ep.* 21, again to Damasus, on the Prodigal Son, etc. This correspondence betrays the same evolution as the treatises; the inspiration at the beginning comes from Origen, and gradually passes over to literary and textual criticism (e.g., *Ep.* 106 from the year 404).

The first attempt at a commentary took place at Antioch in 374, and for reasons known only to God was on the Book of Obadiah. Jerome subsequently made sure that this work disappeared. At Rome, his exegetical works were oral or were limited to the dimensions of a letter as he slowly developed his exegetical method.

1. Commentaries on Paul.

At the beginning of Jerome's sojourn in Bethlehem, or shortly thereafter, his spiritual daughters, who had perhaps heard his oral commentaries, requested a commentary on the Letter to Philemon. It was difficult for him to refuse to take up such a brief work, and the result was a historical and concrete explanation of the epistle. He then went on to Galatians, where he haughtily disdained the commentary of Marius Victorinus and listed as his sources Origen, in the first place, then Didymus, Apollinarius, and Eusebius of Emesa. The Epistle to the Ephesians followed, in which Jerome did not hide (PL 26, 442C) his dependence on Origen (partly preserved), and in which he again made use of Didymus and Apollinarius. With regard to the preexistence of souls, he combats Origen although without naming him. The Pauline cycle, which required only some months, closed with a book on the Letter to Titus. The experience of Palestine and Jerome's growing interest in the *Hexapla* were the reasons for his abandonment of this work. It has been noted above that Jerome was not even concerned with correcting the Latin text of St. Paul.

Editions: PL 26.

Studies: P. Nautin, La date des commentaires de Jérôme sur les épîtres pauliniennes: RHE 74(1979)5-12. — M. A. Schatkin, The Influence of Origen upon St. Jerome's Commentary on Galatians: VC 24(1970)49-58. — V. Bullhart, Textkritisches VII: RB 72(1962)131-132 (on Eph.). — F. Derriau, Le Commentaire de Jérôme sur Ephésiens nous permet-il de connaître celui d'Origène?, in *Origeniana.* Bari 1975, 163-179.

2. *Commentary on Ecclesiastes.*

Already in Rome Jerome had gone through Ecclesiastes orally with

Blesilla. Five years after the death of this young matron (389?), he revised his notes on this book, dedicated to the vanity of the world, in honor of the memory of his pupil. These notes follow the Septuagint text (i.e., the *Vetus Latina*) but also take into account the Hebrew text and the versions of the *Hexapla*. In addition to the Greek commentators, Jerome also places great value in the explanations given by a rabbi. Like his explanation of St. Paul, this written text, which is typical of this stage in his exegetical development, seems often to reproduce a vivid and animated dialogue in which annotations regarding the Hebrew alternate with observations of a spiritual nature.

Editions: M. Adriaen. CCL 72(1959)247-361.

Studies: H. P. Rueger, Hieronymus, die Rabbinen und Paulus. Zur Vorgeschichte des Begriffspaares "innerer und äusserer" Mensch: ZNW 68(1977)132-137.

3. *Notes on the Psalms.*

Excellent manuscripts preserve some isolated notes under the title of *Excerpta,* which for a long time were overlooked by editors. In reality they are not extracts from a more systematic work, but imitate the *Scholia* of Origen and form a worthy complement to those which he dedicated to the Psalter. Only in 1895 were they published in their original form by G. Morin. They are prior to the translation of the Psalter from the Hebrew and also, so it seems, to that made from the *Hexapla,* for which they are a preliminary exercise. They are to be dated around 390.

Editions: G. Morin, CCL 72(1959)163-245.

4. *Quaestiones Hebraicae in Genesim.*

The literary genre of *Quaestiones,* Ζητήματα, dedicated to the philosophical and philological discussion of the classics such as the works of Homer and Plato, was employed by Aristotle, Plutarch, and Porphyry. It was applied to biblical exegesis by Philo, Eusebius, Acacius of Caesarea, and, in the West, by Ambrosiaster. Various monographs in Jerome's correspondence imitate this genre. Toward 392, Jerome began his own bold and personal research, which was quite a different thing from a commentary where the expert could lend a hand to the beginner. He adopted the title *Quaestiones hebraicae* and used as sources the versions of the *Hexapla,* rabbinic traditions, and the works of Origen and Eusebius (cf. *Onomastica, supra*). The subject matter is still the same as the *Scholia,* but method is introduced with greater vigor. The *Quaestiones* were supposed to include the entire Bible, but once Genesis was concluded, Jerome realized the necessity to establish a firm basis for his work with a new translation from the Hebrew.

Editions: De Lagarde, CCL 72(1959)1-56.

5. Commentaries on the Prophets.

The only systematic commentary carried out by Jerome was that on the Prophets. Already in 374 the young biblical scholar had launched himself on the book of Obadiah. In 393, at the period when he was beginning to translate from Hebrew, he devoted himself to commenting on the five minor prophets: Nahum first, then Micah (where the Messianic tradition clashed with the demands of *Hebraica veritas*), Habakuk, then in greater haste, Zephaniah and Haggai. During the same period of time he undoubtedly approached Isaiah in what has been called the *Adbreviatio* concerning the first five verses of chapter I.

In the fall of 396 he commented on Jonah and Obadiah for the second time, then the ten visions of Isaiah, an isolated work which subsequently became book V of the great commentary on that prophet. The immense erudition of Y. M. Duval has inserted the work of Jerome on Jonah into the overall picture of the history of exegesis, and there is no better way of understanding what readings were necessary in order to obtain an initiation into the *status quaestionis* before undertaking a direct examination of the text. Western authors, without access to the libraries of the East, were not able to compete with Jerome, aside from the question of the knowledge of Hebrew.

Only later did Jerome proceed to a general commentary of the Prophets. In 406 he completed the commentaries on the five minor prophets who were still lacking: Zechariah, Malachi, Hosea, Joel, and Amos. Those who seem to be historically more important were left for last. He thus completed his work with Daniel (407), Isaiah (408-409), Ezechiel (411-414), and finally Jeremiah (415-419), which was interrupted by his death. The time required for the editions grew longer as Jerome struggled against his advancing age.

The method was perfectly arranged. First came a dual passage: a translation from the Hebrew (i.e., a citation of the Vulgate, at times revised), then from the Septuagint. The length of the passage depended on the internal demands of the text to be commented on, and could include up to some twenty verses. There followed next a literal commentary which was devoted above all to a discussion of the variants in the versions of the *Hexapla*. Then came a spiritual exposition related to Christ or the church, which was based on the Septuagint version since the exposition was translated or adapted from Origen or another Greek author. For a book such as Zechariah for which a text of Origen was lacking, Jerome requested Didymus to do a commentary, which has been discovered among the Toura papyri. Jerome then contented himself with making a faithful copy, as

L. Doutreleau has demonstrated. The borrowings from Rabbinic tradition are not notable.

Editions: M. Adriaen and F. Glorie, CCL 73-76(1963-1970).

Translations: French: P. Antin, S. Jérôme, Sur Jonas. SCh 43(1956). *Italian:* S. Cola, S. Girolamo. Commento a Daniele. Rome, 1966.

Studies: S. Gozzo, De s. Hieronymi Commentario in Isaiae librum: Ant 35(1960)49-80, 169-214; — L. Doutreleau, Didyme l'Aveugle. Sur Zacharie I: SCh 83(1962)129-137. — J. Braverman, Rabbinic and Patristic Tradition in Jerome's Commentary on Daniel. Diss., Yeshiva U. New York, 1970; *idem,* Jerome's Commentary on Daniel. Washington, 1978. — Y. M. Duval, Le livre de Jonas dans la littérature chrétienne grecque et latine. Sources et influences du Commentaire sur Jonas de s. Jérôme, 2 vols. Paris, 1973; *idem,* S. Cyprien et le roi de Ninive dans l'In Ionam de Jérôme, in *Epektasis,* Mélanges J. Daniélou. Paris 1972, 551-570; *idem,* Origine et diffusion de la recension de l'In prophetas minores hiéronymien de Clairvaux: RH desTextes 11(1981)277-302. — M. Simonetti, Sulle fonti del Commentario a Isaia di Girolamo: Aug 24(1984)441-449.

6. *The Commentary on Matthew.*

Eusebius of Cremona, one of Jerome's companions at Bethlehem, requested a brief and literal commentary on Matthew upon his return to Italy in 398. Jerome, caught by surprise, cited a vast bibliography beginning with Origen, but did not have time actually to read his predecessors. Of the works mentioned by Jerome, the only ones which have survived are the commentary of Hilary and a part of that of Origen. At times Jerome criticizes the former and depends heavily on the latter, but he also shows evidence of a personal knowledge of the biblical sources, of the topography of Palestine and of the methods of literary analysis. He takes from Origen all of what he claims to know firsthand from the Jews, but the valuable citations of the *Gospel According to the Hebrews* seem to come from the work itself. On dogmatic questions, he is already well aware of the errors of Origen, which he criticizes.

Editions: D. Hurst, M. Adriaen. CCL 77(1969).

Translations: French: E. Bonnard. SCh 242, 259(1977, 1979). *Italian:* S. Aliquo. Rome, 1969.

Studies: M. Marin, De corporis puritatem? Hier. "In Mattheum" IV (25, 12): VetChr 14(1977)169-175. — A. Olivar, Trois nouveaux fragments en onciale du Commentaire de Jérôme sur l'Evangile de Matthieu: RB 92(1982)76-81.

7. *The Commentary on the Apocalypse.*

Since this book was not accepted in the East, Jerome did not have a Greek bibliography at his disposal. At a date which cannot be precisely determined, but which cannot have been during his maturity or old age, he revised the Latin commentary of Victorinus of

Pettau (†304), correcting some errors, improving the style and drawing some benefit from the commentary of Tyconius.

Editions: J. Haussleiter, CSEL 49(1916), Victorinus of Pettau, recension Y. — Cf. J. Quasten, Patrology II. Utrecht-Antwerp 1953, 411-413 (Victorinus of Pettau).

HOMILIES

Jerome's first commentaries presuppose his spiritual relationships with erudite acquaintances. However, the substance of the homilies which he was accustomed to give in Bethlehem, especially on Sundays, has been preserved in the form of unrevised stenographic notes, which are not without a certain proportion of faults of memory and dogmatic imprecisions. These monastic texts, which are filled with references to the Hebrew text, never found their way into the medieval homilaries nor into the early printed editions. It was only recently that G. Morin unearthed them and furnished solid proof of their authenticity. Some other texts have subsequently been discovered. The greater part of these homilies are based on the Psalms, others on pericopes from the Gospels (particularly Mark, which is exceptional), and still others are related more specifically to the feasts or to the preparation of the monk-catechumens. Many of them can be connected with the liturgical cycle. It is possible that with these homilies, Jerome was preparing a complete commentary on the Psalter, of which he dreamed his entire life (cf. *In Isaiam* 63, 3-6 and *In Hieremiam* 2, 12-13: CCL 73A, 723, 32-35; CCL 74, 18, 20-21). A mediocre medieval successor completed this work, making use of prior material in the *Breviarium in Psalmos* (PL 26, 821-1270).

R. Grégiore has indicated that in the homilary of Farfa, the only genuine homily is that on Easter (CCL 78, 545), while the other texts are taken from Jerome's *Commentary on Matthew* or from *Ep.* 27. The homilary of Agimund also gives an extract of these and attributes a treatise on St. John of Augustine to Jerome, while a homily of Jerome (CCL 78, 520) appears under the name of Chrysostom. Furthermore, it was under Chrysostom's name that Morin identified various homilies of Jerome.

Many of the homilies make reference to the Origenist controversy, but none of them mention Pelagianism and, in fact, contain imprudent formulas regarding the problem of grace. Morin is inclined to date all of this material from around the year 400.

Editions: G. Morin. CCL 78(1958). — J. P. Bouhot, L'homélie In Joannem Evangelistam de s. Jérôme: REAug 16(1970)227-231 (with an inedited conclusion). — A. Vaccari, Frammento di un perduto Tractatus de S. Girolamo: *Scritti di erudizione e filologia* II. Rome 1958, 75-80.

Translations: English: M. L. Ewald. St. Jerome. The Homilies I-II. FC 48 and 57 (1964, 1966). *Italian:* R. Minuti. S. Girolamo, Commento al Vangelo di S. Marco. Rome, 1965.

THE LIVES OF THE HERMITS

In his commentaries and homilies, Jerome was able to pass from the simple copying of his Greek exemplar to the edition of his own filtered and revised reflections. In three biographic "novelettes" he outlines the monastic ideal in typically Eastern colors and motives such as were exemplified in the famous *Life of Anthony*. At the same time he gives free rein to his personal fantasy, keeping in mind all the while some real information regarding the heroes of the stories and, in any case, of his own lived experiences in Syria and Egypt.

Studies: P. Rousseau, Ascetics, Authority and the Church in the Age of Jerome and Cassian. Oxford, 1978. — I. Opelt, Des Hieronymus Heiligenbiographien als Quellen der historischen Topographie des östlichen Mittelmeerraumes: RQ 74 (1979)145-177. — M. Fuhrmann, Die Mönchsgeschichten des Hieronymus. In *Christianisme et formes littéraires de l'antiquité tardive*. Geneva, 1977. — H. Kech, Hagiographie als christliche Unterhaltungsliteratur. Göttingen, 1977.

1. *The Life of Paul.*

Already at the time of his first contact with the "desert" of Chalcis in 375-379, Jerome was attempting to compete with the *Life of Anthony* by invoking a predecessor of this saint who was supposed to have lived and died unknown, in the greatest solitude. Abstracting from the centaurs and satyrs, it is possible to notice in the background the somewhat fanciful model which the young convert had wanted to realize in the desert, and which his contemporary letters praise.

Editions: PL 23, 17-28.

Translations: English: W. H. Freemantle, LNPF6, ser. 2(1892)299-318 (reprint: 1954) (Paul, Hilarion and Malchus). — R. J. Deferrari, FC 15(1952)225-297 (Paul, Hilarion and Malchus). *French:* P. Antin. Ligugé, 1977 (Paul, Hilarion and Malchus). *Italian:* G. Lanata. Milan, 1975 (Paul, Hilarion and Malchus).

Studies: J. B. Bauer, Novellistisches bei Hieronymus: WSt 74(1961)130-137. — P. C. Hoelle, Commentary on the "Vita Pauli" of St. Jerome. Diss., Ohio State Univ., 1953. — I. S. Kozik, The First Desert Hero. St. Jerome's "Vita Pauli" (with introduction, notes and vocabulary). Mt. Vernon, 1968.

2. *The Life of Hilarion.*

Hilarion of Gaza, the spiritual father of Epiphanius of Salamis, must have been a historical figure, even if his supposed acquaintance with Anthony was legendary. The temptations and miracles attributed to him by this text are the mark of the genius of Jerome, who now wanted to present, in contrast with the *Vita Pauli,* a thaumaturge monk who lived in contact with men. The biography was written at the very beginning of Jerome's residence in Bethlehem, after his travels in Syria and Egypt (386-390).

Editions: PL 23, 29-54. — V. De Buck, Acta Sanctorum Octobris IX. Brussels 1869, 43-69.

Translations: Cf. Vita Pauli, supra.

Studies: J. Rouge, Tempête at littérature dans quelques textes chrétiens: ND 12(1962)55-69.

3. *The Life of Malchus.*

In 390, Jerome again allowed himself some diversion from his erudite labors and recounted the story which had been confided to him by an aged holy man whom he had previously known at Maronia near the desert of Chalcis. This old man, a Syrian originally from Nisibis, practiced perfect chastity with a woman whom the Bedouins had forced him to marry after taking them both as prisoners. Some years earlier, Jerome had not spared his sarcasm against the *virgines subintroductae,* but now in the company of Paula, he perhaps felt the need of a pious model.

Editions: PL 23, 55-62. — C. C. Mierow, Classical Essays Presented to J. A. Kleist. St. Louis 1946, 31-60 (critical text with English transl.).

Translations: Cf. Vita Pauli, *supra.*

POLEMICAL WORKS

There is a lack of good editions of the polemical works which were produced as needed in succeeding instances of Jerome's life. Nevertheless, these works were recently subjected to a critical analysis by I. Opelt, who brought to this work his profound knowledge of the literary genre and a rare sympathy for the polemicist. According to this scholar, Jerome's strong "emotional style" did not hinder him from directing almost all of these debates into the field of exegesis, where he felt at ease. Other excellent studies by Y. M. Duval have revealed how Jerome dusts off the arms forged by other Latin controversialists, e.g., Tertullain or Hilary, in order to use them energetically against his enemies, even at the price of a distorted presentation of the text he was rejecting.

Studies: I. Opelt, Hieronymus Streitschriften. Heidelberg, 1973.

1. *The Dialogue Against the Luciferians.*

This *Altercatio Luciferiani et Orthodoxi* dates back to 382 or, more precisely, somewhat earlier. Lucifer was the Nicene extremist who had consecrated Bishop Paulinus at Antioch, to whom Jerome was connected. However, Lucifer's intransigence in refusing to recognize the ordinations of the neo-Nicenes had finally led him into schism, and his partisans were on poor terms with Damasus. Consequently, as a defender of Paulinus, it was important to separate himself from all suspicion of collusion with the schismatics, while at the same time manifesting sympathy for his adversary. Jerome made use of the argument of the validity of the baptism conferred by the Arians, which Lucifer admitted, as well as of the general attitude of the church and the historical precedents concerning the controversy between Cyprian and Stephen. The tone is exceptionally courteous.

Editions: PL 23, 155-182.

Translations: English: W. H. Freemantle, op. cit., 319-334

Studies: Y. M. Duval, S. Jérôme devant le baptême des hérétiques. D'autres sources de l'Altercatio Luciferiani et Orthodoxi: REAug 14(1968)145-180; *idem,* La "manœuvre frauduleuse" de Rimini: Hilaire et son Temps. Paris 1969, 51-103.

2. *Contra Helvidium.*

Helvidius, a Roman layman connected with the Arian, Auxentius of Milan, had aspired to pick a quarrel with the monk, Carterius, with the intention of proving, against the claims of asceticism, that Mary had lived together with Joseph as husband and wife after the birth of Jesus and had given birth to other children by Joseph. The *De perpetua virginitate beatae Mariae* silenced him, explaining the disputed texts with fiery words and singing the praises of virginity.

Editions: PL 23, 183-206.

Translations: English: W. H. Freemantle, op. cit., 334-346. — J. N. Hritzu, FC 53(1965)3-43.

3. *Adversus Iovinianum.*

The monk Jovinian, who had come to Rome from Milan, attacked virginity and the ascetic life by claiming that the salvation acquired by redemption in Christ was equal for all. His opinions were condemned in 390 and 391 by Pope Siricius (*Ep.* 7) and by Ambrose (*Ep.* 41 and 42). The brilliant refutation of Jerome exceeded the purpose of the work, and the exegesis proposed for 1 Cor. 7 along with the picturesque expressions drawn from pagan antifeminist literature provoked resentment, which Jerome attempted to placate with the *Ep.* 40-50.

Editions: PL 23, 211-338. — E. Bickel, Diatribe in Senecae philosophi fragmenta I. Leipzig 1915, 382-420 (excerpts).

Studies: F. Heimann, The Polemical Application of Scripture in St. Jerome. SP 12. Berlin 1975, 309-316. — Y. M. Duval, Pélage est-il le censeur inconnu de l'Adversus Iovinianum à Rome en 393?: RHE 75(1980)525-557.

Translations: English: W. H. Freemantle, op. cit., 346-416.

4. *Contra Iohannem Hierosolymitanum.*

After the ordination of Paulinian, John had addressed a defense to Theophilus of Alexandria in June of 396 to explain his complaints against Jerome and Epiphanius. The following spring, Jerome composed a biting response. In spite of his gesture of repentance at Easter and the lifting of the excommunication, he hastened to send his information concerning the event to Rome before Rufinus on his arrival back in Italy could spread a version different from his own. With irony and bad faith, the book discusses the errors of Origen.

Editions: PL 23, 355-398.

Translations: English: W. H. Freemantle, op. cit., 424-447.

Studies: S. Jannaccone, La genesi del cliché antiorigenista e il platonismo origeniano nel Contra Johannem Hierosolymitanum di S. Girolamo: *Giornale Ital. Filologia* 17(1964)14-28. — Y. M. Duval, Sur les insinuations de Jérôme contre Jean de Jérusalem: de l'arianisme à l'origénisme: RHE 65(1970)353-374; *idem,* Tertullien contre Origène sur la résurrection de la chair dans le Contre Iohannem Hierosolymitanum: REAug 17(1971)227-278. — P. Nautin, Une citation méconnue des Stromates d'Origène (Contra Iohannem 25), in *Epektasis,* Mélanges Daniélou. Paris 1972, 373-374.

5. *Apologia adversus libros Rufini.*

In his translations of the *Apology for Origen* of Pamphilus and the *De principiis* (397 and 398), Rufinus had offered some words of response to the *Contra Iohannem Hierosolymitanum.* Furthermore, he had presented himself as continuing the work of Jerome, who previously had translated more than 70 homilies of Origen as well as a certain number of books on the Apostle (i.e., Jerome's commentaries) and who was now the author of more original commentaries. In response, Jerome made his own translation of the *De principiis* accompanied by *Ep.* 84, which was insulting to Rufinus, now the object of slander on the part of various friends of Jerome. Rufinus defended himself in 400 with an *Apologia* to Pope Anastasius and in 401 in an *Apologia* against Jerome. The three books of the *Contra Rufinum,* composed in 401 and 402 are a rude response more personal than dogmatic in nature.

Editions: PL 23, 397-492. — P. Lardet. SCh 303(1983).

Translations: English: W. H. Freemantle, op. cit., 482-541. — J. N. Hritzu, op. cit., 47-220.

6. *Contra Vigilantium.*

Vigilantius, a priest from Aquitania, had been a guest at Bethlehem in 395, where he made a rather unpleasant impression. In 406, he was denounced to Jerome as an opponent of the cult of the martyrs, of certain liturgical practices which he considered superstitious, of the claim of monastic poverty, and the celibacy of the clergy. Jerome claimed to have dictated the violent pamphlet stigmatizing his errors in one night.

Editions: PL 23, 339-352.

Translations: English: W. H. Freemantle, op. cit., 417-423.

Studies: Lucassen, De polemicus Hieronymus adversus de priester Vigilantius: *Hermeneus* 32(1960)53-61. — M. Massie, Vigilance de Calagurris face à la polémique hiéronymienne: BLE 81(1980)81-108.

7. *The Dialogue Against the Pelagians.*

Already in 414, Jerome directed the long letter 133 against Pelagius. The following year, he adapted the form of a dialogue in order to discuss, without invective, the limits of man's liberty and consequently the impassibility to which he could aspire. It is a curious fact that at the end of book III, after the discussion of numerous texts, the Pelagian retires without surrendering. The dialogue was composed in the period between the Synod of Jerusalem (July) and that of Diospolis (December), long before the Council of Antioch of 417.

Editions: PL 23, 495-590. Cf. Pelagius, ch. 7 *infra.*

Translations: English: W. H. Freemantle, *op. cit.,* 447-483. J. N. Hritzu, *op. cit.,* 223-378.

Studies: C. Moreschini, Il contributo di Girolamo alla polemica antipelagiana: Cristianesimo nella Storia 3(1982)61-71.

CORRESPONDENCE

After his translation of the Bible, Jerome's correspondence is undoubtedly the part of his work which has received the most attention and has been most widely read. This correspondence does not form a single comprehensive collection, but has been passed down through diverse manuscript traditions (cf. p. *supra*). Martianay has counted 154 "authentic" letters, which include letters addressed to Jerome as well as translations made by him of Greek documents relating to the Origenist controversy. Letters 148-150 are apocryphal. Certain other letters must be included in the body of his correspondence, such as that published by D. De Bruyne and accepted by Hilberg, the so-called *Ep.* 18 of pseudo-Jerome (G. Morin, BALAC 3[1913]51-60), as well as all the prefaces to the translations of biblical and patristic works, which are transmitted and edited with those works. The most famous letters are those regarding virginity (22 and 130), widowhood (46 and 79), monastic life (14, 58 and 122) and the clerical state (52), and the education of young girls (107 and 128). Several of his letters are funeral eulogies, such as those for Nepotian and Lucinus (60 and 75), or for his disciples (23, 24, 33, 39, 66, 77, 108, 127). Others are brief exegetical treatises. The entire collection is marked by the personality and spirit of the author. The edition of Hilberg, which lacks a preface and indices, did not always make use of the earliest manuscripts such as are now indicated by the *Bibliotheca* of B. Lambert.

Editions: I. Hilberg, CSEL 54(1910-1918). — G. J. M. Bartelink, Hieronymus. Liber de optimo genere interpretandi (Ep. 57). Leiden, 1980.

Translations: English: C. C. Mierow, T. C. Lawler, ACW 33(1963). — W. H. Freemantle, op. cit., 1-195. *French:* J. Labourt. 8 vols. (Les Belles Lettres). Paris, 1949-1963. *Italian:* E. Logi. 3 vols. Siena 1935. — S. Cola. 4 vols. Rome, 1960-64. *Portuguese:* Cartas spirituais. Lisbon, 1960. *Spanish:* D. Ruiz Bueno (BAC). Madrid, 1962.

Studies: P. Lardet, Epistolaires médiévaux de s. Jérôme: FreibZPhilTheol 28(1981)271-289. — M. Marcocchi, Motivi umani e cristiani nell'epistolario di s. Girolamo. Milan, 1947. — R. Gründel, Des Hieronymus Briefe. Ihre literarische Bestimmung und ihre Zusammengehörigkeit. Diss., Leipzig, 1958. — P. Antin, Authenticité de Jérôme ep. 53, 1,4: SE 10(1958)359-362. — V. Recchia, Verginità e martirio nei "colores" di s. Girolamo (ep. 24): VetChr 3(1966)45-68. — J. J. Thierry, Some Notes on Ep. 22 of St. Jerome: VC 21(1967)120-127. — E. Hendrikx, S. Jérôme en tant qu'hagiographe (ep. 108): CD 181(1968)661-667. — P. Devos, Une fausse lecture de la lettre 108 de s. Jérôme: AB 87(1969)213. — T. C. Lawler, Jerome's First Letter to Damasus (ep. 15), in *Kyriakon,* Festschrift J. Quasten II. Münster 1970, 548-552. — V. Pavan, Hieronymi praef. ep. 65: VetChr 9(1972)77-92. — C. Schäublin, Textkritisches zu den Briefen des Hieronymus: *Museum Helveticum* 30(1973)55-62. — C. Vitelli, Nota a Girolamo, ep. 60, 14: RFIC 101(1973)352-355. — P. Nautin, Les lettres romaines de S. Jérôme. In *Origène* I. Paris 1977, 284-288 (ep. 20-37 inspired by Origen); *idem,* L'ep. 33, 4 De viris inlustribus: *ibid.,* 214-219, 227-240; *idem,* La date de la mort de Pauline, de l'ép. 66 de Jérôme et de l'ép. 13 de Paulin de Nole: Aug 18(1978)547-550. — H. Donner, St. Sophronius Eusebius Hieronymus. Die Pilgerfahrt der römischen Patrizierin Paula und ihrer Tochter Eustochium nach Bethlehen, in *Zeugnis und Dienst.* Festgabe G. Besch. Bremen 1974, 20-47. — G. Bartelink, Quelques observations sur la lettre 57 de S. Jérôme: RB 85(1976)296-306. — G. Guttila, S. Girolamo, Seneca e la novitas dell'Ad Heliodorum epitaphium Nepotiani: ALGP 14-16(1977-79)217-244. — L. J. van Lof, L'apôtre Paul dans les lettres de saint Jérôme: *Novum Testamentum* 19(1977)150-160. — R. J. O'Connell, When Saintly Fathers Feuded. The Correspondence between Augustine and Jerome: *Thought* 54(1979)344-364.

CULTURE AND THEOLOGY

In the case of Jerome, it is his biography which explains his work more than his doctrinal synthesis. This latter was neither personal nor comprehensive, since Jerome made it his profession to draw from Greek sources and to cite them abundantly for the benefit of the reader, who was left to make his own judgment. Even after he had taken a strong position on particular points, such as the Hebrew canon or the exclusive authority of the *veritas hebraica,* he had no scruples about citing the variants of the Septuagint or citing some deuterocanonical work while following Origen or another Greek writer. He became more cautious after the Origenist and Pelagian controversies, but his earlier writings offered a target, even in connection with the suspect Origenist teachings, for the criticisms of Rufinus.

Many rich and interesting studies have been made of his classical or

Christian culture through which he made such a powerful impact on the Renaissance and the Middle Ages. The identification of the sources from which he drew his spiritual doctrine and his polemic allow a profound appreciation of his true originality in the fields of both exegesis and ascesis.

1. The Greek Classical Authors.

Jerome wanted it to be believed that he had read the Greek poets and philosophers, but this was merely a pretense. Except for some works of Porphyry which he found in the library at Caesarea, he cites Greek authors only second-hand, through the Latin classics or the Greek Fathers. This defect is particularly noticeable in comparison with Eusebius of Caesarea, who was extremely well read.

Studies: P. Courcelle, Les lettres grecques en Occident. Paris, 1948². — M. V. Anastos, Porphyry's Attack on the Bible, in *Studies in Honor of H. Caplan.* Ithaca 1966, 421-450. — B. R. Ross, Vernachlässigte Zeugnisse klassischen Literatur bei Augustin und Hieronymus: RhM 112(1969)154-166; *idem,* Noch einmal Hieronymus und Platon's Protagoras: RhM (1972)290-291. — G. Bartelink, Platons Protagoras bei Hieronymus: RhM 120(1977)192. — W. C. McDermott, St. Jerome and Pagan Greek Literature: VC 36(1982)372-382.

2. The Latin Classics. Jerome's Style.

The famous dream of Chalcis threatened to condemn Jerome for his reading of Cicero (without doubt Cicero was named only as an unconscious censure and could stand for more scabrous authors). In fact, an exceptional mastery of Vergil, Cicero, and many others, without forgetting the satirists, is one of Jerome's strongest qualities. If at times this tended to compromise the balance of his ascetic doctrine (*Contra Iovinianum*) or his polemic (*Contra Rufinum*), it certainly favored his exegetical talents.

Studies: G. Puccioni, Il problema delle fonti storiche di s. Girolamo: *Annali Scuola Norm. Sup.* Pisa 25(1956)191-212. — H. Hagendhal, Latin Fathers and the Classics, Göteborg, 1958 (basic work). — P. Courcelle, La postérité chrétienne du Songe de Scipion: RELA 36(1958)205-234. — F. M. Brignoli, L'oscurità del Timeo platonico secondo Cicerone e Girolamo: *Giornale Ital. Filologia* 12(1959)59-63. — H. T. Rowell, A Quotation from Marcus Caelius Rufus in St. Jerome (=Quintillian): *Eranos* 1959. — L. Alfonsi, La traduzione ciceroniana dell'Economia di Senofonte: *Ciceroniana* 3(1961)7-17. — I. Opelt, Ein Senecazitat bei Hieronymus: JAC 6(1963)175-176. — S. Jannaccone, S. Girolamo e Seneca: *Giornale Ital. Filologia* 16(1963)326-338; *idem,* Sull'uso degli scritti filosofici de Cicerone da parte di s. Girolamo: ibid., 17(1964)329-341. — R. Godel, Réminiscences de poètes profanes dans les Lettres de s. Jérôme: *Museum Helviticum* 21(1964)65-70. — G. Brugnoli, Donato e Girolamo: VetChr 2(1965)139-149. — W. Trillitzsch, Hieronymus und Seneca: *Mittelat. Jahr.* 2(1965)42-54. — A. Cameron, St. Jerome and Claudian: VC 19(1965)111-113. — A. M. Ficke, Hieronymus Ciceronianus: TP 96(1965)119-138. — F. Glorie, Sources de s. Jérôme et de s. Augustin: SE 18(1967-68)451-477. — C. P. Jones, The Younger Pliny and Jerome: *Phoenix* 21(1967)301. — A. Cameron, Echoes of Vergil in St. Jerome's Life of St. Hilarion: CPh 63(1968)55-56. — J. Préaux, Les quatre vertus païnnes et chrétiennes: Hommag. M.

Renard I. Brussels 1969, 639-657. — I. Opelt, Lukrez bei Hieronymus: Hermes 100(1972)76-81. — F. Trisoglio, S. Girolamo e Plinio il Giovane: *Rivista Ital. Studi Classici* 21(1973)343-383. — H. Hagendahl, Jerome and the Latin Classics: VC 28(1974)216-227. — J. J. Thierry, Hieronymus en Ovidius: *Hermeneus* 50(1978).

Jerome's style: J. G. Préaux, Procédés d'invention d'un sobriquet par s. Jérôme: Latomus 17(1958)659-664. — G. Del Ton, De latino scribendi genere s. Hieronymi: *Latinitas* 9(1961)167-174. — P. Nautin, Unius esse: VC 15(1961)40-45. — W. Clausen, Concava verba: CPh 59(1964)38. — D. S. Wiesen, St. Jerome as a Satirist. Ithaca, 1964. — G. Q. A. Meershoek, Le latin biblique d'après s. Jérôme. Nijmegen, 1966. — D. F. Heimann, Latin Word Order in the Writings of St. Jerome, Vita Pauli, Vita Malchi, Vita Hilarionis. Diss., Columbia Univ. 1966. — P. Antin, A la source de "singularitas," vie monastique: ALMA 36(1967-68)111-112; *idem,* Mots "vulgaires" chez s. Jérôme: Latomus 30(1971)708-709. — A. F. Memoli, Diversità di posizioni e apparenti incoerenze degli scrittori latini cristiani di fronte all'eloquenza classica: *Aevum* 43(1969)114-143. — V. Bejarano, San Jerónimo y la Vulgata latina. Distribución de las conjucciones declarativas "quod, quia, quoniam": *Helmantica* 26(1975)51-55. — G. Bartelink, Les observations de Jérôme sur des termes de lange courante et parlée: Latomus (1979)193-222. — L. Holtz, Donat et la tradition de l'enseignement grammatical. Paris 1981.

3. Preceding Christian Literature.

Studies dedicated to the research of Jerome's patristic sources are extremely rare. An exception is provided by those of Y. M. Duval, which have obtained results of notable interest for the polemical works and those regarding Origen. Almost all of these have been mentioned above in connection with the translations and commentaries.

Studies: H. Crouzel, Bibliographie critique d'Origène (Instr. Patr. 8). Steenbrugge, 1971 (index: Origène, Querelle origéniste). — P. Nautin, Une citation méconnue des Stromates d'Origène, in *Epektasis,* Mélanges Daniélou. Paris 1972, 373-374. — G. Bartelink, Les Oxymores "Desertum civitas" et "Dersertum floribus vernans" (ep. 14, 10): *Studia Monastica* 15(1973)7-15. — C. Tibletti, Un Opuscolo perduto di Tertulliano "Ad amicum philosophum": *Acta Acc. Sc. Torino* 95(1960-61)122-126. — Y. M. Duval, La lecture de l'Octavius de Minucius à la fin du IVe s.: REAug 19(1973)56-68 (Silence of Jerome who is not interested in the pagan aristocracy).

Translations from Greek: P. Serra-Zanetti, Sul criterio e il valore della traduzione per Cicerone e s. Girolamo: *Atti I Congr. Studi Ciceroniani* II. Rome 1961, 355-405. — A. Ronconi, Note a s. Girolamo revisore del testo latino dei Vangeli: RCCM 7(1965)962-971. — B. Studer, A propos des traductions d'Origène par Jérôme et Rufin: VetChr 4(1968)137-155. — F. Winkelmann, Einige Bemerkungen zu den Aussagen des Rufinus von Aquileia und des Hieronymus über ihre Übersetzungstheorie und-methode, in *Kyriakon,* Festschrift J. Quasten II. Münster 1970, 532-542.

4. The Philologist of Oriental Languages.

Jerome's curiosity, his interests and his abilities changed during his life, and not always according to a continuous line of development. His contacts with rabbis are better certified at Rome and at the beginning of his sojourn at Bethlehem, although he must have been led to exaggerate their importance and to attribute to himself that which he obtained from books. However the *Hexapla,* which is lost for us, provided him with an exceptional documentation for both his translations and his commentaries.

Studies: J. H. Marks, Der textkritische Wert des Psalteriums Hieronymi iuxta Hebraeos. *Winterthur,* 1956. — W. H. Semple, St. Jerome as a Biblical Translator: BJL 48(1965)227-243. — F. Vattioni, Saggio sulla Volgata dei Proverbi: VetChr 2(1966)143-160; *idem,* S. Girolamo e l'Ecclesiastico: ibid., 3(1967)131-149. — J. Barr, St. Jerome's Appreciation of Hebrew: BJC 49(1967)281-302. — E. Burstein. S. Jérôme. Diss., Paris, 1971. — J. T. Cummings, St. Jerome as Translator and Exegete. SP 12. Berlin 1975, 279-282. — C. Estin, S. Jérôme. De la traduction inspirée à la traduction relativiste: RBibl 88(1981)199-215. — H. P. Rüger, Hieronymus, die Rabbinen und Paulus. Zur Vorgeschichte des Begriffspaars "innere" und "äussere Mensch": ZNW 68(1977)132-137.

5. Hermeneutical and Exegetical Principles.

In Jerome there took place a confluence of a Latin exegetical tradition, which he did not appreciate, with various currents of Greek exegesis and Judaic science. With time, he succeeded in acquiring exceptional experience. His commentaries on the New Testament were few, but his faith in Christ remained a preferred criterion for the interpretation of the Old. It is quite interesting to observe how these diverse factors combined with one another.

Studies: A. Penna, I titoli del Salterio siriaco e s. Girolamo: Bibl 40 (1959)177-187. P. Benoit, L'inspiration de la LXX d'après les Pères: *Exégèse et Théologie* 3. Paris 1968, 69-89. — P. Jay, Le vocabulaire exégétique de s. Jérôme dans le Commentaire sur Zacharie: REAug 14(1968)3-16. — J. F. Hernandez Martin, San Jerónimo y los déuterocanónicas del Antiguo Testamento: CD 182(1969)373-384. — W. Hagemann, Wort als Begegnung mit Christus. Die christozentirsche Schriftauslegung des Kirchenvaters Hieronymus. Trier, 1970. — P. Jay, Remarques sur le vocabulaire exégétique de s. Jérôme. SP 10. Berlin 1970, 187-189; *idem,* Allegoriarum nubilum chez s. Jérôme: REAug 22(1976)82-89. — Y. M. Duval, Jérôme et Origène avant la querelle origéniste: Aug 24(1984)471-494. — P. Jay, Saint Jérôme et le triple sens de l'Écriture: REAug 26(1980) 214-227.

Particular questions: R. Arbesmann, The Daemonium meridianum and Greek and Latin Patristic Exegesis: *Tradition* 14(1958)17-31. — S. Lyonnet, Expiation et intercession. A propos d'une traduction de s. Jérôme: Bibl. 40(1959)885-901. — A. Penna, The Vow of Jephtah in the interpretation of St. Jerome: SP 4. Berlin 1966, 162-170. — R. Cantalamessa, Ratio Paschae. La controversia sul significato della Pasqua nell'Ambrosiaster, in Girolamo e in Agostino: *Aevum* 44(1970)219-241. — J. J. Arce, La epístola 37 de s. Jerónimo y el problema di Tartessos igual a Tarshish bíblica: Latomus 33(1974)943-947.

6. Ecclesiology and Anthropology.

Studies: J. Lecuyer, Le problème des consécrations épiscopales dans l'Eglise d'Alexandrie: BLE 65(1964)242-257. — J. M. Da Cruz Pontes, Le problème de l'origine de l'âme de la Patristique à la solution thomiste: RTAM 31(1964)175-229. — Y. Bodin, S. Jérôme et l'Eglise. Paris, 1966; *idem,* S. Jérôme et les Laïcs: REAug 15(1969)133-147. — J. du Q. Adams, The Populus of Augustine and Jerome. A Study in the Patristic Sense of

Community. New Haven, 1971. — Cf. also the works of Y. M. Duval on the *Altercatio Luciferiani* and on the *Contra Iohannem Hierosolymitanum.*

7. Morality and Asceticism.

Studies: E. Dekkers, Profession, Second Baptême. Qu'a voulu dire s. Jérôme: HJB 77(1958)91-97. — D. Dumm, The Theological Basis of Virginity According to St. Jerome. Latrobe, 1961. — S. Visintainer, La dottrina del peccato in s. Girolamo. Diss., Rome, 1962. — A. Dihle, Buddha und Hieronymus: Mittellat. Jahrb. 2(1965)38-41. — I. S. Nozik, The Ascetical Doctrine of St. Jerome. Diss., Fordham Univ., 1966. — J. Dittburner, A Theology of Temporal Realities. Explanation of St. Jerome. Diss., Rome, 1966. — L. Laurita, Insegnamenti ascetici nelle lettere di s. Girolamo. Diss., Rome, 1967. — P. Antin, S. Jérôme directeur mystique: *Rev. d'Hist. de la spiritualité* 48(1972)25-29. — P. Nautin, Divorce et remariage dans la tradition de l'Eglise latine: RSR 62 (1974)7-54. — C. Micaeli, L'influsso di Tertulliano su Girolamo; le opere sul matrimonio e le seconde nozze: Aug 19(1979)415-429.

POSTHUMOUS AUTHORITY

Jerome's importance can also be measured by the number of manuscripts of his works and by the number of apocryphal writings transmitted under his name (cf. the *Bibliotheca* of B. Lambert, *supra,* p. 220). This same importance is also manifested by the frequency with which he is mentioned in the *florilegia,* such as the *Liber Scintillarum,* by citations and imitations of his works, and by his influence on the liturgy.

Studies: B. Thorsberg, Une hymne en l'honneur de s. Jérôme: Etudes sur l'hymnologie mozarabe. Stockholm 1962, 107-136. — I. Opelt, Quellenstudien zu Eucherius: Hermes 91 (1963)476-483. — S. Pricoco, Sidonio Apollinare, Girolamo e Rufino: *Acta Philologica* 3 (Misc. N. I. Herescu). Rome 1964, 299-306. — J. Schwartz, Arguments philologiques pour dater l'Histoire Auguste: *Historia* 15(1966)454-465. — A. de Vogüé, L'origine d'une interpolation de la Règle bénédictine: *Scriptorium* 21(1967)72. — R. Grégoire, Prières liturgiques médiévales en l'honneur de s. Jérôme: *Studi Medievali* III 9(1968)580-588. — K. S. Frank, Isidor von Sevilla. Das "Mönchskapitel" und seine Quellen: RQ 67(1972)29-48. — R. Etaix, Un ancien florilège hiéronymien: SE 21(1972-73)5-34. — A. de Vogüé, Deux emprunts de la Règle columbanienne: *Rev. d'Hist. de la Spiritualité* 49(1973)129-134. — I. Opelt, Hieronymus bei Dante: Dt. Dante-Jahrb. 51-52(1976-77)65-83. — R. Grégoire, Le succès d'une erreur historique de s. Jérôme. RB 88(1978)91-100, 296.

RUFINUS THE SYRIAN

It has already been noted that the tendency today is to attribute the Vulgate revision of the Pauline Epistles, the Catholic Epistles, and probably the Acts of the Apostles and the Apocalypse to this disciple of Jerome. Nothing is known of the origins of this Rufinus. He is possibly called the "Syrian" because of his sojourn in Bethlehem, whence he carried to Rome Jerome's letters 81 and 84 along with the translation of Origen's *De principiis* in the spring of 399. These letters designate Rufinus as the "holy priest." At the home of Pammachius, he soon made friends with the circle of Pelagius. Before 411 he wrote a *Liber de fide* and perhaps also a *Libellus de fide*. Nothing further is known of him.

Editions: E. Schwartz, Acta Conciliorum Oecumenicorum I, 5. Berlin 1924, 4-5 (Libellus de fide). — M. W. Miller, Rufini presbyteri Liber de fide. Washington, 1964 (Cf. PL 21, 1123-1154).

Studies: A. Vaccari, Rufini presbyteri Liber de Fide: Greg 42(1961)733-736. — F. Refoulé, Le libellus fidei de Rufin: REAug 9(1963)41-49. — H. I. Marrou, Les attaches orientales du pélagianisme: CRI(1968)459-472. — G. Bonner, Rufinus of Syria and African Pelagianism: Aug Studies 1(1970)31-47. — H. Rondet, Rufin le Syrien et le Liber de fide: AugL 22(1972)531-539. — E. TeSelle, Rufinus the Syrian, Caelestius, Pelagius: Aug Studies 3(1972)61-65.

RUFINUS OF AQUILEIA

The life of Tiranius Rufinus, which is bound up in part with the life of Jerome, can only be treated briefly here. He was born at Concordia around 345, studied at Rome around 359-368, was a member of the ascetic community of Aquileia (368-373), and departed for the East at the same time as Jerome but passed the years 373-380 in Egypt in the company of the monks and in the school of Didymus the Blind. Together with Melania the Elder, he took up residence on the Mount of Olives in Jerusalem, where he remained until 397. During this period he gradually grew apart from Jerome, refusing to follow him in the study of Hebrew and taking the side of the bishop of Jerusalem in the Origenist Controversy. During all this time he published nothing—neither translations nor works of his own. This explains in part the scorn with which Jerome attacked him, on the occasion of the first quarrels, as someone lazy who did not succeed in writing. In fact, his Latin is quite correct, though more pious than malicious. He had a weak critical sense and accepted the pseudo-Clementines as the work of that pope who had been a disciple of the Apostles, and took the sentences of Sextus Pythagoricus as the work of the martyred Pope Sixtus. He narrated amazing stories of the monks of Egypt, in comparison with which Jerome's *Vita Pauli* is a monument of historical criticism. His opinions concerning the heresies interpolated into the works of Origen by an unfriendly hand are too simple. All of this did not hinder him from being more honorable than Jerome and from playing an essential role in the transmission of the works of Origen, a large part of which survives thanks only to his work.

Rufinus returned to Rome in 397 and to Aquileia in 399. On his return to the West he dedicated himself to the work of translation along the same lines in which he had urged Jerome to continue his first efforts. At a certain point he felt it necessary to justify this undertaking of his with his apologies. Nevertheless, he had the good taste not to continue, for his part, to fuel the Origenist Controversy.

In 407, the invasion of the Goths forced him to seek refuge at Rome, then at the monastery of *Pinetum* (on the Tyrrhenian Coast, near Terracina) and finally in Sicily, where he died in 410. His friends, Paulinus of Nola, Chromatius of Aquileia, and Gaudentius of Brescia never felt it necessary to break their ties with him merely to please Jerome. Subsequently, Jerome's calumnies brought such discredit on Rufinus' reputation that no attempt was ever made to canonize him. Modern historians, however, no longer allow themselves to be influenced by the libelous press originating from Bethlehem.

Studies: Cf. Jerome's works dealing with the Origenist Controversy *supra* as well as the bibliography provided by M. Simonetti, CCL 20(1961)xii-xx. — M. Villain, Rufin d'Aquilée: NRTh 64(1937)5-33, 139-161; *idem,* Rufin d'Aquilée. La querelle autour d'Origène: RSR 27(1937)5-37, 165-195. — F. X. Murphy, Rufinus of Aquileia. Washington, 1945; *idem,* Rufinus of Aquileia and Paulinus of Nola: REAug 2(1956)79-91; *idem,* Sources of the Moral Teaching of Rufinus of Aquileia. SP 6. Berlin 1962, 147-154. — C. P. Hammond, The Last Ten Years of Rufinus' Life and the Date of his Move South from Aquileia: JThSt 28(1977) 372-429. — Y. M. Duval, Julien d'Eclane et Rufin d'Aquilée: REAug 24(1978) 243-271.

WRITINGS

Nearly all of Rufinus' works are translations and it is not necessary to deal again with their content, which has been treated in previous volumes of Quasten's *Patrology* under Origen, Basil, Eusebius, etc. There are critical editions of almost all of these translations. The prefaces of Rufinus (which is unfortunately all that remains of his correspondence) and his original works have been very well edited by M. Simonetti in CCL 20. A general view of the manuscript tradition can be obtained from the preface of *Il Salterio di Rufino* (ed. F. Merlo, J. Griboment. Rome, 1972), where the numerous citations of the Psalter from the various writings are collected and analyzed.

The value of Rufinus' translations has been widely discussed, since they often represent the only witness to a lost original text. Rufinus, indeed, was concerned with edifying his readers and not with rendering a service to philologists nor with offering them a precise replacement of the Greek work whose destruction he could not foresee; thus he cannot be judged according to these criteria. In the specific case of Origen, he did not hide the fact that he had eliminated or softened heretical passages (i.e., in regard to Trinitarian doctrine), since he considered them to be interpolations. He also confessed to having explained difficult passages on occasion by making recourse to parallel passages of Origen. Within these limits, however, his translation is intelligent and valuable, and the discovery of parallel Greek fragments has gained for him a new respect. An interesting indication of his method of translating is that in general he translated biblical citations by using the existing Latin text, and took note of the peculiarity of his Greek exemplar only when required by the context, undoubtedly with the intention of helping the reader to recognize and profit from the allusions.

Studies: Translations: H. Chadwick, Rufinus and the Tura Papyrus of Origen's Commentary on Romans: JThSt 10(1955)10-42. — B. Studer, A propos des traductions d'Origène par Jérôme de Rufin: VetChr 4(1968)137-155; *idem,* Zur Frage der dogmatischen Terminologie in der lat. Übersetzung von Origines' De Principiis, in *Epektasis,* Mélang. Daniélou. Paris 1972, 403-414. — A. M. Memoli, Fedeltà di interpretazione e libertà espressiva nella traduzione rufiniana dell'Or. XVII di Gregorio Nazianzeno: *Aevum* 43(1969)459-484. — F. Winkelmann, Einige Bemerkungen zu den Aussagen des Rufinus von Aquileia und des Hieronymus über ihre Übersetzungstheorie und -methode, in *Kyriakon,* Festschrift J. Quasten. Münster 1970, II 532-542. — F. Merlo, J. Griboment, Il Salterio di Rufino. Rome, 1972.

Style and literary symbolism: M. Martínez Pastor, Algunas particularidades del latin cristiano di Rufino de Aquileia: *Durius* 1(1973)63-75; *idem,* El simbolismo de umbra en los escritos origenianos de Rufino: ibid., 335-344; *idem,* La simbología de la luz en Origenes-Rufino: *Emerita* 441(1973)183-208; *idem,* Latinidad del vocabulario de Rufino de Aquileia: *Helmantica* 25(1974)181-194. — C. P. Hammond, Products of Fifth Century Scriptoria preserving Conventions Used by Rufinus of Aquileia: JThSt 30(1979)430-462.

1. The *Apologies.*

The Origenist Controversy obliged Rufinus to depart from his role of translator, as it had become urgent that he justify his work. The first step in this direction, in 397-398, was simply a translation of the *Apologia* written by the martyr Pamphilus and by Eusebius in defense of Origen (translation of book I, summary of books IV and V). To this *Apologia,* Rufinus attached a supplement, the *De adulteratione librorum Origenis,* which was an adaptation of Origen's letter to his friends at Alexandria cited in book IV of the *Apologia.* It is indeed true that Origen's Arian disciples had given a very precise interpretation to ambiguous passages of the master, but the generalizations of Rufinus smack of naiveté.

Since he had been accused of Origenism, Rufinus in 400 wrote a four-page letter to defend himself before Anastasius, the bishop of Rome. This *Apologia ad Anastasium* contained a profession of faith in the Trinity, the resurrection and judgment, a discourse on the origin of the soul, and an explanation of the reasons for his translation of Origen.

In 401, he wrote the two books of the *Apologia contra Hieronymum* with the intention of responding to the accusations hurled against him by his former friend and of passing over to the offensive on these personal questions. This was to be his last word in the debate.

Editions: Apologia of Pamphilus PG 17, 539-616. — M. Simonetti, CCL 20(1961), (De adulteratione 1-17, Apologia ad Anastasium 19-28, Contra Hieronymum 29-123). Cf. J. Quasten, Patrology II, Utrecht-Antwerp 1953, 145-146 (Pamphilus' *Apologia*).

Translations: English: W. H. Freemantle, LNPF 3, ser. 2(1892)421-427 (De adulteratione lib. Orig., 430-432 Apol. ad Anastasium, 434-482 Apol. contra Hieronymun.) (reprint: 1969).

Studies: P. Nautin, L'Apologie pour Origène et ses opinions . . . L'adaptation latine de Rufin, in *Origène* I. Paris 1977, 150-153.

2. The Translations of Origen.

Rufinus began in 398 with the most dense and controversial of Origen's works, the treatise *De principiis* (*Peri Archôn)*. In spite of his explicit confession of having deliberately eliminated suspect formulas, the recent studies of M. Simonetti and M. Harl have given more and more credit to his translation. Subsequently, perhaps to respond to suspicions of heresy, he translated, ca. 400, the dialogue *De fide orthodoxa* of Adamantius under the name of Origen, identifying Adamantius with Origen in the tracks of Basil and Gregory Nazienzus (*Philocalia* ch. 24). In 400 Rufinus provided the Latin world with the homilies on Joshua, and in 401 those on Judges along with the nine homilies on Psalms 36-38. In the years 403-404 came the turn for a magnificent series of homilies on Genesis, Exodus, and Leviticus which is today the most prized work of all his translations. There exists also a homily of Origen on Elkanah (1 Kings), but there is no proof that it was actually translated by Rufinus. In his preface to Origen's great commentary on the Letter to the Romans, Rufinus describes his translations as fishing for little fish, deprived of all risks, compared to the departure for the high seas which Heraclius imposed on him in 405-406 by involving him with the fifteen books of commentary on Romans, which would indeed present a fundamental contribution to Latin exegesis. The epilogue to the same work (CCL 20, 276-277) speaks of the lively problems involved in the translation of such an ambitious work, *sed delectavit indulsisse laboribus!* Rufinus remarked how such translations easily circulated under the name of their Latin editor in Hilary, Ambrose, and Jerome, and he refused such an honor for himself, taking care to note the name of his Greek model. Finally, in 410, the last year of his life, Rufinus translated the commentary on the Canticle, and had still time to offer a translation of the beatiful homilies on Numbers, as from Messina he watched Reggio burn across the Straits. He had no further time to add the homilies on Deuteronomy.

Editions: De Principiis: P. Koetschau, Origenes Werke 5(GCS 22). Leipzig, 1913. — H. Crouzel, M. Simonetti. SCh 252, 253, 268, 269, 312(1978-1984). — *Psalms 36-38:* PL 12, 1319-1410. — *Adamantius:* W. H. van de Sande Bakhuyzen. GCS 4. Leipzig, 1901. — V. Buchheit, Tyranni Rufini librorum Adamantii Origenis adversus haereticos interpretatio (*Studia et Testimonia antigua* I). Munich, 1966. — *Octateuch and Canticle:* W. A. Baehrens, Origenes Werke 6-8 (GCS). Leipzig, 1920-1925. — *On Romans:* PG 14, 831-1294(=Delarue).

Translations: English: A. Roberts, J. Donaldson, De Principiis, ANF 4(1885)235-382 (reprint: 1972). — R. P. Lawson, Commentary on the Canticle. ACW 26(1956)21-263. — R. Heine, Homilies on Genesis and Exodus. FC 71(1982).

French: M. Harl, G. Dorival, A. Boulluec. Origène. Traité des Principes. Paris, 1976. — H. Crouzel, M. Simonetti, op. cit. — L. Doutreleau, H. De Lubac, Origène. Homélies sur la Genèse. SCh 7(1943). — P. Fortier, H. De Lubac, Origène. Homélies sur l'Exode. SCh 16(1947). — A. Jaubert, Origène. Homélies sur Josué. SCh 71(1960). A. Méhat, Origène. Homélies sur les Nombres. SCh 29(1951).

Italian: M. Simonetti. I Principi di Origene. Turin, 1968. — G. Gentili. Origene. Omelie sulla Genesi e sull'Esodo. Rome, 1976. — Simonetti, Origene. Commento al Cantico dei Cantici. Rome, 1976.

German: H. Görgemanns, H. Karpp, Origenes, Vier Bücher von den Prinzipien. Darmstadt, 1976.

Studies: C. P. Hammond, Notes on the Manuscripts and Editions of Origen's Commentary on the Epistle to the Romans in the Latin Translation by Rufinus: JThSt 16(1965)338-357. — G. Sanders, Un écrit oublié, le Dialogue d'Adamantius: ACL 37(1968)644-651. — I. Fransen, Un nouveau témoin latin de l'homélie d'Origène sur le livre des Rois: RB 78(1968)108-117. — J. B. Bauer, Benedikt und Origenes: WSt NF 8(1974)182-187. — G. Schroeder, Eusèbe de Césarée, Préparation évangélique VII: SCh 215(1975)111-119.

3. The *Sentences* of Evagrius and Sextus.

A translation of Evagrius, the leader of the Origenists of the desert and friend of Melania, can be attributed to Rufinus' Origenism. It is a wonder that he translated only two series of sentences: *To the Monks* and *To a Virgin.* There exist two Latin translations for each series. For the first series, *To the Monks,* one translation is certainly older and has been subsequently retouched. Since it is known that Rufinus made one translation and that Gennadius subsequently revised one already old, it is customary to attribute to Rufinus the version of Leclercq and to Gennadius the version of Holste. As regards the second series, *To a Virgin,* if Leclercq is correct (op. cit., p. 201, n. 42), the text edited by Holste is that of Rufinus while that published by Wilmart is a later one. It is a curious fact that neither of these versions have a prologue of the translator. They appear to be from the years 403-404.

Prior to 401 Rufinus had also translated other ascetic sentences which he attributed to Pope Sixtus, but which instead were correctly identified by Jerome as the work of the pagan Pythagorean philosopher, Sextus. Origen had cited this collection, and Evagrius had drawn inspiration from it, though without naming it. Rufinus knew only the first 415 sentences out of a series of 610.

Editions: J. Leclercq. L'ancienne version latine des Sentences d'Evagre pour les moines: *Scriptorium* 5(1951)204-213. — A. Wilmart, Les versions latines des Sentences d'Evagre pour les vierges: RB 28(1911)143-153. — PL 40, 1277-1286. — H. Chadwick, The Sentences of Sextus (TSt NS 5). Cambridge, 1959. — H. Silvestre, Trois nouveaux témoins latins des Sentences de Sextus: *Scriptorium* 17(1963)128-129. — P. M. Bogaert, La préface de Rufin aux Sentences de Sexte et à une œuvre inconnue: RB 82(1972)26-46. — J. Bouffartigue, Du grec au latin. La traduction latine des Sentences de Sextus (*Etudes de Littérature ancienne*). Paris 1979, 81-95.

4. *Historia Monachorum in Aegypto.*

This is a collection of picturesque and fantastic tales gathered by travelers from Jerusalem who had toured among the holy monks. There is a Latin version of Rufinus as well as a Greek version. The Greek was previously regarded as a translation, but now is recognized as the original text, edited by a friend of Rufinus. A good Latin edition is unfortunately lacking, thus for this literary genre, in which the copyists felt free to take certain liberties, there is only the edition of Rosweyde, which has no critical apparatus. The translation could have been done in 403.

Editions: PL 21, 387-452. Cf. J. Quasten, Patrology III. Utrecht-Antwerp 1975, 177-179 (Lausiac History).

5. Basil and Gregory Nazienzus.

Before he devoted himself to Origen, the first spiritual text which Rufinus bought to the attention of the West was what he called the "Rule" of St. Basil, which he translated at the monastery of *Pinetum,* where he had stopped on his way to Rome. This was a shorter edition, in 203 questions, of the *Asceticon,* which the Greek manuscripts transmit in a longer version. Rufinus translated faithfully and it can be questioned whether this text did not enjoy a certain authority with the monks in the monastery on the Mount of Olives.

In 399, when he left Rome, Rufinus had begun to translate eight homilies of Basil, which he finished at Aquileia. He counted *Ep.* 46, not without reason, as a homily. In spite of Altaner's opinion to the contrary, the summary translation (inedited) of the homilies on fasting has no claim for being considered as the work of Rufinus.

When he had finished this series the translator turned his attention to nine homilies of Gregory Nazienzus, toward the beginning of 400.

These works of the Cappadocians can be connected with Origenism, but in quite a different sense from that represented by Evagrius.

Editions: Rule: PL 103, 487-554. — *Homilies of Basil:* PG 31, 1723-1794. — *Gregory Nazienzus:* A. Engelbrecht, Tyranni Rufini orationum Gregorii Nazianzeni novem interpretatio: CSEL 46(1910).

Translations: Italian: G. Turbessi. Regole monastiche. Rome, 1974.

Studies: M. Huglo, Les anciennes versions latines des homélies de s. Basile: RB 64(1954)129-132. — B. Altaner, Kleine Patristische Schriften. Berlin 1967, 409-415 (Homilies of Basil).

6. The *Historia Ecclesiastica* of Eusebius.

As a result of the sensible request of Chromatius of Aquileia, Rufinus translated the ten books of Eusebius' *Historia Ecclesiastica* in 402-403, not hesitating to summarize and complete the work. He added two books, either drawing inspiration from or translating the now-lost history of Gelasius of Cesarea, which brought the narration down to the death of Theodosius (395).

Editions: T. Mommsen, in E. Schwartz, Eusebius Werke 2 (GCS). Leipzig, 1903-09 (From more than 100 mss., the editor arbitrarily retains 4). Cf. J. Quasten, Patrology III, 314-317 (Eusebius), 347-348 (Gelasius).

Studies: M. Villain, Rufin d'Aquilée et l'histoire ecclésiastique: RSR 33(1946)164-210. — A. Cameron, A Disguised Manuscript of Rufinus, Translation of Eusebius' Ecclesiastical History: *Scriptorium* 18(1964)270-271. — Y. M. Duval, L'éloge de Théodose dans la Cité de Dieu. Sa place, son sens et ses sources: *Recherches Aug* 4(1966)135-179; *idem,* S. Augustin et les persécutions de la deuxième moitié du IVe s.: MSR 23(1966)175-191; *idem,* Un nouveau lecteur de l'Histoire ecclésiastique de Rufin d'Aquilée, l'auteur du Liber Promissionum et praedictorum Dei: Latomus 26(1967)762-777. — F. Thelamon, Païens et chrétiens au IVe s. L'apport de l'Histoire ecclésiastique de Rufin d'Aquilée. Paris, 1981; *idem,* L'empereur idéal d'après l'Histoire ecclésiastique de Rufin d'Aquilée. SP 10. Berlin 1970, 310-314; *idem,* Recherches sur la valeur historique del'Histoire ecclésiastique de Rufin d'Aquilée: RH 102(1978)522-525. *idem,* Modèles de monachisme oriental selon Rufin d'Aquilée: AnAl 12(1977)323-352. — T. Christenses, Rufinus of Aquileia and the Historia Ecclesiastica, lib. VIII-IX of Eusebius: STh 34(1980)129-152. — M. Pucci, Some Historical Remarks on Rufinus' *Historia Ecclesiastica:* RSA 11(1981)123-128.

7. The Clementine *Recognitiones.*

Possibly in connection with his translation of Eusebius, Rufinus had promised Gaudentius of Brescia that he would translate the *Recognitiones,* which he attributed to Pope St. Clement. He carried out this promise in 406, although he had already translated the brief *Epistula Clementis ad Iacobum.*

Editions: B. Rehm, F. Paschke, Die Pseudoklementinen. II. Rekognitionen (GCS). Berlin, 1965.

Studies: F. Paschke, Zur Pseudoklementinen Ausgabe der Berliner Akademie: *Institut de Recherche et d'Histoire des Textes, Bulletin* 15(1969)57-67.

8. Original Works.

Excluding the *Apologies* and perhaps the final part of the *Historica Ecclesiastica,* Rufinus only twice undertook the composition of an original work. The first attempt in 400 was a commentary on the Apostles' Creed, based on the catechesis he had known in Jerusalem and which was imposing itself everywhere as a model at that time. Then, in 408, after he had been forced to flee from Aquileia, he composed a brief exposition on the *De Benedictionibus Patriarcharum* (Gennadius, 49), in which he made use of the text of Hippolytus (the text preserved in the exegetical chains and not the treatise composed in Greek used by Ambrose and Gregory of Elvira).

Editions: M. Simonetti, CCL 20(1961)125-182, 183-228.

Translations: English: J. N. D. Kelly, Rufinus. A Commentary on the Apostles' Creed.

London, 1955. — W. H. Freemantle, op. cit., 541-563. *French:* M. Simonetti, Rufin d'Aquilée. Les Bénédictions des Patriarches. SCh 140 (1968)

Studies: M. Villain, Rufin d'Aquilée, Commentateur du Symbole des Apôtres: RSR 31(1944)129-156. — M. Simonetti, Osservazioni sul De Benedictionibus Patriarcharum di Rufino di Aquileia: RCCM 4(1962)3-44.

CHAPTER V

CHRISTIAN POETRY

by Angelo DiBerardino

The sections on Paulinus of Nola and Prudentius are by Nello Cipriani. Bibliography by Angelo DiBerardino.

THE BEGINNINGS OF CHRISTIAN POETRY

The first Christian communities, which arose in the world of Palestinian Judaism, modeled their liturgy on that of the synagogue (readings, homilies, chants, and prayers) with the inclusion of the celebration of the Lord's Supper. The Davidic Psalter, which formed an integral part of the liturgy, was regarded as a work of lofty poetry as well. Jerome would later say, "David is our Simonides, Pindar, Alcaeus; and Horatius, Catullus and Serenus as well" (*Ep.* 53, 8: PL 22, 547). The singing of psalms, hymns, and inspired songs was recommended by St. Paul (Col. 3:16; Eph. 5:18). Pliny (*Ep.* 10, 96) stated that the Christians sang a hymn in alternating chorus to Christ as to a god. The first Christian poetry, which was without any literary pretense, was manifest in more or less lengthy hymns connected with chant and prayer, both public and private. (*Const. apost.* 7, 47; Tertullian, *De spect.* 39; Clement Al. *Paedag.* 2, 4; *Strom.* 7, 5). Little remains of the compositions from the first three centuries, and that only in Greek. Heretical sects also made use of songs and poetry to spread their doctrine and help it to be more easily remembered; a practice subsequently adopted by the Arians and Donatists (Irenaeus, *Adv. haer.* I 15, 6; Tertullian, *De carne Chr.* 17 and 20; Origen, *In Iob* 21, 11ff; Athanasius, *Or. c. Arianos* 2, 2-10; *De synod.* 15).

The most ancient Christian poetry, which was popular rather than erudite in character, often contained a doctrinal content, frequently was connected with the liturgy (blessings, litanies, thanksgivings) and was biblical in inspiration. Psalmody was the genre most frequently used, and there were numerous compositions of this type which were not biblical in origin (γ'αλμοὶ ἰδιοτιχοί), the *Odes of Solomon* being among the best known. Clement of Alexandria is the first orthodox writer to be known as an author of hymns. No Latin compositions from the first three centuries have survived, although according to Tertullian (*Adv. Marc.* 3, 22; *De spect.* 19 and 39; *Ad uxorem* 2, 8, 8) such compositions did exist. In any case, these hymns made no other claims than to be an element of prayer. In general, they must have been a particular type of prose which was intended to be sung, and which was characterized by parallelism, biblical inspiration, and an absence of meter.

This form of poetry was traditional in the Roman world (G. B. Pighi, *Poesia religiosa romana. Testi e frammenti.* Bologna, 1958). Poetry in the strict sense was clearly behind prose in making its appearance. Ch. Mohrmann considers that this is due not to a disdain for a classical literary genre, but to the fact that pagan Latin poetry had become a literary exercise for the schools and had lost all contact with everyday life, therefore it was incapable of expressing the life and sentiments of the Christians. In reality, this delay must have been due in part to a certain distrust of poetry for religious and moral reasons, such as can be perceived in Augustine (*Conf.* I 13, 14 and 17). Much later Isidore of Seville would write, "It is prohibited to the Christian to read the compositions of the poets, because these, with their delight in lying fables, stir up the mind with incitements of lust" (*Sent.* 3, 13, 3). It was thus the content of the poetry which aroused such strong concerns in Christian circles (cf. H. I. Marrou, Histoire de l'éducation dans l'antiquité. Paris 1965[6], p. 460-462).

When the Christians began to make use of poetry, they kept as close as possible to the classical rules without making any innovations except in regard to content. This traditionalism was observed in regard to the sources as well as the forms. Horatius, Terentius, Ovid, etc., but especially Vergil, were the expressions of ultimate learning for a Latin and were the basic foundation of all cultural formation. The pagan and Christian centones are the fruit of a particular education and sensitivity. In the Late Empire, instruction and literary education were based almost exclusively on the poets: *Ars grammatica* — secondary education — *praecipue consistit in intellectu poetarum* (Sergius, *Expl. in art. Donati* 4: ed. Keil, p. 486). Vergil was the textbook studied in the smallest details and known to perfection, often by memory; it was the essence of Latin culture and the bible of every student and professor. Because of this, the basic culture was extraordinarily uniform throughout the entire *pars occidentalis* of the empire. For the purpose of instruction, professors and students practiced composing verse, above all in hexameters (heroic verse) on every possible subject. Augustine would remember only the poets he studied (*Conf.* I 13, 14 and 17; *De ordine* 2, 14; *De musica* 2, 1). The composition of poems was a τέχνη, a trade, not a ποίησις. The poets were admired for their technical skill, their metrical virtuosity and their knowledge of the forms, not for the content of their works nor their ideas. Poetry was held in great esteem and many verses were composed, albeit with few truly poetic results. The Christians of the fourth century fit into this cultural tradition.

Christian prose was more creative, more innovative and even

assimilated popular aspects. Poetry was more conservative, more bound to the past and wished to preserve its classical form even with regard to words — it rejected popular terms — in an obviously forced style. The initial literary genre was epic poetry. Only with Paulinus of Nola and especially Prudentius did a poetry appear which, even in its traditionalism, was authentically religious. This poetry almost always had a didactic and pedagogical flavor, as did its pagan counterpart, as well as an occasional apologetic intent, which was a specifically Christian aspect.

On the other hand, the genre of hymnody, from Hilary and Ambrose on, would be that which would best express the new religious sensitivity, and would display more originality, more creativity and enjoy more success. At the beginning, this Christian Latin poetry was of a learned type and was metrical poetry. There soon enough grew up alongside it a poetry which was above all rhythmical, based not on the quantity of the syllables but on the accent, which developed as a sense of meter was gradually lost. There is some question as to the origins of this rhythmic poetry. According to some it is merely the continuation of an ancient Roman tradition (Saturnian verse), while others propose a Semitic origin, and others regard it as the deformation of metrical verse.

Anthologies and Translations: CSEL 16(1898): Poetae christiani minores. — F. Buecheler, A. Riese, Anthologia Latina, sive poesis latinae suppl. Leipzig, 1894-1906, with the suppl. of E. Lommatzsch 1926 (reprint, Amsterdam 1972). — G. M. Dreves, C. Blume, Ein Jahrtausend lateinischer Hymnendichtung, 2 vols., Leipzig, 1902. — S. Colombo, Poeti cristiani latini dei secoli III-VI. Turin, 1913. — A. S. Walpole, A. J. Mason, Early Latin Hymns. Cambridge 1922 (reprint, Hildesheim 1966). — M. Bouchoir, La vie profonde. Pages choisies dans les plus belles oeuvres poétiques de l'Antiquité judéo-chrétienne. Paris, 1924. — S. Gaselee, The Oxford Book of Medieval Latin Verse. Oxford, 1928 (new edition, ed. E. J. F. Raby, Oxford, 1959). — O. J. Kuhnmuench, Early Christian Latin Poets from the Fourth to the Sixth Century. Chicago, 1929. — W. Bulst, Hymni latini antiquissimi LXXV, Psalmi III. Heidelberg, 1956. — J. B. Pighi, Poesia religiosa romana. Testi e frammenti. Bologna, 1958. — G. Vecchi, Poesia latina medievale. Parma, 1952, 1958[2](text, Italian transl. commentary). — G. Schille, Frühchristliche Hymnen. Berlin, 1962 (the best text for a study of the first three centuries). — E. Bolisani, L'innologia cristiana antica. S. Ambrogio e i suoi imitatori. Padua, 1964. — Q. Cataudella, Antologia cristiana dalla cantica ambrosiana alla regola di s. Benedetto. Milan, 1969. — H. Spitzmuller, Poésie latine chrétienne du Moyen Age IIIe-IVe siècle. Paris, 1971 (texts, French transl., commentary; fundamental text).

Studies and Bibliographies: J. Martin, Christliche lateinische Dichter (1900-1927): BJ 221(1929II)65-140 (critical bibliography). — A. Poizat, Les poètes chrétiens; scènes de la vie litteraires du Ie au Ve siècle. Lyons, 1902. — A. J. Mason, The First Latin Christian Poets: JThSt 5(1904)413-432. — S. Colombo, La poesia cristiana antica I: La poesia latina. Turin, 1910. — F. Cabrol, Cantiques: DAL 2(1910)1978-1994. — H. Lietzmann, Lateinische altchristliche Poesie. Bonn, 1910. — Th. Haarhoff, Schools of Gaul: a Study of Pagan and Christian Education in the last Century of the Western Empire. Oxford, 1920. — H. Leclercq, Hymnographie: DAL 6(1925)2901-2928. — C. Weyman, Beiträge zur Gedichte der christlich-lateinischen Poesie. Munich, 1926 (collection of earlier articles; fundamental). — F. J. E. Raby, A History of Christian–Latin Poetry from the Beginnings to the Close of the Middle Ages. Oxford, 1927, 1952[2] (important work). — E. S. Duckett, Latin Writers of the Fifth Century. New York 1930 (reprint Archon Books 1969). — F. A. Wright, T. A. Sinclair, A History of Later Latin Literature. London, 1931, 1969[2]. — Q. Cataudella, Poesia cristiana antica: Did 9(1931)237-354. — S. Gaselee, The Transition from the Late Latin Lyric to the Medieval Love Poem. Cambridge, 1931. — F. J. E. Raby, A History of Secular Latin Poetry in the Middle Ages, 2 vols. Oxford, 1934, 1956[3]. — E. Tea, Pitture ed inni nei primi secoli cristiani: *Atti V Congr. Int. Stud. biz.* 2(1940)432-434. — A. Ferrua, Educazione alla poesia nel IV secolo: CC 88, 3(1937)513-522. — D. Comparetti, Virgilio nel Medioevo. Florence, 1946[3]. — H. Schneider, Die altlateinischen biblischen Cantica. Beuron, 1938; *idem,* Die biblischen Oden: Bibl 30(1949)28-65, 239-272, 433-452, 479-500. G. Lazzati, Idee per una storia della poesia cristiana: SC 69(1941)514-526. — C. Marchesi, Motivi dell'epica antica. Milan-Messina, 1942. — Ch. Mohrmann, La langue et le style de la poésie latine chrétienne: RELA 25(1947)280-297(=Etudes sur le latin des chrétiens I. Rome 1958, 151-168). — S. T. Collins, Corruptions in Christian Latin Poetry (Hilary, Prudentius, V. Fortunatus): JThSt 50(1949)68-70. — U. Sesini, Poesia e musica nella latinità cristiana dal III sec. al X secolo. Turin, 1949. — G. Del Ton, G. Schirò, A. Raes, Innografia: EC 7(1951) 28-39. — M. Simonetti, Studi sull'innologia popolare cristiana dei primi secoli: *Atti Acc. Naz. Lincei, Memorie Sez.* 8, 4(1952)339-485 (fundamental work). — G. Vecchi, Poesia latina medievale. Parma, 1952, 1958[2]. — W. Schmid, Bukolik: RACh 2(1954)786-800. — M. P. Cunningham, The Place of the Hymn of Saint Ambrosius in the Latin Poetic Tradition: *Studies in Philology* 52(1955)510-514. — N. K. Chadwick, Poetry and Letters in Early Christian Gaul. London, 1955 (fundamental work). — Ch. Mohrmann, Le Latin Médiéval: *Cahiers des Civ. Méd.* 1(1958)265-294 (=Etudes sur le latin des chrétiens II. Rome 1961, 181-232). —G. Zannoni, Quid poetica popularis ratio, quid optimorum scriptorum imitatio aetate SS. Patrum ad Latinam christianorum poesin contulerint: *Latinitas* 6 (1958)93-106. — V. J. Herrero Llorente, Lucano en la literature hispanolatina: *Emerita* 27(1959)19-52. — J. W. Duff, A Literary History of Rome in the Silver Age. London, 1960. — P. G. Van der Nat, Divinus vere poeta. Einige beschouwingen over onstaan en karakter der christelijke latijne poezie. Leiden, 1963. — J. Szövérffy, Die Annalen der lateinischen Hymnendichtung I. Berlin, 1964 (important work). — A. Hudson-Williams, Virgil and the Christian Latin Poets: *Proceedings of Vergil Soc. London* 6(1966-67)11-21. — S. Costanza, Avitiana. I. I modelli epici del "De spiritualis historiae gestis." Messina, 1968. — G. Bernt, Das lateinische Epigramm im Übergang von der Spätantike zum frühen Mittelalter. Munich, 1968 (4th-9th century; fundamental work). — Kl. Thraede, Untersuchungen zum Ursprung und zur Geschichte der christlichen Poesie: JAC 4(1961)108-127, 5(1962)125-157; *idem,* Epos: RACh 5(1962)1006-1041. — J. Szövérffy, Weltlich Dichtungen des lateinischen Mittelalters. I. Von den Anfängen bis zum Ende des Karolingenzeit. Berlin, 1970. — G. B. Pighi, Studi di ritmica e metrica. Turin, 1970, — L. Caruso, La poesia figurata nell'Alto Medioevo: *Atti Accad. Napoli* 72(1971)313-376 (4th-10th centuries). — Ch. Witke, Numen litterarum. The Old and the New in Latin Poetry from Constantine to Gregory the Great. Leiden, 1971. — P. Klopsch, Einführung in die mittellateinische Verslehre. Darmstadt, 1972. — H. Rahner, Mater ecclesia. Inni in lode alla Chiesa tratti dal primo millennio della letteratura cristiana. Milan, 1972. — D. Gagliardi, Aspetti della poesia latina tardoantica. Palermo, 1972. — D. Norberg, Au seuil du Moyen Âge. Études linguistiques, métriques et littéraires. Padua, 1974 (useful collection of articles). — J. Fontaine, L'apport de la tradition poétique romaine à la formation de l'hymnodie latine chrétienne: RELA 52(1974)318-354. — L. Alfonsi, Tityrus christianus: una piccola aggiunta: *Sileno* 1(1975)79-81. — M. L. Uhlfeder, Classicism and Christianity. A Poetic Synthesis: Latomus 34(1975)224-231. — R. Herzog, Die Bibelepik der lateinischen Spätantike. Munich, 1975. — D. Kartshoke, Bibeldichtung. Studien zur Geschichte der epischen Bibel paraphrase von Juvencus bis Otfrid von Weissenburg. Munich, 1975. — G. K. Braswell, Kleine Bemerkungen zu frühchristlichen Hymnen: VC 29(1975)222-226.

COMMODIAN

The enigmatic Commodian, the Christian poet without date or country, continues to fascinate scholars, who still have not succeeded in giving a definite response to the numerous questions regarding his person and work. Historical, theological, linguistic, and metrical indications have all been minutely and eruditely scrutinized and the possible literary influences on his work have been researched, all without finding a solution which does not give rise to numerous objections. After a somewhat peaceful tradition which had placed him in the middle of the third century in Africa (Dodwell in 1698 had regarded him as the contemporary and compatriot of Cyprian), Brewer proposed in 1906, with a documented study of linguistic elements and historical allusions (particularly of the *Carmen,* v. 805-822), that Commodian was a layman who lived at Arles in the mid-fifth century and had written in the years 458-466. This opinion was accepted by some as final (Dräseke), but was rejected by the majority (Lejay, Weyman, Zeller, Révay, D'Alès, Martin, DeLabriolle). Brewer responded to these critics with various other writings, and the polemic was quite intense in the first two decades of this century. In 1946, P. Courcelle rendered another opinion and maintained that the famous verses (*Carmen* 805-822) were written in the fifth century and were dependent on Orosius and Salvian, as well as on the Apocalypse. At the same time, Brisson stated that Commodian, who was probably of African origin, was a Donatist from the beginning of the fifth century.

All possible approaches have been attempted but without reaching any certainty: historical comparisons, subtle linguistic analyses, lexicographical elements, theological elements, and possible sources. These methodologies, too, have all been subjected to criticism from the various parties. Commodian must have lived between 238 (Ullrich) and 466 (Brewer). If a poll were taken today, the clear majority of scholars would be in favor of a date in the third century; an opinion which seems preferable for various reasons. Too many passages both of the *Instructiones* as well as of the *Carmen apologeticum* are easily comprehensible only within the context of the third century. To carry the compositions of Commodian beyond 312 can resolve some of the difficulties, but it leaves without solution the majority which suppose a period of distinct persecution: a deceitful peace, persecutions on the horizon, imperial edicts, the attitude of confessors and apostates, exhortations to penance for the *lapsi,* a pagan and persecuting Senate, fearful and pagan Goths, etc. By an analysis of the acrostics 2, 4, 5, 6,

21 and 25 of book II of the *Instructiones* (ed. Martin), A. Salvatore has concluded that Commodian is making reference to the situation created at Carthage by the question of the *lapsi,* to the schism of Felicissimus and in general to the situation of the African Church. All are in agreement that Commodian reechos the teaching of Cyprian in various places.

Gennadius of Marseilles (*De vir. ill.* 15: PL 58, 1068; Czapla, p. 37), writing between 477 and 494, is the first author to mention Commodian when he dedicates a brief note to expressing a severe judgment on his work. His information is abstract and seems to refer only to book I of the *Instructiones.* He writes, in fact, that Commodian had written *adversus paganos* and possessed little knowledge of Christian letters. However, while book I is concerned with the pagans and has little to do with Christianity, book II is concerned solely with the identity of the Christians, their life and their conduct. Nor is the *Carmen* written *adversus paganos,* but contains a lengthy treatment of the Jews and their sympathizers. Furthermore, in book II of the *Instructiones* and in the *Carmen,* Commodian draws abundantly from the Sacred Scripture, which he knew well, and from Cyprian. Gennadius himself writes that Commodian had been converted by reading the Bible. The *Decretum Gelasianum* numbers the writings of Commodian among the apocrypha (PL 59, 163: ed. Dobschütz, p. 56, n. 317). All other information is furnished by the author himself, who, though he often speaks of himself and his surroundings, of the Christians and of the community in which he lives, nevertheless remains vague and gives no precise references to place or time.

The last acrostic of the *Instructiones,* which in the manuscripts bears the title *nomen Gasei,* arbitrarily corrected by ancient editors with *nomen Gazei,* has given rise to the legend that he was originally from Gaza (Palestine). If that interpretation must definitely be rejected, a completely satisfactory one has not yet been proposed. Some have proposed that *gazeus* is actually *custos aerarii* of the community (Greek γάζα, Latin *gazum*; *Instr.* Martin II 10, 12; 27, 14 = treasure). Others have proposed that the word is of Semitic origins and signifies a poet (Sigwalt, Salvatore), and, in fact, the *nomen poetae* would be expected here. Still others propose *homo casae,* a man of the countryside, for his poor lifestyle (Hermann). The possibility has also been advanced that *Gazeus* is a proper name, and in fact it is found in inscriptions as a proper name (cf. E. Diehl, J. Moreau, *Inscr. lat. christianae veteres* I, 1210 = CIL V, 645, 1587). Finally, various other explanations and interpretations have been put forward (e.g., that Commodian was from some African *Casa*).

Furthermore, the same acrostic, when the initial letters are read from bottom to top, reads, "*Commodianus mendicus Christi.*" The poet is revealing his name at the end of the collection. The *mendicus* does not so much designate a poor lifestyle, or a *servus Dei* or someone who is a mendicant out of a love of Christ on behalf of others, but rather indicates a person who is completely dependent on Christ (cf. Augustine, *mendicus est ille, nihil sibi tribuens, totum de misericordia Dei expectans: Enar in sp.* 106, 14, 88: CCL 40, 1582). Even those who suggest a Syrian origin for Commodian maintain that he lived in the West: Illyria (Heer), Gallia Narbonensis (Brewer), probably at Rome (Martin), Africa (the majority of scholars). Too many elements, such as sources, language, style, and topics treated indicate that he should be located in Africa.

Commodian had been a pagan polytheist (*Instr.* I, 1). Because of his notable knowledge of the Jews, whom he criticizes sharply, some have proposed that he passed by way of Judaism to Christianity, which he embraced because of dissatisfaction with his life and religion. He was converted through his reading of the Bible. At a certain point in his life he had to submit to public penance, although no explanation is given for this (*Instr.*, ed. Martin, II 8, 8-9). The manuscript of the *Carmen* terminates with the words: *explicit tractatus sancti episcopi* . . . (the name is missing). The question has thus been raised whether he was a bishop or occupied some high rank in the community. He was certainly well acquainted with the structures of the Christian community and with the rights and duties of each person. Nevertheless, he exercises independence in criticizing abuses, giving counsel to all, exhorting to a generous and unselfish charity, and in reproving the rich and the oppressors, who are responsible for their conduct before God. His ardent and unbending character and his hostility toward compromise and half measures recall Tertullian. It does not seem in any case that he exercised a hierarchical role, and indeed he contrasts his "private" teaching with that of the officially recognized *doctores* (*Instr.*, ed. Martin, II 12, 1-3; 18, 15; *Carmen* 61ff).

Judgments vary concerning his skill and style. Rigault, his first editor wrote, "*stylus (Commodiani) Africanae ferociae rusticitatem sapit, quae tamen in acumina Tertulliani, Cypriani, Minucii, non infrequenter alludit*" (PL 5, 191).

The general opinion is that Commodian was a man of little culture and with little knowledge of classical literature, yet who was quite familiar with Scripture and some Christian authors. He was a popular poet who used the popular language in a manner that was picturesque but not rich, and which was terribly ungrammatical with respect to classical Latin on account of neologisms, barbarisms, confusion in declensions and conjugations, and subversion of the rules of syntax. The meter of his poetry seems rough and difficult to comprehend. Except for some happy circumstances, all traces of skill are absent.

Some (e.g., Boissier, *La fin du paganisme* II, Paris, 1891, p. 41) have regarded this as a deliberate attempt to adapt himself to the people. Amatucci believed that Commodian abandoned classical language as sterile and useful only for erudition because he wanted to be the new Christian poet, and attempted to create a new poetry, close to real life, just as Tertullian had sought to create a new prose (*Storia della Letteratura latinum cristiana.* Turin, 1955[2], p. 91-92). Recently, other scholars such as Perret (1957) and Hoppenbrouwers (1964) have seen in him a great poet of profound faith who, well aware of the particular value of the Christian words, knew how to infuse the genius of the Christian language into traditional poetry. However, this judgment will seem forced to anyone who reads Commodian.

1. *Instructiones.*

This collection of 80 poems (ed. Dombart, 41 + 39; ed. Martin, 45 + 35) of varying length was published for the first time by N. Rigault in 1649 at Toul (France). They consist of acrostic poems, that is, the initial letters of the verses form a name or a motto, except for two alphabetical poems (ed. Martin, I 35; II 15) whose initial letters correspond to the series of the letters of the alphabet. The present division proposed by the editors is inexact, and it perhaps used to be 40 and 40. The author himself arranged them in the order in which they are read. He speaks of his book in several places (ed. Martin I 22, 13; I 25, 19; II 35, 25) and also states the theme of the resurrection and future life (ed. Martin I 25, 19; cf. I 41-45). The first book more or less follows the apologetic tradition, and notes on the Christian religion are interspersed among severe and sarcastic criticisms of the polytheistic religions and the various gods as well as of Judaism and Judaizers. The second book, on the other hand, is concerned with the members of the Christian community. After expounding his eschatological ideas (ed. Martin I 42-45), Commodian outlines the duties of all classes: catechumens (1), the faithful in general (2 and 3), penitents (4), apostates, schismatics, or other evildoers; matrons (14 and 15), the entire people, aspirants to martyrdom, lectors, ministers, and bishops. At the end, the poem gives the name of its author.

2. *Carmen Apologeticum.*

This text was discovered and published by Pitra in 1852 (*Spicilegium Solesmense* I, p. 21-49). Because of the close similarities with the *Instructiones,* he attributed it to Commodian with the title *Carmen apologeticum adversus Iudaeos et gentes.* The only manuscript of the work, which comes from Bobbio, was at Middle Hill (*Codex mediomontanus*) at the time of Pitra and now is in the British Museum with the classification *Additional* 43460. The work does not have a title and terminates with the words *explicit tractatus sancti episcopi . . .* without further indications. Pitra's attribution was confirmed by new arguments advanced by Ebert in 1870 and is no longer a matter of doubt. Pitra obtained the title from Gennadius, who does not seem to have known the work. Révay preferred to call it *Carmen de Antichristo* (PhW 31[1911]1430). In the recent edition of Martin (CCL 128[1960]) it is entitled *Carmen de duobus populis,* i.e., the Hebrews first elected then rejected, and the new people, the Christians. In any case, it is commonly referred to as the *Carmen apologeticum.* It is composed of 1060 hexameters grouped two by two. It is not an apology, but rather a brief exposition of Christianity with an explicit didactic intention. Verses 1-88 introduce the author, a convert from paganism, who desires that other pagans may participate in his own faith in God, who is easily knowable through the prophets and Christ. Verses 89-578 then trace the outline of the history of salvation from creation to the death and resurrection of Christ, while the third part, verses 579-790, is intended to refute the arguments of the pagans and Jews on the divinity of Christ and to give an exhortation to faith, which alone can bring salvation. At the end, verses 791-1060, Commodian, who was tinged with millenarianism, expounds his eschatological ideas. He describes the events of the last days as though he were an eyewitness: the resurrection of the dead, the signs heralding the end, the persecution of the Christians, the capture and destruction of Rome. Rome would suffer in particular in this eschatological context, not only because of the persecution of the "saints," but also because of the oppression of the whole world. "While she exulted, the whole world groaned . . . she weeps eternally, she who boasted to be eternal" (ed. Martin, 921 and 923). At the end comes the defeat of the Antichrist, the triumph of the Christians, and the Last Judgment. The Jews are harshly criticized for not having recognized Christ, for which reason they are rejected by God, and for their opposition to the Christians. Since they separate others from salvation by forcing them to enter the Synagogue, they will arise with others, but for their condemnation. The Christians have taken their place in the plan of God.

More or less the same ideas are found in the *Instructiones.* The exposition of the Christian faith is rather vague. The Trinitarian theology is clearly insufficient, and is, in fact, monarchian; the heresy of the third century. Two verses demonstrate this sufficiently: *Qui pater et filius dicitur et spiritus sanctus* (*Carmen* 94); *Nec pater esset dictus, nisi factus filius esset* (*Carmen* 278). Although its purpose is indeed to instruct, it is above all intended to bestir everyone to take a greater interest and concern for his own lot in the world to come. The satire, the moral exhortation, the apocalyptic fantasies of the man of faith, the frank and caustic language are all directed toward this one goal.

A theme dear to Commodian both in the *Instructiones* and in the *Carmen* is a merciless criticism of the rich. Verses of fire exhort them not to place their hope in their riches, which will instead be the motive for a fearful condemnation without appeal, and look forward to the condition of a heavenly society where all those who have in any way oppressed others on earth will become slaves of the "saints" (*Carmen* 994-998; *Instr.* I 43, 6-19).

Studies on Commodian flourished at the beginning of this century and then again in the last twenty years, and substantial progress has been noted. Nevertheless, Commodian remains a delight for linguists, a torment for students of metrical verse, and a riddle for historians.

Editions: Instructiones: PL 5, 201-262 (ed. Galandi). — E. Ludwig, Leipzig, 1878 (ed. Teubner). — D. Dombart, CSEL 15(1887)1-112. — J. Durel, Les Instructiones de Commodien. Paris, 1912. — J. Martin, CCL 128(1960)1-70. — A. Salvatore. Naples, 1965-1968 (3 vols.). *Carmen:* J. P. Pitra, Spicilegium Soles. I. Paris 1952, 21-49. — E. Ludwig. Leipzig, 1878. — D. Dombart. CSEL 15(1887)144-188. — J. Martin, CCL 128(1960)71-113. — PLS I, 74-101 (ed. Dombart). — A. Salvatore, CPS. Turin, 1977.

Translations: Instructiones: English: ANL vol. 4, 203-219 (reprint, Grand Rapids, Mich., 1972). *French:* J. Durel, op. cit. *Italian:* A. Salvatore, op. cit. *Carmen:* A. Salvatore, op. cit.

Bibliographies: P. de Labriolle: BALAC 2(1912)79-80. — U. Monti, Bibliografia di Commodiano: *Athenaeum* 3(1915)200-208. — J. Martin, BJ 221(1929)88-97.

Studies: For bibliography through 1927, cf. J. Martin, op. cit. — C. Brakman, Commodianea: Mnem 55(1927)121-140, 269-272. — L. Schils, Commodien poèta rythmique?: *Neophilologus* 14-15(1929-30)51-56. — A. F. v. Katwijk, Lexicon Commodianaeum. Amsterdam, 1934 (fundamental work). — M. Müller, Unters. zum Carmen adv. Marcionitas. Würzburg, 1936 (C. is dependent of this Carmen). — L. Herrmann, Qui est saint Alexis?: ACL 11(1942)235-241 (the source for the Syriac legend of Mar Riscia is a lost biography of Commodian). — F. Taillez, Qui est saint Alexis?: OCP 11(1945)216-222. — P. Courcelle, Commodien et les invasions du Ve siècle: RELA 24(1946)227-246. — E. J. Goodspeed, The Date of Commodian: CPh 41(1946)46-47. — J. P. Brisson, Origines du danger social dans l'Afrique chrétienne du IIIe siècle: RSR 33(1946)280-316. — B. Blumenkranz, Die Judenpredigt Augustinus. Basel 1946, 19-25; *idem,* Les auteurs chrétiens latins du moyen âge sur les Juifs et le judaïsme: *Rev. Et. Juifs* NS 9(1948)3-67. — M. Simon, Verus Israel. Paris, 1949, 1964[2]. — P. Scheppens, Commodien (Inst. 2, 17, 19): RSR 36(1949)603. — H. Grégoire, Note sur la survivence chrétienne des Esseniens et des sectes apparentées: NC I-II(1949-50)354-359. — E. Castorina, La poesia di C. nella storia della metrica latina. Catania, 1950. — L. Ferrari, Il problema cronologico di C.: *Gior. it. fil.* 4(1951)59-73. — M. Simonetti, Sulla cronologia di C.: *Aevum* 27(1953)227-239. — J. Vogt. Die Zählung der Christenverfolgung im römischen Reich: *Parola d. Pas.* 9(1954)5-15. — L. Krestan: RACh 3(1957)248-252. — J. Perret, Prosodie et métrique chez Commodien: *Pallas* 5(1957)27-42. — J. Martin, Commodianus: *Traditio* 13(1957)1-71 (fundamental work). — J.-P. Brisson, Autonomisme et Christianisme dans l'Afrique Romaine de Septime Sevère à l'invasion vandale. Paris 1958, 378-410. — K. Thraede, Beiträge zur Datierung Commodianus: JAC 2(1959)90-114. — L. Varcl, Characteristics of Commodian: *Vestnik Drev. Istorij* 68(1959)165-167 (in Russian). — A. Salvatore, Appunti sulla cronologia di C.: Orph 7(1960)161-187. — J. Gagé, Le poème messianique de C. et la crise religieuse de l'Empire romain vers 260 ap. J.-C.: *Bull. Soc. E. Renan* 9(1960)131-133. — A. Salvatore, Elementi commodianei nella praefatio di Prudenzio. Naples, 1960. — J. Gagé, Commodien et le mouvement millénariste du IIIe siècle (258-262 ap. J.-C.): RHPR 41(1961)355-378. — L. Herrmann, Commodien et saint Augustin: *Latomus* 20(1961)312-321. — V. A. Sirago, Gallia Placidia e la trasformazione politica dell'Occidente. Louvain 1961, 484-493. — K. Thraede, Untersuchungen zum Ursprung und Geschichte der christlichen Poesie. I: JAC 4(1961)108-127; II 5(1962)125-157. — H. Hoppenbrouwers, Recherches sur la terminologie du martyre de Tertullien à Lactance. Nijmegen, 1961. — H. Silvestre, Un clichè peu étudié, fortis in armis: ALMA 32(1962)255-257. — A. Salvatore, Su alcuni luoghi delle Instructiones di C.: ND 12(1961)1-20; *idem,* Note sul testo di C.: ibid., 12(1962)21-37. — H. Silvestre, Varia critica, I. Commodianea: SE 13(1962)515-517. — M. Sordi, Dionigi d'Aless., Commodiano e alcuni problemi della storia del III sec.: *Rend. Pont. Acc. Rom. Arch.* 35(1962-63)123-146. — A. Salvatore, Atteggiamenti espressivi nelle Instr. di C.: *Studi Rom* 11(1963)509-525. — H. Hoppenbrouwers, Commodien poète chrétien. Nijmegen, 1964. — A. Salvatore, Note sul testo di Commodiano, in Misc. Oikoumene. Catania 1964, 103-119. — S. Mariner, Enfoques recientes del problema de C. Discusión: *Actas II Cong.* esp. est. clas. Madrid 1964, 121-128. — P. Courcelle, Histoire littéraire des grandes invasions germaniques. Paris, 1964[3] (important text). — G. Pugliese Carratelli, Un'allusione a Mani nel Carmen di C.: RCCM 7(1965)899-905. — G. M. Lee, Note de lecture. Latinisme et graecism: Latomus 24(1965)954. — A. Salvatore, Un Mercurio con l'acryballus in un acrostico di C.: *Vichiana* 2(1965)171-175. — A. H. Visser, Eén of twee antichristen bij Commodianus?: NAKG 47(1965-66)131-136. — L. Callebat, Tradition et novation dans la poèsie de C.: *Pallas* 13(1966)85-94. — A. Salvatore, Lex secunda e interpretazione biblica in C.: VetChr 5(1968)111-130. — K. M. Abbott, Commodian and his Verse: Misc. B. E. Perry. Univ. of Illinois 1969, 272-283. — I. Opelt, Schimpfwörter bei Commodian: VC 24(1970)290-299. — A. Salvatore, Commodianea. Naples, 1970; *idem,* Lettura di un verso di Commodiano (Carmen 1050): *Studi de Falco.* Naples 1971, 486-496; *idem,* Il salmo 110(109 Vulg.) in un passo di Commodiano: VetChr 10(1973)343-350; *idem,* L'enigma di Commodiano. Considerazioni su lo scrittore, il suo ambiente e la sua epoca: *Vichiana* 3(1974)50-81. — A. Salvatore, Interpretazioni commodianee. Naples, 1974. — G. Alföldy, The Crisis of the Third Century as Seen by Contemporaries: *Greek, Rom. Byz. Studies* 15(1974)89-111. — S. Mazzarino, Il carmen contra paganos e il problema dell'era costantiniana: antico, Tardoantico ed era costantiniana. Bari 1974, 398-465. — A. Salvatore, Annotazioni sul Carmen Apol., in *Forma Futuri,* Misc. Pellegrino. Turin 1975, 395-415. — J. Daniélou, Les Testimonia de Commodien, ibid., 59-69. — E. Heck, Juppiter-Jovis bei Commodian: VC 30(1976)72-80. J. Šrutwa, The Life of the Early Christians According to the Writings of Commodian: *Stud. theol. Vars.* 14(1976)233-256 (in Polish, with summary in French). — J. Daniélou, The Origins of Latin Christianity. London 1977, 99-125, 273-288.

IUVENCUS

Around the year 330 (Jerome, *Chronicon,* ed. Helm, year 329), Gaius Vettius Iuvencus composed the first Christian epic poem when he put the Gospels into verse. The only information concerning him is provided by his own works or by Jerome. The latter writes in the *De viris inlustribus* (84: PL 23, 730), "Iuvencus, a Spaniard of noble birth and a priest, composed four books in which he transcribed almost literally the four Gospels in hexameters, and certain other things, in the same verse, relating to the order of the sacraments. He lived at the time of the Emperor Constantine." Jerome also mentions Iuvencus elsewhere and praises his work (*Ep.* 70, *ad Magnum*: PL 22, 668; *Comm. in Matt.* I 2, 11: PL 26, 14). Iuvencus himself states at the end of the poem (IV 806ff) that he is writing under Constantine during a time of peace. These are the only certain notices and the most ancient. Other subsequent ones are amplifications and are not trustworthy. Jerome mentions three other works which have been lost — the ones attributed to Iuvencus are spurious — and nothing further is known of their content.

Given the mentality and tastes of his age and of the Middle Ages, Iuvencus was imitated especially in the fifth century (Paulinus of Nola, Paulinus of Pella, Orientius, C. M. Victorinus, Corripus, Cyprian the Poet, etc.) and was praised throughout the Middle Ages. The *Decretum Gelasianum,* which rejected the centones, nevertheless accepted the work of Iuvencus (c. 4, ed. Dobschütz, n. 253, p. 52). From 1490 until Hümer (1891) 26 editions were published.

The *Evangeliorum libri* are a poem divided into four books with two prologues and comprising 3219 hexameters. This division does not seem to follow any precise criterion but rather is dictated by practical needs (for a different opinion, cf. Amatucci, *Storia lett. lat. cris.* Turin 1956[2], p. 121). At the beginning, Iuvencus refers to the symbols of each of the Evangelists, and gives the eagle for Mark and the lion for John according to earlier tradition (cf. Irenaeus, *Adv. haer.* III 11, 8). This symbolism was reversed only in the fourth century with Ambrose, Jerome, and Augustine. In his preface, he explains his purpose as singing of the life-giving works of Christ: *Nam mihi carmen erit Christi vitalia gesta* (I, 9), which are a gift for mankind. He feels a profound admiration for Homer and Vergil, whose works are immortal, and, as he likewise intends to create a work of art, he is certain that his own work will withstand the attack of time and will be a cause of his salvation (I 21-24). If on the one hand he is a faithful follower of pagan tradition as regards the formal aspect of his exposition of the *divinae gloria legis* by means of human poetry (IV 804), it is nevertheless true that he adheres scrupulously to the sacred text.

These ideas of Iuvencus are of notable historical importance. The ancient poets are objects of great veneration, and only their mythology is repudiated. Iuvencus' intention is to create a Christian epic by the use of pagan literary forms (IV 804), which will form the basic premise of medieval literary theory. Without pomposity, he narrates the life of the Savior in clear and simple language. The value of Iuvencus' work lies not so much in the result obtained as in the fact that he was the first to attempt a composition of this nature. He opened a new path and planted fertile seeds. For some, the simplicity of the Gospel text seems to clash with the solemnity of the hexameter, but this is perhaps more of a psychological difficulty of the reader, such as arises also in the film versions of the life of Christ.

As the first Christian epic poet, Iuvencus cannot neglect the *invocatio* to the god to assist him in his work, and thus he turns to the Holy Spirit (I 25-27) so that *Christo digna loquamur.* The first book deals with the events concerning John the Baptist, the Annunciation, and the beginning of Christ's activity up to the cure of Peter's mother-in-law (770 verses); the second book concerns Jesus' miracles and some parables (the material taken from John's Gospel is inserted here) up to chapter 12 of Matthew (819 verses); the third book includes miracles, parables, and discourses drawn only from Matthew (Mt. 13-21; 773 verses); and the fourth book treats of Jesus' disputes with the Jews, the parables of the ten virgins and of the talents, the death and raising of Lazarus, and the passion, death and resurrection of Christ (812 verses).

Iuvencus is endowed with a good classical culture and an excellent knowledge of the poets such as Plautus, Valerius, Flaccus, Statius and Ovid. Above all he knows Vergil, upon whom he depends heavily for style, language and for many expressions, and from whom he also takes hemistichs. He uses a pure, classical language, but with a new content, and his style is characterized by a literary servility which in his day was considered a merit. Even his Christian vocabulary has a purist character, and he makes use of Greek words or works coming from other genres. He is greatly indebted to the pagan tradition; e.g., he uses *Tonans,* typically pagan, to indicate God. He creates neologisms: *flammicomans* (for "hair of fire"), *flammipes* (from "feet of flame"), *altithronus* (from "lofty throne"). At times, the work gives the impression of being a cento, although, since it is the result of a certain personal reelaboration, it cannot be defined as such. It is not great poetry, but rather the fruit of a good technical skill and a perfect knowledge of the rules of verse. The simplicity and spontaneity of the Gospel accounts at times lose their effect in an epic such as that of Iuvencus; e.g., the *Nunc dimittis* of Simeon (Lk. 2:29-33) and the paraphrase of Iuvencus (I 200-207) and the account of the Last Supper (Mt. 26:20-25) and the verses IV 432-456. The directness and majesty of the Gospel scenes are transformed into an artificial solemnity.

Iuvencus adheres as closely as possible to the text which he sets to verse by means of a paraphrastic technique according to which he amplifies and clarifies obscure passages, expresses his feelings and judgments, and describes certain scenes. He enjoys greater success with his descriptive passages: the Magi (I 224-254), the tempest (II 25-42), and some miracles (II 337-407). Donnini has drawn attention to the use of adjectives to confer a greater expressiveness on the text. Such a use of adjectives permits Iuvencus to better delineate a person or a situation, and he chooses his adjectives with care and refinement.

The *Evangeliorum libri* are important for the *Vetus latina* which it follows faithfully, adhering to the literal sense and clarifying only some obscure passages. Iuvencus basically keeps to the text of Matthew and draws only some details from Mark. From Luke he takes chiefly information pertaining to the Baptist and the infancy of Jesus (with a different chronology from the Gospel: birth, shepherds, presentation in the Temple, circumcision, Nazareth, Egypt, magi, etc.). From John, he takes the Wedding at Cana, the conversation with Nicodemus and with the Samaritan woman, the vocation of Philip and Nathanael, Lazarus and some other episodes (cf. Hanson, *op. cit.*, p. 18 for Gospel sources). He produces something similar to a concordance of the Gospels. His theology, particularly his Christology, is fully orthodox (the Council of Nicea had been held recently). Some manuscripts attribute a *Liber in Genesim* (a work of Cyprian the Poet) to Iuvencus as well as the *Laudes Domini* with the *Triumphus Christi* (a part of the preceding work), which are not his compositions but belong rather to another contemporary Gallic writer.

Editions: PL 19, 53-346 (ed. Arévalo, Rome 1792) with ample commentary. — J. Hümer, CSEL 24(1891). — A. Kanppitsch, Evangeliorum libri quattuor. Graz, 1910-1913 (four fascicles).

Translations: German: A. Knappitsch, op. cit.

Studies: F. Vivona, De Juvenci poetae amplificationibus. Palermo, 1903. — H. Widmann, De Gaio V. A. Juvenco carminis evangelici poeta et Vergili imitatore. Breslau, 1905 (good). — J. Cornu,, Beiträge zur latein. Metrik: SAW 1959/3(1908)1-33. — H. Nestler, Studien über die Messiade des Juv., Passau, 1910. — G. Frank, Vossianus 986 and Reginensis 333:AJPh 44(1923)67-70 (manuscripts). — A. Oreján Calvo, La Historia Evangélica de Juvenco: *Rev. Esp. Est. Bib.* (EB) (1926), July, 3-19. — H. H. Kievits, Ad Juvenci Evv. lib. I commentarius exegeticus. Diss., Gronigen, 1940. — G. Mercati, Il palinsesto bobbiense di Juvenco (Ms. Vat. lat. 5759, sec. VIII), in *Miscellanea Lampros.* Athens 1935 (Cf. Opera Min. 506-512). — A. C. Vega, Capítulos de un libro. Juvenco y Prudencio: CD 157(1945)207-247. — Ch. Mohrmann, La langue et le style de la poésie chrétienne: RELA 25(1947)280-290 (= Etudes sur le latin de chrétiens, I. Rome 1958, 151-168). — F. Laganà, Giovenco. Catania, 1947. — J. De Wit, Ad Juv. Evv. lib. Secundum commentarius exegeticus. Gronigen, 1947. — H. Thoma, The Oldest Manuscript of Juvencus: CR 54(1950)95-96 (Bib. Vat. lat. 13501, saec. VI-VII). — M. A. Norton, Prosopography of Juvencus: Folia 4(1950)36-42 (= J.-M. F. Marique, Leaders of Iberean Christianity, 50-650 A. D. Jamaica Plains, Mass. 1962, 114-120: important study). — H. Hansson, Textkritisches zu Juv. mit einem vollständigen Index verborum. Lund, 1950 (fundamental work). — J. De Wit, De textu Juvenci poetae observationes criticae: VC 8(1954)145-148 (observations on Hansson). — U. Domínguez del Val, in Repertorio Hist. de Ciencias ec. en España I. Salamanca 1967, 29-31 (bibliography). — J. Jiménez Delgado, Juvenco en el códice matritense 10029: *Helmantica* 19(1968)277-332. — P. Flury, Zur Dichtersprache des Juv.: Lemmata W. Ehlers. Munich 1968, 38-47. — A. K. Clarke, Claudian and the Augustinian Circle, in *Misc. Capánaga,* II. Madrid 1968, 125-133. — M. Donnini, Annotazioni sulla tecnica parafrastica negli Evangeliorum libri di Giovenco: *Vichiana* 1(1972)231-249; *idem,* Un aspetto della espressività di Giovenco. L'aggettivazione: *Vichiana* 2(1973)54-67. — P. Flury, Das sechste Gedicht des Paulinus von Nola: VC 27(1973)129-145. — P. G. van der Nat, Die Praefatio der Evangelienparaphrase des Juvencus: *Studia Waszink.* Amsterdam 1973, 249-257. — F. Quadlbauer, Zur Invocatio des Juvencus (praef. 25-27): *Grazer Beiträger* 2(1974)185-212. — I. Opelt, Die Szenerie bei Juvencus. Ein Kapitel historischer Geographie: VC 39(1975)191-207. — M. Donnini, L'allitterazione e l'omoteleuto in Giovenco: *Annali Fac. Lett.* Perugia 12(1974-75)128-159. — A. Longpré, Aspects de métrique et de prosodie chez Juvencus: *Phoenix* 29(1975)128-138. — R. Herzog, Die Bibelepik der Spätantike, I. Munich 1975, 53-98. — R. Palla, "Aterna in saecula" in Giovenco, Praefatio 17: *Studi classici e orientali* 27(1977)277-282. — F. Murru, Analisi semiologica e strutturale della praefatio agli Evangeliorum libri di Giovenco: WS 14(1980)133-151. — J. M. Poinsotte, Juvencus et Israël. La représentation des Juifs dans le premier poème latin chrétien. Paris, 1979.

CENTONES

The cento (Greek χέντρων, Latin *cento*), which was composed of different pieces of cloth and thus adapted for humble use, could be employed as a blanket, a curtain at the door, as a drapery for different uses, like the clothes of servants . . . In all of these meanings there dominates the idea of a composite and varied unity. From this was derived the meaning of a poem composed of words, hemistichs, and verses of another poet taken at random to express another theme. Centones were compiled especially from the poems of Homer (*Homerocentones*) and those of Vergil (*Virgiliocentones*), and were widely diffused throughout the pagan world. Tertullian wrote, "Today I witnessed a totally different narration issue from Vergil, in which the content is adapted to the verse and the verse to the content. Thus Hosidius Geta has completely exaggerated Vergil's tragedy, *Medea.* Also a relative of mine, among other literary pastimes, has explained the *Pinacem Cebetis* of the same poet. It is furthermore customary to give the name *Homerocentones* to those poems which according to the custom of the centones unite in one single work many pieces drawn here and there from the odes of Homer" (*De praescr. haer.* 39, 3-5: CCL 1, 219-220). The centones are works of memory and technical skill more than works of art. In the fourth century the poet Ausonius even ventured into a contest with the Emperor Valentinian, and, when presenting his cento to Axius Paulus, wrote, "*Accipe igitur opusculum de inconnexis continuum, de diversis unum . . . de alieno nostrum*" (Pieper, 207). It is as though a building was destroyed and the remaining materials were used to construct another ediface. Memorization played an important role in the education of that time, and the student was introduced to μίμησις, to the ἀγων with the great poets. The school formed his mental structures and not even the great poet succeeded totally in freeing himself from its influence. The dependency on another was a boast for all, even for a Vergil (*Georg.* 2, 176) and a Propertius (4, 1, 64). The allusion to preceding models was an important part of poetry and necessitated a great familiarity with these models. The authors of these centones had a profound acquaintance with these models which, in any case, were well known to all since they formed part of the common cultural heritage.

Of the Christian centones, the best and most famous presently known is that of the noble and educated Roman lady, Petronia Proba (her name is given in verse 12, "*Arcana ut possim vatis Proba cuncta referre*"). She was the wife of Clodius Adelphius, who held various important imperial posts and became *praefectus urbis* in 351. After having composed a cento, now lost, on the war in 351-353 between Constantius and Magnentius, she converted, or at least returned to Christianity (v. 417-422) and around 360 composed a Vergilian cento inspired by the Old and New Testament in order to celebrate the gifts of Christ by means of Vergil; *Vergilium cecinisse loquar pia munera Christi* (v. 23). This verse expresses her entire program and her new poetic activity: a biblical content paraphrased in Vergilian form. Proba knows Vergil well and also demonstrates a notable technical ability.

The work can be divided into two parts: verses 1-332 narrate episodes from the Old Testament, especially the creation of man, up to the Flood, and verses 333-694 narrate episodes from the New Testament. In the edition of Schenkl, the cento is preceded by a brief *carmen* composed by the *librarius* whom the Emperor Arcadius had requested to transcribe the cento. The *librarius* describes the work as *Maronem/mutatum in melius*! The episode is an example of the enormous dissemination enjoyed by this type of literary composition. The numerous sixteenth-century editions testify to the popularity it enjoyed during the Renaissance.

In a letter to Paulinus of Nola (*Ep*. 53, 7: PL 22, 544-545), Jerome gives a caustic and scornful judgment of this literary genre. He singles out in particular the composition of Proba, which he does not deign to name but of which he cites some verses (*Cento* 34f, 403, 624), and which he defines as puerile and the work of charlatans. A person of deep classical culture yet sincerely Christian felt offended to read verses which in the original text were, for example, in the mouth of Venus, and now were used with a completely different meaning. The work was repudiated by the *Decretum Gelasianum* (PL 59, 162; ed. Dobschütz, n. 287, p. 52). At times, Proba shows a certain daring in making semantic adjustments and some terms take on a new theological value. The lack of suitable Vergilian terms renders her thought imprecise and obscure, and some secondary aspects are excessively developed. I. Opelt has recently drawn attention to her Christology, which from the titles attributed to Christ does not seem to be fully orthodox.

Isidore of Seville (*Etym.* I 39, 26: PL 82, 121) refers to a certain Pomponius who, by borrowing from Vergil, had composed the little poem about Tityrus in honor of Christ. It preserves a poetic dialogue between the Christian, Tityrus, the principal interlocutor, and the pagan, Meliboeus, and is entitled *Versus ad gratiam Domini (incipit: Tityre, tu patulae recubans sub tegmine fagi).* The attribution is confirmed by the fact that the same manuscript, *Vat. Pal.* 1753, joins the cento of Proba and the *Versus ad gratiam Domini,* as Isidore read a manuscript similar to this one. There is no other information regarding Pomponius, who is traditionally placed in the fifth century. The content of the dialogue is simple. Meliboeus, noting that Tityrus is so happy, asks the reason for this. Tityrus responds that he is not singing the prophecies of ancient poets, but things which are true and is uniting himself to the song of all creation, which praises God, the giver of immortality. At Meliboeus' request, he instructs him in Christianity, making reference to the creation of all things, to the conduct of Israel and to the Incarnation. There are ample literary digressions.

The incomplete text, *De Verbi incarnatione,* which is attributed by some to Sedulius (Riese, Hümer) is a work of 111 hexameters composed by an imitator of Proba in the fifth century. God, moved to compassion for man, sends his Son to become incarnate in the womb of Mary, who accepts this mystery with trepidation. A brilliant star announces the birth of Christ. The work then goes on to narrate some of the teachings of Christ and to tell of the Ascension. The descriptions are excessive and truly redundant with respect to the content they intend to present.

In another cento, the *De ecclesia (incipit: Tectum augustum vingens),* of 116 verses, the author begins by describing a Christian temple of 100 columns to which God invites everyone and where mothers and children pray in song day and night. At a certain point silence falls and the priest addresses his exhortation to the faithful, explaining that the Son of God became incarnate, suffered and ascended into heaven, and that whoever does not believe will be punished in the last judgment (there is a lengthy description of this latter event). The author then takes up the celebration of the Eucharist. The *carmen* was recited in public, and the enthusiastic crowd responded, calling the author *Maro iunior* (the new Vergil). In order to thank the crowd, he responded by improvising in the style of a cento other verses taken from Vergil, whom he referred to as "deus." In the manuscript, the section preceding these words reads: *cumque abortio clamaretur "Maro iunior"* . . . Some consider this *abortio* to be the corruption of a substantive (Baehrens: *ab auditorio*) or of a participle (Schenkl: *abituro*), while others (Quichérat, Riese) consider it to be the corruption of a proper name, *Mavortio,* which would make "Mavortius" the name of the poet. This latter interpretation seems preferable and is supported by two reasons in its favor. Quichérat, the first editor of the work in 1840 (*Bibl. École de Chartres* 2 [1840-41]130-131), reads *Mabortio* and claims to have taken it from a copy made by Juret, who neither indicated the manuscript nor made reference to any correction. Furthermore, there is another cento of the poet Mavortius, the *Judgment of Paris,* in the *Anthologia latina* (Riese 1894, n. 10, p. 39-41) which in its primary nucleus contains 12 centos, of which only the *De ecclesia* is Christian in inspiration. The *De ecclesia* was not published by the first editors of the *Anthologia latina* (Bumann 1759 and Meyr 1835), but was brought to light by Suringer in 1867 (*De ecclesia, anonymi cento virgilianus ineditus.* Utrecht, 1867). Suringer believed the supplementary verses were also inedited since he did not know that Quichérat had published them already. The *De ecclesia* is certainly better than the other two centos just now analyzed. The final improvisation shows that the author knew his *deus,* Vergil, perfectly by memory.

Editions: Proba: PL 19, 805-818. — Schenkl, CSEL 16, 1(1888)568-609.

Pomponius: (Versus ad gratiam Domini) Schenkl, CSEL 16, 1(1888)609-615(= PLS I, 773-779). — F. Buecheler, A. Riese, Anthologia latina 1, 2. Leipzig 1906 (reprint, Amsterdam 1972) n.719a, 189-193. De verbi incarnatione (incipit: Omnipotens genitor): PL 19, 773-780. — Hümer, CSEL 10(1885)310-313 (appendix to Sedulius). — Schenkl, CSEL 16, 1(1888)615-620. — F. Buecheler, A. Riese, Anthologia latina 1, 2. n.719. De ecclesia: Schenkl, CSEL 16, 1(1888)621-627. — A. Riese, Anthologia latina I. Leipzig 1894, n.16, 56-61 (the appendix is 16a). — PLS I, 766-771.

Studies: F. Ermini, Ricerche sulla vita e sulla famiglia di Proba: *Riv. Studi crit. Sc. Teol.* 1(1905)742-753; *idem,* Il centone di Proba e la poesia centonaria latina. Rome, 1909 (fundamental work). — A. Olivetti, Osservazioni sui capitoli 45-53 del libro II di Zosimo e sulla loro probabile fonte (Proba): RFIC 43(1915)331-333. — M. L. Lagrange, Le prétendu méssianisque de Virgile: RBibl 31(1922)552-572. — C. Weyman, Zum Cento De ecclesia: HJG 45(1925)75-76. — G. Bellissima, Notizia di due codici inediti del Centone virgiliano di Proba. Siena, 1923. — A. Stanislaus, The Scriptures in Hexameter: *Clas. Weekly* 32(1938)99-100. — D. Comparetti, Virgilio nel Medioevo. Florence, 1937-1941 (reprint 1956). — A. Tuilier, La datation et l'attribution du χριστὸς πάσχω et l'art du centon: *Actes VI Cong. Int. Et. Byz.* I. Paris 1950-51, 403-409. — W. Schmid, Tityrus christianus: RhM 96(1953)101-165. — P. Courcelle, Les exégèses chrétiennes de la quatrième Églogue: REAN 59(1957)294-319. — R. Lamacchia, Tecnica centonaria e critica del testo: RAL 13(1958)258-280; *idem,* Problemi di interpretazione semantica in un centone virgiliano: *Maia* 10(1958)161-188; *idem,* Dall'arte allusiva al centone: *Atene e Roma* 3(1958)193-216. — A. Zannoni, Quid poetica popularis ratio, quid optimorum scriptorum imitatio aetate SS. Patrum ad Latinam christianorum poesim contulerint: *Latinitas* 6 (1958)93-106. — I. Opelt, Der zürnende Christus in Cento der Proba: JAC 7 (1964)106-116. — M. R. Cacioli, Adattamenti semantici e sintattici nel Centone virgiliano di Proba: SIF 41(1969)188-246 (important work). — D. S. Wiesen, Virgil, Minucius Felix and the Bible: Hermes 99(1971)70-91. — M. Bonaria, Appunti per la tradizione vergiliana nel IV secolo, in *Vergiliana.* Leiden 1971, 35-40. — C. Cariddi, Il centone di Proba. Naples, 1971 (fundamental work). — J.

L. Vidal, Observaciones sobre centones virgilianos de tema cristiano. La creación de una poesía cristiana culta: *Boletín Inst. Est. hel.* (Barcelona) 7/2(1973)53-64. — R. Herzog, Die Bibelepik der Spätantike. Munich 1975. — M. L. Ricci, Note al centone Versus ad gratiam Domini attribuito a Pomponio (719a Riese): *Annali della Facoltà di Magisterio,* Univ. of Bari 14(1977)103-121.

DAMASUS

Although it is possible that he was a native of Spain (*natione hispanicus, Liber pontificalis,* ed. Duchesne, I 84), it nevertheless seems that Damasus was born around 304-305 at Rome, where his family was well established and his father was engaged in an ecclesiastical career (Ferrua 7). Jerome (*De. vir. inl.* 103: PL 23, 742) mentions that Damasus died at about eighty years of age in 384. While still a boy at Rome he had received information concerning some martyrs from one of the persecutors (Ferrua 28). Laurentia, his mother, lived for sixty years as a consecrated widow after the death of her husband (Ferrua 10) and his sister, Irene, who was a virgin, died at an early age (Ferrua 11). Damasus was a deacon of Liberius when the latter was sent into exile by Constantius in 355, although he seems to have sympathized for a certain time with the anti-Pope Felix. At the death of Liberius in 366, Damasus, still a deacon, was elected bishop of Rome, while a group of dissidents elected Ursinus. Riots broke out between the two factions and resulted in numerous deaths. Damasus was supported by the majority of the faithful and by the civil authorities as well. Nevertheless, Ursinus and his supporters, although defeated or exiled, were the cause of great difficulties for Damasus in subsequent years with their calumnies, attempts at extortion, and appeals to other authorities. A clamourous lawsuit was directed against Damasus by the converted Jew, Isaac, in 371 and possibly another one was brought in 378. He also had difficulties with other sects at Rome: Donatists, Luciferians, Valentinians, Marcionites, and Novatians. He was also concerned with the Arian question, although not with the capacity and discernment desired by Basil, with whom he corresponded. Basil had spared no efforts in an attempt to obtain peace and he judged Damasus severely. In any case, the relations between the Westerners and the orthodox Easterners were extremely complicated. At Antioch, Basil and the Eastern bishops supported Meletius, while the Westerners together with Damasus backed Paulinus. Matters were aggravated further by real theological difficulties as well as by linguistic differences in which even a man of such elevated culture as Jerome went astray (*Ep.* 1 and 16: PL 22, 325-358). In order to withstand heretics, schismatics, or enemies, Damasus turned to the civil authorities. A man of culture, he took an interest in the pontifical archives (Ferrua 57), undertook various construction projects in the catecombs, and constructed churches such as San Lorenzo in Damaso, the basilicas of the Apostles on the Appian Way, and the Basilica of Saints Mark and Marcellianus in the vicinity of which he was buried along with his mother and sister. He intervened in various questions concerning the Western churches, and almost every year held a synod, which during his pontificate and that of his successor, Siricius, assumed a notable legislative importance. He had a close relationship with Jerome, who was also his "secretary" and collaborator during the years 382-384 (Jerome, *Ep.* 123, 10: PL 22, 1052), and to whom he often turned for an explanation of various exegetical questions. He urged Jerome to write rather than to study (*Ep.* 5, 1: PL 22, 451) and persuaded him to revise the Latin text of the Bible against the Greek, which Jerome did for the Gospels and other books. It should be noted, too, that Damasus enjoyed good relations with the Roman aristocracy.

Studies: J. Wittig, Papst Damasus I. Quellenkritische Studien zu seiner Geschichte und Charakteristik (RQ Suppl.). Rome, 1902. — G. Wilpert, La scoperta delle basiliche cimiteriali dei santi Marco e Marcelliano e Damaso: *Nuov. Boll. Arch. Crist.* 9(1903)43-58. — O. Marucchi, Il pontificato del papa Damaso e la storia della sua famiglia secondo le recenti scoperte archeologiche. Rome, 1905. — C. H. Turner, Ambrosiaster and Damasus: JThSt 7(1905-06)281-284. — J. Wittig, Der Ambrosiaster "Hilarius." Ein Beitrag zur Geschichte des Papstes Damasus I, in M. Sdralek, *Kirchengeschichtliche Abhandlungen* 4(1906)1-66. — S. Charnier, Le premier archéologue chrétien: S. Damase: REAug 8(1906)569-578. — E. Vacanard, Le pape Damase et le culte des saints: *Revue Clergé Fran.* 67(1911)611-614. — J. Wittig, Die Friedenspolitik des Papstes Damasus I. und der Ausgang der arianischen Streitigkeiten. Breslau, 1912. — H. Leclercq, Damase: DAL 4(1920)145-197. — J. Vives, Damasus i Filocalus: AST 2(1926)483-494. — M. Crovini, I malintesi di un famoso episodio storico del IV secolo. S. Basilio e Papa Damaso: SC 56(1928)321-344. — J. Vives, San Damas, compatrici nostre: *Paraula Cristiana* 18(1933)308-326. — G. Roethe, Zur Geschichte der röm. Synoden im 3. u. 4. Jh., Stuttgart, 1937. — A. Ferrua, S. Maria Maggiore e la "basilica Sicinini": CC 89/3(1938)56-61; *idem,* Filocalo, l'amante della bella lettera: CC 90/1(1939)35-47. — G. Ferretto, Note storiche-bibliografiche di archeologia cristiana. Vatican City, 1942. — J. Vives, S. Dámaso papa español y los mártires, Barcelona, 1943. — A. Hoeppfner, Les deux procès du pape Damasus: REAN 50(1948)288-304. — R. Richard, Saint Basile et la mission du diacre Sabine: AB 67(1949)178-202. — A. Penna, S. Girolamo. Rome 1949, 64-74. — A. Ferrua, Damaso I: EC 4(1950)1136-1139. — M. Ann Norton, Prosopography of Pope Damasus: Folia 4(1950)13-31, 5(1951)30-55, 6(1952)16-39 (fundamental work; cf. J.-M. F. Marique, Leaders of Iberean Christianity 50-650 A. D. Jamaica Plains, Mass. 1962, 13-80). — A. Michel, in A. Grillmeier, H. Bacht, Das Konzil von Chalkedon, vol. II. Würzburg 1953, 504-507, 522-524. — H. Marot, Les conciles romains des IVe et Ve siècle et le developpement de la Primauté, in L'Eglise et les Eglises I. Chévetogne 1954, 209-240. — A. de Mandieta, Damase, Athanase, Pierre, Mélèce et Basile. Les rapports de communion ecclésiastique entre l'Église de Rome, d'Alexandrie, d'Antoiche et de Césarée de Cappadoce (370-379). Ibid., 261-281. — P. Borella, S. Damaso e i canti della Messa didattica: EL 72(1958)223-229. — A. van Roy, Damase: DHG 14(1960)48-53. — Ch. Pietri, Concordia Apostolorum et renovatio Urbis (Culte des martyrs et propagande pontificale): MAH 73(1961)275-322. — N. Q. King, The Emperor Theodosius and the Establishment of Christianity. London, 1961. — S. D'Elia, Ammiano Marcellino e il Cristianesimo: *Studi*

Romani 10(1962)372-390. — H. M. Dipier, L'Assumptus Homo patristique III: RT 63(1963)363-388. — A. J. de Costa, São Dãmaso, Dicionario de historia de Portugal 1 (1963)779-781. — S. Morison, An Unacknowledged Hero of the Fourth Century, Damasus I, 366-384; *Studies Ullman.* Rome 1964, 241-263. — A. Lippold, Ursinus und Damasus: *Historia* 14(1965)105-128. — W. H. Semple, St. Jerome as a Biblical Translator: BJR 48(1965)227-243. — A. Lippold, Ursinus: PWK Suppl. 10(1965)1141-1148. — S. Jannaccone, Roma 384 (Struttura sociale spirituale del gruppo geronimiano): *Giov. It. Filologia* 19(1966)32-48. — L. A. Delastre, S. Damase I.er Defenseur de la doctrine de la primauté de Pierre, des Saintes Ecritures et patron des archéologues. Paris, 1965. — V. Peri, Gli inconsistenti archivi pontifici di S. Lorenzo in Damaso: *Rendiconti Pont. Acc. Arch.* 41(1968)192-204. — N. Corneanu, Les efforts des saint Basile pour l'unité de l'Eglise: *Verbum Caro* 23(1969)43-67. — M. H. Shepherd, The Liturgical Reform of Damasus I, in Festschr. Quasten II., Münster 1970, 847-863. — M. Bonaria, Appunti per la tradizione virgiliana nel IV secolo: *Vergiliana.* Leiden 1971, 35-40. — Ch. Piétri, Damase et Théodose. Communion orthodoxe et géographie politique, in *Epektasis,* Mél. Daniélou. Paris 1972, 627-634. — J. Taylor, St. Basil the Great and Pope Damasus I: DR 91(1973)186-203, 262-274. — Ch. Piétri, Roma Christiana, 2 vols. Rome, 1976 (fundamental work for the breadth of its documentation and study).

1. Epigrams (Titles).

Damasus' greatest literary fame is connected with the numerous epigrams he composed to honor the martyrs or deceased relatives and friends, or in memory of various undertakings. Nearly all were intended to be engraved in marble, and the carving, or at least the designs, were done by a true artist, Furius Dionysius Philocalus, a friend of Damasus. Some of the original inscriptions with their unmistakable and artistic characters still exist, bearing the signature of the artist. The majority of the inscriptions, however, are known only from transcriptions made in the Middle Ages. Numerous epigrams as well as other writings have been attributed to Damasus, and De Rossi, Ihm and Ferrua have worked out some criteria for judging their authenticity (cf. *Epigrammata.* Rome, 1942, p. 50-53). On the basis of these criteria, 59 epigrams and 13 fragments are accepted as authentic. The epigrams are an important witness to a sure tradition regarding the martyrs buried at Rome, although the memory of some of them was already obscure at the time of these inscriptions. Damasus is then content to write, "It is said . . ." The content of the epigrams is on the whole not very precise and is expressed in general terms, which often renders the verses obscure. Although he had an excellent knowledge of Vergil and Lucretius, Damasus repeats the customary motifs in the epigrams — martyrdom, time of death, reward — and thus draws on a constant repertoire with few variations. Damasus' verses have more historical and archaeological importance than literary merit, in spite of Jerome's judgment (*De vir. inl.* 103: PL 23, 749). This latter also states that Damasus wrote a work entitled *De virginitate* in prose and poetry (*Ep.* 22, 9: PL 22, 409) of which nothing remains, and which cannot be identified with the epigram in honor of his sister, Irene, and of Agnes. Delisle (*Les manuscripts du comte d'Ashburnham.* Paris 1883, p. 87) mentions a manuscript containing a *De vitiis,* of which nothing further is known.

Editions: Cf. PLS I, 314-423. — PL 13, 375-414. — M. Ihm, Damasi Epigrammata. Leipzig, 1895 (62 authentic, 45 spurious). — A. Ferrua, Epigrammata Damasiana. Rome, 1942 (the best edition, with commentary; 59 authentic, 20 dubious or spurious. Cf. review by A. Vaccari, Biblica 24[1943]190-194).

Translations: French: H. Leclercq, DAL 4(1920)145-197. *Italian:* A. Salvatore, L'epigramma Damasiano In laudem Davidis, in appendix: Antologia degli Epigrammi Damasiani. Naples, 1960.

Studies: G. Ficker, Bemerkungen zu einer Inschrift des Papstes Damasus: ZKG 22(1901)33-342. — G. Mercati, Il carme Damasiano "De Davide" e la falsa corrispondenza di Damaso e Girolamo riguardo al salterio, in Note di letteratura biblica e cristiana antica (ST 5). Rome 1901, 113-126 (reprint 1973). — L. Duchesne, Sur une inscription damasienne: Mélanges Boissier. Paris 1903, 169-172. — O. Marucchi, Osservazioni storiche ed epigrafiche sulla iscrizione recentemente scoperta della madre del papa Damaso: *Nuovo Boll. Arch. Crist.* 9(1903)59-108; *idem,* Breve aggiunta all'articolo sulla iscrizione della madre di papa Damaso: ibid., 9(1903)195-198; *idem,* Di una sconosciuta iscrizione Damasiana in onore del martire S. Valentino: ibid., 11(1905)103-122; *idem,* I frammenti dell'iscrizione damasiana di S. Ippolito aggiunti alla collezione epigrafica del Museo Lateranense: ibid., 18(1912)180-183. — C. Weyman, Vier Epigramme del hl. Papstes Damasus I. Munich, 1905. — P. Franchi de Cavalieri, I santi Nereo e Achilleo nell'epigramma damasiano: Note agiografiche (ST 22). Rome 1909, 41-55, — A. Ferrato, Cronologia costantiniana e die papi S. Eusebio e S. Milziade. Iscrizioni di S. Damaso attribuite erroneamente ae tempi costantiniani spiegati per i tempi di Liberio Papa. Rome, 1910. — G. Bonavenia, Vari frammenti di carmi damasiani: *Nuovo Boll. Arch. Crist.* 16(1910)227-251, 17(1911)23-37, 123-142 (Ihm 9, 10, 8, 40). — S. Colombo, Sull'espressione "superis invisa" in un'iscrnzione: Did 4(1915)209-214; *idem,* Appunti Damasiani: ibid., 1(1912)361-372. E. Schäfer, Die Bedeutung der Epigramme des Papstes Damasus I. für die Geschichte des Heiligenverehrung: EL 46(1932)137-235, 309-378 (subsequent edition; Rome, 1932). — E. Josi, Scoperta di due frammenti del carme damasiano in onore di S. Ermete: RAC 9(1932)147-150; *idem,* Quattro frammenti del carme di Damaso in onore di S. Ippolito: ibid., 13(1936)231-236; *idem,* Altri tre frammenti del carme Damasiano in onore di S. Ippolito: ibid., 16(1939)320-322. — J. Vives, Damasiano: AST 16(1943)1-6. — J. Carcopino, Sur dcux textes controversés de la tradition apostolique romaine: *Comptes Rendues Acc. Ins. Belles Lettres* 1952, 424-433 (hic habitasse, Ferrua 20). — P. Künzle, Del cosidetto "Titulus archivorum" di papa Damaso: RSCI 7(1953)1-26. — A. Ferrua, Intorno ad una dedica damasiano: RAC 29(1953)231-235. — F. Tolotti, Memorie degli apostoli in catacumbas. Vatican City, 1953 (resumé in RAC 22[1954]210-231). — S. Pricoco, Valore letterario degli epigrammi di Damaso: MSLC 4(1954)19-40. — E. Griffe, Hic habitare prius: BLE 58(1957)13-101. — P. Testini, Noterelle sulla Memoria apostolorum: RAC 30(1954)210-231. — H. Chadwick, St. Peter and St. Paul in Rome. The Problem of the Memoria Apostolorum ad Catabumbas: JThSt 8(1957)31-52. — A. Ferrua, Lavori nella catacomba di Domitilla: RAC 33(1957)45-75; *idem,* Qui Filius diceris et pater inveneris. Mosaico novellamente scoperto nella catacomba di Domitilla: *Atti Pont. Acc. Arch.* 33(1960-61)209-224. — L. Vökle, Archäologische Funde und Forschungen, . . . Domitilla-Katakombe. Damasianische Inschrift: RQ 55(1960)114-118. — A. Salvatore, L'epigramma Damasiano in laudem Davidis: *Antologia degli epigrammi Damasiani* (text and translation). Naples, 1960 (first part also in *Annali Fac.*

Lett. Fil. Napoli 8[1958-59]100-133). — E. Griffe, L'inscription damasienne de la catacombe de Saint Sébastien: BLE 62(1961)16-25 (hic habitasse). — J. Knacksteot, Qui filius diceris et pater inveneris. Ein Grabdenkmal in der Domitilla-Katakombe: *Theol. prakt. Quart.* 110(1962)226-231. — N. B. Denis-Boulet, L'inscription damasienne Ad Catacumbas: RAC 43(1967)11-124. — J. Ruysschaert, Pierre et Paul à Rome. Textes et contextes d'une inscription damasienne: *Rendiconti P. Acc. Arch.* 42(1969-70)201-218. — E. Griffe, En relisant l'inscription damasienne "ad Catacumbas": BLE 71(1970)81-91. — H. Chadwick, Pope Damasus and the Peculiar Claim of Rome to St. Peter and St. Paul, in Festschf. Cullmann. Leiden 1962, 313-318. — A. V. Nazzaro, Sui Versus ad fratrem corripiendum di papa Damaso: *Koinonia* 1(1977)195-203.

2. Letters.

Various letters of Damasus have been preserved, including the nine in PL 13. There is some doubt concerning the authenticity of some, such as the first (PL 13, 347-49: *Confidimus quidem*), the original text of which could be that preserved in a manuscript of Verona and edited by Schwartz in 1936. Of particular importance is letter IV (*Tomus Damasi, Confessio fidei*: PL 13, 558-564) composed of 24 articles which is a summary of Trinitarian and Christological errors, and which condemns those who consider the Holy Spirit to be a work of the Son. It concludes by affirming that faith in the Trinity is necessary for salvation. The letter, which has the character of a compiled work, is a Roman profession of faith which was drawn up by a Roman council and sent by Damasus to Paulinus of Antioch. "*C'est le code de l'orthodoxie nicéen en 377*" (Ch. Piétri, *Roma Christiana* I. Rome 1976, p. 839).

The letter *Ad Gallos Episcopos* (Siricius, PL 13, 1181-1194), since it is worded in the singular, is not the work of a synod and does not mention a meeting of bishops. It gives no orders, but rather counsels, exhorts, and presents arguments. The letter is a response to certain persons who wanted to maintain the unity of discipline in questions regarding "law and tradition" such as virgins who do not live up to their calling, clerical continence, the conditions for admission to sacred orders, and monastic vows. Some modern scholars (most recently Piétri) have followed Babut and attribute the letter to Damasus.

The *Decretum Gelasianum (Explanatio fidei)* is composed of two parts different in origin and value. The first and earlier part (ch. I-III) speaks of the sources of authority: 1) of the sevenfold Spirit which rests in Christ; 2) of the biblical canon; 3) of the supremacy of the Roman See. The second part (ch. IV-V) treats of the other authorities: the councils (Nicea, Ephesus, Chalcedon) and the Fathers. A list of heretical or schismatic books is appended to the text. In numerous manuscripts, the title of the work is: *Incipit concilium urbis Romae sub Damaso papa. De explanatione fidei.* In some manuscripts the first three chapters are transmitted independently of the others and are attributed to Damasus. Many scholars (e.g., Thiel, Maassen, Turner,

Zahn, Bardy, Di Capua) admit the possibility that Damasus is responsible for the first part, which would have been composed at the council of Rome in 382 at which it seems Jerome was present, although he does not mention it.

Editions: There is no complete critical edition. Cf. CPL 1633. PL 13, 347-373. *Ep. 1* in PL 69, 1006-7; PG 82, 1051-1055. *Ep 3 and 4* in PL 53, 319-322; PL 56, 686-690; CSEL 71(518-522); PG 82, 122-126; GCS 19, 297-302. *Ep. 7* in PL 69, 1133-1134; PG 82, 1219-1222. *Ep. 8 and 9* in CSEL 54, 103-104, 265-267. *Tomus Damasi:* M. Dossetti, Il Simbolo di Nicea e di Costantinopoli. Rome 1967, 94-111. — *Ad Gallos episcopos:* PL 13, 1181-1194. — E. Babut, La plus ancienne décrétal. Paris 1904, 65-87. *Decretum Gelasianum:* PL 13, 373-376; PL 19, 787-794; PL 59, 157-164, 165-180; PL 84, 843-848. — E. von Dobschütz, TU 38, 4. Leipzig 1912, 3-60 (critical edition).

Studies: C. H. Turner, Latin Lists of the Canonical Books. I: The Roman Council under Damasus, A.D. 382: JThSt 1(1899-1900)554-560. — G. Mercati, Il carme Damasiano "de Davide" e la falsa corrispondenza di Damaso e Girolamo riguardo al salterio, in Note di letterature biblica e cristiana (ST 5). Rome 1901, 113-126 (reprint, 1973). — H. H. Howorth, The Decretal of Damasus: JThSt 14(1912-13)321-337 (Decr. Gelasianum). — H. Leclercq, Gélasien (Décret.): DAL 6(1924)722-747. — P. Galtier, Le "Tome de Damase." Date et origine: RSR 26(1936)385-418, 563-578 (composed by Ambrose in 382). — F. Di Capua, Il ritmo prosaico nelle lettere dei Papi: *Lateranum* 3(1937)251-273 (especially Tomus, confidimus and Decretum Gelas.). — G. Bardy, Gélase (Décret.): DBS 3(1938)579-590. — J. Cochez, Le rythme oratoire des lettres papales: ETL 14(1938)526-534. — M. Richard, La lettre "Confidimus quidem" du pape Damase: AIPh (Mél. Grégoire) 11(1951)323-340. — P. Blanchard, La correspondance apocryphe du pape Damase et de s. Jérôme sure le psautier et le chant de l'Alleluia: EL 63(1949)376-388. — J. Bignani Odier, Une letter apocryphe de saint Damase à saint Jérôme sur la question de Melchisédech: MAH 63(1951)183-190. — F. Scheidweiller, Besitzen wir das lateinische Original des römischen Synodalschreibens von Jahre 371?: AIPh 13(1953[1955])573-586. — A. de Vogüé, La Règle du Maitre et la lettre apocryphe de saint Jérôme sur le chant des Psaumes: *Studia Monastica* 7(1965)357-367. — P. H. Lafontaine, Les conditions de l'accession aux Ordres dans la première législation ecclésiastique. Ottawa, 1963 (Ad Gallos, p. 301-303). — Th. C. Lawler, Jerome's First Letter to Damasus, in Festschrf. Quasten (*Kyriakon*) II. Münster 1970, 548-552. — Ch. Piétri, Roma Christiana. Rome 1976, 831-840, 873-880 (Tomus); 777-682 (Confidimus quidem); 764-778 (Ad Gallos); 881-884 (Decretum Gelas.). — A. Faivre, Naissance d'une hiérarchie. Paris, 1977 (Ad Gallos, p. 310-312).

AUSIONUS

Magnus Decimus Ausonius (ca. 310 - ca. 394), a Gaulo-Roman, was born at Burdigala (Bordeaux), and it was there and at Toulouse that he pursued his studies. He taught in his native city first as *grammaticus* then as *rhetor* until 364 when Valentinian summoned him to Trier to be the tutor of his son, Gratian. He then began a political career which led him to become Praetorian Prefect and Consul in 379. As emperor, Gratian bestowed high honors on many other members of Ausonius' family (e.g., his son-in-law, Talassius, the father of Paulinus of Pella). When Gratian died in 483, Ausonius retired to Burdigala. He was deeply attached to Paulinus of Nola and did not approve of the latter's conversion and retirement to Spain in 389. He wrote Paulinus four letters in verse, which arrived rather late at their destination, to persuade and plead with him to return, but in vain. Four years later, Paulinus responded in his turn with two letters in verse, which displayed, although in terms of profound friendship, his firm intent.

Christian expressions crop up here and there in the vast production of Ausonius (e.g., 27, 113: Pieper, 281), but his work is clearly of a pagan character with passages in complete contradiction to Christian faith and morals. Nevertheless, there are three clearly Christian compositions. The *Oratio matutina* (Pieper 7-11) of 85 verses can be divided into two parts. Verses 1-30 are a prayer of adoration and a profession of faith and are a beautiful synthesis of the Johannine Prologue and the Nicene creed. They speak of the omnipotent, eternal God who can be known only by the Son, who is himself Creator, the Word of God (v. 9, *ipse Dei verbum, verbum Deus*); the Word who became incarnate to call all people to salvation by means of his life. The second part (vv. 31-85) is of a personal character and forms a prayer of petition for forgiveness of sins, and for light and strength to overcome vices, to live in simplicity and friendship with others, and to live in serenity, free from physical and moral harm, in expectation of judgment. The *Oratio matutina* is one of the most ancient Christian prayers. Since it is found in one manuscript among the works of Paulinus of Nola, some scholars have raised doubts concerning its authenticity. Nevertheless, it is closely bound to the *Ephemeris (totius diei negotium)* of which it forms a part. Its theology is fully orthodox. Many subsequent poets have been inspired by it, such as Paulinus of Nola, Paulinus of Pella, Sedulius, and Orientius. In another collection of poems, the *Domestica,* are found the *Versus Paschales* (Pieper 17-19) of 367 and the *Versus rhopalici* (Pieper 19-21) of 379. The former, consisting of 31 verses, are definitely authentic as they are found in all the manuscripts. On the occasion of Easter, they address a prayer to God the Father *(Magne pater rerum)* to whom all things are subject and who has sent his Word into the world, true God and true man. The verses express faith in the Trinity (v. 22: *trina fides auctore uno, spes certa salutis* Pieper 18), which is unhappily compared to the emperor who shares his reign with his brother and his son. The *Versus rhopalici* are in special dactylic hexameters. Each verse is composed of 5 words which have successively one, two, three, four, and five syllables (a total of fifteen) and which give the idea of a progression. The *Versus rhopalici* are also a prayer and include a brief synthesis of Trinitarian faith, of the sacrament of Christian initiation (Baptism) and the redemption accomplished by Christ, of events of early Christianity (Stephen and Paul), and of Christian hope. The doctrine is orthodox, but the technique too refined. Some scholars question the authenticity of the poems (e.g., Schenkl), and Martin has proposed that the author was a priest who knew Ausonius well. In any case, they are contained in the major manuscript of Ausonius, the *Vossianus* 111.

Much has been written and discussed concerning Ausonius' Christianity, and it is questioned whether he was a pagan who composed Christian poems out of opportunism, or a syncretist, or a Christian who by training followed pagan poetical schemes or a pagan who subsequently became a Christian. Ausonius can be situated in the broader context of the political, cultural and religious climate of the second half of the fourth century which cultivated personal characteristics devoid of any extremism. It is certainly not possible to admit that there was a pagan period in his life followed by a Christian period. The opinion which De Labriolle expounded in many writings from 1910 to 1950 (RACh), and which has become a fairly common opinion today, is that Ausonius was a Christian who was not very convinced or engaged in his faith and who remained a pagan by cultural formation and attitude. Ausonius' pagan and Christian periods are intertwined as are his poems themselves and he manifests a fundamental syncretism unlike that of other Christian poets who make use of mythology. Ausonius does not limit himself to merely making use of mythology and does not hesitate to compose prayers to the gods (e.g., *Precatio consulis designati*: Pieper 24-27), even though they contain a new spirit far removed from ancient paganism. The case of Ausonius is extremely important for understanding the thought of many intellectuals of his time, halfway between paganism and Christianity with a prevalence of one aspect of the other. Historical research has accented a dualism (pagans and Christians) and centered its attention on the leaders of the two currents. Instead, it is necessary to take into consideration the intermediate, hazy zone between the two.

Editions PL 19, 823-958 (Oratio mat. also in CSEL 30, 4-7). K. Schenkl. Berlin, 1883(MGH AA V, 2), — H. G. Evely-White, 2 vols., London, 1919-1921 (reprint, 1967) (LCL). — M. Jasinski. Paris, 1935. — A. Pastorino. Turin, 1971. — R. Pieper. Leipzig, 1886 (reprint, Amsterdam, 1976) (Teubner).

Translations (selected): *English:* H. G. Evely-White, op. cit. *French:* M. Jasinki, op. cit. *Italian:* A. Pastorino, op. cit.

Studies: (only regarding Ausonius' Christianity): P. Martino, Ausone et le commencement du christianisme en Gaule. Alger, 1906. — L. Villani, Quelques observations sur les chants chrétiens d'Ausone: REAN 8(1906)325-337. — P. de Labriolle, La correspondence d'Ausone et de Paulin de Nole. Paris, 1910; *idem,* DHGE 5(1931)773-779; *idem,* RACh 1(1950)1020-1023. — P. Fabbri, Il pensiero religioso del poeta D. Magno Ausonio: *Atene e Roma* 17(1914)378-383. — Ch. Guignebert, Les demi-chrétiens et leur place dans l'Église antique: RHR 88(1923)65-102. — G. Weyman, Ausonius und das Christentum: MM 4(1924)274-276. — M. J. Pattist, Ausonius al Christ. Amsterdam, 1925 (fundamental work). — Ch. Mohrmann, Ausonius en zijen verhoudding tot het Christendom: StC 4(1927-28)364-391, 5(1928-29)23-39 (fundamental work). — L.

Jouai, De Magistraat Ausonius. Nijmegen, 1938. — A. Stanislaus, The Christian Ausonius: *Clas. Weekly* 37(1943-44) 156-157. — C. Riggi, Il cristianesimo di Ausonio: *Salesianum* 30(1968)642-695. — P. Langlois, Les poèmes chrétiens et le cristianisme d'Ausone: RPh 43(1969)39-58. — J. Martin, La prière d'Ausone: BAGB 1971, 369-382; *idem,* Textes chrétiens d'Ausone: BAGB 1972, 503-512 (Versus rhopalici).

PRUDENTIUS

The principal, if not the only source of a knowledge of the life of Aurelius Prudentius Clemens is provided by his own works, especially the *Praefatio* of 45 verses with which he introduces the collection of his writings which he published in 405 at age 57.

He was born in 348 in the region of Tarragona, most probably at Calagurris (the modern Calahorra). It is likely that his family was already Christian since the poet is silent about a conversion of his own.

After an ordinary scholastic curriculum he was active as a lawyer, only to pass over to public administration on account of "bitter experiences," and finally as prefect he governed two important cities.

The evidence of excellent government under his administration obtained for Prudentius an unspecified responsibility at the court which crowned his *cursus honorum.*

At this point, a profound crisis of conscience caused him to feel the emptiness of the worldly life he had been leading and led him to consecrate the rest of his days to praising God in poetry. An important factor in the life of Prudentius was his trip to Rome, which impressed him greatly with its classical and Christian monuments. This contact with Rome took place in the first years of the fifth century, between 401 and 403.

During this trip, and especially in the center of Christianity, the Spanish poet found new motives of inspiration for his hymns and was induced to take up an anti-pagan polemic.

All trace of him is lost after 405 and the year of his death remains unknown.

Bibliographies: J. Martin, Christlich lateinische Dichter: BJ 55, 2(1929)124-131 (Prudentius). — C. Magazzù, Rassegna di studi prudenziani (1967-1976): *Bollettino di studi latini* 7(1977)105-134. — M. P. Cunningham, Forty Years of Prudentius Studies, in Aufstieg und Niedergang des römischen Welts. Fest. Vogt. III. Berlin, 1971.

Studies: A. M. Tonna-Barthet, Aurelio Prudencio Clemente. Estudio biográfico crítico: CD 57(1902)25-40, 210-244, 293-307, 567-579; 58(1902)42-55, 297-312, 481-494. — F. Maigret, Le poète chrétien Prudence: *Science Cath.* 17(1903)219-227, 303-313, 393-342. — R. Lejay, Le sabbat juif et les poètes latins: RHL 8(1903)305-335. — G. Krüger, A. Ebert, Prudentius, Aurelius Clemens: RE 16(1905)184-186. — K. Künstle, Antipriscilliana. Freiburg i. B. 1905, 170-184 (Prudentius was not anti-Priscillian). — W. Macholz, Der Dichter Prudentius in den Spuren Marcells von Ancyra: ThStKr 82(1909)577-592. — F. Ermini, Prudenzio. Condizioni e vicende della vita del poeta: *Riv. Storico-crit. Sc. Teol.* 5(1909)835-847. — F. X. Schuster, Studien zu Prudentius. Freising, 1909. — P.

Thomas, Prudence et Caton d'Utique: *Rev. de l'Inst. pub. Bel.* 56(1913)19-20. — E. K. Rand, Prudentius and Christian Humanism: TP (1920)71-83. — E. Porebowicz, L'espagnolisme d'Aur. Prudence: Eos 25(1921)1-12. — J. Bergman, Aurelius Prudentius Clemens, der grösste christliche Dichter des Altertums I (*Acta et commentationes Universitatis Dorpatensis* II). Tartu, 1922. — P. Galindo, Estudios latinos: Quintiliano, Lucrecio, Prudencio. Zaragossa, 1926. — Lucas de San Juan de la Cruz, ¿Done nació . . . Marco Aurelio Prudencio Clemente del siglo IV? Calahorra, 1936. — I. Rodríguez Herrera, Poeta christianus. Prudentius' Auffassung vom Wesen und von der Aufgabe des christlichen Dichters. Speyer, 1936 (Spanish transl. *Helmantica* 32[1981]5-184). — F. Alexander, Beziehungen des Prudentius zu Ovid: WSt(1936)166-173. — J. Vives, Prudentiana: *Homenatge Rubió i Lluch* II. Barcelona 1936, 1-18; *idem,* Prudentiana: AST 12 (1936)1-8; *idem,* Veracidad histórica de Prudencio: AST 17(1945)199-204. — I. Rodríguez Herrero, Mariología en Prudencio: EM 5(1946)347-358; *idem,* Prudencio, poeta de la Hispanidad: *Helmantica* 1(1950)85-101. — G. Bardy, Prudence: DTC 13(1936)1076-1079. — A. C. Vega, Capítulos de un libro: Juvenco y Prudencio: CD 157(1945)209-247; *idem,* Capítulos de un libro: Aurelio Prudencio: CD 158(1946)193-271, 159(1947)421-467, 160(1948)5-34. — C. Rapisarda, La rappresentazione dell'oltretomba in Prudenzio: MSLC 1(1947)41-65; *idem,* Prudenzio e la lingua greca: ibid., 2(1948)21-51. — A. C. Vega, Aurelio Prudencio. Páginas de un libro: CD 160(1948)185-240; *idem,* Aurelio Prudencio. A propósito del centenario de su nacimiento (348): CD 160(1948)381-389. — S. Cirac Estopañan, Los nuevos argumentos sobre la patria de Prudencio: *Publ. Fac. Fil. Letras der* la 8. Zaragossa, 1951. — B. M. Peebles, The Poet Prudentius. New York, 1951. — M. Brozek, De Prudentio Pindaro latino: Eos 47(1954)107-141. — E. Rapisarda, Introduzione alla lettura di Prudenzio, I. Influssi Lucreziani, Catania, 1951. — V. Paronetto, Prudenzio: *Studium* 35(1957)274-280. — F. G. LoPorto, Scoperti i resti del poeta Prudenzio Clemente?: RAC 33(1957)197-202. — A. Kurfess, Prudentius: PWK 23, 1(1957)1039-1071. — A. Salvatore, Studi Prudenziani. Naples, 1958. — L. Alfonsi, Sulla militia di Prudenzio: VC 13(1959)181-183. — W. N. Schumacher, Prudentius an die Via Tiburtina: Spanische Forschungen der Görresgesellschaft, Erste Reihe 16(1960)1-15. — Stella M. Hanley, Prudentius and Juvenal: *Phoenix* 16(1962)41-52. — I. Lana, Due capitoli prudenziani, La biografia, la cronologia, la poetica. Rome, 1962. — R. Ellis Messenger, Aurelius Prudentius Clemens. A Biographical Study. Bibliography, in J.-M. F. Marique, Leaders of Iberean Christianity. Jamaica Plains, Mass. 1962, 81-102. — A. Ferrua, Lavori a S. Sebastiano: RAC 37(1963)203-236. — K. Thraede, Die infantia des christlichen Dichters: Mullus, Festsch. Th. Klauser (= JAC). Münster 1964, 362-365. — R. Cacitti, "Subdita Christo servit Roma deo": osservazioni sulla teologia politica di Prudenzio: *Aevum* 46(1972)402-435. — J. Fontaine, Valeurs antiques et valeurs chrétiennes dans la spiritualité des grands propriétaires terriens à la fin du IVe siècle occidental: *Epektasis,* Mél. Daniélou. Paris 1972, 571-595. — E. Rapisarda, Studi Prudenziani. Catania, 1969 (collection of earlier articles). — R. Argenio, Roma immaginata e veduta dal poeta cristiano Prudenzio: *Studi Romani* 21(1973)25-37. — J. Fontaine, L'Art préroman hispanique I. Paris 1973, 19-42. — W. Evenepoel, Prudentius, ratio et fides: ACL 50(1981)318-327. —L. Padovese. La cristologia di Aurelio Clemente Prudenzio. Rome, 1980. — I. R. Herrera, Poeta Christianus. Esencia y missión del poeta cristiano en la obra de Prudencio. Salamanca, 1981.

WRITINGS

The collection of Prudentius' works was clearly arranged by the poet himself, as is obvious from the preface and the epilogue which open and close the collection.

In the preface, following a succinct autobiography, the poet offers the key for entering into the spirit of his work with a precise allusion to the writings being published: "Now at the end of my life, my sinful soul rids itself of folly. At least with its voice, if it is no longer able with its works, it lifts up its praise to God. Day and night without ceasing I will sing to the Lord with hymns, I will combat heresies and explain the catholic faith, I will destroy the temples of the pagans and will put your idols to death, O Rome. I will dedicate my poems to the martyrs and will exalt the Apostles" (*Praefatio,* v. 34-45).

Considering the mastery displayed by the poet in this collection with regard both to the formal as well as the doctrinal aspects, it is reasonable to suppose the existence of earlier writings of which there is nevertheless no notice.

The extant works all have one aspect in common. According to a fairly ancient custom in Latin literature, the title of each work is in Greek.

Complete editions: CPL 1437-1446. — For early editions, cf. I. Guillén, I. Rodríguez, Obras completas de Aurelio Prudencio (BAC 58). Madrid 1950, 72*-76*. — PL 59, 767-1078. PL 60, 11-594. — J. Bergman, CSEL 61(1926). — M. P. Cunningham, CCL 126(1966). — M. Lavarenne, 4 vols. (Les Belles Lettres). Paris 1944-51. — J. J. Thompson, 2 vols. (LCL) London-Cambridge, Mass. 1949-54 (and subsequent reprints). — J. Guillén, I. Rodríguez, Obras completas de Aurelio Prudencio (BAC 58). Madrid 1950, — I. R. Herrera, Obras completas (BAC 427). Madrid, 1981. — R. J. Deferrari, J. M. Campbell, A Concordance of Prudentius. Cambridge, Mass., 1932.

Studies: Manuscripts: J. Bergman, Neue Prudentiushandschriften: PhW 27 (1896)862-863; *idem,* Neue Prudentius Handschriften von hohen Wert und Alter: *Eranos* 1/2(1902)111-116; *idem,* De interpolationibus codicum Prudentianorum. Narcopiae, 1905; *idem,* De codicum Prudentianorum generibus et virtute: SAW 157, 5(1908); *idem,* De codicibus Prudentianis. Stockholm, 1910; *idem,* Emendationes Prudentianae: *Eranos* 12(1912)111-149. — R. Stettinger, Die illustrierten Prudentius-Handschriften. Berlin, 1895; *idem,* Die illustrierten Prudentius-Handschriften. Tafelband. Berlin, 1905; *idem,* Die Illustrationen der mittelalterlichen Prudentius-Handschriften und ihre spätantike Vorlage, in Verhandlungen der 48. *Versamm. deutscher Philologen und Schulmänner,* 3, bis 6. Hamburg. 1905, 96-120. — J. M. Burnam, Glossemata de Prudentio: *Univ. Studies Cincinnati,* ser. II/1, n.4(1905); *idem,* Commentaire anonyme sur Prudence d'après le ms. 413 de Valenciennes. Paris, 1910. — E. O. Winsted, The Double Recension in the Poems of Prudentius: CR 17(1903)203-207; *idem,* The Spelling in the Sixth Century ms. of Prudentius: CR 18(1904)45-48; *idem,* Mavortius' Copy of Prudentius: CR 18(1904)112ff; *idem,* Mavortius and Prudentius: CQ 1(1907)10ff; *idem,* The Ambrosian ms. of Prudentius: CR 19(1905)54-57; *idem,* Notes on the mss. of Prudentius: *Journal of Philology* 29(1904)165-180. — S. Colombo, De Prudentii codicibus mss. qui in ambrosiana bibliotheca asservantur: Did 5(1927)1-30. — D. de Bruyne, Manuscrits wisigotiques: RB 34(1924)5-20. — C. Mengis, Fragmente einer Freiburger Prudentiushandschrift: Phil 82(1927)89-105. — H. Woodruff, Illustrated mss. of Prudentius: *Art Studies* 1929. Cambridge, Mass. 1930. — G. Meyer, Prudentiana: Phil 87(1932)249-260 (on the manuscripts); ibid., 93(1938)377-403. — S. Jannaccone, Le Par. 8084 de Prudence et la recensio de Mavortius: RELA 26(1948)228-235. — H. Silvestre, Aperçu sur les commentaires carolingiens de Prudence: SE 9(1957)50-75; *idem,* Les manuscrits bruxellois de Prudence: *Scriptorium* 19(1957)102-104. — M. P. Cunningham, Some Facts About the Puteanus of Prudentius: TP 89(1958)32-37; *idem,* A Preliminary Recension of the Older Manuscripts of the Cathemerinon, Apotheosis, and Hamartigenia of Prudentius: SE 13(1962)5-59. — H. D. Meritt, The Old English Prudentius

Glosses at Boulogne-sur-Mer. Stanford, 1959. — A. Bartolucci, Il carme del cod. Paris. 8084 e i problemi della trasmissione delle opere di Prudenzio: *Studi classici ed Orientali* 10(1961)161-178. — M. Ferrari, In Papiam Conveniant ad Dungalum: *Italia Med. e Uman.* 15(1972)1-52.

On the Praefatio: E. Rapisarda, La praefatio di Prudenzio: ND 2(1948)50-61. — M. Brozek, Ad Prudentii praefationem interpretandam: Eos 57(1967-68)149-156; *idem,* De Prudentii Praefatione carminibus praefixa: Forschungen z. rö. Lit, Festschr. Büchner, I. Wiesbaden 1970, 31-316. — C. Magazzù, Rassegna di studi prudenziani (1967-1976): *Boll. Atudi Latini* 7(1977)104-134.

Studies: J. M. Burnam, Prudentius Commentaries: *Amer. Journ. of Archeology* 3 (1900)293-302. — F. Dexel, Des Prudentius Verhältnis zu Vergil. Diss., Erlangen. Landshut, 1907. — S. Colombo, Forme e concetti nella lirica di A. Prudenzio Clemente: Did 2(1913)145-170. — C. Brackman, Quae ratio intercedat inter Lucretium et Prudentium: Mnem 48(1920)434-448; *idem,* Prudentiana: ibid., 49(1921)106-109. — F. Arnaldi, Cristianesimo e sensibilità nell'arte di Prudenzio: *Atene e Roma* 5(1924)89-109. — M. J. Kroll, Die Hymnendichtung des frühen Christentums: *Die Antike* II(1926)258-281. — A. Cugini, La poesia di Aurelio Prudenzio: SC 15(1930)278-296. — L. Strzelecki, Prudentiana: Eos 33(1930-31)490-502 (Prudentius' poetry); *idem,* De Horatio rei metricae Prudentianae auctore: Commentationes Horatianae I. Krakow 1935, 36-49. — M. Lavarenne, Etude sur la langue du poète Prudence. Paris, 1933. — A. Mahoney, Vergil in the Works of Prudentius. Washington, 1934. — E. Martija, Horatii vestigia in Prudentio: *Palaestra latini* 6(1935-36)56-63. — E. Rapisarda, Influssi lucreziani in Prudenzio. Un suo poema lucreziano e antiepicureo: VC 4(1950)46-60. — V. Blanco Garcia, Estética y estilo de Prudencio: *Humanidades* 2(1950)182-191. — J. Pedraz, Filosofía de la historia del imperio romano en los poemas de Prudencio: ibid., 3(1951)22-40. — M. Catalano, L'eroe nel mondo classico e nel mondo cristiano, con particolare riguardo all'eroe cristiano in Prudenzio: *Rivista Studi Classici* 1(1952)5-23. — W. Schmid, Die Darstellung der Menschheitsstufen bei Prudentius und das Problem seiner doppelten Redaktion: VC 7(1953)171-186. — A. Salvatore, Echi ovidiani nella poesia di Prudenzio: *Atti convegno Ovidiano* II. Rome 1959, 257-272. — E. Rapisarda, Poesia e religiosità: Cristo e l'Eucarestia in Prudenzio: *Convivium Dominicum.* Catania 1959, 153-177; *idem,* Gli apostoli Pietro e Paolo e la nave della chiesa in Prudenzio: MSLC 13(1963)61-75. — J. Szövérffy, Die Annalen der lateinischen Hymnendichtung I. Berlin 1964, 78-94. — J. Fontaine, Démons et sybille. La peinture des possédés dans la poésie de Prudence: *Hommages Bayet.* Brussels-Berchem 1964, 196-213. — J. C. Codignani, De A. Prudenti Clementis carminibus: *Latinitas* 12(1964)230-235. — A. Cerri, Aspetti di polemica antimitologica e di composizione poetica in Prudenzio: *Athenaeum* 42(1964)334-360 (=Miscell. Malcovati). — C. Gnilka, Einwachsen der Götterbilder. Ein Missverständnis heidnischer Kultübung bie Prudentius: JAC 7(1964)52-57. — K. Thraede, Studien zu Sprache und Stil des Prudentius. Göttingen, 1965. — S. Gennaro, Prudenzio nella Vita s. Maximi episcopi Reiensis, in *Studi C. Sgroi.* Turin 1965, 561-569. — R. Herzog, Die allegorische Dichtung des Prudentius. Munich, 1966. — A. Hudson-Williams, Vergil and the Christian Latin Poets: *Papers of the Verg. Soc.* 6(1966-67)11-21. — C. Witke, Prudentius and the Tradition of Latin Poetry: TP 99(1968)509-525 (cf. *Numen Litterarum.* Leiden-Cologne 1971, 102-144). — G. Torti, Patriae sua gloria Christus. Aspetti della Romanità cristiana di Prudenzio: RIL 104(1970)337-368. — J. Fontaine, La femme dans la poésie de Prudence, in Mélanges Durry (RELA 47 bis 1970)55-83. — I. B. Pigatus, De Prudentio eiusque poesi: *Latinitas* 18(1970)242-249 (the Christocentrism of Prudentius). — I. Opelt, Prudentius and Oraz: *Forschungen zur röm. Literatur,* Festsch. Büchner II. Wiesbaden 1970, 206-216. — M. P. Cunningham, Notes on the Text of Prudentius: TP 102(1971)59-69. — P. Tordeur, Essai d'analyse statistique de la métrique de Prudence: *Rev. Organis. Intern. étud. Anc. par Ordinateur* 1972 fasc. 2, 19-37 (on Apoth., Hamart., C. Symm., Psych.). —

N. Grasso, Prudenzio e la Bibbia: *Orpheus* 19(1972)79-170. — J. Fontaine, Mélanges des genres dans la poésie de Prudence, in *Forma Futuri,* Misc. Pellegrino. Turin 1975, 755-777. — S. Mariner Bigorra, Prudencio y Venancio Fortunato: influencia de un metro: *Helmantica* 25 (1975)333-340. — M. Díaz y Díaz, Prudencio en la Hispania visigótica. Unas breves notas, in *Corona Gratiarum,* Misc. E. Dekkers II. Bruges 1975, 61-70. — Ch. Gnilka, Das Interpolationen-problem bei Prudentius: *Studien zur Literatur der Spätantike.* Bonn 1975, 86-90. — J. Veremans, L'asclépiade mineur chez Horace . . . Prudence . . . Latomus 35(1975)12-42. — J. Arce, Los versos de Prudencio sobre el emperador Juliano: *Emerita* 44(1976)129-141. — M. P. Cunningham, Contexts of Prudentius' Poems: CPh 71(1976)56-66. — R. Palla, L'interpretazione figurale nelle opere de Prudenzio: SC 106(1978)143-168. — W. Ludwig, Die christliche Dichtung und die Transformation der klassischen Gattung, in *Christianisme et formes littéraires,* ed. A. Cameron. Bern 1977, 303-372.

1. *Cathemerinon (liber).*

The *Cathemerinon,* or hymns for the day, is a collection of 12 humns, of which only the first six, according to the indication of the title, are connected to the hours of the day, while the rest refer to particular occasions in the Christian life or suggest the essential contents of that life.

In particular, the first two hymns refer respectively to dawn and the morning, the third and fourth to noon (before and after the midday meal) and the fifth and sixth the evening (when the lamps are lit and bedtime). The seventh hymn is for periods of fasting and the eighth for the termination of these periods. The ninth hymn is not connected with any specific instance but is a meditation on the life of Christ, while the tenth hymn takes its inspiration from the hope that accompanies Christian death. The final two hymns celebrate the feasts of Christmas and Epiphany.

The poetry presented here draws its inspiration from the liturgy even if it is not destined for use in the liturgy. In fact, only a few of the hymns inspired by Ambrosian models with regard to meter (stanzas of 4 iambic dimeters) are suitable for liturgical chant, while the majority are composed in classical meter in the style of Horace. Finally, the cultivated character of Prudentius' poetry is revealed not only by the variety and classical nature of the forms, but also by the profundity of its content, the multiplicity of its sources and, not least of all, by the notable development of composition.

Editions: CPL 1438. — PL 59, 775-914. — CSEL 61(1926)5-76. — CCL 126(1966)3-72. — M. Lavarenne, I., Livre d'heures. Paris, 1943, 1972³. — H. J. Thompson, LCL(1949)6-114. — J. Guillén, I. Rodríguez, BAC 58(1950)10-170. — M. Pellegrino. Alba, 1954. — F. Sciuto. Catania, 1955. — J. Bergman, Aurelii Prudentii Clementis Carmina. Vienna-Leipzig, 1926 (text of CSEL). — E. Rossi, Inni della giornata. Bologna, 1970. — A. S. Walpole, Early Latin Hymns. Cambridge, 1922 (reprint 1966)115-148 (selection of hymns).

Translations: English: H. J. Thompson, op. cit. — M. C. Eagen, FC 43(1962)3-92. — R. M. Pope, Hymns Translated. London, 1905. *French:* M. Lavarenne, op. cit. *Italian:* U. Monti, Prudenzio. Gli inni della giornata cirstiana. Florence, 1925. — S. Colombo,

Prudenzio. Le odi quotidiane. Turin, 1932. — E. Rossi, Inni della giornata. Bologna, 1970. *Spanish:* J. Guillén, I. Rodríguez, op. cit.

Studies: C. Pascal, Un carme di Venanzio e uno di Prudenzio: BFC 11(1904-05)161-162 (Cath. IV). — E. M. Sanford, Were the Hymns of Prudentius Intended to be Sung?: CPh(1936)71. — I. Rodríguez Herrero, The Oldest Hymn to Mary: *The Eccl. Review* (Philadelphia 1937)485-489 (Cath. XI 53-60); *idem,* El himno más antiguo a la Virgen María: *Ecclesia* 8(1948) n.386, 13. — A. Salvatore, Qua ratione Prudentius aliqua Cathemerinon libri carmina conscribens Horatium Virgiliumque imitatus sit: *Annali Fac. Lett. e Fil.* Napoli 6(1956)119-140; *idem,* Studi prudenziani. Naples 1958, ch. 5. — J. H. Waszink, Prudentius, Cathemerinon III, 95-100: Mnem 11(1943)75-77. — A. G. Amatucci, Sul Liber cathemerinon di Prudenzio: ND 1(1947)35-45. — L. Alfonsi, Il cammino interiore di Prudenzio nelle Odi quotidiane: *Euphrosyne* 3(1961)233-240; *idem,* Poetica e poesia delle Odi quotidiane di Prudenzio: *Saggi e ricerche* in mem. E. Li Gotti, I. Palermo 1961, 5-12. — R. R. Harris, Allegory in Cathemerinon of Prudentius. Diss., Univ. of North Carolina, 1961. — F. Sciuto, Il decimo degli inni quotidiani di Prudenzio. Nota sul suo valore artistico, in *Oikoumene.* Catania 1964, 573-577. — E. Pianezzolla, Sulla doppia redazione, in *Prud. Cath.,* X 9-16, in Misc. critica Teubner II. Leipzig, 1964-65, 269-286. — R. R. Harris, Prudentius, Cathemerinon XII 27-28: *Classical Bulletin* 39(1962)30. — M. Fuhrmann, Ad Galli Cantum. Ein Hymnus des Prudenz als Paradigma christlicher Dichtung: *Der altsprachl. Unterr.* 14(1971)82-106. — J. Fontaine, Trois variations de Prudence sur le thème du Paradis, in *Forschungen zur. röm. Literatur,* Festsch. Büchner, I. Wiesbaden 1970, 96-115 (Hymns III, V, VIII). — L. J. van der Lof, Der Evangelist Johannes bei Prudentius: SP 10(TU 107) Berlin 1970, 247-252 (Cath. VI 77). — B. K. Braswell, Kleine textkritische Bemerkungen au frühchristlichen Hymnen: VC 29(1975)222-226. — M. M. van Assendelft, "Sol ecce surgit igneus." A Commentary on the Morning and Evening Hymns of Prudentius (Cath. I 2, 5 and 6). Groningen, 1976. — W. Evenepoel, Die fünfte Hymne des Liber Cathemerinon des Aurelius Prudentius Clemens: WSt 12(1978)232-248; *idem,* Explanatory and Literary Notes on Prudentius' Hymnus ante somnum: RBPh 56(1978)55-70.

2. *Apotheosis.*

The title refers to the theme treated in the final part of the brief poem, namely the triumph (divinization) of human nature in Jesus Christ. Other titles are nevertheless to be found in the manuscripts: *Hymn of the Most Blessed Trinity, Book of the Most Blessed Trinity, Confession of the Trinity* or, more simply, *On the Trinity.*

In reality, this poem of 1085 hexameters, which is preceded by one preface of 12 hexameters and a second of 28 distichs formed by a senarius and an iambic quaternion, contains an exhibition and a defense of the catholic doctrine of the mystery of God and the divinity of Jesus Christ against the errors of the heretics and the denials of the Jews.

More precisely, following a summary confession of the Trinitarian mystery in the first preface, the second preface proposes the problem of knowing the truth which leads to salvation in the midst of so many errors which lead to perdition. A refutation of heresies follows, directed in the first place against the patripassionism of Sabellius in order to vindicate a correct notion of the divinity (v. 1-177) and, at the same time, the distinction of persons in the one God (v. 178-320).

Attention is next directed to the Jews who did not recognize the Messiah, who instead was received by the pagans and put an end to their idolatrous cults (v. 321-551).

Against the heretics who reduce Christ to a mere man, Prudentius offers a proof of his divinity by making reference to his miraculous origin and his miracles (v. 552-781); and against those who consider all souls to be divine particles, the Christian poet expounds the creationist doctrine (v. 782-952). Finally, he directs his attention to those who deny the reality of Christ's human nature and attribute to him an imaginary, ephemeral body. Prudentius responds that the resurrection of our own bodies is bound to the fact that Jesus was true man and true God who arose after his death (v. 953-1085).

In order to judge fairly this didactic-polemical poem as well as the ones that will follow, it is necessary to depart from modern principles of criticism and aesthetics and make use of the critical criteria of the time. With this necessary premise, it will be possible to avoid the error which unfortunately came about in the past both of demanding from the poet the rigor of a theological discourse as well as of blaming him for the dryness of the treatise. This literary genre does not pretend to be either a theological treatise or a lyric composition. The poetry arises from the poet's ardent adherence to the truth and his passionate defense of this truth against the heretics. There is no lack of invective, of apostrophies proper to a polemicist, of expressions drawn from the classic poets, of fantastic images, and strong robust language. Nor is there any lack of a secure knowledge of doctrine, evidenced, for example, by the clear rejection of spiritual traducianism toward which Augustine would later tend in connection with the confession of Original Sin (cf. v. 915-927). There is furthermore no dearth of truly lyrical expressions such as when Prudentius says that all things sing the name of Christ, and when he ends with an emphasis of sincere piety in the prayer, *O nomen praedulce mihi* . . . (v. 386ff).

Editions: CPL 1439. — PL 59, 915-1006. — CSEL 61(1926)79-124. — CCL 126(1966) 73-115. M. Lavarenne, Prudence, II. Apotheosis. Paris 1945, 1961², 1-39. — J. Guillén, I. Rodríguez, BAC 58(1960)176-238. — H. J. Thomson, LCL(1954)116-198. — E. Rapisarda, L'Apoteosi. Catania, 1950.

Translations: English: H. J. Thomson, op. cit. — M. C. Eagen, FC 52(1955)3-30. *French:* M. Lavarenne, op. cit., 1-39. *Italian:* E. Rapisarda, op. cit. *Spanish:* J. Guillén, I. Rodríguez, op. cit., 177-239.

Studies: R. G. Austin, Prudentius, Apotheosis 895: CQ(1926)46-49. — S. T. Collins, Apotheosis of Prudentius: SE 9(1957)44-49. — R. G. Rank, The Apotheosis of Prudentius. A Structural Analysis: *Classical Folia* 20(1966)18-31. — K. Smolak, Exegetischer Kommentar zu Prudentius, Apotheosis (Hymnus, Praefatio, Apotheosis 1-216). Diss., Typewritten, Vienna, 1968 (cf. *Boll. Studi latini* 7[1977] 119f). — W. Steidle, Die dichterische Konzeption des Prudentius und Gedicht Contra Symmachum:

VC 25(1971)241-281. — M. Simonetti, La crisi ariana e l'inizio della riflessione teologica in Spagna: *Acc. Kincei,* 200(1974)127-147. — K. Smolak, Prudentius, Apotheosis 438-443. Vorstudien zu einem Kommentar zur Apotheosis I: WSt 4(1970)214-241 (text, commentary, German transl.). — J. Arce, Los versos de Prudencio sobre el emperador Juliano: *Emerita* 44(1976)129-141.

3. *Hamartigenia.*

The theme treated in this poem of 966 hexameters, which is preceded by a *praefatio* of 63 iambic senarii, is, as the Greek title indicates, the origin of evil. The tone nevertheless is not that of a theological treatise, but rather of a vigorous and personal polemic against Marcion, as is underlined by the strong opening apostrophe: *Quo te praecipitat rabies tua, perfide Cain, divisor blaspheme Dei?* The Spanish poet attempts to escape, without fully succeeding, the dryness inherent in the subject matter by making frequent recourse to invective and direct discourse.

Prudentius demonstrates the absurdity of Marcionite dualism by vindicating the absolute dominion of the one God over all things and by locating the origin of all the physical and moral evils in the world in the pride of the fallen angel.

The poet is concerned with confirming the moral responsibility of man both with regard to the temptations of the devil as well as to those of the flesh, and he responds to the objection of why God permits sin by making reference to intrinsic human freedom. Numerous examples drawn from the Old Testament (Cain and Abel, Lot, Ruth) impart a liveliness to the poem's descriptions of the natural disturbances which follow sin (v. 206ff), of the condemnation of the "bacchic pleasures of the insane world" (v. 375), and above all of the condemnation of the unbridled luxury of women, where the influence of Lucretius and other classical poets is most clearly recognized.

The final part of the poem offers a colorful description of the realms beyond the tomb, depicted with terms and images drawn from pagan and Christian tradition alike.

In closing, Prudentius raises a humble and sincere prayer, confessing himself worthy of eternal fire but nevertheless expressing the confidence that his purification will take place among fires mitigated by divine clemency.

Editions: CPL 1440. — PL 59, 1007-1078. — CSEL 61(1926)127-163. — CCL 126(1966) 125-163. — M. Lavarenne, Prudence . . . Hamartigenia *Les Belles Lettres,* II. Paris 1945, 1961[2], 41-73. — J. J. Thomson, LCL (1949)200-272. — J. Guillén, I. Rodríguez, BAC 58(1950)244-296. — J. Stam, Prudentius, Hamartigenia (Intro., English Transl. commentary). Amsterdam, 1940.

Translations: English: J. J. Thomson, op. cit., 201-273. — M. C. Eagen, FC 52(1965)43-75. — J. Stam, op. cit. *French:* M. Lavarenne, op. cit. *Spanish:* J. Guillén, I. Rodríguez, op. cit.

Studies: M. Lavarenne, Note sur un passage de l'Hamartigenia, de Prudence: RELA 19(1941)76-79. — S. T. Collins, Corruptions in Christian Latin Poetry: JThSt 1 (1950)69. — N. Goossens, Vilis sapientia (Hamartigenia, 402): Latomus 6(1947)197-205. — N. Grasso, Il testo biblico seguito da Prudenzio in Hamartigenia praef. 11-13: MSCL 3(1951)124-135. — A. Salvatore, Studi prudenziani. Naples, 1958. — G. Stegen, Notes de lecture: Latomus 22(1963)845-847 (Hamar. 730). — Ch. Gnilka, Notizen zu Prudentius: RhM 109(1966)84-94 (Hamar. 12-13; 863-866).

4. *Psychomachia.*

The epic, traditionally regarded as the primary and most glorious of poetic genres, could not be lacking in Prudentius' conscious attempt to produce a vast and organic *corpus* of Christian poetry. Nevertheless, the battles which the new Christian people are called to undertake are no longer those carried out by force of arms for the conquest of the world, but those of the spirit to defend its own liberty against the threats of evil. The *Psychomachia* is thus both an epic and an allegory of spiritual combat, or, more precisely, of the combat for the possession of the soul.

After the customary preface of 68 iambic senarii in which Abraham, who fights for Lot's freedom, is seen as an allegorical figure of the soul which struggles to free itself from the passions, the traditional invocation of the muses is substituted by an invocation to Christ in a slightly modified hexameter: *Christe, graves hominum semper miserate labores* (v. 1).

There then follows, in the heroic style proper to the epic, the account of the clash of the virtues and their opposed vices as though the captains of two armies drawn up on the battlefield were confronting one another in a duel.

Fides fights against the *cultura deorum* (v. 21-39); *Pudicitia* against *Sodomita libido* (v. 40-108); *Patientia* against *Ira* (v. 109-177); the *Humilis mens* against *Superbia* (v. 178-309); *Sobrietas* against *Luxuria* (v. 310-453); *Operatio benefica* against *Avaritia* (v. 454-664); and finally, *Concordia* against *Discordia-Heresis* (v. 665-887).

The monotony of this scheme is broken by the numerous examples of biblical figures who were victorious in this battle against the vices, beginning with the Virgin, the absolute conqueror of *luxuria;* Job, victor over *ira*; David of *superbia,* etc.

Furthermore, there is no lack of references to the contemporary situation as when, speaking of the extensive hold of avarice over all the social classes, he laments that victims are to be found even among the priests, who "as captains were sustaining the first line of battle" (v. 498-499).

Finally, the happy intuitions of the Christian poet are undeniable in his personification of the individual virtues and vices, even in the context of the repetition of traditional motifs. He succeeds in creating unforgettable moral types which contributed to the good fortune enjoyed by this poem in medieval literature.

Editions: CPL 1441. — PL 60, 11-90. — CSEL 61(1926)167-211. — CCL 126(1966)390-400. — M. Lavarenne, Psychomachie. Paris, 1933; *idem,* Psychomachie . . . (*Les Belles Lettres*). Paris 1948, 1963[2], 1-82. — U. von Englemann, Die Psychomachie des Prudentius. Freiburg i. Br.-Basel, 1949. — J. J. Thomson, LCL(1949,1961[2])274-342. — E. Rapisarda, Psychomachia. Catania, 1962. — J. Guillén, I. Rodríguez, BAC 58(1950)304-356.

Translations: English: J. J. Thomson, op. cit. — M. C. Eagen, FC 52(1965)79-110. *French:* M. Lavarenne, op. cit. *German:* U. von Engelmann, op. cit. *Italian:* E. Rapisarda, op. cit. *Spanish:* J. Guillén, I. Rodríguez, op cit.

Studies: A. Melardi, La Psychomachia di Prudenzio. Poema eroico-allegorico del V secolo. Studio filologico. Pistoia, 1900; *idem,* Quid rationis Prudentii Psychomachia cum Cebetis tabula habere videatur. Potenza, 1901. — L. Hench, Sources of Prudentius' Psychomachia: CPh 19(1924)78-90. — H. J. Thomson, The Psychomachia of Prudentius: *Classical Review* 44(1930)109-112; *idem,* Prudentius Psychomachia: *Proceedings Class. Ass.* (1929)37-38. — G. Bardy, Prudence, Psychomachia, Praef. 31: RSR 25(1935)363. — L. Cotogni, Sovrapposizioni di visioni e di allegorie sulla Psychomachia di Prudenzio: RAL(1936)441-461. — M. W. Bloomfield, A Source of Prudentius Psychomachia: *Speculum* 18(1943)87-90. — R. Argenio, La Psychomachia di Prudenzio: *Rivista Studi Classici* 8(1960)267-280. — H. R. Jauss, Form and Auffassung der Allegorie in der Tradition der Psychomachia (von Prudentius zum ersten Roman de la Rose), in *Medium Aevum Vivum,* Festsch. W. Bulst. Heidelberg 1960, 179-206. — Ch. Gnilka, Studien zur Psychomachie des Prudentius, Wiesbaden, 1963. — P. F. Beatrice, L'allegoria nella Psychomachia di Prudenzio: StP 18(1971)25-73. — E. J. Mickel, Jr., Parallels in Prudentius' Psychomachia and La Chanson de Roland: *Stud. in Philol.* 67(1970)439-452. — M. Ch. Ward, Allegory as Satire: A Consideration of Henri d'Andeli's Bataile des VII Ars in Relation to the Psychomachia: *Rivista Studi Classici* 21(1973)103-113. — R. Katscher, Waltharius-Dichtung und dichter: *Mittellateinisches Jahrb.* 9(1973)48-120 (a portion is dedicated to the influence of the Psychomachia in the poetry of Waltharius). — C. Magazzù, L'utilizzazione di Virgilio nella Psychomachia di Prudenzio: *Boll. Studi Latini* 5(1975)13-23. — M. Smith, Prudentius' Psychomachia. A Reexamination. Princeton, 1976. — J. P. Hermann, The Pater noster Battle Sequence in Solomon and Saturn and the "Psychomachia" of Prudentius: *Neuphilologische Mitteilungen* 77(1976)206-210. — R. Hanna, The Sources and the Art of Prudentius' "Psychomachia": CPh 72(1977)108-115. — K. R. Haworth, Deified Virtues, Demonic Vices and Descriptive Allegory in Prudentius' Psychomachia. Diss., Mich. State Univ., Lansing, 1979. — S. G. Nugent, Vice and Virtue in Allegory. Reading Prudentius' Psychomachia. Diss., Cornell Univ., Ithaca, 1980.

5. *Contra Symmachum.*

When Prudentius decided to write in verse the two books *Contra Symmachum,* almost twenty years had passed since the spirited debate between the powerful pagan senator and the equally powerful Christian bishop, Saint Ambrose. It has been suggested that Prudentius' polemic was caused by a second appeal on the part of Symmachus to the Emperor Honorius, but there is no record of this.

What is certain is that the Spanish poet made use in his work of the two letters which the Bishop of Milan addressed to the Emperor

Valentinian II in 384 to counter the *Relatio* of Symmachus. It was during his Roman sojourn, before the spectacle of Christian Rome, that Prudentius became convinced of the anachronistic nature of the attempt to give new life to paganism. Just as the viper which bit Saint Paul when he had reached safety after the storm (cf. preface, book I), so does the pagan reaction attack the church when the persecutions are already a distant memory and triumph appears assured.

Prudentius' anti-pagan polemic does not have an anti-Roman character. To the contrary, the Spanish poet cherishes a profound and sincere love for Rome, the *egregium caput orbis* (I, 497). His polemic arises instead out of the certainty that the government of a Christian prince, who has in mind the future welfare of the citizens as well as their present material needs, marks an undeniable progress over the pagan government (I, 22-24), and that it would be folly to return to the error and superstition of the ancestors (ibid., 35-39). The ancient gods were not able to teach justice because they were themselves criminals who incited to vice, from Saturn to Jupiter, Mercury, Priapus, Hercules, Bacchus, Mars, Venus, Juno, and Cybele (ibid., 42-196). "The vain superstition poorly begun by the ancestors in former times was developed, transmitted to following ages and increased by posterity; men rashly carried on this long series and dark customs were spread through the centuries marked by vice" (ibid., 240-244).

Their descendants did worse, prostrating themselves before Augustus, raising temples to Livia, and rendering divine honors to Hadrian along with his Antinoos (ibid., 245ff). The greatness of Rome did not depend on the cult offered to the gods, but everything was disposed by Christ, who "desires that kingdoms would succeed one another according to an established order and that the triumphs of the Romans would be multiplied" (ibid., 387-390).

After he has also refuted the cult rendered to the sun and the moon and the infernal deities (ibid., 309-407), Prudentius recalls in stirring tones the victory gained by Constantine in the name of Christ, which marked the end of a miserable slavery, both civil and religious (I, 468).

In the final part of the book, the poet addresses Symmachus directly and, while admiring his oratorical skill, invites him to consider the immense majority of the Roman Senate and people who have already become Christians and also to consider his own *honores* as coming from the munificence of Christian emperors and as gifts of God.

The 658 hexameters of book I are supplemented by the 1131 of book II. The second book also opens with a preface (66 lines of glyconic verse) in which, in parallel fashion to the first book which recalls the Apostle Paul, the figure of Peter is presented, who overcomes the menace of the waves of the storm by faith in Jesus Christ.

The book begins by summarizing briefly the contents of the preceding book and announcing the material yet to be treated: "Up to now I have sung of the primordial origins of the ancient gods, of the reasons why this foolish error was propagated in the world and of the conversion of Rome to Christ. Now I will give the objections and will deflect them blow by blow" (II, 1-4).

The plan of the book is simple. The poet reproduces almost to the letter the most important statements of Symmachus' *Relatio* III and follows them with his own refutations.

The Roman orator had attributed the merit for the past and future fortunes of Rome to victory. Through the mouth of Honorius and Arcadius, Prudentius responds that the victories are the result of military valor and divine protection (II, 7-66).

Symmachus had appealed to the principle of cultural and religious tolerance, *suus enim cuique mos, suus ritus* (*Relatio* III, 8), supported by the shrewd consideration that it was not possible to reach the profound mystery of the divinity by one single path: *uno itinere non potest perveniri ad tam grande secretum* (*Relatio* III, 10). Prudentius responds first by making reference to the insufficiency of reason to penetrate the mystery of God, and then by showing the facility of the way of faith, which is open to all (II, 67-269). He then attacks in principle the recourse to tradition as a valid mode of conduct. All traditions change with time. At Rome itself, the religious rites have changed continuously over the centuries, and the cults of primitive Latium have been supplemented and supplanted by new cults imported from subjugated nations (II, 270-368).

Another statement which occupies the attention of the Christian poet is the one according to which the divinity assigned different guardians to individual cities and *genii fatales* to individual people (*Relatio* III, 8). It had not been fate nor an undefined genius nor the ancient gods who had caused Rome to prosper, but the divine will to unite the peoples of the world under the same laws and the same prince in order to prepare the way for Christ (II, 369-647).

At this point, Rome herself appears on the scene to underscore the political and moral rebirth which coincided with her conversion to Christianity (II, 648-767).

Finally, another lament of Symmachus, namely that the abandonment of the cult of Pallas and of Vesta (the Vestals and the sacred fire) is the cause of calamitous droughts, is rejected either by denying the reality of such occurrences or by providing natural explanations (II, 909-1121).

The book concludes with an apostrophe to Honorius that he may carry to completion the work begun by his father in prohibiting the gladiatorial contests (II, 1122-1131).

Editions: CPL 1442. — PL 60, 111-276. — CSEL 61(1926)215-288. — CCL 125(1966) 185-250. — G. L. Bisoffi, Il contra Symmachum di Aurelio Prudenzio Clemente. Treviso, 1914. — M. Lavarenne, Prudence III . . . Contre Symmaque (*Les Belles Lettres*). Paris 1948, 1963², 83-196. — J. J. Thomson, LCL(1949, 1961²)344-400; II(1953,1962²)2-96. — J. Guillén, I. Rodríguez, BAC 58(1950)362-470. — E. Rapisarda, Contra Symmachum. Catania, 1954.

Translations: English: J. J. Thomson, op. cit. — M. C. Eagen, FC52(1965)113-176. *French:* M. Lavarenne, op. cit. *German:* M. Manitius, Mären und Satiren aus dem Lateinischen. Stuttgart 1905. *Italian:* E. Rapisarda, op. cit. — L. Taormina, G. Stramondo, 2 vols. Catania, 1956. *Spanish:* J. Guillén, I. Rodríguez, op. cit.

Studies: C. Pascal, Il poemetto "contra orationem Symmachi" in un codice antichissimo di Prudenzio: SIF 13(1905)75-81. — J. Révay, Symmachus és Prudentius: *Egyetemes Phil. Közl.* 35(1911)219-229, 438-450. — F. Di Capua, A. Prudenzio: Contra Symmachum II, 1059: BFC 25(1917-18)44-45. — Joutard, Le Poème de Prudence "Contre Symmache": sa composition et ses sources. Paris, 1930 (cf. RELA 12[1934]416). — M. Ligouri Ewald, Ovid in the contra Symmachum of Prudentius. Washington, 1942 (sources). — D. Romano, Carattere e significato del Contra Symmachum. Palermo, 1955. — A. Cerri, Archeologia romana nel Contra Symmachum di Prudenzio: *Athenaeum* 41(1963)304-317. — N. Casini, Le discussioni sull' "Ara Victoriae" nella curia romana: *Studi romani* 5(1957)501-517. — F. Solmsen, The Conclusion of Theodosius' Oration in Prudentius' Contra Symmachum: Phil 109(1965)310-313; *idem,* The Powers of Darkness in Prudentius' Contra Symmachum. A Study of his Poetic Imagination: VC 19(1965)237-257. — Ch. Gnilka, Zwei Textprobleme bei Prudentius: Phil 109(1965)246-258 (C. Symm. II, 423-427). — A. Cameron, Aeneus and Aenipes. Two notes on Prudentius: Phil 111(1967)147-150 (I, 102 and 351 interpolations). — R. Argenio, Il contra Symmachum di Prudenzio fu uno scritto di attualità?: *Rivista Studi Classici* 16(1968)153-163. — V. Zappacosta, De Prudentii libro I Contra Symmachum: *Latinitas* 15(1967)202-218; *idem,* De Prudentii libro I Contra Symmachum et L. Pacati Drepanii Panegyrico Theodosio Augusto dicto: ibid., 15(1967)277-292. — A. Cerri, Prudenzio e la battaglia di Azio: *Athenaeum* 46(1968)261-272. — H. Le Bonniec, Sur deux vers énigmatiques de Prudence (C. Symm. II, 1107-1108), in Mélanges Durry (=RELA 47 bis 1970)55-83. — W. Steidle, Die dichterische Konzeption des Prudentius und das Gedicht Contra Symmachum: VC 25(1971)241-281 (cf. *Boll. Studi Latini* 7[1977]127). — R. Klein, Symmachus. Eine tragische Gestalt des ausgehenden Heidentums. Darmstadt, 1971. — R. Verdière, Notes de lecture: Latomus 30(1971)390-392. — R. Cacitti, Subdita Christo servit Roma Deo: Osservazioni sulla teologia politica di Prudenzio: *Aevum* 46(1972)402-435. — S. Mazzarino, Tolleranza e Intolleranza: la polemica sull'Ara della Vittoria, in *Antico, Tardoantico ed èra costantiniana,* I. Bari 1974, 339-377. — T. D. Barnes, The Historical Setting of Prudentius' Contra Symmachum: AJPh 97(1976)373-386. — S. Doepp, Prudentius' Gedicht gegen Symmachus. Anlass und Struktur: JAC 23(1980)65-81.

6. *Peristephanon.*

This collection consists of 14 hymns in honor of the Christian martyrs who have merited a crown for the victory won in the struggle of life. The first half (hymns 1-7) was composed before the poet's journey to Rome, while the second half (hymns 8-14) was composed during the journey and upon his return home.

Prudentius' purpose is to narrate the historical truth concerning martyrdom (thus his lament for the disappearance of the Acts of the Martyrs under Diocletian: I, 73ff), to extol the efficacy of the intercession of the martyrs as demonstrated by the miracles and graces obtained through them and, finally, to promote the solemn celebration of their feasts and the visitation of their tombs.

However, the use of oral and written sources of a predominantly laudatory and edifying nature is certainly no help to remaining faithful to the sources. Furthermore, the poet's enthusiastic admiration for the Christian hero, although it helps on the one hand to give warmth and life to the poetry, nevertheless, leads invariably on the other to rhetorical amplifications and to forced tones and accents of color; all elements which already are present in the natural tendencies of Prudentius' poetry.

The hymns, which are different enough in length — ranging from the brief hymn VIII of only 18 verses (9 elegiac distichs) to the very long hymn X of 1140 iambic senarii in honor of Saint Romanus — vary also in meter, which is Horatian for the most part.

The martyrs who are celebrated are those venerated for the most part in Spain: Hemeterius and Chelidonius of *Calagurris* (hymn I), Eulalia of Mérida (hymn III), the 18 martyrs of Saragossa (hymn IV), the deacon, Vincent, also of Saragossa (hymn V), Fructuosus, Augurius, and Eulogius of Tarragona (hymn VI); and at Rome: Lawrence (hymn II), Hippolytus (hymn XI), Peter and Paul (hymn XII), and Agnes (hymn XIV). To these must be added Quirinus, an Illyrian martyr (hymn VII), Cassian, whose tomb at Imola Prudentius visited on his way to Rome (hymn IX), and Romanus of Antioch, who was venerated also in the West (hymn X).

This final hymn merits special notice not so much for its unusual length, noted above, as for its very peculiar structure, which gives it the appearance of a work apart, of a theatrical composition. In effect, the poem develops through various scenes and interminable monologues of various personages, and passes from savage descriptions to tender episodes such as that of the martyrdom of an infant (v. 656-845), and from strokes of refined irony to outright sarcasm. Hymn II in honor of Saint Lawrence is another composition which merits mention for its distinguished poetic value, for which it has been compared with the *Carmen saeculare* of Horace.

As in the *Cathemerinon* so also in the *Peristephanon,* Prudentius reveals his indubitable poetic abilities, even if his more successful lyrical passages are generally submerged in pomposity and rhetorical diatribes. The best elements, from a poetical point of view, are to be found in the rather realistic and colorful descriptions. The great versifying talent of the Spanish poet, his domination of the modes of expression, his knowledge of the classical poets, and his consummate skill are obvious throughout the work.

Editions: CPL 1443. — PL 60, 275-590. — CSEL 61(1926)291-431. — CCL 126(1966)251-389. — M. Lavarenne, Peristephanon Liber (*Les Belles Lettres*). Paris 1951, 1962^{2}, 1-200. — M. J. Bayo, Prudencio. Himnos a los Mártires. Madrid, 1946. — J. J. Thomson, Prudentius, II, LCL (1953, 1962^{2})98-344. — J. Guillén, I. Rodríguez, BAC 58(1950)476-754.

Translations: English J. J. Thomson, op. cit. — M. C. Eagen, FC 43(1962)95-280. *French:* M. Lavarenne, op. cit. *Italian:* C. Marchesi, Le corone di Prudenzio tradotte e illustrate. Rome, 1917. — E. Nesi, Siena, 1932. — V. Paronetto, Le corone. Turin, 1957 (selection). *Spanish:* J. Planella, El Píndaro cristiano. Buenos Aires-México, 1942. — M. J. Bayo, op. cit. — J. Guillén, I. Rodríguez, op. cit.

Studies: F. Ermini, Peristephanon. Studi prudenziani. Rome, 1914. — F. Dölger, Die religiöse Brandmarkung in den Kybele-Attis-Mysterien nach einem Texte des christlichen Dichters Prudentius: AC 1(1929)55-72, 317 (Perist. 1076-1090). — M. Alamo, Un texte du poète Prudence: "ad Valerium episcopum" (Perist. hymnus XI): RHE 35(1939)750-756. — M. J. Bayo, Sobre el Peristephanon de Aurelio Prudencio Cl.: *Rev. Nacional Educación* 2(1942)35-54. — A. Pérez de Toledo, Un poema de Prudencio. Himno en honor de la pasión del beatisimo mártir Lorenzo: CD 160(1948)241-280 (translation and commentary). — L. Casanoves Arnandis, Prudencio en el Peristephanon. Valencia, 1948. — P. Künzle, Bemerkungen zum Lob auf Sankt Peter und Sankt Paulus von Prudentius (Perist. XII): RSCI 11(1957)309-370. — M. Pellegrino, Structure et inspiration des "Peristephanon" de Prudence: *Bull. Faculté des Lettres de Strasbourg* 39(1961)437-450. — F. Kudlien, Krankheitsmetaphorik im Laurentiushymnus des Prudentius: Hermes 90(1962)104-115. — M. P. Cunningham, The Nature and Purpose of the Peristephanon of Prudentius: SE 14(1963)40-45. — A. Ferrua, Lavori a S. Sebastiano: RAC 37(1963)203-236. — V. Buchheit, Christliche Romideologie im Laurentius-Hymnus des Prudentius, in Polychronion F. Dölger. Heidelberg 1966, 121-144. — Kl. Thraede, Die Infantia des christlichen Dichters, Festsch. Klauser. Münster 1964, 352-365. — R. Argenio, Prudenzio a Roma visita le Basiliche di S. Pietro e S. Paolo: *Rivista Studi Classici* 15(1967)170-175. — I. Opelt, Der Christenverfolger bei Prudentius: Phil 111(1967)242-257. — J. Ruysschaert, Prudence l'Espagnol poète des deux basiliques romaines de S. Pierre et de S. Paul: RAC 42(1968)267-286. — G. Richard, l'apport de Virgile à la création épique de Prudence dans le Peristephanon liber: *Caesarodonum* 4(1969)187-193. — R. Argenio, Due corone di Prudenzio: Quirino e San Cassiano, ibid., 18(1970)58-79 (study and translation of hymns VII and IX). — P. T. A. Sabatini, Storia e leggenda nei Peristephanon di Prudenzio: ibid., 20(1972)32-53; 187-221; 21(1973)39-77. — Kl. Thraede, Rom und die Märtyrer in Prudentius "Peristephanon." II, 1-20, in Studia J. H. Waszink. Amsterdam, 1973, 317-327. — M. A. H. Maestre Yenes, Prudencio, Peristephanon XII, 37: Estudio estilístico-estructural: *Estudios Clásicos* 17(1973)303-319. — R. Gelsomino, Da Cicerone a Prudenzio: genesi di un'invenzione dantesca: *Gironale ital. Fil.* 4(1973)1-14. — R. Pillinger, Ein Textproblem bei Prudentius (Per. XII, 31-34): VetChr 13(1976)113-115. — S. Costanza, Il catalogo dei pellegrini. Confronto di due tecniche narrative (Prud. "Per." XI, 189-213; Paolino di Nola, "Carm." XIV, 44-85): *Boll. di studi latini* 7(1977)316-326. — B. Riposati, La struttura degli Inni alle tre vergini martiri del Peristephanon di Prudenzio, in *Studi Lazzati* (SPMed 10). Milan 1980, 25-41.

7. *Dittochaeon.*

This composition, which closes the collection of Prudentius' works, is the most peculiar of them all, including the title, which is difficult to interpret.

It consists of 49 verses, each of four hexameters, which illustrate a like number of biblical scenes and personalities (24 from the Old Testament and 25 from the New). Although they are clearly related to some pictoral work, it is not known whether they refer to a scene depicted in some church or whether they were written to provide inspiration for some artist. In any case, their importance is not to be sought so much in the field of poetry as in the history of early Christian art.

Editions: CPL 1444 and 1445. — PL 60, 89-112, 591-594. — CSEL 61(1926)433-447, 448-449. — CCL 126(1966)390-400, 401-402. — M. Lavarenne, Prudence IV (*Les Belles Lettres*). Paris 1951, 1962², 205-216, 217-218. — J. J. Thomson, Prudentius II. LCL(1953, 1962²)346-374. — J. Guillén, I. Rodríguez, BAC 58(1950)738-754, 760-762.

Translations: English J. J. Thomson, op. cit. — M. C. Eagen, FC 52(1965)179-196, 199-200. *French:* M. Lavarenne, op. cit. *Italian* R. Argenio, Il Dittocheo e l'epilogo di Prudenzio: *Rivista Studi Classici* 15(1967)40-77. *Spanish:* J. Guillén, I. Rodríguez, op. cit.

Studies: J. P. Kirsch, Le "Dittochaeum" de Prudence et les monuments de l'antiquité chrétienne: *Atti II Cong. Archeologia crist.* Rome 1902, 127-131. — G. Mannelli, La personalità prudenziana nel Dittochaeum: MSLC 1(1947)79-126. — F. Ogara, El "Dittochaeum" de Prudencio: EE 1(1922)135ff. — M. Brozek, De Prudentii Epilogo mutilo: Eos 49(1957-58)151-154. — R. Argenio, Il Dittocheo e l'epilogo di Prudenzio: *Rivista Studi Classici* 15(1967)40-77. — J. L. Charlet, Prudence lecteur de Paulin de Nole. A propos du 23e quatrain du Dittochaeum: REAug 21(1975)55-62. — R. Pillinger, Die Tituli Historiarum oder das sogenannte "Dittochaeos" des Prudentius. Versuch einer archäologisch-philologischen Kommentars. Diss., Vienna, 1976; *idem,* Die Tituli Historiarum oder das sogenannte Dittochaeon des Prudentius. Vienna, 1980.

PAULINUS OF NOLA

Meropius Pontius Anicius Paulinus belonged to a family of the Senatorial aristocracy which possessed vast landholdings in Italy and in Aquatania, where he lived. It was in the capital of this province, Burdigala (Bordeaux) that Paulinus was born at a date which cannot be exactly determined but which must have been around 353.

Nothing is known of his parents, who were certainly Christians by the time of their death, and perhaps already at the time of the birth of their son. Paulinus received an excellent liberal education such as was suited for one who by his social position was destined for important official positions and was possible in such a renowned center of studies such as Bordeaux. To this was added the good fortune of having Ausonius, the most celebrated rhetor of the age and a refined poet, as a teacher. Although it has been ascertained that the scholastic influence of Ausonius on Paulinus was of a private nature and lasted only a few years at the very beginning of his studies (cf. P. Fabre, *S. Paulin de Nole et l'amitié chrétienne,* p. 22), the bond of friendship that developed was nevertheless profound and enduring. At about twenty years of age he left his home to go to Rome, probably in order to succeed his father in the Senate and to begin the *cursus honorum.* In 379, through the support of Ausonius, he received the post of governor of Campania. It was in this period, on the occasion of the feast of the saint, that the first encounter of Paulinus with Saint Felix took place at Nola and the question of religion was seriously raised in Paulinus' life (*Carmen* XXI, 365ff).

Paulinus is next found in Aquitania, free of political responsibilities, and shortly thereafter in Spain, where he was married to Therasia and led a life similar to that of the great proprietors of the time, with journeys to his various estates, visits to noble friends, encounters with men of letters (Sulpicius Severus, Iovius, etc.), and poetical exercises.

On the basis of a statement of Ausonius, a decisive influence of his wife has been proposed for the religiosity of Paulinus, but this is impossible to ascertain. However, no small contribution to his withdrawal from the world must have come from the obscure episode of the violent death of his brother and from the dangers to which he himself was exposed, and not in the least from the premature death of his young son, Celsus. Nor can there be forgotten the influence of men such as Delphinus and Amandus of Bordeaux, Martin of Tours, Victricious of Rouen and Ambrose of Milan (*Ep.* III *ad Alypium*).

He was baptized in 389 at Bordeaux and agreed to be ordained priest while at Barcelona at Christmas of 394, on the condition that he be free to establish his residence elsewhere. He had, in fact, already come to the decision to sell his immense riches, embrace the monastic life and retire to Nola near the tomb of Saint Felix.

The decision was received with great disappointment by Ausonius, but with exultation by Ambrose and with amazement by people in general (Ambrose, *Ep* 58, XIII: PL 16, 1228-1229). Thus, in the spring of 395, Paulinus departed for Italy where, after a stop in Rome as brief as it was bitter (*Ep* 5, *ad Severum,* 13-14), he returned to the city in Campania.

From this point on, the life of Paulinus continued tranquilly in the silence of the monastery, where he was occupied by the construction of new buildings for the reception of pilgrims, by correspondence with many friends new and old, and by his poetic activity, especially in honor of his patron saint. Political events and the heated religious controversies found scarcely an echo in the spirit of Paulinus. The date of his episcopal ordination is uncertain (probably in 409, and in any case before 413) as is that of the death of his wife who also lived at

Nola in a monastery of women. There are also no clear and precise documents concerning his long episcopate, although the date of his death in 431 is certain.

Studies: F. Maigret, St. Paulin de Nole: *Revue de Lille* 21(1903)944-959. — A. Baudrillart, Saint Paulin, évêque de Nole (353-431). Paris, 1904, 1905[2]. — A. Hauch, Paulinus von Nola: RE 15(1904)55-59. — G. Popescu-Fratilesti, Paulin de Nola. Bucharest, 1904. — E. Ch. Babut, Paulin de Nole et Priscillien: RHL 1(1910)97-130, 252-275. — J. De Smet, Poètes latins chrétiens. I: Saint Paulin de Nole. Poésies choisies. Introduction à l'étude des auteurs chrétiens. Vue d'ensemble sur le IVe siècle. Brussels, 1912. — C. Weyman, Paulinus und Prudentius bei Faustus von Reji, in *Beiträge zur Geschichte der christlich-lateinischen Poesie.* Munich 1926, 102; *idem,* Paulinus von Nola und Cyprian: MM 4(1923-24)188-286. — U. Moricca, Il Votum di Sulpicio Severo e di S. Paolino da Nola: Did 3(1925)89-96; *idem,* Analecta: La morte violenta di un fratello di Paolino di Nola: ibid., 4(1926)85-90 (Carm. 21, 416-420). — H. Leclercq: DALC 8(1929)2824-26 (letters). — A. W. Bijvanck, De gebouwen aan het graf von Sint Felix bij Nola in Campanië, in *Mededeelingen v. het Neder. hist. Inst.* Rome 1929, 49-50. — V. Jodice, Profilo storico ed estetico de S. Paolino. Rome, 1931. — L. Allevi, S. Paolino di Nola e il tramonto della civiltà antica: SC 17(1931)161-175. — E. Amann, Paulin de Nole: DTC 12(1933)68-71. — Ch. Favez, La consolation latine chrétienne. Paris, 1937. — M. Vilain, Rufin d'Aquilée. La querelle autour d'Origène: RSR 27(1937)5-37, 165-195. — G. Chierici, Lo stato degli studi intorno alle basiliche paoliniane di Cimitile: *Atti IV Congresso naz. Studi Romani,* Rome 1938, 236-243; *idem,* Di alcuni risultati intorno . . . alle basiliche Paoliniane a Cimitile: RAC 16(1939)59-72; *idem,* Sant'Ambrogio e le costruzioni Paoliniane a Cimitile, in *Ambrosiana.* Rome 1942, 315-331. — G. Rizza, Paolino di Nola. Catania, 1947. — A. Boulanger, Saint Paulin de Nole et l'amitié chrétienne: VC 1(1947)183-185 (on the book of Fabre, infra). — P. Courcelle, Paulin de Nole et saint Jérôme: RELA 25(1947)250-280. — P. Fabre, S. Paulin de Nole et l'amitié chrétienne. Paris, 1949 (fundamental work). — G. Bardy, Un élève de Augustin, Licentius: *L'Année Théol. August.* 14(1954)55-79. — D. Mallardo, Presunto rinvenimento a Cimitile del sarcofago di S. Paolino vescovo de Nola: *Rendiconti Acc. Arch. Lett. Arti Napoli* 30(1955)193-198. — F. X. Murphy, Rufinus of Aquileia and Paulinus of Nola: REAug 2(1956)79-91. — W. Meany, The Humanism of the Paulinus of Nola. Diss. (typewritten), Freiburg, 1956. — G. Chierici, Cimitile: *Palladio* 7(1957)69-73. — A. Weis, Die Verteilung der Bildzyklen des Paulin von Nola in den Kirchen von Cimitile: RQ 52(1957)129-150. — Ch. H. Coster, Christianity and the Invasions. Two Sketches: CJ 55(1959)146-159. — D. Gorce, Paulin de Nole. Paris, 1959. — J. Doignon, Nos bons hommes de foi, De doctr. christ. IV, 40, 61: Latomus 22(1963)795-805 (regarding the vocation of Paulinus). — S. Prete, Paolino di Nola e l'umanesimo crisiano. Bologna 1964. — S. Prete, M. C. Celletti: *Bibliotheca Sanctorum* 10(1968)156-162. — W. H. C. Frend, Paulinus of Nola and the Last Century of the Western Empire: JRS 59(1969)1-11. — P. C. Walsh, Paulinus of Nola and the Conflict of Ideologies in the Fourth Century, in *Kyriakon,* Festsch. Quasten II. Münster 1970, 565-571. — A. Mencucci, S. Paolino e Senigallia. Senigallia, 1971. — J. Martínez Gázques, Paolino de Nola e Hispania: *Bol. Instit. est. helen* 7(1973)27-33. — D. Marin, La testimonianza di Paolino de Nola sul cristianesimo nell'Italia meridionale: *Archivio St. Pugliese* 27(1974)161-190. — J. C. Wright, Saint Paulinus of Nola, in *Class. et Iberica,* Festsch. J. M.-F. Marique, Worcester 1975, 417-425. — F. Corsaro, L'autore del "de mortibus boum," Paulino di Nola e la politica religiosa di Teodosio: Orpheus 22(1975)3-26. — S. Costanza, I rapporti tra Ambrogio e Paolino di Nola, in Ambrosius Episcopus II. Milan 1976, 220-232. — W. Erdt, Christentum und heidnisch-antike Bildung bei Paulin von Nola. Meisenheim am Glan, 1976. — J. T. Lienhard, Paulinus of Nola and Early Western Monasticism. With a Study of the Chronology of His Works and an Annotated

Bibliography, 1879-1976. Bonn, 1977; *idem,* Some Fragments of Paulinus of Nola: Latomus 36(1977)438-439. — P. Courcelle, Grégoire le Grand devant les conversions de Marius Victorinus, Augustin et Paulin de Nole: Latomus 36(1977)942-950.

WRITINGS

Paulinus' writings include his letters and a collection of poems. Saint Jerome mentions a panegyric in prose in honor of the Emperor Theodosius, but it has been lost. Saint Augustine (*Ep.* 31, 8) speaks of a polemical work which Paulinus was writing against the pagans, but it is not known if this work was ever completed.

Editions: CPL 202-206. — PL 61 (L. A. Muratori with commentary of J. Le Brun). — W. Hartel, CSEL 29 & 30(1894).

Translations: English: R. C. Goldsmith, Paulinus' Churches at Nola. Amsterdam, 1940 (*Ep.* 32; *carmina* 27 and 28). *French:* Ch. Pietri, St. Paulin de Nole. Poèmes, Lettres et Sermon. Namur, 1964. *Italian:* L. Pizzolato, L'amicizia cristiana. Antologia delle opere di Agostino di Ippona e altre testi di Ambrogio, Girolamo e Paolino di Nola. Turin, 1973.

Studies: M. Philipp, Zum Sprachgebrauch des Paulinus von Nola. Erlangen, 1904. — B. Botte, Consummare: ALMA 12(1937)43-44. — I. Morelli, De s. Paulini Nolani doctrina christologica. Naples, 1945. — G. Rizza, Interpretazioni bibliche ed influenza retorica nell'opera di Paolino da Nola: MSLC 1(1947)153-164. — P. Fabre, Essai sur la chronologie de l'oeuvre de s. Paulin de Nole. Paris, 1948 (fundamental work). — G. Rizza, Pitture e mosaici nelle basiliche paoliniane di Nola e Fondi: *Siculorum Gymnasium* 1(1948)311-321. — P. Courcelle, Fragments historiques de Paulin de Nole conservés par Grégoire de Tours, in Mélanges Halphen. Paris 1951, 143-153 (= Histoire Litt. des grandes inv. germ. Paris 1964[3], 283-302). — F. G. Sirma, Ausonio, Paolino e il problema del Testo ausoniano: *Aevum* 37(1963)124-135. — A. Ferrua, Cancelli di Cimitile con scritte bibliche: RQ 68(1973)50-68. — A. Lepinsky, Le decorazioni per la basilica di S. Felice negli scritti di Paolino di Nola: VetChr 13(1976)65-80. — S. Prete, Paolino di Nola: la storia umana come provvidenza e salvezza: Aug 16(1976)145-157; *idem,* I temi della proprietà e della famiglia negli scritti di Paolino di Nola: Aug 17(1977)257-282. — R. Herzog, Probleme der heidnisch-christlichen Gattunskontinuität am Beispiel des Paulinus von Nola, in *Christianism et formes littéraires* (Entretiens sur l'Antiquité classique 23). Bern 1977, 273-423. — K. Kohlwas, Christliche Dichtung und stilistische Form bei Paulinus von Nola. Bonn, 1979.

1. Letters.

Of the numerous letters written by Paulinus to friends and famous persons of his time, only fifty are extant today. These letters, which were so much admired by his contemporaries as to be compared by Jerome to those of Cicero (*Ep.* 85, 1: PL 22, 752), do not hold great interest for modern scholars since their author does not take part, or does so only in a marginal manner, in the cultural debates of his time, does not speak of the troubles of his era and does not even offer an interesting biographical sketch.

He addressed himself to Jerome and to Augustine (four letters) to request explanations of Scriptural passages or doctrinal clarifications of minor importance. To Delphinus (five letters) he expressed his gratitude for having been baptized by him and wards off the request to write works of greater depth of which his friend considers him to be capable. With Amandus (six letters) he manifests a greater frankness and confidence and risks confronting theological themes (*Ep.* 12 on the purpose of the Incarnation) which he did not dare touch in his correspondence with Augustine or Delphinus.

The most substantial and lively group of letters from the collection is furnished by the 13 letters addressed to Sulpicius Severus. Some of the most significant moments of Paulinus' spiritual adventure are relived in these letters, from his troubled ordination as a priest, to the expectation of departing for his retreat at Nola (*Ep.* 1 *ad Severum*), the bitterness he suffered at Rome from the hostility of the Roman clergy and the coldness of Pope Siricius, and the warm reception given him by the bishops of Campania (*Ep.* 5 *ad Severum*). To the great joy of Paulinus, Severus at a certain point confided to his friend his intention of coming to live at Nola. However, he subsequently reconsidered and contented himself with sending Paulinus a copy of the *Vita Martini* which he had just finished. In spite of his disappointment, Paulinus recalls the perfect harmony which already bound them in the world and which could not diminish now that they were dedicated to Christ. "Now you are in truth father, brother and kinsman to me . . . You are my friend in the love of Christ and brother in the divine rebirth."

The opportunities for remaining in close contact with his friends through letters were numerous even if not in themselves outstanding: monk couriers who were less than spiritual, the sending of a cook who was holy but totally inexperienced in cooking (*Ep.* 23), the exchange of a cloak and a tunic (*Ep.* 29), the incredible request for a portrait of Paulinus to be placed in the baptistry beside that of Martin (*Ep.* 30), and the discouraging news that this request would not be honored (*Ep.* 32).

The interest of the correspondence with Severus lies not only in the documentation of a sincere and fraternal friendship, but also in the revelation of the richness of Paulinus' asceticism, of his perfect orthodoxy in relation to the Pelagian heresy (*Ep.* 33 and 34), his elevated mysticism (*Ep.* 28), and in the information concerning Paulinus' pilgrimage to the Holy Land and his veneration of the relics (*Ep.* 29 and 32).

Letter 34 is a discourse on benevolence, and letter 16 to Iovius treats of providence and fate and, in a rather superficial manner without further investigation, the use of pagan literature by Christians.

Letter 48 exists only in a fragment, while the authenticity of letters 46 and 47 *Ad Rufinum* has been questioned.

The literary merit of the letters, so much admired by Jerome, does not carry the same weight in the judgment of modern scholars as it did with the ancients. From this point of view, the judgment is not particularly flattering since Paulinus does not possess an original style and tends to be boring and tedious because of the excessive citations from Scripture.

Translations: English: P. G. Walsh, ACW 35 & 36(1967)(letters 1-22 and 23-51). *Dutch:* A. P. Muys, De briefwisseling van Paulinus van Nola en Augustinus. Diss., Hilversum, 1941. *French:* Ch. Pietri, op. cit. *German:* G. Burke, Paulinus von Nola. Das Einige Notwendige. Einsiedeln, 1961 (Anthology). — A. Kurfess, Ausonius und Paulinus. Zwei poetische Briefe (*Ep.* 27 and 40), Gebet des Paulinus (*Ep.* 32); *Gymnasium* 62(1955)543-546. — W. Erdt, Christentum und heidnisch-antike bei Paulin von Nola, mit Kommentar u. Übersetzung des 16. Briefes. Meisenheim am Glan, 1976.

Studies: L. Villani, Osservazioni intorno alle epistole scambiate tra Ausonio e Paulino Nolano durante la dimora di questo in Ispagna. Vercelli, 1902. — P. Reinelt, Studien über die Briefe des heiligen Paulinus von Nola. Diss., Breslau, 1904. — J. Brochet, La correspondence de saint Paulin de Nole et de Sulpice Sévère. Paris, 1906. — E. C. Babut, Paulin de Nole, Sulpice Sévère et St. Martin. Recherches de chronologie. I: Date des Lettres de Paulin de Nole à Sulpice Sévère: *Annales du Midi* 20(1908)18-44. — C. Weyman, Caput unguento deducere (*Ep.* 13, 7): *Arch. für latein. Lexik.* 15(1906-08)260. — P. De Labriolle, Un épisode de la fin du paganisme. La correspondence d'Ausone et de Paulin de Nole (Chefs-d'œuvre de la littérature religieuse). Paris, 1910. — J. Mantuoni, Paulinische Studien, in *Strena Buliciana.* Zagreb 1924, 345-366 (*Ep.* 32, 10). — L. Villani, Sur l'ordre des Lettres échangées par Ausone et Paulin de Nole: REAN 29(1927)35-44. — F. Fabre, Les citations dans la correspondence de Paulin, in Mélanges 1945 II. Paris, 1946, 17-38. — P. Courcelle, Sur la correspondence entre saint Augustin et saint Paulin de Nole: *Bull. Société nat. Antiquaire de France* (1950-51)204; *idem,* Les lacunes de la correspondence entre saint Augustin et Paulin de Nole: REAN 53(1951)253-300. — P. G. Cirillo, Hieronymus. Le tre lettere del S. dottore a s. Paolino di Nola. Tivoli, 1958. — A. Russo, Caratteristiche di lingua e di stile nell'Epistolario di S. Paolino di Nola: *Atti Acc. Pontaniana Napoli* 8(1958-59)153-185; *idem,* Osservazioni intorno allo stile dell'Epistolario di s. Paolino di Nola: *Asprenas* 7(1960)158-170. — S. Prete, The Textual Tradition of the Correspondence between Ausonius and Paulinus: *Collect. Vaticana Miscel.* Albareda (ST 220). Vatican City 1962, II, 309-330. — L. Alfonsi, Cultura classica e cristianesimo. L'impostazione del problema nel proemio delle Div. Instit. di Lattanzio e nell'*Ep.* XVI di Paolino di Nola: *Le Parole e le Idee* 8(1966)163-176. — P. G. Walsh, Textual Notes on the Epistulae of Paulinus Nolanus: Orpheus 13(1966)153-158. — G. Casati, S. Agostino e S. Paolino di Nola: Aug 8(1968)40-57. — A. Salvatore, Due omelie su Sansone di Cesario di Arles e l'Epistola 23 di Paolino di Nola: VetChr 7(1970)83-113. — A. Esposito, Studio su l'Epistolario di S. Paolino Vescovo di Nola. Naples-Rome, 1971.

2. Poems.

Of the 33 poems edited by Hartel in CSEL 30, the fourth has been claimed for Paulinus of Pella, the fifth is a work of Ausonius, and neither the thirty-second, the so-called *Carmen ultimum,* nor the thirty-third, *Obitus Baebiani* are any longer considered authentic. There thus remain twenty-nine poems which can definitely be attributed to Paulinus.

Of these, three are from the period prior to 389, the year of his baptism. The first two are brief notes in verse which, according to the custom of the time, accompanied the exchange of small gifts with Gestidius, a rich landowner in Gaul. The third is a fragment of 11 hexameters, cited with approval by Ausonius, coming from a more ambitious project of rendering in verse the *De regibus* of Suetonius.

After his baptism, Paulinus' poetical interest, while remaining faithful to the language of the classical poets, turns to religious themes of biblical inspiration after the example of Iuvencus.

Thus poem six, 330 hexameters in honor of John the Baptist, draws material from the Gospel account to reconstruct the important episodes in the life of the saint, which are interrupted by frequent moralizing digressions. Poems seven, eight and nine, which paraphrase respectively Psalms 1, 2 and 136, belong to the same genre. These poems did not turn out well, as Paulinus himself recognized, and he made no further attempts along the same lines. On the one hand, the strong and austere figure of the Baptist emerges as colorless, while on the other, the Psalms lose their hieratic solemnity.

A different evaluation is merited by the two poetic epistles (poems ten and eleven). These were written in response to the letters in which Ausonius had invited him in sorrowful tones to return to his native land, to his poetry and his friend, and had even gone so far as to blame Therasia for the silence of Paulinus.

The replies of the monk of Nola, always in keeping with the literary canons then in vogue (alternation of meter, frequent reminiscences of the classical poets), are sincere expressions of affectionate gratitude for his old teacher, friend and protector, but they confirm his firm adherence to Christ in his poetry and his life. "I was once in accord with you in invoking with equal love, if not with equal strength, the deaf Phoebus in the Delphic cave; in invoking the divine muses and in asking of the forests and the mountains the divine gift of the word. Now another force, a greater God, directs my spirit" (*Carm.* 10, 23-29). "When Christ from heaven hurls his light into our hearts, he purifies the slothful body from painful torpor and renews the disposition of the mind; destroying all that once gave pleasure in place of chaste joys and, as a rightful master, claims our all: our heart, our mouth, our time" (ibid., 57-64). It was precisely this total consecration that the idle Ausonius was unable to comprehend. It was not a question of denying homeland, or friends, or poetry, but of a higher love which transcended and transformed all things.

Paulinus would always remain faithful to his new poetic ideal.

"Stretch the cords of your lyre," he would write to Iovius in verse. "Move your fruitful mind to consider noble topics and do not sacrifice your genius in the customary poems. A higher order of things is revealing itself to you. Sing no more of the Judgment of Paris nor of the fanciful wars of the giants. This was your entertainment as an infant and the game was not unbecoming to small children" (*Carm.* 23, 9-14).

The prolix poem twenty-four (942 iambic trimeters) directed to Citerius, easily divisible into two parts, also belongs to this epistolary genre. The first part narrates the adventuresome voyage of an Aquitanian monk to bring him the news of the offer of Citerius and his wife of one of their sons for the priesthood. The second part contains, in addition to the praises directed to the parents, an exhortation to the young man who has been consecrated.

On the other hand, poem thirty-one, of 316 elegiac distichs composed at the death of the young boy Celsus, belongs to the genre of *consolationes.* It is one of the most inspired poetic compositions of the age, where faith and affection suggest elements of a new and authentic poetry. The emotion reaches its height when the repeated name of Celsus recalls to the poet's mind his own little son of the same name who had lived only a brief time.

Poem seventeen, of 340 lines in sapphic verse, belongs to the genre of the *propempticon* (a song of accompaniment). It was written in 398 for Nicetas, bishop of Remesiana in Dacia, who on the occasion of one of his visits to Rome had called on Paulinus and become his friend. The customary tedious speeches and digressions are not able to suffocate the warmth of the farewell and the joy of the believer and Roman citizen. "Because of your work in this mute region of the world, the barbarians have learned to sing the praises of Christ with a Roman heart and to live in purity the tranquil Christian peace" (*Carm.* 17, 262-264).

Another attempt at giving Christian content and spirit to the classical literary forms is provided by *Carmen* 25, which is an epthalamium composed for the marriage of Julian (the future bishop of Eclanum and leader of Pelagianism) and Ja (or Tizia). The poem, which extends through 119 elegiac distichs and terminates with three pentameters is suffused by a quiet joy, but lingers too long in moralizing exhortations and is weighed down by numerous obscurities.

A unique place in Paulinus' poetry is occupied by the *Carmina natalicia,* 14 poems composed for the feast of Saint Felix (January 14) uninterruptedly, according to a precise plan, from 395 to 408. While the first two of these poems are brief invocations to the saint to obtain a good voyage (*Carm.* 12) or to manifest the poet's own joy at living close to his shrine (*Carm.* 13), the poet begins in the third poem (*Carm.* 14) to extend his interest to the crowds of pilgrims who come from nearby regions to honor the saint. Paulinus follows them in their travels, recalls their songs and describes concretely and sympathetically the manifestations of their simple and superstitious piety.

With the fourth of these poems (*Carm.* 15), the life and miracles of the saint become the theme of the verse in such a way as to form, along with the following poems (*Carm.* 16, 18, and 23), an encomiastic poetic biography. Paulinus is not concerned with the historicity of the facts he narrates. In a similar manner to his friend, Sulpicius Severus, in the *Vita Martini,* his purpose is to edify by seeing miracles even where they do not exist, just like the people devoted to Saint Felix.

Carmen 26, from 402, reflects Paulinus' anxiety and fear in the face of the barbarian invasions, while the following poem (*Carm.* 27) returns to a joyful tone on account of the improved situation, the return of his friend Nicetas, and the completion of new buildings. *Carmen* 28 is of more archeological than poetic interest, as it continues the description, begun in the preceding poem, of the constructions Paulinus wanted around the tomb of his patron saint. The triumph of Christianity over paganism is the theme of the first part of *Carmen* 29 (composed in 405), while the second part recounts with the usual narrative skill and psychological observations an incident of theft at the shrine of St. Felix and the discovery of the thief.

By this time, the repetition of the same theme had exhausted both the material and the poet, and, in order to maintain the promise of an annual hymn, he is forced to have recourse to insignificant facts, attempting to make them appear marvelous (*Carm.* 20).

There is, nevertheless, a new spark of life in *Carmen* 21, from the year 407, on account of the escape from the barbarian menace and the visit of certain illustrious personages and friends, whose praises he sings. This poem is important above all because of the valuable, although obscure, biographical notices it provides.

Finally three brief fragments totaling 35 verses have survived from the final poem for the feast of Saint Felix, *Carmen* 29.

On the whole, the attempt of Paulinus to make use of profane literary forms to celebrate Christ and his saints can be judged as at least partially successful.

Although he does not reach great heights, Paulinus nevertheless always knows how to maintain a dignified level with regard to the delicacy of sentiments, the serenity of content, the purity of language, and the fluidity and harmony of verse, and the good taste of a refined education. The things which are most jarring are his prolixity, on the one hand, and the clearly forced attempt to find new material for his verses, on the other. Paulinus' artistic talent is most successful in his description and sketches of popular scenes which offer a valuable testimony to the customs and religiosity of his time.

Translations: English: P. G. Walsh, ACW 40(1975). *Dutch:* J. A. Bouma, Het epthalamium van Paulinus van Nola. Carmen XXV. Assen, 1968. *French:* J. De Smet, Poètes latins chrétiens. I: Saint Paulin de Nole. Poésies choisies. Brussels, 1912 (anthology). — Ch. Pietri, op. cit. *Italian:* S. Costanza, Meropio Ponzio Paolino. Antologia di carmi. I. Messina, 1971. — A. Mencucci, S. Paolino di Nola. I carmi. Siena, 1973.

Studies: A. Huemer, De Pontii Paulini Nolani re metrica. Vienna, 1903. — Ph. Martin, Le cursus dans saint Paulin de Nole: *Revue August.* Louvain 5(1904)33-34. — W. Meyer, Die rhytmischen Jamben des Auspicius: NGWG(1906)207. — R. Pichon, Observations sur le VIIIe Natalicium de Paulin de Nole: REAN 9(1909)337-342. — C. Morelli, L'epitalamio nella tarda poesia latina: SIF 8(1910)319-342. — J. Fries, Beitrag zu Aesthetik der römischen Hochzeitpoesie. Aschaffenburg, 1910. — F. Jäger, Das antike Propemptikon und das 17. Gedicht des Paulinus von Nola. Rosenheim, 1913. — P. L. Kraus, Die poetische Sprache des Paulinus Nolanus. Augsburg, 1918. — C. Weyman, Paulinus von Nola und Ambrosius: MM 3(1922)167ff. — A. Wilmart, L'hymne de Paulin sur Lazare dans un manuscrit d'Autun: RB 32(1922)27-45. — A. H. Chase, The Metrical Lives of S. Martin of Tours by Paulinus and Fortunatus and by Sulpicius Severus: HSCP(1932)51-76. — G. B. A. Fletcher, Imitationes vel loci similes in poetis latinis: Paulinus Nolanus: Mnem 1(1933-34)208-210. — P. Fabre, Sur l'ordre chronologique de deux Natalicia de saint Paulin de Nole: REAN(1934)178-188. — G. Wiman, Till Paulinus Nolanus' Carmina: *Eranos* 32(1934)98-103 (textual criticism). — Ch. Favez, A propos de consolation. Note sur la composition du carmen 31 de Paulin de Nole: RELA 13(1935)226-268. — S. Blomgren, On mågra ställen i Paulini Nolani carmina: *Eranos* (1940)62-67. — P. Courcelle, Un nouveau poème de Paulin de Pella: VC 1(1947)101-113 (Carmen 19). — J. Kornprobst, Das carmen XXXII des Paulinus von Nola. Diss. Typewritten, Innsbruck, 1947. — A. Hudson-Williams, Influus: *Eranos* 48(1950)70-71 (*Carmen* 31, 444). — W. Schmid, Tityrus christianus: RhM 96(1953)101-165. — P. Menna, Illud carmen quod ad coniugem inscribitur divi Paulini Nolani sitne an divi Prosperi Aquitani: *Latinitas* 10(1962)208-232. — R. Argenio, Il miracolo dei buoi nel XX natalizio di S. Paolino di Nola: *Rivista Studi Class.* 17(1969)330-338. — A. Salvatore, L'aspetto biblico-religioso nel programma poetico di Paolino di Nola, in *Annuario Liceo.* P. Giannone. Caserta 1960-69, 3-22. — R. Argenio, S. Paolino da Nola cantore de miracoli. Rome, 1970. — R. P. H. Green, The Poetry of Paulinus of Nola. A Study of his Latinity. Brussels, 1971 (fundamental work). — R. Argenio, Una rettificazione sul martirio di S. Felice: *Rivista Studi Class.* 19(1971)24-25 (*carm.* XIV 9f; XXVII). — W. Wieland, Obses πάρεδρος (Paul. Nol. *carm.* 22, 54): *Museum Helveticum* 28(1971)115-117. — S. Costanza, Dottrina e poesia nel carme XXXI di Paolino da Nola: *Giornale Ital. Filogia* 24(1972)346-353; *idem,* La poetica di Paolino di Nola, in *Studi in onore Q. Catandella.* II. Catania 1972, 593-613. — J. Doignon, Un récit de miracle dans les "Carmina" de Paulin de Nole. Poétique virgilienne et leçon apologétique: *Revue Hist. Spiritual.* 48(1972)129-144 (Natalicium XIII). — A. Ruggiero, Il messaggio umano e cristiano nella poesia di Paolino di Nola. Nola, 1972. — J. Fontaine, Le symbolisme de la cithare dans poésie de Paulin de Nole, in *Studia Waszink.* Amsterdam 1973, 123-143. — P. Flury, Das sechste Gedicht des Paulinus von Nola: VC 27(1973)129-145. — H. Green, Paulinus of Nola and the Diction of Christian Latin Poetry: Latomus 32(1973)79-85; *idem,* Some Types of Imagery in the Poetry of Paulinus of Nola: VC 27(1973)50-52. — S. Costanza, I generi letterari nell'opera poetica di Paolino di Nola: Aug 14(1974)637-650. — S. Prete, Paolino di Nola: La parafrasi biblica della laus Johannis (*carm.* 6): Aug 14(1974)625-635. — S. Costanza, Il paesaggio nell'opera poetica di Paolino di Nola, in *Forma Futuri,* Miscel. Pellegrino. Turin 1975, 741-754; *idem,* Aspetti autobiografici nell'opera poetica di Paolino di Nola:

Giornale Ital. Filogia 6(1975)265-277. — H. Junod-Ammerbauer, Le poète chrétien selon Paulin de Nole: REAug 21(1975)13-62. — D. R. Schackleton Bailey, Critical Notes on the Poems of Paulinus Nolanus: AJPh 97(1976)3-19. — J. T. Lienhard, Textual Notes on Paulinus of Nola, *carm.* 6, 256-330: VC 31(1977)53-54. — P. G. Walsh, Paulinus of Nola and Virgil: *Proceedings of the Virgil Society* 15(1975-76)7-15. — C. Tibiletti, Nota teologica a Paolino di Nola (Carmen 25, 189): Aug 18(1978)389-395. — J. R. Wachel, Classical and Biblical Elements in Selected Poems of Paulinus of Nola. Diss., Univ. of Iowa, 1978. — A. Sbrancia, L'eptalamio di S. Paolino di Nola (Carmen 25): *Annal. Fac. Phil. Univ. di Macerata* 11(1978)83-129. — S. Prete, Il carme 20 di Paolino di Nola. Alcuni aspetti letterari e culturali: Aug 21(1981)169-177.

APPENDIX

1. *Sacramentorum liber.*

Gennadius also attributes a sacramentary to Paulinus (*De vir. ill.* 49: *fecit et sacramentarium*). Kl. Gamber, who has studied this question carefully, has concluded that the ancestor of the Gelasian Sacramentary is probably that composed by Paulinus of Nola (*Urgelasianum*), and he has attempted a reconstruction. His opinion has met with much doubt on the part of other scholars.

Studies: Kl. Gamber, Das kampanische Messbuch als Vorläufer des Gelasianum. Ist der hl. Paulinus von Nola der Verfasser?: SE 12(1961)5-111. — V. Raffa, S. Paulinus Nolanus auctor sacramentarii Gelasiani primigeni?: EL 76(1962)345-348. — Kl. Gamber, Das Messbuch des hl. Paulinus von Nola: *Heiliger Dienst.* 20(1966)17-25; *idem,* Das altkampanische Sakramentar. Neue Fragmente in angelsächsicher Überlieferung: RB 79(1969)329-342.

2. *Poema ultimum.*

This poem is designated as *ultimum* since, as *Carmen* 32, it is the last of the series. It was discovered and published by Muratori in 1697 under the name of Paulinus. Because of linguistic and metrical errors in the text, Muratori's opinion has not won general acceptance. F. G. Sirna attributes it to the circle around Paulinus, possibly to the same Iovius to whom letter 16 and *Carmen* 22 are addressed. According to Chastagnol, the poem could be addressed to the Senator R. Antonius Volusianus, *Praefectus urbis* in 417-418.

The poem, which is composed of 255 hexameters, belongs to the genre of apologetic literature. The author, while professing his Christian faith and singing at length of divine mercy, rejects Judaism, mocks the cult and gods of the pagans, and renounces pagan philosophy and wisdom.

Editions: CPL 206. — PL 5, 261-282 (*Antonii Carmen*). — PL 61, 691-710. — W. De Hartel, CSEL 30(1894)329-338.

Translations: Italian: A. Menciucci. Sienna, 1973 (incomplete).

Studies: G. Morelli, L'autore del cosidetto Poema Ultimum attribuito a Paolino di Nola: Did 1(1912)481-498. — A. Chastagnol, Le sénateur Volusien et la conversion d'une famille de l'aristocratie romaine au bas empire: REAN 58(1956)241-253. — F. G. Sirna, Sul cosiddetto poema ultimum Ps. Paoliniano: *Aevum* 35(1961)87-107.

3. *De obitu Baebiani.*

De obitu Baebiani is the title of *Carmen* 33, which is composed in different meters: iambic trimeters, hexameters, asclecpiads, etc. It was first published by Brandes in 1890. Although the work is anonymous in the manuscripts, Brandes attributed it to Paulinus because of similarities in style and content. This opinion, which was accepted by Havet, has been firmly rejected by Fabre.

Verius Baebianus, a wealthy man, is baptized on account of illness. Filled with joy because of this, he falls into a deep sleep in which he receives heavenly visions. When he awakes after two days, he tells of the things he has seen and dies peacefully. The final moments of his life and the visions, furnished with explanations, were reproduced as pictures in the home of his widow.

Editions: CPL 205. — W. Hartel, CSEL 30(1894)338-343. — PLS III, 111-1114 (ed. Hartel).

Translations: Italian: A. Menciucci. Sienna 1973, 156-161.

Studies: W. Brandes, Obitus Baebiani, ein unerkanntes Gedicht des Paulinus von Nola: WSt 21(1890)280-297. — L. Havet, Paulinus Nolanus. Obitus Baebiani: RPh 24(1900)144-145.

CLAUDIANUS

Little is known of the life of Claudius Claudianus. Born, or at least educated, at Alexandria in Egypt, he was still a young man when he arrived in Rome in 394. He was a poet who composed first in Greek and then in Latin and who learned the classical authors. For this reason, his language is unusually pure. He became the court poet of Honorius and the panegyrist of Stilicho, and was so famous in his own time as to be considered the equal of Homer and Vergil (Dessau, ILS 1, 2949). He died around 404. Aside from his secular poetry, compositions of a Christian inspiration have also been attributed to Claudianus: two epigrams in Greek totaling 15 verses (VI and VII; ed. Birt, p. 421-422); an ironic epigram, *In Jacobum magistrum equitum,* written to exhort this *magister equitum* not to scorn his verse and to wish him the help of the saints in battle (Birt, 50, p. 340); the *Miracula Christi* (Birt XXI, p. 412) and the *De Salvatore* (Birt XX; p. 411-412). Critics are for the most part in agreement on denying the authenticity of the *Miracula Christi,* an epigram of 9 distichs which, according to Turco, described the pictures or mosaics of a Roman basilica or baptistry, each distich describing an event from the Gospel (the Annunciation, the Magi, Cana, Peter walking on the water, Lazarus, etc.). The critics have given little consideration to the Greek epigrams, but have directed their attention to the *De Salvatore* (or *Carmen Paschale*), where they raise two distinct questions: the authenticity of the work and the Christianity of Claudianus. In general, the authenticity of the work has been accepted, although with some hesitation (for example, Fabricius and Manitius attribute it to Damasus, Niehbur to Merobaude, and Fargues possibly to Claudianus Mamertus). An important factor is that the poem is found in the most ancient manuscript of the works of Claudianus (*saec.* VIII). The *De Salvatore,* a poem of 20 verses, presents a wonderful sketch of Christology. Christ the Creator of all things assumes a human nature in the virgin womb of Mary, a young unmarried girl, who gives birth to her maker. He whom the world could not contain lived as a man among men in order that by his own death he might put death to flight. The poem concludes with a prayer for the well-being of the emperor.

The conclusion introduces the question of the Christianity of Claudianus. Birt and Pellegrino admit that he was a Christian; others (Geffken, Rolfe, Schmid) believe that he was a Christian in name only and not by conviction; still others (Vollmer, Rauschen, Helm, Fargues, Mazzarino, Cameron) sharply deny his Christianity. Various reasons militate in favor of this latter opinion. The content of his vast poetic production is clearly pagan and involves an ample use of mythology. However — and this is a phenomenon of considerable interest — in the plastic arts and in Christian poetry, abundant reference was made to pagan mythology even on the part of convinced Christians (e.g., Prudentius, Sidonius Apollinaris). Nevertheless, there exists a precise judgment of Augustine according to which Claudianus was *a Christi nomine alienus* (*De civ. Dei* 5, 26: CSEL 47, 162), and he is remembered by Orosius as *poeta quidem eximius, sed paganus pervicacissimus* (*Hist.* 7, 35: PL 31, 1154). The final invocation reveals that the work was composed specifically for Easter, and thus is an occasional piece written for a particular circumstance. It seems to belong to a particular literary genre which includes the *Versus paschales* of Ausonius, the *De Christo* of Merobaude and the *Carmen paschale* of Sedulius, and which follows the ancient pagan tradition of composing hymns to the divinity (e.g., the hymn to Zeus of Cleanthes and that to Isis of Apuleius). The court poet of a Christian court, while remaining a pagan — albeit a more superficial than convinced pagan — could have composed pieces to offer to his patrons on the occasion of certain particular anniversaries (Easter was almost an official feast within the state).

Editions: CPL 1461f (Ps. Claudius Claudianus). — J. M. Gesner. Leipzig, 1759 (reprint, Hildesheim, 1969). — L. Jeep. Leipzig, 1876-79. — J. Koch. Leipzig, 1893. — Th. Birt, MGH, AA 10. Berlin, 1892 (Greek epigrams VI and VII, 421-422; *Miracula Christi*

XXI, 412-413; *De Salvatore,* XX, 411-412). *De Salvatore:* PL 13, 376-77; PL 53, 788-89. — M. Ihm, Epigrammata Damasiana. Leipzig, 1895, 69-71, n. 68. *Greek epigrams*: PL 53, 789. *Miracula Christi:* PL 53, 790. F. Buechler, A. Riese, Anthologia Latina I, 2. Leipzig 1906, 329, n. 879 (reprint, Amsterdam 1972).

Studies: (only the religious aspect of Claudianus and his work) E. Arens, Quaestiones Claudianeae. Münster, 1894. — T. G. Glover, Life and Letters in the Fourth Century. Cambridge, 1901. — G. Turcio, Sull'Epigramma "Miracula Christi" attribuito a Claudio Claudiano: RAC 5(1928)337-344. — R. Helm, Heidnisches und Christliches bei spätlateinischen Dichtern, in *Natalicium Geffcken,* Heidelberg 1931, 1-46. — P. Fargues, Claudien. Études sur sa poésie et son temps. Paris, 1933. — S. Mazzarino, La politica religiosa di Stilicone: RIL 71(1938)235-262; *idem,* Stilicone: la crisi imperiale dopo Teodosio. Rome, 1942. — P. Courcelle, Les lettres grecques en Occident. Paris, 1943. — O. Jannssen, A. Galama, Uit de Romeine Keizertijd, 's Hertogenbosch, 1951. — W. Schmid, Ein verschollener Kodex des Cuias und seine Bedeutung für die Claudiankritik: SIF 37-38(1956)498-518; *idem,* Claudianus I: RACh 3(1957)152-167 (fundamental work). — D. Romano, Appendix Claudianea. Palermo, 1958. — L. Alfonsi, Su una fonte del Carmen De Christo Jesu beneficiis di Elpidio Rusitco: RFIC 34(1956)173-178. — S. Gennaro, Lucrezio e l'apologetica latina in Claudiano: MSLC 7(1957)5-60; *idem,* Da Claudiano a Merobaude. Aspetti della poesia cristiana de Merobaude: MSLC 8(1958). — G. Martin, Claudian, an Intellectual Pagan of the Fourth Century, in *Studies Ullman.* Missouri 1960, 69-80. — A. Cameron, St. Jerome and Claudian: VC 19(1965)111-113; *idem,* Rutilius N., St. Augustine, and the Date of the De Reditu: JRS 58(1967)31-39; *idem,* Poetry and Propaganda at Court of Honorius. Oxford, 1970 (fundamental, esp. ch. 8, 189-227). — F. Casaceli, Recenti studi Claudiani: *Bollettino di studi latini* 2(1972)318-326. — A. K. Clarke, Claudian and the Augustinian Circle: Augustinus 13(1968)125-133. M. Wacht, Lemmatisierter Index zu den Carmina maiora Claudians mit statistischen Anhängen zu Sprache und Metrik. Nuremberg Microfilm Computer Service, 1980. — S. Doepp, Zeitgeschichte in Dichtungen Claudians. Wiesbaden, 1980. — J. L. Sebesta, Claudian's credo. The De Salvatore: *Classical Bulletin* 56(1980)33-36.

LICENTIUS

Licentius, who was born at Thagaste, was a fellow citizen of Augustine (Aug. *De beata vita* 1, 5; *Carm.* 137) and his disciple and friend. He was the son of Augustine's benefactor, Romanianus, and a relative of Alypius (Aug. *Ep.* 27, 5 and 6). He was present at Cassiciacum in 386 as the guest of Verecundus and although he was quite young (he is called *puer* by Augustine) he took part in the philosophical discussions held during that retreat, and is an interlocutor of Augustine in the *Contra Academicos,* the *De beata vita* and the *De ordine.* He converted to Christianity along with his teacher, but it is not known when he was baptized. Since he wished to complete the civil and military *cursus honorum,* he remained in Italy after Augustine's departure and lived for a time at Rome (*Ep.* 32, 4 and 5; *Carm.* 71). Augustine valued his talent and placed much hope in him. Already during the stay at Cassiciacum Licentius he dedicated himself enthusiastically to the composition of poetry and was described by Augustine as *poeta paene perfectus* (*Contra acad.* II 3, 7; cf. II 4, 10; III 4, 7; *De ord.* I 3, 8). It is known that he composed a poem about

Pyramus and Thisbe following a theme of Ovid (*De ord.* I 8, 24). Around 395 he sent Augustine a letter from Rome accompanied by a poem of 154 hexameters. This poem, preserved among the works of Augustine, is definitely authentic since Augustine quotes it himself (*Ep.* 26, 4). The poet wrote to Augustine to place before him the difficulties he was experiencing in reading Varro without the help of his master, and he requested of Augustine the *De musica.* Licentius experienced a nostalgia for the past at the same time that he was searching in the spiritual life. He showed a desire to dedicate his life to higher things, but pointed out the difficulty of succeeding in this without the expert guide of his teacher, for whom he nourished a great admiration and to whom he remained closely attached by friendship, their common home of Thagaste and their Christian faith (*Carm.* 137-139).

Augustine responded by severely reproaching him for his manner of life. Licentius placed great importance on the technical perfection of his verse and did not rest until it was in accord with the laws of prosody, yet he did not care if his life was in accord with the divine laws. If Licentius did not wish to listen to his advice, at least he should heed the better aspirations of his own heart, expressed here and there in his poem, and dedicate his talent to God. Augustine advised him to go to Paulinus of Nola in Campania to learn from his example, and wrote a worried letter to Paulinus (*Ep.* 27). Paulinus, who was a friend of both Augustine and Romanianus, sent Licentius 5 blessed loaves and wrote a letter exhorting him to abandon his present way of life. To this letter he added an elegiac poem in which he continued his exhortations at greater length. Contrary to what is often affirmed on the basis of *Carmen* 74, Licentius was not yet married at that time, although he was thinking seriously of marriage (cf. the *Carmen* of Paulinus, v. 20f and v. 89). Nothing is known concerning the result of these interventions, just as nothing is known concerning the subsequent career of Licentius or of other writings of his. Aside from the expressions of sincerity and nostalgia, his poem is an excellent scholastic exercise, packed with mythology of which he makes much display, such as when he calls Christ *noster Apollo* and *sobolus Tonantis.* He has a good knowledge of the classical authors (Vergil, Ovid, Horace) and is familiar with Christian writers as well. In his reply, Augustine did not judge the value of his poetry, but dwelt solely on the style of the author's life. There are some connections between the *Carmen* of Licentius and Claudianus, especially with the *De raptu Proserpinae* and the *Panegyricus Probini et Olybrii.* It is commonly accepted that Licentius depends on Claudianus. However, A. K. Clarke has correctly observed that in certain cases the contrary could also be true. Licentius and Claudianus could also have been friends who met at Milan and Rome.

Editions: PL 33, 103-107. — E. Baehrens, Poetae lat. minores VI. Leipzig 1886, 413-420. — A. Goldbacher, CSEL 34, 1(1895)89-95.

Translations: Italian: NBA XXI. Rome 1969, 149-157.

Studies: M. Zelzner, De carmine Licentii ad Augustinum. Arnsberg, 1915 (text, manuscripts, critical notes, meter, sources). — C. I. Balmus, La Lettre de saint Augustin à Licentius, in *Memoria Lui Vasile Parvan.* Bucharest 1934, 21-27. — G. Bardy, Un élève de saint Augustin, Licentius: *L'Année Theol. Augustin.* 14(1954)55-79. — D. Romano, Licenzio poeta. Sulla posizione di Agostino verso la poesia: ND 11(1962)1-22. — A. K. Clarke, Claudian and the Augustinian Circle of Milan: *Augustinus* 13(1968)125-133 (relations between Claudianus and Licentius).

ENDELECHIUS

Almost nothing is known about Severus Endelechius. It seems that Endelechius the poet (in the manuscripts it appears *Carmen Severi Sancti id est Endelechi rhetoris = oratoris*), the friend of Paulinus of Nola who requested a panegyric on the death of Theodosius (Paulinus, *Ep.* 28), was the same person as the orator active at Rome in the *Forum Martis* at the close of the fourth century. This identification, proposed by J. Sirmond in 1614, has won general acceptance today. The poet was likely of Gallic origin as was Saint Paulinus.

The *Carmen de mortibus boum* of 132 verses in 33 stanzas draws its inspiration from the virgilian *Bucolics.* The pagan herdsman Buculus recounts to his friend, Egon, how the outbreak of the plague, widespread in numerous other regions of the empire, had destroyed all his oxen and how he had abandoned all hope. Meanwhile, they encounter the Christian herdsman, Tityrus, who had suffered no damages, peacefully leading his own animals. To the request of the two pagans for an explanation, Tityrus responds, to their amazement, that he had placed the sign of the cross (guarantee of *certa salus*) on the forehead of his animals, for which he owes his good fortune to God: *magnis qui colitur solus in urbibus, Christus.* In the face of this miracle, Buculus and Egon are converted. Within the poem the protreptic (paganism was rather a phenomenon of the countryside, of the *pagi*) and apologetic (in the first centuries the cause of the plague was one of the chief accusations against the *superstitio* of the Christians) motives are obvious. The description of the plague is effective and the feelings of Buculus are portrayed well. The entire scene is set in Gaul (for which reason a Gallic origin is supposed for the author). There is a notable dependence on the *Bucolics* and *Georgics* of Vergil.

Editions: PL 19, 797-800. — F. Buecheler, A. Riese, Anthologia Latina I, 2. Leipzig 1906 (reprint, Amsterdam 1972), 334-339, n. 893.

Studies: J. Martin: BJ 221(1929)105-106 (bibliography 1900-1927). — H. De La Ville De Mirmont, L'astrologie chez les Gallo Romains: REAN 8(1906)135-137. — J. Ziehen, Neue Studien zur lateinischen Anthologie. Frankfurt-Leipzig, 1909 (*Endelechius,* p. 20).

— C. Morelli, Frustula: SIF 21(1915)184-185. — C. Weyman, Das Gedicht des Severus Santus Endelechius De mortibus boum: MM 4(1924)277-284 (= Beiträge zur Geschichte der chr.-lat. Poesie. Munich 1826, 103-110). — U. Moricca, Endelechius o sanctus Endelecius?: Did 4-3(1926)91-94. — W. Schmid, Tityrus Christianus: RhM 96(1953)101-165 (fundamental work); *idem,* RACh 5(1962)1-3. — M. Cock, A propos de la tradition manuscrite du Carmen de m. b. d'Endéléchius: Latomus 30(1971)151-160. — F. Corsaro, L'autore del "De mortibus boum," Paolino di Nola e la poetica religiosa de Teodosio: Orpheus 22(1975)3-26. — T. Alimonti, Struttura, ideologia ed imitazione virgiliana nel "De mortibus boum" de Endelechio. Turin, 1976 (fundamental work).

CYPRIAN THE POET

In 1891 Pieper published a critical edition, in the Corpus Vindobonense, of a series of poetic compositions on the historical books of the Old Testament under the name of Cyprianus Gallus. In doing this he provided a more or less precise paternity for works which had been circulating under various names in various editions. In 1560, Morel had published 165 verses with the title *Genesis* together with the *De Sodoma* which in the manuscript (today the *Paris.* 14758) are attributed to Cyprian. Sirmond added further passages in 1643, while Martène in 1724 published another 1276 verses from a ninth-century manuscript under the name of Iuvencus. These fragments were published numerous times under the names of Tertullian, Cyprian, Iuvencus, Salvian, Alcimus Avitus, and even Prudentius. In PL 19, 345-380, with the annotations of Martène and Arévalo, they are found under the name of Iuvencus. In 1852 Pitra (*Spic. Solesm.* I. Paris 1852, p. 171-258) completed *Genesis* from two manuscripts of the ninth and the tenth centuries, and published for the first time *Exodus, Deuteronomy, Joshua,* and parts of *Leviticus* and *Numbers.* In 1888, he added the *Book of Judges* and other passages of *Leviticus, Numbers,* and *Deuteronomy* (*Analecta sacra et class.* I. Paris-Rome 1888. p. 181-207). Because of the attribution of the two manuscripts as well as similarities of vocabulary, syntax, idioms, poetic license, and meter, Pitra attributed this vast work to Iuvencus. Pieper published it (CSEL 23) with the title, *Heptateucos* (7 books). Ancient manuscripts had already spoken of the *Heptateucos,* while a catalogue from the monastery of Saint Nazarius at Lorsch added other historical books such as *Kings, Esther, Judith,* and *Maccabees* and, according to a catalogue from Cluny, also *Paralipomenon.* Verses of *Job* are to be found as well in Pieper. From the seventh century, the works of Cyprian were joined to others of similar content, especially those of Avitus, which has been the cause of confusion in the manuscript tradition.

At the end of the last century and the beginning of the present, the discussions centering around the works attributed to Cyprian were lively and fruitful and led to a certain concordance in judgment.

Müller posed the problem in new terms (RhM 21[1886]123-133), and for linguistic reasons considered the poet to be a Gallo-Roman of the fourth to sixth century. Best (*De Cypriani quae feruntur.* Marburg, 1891) proposed two authors; one for *Genesis,* composed in Italy around 410, and an unidentified Gallo-Roman for the other books. Since his previous attribution to Cyprian of Toulon had been refuted, Pieper moved the date of composition up to the beginning of the fifth century and for the first time described the author as *Gallus,* which finds no justification in the manuscripts, even though they are widespread in France and England. Following the studies of Ebert, Harnack, Stutzenberger, Brewer, and Hass, certain points have been clarified. The entire *Heptateucos* is the work of a single author by the name of Cyprian who lived around the year 400. He was familiar with the work of Ausonius (*Mosella* 47 = Cyp., *Iesu Nave* 89) and Claudianus (*Paneg. III cons. Hon.* 90-97 = Ex. 474f, *Iudic.* 131; *Paneg. IV cons. Hon.* 118 = *Ex.* 152). Genesis is well known to Claudius M. Victorius, who died before 450 (*Cypr., Gen.* 105 = *Vict., Aleth.* 1, 419; *Gen.* 238 = *Aleth.* 2, 364; *Gen.* 255 = *Aleth.* 2, 402; *Gen.* 486f = *Aleth.* 3, 433; *Gen.* 585 = *Aleth.* 607). Furthermore, Cyprian made use of a biblical text antecedent to that of Jerome and at times had recourse to the Greek text. It is not known whether some inaccuracies are to be attributed to an already corrupt *Vetus* which he used or to his own misunderstanding. Brewer thought the poet might be the learned presbyter and biblicist Cyprian, the addressee of Jerome's letter 140, whom Jerome praises and at whose explicit request explains Psalm 89(90), which is a prayer attributed to Moses. Furthermore, since he agreed with Harnack in identifying the author of the *Heptateucos* with the author of the *Cena Cypriani,* which was composed toward the end of the fourth century in the region of Brescia-Verona, he concluded that the poet had lived in northern Italy. Since he was a learned presbyter according to the letter of Jerome, he placed his skill at the service of the religious instruction of the people.

1. *Heptateucos.*

Although some passages are still missing, the *Heptateucos* as reconstructed by Pitra is a combination of some 5250 verses, almost all of which are hexameters. There are three hendecasyllabic canticles: that of Moses after the crossing of the Red Sea (*Ex.* 15 = *Cypr., Ex.* 507-542), that of the people at the well of Beer (*Num.* 21 = *Cypr., Num.* 557-568) and that of Moses prior to his death (*Deut.* 32 = *Cypr., Deut.* 152-278). These passages contain possibly the best poetry of Cyprian. The different books are of varying lengths: *Genesis* 1498 verses, *Exodus* 1338, *Leviticus* 309, *Numbers* 777, *Deuteronomy* 288, *Joshua (Jesu Nave)* 585, and *Judges* 760. The figures illustrate the poet's clear preference for the narrative sections. Leviticus and Deuteronomy are noticeably shorter since Cyprian passes over the cultic ordinances, which were archaic and of little pedagogic value, and referred only to regulations of purity and impurity and such things as would have been of interest to the reader. If in general Cyprian merely sets the biblical text to verse, as did Iuvencus, he does nevertheless omit entire sections: e.g., *Ex.* 26-31 = *Cypr., Ex.* 1090-1133; *Ex.* 35-40 = *Cypr., Ex.* 1322-1333 (description of the Tent). On the other hand, he does not leave out the incest of the daughters of Lot, which he recounts in all simplicity. On rare occasions, he allows himself amplifications and expansions of the text; e.g., the crossing of the Red Sea (*Ex.* 14 = *Cypr., Ex.* 418-507), the golden calf (*Ex.* 32 = *Cypr., Ex.* 1134-1246) and the departure from Sinai (*Num.* 10:32-34 = *Cypr., Num.* 205-240). Claudius M. Victorius uses 390 verses to describe creation and paradise, Cyprian only 72; although the latter gives ample space to the story of Joseph (*Gen.* 37-47 = *Cypr., Gen.* 1129-1468).

Contrary to the practice of Victorius, Cyprian, in his fidelity to the text, retains and latinizes almost all the biblical names: Noah = Noelus, Lamech = Lamechus, Shem and Ham = Sechus and Chammus, Lot = Lodus, etc.

Cyprian shows a remarkable familiarity with the classical authors, Horace, Ovid, Persius, and Catullus, but above all with Lucretius and Vergil from whom he at times cites entire verses. He is also familiar with the Christian poets, Iuvencus, Prudentius, and Paulinus of Nola. He created numerous neologisms: *celsiiugus* (*Gen.* 291 and 375), *clepto* (*Ex.* 827 and 881), *ditificus* (*Num.* 677), *emitigo* (*Lev.* 160), *lentigradus* (*Gen.* 1064). *Tonans* is frequently used to indicate God, but there are no mythological recollections. Cyprian constructs some good verses, even though at times he does not adhere scrupulously to the laws of meter and makes frequent recourse to alliteration in keeping with the fashion of the time. The knowledge of the classics and of Scripture, the doctrinal purity, the lack of mythology (of which the Christian poets were already making use), and the time of composition of the *Heptateucos* all render Brewer's opinion highly probable that Cyprian the Poet is to be identified with the Cyprian who was the addressee of Jerome's letter 140. In order to avoid confusion, it would be well to eliminate the epithet *Gallus*. Following the research at the end of the last century and the beginning of the present, Cyprian has emerged as an author in his own right whose work merits a renewed and deepened interest today.

Editions: R. Pieper, CSEL 23(1891). — PLS III, 1151-1245.

Studies: J. E. B. Mayor, The Latin Heptateuch . . . Critically Reviewed. London-

Cambridge, 1899. — A. Stutzenberger, Der Heptateuch des gallischen Dichters Cyprianus. Zweibrücken, 1903. — J. Cornu, Zum Heptateuchos Cypriani: *Archiv f. lat. Lex. Gram.* 13(1904)192. — H. Brewer, Über den Heptateuchdichter Cyprian und die Caena Cypriani: ZkTh 28(1904)92-115. — O. Hey, Textkritische Bemerkungen zu lateinischen Schriftstellern, in *Festschr. z. 25. Stiftungfest d. hist. phil.* Vereins d. Un. Munich 1905, 44. — J. Cornu, Zwei Beiträge zur lateinischen Metrik: *Prager deutsche Studien* 8(1908)50-57. — W. Hass, Studien zum Heptateuchdichter Cyprian. Berlin, 1912. — F. Vernet, Cyprien, poèt italien ou gallo-roamin, vers l'an 400: DTC 3(1923)2470-2472. — L. Krestan, RACh 3(1957)477-481. — D. Kuijper, Maxilla per via (emendatio): VC 6(1952)44-46. — A. Longpré, Traitement de l'élision chez le poèt Cyprianus Gallus: *Phoenix* 26(1972)62-67; *idem,* Structure de l'hexamètre de Cyprianus Gallus: Cahiers EtAn 1(1972)75-100. — S. Smolak, Lateinische Umdichtungen des biblischen Schöpfungsberichtes: SP 12 (TU 115). Berlin 1975, 350-360. — A. Longpré, L'étude de l'hexamètre de Venantius Fortunatus: *Cahiers des études anciennes* 5(1976)45-58.

2. Dubious or Spurious Works.

a) *Orationes.*

There are two prayers found in the manuscripts under Cyprian's name with the title, *orationes Cypriani.* According to Harnack, the second of these is a biblical cento written by the author of the *Caena* since it mentions Thecla, and comes from the South of Gaul. According to K. Michel, the two prayers date to the post-Constantinian period but depend on a Greek text from the second or third century.

Editions: PL 5, 985-990 (Cyprian of Antioch). — W. Hartel, CSEL 3, 3(1871)144-151. A. von Harnack, TU 19, 3. Leipzig 1899, 25-28.

Studies: K. Michel, Gebet und Bild in frühchristlicher Zeit. Leipzig 1902, 2-22. — Th. Schermann, Die griech. Kyprianosgebete: OC 3(1903)303-323. — H. von Soden, TU 25, 3. Leipzig 1904, 222 (manuscripts).

b) *Caena Cypriani.*

(Cf. J. Quasten, *Patrology* II. Utrecht-Antwerp 1953, p. 371f.) According to Harnack and Brewer, it is a work of the same author of the *Heptateucos* and was written around the year 400. In the opinion of Brewer, the work is dependent on Zeno of Verona (†380). The author knows the *Acta Pauli,* a work almost unknown in the West, but recommended by Philastrius of Brescia. The geographical references, allusions to wines, and the interest for the Po River all point to the region around Brescia and Verona. W. Hass, although accepting the location in northern Italy, rejects the attribution to the author of the *Heptateucos* because of the use of a different biblical text. Lapôtre considers it to be the work of the Spaniard Bacharius, written at the time of Julian the Apostate. The *Caena Cypriani* is a parody in prose which draws its inspiration from the characteristics of biblical personalities. It enjoyed a great success in the Middle Ages, where it was read at the coronation of Charles the Bald, and existed in at least three poetic versions.

Editions: CPL 1430. To the bibliography of Quasten, *op. cit.* p. 372, add: PL 4, 1007-1014 (among the works of Cyprian).

Studies: A. Lapôtre, Le souper de Jean Diacre: MAH 21(1901)305-385. — K. Strecker, Die Cena Cypriani und ihr Bibeltext: *Zeitsch. f. wiss. Theol.* 54(1912)61-68. — W. Hass, Studien zum Heptateuchdichter Cyprian mit Beiträgen zu den vorhieronymianischen Bibelüberstezungen. Berlin, 1912. — G. Bardy: RBibl 11(1914)117-121. — A. Lampert, Bachiarius: DHGE 6(1932)58-61. — F. X. Murphy, Bacharius: *Classical Folia* 5(1951)24-29 (= J.-M. F. Maruque, Leaders of Iberean Christianity, 50-650 A.D., Jamaica Plains, Mass. 1962, 121-126).

c) *De Sodoma* and *De Jona.*

The first of these poems, consisting of 167 hexameters, was first published by Morel in 1560, and is found in some manuscripts (*Paris.* 14758) under the name of Cyprian and in others (*Paris.* 2772) under the name of Tertullian. The *De Jona (De Ninive),* of 105 verses, was published by Juret in the *Bibliotheca Patrum* of Margarin de la Bigne. It is closely bound to the preceding poem not only in some instances of the manuscript tradition (*Paris.* 2772, *saec.* X) and by an explicit reference to the *De Sodoma,* but also by reasons of form and stylistic procedure. It is possible that the two works were parts of a larger treatise. The text of the *De Jona* is mutilated. After making reference to the patience of God who waits for the repentance of men and presenting the invitation to Jonah to go and preach at Nineveh, the author describes the vicissitudes of Jonah's fate up to the calming of the storm, with nothing about the preaching in Nineveh. Nevertheless, in some manuscripts the title is given as *De Ninive.* The longer *De Sodoma* (Gen. 19) has as its theme the destruction of the two sinful cities, the transformation of Lot's wife into a pillar of salt and God's conduct with regard to these events. Both poems have in common the penitential theme of a strong appeal to conversion. The poet, immersed in classical culture, elaborates the biblical themes with greater liberty than either Iuvencus or Cyprian. According to Pieper, the poems are not the work of Cyprian the Poet, but come from the same time and place. Hall also rejects the attribution to Cyprian, which instead is admitted by Brewer. M. Dando recently attributed the two poems to Avitus on the basis of a series of parallelisms between these poems and the *libelli* of Avitus. A. Roncoroni has correctly observed that, in spite of the exaggerated importance of Dando's references, this could indicate that Avitus knew these poems, but it does not show that he was their author.

Editions: PL 2, 1159-1162 (*De Sodoma*); PL 2, 1166-1172 (*De Jona*) both under the name of Tertullian. — W. Hartel, CSEL 3, 3(1871)289-301 (Ps. Cyprian). — R. Pieper, CSEL 23(1891)212-226.

Studies: H. Brewer, Über den Heptateuchdichter Cyprian und die Caena Cypriani: ZkTh 23(1904)92-115. — W. Hass, Studien zum Heptateuchdichter Cyprian. Berlin, 1912. — O. Ferrari, Intorno alle fonti del poema di Cl. M. Vittore: Did 1(1912)57-74. — M. Dando, Alcimus Avitus as the Author of . . . De Sodoma and De Jona formerly Attributed to Tertullian and Cyprian: *Classica et Mediev.* 26(1967)258-275. — A. Roncoroni, L'epica lirica di Avito di Vienna: VetChr 9(1972)303-329.

d) *Ad quendam senatorem (Incipit: cum te diversis).*

Some manuscripts (e.g., *Vat. Reg.* 116 fol. 114 and *Paris.* 2772) attribute a poem of 85 hexameters to Cyprian with the title, *Cypriani ad quendam senatorem ex christiana religione ad idolorum cultum conversum.* The anonymous author addresses himself in verse — according to verses 3f the addressee loved poetry — to an ex-consul who had become dissatisfied with Christianity and had passed over to the cult of the *Magna Mater* and of Isis, and had become a priest of the latter. He criticizes the immoral life of the priests of Cybele and exhorts the unhappy and ridiculous senator to change and not remain in error (v. 84 *suffecit peccare semel*). The poem, which is written in good language (two neologisms: V. 43 *vericola,* v. 83 *fidamen*) and according to the rules of meter, fits into the spiritual climate of the end of the fourth century. From various indications it can be deduced that the poem was written at Rome (e.g., v. 11f).

Editions: CPL 1432. — PL 2, 1163-1166 (Tertullian). — W. Harter, CSEL 3, 3(1871) 302-305. — R. Pieper, CSEL 23(1891)227-230.

Studies: H. Brewer, Über den Heptateuchdichter Cyprian und die Caena Cypriani: ZkTh 23(1904)92-115.

SPES

Spes, who according to De Rossi and Frutaz was bishop of Spoleto at the end of the fourth and beginning of the fifth century and the predecessor of Achilles (successor, according to Lanzoni), wrote a poem of 12 verses in honor of the martyr Vitalis. The body of the martyr, who died by crucifixion, was found by Spes. The original title is preserved only in fragments, and the text, which was published by De Rossi in 1871, is found in the *Codex Vallicellianus* H, 8, 1 f. 528 (*Incipit: Martyris hic locus*). The poem, which is written in good language and perfect meter, recommends to the intercession of the saint the author and the virgin, Calventia, almost certainly the bishop's daughter, in order that she may persevere in her acceptance of a life of virginity. After 32 years of his episcopate, Spes died on November 23. His epitaph is still preserved. His relics were transferred to Aachen by Charlemagne to adorn the royal chapel.

Editions: G. B. De Rossi, *Bullettino Arch. cristiana,* II serie 2(1871)95. — CIL XI, 2, p. 723 n. 4966. — Diehl, Inscriptiones christ. lat. veteres I. p. 364, n. 1851.

Studies: G. B. De Rossi, Spicilegio d'archelogia cristiana nell'Umbria, op. cit., 94-120. — F. Lanzoni, Le Diocesi d'Italia dalle origini al principio del secolo VII. Faenza 1927, 1, 436-438. — C. Pietrangeli, Spoletium. Rome 1939, 79-80. — H. Leclercq, DACL 15(1953)1639-1640. — A. Rambaldi, B. Toscano, Spoleto. Immagini e memorie. Spoleto, 1963. — A. P. Frutaz, Spes e Achilleo vescovi di Spoleto, in *Atti II Conv. Studi Umbri.* Perugia 1964, 362-365.

ACHILLES

Achilles (in the poems, *Achilles* or *Achillis*) was bishop of Spoleto at the beginning of the fifth century. In 419, as a result of the dissensions in the Roman Church between Pope Boniface I, who had been elected on December 27, 418, and the rival candidate Eulalius, Achilles was sent to Rome by the court at Ravenna to preside at the celebration of Easter since the two rival candidates had been banned from the city by the civil authorities. The *Collectio Avellana* (ed. O. Günther, CSEL 35) preserves a collection of eight letters regarding this lamentable episode. Letter 22 (p. 69), dated March 15, addresses the invitation to Achilles to come to Rome, where he arrived on March 21, in time for Easter which was celebrated on March 30. The choice of Achilles for this delicate mission indicates the prestige which he enjoyed at the court.

Achilles had a church dedicated to Saint Peter built *extra moenia* to the east of Spoleto along the Via Flaminia, and placed there relics of the Apostle. Of the poems which he composed for the church, four are preserved in the collection *Laureshasmense* IV from the seventh century (Cod. *Vat. Pal. lat.* 833, *saec.* IX-X), and in a fragmentary state in the *Centulense* of the seventh century (manuscript of Corbie, now *Petropolitanus, saec.* VIII-IX). The first poem, of 14 verses (*Incipit: antistes Xti;* ed. De Rossi, n. 79, p. 113-114), praises the greatness of the church which contains the relics of the Apostle Peter. The second poem (*Incipit: Quidnam igitur,* ed. De Rossi, n. 80, p. 114), which is a broad paraphrase of Mt. 16:16-19, begins with the idea that all the churches depend on Peter and praises his universal primacy whose efficacy reaches to heaven. Poem three, of six verses (*Incipit: Qui Romam,* ed. De Rossi, n. 81, p. 114), informs the traveler that this church is a *sedes Petri* since it contains his relics, while the fourth poem, (*Incipit: Solvente, iuvante,* ed. De Rossi, n. 82, p. 114) speaks of Peter's ability to loosen chains on earth and open the gates of heaven. The poems of Achilles, which are inferior in language and meter to those of Spes, are of great importance for their doctrine on the primacy of Peter and his offices as *arbiter* on earth and *ianitor* in heaven.

Editions: CPL 1484. — J. B. De Rossi, Inscriptiones chr. Urbis Romae II-1. Rome 1888, n. 79-82, p. 113-114. — CIL XI, 2, 1, 698-699 (in PLS III, 1246 only n. 82).

Studies: U. Rouziès: DHGE 1(1912)314-315. — C. Pietrangeli, Spoletium. Rome, 1939.

— H. Leclercq: DACL 15(1953)1639-1640. — A. Rambaldi, B. Toscano, Spoleto. Immagini e memorie. Spoleto 1963, 17-74. — A. P. Frutaz, Spes e Achilleo vescovi di Spoleto, in *Atti del II Conv. Studi Umbri*. Perugia 1964, 352-377.

CLAUDIUS MARIUS VICTORIUS

The only certain information concerning this poet is provided by Gennadius in his *De vir. ill.* 61, where he writes, "Victorius, a rhetor of Marseilles, composed in a true and pious Christian spirit for his son, Etherius, a commentary of four books in verse on Genesis, from the beginning up to the death of the Patriarch Abraham. But since the author was accustomed to working with literature and had not been instructed by any teacher in the divine Scriptures, he expresses thoughts of little value in his poetry. He died under the reign of Theodosius (II) and Valentinian (III)." Sidonius Apollinaris (*Ep.* 5, 21: PL 58, 550, ed. Loyen 2, 211) praises a poet by the name Victorius, who could be either Claudius Marius or Victorius of Aquitania who composed an Easter table in 457. The text of Gennadius gives the name Victorius or Victorinus, never Victor, while the only extant manuscript of the *Alethia* (*Par. lat.* 7558, *saec.* IX) gives Victor and Victorius. The name Victorius is preferred today (Hovingh in the CCL and the CPL 1455) over Victor (Schenkl in the CSEL). A married layman and an orator by profession, Victorius was a contemporary of Prudentius and died, according to Gennadius, between 425 and 450. The reference to the Alani and the vigorous defense of free will suggest that the composition of the *Alethia* is to be dated between 420 and 440. Furthermore, Gennadius mentions four books (in some manuscripts three), while only three are extant today, although the third book contains the *explicit* of book four and does not include the death of Abraham but concludes with the destruction of Sodom and Gomorrah (Gen. 19:28). Some scholars (Gagny, Ceillier, Clément) have proposed the *Epistola ad Salmonem (= Epigramma Paulini)*, which follows the *Alethia* in the manuscripts, as the fourth book, while others (Schenkl) suppose that there were originally only three books. The reference of Gennadius ("three" of certain manuscripts could have been introduced by a scribe who was familiar with an already mutilated manuscript), the *explicit* and Victorius' intention as stated in the *Precatio* (v. 106) all indicate that the fourth book has been lost. There is no reference to Victorius' son Etherius in the entire *Alethia,* but it is possible that the initial dedication has been lost. Nevertheless, there is an explicit didactic intention (*Precatio* 104f: *dum teneros formare animos et corda paramus / ad verum virtutis iter puerilibus animis*). Indecent episodes are either avoided (the daughters of Lot, Gen. 19:31-38) or given a brief treatment (the vices of the inhabitants of Sodom), and the reader's pardon is requested (*Alethia* 3, 695ff).

The *Alethia* (the name is a latinized form of the Greek ἀλήθεια = truth) begins with a long and fervent prayer (126 verses) which is both a profession of faith (*in tribus esse deum, sed tres sic credimus unum,* v. 5) and a glorification of God's creating and conserving power. The author makes his entreaty that even in the imprecision of verse there be no danger to faith (v. 119-122), and concludes in a certain liturgical style. Book I (523 verses) covers the first three chapters of Genesis from the creation to the expulsion of Adam and Eve from the earthly paradise. Book II (457 verses) takes in another four chapters concerning the sin of Cain as well as Noah and the Flood, while book III (741 verses) treats chapters 8-19, including Noah and his descendants, Abraham and the destruction of Sodom and Gomorrah.

Victorius, who was endowed with a good classical formation, is not content merely with setting the biblical text to verse like Iuvencus, but he explains and amplifies the narrative and introduces material of his own drawn from various traditions and legends. He refutes the atomistic doctrine (I 22-32) and the astrology which was widespread in Gaul (III 139-148). He gives a series of interpretations, such as that in the beginning God created only the genera (I 171f) and that when God pronounced the sentence of condemnation the earth trembled and Tartarus was formed (I 474). The construction of the Ark lasted a hundred years in order to allow an opportunity for repentance, but men became yet more guilty (II 425-433). Adam and Eve were not clothed because their eyes were turned toward heaven and they were not concerned with the affairs of the flesh (I 423-428), but sin weakened the body and they began to notice cold and heat (I 434-438). He embarks on numerous digressions such as that on polytheism, begun by Nimrod, who was so grieved by the loss of his son that he erected an altar to him and offered him worship, thus giving a terrible example (III 170-209). The longest digression, a beautiful description of man's condition after his expulsion from paradise, is found at the beginning of book II. Adam finds himself confronted with a hostile world and remembers the fruitfulness of the soil of paradise. Victorius develops here a theory of civilization deriving from Lucretius. The serpent-tempter returns, and when Adam and Eve attempt to stone him, sparks fly from the rocks and set the forest ablaze, providing for the invention of fire.

Gennadius accuses Victorius of a certain theological ignorance; an accusation which, though severe, is partly true. Victorius preserves many ideas from the best of pagan tradition, especially from Platonism. He defends human freedom, the true glory of man which imparts value to human actions (*Precatio* 69-71; I 328-331). Creation itself receives meaning only in relation to man, for in themselves things have no glory. Man, the *spectator avidus* (cf. I 155f) is the goal of creation: *possesio nulla est si rerum possessor abest* (I 157). Plinval accused Victorius of Semi-Pelagianism, although this accusation was rejected by Ferrari and, more recently, by Hovingh.

Victorius imitates and draws abundantly from pagan sources such as Ovid, Vergil, and especially Lucretius, as well as from Christian models such as Lactantius, Prudentius, Ambrose, Augustine and the *Carmen de Providentia divina.* His language and style are sufficiently correct, even if his expressions are at times obscure and difficult to translate. There are passages of true poetic merit, especially in his descriptions. The work was not destined to have a wide circulation, perhaps because of Gennadius' judgment and because of a content which contributed little to edification. The *Decretum gelasianum* does not mention it. A. Mai attributed to Victorius also the poem *De nativitate vita passione et resurrectione Domini* (*Classici auctores e Vat. cod. ed.* Rome 1833, p. 385).

Editions: PL 61, 937-972 (ed. Gagny). — C. Schenkl, CSEL 16(1888)335-498. — P. F. Hovingh, CCL 128(1960)111-198 (best edition).

Translations: Dutch: A. Staat, De cultuurbeschouwing van Cl. M. Victor. Comm. op. Alethìa II, 1-202. Amsterdam, 1952 (first part of book II). *French:* P. F. Hovingh, Cl. Marius Victorius. Alethìa, La prière et les vers 1-170 du livre I. Gronigen, 1955 (intro. and commentary).

Studies: A. Bourgoin, De Cl. M. Victore rhetore christiano quinti saeculi. Paris, 1883. — S. Gamber, Un rhéteur chrétien au Ve siècle. Marseille, 1884. — C. Pascal, Sopra alcuni passi delle Metamorfosi ovidiane imitati dai primi scrittori cristiani: RFIC 37(1909)1-6. — F. E. Robbins, The Hexaemeral Literature. A Study of the Greek and Latin Commentaries on Genesis. Chicago, 1912. — F. Falcidia Riggio, Cl. M. Vittore, retore e poeta. Saggio critico. Nicosia, 1912. — O. Ferrari, Un poeta cristiano del quinto secolo: Cl. M. Vittore. Pavia, 1912 (fundamental work); *idem,* Intorno alle fonti del poema di C. M. Vittore: Did 1(1912)57-74. — A. H. Krappe, A Persian Myth in the Alethìa of C. M. Victor: SJMS 17(1942)255-260. — G. Bardy, DTC 15(1948)2877-2880. — D. R. S. Bailey, Echoes of Propertius: Mnem 5(1952)307-333. — P. F. Hovingh, La fumée du sacrifice de Caïn et Abel et l'Alethìa de C. M. Victorius: VC 10(1956)43-48; *idem,* Cl. M. Victorius, Alethìa 1, 188: VC 13(1969)187-189; *idem,* A propos de l'édition de Cl. M. Victorius, parue dans le CCL: SE 11(1960)193-211. — H. Silvestre, Loci paralleli entre l'Alethìa de C. M. Victorius et la Consolation de Boèce: SE 13(1962)517-518. — A. Hudson-Williams, Notes on Cl. M. Victor: CQ 14(1964)296-310; *idem,* Ne ἅπαξ quidem λεγόμενον: *Eranos* 61(1963)176-177. — J. M. Duval, Un texte du Ve siècle relatif au santuaire apollinien des Leuci, in Miscel. Renard, II. Brussels 1969, 256-261. — J. M. Evans, Paradise Lost and the Genesis Tradition. Oxford-London, 1968. — H. H. Horney, Studium sur Alethìa des M. Victorius (poëma de Gen. 1-19). Diss., Bonn, 1972 (cf. *Boll. Studie Latini* 4[1974]312-314). — K. Smolak, Unentdeckte Lukrezspuren: WSt 8(1974)216-273. — M. D. Metzger, Marius Victorius and the Substantive Infinitive: *Eranos* 72(1974)65-67. — R. Herzog, Die Bibelepik der lateinischen Spätantike. Munich, 1975.

SEDULIUS

Only the briefest information is available concerning this poet, who was much esteemed in the Middle Ages as well as in modern times.

His name, *Caelius* or *Coelius,* is found only in the more recent manuscripts and is lacking in the first editions. Some manuscripts (e.g., the *Gothanus, saec.* VIII) contain an inscription stating that he was an orator and *laicus,* a student of philosophy in Italy, who at the advice of the presbyter Macedonius taught metrics and who composed two books in verse in Achaia at the time of Valentinian III and Theodosius II (425-450). The poet himself, in the dedicatory letter of his *Carmen* to Macedonius, makes brief references, which partially confirm the information from the manuscripts, to his "conversion" from the practice of pagan letters (Was he a pagan or a nominal Christian?). The information concerning his place of birth and residence is of a relatively recent date. The *cod. Marcianus* of Venice describes him as *genere italicus,* which is confirmed by Adelmo, who writes *Romae urbis indigena.* The thesis of Sigerson, who on the basis of Trithemius (*Script. eccl.* 142) considers that he was Irish *(scotus)* and offers an incredible description of the poet's life, is pure fantasy.

The chronology provided by the manuscripts seems to be reliable and is supported by corroborating arguments. Sedulius is quoted by poets and writers of the second half of the fifth century, such as Paulinus of Périgueux, Avitus, Dracontius, Ennodius, etc. According to the testimony of certain manuscripts, Turcius Rufus Asterius, consul in 494 and editor of Vergil (Medici codex of Vergil), was responsible for the publication of the *Carmen* (probably a new edition). In the same manuscripts is found an epigram which refers to the edition and commends the poem (*Anthologia latina* I, 2, 491; CSEL 10, 307). The *Decretum gelasianum* at the end of the fifth century praises the work of Sedulius, who is not mentioned by Gennadius, and describes him as *vir venerabilis* (34, allusion to priesthood). Liberius Bellisarius, a sixth-century poet, gives him the title of *antistes* (*Anthologia latina* I, 2, 492-493; CSEL 10, 307-310), while Isidore of Seville calls him *presbyter* (*De vir. ill.* 20: PL 83, 1094). For these reasons it seems that he was a priest and carried out the functions of cantor in the liturgical celebrations (*Carmen* I, 23-26). Apart from the ambiguous *antistes* of Liberius, the information that he was a bishop is repeated by Alcuin (PL 101, 609B) and by Sigebert of Gembloux (PL 160, 549A), who in fact dates him at the time of the sons of Constantine; but this information is of too late a date to be reliable. The *ministra,* Syncletica, for whom Sedulius employed such expressions of esteem and praise and to whom he had considered dedicating the *Carmen,* was still alive at this time. Most likely she is to be identified with Syncletica, the sister of Eustathius, who translated Basil's *Hexaemeron* into Latin in Italy toward the end of the fourth century. Furthermore, Sedulius speaks of Jerome, *divinae legis interpretis et caelestis bibliothecae cultoris* (*Ad Maced.;* Huemer 8, 10f) in such a way that it seems he was already dead (419-420). It has been noted, too, that the poet speaks of Sabellianism and Arianism, but does not mention Nestorianism. All of these factors, as well as the language and metrical structure of his poetry, indicate that he is to be located in Italy during the first half of the fifth century between 420 and 430.

Paschale carmen is the name the poet himself, drawing his inspiration from Saint Paul; *pascha nostrum immolatus est Christus* (*Ep. ad Maced.;* ed. Huemer 19, 9f), gave to the poem which was intended to praise the *mirabilia* of the Savior. Sedulius divided the work into four books, possibly because he considered book I, on the Old Testament, as an introduction. Isidore of Seville, however, speaks of three books (*De vir. ill.* 20: PL 83, 1094); a tradition which is confirmed by some manuscripts (i.e., 1-2, 3-4, 5). The normal division in the printed editions is in five books.

In order to understand the poem, it is necessary to keep in mind the ideas expressed by Sedulius in the dedicatory letter addressed to Macedonius, a priest whom he esteemed and revered. It is possible, however, that Macedonius is only a literary fiction created by the author to justify his composition of the *Carmen* and the literary genre he employed. Sedulius says that, since he has turned to God from the vanities of worldly wisdom, he wants to place his talents, formerly employed in profane studies, at the service of good and to lead others to the truth. Furthermore, it seems to him a crime not to make use of the gifts given him by God. He turns to poetry because people do not tend to read prose *(rhetorica facundia)* but are rather attracted by the pleasure of verse. A poetic work, read over and over, impresses itself on the memory. This taste is not to be despised nor is the opportunity to be lost of drawing others to the faith.

The ideas of Sedulius are situated within the contemporary cultural debate on Christian *rusticitas,* which constituted a great obstacle to cultivated persons embracing Christianity (e.g., Augustine). Sedulius intended to avoid this difficulty and even considered himself a pioneer in this task: *raro, pater optime, . . . divinae munera potestatis stilo quisquam huius modulationis aptavit* (Huemer, 5, 2ff). There is found here a touch of pride, of literary vanity, and an overestimation of his artistic capacities. Epic poetry is only a means, an instrument at the service of the faith, and he felt the need to justify himself before possible detractors and critics.

In the first verses of the poem too, in other terms, he gives the reasons for his poetic compositions: if the pagans make use of the poetic art to praise their literary fictions, why should he, who is accustomed to making the ten-stringed lyre resound to the songs of David and to standing reverently in the choir, be silent about the renowned feats of the savior?

In the first book, after these verses, Sedulius addresses a prayer to God for divine guidance and thus extols the divine creative power which orders and guides the entire universe. The numerous *mirabilia* of the Old Testament speak of such a power. He then goes on to narrate the wonders of the New Law and ventures to criticize Arius and give an exposition of the orthodox faith. After a reference to Original Sin, the second book goes on to present the infancy of Jesus, his baptism, the choice of the Apostles and a long commentary on the *Pater* (231-300). The third and fourth books deal with the miracles of Jesus, drawn mostly from Matthew, and with the content of some of his discourses. The fifth and longest book goes from the Last Supper to the Ascension.

Sedulius himself, in a scholastic exercise much in vogue at the time, transcribed the *Paschale carmen* into a prose composition entitled *Opus: priores igitur libri, qui versu digesti sunt, nomen Paschalis carminis acceperunt, sequentes autem in prosam nulla cursus varietati conversi, Paschalis designantur operis vocabulo nuncupati* (Huemer 173, 16-19). The question has been raised as to the reason for this *translatio* (2 *Ad Maced.;* Huemer 172, 5). Some scholars believe that Sedulius was reprimanded by Macedonius for reasons of doctrinal clarity or because he had treated the sacred text too freely. In the second letter to Macedonius he makes reference to the latter's request: *Praecepisti . . . paschalis carminis textum . . . in rhetoricum me trasferre sermonem* (Huemer 171, 3-5), but he does not mention the motive for the request, whether he had been pleased with the work or whether he had written *stilo . . . liberiore.* Curtius judges the latter motive as highly improbable as it presupposes the sensitivity of Macedonius. Iuvencus was not reprimanded for his "harmonization" of the Gospels. Furthermore, the *Opus* has used the same liberty as the *Carmen* with regard to the Scriptures. It is not a question of a total revision of the work, but only the *sermo* has changed while the ideas and content remain the same; it is a question of form rather than of content.

Theological reasons are certainly not behind this transcription. Sedulius himself justifies the double edition only by citing previous examples and not by adducing other motives. More than once he makes a profession of humility, but it is possible to read between the lines a complacency with his literary skills which allow him to compose the same thing both in poetry and in prose.

Unlike the *Opus,* of which few manuscripts have survived, the *Carmen* was a scholastic text in the Middle Ages and was found in all monastic libraries. During the Renaissance, Sedulius came to be called the *christianissimus poeta* even by Luther (P. Drews, *Disput. M. Luthers.* Göttingen 1895, p. 588). Sigerson has counted 75 editions of the Carmen up to 1886.

Sedulius handled the biblical text with a greater liberty than other poets, often made recourse to allegorical explanations and twice cited apocryphal works. He does not hesitate to express his feelings and thoughts. As a *scholasticus* he manifests a clear didactic tendency aimed at edification and makes ample use of rhetorical rules and an oratorical tone. Since he was formed on the classics (Vergil, Ovid, Lucanus, Claudianus) his language and syntax are largely correct. All of these traits rendered him suitable for use in the schools. He is undoubtedly the best among the versifiers of the Bible.

Two other poetic compositions of Sedulius have been preserved. The first (*cantemus, socii . . .*) is an elegy of 55 distichs in an epanaleptic scheme: at the end of the second verse there is repeated a word already used in the first half of the preceding verse of the distich. This elegy is a brief history of salvation which begins with the sin of Adam and interprets Christologically the episodes of the Old Testament, finally ending with the marvels and the life of Christ. The work finishes with a Trinitarian conclusion.

The second composition is a very famous hymn *(A solis ortus cardine)* of 23 verses in iambic dimeters on an alphabetical scheme. It is a hymn to Christ of his life and miracles and of his saving deed for men. The hymn has been taken over into the liturgy with verses A - G (7) used at Christmas, and verses H - I - L - N (in some hymnals also verses K and M) at Epiphany, while some rites give the entire poem. The hymn is also used on other feasts.

Editions: PL 19, 549-752 (The texts of the *Carmen* and of the *Opus* are printed on the same page; from Arévalo's edition with its useful notes). — *Hymns:* PL 19, 753-770. — J. Huemer, CSEL 10(1885). — G. Dreves, Analecta hymnica I. Leipzig 1907, 53-60. — A. S. Walpole, Early Latin Hymns. Cambridge 1922, 151-158 (reprint, Hildesheim, 1966).

Translations: Dutch: N. Schefs, Sedulius Paschale Carmen, boek I en II. Delft, 1938. *English:* G. Sigerson, The Easter Song of Sedulius. Dublin, 1922. — R. A. Swanson, Carmen Paschale I: CJ 52(1957)289-298. — A. J. O. J. Kuhnmuench, Early Christian Latin Poets. Chicago 1929, 252-272 (excerpts). *Italian:* F. Corsaro, L'opera poetica di Sedulis. Catania, 1948; *idem,* Sedulio poeta. Catania, 1956.

Studies: C. Caesar, Die Antwerpener Hs. des Sedulius: RhM 56(1901)247-271 (saec. X). — J. Candel, Un vouveau manuscrit de l'"Opus Paschale" de Sedulius: *Rev. phil. Litt. hist. an.* 28(1904)283-292; *idem,* De clausolis a Sedulio in eis libris qui iscribuntur Paschale Opus adhibitis. Toulouse, 1904. — J. van den Gheyn, Les feuillets de garde du ms. 246 de la bibliothèque de l'Université de Gand: *Rev. des Bibliot. Arch. Belg.* 5(1907)415-419. — S. De Ricci, Inventaire sommaire des mss du Musée Palatin d'Anvers: *Rev. des Bibliot.* 20(1910)231 (ms. saec. X). — J. Loth, Glosses bretonnes inédites du IX siècles: *Revue celtique* 33(1912)417-431. — H. Nestler, Studien über die Messiade des Iuvencus. Diss., Munich-Passau, 1910. — P. Th. Mayr, Studien zu dem Paschale Carmen des christlichen Dichters Sedulius. Munich 1916 (fundamental work). — W. Meyer, Rhytmische Paraphrase des Sedulius von einem Iren: NGWG(1917)589-624. — H. Brewer, Der zeitliche Ursprung und der Verfasser des Moneschen Messen: ZkTh 43(1919)697. — C. Weyman, Der Preis der Gottesmutter bei Sedulius, VII: Sedulius und "gute Schächer": MM 3(1923)186-189; *idem,* Sedulius über Judas: MM

4(1924)289-291. — A. D. McDonald, The Iconographic Tradition of Sedulius: *Speculum* 8(1933)150-156. — K. B. Gladysz, De extremis quibus Sedulliana carmina ornantur verborum syllabis inter se consonantibus: Eos Suppl 17(1934) (extensive bibliography). — H. Meritt, Old English Sedulius Glosses from 8th-9th cent. mss at Corpus Christi College, Cambridge: AJPh 57(1936)140-150. — N. R. Ker, British Museum, Burney mass: *Brit. Mus. Quat.* 12(1938)134-135 (mss.). — N. Schefs, Sedulius' Paschale Carmen. Delft, 1938. — G. R. Manton, The Cambridge Ms. of Sedulius' Carmen Paschale: JThSt 40(1939)365-370. — H. Meritt, The Context for Some Latin Words in the Harleion Glossary: AJPh 62(1941)331-334. — B. Altaner, Eustathius, der lateinische Übersetzer der Hexaëmeron-Homilien Basilius des Grossen: ZNW 39(1941)162-168 (Syncletica is sister of Eustathius). — F. Corsaro, Sedulio. Catania, 1945; *idem,* La poesia di Sedulio, Catania 1945, 1949[2]; *idem,* La lingua di Sedulio. Catania 1949; *idem,* Sedulio poeta. Catania, 1956. — P. Courcelle, Fragmentes non identifiés de Fleury-sur-Loire: REAug 2(1956)447-455. — W. Jungandreas, Die Runen des Codex seminarii Trevirensis R. III, 61: TThZ 30(1967)161-169. — H. Luelfing, Ein Brief Siegmund Hellmanns am Emil Jacob zur Seduliusüberlieferung: Phil 115(1971)179-182. — A. Bastiaenses, L'antienne Genuit puerpera regem, adaptation liturgique du Pasch. Carmen des Sedulius: RB 83(1973)388-397. — C. Tibiletti, Note al testo del Paschale Carmen di Sedulio, in *Forma Futuri,* Misc. Pellegrino. Turin 1975, 778-785. — R. Herzog, Die Bibelepik der lateinischen Spätantike. Munich, 1975. — I. Opelt, Die Szenerie bei Sedulius: JAC 19(1976)109-119.

ORIENTIUS

Orientius is the name which the poem itself (*Comm.* 2, 417) and the manuscript containing it give to the author of a poetic composition known as the *Commonitorum,* which has to be subsequent to the *Carmen de Providentia* composed around 415 in southern Gaul (*Carm. de Prov.* 35-38 = *Comm.* 2, 167-172). The first writer to mention Orientius is Venantius Fortunatus (*Vita s. Martini* 1, 17: PL 88, 366) in the second half of the sixth century, who locates him between Sedulius and Prudentius. Other subsequent notices concerning him are of no value. Paul the Deacon quotes one of his verses, which was often quoted in the Middle Ages, without knowing the author (*Comm.* 1, 567 = *Hom. de tempore* 153: PL 95, 1347). Orientius definitely lived in Gaul (*Comm.* 2, 184), which had been devastated by the numerous barbarian invasions of the fifth century. He speaks at length of these incursions but does not name the invaders (*Comm.* 2, 165-202). We have a summary knowledge of the life (there exist three biographies) of a certain Orientius, bishop of *Augusta Ausciorum* (Auch, in Gascony), who in 439 acted as intermediary between the king of the Visigoths and the Roman generals Aetius and Lictorius. The biography reports that Orientius, after having abandoned the changeable things of this world, had dedicated himself totally to God, and that he was an educated man who was completely engaged in the conversion and instruction of his people (ASS, Mai I, 61A). These ideas recur often in the *Commonitorium.* The author often refers to the fact that he is a sinner (1, 611; 2, 393-402, 417-418) and that his purpose is that of instructing (1, 16-18). The identification of the poet with this bishop of Auch is commonly accepted today, in spite of some valid objections. The biography, although it states he was a bishop, is silent about his literary activity, while the *inscriptio* of the manuscript makes no mention of the episcopacy. Both sources however agree in calling him a saint. He is not mentioned by Gennadius of Marseilles or by Isidore of Seville.

The *Commonitorium* — the name does not come from the manuscript but was given by the first editor, Delrio, in 1600 — is composed of 518 elegiac distichs in two books (309 and 209 verses). Some have proposed that the title be changed to *Monita,* a word which occurs frequently in the text, but it is better to leave the present title *Commonitorium,* which was a common term in the fifth century, in preference to the more generic *monita.* The work is a long exhortation to live the Christian life: *vita docenda mihi est, vita petenda tibi* (1, 16), and for this reason the author addresses an invocation to Christ that his teaching may be efficacious (1, 17-42). The life of man is characterized by a dual aspect; the first being earthly, brief and fragile, inclining toward evil and toward pilgrimage in the second, which is heavenly, eternal and founded in God (1, 43-64). Man must honor God, the giver of every good thing, not with externals but with his own life and with his love for others (1, 65-256). The resurrection (*vivet homo* 1, 299) conducts man to glory or to the just punishment for his crimes. The poem dwells at length on the various vices: lust, envy, greed (*radix causa caput fons et origo mali* 1, 490), pride, falsehood, gluttony, and drunkenness. It is possible that he is dependent on Cassian for his description of these vices (*Coll.* 5 Abbatis Serapionis). The themes of the inevitability of death and of the divine judgment occur constantly in order to render the exhortation more effective.

Orientius speaks with sincerity and humility, and is completely taken up in giving counsels and teachings. The *Commonitorium* is a homily in verse. The author is not concerned with theological issues and makes only a brief reference to faith in the Trinity (2, 403-406). The poem is concerned totally with moral doctrine and with the exhortation to a good life in order to receive a divine reward. The examples employed by Orientius are taken almost exclusively from the Bible, and he draws his inspiration from the Scriptures, Lactantius, and Hilary, while at the same time giving evidence of a good classical foundation. His ideal is peace with all people (1, 593-618): *pacem placatus, pacem quoque laesus amato: pax in visceribus, pax sit in ore tuo* (1, 613f).

Although Orientius is not a great poet, his originality is evident in his many descriptive passages and his verses are generally well constructed, but with frequent use of rhyme. Plinval (*Pélage,* Lausanne 1943, p. 240) notices traces of Pelagianism, but only in regard to the moral teaching and not the theology. The *Commonitorium* is preserved in a single manuscript, the *Turonensis* (Paris, Bibl. Nat. *Nouv. acq. lat.* 457), which also contains other poetic compositions of dubious authenticity: the *De nativitate Domini* (epigram of 7 hexameters), the *De epithetis Salvatoris* (5 distichs), the *De Trinitate* (95 hexameters; of interest for the symbolism of the cross), the *Explanatio nominum Domini* (51 hexameters; explanation of Christological titles), the *Laudatio* (33 hexameters; a continuation of the preceding together with a concluding prayer), and two *orationes* (part of a collection of 24) in stanzas of 5 iambic verses (7 + 6). The *De Trinitate,* the *Explanatio* and the *Laudatio* form a certain literary and thematic unity, for which reason they are regarded by some as one single poem (Ellis and Rapisarda have edited them with a progressive numeration of the verses).

Editions: PL 61, 977-1006 (Gallandi). — R. Ellis, CSEL 16(1881)191-261. — L. Bellanger, Le poème d'Orientius. Paris-Toulouse 1903. — M. D. Tobin, PSt 74 (1945) (text of Ellis). — C. A. Rapisarda, Orientii Comm., Carmina Orientio tributa. Catania, 1958, 1970[2]. (Only the text: ND 10[1960]xii-36.)

Translations: English: M. D. Tobin, op. cit. *Italian:* C. A. Rapisarda, op. cit.

Studies: L. Havet: *Rev. phil. litt. hist. anc.* 26(1902)149-157. — P. Lahargou, Saint Orient, évêque et poète du cinquième siècle. Dax, 1902. — L. Bellanger, Étude sur le poème d'Orientius. Toulouse, 1902 (fundamental work). — R. Ellis, The Comm. of Orientius. A Lecture. Oxford, 1903. — L. Bellanger, Le poème d'Orientius. Paris-Toulouse, 1903 (a revision and extension of the work listed above); *idem,* Recherches sur saint Orence, évêque d'Auche: *Bull. Soc. Archéol. du Gers.* Auch, 1903. — L. Guérard, Les derniers traveaux sur St. Orens: *Rev. de Gascogne* 44(1903)385-396, 45(1904)97-115. — L. C. Purser, M. Bellanger's Orientius: *Hermathena* 13(1904)36-69. — C. Pascal, Orientiana: BFC 12(1905-06)134-136. — F. Haverfield, Recent Literature on Orientius: CR 19(1905)126-128 (review of Bellanger, Ellis, Guerard). — H. Delahaye: AB 24(1905)147-149 (review of Lahargou, Bellanger, Guerard). — C. Pascal, Sopra alcuni passi delle metamorfosi ovidiane imitati dai primi scrittori cristiani: RFIC 37(1909)1-6. — C. Weyman, Lexikalische Notizen: *Glotta* 3(1912)193. — F. R. Montgomery Hitchcock, Notes on the Comm. of Orientius: CR 28(1914)41-42. — P. Thomas, Observations ad Orientium: Mnem 49(1921)69-70. — U. Moricca, Observationum in aliquot Orientii . . . carminum locos specimen: Did 5(1927)31-33. — M. Galdi, Orientiana: *Athenaeum* 6(1928)32-47. — A. Hudson-Williams, Orientius and Lactantius: VC 3(1949)32-47; *idem,* Notes on Orientius' Comm I: CQ 43(1949)130-137; *idem,* Notes on Orientius' Comm. II: CQ 44(1950)25-30, 120; *idem,* Imitative Echoes and Textual Criticism: CQ 9(1959)67-68. — H. MacL. Currie, Notes de Lecture: Latomus 16(1957)141 (*Comm.* I, 493-494). — G. Brugnoli, L'oltretomba in O.: Orpheus 4(1957)131-137 (important study). — C. A. Rapisarda, Introduzione critica ad Orienzio con bibliografia: ND 8(1958)1-78; *idem,* Due note al testo del Comm. di O., in Misc. *Convivium dominicum.* Catania 1959, 407-413. — F. Sciuto, Tertulliano e O., ibid., 415-422; *idem,* Ancora su Tertulliano e O.: MSCI 9(1959)25-32. — B. Luiselli, Orientiana: *Atene e Roma* 6(1961)173-180. — P. Courcelle, Histoire litteraire des grandes invasiones germaniques. Paris 1964[3], 98-100. — F. Sgarlata, Nota orienziana: *Helikon* 9-10(1969)695-697 (*Comm.* II, 225f). — K. Smolak, Poetische Ausdrüke im sogenannten ersten Gebet des Orientius: WSt 8(1974)188-200 (expressions of Plautus, Ovid and Lucretius). — D. R. S. Bailey, Emendations of the "Commonitorium" of Orientius: CPh 72(1977) 130-133.

AGRESTIUS

In the Bibliothèque Nationale at Paris there is a manuscript (*Cod. lat.* 8093, *saec.* VIII-IX) containing a poem of 49 verses with the title, *Versus Agresti ep. de fide ad Avitum ep.* There are various persons of the fifth century with the name Avitus, including three contemporaries of Orosius at Braga (CSEL 18, 155-157), one of whom was a good friend of Jerome (*Ep.* 124: PL 22, 1059-1072). On the other hand, only one Agrestius is known from the fifth century, while another was bishop of Tours in the mid–sixth-century. Hydatius noted in his Chronicle (ed. Tranoy, SCh 218, Paris, 1974, n. 102) for the year 433 that "in the district of Lugo, Pastor and Syagrius were ordained bishops against the will of Agrestius, bishop of Lugo." In 441, the same Agrestius signed the Acts of the Council of Orange (ed. Munier, CCL 148, 1963, 87.17). Smolak's careful and detailed analysis has shown that the poem was composed in a Franco-Spanish region around the middle of the fifth century. The text is also found in the famous Visigothic Latin manuscript (the first part of which is at Paris) which contains many works of Spanish origin preserved only in this manuscript. The content of the poem, which is a profession of faith, lends credence to the information provided by Hydacius, who seems to imply that Agrestius had Priscillianist leanings and thus could have intended the poem as an attempt to justify himself. All indications point to the identification of the author with Agrestius, bishop of Lugo and thus decisively oppose the opinion of Dekkers (CPL 1463), who identifies the poet with Agrecius, bishop of Sens (*Sinones*) in Gaul in the middle of the fifth century.

The structure of the poem is that of a didactic letter, with the title, preface and profession of faith before the community. The author begins by greeting his friend, Avitus, and thanking him for the benefits he has received and then launches on a long digression of a personal and literary character. In the body of the poem he gives the profession of faith which in some way had been requested of him: faith in the Trinity, God as Creator of all things from nothing (with a long description of creation and the transgression of Eve). The *De fide,* with its dependence on the *Georgics* of Vergil, has almost the character of a cento with its proper use of meter. It is possible that Agrestius composed the work to defend himself against charges of sympathy for Priscillianism, which was strong in Galicia at that time. Pastor and Syagrius were uncompromising adversaries of this heresy, and it is probably on account of this that they were opposed by Agrestius. The poem, which has long been known in an incomplete form, was published only recently. Within a short time, two editions have appeared: that of A. C. Vega in 1966 and the edition by K. Smolak, which is the better of the two, in 1973.

Editions: PLS V, 400-401. — A. C. Vega, Un poema inédito tutulado "De fide" de Agrestio, obispo de Lugo, siglo V: *Boletín de la R. Academia de la Historia* 159(1966)167-209. — K. Smolak, Das Gedicht des Bischofs Agrestius. Eine theologische Lehrepistel aus der Spätantike. Einleitung, Text, Übersetzung und Kommentar: SAW 2(1973).

PAULINUS OF PELLA

Nearly everything that is known concerning Paulinus, known also as the Penitent, comes from his autobiographical poem, the *Eucharisticos*. He was born at Pella (Macedonia) at the end of 376 or beginning of 377 while his father was *vicarius* of that imperial diocese, and then at the age of nine months he moved to Carthage, where his father held the office of proconsul for 18 months. Following this, he passed through Rome and, together with his family, settled in Burdigala (Bordeaux), which was the native country of his parents. It was here that Paulinus pursued his studies, which had to be interrupted for reasons of health. Since he was accustomed to speaking Greek, he encountered difficulties in his study of Latin (*Euch.* 72-84). He married at age twenty. As a member of the Gallic upper-middle class, he suffered much from the Gothic invasions and, since he had in some way collaborated with the invaders (he had the nominal title of head of finances under the usurper Attalus in 414), he was also the object of the revenge of the Gallo-Romans. He, therefore, retired to Bazas (*Vasates*), the land of his ancestors where he possessed some property which subsequently he lost together with his holdings at Bordeaux. His "conversion," i.e., his return to the faith of his childhood, took place in 421-422. He passed the final decades of his life at Marseilles, where he owned a small estate. Nevertheless, it seems that at the end of his life he returned to his adopted city (v. 572-574 are in the past tense). He died sometime after 459. On his mother's side, Paulinus was the nephew of the poet Ausonius, who, however, never mentions him. It cannot be ruled out that Paulinus was born of a previous marriage of his father, Talassius.

The *Eucharisticos* is an autobiographical poem which was published in 459 when the author was 83 (v. 12f). According to Courcelle, the essential nucleus of the poem was composed in 455, and the verses 1-23 and 564-616 were added in 459. The *Eucharisticos* (λόγος is implied) designates the poem as one of thanksgiving: *Eucharisticos Deo sub ephemeridis meae textu* = "Thanksgiving to God woven from the account of my life." The author, as he states in the preface, does not in any way intend to narrate his biography for the curiosity of others, but rather to give thanks to God who has always protected and guided him. God has watched over him, at times by means of trials (v. 431f; 438ff, 457-550), but especially by means of His special protection in various circumstances (v. 22f, 150ff, 173ff).

triclinium of the imperial palace at Ravenna in a *nymphaeum* which had been transformed into a baptistry. This hypothesis, however, is unacceptable. The third fragment (8 verses) describes a garden and the fourth (46 hendecasyllables) was written to celebrate the first birthday of Aetius' son, Gaudentius, in 442. All of these fragments were discovered in 1823 by Niehbur in a palimpsest of the fifth or sixth century at Sankt Gall.

The poem *De Christo,* published by Camers in 1510 with the works of Claudianus, was published under the name of Merobaudes by Fabricius in 1564, who followed the inscription of the manuscript he was using. In spite of some uncertainties, Fabricius' attribution has gained general acceptance. More recently, S. Gennaro has been able to demonstrate a close relation between the secular poems of Merobaudes, which are rich in mythology, and the *De Christo* on the basis of similarities in form, expression and rhetorical ornamentation. Furthermore, Christian motifs and attitudes contained already in the poems *natalicii* are made more explicit in the *De Christo,* which marks a continuation and a development in the poetic world of Merobaudes. The poem is orthodox in its Christology: Christ is truly the Son of God, is eternal yet born in time, is the Creator together with the Father, and became incarnate to reveal the true countenance of God, of which event his mother, the shepherds and the Magi were the first witnesses. His Incarnation is our means of salvation and his death the cause of our life. Merobaudes, who imitated Prudentius, was in turn imitated both by Elpidius Rusticus and by Dracontius.

Editions: F. Vollmer, MGH, AA 14. Berlin 1905, 1-20; the *De Christo* is also found in PL 53, 789-790; PL 61, 971-974. — M. Ihm, Damasi Epigrammata. Leipzig 1895, 71-73. — F. Bücheler, A. Riese, Anthologia Lat. I, 2. Leipzig 1906, 327-328, n. 878.

Translations: English: F. M. Clover, TP 51, 1. Philadelphia, 1971. *Hungarian:* Th. Olajos, Merobaudes Müvei: *Antik Tanulmányok* 13(1966)172-188.

Studies: A. Testi-Rasponi, Frammenti poetici de Merobaude: *Felix Ravenna* 31(1926)43-47. — F. Lot, Un diplôme de Clovis confirmatif d'une donation de patrice romain: RBPh 17(1938)906-911. — A. Loyen, Recherches historiques sur les panégyriques de Sidoine Apollinaire. Paris, 1942. — S. Gennaro, Da Claudiano a Merobaude. Aspetti della poesia cristiana di Merobaude: MSLC 8(1958) (fundamental work). — A. V. Sirago, Galla Placidia e la trasformazione politica d'Occidente. Louvain, 1961. — K. F. Stroheker, Spanische Senatoren der spatrömischen und westgotischen Zeit: *Madrider Mitteilungen* 4(1963)107-132 (= Germanentum und Spätantike, Zurich 1965, 54-87). — S. I. Oost, Some Problems in the History of Galla Placidia: CPh 60(1965)1-10. — S. Monti, Per l'esegesi dei carmi 1 e 2 di Merobaude: *Ren. R. Acc. Arch. Lett. Belle Arti,* Naples, Ser. 2, 41(1966)3-21. — Th. Olajos, PWK Sup. 12(1970)863-866. — M. M. Clover, Toward an Understanding of Merobaudes, Panegyric I: *Historia* 20(1971)354-367. — Th. Olajos, L'inscription de la statue d'Aetius et Merobaudes, in *Acta V Cong. Inter Epig. Gr. La.,* Oxford 1971, 469-472. — A. Loyen, L'œuvre de Fl. Merobaudes et l'histoire de l'Occident de 430 à 450: REAN 74(1972)153-174. — T. D. Barnes,

Merobaudes on the Imperial Family: *Phoenix* 28(1974)314-319; *idem,* Patricii under Valentinian III: *Phoenix* 29(1975)155-170.

ANONYMOUS POEMS

1. *Laudes Domini.*

The same manuscript (*Paris.* 7558, *saec.* IX) which contains the *Alethia* of Cl. M. Victorius also contains a poem of 148 hexameters in the Vergilian style which is notable for its beautiful composition and unusually pure language. The anonymous poet narrates the account of a miracle which took place in the territory of the Haedui (modern Autun) in Gaul. A man had placed the body of his wife in a tomb large enough to permit him to be buried beside her. At the time of his death, when the tomb was opened, the woman raised her hand in a gesture of greeting to receive him. The author takes this as his cue to sing the *laudes* of Christ the *incorrupta Dei soboles,* the Creator along with the Father of all things (lengthy description, v. 36-88) who, having been sent as Lord and master of life, was born of a virgin and worked miracles. The poem closes with a prayer for the victorious Constantine and for his family. Gregory of Tours (*In gloria conf.* 75: PL 61, 882) refers to a similar incident in connection with Reticius, bishop of Autun at the beginning of the fourth century. The two accounts, however, differ with regard to the details.

The author of the *Laudes* has a good classical and biblical background. The poem, which was imitated by Iuvencus, was composed between 316-324 by an inhabitant of the region.

Editions: PL 6, 45-50; PL 19, 379-386 (ed. Arévalo); PL 61, 1091-1094 (ed. Fabricius). — W. Brandes, Über das frühchristliche Gedichte Laudes Domini. Braunschweig, 1887. — P. van der Weijden, Laudes Domini. Paris, 1967.

Translations: Dutch: P. van der Weijden, op. cit.

Studies: G. Bardy, Les "Laudes Domini" poème autunois du commencement du IVe siècle, in *Mémoires Ac. de Dijon* (1933). Dijon 1934, 36-51. — A. Frisone, Sancti poetae: *Helikon* 9-10(1969)673-676. — I. Opelt, Das Carmen "De laudibus Domini" als Zeugnis des Christentums bei den Gallen: *Romanobarbarica* 3(1978)159-166.

2. *Carmen contra paganos* (*Cod. Par.* 8084).

In the most ancient manuscript of Prudentius (Paris, Bib. Nat. *Par. lat.* 8084, *saec.* VI) there is an anonymous poem of 122 verses which was published for the first time in its entirety by Delisle in 1867. The poem, which attracted immediate attention, presents a passionate invective against the pagan cult in general (v. 1-24) and against a well-known figure of the time in particular. With insistent questions the poem addresses both this person as well as all pagans. It criticizes the ridiculous cult of the gods, their quarrels and their immodest life and uses irony in speaking of a personage recently deceased who was devoted to the various cults, especially that of Cybele. The poem is of little literary merit as the author allows himself to be so caught up in his biting sarcasm as to return to everyday speech. There are various implicit indications that the author was a Christian, such as the traditional motifs of Christian apologetic, the *verus deus* of v. 54 and the *christicolae* of v. 78.

Given the heat of the polemic, the author is certainly a contemporary of the person he is attacking. However the obscure language and the numerous allusions to precise situations which were understandable only in the contemporary context render it difficult to distinguish who is the object of the attack. Furthermore the mutilated and fragmentary state of the text render many interpretations dependent on hypothetical corrections. Morel, in 1868 ("Recherches sur un poème latin du IVe siècle, retrouvé par Delisle": *Revue Arch.*, June 1868, 451-459; July 1868, 44-55) proposed the following as likely candidates: V. Agorius Praetextatus, V. Nicomachus Flavianus, Symmachus the *praef. urbis* in 384, and G. B. Pompeianus, *praef. urbis* in 408-409. He finally settled on Nicomachus Flavianus (to whom is due the title of the poem: *Adv. Nicomachum, Adv. Flavianum*), and dated the poem to the end of 394 or the beginning of 395. This thesis was eruditely supported by De Rossi and Mommsen and became the common opinion. Ellis ("On a Recently Discovered Latin Poem of the Fourth Century": *Journal of Philol.* 1[1868]66-80) and Moricca opted for Praetextatus and in 1960 Manganaro came out in favor of Pompeianus. Recently, Mazzarino, in a careful and precise study, decisively proposed the elder Symmachus, *praef. urbis* in 364-365 and consul-designate for 377, who died in 376. Like other compositions which bear witness to the polemic between pagans and Christians (e.g., the *Ad quendam senatorem* and the *Poema ultimum,* no. 32 in the collection of Paulinus of Nola), the poem was composed at Rome.

Editions: Th. Mommsen: Hermes 4(1870)350-363 (= Gesammelte Schriften VII. Berlin 1909, 485-493; critical text of M. Haupt and G. Krüger). — E. Baehrens, Poetae latini minores III. Leipzig 1881, 287-292. — F. Buechler, A. Riese, Anthologia Latina I., Leipzig 1894, 20-25, n. 4. — PLS I, 780-784 (ed. Haupt-Krüger). — G. Manganaro: ND 11(1961)26-45. — F. Roncoroni: RSLR 8(1972)61-65.

Translations: Italian: G. Manganaro, op. cit.

Studies: Seefelder, Abhandlung über das Carmen adv. Flavianum. Gmünd, 1901. — C. Morelli, L'autore del cosiddetto poema ultimum attribuito a Paolino di Nola: Did 1(1912)481-498. — O. Barkowski, De carmine adv. Flavianum anonymo. Koenisberg, 1912. — U. Moricca, Il carme del cod. Paris 8084: Did 4(1926)94-107. — G. Manganaro, La reazione pagana a Roma nel 408-409 d. C. e il poemetto anonimo Contra paganos: *Giornale It. Filol.* 13(1960)210-224. — H. von Geisau: PWK Sup 10(1965)121-124. — D. Romano, Una interpretazione di Flaviano: *Annali Liceo cl. Garibaldi Palermo* 7-8(1970-71)105-114 (v. 55-56 refer to Flavianus). — J. F. Matthews,

The Historical Setting of the Carmen *contra paganos: Historia* 19(1970)464-479 (important study; V. N. Flavianus). — F. Roncoroni, Carmen codicis Par. 8084: RSLR 8(1972)58-72 (important for metrical, grammatical, and linguistic aspects). — G. Picone, Il problema della datazione del Liber prodigiorum di Giulio Oss.: *Pan. Studi Ist. Fil. lat.* 2(1974)71-77. — S. Mazzarino, Tolleranza e intolleranza: la polemica sull'ara della Vittoria, in *Antico, Tardoantico ed era costantiniana.* Bari 1974, 339-377; *idem,* Il carmen "contro i pagani" e il problema dell'era costantiniana, ibid., 398-465 (fundamental study, including the text). — C. Salemme, Nota al Carmen Codicis Parisini 8084, 23ff: *Bollettino Studi latini* 6(1976)91-93.

3. *Epigramma Paulini.*

In the *Codex Par. lat.* 7558, *saec* IX, together with the *Alethia* of Cl. Marius Victorius, there is found a poem of 110 hexameters entitled *Epigramma Paulini.* Jean de Gagny, who first edited the poem in 1536 from a manuscript of Lyons, now lost, attributed it to Victorius with the title: *Cl. M. Victoris . . . de perversis aetatis suae moribus. Liber quartus ad Salmonem.* G. Fabricius substituted the *Liber quartus* with *Epistola.* Schenkl, the most recent editor, restored the title as found in the manuscript, although he omitted the *sancti* which had possibly been added by a scribe owing to a confusion with Paulinus of Nola. The editors and scholars subsequent to Gagny were nearly all agreed on attributing the poem to Victorius (e.g., Fabricius, Ceillier, Bourgoin, Ebert). Petschenig suggested to Schenkl (CSEL 16, 1, p. 502) Paulinus, bishop of Béziers (Gallia Narbonensis), on the basis of a brief reference for the year 419 in the chronicle of Hydatius: "In the region of Gaul in the city of Béziers (Biterrae), Paulinus, the bishop of that city, recounted the many and terrible events which had taken place in a letter sent to all regions" (SCh 218, ed. Tranoy, n. 73, p. 125). If Schenkl's proposed correction, which has been refuted by Griffe, of reading *Tecumque* (a river of Narbonne) instead of *tecumque* is true, then this identification, which at present is merely considered probable, would be almost certain (P. Courcelle, *Histoire litt. des grandes invasions germaniques.* Paris 1964³, p. 87-88).

The poem was composed after the invasions of 407-409, at a time when the population was occupied with the business of reconstruction after the departure of the barbarians (v. 19-29, ed. Schenkl). The poem develops as a Dialogue between three speakers: two monks, of whom one must be an abbot (he is called *magister* and *pater*), and a guest by the name of Salmon who had once lived in the monastery but is now presented as *supplex peccator* (v. 1). The monk, Tesbon, a friend of the abbot, asks Salmon for information concerning the condition of the country. The guest responds that the barbarians, having broken their treaty, have for the first time invaded the whole country. The marble villas as well as the theaters are ruined, and everyone is involved in the work of reconstruction while the interests of the soul are neglected. Salmon, who expresses the poet's point of view, observes that in spite of so many calamities caused by sins, men have not changed. There are still the same vices, the same hypocrisies, the same astrological practices. The women give themselves over to luxury, to frivolities, to feasts, and to reading the pagan poets, all with the complicity of the men. He concludes the indictment by saying that if people, free from the old vices, would open themselves to Christ, no violence would prevail against his servants (v. 89-93). The abbot responds to this pessimistic and critical statement of Salmon by saying that there are, nevertheless, many pious persons among the people. Salmon recognizes the truth of this observation and requests to speak to him about the peace of his monastic life. Since the hour for prayer had arrived, the continuation of the conversation is postponed until the following day.

The epigram, which is linguistically and stylistically correct and written in a satiric tone in the style of Horace, is partially incomplete. It bears a notable resemblance to the *Carmen de providentia divina* inasmuch as it refers to the same events. It is valuable for its information concerning life in Gaul at the beginning of the fifth century. It is customary to attribute to the author of the *Epigramma Paulini* also the *Passio s. Genesii,* a work from the first half of the fifth century, sometimes attributed to Paulinus of Nola, dealing with the piety of Saint Genesius and the circumstances of his martyrdom (under Decius?). Homily 50 of the *Collectio gallicana* draws its inspiration from this work.

Editions: Epigramma: PL 61, 969-972 (ed. Gagny, defective). — C. Schenkl, CSEL 16, 1(1888)503-510. *Passio:* PL 61, 418-420. — W. Hartel, CSEL 29(1894)425-428. — S. Cavallin: *Eranos Löfstedtianus* 43(1945)160-164.

Translations: French: Epigramma; E. Griffe: REAug 2(1956)189-194 (nearly complete translation). *Passio;* P. Monceaux, La vraie légende dorée. Relations de martyre. Paris, 1938.

Studies: E. Griffe, L'Epigramma Paulini, poème gallo-romain du Ve siècle: REAug 2(1956)187-194. — W. Schmid, Ein verschollener Kodex des Cuias und seine Bedeuting für Claudiankritik: SIF 27-28(1957)498-518. — P. Courcelle, Histoire littéraire des grandes invasiones germaniques. Paris, 1964[3]. For St. Genesius, cf. *Bibliotheca Sanctorum* 6(1965)115-117.

4. *Carmen de Providentia.*

The barbarian invasions at the beginning of the fifth century spread ruin and death throughout Gaul. A poet, an eyewitness of these events, was profoundly moved by the calamities of his people. Some Christians, who could understand why adults would have to suffer such dreadful chastisements, but not children, were wondering about the reality of divine providence. They were asking, "But what have these innocent little boys and girls done, who committed no evil in their lives? Why has it been permitted that the temples of God be devastated by fire? Neither has the honor of a consecrated chastity protected the virgins, nor the love of a sacred sentiment the widows . . ." (v. 43-48). It was to these anguished questions that the poet wanted to respond in the years 415-416, at a time when the barbarians had already been occupying the country for ten years (*caede decenni Vandalicis gladiis sternimur et Geticis,* v. 33f). The poem is composed of 48 elegiac distichs (the description of devasted Gaul and the doubts of the Christians) and 876 hexameters (the long response). The poet, who is the author of other lost works (v. 1-7), responds to all these doubts by means of Scripture. God is the wise Creator of the world and of mankind, and, though the latter has fallen into sin through the devil's temptation, there have always been people who are just. God has always cared for the world and for mankind (numerous examples are cited from the Bible) and has imprinted His law in the heart of man: *Incisos apices ac scripta volumina cordis inspicite, et genitam vobiscum agnoscite legem,* v. 420f). Christ truly became incarnate, and thus the law is easy to observe with his grace, since he has given an example. Man was created and endowed with a free will. The saints suffered the same temptations as other men, and thus the difficulties in leading a good life are not to be attributed to the stars, which exercise no influence over us, but to the free human will. The same things happen to the good and to the bad; the lot of the second being punishment while the crown of virtue is that of the former.

This *Carmen,* which was published by Gryphius in 1539 under the name of Prosper of Aquitaine, is preserved in a single incomplete manuscript (*Paris Mazarinensis* 3896) of only 340 verses. It is disputed whether it is anterior to or dependent upon the *editio princeps.* It is generally accepted that the poem is not a work of Prosper because it is infected with Pelagianism, an aspect which was already noted by early editors (e.g., Soteaux, Louvain 1565; and Olivier, Douai 1577) and several scholars (Bellarmine, Noris, De Plinval) but which recently has been denied by Valentin. The charge of Pelagianism has weighed heavily on this important poem, and for this reason it has been studied little. The poem was only recently translated by McHugh, who has provided the best study of the work currently available.

The author is acquainted with the classical authors (Lucretius, Vergil, Ovid, Cicero, and Livy) as well as with Christian writers (Augustine, Prudentius, and Paulinus of Nola), possesses a good technique of versification, and writes in a clear and elegant style. Even though it is a didactic and polemical poem, there are instances of true poetry. In the *editio princeps* the title is given as *Carmen de Providentia Dei,* while the heading in the text is *Carmen de Providentia divina,* under which title it is known to Hincmar of Rheims, who attributed it to Prosper (*De praedestinatione diss. post.*, 38, 4-5: PL 125, 442-445).

[The attribution and dating of the *Carmen* has recently (1977) been submitted to a meticulous examination by G. Gallo, who recognized its Pelagian character and proposed that it is a work of Hilary of Arles, composed in 429. Prosper of Aquitaine's *Carmen de ingratis* is thus to be considered a reply to this work of Hilary's. (From the Spanish edition.)]

Editions: PL 51, 617-638 (Maurist text). — M. P. McHugh, The Carmen de Providentia Dei attributed to Prosper of Aquitaine (PSt 98). Washington 1964, 260-308.

Translations: English: M. P. McHugh, op. cit.

Studies: L. Valentin, Saint Prosper d'Aquitaine, étude sur la littérature latine ecc. au IVe siècle en Gaule. Toulouse-Paris, 1900 (important study; attributes the Carmen to Prosper). — G. de Plinval, Pélage. Lausanne, 1943. — M. P. McHugh, Observations on the Text of the "Carmen de Providentia dei": *Manuscripta* 12(1968)3-9. — Cf. Bibliography under Prosper of Aquitaine. — G. Gallo, Uno scritto filo-pelagiano attribuibile a Ilario di Arles: *Aevum* 57(1977)333-348 (cf. L. Brix: REAug 24[1978]365).

5. *De ligno crucis.*

The manuscript tradition attributes to Cyprian or Tertullian this poem of 69 hexameters, which subsequent criticism has assigned variously to Victorius, Prudentius, Avitus, or an anonymous fifth-century author who was imitating classical poetry. It has been assigned several different titles: *De Pascha, De cruce, De ligno vitae.* It is an allegorical poem which likens Christ to a bough planted on Golgotha which after three days becomes a tree and after forty days reaches to heaven. Twelve smaller branches (the Apostles) are detached from the tree and scattered abroad to preach the Gospel. A fountain springs up in the shade of the tree which brings salvation to all who are able to taste the fruit of this tree of life.

The prosody and meter are correct. According to Roncoroni it was possibly composed in Gaul. The text has been handed down in two versions, since v. 47-52 are lacking in some manuscripts.

Editions: CPL 1458. — *incipit:* Est locus ex omni . . .: PL 2, 1113-1114 (among the works of Tertullian). — G. Hartel, CSEL 3, 3(1871)305-308 (among the works of Cyprian). — R. Roncoroni: RSLR 12(1976)388-390.

Studies: C. Pascal, Un carme pseudociprianeo: BFC 10(1904)282. — P. Rasi, I "Versus de ligno crucis" in un codice della Biblioteca Ambrosiana: RIL 39(1906) 657-665; *idem,* De codice quodam Ticinensi quo incerti scriptoris carme "De Pascha" continetur. Accedunt ad carmen upsum Adnotationes at Appendix metrica: RFIC 34(1906)426-459; *idem,* Nuove osservazioni sul "Carmen de Pascha," in *Miscell. Ceriani.* Milan 1910, 577-604. — S. Brandt, Zu Ps. Cyprian de Pascha: PhW 40(1920)424-432. — M. Dando, Alcimus Avitus as the Author of . . . De Pascha (De cruce) . . . formerly Attributed to Tertullian and Cyprian: *Classica et Mediev.* 26(1967)258-275

6. *Psalmus responsorius.*

Psalmus responsorius is the title, perhaps original, of a text recently published, which has been handed down in an incomplete form in a papyrus manuscript preserved in Barcelona (*Pap. Barcin.* 149b-153). The five surviving pages, written on both *verso* and *retro* are part of a larger manuscript containing Latin and Greek compositions. The editor of the text, Roca-Puig, does not mention its place of origin. It could be of Egyptian origin, although Naldini has also proposed that it was written in *Africa proconsularis* whence it passed into Egypt.

Roca-Puig dates the text to the first half of the fourth century, and this proposal is accepted by Naldini, who prefers to place the time of composition between 340-350. After the title, there follow four verses of an invocation (*Pater qui omnia regis . . .*) and twelve verses in an alphabetical order up to the letter "m." There are traces of the beginning of a verse for "o," and if it was indeed an alphabetical poem, there must have been a total of 23 verses. The title *Psalmus responsorius* suggests the poem's liturgical use in some Latin community in Egypt. The four opening verses are not an introduction, as the editor believes, but rather are the *responsio* of the faithful to each verse sung or recited by the soloist (cf. the *responsorii psalmi,* psalms with a response of Egeria, *Peregrinatio* 27, 8; the word *psalmus* can mean either "a religious poem" or "a narration in verse"). The composition does not follow the rules either of quantitative or of rhythmic meter. It bears resemblance in structure with the much more polished *Psalmus abecedarius* of Saint Augustine.

The author's purpose is to praise the *magnalia Dei* (v. 5). After a brief reference to David and the prophets, the poem continues with a description of the first part of the life of Christ: the sterility of Mary's mother, Anne, her prayer, Mary's secluded life in the Temple, her marriage with Joseph, the Annunciation beside a fountain, the birth of Jesus in the open countryside, the visit of the Magi kings (called *graeci,* v. 61) to Bethlehem with their gifts, the slaughter of the Innocents, the flight into Egypt, and the Miracle at Cana (stanza 22). The other stanzas must have treated other episodes from the life of Christ. It was evidently a Christological hymn.

The author draws his information principally from the canonical Gospels of Matthew and John (the Wedding at Cana), and especially from the apocryphal Protoevangelium of James for the first seven stanzas. Strangely enough, the Gospel of Luke, so rich in information on the life of Mary and the infancy of Jesus, is not used. This *Psalmus* is an important ancient witness to the cult of the Madonna, her virginity, her divine maternity and her intercession at the Wedding at Cana.

Editions: R. Roca-Puig, Himne a la Vierge Marie. Psalmus responsorius. Papir llati del segle IV. Barcelona, 1965[2] (the text is found also in: Marianum 39[1967]258-260 and RSLR 4[1968]155-157[better reading of the text]).

Translations: Catalan: R. Roca-Puig, op. cit.

Studies: L. M. Peretto, Psalmus responsorius. Un inno alla Vergine Maria di un papiro del IV secolo: Marianum 39[1967]255-265. — M. Naldini: RSLR 4[1968]154-161(review of the volume of Roca-Puig).

CHAPTER VI

SAINT AUGUSTINE

by Agostino Trapè

Augustine is undoubtedly the greatest of the Fathers and one of the great geniuses of humanity, whose influence on posterity has been continuous and profound. Studies on Augustine have multiplied in the past and continue to multiply today to such an extent that it becomes impossible to give a complete review of them all. Only the more significant works are listed here, and the reader is referred to the collections of bibliographies which are indicated below.

Bibliographies: E. Nebreda, Bibl. Augustiniana. Rome, 1928. — Bulletin de Théologie Ancienne et Médiévale. Mont César-Louvain, 1929ff. — R. Gonzales, Bibl. agustiniana del Centenario: *Religión y Cultura* 15(1931)461-509. — E. Krebs, Neuere Augustinusliteratur: ThR(1932)137ff. — F. van Steenberghen, La philosophie de St. Aug. d'après les travaux du centenaire: *Revue Néoscol Phil* 1932-33. — G. Kruger, A Decade of Research in Early Christian Literature (1921-1930): HThR 26(1933)173-321. — M. F. Sciacca, Augustinus, in *Bibl. Einführungen in das Studium d. Phil.* Bern, 1948. — Bulletin Augustinien: AnThA 1949-53, subsequently REAug 1955ff. — E. Lamirande, Un siècle et demi d'études sur l'ecclésiologie de St. Aug. Essai bibliographique: REAug 8(1962)1-125. — C. Andresen, Das Augustinus-Gespräch der Gegenwart. Cologne, 1962. — T. van Bavel, Répertoire bibliographique de Saint Aug. (1950-1960). Steenbrugge, 1963. — A. Rigobello, Studi agostiniani in Italia nell'ultimo ventennio: *Cultura e Scuola* 32(1969)73-84. — C. Andresen, Bibliographia Augustiniana: *Wissenschaftliche Buchgesellschaft.* Darmstadt, 1973[2]. — R. Lorenz, Zwölf Jahre Augustinusforschung (1959-1970): *Theol Rundschau* 38(1974)292-333; 39(1974)95-138, 253-286, 331-364; 40(1975)1-41, 97-149, 227-261. — Fichier augustinien (Augustine Bibliography). Fichier Auteurs, I-II; Fichier Matières, I-II. Boston, 1972. — E. S. Lodovici, Agostino, in *Questioni di Storiografia fil.* I. Brescia 1975, 445-501. — T. Halton, R. Sider, A Decade of Patristic Scholarship 1970-1979 II: *Classical World* 76(July-August 1983)362-379.

Encyclopedias: C. Boyer, S. Agostino: EC 1, 519-567. — E. Portalié, Augustin: DTC 1, 2268-2472. — A. Trapè, S. Agostion: Biblioteca Sanctorum I, 428-596. — A. Schindler, Theologische Realenzyklopädie IV, 646-698. — O. J-B. de Roy, St. Augustine, The New Catholic Encyclopedia 1(1967)1041-1058.

Miscellanea: Miscellanea agostiniana (MSCA) I (S. A. sermones post Maurinos reperti), II (Studi agostiniani). Rome, 1931. — Miscellanea augustiniana. Nijmegen, 1930. — Aurelius Augustinus. Die Festschrift der Görres-Gesellschaft zum 1500 Todestage des hl. A. Cologne, 1930(AurAug). — Mélanges augustiniennes. Paris, 1931. — Augustinus Magister I-III (AugMag). Paris, 1954. — Recherches Augustiniennes. Paris, 1958ff. — Estudios sobre la "ciudad de Dios" I-II. El Escorial, 1954.

The treatment of Augustine will be divided into four parts: Life, person, works and doctrine.

LIFE

It is important to know with precision the facts of Augustine's life, especially those concerning his return to the Catholic faith, for they are often employed, rightly or wrongly, to interpret his thought. Those facts are, for those times, well known both because Augustine himself "confessed" at length and because his friend and disciple, Possidius, wrote his biography.

SOURCES

Autobiographical Sources.

1. The *Dialogues* of Cassiciacum. The *Dialogues* can be considered as the first "Confessions." Composed between November 386 and March 387, they offer in the prologues (*De beata vita* 1-5; *Contra Acad.* 2, 3-6; *De ord.* 1, 2, 5) the first important notices concerning Augustine's life, and, in the works themselves, indications of his interior disposition prior to baptism. This remains true even in the event that, as some affirm, the dialogical form is not historical but is merely a literary construction.

For the editions and bibliography, see below pp. 344–45.

2. The *Confessions*. These are both an autobiographical composition as well as a work of philosophy, of theology, of mysticism, and of poetry. They are among the most widely read and studied of Augustine's works today. The objects of study are, in particular, the origin, date, division, unity, and historical value of the work. Concerning this final point, a lively discussion broke out a century ago, which can be said to have been concluded in favor of the historical credibility of the *Confessions* and thus of the presentation of Augustine's interior evolution described therein. As a result of this discussion a valuable distinction has been established between facts and judgments: the former Augustine narrates with precision whereas the latter are connected, not with the Augustine presented in the narration, but with Augustine the author, who by that time was already a monk and bishop. Thus a supposed opposition between the *Confessions* and the *Dialogues* does not stand up to criticism. Rather, although different in tone and subject matter, the two sets of works complement each other and present the same *iter* toward conversion.

The *Confessions* are divided into two parts: the first part (I-IX) describes Augustine up to the time of his conversion and the death of his mother; the second part (X-XIII), added at a later date (*Conf.* 10 3, 4), describes Augustine as he is writing (*Conf.* 10 4, 6). The unity of the work is to be sought in the aspect of praise of God "for the good things and for the bad" (*Retract.* 2, 6) common to the entire work (*confessio* = praise), and in the autobiographical aspect, present also in the second part.

The *Confessions* were begun after April 4, 397 (the death of Ambrose) and were completed around 400.

Editions: M 1, 69-244. — PL 32, 659-868(Paris 1841). — P. Knöll, CSEL 33, 1(1896) (=BT, Leipzig 1898). — F. Skutella, BT. Leipzig 1934. — F. Skutella, H. Jürgens, W. Schaub, BT. Stuttgart 1969 (*editio correctior*); BA 13-14; BAC 2(11); NBA 1. — Cf. L. M. J. Verheijen, Contribution à une édition critique améliorée des Confessions de saint Augustin: AugL 20(1970)35-53; *idem,* Aug 17(1977)35-53; *idem,* CCL 27(1981).

Translations: English: W. Montgomery, Cambridge 1908. — P. Schaff, LNPF 1 ser. 1(1886)27-207 (reprint 1956). — V. J. Bourke, FC 21(1953). — F. J. Sheed, New York 1944. *French:* P. De Labriolle, Paris 1961[8]. — G. Combès, Paris 1957. — L. de Mondadon, Paris 1961. — E. Tréhorel, BA 13-14. *German:* C. J. Perl, Paderborn 1955[4]. — H. Schiel, Freiburg i. Br. 1959[6]. — C. J. Perl, Paderborn 1964. — W. Thimme, Stuttgart 1967. *Italian:* G. Capello, Turin 1969[4]. — A. Bussoni, Parma 1973. — C. Vitali, Milan 1974. — C. Carena, NBA 1. Rome, 1975[3]. *Spanish:* E. de Zeballos, Barcelona 1957[2]. — L. Riber, Madrid 1957. — V. Sánchez Ruiz, Madrid 1958[3]. — A. C. Vega, BAC 2(11). Madrid, 1968.

Studies: (General studies) G. Wunderle, Einführung in Aug. Konfessionen. Augsburg, 1930. — J. M. Le Blond, Les conversions de st. Aug. Paris, 1950. — A. Solignac, Introd. aux confessions: BA 13. — R. Guardini, Die Bekehrung des hl. Aur. Aug. Munich, 1959[3]. — M. Pellegrino, Per un commento alle Conf.: REAug 5(1959)439-446. — P. Courcelle, Rech. sur les Conf. Paris, 1968[2]. — A. Mandouze, Saint Aug., l'aventure de la raison et de la grâce: ETAug. Paris, 1968. — M. Pellegrino, Le Conf. di S. Ag. Studio introduttivo. Rome, 1972[2]. — A. Trapè, Introduzione alle Conf.: NBA 1(1975[3]). (Opinions on the purpose and unity of the Confessions) M. Wundt, Augustins Konfessionen: ZNW 22(1923)161-206. — P. De Labriolle, Pourquoi St. Aug. a-t-il rédigé les Conf.?: BAGB (1926)43-47. — M. Zepf, Augustins Confessiones. Tübingen, 1926. — E. Willinger, Der Aufbau der Konfessionen Aug.: ZNW 28(1929)81-106. — O. Pincherle, Sant'Agostino. Bari, 1930. — J. Stiglmayr, Das Werk der Aug. Konfessionen mit ein Opfergelübde besiegelt: ZAM 5(1930)234-245. — L. Landsberg, La conversion de St. Aug.: VS Suppl(1936)31-56. — J. Freyer, Erlebte und systematische Gestaltung in Aug. Konf., in *Neue deutsche Forsch.* 4. Berlin, 1937. — M. M. Wagner, Plan in the Confessions of St. Aug.: *Phil Quarterly* 23(1944)1-23. — F. Cayré, Le sens et l'unité des Conf.: AnThA 13(1953)13-32. — H. Kusch, Studien über Aug., in Festschr. F. Dornseiff. Leipzig 1953, 124-200. — J. J. O'Meara, The Young Augustine. London, 1954. — F. Cayré, Le Livre XIII des Conf.: REAug 2(1956)143-161. — N. G. Knauer, Psalmenzitate in Aug. Konf. Göttingen, 1955; *idem,* "Peregrinatio animae." — Zur Frage der Einheit der augustinischen Konf.: Hermes 85(1957)216-248. — R. O'Connell, The Plotinian Fall of the Soul in St. A.: *Traditio* 19(1963)129-164; *idem,* The Riddle of Aug.'s Conf. A Plotinian Key: *Int Phil Quarterly* 4(1964)327-372; *idem,* St. Aug.'s Early Theory of Man. Cambridge, 1968; *idem,* St. Aug.'s Conf. The Odyssey of Soul. Cambridge, 1969. — E. Dönt, Aufbau und Glaubwürdigkeit der Konf. und die Cassiciacumgespräche des Aug.: WSt 3(1969)181-197; *idem,* Zur Frage der Einheit von Aug. Konf.: Hermes 99(1971)350-361. — G. Pfligersdorfer, Das Bauprinzip von Aug. Confessiones, Festschf. K. Kretska. Heidelberg 1970, 124-147. — O. Meo, Memoria e linguaggio nel libro X delle Confessioni: *Laurentianum* 17(1976)388-407. — D. A. Cress, Hierius and St. A.'s Account of the lost "De pulchro et apto" (Conf. IV 13-15): Aug Studies 7(1976)47-58. — G. Luongo, Autobiografia ed esegesi biblica nelle "Confessioni" di A.: *La parola del passato* 31(1976)286-306. — I. Opelt, Sallust in A.'s "Confessiones," in *Latinität und alte Kirche.* Festsch. R. Hanslik, Vienna 1977, 196-204. — J. Oroz Reta, Prière et recherche de Dieu dans les "Confessions" de S. A.: Aug Studies 7(1976)99-118. — A. Pincherle, The "Confessions" of S. A.: Aug Studies 7(1976)119-133. — H. J. Sieben, Der Psalter und die Bekehrung der voces und affectus. Zu A. "Conf." IX 4. 6 und X 33: *Theologie und Philosophie* 52(1977)481-497. — C. Starnes, S. A. and the Vision of the Truth: *Dionysius* 1(1977)85-126. — G. P. Lawless, Interior Peace in the Confessions of St. Augustine: REAug 26(1980)45-61.

3. The *Retractations*. These are a fundamental work for a study of Augustine's writings, but are important also for a knowledge of the spirit and the religious motives which inspired him. They are a long examination of conscience of the elderly writer on his own literary activity; the final "Confessions." (See above, p. 343).

4. *Sermons* 355 and 356. Given, respectively, on December 18, 425 and shortly after Epiphany the following year, these sermons make up in part for the silence of the *Confessions* concerning the time between Augustine's return to Africa and the beginning of his episcopate. They provide information on the foundation of the monasteries at Hippo and present a sketch of the life lived there.

Biographical Sources

1. The *Vita Sancti Augustini* by Possidius. Written between 431-439 (*Vita* 28, 10-11), the *Vita* was composed on the basis of personal reminiscences (*quae in eodem vidi et audivi: praef.* 1) and the written sources available in the library at Hippo. It possesses an exceptional historical value and is an indispensable guide for a knowledge of the life and activity of Augustine from his ordination as a priest until his death.

Editions: PL 32, 33-66. — H. T. Weiskotten, Princeton 1919. — A. C. Vega, El Escorial 1934. — M. Pellegrino, Alba 1955. — F. R. Hoare, New York 1965. — A. A. R. Bastiansen, C. Carena, Milan 1975, 130-140.

Translations: English: H. T. Weiskotten, op. cit. — F. R. Hoare, op. cit. — M. M. Muller, R. Deferrari, FC 15(1952)67-124. *French:* L. Moreau, Paris 1940. *German:* A. von Harnack, Berlin 1930. — K. Romeis, Berlin 1930. *Italian:* M. Pellegrino, op. cit. — M. Simonetti, Rome 1977. *Spanish:* V. Capánega, BAC 1(1958)359-429. — P. B. Hospital, El Escorial 1959.

AUGUSTINE'S LIFE

1. From birth to conversion (354-386)

Augustine was born on November 13, 354, the son — perhaps the eldest — of a municipal counsellor and small property holder at Thagaste in Numidia. If, as seems probable, he was African by race as well as by birth, he was nevertheless Roman by language, culture and persuasion. He studied at Thagaste, at Madaura and, with the aid of his fellow-citizen Romanianus, also at Carthage. Augustine taught grammar at Thagaste (374), and rhetoric at Carthage (375-383), Rome (384) and at Milan (fall 384-summer 386), in this latter city as an official professor. He had a profound knowledge of the Latin language and culture, but was not proficient in Greek and did not know Punic.

Having received a Christian education from his very pious mother,

Monica, Augustine always remained a Christian at heart, even when, aged 19, he abandoned the Catholic faith.

Augustine's long and tormented interior evolution (373-386) began with the reading of Cicero's *Hortentius,* which stirred his enthusiasm for wisdom, but tinged his thought with rationalism and naturalism. Shortly thereafter, having read the Scriptures without profit, he encountered, listened to and followed the Manichaeans. There were three principal reasons for this development: the declared rationalism which excluded faith, the open profession of a pure and spiritual Christianity which excluded the Old Testament, and the radical solution to the problem of evil offered by the Manichaeans.

He was not a convinced Manichaean, but rather was confident that the wisdom promised would be shown to him (*De beata vita* 4). He was, on the other hand, a convinced anti-Catholic. Augustine accepted the methodological and metaphysical presuppositions of Manichaeism: rationalism, materialism, and dualism. When he gradually realized through the study of the liberal arts, particularly philosophy, the inconsistency of the religion of Mani — the Manichaean bishop Faustus provided the conclusive evidence — Augustine did not consider returning to the Catholic Church nor did he take up with any school of philosophers "because they were without the saving name of Christ" (*Conf.* 5 14, 25). Instead, he fell into the temptation of skepticism: "For a long while the Academics were at the helm of my ship" (*De beata vita* 4). The road back began at Milan with the preaching of Ambrose, which dispersed the Manichaean difficulties and provided the key for the interpretation of the Old Testament. It continued with personal reflection on the necessity of faith to arrive at wisdom and terminated in the conviction that the authority on which faith rested was the Scriptures; the Scriptures guaranteed and read by the Church. Now he became aware that the way which led to Christ was precisely the Church.

The importance of Augustine's conversion and the role played in it by his reading of the Platonists has been the object of much discussion in the past and continues to be so today. If one is to remain faithful to the writings of Augustine, it is necessary to make a distinction between the motive of faith and the content of faith: the former he had obtained prior to his reading of the Platonists; the latter he clarified, in part, afterwards. In spite of the many questions which remained obscure, he adhered as he had always done to the authority of Christ and once again, at last, to the authority of the church. "Yet the faith of your Christ found in the Catholic church remained firmly rooted in my heart . . . It was, to be sure, a faith still rough in many points and fluctuating beyond the bounds of sound doctrine, nevertheless my spirit never abandoned it, rather it imbibed a little more each day" (*Conf.* 7 5, 7).

The Platonists helped Augustine resolve two major philosophical problems: materialism and the nature of evil. He learned to overcome the first of these following precisely the advice of the Platonists (*Conf.* 7 10, 16), by discovering within himself the intelligible light of the truth. He solved the second by coming to the notion of evil as a defect or privation of good. There remained, however, the theological problem of mediation and grace. In order to resolve this he turned to Saint Paul, from whom he grasped that Christ is not only Teacher but also Redeemer. When he had thus overcome the final error, naturalism, his return to Catholic faith was complete.

However, at this point there appeared, or better, reappeared, another problem: namely, the choice of the way to live the Christian ideal of wisdom and the question of whether it was necessary to renounce for this every earthly hope, including a career and marriage. The giving up of his career, even though it promised to be a brilliant one (he was being considered for the presidency of a tribunal or of a province) was not difficult. The giving up of marriage cost him dearly. At age seventeen in order to place some check on the passions of adolescence and to remain in vogue with the popular society (*Solil.* 1 11, 19), Augustine had begun to live with a woman by whom he had a son (who died between 389 and 391) and to whom he had always remained faithful (*Conf.* 4 2, 2). After long hesitation (*Conf.* 6 11, 18; 16, 26) and intense inner conflict, and not without an extraordinary assistance of grace (*Conf.* 8 6, 13; 12, 30), Augustine made his choice according to the counsel of the Apostle and his own most profound aspirations: "I turned myself fully to you and no longer sought either wife or any other hope in this world" (*Conf.* 8 12, 30). It was the beginning of August, 386.

Studies regarding Augustine's conversion and the historical value of the *Confessions:*

1. A history of the question: J. Nörregaard, Augustins Bekehrung. Tübingen, 1923, 1-19. — H. Gros, La valeur documentaire des Conf. de St. Aug. (Diss., Fribourg 1927); VS 1926-27. — U. Mannucci, S. Ag. e la critica recente: MSCA II, 23-48. — M. P. Garvey, St. Aug. Christian or Neoplatonist? Milwaukee 1939, 1-40. — M. F. Sciacca, S. Agostino. Brescia 1949, 111-115. — P. Courcelle, Recherches sur les Confess. Paris 1950, 1968[2], 7-10. — A. Solignac, Introd. Conf.: BA 13, 55-84. — C. Boyer, Christianisme et néo-platonisme dans la formation de St. Aug. Rome, 1953[2].

2. Conversion to Platonism: A. von Harnack, Augustins Konfessionen. Giessen, 1888 (reprint: Reden und Aufsätze I. 1904, 51-79). — G. Boissier, La conversion de St. Aug.: *Revue Deux-Mondes* 85(1888)43-69. — L. Gourdon, Essai sur la conversion de St. Aug. Cahors, 1900. — O. Scheel, Die Anschauung Augustins über Christi Person und Werke. Tübingen, 1901. — H. Becker, Aug. Studien zür seine geistigen Entwicklung. Leipzig, 1908. — W. Thimme, Aug. geistige Entwicklung in den ersten Jahren nach seineer Bekehrung 389-391: *Neue Studien zur Geschichte der Theologie* 3(1908); *idem,* Grundlinien der geistigen Entwicklung Aug.: ZKG 31(1910)172-213. — P. Alfaric, L'évolution intellectuelle de St. Aug. I (Du manicheisme au Néo-platonisme). Paris,

1918. — M. Peters, A.s' erste Bekehrung, in Harnack-Ehrung. Leipzig, 1921, 195-211. — M. Wundt, Ein Wendepunkt in Aug. Entwicklung: ZNW 21(1922)53-64. — M. Nédoncelle, L'abandon de Mani par A. ou la logique de l'optimisme: RAug 2(1962)17-32. — P. J. de Menasce, Augustin Manichéen, in Festschrift R. Curtius. Bern 1966, 79-93.

3. Conversion to Christianity: J. Nörregaard, op. cit. — C. Boyer, La conversion de St. Aug.: SC 9(1927)401-414. — J. Mausbach, Die Etik des hl. Aug. Freiburg i. Br. 1929, I. 6-16. — W. J. S. Simpson, Saint Augustine's Conversion. London, 1930. — U. Mannucci, La conversione di S. Ag. e la critica recente: MSCA II, Rome, 1931, 23-48. — P. Monceaux, S. A. et saint Antoine: MSCA II, 61-89. — J. Geffcken, Tolle-Lege Erlebnis: ARW 31(1934)1-13. — R. Guardini, Die Bekehrung des hl. A. Leipzig, 1935, Munich 1959[3]. — M. P. Garvey, St. Aug., Christian or Neo-platonist? Milwaukee, 1939. — P. Muñoz-Vega, Psicología de la conversión de S. A.: Greg 22(1941), 23(1942). — P. Courcelle, Les premières "Confessions" de s. A.: RELA 21-22(1943-44)155-174. — J. M. Le Blond, Les conversions de s. A. Paris, 1950. — M. F. Sciacca, St. Aug et le néo-platonisme. La possibilité d'une phil. chretienne. Louvain, 1961. — M. Pellegrino, Problemi vitali nelle Conf. di S. Ag., Tolentino, 1961; *idem,* S. Paolo nelle Confessioni di S. Ag.: AnalBibl 17-18(1963)503-512; *idem,* Le Confessioni. Studio introduttivo. Rome, 1972[2]. — W. Mallard, The Incarnation in Augustine's Conversion: RAug 15(1980)80-98.

4. For the question raised by P. Courcelle regarding A.s' conversion to Christianity after the reading of the Platonists and the experience in the garden: P. Courcelle, Recherches sur les Confessions. Paris, 1950, 1968[2]; *idem,* Litiges sur la lecture des "libri platonicorum" par s. A.: AugL 4(1954)225-239. — C. Boyer: *Doctor Communis* 4(1951)109-111. — C. Mohrmann, Recensione: VC5(1951)213-231. — F. Cayré: AthR 10(1949)116-132; 12(1951)144-151, 244-252, 261-271. — J. O'Meara, The Young Augustine. London 1954, 116-119; *idem,* Arrupui, aperui et legi: AugMag I, 59-61. — A. Mandouze, L'extase d'Ostie: AugMag II, 67-84. — C. Boyer, Le retour à la foi de St. Aug: *Doctor Communis* 8(1955)1-6. — G. Mathon, Quand faut-il placer le retour d'Aug. à la foi catholique?: ReAug 1(1955)107-127. — F. Bolgiana, La conversione di S. Ag., Turin, 1956. — C. Mohrmann, Considerazioni sulle Conf. di S. A.: *Convivium* 25(1957)257-267; 27(1959)1-11, 129-139. — J. O'Meara, Aug. and Neoplatonism: RAug 1(1958)91-111. — E. Kevane, Philosophy, Education and the Controversy on S. A.'s Conversion, in *Studies in Philosophy and the History of Philosophy* II. Washington 1963, 61-103. — L. Rodriguez, La conversión de S. A. a través de los diálogos de Casiciaco: CD 176(1963)303-318. — E. Dönt, Aufbau und Glaubwürdigkeit der Konf: WSt 3(1969)181-197. — M. Testard, Observations sur la conversion d'A. et d'Alypius au jardin de Milan, in Festsch. K. Büchner II. Wiesbaden 1970, 266-273. — A. Trapè, La Chiesa milanese e la conversione di S. Agostino: *Archivio Ambrosiano* 27(1974)5-24.

2. From Conversion to Episcopate (386-396)

The span of less than ten years between Augustine's conversion and the beginning of his episcopate was a time of exceeding spiritual and theological richness. Having taken the decision to give up teaching and to forgo marriage, he retired toward the end of October to Cassiciacum (probably the modern Cassago in Brianza) in order to prepare for baptism. He returned to Milan at the beginning of March, enrolled himself among the catechumens, followed the catechetical instructions of Ambrose and, together with his friend Alypius and his son Adeodatus, was baptized by him at the Easter

Vigil during the night of April 24-25, 387: "And there fled from us all the anxiety of our past life" (*Conf.* 9 6, 14). After Baptism, the little band decided to return to Africa to put into practice there "the holy proposal" to live together in the service of God. Before the end of August, they departed from Milan and reached Ostia where Augustine's mother, Monica, suddenly took ill and died. After the death of his mother Augustine decided to return to Rome, where he remained until after the death of the usurper Maximus (July or August 388), concerning himself with the monastic life and continuing to write books. He then returned to Africa, retired to Thagaste and together with his friends put into practice his program of the ascetic life (cf. Possidius, *Vita* 3, 1-2).

In 391, he went down to Hippo in order "to find a place to found a monastery and live with my brothers," but he found there the surprise of his priestly ordination, which he accepted reluctantly (*Serm.* 355, 2; *Ep.* 21; Possidius, *Vita* 4, 2). Once he had been ordained a priest, he received permission from the bishop to found, according to his plan, a monastery where "he began to live according to the manner and rule established in the times of the Holy Apostles" (Possidius, *Vita* 5, 1), intensifying his asceticism, developing further his theological studies and beginning his apostolate of preaching. His episcopal consecration took place in 395 or, according to some, in 396. He was for some time coadjutor of Hippo then — at least from August 397 — bishop. At that time he left the community of laymen where he had lived as the head of the community, and in order to free himself to show hospitality to all, he moved to the "house of the bishop," establishing there a monastery of clerics (*Serm.* 355, 2).

Studies: For the date of the episcopal ordination, cf. A. Casamassa, Enciclopedia italiana, 2, 915; *idem,* Scritti patristici II (*Lateranum* 22). Rome 1956, 285-286. — O. Perler, Les voyages de St. Aug., Paris 1969, 164-178. — A. Pincherle, La formazione teologica di sant'Agostino. Rome, 1947. — G. P. Lawless, Augustine's First Monastery: Thagaste or Hippo?: Aug 25(1985)65-78 (Misc. Trapè).

3. From Episcopate to Death (396-430)

Augustine's episcopal activity was prodigious indeed, both with regard to the ordinary care for his own diocese as well as the extraordinary work in which he engaged for the African Church and the church universal.

Among his ordinary duties must be numbered the following: the ministry of the word (he preached uninterruptedly two times a week — Saturday and Sunday — and often for several consecutive days and even twice a day); the *audientia episcopi* in which he heard and rendered judgments in lawsuits, which not infrequently occupied him for the entire day; the care of the poor and of orphans; the formation of the clergy, in which he proved himself paternal yet strict; the organization of monasteries for men and women; the visitation of the sick; the intervention on behalf of the faithful with the civil authorities (*apud saeculi potestates*), in which he did not like to engage, but nevertheless undertook when he considered it proper; and the administration of the material goods of the church, with which he would gladly have concerned himself less except that he did not find any layman who was willing to take up the task.

His special activities are even more impressive: the numerous and long journeys to attend the frequent councils in Africa or to respond to the requests of his colleagues; the dictation of letters to respond to as many as addressed themselves to him from every region and social class; and the explanation and defense of the faith. This last duty led him to intervene without respite against Manichaeans, Donatists, Pelagians, Arians, and pagans. He was the moving force of the conference in 411 between Catholic and Donatist bishops, and was the principal architect of the solution of the Donatist Schism and the Pelagian Controversy. When he died on August 28, 430, in the third month of the siege of Hippo by the Vandals, he left three important works incomplete, among them his second response to Julian, the chief theorist of Pelagianism. His last work was a letter (*Ep.* 228), perhaps dictated from his deathbed, concerning the responsibilities of his priests in the face of the barbarian invasion. Augustine presumably was buried in his cathedral, the *Basilica Pacis.* At an uncertain date, his remains were transported to Sardinia and from there, around the year 725, to Pavia, where they rest in the Basilica of San Pietro in Ciel d'Oro.

Studies (Augustine's life): N. Concetti, S. Aug. Vita. Tolentino, 1930. — F. Meda, S. Agostino, in *Coll. Athena Studi Rel.*, Milan, 1930. — U. Moricca, S. Ag. l'uomo, lo scrittore. Turin, 1930. — A. Pincherle, S. Ag. d'Ippona, vescovo e teologo. Bari, 1930. — G. Bardy, St. Aug., l'homme et l'œuvre. Paris, 1940[3]. — J. O'Meara, The Young Augustine. London, 1954. — A. Sizoo, Aug. Leven en Werken. Kampen, 1957. — G. Bonner, St. Aug. of Hippo. Life and Controversies. Philadelphia, 1963. — J. O'Meara, The Young Aug. the Growth of St. Aug.'s Mind up to His Conversion. Staten Island, 1965. — P. Brown, Aug. of Hippo. A Biography. London, 1967. — G. Papini, S. Agostino. Milan, 1970[2]. — A. Trapè, S. Ag. l'uomo, il pastore, il mistico. Fossano, 1976. — K. Flasch, Augustin, Einführung in sein Denken. Stuttgart, 1980. — R. E. Meagher, An Introduction to Aug., New York, 1978. — A. Pincherle, Vita di sant' Ag., Bari, 1980.

PERSONALITY

Augustine possessed a complex and profound personality; he was at the same time philosopher, theologian, mystic, poet, orator, polemicist, writer, and pastor. These qualities all complemented one another and made of Augustine a man "to the likes of whom almost no one, or certainly very few, can be compared of all those who have lived since the beginning of the human race until today" (Pius XI, AAS 22[1930]223). Altaner writes: "The great bishop united in himself the creative energy of Tertullian and the breadth of spirit of Origen with the ecclesiastical sensitivity of Cyprian; the dialectical acumen of Aristotle with the soaring idealism and speculation of Plato; the practical sense of the Latins with the spiritual subtlety of the Greeks. He was the greatest philosopher of the patristic era and, without doubt, the most important and influential theologian of the Church in general. Since his own time, his works have found enthusiastic admirers" (*Patrologia,* Italian translation, Turin 1976, p. 433).

Augustine created in the Christian milieu the first great philosophical synthesis, which remains an essential component of Western thought. Departing from the evidence of his knowledge of himself, he expounded on the themes of being, of truth, and of love, and contributed much to the understanding of the problems of the search for God and the nature of man, of eternity and time, of liberty and evil, of providence and history, of beatitude, of justice and of peace.

With humility yet assurance, he expounded on the Christian mysteries, bringing about the greatest progress in dogma in the history of theology, not only with regard to the doctrine of grace, but also concerning the Trinity, Redemption, the Church, the sacraments, and eschatology. It could well be said that there is no theological question which Augustine has not illuminated. He explained at length a moral doctrine centered on love as well as a social and political theory. He defended Christian asceticism and pointed out the highest summits of mysticism.

As an orator, Augustine knew how to weave together the profound and dogmatic precision of the teacher, the lyric exuberance of the poet, the vibrant emotion of the mystic, and the evangelical simplicity of the pastor who desired to be all things to all men. He was acquainted with the various oratorical styles, which he described toward the end of his life in the *De doctrina christiana.* He made use of these styles himself, passing with ease from the simple to the more complex and, often, to the sublime.

Augustine was a formidable polemicist. Profoundly convinced of the truth and freshness of Catholic teaching, he defended it against all — pagans, Jews, schismatics, heretics — with the weapons of dialectics and the resources deriving from faith and reason. He always respected his adversaries, however. He studied their works, related their texts which he was refuting and recognized their merits, yet did not conceal or pass over their errors. He learned from his own painful experience of error to be gentle with those who were going astray.

He was a consummate master of rhetoric. He made use of it himself and taught others to do the same (cf. *De doctr. christ.* 4), subordinating it always, however, to the content. "It is necessary to consider the content over the words just as the soul is over the body" (*De cat. rud.* 9, 13). When it was necessary in order to make himself understood, Augustine did not hesitate to make use of neologisms or irregular grammar. "I prefer to be criticized by the grammarians than not to be understood by the people" (*In ps.* 36; 138, 19; *Serm.* 3, 6; 37, 14). If his style in the early works is still marked by the imitation of classical models — "inflated by the usage of secular writings" (*Retract. prol.* 3) — he draws his inspiration in the other works more and more from the Bible and ecclesiastical writers, thus making an effective contribution to the formation of Christian Latin. Augustine did not have one single style, but rather many; as many, it can be said, as the contents of his works demanded: the *Confessions,* the *City of God,* the *Sermons* and the *Letters.* These latter works have a style clearly different with regard to vocabulary and sentence structure, which are adapted to the character of each individual work according to the diversity of the subject.

Studies (language and style): F. DiCapua, Le clausole in s. Ag. con tre sillabe atone fra i due accenti: BFC 19(1912)12-16. — M. C. Colbert, The syntax of the "De civitate Dei" of S. Aug. (PSt 4). Washington, 1923. — G. Reynolds, The Clausulae in the "De civitate Dei" of S. Aug. (PSt 7). Washington, 1924. — M. R. Arts, The Syntax of the "Confessions" of S. Aug. (PSt 14). Washington, 1927. — J. C. Balmus, Étude sur le style de St. Aug. dans les "Confessions" et la "Cité de Dieu." Paris, 1930. — F. DiCapua, Il ritmo prosiaco in s. Ag.: MSCA II, 607-764. — B. H. J. Weerenbeck, Sur la langue de s. A., in Rotterdam 1930, 463-483. — M. Comeau, La rhétorique de s. A d'après les "Tractatus in Ioannem." Paris, 1930. — M. J. Holman, Nature-Imagery in the Works of St. A. (PSt 44). Washington, 1935. — A. B. Paluszak, The Subjunctive in the Letters of St. A. (PSt 46). Washington, 1935. — M. S. Muldowney, Word-order in the Works of St. A. (PSt 52). Washington, 1938. — M. B. Schieman, The Rare and Late Verbs in St. A.'s "De civitate Dei" (PSt 53). Washington, 1938. — J. Finaert, L'évolution littéraire de s. A., Paris, 1939; *idem,* S. A. rhéteur. Paris, 1939. — M. B. Carroll, The Clausulae in the "Confessions" of St. A. (PSt62). Washington, 1940. — B. L. Meulenbroek, Metriek en rhythmiek in A.' Cassiciacum-dialogen. Nijmegen, n.d. — J. Brennan, A Study of the Clausulae in the Sermons of St. Aug. (PSt 77). Washington, 1947. — L. Verheijen, "Eloquentia pedissequa." Observations sur le style des "Confessions" de s. A., Nijmegen, 1949. — I. Fontaine, Sens et valeur des images dans les "Confessions": AugMag I, 117-126. — M. Pellegrino, Atteggiamenti stilistici nelle "Confessioni" di s. A.: *Humanitas* 9(1954)1040-1049; *idem,* Le "Confessioni" di s. Ag., Rome 1972[2], 175-214. — U. Mariani, S. A. oratore e scrittore, in *Augustiniana.* Naples 1955, 121-140. — F. DiCapua, S. A. Poeta, ibid., 111-120. — S. Ioseph-Arthur, El estilo de San Agustín en las "Confessiones": *Augustinus* 2(1957)31-48, 3(1958)503-528. — Ch. Mohrmann, Études sur le latin des chrétiens I-IV. Rome, 1958-1977; *idem,* Saint Aug. écrivain: Recherches Aug. (1958)43-66; *idem,* Die altchristliche Sondersprache in den "Sermones" de Hl A. Nijmegen, 1965[2]. — V. Blanco García, La lengua latina en las obras de S. A., Saragossa, 1959. — J. Oroz Reta, La retórica en los "Sermones" de S. A., Madrid, 1963. — L. F. Pizzolato, Le fondazioni dello stile delle "Confessioni" di s. A., Milan, 1972; *idem,* Le

"Confessioni" di s. A. Da biografia a confessio. Milan, 1968. — W. Hensellek, Lexikologische Beobachtungen in A.s Frühschrift "Contra academicos." AAWW 114(1977)46-175; *idem,* Beobachtungen zur Sprache von A.s De utilitate credendi": ibid., 115(1978)16-41.

Of particular interest is the study of Augustine's character, for his outstanding moral qualities corresponded to his extraordinary intellectual abilities. He possessed a generous and strong constitution, and was endowed with an insatiable thirst for wisdom, a profound need for friendship, a vibrant love for Christ, the church and the faithful, and an astonishing devotion and stamina for work. Augustine was further marked by a moderate yet austere asceticism, a sincere humility which did not hesitate to acknowledge his own errors (cf. the *Confessions* and the *Retractations*), and an assiduous dedication to the study of Scripture, to prayer, to the interior life and to contemplation.

The Bishop of Hippo was a pastor who considered himself to be and defined himself as "servant of Christ and servant of the servants of Christ" (*Ep.* 117), and who accepted the full consequences of such a definition: complete availability for the needs of the faithful, the desire not to be saved without them ("I do not wish to be saved without you" *Serm.* 17, 2), prayer to God to be ever ready to die for them *aut effectu aut affectu* (MSCA I 404), love for those gone astray even if they did not desire love and even if they gave offense ("Let them say against us whatever they will; we love them even if they do not want us to." *In ps.* 36 3, 19). He was a pastor in the full sense of the word.

Augustine was a master who nevertheless considered himself a disciple and desired that all be disciples with him of the truth which is Christ. In his controversies he desired but one victory: that, namely, of the *City of God,* the victory of the truth (*De civ. Dei.* 2 29, 2). "As far as I am concerned, I will not hesitate to search if I find myself in doubt; I will not be ashamed to learn if I find myself in error. Therefore . . . let him continue along with me, whoever with me is certain; let him search with me, whoever shares my doubts; let him turn to me, whoever acknowledges his own error; let him rebuke me, whoever perceives my own" (*De Trin.* I 2, 4-3, 5). He considered it a great favor to be corrected, even if he did not hide the fact that whoever wished to correct him must himself be on guard against error (*De dono persev.* 21, 55; 24, 68). Above all, he did not wish to be identified as the church, of which he considered himself to be merely a humble and devoted son. "Am I perhaps the Catholic church? . . . It is sufficient for me to be found in her" (*In ps.* 36 3, 19).

Studies: O. Fusi Pecci, Il pastore d'anime in S. A., Turin, 1956. — M. Pellegrino, S. A. pastore d'anime: RAug 1(1958)317-338; *idem,* Verus Sacerdos. Fossano, 1965. — F. Van der Meer, De Zielzorger. Utrecht, 1946 (English transl: Augustine the Bishop. London-New York, 1961). — A. Trapè, Il sacerdote uomo di Dio e servo della Chiesa. Milan, 1968.

This, in short, was the man who has been the most widely followed teacher in the West, and who can well be called *Pater communis*. "That which Origen was for theological science in the third and fourth centuries, Augustine has been in a more lasting and effective manner for the entire life of the church in the succeeding centuries down to the present time. His influence extends not only to the domains of philosophy, of dogmatics, and of moral and mystical theology, but also to social life and welfare, ecclesiastical policy and public jurisprudence. He was, in a word, the great craftsman of the Western culture of the Middle Ages" (Altaner, *Patrologia.* Turin 1976, p. 433).

As scholar and polemicist, Augustine desired to be a faithful interpreter of Catholic teaching, and this teaching remains the best key to the interpretation of his thought. "And if at times on the part of Protestants it has been attempted and is attempted to interpret his thought as partially not in accord with the thought of the church, it must be noted to the contrary with K. Holl (*A. innere Entwicklung.* 1922, p. 51) that 'the Catholic Church has always understood him better than her adversaries.' The ecclesiastical magisterium has followed no other theological author in its decisions as much as Augustine, even for the doctrine of grace" (Altaner, *op. cit.,* p. 433-434).

Celestine I defended the memory of Augustine and numbered him among the "best teachers," declaring that he had always been loved and honored by all (DS 237). Hormisdas (DS 366), Boniface II (DS 399), and John II refer in questions concerning grace to Augustine, "whose doctrine, according to the decisions of my predecessors, the Roman Church follows and preserves" (PL 66, 21), as the latter of the above-mentioned pontiffs noted. Popes nearer to our own day — Leo XIII (*Acta* I 270), Pius XI (AAS 22, 233), and Paul VI (AAS 62, 420) — have extolled Augustine's doctrine and holiness. The councils of the church too — notably Orange, on original sin and grace; but also Trent, on justification; Vatican I on the relation between reason and faith; and Vatican II on the mystery of the church, on revelation, and on the mystery of man — have drawn abundantly from his teaching. They have thus demonstrated that this teaching is not merely that of Augustine, but of the church, which consequently has acknowledged it to be her own. It is hardly necessary to note that in these cases it is no longer the Bishop of Hippo under discussion, but the church herself.

Augustine thus remains a thinker and writer on whom the repeated declarations of the magisterium and the continued esteem of subsequent theologians — not least among them Aquinas — have conferred a particular authority. This authority, while it does not allow anyone to prefer his teaching to that of the church (DS 2330; AAS 22, 232), likewise does not permit anyone to call Augustine's orthodoxy into question or to deny the incomparable service he rendered to the church and to Christian culture.

The fact that Augustine's thought has been interpreted through the centuries in widely diverse ways is not a sign of obscurity. Augustine is not an obscure author, but neither is he an easy one. The difficulties arise from various sources: the profundity of his thought, the multiplicity of his works, the breadth of the questions treated and the different ways in which they are approached, the diversity of his language. One must also take into account the uncertainty characteristic of anyone taking the first steps in new and difficult questions, the evolution of his thought, the lack of systematization and, finally, the limits which Augustine, like any other writer, possessed. Only the one who succeeds in patiently overcoming these difficulties will discover the *true* Augustine, the author of those writings "in which the faithful always find him alive" (Possidius, *Vita* 31, 8); the historical Augustine, far richer and more balanced than he appears through hasty interpretations or "popular" Augustinianism.

After the list of his writings, a brief résumé of Augustine's thought will be presented making use of numerous citations, so that the reader may repeat on his own this work of summarizing his thought.

WRITINGS

SOURCES

There are two sources listing Augustine's works, each of them incomplete: the *Retractationes* of Augustine himself and the *Indiculus* of Possidius. Augustine was already considering the *Retractationes* in 412 (*Ep.* 143, 2) but actually began the work only in 426-427 (*Retract.* 2, 51; *De doct. chr.* 4 26, 53). These proved to be a long and detailed examination of conscience concerning his entire literary production. He divided his works according to literary genre into books, letters, and treatises. He was able to review only the books, which he found to be 232 in number, divided among 93 works. He reviewed them according to their chronological order that the reader might be able to recognize "how I have made progress by writing" (*Retract. prol.* 1). He lacked the time to review his letters and treatises, which constitute a large, if not also the most important, part of his works. In addition to their bibliographical value, the *Retractationes* are equally important for their doctrinal aspect (they offer the key for understanding the works and for knowing the final form of Augustine's thought) and their autobiographical content, mentioned above (p. 345).

Editions: M 1, 1-64. — PL 32, 583-656. — P. Knöll, CSEL 36, 2(1902). — A. Mutzenbecher, CCL 57(1984).

Translations: English: M. I. Bogan, FC 60(1968)1-322. *French:* G. Bardy, BA, 274-446. *German:* C. J. Perl. Paderborn, 1976. *Italian:* P. Montanari. Florence, 1949.

Studies: A. Harnack, Die Retraktationen A.'s: Sitzungsberichte des Hgl. Preuss. A der W. (1905)1096-1131. — J. De Ghellinck, Les Rétractations de St. A.: NRTh 57(1930)481-500 (= Patristique et moyen âge III. Gembloux 1948, 341-365). — M. J. Lagrange, Les Rétractations exégétiques de St. A: MSCA II, 373-396. — M. F. Eller, The Retractationes of Saint Augustine: CH 18(1949)172-184. — J. Burnaby, The Retractationes of Saint Augustine: Self-criticism or Apologia?: AugMag I, 85-92. — L. J. van der Lof, Augustin a-t-il changé d'intention pendant la composition des Retractations: AugL 16(1966)5-10.

To his *Vita Augustini,* Possidius also attached an *Indiculus* of Augustine's works (PL 46, 5-22; ed. crit. A. Wilmart, MSCA II, 161-208) in which he listed a table of 1,030 books, letters, and treatises, "omitting those which cannot be counted because they have not been assigned a number." Possidius is probably referring here to the catalogue of the works in the library at Hippo (*Retract.* 2, 41) on which both the *Indiculus* and the *Retractationes* depend. Even with its omissions and a few mistakes, the *Indiculus* remains a valuable document.

In the presentation of Augustine's works, the distinction of literary genre as established by Augustine — books, letters, treatises — has been preserved. For the sake of convenience, however, the books have been divided according to a systematic order into autobiographical, philosophical, apologetic, dogmatic, moral-pastoral, monastic, exegetical, and polemical works.

BOOKS

1. Autobiographical.

Augustine's autobiographical compositions include two of his most original works, the *Confessiones* and the *Retractationes.* Cf. *supra* p. 344 and p. 345.

2. Philosophical.

The *Dialogues* represent Augustine's philosophical works and were written between his conversion and ordination to the priesthood (386-391) at Cassiciacum, Milan, Rome, and Thagaste. They deal with the great problems of philosophy: certitude, happiness, order, the immortality and greatness of the soul, the existence of God, human liberty, the cause of evil, the interior teacher. As these are works of his youth, it is necessary to refer to his mature works for further clarification or confirmation of the thoughts expressed in these compositions.

Studies: Historicity: A. Gudeman, Sind die Dialoge Augustins historisch?, in *Festschrift der phil hist.,* Vereins. Munich 1926, 16-17. — R. Philippson, Sind die Dialoge Augustins historisch?: RhM (1931)144-150. — B. L. Meulebroeck, The Historical Character of Augustine's Cassiciacum Dialogues: Mnem 14(1947)203-229. — J. J. O'Meara, The Historicity of the Early Dialogues of Saint Augustine: VC 5(1951)150-178. — O. Perler, Recherches sur les Dialogues et le site de Cassiciacum: Aug 13(1968)345-352.

Content: D. E. Roberts, in R. W. Battenhouse, ed., The Earliest Writings: A Companion to the Study of St. A. New York 1955, 93-126. — A. Guzzo, Dal Contra Academicos al De vera religione. Turin, 1957. — J. Morán, La teoría de la "admonición" en los Diálogos de san Agustín: Aug 13(1968)257-271. — J. Oroz Reta, Los diálogos de Casiciaco. Algunas observaciones estilísticas: *Augustinus* 13(1968)327-344. — V. Pratola, Problemi agostiniani. L'Aquila, 1969. — R. Voss Bernd, Der Dialog in der frühchristlichen Literatur (*Studia et Testimonia Antiqua* 9). Munich, 1970. — M. A. Molina, Felicidad y sabiduría: Agustín en noviembre de 386: *Augustinus* 18(1973)355-372.

a) at Cassiciacum (November 386 - March 387):

1. *Contra Academicos* or *De Academicis libri* III. This work is a refutation of skepticism, written for the purpose of returning to man the hope of arriving at the truth (*Retract.* 1 1, 1; *Ep.* 1).

Editions: M 1, 249-296. — PL 32, 905-958. — P. Knöll, CSEL 63, 3(1922). — W. M. Green, *Strom. Patr. et Mediaev.* 2. Utrecht, 1956; *idem,* CCL 29(1970)1-61.

Translations: English: M. P. Garvey. Milwaukee, 1942. — D. J. Kavanagh, E. Arbesmann, FC 1(1948)103-222. — J. J. O'Meara, ACW 12(1951). *French:* R. Jolivet, BA 4(1948)15-203. R. Jolivet, E. Gilson. Paris, 1955. *German:* E. Mühlenberg. Zurich-Munich, 1972. *Italian:* L. Nutrimento. Treviso, 1957. — D. Gentili, NBA 3(1970)25-165 (with text). *Polish:* K. Augustyniak, SAPF 1. Warsaw, 1953. *Portuguese:* V. De Almeida. Coimbra, 1957. *Spanish:* V. Capánaga, BAC 3(21)(1947)1-234(with text).

Studies: B. J. Diggs, St. Augustine Against the Academicians: *Traditio* 7(1949-50)73-93. — J. Oroz Reta: "Contra Academicos" de San Agustín-Estudio literario: *Helmantica* 6(1955)131-149. — G. Pfligersdorfer, Notas sobre algunos textos de san Agustín en sus obras: "Contra Academicos" y "De beata vita": CD 176(1963)464-488. — J. A. Mourant, Augustine and the Academics: RAug 4(1966)67-96. — C. Andresen, Gedenken zum philosophischen Bildungshorizont vor und in Cassiciacum: *Augustinus* 13(1968)77-98. — L. Cilleruelo, La primera meditación agustiniana: Aug 13(1968)109-123. — P. Valentin, Un "protreptique" conservé de l'Antiquité: le "Contra Academicos" de saint Augustin: RSR 43(1969)1-26, 97-117. — P. Hadot, Le "Contra Academicos" de saint Augustin et l'histoire de l'Académie: *École pratique de Hautes Études,* sect. V, *Annuaire* 77(1969-70)291-297. — J. O'Meara, Plotinus and Augustine. Exegesis of "Contra Academicos" 2, 5: *Revue Internat. de Philosophie* 92(1970)321-337. — G. Madec, Pour l'interpretation de "Contra Academicos" 2, 5: REAug 17(1971)322-328. — A. M. Nieman, The Arguments of Augustine's "Contra academicos": *The Modern Schoolman* 59(1981-82)255-279.

2. *Beata vita liber* I. The dialogue took place November 13-15, 386 and demonstrates that the blessed life consists in the knowledge of God (*Retract.* 1, 2).

Editions: M 1, 298. — PL 32, 959-976. — P. Knöll, CSEL 63, 3(1922)89-116. — W. M. Green, *Strom. Patrist. et Mediaev.* 2. Utrecht 1955, 79-95; *idem,* CCL 29(1970)65-85.

Translations: English: E. Touscher. Philadelphia, 1937. — L. Schopp, FC 1(1948). *French:* R. Jolivet, BA 4(1948)223-284 (with text). — R. Jolivet, E. Gilson. Paris, 1955. *German:* I. Schwarz-Kirchenbauer, W. Schwarz. Zurich-Munich, 1972. *Italian:* B. Neri. Florence, 1930. — S. Candela. Naples, 1954. — A. M. D'Angelo. Rome, 1959. — D. Gentili, NBA 3, 1(1970)183-225 (with text). *Polish:* A. Swiderek: SAPF 1(1953). *Spanish:* V. Capánaga, BAC 1(10), 522-666.

Studies: E. Dutoit, Augustin et le dialogue du "De beata vita": *Mus Helveticum* 6(1949)33-48. — A. van Duinkerken, Sint Augustinus over het Gelukkige Leven: Mensen en Meningen (1951)113-151. — L. Alfonsi, Sant'Agostino "De beata vita c. 4": RFIC 36(1958)249-254. — J. Doignon, Notes de critique testuelle sur le "De beata vita" de s. A.: REAug 23(1977)63-82.

3. *De ordine libri* II. Augustine proposes to examine whether evil enters into the order of providence, but in the face of the difficulties raised by this question for the partners in the dialogue, he passes to a description of the order to be followed in studies (*Retract.* 1, 3).

Editions: M 1, 315-352. — PL 32, 977-1020. — P. Knöll, CSEL 63, 3(1922)121-185. — W. M. Green, *Strom. Pat. et Mediaev.* 2. Utrecht 1955, 97-148; *idem,* CCL 29(1970)87-137.

Translations: English: R. P. Russell, FC 1(1948). *French:* R. Jolivet, BA 3(1948)302f (with text). — R. Jolivet, E. Gilson. Paris, 1955. *German:* C. J. Perl. Paderborn, 1953. — E. Mühlenberg. Zurich-Munich, 1972. *Italian:* A. M. Moschetti. Florence, 1941. — D. Gentili, NBA 3(1970) (with text). *Japanese:* W. Takahashi. Tokyo, 1954. *Polish:* J. Modrzejewski, SAPF 1(1953). *Spanish:* V. Capánaga, BAC 1(10), 673-812 (with text).

Studies: A. Dyroff, Über Form und Begriffsgehalt des augustinischen Schrift "De ordine": AurAug I, 15-62. — I. Quiles, La interioridad en el Diálogo agustiniano "Del Orden": *Ciencia Y Fe* 11(1955)75-94. — A. Solignac, Réminiscences plotiniennes et porphyriennes dans le début du "De ordine" de saint Augustin: APh 20(1957)446-465. — S. U. Zuidema, De ordo-idee in Augustinus dialog "De ordine": *Phil Reformata* 28(1963)1-18. — K. A. Wohlfarth, Der metaphysische Ansatz bei A., Meisenheim, 1969. — H. H. Gunermann, Literarische und philosophische Tradition im ersten Tagesgespräch von A.' "De ordine": RAug 9(1974)183-226.

4. *Soliloquiorum libri* II. The Soliloquies treat of the conditions of the quest for and possession of God and present an argument in favor of the immortality of the soul, *viz.* the presence in the soul of immortal truth (*Retract.* 1, 4).

Editions: M 1, 355-386. — PL 32, 869-904. — W. H. P. Müller. Bern, 1954.

Translations: English: C. C. Starburk, LNPF 7, ser. 1 (1883)538-560 (reprint: 1956). — R. E. Cleveland. Boston, 1910. — Th. F. Gilligan, FC 2(1948). — J. H. S. Burleigh. London, 1953. *French:* P. De Labriolle, BA 5(1948)24-163 (with text). — P. De Labriolle, E. Gilson. Paris, 1955. *German:* L. Schopp, A. Dyroff. Munich, 1938. — P. Remark. Munich, 1953[2]. — H. Müller. Bern, 1954. — C. J. Perl. Paderborn, 1955. *Italian:* P. Montanari. Florence, 1930. — G. Sandri. Brescia, 1950. — A. M. D'Angelo. Rome, 1956. — D. Gentili, NBA 3, 1(1970)361-487 (with text). — A. Marzullo. Varese-Milan, 1972 (with text). *Polish:* A. Swiderek, SAPF 2(1953). *Spanish:* A. Capánaga, BAC 1(10)(1957)489-614 (with text).

Studies: V. Luque, La oración agustiniana de ayer y de siempre: *Crisis* 1(1954)551-572.

— I. Quiles, La interioridad agustiniana en los Soliloquios: *Ciencia Y Fe* 10(1954)25-48. — R. Acworth, St. Augustine and the Theological Argument for the Immortality of the Soul: DR 75(1957)215-221. — A. Viñayo Gonzáles, Angustia y ansiedad del hombre pecador: Fenomenología de la angustia en los "Soliloquios" de San Agustín: *Studium Legionense* 1(1960)137-256. — Q. Cataudella, I "Soliloqui" di Agostino e il libro 1° delle "Tusculanae": *Aevum* 40(1966)550-552. — G. Raeithel, Das Gebet in den Soliloquien Augustin: ZRG 20(1968)139-153 (cf. REAug 15[1969]285).

b) at Milan (before his baptism):

5. *De immortalitate animae liber I.* These are a series of extremely concise and, therefore, obscure notes which were intended as a completion of the preceding work (*Retract.* 1, 5).

Editions: M 1, 387-389. — PL 32, 1021-1034. — H. Fuchs. Zurich, 1954.

Translations: English: E. Tourscher. Philadelphia, 1937. — L. Schopp, FC 2b (1947)1-47. *French:* P. De Labriolle, BA 5(1948)170f (with text). — P. De Labriolle, E. Gilson. Paris, 1955. *German:* H. P. Müller, Zurich-Bern, 1954. *Italian:* D. Gentili, NBA 3, 2(1970)15-133 (with text). *Polish:* M. Tomaszewski, SAPF 2(1953). *Spanish:* J. Bezic. Buenos Aires, 1954.

Studies: I. A. Mourant, Remarks on the "De immortalitate animae": AugStudies 2(1971)213-217. — C. W. Wolfskeel, Augustin über die Weltseele in der Schrift "De immortalitate animae": THETA-PI 1(1972)81-103; *idem,* Ist Augustin in "De immortalitate animae" von der Gedankenwelt des Porphyrios beeinflusst worden?: VC 26(1972)130-145. — R. Penaskovic, An Analysis of Saint Augustine's De immortalitate animae: AugStudies 11(1980)167-176.

6. *Disciplinarum libri.* These books were intended as a vast encyclopedia on the model of Varro to demonstrate how one could and ought to ascend from material things to God. Augustine completed only the *De grammatica* (lost) and, subsequently, the *De musica.* Concerning the other intended books (dialectics, rhetoric, geometry, arithmetic, philosophy) he only sketched a few notes which were also lost, although he noted, "I think some people have them" (*Retract.* 1, 6).

c) at Rome (autumn 387 - July or August 388):

7. *De quantitate animae liber I.* Augustine discusses various questions concerning the soul, especially those concerning the spiritual nature of the soul and its ascent toward contemplation (*Retract.* 1, 8).

Editions: M 1, 401-440. — PL 32, 1035-1080.

Translations: English: J. J. McMahon, FC 2b(1947). — J. M. Colleran, ACW 9(1950). — F. E. Tourscher. Philadelphia, 1933 (with text). *French:* P. De Labriolle, BA 5(1948)221-396 (with text). — P. De Labriolle, E. Gilson. Paris, 1955. *German:* C. J. Perl. Paderborn, 1960. — K. H. Lutcke, G. Weigel. Zurich-Munich, 1973. *Italian:* D. Gentili, NBA 3, 2(1976) (with text). *Polish:* D. Turkowska, SAPF 2(1953). *Spanish:* E. Cuevas, BAC 3(21)(1947)523-665 (with text).

Studies: A. Caturelli, Los grados de perfección del alma según San Agustín: *Sapientia* 9(1954)254-271. — A. Benito y Durán, El diálogo de la cuantivalencia del alma de San Agustín: *Augustinus* 7(1962)175-202.

8. *De libero arbitrio libri III.* This work, begun at Rome and completed at Hippo between 391-395, deals at length with the origin of evil and such related problems as freedom, the moral law, the existence of God and divine foreknowledge. This much-discussed work is very important for a comparison between Augustine's positions before and after the Pelagian Controversy (*Retract.* 1, 9).

Editions: M 1, 560-564. — PL 32, 1221-1310. — W. M. Green, CSEL 74(1956); *idem,* CCL 29(1970)211-321.

Translations: English: M. Pontifex, ACW 22(1955). — A. S. Benjamin, L. H. Hackstaff. Indianapolis, 1964. — R. P. Russell, FC 59(1968)63-241. *French:* F. J. Thonnard, BA 6, 1952 (with text). — G. Madec, BA 6²(1976)155-529 (with text). — F. J. Thonnard, E. Gilson. Paris, 1955. *German:* C. J. Perl. Paderborn, 1962². — W. Thimme. Zurich, 1952. *Italian:* P. Montanari. Florence, 1939. — G. Baravalle. Rome, 1960. — D. Gentili, NBA 3, 2(1976)156-376 (with text). *Japanese:* Imaizumi Sâburô. Tokyo, 1966. *Polish:* E. Trombala, SAPF 3(1953). *Spanish:* E. Seijas, BAC 3(21), 248-521 (with text).

Studies: P. Séjourné, Les conversions de saint Augustin d'après de "De libero arbitrio": RSR 25(1951)243-264, 333-363. — H. De Lubac, Note sur saint Aug. "De libero arbitrio 3 20, 65": AugMag III, 279-286. — A. Trapè, Un celebre testo di S. Ag. su "l'ignoranza e la difficoltà" e l' "op. imp. contra Jul": AugMag II, 795-803. — R. J. O'Connell, "De libero arbitrio" I, Stoicism Revisited: AugStudies 1(1970)49-68. — A. Trapè, Introd. gen: NBA 3, 2(1976)7-29. — Cf. *infra,* bibliography under the headings "freedom," "evil" and "the existence of God."

d) at Thagaste (388-391).

9. *De musica libri VI.* The *De musica* is a treatise on rhythm which was to have been completed by another treatise on melody (*Ep.* 101, 3-4). Book VI teaches the manner of ascending from mutable numbers to the immutable number which is God (*Retract.* 1, 6, 11).

Editions: M 1, 443-540. — PL 32, 1081-1194. — G. Marzi. Florence, 1969.

Translations: English: R. C. Taliaferro, FC 2b(1948)151-379. *French:* G. Finaert, F. J. Thonnard, BA7(1947)20-478 (with text). *German:* C. J. Perl. Paderborn, 1940, 1962². *Italian:* G. Marzi. Florence, 1969. — D. Gentili, NBA 3, 2(1976)379-708 (with text). *Polish:* D. Turkowska, SAPF 4(1954).

Studies: F. Amerio, Il "De musica" di Sant' Agostino. Turin, 1929. — K. Svoboda, L'esthétique de saint Augustin et ses sources. Paris, 1933. — H. Davenson, Traité de la musique selon l'esprit de Saint Augustin. Neuchâtel, 1942. — A. I. H. Vincent, Analyse du traité de métrique et de rythmique de st. Aug. intitulé "De musica." Paris, 1949. — K. Mayer Baer, Psychologic and Ontologic Ideas in Augustine's "De musica": *Journal of Aesth. and Art Criticism* 11(1952-53)224-230. — C. Del Grande, S. Agostino e la musica: *Rassegna Musicale* 3(1953)269-277. — A. Squire, The Cosmic Dance. Reflections on the "De musica" of St. Augustine: *Blackfriars* 35(1954)477-484. — C. J. Perl, Augustinus und die Musik: AugMag III, 439-452. — H. I. Marrou, Saint Augustin et la fin de la culture antique. Paris, 1958. — W. Takahashi, On St. Augustine's "De musica": *Sophia* (Tokyo) 8(1959)79-89. — U. Pizzani, Spunti escatologici nel "De musica" di S. Agostino: Aug 18(1978)209-218.

10. *De magistro liber I.* This work presents a dialogue between Augustine and his son, Adeodatus, demonstrating that one learns

wisdom only from the interior teacher, God. It is an important study of pedagogy (*Retract.* 1, 12).

Editions: M 1, 541-564. — PL 32, 1193-1220. — G. Weigel, CSEL 77, 4(1961)3-55. — K. D. Daur, CCL 29(1970)157-203.

Translations: Dutch: G. Wijdeveld. Amsterdam, 1937 (with text). *English:* J. M. Colleran, ACW 9(1950). — R. P. Russell, FC 59(1968)1-61. *French:* F. J. Thonnard, BA 6(1952)42-152 (with text). — F. J. Thonnard, E. Gilson. Paris, 1955. *German:* H. Hornstein. Düsseldorf, 1957. — C. J. Perl. Paderborn, 1974[2]. — G. Weigel, in *A. Philosophische Spätdialoge.* Zurich-Munich 1973, 247-385 (with text). *Italian:* D. Bassi, CPS 11(1941) (with text). — A. Guzzo. Florence, 1927. — G. Capasso. Rome, 1953. — A. Mura. Rome, 1965 (with text). — M. Casotti, Brescia, 1968 (with text). V. Lombardo. Padua, 1968. — D. Gentili, NBA 3, 2(1976)726-794 (with text). *Polish:* J. Modrejewski, SAPF 3(1953). *Portuguese:* R. Ricci. Porto Alegre, 1956. *Spanish:* M. Martínez, BAC 3(21)(1971)667-757. — L. Baciero. Salamanca, 1972.

Studies: F. X. Eggersdorfer, Die hl. Augustinus als Pädagoge und seine Bedeutung fur der Geschichte der Bildung. Freiburg Br., 1907. — M. Casotti, Il "De magistro" di Sant' Agostino e il metodo induttivo, in *SAg XV cent.*, Milan 1931, 57-74. — L. Allevi, I fondamenti della pedagogia nel "De magistro" di S. Ag. e San Tommaso: SC 45(1937)545-561. — J. M. Colleran, The Treatises "De magistro" of St. Augustine and St. Thomas. Rome, 1945. — B. Nardi, Il pensiero pedagogico del Medioevo. Florence, 1956. — G. Bellotti, L'educazione in s. Agostino. Bergamo, 1963. — M. Casotti, Il "De magistro" di S. Ag. e San Tommaso. Brescia, 1963. — L. R. Patanè, Il pensiero pedagogico de S. Ag. Bologna, 1967. — L. Alfonsi, S. Ag. e i metodi educativi dell'antichità: *Studi Romani* 19(1971)253-263. — G. Madec, Analyse du "De magistro": REAug 21(1975)63-71. — A. K. Clard, Unity and Method in Augustine's "De magistro": AugStudies 8(1977)1-10.

3. Apologetics

Under this heading are included the works written in defense of the Christian faith against the pagans or against those who denied the faith in the name of reason.

1. *De vera religione liber* I. Augustine composed this book at Thagaste in 390 to show that the Triune God must be worshipped with the true religion which is found, not with the pagans or the heretics, but in the Catholic church, the one "orthodox" church which is the "full guardian of the truth." He shows that Manichaean dualism is absurd and that God guides men to salvation with the force of reason and the authority of the faith, making use even of vices to admonish man to seek God. The plan of salvation, according to Augustine, is realized through history and prophecy. The work is a little masterpiece which contains the seeds of many ideas found in *The City of God* (*Retract.* 1, 13).

Editions: M 1, 747-788. — PL 34, 121-172. — W. M. Green, CSEL 77(1961). — K.-D. Daur, CCL 32(1962)169-260.

Translations: English: J. H. Burleigh. Of True Religion. London-Philadelphia, 1953, 218-283. *French:* J. Pegon, BA 8(1951)22-190 (with text). *German:* C. J. Perl. Paderborn, 1957, 1974[3]. — W. Thimme. Zurich-Stuttgart, 1962. *Italian:* S. Colombo. Turin, 1925,

1945[8]. — S. Corassali. Turin, 1930 (with text). — A. Neno. Florence, 1933. — C. Marizioni. Florence, 1935; *idem,* Florence 1937 and Rome 1954 (with text). D. Bassi, CPS 11. Turin, 1942 (with text). *Spanish:* V. Capánaga, BAC 4(30)(1956)69-209 (with text).

Studies: A. Vecchi, Il concetto di filosofia e il problema del corso storico nel "De vera religione" di S. Ag.: *Actes XIe Congr. Int. Phil.* 14(1953)282-291. — G. Folliet, "Miscela" ou "Miseria" (Aug. "De vera rel." 9, 16); REAug 14(1968)27-46.

2. *De utilitate credendi liber* I. Composed in 391, this is the first of Augustine's works after his ordination as a priest. It is an acute analysis of the relations between reason and faith and demonstrates the truth of the Catholic faith, which is not a blind faith since it is founded upon indisputable reasons (*Retract.* 1, 14).

Editions: M 8, 45-70. — PL 42, 65-92. — J. Zycha, CSEL 25, 1(1891)3-48.

Translations: English: C. L. Cornish, LNPF 3, ser. 1(1887)347-366 (reprint: 1956). — L. Meagher, FC 2b(1948). J. Burleigh, Earlier Writings. Philadelphia-London, 1953. *French:* J. Pigon, BA 8, 209-301 (with text). *German:* C. J. Perl. Paderborn, 1966. *Italian:* N. Casacca. Bologna 1918, Florence 1930. — D. Bassi, CPL 3. Turin, 1936 (with text). *Spanish:* BAC 4(30)(1956)829-899.

Studies: P. Batiffol, Autour du "De utilitate credendi" de St. Aug.: RBibl 14(1917)9-53. — T. De Castro, El método apologético agust. en el libro "De util. credendi": ReIC 4(1931)112-119.

3. *De fide rerum quae non videntur liber* I. This treatise, written after the laws of Honorius of 399, concerns the same topic as the preceding work. Concerning its authenticity, cf. *Ep.* 231, 4.

Editions: M 6, 141-150. — PL 40, 171-180. — M. F. McDonald, PSt 84. Washington, 1950 (with text).

Translations: English: C. L. Cornish, LNPF 3, ser. 1(1887)337-343 (reprint: 1956). — M. F. McDonald, op. cit. — R. Deferrari, M. F. McDonald, FC 2b(1947)445-469. *French:* J. Pegon, BA 8, 311-341 (with text). *Spanish:* H. Rodríguez, BAC 4(30)(1956)795-817 (with text).

4. *De divinatione daemonum liber* I. The book dates from 406-408 and presents a comparison between the predictions attributed to demons and prophecies (*Retract.* 2, 30).

Editions: M 6, 505-514. — PL 40, 581-592. — J. Zycha, CSEL 41(1900)597-618.

Translations: Dutch: H. J. Geerlings, De antieke daemonologie en A.' schrijft "De divinatione daemonum." 's Gravenhage, 1953, 113-139. *English:* R. Wentworth Brown, FC 27(1955)417-440. *French:* J. Boutet, BA 10(1952)655-693 (with text).

Studies: T. G. Ter Haar, De divinatione daemonum, in MiscAug., Rotterdam 1930, 323-340.

5. *Quaestiones expositae contra paganos* VI. These were composed between 406 and 412 and are published among Augustine's letters as *Ep.* 102 (*Retract.* 2, 31). They are a response to six questions (on the

resurrection, the time of the Christian religion, the distinction between pagan and Christian sacrifices, etc.) posed by the philosopher Porphyry (against whom many pages of *The City of God* will be directed).

Editions: M 121, 273-287. — PL 33, 370-386. A. Goldbacher, CSEL 34, 2(1898)554-577.

Translations: English: W. Parsons, FC 18(1953)148-177. *Italian:* L. Carrozzi, NBA 21, 951-993.

6. *De civitate Dei libri* XXII. This work numbers among Augustine's masterpieces, of which it is possibly the greatest. It presents a synthesis of his philosophical, theological, and political thought, and is one of the most significant works of Christian and world literature. Augustine himself describes it as "a great and arduous work," "a gigantic work." He labored on the treatise from 413 to 426 and published it at intervals (414 the first three books, 415 books 4 and 5, 417 books 6-10, and in 418-419 he was working on book 14). From the beginning, however, the work was composed according to a comprehensive plan (*De civ. Dei* 1, 35-36). The occasion for the treatise was provided by the accusations of the pagans against Christianity which were renewed with increased bitterness after the sack of Rome in 410. The work is divided into two parts: the first (books 1-10) is a refutation of paganism, the second (books 11-22) is an exposition and defense of Christian doctrine. The first part is further subdivided into two sections, of which the first (books 1-5) shows the social sterility and the second (books 6-10) the spiritual sterility of paganism. The second part is subdivided into three sections of four books each of which expound, respectively, the origin, the course, and the destinies of the two cities, that of God and that of the world. The structure of the work is perfect, even though there are numerous digressions concerning incidental matters (*Retract.* 2, 43; *Ep.* 212A; 184A).

The central idea of the composition is that of divine providence which illuminates and guides human history. This history is divided into two cities founded on two loves: the love of self and the love of God. The drama of this history contains five acts: creation, the sin of the angels and of man, the preparation for the coming of Christ, the Incarnation and the church, and the final destiny. In each of these acts, Augustine confronts and resolves in the light of reason and faith — thus by philosophy and theology together — the great problems of history: origins, the presence of evil, the struggle between good and evil, the victory of good over evil, the eternal destinies of good and evil. *The City of God* was widely read and exercised considerable influence in the Middle Ages. The bibliography relating to this work is extraordinarily complex and extensive, which gives proof of its perennial value and modernity.

Editions: M 7, 1. — PL 41, 13-804. — B. Dombart, A. Kalb. Leipzig, 1928-29[4] (= CCL 47-48[1955]). — E. Hoffmann, CSEL 40(1899-1900). — J. E. C. Weldon. London, 1924.

Translations: Dutch: J. Wytzes. Kampen, 1947. *English:* P. Schaff, ed., LNPF 2, ser. 1(1886)1-511 (reprint: 1956). — J. Healey, E. Barker. London-Toronto, 1945[3]. — M. Dods. New York, 1950[2]. — D. B. Zema, G. Walsh, G. Monahan, D. J. Honan, FC 8 14 24(1950-54). — E. Barker, New York-London, 1957. — G. E. McCracken, et al., LCL 411-417(1972) (with text). *French:* P. De Labriolle, J. Perret. Paris, 1941-46. — L. Moreau, G. Bardy. Corbeil, 1949. — G. Bardy, G. Combes, BA 33-37(1959-60) (with text). *German:* A. Schröder, BKV[2], 1911-16. — C. J. Perl. Salzburg, 1951-53. — W. Thimme. Zurich, 1955. — J. Bernhart. Stuttgart, 1955. *Greek:* A. Dalezios. Athens, 1954-56. *Italian:* C. Giorgi. Florence, 1927-30. — C. A. Costa, CPS. Turin, 1939 (books 1-5 with text). — C. Borgogno. Rome, 1963[3]. — D. Bentili, NBA 5, 1(1978) (books 1-10 with text). *Polish:* W. Kubicki. Poznan, 1930-34. *Portuguese:* O. Paes Leme, R. Azzi. São Paulo, 1961. *Russian:* Academy of Kiev. Kiev, 1890 (reprint: Brussels, 1974). *Slovak:* M. Patoprsty. Vojtecha, 1948. *Spanish:* L. Riber. Barcelona, 1953 (books 1-5 with text). — J. Morán, BAC 17-18 (177-178) and S. Santamarta, M. Fuertes, BAC 17-18[3] (177-178) (both with text). *Swedish:* Sv. Lidman. Om Gudsstaten, 1944[5].

Anthologies: Dutch: A. Sizoo. Kampen, 1947. — J. Wytzes. Kampen, 1950. *English:* W. G. Most. Washington, 1949. — R. H. Barrow. New York, 1951. — F. R. M. Hitchcock. New York-London, 1951. — J. W. C. Wand. Oxford-London, 1963. *French:* L. Bertrand. Paris, 1914. — G. Vidal. Avignon, 1930. — G. Bardy. Paris, 1949. *German:* A. Harnack. Tübingen, 1922. — J. Bernhart. Leipzig, 1930. Stuttgart, 1965[3]. — H. Klöser. Paderborn, 1953. — M. Zepf. Heidelberg, 1954. — J. Fischer. Münster, 1954. *Italian:* V. Giovanniello. Florence, 1951, 1963[2]. — G. Capasso. Naples, 1952. — D. Pesce. Florence, 1954. — C. Moreschini. Florence, 1970. — F. V. Joannes. Milan, 1976. *Japanese:* M. Nakayama. Tokyo, 1932 (with summary in English). *Latin:* M. Verheijen, K. Woldring, L. Hogveld. Scriptores Graeci et Romani 45-46. Zwolle, 1950-51. *Polish:* S. Bross. Poznan, 1935[2]. *Spanish:* L. Nueda. Barcelona, 1943. — J. Marias. Barcelona, 1950.

Bibliographies: S. M. Del Estal, Historiografía de la Ciudad de Dios de 1928 a 1954: CD 167(1955)647-774. — E. Lamirande, Un siecle et demi d'études sur l'ecclésiologie de St. Aug.: REAug 8(1962)1-125; *idem,* Supplément bibl. sur l'ecclésiologie de St. Aug.: REAug 17(1971)177-182. — G. Hasenhor, Les traductiones romanes du De civ. Dei. I La traduction italienne: *Rev Hist Textes* 5(1975)169-238.

Motives and structure: F. Cayré, La "cité de Dieu": RT 35(1930)487-507. — E. Gilson, Les métamorphoses de la Cité de Dieu. Paris-Louvain, 1952. — A. C. Vega, Estructura literaria de la Ciudad di Dios: CD 167(1955)13-51. — A. Vecchi, Introduzione al "De civ. Dei." Modena, 1957. — P. Brezzi, Analisi e interpretazione del "De civ. Dei" di S. A., Tolentino, 1960. — J. Lamotte, But et adversaires de s. A. dans le "De civitate Dei": AugL 11(1961)434-469. — J. Divjak, A.s erster Brief an Firmus und die revidierte Ausgabe der Civitas Dei, in *Latinität und Alte Kirche.* Vienna 1977, 56-70.

Philosophical questions: E. Winter, De doctrinae neoplatonicae in Aug. De civ. Dei vestigiis. Freiburg, 1928. — P. Monnot, Essai de synthèse philosophique d'après le XIeme libre de la Cité de Dieu: APh 7(1930)142-185. — J. H. S. Burleigh, The City of God. A Study of St. Aug.'s Philosophy. London, 1949. — U. A. Padovani, Filosofia e teologia della storia. Brescia, 1953. — C. Boyer, La Cité de Dieu source de la phil. aug.: CD 167(1955)53-65. — G. Bueno Martínez, Lectura lógica de la CdD, in *S. A. Estudios y Coloquios.* Saragossa 1960, 147-173. — F. Casado, El repudio de la filosofía antigua en la

CdD: CD 167(1955)67-93. — C. Vaca, Puntos para una psicología del pecado en la CdD: CD 167(1955)269-282. — F. J. Thonnard, La philosophie de la CdD: REAug 2(1956)403-426. — A. Muñoz Alonso, Concepto agustiniano de la filosofía en la CdD, in *S. A. Esutdios y Coloquios.* Saragossa 1960, 35-47. — R. Martin, The Two Cities in Aug.'s Political Philosophy: *Journal Hist. of Ideas* 33(1972)195-216. — W. Rordorf, St. Aug. et la tradition philosophique antifataliste à propos du De civ. Dei 5, 1-11: RELA 51(1973)23-24. — M. F. Sciacca, Filosofia e teologia della storia in S. A., in *Provvidenza e storia.* Pavia 1974, 29-42.

Religious questions: Th. F. Carlson, De contentione Aur. Aug. cum paganis in libro eius De Civ. Dei., Lund, 1847. — G. Lüttgert, Theologumena Varroniana a S. Aug. in iudicium vocata. Sorau, 1858-59. — H. Scholz, Fruitio Dei: Glaube und Unglaube in der Weltgeschichte. Leipzig, 1911. — G. Busnelli, L'avvocato dei tempi moderni: CC 65(1914)514-531. — F. G. Sihler, From Augustus to Augustine. Cambridge, 1923. — P. De Labriolle, La réaction païenne. Paris, 1934. — A. Schütz, Gott in der Geschichte. Salzburg-Leipzig, 1936. — H. Fuchs, Der geistige Widerstand gegen Rom in der antiken Welt. Berlin, 1938. — C. Zimara, Die Lehre des hl. Aug. über die sogennante Zulassungen Gottes: DT 19(1941)269-294. — W. Ziegenfuss, Aug. Christliche Transzendenz in Gesellschaft und Geschichte. Berlin, 1948. — A. Quaquarelli, La polemica pagano-cristiana da Plotino ad Ag., Milan, 1952. — R. Lorenz, Die Herkunft des augustin. "Frui Deo": ZKG 64(1952-53)34-60. — E. Castelli, I presupposti di una teologia della storia. Milan, 1952. — G. Soleri, Alla ricerca di una teologia della storia: *Città di Vita* 9(1954)19-37. — F. J. Thonnard, Science et Sagesse dans la CdD: CD 167(1955)511-524. — E. Stakemeier, Civitas Dei. Die Geschichtstheologie des hl. Aug. als Apologie der Kirche. Paderborn, 1955. — J. Oroz de la Consolación, Introducción a una "Theologia" agustino-varroniana, vista desde la CdD: CD 167(1955)151-178. — J. I. Alcorta Echevarria, El ordo amoris y la aversio a Deo en la Diálectica de las dos ciudades: CD 167(1955)125-150. — E. D. Carretero, Antropología teológica de la CdD: CD 167(1955)193-268. — U. Domínguez del Val, El martirio argumento apologético en la CdD: CD 167(1955)527-542. — J. Pépin, La théologie tripartite de Varron: REAug 2(1956)265-295. — P. Courcelle, Propos antichrétiens rapportés par st. Aug.: RAug 1(1958)149-184. — A. Wachtel, Beiträge zur Geschichtstheologie des Aur. Aug., Bonn, 1960. — A. von Campenhausen, Aug. und der Fall von Rom, in *Tradition und Leben.* Tübingen 1960, 253-271. — A. D. R. Polman, The Word of God According to St. Aug., London, 1962. — R. Thouvenot, St. Aug. et les Païens: Latomus 70(1964)682-690. — Y. M. Duval, St. Aug. et les persécutions de la deuxième motié du IVe siècle: MSR 23(1966)175-191. — J. A. McCallin, The Christological Unity of St. Aug.'s De civ. Dei: REAug 12(1966)85-109. — J. F. Ortega Muñoz, Doctrina de s. Ag. sobre la tolerancia en materia de religión: CD 179(1966)618-646. — D. Lange, Zum Verhältnis von Geschichtsbild und Christologie in Aug. De civ. Dei: EvangTh 28(1968)430-441. — A. Benoit, Remarque sur l'eschatologie de St. Aug., in Festschr. E. Stähelin. Basel 1969, 1-9. — R. A. Markus, Saeculum: History and Society in the Theology of St. Aug., Cambridge, 1970. — E. Teselle, Aug. the Theologian. London, 1970. — J. F. O'Grady, Priesthood and Sacrifice in the City of God: *Augustinus* 11(1971)27-44. — A. Schindler, Querverbindungen zwischen Aug. theologischer und Kirchenpolitischer Entwicklung 390-400: ThZ 29(1973)95-116. — E. Teselle, Aug.'s Strategy as an Apologist. Villanova, 1974. — G. Madec, Tempora Christiana, in *Scientia augustiniana.* Festschr. A. Zumkeller. Würzburg 1975, 112-136.

Ecclesiology: G. Walter, Die Heidenmission nach der Lehre des hl. Aug., Leipzig, 1921. — H. Leisegang, Der Ursprung der Lehre A.s von der Civ. Dei: *Archiv f. Kulturgeschichte* 16(1925)127-158. — E. Salin, Civitas Dei. Tübingen, 1926. — V. Stegemann, Aug. Gottesstaat. Tübingen, 1926. — R. Frick, Die Geschichte der Reich-Gottesgedanken in der alten Kirche bis zu Origenes und Aug., Giessen, 1928. — F. Cayré, La Cité de Dieu: RT 35(1930)487-507. — W. J. M. Mulder, Gottesstaat und Gottesreich, in MiscAug.

Rotterdam 1930, 212-219. — J. Pange, La Cité de Dieu de St. Aug., Paris, 1930. — P. M. Vélez, Las dos ciudades de s. Ag.: *Religión y Cultura* 23(1933)161-192. — W. Kamlah, Christentum und Geschichtlichkeit. Stuttgart, 1951. — E. Hippel, Aug. Lehre vom Gottesstaat: *Neues Abendland* 6(1956)476-485. — J. Götte, Vorsehungsgedanke und Vorsehungsglaube des hl. Aug.: *Jahresbericht des Canisius Kollege* (1950-51)22-71. — P. Galeani, Provvidenza e beni temporali secondo S. Ag., Rome, 1952. — A. Adam, Der manichäische Ursprung der Lehre von der zwei Reiche bei Aug.: ThLZ 77(1952)385-390. — B. M. Melchior, Two Loves that Built Two Cities: *Teacher's Scrapbook* 48(1953)237-240. — A. Lauras, H. Rondet, Le théme des deux cités dans l'œuvre de St. Aug.: ÉtAug. Paris 1953, 97-160. — E. Hendrikx, Der betekenis van Aug.'s De civ. Dei voor Kerk en Staat. Groningen-Djakarta, 1954. — J. Ratzinger, Herkunft und Sinn der Civitas-Lehre Aug.: AugMag II, 965-979. — A. Lauras, H. Rondet, Deux cités: Jerusalem et Babylone: CD 167(1954)117-150. — J. Straub, Die geschichtliche Stunde des hl. Aug.: CD 167(1954)571-583. — D. Pesce, Città terrena e città celeste nel pensiero antico. Florence, 1957. — E. Hendrikx, Die Bedeutung von Aug. De civ. Dei für kirche und Staat: Aug 1(1961)79-93. — H. Rahner, Kirche und Staat im frühen Christentum. Munich, 1961. — R. B. Barr, The Two Cities in St. Aug.: *Laval* 18(1962)211-229. — M. Campelo, Los dos mundos de s. Ag: RFE 23(1964)347-360. — E. Gilson, Les métamorphoses de la CdD. Paris-Louvain. 1952, — H. Holstein, Le peuple de Dieu d'après la Cité de Dieu, in *Mel. V. Capánaga,* I. Madrid 1967, 193-208. — T. Matsuda, The City of God in Aug.: *Med Thought* 10(1968)23-41. — J. Campos, La CdD según la mente y sentir de los Padres de la Iglesia: CD 184(1971)495-579.

Moral, social and political questions: B. Seidel, Die Lehre des hl. Aug. vom Staate. Breslau, 1909. — O. Schilling, Die Staat und Soziallehre des hl. Aug., Freiburg Br, 1910². — P. Monceaux, St. Aug. et la guerre: L'Eglise et le droit de guerre. Paris, 1913. — O. Schilling, Naturrecht und Staat nach der Lehre der alten Kirche. Freiburg Br, 1914. — J. M. Figgis, The Political Aspect of St. Aug.'s De civ. Dei. London, 1921. — U. Schroeder, Aug. Ansicht vom christlichen Staat als Glied der Civ. Dei. Greifswald, 1922. — J. Bourgeot, Aug. Phil. des Friedens und des Kriegs. Leipzig, 1926. — G. Combès, La doctrine politique de st. Aug. Paris, 1927. — A. Jäger, Aug. und der antike Friedensgedanke: *NPhilUntersuch* 3(1928)5-15. — Ch. Dawson, St. Aug. and His Age, in *A Monument to St. Aug. XV cent.* London, 1930. — Y. De La Brière, La conceptión de la paix et de la guerre chez st. Aug.: *Rev. Fil.* 30(1930)557-572. — A. Zivkovic, Civitas terrena kod Sw. Aug.: *Bogoslov Smotra* 18(1930)51-66. — L. Teixidor, La libertad humana en san. Ag.: EE 9(1930)433-461. — O. Schilling, Die Staatslehre des hl. Aug. nach De civ. Dei: AurAug (1930)301-313. — F. X. Millar, The Significance of St. Aug.'s Criticism of Cicero's Definition of the State: *Phil Perennis.* Regensburg, 1930, 22-112. — H. X. Arguillière, Observations sur l'augustinisme politique: RevPhil 30(1930)539-556. — G. Roberti, Il diritto romano in S. Ag.: RFN 23(1931)305-366. — V. Grabar, Le doctrine du droit intern. chez st. Aug.: *Arch Phil du Droit* 2(1932)428-446. — L. Kosters, Le droit des gens chez st Aug.: *Rev Droit Int Leg* 14(1933)31-61, 282-317, 637-676. — C. V. von Horn, Beiträge zur Staatslehre St. Aug. nach De civ. Dei. Breslau, 1934. — F. E. Tourscher, War and Peace in St. Aug.'s De civ. Dei. Washington, 1934. — R. Regout, La doctrine de la guerre juste de st. Aug. à nos jours. Paris, 1935. — E. Peterson, Der Monotheismus als politisches Problem. Leipzig, 1935. — N. H. Baynes, The Political Ideas of St. Aug.'s De civ. Dei. London, 1936. — G. Ceriani, Giustizia e libertà nella CdD. Venegono Inf, 1941. — L. Pinorma, Jumalan valtakunta ja maallinen Yhteisö Aug. teoksessa De civ. Dei. Oslo, 1941. — A. G. Kis, Gedanken des hl. Aug. über die Sklaverei. Vienna, 1942. — A. S. Truyoly Serra, El derecho y el Estado en S. A., Madrid, 1944; *idem,* Supuestos y conceptos fundamentales del pensamiento jurídico de S. A.: *Verdad y Vida* 2(1944)308-336, 513-531. — H. F. Friberg, Love and Justice in Political Theory. A Study of Aug.'s Definition of the Commonwealth. Chicago, 1944. — J. Hidalgo, El concepto de Imperio en s. Ag.: *Arbor* 1(1944)430-438. — F. Cayré, La philosophie de la paix: AnThA 6(1945)149-173. — M. L. Vanesse, Le concept de societas et quelques notions connexes dans le De civ. Dei: Diss., Louvain, cf. RBPh 25(1946-47)370. — M. Lanseros, El Derecho y el Estado en s. Ag.: *Rev Esp Der Can* 1(1946)521-530. — J. K. Ryan, The Augustinian Doctrine of Peace and War: AER 116(1947)401-421. — M. G. Ribera, El concepto de la Ley eterna, ley natural y ley positiva en la CdD: *Jus* 18(1947)121-127. — R. Melli, Il concetto di autorità in S. Ag., Lecce, 1948. — A. Ferraiolo, Il pensiero politico de S. Ag. e S. Tommaso., S. Agata di Puglia, 1950. — V. Giorgianni, Il concetto del diritto e dello stato in s. Ag., Padua, 1951. — F. E. Cranz, The Development of Aug.'s Ideas on Society Before the Donatist Controversy: HThR 47(1954)255-316. — H. J. Diesner, Studien zur Gesellschaftslehre und sozialen Haltung Aug., Halle, 1954. — P. Brezzi, Una civitas terrena spiritualis come ideale storico-politico di S. Ag.: AugMag II, 915-922. — P. Th. Camelot, St. Aug. Doctor of Peace: *Cross and Crown* 6(1954)69-80. — C. Cary-Elwes, Peace in the City of God: CD 167(1955)417-430. — J. Zaragüeta, Perspectiva ética de la CdD: CD 167(1955)285-311. — H. Rondet, Pax, tranquillitas ordinis: CD 167(1955)343-364. — P. L. Verdú, Persona y communidad en la CdD: CD 167(1955)299-309. — Q. Tosatti, Ag. e lo stato Romano: *Studi Romani* 3(1955)532-547. — C. J. Perl, Über die Wertphilosophie Aug. Ein Versuch axiologischer Einführung in den Gottenstaat: CD 167(1955)113-123. — G. Kehnscherper, Die Stellung der Bibel und der alten christlichen Kirche zur Sklaverei. Halle, 1957. — E. H. Brookes, The City of God and the Politics of Crisis. Toronto, 1960. — D. X. Burt, Teoría agustiniana sobre la tolerancia en materia religiosa: *Augustinus* 5(1960)369-404. — S. Cotta, La città politica di S. Ag., Milan, 1960. — H. J. Diesner, Die Ambivalenz des Friedensgedankens und der Friedenspolitik bei A., in *Kirche und Staat.* Berlin 1963, 46-52. — B. Lohse, Aug. Wandlung in seiner Beurteilung des Staates: SP 6(1962)447-475. — A. Coccia, La schiavitù nel pensiero di S. Ag.: *Città di Vita* 17(1962)586-597. — A. H. Deane, The Political and Social Ideas of St. Aug., New York-London, 1963. — R. A. Markus, Saeculum, History and Society in the Theology of St. Aug., London, 1970. — E. Soto, Lineamenta iuris crim. in doctrina S. Aug., Rome, 1972. — E. L. Fortin, Idealisme politique et foi chrétienne dans le pensée de st. Aug.: RAug 8(1972)231-260.

Time and Historiography: G. von Hertling, Aug. Der Untergang der antiken Kultur. Mainz, 1911[3]. — U. A. Padovani, La CdD di S. Ag. Teologia e non filosofia della storia, in *S. Ag.,* Milan 1931, 220-263. — P. Brünner, Zur Auseinandersetzung zwischen antiken und christlichen Zeit und Geschichtsverständnis bei Aug.: ZThK 14(1933)55-81. — P. Courcelle, Histoire littéraire des grandes invasions germaniques. Paris, 1964[3]. — G. Cataldo, la filosofia della storia nel De civ. Dei., Bari, 1950. — H. I. Marrou, L'ambivalence du temps de l'histoire chez St. Aug., Paris-Montreal, 1950. — G. Amari, Il concetto di storia in S. Ag., Rome, 1951. — J. Daniélou, Philosophie ou Théologie de l'Histoire?: *Dieu vivant* 19(1951)127-136. — R. Berlinger, Zeit und Zeitlichkeit bei Aur. Aug.: AnThA 13(1953)260-279. — E. Castelli, I presupposti di una teologia della storia. Milan, 1953. — P. Chiocchetta, Teologia della storia. Rome, 1953. — A. Ferrabino, S. Ag. e la religione della storia: *Humanitas* 9(1954)959-965. — J. Hubaux, St. Aug. et la crise cyclique: AugMag II, 943-950. — P. Leturia, Las coordenadas de la historia universal en la historiología de s. Ag.: *Misiones Extr.,* Burgos 1954, 16-32. — J. Chaix Ruy, Anti-historisme et théologie de l'histoire: RAug 1(1958)301-315. — A. H. Wachtel, Beiträge zur Geschichtstheologie des Aur. Aug., Bonn, 1960. — F. M. Schmölz, Historia sacra et profana bei Aug.: FThSt 8(1961)308-321. — M. Elices, Función historiológica de paz, principalmente en el libro XIX de la CdD: CD 177(1964)77-85. — G. L. Keyes, Christian Faith and the Interpretation of History. A Study of St. Aug.'s Phil. of History. Lincoln, 1966. — F. Diaz de Cerio, La hist. según s. Ag.: *Perfecit* 1(1968)351-402. — D. Lange, Zum Verhältnis von Geschichtsbild und Christologie in Aug. De civ. Dei: *Evang Theol* 28(1968)430-441. — H. I. Marrou, Théologie de l'Histoire. Paris, 1968, — T. Orlandi, Il De civ. Dei di Ag. e la storiografia di Roma: *Studi Romani* 16(1968)17-29. — J. Pegueroles, Sentido de la historia según s. Ag.: *Augustinus* 16(1971)239-261. — P. Prini, Autobiografia e storia del mondo nel pensiero di s. Ag.: *Provvidenza e Storia*. Pavia 1974, 15-17. — M. Ferrini, La visione agostiniana della città politica: *Humanitas* 32(1977)3-17. — E. L. Fortin, Augustine's City of God and the Modern Historical Consciousness: *Review of Politics* 41(1979)323-343.

St. Augustine and Rome: P. Gerosa, S. Ag. e l'imperialismo romano: MSCA II (1931) 977-1040. — J. D. Burger, Aug. et la ruine de Rome: *RevThPh* 30(1942)177-194. — H. von Campenhausen, Aug. und der Fall von Rom: *Universitas* 2(1947)257-268. — V. Pöschl, Aug. und die Röm. Geschichtsauffassung: AugMag II (1955)957-963. — J. Straub, Aug. Sorge um die Regeneratio Imperii: HGJ 73(1954)34-60. — J. Wytzes, Aug. en Rome: *Hermeneus* 26(1954)41-50, 68-73. — F. G. Mayer, Aug. und das antike Rom., Stuttgart, 1955. — A. Mandouze, St. Aug. et la religion romaine: RAug 1(1958)187-223. — M. J. Wilks, Roman Empire and Christian State in the De civ. Dei: *Augustinus* 12(1967)489-510. — P. Courcelle, Mille nocendi artes, in Mel. P. Boyancé. Rome, 1974, 219-227. — G. Cannone, Il sermo de exc. Urbis di S. Ag.: VetChr 12(1975)325-346. — J. Oroz Reta, La romanidad de S. A.: *Estudios clásicos* 20(1976)353-360.

Influence: F. Tournier, Les deux cités dans la littérature chrétienne: *Etudes* 123(1910)644-665. — E. Troeltsch, A. die christliche Antike und das Mittelalter. Munich, 1915. — E. Bernheim, Die augustinische Geschichtsauschauung: *Zeitschr. der Savigny-Stiftung für Rechtsgesch.* 33(1912)309-335. — C. Calcaterra, S. Ag. nelle opere di Dante e del Petrarca: RFN suppl 23(1931)422-499. — S. Vismara, La storia in S. Ag. e in G. B. Vico: RFN suppl 23(1931)115-166. — U. Mariani, Le teorie politiche di S. Ag. e il loro influsso sulla scuola agostin. del sec. XIV. Florence, 1933. — R. Régout, La doctrine de la guerre juste de St. Aug. à nos jours. Paris, 1935. — Th. Deman, St. Aug. maître de culture chrétienne: VS 62(1940)158*-187*. — P. Jaccard, De st. Aug. à Pascal: RTP(1940)41-55. — H. X. Arquillière, L'Augustinisme politique. Paris, 1956². — P. Brezzi, L'influenza di S. Ag. sulla storiografia e sulle dottrine politiche del medio evo: *Humanitas* 9(1954)977-989. — F. Cayré, St. Aug. initiateur de l'école d'Occident: *Giorn. Metaf.* 9(1954)449-463. — U. A. Padovani, Storicismo teologico agostin.: *Humanitas* 9(1954)966-977. — A. Ramos Motta, S. Ag. na obra de P. Oròsio: *Filosofia* 1(1954)35-40. — B. Smalley, John Ridewall's Commentary on De civ. Dei: *Medium Aevum* 25(1956)140-153. — U. Mariani, Chiesa e Stato nei teologi agostiniani del s. XIV. Rome, 1957. — J. Ratzinger, Die Geschichtstheol. des hl. Bonaventura. Munich, 1959. — G. Tavard, Le thème de la Cité de Dieu dans le protestantisme americain: REAug 5(1959)207-221. — P. P. Gerosa, Umanesimo cristiano del Petrarca. Influenza agostiniana. Turin, 1966. — P. Brezzi, Il superamento dello schema agostin. nella storiogr. medievale. Turin, 1975. — G. Morra, L'agostinismo medievale e S. Bonaventura: *Quest Stor Filos* I. Brescia 1975, 579-615. — M. C. Rose, Aug.'s Thought and Present Day Christianity: *Thomist* 39(1975)49-64.

Contemporary Significance: W. Cunningham, St. Aug. and His Place in the History of Christian Thought. London, 1886. — A. Harnack, Was verdankt unsere Kultur den Kirchenvätern. Leipzig, 1911. — J. Geyser, Aug. und die phänomenologische Religionsphilosophie der Gegenwart. Münster, 1923. — J. Hessen, Aug. und seine Bedeutung für die Gegenwart. Stuttgart, 1924. — R. Mehl, Notes sur l'actualité de st. Aug.: RHPR 31(1951)224-233. — J. Guitton, Attualità de S. Ag. (Italian transl.) Rome, 1963. — R. Ciucci, S. Ag. oggi. Florence, 1969. — J. Préaux, De la cité de Dieu à la cité séculière de H. Cox, in *Probl Hist Christ* 3. Brussels 1973, 73-97. — W. Takahashi, The Contemporary Significance of Aug.'s De civ. Dei: *St Med Thought* 14(1972)1-15 (in Japanese with an English summary). — G. Del Ton, Timori e speranze per l'avvenire: *Divinitas* 17(1973)5-18. — S. A. Kamer, Orthodox and Revolutionary Theology of History in the Middle Ages. Diss., Louisville, 1976.

4. Dogmatic

1. *De fide et symbolo liber* I. This work contains the explanation of the creed given by Augustine in October 393 before the African bishops who were meeting at Hippo *in secretario Basilicae Pacis* (*Retract* 1, 17). This book is an important witness to the beginnings of Augustine's Trinitarian doctrine.

Editions: M 6, 151-164. — PL 40, 181-196. — J. Zycha, CSEL 41(1900)1-32

Translations: English: J. Burleigh, Earlier Writings. Philadelphia-London, 1953. — P. Schaff, ed., LNPF 3, ser. 1(1887)321-333 (reprint: 1956). — R. P. Russell, FC 27(1955)311-345. *French:* J. Rivière, BA 9(1947)19-75 (with text). *German:* C. J. Perl. Paderborn, 1968.

2. *De diversis quaestionibus octoginta tribus liber* I. Augustine composed this work, which consists of responses to questions of a philosophical, dogmatic, or exegetical nature placed to him by friends, between the years 388-396. He was already a bishop at the time when he had these various responses put together in a single book *Retract.* 2, 26.

Editions: M 6, 1-80. — PL 40, 11-100. — A. Mutzenbecher, CCL 44A(1975)11-249.

Translations: English: J. Burleigh, op. cit. — D. L. Mosher, FC 70(1982). *French:* J.-A. Bechaert, BA 10(1952)53-379 (with text).

Studies: A. Solignac, Analyse et sources de la Question "De ideis": AugMag I, 307-315. — R. Flórez, Sobre la mentalidad de Agustín en los primeros años de su monacato. El libro de las ochenta y tres cuestiones: CD 169(1956)464-477.

3. *De diversis quaestionibus ad Simplicianum libri* II. Although this is an exegetical work, it has a fundamental dogmatic importance. It is addressed to Simplicianus, bishop of Milan and successor of Ambrose (it thus dates from after April 4, 397), and contains the explanation of questions drawn from the Letter to the Romans and II Kings. Book I is indispensable for an understanding of Augustine's doctrine of grace, for in it he corrects his previous error and clearly affirms the necessity and gratuitousness of grace, even for the beginning of faith and the desire for conversion (*Retract.* 2, 1).

Editions: M 6, 81-120. — PL 40, 101-148. — A. Mutzenbecher, CCL 44(1970).

Translations: English: J. Burleigh, op. cit., 370-406 (book I). *French:* J. Boutet, BA 10(1952)410-579 (with text). *Spanish:* V. Capánaga, BAC 9(79)(1952)60-169 (with text).

Studies: A. Casamassa, Il pensiero di S. Ag. nel 396-397. Rome, 1919. — A. Pincherle, La formazione teologica di S. Ag., Rome, 1948. — A. Zeoli, La teologia agostiniana della grazia fino alle "Quaest. ad Simplicianum" (396). Naples, 1963 (cf. review by F. J. Thonnard, REAug 12[1966]361-362). — A. Pincherle, Sulla formazione della dottrina agostiniana della grazia: RSLR 11(1975)1-23. — W. Babcock, Augustine's Interpretation of Romans (A. D. 394-396): AugStudies 10(1979)55-74.

4. *Ad inquisitionem Ianuarii libri* II (*Ep.* 54-55). These two books were

written around 400 concerning the customs and rites of the church (*Retract.* 2, 20).

Editions: M 2, 123. — PL 33, 199-223. — A. Goldbacher, CSEL 34, 2(1898)158-213.

Translations: English: W. Parsons, FC 12(1951)252-293. *Italian:* L. Carrozzi, NBA 21(1969)437-497 (with text).

5. *De fide et operibus liber* I. Augustine composed this work in 413 to show that faith must be accompanied by works, and to propose this fact as a fundamental principle of pre- and postbaptismal catechesis (*Retract.* 2, 38).

Editions: M 6, 165-192. — PL 40, 197-230. — J. Zycha, CSEL 41(1900)33-97.

Translations: English: G. Lombardo, S. Augustine's "De Fide et operibus." Cath. Univ. of America, Washington, 1951. — R. J. Deferrari, FC 27(1955)215-282. *French:* J. Rigon, BA 8, 355-460 (with text). *Italian:* R. Calzecchi Onesti, Sant' Agostino. Fede operante. Vicenza, 1965.

6. *De videndo Deo liber* I (*Ep.* 147). Written in 413, this book treats the question of the vision of God with bodily eyes (cf. *De civ. Dei* 22, 29; *Retract.* 2, 41).

Editions: M 2, 473-496. — PL 33, 596-622. — A. Goldbacher, CSEL 44(1904)275-231. — M. Schmaus, FP 23(1930).

Translations: Dutch: L. Coppens. Nijmegen, 1949. *English:* W. Parsons, FC 20(1953)170-224. *Italian:* L. Carrozzi, NBA 22(1971)367-433 (with text).

7. *De praesentia Dei liber* I (*Ep.* 187). This treatise from 417 deals with the inhabitation of the Holy Spirit in the souls of the just (*Retract.* 2, 49).

Editions: M 2, 687-692. — PL 33, 832-848. — A. Goldbacher, CSEL 57(1923)81-119.

Translations: English: W. Parsons, FC 30(1955)221-255. *Italian:* L. Carrozzi, NBA 23(1974)131-175 (with text).

8. *Enchiridion ad Laurentium* or *De fide, spe et caritate liber* I. This manual from the year 421, arranged according to the scheme of the three theological virtues, contains an explanation of the creed (faith), of the Lord's Prayer (hope) and of the moral precepts (love). It presents a brief and clear synthesis of Augustine's theology (*Retract.* 2, 63).

Editions: M 6, 195-242. — PL 40, 231-290. — O. Scheel. Tübingen, 1903, 1937[3]. — E. Evans, CCL 46(1966)49-114.

Translations: Dutch: C. Bloemen. Roermond, 1930. — A. Sizoo, G. C. Berkouver, Augustinus over het Credo. Het Enchiridion en andere geschriften over het apostolisch Symbol. Kampen, 1941. *English:* J. F. Shaw, LNPF 3, ser. 1(1887)237-276 (reprint: 1956). — L. A. Arand, ACW 3(1947). — B. M. Peebels, FC 2(1947)369-472. — E. Evans. London, 1953. — A. C. Outler. London-Philadelphia, 1955. — H. Paolucci. Chicago, 1961. *French:* A. Rivière, BA 9(1947)103-327 (with text). *German:* P. Simon. Paderborn, 1962[2]. — J. Barbel. Düsseldorf, 1960. — S. Mitterer, BKV[3](1925). *Italian:* A. Thonna-Barthet. Florence, 1931. — E. De Nicola, M. F. Sciacca. Fossano, 1971.

Polish: Wl. Budzik. Warsaw, 1952. *Spanish:* V. Capánaga, BAC 4(30)(1956)463-635 (with text).

Studies: M. F. Sciacca, Riflessioni sull' "Enchiridion" di S. Ag.: AugStudies 2(1971)105-113.

9. *De cura pro mortuis gerenda liber* I. Augustine wrote this response to Paulinus of Nola in 424-25 concerning solicitude for the dead and the benefit which derives to the deceased from being buried near the memorials of the martyrs (*Retract.* 2, 64).

Editions: M 6, 515-532. — PL 40, 591-610. — J. Zycha, CSEL 41(1900)619-660.

Translations: English: M. H. Allies. London, 1914. — H. Browne, LNPF 3, ser. 1(1887)539-551 (reprint: 1956). — R. J. Deferrari, FC 27(1955)347-384. *French:* G. Combès, BA 2(1937)384-452 (with text). *German:* G. Schlachter, R. Arbesmann. Würzburg, 1975. *Italian:* C. Giorgi. Florence, 1927. — R. Calzecchi Onesti. Vicenza, 1962.

Studies: N. Spaccapelo, Il "De cura pro mortuis gerenda" di S. Ag. Annotazioni di antropologia: SC 100(1972)98-115. — L. J. van der Lof, De san Agustín a san Gregorio de Tours. Sobre le intervención de los mártires: *Augustinus* 19(1974)35-43.

10. *De octo Dulcitii quaestionibus liber* I. This work was composed shortly after the preceding one. The responses, with the exception of the fifth, concerning the election of David, are drawn from previous works (*Retract.* 2, 65).

Editions: M 6, 121-140. — PL 40, 147-170.

Translations: English: R. J. Deferrari, FC 16(1952)423-466. *French:* G. Bardy, BA 10(1952)583-642 (with text).

Studies: A. Mutzenbecher, Zur Datierung von Augustinus "De octo Dulcitii qq.": SE 19(1969-70)365-379.

11. *De Trinitate libri* XV. This is Augustine's principal dogmatic work; a true masterpiece which has exercised a decisive influence on Western Trinitarian theology. The treatise was composed in two stages: the first twelve books (published, to his chagrin, without Augustine's knowledge) between 399 and 412; the remaining books and final edition around 420. The *De Trinitate* is structured according to the following plan: books 1-4, biblical theology of the Trinity; books 5-7, speculative theology and defense of the dogma; book 8, introduction to the mystical knowledge of God; books 9-14, search for the image of the Trinity in man; book 15, summary and conclusion of the work. It thus presents at one and the same time the exposition, defense, formulation, illustration and contemplation of the dogma. Some of the more original aspects of Augustine's presentation are the doctrine of the relations, the "psychological" explanation of the Trinity, the personal properties of the Holy Spirit (the Holy Spirit proceeds as love) and the connection between the mystery of the Trinity and the life of grace (*Retract.* 2, 15).

Editions: M 8, 749-1004. — PL 42, 819-1098. — W. J. Mountain, CCL 50, 50A (1968).

Translations: Danish: J. Pedersen. Copenhagen, 1965 (Anthology). *English:* W. G. T. Shedd, LNPF 3, ser. 1(1887)1-228 (reprint: 1956). — J. F. Shaw. New York, 1905. — J. Burnaby. Philadelphia, 1955. — S. McKenna, FC 45(1963). *French:* M. Mellet, T. Camelot, E. Hendrikx, P. Agëasse, J. Moingt, BA 15-16(1955) (with text). *German:* M. Schmaus, BKV^3 (1935); *idem,* Munich, 1951 (anthology). *Italian:* P. Montanari, *Bibl Ag* 10. Florence, 1932-35. — G. Beschin, NBA 4(1973). *Polish:* M. Stokowska, J. M. Szymusiak, *Prisma Ojcòw Kòsciola* 25. Poznan, 1962. *Spanish:* L. Arias, BAC 5(39) (1956^2) (with text).

Studies: J. Stiglmayr, Zur Trinitätspekulation und Trinitätsmystik des hl. Augustinus: ZAM 4(1929)168-172. — J. Plagnieux, Influence de la lutte antipelagienne sur le "De Trinitate" ou Christocentrisme de Saint Augustin: AugMag II, 817-826. — M. Schmaus, Die Denkform Augustins in seinem Werk "De Trinitate": SAM. Munich, 1962. — D. I. Hassel, Method and Scientia in St. Aug. A Study of Books VIII to XV in his "De Trinitate." St. Louis, 1963. — A. M. La Bonnardière, Recherches de chronologie augustinienne. Paris, 1965. — A. Schindler, Wort und Analogie in Augustins Trinitätslehre: *Hermeneutische Untersuchungen zur Theologie,* IV. Tübingen, 1965. — K. Rahner, Bemerkungen zum dogmatischen Traktat "De Trinitate," in *Schriften sur Theologie* 4(1964)103-133. — B. Altaner, Kleine Patristische Schriften (TU 83). Berlin 1967 (collection of writings on Augustine's sources). — E. Hill, Karl Rahner's Remarks on the Dogmatic Treatise "De Trinitate" and St. Augustine: AugStudies 2(1971)67-80; *idem,* St. Augustine's "De Trinitate." The Doctrinal Significance of its Structure: REAug 19(1973)277-286. — R. J. Teske, Properties of God and the Predicaments in De Trinitate V: *The Modern Schoolman* 59(1981-82)1-19. — D. E. Daniels, The Argument of the De Trinitate and Augustine's Theory of Signs: AugStudies 8(1977)33-54.

5. Moral and Pastoral

1. *De mendacio liber* I. Written in 395 and considered by Augustine himself as "obscure and complicated" (*Retract.* 1, 27), it is, nevertheless, not without merit.

Editions: M 6, 419-446. — PL 40, 487-518. — J. Zycha, CSEL 41(1900)411-466.

Translations: English: P. Schaff, ed., LNPF 3, ser. 1(1887)457-477 (reprint: 1956). — M. S. Muldowney, FC 16(1952)47-110. *French:* G. Combès, BA 2(1937)235-305 (with text). *German:* P. Keseling. Würzburg, 1953, 62-124. *Italian:* N. Casacca. Bologna, 1920. — D. Bassi. Rome, 1930. *Spanish:* R. Flórez, BAC 12(121) (1954)531-607 (with text).

2. *Contra mendacium liber* I. This book, written in 420-21, takes up again the theme of mendacity and demonstrates its illicit nature (*Retract.* 2, 60).

Editions: M 6, 447-474. — PL 40, 517-548. — J. Zycha, op. cit., 469-528.

Translations: English: H. Browne, LNPF 3, ser. 1(1887)481-500 (reprint: 1956). — J. Jaffee, FC 16(1952)111-138. *French:* G. Combès, op. cit., 315-375 (with text). *German:* P. Keseling. Würzburg 1953, 62-124. *Spanish:* R. Flórez, BAC 12(121)(1954)615-689 (with text).

3. *De agone christiano liber* I. Augustine composed this work at the beginning of his episcopate as a manual of Christian life for

instructing uneducated people in the faith. It contains an explanation of the creed (a list of errors to be avoided) and of the moral precepts drawn from the example of the Son of God (*Retract.* 2, 3).

Editions: M 6, 245-262. — PL 40, 289-310. — J. Zycha, op. cit., 101-138.

Translations: English: R. P. Russel, FC 2(1947)315-353. *French:* B. Roland-Gosselin, BA 1(1949)373-435 (with text). *German:* C. J. Perl. Vienna, 1948. — A. Habitzki. Würzburg, 1961. *Polish:* W. Budzik. Warsaw, 1952. *Spanish:* L. Cilleruelo, BAC 12(1954)476-528 (with text).

Studies: A. D'Alès, De agone christiano: Greg 11(1930)131-135.

4. *De catechizandis rudibus liber* I. This manual of catechetical instruction, composed around 400, is rich in pedagogical insights (*Retract.* 2, 14).

Editions: M 6, 263-296. — PL 40, 309-348. — G. Krüger. Tübingen, 1909. — W. Y. Fausset. London, 1915[3]. — J. Christopher (PSt 8). Washington, 1926. — J. B. Bauer, CCL 46(1969)121-178.

Translations: Dutch: F. Vermuyter. Antwerp-Eindhoven, 1928. — The Augustinian Fathers, Sint Augustinus. Het eerste geloofsonderricht. Nijmegen, 1955. — H. Robbers. 's-Hertegenbosch, 1955. *English:* S. D. F. Salmond, LNPF 3, ser. 1(1887)282-314 (reprint: 1956). — E. Ph. Barker. London, 1912. — J. Christopher, op. cit. (with text); *idem,* ACW 2(1946, 1966). H. Farmer, St. Augustine on Catechizing: *The Life of the Spirit* 13(1958-59)172-181. *French:* J. Combès, J. Fargues, BA 11(1949)19-147 (with text). *German:* E. Ernesti. Paderborn, 1902. — S. Mitterer, BKV[3](1925). — F. Auer. Innsbruck, 1927. — H. Rohde. Heidelberg, 1965. *Italian:* N. Casacca. Bologna, 1918. — G. de Luca. Florence, 1923 (with text). — G. Gravina, in B. Nardi, ed., Il pensiero pedagogico del medioevo. Florence, 1956. — A. Mura. Brescia, 1956. — R. Calzecchi Onesti. Vicenza, 1967. *Polish:* W. Budzik. Warsaw, 1929, 1952[2]. *Spanish:* J. Oroz Reta: *Helmantica* 22(1971)5-176.

Studies: G. C. Negri, La disposizione del contenuto dottrinale nel "De catech. rudibus" di S. Ag., Diss., Rome, 1961. — L. J. van der Lof, The Date of the "Catechizandis rudibus": VC 14(1962)198-204. — D. Grasso, Saint Augustin évangélisateur: *Parole et Mission* 6(1963)357-378. — G. Oggioni, Il "De catech. rudibus" di S. Ag., catechesi per i lontani: SC 91(1963)117-126. — R. Cordovani, Il "De catech. rudibus" di S. Ag. Questioni di contenuto e di stile: Aug 6(1966)489-527; *idem,* Lo stile nel "De catech. rudibus" di S. Agostino: Aug 8(1968)280-311. — C. Przydatek, L'annuncio del Vangelo nello spirito del dialogo. Studio storico-teologico sulla predicazione missionaria secondo l'opuscolo di S. Ag. "De catech. Rudibus." Rome, 1971. — F. Campo del Pozo, La catequesis pastoral en el "De catech. rudibus": *Estudio Agustiniano* 7(1972)105-127. — A. Etchegaray Cruz, Le rôle du "De catech. rudibus" de saint Augustin dans le catéchèse missionnaire dès 710 jusqu'à 847: SP 11(TU 108). Berlin 1972, 316-321. — P. Siniscalco, Christum narrare et dilectionem monere. Osservazioni sulla "narratio" del "De catech. rudibus" di S. Ag.: Aug 14(1974)605-623. — J. B. Allard, La natura du "De cat. rud." de s. A., Rome, 1976 (Diss., Lateran Univ.). — J. P. Belche, Die Bekehrung zum Christentum nach des hl. Aug. Büchlein "De catech. rudibus": AugL 27(1977)26-69, 333-363; 28(1978)255-287. — A. Trapè, S. Agostino e la catechesi; teoria e prassi: *Salesianum* 41(1979)323-331.

5. *De bono coniugale liber* I. Written around 401 in response to the controversy begun by Jovinian, the work emphasizes the dignity and the goods of marriage (*Retract.* 2, 22).

Editions: M 6, 319-340. — PL 40, 373-396. — J. Zycha, op. cit., 185-231.

Translations: Dutch: M. Ruhe. Amsterdam, 1941. *English* C. L. Cornish, LNPF 3, ser. 1(1887)397-413 (reprint: 1956). — T. Wilcox, FC 27(1955)1-51. *French:* G. Combès, BA 2(1937)25-87 (with text). *German:* A. Maxsein. Würzburg, 1949. *Italian:* R. Calzecchi Onesti. Vicenza, 1966. — M. Palmieri, NBA 7, 1(1978)11-63 (with text). *Spanish:* G. García, BAC 12(121)(1954)33-119 (with text).

6. *De sancta virginitate liber* I. Written immediately after the preceding work, the *De virginitate* teaches esteem of virginity without slighting matrimony, and the necessity for the cultivation of humility to persevere in virginity (*Retract.* 2, 23).

Editions: M 6, 341-368. — PL 40, 397-428. — J. Zycha, op. cit., 233-343.

Translations: English: C. L. Cornish, op. cit., 417-438 (reprint: 1956). — J. McQuade, FC 27(1955)133-212; *idem,* Boston, 1962. *French:* J. Saint-Martin, J.-M. Perrin, La virginité chrétienne. Paris, 1955, 121-176. — J. Saint-Martin, BA 3(1939)197-312 (with text). *German:* I. Dietz. Würzburg, 1952. *Italian:* R. Calzecchi Onesti. Vicenza, 1966. V. Tarulli, NBA 7, 1(1978)75-159 (with text). *Spanish:* M. de Aranzadi, G. Oteo. Madrid, 1948. — F. de B. Vizmanos, Las vírgenes cristianas de la Iglesia primitiva (BAC 45). Madrid, 1949, 870-922. — L. Cilleruelo, BAC 12(121)(1954)139-227 (with text). — G. Erce. Monachil, 1955.

Studies: P. J. Heerinckx, Divi Aug. tractatus "De sancta virginitate": Ant 6(1931)37-58. — D. Riccardi, Verginità nella vita religiosa secondo la dottrina de S. Agostino. Rome, 1961. — G. Oggioni, Matrimonio e verginità presso i Padri. Venegono, 1963. — J. M. Leonet, Situación de la virginidad en la espiritualidad agustiniana: RAE 6(1965)215-245. — J. Fernandez Gonzales, Teologia de la virginidad en san Agustín: RAE 7(1966)231-250.

7. *De bono viduitatis liber seu epistola.* This is a letter written in 414 to Juliana, mother of the virgin Demetriades, on the merits of widowhood (Possidius, *Ind.* 10, 5).

Editions: M 6, 369-386. — PL 40, 429-430. — J. Zycha, op. cit., 303-343.

Translations: English: L. Cornish, op. cit., 457-477 (reprint: 1956). — M. C. Eagen, FC 16(1952)265-319. *French:* J. Saint-Martin, BA 3(1949²)321-291 (with text). *German:* A. Maxsein. Würzburg, 1952. *Italian:* V. Tarulli, NBA 7, 1(1978)169-219 (with text). *Spanish:* M. de Aranzadi, J. Oteo. Madrid, 1946. — L. Cilleruelo, BAC 12(121)(1954)233-279 (with text).

8. *De continentia liber* I. This is a treatise on the virtue and charism of continence (*Ep.* 231, 7; Possidius, *Ind.* 10, 6), and was composed in 395 or, according to more recent studies, after 412 (cf. REAug 5[1959]121-127).

Editions: M 6, 297-318. — PL 40, 349-372. — J. Zycha, op. cit., 139-183.

Translations: Dutch: M. Ruhe. Amsterdam, 1941. *English:* C. L. Cornish, op. cit., 379-393 (reprint: 1956). — M. F. McDonald, FC 16(1952)181-231; *idem,* Boston 1962. *French:* J. Saint-Martin, op. cit., 111-189 (with text). *German:* P. Keseling. Würzburg, 1949. *Spanish:* L. Cilleruelo, op. cit., 285-337 (with text).

9. *De patientia liber* I. This treatise (415) is a parallel work to the

preceding one and is concerned with the virtue and charism of patience (*Ep.* 231, 7).

Editions: M 6, 533-546. — PL 40, 611-626. — J. Zycha, op. cit., 633-691.

Translations: English: H. Browne, LNPF 3, ser. 1(1887)527-536 (reprint: 1956). — L. Meagher, FC 16(1952)233-264. *French:* G. Combès, BA 2(1939)463-511 (with text). *German:* J. Martin. Würzburg, 1956. *Spanish:* L. Cilleruelo, op. cit., 437-473 (with text).

10. *De coniugiis adulterinis libri* II. Augustine wrote these books around 420 in order to prove the indissolubility of marriage even in cases of adultery, but he doubts whether he has succeeded in providing a complete proof (*Retract.* 2, 57).

Editions: M 6, 387-418. — PL 40, 451-486. — J. Zycha, op. cit., 347-410.

Translations: English: C. T. Huegelmeyr, FC 27(1955)53-132. *French:* G. Combès, op. cit., 97-227 (with text). *German:* J. Schmid. Würzburg, 1949. *Spanish:* L. Cilleruelo, BAC 12(121)(1954)339-431 (with text). *Italian:* A. Festa. Vicenza, 1967. — M. Palmieri, NBA 7, 1(1978)231-317 (with text).

Studies: H. Crouzel, L'Eglise primitive face au divorce. Paris, 1971.

11. *Contra Hilarium liber* I (lost). The work was written in 399 in defense of the practice of singing the psalms during the Eucharistic celebration (*Retract.* 2, 11).

Studies: J. M. Murphy, The Contra Hilarium of Augustine, Its Liturgical and Musical Implications: AugStudies 10(1979)133-143.

6. Monastic

1. *Regula ad servos Dei.* This work, the first of its kind in the West, is brief but rich in wise monastic principles. The discussions centering around this valuable "booklet" are not concerned with the authenticity of the text but with its original purpose; i.e., whether it was addressed to nuns (*Ep.* 211) or to the "servants of God" of the first community at Hippo (Possidius, *Vita* 5, 11). With the exception of a few variations and the use of either the feminine or the masculine gender, the text is identical. Modern criticism tends to hold the latter hypothesis as the more probable of the two, although no definitive solution has yet been reached.

Editions: M 1, 789-794. — PL 32, 1377-1384. — A. C. Vega. El Escorial, 1933. — L. Verheijen, La Règle de S. A.: I, Tradition manuscrite, II, Recherches historiques. Paris, 1967 (text: I, 417-437, the best edition). Cf. *idem,* Nouvelle approche de la Règle de S. A., Abbaye de Bellefontaine, 1980.

Translations and Commentaries: English: J. C. Resch. De Pere (Wisc.), 1961. — T. A. Hand. Dublin, 1956. — F. E. Tourcher, R. P. Russel. Villanova, 1942. *Dutch:* K. Ruts. Westmalle, 1932. — T. J. van Bavel. Averbode (Belgium), 1971. *French:* F. Cayré. Paris, 1943. — A. Sage. Paris, 1971². *German:* A. Zumkeller. Würzburg, 1956. — W. Hümpfner, in H. U. von Balthasar, *Die grosse Ordensregel.* Einsiedeln, 1961², 137-171; *idem,* in A. Zumkeller, *Das Mönchtum des hl. A.,* Würzburg 1968², 333-342. *Italian:* R.

Calzecchi Onesti. Vicenza, 1966. A. Trapè. Milan, 1971. — G. Turbessi, Regole monastiche antiche. Rome, 1974. *Polish:* P. Markiewicz. Czestochowa, 1948. *Spanish:* A. Manrique. Madrid-El Escorial, 1965. — A. Trapè. Madrid, 1978.

Studies: T. J. van Bavel, De evangelische betekenis van de Regel van Sint Augustinus, in Gedenkboek Orde van Prémontré 1121-1971. Averbode (Belgium) 1971, 97-113. — L. Verheijen, Élements d'un commentaire de la Règle de Saint Augustine: AugL 21(1971)5-23, 357-404; 22(1972)5-34, 469-510; 23(1973)306-333; 24(1974)5-9; 25(1975)119-204; 27(1977)5-25; 29(1979)43-86; *idem,* Nouvelle approche de la Règle de S. Augustine. Abbaye de Bellefontaine, 1980. — G. Lawless, The Rule of St. Augustine as a Mirror of Perfection: Ang 58(1981)460-474. — ibid., Ordo Monasterii. Structure, Style and Rhetoric: Aug 22(1982)469-491.

2. *De opere monachorum liber* I. Augustine addressed this work to the monks at Carthage in 401. It shows the necessity for monks to be engaged in manual labor as well as in prayer as long as they are not prevented by reasons of infirmity, pastoral ministry, or study. It contains the theology of *ora et labora* which has exercised no small influence in the development of Western monasticism (*Retract.* 2, 21).

Editions: M 6, 475-504. — PL 40, 547-582. — J. Zycha, CSEL 41(1900)529-596.

Translations: English: H. Browne, LNPF 3, ser 1(1887)503-524 (reprint: 1956). — M. S. Muldowney, FC 16(1952)321-294; *idem,* Boston 1962. *French:* J. Saint-Martin, BA 3(1946²)401-515 (with text). *German:* R. Arbesmann. Würzburg, 1972. — K. S. Frank, Frühes Mönchtum im Abendland. Zurich-Munich, 1975, 35-106. *Spanish:* L. Cilleruelo, BAC 12(121)(1954)697-771 (with text).

Studies: J. Popa, The Manual Work of Monks According to the Treatise "De opere monachorum": of St. Aug.: *Studii Teologice* 5(1953)495-512 (in Romanian). — L. Cilleruelo, Los monjes de Carthago y S. Ag.: CD 169(1956)456-463. — G. Folliet, Des moines euchites à Cartage en 400-401: SP 2(TU 64). Berlin 1957, 386-399. — L. Cilleruelo, Nota sobre el agostinismo de los monjes de Cartago: CD 172(1959)365-370. — J. M. del Estal, Desacertada opinión moderna sobre los monjes de Cartago: CD 172(1959)596-616. — R. Arbesmann, The Attitude of S. A. Toward Labour, in *The Heritage of the Early Church.* Rome 1973, 245-259 (*Orientalia Chr. Analecta* 195). — A. Sànchez Carago, Retórica, evangelio y tradición ecclesiástica en el De opere monachorum de S. Agustín: *Recollectio* 4(1981)5-57.

7. Exegetical

a) General Works

1. *De doctrina christiana libri* IV. Augustine wrote the first part, up to 3 25, 36, in 397, and the second part in 426-27, when he published the complete work. It is important for the dogmatic synthesis, based on the distinction between *uti* and *frui* (1, 1) which served as the model for the medieval *Sententiae,* for the doctrine of the sign and biblical hermeneutic (1, 2-3) and for the principles and examples of sacred oratory (1, 4) (*Retract.* 2, 4).

Editions: M 3, 1, 1-92. — PL 34, 15-122 (cf. 47, 1221f). — G. M. Green, CSEL 89 (1963)3-169. — J. Martin, CCL 32(1962)1-167. — H. J. Vogels, FP 24(1930).

Translations: Dutch: F. Vermuyten. Brussels-Mechelen, 1924. — A. Sizoo. Delft, 1933. *English:* P. Schaff, ed., LNPF 2, ser. 1(1886)522-597 (reprint: 1956). — J. J. Cavigan, FC 2(1947)19-235. — J. F. Shaw. Chicago-London, 1952. — D. W. Robertson. New York, 1958. *French:* G. Combès, J. Fargues, BA 11(1949)169-539 (with text). *German:* P. S. Mitterer, BKV3 49(1925, 19322). — G. Arbesmann. Würzburg, 1972. *Italian:* M. Belli. Milan, 1920. *Spanish:* D. Ruiz Bueno. Madrid, 1947. — B. Martín Pérez, BAC 15(168)(1957)55-349 (with text).

Studies: G. Istace, Le livre 1er du "De doctrina christiana" de saint Augustin. Organisation synthétique et méthode mise in œuvre: ETL 32(1956)289-330. — J. Oroz Reta, El "De doctrina christiana" o la retórica cristiana: EC 32(1956)452-459. — E. Hill, De doctrina christiana. A Suggestion. SP 6(1962)443-446: U. Duchrow, Zum Prolog von Augustins "De Doctrina Christiana": VC 17(1963)165-172; *idem,* Sprachverständnis u. biblisches Hören bei A., Tübingen, 1965. — G. Casati, De Doctrina Christiana: Aug 6(1966)18-44. — E. Kevane, Augustine's "De doctrina Christiana"; A Treatise on Christian Education: RAug 4(1966)97-133. — C. P. Mayer, "Res per signa." Der Grundgedanke des Prologs in Augustins Schrift "De doctr. christiana" und das Problem seiner Datierung: REAug 20(1974)100-112. — C. Schäublin, Zum Text von Augustin "De doctrina christiana": WSt 8(1974)173-181. — A. Pincherle, Sulla composizione del "De doctrina christiana" di s. A., in *Storiografia e Storia,* Misc. E. Duprè Theseider. Rome 1974, 541-559; *idem,* S. Agostino: tra il "De doctrina christiana" e le "Confessioni": *Archeologia classica* 16-17(1973-74)555-574 (= Misc. M. Guarducci). — M. Avilés Bartina, Algunos problemas fundamentales del "De doctrina christiana": *Augustinus* 20(1975)83-105. — H. J. Sieben, Die "res" der Bibel. Eine Analyse von Augustinus "De doctr. christ. I-III": REAug 21(1975)72-90. — M. Avilés Bartina, Prontuario agustiniano de ideas retóricas: *Augustinus* 22(1977)101-149. — O. O'Donovan, Usus and Fruitio in Augustine, De Doctrina Christiana I: JThSt 33(1982)361-387. — G. A. Press, The Content and Argument of Augustine's De doctrina christiana: AugL 31(1981)165-182. — M. D. Jordan, Words and Word. Incarnation and Signification in Augustine's De doctrina christiana: AugStudies 11(1980)177-196. — G. A. Press, The Subject and Structure of Augustine's De Doctrina Christiana: AugStudies 11(1980)99-124.

b) On the Old Testament

Among the books of the Old Testament, it was Genesis which particularly attracted Augustine's attention. He undertook to interpret this book four times, twice in an allegorical manner (in addition to the works indicated below cf. *Conf.* 12-13), and twice according to the literal sense.

2. *De Genesi adversus Manichaeos libri* II. Augustine wrote this work at Thagaste around 389 with the intention of depriving the Manichaeans of their arguments against Genesis. He encountered much difficulty in the literal interpretation and often had recourse to allegory (*Retract.* 1, 10; *De Gen. ad litt.* 8, 2, 5).

Editions: M 1, 645-684. — PL 34, 173-220.

Translations: Spanish: B. Martín, BAC 15(168)(1957)361-491 (with text).

Studies: A. Zacher, De Genesi contra Manichaeos. Ein Versuch Augustinus, die ersten drei Kapitel von Genesis zu erklären und zu verteidigen. Diss., Gregorian Univ. Rome,

1962 (typed manuscript). — P. Abulesz, Aur. Aug. "De Genesi contra Manichaeos libri duo." Diss., Vienna, 1972 (typed manuscript).

3. *De Genesi ad litteram liber imperfectus.* This represents Augustine's first attempt at a literal interpretation which he began in 393 and immediately abandoned, reaching only Gen. 1:26 (*Retract.* 1, 18).

Editions: M 3, 1, 93-116. — PL 34, 219-246. — J. Zycha, CSEL 28, 1(1894)457-503.

Translations: Spanish: B. Martín, BAC 15(168)(1957)501-565 (with text).

4. *De Genesi ad litteram libri* XII. The composition of this work, which is among the more important of Augustine's writings, lasted from 401 to 415, although there is reason to believe that the first nine books (possibly the first eleven) were composed at a time very near to the first date (*De Gen. ad litt.* 9, 7, 12). The exegesis extended to Gen. 3:24. Books 6, 7 and 10 contain an ample treatise on anthropology, and much space is devoted in the work to the doctrine of simultaneous creation and the *rationes seminales* (*Retract.* 2, 24).

Editions: M 3/1, 117-234. — PL 34, 245-486. — J. Zycha, op. cit., 3-435.

Translations: English: J. H. Taylor, ACW 41(1982)books 1-6; 42(1982)books 7-12. *French:* P. Agaësse, A. Solignac, BA 48-49(1972) (with text). *German:* H. U. von Balthasar, Psychologie und Mystik ("De Gen. al litt." XII). Einsiedeln, 1960 (only book 12). — C. J. Perl. Paderborn, 1961 (books 1-6); 1964 (books 7-12). *Russian:* Kiev, 1893-95. *Spanish:* B. Martín Pérez, BAC 15(168)(1957)577-1271 (with text).

Studies: J. H. Taylor, The Text of Augustine's "De Genesi ad Litteram": SJMS 25(1950)87-93. — J. Pepin, Une curiose déclaration idéaliste du "De Genesi ad Litteram" (XII 10, 21) de Saint Aug., et ses origines plotiniennes: RHPR 34(1954)373-400. — J. Pegueroles, La teoría agustiniana de la illuminación en el "De Genesi ad litt." (Libro XII): *Estudio Ag* 7(1972)575-588. — G. Pelland, Cinq études d'Augustin sur le début de la Genèse. Paris, 1972. — M. M. Gorman, A Study of the Literal Interpretation of Genesis ("De Genesi ad litteram") Diss., Toronto, 1975. — J. Doignon, Une définition oubliée de l'amour conjugal édénique chez Augustin: piae caritatis adfectus (Gen. ad litt. 3 21, 33): VC 19(1982)25-36.

5. *Locutionum in Heptateuchum libri* VII and *Quaestionum in Heptateuchum libri* VII. Augustine explains here the less commonly used and thus less intelligible expressions of the first seven books of Scripture, and proposes and often solves questions relating to the reading of the same books (*Retract.* 2, 54-55).

Editions: a) M 3/1, 325. — PL 34, 485-546. — J. Zycha, op. cit., 507-629. — J. Fraipont, CCL 33(1958)381-465. b) M 3/1, 379. — PL 34, 547-824. — J. Zycha, CSEL 28, 2(1895)1-506. — J. Fraipont, op. cit., 1-377.

6. *Adnotationes in Iob liber* I. These marginal notes to the Book of Job, transcribed and collected into a volume by others, are "delightful to those who are able to understand them" (*Retract.* 2, 13).

Editions: M 3/1, 625-680. — PL 34, 825-886. — J. Zycha, CSEL 28, 2(1895)509-628.

7. *De octo quaestionibus ex Veteri Testamento.* These are a brief explanation of 8 passages from the Old Testament which D. De Bruyne identified as belonging to Augustine.

Editions: PLS II, 386-389. — J. Fraipont, CCL 33(1958)469-472. — D. De Bruyne, MSCA II, 334-340.

c) On the New Testament

The works on the New Testament demonstrate, no less than those on the Old, the advances achieved by Augustine in his understanding of Scripture.

8. *De sermone Domini in monte libri* II. These two books, which date from the first years of Augustine's priesthood, are an exposition of the Sermon on the Mount, containing a synthesis of moral doctrine and an explanation of the Beatitudes and the Gifts of the Holy Spirit (*Retract.* 1, 19).

Editions: M 3/2, 165-236. — PL 34, 1229-1308. — A. Mutzenbecher, CCL 35(1967).

Translations: Arabic: J. Fayiz. Alexandria, 1962. *English:* W. Findley, P. Schaff, LNPF 6, ser. 1(1888)1-70 (reprint: 1956). — J. Jepson, ACW 5(1948). — D. J. Kavanagh, FC 11(1951). — J. Pelikan. Philadelphia, 1973. *German:* A. Schmitt. St. Ottilien, 1952. *Italian:* B. Neri. Florence, 1928. — D. Bassi, CPS 1. Turin, 1955, 1965[2] (with text). *Spanish:* F. García, L. Cilleruelo, R. Flórez, BAC 12(121)(1954)773-995 (with text).

Studies: A. Holl, Augustinus Bergpredigtexegese nach seinem Frühwerk "De sermone Domini in monte libri duo." Vienna, 1960.

9. *Expositio 84 propositionum ex epistola ad Romanos; Expositio epistolae ad Galatas; Epistolae ad Romanos inchoata expositio.* These three works, the last of which was abandoned because of the difficulty of the undertaking, represent Augustine's first attempts at a literal interpretation of the letters of Saint Paul. The same subject was taken up again after a short time regarding the questions on grace in the *Quaest. ad Simplicianum* (cf. p. 369) and again at a later date during the Pelagian Controversy, especially in the work *De spiritu et littera* (p. 386). (*Retract.* 1, 23-25).

Editions: a) M3/2, 903-942. — PL 35, 2063-2084. — J. Divjak, CSEL 84(1971)3-52. — J. Martín Pérez, BAC 18(187)(1959)14-63 (with Spanish translation). b) M 3/2, 941, — PL 35, 2105-2148. — J. Divjak, op. cit., 55-141. — B. Martín Pérez, op. cit., 105-191 (with Spanish translation). c) M 3/2, 925. — PL 35, 2087-2106. — J. Divjak, op. cit., 145-181. — B. Martín Pérez, op. cit., 65-101 (with Spanish translation). — A. Sizoo. Kampen, 1954 (Dutch translation).

Studies: S. Iodice, Legge e Grazia in S. Agostino. Naples, 1977 (with Italian translation of the three works). — W. Babcock, Augustine's Interpretation of Romans (A.D. 394-396): AugStudies 10(1979)55-74.

10. *Quaestiones Evangeliorum libri* II. These explanations of certain difficult passages of Matthew (47) and Luke (51) were occasioned by

questions proposed to Augustine in friendly conversation (*idem, prol: Retract.* 2, 12).

Editions: M 3/2, 237-276. — PL 35, 1321-1364. — A. Mutzenberger, CCL 44B(1980).

11. *De consensu Evangelistarum libri* IV. Augustine wrote this work around 400 to refute those who accused the Evangelists of contradictions. He proves their authority (against the pagan philosophers who accused them of having falsely attributed divinity to Christ: book I) and the historicity and harmony of their accounts. This is a valuable study on the concordance of the Gospels (*Retract.* 2, 16).

Editions: M 3/2, 1-162. — PL 34, 1041-1230. — F. Weihrich, CSEL 43(1904).

Translations: English: W. Findley, P. Schaff, LNPF 6, ser. 1(1888)77-236 (reprint: 1956).

Studies: A. Penna, Il "De consensu Evangelistarum" ed i "Canoni Eusebiani": Bib 36(1955)1-19. — H. Merkel, Die Widersprüche zwischen den Evangelien. Ihre polemische und apologetische Behandlung in der Alten Kirche bis zu Augustin. Tübingen, 1971.

12. *Expositio epistolae Jacobi ad duodecim tribus* (lost). These were a collection of marginal notes collected by others as in the case of the *Adnot. Iob* (*Retract.* 2, 32).

13. *Speculum de Scriptura sacra.* These are a collection of moral precepts from the Old and New Testament (Possidius, *Vita* 28) compiled around 427. G. de Plinval denies the Augustinian paternity of this collection (AugMag I, 187-192).

Editions: M 3/1, 681-818. — PL 34, 887-1040. — F. Weihrich, CSEL 12(1887)3-285.

Studies: J. Belsheim, Fragmenta Novi Testamenti in translatione latina antehieronymiana ex libro qui vocatur Speculum. Christiana (Oslo), 1899.

14. *Quaestionum septemdecim in Evangelium secundum Matthaeum liber* I. These are explanations, some very brief, of 17 passages of Matthew. Their date of composition is uncertain, and they are not mentioned in the *Retractationes* and the *Indiculus* of Possidius. The Maurists doubted the authenticity of the work, which is nevertheless defended by G. Morin.

Editions: PL 35, 1365-1374. — A. Mutzenbecher, CCL 44B(1980).

Studies: G. Morin, RB 28(1911)1-10.

8. Polemical

a) Against the Manichaeans.

The themes treated in these works include metaphysics (the immutability of God, creation, evil), apologetics (the credibility of the faith) and Scripture (the harmony between the Old and the New Testament).

1. *De moribus Ecclesiae catholicae et de moribus Manichaeorum libri* II. This first apology for the faith was written by the new convert in Rome in 388 and published in Africa, probably the following year (1 1, 1; 2 1, 26). The work is based on a comparison between the doctrine and life of the Catholic church, centered on and formed by love, and that of the Manichaeans, whose doctrine was untenable and whose life was inconsistent (*Retract.* 1, 7).

Editions: M 1, 687-744. — PL 32, 1309-1378.

Translations: Danish: J. Pedersen. Copenhagen, 1965. *English:* R. Stothert, LNPF 4, ser. 1(1887)41-89 (reprint: 1956); *idem,* New York, 1948. — D. A. Gallagher, I. J. Gallagher, FC 56(1966). *French:* B. Roland-Gosselin, BA 1(1949)137-337 (with text). *German:* P. Keseling. Regensburg, 1948. *Italian:* A. Neno. Florence, 1935. — D. Bassi, CPS 3(1936)119-267 (with text). *Japanese:* K. Kenji. Tokyo, 1963. *Spanish:* T. Prieto, BAC 4(30)(1956)235-447 (with text).

Studies: Th. Deman, Héritage antique et innovation chrétienne dans le "De moribus Ecclesiae catholicae": AugMag II, 713-726. — J. K. Coyle, Augustine's De oribus Ecclesiae Catholicae (Paradosis 25). Fribourg, 1978.

2. *De duabus animabus liber* I. This work from 392 is a refutation of the fundamental Manichaean thesis of the two souls, one deriving from the principle of good and the other from the principle of evil, which denies human freedom. Augustine maintains that in each man there is one single soul endowed with free will from which evil arises (*Retract.* 1, 15).

Editions: M 8, 75-92. — PL 42, 93-112. — J. Zycha, CSEL 25, 1(1891)51-80.

Translations: English: A. H. Newman, LNPF 4, ser. 1(1887)95-107 (reprint: 1956). *French:* R. Jolivet, BA 17(1961)53-115 (with text). *German:* C. J. Perl. Paderborn, 1966.

3. *Acta contra Fortunatum Manichaeum.* These are the minutes of a debate on the origin of evil held at Hippo the 28-29 of August, 392. Augustine shows that evil proceeds from the freely chosen sin of man. Fortunatus was unable to respond and left Hippo (*Retract.* 1, 16).

Editions: M 8, 93-108. — PL 42, 111-130. — J. Zycha, CSEL 25, 1(1889)83-112.

Translations: English: A. H. Newman, op. cit., 113-124 (reprint: 1956). *French:* R. Jolivet, BA 17(1961)133-191 (with text).

4. *Contra Adimantum Manichaei discipulum liber* I. Augustine composed this treatise in 392 to refute the manichaean thesis of a supposed opposition between the Old and the New Testament (*Retract.* 1, 22).

Editions: M 8, 111-150. — PL 42, 129-172. — J. Zycha, CSEL 25, 1(1891)115-190.

Translations: French: R. Jolivet, BA 17(1961)219-375.

5. *Contra epistolam Manichaei quam vocant fundamenti liber* I. Augustine wrote this work at the beginning of his episcopate against the letter which was a type of catechism of the sect. He refutes its commence-

ment and general principles by showing that Mani has no reason to refer to Christ (while the Catholic church has many and valid reasons) and by illustrating the absurdity of Manichaean dualism (*Retract.* 2, 2).

Editions: M 8, 151-182. — PL 42, 173-206. — J. Zycha, op. cit., 193-248.

Translations: English: R. Stothert, LNPF 4, ser. 1(1887)129-150 (reprint: 1956). *French:* R. Jolivet, BA 17(1961)391-507 (with text).

6. *Contra Faustum Manichaeum libri* XXXIII. In this work of 397-398, Augustine presents an ample defense of the Old and the New Testament by citing the words of his adversary and refuting them. He denies that the Manichaeans are able to call themselves Christians (*Retract.* 2, 7).

Editions: M 8, 183-470. — PL 42, 207-518. — J. Zycha, op. cit., 251-797.

Translations: English: R. Stothert, op. cit., 155-345 (reprint: 1956).

7. *De actis cum Felice Manichaeo libri* II. These are the minutes of a debate held on December 7 and 12, 404 (sixth consulate of Honorius), in which the discussion centers on the immutability of God, creation, and the origin of evil. Felix yields the victory to Augustine (*Retract.* 2, 8).

Editions: M 8, 471-500. — PL 42, 519-522. — J. Zycha, CSEL 25, 2(1892)801-852.

Translations: French: M. Jourjon, BA 17(1961)645-757 (with text).

Chronology: Regarding the date of this work (4th or 6th consulate of Honorius?), which is important for the chronology of Augustine's works, cf. P. Monceaux, Sur la date des Confessions: CRI(1908)51-53. — A. Casamassa, Scritti Patristici, Lateranum II. Rome 1956, 240-243. — M. Pellegrino, Le Confessioni di S. Agostino. Studio introduttivo. Rome, 1972[2]. — M. Jourjon, Oeuvres de St. A., Contre le Man. Felix: BA 17(1961)787-788. — A. Solignac, Les Confessions: BA 13(1962)45-54.

8. *De natura boni liber* I. This work, composed in 399, shows once again that all things, inasmuch as they exist, are good and that evil is nothing but a privation of good. The Manichaean principle of absolute evil is absurd (*Retract.* 2, 9).

Editions: M 8, 501-518. — PL 42, 551-572. — J. Zycha, op. cit., 855-889.

Translations: English: A. H. Newman, LNPF 4, ser. 1(1887)351-365 (reprint: 1956). — *idem,* New York, 1948. — H. S. Burleigh. Philadelphia, 1953. — A. A. Moon, (PSt 88). Washington, 1955 (with text). *French:* B. Roland-Gasselin, BA 1(1949)441-509 (with text). *Spanish:* M. D. Paladini. Tucumán, 1945 (with text); *idem,* in Ideas y valores 2. Bogotá 1952, 498-524. — M. Lanseros, BAC 3(21)979-1047 (with text).

9. *Contra Secundinum Manichaeum liber* I. This is a response to a Manichaean "auditor" who had invited him to return to Manichaeism. Augustine considered this work of 399 one of his best writings against the Manichaeans (*Retract.* 1, 10).

Editions: M 8, 523-548. — PL 42, 577-602. — J. Zycha, op. cit., 905-975.

Translations: French: R. Jolivet, BA 17(1961)539-633 (with text).

b) Against the Donatists.

The long and difficult polemic against the Donatists forced Augustine to compose numerous works in which, by clarifying the terms of the controversy, he contributed to a deeper understanding of ecclesiology and sacramental theology.

1. *Psalmus contra partem Donati.* This alphabetical psalm was intended to be sung to the people, who responded with a refrain. It narrates the history of the schism and invites the Donatists to return to unity with the Catholics (*Retract.* 1, 20).

Editions: M 9, 1-8. — PL 43-23-32. — M. Petschenig, CSEL 51(1908)3-15. — H. Vroom, Le psaume abécédaire de s. A. et la poésie rythmique (Latinitas christianorum primaeva 4). Nijmegen, 1933 (with a detailed study). — C. Lambot: RB 47(1935)312-330. — W. Bulst, Hymni latini antiquissimi LXXV Psalmi III. Heidelberg 1956, 139-147, 197-198. R. Anastasi. Padua, 1957 (crit. text).

Translations: French: G. Finaert, BA 28(1963)150-191 (with text of Anastasi). *Italian:* R. Anastasi, op. cit. — F. Ermini, MSCA II (1931)341-352.

Studies: F. Ermini, Il "Psalmus contra partem Donati": MSCA II, 341-352. — D. Norbert, Ad s. A. Psalmum abecedarium adnotationes: SIF 27-28(= Studi G. Pasquali). Florence 1956, 315-317.

2. *Contra epistolam Parmeniani libri* III. This first major work on the Donatist Controversy, written in 400, establishes the fundamental thesis that in the unity of the Catholic church and in the communion in the sacraments, the wicked do not contaminate the good (*Retract.* 2, 17).

Editions: M 9, 11-78. — PL 43, 33-108. — M. Petschenig, op. cit., 19-141.

Translations: French: G. Finaert, BA 28(1963)209-409 (with text).

3. *De baptismo libri* VII. This fundamental treatise was composed immediately after the previous work. It demonstrates the validity of baptism administered by heretics and takes away from the Donatists the authority of Cyprian, to whom they were appealing (*Retract.* 2, 18).

Editions: M 9, 79-204. — PL 43, 107-244. — M. Petschenig, op. cit., 145-375.

Translations: English: J. R. King, LNPF 4, ser. 1(1887)411-514 (reprint: 1956). *French:* G. Finaert, BA 29(1964)57-575 (with text).

4. *De unitate ecclesiae liber* I. or *Epistola ad catholicos de secta donatistarum.* This was composed at the same time as the following work (1, 1) and insists on the basic proposition that the true church of Christ is the universal church. Possidius lists this work among the letters (*Ind.* 6, 20) and as such it is cited by the Council of Constantinople of 553 (Mansi IX 261). Concerning the authenticity cf. CPL 334.

Editions: M 9, 337-388. — PL 43, 391-446. — M. Petschenig, CSEL 52(1909)231-1873.

Translations: French: G. Finaert, BA 28, 503-707 (with text). *Spanish:* S. Santamarta, BAC 4(30)(1956)649-787 (with text).

5. *Contra litteras Petiliani libri* III. These three books were written during the pontificate of Pope Anastasium (398-401) as a response to the letter of the Donatist bishop of Cirta, Petilianus, and the reply of the same to Augustine's response (*Retract.* 2, 25).

Editions: M 9, 205-336. — PL 43, 245-383. — M. Petschenig, op. cit., 3-277.

Translations: J. R. King, C. D. Hartranft, LNPF 4, ser. 1(1887)519-628 (reprint: 1956). *French:* G. Finaert, BA 30(1967)133-745 (with text).

6. *Contra Cresconium grammaticum partis Donati libri* IV. The *Contra Cresconium* was written at a time when the laws of Honorius of 405 against the Donatists were of "very recent"date. They are a response to Cresconius, who had come to the defense of Petilianus. In book IV, Augustine bases his argument on the schism among the Donatists between the partisans of Primianus and those of Maximinus (*Retract.* 2, 26).

Editions: M 9, 389-526. — PL 43, 445-594. — M. Petschenig, op. cit., 325-382.

Translations: French: G. Finaert, BA 31(1968)71-643 (with text).

Studies: A. Bruckmayr, Studie zu St. A.'s Contra Cresconium, in Festschr. zum 400 jähr. Bestande des Obergymnasiums zu Kremsmünster. Wels 1949, 201-219. — F. Weissengruber, A.s Wertung von Grammatik und Rhetorik in Traktat "Contra Cresconium": Hermes 105(1977)101-124.

7. *De unico baptismo contra Petilianum liber* I. This work, from around the year 411, is the refutation of a composition of Petilianus of the same title (*Retract.* 2, 34).

Editions: M 9, 527-544. — PL 43, 595-614. — M. Petschenig, CSEL 53(1910)3-34.

Translations: French: G. Finaert, BA 31(1968)665-737 (with text).

8. *Breviculus collationis cum Donatistis libri* III. These three books contain a summary of the official minutes (long and confused) of the conference between the Catholics and the Donatists held at Carthage on June 1, 3 and 8, 411 (*Retract.* 2, 39).

Editions: M 9, 545-580. — PL 43, 613-706. — M. Petschenig, op. cit., 39-92. S. Lancel, CCL 149(1974)259-306.

Translations: French: G. Finaert, BA 32(1965)95-243 (with text). — S. Lancel, SCh 194, 195, 224(1972, 1975) (with text).

9. *Post collationem contra Donatistas liber* I. The book is Augustine's passionate appeal to the Donatists after the conference of 411 to return to the Catholic church. It is at the same time a defense against the lies which were being spread by the Donatist bishops. It is the best

of Augustine's anti-Donatist compositions, a "great" work written "with much care" (*Retract.* 2, 40).

Editions: M 9, 581-616. — PL 43, 651-690. — M. Petschenig, op. cit., 97-162.

Translations: French: G. Finaert, op. cit., 249-393 (with text).

10. *De correptione donatistarum liber* I. (*Ep.* 185) Augustine wrote this work in 417 in defense of the imperial legislation against the Donatists (*Retract.* 2, 48).

Editions: M 2, 643-663. — PL 33, 792-815. — A. Goldbacher, CSEL 57, 2(1911)1-44.

Translations: English: J. R. King, C. D. Hartranft, LNPF 4, ser. 1(1887)633-651 (reprint: 1956). — W. Parsons, FC 30(1955)141-190. *Italian:* L. Carrozzi, NBA 23(1974)9-75 (with text).

11. *Gesta cum Emerito donatista liber* I. These are the minutes of the debate held on September 20, 418 between Emeritus and Augustine on the occasion of the latter's visit to Caesarea in Mauretania at the request of Pope Zosimus (*Retract.* 2, 51).

Editions: M 9, 625-643. — PL 43, 697-706. — M. Petschenig, op. cit., 181-191.

Translations: French: G. Finaert, op. cit., 451-487 (with text).

Studies: A. Turrado, Le renuncia de los obispos. San Agustín, alma de un episodio: *RevAgEspir* 8(1967)277-286.

12. *Sermo ad Caesariensis ecclesiae plebem.* This sermon was given on the same occasion as the preceding work and insists on the necessity of the Catholic church for salvation.

Editions: M 9, 617-624. — PL 43, 689-698. — M. Petschenig, op. cit., 167-178.

Translations: French: G. Finaert, op. cit., 417-445.

13. *Contra Gaudentium donatistarum episcopum libri* II. This final anti-Donatist work is a response to two letters sent by the Donatist bishop of Tamugadi to the Tribune Dulcitius, who passed them on to Augustine (*Retract.* 2, 59).

Editions: M 9, 635-676. — PL 43, 707-758. — M. Petschenig, CSEL 53(1910)201-274.

Translations: French: G. Finaert, op. cit., 511-685 (with text).

14. Other of Augustine's anti-Donatist works have been lost. They include: *Contra epistolam Donati haeretici liber* I (*Retract.* 1, 21); *Contra partem Donati,* in which he maintains that the imperial authority must not intervene to force the Donatists to return to the Catholic communion (*Retract.* 2, 5); *Contra quod attulit Centurius a Donatistis liber* I (*Retract.* 2, 19); *Probationum et testimoniorum contra Donatistas liber* I (*Retract.* 2, 27); *Contra Donatistam nescio quem liber* I (*Retract.* 2, 28); *Admonitio Donatistarum de Maximianistis liber* I (*Retract.* 2, 29); *De*

Maximianistis contra Donatistas liber I (*Retract.* 2, 35); *Ad Emeritum Donatistarum episcopum post collationem liber* I (*Retract.* 2, 45).

c) Against the Pelagians.

The numerous works relating to the Pelagian Controversy, which forced Augustine to develop his theology of redemption, sin and grace, can be divided for the sake of convenience into three sections according to the persons with whom they are concerned: those dealing with Pelagianism in general (Pelagius and Caelestius), those directed against Julian and those addressed to the monks at Hadrumetum and Marseilles. The works in each of these sections are characterized by a particular form and style. The first section includes works of positive and calm theological investigation and exposition, the second is characterized by strongly polemical works and the third brings the final clarifications and positions regarding the mystery of predestination and grace.

c[1]) Concerning Pelagianism in general

1. *De peccatorum meritis et remissione et de baptismo parvulorum ad Marcellinum libri* III. A fundamental work written in 412, it contains the first biblical theology of redemption and original sin and the necessity of baptism, the doctrine of the necessity of grace for observing the commandments of God and the response (1, 3) to the difficulties against the notion of hereditary sin proposed by Pelagius in his explanation of Rom. 5:12 (*Retract.* 2, 33).

Editions: M 10/1, 1-84. — PL 44, 109-200. — C. F. Urba, J. Zycha, CSEL 60(1913)3-151.

Translations: English: P. Holmes, R. E. Wallis, LNPF 5, ser. 1(1887)15-78 (reprint: 1971). *Spanish:* V. Capánaga, BAC 9(79)(1952)201-439 (with text).

Studies: V. Grossi, Il battesimo e la polemica pelagiana negli anni 411/413 (De pecc. meritis et remissione — Ep. 88 ad Bonifacium): Aug 9(1969)30-61.

2. *De gratia Novi Testamenti ad Honoratum liber* I (*Ep.* 140). Written about the same time as the preceding work, this composition contains the response to five Scriptural questions sent to Augustine from Carthage by his friend, Honoratus. Augustine adds a sixth question regarding the grace particular to the New Testament, which he explains at length (*Retract.* 2, 36).

Editions: M 2, 422-456. — PL 33, 538-577. — A. Goldbacher, CSEL 44(1904)155-234.

Translations: English: W. Parsons, FC 20(1953)58-136. *Italian:* L. Carrozzi, NBA 22(1971)205-307 (with text).

3. *De spiritu et littera ad Marcellinum liber* I. This book, written shortly after the first work to Marcellinus, which provided the occasion for its composition, is a key work for Augustine's doctrine of grace.

Augustine discusses the relation between the law (letter) and grace (spirit) at length and maintains that without grace, which inspires the love of God in the heart, the knowledge of the law does not justify anyone. The law has been given that we may look for grace and grace has been given that we may observe the law. The law, by commanding, is an occasion of death; grace, by helping, is a source of life (*Retract.* 2, 37).

Editions: M 10/1, 86-126. — PL 44, 201-246. — C. F. Urba, J. Zycha, CSEL 60(1913)155-229. — W. Bright. Oxford, 1914.

Translations: English: P. Holmes, R. E. Wallis, op. cit., 83-114 (reprint: 1971). — W. J. S. Simpson. London, 1928. — J. Burnaby. LCC 8(1955) (selections). *French:* J.-D. Burger. Neuchâtel, 1951 (with text). *German:* E. Kochs. Neukirchen-Vluyn, 1962. — A. Forster. Paderborn, 1968 (with text). S. Kopp, ALG 1(1971)302-434 (with text). *Italian:* S. Iodice. Naples, 1979. *Spanish:* E. López, BAC 6(50)(1956)687-810 (with text).

Studies: J. Plagnieux, Le chrétien en face de la Loi d'après le "De spiritu et littera" de s. A., in Festschr. M. Schmaus. Munich 1957, 725-754. — Ch. Boyer, Luther et le "De spiritu et littera" de s. A.: *Doctor Communis* 21(1968)167-187 (= Luther et sa doctrine. Rome 1970, 15-44).

4. *De natura et gratia liber* I. Augustine composed this around 415 as a response to the *De natura* of Pelagius. He shows that it is necessary neither to defend nature against grace nor grace against nature but rather to defend nature and grace together. It is grace which frees and heals nature (*Retract.* 2, 42).

Editions: M 10/1, 127-164. — PL 44, 247-290. — C. F. Urba, J. Zycha, CSEL 60(1913)233-299.

Translations: English: P. Holmes, R. E. Wallis, op. cit., 121-151 (reprint: 1971). P. Holmes. New York, I 519-579 (reprint). *French:* J. de la Tullaye, BA 21(1966)245-413 (with text). *German:* A. Maxsein, ALG 1(1971)519-579 (with text). *Spanish:* V. Capánaga, BAC 6(50)(1956)813-953 (with text).

Studies: G. de Plinval, Corrections aux "De gestis Pelagii" et "De natura et gratia": REAug 11(1965)291-292. — F.-J. Thonnard, La notion de "nature" chez s. A. Ses progrès dans la polémique antipélagienne: REAug 11(1965)239-265. — L. Merino, La Inmaculada en el libro "De natura et gratia" de San Agustín: *Casiciaco* 22(Valladolid 1968)243-249.

5. *De perfectione iustitiae hominis epistola sive liber.* This was written at the same time as the *De natura et gratia* as a response to the *Definitiones* of Caelestius in which the disciple of Pelagius was defending *impeccantia* and denying the necessity of grace. Augustine denies the former and affirms the latter. He states that full justice is never able to be obtained on this earth and that the precept to love God with one's whole heart is the ideal to which one aspires not the goal to be reached (*Indic.* 7, 4 and 10 3, 21).

Editions: M 10/1, 167-190. — PL 44, 291-318. — C. F. Urba, J. Zycha, CSEL 42(1902)3-48.

Translations: English: P. Holmes, R. E. Wallis, op. cit., 151-176 (reprint: 1971). *French:* J. de la Tullaye, BA 21(1966)127-219 (with text). *German:* A. Fingerle, ALG 2(1964)129-197 (with text).

6. *Ad Hieronymum presbyterum libri* II (*Ep.* 166-167). Augustine wrote to Jerome in 415 asking his opinion regarding the origin of the soul (1, 1) in view of the doctrine of original sin (whether the soul came to be by creation or by spiritual generation) and regarding the interpretation of James 2:10 (*Retract.* 2, 45).

Editions: M 2, 583-602. — PL 33, 720-741. — A. Goldbacher, CSEL 44(1904)545-609.

Translations: English: W. Parsons, FC 30(1955)6-49. *Italian:* L. Carrozzi, NBA 22(1971)717-781 (with text).

7. *De gestis Pelagii liber* I. This is an examination of the proceedings of the Synod of Diospolis, written toward the end of 417, which shows that Pelagius himself was absolved but that Pelagianism was condemned. (*Retract.* 2, 47).

Editions: M 10/1, 191-228. — PL 44, 319-360. — C. F. Urba, J. Zycha, CSEL 42(1902)51-122.

Translations: English: P. Holmes, R. E. Wallis, op. cit., 183-212 (reprint: 1971). *French:* J. de la Tullaye, BA 21(1966)433-479 (with text). *German:* B. Altaner, ALG 2(1964)199-319 (with text). *Spanish:* G. Erce Osaba, BAC 9(79)(1952)685-779 (with text).

Studies: G. de Plinval, Corrections aux "De gestis Pelagii" et "De corr. et gratia": REAug 11(1965)291-292.

8. *De gratia Christi et de peccato originali libri* II. Augustine composed this work toward the middle of 418 at the request of Albina, Pinianus and Melania. He denounced the error of Pelagius, who called freedom the law and revelation grace, but denied the interior help of grace except as an aid to observing *facilius* God's commandments (1, 1). He shows that neither Pelagius nor his disciple Caelestius professed the doctrine of original sin, one of the fundamental truths of the faith (*Retract.* 2, 50).

Editions: M 10/1, 229-252. — PL 44, 359-416. — C. F. Urba, J. Zycha, CSEL 42(1902)125-206.

Translations: English: R. Holmes, R. E. Wallis, op. cit., 217-236 (reprint: 1971). *French:* H. Chirat, J. Plagnieux, BA 22(1975)53-269 (with text). *German:* A. Fingerle, ALG 2(1964)321-467 (with text). *Spanish:* A. Centeno, BAC 6(50)(1956)308-458 (with text).

9. *De anima et eius origine libri* IV. Augustine directed this work against the error of the young Vincentius Victor who had reproved Augustine for his hesitation between creationism and (spiritual) traducianism. He rejects the Manichaean theory of emanation and the Origenist preexistence of the soul and defends his hesitation (*Retract.* 2, 56).

Editions: M 10/1, 337-408. — PL 44, 475-548. — C. F. Urba, J. Zycha, CSEL 60(1913)303-419.

Translations: English: R. Holmes, R. E. Wallis, op. cit., 315-371 (reprint: 1971). *French:* F. J. Thonnard, E. Bleuzen, A. de Veer, BA 22(1975)376-667 (with text). *German:* A. Maxsein, D. Morick, ALG 3(1977)167-282. *Spanish:* M. Lanseros, BAC 3(21), 769-973 (with text).

Studies: A. J. Geiger, The Origin of the Soul. An Augustinian Dilemma. (Diss., Angelicum). Rome, 1957.

c²) Against Julian

10. *Contra duas epistolas pelagianorum libri* IV. This work was written around 420 and dedicated to Pope Boniface, who had sent Augustine the two letters of Julian and the bishops who together with him had refused to sign the *Tractoria* of Pope Zosimus. Augustine refutes the slanderous accusations of denying free will, condemning matrimony, censuring the saints, diminishing the law, denigrating baptism, and reviving Manichaeism (*Retract.* 2, 61).

Editions: M 10/1, 411-492. — PL 44, 549-638. — C. F. Urba, J. Zycha, CSEL 60(1913)423-470.

Translations: English: R. Holmes, R. E. Wallis, op. cit., 377-434 (reprint: 1971). *French:* F.-J. Thonnard, É. Bleuzen, BA 23(1974)313-657 (with text). *German:* D. Morick, ALG 3(1977)283-408. *Spanish:* G. Erce Osaba, BAC 9(79)(1952)461-671 (with text).

11. *De nuptiis et concupiscentia libri* II. Augustine composed this work, with some interruptions, between 419-420 in order to respond to Julian, who accused him of denying the goodness of matrimony because he taught the doctrine of original sin and defended the proposition that disordered concupiscence as an evil. In response to the first book, Julian composed four of his own. When Augustine received an extract of these he added book two (*Retract.* 2, 53).

Editions: M 10/1, 338-408. — PL 44, 413-474. — C. F. Urba, J. Zycha, CSEL 42(1902)14-319.

Translations: English: R. Holmes, R. E. Wallis, op. cit., 263-308 (reprint: 1971). *French:* F.-J. Thonnard, É. Bleuzen, BA 23(1974)53-289 (with text). *German:* A. Fingerle, ALG 3(1977)77-166. *Italian:* N. Cipriani, NBA 7, 1(1978)394-453 (with text).

12. *Contra Iulianum libri* VI. This work, composed around 421, is the greatest and most important work of the Pelagian Controversy. In it, Augustine responds to the four books Julian had written against the first book of *De nuptiis* and refutes point by point the statements on original sin, marriage, concupiscence, the baptism of children, and the virtue of the infidels. In two books added at the beginning, he develops the argument of tradition and responds to the accusation of novelty (*Retract.* 2, 62).

Editions: M 10/1, 498-710. — PL 44, 641-874.

Translations: English: M. A. Schumacher, FC 35(1957).

Studies: A. Bruckner, Die vier Bücher Julians von Aeclanum an Turbantius. Ein Beitrag zur Charakteristik Julians und Augustins. Berlin, 1910. — W. Eborwicz, Quelques remarques sur le "Contra Julianum" de saint Augustin: *Augustinus* 12(1967)161-164 (= Strenas V. Capánaga).

13. *Contra secundam Iuliani responsionem opus imperfectum.* Julian, who had taken refuge in Cilicia, composed eight books against the second book of *De nuptiis et concupiscentia.* Augustine slowed the drafting of the *Retractationes* and undertook a detailed refutation of Julian, relating the text of his adversary passage by passage and adding his response. All the themes of the Pelagian controversy are treated anew with transparent clarity and a new depth. The work was interrupted after the sixth of the projected eight books by Augustine's death (*Indic.* 7, 16; *Vita* 28, 3).

Editions: M 10/2, 874-1386. — PL 45, 1049-1608. — M. Zelzer, CSEL 85, 1(1974)(books 1-3).

Studies: A Trapè, Un celebre testo di s. A. sull'ignoranza e la difficoltà (*Retract.* I, 9, 6) e l'Opus imp. c. Iul.: AugMag II, 795-803. — Y. de Montcheuil, La polémique de Saint Augustin contre Julien d'Éclane: RSR 44(1956)193-218. — F. Clodius, El libre albedrío según el "Opus Imperfectum" de San Agustín: *Annales Fac Teol.* Santiago (Chile) 13(1961)5-51, 273-287; *idem,* El libre albedrío según Julián de Eclano: ibid., 14(1962)99-134. — A. Primmer, Textvorschläge zu Augustins "Opus imperfectum," in *Latinität und alte Kirche.* Vienna 1977, 235-250.

c^3) To the monks of Hadrumetum and Marseilles

14. *De gratia et libero arbitrio liber* I. Augustine addressed this work to the monks at Hadrumetum to allay the difficulties caused by his *Ep.* 194, which some of them had read and transcribed at Rome, concerning the problem of the coexistence of grace and free will. In this noble book he proves the two truths — the necessity of grace and the existence of free will — according to the teaching of Scripture and exhorts the monks to remember them and profess them together even if they do not understand how they are to be reconciled with one another. Augustine defends the gratuity of grace and shows how God, by crowning our merits, crowns His own gifts (*Retract.* 2, 66: *Ep.* 214-216).

Editions: M 10/1, 718-744. — PL 44, 881-912.

Translations: English: P. Holmes, R. E. Wallis, op. cit., 443-465 (reprint: 1971). — P. R. Russell, FC 59(1968)250-308. *French:* M. J. Pintard, BA 24, 91-207 (with text). *German:* S. Kopp, ALG 7(1955)77-159 (with text). *Italian:* L. Galati. Rome, 1959. *Spanish:* G. E. de Vega, BAC 6(50)(1956)226-300 (with text).

Studies: A.-M. La Bonnardière, Quelques remarques sur les citations scripturaires du "De gratia et libero arbitrio": REAug 9(1963)77-85.

15. *De correptione et gratia liber* I. This work was written shortly after

the preceding and again for the monks of Hadrumetum, some of whom had drawn the false conclusion that, if grace was necessary, fraternal correction was useless. Augustine responds that it is not useless and then goes on to treat the more profound questions of predestination and the efficacy of grace, which is different before and after original sin — the famous distinction between *adiutorium sine quo* and *adiutorium quo*. He maintains that grace, although rendering correction beneficial, does not take away free will, and by comprehending the history of salvation in terms of freedom, he distinguishes between the freedom of Adam, our own, and that of the blessed in heaven. This is the most important of Augustine's works for his doctrine on grace (*Retract.* 2, 67).

Editions: M 10/1, 750-778. — PL 44, 915-946. — C. Boyer. Rome, 1932, 1951[2] (Maurist text).

Translations: English: P. Holmes, R. E. Wallis, op. cit., 471-479 (reprint: 1971). — J. Courtney Murray, FC 2(1947)245-305. *French:* J. Pintard, BA 24, 269-381 (with text). *German:* S. Kopp, ALG 7(1955)161-239 (with text). *Spanish:* V. Capánaga, BAC 6(50)(1956)127-223 (with text).

Studies: L. Bovy, Grâce et liberté chez saint Augustin. Montreal, 1938. — J. Schmucker, Die Gnade des Urstandes und die Gnade der Auserwählten in Augustins De corr. et gratia (Diss., Greg. Univ.) Rome, 1943. — O. Chadwick, Eulalius of Arles: JThSt 46(1945)200-205. — Guy de Broglie, Pour une meilleure intelligence du "De corr. et gratia": AugMag III, 317-337. — J. Lebourlier, Essai sur la responsabilité du pecheur. Grâce et liberté chez saint Augustin. La grâce d'Adam dans le "De corr. et gratia": AugMag II, 789-793. — F. Capponi, "Insuperabiliter" o "Inseparabiliter"? (Aug. De corr. et gratia 12, 38): Latomus 28(1969)681-684.

16. *De praedestinatione sanctorum* and *De dono perseverantiae.* These works were written to Prosper and Hilary, who had informed Augustine from Gaul of the disturbance among the monks of Marseilles (known later as Semi-Pelagians) caused by the two preceding works, which had given rise to a vigorous opposition to the doctrine contained therein. In his response Augustine shows that both the beginning of faith as well as perseverance in goodness are gifts of God and not, as the monks affirmed (*Ep.* 225-226), the work of the free will alone.

Editions: a) M 10/1, 790. — PL 44, 959-992. b) M 10/2, 822. — PL 45, 993-1034.

Translations: English: a) R. Holmes, R. E. Wallis, op. cit., 497-519 (reprint: 1971). b) *idem,* ibid., 525-552. — M. A. Lesousky (PSt 91). Washington, 1956 (with text). *French:* a & b) M. J. Chéné, BA 24, 465-597, 601-765 (with text). *German:* a & b) A. Zumkeller, ALG 7(1955)241-327, 329-439 (with text). *Spanish:* a) E. López, BAC 6(50)(1956)479-567 (with text). b) T. de Castro, ibid., 573-671 (with text).

Studies: J. Chéné, Les origenes de la controverse semi-pélagienne: AnThA 13(1953)56-109; *idem,* Le semipélagianisme du midi de la Gaule d'après les lettres de Prosper d'Aquitaine et Hilaire à Saint Augustin: RSR 43(1955)321-341. — J. M. Dalman,

"Praedestinatio, electio" en el libro "De pradest. sanct." Contribution a un Lexikon augustinianum: AugMag I, 127-136.

d) Against Arianism

1. *Contra sermonem Arianorum liber* I. Augustine composed this work, in which he proves the consubstantial nature of the divine persons, against an anonymous Arian sermon in 418 (*Retract.* 2, 52).

Editions: M 8, 625-648. — PL 42, 683-708 (Clavis 702).

2. *Collatio cum Maximino Arianorum episcopum.* This is the record of a conference held with the Arian bishop, Maximinus, who had been sent to Hippo by the governor Sigisvultus, "for the sake of peace," probably in 427 (Possidius, *Vita* 17).

Editions: M 8, 649-676. — PL 42, 709-742 (Clavis 699).

3. *Contra Maximinum arianum libri* II. Augustine composed this work because Maximinus, upon his return to Carthage from Hippo, boasted of having won his debate with Augustine. In the preface Augustine wrote, "First I will show that you have not been able to refute what I said; then, as is necessary, I will refute what you said" (Possidius, *Vita* 17, 9).

Editions: M 8, 677-744. — PL 42, 743-814.

Studies: A Pincherle, L'arianesimo e la Chiesa africana nel sec. IV: Bilychnis 35(1925)97-106. — J. Zeiller, L'arianisme en Afrique avant l'invasion vandale: RH 173(1934)535-540. — M. Simonetti, S. Agostino e gli Ariani: REAug 13(1967)55-84. — A. Pincherle, Ancora aull'arianesimo e la Chiesa africana del IV secolo: *Studi MatStRel* 39(1968)169-182.

e) Against the Priscillianists, the Marcionites and the Jews

1. *Ad Orosium contra Priscillianistas et Origenistas liber* I. This is a brief response to Orosius regarding certain doctrinal points of the Priscillianists and the Origenists such as the creation *ex nihilo* and the eternity of punishment (*Retract.* 2, 44).

Editions: M 8, 611-620. — PL 42, 669-678.

Studies: J. A. Davids, De Orosio et s. Augustino Priscillianistarum adversariis. The Hague, 1930. — B. Altaner, Augustinus und Origenes. Eine quellenkritische Untersuchung: HJG 70(1951)15-41 (= TU 83[1967]224-252). — Th. E. Mommsen, Orosius and Augustine, in *Medieval and Renais. Studies,* E. F. Rice, ed. Ithaca 1959, 325-348. — H. J. Diesnier, Orosius und Augustinus: *Acta Antiqua Ac Sc Hungaricae* 9(1963)89-102. — B. Studer, Zu einer Teufelserscheinung in der Vita Martini des Sulpicius Severus, in *Oikoumene, Misc. Vat. Conc. II.* Catania 1964, 351-404. — W. Theiler, Augustin und Origenes: *Augustinus* 13(1968)423-432 (= Strenas V. Capánaga).

2. *Contra adversarium legis et prophetarum libri* II. Augustine wrote these books around 420 to defend the Old Testament from accusations

contained in a Marcionite work which was being eagerly read and listened to in the squares of Carthage (*Retract.* 2, 58).

Editions: M 8, 549-606. — PL 42, 603-666. — M. P. Ciccarese. Rome, 1981 (with Italian translation).

Studies: M. P. Ciccarese, La tradizione manoscritta del "Contra adversarium legis et prophetarum": SSR 1(1977)325-338 (cf. REAug 25[1979]324).

3. *Tractatus adversus Iudaeos.* This work of an uncertain date is an explanation of Rom. 11:22. Augustine maintains that the prophecies of the Old Testament have been fulfilled in Christ and the church, and urges an attitude of humility and charity toward the Jews (*Indic.* 3, 4).

Editions: M 8, 29-43. — PL 42, 51-64.

Translations: English: M. Ligouri, FC 27(1955)387-414.

Studies: B. Blumenkranz, Die Judenpredigt Augustins. Basil, 1946; *idem,* Augustin et les juifs. Augustine et le Judaïsme: RAug 1(1958)225-241.

f) Against heresies in general

1. *De haeresibus.* Augustine composed this work in 428-429 at the request of the Carthaginian deacon, Quodvultdeus (*Ep.* 121-124). Drawing on Epiphanius and Philaster as well as on his own personal knowledge, he lists 88 heresies from Simon Magus to Pelagius and Caelestius. The work remained incomplete owing to the death of Augustine. The second and most important part was intended to deal with the manner of recognizing, judging and thus of avoiding, heresy, known or unknown. It would have provided a complete treatise of ecclesiology, which is lacking in patristic literature (ibid., *proem.*).

Editions: M 8, 1-28. — PL 42, 21-50. — R. Vander-Plaetse, C. Beukers, CCL 46(1969)283-351. — F. Oehler, Corpus haeresiol. I. Berlin, 1856, 192-225.

Translations: English: G. Müller, The "De haeresibus" of St. Aug. (PSt 90). Washington, 1956.

Studies: G. Bardy, Le "De haeresibus" et ses sources: MSCA II, 397. — S. Jannaccone, La dottrina eresiologica di S. Ag. . . . a proposito del trattato "De haeresibus." Catania, 1952. (For further bibliography, cf. CCL 46(1969)xxx-xxxii.)

LETTERS

Augustine's correspondence, the mark and expression of the influential personality and apostolic zeal of the author, is rich in historical, philosophical, theological, exegetical, spiritual, literary, and autobiographical content. His letters, which are numerous and often the length of a treatise, constitute a valuable commentary on his works *in libris* and provide an irreplaceable aid for understanding the questions and controversies of that turbulent and decisive period of the history of the church, especially in regard to the Donatist and Pelagian Conflicts. The Maurists published 270 letters, of which 53 were addressed to Augustine and 9 written by him were included among the *opuscula in libris*. Subsequently 6 further letters have been discovered: two by G. Bessel (184/1 and 202A in PL 33); two by A. Goldbacher (92A and 173A in CSEL 44); one by G. Morin (215A in CSEL 58, p. xciii) and one by C. Lambot (212A in RB 51[1939]109-121 and NBA 23, p. 532, which currently offers the most complete collection). J. Divjak has announced the discovery of further letters (cf. REAug 24[1978]343 n. 54) which will be published in CSEL 88.

The correspondence covers a period of more than 40 years (from the end of 386 until 430). The Maurists divided the letters into four classes:

1. *Epistolae* 1-30 from his conversion to his episcopal ordination;
2. *Epistolae* 31-123 from his episcopal ordination until the conference of 411;
3. *Epistolae* 124-231 from 411 until his death;
4. *Epistolae* 232-270 of uncertain date.

Editions: M 2. — PL 33. —A. Goldbacher, CSEL 34, 1(1895), 34, 2(1898), 44(1904), 57(1911), 58(1923). — J. Schmid, SS. Eus. Hieronymi et Aur. Augustini Epistulae mutua (FP 22). Bonn, 1930. — PLS II, 359-363 (Letters discovered by Goldbacher and Morin). — J. Divjak, CSEL 88(1981).

Translations: Dutch: H. Huisman. Amsterdam, 1956 (Ep. 90, 91, 103, 104). *English:* J. C. Cunningham, LNPF 1, ser. 1(1886)219-593 (reprint: 1956) (160 letters). — W. Parsons, FC 12, 18, 20, 30, 32(1951-1956). — J. H. Baxter, LCL 239(1965³) (62 letters with text). *French:* F. Pojulat. Paris, 1858. *German:* A. Hoffmann. BKV 29-30(1917) (selected letters). *Italian:* G. Rinaldi, L. Carrozzi, CPS 10-11(1939-40) (61 letters with text). — L. Carrozzi, NBA 21-23(1969, 1971, 1973) (with text). *Spanish:* L. Cilleruelo, BAC 8, 11, 11A (with text).

Chronology: P. Monceaux, Histoire littéraire de l'Afrique chrétienne, vol. 7. Paris, 1923. — H. Lietzmann, Zur Entstehungsgeschichte der Briefsammlung Augustins. Berlin, 1930 (= TU 67, 260-304). — D. de Bruyne, Les anciennes collections des épitres de Saint Augustin: RB 43(1931)284-295. — H. J. Diesner, Zur Datierung der Augustinbriefe 228-331: FF 35(1961)184-185; *idem,* Zur Datierung des Briefes 220 und anderer Spätschriften Augustins: FF 35(1961)281-283. — V. Paronetto, Nota sulla datazione dell'epistoloario agostiniano: Aug 14(1974)363-367. — A. Goldbacher, CSEL 58(1923)12-63.

Studies: A. Vaccari, Cuore e stile di S. Ag. nella Lettera 73: MSCA II, 353-358. — M. E. Keenan, The Life and Times of St. Augustine as Revealed in his Letters (PSt 83). Washington, 1935; *idem,* Classical Writers in the Letters of Aug.: CJ 32(1936)35-37. — C. Jenkins, Augustine's Classical Quotations in His Letters: JThSt 39(1938)59-65. — V. Nolte, Augustins Freundschaftsideal in seinen Briefen (Cassiciacum VI). Würzburg, 1939. — Ch. Morel, La vie de prière de saint Augustin d'après sa correspondance. Paris, 1954. — J. C. Didier, St. A. et le baptême des enfants: REAug 2(1956)109-129. — H. Rondet, La théologie de la grâce dans la correspondance de saint Augustin: RAug 1(1958)303-315. — G. Folliet, Deificari in otio. Aug. ep. 10, 2: RAug 2(1962)225-236. — H. Ulbrich, Augustins Briefe zur entscheidenden Phase des Pelagianischen Streites: REAug 9(1963)51-75, 235-258. — M. Pellegrino, Introduzione alle Lettere di S. Ag.:

NBA 21(1969)7-107. — M. P. Ciccarese, La tipologia delle Lettere di S. Agostino: Aug 11(1971)471-507. — M. Moreau, Le dossier Marcellinus dans la Correspondence de saint Augustin: RAug 9(1973)3-181. — H. Chadwick, New Letters of St. Augustine: JThSt 34(1983)425-452. — J. O'Connell, When Saintly Fathers Feuded. The Correspondence between Augustine and Jerome: *Thought* 54(1979)344-364. — G. Madec, Du nouveau dans la correspondance augustinienne: REAug 27(1981)56-66. — For further bibliography, cf. NBA 21(1969)cv-cx.

TREATISES

The treatises can and must be divided into three sections: *The Commentaries on Saint John,* the *Exposition of the Psalms* and *The Sermons.*

1. Commentaries on Saint John

1. *Tractatus in evangelium Ioannis.* The commentary consists of 124 sermons, some of which were actually given, others of which were merely dictated. They can be divided into two groups: 1-54 and 55-124. There is much debate concerning the date of composition. The second group of sermons is dated to 416 by Le Landais, to 418 by Zarb, and after 419-20 by La Bonnardière; and the first group is assigned to 411 by De Ferrari, 413 by Zarb, 414 by Le Landais. La Bonnardiére assigns 1-16 to the years 406-408 and places 17-54 after 418.

The entire commentary is marked by a pastoral character but is also extraordinarily rich in theological, philosophical, and spiritual content.

Editions: M 3/2, 1-826. — PL 35, 1379-1970. — R. Willems, CCL 36(1954).

Translations: Dutch: H. J. Scheerman, Verhandelingen over het Evangelie van Sint Jan I-II. Amsterdam, 1940. *English:* H. Browne, 2 vols. Oxford, 1848-1849. — J. Gibb, J. Innes, LNPF 7, ser. 1(1888)7-452 (reprint: 1956). *French:* M. Pontet. Namur, 1958 (selections). — M. F. Berrouard, BA 71-72(1969, 1977) (up to tr. 33 with text). *German:* T. Specht, BKV 8, 11, 19(1913-14). *Italian:* A. Tonna Barthet. Florence, 1938 (selection). — R. Minuti, R. Marsiglio. Rome, 1965. — E. Gandolfo, V. Tarulli, NBA 24(1968) (with text). *Spanish:* T. Prieto, BAC 13(139)(1955), V. Rabanal, BAC 14(165) (with text). *Portuguese:* P. Amado. Oporto, 1950-54.

Chronology: R. J. Deferrari, On the Date and Order of Delivery of St. Augustine's Tractatus on the Gospel and Epistle of St. John: CPh 12(1917)191-194. — S. Zarb, Chronologia tractatuum S. Augustini in evang. primamque ep Io. apostoli: Ang 10(1933)50-110. — M. Le Landais, Deux années de prédication de saint Augustin. Paris, 1953. — A. M. La Bonnardière, Recherches de chronologie augustinienne. Paris, 1965. — M. F. Berrouard, La date des tractatus I-LIV in Ioannis Evang. de saint Augustin: RAug 7(1971)105-168.

Studies: M. Comeau, La vie intérieure de chrétien d'après les "Tract. in Io." de saint Augustin: RSR 20(1930)5-25, 125-149; *idem,* Saint Augustin. Exégète du quatrième évangile. Paris, 1930. — M. Pontet, Saint Augustin: sermons sur saint Jean. Namur, 1958. — A. Tamayo, La mediación reveladora de Cristo en la escatología definitiva según la exégesis agustiniana de los escritos de san Juan. Diss., Innsbruck, 1962 (typewritten). — D. F. Wright, The Manuscripts of St. Aug.'s "Tractatus in Evangelium Iohannis." A Preliminary Survey: RAug 8(1972)55-143. — G. Folliet, Un fragment de manuscrit des "Tractatus in Evang. Io" de saint Aug. découvert à Vézelay en 1966: RAug 8(1972)145-147. — R. P. Hardy, The Incarnation and Revelation in Augustine's "Tract. in Io Evang.": *Eglise et théologie* 3(1972)193-200; *idem,* Actualité de la Révélation Divine. Paris, 1974.

2. *Tractatus in epistolam Ioannis ad Parthos.* These are ten sermons on charity, of which John "has sung the praises, saying many things; in fact, nearly everything": (*prol.*). They were given during the festivities at Easter in a year between 413 and 418, and interrupted the commentary on the Gospel. They are the most beautiful treatment of this theme in patristic literature.

Editions: M 3/2, 825-900. — PL 35, 1977-2062.

Translations: Arabic: J. Helou. Beirut, 1967. *Dutch:* T. J. van Bavel. Heverlee-Leuwen, 1969. *English:* H. Browne, J. H. Myers, LNPF 7, ser. 1(1888)450-529 (reprint: 1956). *French:* P. Agaësse, SCh 75(1967) (with text). *German:* F. Hoffmann. Freiburg Br, 1938, 1954[3] (incomplete). *Italian:* P. Tablino. Rome, 1954. — G. Madurini, L. Muscolino, NBA 24(1968)1628-1856 (with text). — S. Aliquò. Rome, 1971[3]. *Portuguese:* J. A. Rodrigues Amado. Coimbra, 1959. *Spanish:* B. Martín Pérez, BAC 18(187)(1959)192-362 (with text).

Studies: G. Combès, La charité d'après saint Augustin. Paris, 1934. — M. Mellet, Saint Augustin prédicateur de la charité fraternelle dans ses commentaires sur saint Jean: VS 83(1945)304-325, 556-576; 84(1946)69-91. — J. Gallay, La charité fraternelle selon les Tractatus in Iam Ioannis de saint Aug. Lyons, 1953. — F. Hoffmann, Gott ist die Liebe. Die Predigten des hl. Augustinus über den 1. Johannesbrief. Freiburg Br., 1954[3]. — J. Gallay, La conscience de la charité fraternelle d'après les tract. in Iam Ioannis de saint Aug.: REAug 1(1955)1-20; *idem,* "Dilige et quod vis fac." Notes d'exégèse augustinienne: RSR 43(1955)545-555. — J. Grabowski, The Role of Charity in the Mystical Body: REAug 3(1957)29-63. — J. B. Bauer, Dilige et quod vis fac (zu Aug. Tract. in I Jo. 7, 81): *Wissenschaft und Weisheit* 20(1957)64-65. — J. A. R. Amado, Santo Agostino. Quem è Dios. Comentário à Primeira Carta de S. Joào. Coimbra, 1959. — M. Huftier, La charité dans l'enseignement de saint Augustin. Tournai, 1959. — J. Burnaby, Amor Dei. A Study of St. Augustine's Teaching on the Love of God as the Motive of the Christian Life. London, 1960[3]. — O. Roy, L'expérience de l'amour et l'intelligence de la foi trinitaire selon saint Augustin: RAug 2(1962)415-445. — S. Poque, Les lectures liturgiques de l'Octave pascale à Hippone d'après les Traités de saint Augustin sur la Première Épitre de S. Jean: RB 74(1964)217-241. — T. J. van Bavel, Eenheid en liefde. Augustinus preken over de eerste brief van Johannes. Louvain, 1969. — V. Capánaga, Interpretación agustiniana del Amor. Eros y Agapè: AugL 18(1973)213-278. — D. Dideberg, S. A. et la Première Épitre de S. Jean. Paris, 1975.

2. *Exposition of the Psalms.*

This is the longest of Augustine's works and the richest in spiritual doctrine, and forms the only complete treatise on the Psalms in patristic literature. The composition of the work extended over a period of time from 392 (1-32) until 416 or, according to some, up until 422 for Psalm 118. The work can be divided into two classes: expositions which were dictated and expositions which were preached. The dictated expositions can be further subdivided into three groups (cf. *Ep.* 169, 1 and Possidius, *Indic.* 7, 4): brief exegetical notes (Psalms 1-31, with a few exceptions), longer expositions (67, 71, 77 and others) and homilies intended to be read to the people (32 homilies on Psalm 118). All the rest are sermons delivered before the people in various cities, mostly Carthage. They do not present an historical-philological interpretation, but rather a theological-spiritual one based on the doctrine of the *Christus totus:* the Psalms resound with the voice of Christ, of the church, and of the individual faithful (*In ps.* 3 1, 9-10). The content treats all the important themes of Christian doctrine and includes philosophy, theology, spiritual doctrine, and mysticism. Augustine has particularly developed the themes of the mystical body, of the two cities, and of the ascent of the soul to God for which the lyric tone of the Psalms provides the wings. The text on which the commentary is based is a Latin translation of the Septuagint revised by Augustine himself.

Editions: M 4. — PL 36-37. — E. Dekkers, J. Fraipont, CCL 38-40(1956). — Catalogus verborum quae in operibus S. Augustini inveniuntur, vol. 2 Enarrationes in Psalmos 1-50: CCL 38(1978); Enarrationes in Psalmos 51-100: CCL 39(1981).

Translations: Dutch: L. Grollenberg, P. Struik: *Tijdscrift voor Geestelijk leven* 14(1958)665-676 (Psalm 60). *English:* A. Cleveland Coxe, LNPF 8, ser. 1(1888) (reprint: 1956). — S. Hebgin, F. Corrigan, ACW 29-30(1960). *French:* G. Humeau. Paris, 1948. — G. Gorce. Namur, 1960 (anthology). — J. Petet. Paris, 1964 (anthology). *German:* H. von Balthasar. Leipzig, 1935. — H. Weber. Paderborn, 1964 (Ps. 1-17). *Italian:* E. Logi. Siena, 1931-32. — V. Tarulli, R. Minuti, T. Mariucci, NBA 25-28(1967-1977) (with text). *Spanish:* B. Martín Pérez, BAC 19-22(235, 246, 255, 264)(1964-1967) (with text).

Chronology: S. Zarb, Chronologia Enarraionum S. Aug. in Psalmos. Malta, 1948 (cf. L. Brix, REAug 10[1964]193). — M. Le Landais, Quatre mois de prédication de Saint Aug.: RSR 36(1948)226-250; *idem,* Deux années de prédication de S. Augustin, in *Etudes Augustiniennes.* Paris 1953, 7-95. — A. Lauras, H. Rondet, Le thème des deux cités dans l'œuvre de Saint Augustin, in *Etudes Augustiniennes.* Paris 1953, 99-160. — A. M. La Bonnardière, Note de chronologie augustinienne. Notice sur le psaume 25: RSR 45(1957)91-93; *idem,* Les "Enarrationes in psalmos" prêchés par st. A. à Carthage en décembre 409: RAug 11(1976)52-90; *idem,* Recherches de chronologie augustinienne. Paris 1965, 119-164. — H. Rondet, Essais sur la chronologie des "Enarrationes in psalmos" de saint Augustin: BLE 61(1960)11-127, 258-286; 65(1964)110-136; 68(1967)180-202; 71(1970)174-200; 77(1976)99-118. — S. Poque, L'énigme des enarrationes in Psalmos 110-117 de st. A.: BLE 77(1976)241-246.

Manuscript Tradition: A. Wilmart, La tradition des grands ouvrages de St. Ag. IV Les Enarrations: MSCA II, 295-315.

Biblical text: P. Capelle, Le texte du Psautier Latin en Afrique. Rome, 1913. — D. de Bruyne, St. Augustin reviseur de la Bible. II, Psaumes: MSCA II, 544-578; *idem,* Notes sur le Psautier de Saint Augustin: RB 45(1933)20-28. — A. Vaccari, I Salteri di S. Girolamo e di S. Agostino. Rome, 1952; *idem,* Psalterium Sancti Aug. in M. Sinai repertum: Bibl 36(1955)260. — S. Ongaro, Salterio veronese e revisione agostiniana: Bibl 35(1954)443-474.

Studies: E. Bouby, St. Augustin. Les Enarrationes sur les Psaumes: RevAug 3(1903)418-436. — M. Pontet, L'exégèse de St. Augustin predicateur. Paris, 1945. — T. Delamare,

Lorsque St. Augustin expliquait les Psaumes: VS 82(1950)115-136. — C. Kannengiesser, Enarratio in psalmum 118. Sciences de la révelation et progrès spirituel: RAug 2(1962)359-381. — J. F. Cordelier, La pédogogie de saint Augustin dans les "Ennarationes in Psalmos." Dijon, 1971. — S. Poque, L'énigme des Enarr. in psalmos 110-117 de s. A.: BLE 77(1976)241-264. Cf. *infra,* 4. Spiritual Doctrine.

3. Sermons

The Sermons are the fruit of a career of preaching which continued without interruption for almost forty years. The library at Hippo must have contained very many sermons, perhaps three or four thousand, the greater part of which were probably never revised and published by Augustine and have perished. The Maurists edited 363 sermons as genuine, divided into four classes (on the Scripture, on the liturgical seasons, on the saints, on various topics), judged others to be of doubtful authenticity and still others to be spurious. G. Morin published a further 138 sermons which he considered authentic (MSCA I), although other scholars have raised doubts regarding the authenticity of some of these (CPL 284-287; PLS II, 417ff). Lambot subsequently discovered and published further homilies (RB 1933-1958; PLS II, 744). The total number of Augustine's sermons now numbers slightly more than 500. As a result of the efforts of Lambot, the CCL has undertaken a long-awaited critical edition of the sermons of Augustine and the first volume (CCL 41) has been published containing the sermons on the Old Testament (1-50).

The content of the sermons is rich and varied, embraces all the themes of Scripture and the liturgy and serves as a valuable commentary on the great dogmatic and exegetical works. They are a model of popular eloquence which is at the same time clear yet profound, lively and incisive, direct and effective.

Editions: M 5. — PL 38-39. — Lambot, CCL 41 (the first 50 on the Old Testament). *Partial editions:* C. Lambot, Strom. Patr. et Medioev. I, Utrecht, 1950 (serm. 14, 15, 34, 60, 101, 104, 166, 177, 184, 221, 254, 261, 298, 302, 355, 356, 358). — G. Morin: MSCA I. — PLS II, 398-1360. — CPL 284-288, 368-372. Cf. P.-P. Verbraken, Études critiques sur les Sermons authentiques de S. A. (Instrumenta patristica 12). Steenbrugge, 1976.

Translations: English: R. G. MacMullen, LNPF 6, ser. 1(1887)245-545 (Serm. 51-147 on the Gospel) (reprint: 1956). — Q. Howe. New York, 1956 (selections). — Ph. T. Weller. St. Louis, 1959 (serm. on Easter). — D. J. Kavanagh, FC 11(1951, 1963[2]) (17 serm.). — S. Muldowney, FC 38(1959) (selections). — Th. Comerford Lawler, ACW 15(1952, 1963[2]) (Serm. for Christmas and Epiphany). *French:* G. Humau, 3 vols. Paris, 1932-1934. — S. Poque, SCh 116(1966) (Serm. on Easter: with text). *German:* A. Schmitt. Mannheim, 1947 (selections); *idem.* Bern, 1967 (40 serm.). *Italian:* E. Logi. Siena, 1930 (selections); *idem,* I Vangeli domenicali commentati. Florence, 1933. *Spanish:* L. Alvarez (vols. 1-4) and A. del Fueyo (vols. 5-8). Madrid, 1923-1931. — A. del Fueyo, BAC 7 and 10(1981[4], 1983); A. del Fueyo, P. de Luis, BAC 23-25(1983-84) (with text).

Chronology: A. Kunzelmann, Die Chronologie der Sermones des hl. A.: MSCA II, 417-520. — A. de Veer, La date des Sermons de st. A.: REAug 15(1969)241-346.

Studies: C. Lambot, Le catalogue de Possidius et la collection carthusienne de sermons de saint Augustin: RB 60(1950)3-7. — M. Simonetti, Studi sulla letteratura cristiana d'Africa in età vandalica: RIL 83(1950)407-424; *idem,* Alcune osservazioni sulla struttura dei "Sermones de Sanctis" agostiniani: AugMag I, 141-149. — C. Lambot, Critique interne et sermons de saint Augustin: SP 1. Berlin 1957, 112-127 (= TU 63). — C. Mohrmann, Das Wortspiel in den augustinischen Sermones, in *Études sur le latin des Chrétiens.* I, Rome, 1958, 323-349. — M. Pellegrino, S. Agostino. Il pastore d'anime. Fossano, 1960. — P. Borgomeo, L'église de ce temps dans la prédication de St. A., Paris, 1972 (bibl. 423-433). — V. Loi, Struttura e "topoi" del panegirico classico nei "sermones de sanctis" di S. Agostino: Aug 14(1974)591-604. — P.-P. Verbraken, Les fragments conservés de sermons perdus de saint Augustin: RB 84(1974)245-270. — M. Avilés Bartina, Estudio de diez sermones agustinianos: *Perficit* (Spain) 7(1976)33-71. — P. Vismara Chiappa, Il tema della povertà nella predicazione di S. A. Milan, 1975.

Special mention is given here to certain sermons whose authenticity has been questioned and which the editors have printed separately:

1. *Sermo de Urbis excidio.* This sermon was given "Recenti excidio tantae urbis," thus in 410 or shortly thereafter. It contains expressions of sorrow as well as of hope in the face of what has taken place and gives an explanation of the utility of tribulation. It resembles Augustine's sermons in form and content.

Editions: PL 40, 715-724. — M.-V. O'Reilly, PSt 89. Washington, 1955 (= CCL 46 [1969]249-262).

Translations: English: M.-V. O'Reilly, op. cit. (with text). *German:* J. Fischer, in *Die Völkswanderung im Urteil.* Heidelberg 1945, 66-68.

Studies: G. Cannone, Il sermo de excidio urbis Romae di S. Agostino: VetChr 12(1975)322-345.

2. *Sermo ad catechumenos de symbolo.* This explanation of the creed is of an uncertain date (cf. *Serm.* 213 [Guelph. 1: MSCA I, 441-445], 214, 215). The other three sermons which follow this one in the manuscripts and printed editions are not authentic and have been attributed by some to Quodvultdeus, the bishop of Carthage.

Editions: CPL 401-403. — PL 40, 627-636. — R. Vander Plaetse, CCL 46, 185-199.

Translations: Dutch: A. Sizoo. Kampen, 1941. *English:* R. W. Muncey. Condon, 1931. — M. Ligouri, FC 27(1955)285-307.

Studies: A. Sizoo, De ectheid van Augustinus' Sermo de Symbolo ad cat.: *Gereformeerd Theol. Tijd.* 41(1940)286-300. — C. Eichenseer, Das Symbolum Apostolicum beim hl. Aug., St. Ottilien, 1960.

3. *Sermo de disciplina christiana.* This is a homily of uncertain date on the true love of God and neighbor which constitutes the summation of the Christian precepts.

Editions: M 6, 581-590. — PL 40, 669-678. — R. Vander Plaetse, CCL 46(1969)707-724.

Translations: German: A. Habitzky. Würzburg, 1961.

4. *Sermo de utilitate ieiunii.* This sermon on the nature of Christian

fasting is mentioned by Possidius (*Indic.* 10 6, 55: MSCA II, 195) and was given perhaps in 411 (cf. ibid., 13). It is a polemic against the Manichaeans and a sorrowful appeal to the Donatists.

Editions: M 6, 613-622. — PL 40, 707-718. — S. D. Ruegg, PSt 85. Washington, 1951 (= CCL 46, 231-241).

Translations: English: S. D. Ruegg, op. cit. (with text). — M. S. Muldowney, FC 16(1952)397-422. *French:* G. Combès, BA 2, 515-539 (with text).

Studies: C. Lambot, Un "Ieiunium Quinquagesimae" en Afrique au IVe siècle et date de quelque sermons de St. A.: RB 47(1935)114-124.

DUBIOUS WORKS

The authenticity of the following works has been seriously questioned or is only more or less probable.

1. *De grammatica liber.* The work is mentioned by both Augustine (*Retract.* 1, 6) and Possidius (*Indic.* 10 1, 3: MSCA II, 175). Augustine claims to no longer have it in his library although he thinks that some people may have it. The present text has come down in a longer and a shorter version, neither of which can be considered authentic. However, some believe, not without some probability, that these two works are excerpts from the genuine text.

Editions: Longer version: PL 32, 1385-1408. — H. Keil, Grammatici latini V., Leipzig 1868, 496-524. Shorter version: A. Mai, Nova Patrum bibliotheca I 2, p. 167-181. — C. F. Weber, Augustini ars grammatica breviata. Marburg, 1961.

Studies: H.-I. Marrou, St. A. et la fin de la culture antique. Paris 1938, 570-576.

2. *Principia dialecticae.* These are mentioned in the *Retractationes* (1, 6) with the words, "Of the Dialectica . . . only the *principia* were left, which we have nevertheless lost." Contrary to the opinion of the Maurists, many consider the present text to be authentic.

Editions: PL 32, 1409-1420. — G. Crecelius, A. Augustini de dialectica liber. Eberfeld, 1857. — B. Darrell Jackson, J. Pinborg. Dordrecht-Boston, 1975 (with English transl.).

Studies: B. Fischer, De Augustini disciplinarum libro qui est de dialectica. Iena, 1912. — H.-I. Marrou, op. cit. 576-578. — J. Pepin, St. A. et la dialectique. Villanova Univ., 1976.

3. *Principia rhetorices (Retract.* 1, 6).

Editions: PL 32, 1439-1448. — C. Halm, Rhetores latini minores. Leipzig, 1863, 137-151. In addition to the Maurists, the authenticity of the work is also denied by J. Zurek, De S. Augustini praeceptis rhetoricis. Vienna, 1905, 69-110. — H.-I. Marrou, op. cit. 578-579. — CPL 1556. The authenticity is defended by B. Riposati, Studi in onore di G. Funaioli. Rome 1955, 378-393.

4. *Oratio s. Augustini in librum de Trinitate.* This work is a long prayer to the One and Triune God.

Editions: G. Morin: RB 21(1904)129-132. — PLS II, 1543-1545. — B. Fischer: ThLZ 77(1952)288 (denies authenticity). W. S. Mountain, CCL 50, lxxvii-lxxxii (denies authenticity).

5. *Versus de s. Nabore.* These are eight verses in honor of a martyr who returned to the unity of the Catholic church from schism and for this reason was killed by the Donatists.

Editions: F. Büchler, A. Riese, Anthologia Latina I, 2. Leipzig, 1906, n. 484a (reprint: 1972). — PLS II, 356-357. — A. Vaccari, I versi di S. Agostino: CC 98/1(1947)213-214 (= Scritti II, Rome 1958, 245-247).

6. *Capita* or *Breviculi.* These are titles or summaries of the different chapters which make up the books of the more important works: *De civitate Dei* (CCL 47, V-XLV; cf. *Ep.* 212A to Firmus, NBA 23, 535); *De Trinitate* (CCL 50, 4-23; PLS II, 1546-1555) and *De Genesi ad litteram* (CSEL 28/1, 436-456; PLS II, 363-385; BA 49, 461-493, cf. observations *ibid.,* 461-463).

SPURIOUS WORKS

Through the centuries many works — books, letters and, above all, sermons — have been attributed to the Bishop of Hippo and published under his name. A knowledge of these is useful, indeed important, not only for reasons of textual criticism in determining the true author to the extent possible, but also for evaluating more precisely the influence of Augustine on his posterity. It is known in fact that Augustine has been known and cited through these works which, since they are not authentic, have not always permitted an access to his genuine thought. These works will be given only a brief presentation here.

1. Books

Some of these are works dealing with theology: a) general theology such as the *De fide ad Petrum* (PL 40, 753-789) which is a dogmatic collection much used in the Middle Ages (it is a work of Fulgentius of Ruspe: PL 65, 671-705); b) Trinitarian theology, such as the *De unitate Trinitatis* (PL 42, 1207-1212) "of an unknown but ancient author" and the *De unitate Trinitatis contra Felicianum arianum* (PL 42, 1157-1176) which was considered authentic by the theologians of Louvain (ed. Lov. t. VI) but was restored to Vergil of Tapso by the Maurists (CPL 808); c) the theology of grace, such as the *Hypomnesticon contra Pelagianos et Caelestianos* (PL 45, 1611-1664), a work in six books which refutes five errors of the Pelagians and illustrates the doctrine of predestination in the sixth book (the author is unknown, but is definitely later than Augustine: CPL 381), the *De praedestinatione et gratia* (PL 45, 1665-1678) which contains principles openly contrary to those of Augustine (16, 18) and the very brief *De praedestinatione Dei* (PL 45, 1677-1680).

Other of the spurious works are exegetical: the *De mirabilibus sacrae Scripture* (PL 35, 2149-2200), three books on the more amazing episodes of Scripture composed by an unidentified "Augustinus Hibernicus" (CPL 1123); the *Quaestiones Veteris et Novi Testamenti* (PL 35, 2207-2416; CSEL 50; PLS II, 390), an explanation of 115 questions attributed to Ambrosiaster (CPL 185); the *Expositio in Apocalypsim* (PL 35, 2417-2452) of Caesarius of Arles (CPL 1016) and the *Liber de divinis Scripturis* (CSEL 12), a work on 142 topics (titles in PLS II, 392-396) by an anonymous fifth-century author (CPL 384).

Still other numerous and widely diffused works deal with questions of spirituality: the *De spiritu et anima; Soliloquiorum animae ad Deum liber* (not to be confused with the two books of the *Soliloquii,* cf. p. 358), *De diligendo Deo; Meditationum liber* and the *Manuale* (PL 40). These works are all intended to nourish piety and their authors (author?) demonstrate a knowledge of Augustine and of the medieval doctors. For other works, cf. CPL, p. 530-531; PLS II, 1363-1378.

Editions: J. E. Chisholm, The Pseudo-Augustinian Hypomnesticon against the Pelagians and Caelestians, 2 vols. Fribourg, 1967, 1980.

2. Letters

Few letters have been falsely attributed to Augustine although scholars are unceasingly searching for and finding authentic letters (cf. p. 393). Among the spurious letters are the following: *Epistulae Augustini et Bonifacii comitis* (PL 33, 1093-1098), 16 very brief letters from a supposed correspondence between the two figures (cf. J. De Lepper, *De rebus gestis Bonifatii.* Tilburg 1941, 9-17; CPL 367); *Altercatio cum Pascentio Ariano* (*Ep.* 20: PL 33, 1156-1162) the false attribution of which is probably due to the *Ep.* 238, 239 and 241 of Augustine to Pascentius which are authentic; *Epistula s. Augustini ad sororem de obitu s. Monicae* (ed. Lov. X, p. 764ff).

3. Sermons

The dubious or pseudoaugustinian sermons are numerous. The Maurists published 317 divided, like the authentic sermons, into four categories: on Scripture, on the liturgical seasons, on the saints, and on various topics (PL 39, 1735-2354). Many others have subsequently been published: 269 by A. B. Caillau and B. Saint-Yves, *S. Augustini operum supplementum.* Paris 1836-39; 200 by A. Mai, *Nova Patrum Bibliotheca,* I. Rome, 1852; others by G. Morin, *Tractatus sive sermones s. Augustini.* Kempten, 1917, App. p. 165-218; (PLS II, 841-1360). From this vast quantity the work in particular of G. Morin, C. Lambot and P.-P. Verbraken has made it possible to establish the authenticity of many of Augustine's sermons (in addition to those of the Maurist edition) or to recognize their true author. Regarding all of this material, cf. G. Morin, MSCA I, 721-769; CPL 368-372; P.-P. Verbraken, op. cit. (p. 398).

Studies: E. Portalié: DTC I, 2306-2310. — F. Cavallera: DSp I, 1130-1135. — B. Blumenkranz, La survie médiévale de St. A. à travers ses apocryphes: AugMag II, 1003-1018.

DOCTRINE

REASON AND FAITH

With regard to methodology, Augustine's thought can be summed up in these two terms: reason and faith. At age 19 he adopted a mistaken attitude. Since he had been ensnared by the Manichaean propaganda, he turned the pair into a dilemma and rejected faith in the name of reason. His return to the Catholic church began with the discovery that the relation between reason and faith did not have to be seen in terms of opposition but of collaboration. There were, in fact, two ways which led man to a knowledge of the truth: authority and reason. Chronologically, authority came first, i.e., faith; but in order of importance, the first place was occupied by reason, i.e., knowledge (*C. acad.* 3 20, 43; *De ord.* 2 9, 26; *De mor. eccl. cath.* 1 2, 3).

His doctrinal life passed between fideism and rationalism. To anyone who wanted to understand without believing, he repeated his saying: *crede ut intelligas,* because understanding was a reward of faith. He defended the justice of this principle and of this method and wrote a book on the utility of believing. Faith is useful for all, even for the philosopher. It is, in fact, a medicine which heals (*Conf.* 6 4, 6), a fortress which protects (*Ep.* 118, 32), a nest where plumage is developed for flight (*Serm.* 51 5, 6), a shortcut which allows one to know quickly and without effort the truths necessary for leading a wise life (*Ep.* 102, 38; *De cons. evang.* 1 35, 53). But to anyone who thought it necessary to dismiss reason he repeated: *intellige ut credas,* for one is not able to believe without reason. No one in fact believes "if he has not first thought it necessary to believe" (*De praed. sanc.* 2, 5). It is reason which shows "who is to be believed" (*De v. rel.* 24, 45), and thus "even faith has eyes with which it sees that what it does not yet see is nevertheless true" (*Ep.* 120, 2, 8). He furthermore repeated: *intellectum valde ama,* love greatly to understand the content of faith (*Ep.* 120, 3, 13).

For his own part, he strove to demonstrate the credibility of the faith and to study thoroughly the teaching of the same. The scope of his efforts: "to lead men back to the hope of finding the truth" (*Ep.* 1, 1); and the program: adherence to Christ and philosophical reflection.

For a résumé of the motives for the credibility of the Catholic faith cf. *Conf.* 6 11, 19; *De mor. eccl. cath.* 1 7, 12; *De util. cred.* 14, 30-17, 35; *Ep.* 137, 4, 15-16; *C. ep. Man.* 4, 5. In this latter work Augustine wrote, "Aside from the sincere and genuine wisdom . . . which you do not believe exists in the Catholic church, there are many reasons which hold me in her bosom. The concurrence of peoples and nations holds me, the authority established by the miracles, nourished by hope, increased by charity, strengthened by antiquity, holds me; the succession of bishops, from the very see of the Apostle Peter, to whom the Lord, after his resurrection, entrusted the feeding of his sheep, up to the present episcopate holds me; finally, the very name of *catholica,* which not without reason this church alone has obtained, holds me . . . These bonds of the Christian name — so many, so great and so very gentle — hold the believer in the bosom of the Catholic church, even if, owing to the slowness of our mind and the unworthiness of our life, the truth does not yet appear." To anyone who denied the miracles Augustine responded; "This one great miracle is sufficient for us: that the whole world has believed without miracles" (*De div. Dei* 22, 5).

The program of reflection has been summarized thus in the *Contra academicos,* the first of his works: "Everyone knows that we are moved to knowledge by the dual weight of authority and reason. I therefore consider it as definitely certain that I must not stray from the authority of Christ, for I do not find any other which is more valid. With regard to that which must be reached with the discernment of reason, I am confident to find meanwhile in the Platonists that which is not inconsistent with the sacred mysteries of the faith. In fact my present disposition is such that I desire to learn without delay that which is true, not only by means of faith but also by means of understanding" (*C. acad.* 3 20, 43). This reflection will be at the same time philosophical, theological and mystical; the three moments in the ascent toward the truth which Augustine never separates from one another. His method is, in fact, based on three premises: the utility of faith; the appeal to the evidence of reason when possible; the aspiration for wisdom, which is not only understanding, but also the love, possession and enjoyment of the truth, which constitutes the highest good for man. The brief summary which follows will be divided into three sections: philosophy, theology, and spiritual doctrine.

Studies: B. Pergamo, De S. Aug. methodo apologetico: Ant 6(1931)3-36. — I. Stoszko, L'Apologétique de St. Aug., Strasbourg, 1932. — R. E. Cushman, Faith and Reason in the Thought of St. Aug.: CH 19(1950)271-294. — R. Aubert, Le problème de l'acte de foi. Louvain, 1950. — R. Paciorkowsky, Christianity in the Apologetic Thought of St. Aug., Poznan, 1952 (in Polish with a summary in French). — J. P. Bonnefoy, Le docteur chrétien selon Augustin: foi, raison et autorité: RET 13(1953)25-54. — G. Oggioni,

L'esperienza della fede nella conversione di S. Ag.: *Scrinium Theol* 1(1953)125-181. — M. T. Antonelli, Aspetti agostiniani del problema del filosofare: AugMag I, 335-346. — E. Oggioni, Dualismo paradossale dell'Agostinismo speculativo: AugMag I, 381-388. — R. E. Cushman, Faith and Reason. New York, 1955. — M. Löhrer, Der Glaubensbegriff des hl. Aug. in seinen ersten Schriften bis zu den Confessiones. Einsiedeln, 1955. — H. A. Wolfson, The Philosophy of the Church Fathers. Cambridge, Mass., 1956. — B. M. G. Reardon, The Relation of Philosophy to Faith in the Teaching of St. Aug.: SP 2 (TU 64), Berlin 1957, 288-294. — M. Blondel, The Latent Resources in St. Aug.'s Thought (originally: A Monument to St. Aug.). New York 1957[3], 317-353. — M. Löhrer, Glaube und Heilsgeschichte in De Trin. Aug.: FreibZPhTh 4(1957)385-419. — A. Aróstegui, Interpretación agustiniana del "Nisi credideritis, non intelligetis": RevFil (Madrid) 24(1965)277-283. — M. Huftier, Les yeux de la foi chez s. Aug.: MSR 25(1968)57-66, 105-114. — W. G. von Jess, Reason and Propedeutic to Faith in Aug.: IntJourPhilRel 5(1974)225-233. — K. Flasch, Augustin, Einführung in sein Denken. Stuttgart, 1980. — E. S. Mead, St. Augustine on God as Known by Human Reason. Collegeville, 1980.

PHILOSOPHY

1. Sources

Augustine possessed no mean knowledge of the history of philosophy (*C. acad.* 2 4, 10-6, 15; *Ep.* 118; *De civ. Dei* 8). As a young professor he read and knew by heart many works of the philosophers (*Conf.* 5 3, 3). Among these were the philosophical works of Cicero, Varro's erudite works, those of Apuleius, of Seneca, and of Aulus Gellius and Celsus (concerning the latter, cf. *De haer., praef.*). Later, at Milan, he read Plotinus and Porphyry, who immediately became and remained his favorite authors.

That Augustine preferred the Neoplatonists to all other philosophers is well known; less well known is the extent to which he corrected and went beyond their teaching. He preferred them for two reasons: because they were closer "to us," i.e., to Christian doctrine (*De civ. Dei* 8, 5: 11, 5; *De v. rel.* 4, 7), and because they had created "a common teaching of the true philosophy" in which they maintained, among other things, that Plato and Aristotle, the two greatest philosophers (*De civ. Dei* 8 4, 12), were in such complete agreement that only to the less discerning could there seem to be discord between them (*C. acad.* 3 19, 42). If in his first enthusiasm, for which he would later make amends (*Retract.* 1 1, 4), he believed to find in them connections with Christian teaching which, in fact, do not exist — such as the generation of the Word (*Conf.* 7 9, 13-15) and the notion of the Kingdom of Christ which is not of this world (*Retract.* 1 3, 2)—or attributed to them doctrines which in reality they did not hold, such as that of creation (*De civ. Dei* 8, 6), he nevertheless combatted and rejected their "great errors" (*Retract.* 1 1, 4). Among these errors were the existence of minor deities (*De civ. Dei* 12, 24-26), the necessity and eternity of creation (*ibid.*, 11, 4-6; 12, 15-20; *C. Prisc. et Orig.* 2 8, 9), the preexistence and the sin of souls (*De Gen. ad litt.* 10

15, 27; *Ep.* 164, 7, 20; 166, 9, 27), the cyclical and metempsychotic theory of history (*De civ. Dei* 10, 30; 12, 26) and the concept of the unnatural and therefore violent union of the soul with the body (*De Trin.* 15, 7, 11; *De Gen. ad litt.* 7, 27, 38). Indeed, on some points his attitude became unusually hard, as when he stated that it was foolishness to separate the body from man's nature (*De an. et eius orig.* 4, 2, 3) or that the doctrines of reincarnation were ravings of great teachers: *magna magnorum deliramenta doctorum* (*Serm.* 241, 6).

He was sustained in this steadfast attitude by the rule he had imposed on himself (cf. p. 349) and in particular by those teachings of the Scripture which concerned the field of pure reason such as the doctrine of creation (Gen. 1:1; John 1:3), the creation of man in the image of God (Gen. 1:27), the notion of God as subsistent Being (Ex. 3:14) and the possibility of the knowledge of the Creator through created things (Rom. 1:20). Themes such as this latter one were often recalled by Augustine even in the very midst of the loftiest philosophical speculations (*Conf.* 7, 10, 16) and they stimulated him to further develop some of the fundamental themes of his philosophy and to resolve the difficulties of the Platonists (*De civ. Dei* 12, 17). A new philosophy was thus born among the sources of which it is not improper to number the numerous incentives provided by Christian teaching. This philosophy can no longer be described as Platonic or Neoplatonic — Augustine was as much anti-Platonic as he was Platonic — and can be described only as Christian. A synthesis of the principles, themes and essential solutions of this philosophy will be given below.

Studies: A. Casamassa, Le fonti della fil. di S. Ag., in *Acta hebddomadae augustiniano-thomisticae.* Turin 1931, 88-96 (= Scritti patristic. Lateranum 1955). — R. Jolivet, St. Aug. et le néoplatonisme chrétien. Paris, 1932. — P. Henry, Plotin et l'Occident. Louvain, 1934; *idem,* Aug. and Plotinus: JThSt 38(1937)1-23. — J. De Blic, Platonisme et christianisme dans la conception augustinienne du Dieu Créateur: RSR 30(1940)172-190. — H. J. Marrou, St. Aug. et la fin de la culture antique. Paris, 1938, 1946². — A. Dahl, Aug. und Plotin. Lund, 1945. — B. Switalski, Plotinus and the Ethics of St. Aug., New York, 1946. — R. M. Bushmann, St. Aug.'s Metaphysics and Stoic Doctrine: NSch 26(1952)283-304. — G. Faggin, S. Ag. e Porfirio, in S. Ag. e le grandi correnti della fil. contemporanea. Tolentino, 1956, 376-382. — R. Jolivet, Essai sur les rapports entre la pensée grecque et la pensée chrétienne. Paris, 1955². — E. Fortin, St. Aug. et la doctrine néo-platonicienne de l'âme: AugMag III, 371-380. — A. Solignac, Réminiscences plotiniennes et porphiriennes dans le début du "De ordine" de St. Aug.: APh 20(1957)446-465; *idem,* Doxographies et manuels dans la formation philosophique de s. A.: RAug 1(1958)113-148. — M. Testard, St. Aug. et Ciceron. Paris, 1958. — E. Fortin, Christianisme et culture philos. au Ve siècle. Paris, 1959. — J. J. O'Meara, Porphiry's Philosophy from Oracles in Aug., Paris, 1959. — P. Hadot, Citations de Porphyre chez Aug.: REAug 6(1960)205-244. — F. Masai, Les conversions de St. Aug. et les débuts du spiritualisme en Occident: *Le Moyen Age* 67(1961)1-40. — R. J. O'Connell, The Enneads and St. Aug.'s Image of Happiness: VC 17(1963)129-164; *idem,* Enneads VI, 4 and 5 in the Works of St. Aug.: REAug 9(1963)1-39; *idem,* The Plotinian Fall of the Soul in St. Aug.: *Traditio* 19(1963)1-35. — J. N. Bezançon, Le mal et l'existence temporelle chez Plotin et chez St. Aug.: RAug 3(1965)133-160. — K. Jasper, Plato and Aug., New York, 1966. — A. H. Armstrong, St. Aug. and Christian Platonism. Villanova, 1967. — C. Baguette, Le stoïcisme dans la formation de St. Aug., Diss., Louvain, 1968. — R. J. O'Connell, St. Aug. Early Theory of Man A.D. 386-391. Cambridge, 1968; *idem,* St. Aug.'s Confessions. The Odyssey of Soul. Cambridge, 1969. — G. Barra, La figura e l'opera di Terenzio Varrone nel *De civ. Dei.* Naples, 1969. — C. Baguette, Une période stoïcienne dans l'évolution de la pensée de St. Aug.: REAug 16(1970)47-77. — F. P. Hager, Metaphysik und Menschenbild bei Plotin und bei Aug.: StPhil 33(1973)85-111. — A. Trapè, Aug. et Varro, in *Atti Congr. Studi Varroniani.* Rieti 1976, 553-563; *idem,* Introduzione generale: NBA 3, 2. — J. F. Ortega Muñoz, Agustín de Hipona, filósofo de la historia: CD 189(1976)163-205. — B. Bubacz, St. Augustine's Theory of Perception *Visio corporis* and *Visio spiritualis: The Modern Schoolman* 57(1979-80)313-337. — J. J. O'Donnell, Augustine's Classical Readings: RAug 15(1980)144-175.

2. Principles

In order to reconstruct the fundamental lines of Augustine's philosophy it is useful to keep in mind the principles which inspired and qualified it. In the judgment of the present author these principles are substantially the following three: interiority, participation, immutability.

1. The first is the best known of the three. Augustine discovered it through his reading of the Platonists and developed it in the light of his creationist doctrine (*Conf.* 7, 10, 16). Augustine began his philosophical activity with an admonition to the subject: "Return into yourself." His purpose was not to stop with the subject, but rather to verify that there was in the subject something which transcended him, viz. the presence of the truth. "Truth dwells in the interior man" (*De v. rel.* 39, 72). This truth, which is interior and superior to the mind, is not perceptible to the senses but only to the intellect and presents itself with definite characteristics which are objectivity, necessity, universality and, thus, undeniableness.

The human mind is, in fact, intelligible by nature and is connected with realities which are not only intelligible but also immutable, and it perceives them with certainty as soon as it turns toward them (*Retract.* 1, 8, 2; 1, 4, 4). Mathematical axioms, the rules of dialectic and the basic principles of ethics are proof of this. "Even if the entire human race were submerged in sleep, it would still be true that three times three equals nine" (*C. acad.* 3, 11, 25). A specific instance of this undeniable perception of the truth is the certainty of living and of thinking. "I know that I live, I know that I think" (*De b. vita* 7; *Solil.* 2, 1, 1). This is a certainty which doubt cannot shake nor error dispel. In fact, "If I doubt, I am alive" (*De Trin.* 10, 10, 14; 15, 11, 21); "If I am mistaken, I exist" (*De civ. Dei* 11, 26).

This is the response to be given to the insidious question of the skeptics.

"And if you are mistaken?" they said. Augustine responded, "If I am mistaken, that means I exist. He who does not exist cannot be mistaken; therefore I exist if I am mistaken. And if it is true that I exist if I am mistaken, how can I be mistaken about existing when it is certain that I exist when I am mistaken? Since I therefore would be the one who is mistaken even if I were mistaken, when I know that I exist I am certainly not mistaken" (ibid.). With the same certainty he knew that he thought and loved. It was thus this triple certainty which constituted an effective weapon against skepticism, because it was undeniable; against materialism, because it revealed the intelligible nature of truth; against subjectivism, because the certainty of truth was something which the mind "discovers, does not create" (*De v. rel.* 39, 73), which it recognizes that it exists, does not cause to exist (*Ep.* 162, 2; *De lib. arb.* 2, 12, 34).

To this principle of interiority, which has a metaphysical and not, as some would think, a psychological significance, are linked three of the fundamental theses of Augustinian philosophy: the demonstration of the existence of God (*De lib. arb.* 2, 15, 39), the proof of the spiritual nature of the soul (*De Trin.* 10, 8, 11-10, 16) and the proof of the soul's immortality (*Solil.* 2, 13, 24). There is likewise connected to it the "psychological" explanation of the Trinity, which is one of the most original doctrines of the Bishop of Hippo.

2. The second principle which enters into the essential nucleus of Augustine's philosophy is that of participation, which is also a well-known doctrine. Following the *De mor. eccl. cath.* 2, 4, 6 the principle can be stated as follows: every good is either good by its nature and essence or is good by participation; in the first case it is the Highest Good, in the second it is a limited good. The same principle, with explicit reference to creation, can also be stated in another way: "Every good either is God or proceeds from God" (*De v. rel.* 18, 35). But since in the unity of the human spirit life takes on a triple form, i.e., being, knowing and loving, so does the principle of participation take on the same form and thus becomes the participation in being, in truth and in love. From this triple form of participation there arises the notion, which is so frequent in Augustine, of God as the cause of being, the light of understanding and the source of love (*De civ. Dei* 8, 4; 8, 10, 2). There also arises the three-fold division of philosophy into natural, rational and moral (*De civ. Dei* 2, 7; 8, 4) and, finally, the essential solution of each of these three parts in creation, illumination and beatitude which are, then, the three modes of expressing the one doctrine of participation.

3. The third principle, on which scholars have placed little or no emphasis but which nevertheless illuminates and clarifies the other two, is the principle of immutability. Augustine states it thus: "Only immutable being is genuine, true and authentic being" (*Serm.* 7, 7; *Conf.* 7, 11, 17), because it alone is absolutely simple (*De civ. Dei* 11, 10,

1), it alone is Being in essence, the *ipsum esse* (*De Trin.* 5, 2, 3): "He is everything which He possesses" (*De div. Dei* 11, 10, 1). In fact He does not exist in some manner, in a certain measure, but He is Being (*non aliquo modo est, sed est est: Conf.* 13, 31, 46). "What is your name, O Lord our God? My name is 'He is.' But what does it mean that my name is 'He is'? It means that I live forever, that I cannot change" (*Serm.* 6, 3). It follows from this that "anything whatever, however excellent it may be, if it is changeable, does not truly exist, because where there is also non-being, there is no true being" (*In Io.* 38, 10). Non-being is limitation, complexity, mutability.

This principle therefore serves to distinguish essential being from participative being, i.e., the Creator from creatures: "Heaven and earth exist and proclaim that they have been created, *mutantur enim atque variantur*" (*Conf.* 11, 4, 6). It serves to ascend to God through the degrees of beings (*Serm.* 241, 2; *In Io.* 20, 12); it serves to establish the very degrees of beings which are the degrees of their mutability in time and space or only in time (*Ep.* 18, 2; *De Gen. ad litt.* 8, 20, 39-21, 41).

Studies: R. Amerio, Forme e significato del principio di autocoscienza in S. Ag. RFN Suppl 23(1931)75-114. — Ch. Boyer, L'idée de vérité dans la phil. di St. Aug., Paris, 1941. — F. Cayré, Initiation à la phil. de St. Aug., Paris, 1947. — E. Gilson, Introduction à l'étude de St. Aug., Paris, 1969[4] (English transl.: The Christian Philosophy of St. Aug., New York, 1960). — G. Capasso, Il pensiero filosofico de s. Ag., Naples, 1952. — L. Cilleruelo, Introducción al estudio della memoria in San. Ag.: CD 164(1952)5-24; *idem,* La memoria Dei según san Ag.: AugMag I, 499-510; *idem,* La memoria sui: *Giorn Metaf* 9(1954)428-429. — A. Maxsein, "Philosophia cordis" bei Aug.: AugMag I, 357-371. — R. Allers, Illumination et vérité éternelle. Une étude sur l'a priori augustinien: AugMag I, 421-462. — F. Sciacca, Il principio della metafisica di S. Ag. e i tentativi metafisici del pensiero moderno, in S. Ag. e le grandi correnti . . . Tolentino, 1954; *idem,* Trinité et unité de l'esprit: AugMag I, 521-533. — A. Trapè, La nozione del mutabile e dell'immutabile secondo S. Ag., Tolentino, 1959. — T. Manfredini, Unità del vero e pluralità delle menti in S. Ag., Bologna, 1960. — Ch. Boyer, S. Ag. filosofo. Bologna, 1965. — E. Zum Brunn, Être ou ne pas être d'après st. Aug.: REAug 14(1968)91-98. — S. Biolo, La coscienza nel De Trin. di S. Ag., Rome, 1969. — V. Pratola, Problemi agostiniani. L'Aquila, 1969. — A. Schöpf, Aug. Einführung in sein Philosophieren. Munich, 1970. — N. Blazques, El concepto de substancia según san Ag.: *Augustinus* 15(1970)369-383.

3. Themes

Inspired by these fundamental principles, Augustine's philosophy developed around two essential themes: God and man. "I desire to know God and the soul. Nothing else? Absolutely nothing" (*Solil.* 1, 2, 7). The famous prayer: "O God, who are always the same, may I know myself and know You" (Solil. 2, 1, 1), has its origin in this attitude, which does not exclude the knowledge of the sensible universe, but which places it within a hierarchy and orders it toward man who is its crown and end (*Conf.* 10, 8, 15; 13, 33, 48).

The two themes, though distinct, are inseparably bound in the doctrine of man as the image of God: the image is inseparable from the exemplar and vice versa. Augustine thus studies man in order to know God as in the final books of the *De Trinitate,* he studies God in order to know man and his history as in the *De civitate Dei,* and he studies God and man together as in many pages of the *Confessiones* which are introduced, it could be said, by these two questions: "What are you for me, (O Lord)? . . . What am I for You?" (*Conf.* 1, 5, 5).

Hence there arises that simultaneous insistence, which is a typical Augustinian characteristic, on the divine immanence and transcendence: God is the *"internum aeternum"* (*Conf.* 9, 4, 10), "very remote and very present" (ibid., 1, 4, 4), "extremely exalted and extremely close" (ibid., 6, 3, 3), "more intimate than my greatest intimacy and higher than my greatest height" (ibid., 3, 6, 11), "the most internal of everything, because all things exist in Him, and the most external, because He is above all things" (*De Gen. ad litt.* 8, 26, 48). Consequently He is both present and absent: we known Him because He is present, we seek him because he is absent.

a) God

The route of the mind to God is often described in Augustine's works (*De lib. arb.* 2, 3, 7-15, 39, the first and most extensive exposition; *De v. rel.* 29, 52, 39-73; *In ps.* 41, 7-8; *Serm.* 141, 1-3; *In Io.* 20, 12-13; *De civ. Dei* 8, 6) and always has a movement which proceeds "from external to internal, from inferior to superior realities" (*In ps.* 14, 5, 5) or, in a more general manner, from the mutable to the immutable (*Conf.* 7, 10, 16). There are three essential moments in this process: examine the world (*Serm.* 141, 2), return into oneself, transcend oneself (*De v. rel.* 39, 72).

The world, when it is examined with our attention fixed on it, responds with its very nature (*Conf.* 10, 6, 9), a nature which proclaims through the mutability to which it is subject that it has been created. When this message has been accepted, the mind could conclude that God, the necessary Being who has created the world, therefore exists (ibid., 11, 4, 6). The Augustinian route however continues, since it is never merely a metaphysical proof but also an interior ascent which involves the whole man who must know himself in order to find God. He knows himself when he perceives himself as a being who exists, thinks and loves. He can thus ascend to God by three paths: being, truth and love. The fact that the second of these ways is more frequent and, therefore, typical arises from the fact that Augustine loves to depart from the more indubitable truths such as self-knowledge and the autonomy of the will in order to preclude any escape into skepticism. The most famous text indicating this way is that of *De v. rel* 39, 72: "Do not go outside, but return into yourself, for the truth dwells in the interior man; and if you discover that your nature is mutable, transcend yourself. But remember that when you transcend yourself you are transcending a soul which is rational. Tend, therefore, towards that place where the light of reason is enkindled."

With regard to a knowledge of divine nature, Augustine emphasized its incomprehensibility and ineffability. "The preeminent excellence of divinity transcends the capacity of human speech. When it concerns God the thought is truer than the word and the reality is truer than the thought" (*De Trin.* 7, 4, 7). It is thus no small beginning of wisdom to know what God is not (*Ep.* 120,13). "Let us then think of God, if we are able and inasmuch as we are able, as good without quality, great without quantity, creator without necessity, in the first place without arrangement, containing all things without outward appearance, entirely omnipresent without extension, eternal without time, author of things mutable while remaining absolutely immutable and extraneous to any passibility. Whoever conceives of God in this manner, even if he is not yet able to discover perfectly that which He is, at least avoids by pious diligence, as much as possible, attributing to Him that which He is not" (*De Trin.* 5, 1, 2). This is the *docta ignorantia* (*Ep.* 130, 28).

This notwithstanding he indicated the paths for arriving at a positive knowledge of God — they are the way of affirmation, of negation and of eminence which he frequently traveled himself (*Conf.* 11, 4, 6) — and wrote sublime pages on the divine perfections (*Conf.* 1, 4, 4; 10, 6, 8; *De div. qq. ad S.* 2 q. 2, 3 *scientia divina*).

The notion of God which he habitually expounded was of a triple nature, as was the way of ascending to Him. God is supreme Being, first Truth, eternal Love. It is impossible to say on which aspect he placed the greatest emphasis. Often an effort to bind them together is apparent, as when he invokes God as "eternal truth, true love and lovable eternity" (*Conf.* 7, 10, 16).

Studies: J. Hessen, Der augustinische Gottesbeweis. Münster, 1920. — W. P. Tolley, The Idea of God in the Philosophy of St. Aug., London, 1930. — W. Gäbel, Aug. Beweis für das Dasein Gottes auf Grund der Veränderlichkeit der Welt. Breslau, 1924. — I. Sestili, Aug. philosophia pro existentia Dei: MSCA II, 765-793; *idem,* Argumentum august. de existentia Dei, in *Acta hebdomadae augustiniano-thomisticae.* Turin 1931, 241-270. — Ch. Boyer, La preuve de Dieu augustin.: Essai sur la doctrine de St. Aug., Paris, 1932, 46-96. — A. Masnovo, L'ascesa a Dio in S. Ag., in *S. Ag. e S. Tom.,* Milan, 1942, 108-128. — E. Gilson, Philosophie et Incarnation selon St. Aug., Montreal, 1947. — M. F. Sciacca, L'esistenza di Dio, in *Filosofia e metafisica.* Milan, 1962², II 77-235. — F. Cayré, Dieu présent dans la vie de l'esprit. Paris, 1951; *idem,* Réponse à un critique sur "Dieu présent dans la vie de l'esprit" ou preuve august. de l'existence de Dieu: AnThA 14(1954)119-122. — Ch. Boyer, L'esistenza di Dio secondo S. Agostino: RFN 46(1954)321-331. — S. Connolly, St. Aug.'s "Ascent" to God: IER 81(1954)120-133,

260-269. — G. Giannini, L'implicazione della prova di Dio agostin. nelle "Vie" tomistiche: *Doctor Communis* 8(1955)52-58. — E. Gilson, L'infinité divine chez St. Aug.: AugMag I, 569-574. — J. Grabowski, The All-present God: A Study in St. Aug., London, 1954. — B. M. Xiberta, El itinerario augustiniano para alcanzar el conocimiento de Dios: *Convivium* 1(1956)137-179. — J. van Gerven, Liberté humaine et prescience divine d'après st. Aug.: RevPhilosLouv 55(1957)317-330. — G. Madec, Note sur la vision august. du monde: REAug 9(1963)139-146. — A. D. R. Polman, De leer van God bij Aug., Kampen, 1965. — E. Z. Brunn, L'immutabilité de Dieu selon st. Aug.: *Nova et Vetera* 41(1966)219-225. — G. Giannini, Rilievi ad una critica della prova di Dio agost.: *Doctor Communis* 22(1969)45-56. — J. Ratzinger, Der Weg der religiösen Erkenntnis nach dem hl. Aug., in *Kyriakon,* II. Münster 1970, 553-564.

b) Man

Man forms the other epicenter of Augustine's thought. He studies the mystery, nature, spirituality and liberty of man with true passion. For Augustine, man is a *"grande profundum"* (*Conf.* 4, 12, 22) and often a *"magna quaestio"* (ibid., 4, 4, 9): an abyss because of the multiplicity of contrasting sentiments and the inexhaustible riches of memory, a great problem because of the enigma of suffering and death. "The faculty of memory is magnificent. My God, its infinite and profound complexity almost inspires a sense of dread. It is my spirit; it is what I am myself. What then am I, O my God? What is my nature? A varied and multiform life of powerful immensity" (*Conf.* 10, 17, 26). "In reality I do not succeed in comprehending all that I am" (ibid., 10, 8, 5).

A particular instance of this mystery is the nature of man as a composite being, which would remain incomprehensible to us were not we ourselves composed of two such diverse elements as body and spirit (*Ep.* 137, 3, 11). Contrary to what is often written, Augustine overcame by far, as has been mentioned above, the spiritualism of an Hellenic type regarding the union of these two elements, even though he continued here and there to use this type of language, especially in his preaching. It is not the body as such, but the corruptible body which is the prison of the soul (*De civ. Dei* 13, 16; *In ps.* 141, 18-19), which has been born to inform the body, which by its nature is ordered to the body and which is not able to achieve beatitude without the body (*De Gen. ad litt.* 7, 28, 38; 12, 35, 68). This does not prevent him from insisting on the spiritual nature and personal immorality of the soul, the first of which he demonstrates with the intuition which the mind has of itself — "When the mind knows itself, it knows its substance" (*De Trin.* 10, 10, 13-16) — and the second of which he proves by the presence of immortal truth in the soul (*Solil.* 2, 13, 24): "And if the soul dies? Then truth dies too" (*Ep.* 3, 4).

The origin of the soul proved to be a long and tormented question. Against the Manichaeans he asserted the principle that the soul is neither a particle of the divine substance nor does it proceed from the transformation of another nature but has been created from nothing (*De Gen. ad litt.* 7, 28, 43; *Ep.* 166, 2, 3), and he forcibly rejected material traducianism "than which nothing more erroneous can be maintained" (*Ep.* 190, 4, 14). As for his own view, he continued to fluctuate between a form of spiritual traducianism and creationism (*Retract.* 1, 1, 3). Although it seemed to him that neither reason nor Scripture provided decisive arguments (*De anima et eius orig.* 1), he nevertheless did not disguise his sympathy for the second opinion (*Ep.* 166, 8, 25; 190, 4, 15) although he sought to understand the propagation of original sin according to both theories (*C. Iul.* 5, 4, 17).

However, the fundamental thesis which illumines the mystery of man and reveals his greatness is his creation in the image of God. This thesis can indeed be called the synthesis of Augustine's thought. Augustine studied the notion of image (*De Gen. ad litt. op. imp.* 57), proved that it is a property of the interior man, i.e., of the mind and not of the body (*De Trin.* 12, 7, 12; *In Io.* 8, 6), which is immortally impressed in the immortal nature of the soul (*De Trin.* 14, 4, 6). It consists of the capacity, which is deformed by sin and restored by grace, to be elevated to the immediate possession of God (ibid., 14, 14, 18; 14, 16, 22; 15, 8, 14). Consequently, man "is the image of God to the extent that he is capable of receiving God and of participating in Him" (ibid., 14, 8, 11). "Because it is able to participate in the highest nature, it is in fact a great nature" (ibid., 14, 4, 6). Inasmuch as man is *capax Dei* he is also *indigens Deo* to the extent that "he is established in such a great dignity that, even though mutable, he is able to achieve beatitude only by adhering to the immutable good, i.e., to God. Nor is he able to satisfy his indigence except in beatitude, but only God is sufficient to satisfy it" (*De civ. Dei* 12, 1, 3). This is the profound sense behind the celebrated saying: "You have made us for yourself and our heart is restless until it rests in You" (*Conf.* 1, 1, 1).

But if image signifies similarity, the created image which is man also signifies dissimilarity (*De Trin.* 15, 11, 21; *Conf.* 11, 9, 11). The similarity explains the supreme suitability of grace, while the dissimilarity establishes its gratuitousness and transcendence. Augustine sees the delicate question of the encounter of man with God under these two aspects which cannot be separated (*Serm.* 7, 7; *In ps.* 101, 2, 10). He insists on this when, as a theologian, he explains that man is the image not only of the one God but of the triune God inasmuch as in man "his spirit, love and knowledge are three things, and these three are one, and, when perfect, are equal" (*De Trin.* 9, 4, 4).

Other chapters of Augustinian anthropology are those concerning liberty, the passions and language. He energetically defended freedom against the Manichaeans nor did he deny it, as we will see (cf. p.

435), against the Pelagians. He experienced it dramatically during the interior struggle which preceded his conversion and made it the object of his study in the *De libero arbitrio* and in other anti-Manichaean works. At that time he observed that there were not two souls in him, as the Manichaeans claimed, but one single soul and one single will. "It will be I who wills and I who does not will; I, I will be the one. I did not used to fully will nor did I used to fully not will. Hence there arose my struggle with myself . . ." (*Conf.* 8, 10, 22). He would later admonish people to not seek excuses for their own sins, but to say simply: "God has created me with free will; if I have sinned, I have sinned . . . I, I; not fate, not chance, not the devil" (*In ps.* 31, 2, 6). In the *De libero arbitrio* (3, 3, 8) he wrote: "Our will would not be a will were it not in our power. Precisely because it is within our power it is free for us." For the definitions of liberty and of sin, which were clarified and confirmed in the *Retractationes* (1, 15), cf. *De duab. an. c. man.* 10, 14-11, 15.

As a subtle psychologist, Augustine developed the theme of the passions, reduced them to the common root of love (*De civ. Dei* 14, 6) and distinguished between feeling and passion (*C. Iul. op. imp.* 4, 29; 4, 69). With regard to passion he described three possibilities: absence of passion, ordered passion which is subject to reason, and disordered passion or concupiscence. Only the latter of these is an evil because it stirs up a "civil war" in man and attempts to draw him to moral evil.

Much attention is given today to the doctrine of sign (*De doctr. chr.* 1, 2, 2; 2, 1, 1) and of language *(De magistro)* in a modern rereading of Augustine.

Studies: 1. *The union between body and soul:* L. Cilleruelo, La formación del cuerpo según San Ag.: CD 162(1950)445-473. — M. F. Sciacca, La persona umana secondo S. Ag., in *Umanesimo e mondo cristiano.* Rome 1951, 151-160. — Ch. Couturier, La structure métaphysique de l'homme d'après st. Aug.: AugMag I, 543-550. — R. Schwarz, Die leibseelische Existenz bei Aur. Aug.: PhJ 63(1954)323-360. — E. L. Fortin, Christianisme et culture philosophique au V éme s., Paris, 1959. — R. Champoux, L'union du corps et de l'âme selon st. Aug.: *Dialogue* 1(1962)309-315. — J. Pepin, Une nouvelle source de St. Aug.: Le "zetemata" de Porphyre sur l'union de l'âme et du corps: REAN 66(1964)53-107. — A. Rigobello, Linee per una antropologia prescolastica. Padua, 1972. — G. Iammarrone, Attualità e inattualità di S. Ag., Florence, 1975.

2. *Anthropology:* F. Thonnard, La vie affective de l'âme selon St. Aug.: AnThA 14(1953)33-55. — Segundo de Jesús, Las pasiones en la concepción agustiniana de la vida espiritual: *Rev Espirid* 14(1955)251-280. — B. Bravo, Angustia y gozo en el hombre. Madrid, 1957. — R. Flórez, Las dos dimensiones del hombre agustiniano. Madrid, 1958. — J. Laporte, Le problème de l'origine de l'âme chez st. Aug., Diss., Paris, 1961. — A. Di Giovanni, L'inquietudine dell'anima. Rome, 1964; *idem,* La dialettica dell'amore. Rome, 1965. — R. J. O'Connell, St. Aug.'s Early Theory of Man. Cambridge, 1968. — A. Rigobello, Intentio-extensio distentio, in Misc. C. Giacon. Padua 1972, 135-142 (= Linee per un'antropologia prescolastica. Padua 1972, 15-27). — A. Di Giovanni, Per una morale antropologica. Rome, 1973. — R. J. O'Connell,

Aug.'s Rejection of the Fall of the Soul: AugStudies 4(1973)1-32. — J. van Bavel, The Anthropology of Augustine: LouvStudios 5(1974)34-47. — A. Trapè, Introd. generale: NBA 3, 2; *idem*, S. Agostino filosofo e teologo dell'uomo: *Divinitas* 24(1980)53-67. — V. Grossi, l'antropologia cristiana negli scritti di Agostino: SSR 4(1980)89-113.

3. *Freedom:* A. Martínez, Introducción a la filosofía del espiritu de S. Ag.: RevFil 1(1950)315-326. — H. Barth, Die Bedeutung der Freiheit bei Epiktet und Aug., in Festschr. E. Brunner. Zurich 1950, 49-64. — H. Daudin, La liberté et la volonté. Paris, 1950. — K. H. Schelkle, Erwählung und Freiheit im Römerbrief nach der Auslegung der Väter: ThQ 131(1951)17-31, 189-207. — P. Lenicque, La liberté des Enfants de Dieu selon st. Aug.: AnThA 14 (1953)110-144. — P. Palmeri, La persona umana nel pensiero di S. Ag.: StP 1. Berlin 1954, 270-399. — A. Muñoz Alonso, La libertad en S. Ag.: Rev Calasancia 1(1955)127-136. — G. De Plinval, Aspects du déterminisme et de la liberté dans la doctrine de St. Aug.: REAug 1(1955)345-378. — E. Frutos Cortés, Destino y libertad del hombre en el providencialismo agustiniano: *Augustinus* 1(1956)225-233. — J. van Gerven, Liberté humaine et prescience divine d'après st. Aug.: RevPhilLouv 55(1957)317-330. — A. Muñoz Alonso, La libertad en San Ag., in *Sem. Esp. Fil.* Madrid 1957, 221-232. — M. T. Clark, Aug. Philosopher of Freedom. New York-Paris, 1958. — A. Coccia, Unità del genere umano e dignità dell'uomo nel pensiero di S. Ag.: *Città di Vita* 16(1961)729-738. — F. Haider, Aug. und das psychologische Problem des freien Willens, in *Gedenkschrift Betschart* I. Munich 1963, 231-255. — V. Boublik, La liberté d'après St. Aug.: *Pensée Cath* 92(1964)22-36. — S. Alvarez Turienzo, La libertad como implicación ética: *Rev. Humanidades* 6(1966)89-130. — M. Huftier, Libre arbitre, liberté et péché chez st. Aug.: RTAM 33(1966)187-281. — V. Melchiorre, Sartre, Spinoza, S. Ag. Libertà e responsabilità. Padua 1967, 14-28. — F. Sontag, Aug.'s Metaphysics and Free Will: HThR 60(1967)297-306. — F. J. Thonnard, La notion de liberté en philosophie august.: REAug 16(1970)243-270. — D. J. McQueen, Aug. on Free Will and Predestination: *Museum Africum* 3(1974)17-27. — D. De Celles, Divine Prescience and Human Freedom in Augustine: AugStudies 8(1977)151-160.

4. *Language:* J. Pépin, Note nouvelle sur le problème de la communication des consciences chez Plotin et st. Aug.: *Revue de métaphysique et morale* 56(1951)316-326. — R. A. Markus, Aug. on Signs: *Phronesis* 2(1957)60-83. — J. Engels, La doctrine du signe chez st. Aug.: SP 6 (TU 81). Berlin 1962, 366-373. — R. A. Markus, Imago et similitudo in Aug.: REAug 10(1964)125-143. — F. Soria, La teoría del signo en S. Ag.: *Ciencia Tomista* 92(1965)357-396. — U. Duchrow, Sprachverständnis und biblisches Hören bei Aug., Tübingen, 1965. — C. P. Mayer, Die Zeichen in der Geistigen Entwicklung und in der Theologie des jungen Aug., 2 vols. Würzburg, 1969, 1974. — U. Simone, Semiologia agostiniana: *La Cultura* 7(1969)89-95. — G. H. Allard, Art libéraux et langage chez st. Aug., in *Art liber. et phil. Moyen Âge*. Paris 1969, 481-492. — G. B. Cataldo, Semantica e intersoggestività della parola in S. Ag.: *Sapienza* 26(1973)170-184. — G. Ripanti, Il problema della comprensione nell'ermeneutica agostiniana: REAug 20(1974)88-99. — L. Alici, Il linguaggio come segno e come testimonianza. Una rilettura de Agostino. Rome, 1976.

4. Solutions

To the great problems of being, of knowing and of loving, which are the three great problems of philosophy, Augustine offers three fundamental solutions: creation, illumination and wisdom or beatitude.

a) Creation.

Augustine's doctrine is at the same time a doctrine of faith and of reason (*De Gen. ad litt.* 1, 14, 28) which clarifies the problem of the origin of things. He developed and defended his doctrine against the Manichaeans, who were pantheists, and against the Neoplatonists who, although they seemed to him to admit the reality of creation, nevertheless affirmed its eternity and necessity. God created all things "not from His own substance, nor from something which He had not made, but from nothing" (*C. Fel. man.* 2, 19). He created all things according to all the components of their nature in such a way that nothing in them was independent of His action. Indeed, one thing can proceed from another by generation, by fabrication, or by creation. In the first instance it is equal to that which generated it and in the second it presupposes the material from which it has been made. Only in the third instance does the action reach the roots of being and make to come into being that which absolutely did not exist. "That which one makes either he makes from his own substance, or from something outside of himself or from nothing. Man, who is not omnipotent, generates a child from his own substance and, as a craftsman, makes a chest out of wood, but does not make the wood; produces a vase but not the silver. No man is able to make something out of nothing; that is, cause that which absolutely does not exist to be. God, on the other hand, because He is omnipotent, has generated the Son from His own substance, has created the world out of nothing and from the earth has formed man. There is a great difference between that which God has generated from His own substance and that which He has made not from His own substance but from nothing; that is, has made that it might receive being and that there might be placed among those things that exist, that which absolutely did not exist" (*C. Fel. man.* 2, 18). God has therefore created together, has "co-created" matter and form, between which there is no difference in relation to time but only in relation to origin and causality (*De Gen. ad litt.* 5, 513-16; *Conf.* 12, 29, 40).

Augustine further maintains, according to the teaching of Christian faith, that creation took place *in tempore,* indeed *cum tempore* (*De civ. Dei* 11, 6), because nothing can be co-eternal with God (ibid., 12, 15-16; *Conf.* 12, 11, 11). The difficulties of his adversaries, who bring the discussion to bear on the difficult question of the relations between time and eternity, are considerable but not insoluble. There does not exist, he replies, a time before creation because God does not precede time with time but with eternity (*Conf.* 11, 10, 12-13, 16). Nor does creation in time imply any mutability in God, because God "knows how to work while at repose and to repose while working and is able to apply to a new work a plan which is not old but eternal": the "before" and "after" are not to be found in Him, but in the things which first did not exist and then began to be (*De civ. Dei* 12, 17, 2). These are difficult explanations but they are not absurd. "How can I help it if others do not understand?" (*Conf.* 1, 6, 10), asked Augustine, aware of his speculative force.

God creates from nothing and creates according to the eternal reasons which are nothing else than the exemplary ideas existing in the divine mind by participation in which all things are which exist. Each thing is created according to a particular idea (*De div. qq.* 83, *q.* 46, 2). Divine exemplarism is one of the fundamental Augustinian theses and has both a metaphysical and a gnoseological value (cf. p. 416).

Another chapter of the creationist doctrine is that of the *rationes seminales* or causal reasons. God created all things simultaneously but not all in the same way: some things He created in themselves such as matter and the human soul, others he created virtually in invisible germs, almost as "the seeds of seeds." It is on these that the progressive development of the universe depends (*De Gen. ad litt.* 5, 23, 44-45; 6, 6, 10-18, 29; *De Trin.* 3, 8, 13-9, 16). This doctrine aroused and continues to arouse much interest in an age of evolutionism.

From the creationist doctrine there derives the doctrine of the goodness of created things, and from this latter teaching derives the doctrine of evil. God created not because of need nor necessity but "because He wanted to," and He wanted to because He is good and created things are good. "There is no more correct reason than this, that a good God created good things" (*De civ. Dei* 11, 21). Therefore evil natures do not exist (ibid., 12, 8), and "it is a great error, a great madness, to transfer to things which men use in an evil way the evil of the one who misuses them" (*Serm.* 50, 7). Manichaean pessimism is thus absurd.

Evil is not a substance (*Conf.* 7, 16, 22) — Augustine reached this conclusion after painful searching (ibid., 7, 5, 7-7, 11) — but is the defect, the corruption, the privation "either of moderation, or of beauty or of the natural order" (*De nat. boni* 4). Evil thus cannot exist except in the good; not in the supreme Good which is incorruptible, but in the mutable good which is created from nothing. "We are asked: What then is the origin of evil? We respond: The good, but not the supreme and immutable good. Evils have their origin from inferior and mutable goods. . . . But a nature would not be mutable if it came from God without having been created from nothing. Therefore, God, the author of nature, is the author of good. The things which suffer by their condition a privation of good do not show by whom they have been made but from where they have been made.

Now where they have been made from is not something, but is absolutely nothing" (*C. Iul.* 1, 8, 36-37).

Evil is of two sorts: that which man involuntarily suffers and that which he voluntarily commits. The former is physical evil such as suffering and death or the evil of ignorance and of concupiscence; the latter is moral evil such as sin, which is iniquity and injustice. They both depend on the defectibility of the creature and therefore have not an efficient but a deficient cause. "No one seeks the efficient cause of the bad will. This cause is not efficient but deficient because the bad will is not an effect but a defect . . . To want to find the cause of this defect . . . is like wanting to see darkness or to hear silence" (*De civ. Dei* 12, 7).

Augustine demonstrates against the Manichaeans that the existence of evil is not an argument against the goodness of God, because God is not its cause, but merely permits it. He permits it because "He is so omnipotent and good as to be able to draw good even out of evil" (*Ench.* 3, 11). On the other hand, speaking no longer on a metaphysical but on an existential and historical plane, he maintains against the Pelagians that the evils in the world have a clearly penal character and therefore presuppose some blow at the beginning, as the Catholic faith teaches. In this difficult question the Augustinian doctrine passes between opposed adversaries and avoids the difficulties of opposite errors. It is this doctrine which would be substantially accepted by the Scholastics.

To the doctrine of creation is bound another difficult doctrine, that of time, which is treated extensively in the eleventh book of the *Confessions*. In reality, time is "a most complicated enigma" (*Conf.* 11, 22, 28). The past, in fact, no longer exists, the future does not yet exist, and the present "owes its existence to not being able to continue in existence." One thing is certain: if it were not for motion, there would not be time. (ibid., 11, 14, 17). It is likewise certain that there would not be time if there were not memory of the past, intuition of the present, and expectation of the future (ibid., 11, 20, 26). Thus time does not properly exist in things but in the mind. It is nothing other than a "distension," the "distension" of the mind which remembers, intuits and awaits (ibid., 11, 26, 33-28, 37). It is in the mind, therefore, that time is measured, that there exists "the present of the past, the present of the present, the present of the future" (ibid., 11, 20, 26): "a long future is the long expectation of the future; likewise . . . a long past is a long memory of the past" while the present "is my attention through which the future turns itself into the past" (ibid., 11, 28, 38).

These philosophical considerations of time served to introduce others to the *"intentio-distentio-extensio"* proper to the human mind turned toward eternity (ibid., 11, 29, 39) or to life which, bound up by time, is nothing else than a sound between two great silences (*In ps.* 190, 20), the silence of the future which does not yet exist and the silence of the past which is no more (*De lib. arb.* 3, 7, 20).

Studies: 1. *Creation:* J. de Blic, Les arguments de st. Aug. contre l'éternité du monde: MSR 2(1945)33-44; *idem,* Le processus de la création d'après st. Aug., in Mel Cavallera. Toulouse 1948, 179-189. — W. A. Christian, Aug. on the Creation of the World: HThR 46(1953)1-25. — Ch. Boyer, Éternité et création dans les derniers livres des Confessions: *Giorn Metaf* 9(1954)441-448. — V. J. Bourke, St. Aug. and the Cosmic Soul: *Giorn Metaf* 9(1954)431-440. — F. von Rintelen, Bonitas creationis: *Giorn Metaf* 9(1954)523-541. — G. Capone Braga, Il mondo delle idee. Milan, 1954[2]. — Ch. Couturier, Structure métaphysique de l'être créé d'après st. Aug., in *Histoire de la philosophie et métaphysique* (Recherches philosophiques 1). Bruges 1955, 57-84. — E. Gilson, Notes sur l'être et le temps chez st. Aug.: RAug 2(1962)205-223. — R. H. Cusineau, Creation and Freedom: RAug 2(1962)253-271. — R. E. de Roux, El Amor de Dios al hombre en san Ag.: *Eccles Xaveriana* 12(1962)3-41. — J. Chaix-Ruy, La création du monde d'après st. Aug.: REAug 11(1965)85-88. — E. zum Brunn, Le dilemme de l'être et du néant chez st. Aug., Paris, 1969. — A. di Giovanni, Creazione ed essere nelle Confessioni di s. Ag.: REAug 20(1974)285-312.

2. *Creation and Time:* J. Chaix-Ruy, La perception du temps chez St. Aug., in *Cah de la nouv Journ* 17. Paris 1930, 73-93. — J. F. Callahan, Four Views of Time in Anc. Phil. Cambridge, 1948. — H. –I. Marrou, L'ambivalence du temps de l'histoire chez st. Aug., Paris, 1950. — J. Gillet, Temps et exemplarisme chez st. Aug.: AugMag II, 933-942; J. Chaix-Ruy, La cité de Dieu et la structure du temps chez st. Aug.: AugMag II, 923-932; *idem,* Le problème du temps dans les Conf. et dans la Cité de Dieu: *Giorn Metaf* 9(1954)464-477. — S. Caramella, Validità scientifica della concezione agostin. del tempo, in S. Ag. e le grandi correnti. Tolentino 1956, 335-340. — J. Chaix-Ruy, St. Aug. Temps et histoire. Paris, 1956; *idem,* Existence et temporalité selon st. Aug.: *Augustinus* 3(1958)337-349. — E. Lampey, Das Zeitproblem nach den Bekenntnissen Aug.: *Wissenschaft und Weisheit* 22(1959)1-16, 109-118, 190-203. — M. E. Ravicz, Time and Eternity: *Thomist* 22(1959)542-554. — O. Lechner, Idee und Zeit in der Metaphysik Aug., Munich, 1964. — J. M. Quinn, The Concept of Time in St. Aug.: Aug 5(1965)5-57. — W. B. Green, St. Aug. on Time: Scottish J Th 18(1965)148-163. — J. Moreau, Le temps et la création selon st. Aug.: *Giorn Metaf* 20(1965)276-290. — R. Suter, El concepto del tiempo según san Ag.: *Convivium* 19-20(1965)97-111. — H. J. Kaiser, Aug. Zeit und "memoria." Bonn, 1969. — A. Solignac, La conception du temps chez Augustin: BA 14, 581-591. — A. Rigobello, Intentio-distentio-extensio, modello ermeneutico dell-antrop. ag., in Scritti A. Giacon. Padua 1972, 135-146 (= Linee per un'antropologia prescolastica. Padua 1972, 15-27). — W. G. van Jess, Augustine: A Consistent and Unitary Theory of Time: NSch 46(1972)337-351. — P. Janich, Aug. Zeitparadox und seine Frage nach einem Standard der Zeitmessung: AGP 54(1972)168-186. — J. Pegueroles, El ser y el tiempo: *Pensamiento* 28(1972)165-191. — P. Mazzeo, Il problema ag. del tempo nelle Conf. e nel De civ. Dei: *Annali Univ Bari* 15(1972)279-313. — L. Alici, Genesi del problema ag. del tempo: StP 22(1975)43-67; *idem,* La funzione della "distentio" nella dottrina agostiniana del tempo: Aug 15(1975)325-345. — A. J. Bucher, Der Ursprung der Zeit aus dem Nichts: RAug 11(1976)35-51.

3. *The Problem of Evil:* G. Philips, La raison d'être du mal d'après st. Aug., Louvain, 1927. — R. Jolivet, Le problème du mal d'après st. Aug., Paris, 1936. — L. Macali, Il problema del dolore secondo S. Ag., Rome, 1943. — F. Châtillon, Regio dissimilitudinis, in Mél. F. Podechard. Lyons 1945, 85-102. — G. Soleri, Il problema metafisico del

male: *Sapienza* 5(1952)289-306, 415-442; *idem,* La soluzione ag. del problema del male, in S. Ag. e le grandi correnti. Tolentino 1956, 341-348. — L. Pelloux, Riflessi della soluzione ag. del problema del male nella fil. contemporanea, in S. Ag. e le grandi correnti . . . Tolentino 1956, 33-49. — C. Vaca, El pecado y los pecados en las Conf. de san Ag.: *Rev. Calasancia* 1(1955)67-72. — F. M. Verde, Il problema del male da Plutarco a S. Ag.: *Sapienza* 11(1958)231-268. — A. Solignac, La condition de l'homme pécheur d'après st. Aug.: NRTh 68(1956)359-387. — V. Capánaga, Materia y espíritu en el problema del mal según san Ag.: *Augustinus* 6(1961)169-178. — J. N. Bezançon, Le mal et l'existence temporelle chez Plotin et St. Aug.: RAug 3(1965)133-160. — F. De Capitani, Concetti presupposti alla definizione del male in alcuni scritti contro i Manichei di S. Ag., Diss., Univ. S. Cuore, Milan, 1971. — G. R. Evans, Augustine on Evil. New York, 1983.

4. *Rationes Seminales:* A. Solignac, Le double moment de la création et les raisons causales: BA 48, 653-668 (cf. bibl. p. 667-668). — L. Pera, La creazione simultanea e virtuale secondo S. Ag., Florence, 1928-1929. — P. Galtier, St. Aug. et l'origine de l'homme: Greg 11(1930)5-31.

5. *Miracles:* P. D. Vooght, La notion phil. du miracle chez St. Aug.: RTAM 10(1938)317-343; *idem,* La théologie du miracle selon St. Aug.: RTAM 11(1939)197-222. — F. Brazzale, La dottrina del miracolo in S. Ag., Rome, 1964.

b) Illumination.

The second fundamental solution of Augustinian philosophy which is closely bound to the first is the theory of illumination. It is another aspect — the second — of the doctrine of participation (cf. p. 408). "Our illumination is a participation in the Word, that is, in that life which is the Light of men" (*De Trin.* 4, 2, 4). In order to facilitate the understanding of this theory, which has proved to be a constant problem for interpreters, some of its essential points will be presented here.

Since it is an aspect of participation, illumination cannot be understood apart from that doctrine: if God is the source of being, He is also the light of understanding. He is, therefore, the interior teacher who instructs man in the truth (*De mag.* 12, 39-14, 46), He is "the sun" of the soul (*Solil.* 1, 8, 15) "in which and from which and through which all intelligible things shine in an intelligible way on the soul who understands" (ibid., 1, 1, 3). It is "in the Truth itself . . . in God that we see the immutable ideal of justice according to which we judge it is necessary to live" (*De Trin.* 8, 9, 13). Indeed, "If we both see the truth of your assertions and both see the truth of mine, where do we see this? Certainly not you in me, nor I in you but both precisely in the immutable truth which is above our understanding" (*Conf.* 12, 25, 35). The classical text on this matter is the following: ". . . the nature of the rational soul has been made in such a way that united to intelligible things according to the natural order arranged by the Creator, it perceives them in a special incorporeal light in the same way that the bodily eye perceives that which surrounds it in ordinary light since it has been created capable of receiving this light and has been disposed towards it" (*De Trin.* 12, 15, 24).

This doctrine has been interpreted in terms of Platonic memory, of ontological intuition, of innate ideas and of the scholastic concept of abstraction. The first three interpretations do not correspond to the texts. In fact, the doctrine of illumination: a) was proposed in order to take the place of that of Platonic reminiscence (ibid.); b) excludes the immediate knowledge of God — we know God *per speculum,* i.e., through images (ibid., 12, 8, 14) — and thus excludes the knowledge in God of both sensible (*De Gen. ad litt.* 5, 16, 34) and intelligible realities (ibid., 4, 32, 49); c) supposes that the mind does not have ideas preformed in itself, but rather acquires them: "The human mind has thus been made that it first recognizes created things as it is able, then seeks their causes, existing as immutable exemplars in the Word of God, and seeks in some way to perceive them and thus to see the invisible realities by means of created things" (ibid.).

With regard to the fourth interpretation, however, a distinction must be made. If there is intended the illuminative function of the active intellect of the scholastics conceived as a "participated similarity of uncreated light" the comparison can be maintained, and it is truly a case of doctrinal continuity. Augustine insists that the human mind cannot be a light for itself (*Serm.* 67, 8; 183, 5). It is a light which illumines because it has itself been illuminated (*In Io.* 25, 3), that is, it has been created (*C. Faustum* 20, 7; *De pec. mer. rem.* 1, 25, 36-38). God alone is light unto Himself, and thus is the true light (*In Io.* 14, 1). The divine illumination establishes the certainty of our judgments and attributes to them the characteristics of universality and necessity, and thus Augustine is insistent on this illumination.

But if it is a question of the passage from sensible to intelligible perception, that is, no longer a question of the value but of the origin of ideas, the situation changes. Augustine distinguishes three types of perception: *corporeal,* proper to the senses; *spiritual,* proper to the imagination; and *intellectual,* proper to the intellect (*De Gen. ad litt.* 12, 7, 16). He describes the first and explains both the certainty (*C. acad.* 3, 14, 26; *De v. rel.* 33, 62; *De civ. Dei* 19, 18) and the process (*De Trin.* 11, 9, 16) of sense perception. He describes the second in *Conf.* 10, 8, 12-14, 21 where he speaks of memory and indicates the passage from one to the other. However, he does not speak of the passage from imaginative to intellectual perception, but rather emphasizes the distance: "Just as the mind gathers knowledge of corporeal realities from the bodily senses, so does it gather knowledge of the incorporeal realities by means of itself" (*De Trin.* 9, 3, 3). The mind contemplates those realities which are "neither corporeal nor similar to corporeal realities" (*De Gen. ad litt.* 12, 24, 51) "either by gazing into itself or by gazing into that truth which is the guide of the spirit" (*De Trin.* 14, 7, 9). There can be added here the well-known distinction between wisdom and knowledge — "to wisdom there pertains the intellectual perception of eternal realities, but to knowledge pertains the rational perception of temporal realities" (*De Trin.* 12, 15, 25) — and the other distinction which is the foundation of the former, between intellect and reason: the first intuits intelligible and immutable truth; the second derives from this the light for judging and guiding actions (*De Trin.* 12, 3, 3).

Studies: B. Kaelin, Die Erkenntnislehre des hl. Aug. Sarnen, 1920. — F. Cayré, Contuition et vision médiate de Dieu d'après st. Aug.: ETL 6(1929)29-39, 205-229. — E. Gilson, Introduction à l'étude de st. Aug., Paris, 1969[4] (English transl.: The Christian Philosophy of St. Augustine. New York, 1960). — I. Sestili, Thomae Aquinatis cum Augustino de illuminatione concordia. Isola del Liri, 1929. — B. Romeyer, Études sur st. Aug. Trois problèmes de philosophie augustinienne. Athens, 1930. — Ch. Boyer, La philosophie aug. ignore-t-elle l'abstraction?: NRTh 57(1930)817-830 (= Essai sur la doctrine de s. A. Paris 1932, 166-183). — R. Jolivet, Dieu soleil des esprits. Paris, 1934. — J. Gonzales-Quevedo, Ideas innatas e illuminación divina. Comillas, 1951. — R. Allers, St. Aug.'s Doctrine on Illumination: FS 12(1952)27-46. — F. Cayré, Initiation à la philosophie de St. Aug. Paris, 1947. — G. Capone Braga, Il significato della teoria dell'illuminazione di S. Ag., in S. Ag. e le grandi correnti . . . Tolentino 1956, 306-311. — Ch. Boyer, S. Ag. e il neotomismo, in S. Ag. e le grandi correnti . . . Tolentino 1956, 119-140. — H. Somers, Image de Dieu et illumination divine: AugMag I, 451-462. — V. Warnach, Erleuchtung und Einsprechung bei Aug: AugMag I, 429-450. — I Quiles, Interpretación integral de la "illuminación agustiniana": AugL 3(1958)255-268. — A. Sage, La dialectique de l'illumination: RAug 2(1962)111-123. — F. J. Thonnard, La notion de lumière en philosophie augustinienne: RAug 2(1962)125-175. — F. Piemontese, La veritas agostiniana e l'agostinismo perenne. Milan, 1963. — G. Bracci, Tentativo di una nuova interpretazione dell'illuminazione agostiniana: *Riv. Rosminiana* 58(1964)35-50.

c) Beatitude.

Man has his beatitude from the same source from which he has the strength of being and the light of knowing, i.e., from God (*De civ. Dei* 11, 25), and this beatitude cannot be anything other than God Himself. This is the third major principle of Augustinian philosophy which Augustine develops at length and applies in the fields of morals, pedagogy and history.

He takes up the Platonic notion of philosophy as a search for the happy life, but departs radically from the Platonists on the nature and properties of happiness (*Serm.* 141, 6). He defines it as "the joy of the truth" (*Conf.* 10, 23, 33) and explains that he is not able to be happy "who either does not have what he loves, whatever it may be; or who has what he loves but loves what is harmful; or who does not love what he has, even though it be extremely good" (*De mor. Eccl. cath.* 1, 3, 4). However, he alone is happy who has everything he wants and who wants nothing evil (*De Trin.* 13, 5, 8), since, he says, quoting

Cicero, "nothing is more pitiable than to want that which is not suitable" (*De Trin.* 13, 5, 8; *Ep.* 130, 5, 10). He identifies happiness with wisdom — "no one is wise except one who is happy" (*De b. vita* 2, 14) and "no one is happy except one who is wise" (*C. acad.* 1, 9, 24) — and maintains against the Neoplatonists that there is no true happiness which is not eternal (*De Trin.* 13, 7, 10-8, 11). Nevertheless, he energetically excludes the theory of eternal rebirths "than which nothing more dreadful can be thought" (*Ep.* 166, 9, 27). He shows that the pagan concept is illusory which places happiness in the goods of the body or the mind or both, or in the social welfare of the family, in friendship, in the state, or, in any case, in this world (*De civ. Dei* 19, 4-9). Here we possess happiness only in hope, without which the present life would be one great misery (ibid., 19, 20). Happiness allows for the memory but not the experience of evil (*De civ. Dei* 22, 30, 4). The body, too, must participate in this happiness, since it is something which involves the whole man (*De Gen. ad litt.* 7, 27, 38).

Augustine reduces the virtues to the *ordo amoris* (*De civ. Dei* 15, 22), a love directed to a life which conforms to the very order of things, which are to be loved to a greater or lesser degree according to their perfection and merit (*De doct. Chr.* 1, 27, 28); the order of things conformed to the eternal law which "commands that the natural order be preserved and forbids that it be disturbed" (*C. Faustum* 22, 27). He emphasizes that the eternal law clarifies and expresses the supreme good and perfection of the creatures, since "God does not command anything which benefits Himself, but only that which benefits him whom He commands" (*Ep.* 138, 6); a supreme good and perfection which are summed up in that peace which is precisely "the tranquility of order" (*De civ. Dei* 19, 13).

He formulates the doctrine of *frui* and *uti* and distinguishes, on the one hand, those things which render a person happy and which must be loved in themselves as the end to which one tends and in which one takes delight, and, on the other, those things which are only the means to this end which must be used as such. It follows that moral disorder consists completely in inverting the order of things, i.e., in *"fruendo uti velle atque utendis frui"* (*De div. qq.* 83, *q.* 30), through which "human life is rendered evil and guilty only of the wrong use and wrong enjoyment of things" (*De Trin.* 10, 10, 13). It is on this basis that the famous Augustinian aphorism, "Love, and do what you will" (*Exp. ep. ad Gal.* 57; *In ep. Io.* 7, 8) must be understood, which expresses not autonomy, but the primacy and dynamism of love.

Once he has established these principles, Augustine indicates the course toward happiness on the individual *(Confessiones)* as well as on the social plane *(De civitate Dei)*. This course is prompted by divine providence and has as its immanent principle that love which is the "weight" which moves the mind wherever it goes (*Conf.* 13, 9, 10). Love and providence are the two hinges of the personal history of each man and of the universal history of humanity.

Morality is centered on the love of God which is identified with authentic love of self: "Only one who loves God knows how to love himself" (*De mor. Eccl. cath.* 1, 26, 48), and likewise, "One who loves himself but not God does not love himself (*In Io.* 123, 5). Education (cf. *De magistro* and *De catechizandis rudibus*) is based on love — the aphorism mentioned above is presented in an educational context with an educational purpose — and has as its goal the discovery and arousing of love (*De cat. rud.* 4, 8; 10, 15-15, 23: remedy against the six causes of boredom). In education, therefore, "free curiosity is more valuable than pedantic compulsion" (*Conf.* 1, 14, 23).

History, both on a personal and a universal level, has as its guiding idea the dramatic contrast between the two loves, that of self and that of God (*De civ. Dei* 14, 28) or, better, as Augustine himself says, between private love and social love (*De Gen. ad litt.* 11, 15, 20). This drama, applied to humanity, can be summed up, as has been said, in five acts which unfold between the beginning and the end of time and resolve the five great problems proposed and imposed by history.

The solutions offered by Augustine enter into the realm of theology although without abandoning that of pure philosophy. Indeed, if it is true that the full intelligibility of history derives from faith, it is nevertheless true that reason — and everything which has been said up to this point shows this — provides principles which illuminate the beginning, the course and the end of this history. Thus philosophy together with a theology of history form a reciprocal relationship dear to Augustine. A brief synthesis of his philosophy has been offered and the same will be attempted for his theology. It must also be noted, however, that in the *De civitate Dei* Augustine offers an important sociological and political doctrine: the two cities are not to be identified with the church, on the one hand, or with the state on the other. Augustine's concept is "mystical" (*De civ. Dei* 15, 1, 1), that is, spiritual and ideal. It provides a place for a "political city" which arises out of the social nature of man (*De bono coniug.* 1, 1) and has its own proper responsibilities; the principal among them being that of securing peace on earth, from which the pilgrim city of God on its way to eternal beatitude also benefits (*De civ. Dei* 19, 26).

Studies: (Cf. the bibliography on the *De civ. Dei,* p. 364). — J. Mausbach, Die Etik des hl. Aug. Freiburg Br., 1909. — J. Martin, La doctrine sociale de St. Aug. Paris, 1912. — B. Rolland-Gosselin, La morale de S. Ag. Paris, 1925. — Ch. Boyer, St. Aug. moraliste. Paris, 1932. — A. Brucculeri, Il pensiero sociale di S. Ag. Rome, 1932. — T. Rohmer, La finalité morale chez les Théologiens de st. Aug. à Duns Scot. Paris, 1939. — V. Bourke, Augustine's Quest of Wisdom. Milwaukee, 1945. — A. Vecchi, Filosofia e teologia nella morale agostiniana: *Giorn Metaf* 9(1954)555-574. — K. Foster, Metaphysische und heilsgeschichtliche Betrachtungsweise in Aug. Weisheitsbegriff: AugMag II, 381-389. — R. Holte, Beatitude et sagesse. Paris, 1962. — A. Becker, De l'instinct du bonheur à l'extase de la béatitude. Paris, 1967. — F. Campo del Pozo, Filosofia del derecho según s. Ag. Valladolid, 1968. — F. Cavalla, Scientia, sapientia et esperienza sociale. Padua, 1974. — A. Becker, L'appel des béatitudes. À l'écoute de s. A. Paris, 1977. — F. L. Miller, The Fundamental Option in the Thought of S. A.: DR 95(1977)271-283.

THEOLOGY

Augustine defines theology as "the science which generates, nourishes, defends and fortifies faith . . . Many of the faithful do not possess this science, even though they have a great deal of faith. For it is one thing to know only that which must be believed in order to obtain the blessed life . . . and another to know it in such a way as to be able to place it at the service of the good and to defend it against the bad (*De Trin.* 14, 1, 3).

1. Theological method

It is important to know first of all the method which Augustine followed, i.e., the principles by which he was inspired in contributing to the progress of theology as he did. These principles are:

1. The first principle is the strict adherence to the authority of the faith which, one in its origins, the authority of Christ (*C. acad.* 3, 20, 43), is expressed in Scripture, in tradition and in the church.

a) With regard to Scripture, he emphasizes its divine origin (*In ps.* 90, 2, 1), inerrancy (*Ep.* 28, 3, 3; 82, 1, 3), profundity (*Ep.* 137, 1, 3) and richness (*Conf.* 12, 14, 17-32, 43). He has a famous saying: regarding the Scripture "it is not lawful to say, 'The author of this book has not spoken the truth.' Instead, either the manuscript is incorrect, the translator has made a mistake or you do not understand" (*C. Faustum* 11, 5).

The Scripture is the soul of Augustine's theology. He loved and studied it with real passion (*Conf.* 11, 2, 2-4), made a critical revision of the text when he was able (particularly with regard to the Psalms: *Ep.* 261, 5), wrote commentaries on several of the biblical books (cf. p. 377) and defended the harmony of the Scriptures (*De consensu Ev.*: cf. p. 380).

In all of his theological controversies he referred to the Scripture and penetrated its thought, and illustrated his solution first of all by a synthesis of biblical theology (on the Trinity, *De Trin.* 1-4; on redemption and original sin, *De pecc. mer. et rem.* 1, 13, 33-28, 56; on the necessity of grace, *De spir. et litt.;* on grace and free will, *De gr. et lib. arb.;* on the church, *De unitate Eccl.*). If he indulged in the allegorical sense in his discourses to the people, he sought out the literal sense, i.e., the sense intended by the author, in his dogmatic argumentation and biblical works (*De Gen. ad litt.* 1, 21, 41).

b) Augustine read the Scriptures in the church and according to tradition. To the Manichaeans he said, "I would not believe in the Gospel if the authority of the Catholic church did not lead me to do so" (*C. ep. Man.* 5, 6; cf. *C. Faustum* 28, 2), and he reminded the Donatists of the two qualities of Apostolic tradition: universality and antiquity (*De bapt.* 4, 24, 31). He replied to the Pelagians that it was necessary to hold as true that which tradition has passed on even if one does not succeed in explaining it (*C. Iul.* 6, 5, 11), because the Fathers "taught the church that which they learned in the church" (*C. Iul. op. imp.* 1, 117; cf. *C. Iul.* 2, 10, 34).

c) It is in fact the church which determines the canon of Scripture (*De doct. chr.* 2, 7, 12), which transmits tradition and interprets both of the above (*De Gen. ad litt. op. imp.* 1, 1), which settles controversies (*De bapt.* 2, 4, 5) and prescribes the *regula fidei* (*De doctr. chr.* 3, 1, 2). Therefore, "I will rest secure in the church," writes Augustine, "whatever difficulties arise" (*De bapt.* 3, 2, 2), because "God has established the doctrine of truth in the cathedra of unity" (*Ep.* 105, 16).

2. A second principle was provided by the ardent desire to arrive at an understanding of the faith and the employment toward this end of all human resources to understand the teaching of Scripture. These resources are described in the *De doctrina christiana:* textual criticism (2, 14, 21-22), and an understanding of languages (2, 11, 16), of sacred and secular history (2, 31, 48), of hermeneutics (3), of dialectics (2, 31, 48) and of philosophy. "If those who are called philosophers have said something in harmony with our faith, not only are they to be feared, but they are to be claimed for our use . . ." (2, 40, 60).

Furthermore, there is need of great love (*De mor. Eccl. cath.* 1, 17, 31), great humility (*Ep.* 118, 22) and much study (*De Trin.* 15, 28, 51).

3. The third principle was the firm conviction of the originality of Christian doctrine which he affirmed and defended before all: pagans, heretics and Judaizers (*De v. rel.* 6, 10; *De ag. chr.* 12, 13). He therefore approved of the philosophers with regard to those teachings which they held "in common with us," but he boldly opposed them, including the Platonists, the most noble among them "in that which they think contrary to us" (*De civ. Dei* 1, 36; cf. ibid., 12, 17, 2 and *Serm.* 242, 5-6), and perceived in their doctrines "great errors against which it is necessary to defend Christian doctrine" (*Retract.* 1, 1, 4). He upheld the identity of this doctrine against the heretics who had a wrong understanding of the Scripture. However, he recognized the progress in the understanding of the faith and the usefulness of

their controversies, because "many truths of the faith, in order to be defended against them, are studied more diligently, understood more clearly, preached more insistently in such a way that the question raised by the adversary becomes an occasion of progress" (*De civ. Dei* 16, 2, 1; *In ps.* 54, 21).

4. A fourth principle was a profound sense of mystery which rendered theological investigation both bold yet discreet and disposed it to respect the threshold of divine transcendence. Augustine repeatedly preached this sense of mystery — "trusting ignorance is better than reckless wisdom" (*Serm.* 27, 4) — and applied it to all the Christian mysteries: to the incomprehensibility of God, "If you understand it, it is not God" (*Serm.* 122, 5; cf. *Ep.* 120, 3, 13; *De Trin.* 5, 3, 4; 7, 4, 7); to the Trinity (*De Trin.* 1, 1, 1); to the Incarnation (*Ench.* 13, 41; *Ep.* 137, 2, 8); to original sin (*De pecc. mer. et rem.* 3, 4, 7); to liberty and grace (ibid., 2, 18, 28; *De gr. Christi* 47, 52) and to predestination (*De sp. et litt.* 34, 60; *Serm.* 27, 7). Therefore it was necessary to search and to debate "with holy humility, with catholic peace, with Christian charity" (*De bapt.* 2, 3, 4), always ready to be corrected either by brothers or, when they speak the truth, by adversaries (*De Trin.* 2, 9, 16).

5. The fifth principle was the subordination of theology to charity and thus to the life of the church, because "the fullness and the end of all the Scriptures is love" (*De doctr. chr.* 1, 35, 39), and love is also the end of theology (ibid., 1, 3, 3-40, 44) which in its turn finds a source of illumination in the love which animates the theologian (*De quant. an.* 33, 76).

6. The final principle was a vigilant care for a precise theological language. "The philosophers speak with undisciplined words . . . but we must speak according to a definite rule in order that the freedom of the words may not generate false opinions concerning those things which the words signify" (*De civ. Dei* 10, 23).

Studies: Ch. Boyer, Philosophie et théologie chez St. Aug., in *Essais sur la Doctrine de St. Aug.* Paris 1932, 184-205. — B. M. G. Reardon, The Relation of Philosophy to Faith in the Teaching of St. Aug.: SP 2 (TU 64). Berlin 1957, 288-294. — E. González, El concepto y método de la teologia en De Trin. de St. Aug.: *Augustinus* 1(1956)379-398. — T. Camelot, Quod intelligimus debemus rationi. Note sur la méthode théol. de St. Aug.: HJG 77(1958)397-402. — D. J. Hassel, Conversion, Theory and Scientia in De Trin.: RAug 2(1962)383-401; *idem,* Method and Scientia in St. Aug., Diss., St. Louis, 1963.

2. Trinitarian Doctrine

Augustine's Trinitarian doctrine represented a great progress for theology along the lines of tradition and determined the development of Trinitarian theology in the West.

He began with a profession of faith ("This is my faith because it is the Catholic faith": *De Trin.* 1, 4, 7), presented the difficulties raised by reason (ibid., 1, 5, 8) and examined the Scriptures to explain these difficulties. He studied the distinctive properties of the three persons (*De Trin.* 1-4), explained that the processions and missions of which the Scripture speaks indicate the order of origin of one person from another and not their subordination one to another (ibid., 4, 20, 27; cf. *C. Max.* 2, 14, 2-8), emphasized that all the actions of the Trinity *ad extra* are common to all three persons (such as creation and the theophanies of the Old Testament) even though only the Son became Incarnate (*De Trin.* 2, 10, 18) and indicated in the doctrine of the relations the only way to avoid the errors of Arius and Sabellius (ibid., 5-7). He established the rules for speaking correctly of this mystery (ibid., 5-7), illustrated its nature against the "garrulous rationalists" by making recourse to the image of the Trinity in man, explained the spiritual fruitfulness of this mystery and led the reader to a love and contemplation of it (ibid., 9-15).

The principle of the equality and the distinction of the persons is stated with these words: "God is everything which He has except for the relations by which each person is related to another. There is no doubt that the Father has the Son, but the Father is not the Son . . ." (*De civ. Dei* 11, 10, 1). The first part of this principle expresses the absolute simplicity of God by which the persons are identified with the divine nature which is therefore not something common to them "as though a fourth part," but is itself the Trinity (*Ep.* 120, 3, 13-17). The second part indicates in the doctrine of the relations the distinction of the three persons: "Even though it is not the same thing to be the Father and to be the Son, nevertheless the substance is not different because these designations do not belong to the order of substance but of relation; a relation which is not accidental because it is not mutable" (*De Trin.* 5, 5, 6).

In addition to the doctrine of the relations, Augustine's contribution to an understanding of the Trinitarian mystery was also decisive in two other points which, together with that of the relations, were taken up by the Scholastics: the theology of the Holy Spirit and the "psychological" explanation of the Trinity.

The Holy Spirit proceeds from the Father and the Son as from a single principle (*De Trin.* 5, 14, 15), but *principaliter* from the Father, because the Father, who is the "origin of the divinity" (ibid., 4, 20, 29) has conceded it to the Son to emanate the Holy Spirit (ibid., 15, 17, 29; *In Io.* 99, 8-9). The Spirit proceeds as Love and thus is not begotten since it is proper to love not to be an image but an inclination, a gift and a communion. Augustine thus provided the theological reason — taken up later by Thomas — which in some way demonstrates the distinction which exists between the generation of the Son and the procession of the Holy Spirit, which was one of the three questions he had promised to illustrate from the very beginning of the *De Trinitate* (1, 5, 8) and to which he returned frequently in the composition of the work. "The will (love) proceeds from the intellect but not as the image of the intellect. There is thereby indicated a certain distinction between generation and procession since it is not the same thing to see with the intellect as to desire and enjoy with the will" (ibid., 15, 27, 50; cf. 9, 12, 18). On the other hand, "the Son is Son inasmuch as he is the Word and is the Word inasmuch as he is the Son" (ibid., 7, 2, 3).

The "psychological" explanation of the Trinity then illustrates both the mystery of God the Trinity as well as the mystery of man, created in the image of God. This Augustinian investigation is original and profound. It seeks this image in the exterior man (ibid., 11), but finds it only in the interior man, in the mind, and it expresses this image in the formula *mens, notitia, amor,* or in a second formula which is "a more evident trinity" (ibid., 15, 3, 5); *memoria, intelligentia, voluntas.* This latter, since it has a dual object — God and man — becomes memory, understanding and love of self (ibid., 10) or memory, understanding and love of God (ibid., 14-15) which is the most similar likeness, but which nevertheless always remains "a dissimilar likeness" (*Ep.* 169, 6; *De Trin.* 15, 14, 24-16, 26).

Studies: M. Schmaus, Die psychologische Trinitätslehre des hl. A. Münster, 1927. — F. Cavallera, Les Premières formules trinitaires de saint Augustin: BLE 31(1930)97-123. — J. Lebreton, St. Augustin théologien de la Trinité. Son exégèse des théophanies: MSCA II, 821-836. — I. Chevalier, La théorie augustinienne des relations trinitaires. Analyse explicative des textes: DT 18(1940)317-384; *idem,* St. A. et la pensée grecque. Les relationes trinitaires. Fribourg, 1940. — R. Remblay, La théorie psycologique de la Trinité chez St. A., in *Études et Recherches* VIII. Paris-Ottawa 1952, 83-109; *idem,* Les processions du Verbe et de l'amour humain chez St. A.: RUO 24(1954)93-117. — M. Nédoncelle, L'intersubjectivité humaine est-elle pour St. A. une image de la Trinité?: AugMag I, 595-602. — G. Mascia, La teoria della relazione nel De Trinitate di S. A., Naples, 1955. — M. Löhrer, Glaube und Heilsgeschichte in De Trinitate Augustins: FreibZPhTh 4(1954)385-419. — J. Morán, Acción y contemplación en el libro XII De Trinitate de San A.: SP 9 (TU 94). Berlin 1966, 451-468; *idem,* Las relaciones divinas según San A.: *Augustinus* 4(1959)353-372. — P. Smulders, Esprit Saint chez les Pères latins: DSp 4(1960)1272-1283. — E. Bailleux, La sotériologie de St. A. dans le De Trinitate: MSR 23(1966)149-173; *idem,* Dieu Trinité et son œuvres: RAug 7(1971)189-218; *idem,* La christologie de St. A. dans le De Trinitate: RAug 7(1971)219-243. — F. Bourassa, Appropriation ou "propriété": SE 7(1930)57-85; *idem,* Questions de théologie trinitaire. Rome, 1970. — B. De Margerie, La doctrine de St. A. sur l'Esprit-Saint comme communion et source de communion: Aug 12(1972)107-119. — J. B. Du Roy, L'espérience de l'amour et l'intelligence de la foi trinitaire selon St. A.: RAug 2(1962)415-445. — O. Du Roy, L'intelligence de la foi en la Trinité selon St. A. Genèse de la théologie trinitaire jusqu'en 391. Paris, 1966. — P. Hadot, La structure de l'âme, image de la Trinité chez Victorinus et chez A.: SP 6 (TU 81). Berlin 1962, 409-442. — M. Simonetti, La processione dello Spirito Santo nei Padri latini: *Maia* 7(1954)201-217; 8(1955)308-324; *idem,* S. A. e gli Ariani: REAug 13(1967)55-84. — A. Trapè, Nota sulla processione dello Spirito Santo nella teologia trinitaria de S. A.: *Studi Tom.* I. Rome

1974, 119-125. — A. Trapè, M. F. Sciacca, Introduzione a La Trinità: NBA 4, 7-127. — J. Verhees, Augustins Trinitätsverständnis in den Schriften aus Cassiciacum: RAug 10(1975)45-75. — F. Bourassa, Théologie trinitaire de saint Augustin: Greg 58(1977)675-718, 59(1978)375-412. — J. S. O'Leary, Dieu-Esprit et Dieu-substance chez saint Augustin: RSR 69(1981)357-390.

3. Christological Doctrine

Augustine came to an understanding of the Catholic doctrine on the Incarnation of the Word on the eve of his conversion (*Conf.* 7, 19, 25), and from that point onward he defended this doctrine with vigor and tenacity.

His doctrine is distinguished from traditional teaching only by the clarity of its language (in particular the formula *"una persona in utraque natura": Serm.* 294, 9), by the recurrence of the ever more insistent and clearly developed example of the union between the body and the soul, by the defense against all heresies which denied or obscured the perfect human and divine nature of Christ and by the presentation of the Christ-man as the shining example of the gratuity of grace.

The most suitable formulae on the unity of person and duality of nature in Christ—formulae which anticipate that of Chalcedon — are found in the sermons. In addition to that mentioned above, the following are also to be found: "He who is man is the very one who is God, and he who is God is the very one who is man; not by the confusion of nature but by the unity of person" (*Serm.* 186, 1, 1). ". . . not two persons, God and man. In Christ there are certainly two substances, God and man, but one single person" (*Serm.* 130, 30). Or elsewhere: *idemque ipse utrumque ex utroque unus Christus;* the same identical person is both, constituted by one and the other, one single Christ (God and man) (*Ench.* 10, 35; *De Trin.* 1, 7, 14). But there is no confusion: "God remains God; man is united to God and forms one single person; not a demigod, God for the part of God and man for the part of man, but entirely God and entirely man: *totus Deus et totus homo*" (*Serm.* 293, 7).

This union is "marvelous and ineffable" (*Ench.* 13, 41). Augustine vigorously emphasizes the difference between men sanctified by God and the God-man: "The Word in flesh is one thing, and the Word made flesh is another. That is, the Word in man is one thing, the Word become man is another" (*De Trin.* 2, 6, 11; cf. *De ag. chr.* 20, 22; *Ep.* 184, 40). The best example of this singular union is the union of the soul and the body in man which is itself marvelous and mysterious. "Indeed, as in the unity of the person the soul is united to the body and there is man, likewise in the unity of the person God is united to man and there is Christ" (*Ep.* 137, 3, 11). Therefore, "as each man is one single person, rational soul and body, Christ is likewise one single person, Word and man" (*Ench.* 11, 36).

Hence there arises the *communicatio idiomatum* which Augustine employs and defends. "God who was born," "the Crucified God" and "the God who died" are frequent expressions in Augustine. The reason for this is the unity of the person because of which God is man and man is God (*Ep.* 169, 2, 8). Thus, "God has not been killed, yet nevertheless according to the man he has been killed" (*Serm.* 213, 4: MSCA I, 444). Augustine states a general principle in commenting on John 3:13: "because of the unity of person the Son of God is on earth and because of the same unity of person the son of man is in heaven . . ." (*Serm.* 194, 9). Augustine insists that the man (or the human nature; the two terms are equivalent in Augustine) was assumed to the personal union with the Word in the very moment in which it was created, since it was created *"ipsa assumptione"* (*Con. serm. ar.* 8) in such a way that "from the time he began to be man, nothing other than the only Son of God began to be man" (*Ench.* 11, 36). For this reason Christ is the resplendent example of the absolute gratuity of grace (*Ench.* 12, 40; *De praed. s.* 15, 30; *De don. pers.* 24, 67).

A summary of Augustine's Christological doctrine is provided by a text written at the end of his life: "The faithful Christian believes and confesses that there is in Christ a true human nature, that is, our own, although it is exalted to the dignity of the only Son of God, inasmuch as God the Word has assumed it in an incomparable union in such a way that He who assumed and that which is assumed is one person in the heart of the Trinity . . . Because we do not say that Christ is only God as do the heretical Manichaeans, nor that he is only man as do the heretical Photinians; nor that he is man but is lacking in something which belongs to human nature, either the soul or, in the soul, the rational mind, or that he has a body not formed from woman but derived from the conversion and mutation of the Word into flesh, which are three false and empty opinions of the heretical Apollinarians . . . But we say that Christ is true God, born of God the Father . . . and that the same Christ is true man, born of a woman, his mother . . . and that his humanity, by which he is less than the Father, takes nothing away from his divinity by which he is equal to the Father. A dual nature, one single Christ . . ." (*De praed. s.* 24, 67).

Studies: O. Scheel, Die Anschauung Aug. über Christi Person und Werk. Tübingen, 1901. — H. Paissac, Théologie du Verbe, st. Aug. et st. Thomas. Paris, 1951. — E. Scano, Il cristocentrismo e i suoi fondamenti dommatici in S. Agostino. Turin, 1951. — T. J. van Bavel, Recherches sur la christologie de St. Aug. (*Paradosis* 9). Fribourg, 1954. — E. Braem, Christus als model en genadebron van onze praedestinatie volgens St. Aug.: AugL 4(1954)356-361. — G. Philips, L'influence du Christ-Chef sur son Corps mystique suivant st. Aug.: AugMag II, 805-815; *idem,* Le mystère du Christ: AugMag

III, 213-229. — L. Galati, Cristo la Via nel pensiero di S. Ag. Rome, 1956. — A. Piolanti, Il mistero del "Cristo totale" in S. Ag.: AugMag III, 453-469. — T. van Bavel, L'humanité du Christ comme "lac parvulorum" et comme "via" dans la spiritualité de st. Aug.: AugL 7(1957)245-281. — F. Da Cagliari, Cristo glorificato datore di Spirito Santo nel pensiero de S. Ag. e di S. Cirillo Alessandrino. Grottaferrata, 1961. — G. Bavaud, Un theme aug.: le mystère de l'Incarnation: REAug 9(1963)95-101. — H. M. Diepen, L'"Assumptus Homo" patristique: RT 64(1964)32-52. — O. Brabant, Le Christ centre et source de la vie morale chez st. Aug. Gembloux, 1971. — G. Madec, Christus scientia et sapientia nostra: RAug 10(1975)77-85. — W. Geerlings, Christus exemplum. Studien zur Christologie und christusverkündigung Augustins. Mainz, 1978 (cf. B. Studer: Aug 19[1979]539-546). — G. Rémy, Le Christ médiateur dans l'œuvre de s. A. Lille-Paris, 1979. — B. Studer, Le Christ notre justice selon st. Augustin: RAug 15(1980)99-143.

4. Mariology

For the patristic age, Augustine presents a broad and rich Mariology. Already in 389 he wrote that the Mother of the Lord, the Virgin Mary, is the "*dignitas terrae*" (*De Gen. c. man.* 2, 24, 37). There are four principal points in his Mariology:

1. *Divine maternity.* It is not necessary to insist on this point following all that has been said above concerning the unity of person in Christ. Augustine does not hesitate to affirm, "God was born of a woman" (*De Trin.* 8, 4, 7), and explains, "How could we confess in the *regula fidei* that we believe in the Son of God who was born of the Virgin Mary if not the Son of God but the son of man was born of the Virgin Mary? Who among the Christians denies that the son of man was born of that woman? Nevertheless, it was the God become man and thus the man become God" (*Serm.* 186, 2).

2. *Perpetual virginity.* Augustine states and defends this with particular energy: "A virgin she conceived, a virgin she gave birth, a virgin she remained" (*Serm.* 51, 18). To Volusianus, who presented the obvious difficulties which reason proposes, he responded, "Let us concede that God is able to do something which we must admit that we are not able to fathom. In such things the entire explanation of the event lies in the power of the one who is at work" (*Ep.* 137, 2, 8). Mary expressed her intention to embrace virginity before the announcement of the angel and thus gave rise to the Christian ideal of virginity (*Serm.* 51, 26). That does not take away from the fact that Mary was truly the spouse of Joseph and that it was a true marriage and true conjugal affection which bound her to him (*De nupt. et conc.* 1, 11, 12).

3. *Holiness.* In polemic with the Pelagians Augustine decisively affirms Mary's immunity from all sin. This is certainly true with regard to all personal sin: "Except the holy Virgin Mary, of whom, out of honor for the Lord, I absolutely do not want there to be any question when sin is spoken of . . ." (*De nat. et gr.* 36, 42). The question is whether these words are to be understood with regard to immunity from original sin. It seems that they are, as the principle is universal.

There is the response to Julian, who accused Augustine of the contrary, where, according to the text and context, there is both the affirmation of the universality of original sin and the exception made for Mary. "We do not consign Mary to the devil because of the condition of her birth" — this was the accusation — "since" — and this is the response — "the condition of birth was removed by the grace of rebirth" (*C. Iul. op. imp.* 4, 122).

4. *The relation of Mary to the church.* This is a beautiful principle of Augustine's Mariology. Mary is the model of the church. She is a model through the splendor of virtues and for the gift of being corporally that which the church must be spiritually, i.e., virgin and mother: virgin in integrity of faith, mother in the warmth of charity (*Serm.* 188, 4; 191, 4; 192, 2). But she is also the mother of the church (Augustine calls her "mother of the members of Christ") "because she cooperated with charity in order that children might be born in the church" (*De s. virg.* 6, 6).

Studies: Ph. Friedrich, Die Mariologie des hl. Aug. Cologne, 1907. — F. S. Müller, Aug. amicus aut adversarius immaculatae conceptionis?: MSCA II, 885-914. — F. Hofmann, Mariens Stellung in der Erlösungsordnung nach dem hl. Aug. Düsseldorf, 1952. — Y. Congar, Marie et l'Église dans la pensée patristique: RSPT 38(1954)3-38. — M. Pellegrino, La Vergine Maria. Pagine scelte di S. A. Rome, 1954. — J. Dietz, Ist die hl. Jungfrau nach Aug. "Immaculata ab initio"?, in *Virgo Immaculata* 4. Rome 1955, 61-112 (= AugL 5[1954]362-411); *idem,* Maria und die Kirche nach dem hl. Aug., in *Maria et Ecclesia* 3. Rome 1959, 201-239. — P. Frua, L'immacolata concezione e S. A. Saluzzo, 1960. — J. Morán, La Mariología de st. Aug. a travérs de la bibliografía (1900-1950): RET 23(1963)333-366. — Ch. Boyer, La controverse sur l'opinion de st. Aug. touchant la conception de la Vierge, in *Essais a. et n. sur la doctrine de St. Aug.*, Milan 1970, 345-359. — E. Lamirande, En quel sens peut-on parler de dévotion mariale chez st. Aug.?, in *De primordis cultus mariana* 3. Rome 1970, 17-35. — J. Morán, Puede hablarse de culto a María en san Ag.?: Aug 7(1967)514-521. — J. Falgueras Salinas, La contribución de San A. al dogma de la Immaculada Concepción de María: *Scripta Theologica* (Pamplona) 4(1972)355-433.

5. Soteriology

The two areas in which Augustine's developments had the greatest influence are soteriology and grace. He expounded these doctrines against the Pelagians and the pagans so that the cross of Christ might not be rendered empty (1 Cor. 1:17).

1. Augustine emphasizes first of all the nature and uniqueness of the mediation. Christ is mediator as man (*Conf.* 10, 43, 68; *De civ. Dei* 9, 15, 2) or, more precisely, as the God-man: "Man is not mediator without divinity, nor is God mediator without humanity . . . but between the one divinity and the one humanity the human divinity and divine humanity of Christ is mediator" (*Serm.* 47, 12, 21). Indeed only the God-man could be mediator. Augustine maintains this strongly against the Platonic demonology (*De civ. Dei* 9-10). The mediator must be in the middle between the two extremes to be

united, joined to them but distinct from them: between the just and immortal God and unjust and mortal men there must be one who is just and mortal; just like God, mortal like men (*Conf.* 10, 42, 67). Therefore Christ, the God-man, is the mediator of freedom, of life, of unity and of salvation for all men (*De Trin.* 4). Outside of this universal way, "which has never been lacking to the human race, no one has ever been liberated, no one is being liberated, no one will be liberated" (*De civ. Dei* 10, 32, 2). Augustine notes explicitly that this way was opened even to the Gentiles, outside of Israel, before the coming of Christ (*De civ. Dei* 18, 47).

2. Christ is mediator because he is redeemer. In this regard Augustine offers the first essay of biblical theology in which he shows that the motive of the Incarnation, according to the Scripture, is nothing other than the redemption of man. When he has examined the texts — and he examined many, over sixty — he concludes: "The Lord Jesus Christ has come in the flesh for no other reason . . . than to vivify, save, liberate, redeem and illuminate those who formerly were in death, weakness, slavery, prison and in the shadow of sins." From this it therefore follows that no one can belong to Christ who does not have need of life, salvation, liberation, redemption and illumination (*De pecc. mer. et rem.* 1, 26, 39). To this conclusion are bound the three essential properties of redemption, which are *necessity,* because no one can be saved without Christ; *objectivity,* because it does not consist only in the example of virtue to be imitated but in reconciliation with God; *universality,* because Christ died for all, none excepted.

It is from the theology of redemption that Augustine deduces the theology of original sin, and not vice versa as is often thought. Original sin constitutes a separation from God because Christ has reconciled us with God, all are subject to original sin because Christ has redeemed all. It is not merely the imitation of the bad example of Adam because redemption is not merely the imitation of the good example of Christ. They are thus two solidarities, opposite in character but necessarily joined together, with Adam and Christ. "The entire Christian faith consists in the cause of two men" (*De pecc. orig.* 24, 28). "One man and one man: one who leads to death, one who gives life" (*Serm.* 151, 5). "Each man is Adam, just as in those who believe each man is Christ" (*In ps.* 70, 2, 1). The Augustinian expression *massa damnata* is often brought forward as a proof of pessimism, but one forgets that for Augustine humanity is also the *massa redempta,* i.e., reconciled to God, as is seen from the texts cited here and even more clearly in the following: "Through this Mediator there is reconciled to God the mass of the entire human race which is alienated from Him through Adam" (*Serm.* 293, 8). In fact, on the level of theological argumentation the sequence moves from the *massa redempta* to the *massa damnata,* i.e., from the universality of redemption to the universality of sin: "If one has died for all, then all have died" (2 Cor. 5:14); died — and thus he intends this Pauline text which he frequently cites — because of sin which in infants can only be original sin (cf., e.g., *C. Iul.* 6, 4, 8). There is thus in Augustine a basic optimism rooted in his Christological doctrine, which illuminates the mystery of grace summarized in the dual solidarity with Adam and with Christ.

3. Christ is the redeemer because he is the priest and the sacrifice. Christ was anointed priest not with a visible anointing but "with the mystical and invisible unction when the Word of God became flesh, that is, when the human nature . . . was united to God the Word, in the womb of Mary, in such a way as to form with Him one single person" (*De Trin.* 15, 25, 46). But Christ willed to be not only the priest, but also the sacrifice: "For us, in your sight, priest and sacrifice, and priest inasmuch as sacrifice" (*Conf.* 10, 43, 69). He offered to the Father a sacrifice which was true, free, and perfect in every way, by means of which "he has atoned for, abolished and redeemed all the faults of humanity, ransoming us from the power of the demon" (*De Trin.* 4, 13, 16-14, 19).

As regards the theory of the devil's rights on which Augustine often dwells, it must be remembered that, according to Augustine, Christ died "to fulfill the will of a good Father, not to pay a debt to an evil principle" (*Serm.* Morin 17: MSCA I, 662).

Studies: O. Scheel, Zu Aug. Anschauung von Erlösung durch Christus: ThStKr 77(1904)401-433, 491-554. — C. van Crombrugge, La doctrine christologique et sotériologique de St. Aug. et ses rapports avec le néo-platonisme: RHE 5(1904)237-257, 477-503. — J. Rivière, Le dogme de la rédemption chez St. Aug. Paris, 1933[3]. — A. F. Krüger, Synthesis of Sacrifice According to St. Aug. Mundelein (Illinois), 1950). — H. E. W. Turner, A. R. Mowbray, The Patristic Doctrine of Redemption. London, 1952. — J. Lécuyer, Le sacrifice selon St. Aug.: AugMag II, 905-914. — R. Arbesmann, The Concept of "Christus medicus" in St. Aug.: *Traditio* 10(1954)1-28. — B. Speekenbrink, Christ the "medicus humilis" in St. Aug.: AugMag II, 623-629; *idem,* De Heilsbetekenis van Christus' Verrijzenis; Formulering en betekenis van een verrijzenis adagium vanaf st. Aug. tot st. Thomas: StC 30(1955)1-34, 81-98, 161-184. — J. Kremer, Was an den Leiden Christi noch mangelt. Bonn, 1956. — R. Schneider, Was hat uns Aug. "Theologia medicinalis" heute zu sagen?: *KerygDog* 3(1957)307-315. — P. C. J. Eijkenboom, Het Christus-Medicusmotief in de Preken van sint Aug. Assen, 1960. — F. Nikolash, Das Lamm als Christussymbol in den Schriften der Väter. Vienna, 1963. — J. P. Jossua, Le salut, incarnation ou mystére pascal. Paris, 1968. — G. Ferraro, L'interpretazione di S. Ag. della passione di Cristo nel commento al quarto Vangelo, in *Atti Congr. Intern. a Roma* 1975. Turin, 1976.

6. Supernatural Anthropology

To Augustine's doctrine of redemption are bound four fundamental questions of supernatural anthropology: original sin, justification, helping grace, and predestination. Augustine developed these questions in polemic with the Pelagians and contributed a decisive progress with regard to these topics in Catholic theology. In order to understand this development it is necessary to keep in mind the terms as well as the nature of the polemic. Augustine did not deny what the Pelagians affirmed — the goodness of created things, free will, the utility of the law, the merit of good works — but he affirmed what they denied: redemption, grace, Christian liberty, and the free gift of salvation. It is clear that polemical necessities drove him to insist on that which the Pelagians were denying, but his stated purpose was that of a synthesis and harmony of contraries. The Catholic teaching, as he repeatedly said, passes between the opposed errors of the Pelagians and the Manichaeans, as far from the one group as from the other (*C. d. epp. pel.* 2, 1, 1-2, 4; *De nupt. et conc.* 2, 3, 9, etc.), just as at one time it had passed between the opposed doctrines of the Sabellians and the Arians (*De nupt. et conc.* 2, 23, 38) and, during his own lifetime, between those of the Manichaeans and the Jovinians (*C. Iul.* 1, 2, 4). It is necessary to recognize that he maintained his purpose even amidst the snares of the polemic and the difficulty of the language by constantly defending the *veritatis medium* (*De s. virg.* 19), i.e., the *via media* of the truth which passes safely between opposite extremes. Indeed, he defends the existence of original sin against the Pelagians but confirms the goodness of all things against the Manichaeans; he upholds the total and perfect remission of sins in baptism but opposes the Pelagian thesis of *impeccantia* and clarified that the fullness of justification is never able to be realized here on earth; he taught the necessity of grace as well as the free cooperation of man, the gratuity of the divine election to eternal life and the culpability of those who are not saved.

The same equilibrium is encountered in his doctrine on the church, on the sacraments, and on eschatology.

1. With regard to original (native) sin he drew an important distinction between its existence and its nature: he vigorously defended the first and was cautious and prudent with regard to the second.

a) He defends the existence of original sin with all the arguments available to theology: biblical, liturgical, patristic, and rational.

The first biblical texts to appear in his writings, in 388 and 392 respectively, are: 1 Cor. 15:22 (*De mor. Eccl. cath.* 1, 19, 35) and Rom. 5:19 (*C. Fort.* 2, 22), thus not Rom. 5:12. Once the Pelagian Controversy had arisen he developed the biblical argument concerning the soteriological purpose of the Incarnation (cf. p. 433). Even when he cites Rom. 5 he does not insist only on verse 12 but rather on the entire passage 5:12-29 (*De nupt. et conc.* 2, 28, 47).

The liturgical argument of the baptism of infants (*Serm.* 294) confirms and clarifies the biblical argument (*De pecc. mer. et rem.* 3, 4, 7) while the patristic argument demonstrates the traditional nature of the doctrine (*C. Iul.* 1-2). In force of this argument Augustine is able to state: "I am not the one who has invented original sin which the Catholic faith has believed from antiquity" (*De nupt. et conc.* 2, 12, 25). When Julian accuses him of having changed his opinion, Augustine bluntly denies the charge and refers his adversary to the writings of his youth (*C. Iul.* 6, 12, 39). The attentive study of these writings proves Augustine correct. The change, which Augustine plainly admits (*Retract.* 2, 1, 1; *De praed. s.* 3, 7-4, 8) concerns the beginning of faith, not original sin. With regard to this latter point there was a development of theology which was provoked by the Pelagian Controversy, but no change of doctrine. If there is a question of change, it concerns secondary matters, such as the interpretation of the passage in Rom. 7:14-25 (*Retract.* 1, 23; 2, 1, 1).

Finally, the rational argument offers an invitation to reflect on the teaching of the faith and shows that the problem of evil, on the existential and historical plane, cannot be understood without original sin (just as it cannot be overcome without the Redemption). Indeed man, subject to so many evils — suffering, death, ignorance, concupiscence — is obviously wretched, but "under the just God no one is able to be wretched who has not merited it" (*C. Iul. op imp.* 1, 3, 9; cf. *De civ. Dei* 22, 22; *C. Iul.* 4, 16, 83; *C. Iul. op. imp.* 6, 5; for the evils suffered by infants, ibid., 6, 27; 6, 36, 41; *Ep.* 166, 16-20).

b) Regarding the nature of original sin, he is profoundly aware of its mysterious quality (cf. above), clarifies the basic point that it is transmitted not by imitation but by propagation (*De pecc. mer. et rem.* 1, 9, 9-11), and gives the following idea of it: original sin is concupiscence joined to guilt (*De nupt. et conc.* 1, 25, 28-26, 29), meaning by concupiscence the inclination of the soul to prefer temporal goods to eternal (*De mend.* 7, 10) and by guilt the state of enmity with God and the privation of divine life (*De pecc. mer. et rem.* 1, 11, 13-39, 70; 2, 28, 45). It is wrongly claimed that he identified original sin with concupiscence, for such a claim does not correspond to the truth. Augustine distinguished between appetite and concupiscence; the former a good thing, the latter, if disordered, bad (*C. Iul. op. imp.* 4, 29). He distinguished between ordered concupiscence, i.e., subject to reason, and disordered concupiscence (*C. d. epp. pel.* 1, 17, 34-35; *C. Iul. op. imp.* 1, 70; 2, 18) and maintained clearly and firmly that the latter in itself, i.e., without the guilt, which is taken away in baptism, or without personal consent, is not a sin, even if it is an evil; if it is called sin it is only because it arises from and tends toward sin (*De pecc.*

mer. et rem. 2, 4, 4; 2, 28, 45; *De nupt. et conc.* 1, 23, 25; *C. d. epp. pel.* 11, 13, 27). The Council of Trent used these same words to express the Catholic teaching (DS 1515).

2. To the doctrine of original sin is connected that of justification which clarifies and confirms it. In order to understand this second doctrine it is necessary to make, as did Augustine, two basic distinctions: the first between remission of sins and interior renewal (*De Trin.* 14, 17, 23), the second between initial justification and total and conclusive justification (*C. d. epp. pel.* 3, 3, 4-5).

The remission of sins is "total and full," "full and perfect" (*De pecc. mer. et rem.* 2, 7, 9). All sins are forgiven, none excluded (*De g. pel.* 12, 28), and man is restored to innocence (*C. Iul. op. imp.* 6, 19). Augustine is steadfast in his insistence on this point. Interior renewal, on the other hand, is progressive and is never perfect except in the resurrection when, once baptism has fully born fruit, "mortality" and "sickness" will cease; the two evils against which man, even justified man, must struggle and, by struggling, advance in justification (*C. d. epp. pel.* 3, 3, 5). But even though it is only a beginning, Christian justification introduces already here on earth the restoration of the image of God which "immortality imprinted in the immortal nature of the soul" (*De Trin.* 14, 4, 6), sin had obscured although not destroyed (ibid., 14, 3, 18; 15, 8, 14); the divine life of grace (*In ps.* 70, 2, 3), which the Holy Spirit "infuses in a hidden manner even in children" (*De pecc. mer. et rem.* 1, 9, 10), the "deification" (*In ps.* 49, 2); *Serm.* 166, 4), the inhabitation of the Holy Spirit which makes of the baptized his temple, even if they are not aware of it, as in the case of children (*Ep.* 187; cf. p. 370).

In spite of these sublime gifts, justification will be completed only in the next life. The idea which Augustine offers of this, after an attentive reading of the Gospel and of St. Paul, is essentially, even if not exclusively, eschatological. It embraces the entire sweep of salvation history seen by Augustine from the viewpoint of freedom. Before sin there was the *libertas minor* which consisted in the "ability not to sin" and "the ability not to die." There followed the loss of these freedoms, which are gradually restored to us by Christ. Finally, after the resurrection, there will be the *libertas maior,* i.e., "the inability to sin" and "the inability to die," which are essential properties of the divine nature of which man, fully justified, becomes a partaker (*De c. et gr.* 12, 32).

3. On this theme of justification depends the entire doctrine of helping grace, which was the crucial point of the Pelagian controversy. Augustine defended the nature, necessity, efficacy and gratuity of this grace. It was this defense which earned him the title of Doctor of grace.

a) Nature

Grace in a Christian sense is not the creation as the Pelagians thought, even though this is a free gift of God (*De n. et gr.*; cf. p. 387; *Serm.* 26, 4; *Ep.* 177, 7); nor the law, even if the law, by indicating the way of salvation, is a benefit and a sign of favor (*De sp. et litt.*; cf. p. 386); nor justification alone. To these three manners of speaking of grace, which Augustine knows and acknowledges, it is necessary, he says, to add a fourth, i.e., the divine aid for fulfilling what the law commands, for attaining justification and persevering in it. "Pelagius must concede the existence of this grace if he wants not only to be called but really to be a Christian" (*De gr. Chr.* 16, 11).

The task of this grace is to remove the obstacles which impede the will from carrying out the good and fleeing from evil. These obstacles, which are the consequence of original sin, are two in number: "ignorance and weakness" (*De pecc. mer. et rem.* 2, 17, 26). But since the second of these obstacles is the greater of the two (*De sp. et litt.* 3, 5), helping grace is rather the motion of the will than the illumination of the intellect. According to the Augustinian definition, it is "the inspiration of charity by which we do with holy love that which we recognize must be done" (*C. d. epp. pel.* 4, 5, 11). The opposition to the naturalistic conception of the Pelagians is clear: ". . . from where does the love of God and neighbor in man come if not from God Himself? In fact, if it does not come from God but from men, the Pelagians have won; if on the other hand it comes from God we have defeated the Pelagians" (*De gr. et lib. arb.* 18, 37).

b) Necessity

Augustine defends the absolute necessity of this grace, both for avoiding sin and for turning to God and attaining salvation. The contrast with the Pelagians on this point lay in the conclusions rather than the principles. The common presupposition was that God does not command the impossible. From this the Pelagians concluded that grace is not necessary; Augustine concluded that prayer is therefore necessary to obtain grace. Indeed, only grace renders the observance of the commandments possible while only prayer obtains grace. "God does not command the impossible, but in commanding He admonishes you to do that which you can and to ask for that which you cannot" (*De nat. et gr.* 43, 50), and He helps you in order that you may be able, since "He does not abandon one if He is not abandoned" (ibid., 26, 29). This principle and conclusion were adopted by the Council of Trent (*Decr.* de *iust.* c. 11).

Augustine's argumentation is based, in addition to the Scripture, on the liturgy and gives the theological reason for the liturgy of petition, which is no less important than that of praise. Polemical motives led him to insist on that of which human nature is *incapable* without grace. With regard to the positive, largely philosophical aspect of the question, which was discussed by the Scholastics and in an anti-Scholastic vein by the Reformers and the Jansenists, his thought is definitely more subtle. Regarding the virtues of the pagans cf. *C. Iul.* 4, 3, 21-33; *De div. Dei* 19, 25; *De sp. et litt.* 28, 48.

c) Efficacy

The theme of the efficacy of grace is a more difficult one since it touches on the question of liberty. Augustine is aware of this and thus his view is that of the Gospel and his motto is taken from the words of Christ, "If the Son will set you free, you will truly be free" (John 8:36). The Christian freedoms are four in number: freedom from sin, from the inclination to evil, from death, and from time: and they bestow justice, order, immortality, and eternity (*In Io.* 41, 9-13). He defended and praised these freedoms and took freedom as the key for his interpretation of history (cf. p. 405). The following text summarizes Augustine's thought with regard to the first point, that of sin: "Do we thus render free will void by means of grace? Far be it! Rather, we establish the value of the free will. Indeed, as the law is not made void by means of faith but is confirmed in its value (Rom. 3:31), so is the same true for the free will and grace. The law is only observed by means of the free will. But from the law arises the awareness of sin, from grace the health of the soul from the vice of sin, from the health of the soul the liberty of the free will, from the liberty of the free will the love of justice, from the love of justice the fulfillment of the law. Therefore, just as the law is not made void but is established by means of faith, since faith obtains the grace by which the law is observed, thus is the free will not made void but is established by means of grace, because grace heals the will, and the will, having been made whole, freely loves justice" (*De sp. et litt.* 30, 52).

If, however, his outlook was that of evangelical freedom — the freedom from evil — he was not ignorant of the problem posed by freedom of choice which would subsequently be the predominant subject of Scholastic discussions. He was therefore firm in his principles, clear in his admonitions and cautious in his solutions. He maintained that the two truths — the freedom of choice and the efficacy of grace — must be defended together. For this purpose he wrote his work *De gratia et libero arbitrio* (cf. p. 390). "Free will is not taken away because it is assisted, but is assisted in order that it not be taken away" (*Ep.* 152, 2, 10). Therefore, "He who created you without your cooperation does not justify you without your cooperation. He created you without your knowing it, he does not justify you without your wanting it" (*Serm.* 11, 13). The proof can be reduced to the

Christological motive that Christ, according to Scripture, is judge and savior: "If grace does not exist, how does he save the world? If there is no free will, how does he judge the world?" (*Ep.* 214, 2).

He likewise maintained that the harmony between these two truths, each certain and undeniable, "is a most difficult question, intelligible to few" (*Ep.* 214, 6) and a cause of distress to all (*De pecc. mer. et rem.* 2, 18, 28) because in defending the one the impression is given of denying the other (*De gr. Chr.* 47, 52; *De gr. et l. arb.* 1, 1). From this conviction arose his warning — often too much ignored — to hold fast to the terms of the problem even when their harmony is not obvious (*Ep.* 214, 2).

As for himself, he preferred as usual to halt at the threshold of the mystery: "Man is drawn by grace *miris modis*" (*C. d. epp. pel.* 1, 37). Nevertheless he did not refuse to offer principles and indications to illuminate the mystery. Above all he insists on the "most omnipotent" divine action which has our free will in its power more than we do in our own (*De c. et gr.* 14, 45) and in the "tender generosity of love" which is characteristic of grace (*C. Iul. op. imp.* 3, 112; *De pecc. mer. et rem.* 2, 17, 26) which consequently moves the will, rendering it inviolate against evil without violating its liberty.

d) Gratuitousness

The fact that grace is a free gift of divine benevolence is another doctrine which Augustine defends against the Pelagians (*De d. pers.* 2, 4; *C. d. epp. pel.* 3, 8, 24; 4, 7, 19; *C. Iul.* 3, 1, 2), who maintained to the contrary that it was granted according to our merits (*De gestis Pel.* 14, 30; *De gr. et l. arb.* 5, 10; 14, 27). The beginning of faith is a gift of God (*De praed. s.*, cf. p. 391) — on this point he admits that he had once erred himself (ibid., 3, 7; 4, 8) — as is likewise the gift of final perseverance (*De d. pers.*, cf. p. 391).

This does not exclude the merits of man, but it renders them dependent on the gift of grace: "Do the merits of the just therefore not exist? Undoubtedly they do, because they are just. But as to the fact that they are just, it was not a matter of merit, for they became just when they were justified" (*Ep.* 194, 6). Therefore, "When God crowns our merits he is crowning nothing other than his gifts" (*Ep.* 194, 19). "The merits themselves are a free gift" (*Ep.* 186, 10; *De gr. et l. arb.* 5, 10-8, 20).

4. The necessity of defending the gratuitousness of grace led Augustine to develop the theme of predestination, which is its cause and impregnable rock of defense (*De d. pers.* 21, 54). Predestination is, in fact, according to Augustine's definition, "the foreknowledge and preparation of the favors of God by which all those who are set free are set free with certainty" (ibid., 14, 35). None other of his doctrinal

points has been as much discussed at this one, from the time of the monks of Marseilles (Semi-Pelagians) down to our own day. Many, from Gottschalk (ninth cent.) on, have wrongly interpreted the sense of this predestination. In order to understand Augustine's thought it is necessary to attend to his writings and to forget for the moment the later controversies. It will then be apparent that also on this subject, the most difficult and obscure of all, Augustine endeavored to render the meaning of the Scriptures, that he expounded the two apparently contradictory truths which express the content of the matter, developed the pastoral consequences and halted, more than ever in this matter, at the threshold of the mystery, inviting others to do the same.

He was confronted by the problem and developed his thought on the matter at the beginning of his episcopate (cf. p. 349). From that point on he had no further doubts regarding the absolute gratuity of predestination. The example of this gratuity is our Savior, the man Jesus Christ.

The apparently contradictory terms (as in every Christian mystery) are: The gratuitous predelection of God for the elect and the love of God for all men. Therefore, "the fact that some are saved is the gift of the one who saves; the fact that some perish is the merit of those who perish" (DS 623). These words of the Council of Quiercy, which reject a dual predestination, express the authentic thought of Augustine. It is obvious that he insisted more on the first of the two terms, but it is certain that he did not deny but rather affirmed the second also.

Indeed, a) he stated the universal principle according to which God is "the one who provides for and creates all things, but only provides for sin" (*Conf.* 1, 10, 16; *De Gen. ad litt.* 3, 14, 37). God can therefore condemn but cannot cause wickedness (*Ep.* 194, 6, 30). b) He distinguished between predestination and foreknowledge and explained that sins are the object of divine foreknowledge, not of predestination (*De an. et eius or.* 1, 7, 7; *De praed. s.* 10, 19). c) He maintained that the justice of God demands that there not be penalty without guilt: "God is good, God is just. Because He is good, He can set free without any merits; because He is just, He cannot condemn anyone without blameworthy actions" (*C. Iul.* 3, 18, 36). d) He emphasized, above all, that Christ, the supreme witness of God's love toward men (*De Trin.* 4, 1, 2), died for all, even for those who will not be saved. God is thus the Father of all and wants that all be saved. This conclusion is so obvious that predestinationists down the ages have denied it, i.e., have denied the universality of the redemption which instead the Catholic teaching has reaffirmed against them.

It is further necessary to remember that the Augustinian doctrine on the gratuitousness of predestination is dominated by three premises: an exegetical premise, the interpretation of Saint Paul (*De div. qq. ad S.* 1, *q.* 2); an eschatological premise, the *debiti fines* of the two cities, which differ from one another and which are both eternal (*De civ. Dei* 21); and a theological-metaphysical principle, the omnipotence of the divine action which, although no one can be saved who does not wish to be, can transform every person, without violating his freedom, from one who does not wish to be saved to one who does (*Ench.* 25, 98; *C. d. epp. pel.* 1, 19, 37; *De praed. s.* 8, 15; *C. Iul. op. imp.* 2, 157; 3, 122; 6, 10). His doctrine must be examined on the basis of these principles if it is not to be misunderstood.

On these same principles, particularly the final one, which reveals the more profound aspect of the mystery, there depends the exegetically restrictive interpretation which he gives in his later years to the Pauline passage of 1 Tim. 2:4 (*Ench.* 27, 103; *De praed. s.* 18, 36). God always has in reserve a grace which no heart, no matter how hard, resists, since it is given precisely for taking away the hardness of the heart (*De praed. s.* 8, 13). The question then arises as to why He does not use this grace for all, but permits that some be lost? This is the tortuous question which Augustine asks himself and to which he confesses not to know how to respond. Who could? He therefore bows humbly to the mystery (*Serm.* 27, 7) and repeats his act of faith with the words of Paul, "Is there perhaps injustice in God?" (*De div. qq. ad S.* 1, *q.* 2; *De pecc. mer. et rem.* 1, 21, 23-30; etc.), adding to this his own comment, "Grace cannot be unjust, nor can justice be cruel" (*De civ. Dei* 12, 27).

He does not fail, however, to show the pastoral significance of the mystery itself. It aids the Christian in avoiding presumption and despair, the apposite stumbling-blocks to salvation (*In Io.* 53, 8); increases his humility and trust — "We live more securely if we abandon ourselves in everything to God" (*De d. pers.* 6, 12) — and invites him to prayer (*In Io.* 26, 2; *De d. pers.* 16, 39) and to action (ibid., 22, 59).

It is this pastoral aspect, among the most profound aspects of Augustinianism, which unfortunately has been often neglected, not without grave consequences for the exact interpretation of Augustine's thought.

This, in its essential points, is the Augustinian doctrine on grace. Its true significance will be more easily understood the more one removes it from the context of later discussions, whether Scholastic or Controversialist.

Studies: 1. *Original sin:* J. Clémence, St. Aug. et le péché originel: NRTh 70(1948)727-754. — F. Floëri, Le Pape Zosime et la doctrine aug. du péché originel: AugMag II, 755-761. — J. Gross, Das Wesen der Erbsünde nach Aug.: AugMag II, 773-787. — G.

Armas, Teología agost. del pecado: *Augustinus* 1(1956)169-186. — A. Solignac, La condition de l'homme pécheur d'après st. Aug.: NRTh 78(1956)359-387. — E. Bonaiuti, Ag. e la colpa ereditaria. Venice, 1957 (reprint from *Rich Rel* 2[1926]401-427, cf. response of A. Casamassa, Il pensiero di S. Ag. nel 396-397. Rome, 1929). — A. M. Dubarle, La pluralité des péchés héréditaires dans la tradition aug.: REAug 3(1957)113-136. — H. Staffner, Die Lehre des hl. Aug. über das Wesen der Erbsünde: ZKTh 79(1957)385-416. — Ch. Boyer, Le péché originel, in *Theologie du péché.* Tournai 1960, 243-291. — J. Gross, Entstehungsgeschichte des Erbsündendogmas. Von der Bibel bis Aug. Munich-Basel, 1960 (Cf. review in REAug 9[1963]383-387). — G. Díaz, De peccati originalis essentia, in *Schola Augustiniana praetridentia.* Madrid, 1961. — F. Refoulé, Misère des enfants et péché originel d'après St. Aug.: RT 63(1963)341-362. — A. Vanneste, Saint Paul et la doctrine August. du péché originel: *Anal Biblica* 18(1963)513-522. — F. Floëri, Remarques sur la doctrine august. du péché originel: SP 9 (TU 94). Berlin 1966, 416-421. — H. Rondet, Le péché originel dans la tradition patristique et théologique. Paris, 1967 (Eng. Transl.: Original Sin. New York, 1972). — A. Sage, Le péché originel dans la pensée de saint Aug. de 412 à 430: REAug 15(1969)75-112; *idem,* Péché originel. Naissance d'un dogme: REAug 13(1967)211-248. — V. Grossi, Il peccato originale nella catechesi di S. Ag. prima della polemica pelagiana: Aug 10(1970)325-359, 458-492; *idem,* La liturgia battesimale in S. A. Rome, 1970. — S. Lyonnet, A. et Rom. 5, 12 avant la controverse pélagienne: NRTh 89(1967)842-849. — V. Capánaga, Tres adjectivos en la antropología religiosa agustiniana: *Augustinus* 22(1977)3-37.

2. *Justification:* E. Braem, Aug.' Leer over de heiligmakende Genade: AugL 1(1951)7-20, 77-90, 153-174; *idem,* AugL 2(1952)201-204; *idem,* AugL 3(1953)5-20, 328-340. — V. Capánaga, La deificación en la soteriología agustiniana: AugMag II, 745-754. — E. Braem, Ons Goddelijk Kindschap volgens Sint Aug. Filii in Filio: AugL 4(1954)196-204. — L. Cristiani, Luther et St. Aug.: AugMag II, 1029-1038. — J. Cadièr, Calvin et St. Aug.: AugMag II, 1039-1056. — U. Saarnivaara, Die Rechtfertigung nach Aug. und nach Luther: *Luth Rundblick* 3(1955)164-172. — G. Bavaud, La doctrine de la justification d'après st. Aug. e la Reforme: REAug 5(1959)21-32. — A. Turrado, La inhabitación de la Sma. Trinidad en los justos según la doctrina de S. A.: AugMag I, 583-593; *idem,* Dios en el hombre. Plenitud o tragedia. Madrid, 1971. — V. Carbone, La inabitazione dello Sp. S. nelle anime dei giusti secondo la dottrina de S. Ag. Rome, 1961. — G. De Ru, De rechvaardiging bij Aug. verleken met de leer der iustificatio bij Luther en Calvin. Wageningen, 1966. — J. Baur, Salus Christiana. Gütersloh, 1968. — G. Bavaud, Le mystère de la justification: FreibZPhTh 19(1972)127-143. — P. Wilson-Kastner, Grace as Participation in the Divine Life in the Theology of A.: AugStudies 7(1976)135-152.

3. *Helping Grace:* H. Rondet, Gratia Christi. Paris, 1948. — A. Trapè, S. Ag. e le correnti teol. eterodosse, in s. Ag. e le grandi correnti. Tolentino 1956, 221-260. — H. Rondet, La liberté et la grâce dans la théologie augustinienne, in St. Aug. parmi nous. Paris 1954, 199-222. — R. Garrigou-Lagrange, La grâce efficace et la grâce suffisante selon st. Aug.: Ang 31(1954)243-251; *idem,* L'équilibre supérieur de la pensée de saint Aug. dans la question de la grâce: AugMag II, 763-771. — J. Lebourlier, Grâce et liberté chez st. Aug.: AugMag II, 789-793. — Th. Deman, La théologie de la grâce: AugMag III, 247-263. — G. Nygren, The Augustinian Conception of Grace: SP 2 (TU 64). Berlin 1957, 258-269. — H. Rondet, La théologie de la grâce dans la correspondance de st. Aug.: RAug 1(1958)303-315. — Ch. Boyer, L'auditorium sine quo non: *Doct. Communis* 13(1960)5-18. — A. Sage, Les deux temps de grâce: REAug 7(1961)209-230: *idem,* De la grâce du Christ, modèle et principe de la grâce: REAug 7(1961)17-34. — E. Gailleux, La liberté augustin. et la grâce: MSL 19(1962)30-48. — P. Y. Emery, Le Christ notre récompense: Grâce de Dieu et responsabilité de l'homme.

Neuchâtel, 1962. — A. Trapè, Verso la riabilitazione del pelagianesimo?: Aug 3(1963)482-516. — A. Zeoli, La teol. Agost. della Grazia fino alle "Quaest. ad Simpl." Naples, 1963 (cf. REAug 12[1966]361-362). — R. Lorenz, Gnade und Erkenntnis bei Aug.: ZKG 75(1964)21-78. — A. Sage, Praeparatur voluntas a Domino: REAug 10(1964)1-20. — H. García Ochoa, Hacia una síntesis de la "gracia agustiniana." Madrid, 1965. — A. Sage, Augustinisme et théol. moderne: REAug 12(1966)137-156. — J. Pegueroles, La libertad y la gracia en S. Ag.: EE 46(1971)207-231. — G. Greschake, Gnade als konkrete Freiheit. Mainz, 1972 (cf. A. Zumkeller: AugStudies 5[1974]209-226 and B. Studer: FreibZThPh 21[1974]459-467). — G. Philops, L'Union personnelle avec le Dieu vivant. Gembloux, 1974. — A. Trapè, Libertà e grazia nella storia della salvezza, in *Provv. e Storia, Atti Sett Ag Pavese.* Paiva 1974, 45-57. — A. Vanneste, Nature et grâce dans la théologie de st. Aug.: RAug 10(1975)143-169. — J. Patout Burns, The Development of Augustine's Doctrine of Operative Grace. Paris, 1980.

4. *Predestination:* J. M. Dalmau, Predestinatio, Electio en el libro "De praed. sanctorum": AugMag I, 127-136. — L. Ciappi, La predestinazione. Rome, 1954. — G. Nygren, Das Prädestinationsproblem in der Theologie Aug. Göttingen, 1956. — J. F. Thomas, St. Aug. s'est-il trompé? Essai sur la prédestination. Paris, 1959. — G. Bavaud, La doctrine de la prédestination et de la réprobation d'après st. Aug. et Calvin: REAug 5(1959)431-438. — J. Chéné, St. Aug. enseigne-t-il dans le "De sp. et litt." l'universalité de la volonté salvifique de Dieu?: RSR 47(1959)215-224. — A. Sage, La prédestination chez st. Aug. d'après une thése récente: REAug 6(1960)31-40. — W. Boublik, La predestinazione. S. Paolo e S. Ag. Rome, 1961; *idem,* La predestinazione in St. Ag. Una risposta al P. Sage: *Divinitas* 5(1961)149-164. — J. Chéné, La théologie de St. Aug. Grâce et prédestination. Lyons, 1962. — J. Morán, El difícil equilibrio en el problema de la predestinación: Aug 2(1962)325-350. — A. Sage, Faut-il anathématiser la doctrine aug. de la Prédestination?: REAug 8(1962)233-242. — A. Trapè, A proposito di predestinazione: S. Ag. e i suoi critici moderni: *Divinitas* 7(1963)243-284. — F. J. Thonnard, La prédestination aug. et l'interprétation de O. Rottmanner: REAug 9(1963)259-287; *idem,* La prédestination aug. Sa place en phil. aug.: REAug 10(1964)97-123. — A. Sage, "Praeparatur voluntas a Domino": REAug 10(1964)1-20; *idem,* La volonté salvifique universelle de Dieu dans la pensée de St. Aug.: RAug 3(1965)107-131. — R. Bernard, La prédestination du Christ total selon St. Aug.: RAug 3(1965)1-58. — H. Rondet, La prédestination augustinienne: ScEccles 18(1966)229-251. — J. M. Rist, Aug. on Free Will and Predestination: JThSt 20(1969)420-447. — A. Zumkeller, Aug. über die Zahl der Guten bzw. Auserwählten: Aug 10(1970)421-457. — V. Grossi, Il termine "praedestinatio" tra il 420-435: Dalla lilnea agostiniana dei "salvata" a quella dei "salvati e dannati": Aug 25(1985)27-64 (Miscl. Trapè).

7. The Church

This is another cornerstone of Augustinian doctrine which is singularly rich and modern. Augustine developed his thought on the nature of the church in the Manichaean and Donatist Controversies; in the former he studies it as an historical fact and a motive of credibility, in the latter as a communion and as the mystical body of Christ. The difficulty encountered by some in interpreting his thought arises from the complex and mysterious reality of the church itself, a reality which is at the same time historical and eschatological, hierarchical and spiritual, visible and invisible, as Augustine always keeps in mind. Therefore, when he speaks of the church, he means either the community of the faithful built on the foundation of the Apostles, or the community of the just in pilgrimage through the world from Abel until the end of time, or, finally, the community of the predestined living in blessed immortality. It is necessary to distinguish and to combine these aspects as Augustine does.

With regard to the first aspect he defends the unity and universality, the apostolicity and the holiness of the church. He was above all the apostle and theologian of unity which supposes, when it is complete, the communion of faith, sacraments, and charity. To this triple communion is thus opposed heresy, schism, and sin, which is always a lack of love. The heretic is not the one who errs in faith (*Ep.* 43, 1), but the one who "opposes the Catholic doctrine manifested to him" (*De bapt.* 16, 23), i.e., opposes the *regula fidei* proposed by the church. This *regula* resounds in the baptismal symbol (*Serm.* 212-215: explanation and *redditio* of the symbol), in the councils "which have an eminently salutary authority in the church" (*Ep.* 54, 1) and in the *Sedes Petri,* "in which the primacy of the apostolic cathedra was always active" (*Ep.* 43, 7). Augustine has recourse to this cathedra both to recognize "with greater certainty and salutary utility" the true church (*Ep.* 53, 2) and to resolve doctrinal questions in an authoritative manner (*Serm.* 131, 10: the famous formula *"Causa finita est"* which recurs in other words in *C. duas epp. pel.* 2, 3, 5).

With regard to the communion of the sacraments, i.e., the church gathered together in the unity of sacramental signs (*Ep.* 54, 1), he resolves the old problem posed by Cyprian and makes a decisive contribution to ecclesiological and sacramental theology. He distinguishes between a valid sacrament and a fruitful sacrament and shows that baptism (the same must be said for orders) is valid even outside of the church, but is fruitful only within the church: "It is one thing not to possess it, another not to possess it in a useful manner" (*De bapt.* 4, 17, 24; 6, 1, 1).

The reason for the first assertion is that "baptism possesses its own holiness and truth because of Him who instituted it" (*C. Cre.* 4, 16, 19), who is its principal minister (*In Io.* 6, 7) and whose character it imprints (*In Io.* 6, 15-16; *In Ep. Io.* 7, 11; etc.).

The reason for the second is that he is not able to possess the grace proper to baptism who does not have charity, but he does not possess charity who rends apart unity: "Those who do not love the unity of the church do not have the charity of God" (*De bapt.* 3, 16, 21).

Another problem arises at this point, namely, that of the presence of sinners in the church because the church is not only the communion of sacraments but also the communion of saints. In connection with this difficult subject Augustine defends and illustrates, again, two points: a) the church is holy but this does not impede there being sinners within the church, for it is a "mixed" body; b) sinners do not contaminate the virtue of the good (*De fid. et op.* 5, 7; *Ep.* 105, 16-17) even if these sinners are the very ministers of the church. "I have said it often and I repeat it insistently; whatever we are, you can rest secure, you who have God as your Father and the church as your mother" (*C. lett. Pet.* 3, 9, 10).

This doctrine and that expounded above are based on two others which form the heart of Augustine's ecclesiology. The first is a Christological principle, that of the *Christus totus,* according to which Christ, as head, is always present and active in his body, the church; the church and Christ from one single person (*In Io.* 21, 8; *In ps.* 55, 3; *Ep.* 187, 40). The second is a pneumatological principle, that of the Holy Spirit as the soul of the mystical body (*Serm.* 267, 4), according to which the principle "of the communion which constitutes the unity of the church of God" is He who in God is the "communion of the Father and the Son" (*Serm.* 71, 20, 30). Therefore, "Only the Catholic church is the body of Christ . . . Outside of this body, no one is animated by the Holy Spirit (*Ep.* 185, 11, 50; *In Io.* 26, 13). Augustine is thinking here of one who is knowingly outside of the church, in which case "he can have everything but salvation" (*S. ad Caes. eccl. pleb.* 6).

But the church has broader dimensions than the institutional ones. It traverses all the ages and stretches towards eternity where it finds its fulfillment. Only then, in fact, will she be "without blemish, without wrinkle" (Eph. 5:27) since only then will the sinners be separated also exteriorly from the just (*Retract.* 1, 198; 2, 18). The church is thus essentially, though not exclusively, eschatological, just as is the Christian justification which it brings. Therefore he often describes the church as the community of the just or the people of God which traverses and writes the history of salvation. "Thus in this world, in these evil days, not only since the time of the bodily presence of Christ . . . but from the time of Abel, the first of the just, who was killed by his wicked brother, the church continues on her pilgrimage until the end of time between the persecutions of the world and the consolations of God" (*De civ. Dei* 18, 51, 2).

At other times, he sees the church as the community of the elect which includes all of the predestined, and them alone (*De cat. rud.* 20, 31). Because of this vision, which fits in well with his philosophical outlook, he sometimes seems to say that sinners are only "apparently" in the church (*De bapt.* 6, 14, 23; *C. litt. Pet.* 2, 108, 247), or that the just who do not persevere are not children of God. However, it cannot be doubted that for Augustine the former are really "in the bosom of the church" (*In ps.* 103, 3, 5), in its "interior" (*In ps.* 128, 8) and live in the same "congregation" under the "same shepherd" (*C. ep. Pet.* 3, 3, 19) *ipsa communione catholica continentur* (*Serm.* 5, 1); and that the latter, as long as they are just, really do possess justice, i.e., really are children of God, even if God foresees that they will not always be so (*De c. et gr.* 9, 20, 23). It cannot be doubted, likewise, that the church already here on earth is the Kingdom of God, even though not yet in a perfect manner: "Where there are found the two categories (bad and good), it is the church which is present; where there is only the second, it is the church of the future . . . Therefore even in the present age the church is the Kingdom of Christ and the Kingdom of Heaven" (*De civ. Dei* 20, 9, 1). Thus these are two stages of the same church (*Brev. coll.* 9, 16), Augustine repeats with insistence, not two churches (ibid., 10, 20).

In conclusion it can be said that Augustine had the great merit of analyzing and defining the reciprocal rapports of four realities essential to salvation: faith, the church, the sacraments, and charity. In this way, he created that synthesis which served as a guide to subsequent theologians.

Studies: K. Müller, Kirche und Reich Gottes bei Aug.: ZNW 27(1928)202-211. — P. Battifol, Le catholicisme de st. Aug. Paris, 1928[4]. — H. A. van Bakel, "Tyconius, Augustinus ante Aug.": NTT 19(1930-31)36-57. — F. Hofmann, Der Kirchenbegriff des hl. Aug. in seinem Grundlagen und seiner Entwicklung. Munich, 1933. — Th. Michels, Das Heilswerk der Kirche. Ein Beitrag zu einer Theologie der Geschichte. Salzburg, 1935. — E. Mersch, Le corps mystique du Christ, in *Ét. théol. hist.* II. Brussels 1936, 35-138. — W. Rambach, Ecclesia und Regnum Dei bei Aug.: Phil 93(1938)248-265. — G. Spanedda, Il mistero della Chiesa nel pensiero di S. Ag. Sassari, 1944. — P. Dabin, Le sacerdoce royal des fidèles dans la tradition ancienne et moderne. Paris, 1950. — G. Favara, La necessità della Chiesa secondo S. Ag. Acireale, 1950. — A. Oepke, Das neue Gottesvolk in Schrifttum. Gütersloh, 1950. — A. Müller, Ecclesia-Maria. Freibourg, 1951. — W. Kamlah, Christentum und Geschichtlichkeit. Stuttgart-Cologne, 1951[2]. — H. Eibl, Vom Götterreich zum Gottesstaat. Freiburg Br, 1951. — E. Staehlin, Die Verkündigung des Reiches Gottes in der Kirche J. Christi. Basel, 1951. — J. Beumer, Die Idee einer vorchristlichen Kirche bei Aug.: MTZ 3(1952)161-175. — A. M. La Bonnardière, Marthe et Marie figures de l'Eglise d'après st. Aug.: VS 34(1952)404-427. — Y. Congar, Ecclesia ab Abel, in Festschr. K. Adam. Düsseldorf 1952, 79-108. — G. Favara, Chiesa e grazia in S. Ag.: DT 55(1952)375-395. — E. Gilson, Église et Cité de Dieu chez st. Aug.: AHD 20(1953)5-23. — E. Benz, Aug. Lehre von der Kirche. Wiesbaden, 1954. — J. Ratzinger, Volk und Haus Gottes in Aug. Lehre von der Kirche. Munich, 1954; *idem,* Herkunft und Sinn der "Civitas-Lehre" Aug.: AugMag II, 965-979 (a response to A. Kamlah, op. cit. *supra*). — A. Poppi, Lo Spirito S. e l'unità del Corpo Mistoco in Ag.: *MFrancescana* 54(1954)345-398. — E. Hendrikx, Die Bedeutung von A. "De civitate Dei" für Kirche und Staat: Aug 1(1961)79-93. — E. Kinder, Reich Gottes und Kirche bei Aug. Berlin, 1954. — Th. Parker, St. Aug. and the Conception of Unitary Sovereignty: AugMag II, 951-955. — F. Refoulé, Situation des pécheurs dans l'Église d'après st. Aug.: STh 8(1954)86-102. — P. Rinetti, S. Ag. e l'"Ecclesia Mater": AugMag II, 827-834. — H. U. von Balthasar, Aug. Das Antlitz der Kirche. Einsiedeln, 1955. — K. Forster, Die ekklesiologische Bedeutung des corpus Begriffes im "Liber Regularum" des Tyconius: MTZ 7(1956)173-183. — J. Ratzinger, Beobachtungen zum Kirchenbegriff des Tyconius im "Lib. Regularum": REAug 2(1956)173-185. — Y. Congar, Civ. Dei et Ecclesia chez st. Aug.: REAug 3(1957)1-14. — J. Grabowski, The Church. St. Louis-London, 1957. — A. Piolanti, Il mistero della Communione dei Santi nella Rivelazione e nella Teologia. Paris-Rome, 1957. — M.

Pellegrino, Espíritu e institución en la eclesiología de s. Ag.: CD 171(1958)444-469. — S. J. Grabowski, La Iglesia y la Predestinación en los escritos de s. Ag.: *Augustinus* 4(1959)329-352. — M. Agterberg, Ecclesia-Virgo. Louvain, 1960. — D. X. Burt, Teoría agustiniana sobre la tolerancia en materia de religión: *Augustinus* 5(1960)369-404. — F. Hofmann, Die Bedeutung der Konzilien für die kirchliche Lehrentwicklung nach dem hl. Aug., in *Kirche und Überlieferung*. Freiburg-Basel-Vienna, 1960. — J. Ratzinger, Die Kirche in der Frömmigkeit des hl. Aug., in *Sentire Ecclesiam*. Freiburg-Basel-Vienna 1961, 152-175. — E. Lamirande, Un siècle et demi d'études sur l'eccles. de St. Aug.: REAug 8(1962)1-125; *idem*, Le temps de l'Église: RUO 32(1962)25-44, 73-87; *idem*, L'Église celeste selon St. Aug.: Ét Aug, Paris, 1963. — G. Bavaud, Le pécheur n'appartien pas à l'Église: *Orpheus* 10(1963)187-193. — A. Trapè, La "Sedes Petri" in s. Aug., in Misc. A. Piolanti. Rome, 1964, 57-75. — R. Crespin, Ministère et Sainteté. Paris, 1965. — M. Pellegrino, Chiesa e martirio in S. Ag.: RSLR 1(1965)191-227. — H. B. Weijland, Aug. en de kerkelijke tucht. Kampen, 1965. — D. Faul, Sinners in the Holy Church: SP 9 (TU 94). Berlin 1966, 404-415. — E. Lamirande, Anima Ecclesiae chez St. Aug.: REAug 13(1967)319-320. — U. Duchrow, Reino de Dios: *Augustinus* 12(1967)139-160. — H. Holstein, Le peuple de Dieu d'après la Cité de Dieu: *Augustinus* 12(1967)193-208. — H. M. Klinkenberg, Unus Petrus, in Ms. Mediaev. Berlin 1968, 216-242. — H. Petersen, Helligbed og autoritet i oldkirken. Copenhagen, 1968. — M. Reveillaud, Le Christ-Homme tête de l'Église: RAug 5(1968)67-94. — E. Sauser, Zum Bild der unselbständigen Kirche in der Theologie des hl. Aug.: CD 181(1968)474-801. — W. Simonis, Heilsnotwendigkeit der Kirche und Erbsünde bei Aug.: *Theologie und Philosophie* 43(1968)481-501. — J. F. Centeno, La dimensión sacramental de la Iglesia según s. Ag.: EstAg 3(1968)491-503. — E. Lamirande, Études sur l'Ecclésiologie de st. Aug. Ottawa, 1969. — S. Verges, La Iglesia Esposa de Cristo. Barcelona, 1969. — R. Palmero Ramos, Ecclesia Mater en s. Ag. Madrid, 1970. — S. Folgado Flórez, Principios de eclesiología agustiniana: Aug 10(1970)285-324. — W. Simonis, Ecclesia visibilis et invisibilis. Frankfurt, 1970. — H. J. Sieben, Zur Entwicklung der Konzilsidee: IV, Konsilien in Leben und Lehre des A. von Hippo. TheolPhilos 46(1971)496-528. — P. Zmire, Rech. sur la collégialité episcopale dans l'Église d'Afrique: RAug 7(1971)3-72. — H. Rahner, Symbole der Kirche. Salzburg, 1964. — P. Borgomeo, L'Église de ces temps dans la prédication de saint Aug. Paris, 1972. — S. Folgado Flórez, Sentido eclesial católico de la "Civitas Dei": Aug 14(1974)91-146. — T. J. van Bavel, B. Bruning, Die Einheit des "totus Christus" bei A., in *Scientia Augustiniana*. Festschr. A. Zumkeller. Würzburg 1975, 43-75. — S. Folgado Flórez, Dinamismo católico de la Iglesia en san Agustin. El Escorial, 1977. — J. Verhees, Heiliger Geist und Gemeinschaft bei A.: TEAug 23(1977)245-264. — J. Salaverri, Presencia dinámica de Jesucristo en la Iglesia según S. A.: *Misc. Comillas* 24(1976)125-143. — N. Escobar, Donatismo y santidad de la Iglesia: *Augustinus* 22(1977)323-330.

8. Sacraments

In addition to the general doctrine on the nature of the sacraments, Augustine expounded at length for polemical and pastoral reasons the particular doctrine of baptism, reconciliation, eucharist, and matrimony.

His thought has been widely studied but has not always been expounded in an unequivocal manner. Here as in other instances, it is necessary to keep in mind the various aspects of the dogma which he illustrates and defends. Thus his insistence on the necessity of baptism does not take away the efficacy of baptism of desire (*De bapt.* 4, 22, 29); or his insistence on the ecclesiological symbolism of the

Eucharist does not obscure his explicit affirmations of the real presence (the bread is the Body of Christ and the wine is the Blood of Christ: *Serm.* 227; 272; *In ps.* 98, 9; 33, 1, 10) and of the sacrificial nature of the Eucharist (*De civ. Dei* 10, 19-20; *Conf.* 9, 12, 32; 13-36). His words on public penance do not exclude the references to that penance which is not public, or *correptio secreta* (*De div. qq.* 83, *q.* 26; *De fide et oper.* 26, 48), just as the doctrine on the evil of concupiscence does not invalidate that on the goods of matrimony expressed in the well-known trinity of offspring, faith and the sacrament (*De b. con.* 24, 32; *De s. virg.* 12; etc.).

A select bibliography is provided below for further study.

Studies 1. *Sacraments in general:* E. Hocedez, La conception aug. du sacram. dans le tr. 80eme in Io: RSR 2(1913)1-29. — E. Nevent, La théologie sacramentaire de St. Aug.: DT 34(1931)3-27. — P. V. Kormyljak, S. Aug. i de efficacitate sacramentorum doctrina contra Donatistas. Rome, 1953. — M. N. Häring, The August. Axiom. Nulli sacramento iniuria facienda est: MS 16(1954)87-117. — P. Th. Camelot, "Sacramentum." Notes de théol. sacram. aug.: RT 57(1957)429-449. — J. Gaillard, St. Aug. et les sacrements de la foi: RT 59(1959)664-703. — L. Villette, Foi et Sacrement. I: Du Noveau Testament à st. Aug. Paris, 1959. — A. Vanneste, La sainteté et la foi du ministre et du sujet des Sacraments: ETL 39(1963)5-29. — P. Crespin, Ministère et Sainteté. Paris, 1965. — J. Morán, La concepción de sacramento en S. Ag.: EstAg 4(1969)321-364. — B. Bobrinskon, L'Esprit du Christ dans les sacraments chez Jean Chrys. et Aug., in Jean Chrys. et Aug. Paris 1975, 247-249. — B. Studer, "Sacramentum" et "Exemplum" chez saint Augustin: RAug 10(1975)87-141.

2. *Baptism:* P. Th. Camelot, "Sacramentum fidei": AugMag II, 891-896. — E. R. Fairweather, St. Aug.'s Interpretation of Infant Baptism: AugMag II, 897-903. — B. Leeming, Is Their Baptism really Necessary?: *The Clergy R.* 39(1954)66-85, 193-212, 321-340. — J. -C. Didier, St. Aug. et le baptême des enfants: REAug 2(1956)109-129; *idem,* Le baptême des enfants dans la tradition de l'Église. Tournai, 1959 (texts); *idem,* Faut-il baptiser les enfants? La reponse de la Tradition. Paris, 1967 (texts). — E. Sauser, Baptismus — baptismus cottidianus — u. Sündenvergebund in der Théol. des hl. Aug., in *Zeichen des Glaubens.* Freiburg 1972, 83-94. — J. Fernández Gonzáles, Antropología y sacramentos en San Agustín. Bases para la renovación del orden sacramental: RevAgustEsp 17(1976)193-216.

3. *Penance:* F. Hünermann, Die Busslehre des hl. Aug. Paderborn, 1913. — K. Adam, Die kirch. Sündenvergebung nach dem hl. Aug. Paderborn, 1917; *idem,* Die geheime Kirchenbusse nach dem hl. Aug. Paderborn, 1921. — P. Galtier, St. Aug. aut-il confessé: RAp 32(1921)221-224, 257-269. — B. Poschmann, Kirchenbusse u. correptio secreta bei A. Braunsberg, 1925. — P. Batifol, Études d'histoire et de théol. pos. Les origines de la pénitence. Paris, 1926[8]. — P. Galtier, Comment on écarte la pénitence privé: Greg 21(1940)183-202. — J. Vermeylen, Le cheminement de la pénitence selon st. Aug.: CollMech 51(1966)514-546. — A. M. La Bonnardière, Pénitence et réconciliation des Pénitents d'après st. Aug.: REAug 13(1967)31-53, 249-283; 14(1968)181-204.

4. *Eucharist:* L. Tarchier, Le sacrement d'E. d'après st. Aug. Lyons, 1904. — M. Blein, Le sacrifice de l'E. chez St. Aug. Lyons, 1906. — O. Blank, Die Lehre des hl. Aug. v. Sakramente der Eucharistie. Dogmengeschichtliche Studie. Paderborn, 1907. — K. Adam, Die Eucharistielehre des hl. Aug. Paderborn, 1908. — J. Vetter, Der hl. Aug. und das Geheimnis des Leibes Christi. Mainz, 1929. — G. Lecordier, La doctrine de l'E. chez st. Aug. Paris, 1930. — P. Batiffol, Études d'histoire et de théol. positive.

L'Eucharistie. Paris. 1930. — P. Bertocchi. Il simolismo ecclesiologico della E. in s. Ag. Bergamo, 1937. — Ch. Boyer, L'Eucarestia e i Padri africani, in A. Piolanti, *L'Eucaristia.* Rome 1957, 165-171. — L. J. van der Loof, Euch. et présence réelle selòn st. Aug.: REAug 10(1964)295-304. — W. Gessel, Eucharistische Gemeinschaft bei Aug. Würzburg, 1966. — A. Sage, L'Euch. dans la pensée de st. Aug.: REAug 15(1969)209-240.

5. *Matrimony* — a) *Matrimony & sexuality:* J. Peters, Die Ehe nach der Lehre des hl. Aug. Paderborn, 1918. — B. Alves Pereira, La doctrine du mariage selon st. Aug. Paris, 1930. — R. Orbe, S. Ag. y el problema de la concupiscencia en su marco historíco: RET 1(1941)313-337. — N. Ladomerszky, St. Aug., docteur du mariage chrétien. Rome, 1942. — M. Müller, Die Lehre des hl. Aug. von der Paradiesesehe und ihre Auswirkung in der Sexualethic des 12. und 13 Jahrh. bis Thomas von Aquin., Regensburg, 1954. — G. Bonner, "Libido and Concupiscentia" in St. Aug.: SP 6 (TU 81). Berlin 1962, 303-314. — G. Oggioni, Il matrimonio nei Padri. Venegono, 1963. — L. Janssens, Morale conjugale et progestogènes: ETL 39(1963)787-826. — F. Thonnard, La notion de concupiscence en phil. aug.: RAug 15(1969)113-131. — B. Honings, Morale agost. coniugale: Eph. Carmel 20(1969)259-319. — J. J. Hugo, St. Aug. on Nature, Sex and Marriage. Chicago, 1969. — M. Zalba, En torno a une interpretación agust.: *Augustinus* 15(1970)3-18. — A. Zumkeller, Aug. in der Diskussion unsere Zeit. *Cor Unum* 27(1969)83-91; 28(1970)12-24. — D. Covi, Il fondamento ontol. della sessualità umana secondo S. Ag.: *Laurentianum* 11(1970)375-395; *idem,* El fin de la actividad sexual según s. Ag.: *Augustinus* 17(1972)47-65; *idem,* La ética sexual según s. Ag.: *Augustinus* 18(1973)303-315; *idem,* El valor y el fin de la actividad sexual matrimonial según s. Ag.: *Augustinus* 19(1974)113-126. — C. Morán, Un capítulo en la historia de la moral matrimonial: EstAg 8(1973)329-353. — N. Cipriani, Una teoria neoplatonica alla base dell'etica sessuale di S. Ag.: Aug 14(1974)351-361. — E. S. Lodovici, Sessualità matrimonio e concupiscenza in s. Ag., in *Etica sess. e matr. nel crist. delle orig.* Milan 1976, 212-272. — J. Doignon, Une définition oubliée de l'amour conjugal édénique chez Augustin: piae caritatis adfectus (Gen. ad. litt. 3, 21, 33): VC 19(1982)25-36.

b) *Indissolubility of marriage:* M. F. Berrouard, St. Aug. et l'indissolubilité du mariage: RAug 5(1968)139-155. — H. Crouzel, L'Église primitive face au divorce. Paris, 1971. — G. Pelland, Le dossier patristique relatif au divorce: Sc et Esprit 24(1972)285-312; 25(1973)99-119. — B. Gherardini, Appunti per uno studio della sacramentalità del matrimonio in s. Agostino: *Lateranum* 52(1976)122-149.

c) *The goods of matrimony:* A. Reuter, S. Aur. Aug. doctrina de bonis matrimonii. Rome, 1942. — G. Armas, Hacia una ética agustiniana del hogar: *Augustinus* 3(1958)461-477; 4(1959)519-527; 6(1961)499-512; 7(1962)145-164. — J. Noonan, Contraception. A History of its Treatment by Cath. Theologians and Canonists. Cambridge, Mass., 1966[2].

d) *Virginity:* R. Hesbert, St. Aug. et la virginité de la foi: AugMag II, 645-655. — M. Agterbert, St. Aug. Exégète de l'"Ecclesia-Virgo": Aug 8(1958)237-266; *idem,* Ecclesia Virgo. Louvain, 1960. — J. M. Del Estal, El voto de virginidad en la primitiva iglesia de Africa: CD 175(1962)593-623. — D. Riccardi, Verginità nella vita religiosa secondo la dottrina de S. Ag. Rome, 1962. — J. Leonet, Situación de la verginidad en la espiritualidad augustiniana: RAEsp 6(1965)215-245. — A. Trapè, Introduzione generale: NBA 7, 1(1978)9-104.

9. Eschatology

Augustinian theology — of grace, of the church, of history — is decidedly eschatological inasmuch as it takes its orientation, illumination and significance from eschatology. The four final books of the *De civitate Dei* are concerned with eschatology (cf. p. 364). Some of

Augustine's positions were conclusive in this question and he gave a definitive form to Christian eschatology. He strongly opposed, in the name of faith and reason, the Platonic concept of history which ran contrary to the very nature of man and of happiness (cf. p. 403); made short shrift of millenarianism after having accepted it at first himself (*De civ. Dei* 20, 7; *Serm.* 259, 2) by explaining Apoc. 20:1-5 in an allegorical sense (it regards the spiritual resurrection and the Kingdom of God which is the church already here on earth); and especially against the Platonists he defended the resurrection of the body — real bodies even though no longer corruptible (*De civ. Dei* 22, 1-28). Repeatedly he clarified the tortuous problem of the eternity of punishment (*De civ. Dei* 21; *De fide et op.* 14, 21f; *Ench.* 67f; *Ad Orosium c. Pr. et Or.*) by observing that the words of Scripture must be taken "as speaking the truth" *(veraciter)* and not merely "as a threat" *(minaciter)* (*De civ. Dei* 21, 24, 4); considered that the church had correctly condemned Origen's apocatastasis (ibid., 21, 17); responded to the arguments of the "merciful" who defended various forms (six) of mitigation of punishment (ibid., 21, 17f); and said the final word on the question of whether those who shared in the resurrection would see God with their bodily eyes (ibid., 22, 29; cf. *Ep.* 92; 147; 148; *Retract.* 2, 41). He attempted to give an idea of celestial beatitude (ibid., 22, 30) by insisting on its social (ibid., 19, 5, 13; *In Io.* 67, 2) and Christological aspect (*De civ. Dei* 22, 30, 4) and on the character of "insatiable satiety" (*Serm.* 362, 29; *In Io.* 3, 21).

With regard to intermediate eschatology it is sufficient to note that Augustine does not hesitate to admit the existence of purgatory (*Ench.* 69; *De civ. Dei* 21, 13; 21, 16; *In ps.* 37, 3) in which, according to what "has been handed down by the fathers and is upheld by the custom of the universal church," souls are aided by the "saving sacrifice" and by the good works of the faithful (*Serm.* 172, 2; cf. *Conf.* 9, 12, 32). But he also admits that these souls will not enjoy beatitude before the resurrection, but only a "consolation of deferment": *solacium dilationis* (*Serm.* 280, 5; cf. *Ench.* 109; *De Gen. ad litt.* 12, 35, 68).

Studies: A. Lehaut, L'éternité des peines de l'enfer dans st. Aug. Paris, 1912. — C. Hartmann, Der Tode in seiner Beziehung zum menschl. Dasein bei Aug. Giessen, 1932. — H. Eger, Die Eschatologie Augustinus. Greifswald, 1933. — E. Lewalter, Eschatologie u. Weltgeschichte in der Gedankenwelt Aug.'s: ZKG 53(1934)1-51. — R. Lorenz, Fruitio Dei bei Aug.: ZKG 64(1950)75-132. — J. C. Plumpe, Mors secunda, in Mél. De Ghellinck, I. Gembloux, 1951, 387-403. — M. Lods, L'espérance chrétienne d'Origène à Aug.: *Bull Fac libre Th Paris* 15(1952)18-39. — N. Wicki, Die Lehre von der himmlischen Seligkeit in der Mittelalt. Scholastik. Freibourg, 1954. — J. Gavigan, S. Aug. doctrina de purgatorio praesertim in opere *De civ. Dei:* CD 167(1954)283-296. — J. Hubaux, St. Aug. et la crise eschatologique à la fin du IV s.: *Ac Roy Belgique Bil Let Sc* 40(1954)658-673; *idem,* St. Aug. et la crise cyclique: AugMag II, 943-950. — G. Folliet, La typologie du sabbat chez st. Aug.: REAug 2(1956)371-390. — J. Hubaux, Rome et

Véies. Paris, 1958. — Th. E. Clarke, St. Aug. and Cosmic Redemption: TS 19(1958)133-164. — Ch. Mohrmann, Locus refrigerii lucis et pacis: QLP 39(1958)196-214. — J. Ntedika, L'évolution de la doctrine du purgatoire chez st. Aug. Paris, 1966. — B. Lohse, Zur eschatologie des älteren Aug. (*De civ. Dei* 20, 9): VC 21(1967)221-240. — J. Ntedika, L'évocation de l'au-delà dans la prière pour les morts. Paris, 1971.

SPIRITUAL DOCTRINE

1. Characteristics

Augustine has exercised a decisive and continuous influence on Western Christian spirituality. This is due not only to the fact that he defended the theological foundations of the spiritual life, especially with regard to the doctrine of grace, but also to the fact that he developed and carefully examined the essential points of this life and showed their intimate relation to the great Christian mysteries: the Trinity, Christ, the church, and justification. It can therefore be said that Augustinian spirituality is at once Trinitarian, Christological, ecclesiological, anthropological, and — because of the source from which it is continuously nourished — biblical. It is therefore characterized by the following points:

1. It is completely oriented to the worship and love of the Trinity: "(Man) must relate every living thing to recollection, contemplation and love of the sublime Trinity in such a way that the Trinity becomes the object of his recollection, of his contemplation, of his love" (*De Trin.* 15, 20, 39). The concluding prayer of the *De Trinitate* — a work undertaken for this practical motive as well as for the speculative aspect — responds to this fundamental precept as it says among other things, "(Lord, God Trinity) may I be mindful of you, understand you, love you. Increase these gifts in me until you have entirely reformed me" (ibid., 15, 28, 51).

2. Augustine's spirituality finds its center in Christ who is *via* and patria; *via* as man, *patria* as God. We go to him by means of him (*Serm.* 123, 3). "There was not nor could there have been a more suitable way for healing our distress" than the incarnation and death of Christ (*De Trin.* 13, 10, 13). His example is the most effective remedy against our ills (*De ag. chr.* 11, 12), the example of all the virtues (*De v. rel.* 16, 32; *Conf.* 4, 12, 18) and of the beatitudes of the Gospel (*De s. virg.* 28). In him, God has shown us "how much He has loved us and as what type of people He has loved us: how much so that we might not despair, as what type of people in order that we might not become proud" (*De Trin.* 4, 1, 2). Christ is the entire life of the Christian: "Our knowledge is Christ; our wisdom is again the same Christ . . . By means of him we tend towards him, by means of knowledge we tend towards wisdom, all the same without departing from one and the same Christ" (*De Trin.* 13, 19, 24).

3. This spirituality is inserted into the life of the church to such an extent that love for the church becomes the measure of Christian perfection. "We are convinced, brothers, that one possess the Holy Spirit to the extent which he loves the church of Christ" (*In Io.* 32, 8). From this conviction arises his sorrowful appeal: "Let us love the Lord our God, let us love His church; God as Father, the church as mother . . . no one is able to offend the bride and merit the friendship of the bridegroom" (*In ps.* 88, 2, 14).

4. The essential task of Augustinian spirituality is the restoration of the image of God in man. Sin discolors this image, deforms and obscures it and renders it worn out, old, imprisoned and sick. The Holy Spirit, on the other hand, revives, reforms, illuminates, renews, frees, heals, and restores it. These are all images Augustine uses to express the mysterious action of grace. This is the theme of many precious pages of the *De Trinitate* (especially in books XIV and XV), the structure of which, in the second part, is designed in such a way as to lead the reader from the consideration of the natural image to the restoration of the supernatural image which is wisdom (*De Trin.* 15, 6, 10). "The likeness to God will be perfect in this image when the vision of God will be perfect" (ibid., 14, 17, 23).

5. This is a spirituality which draws its nourishment from meditation on Scripture. Augustine dedicated to this meditation all the hours which he found free "from the necessity of restoring the body and of attending to the spirit and from the services which we owe people, or which we do not owe, but render nevertheless" (*Conf.* 11, 2, 2), and he prayed that the Lord might open for him the secrets of the Scripture (ibid.). The last three books of the *Confessions* are a notable example of this love and this method of his. Scripture is the teacher of virtue and a mirror without illusion (*Serm.* 49, 5) whose content is summed up in two themes: Christ (*Conf.* 11, 2, 4) and charity (*Serm.* 350, 2). Indeed, all of Scripture "speaks of Christ and commends charity" (*De cat. rud.* 4, 8).

2. Essential Points

The essential points of Augustine's spiritual doctrine can be summarized under the following headings: the universal vocation to holiness; charity as the center, soul and measure of Christian perfection; humility as the indispensable condition for the development of charity; purification as the law of interior ascent; prayer as a duty and a necessity, the means and the end of spiritual life; and the degrees of the spiritual life.

Each of these headings opens onto a vast doctrinal horizon which can scarcely be indicated, much less summarized, except by brief references.

1. With regard to the universal vocation to holiness, Augustine displayed an admirable equilibrium. If on the one hand he, like many of the Fathers, praised consecrated virginity and maintained against Jovinian that it is, *iure divino,* superior to matrimony (*De s. virg.* 1, 1), if he enthusiastically propagated and organized monastic life for men and women (*De op. mon.; Serm.* 355 and 356) and emphasized voluntary poverty, he also, on the other hand, defended the fact against certain Pelagian theses that all Christians, including the rich, if they live according to the Gospel, can obtain salvation (*Ep.* 157, 4, 23-29) and even perfection. Indeed, he does not compare the states of life but rather the persons who embrace these states and repeats in no uncertain terms that a married person can be more perfect than one consecrated to virginity if he is more obedient, more humble and more devout. "Not only is one who is obedient to be preferred to one who is disobedient, but even the married person who is more obedient is to be preferred to the virgin who is less obedient" (*De b. con.* 23, 28, 30). Likewise, it is certain that "humble spouses follow the Lamb more easily than do proud virgins" (*De s. virg.* 51, 52).

Even more, it is possible that spouses, but not virgins, can be ripe for martyrdom, the supreme degree of Christian perfection (ibid., 45-47; *Serm.* 354, 5). All depends on the degree of charity which each attains.

2. With regard to his teaching on charity, Augustine has two great merits: that of having made clear the essential prerogatives of charity by organizing Christian knowledge and wisdom around it, and that no less important of having analyzed the sentiment of fear which either accompanies or is opposed to charity.

Augustine's teaching on love has been indicated above. It can be added here that Augustine sees in charity the content of Scripture (*De d. chr.* 1, 35, 39; 3, 10, 15; *Serm.* 350), the goal of theology (*De Trin.* 14, 1, 3), the synthesis of philosophy and the secret of good government (*Ep.* 137, 5, 17), the essence and the measure of Christian perfection (*De nat. et gr.* 70, 84), the sum of all the virtues (*De mor. Eccl. cath.* 1, 15, 25; *Ep.* 155, 4, 13), the inspiration of grace (*C. duas epp. Pel.* 4, 5, 11; *In Io.* 26, 4-5), the gift on which all the gifts of the Holy Spirit depend (ibid., 87, 1), the single virtue with which no one can be evil (ibid., 32, 8), the one thing which distinguishes good works from bad (*In ep. Io.* 7, 8; 8, 9).

He emphasizes the dynamism of charity which is expressed in the constant desire for growth (*De perf. iu. hom.; Serm.* 169, 15, 18), its radical nature which excludes all compromise and demands total dedication (*Serm.* 34, 4, 7; 334, 3), its selflessness, which does not permit one to love for any motive other than the person loved, since "that which is not loved for itself is not loved" (*Sol.* 1, 13, 22). This does not exclude the desire for reward when this reward is God Himself. To love God "freely," a fundamental thesis of spiritual Augustinianism, means not to desire anything from God other than God (*In ps.* 55, 17; 85, 11; 127, 9): "This is what it means to love God freely, to hope for God from God" (*Serm.* 334, 3). Hence there arises his insistence on the theme of fear. He distinguishes clearly between servile fear — the fear of punishment — and chaste or filial fear: the former is opposed to charity and the latter is inseparable from it (*In Io.* 43, 7). He further distinguishes, though less explicitly, between the servile fear which does not exclude the will to sin and which is similar to the fear of a thief or a wolf (*De nat. et gr.* 57, 67; *Serm.* 161, 8; 178, 10), and that which does exclude this will and is therefore "good and useful" (*In ps.* 127, 8) and prepares a place for charity (*Serm.* 156, 14; *In ep. Io.* 9, 4).

He furthermore emphasizes the assimilative faculty of love by which "each person is like unto that which he loves" (*In ep. Io.* 2, 14).

The outline given here, which was filled out in many pages — the Bishop of Hippo never tired of speaking of this subject (*In ep. Io.* 9, 8) — merited for him the title of Doctor of Charity. To this there can rightly be added that of Doctor of Humility, since he spoke of this virtue with the same insistence.

3. In Augustine's judgment humility is inseparable from charity — *ubi humilitas ibi caritas (In ep. Io., prol.)* — for which it constitutes the foundation (*Serm.* 69, 1), the approach (*Ep.* 118, 22) and the dwelling (*De s. virg.* 51, 52). It is humility which distinguishes the city of God from the city of this world (*De civ. Dei, praef.;* 14, 13, 2; 14, 28). He describes the nature, roots and the fruit of humility. Its nature consists in recognizing ourselves for what we are (*Ep.* 137, 4). Its roots are, essentially, three: the metaphysical root or creation, because of which we have of our own accord only limits and thus error and sin (*In Io.* 5, 1); the theological root or gratuitousness of grace, by which even our merits are a gift of God (*Ep.* 186, 10), who forgives us even the sins we have not committed (*Conf.* 2, 7, 15; *Serm.* 99, 6); and the Christological root or the teaching and example of Christ, who brought this virtue into the world (*In ps.* 31, 18). The fruits of humility are many but can likewise be reduced to three: fortitude (*In ps.* 92, 3), victory (*Serm.* 163, 9), magnanimity: *ubi humilitas, ibi maiestas (Serm.* 160, 4).

4. Another condition for the development of charity is purification or asceticism. He rejects the metaphysical basis of asceticism as provided by the Manichaeans and the Platonists, but recognizes and emphasizes that of Saint Paul (Gal. 5:17; Rom. 7:14-25). He states the rule in these terms: "The nourishment of charity is the diminution of greed, its perfection (which is not of this world) is the absence of

greed" (*De div. qq.* 83, *q.* 36, 1; *De doct. chr.* 3, 10, 16). On the basis of this rule he twice presents a detailed self-examination (*Sol.* 1, 6, 12-14, 26; *Conf.* 10, 28, 39-39, 64) — Augustine was a true ascetic — and taught the faithful to do likewise (*In ps.* 31, 2, 5; 143, 6, etc.) by summarizing his teaching in this aphorism: "All our striving in this life consists in healing the eye of the heart in order that it may see God" (*Serm.* 88, 5). But he admonishes that "the strivings of lovers are not burdensome . . . because when one is in love either he does not feel the burden or he loves to feel it" (*De b. vid.* 21, 26).

5. The most important chapter of Augustinian spiritual doctrine, and that which has exercised the most continuous and efficacious influence on succeeding generations is the chapter on prayer. Augustine was a man of prayer and a great teacher of prayer even though, aside from *Ep.* 130, he did not compose a treatise on the subject. He nevertheless developed all the aspects of the theology of prayer: its nature, which he identified with conversion of heart (*De serm. Dni.* 2, 3, 14) and with desire (*In ps.* 37, 13; *Serm.* 80, 7); the motive or reason for prayer, which does not lie in informing God of what He knows but in preparing the soul for what He wants to give to it (*Ep.* 130, 17); the necessity of prayer which is bound essentially to the necessity of grace, since "God has desired that in spiritual combat we might fight rather with prayers than with our own strength" (*C. Iul. op. imp.* 6, 15); interiority, which resolves many of the problems inherent in prayer (*Ep.* 130, 22); and the social nature of prayer or the utility of prayer for others. Indeed he wrote that it was necessary to pray "for those who have not yet been called in order that they may be: perhaps they have been predestined in such a way that they be admitted by our prayers" (*De d. pers.* 22, 60). Augustine also studied the supernatural aspect or grace of prayer inasmuch as prayer is the means for obtaining grace but is, in its turn, the effect of grace: "It is known that there are divine gifts which God gives also to those who do not pray, such as the beginning of faith, and divine gifts which He gives only to those who pray, such as final perseverance" (ibid., 16, 39); its efficacy, which is conditioned by petitioning in the name of the Savior and thus according to the order of salvation (*In Io.* 73); and its Christocentricity or the presence of Christ in the one who prays. On this last point he offers the following effective synthesis: "Christ prays for us, prays in us, is prayed to by us; he prays for us as our Priest, he prays in us as our Head, is prayed to by us as our God. We therefore recognize our voice in him and his in us" (*In ps.* 85, 1).

6. Prayer accompanies the gradual ascent of the soul toward God. Augustine often spoke of the degrees of the spiritual life. He speaks of these for the first time in the *De quantitate animae* where he distinguishes and describes the four degrees which he calls virtue,

serenity, entrance (into light), and repose (in light) or contemplation. The first degree involves the effort of purification, especially the practice of temperance and justice; the second, constancy and quiet or interior health; the third, the directing of the sight toward the object of vision; the fourth, a prolonged repose in the contemplation of truth (*De q. an.* 33, 73-76). To these degrees there correspond those of beginning, proficient, great or fortified, and perfect charity (*De n. et gr.* 70, 84; *In ep. Io.* 5, 4). He returns to them a second time in the *De sermone Domini in monte* where he draws a relation between the beatitudes, the gifts of the Holy Spirit and the petitions of the Our Father and offers a program of spiritual life which goes from the foundation, which is the poverty of spirit to which is related the gift of fear, the beginning of wisdom, to the summit which is the blessedness of peace, the fruit of the possession of wisdom (*De serm. Dni.* 1, 1, 3-4, 12; 2, 5, 17-11, 39). He returns in the *De doctrina christiana* 2, 7, 9-11 to the gifts of the Holy Spirit as a progressive ascent from fear to wisdom.

3. Summit

Augustine dwells insistently and at length on contemplation, the summit of the spiritual life, for in addition to being an ascetic, he was also a mystic and his experience resounds in his words. He speaks of this directly in several places in the *Confessions:* 7, 17, 23 (before his conversion); 9, 10, 23-26 (the well-known ecstasy at Ostia); and 10, 40, 65 (not infrequent mystical experiences). He describes this contemplation by means of a philosophical scheme, but one filled with Christian content. He uses the same scheme and the same content in his addresses to the people (*In ps.* 41, 7-10).

Augustine made a dual contribution to the delicate and difficult question of contemplation: he described the nature and the fruits of contemplation and proposed the principles for reducing contemplation and action, or, in other words, interior life and active apostolate, to a unity. Contemplation is the "highest and most secret" reward of the strivings of asceticism (*De q. an* 33, 74) and consists in an experiential knowledge, i.e., one that is loving and, although in obscurity, full of the light of divine things: an "attaining them," a "touching them," a "gathering together" in them of all the faculties of the soul and of one's own being (*De lib. arb.* 2, 16, 41). He constantly describes contemplation in three instances: acesis, perception, and relapse. The ascesis is generally long and difficult, passes through detachment, recollection, silence, and demands all of one's interior strength. "And we were ascending by interiorly considering, exalting and wondering at your works; and we united to our spirits and transcended them in order to reach the region of inexhaustible abundance" (*Conf.* 9, 10, 24). The attainment of the goal is, on the other hand, sudden and dazzling, a fleeting perception: "And (the mind) arrived at Being itself in an impetus of trembling vision" (ibid., 7, 17, 23); "We grasped it a little (the source of wisdom) with all the impetus of our heart, and we longed for it" (ibid., 9, 10, 24); "For a moment only and in haste" (*In ps.* 41, 10). Then the "relapse" or the "return" to the tumult of words and to the demanding occupations which weigh down the flight of the soul (*Conf.* 9, 10, 24; 10, 40, 65).

These are fleeting but precious moments for the life of the spirit (*De q. an.* 33, 76) and for the apostolate (*Ep.* 48). They are a particular gift of grace, almost a call from above: "Following a mysterious sweetness, I know not what kind of hidden and interior delight, as though an organ were sounding sweetly from the house of God . . . we detached ourselves from the clamor of flesh and blood and reached the house of God" (*In ps.* 41, 9). But it is not a question here of an immediate vision of God (*Ep.* 92; 3; 147, 31; *De Gen. ad litt.* 12, 26, 53-28, 56), but of a profound experience by means of faith "as though in a mirror, in a vague manner" in anticipation that God may reveal Himself to us "face to face" (1 Cor. 13:12; *De cons. ev.* 1, 5, 8).

2. The theological equilibrium and personal experience which emerge in his teaching on contemplation come out to an even greater degree in his teaching on the relations between the two modes of Christian life, active and contemplative, of which he often speaks. He sees them symbolized in Martha and Mary (*Serm.* 103; 104; 179, 4-5) or in Leah and Rachel, the wives of Jacob, of whom the first is loved in view of the second (*C. Faust.* 22, 54-58), or in the Apostles Peter and John (*In Io.* 124), and he describes in detail the characteristics of these relations. He sees a profound tension between the one and the other of these ways of life (*Ep.* 10; 21; 48; *Serm.* 339, 4; MSCA I, 193) which is that which exists between *caritas veritatis* and the *necessitas caritatis.* He strives to resolve this tension with three principles. a) The first is the primacy of the contemplative life or life of prayer, study and an intellectual apostolate (he had chosen this life for himself after his conversion, cf. p. 348). b) The second is the obligation to accept the active life when the necessities of the church demand it. By active life he directly intends the priesthood: "If the church, your mother," he says to the monks, "will require your work, do not accept it out of eager pride, do not reject her out of cherishing indolence . . . do not prefer your life of quiet *(vestrum otium)* to the necessities of the church" (*Ep.* 48, 2). c) The third principle is the necessity to preserve in action the enjoyment of contemplation, the *dilectio veritatis.*

The text which summarizes these principles and is his most mature synthesis on this topic is found in *De civ. Dei* 19, 19. The text is worth citing: "No one must be so contemplative as to forget in the course of his contemplation that he must be of service to his neighbor, and no one must be so active as not to seek the contemplation of God. In contemplation, one must not seek an inert repose, but the discovery of the truth with the purpose of progressing in it without hesitating to share what has been discovered with others. In action, then, one must seek neither honor nor power in this life, since everything is vanity under the sun, but rather the goodness of the work itself." Therefore, "the love of the truth seeks out the quiet of contemplation *(otium sanctum);* the necessity of love accepts the activity of the apostolate *(negotium iustum).* If no one imposes this burden on us, let us apply ourselves to the study and to the contemplation of the truth; but if it is imposed on us we must accept it because of the necessity of charity. Nevertheless, even in this case, we must not completely renounce the joy of the truth in order that it does not happen that, deprived of that sweetness, we be oppressed by this necessity."

Studies: 1. *Spiritual doctrine in general:* A. Tonna-Barthet, De vita christiana. Rome, 1927[2]. — G. Hök, Trappstegskristendom, Ett arv fran Aug.: *Svensk Teol Kvartalskrift* 30(1954)262-272. — R. Hazelton, The Devotional Life, in *A Companion to the Study of St. Aug.* New York 1955, 398-416. — Román de la Inmaculada, La Sagrada Escritura domo fuente de vida espiritual según S. Ag.: RevEsp 14(1955)281-298. — Segundo de Jesús, Las pasiones en la concepción agustiniana de la vida espiritual: RevEsp 14(1955)251-280. — E. Boularand, Désintéressement: DSp III(1957)566-571. — F. R. Refoulé, Sens de Dieu et Sens de l'Église chez st. Aug.: NRTh 78(1956)262-270. — L. Chevallier, H. Rondet, L'idée de vanité dans l'œuvre de st. Aug.: REAug 3(1957)221-234. — O. Perler, Le pélerin de la Cité de Dieu. Paris, 1957. — A. Alcalá Galve, Interioridad y conversión a través de la experiencia de San Ag.: CD 170(1957)592-624; 171(1958)375-418. — F. J. Thonnard, Traité de vie spirituelle à l'école de st. Aug. Paris, 1959. — A. Penna, Lo studio della Bibbia nella spiritualità di s. Ag., in *S. A. vitae spir mag* I. Rome 1959, 147-168. — J. Morán, Apuntes para la Espiritualidad agustiniana: Rev Ag Esp 1(1960)360-403. — A. Tissot, St. Aug. maître de vie spirituelle. Le Puy, 1960. — A. C. Vega, S. Ag. padre de la espiritualidad occidental: Rev Ag. Esp 1(1960)95-106. — D. Riccardi, La verginità nella vita religiosa secondo S. Ag. Turin, 1961. — J. Morán, A. G. Niño, Ejercicios espirituales agustinianos: Rev Ag Esp 4(1963)17-51, 221-252; 5(1964)38-79, 362-427. — V. Capánaga, Ag. de Hipona, Maestro de la conversión cristiana. Madrid, 1974.

2. Charity: A. Teixidor, De mente S. A. circa timorem servilem: Greg 10(1929)501-536. — G. Combès, La charité d'après st. Aug. Paris, 1932. — G. Hultgren, Le commandment d'amour chez A. Interpr. phil. et théol. d'après les escrits 386-400. Paris, 1939. — R. Balducelli, Il concetto teol. di carità attraverso le maggiori interpretazioni patristiche e medievali di I Cor. 13. Rome, 1951. — O. Perler, Weisheit und Liebe. Olter-Freiburg Br., 1952. — A. Nygren, Eros et Agapé. Gütersloh, 1930-1937. — P. Adnès, L'humilité vertu spécifiquement chrétienne d'après st. Aug.: RAM 28(1952)208-233; *idem,* La doctrine de l'humilité chez st. Aug. Toulouse, 1953. — G. Doumain, Charité et vertu d'après st. Aug. Lille, 1953. — E. Boularand, La crainte servile et la crainte filiale dans st. Aug.: DSp II(1953)2483-2487. — S. Cuesta, La concepción agustiniana del mundo a través del amor: AugMag I, 347-356. — P. Adnès, L'humilité à l'école de st. Aug.: RAM 31(1955)28-46. — J. I. Alcorta, El mansaje agustiniano del amor: AugMag III, 357-364. — J. B. Bauer, Aug. und die Liebe. Die Funktion der Liebe im Leben in der Lehre Aug.: *Der Seelsorger* 25(1954-55)241-248,

295-299. — R. Brunet, Charité et Communion des Saints chez S. Aug.: RAM 31(1955)386-398. — N. Hartmann, Ordo amoris: Wissenschaft und Weisheit 18(1955)1-23, 108-121. — A. van der Zeijden, De liefde tot God volgens St. Aug. en Sint Bernardus: *Cîteaux in de Nederlanden* 6(1955)179-205, 241-258. — A. Turrado, La teología de la Caridad en san Tómas de Villanueva, maestro de espiritualidad agustiniana: CD 171(1958)564-598. — M. Huftier, La charité dans l'enseignement de st. Aug. Paris, 1960. — O. Schaffner, Christliche Demut. Des hl A. Lehre von der humilitas. Würzburg, 1959. — J. Burnaby, Amor Dei. London, 1960. — F. Ohly, Goethes "Ehrfurchten" — ein "ordo caritatis": *Euphorion* 55(1961)113-145. — J. B. du Roy, L'expérience de l'amour et l'intelligence de la foi trinitaire selon st. Aug.: RAug 2(1962)415-445. — A. Di Giovanni, La dialettica dell'amore. "Uti-frui" nelle preconfessioni de S. Ag. Rome, 1965. — J. Brechtken, Fruitio und Agape: ThGl 59(1969)446-463. — V. Capánaga, Interpretación agustiniana del amor. Eros y Agape: *Augustinus* 18(1973)213-278. — R. Johannesson, Caritas in Augustine and Medieval Theology, in Ch. W. Kegley, ed., *Phil. and Theol. of A. Nygren.* London-Amsterdam 1974, 187-202. — J. Burnaby, Amor in St. Augustine, ibid., 174-186. — O. O'Donovan, The Problem of Self-Love in St. Augustine. New Haven, 1980.

3. *Prayer:* F. Brambilla, Necessità della preghiera: la dottrina cattolica alla luce del pensiero de A. Rome, 1943. — Ch. Morel, La vie de prière de st. Aug. d'après sa correspondance: RAM 23(1947)222-258. — J. Delamare, La prière à l'école de st. Aug.: VS 86(1952)477-493. — G. Favara, Chiesa e preghiera in S. ag.: *Palestra del Clero* 36(1957)454-468, 489-499. — A. M. Besnard, Les grandes lois de la prière. St. Aug. maître de prière: VS 41(1959)237-280. — M. Villegas, La oración en san Ag.: CD 175(1962)624-639. — T. A. Hand, St. Aug. on Prayer. Dublin, 1963. — M. Abad, La oración misionera y sus fuentes según san Ag. Madrid, 1964. — C. Vagaggini, La teologia della lode secondo s. A., in *La preghiera nella Bibbia e nella tradizione patristica e monastica.* Rome 1964, 399-467. — G. García Montaño, La eficacia de la oración según la doctrina de San Ag. Madrid, 1966; *idem,* La oración y la voluntad salvífica de Dios según san Ag.: *Augustinus* 14(1969)295-304; *idem,* Doctrina agustiniana de la oración: *Augustinus* 18(1973)279-302. — M. F. Berrouard, Mystère et recherche. Une prière de saint Aug.: VS 128(1974)669-686. — G. García Montaño, La oración y sus efectos en la doctrina agustiniana: *Augustinus* 22(1977)151-179.

4. *Mysticism:* G. Gardeil, La structure de l'âme et l'expérience mystique. Paris, 1972[2]. — J. Marechal, La vision de Dieu au sommet de la contemplation d'après St. Aug.: NRTh 57(1930)81-109. — E. Hendrickx, Aug. Verhältnis zur Mystik. Würzburg, 1936. — G. Della Volpe, La mistica de Plotino a S. Ag. e la sua scuola. Messina, 1950. — F. Cayré, Mystique et Sagesse dans les Conf. de st. Aug: RSR 39(1951)443-460. — C. Butler, Western Mysticism. London, 1951. — M. Olphe-Galliard, Contemplation augustinienne: DSp II(1952)1911-1921. — A. Grilli, Il problema della vita contemplativa nel mondo greco-romano. Milan, 1953. — F. Cayré, La contemplation augustinienne. Paris, 1954[2]; *idem,* Notion de la mystique d'après les grands traités de st. Aug.: AugMag II, 609-622. — P. Courcelle, La première expérience august. de l'extase: AugMag I, 53-57. — P. Muñoz Vega, Los problemas de la experiencia mística a la luz del pensamiento agustiniano: AugMag I, 603-607. — A. Mandouze, Où en est la question de la mystique augustinienne?: AugMag III, 163-168. — H. Meyer, War Aug. Intellectualist oder Mystiker?: AugMag III, 429-437. — E. I. Watkin, The Mysticism of St. Aug., New York, 1957. — P. Blanchard, Connaissance religieuse et connaissance mystique chez st. Aug. dans les Conf.: RAug 2(1962)311-330. — L. Cilleruelo, Deum videre en san Ag.: *Salmanticenses* 12(1965)3-31; 13(1966)231-281. — E. Hendrikx, Aug. Verhältnis zur Mystik: *Scientia Aug.,* Festschr. A. Zumkeller. Würzburg 1975, 107-111. — I. Bochet, Saint Augustin et le désir de Dieu. Paris, 1982.

5. *Monasticism:* R. Arbesmann, Aug., der Vater der nordafrikanischen Mönchtums, in

St. Aug. Würzburg 1930, 35-61. — P. Monceaux, St. Aug. et St. Antoine: MSCA II, 61-89. — U. Moricca, Spunti polemici de S. Ag. contro i nemici e i falsi interpreti del suo ideale monastico: MSCA II, 933-975. — M. Mellet, L'itinéraire et idéal monastique de st. Aug. Paris, 1934. — N. Merlin, St. Aug. et la vie monastique. Albi, 1935. — G. Giardini, Ideale monastico de S. Ag. Rome, 1954. — A. Trapè, Il principio fondamentale della spiritualità agost. e la vita monastica, in *S. Ag. vitae spir magister* I. Rome 1956, 1-46. — L. Cilleruelo, Caratteri del monacato agostiniano, in *St. aug. vitae spir magister* I. Rome 1956, 43-75. — U. Domínguez del Val, Cultura y formación intelectual en los monasterios agustinianos: CD 169(1956)428-501. — D. Sanchis, Pauvreté monastique et charité fraternelle chez st. Aug.: *Augustinus* 8(1958)1-21. — J. J. Gavigan, De vita monastica in Africa Septentrionali inde a temporibus s. Augustini usque ad invasiones Arabum. Turin, 1962. — A. Manrique, Teología agustiniana de la vida religiosa. El Escorial, 1964. — L. Cilleruelo, El monacato de san Ag. Valladolid, 1966. — A. Zumkeller, Das Mönchtum des hl. Aug. Würzburg, 1968[2]. — A. Sage, La vie religieuse selon st. Aug. Paris, 1972. — G. P. Lawless, The Rule of St. Augustine as a Mirror of Perfection: Ang 58(1981)460-474.

CHAPTER VII

ADVERSARIES AND FRIENDS OF AUGUSTINE

by Vittorino Grossi

THE PELAGIAN CONTROVERSY FRIENDS AND ADVERSARIES OF AUGUSTINE

The Pelagian Controversy has gone down in history as essentially a question concerning the manner of understanding Christian anthropology. On the basis of Augustine's writings, of those of his friends who repeated his thought and of the doctrine of the church, it has been viewed through the course of the centuries primarily as a heresy condemned by the church. The current status of studies, from those of Plinval (1943) to the more recent ones of Greshake (1972) and Wermelinger (1976), makes it possible to distinguish better the logic underlying the polemic of the Pelagians from that of Augustine and his friends and offers a broader possibility than in the past of isolating their respective positions and rendering to each his due. All parties concerned stand to benefit from this, not least of all Augustine, whose thought is being freed both from Pelagian formulations refuted by him in the manner of *ad hominem* arguments but which did not express his true thought as well as from formulations of his thought which, although made by his disciples and not by Augustine himself, have nevertheless circulated as his own and have conditioned subsequent theological research to a great extent.

ADVERSARIES OF AUGUSTINE

The Pelagian Controversy arose with Pelagius, the figure who has gone down in history as the adversary who stood up to Augustine and who was the theorist of Pelagianism. Alongside Pelagius there is Caelestius, a figure who crops up continuously in the question, and Julian of Eclanum, active in the final stage of the polemic. These three individuals were the leading figures of a whole current of thought of the first half of the fifth century, known today as Pelagianism, which was connected with the intellectual circles of the age, especially Roman, and which extended itself almost everywhere: at Rome in Italy, in Sicily (Syracuse), in the Campania (Nola and Eclanum), in Northern Italy (Aquileia); in Gaul and Britain; in Africa, where, beginning at Carthage with the accusation of Caelestius by Paulinus of Milan, it encountered its decisive opponents in Augustine and his friends; and in the East, especially at Jerusalem, where it was received with greater sympathy. Given the vast diffusion of the Pelagian movement, often including mutual friends of Augustine and Pelagius, there grew up an anonymous mass of ideas and persons which obscured individual points and personalities. This rendered it difficult for contemporaries of the controversy to obtain a clear idea of the questions, and for us to distinguish the nuances of the polemic and to get a precise idea of the thought and personality of Pelagius himself.

In Roman intellectual circles, the ideas inherent in Origenism were carefully studied as were the positions of Jovinian, who, on the basis of the same baptismal grace granted to all, denied any difference of merit in the conduct of Christians, especially of the ascetics, monks and virgins. From the discussions which took place in those circles, there remain above all the commentaries on the Pauline epistles of Pelagius, Ambrosiaster and Augustine; Jerome's polemic against Jovinian, the *Quaestiones 83* of Augustine, etc. These were intellectual circles composed for the most part of laymen who were interested in questions of doctrine and who studied Scripture. Augustine, who together with his friends had formed one of those circles, mentions in *Retract.* 2, 38 "how some writings had been sent by some of the lay brethren who were students of Scripture."

The anti-Origenist and anti-traducianist *Liber de fide* of Rufinus the Syrian remains as a witness of the anti-Origenist circles at Rome. Jerome places Pelagius in the Roman Origenist circle, bound to Rufinus and Melania who, with Rufinus' translation of Evagrius Ponticus (SCh 170-171) and the *Historia monachorum,* had transmitted Origenism into the West. Furthermore, the layman, Lactantius, had given Rome an idea of Christianity founded on the human responsibility of freedom.

The Pelagian movement gathered many of these strains into one in the denial of original sin and the resulting opposition to any sort of traducianism with regard to the sin of Adam, and in its ambiguous attitude toward the practice of infant baptism and the understanding of divine grace. The themes discussed in these Roman circles and their Pelagian solutions, when they spread to Africa and came into contact with Augustine's ecclesiological-sacramental solutions for the Donatist problem, then drawing to a close, and the question of traducianism tied to the problem of the origin of the soul, came into conflict with the practice of infant baptism, given *in remissionem peccatorum.* There thus arose the African position in regard to Pelagianism which, in the history of theology, contributed to a deeper understanding of Christian anthropology understood in a necessary rapport with the grace of Christ for every person.

The Pelagian positions were received in Africa as "a new scandal in the church" (Aug., *Ep.* 177, 15), a new heresy (*Retract.* 2, 33). Pelagius and Caelestius were regarded as the leaders of the movement, men endowed with considerable persuasive skill (*Ep.* 175, 1) but "sinister authors of a new heresy" (*Ep.* 175, 1; *Ep.* 182, 3) and of the most pernicious of errors.

Studies: M. W. Miller, Rufini presbyreri Liber de Fide. A Critical Text and Translation with Introduction and Commentary (PSt 96). Washington, 1964 (cf. H. Rondet, Rufin le Syrien et le Liber de fide: AugL 22[1972]531-539, who does not accept Miller's conclusions and attributes the work possibly to Caelestius). — G. Bonner, Les origines africaines de la doctrine augustinienne sur la chute et le péché orig.: *Augustinus* 12(1967)97-116. — H. I. Marrou, J. R. Palanque, Prosopographie pélagienne, in *Prosopographie chrétienne du Bas-Empire,* I. Paris, 1967. — V. Grossi, Il battesimo e la polemica pelagiana negli anni 411-412(413): Aug 9(1969)30-61. — G. Bonner, Rufinus of Syria and African Pelagianism: AugStudies 1(1970)31-47. — G. Martinetto, Les premières réaction anti-augustiniennes de Pélage: REAug 17(1971)83-117. — E. TeSelle, Rufinus the Syrian, Caelestius, Pelagius: Explorations in the Prehistory of the Pelagian Controversy: AugStudies 3(1972)61-95 (Rufinus the Syrian is identified with Rufinus the Presbyter, companion of Jerome at Bethlehem). — G. Bonner, Augustine and Modern Research on Pelagianism. Villanova (Penna.), 1972. — P. Brown, Religion and Society in the Age of Saint Augustine. London, 1972 (especially p. 168-226: Pelagius and his Supporters: Aims and Environment, published from JThSt 19[1968]93-114): *idem,* The Patrons of Pelagius. The Roman Aristocracy between East and West: JThSt 21(1970)56-72; *idem,* Aspects of the Christianization of the Roman Aristocracy: JRS 51(1961)1-11. — A. Peñamaría, Libertad, mérito y gracia, en la soteriología de Hilario de Poitiers. Precursor de Pelagio o Agustín?: REAug 20(1974)234-250 (there is perhaps imposed on Pelagius and Augustine a formulation of the question which is foreign to them). — K. C. Huber, The Pelagian Heresy. Observations on its Social Context, Diss., Oklahoma St. Univ., 1979.

PELAGIUS

LIFE

Pelagius was born in Britain around 354. Given his cultural formation, he was probably the son of Roman officials who had emigrated there. He was large and clumsy in stature — for this reason he was easily the object of laughter — extremely polemical in character, a man of a fairly high cultural level (he spoke Greek), trenchant and concise as a writer. He came to Rome between 380-384 under Pope Anastasius, at which time he was baptized, or else between 375-380 during the first years of Gratian. He most likely studied law. Some sources (e.g., Marius Mercator) indicate that he was a monk, and he had to have followed this style of life as an individual rather than a cenobite. At Rome, he had the ear of the great Roman families, such as the *gens Anicia.* With the fall of Rome in the summer of 410 he sought refuge in Africa, at Carthage to be exact (Aug., *De gestis* 22, 46), perhaps in the company of Melania the Younger, Pinianus, and Albina. From there he continued to Jerusalem where he earned the friendship of the bishop, John, who defended him against the accusations brought against him by Orosius and the Latin exiles in 415. The discussions from Rome between Origenists (under the leadership of Pelagius) and anti-Origenists (under the leadership of Jerome) took place all over again in Jerusalem.

At the end of 415 a new charge was brought against Pelagius at Diospolis by two exiled Gallic bishops, Eros and Lazarus of Aix, on the basis of six propositions drawn from Pelagius' *Liber Testimoniorum* which affirmed the real possibility of man's impeccability in virtue of his free will on the basis of the possibility given in creation of acting according to God's commands. By speaking of this in terms of a theoretical possibility in man and by distancing himself from Caelestius, Pelagius avoided condemnation at Diospolis. After his acquittal which his friends extolled as a vindication of the Pelagian theses themselves, Pelagius wrote his *Chartula defensionis* as a piece of personal propaganda, which the deacon from Hippo, Carus, forwarded to Augustine (*De gestis* 1, 1; *Ep.* 177 and 179) and the *De libero arbitrio*.

In addition to Augustine's *De gestis* and his letters to the bishop Hilary (*Ep.* 178), to John of Jerusalem (*Ep.* 179) and Paulinus of Nola (*Ep.* 186), the Africans turned to Innocent I in a letter signed by five bishops (*Ep.* 175, 176, 177) explaining the error into which the bishops at Diospolis had fallen. Pope Innocent responded with three letters (*Ep.* 181, 182, 183 among the letters of Augustine: CSEL 44, 701-730) condemning Pelagius and Caelestius, though expressing hope for their recovery. Pelagius reacted by a letter to Pope Innocent (Aug., *De gr. Christi* 4, 5 and 30, 32) in which he claimed to be the victim of calumny. Innocent died in March of 417 and was succeeded by Zosimus, an Easterner, who, according to information supplied by Praylius, John's successor in Jerusalem, summoned Pelagius and Caelestius to the Basilica of Saint Clement toward the end of summer, 417. When a *libellus fidei* of theirs (in PL 48, 497-505) had been read, they were considered to be in conformity with the faith and were absolved from the condemnation which had been passed against Caelestius in 411. The charge brought against them at Diospolis was considered unjustified (*Ep.* 2 and 3 of Zosimus).

The African reaction took the form of a *concilium africanum,* the decisions of which *(Volumen)* were sent to Rome with the deacon, Marcellinus of Carthage. These decisions were based on the *libellus* containing the charge from Diospolis and on the *De natura* of Pelagius (the anti-Pelagian *libellus* contained in Augustine's *Ep.* 186?). From this period comes also the *libellus* of Paulinus to Zosimus concerning the Pelagian questions currently under discussion (CSEL 35, 108). Zosimus replied with *Ep.* 12 of March 21, 418, inviting all to establish peace and concord and *Ep.* 21, in which he did not accede to the Africans' desire for a revision of the absolution of Pelagius and

Caelestius. In addition to Rome, the Africans also turned to Ravenna, which issued a rescript of condemnation on April 30, 418, followed by a second one in the fall of the same year. The Pelagian movement was condemned as *superstitio* subject to the penalties of the *praescriptio* (PL 56, 490-492 and 499-500).

In the meanwhile, the Africans held a *concilium plenarium,* or general council, on May 1, 418, in the Basilica Faustus at Carthage under the presidency of Aurelius of Carthage and Donatianus of Telepte. Three representatives were elected from each province, including Alypius, Augustine, and Restitutus for Numidia. In eight or nine canons, according to the manner in which they are divided, they reaffirmed the positions of the *concilium africanum* and the condemnation of 411, i.e., they condemned the following Pelagian theses: that children are not also guilty in Adam (canons 1-3), that grace can be reduced to the possibilities of nature and free will (canons 4-6), that prayer is not necessary for the saints (canons 7-9) (CCL 149, 69-73; PL 56, 497-499 the anti-Pelagian *libellus* which, possibly together with the *De gestis* of Augustine and the *Ep.* 186 to Paulinus, constituted the material of the Council of Carthage).

In view of the imperial resoluteness against the Pelagians, Pope Zosimus sent his famous *Tractoria* (circular letter) to all the major episcopal sees both East and West in July 418. In this, he reaffirmed the position of his predecessor, Innocent, with regard to Pelagius and Caelestius, and requested all the bishops to subscribe to this.

Julian of Eclanum wrote two letters to Zosimus (Aug., *C. Iul. op. imp.* 1, 18) requesting explanations which did not prove acceptable. Together with eighteen other bishops he refused to sign the *Tractoria* and was condemned. There was also a *libellus* of the bishops of Northern Italy addressed to Augustine, the metropolitan at Aquileia, requesting a council against the *Tractoria* (PL 48, 508-526 and 45, 1732-1736). On the part of the court, another rescript of Honorius was issued on June 9, 419 against delays in applying the imperial decrees (PL 56, 493-494). Julian departed for the East along with some of his followers and Pelagius likewise left for Egypt. On July 9, 425, Valentinian III issued a rescript against Pelagianism in Southern Gaul (*Codex Theodosianus,* ed. Mommsen-Krüger 911-912). The Council of Ephesus explicitly anathematized the Pelagian teaching and its supporters.

Boniface and Celestine, the successors of Zosimus, continued the policy of their predecessors along the lines of the Council of Carthage and the *Tractoria* of Zosimus. The *Indiculus Coelestini* or *Capitula Coelestini* (called thus because transmitted with *Ep.* 21 of Celestine), an official document presenting the Roman position, is to be dated no later than 442. It contains three canons of the Council of Carthage (4-

6) which in turn, on the question of the *tradux peccati,* are derived from the letters of Innocent.

WRITINGS

The Pelagian writings, regarded in the past as a single *corpus,* are divided today into three groups: works definitely attributed to Pelagius, dubious works, works of other authors. The major contributions to the clarification of this problem were made by the following: C. P. Caspari (*Briefe, Abhandlungen und Predigten aus den zwei letzten Jahrhunderten des kirchlichen Altertums und dem Anfang des Mittelalters.* Christiana [Oslo], 1980). The Pelagian *corpus* published by Caspari is considered to be the work of the bishop Fastidius, who was also the object of studies by J. Baer (*De operibus Fastidii, britannorum episcopi.* Nuremberg, 1902). Followed by A. Souter (*Pelagius' Expositions of Thirteen Epistles of Saint Paul.* Cambridge, 1926), G. Morin (RB 15[1898]481-493; 34[1922]265-275, reprinted in RB 51[1939]128-136; 46[1934]3-17), and G. Plinval ("Recherches sur l'œuvre littéraire de Pélage": RPh 60[1934]9-42; *Pélage.* Lausanne, 1943; and especially "Vue d'ensemble sur la littérature pélagienne": RELA 29[1951]284-294). The approach adopted by A. Hammer in PLS I, 1101ff, based on the similarity of style, has been criticized by Morris ("Pelagian Literature": JThSt 16[1965]25-60), who insists rather on unity of content and the manner of citing the Scriptures. Further remarks and specifications were added by the CPL 728-766 and the contributions of the *Vetus Latina* I, 1 (B. Fischer, Verzeichnis der Siegel für Kirchenschriftsteller. Freiburg im Br., 1963²). A return closer to the positions of Plinval is noticeable in R. F. Evans ("Pelagius, Fastidius and the Pseudoaugustinian *'De vita christiana'* ": JThSt 13[1962]72-98; *Four Letters of Pelagius.* London, 1968). P. Courcelle's attributions to Eutropius should also be mentioned (*Histoire littéraire des grandes invasions germaniques.* Paris 1964³, 303-317).

The difficulty of a precise attribution of the Pelagian works existed already at the time of the polemic itself since, as Jerome states, Pelagius and his sympathizers often refused to assume responsibility for the Pelagian writings which were in circulation (*Dial. adv. Pelag.* 3, 14-16). On the other hand, the works of Pelagius himself show a certain consistency since it was difficult for him to abandon his original positions which he continued to propose anew in different words; a procedure pointed out by Augustine on various occasions (*De gratia Christi* 3, 13; *De gestis* 2; 23; 30; 54).

The works of Pelagius have been transmitted for the most part under the name of Jerome, although today part of them are attributed to Fastidius and part to Eutropius (Cf. "Eutropius," *infra*). The ascetical-moral writings which reflect the asceticism and the social conditions of the fourth and fifth centuries are attributed to the bishop Fastidius: *De vita christiana, De divitiis, De malis doctoribus, De castitate, Qualiter religionis* also known as *De possibilitate non peccandi* (Caspari, 114-119), and the *Epistulae* published by Morin (RB 1922, 1934 and 1939). Baer brought to light the unity of language and style in this literary production and Caspari and Ivo Kermer (*Das Eigentum des Fastidius im pelagianischen Schrift.* St. Ottilien, 1938) did the same for the unity of content, as did Morris, who attributes the *De Vita christiana, De divina lege* and the *De virginitate* to Fastidius. R. S. T. Haslehurst published an unsatisfactory English edition of Fastidius' writings in 1927 (*The Works of Fastidius.* London, 1927, text and translation).

There also appear under a false attribution the *De divina lege, De virginitate, De opprobriis,* the two *Epistulae* to the daughters of Gerontius: *De contemnenda haereditate* and *De vera circumcisione* (according to a hypothesis of Plinval, *Recherches* 33, 4, subsequently confirmed by J. Madoz in EE [1942]27-54, the second letter is a continuation of the first), the *Ep. ad Tyrasium* or *Titianum* (PL 38, 278 and 33, 1175) which Plinval (p. 43) attributes to Caelestius, and the *Commentary on the Epistles of Paul,* the best manuscript of which, published in 1550 under the name of Primasius, bishop of Utica, begins, *"incipit explanatio sancti Hieronymi in ep. ad Romanos."*

An overall treatment of the Pelagian writings can be found in PLS I, 1101ff, G. de Plinval (*Pélage,* p. 44-45) and Morris (JThSt 16[1965]25-60).

THE WORKS OF THE PELAGIAN "CORPUS"
(CPL 728-766; Greshake, p. 311-312)

A. *Authentic Works:*

Expositiones XIII epistularum Pauli: A. Souter, ed., *Pelagius' Expositions of Thirteen Epistles of St. Paul* (TSt 9, 2). Cambridge, 1926 (PLS I, 1110-1374).

Liber de induratione cordis Pharaonis: G. Morin, ed., in G. de Plinval, *Essai sur le style et la langue de Pélage.* Fribourg 1917, p. 137-203 (PLS I, 1506-1539).

Expositio interlinearis libri Iob: PL 23, 1475-1538 as distinct from that attributed to the priest Philop PL 26, 619-802 and from that of Julian of Eclanum studied by Vaccari (*Un commento a Giobbe di Giuliano di Eclano.* Rome, 1915).

De vita christiana: PL 50, 383-402.

Epistula ad Demetriadem: PL 30, 15-45.

De divina lege: PL 30, 105-116.

Epistula de virginitate: CSEL 1, 224-250.

Epistula ad Marcellam: CSEL 29, 429-436.

Epistula ad Celantiam: CSEL 29, 436-459.

Libellus fidei: J. Garnier, ed., PL 48, 488-491 and PL 45, 1716-1718.
Fragments are preserved of other writings of Pelagius, transmitted mainly by Augustine:

De fide trinitatis or *Libri tres de Trinitate,* frag. VI, in C. Martini, ed., *Ambrosiaster, de auctore, operibus, theologia.* Rome 1944, p. 189-210 (PLS I, 1544-1560).

Liber testimoniorum or *Eglogarum liber,* in Jerome, *Dial. adv. Pel.* 1, 25-32: PL 23, 542-550.

Augustine, *De gestis Pel.* 3, 6-7: CSEL 42, 57-59 and J. Garnier, ed., PL 48, 594-596.

De libero arbitrio, in Augustine, *De gr. Christi:* CSEL 42, 125-206; J. Garnier, ed., PL 48, 611-613; *Fram.* III *ms. parisiensis* 633, A. Souter, ed., *Proceedings of the British Acad.* 11(1910-11)32-35 (PLS I, 1539-1543).

De natura, in Augustine, *De natura et gratia:* CSEL 60, 233-299; J. Garnier, ed., PL 48, 599-606 (incomplete).

De amore; De bono constantiae, in Bede, *In Cantica Canticorum:* PL 91, 1065-1077; A. Brückner, *Julian von Aeclanum* (TU 15, 3). Leipzig 1877, p. 72-75.

Epistula ad Livaniam, in Augustine, *De gestis* 6, 16 (interpolated): CSEL 42, 68; in M. Mercator, *Commonitorium* II: ACO 1, 5, 1, p. 69.

Epistula ad Innocentium, in Augustine, *De gr. Christi* 1, 31, 33: J. Garnier, ed., PL 48, 610-611.

Epistula ad amicum, in Augustine, *De gestis Pel.* 30, 54: CSEL 42, 107.

Epistula ad discipulos, in Augustine, *De pecc. or.* 15, 16: CSEL 42, 177-178.

Fragmenta Vindobonensia: PLS I, 1561-1570.

B. *Writings similar to Pelagius:*

Epistula ad adolescentem: PLS I, 1375-1380.
Tractatus de divitiis: PLS I, 1380-1418.
Epistula de malis doctoribus: PLS I, 1418-1457.
Epistula de possibilitate non peccandi: PLS I, 1457-1464.
Epistula de castitate: PLS I, 1464-1505.
Consolatio ad virginem: PL 30, 55-60.
Epistula ad Claudiam: CSEL 1, 219-223.
Epistula ad Oceanum: PL 30, 282-288.

C. *"Pelagian" writings by other authors:*

Epistula ad virginem devotam: PL 17, 579-598.
Epistula de contemnenda haereditate: PL 30, 45-50.
Epistula de vera circumcisione: PL 30, 188-210.
Epistula ad Pammachium et Oceanum de renuntiatione saeculi: PL 30, 239-242.

Epistula de vera paenitentia: PL 30, 242-245.
Epistula "Honorificentiae tuae," in C. Caspari, *op. cit.*, p. 3-13.

With regard to their content, the writings of Pelagius can be divided into three categories:

1. Exegetical works.
2. Theological works.
3. Ascetical-moral works.

1. Exegetical Works

Pelagius' exegetical works, which are concise in their exposition, are useful above all for the question of contemporary translations of the Bible and their popularization of the Vulgate. The exegesis contained in these works is developed according to two rules: 1) The Scriptures, being the work of one and the same Spirit, cannot contain contradictions (*De Trin.; De induratione* 21); 2) The obscure passages are to be explained on the basis of clear ones (*De induratione* 9 and 11). Both of these principles must in turn be understood in light of the necessary justice of God which excludes every preference of persons and does not demand the impossible (*De castitate* 13; *Qualiter* 2; *De natura* 83).

Studies: Pelagius' Origins and Life: H. Zimmer, Pelagius in Irland. Berlin, 1901 (thesis of Pelagius' Irish origin). — J. B. Bury, The Origin of Pelagius: Hermathema 13(1905)26-35. — K. Adam, Causa finita est, in Festgabe A. Ehrhard. Bonn 1922, 1-23. — K. Müller, Der heilige Patrick, Anhang: Pelagius' Heimat: NGWG 1931, 113-115. — G. de Plinval, Le problème de Pélage sous son denier état: RHE 35(1939)5-21. — G. Bardy, Grecs et Latins dans le premières controverses pélagiennes: BLE 49(1948)3-20. — P. Grosjean, Notes d'hagiographie céltique 34. S. Jérôme, Pélage et Gildas: AB 75(1957)206-211. — R. F. Evans, Pelagius' Veracity at the Synod of Diospolis, in *Studies in Medieval Culture.* Western Michigan Univ. 1964, 21-30. — H. Ulbrich, Augustins Briefe zur entscheidenden Phase des pelagianischen Streites: REAug 9(1963)51-75, 235-258 (on the events of the years 415-418). — L. W. Barnard, Pelagius and Early Syrian Christianity: RTAM 35(1968)193-196.

Editions: Commentary on Paul: A. Souter, TSt 9, 2. Cambridge, 1926 (PLS I, 1110-1374). *Commentary on Job:* PL 23, 1047-1475. *Commentary on the Canticle of Canticles:* fragments in A. Brückner, Julian von Eclanum (TU 15, 3). Leipzig 1897, 74-75. *De malis doctoribus:* PLS I, 1418-1457, ed. Caspari, on the false interpretation of Scripture.

Studies: Sources: A. Souter, Pelagius' Expositions of 13 Epistles of St. Paul (TSt 9, 1). Cambridge 1922, 174-200. — A. J. Smith, The Latin Sources of the Commentary of Pelagius in the Epistles of St. Paul to the Romans: JThSt 19(1918)162-230 (Ambrosiaster); 20(1919)55-65 (Augustine); 127-177 (Rufinus). — H. J. Chapman, Pélage et le texte de S. Paul: RHE 18(1922)469-481; 19(1923)25-42. — H. Vogels, Der Pelagiuskommentar zu den Briefen des hl. Paulus: ThR 25(1926)121-126.

The Latin Text Used by Pelagius: (a text of Northern Italy? = Aquileia?) E. Nellessen: ZNW 59(1968)220-224. — W. Thiele: ZNW 60(1969)269. — H. J. Frede: *Vetus Latina* 24, 2(1969)283-284 (questions regarding the Pauline text used by Pelagius); *idem,* Pelagius, Der irische Paulustext, Sedulius Scottus (*Vetus Latina* 3). Freiburg, 1961; *idem,* Ein neuer Paulustext und Kommentar I-II. Freiburg, 1973-74 (regarding the necessity of a new critical edition of the Commentary on Paul of Pelagius on account of the numerous interpolations of pseudo-Jerome).

On the Latin Text of Paul Used by Pelagius and the Latin Translation of Theodore of Mopsuestia: H. B. Swete, Theodori episcopi Mopsuesteni in epistolas B. Pauli Commentarii. The Latin Version with the Greek Fragments I-II. Cambridge, 1880-1882. — E. Dekkers, Traductions grecques des écrits patristiques latins: SE 5(1953)193-233 (cf. 208-210 for Pelagian biblical texts). — F. H. Tinnefeld, Untersuchungen zur altlateinischen Überlieferung des I Tim. Der lateinische Paulustext in den Handschriften D E F G und in den Kommentaren des Ambrosiaster und des Pelagius. Wiesbaden, 1963. — C. Charlier, Cassiodore, Pélage et les origens de la Vulgate paulinienne, in *Stud. Paulinorum Congressus.* Rome 1963, 461-470. — K. Th. Schäfer, Der Paulustext des Pelagius, ibid., 453-460.

On the Prologue: G. De Plinval, Précisions sur l'authenticité d'un prologue de Pélage: Primum quaeritur: REAug 12(1966)247-253.

On the Pelagian Interpretation of Paul: H. H. Esser, Das Paulusverständnis des Pelagius nach seinem Pauluskommentar. Bonn, 1961; *idem,* Thesen und Anmerkungen zum exegetischen Paulusverständnis des Pelagius, in *Zwischenstation,* Festschrift K. Kupisch. Munich 1963, 27-42; *idem,* SP 7 (TU 93). Berlin 1966, 443-461.

Other Studies: C. H. Turner, Pelagius' Commentary on the Pauline Epistles and its History: JThSt 4(1903)132-141 (review of H. Zimmer, Pelagius in Irland). — E. Riggenbach, Unbeachtet gebliebene Fragmente des Pelagius-Kommentar zu den paulinischen Briefen. Gütersloh, 1905. — A. Souter, Prolegomena to the Commentary of Pelagius on the Epistles of St. Paul: JThSt 7(1906)568-575; *idem,* The Commentary of Pelagius on the Epistles of Paul: the Problem of its Restoration: *Proceedings British Academy* 2(1905-06)409-439; *idem,* The Relation of the Roman Fragments to the Commentary in the Karlsruhe ms.: JThSt 8(1907)535-536. — D. De Bruyne, Le prologue inédit de Pélage à la 1 Cor.: RB 24(1907)257-263. — E. Riggenbach, Eine wichtige Entdeckung für die Pelagiusforschung: ThLB 28(1907)73-75; *idem,* Neues über Pelagius: ThLB 28(1907)425. — A. Souter, The Commentary of Pelagius on the Epistles of St. Paul: *Expositor* 1(1907)455-467; *idem,* Another New Fragment of Pelagius: JThSt 12(1911)32-35; *idem,* Freiburg Fragments of ms. of the Pelagius commentary on the epistles of St. Paul: JThSt 13(1912)515-545 (résumé in ThLB 38[1913]42: New Manuscripts of Pelagius); *idem,* Pelagius and the Pauline Text in the Book of Armagh: JThSt 16(1915)105; — The Character and History of Pelagius' Commentary on the Epistles of St. Paul: *Proceedings British Academy* 7(1915-16)261-296. — D. De Bruyne, Étude sur les origines de notre Texte latin de saint Paul: RBibl 12(1915)358-392. — E. Mangenot, Saint Jérôme ou Pélage editeur des Epitres de St. Paul dans la Vulgate: *RevClergéfrançais* 1916. — H. Koch, Pelagio e la lettera agli Ebrei: Religio 11(1935)21-30.

2. Theological Writings

These works can be centered around the *De natura* of 414, the work which Pelagius' disciples Timasius and James sent to Augustine, who for the first time wrote publicly against Pelagius. The *De natura* upholds the fundamental possibility inherent in man's nature from creation to live according to the commandments of God and to be able to live without sin. Pelagius developed this idea in the *De libero arbitrio,* written after his acquittal at Diospolis. Free will is viewed as a *radix* implanted in man in a neutral state at creation which he then determines by his own choice. God's grace always enters in to aid this primary decision which, for Pelagius, is generally understood in terms of a challenge to follow the example of Christ. The other writings provide a concrete definition of these ideas: one group treats the question of what it means to be a Christian *(Ad adulescentem, De possibilitate no peccandi, De vita christiana);* another deals with the question of justice in man *(Ad Celantiam);* the writings on virginity take up the question of the nature of virginity, the possibility of virginity based in nature and the merit of such a choice *(Ad Demetriadem, De castitate, De virginitate);* and another group takes up the topic of freedom as the mediation of salvation for man and rejects all external fatalism *(De induratione cordis Pharaonis, De divina lege, Testimonia).* Specifically Trinitarian and Christological questions are contained in the *De Trinitate* and the *Libellus fidei* sent to Pope Innocent.

I. a) *De natura.* Fragments in Augustine (*De nat. gr.:* PL 44, 247-290; CSEL 50, 231-299), collected by J. Garnier (PL 48, 590-606 incomplete) and A. Brückner (Quellen, p. 60-64).

De libero arbitrio. Fragments in Augustine (*De gr. Christi:* PL 44, 359-410; CSEL 42, 123-206), collected by J. Garnier in PL 48, 611-613; three fragments of A. Souter in PLS I, 1539-1543.

b) *Testimonia* or *capitula* or *eglogae,* in PL 23, 542-550; French translation in BA 21, German translation in ALG II.

De vita christiana: PL 40, 1031-1046. In the manuscript tradition this work is always attributed to St. Augustine except in the ms. of Sankt Gallen and the ms. 232 of Monte Cassino. In the former, the *incipit* and the *explicit* attribute it to Pelagius: *incipit liber pelagii heretici . . . explicit de vita christiana pelagii heretici.* In the latter, the *incipit* and *explicit* give the name of Fastidius, perhaps under the influence of Gennadius (*De vir. ill.* 57: *Fastidius scripsit ad Fatalem quendam De vita christiana librum*). In both cases it is a question of an obvious correction. The considerable difference of a literary nature in comparison with the *Ep. ad Demetriadem* indicates that this work of a popular nature is to be attributed to a contemporary of Pelagius.

Studies: C. P. Caspari, *Briefe* . . . attributes the work to Fastidius. — R. F. Evans attempted the attribution to Pelagius in the article: Pelagius, Fastidius and the pseudo-Augustinian "De vita christiana": JThSt 13(1962)72-98. He points out that only in the 13th cent. did Pelagius' name disappear from all the mss. of the Expositiones. — G. Morin, Le De vita christiana: RB 15(1898)481-493 attributes the work to Pelagius, then in the article: Pélage ou Fastidius?: RHE 5(1904)258-264 accepts the thesis of Baer that it is a work of Fastidius (J. Baer, De operibus Fastidii britannorum episcopi. Nuremberg, 1902) which circulated under the name of Pelagius. — G. De Plinval, Recherches sur l'œuvre littéraire de Pélage: RPh 60(1934)9-42 considers it to be a work from the Pelagian circle but not of Pelagius. — I. Kirmer, Das Eigentum des Fastidius im pelagianischen Schriften. St. Ottilien, 1938, considers it to be a work of Fastidius.

c) *De divina lege:* PL 30, 105-116. The themes contained in this work, freedom, the sacraments, and the polemic with Jovinian, are similar to those treated in the *Ep. ad Demetriadem.* J. Morris (JThSt 13[1962]72-98) rejects the attribution to Pelagius because the text, "*Ego te Christianum volo esse, non monachum dici*" seems to contradict Pelagius' esteem for monasticism.

d) *De induratione cordis Pharaonis:* PLS I, 1506-1539, G. Morin, ed. The work bears the subtitle "Treatise on the vessels of honor and of shame" and was written after lengthy provocation (by Ambrosiaster?). The author addresses himself to whomever desires to reform his own life by rejecting all pagan fatalism according to which God created two categories of people, good and bad in themselves and incapable of change. The topics are introduced in n. 2: the interpretation of Ex. 20:5 *(reddam peccata patrum in filios)* n. 1-12; Esau and Jacob n. 13-21; Pharaoh n. 22-23; the vessels of honor and of shame n. 34-48; the *praesciti* and the predestined n. 49-55.

Studies: G. Martinetto, Les premières réactions antiaugustiniennes de Pélage: REAug 17(1971)83-117: the *De induratione* is seen as the first reaction of Pelagius to Augustine, especially to the *Quaestiones 83*.

e) *Epistula ad Demetriadem:* PL 30, 15-45. This letter, written after the fall of Rome (*Ad Dem.* 30), is one of the fundamental works for a knowledge of Pelagius' anthropology. He speaks of a "certain natural soundness" inherent in each person which presides in the stronghold of the soul to train it in the judgment of good and evil (c. 4). In nature there is not found so much a vice which impels to evil as a dual possibility of choice (c. 8). The darkening which has entered into nature from the habit of sin is overcome by God's grace: the *Lex* before Christ and then the example of Christ himself. Virginity enters into the life of justification over and above that which is demanded of all; it is possible to be educated for it and it receives a particular reward (c. 9-13).

Editions: PL 30, 15-45. — K. C. Krabbe, Epistula ad Demetriadem de vera humilitate (PSt 97). Washington, 1965 (crit. text with English transl.). — The best manuscript, the Augiensis 105 saec. IX from Reichenau attributes the work to Julian of Eclanum.

Studies: L. Valentin, Saint Prosper d'Aquitaine, in Étude sur la littérature latine ecclésiastique au V siècle en Gaule. Toulouse 1900, 714-725 (attributes it to Prosper). — M. Gonsette, Les directeurs spirituels de Démétriade. Episode de la lutte antipélagienne: NRTh 60(1933)783-801.

II. Two other Pelagian writings on virginity can be connected with the *Ep. ad Demetriadem.* These develop the question not only with regard to the merit of virginity but also with respect to its Christological and ecclesiological dimensions.

a) *Epistula de castitate:* PLS I, 1464-1505, G. Morin, ed. Chastity, for both men and women, is the abstinence from all sexual relations in thought and in deed. Furthermore, the virginity of the woman is intended as the preservation intact of the nature received in creation which possesses in itself the norm of the future life — there will be no more marriage — and it likens her to the priest who carries out his service at the altar in continence. The relation of the virgin with Jesus Christ is such as to be a living expression of him. There is a certain disparagement of matrimony in comparison to virginity, and its relations are seen as animal lust.

Studies: G. De Plinval, Pélage, p. 44-45, attribution to Pelagius. — S. Prete, Lo scritto pelagiano De castitate è di Pelagio?: *Aevum* 35(1961)315-322, questions the thesis of Plinval. — R. F. Evans, Four Letters of Pelagius. London 1968, 24ff, attribution to an anonymous Sicilian.

b) *Ad Claudium sororem De virginitate:* CSEL 1, 225-250, C. Halm, ed. Halm attributes the work to Sulpicius Severus, but it is a composition of Pelagius. It is directed against Jovinian, who, on the basis of a common baptismal grace, upheld the equality of merit for all. Virginity is confirmed from the Scriptures and from the custom of the church and is seen in the context of a Christian life already firmly established. Theologically, virginity is seen as a spiritual marriage with Jesus Christ, who chose a virginal heart when he became incarnate. The relationship with Christ allows the virgin to develop within herself the features characteristic of the church without spot or wrinkle and thus to become for others an example of participation in holiness. This letter is one of the better treatises on virginity from the fifth century.

3. Ascetical-Moral Writings

a) These works are exhortations to sustain adversities with Christian constancy (*Ep. ad Marcelam, ad Oceanum, ad virginem in exilium missam, De bono constantiae,* fragments in A. Brückner, *Julian von Eclanum* [TU 15, 3]. Leipzig 1897, p. 74-75). The treatise *De divitiis,* although it follows the literary form of a scholastic exercise on a given theme, nevertheless is in content and arguments one of the most radical treatises of the fifth century on the question of the distribution of goods.

b) *De divitiis:* PLS I, 1380-1418. This work rejects the possession of riches as a discrimination between rich and poor which comes about whenever anyone has more than what is sufficient for necessities. The accumulation of possessions whether as real estate or as money is considered unjust because, according to the author, it always comes either from unjust possession or from robbery. As proof of his position the writer cites the conduct of God who gives spiritual goods — forgiveness of sins, the Eucharist, sanctification — without discrimination of persons. If this is the case on the spiritual plane, which is of a higher order, how much more ought it be the case on the plane of material goods, which is of a lower order. There are people who are poor because there are people who are rich. The example of Christ, who was poor, is proposed to the Christians of the New Testament. In this work poverty is viewed according to the theory of sufficiency, i.e., of not possessing more than what is necessary. The possession of legitimate wealth, e.g., the inheritance left by parents, is not denied although it is considered to be an occasion of sin.

Studies: R. F. Evans, Four Letters of Pelagius. London, 1968 (the *De divitiis* is the work of an anonymous Sicilian Pelagian, as it echoes the questions of Hilary to Augustine in *Ep.* 156).

THE DOCTRINE OF PELAGIUS

The doctrine of Pelagius and, in its nuances, of others who claimed as their own the various propositions which have gone down in history as the Pelagian concept of Christianity, must be divided into three periods: Pelagianism before 411 (the date of the first condemnation of the movement); Pelagianism of the years 411-418 (the condemnation of Caelestius of 411, the synod of Diospolis, the Plenary Council of Carthage of 418 and the *Tractoria* of Zosimus); Pelagianism after 418, also known as Semi-Pelagianism.

1. Before 411: *De induratione cordis Pharaonis*

This work of Pelagius was written perhaps against Ambrosiaster, against Augustine's *Quaestiones 83* and in polemic with other similar works of the time. It reflects the disputes within Christian intellectual circles in Italy who, in the interpretation of certain passages of Scripture, especially of Paul, searched for their understanding of Christianity under the stimulus of Origenism, the Latin translation of the works of Plotinus, Jovinian's polemics against monastic asceticism, and the persistence of Manichaean circles considered as defenders of pagan fatalism who, in the Christian camp, presented God as the creator of two categories of humanity: the one destined to damnation because it was bad and the other to life because it was good. The scriptural passages considered were Ex. 20:5, *reddam peccata patrum in filios;* Ex. 7:3, *Ego indurabo cor pharaonis;* Rom. 2:11, *cui vult miseretur, et quem vult indurat;* Rom. 9:11-21, *Iacob dilexi, Esau autem odio habui;* Rom. 9:21-24 on *vasa honoris et ignominiae;* and on the *praesciti* and the *praedestinati* (cf. Rom. 8:29).

Such questions are treated by Pelagius in the *De induratione cordis Pharaonis* and are resolved by him not on the basis of predestination to a destiny but on the basis of meriting a destiny by observing the commands of God with one's own freedom. This is inherent in human nature: *insertum est in natura* (*De ind.* 46). He concludes (*De ind.* 51), "Known beforehand, the predestined, the elect, the justified are those whom He foresaw would, with a steady mind, remain steadfast in all that they would have to suffer for His name."

2. The Pelagianism of the Years 411-418

a) The Condemnation of 411

In this period the Pelagian Dispute was publicly begun and concluded. With regard to this question there came about: the *collatio carthaginensis* against Caelestius in 411; the Synod of Diospolis against Pelagius in 415; the *concilium africanum* of 417; the Plenary Council of Carthage in 418 and the *Tractoria* of Pope Zosimus. To these can be added the principal writings of Pelagius: *Ad Demetriadem, Liber Testimoniorum, De natura, De libero arbitrio,* and the *Definitiones* of Caelestius. Largely on the basis of this documentation it will be attempted to outline Pelagius' doctrine which, when it came into contact with the African Church emerging from the experience of the Donatist Schism, entered into a new phase and perhaps a different development in its history. The questions of the *De induratione cordis Pharaonis* against the fatalism of Manichaean extraction were no longer placed on the theoretical level but on the level of the practice of infant baptism (Augustine's *De peccatorum meritis et remissione et de baptismo parvulorum* dates from 411-412). Baptism was administered to them *in remissionem peccatorum* in the context of traducianism in regard to the question of the origin of the soul. The African Church made its contribution to the explanation of the effect of Adam's sin in his descendants and of Christian redemption especially in regard to the questions of the death of the body and of the soul, the weakening of the power of the will which needs to be healed by the grace of the Redeemer, the liberation necessary *per Christum* for all people of every age and thus the necessity of baptism even for children.

Pelagius and his followers, fugitives from Rome after 410, continued the Roman discussion of the *De induratione cordis Pharaonis* by proposing their conclusions on human liberty as the only decisive thing in determining one's own destiny, and by rejecting any form of traducianism with regard to the sin of Adam. They considered corporal death to be natural to man and placed the possibility of spiritual death in the realm of freedom which imitates the sinful Adam by not obeying the laws of God. Every person is thus born in the state in which Adam was created, and if the church baptizes children it does so for the purpose of regeneration not for the forgiveness of their sins. The Pelagian positions were drawn up in the six points of the accusation by Paulinus, the deacon of Milan, who was at Carthage at that time to expedite certain affairs of the Church of Milan. Caelestius, who was also present, was accused before bishop Aurelius and the clergy of Carthage. He replied that the accusations brought against him were the teaching he had learned from the Roman priest, Rufinus (Mercator, ACO I, 5, 1, p. 5). The six points of the accusation concerning the Pelagian positions were regarded by the Africans as inadmissible presuppositions. These points were the following: death was natural for Adam; his sin was a personal matter without consequences for anyone else; children are therefore born in the state of Adam before his sin; no one dies because of the sin of Adam or rises because of the resurrection of Christ; the Old Testament and the New Testament lead both alike to heaven; there were also just persons in the Old Testament who did not sin.

The accusation of 411 against Caelestius has come down in two independent sources: one from the *De gestis Pelagii* of Augustine, who cites the record of the proceedings of Diospolis translated into Latin by Marius Mercator, the other from Mercator himself in his *Commonitorium super nomine Coelestii* (ACO I, 5, 1, p. 66). The written source for Paulinus seems to have been Rufinus' *Liber de fide.* The condemnation of 411 was of fundamental importance in the Pelagian Controversy. It was referred to constantly, by the one party in order to confirm it and by the other to escape from under it. In proposition 6 is found the word "impeccable" which was a key term in the polemic subsequent to 411.

Sources: Minutes of the condemnation of 411 in: Augustine, De gestis Pelagii 11, 23 (CSEL 42, 76f). — M. Mercator, Commonitorium II (ACO I, 5, 1, p. 66). — *The Liber de fide of Rufinus:* PL 21, 1123-1154 and PL 48, 451-488. — M. W. Miller, Rufini presbyteri Liber de Fide (PSt 96). Washington, 1964 (critical text with English translation).

Studies: F. Loofs, Pelagius und der pelagianische Streit: RE 15(1904)759. — B. Altaner, De Liber De fide, ein Werk des Pelagianers Rufinus des "Syrers": ThQ 130(1950)432-449 (= TU 83, Berlin 1967, 467-482) his dating of the work to around 414 seems hardly probable. — J. H. Koopmans, Augustine's First Contact with Pelagius and the Dating of the Condemnation of Caelestius at Carthage: VC 8(1954)149-163. — F. Refoulé, Datation du premier concile de Carthage contre les pélagiens et du Libellus fidei: REAug 9(1963)41-49. — G. Bonner, Les origines africaines de la doctrine augustinienne sur la chute et le péché originel: *Augustinus* 12(1967)97-116. — H. I. Marrou, Les attaches orientales du Pélagianisme: CRI (1968)461-472. — V. Grossi, Il battesimo e la polemica pelagiana negli anni 411-413: Aug 9(1969)30-61. — G. Bonner, Rufinus of Syria and African Pelagianism: AugStudies 1(1970)31-47 (with parallel texts of Rufinus and the *De pecc. meritis* of Augustine). — C. García-Sánchez, Pelagius and Christian Initiation. Diss., Catholic Univ. of America, Washington, 1978.

b) The Events from 411 to 418

The six points of the accusation presented by Paulinus at Carthage provided the impetus for the development of the questions of the presence of original sin in each individual (the first four points), the relation between the Old and the New Testament in the Pauline terminology of law and grace (n. 5) and the real possibility of living without sin or the thesis of *impeccantia* (n. 6). In 414 Augustine was sent five Pelagian propositions which were circulating in Sicily (*Ep.* 156 of Hilary of Syracuse), Caelestius' *Definitiones* on the *impeccantia* of man by the Spanish bishops Eutropius and Paul (Augustine responded with the *De perfectione iustitiae hominis*) and the *De natura* of Pelagius (to which Augustine replied with the *De natura et gratia*) on the goodness of human nature and thus the real possibility inherent in it of doing good and avoiding evil. In this work, grace is the law in the sense that God has revealed to man the things which must be done; the doing of them is thus within the possibility of his nature and in this lies the discriminating factor of different merit among the Christians. Pelagius had already applied these principles to the choice of virginity in the *Ep. ad Demetriadem,* which was written shortly after his exile from Rome.

Pelagius had meanwhile won the friendship of John, bishop of Jerusalem, and Orosius went to him there, sent by Augustine, to seek clarifications on the questions of the baptism of infants, of original sin, and of *impeccantia.* When he did not obtain the desired results, Orosius called together the Latin exiles at Jerusalem and brought about a meeting with bishop John and the local clergy. They were aided by an interpreter, but the whole thing turned into a confrontation between the anti-Origenists of Jerome and the Origenists of Pelagius who had now transferred themselves from Rome to the East. Since no understanding was reached, the accusation was drawn up against Pelagius at Diospolis in December of 415, this time by Eros and Lazarus of Aix, Gallic bishops in exile. The attempt was made to apply the condemnation of Caelestius of 411 to Pelagius. The substance of the accusation was formed by six propositions drawn from the 160 headings of Pelagius' *Liber testimoniorum.* These propositions were a synthesis of the Pelagian ideas which were going around but for which the Pelagians themselves often denied responsibility (Jerome, *Dial. adv. Pelag.* 3, 14-16), as Pelagius did on this occasion even though the propositions had been taken from his own work. The principal charge brought against him was that "man can, if he so wills, be without sin." Pelagius himself explained that man receives from God the potential of orienting himself according to God's commands (*De gestis* 30, 54). The *Lex,* or revelation, is one of the divine aids for realizing such a possibility. Pelagius was acquitted from the accusations brought against him. He then explained his thought more systematically by writing the *De libero arbitrio.* Augustine was convinced that at Diospolis Pelagius had reduced grace to freedom (*De gestis* 10, 22). In the *De libero arbitrio* the relationship grace-freedom is limited by the adverb *facile*. For the free will, grace is a *facilitas non peccandi* rather than a *possibilitas non peccandi,* and belongs to human nature as such. Pelagius' explanations concerning grace at Diospolis (*De gestis* 14, 30), his distancing himself from Caelestius, and the *De libero arbitrio* indicate that he did not identify grace with nature or free will or consider prayer as useless for the Christian, only that he reduced grace to a stimulus for the will.

For Augustine, the Pelagian concept reduced grace to nature or free will and thus he saw in Pelagius the enemy of the grace of God (*De gestis* 22, 46). Such a position reflects on the one hand the lack of distinction within Pelagian theology between the positions of Pelagius, of Caelestius, of the Sicilian Pelagians and of other related groups and, on the other, the consequences which could be drawn from the Pelagian concept of Christian anthropology. If the *impeccantia* of man were placed on the plane of the theoretically possible, such an affirmation could be sustained. It was on this plane, on which the Easterners were masters, that Pelagius was understood at Jerusalem and Diospolis and thus was acquitted on every charge of the accusation. The Africans responded that the theoretical man of the Pelagians did not belong to history: to the history of sin in Adam, of the sacraments of the church, of the redemption of Jesus Christ. The assertions of Pelagius could not be applied to history and therefore were heretical. Whenever they were applied it resulted in the uselessness of the sacraments, hypocrisy in their administration and the uselessness for man of the Redeemer (these conclusions were already to be found in the *De peccatorum meritis* of 411-412). When an attempt was made to pass from the theoretical to the practical plane, Pelagius became evasive, such as in the question of the just of the Old Testament where he substituted "in a holy and just manner" for "just without sin" (*De gestis* 11, 26). It is in this context that Augustine's accusation that Pelagius had deceived the Oriental bishops with regard to his real thought must be understood (*De gestis* 3, 8; 6, 10-20, 22; 14, 30-31, etc.).

For Pelagius, the potential for good which God placed in man, which formed the basis of Pelagian anthropology, was the very image of God of Gen. 1:26. Contained in the nature of this image was the possibility for man to be able to live without sin, to be able to conduct himself in keeping with the observance of God's precepts. When he sinned, Adam did not spoil this image and thus the *posse* of the free will by his transgression either for his body or for his soul. Nevertheless, because of Adam's transgression his example of sinner spread, and from such a habit the image of God in man was obscured. God, therefore, gave man first the Law then sent Jesus Christ to him so that his example might free the image from its torpor. It was thus a question of an example which would arouse freedom, called to choose the precepts of the Lord on its own accord. Pelagius defines the Law of the Old Testament as the *correctorium* for the image and the example of Jesus Christ as the grace given to men (*De induratione* 3; 5; 4; 8; 11; 34; *De malis doctoribus* 18, 2; *De lib. arb. frag.* 3: PLS I, 1543; *De vita christiana* 14: PLS I, 1044; *De castitate* 6, 2: PLS I, 1474; *De virginitate* 7: CSEL 1, 234; *Ad Demetriadem* 23, a fundamental text for Pelagius' anthropology). There is not much evidence in Pelagius of a dynamic understanding of the image (Greshake) as a force *trahens* which moves man to make a choice. Instead, by developing the concept of creation *de potentia Dei ordinata,* he sees the possibility of choice as given to human nature with creation. This theology of creation is the crux of Pelagius' thought. His insistence on the *exemplum* is in accord with sound Christian tradition. Christianity is always handed on, it is a *tradere* bound to one who possesses it already and as such is always on the order of an *exemplum.* Pelagius did well to single out the category of *exemplum,* but went astray when he applied to it the power of stimulating of itself man's freedom to be able to appropriate the example. Augustine recognized this faulty concept very well and gave a fundamental explanation of it both for the example of Christ as for that of Adam. Furthermore, the African Church already with Tertullian (*De oratione* 4 and 8) had clarified its thought on the importance of the example of Christ in the manner in which Augustine explained it in the Pelagian polemic.

After his acquittal at Diospolis, Pelagius, in a letter to Pope Innocent (in Augustine, *De gratia Christi* 30, 32), judged the process against himself and his thought as an involved calumny. The African reaction to the acquittal led to the *concilium africanum,* the Council of Carthage of 418 and the *Tractoria* of Zosimus which decisively condemned the Pelagians.

The charges condemned in the accusation of 418 at Carthage are as follows: canon 1 corresponds to the first point of the condemnation of 411 regarding the natural death of Adam; can. 2 corresponds to points 2-4 of 411 on the baptism of infants except that Rom. 5:12 is substituted for 1 Cor. 5:21; can. 3 concerns infants who have died without baptism and the lack of distinction between eternal life and the Kingdom of God (this is the least known proposition among the Pelagian sources); canons 4-6 deal with the question of grace which is necessary for keeping the commandments (can. 4), for every good action (can. 6) and which is not merely an external aid (can. 5); canons 7-9 are directed against the concept of *impeccantia.*

The questions of baptism (can. 1-3), of grace which is not only *remissio* (can. 4), *revelatio* (can. 5) or *creatio* (can. 6), and of the impossibility of being without sin (can. 7-9) together with their related consequences formed the object of the Council of Carthage and can be considered as a development both of the thought of Pelagius and the Pelagians and, above all, of the implications of such thought such as the reduction of grace to a partial perspective. A development of the relation between grace and freedom did not take place in this council. The *Tractoria* of Zosimus, albeit with some variation in terminology, confirmed the judgment of the Council of Carthage on Pelagius and the Pelagians and their teaching. The reaction to the *Tractoria* and the polemic with Julian brought no new contributions to the question except a development of the consequences for Christian marriage in light of the thesis regarding the transmission of original sin. Just as Augustine had led the Pelagians to draw the full implications of their ideas, so did Julian compel Augustine to consider all the consequences deriving from the thesis of the transmission of original sin.

Sources: (cf. the general bibliography, *infra*): Orosius, Liber apologeticus contra Pelagianos: CSEL 5, 603-664. — Prosper of Aquitaine, Epitoma Chronicorum: Mommsen, MGH AA IX, 385-485. — *Conventus Hierosolymitanus:* Mansi IV, 307-312. — *Council of Diospolis:* Mansi IV, 311-320. — Augustine, De gestis Pelagii: CSEL 42, 49-122. — A. Brückner, Quellen zur Geschichte des pelagianischen Streites. Tübingen 1906, 14-20. — O. Wermelinger, Rom und Pelagius. Stuttgart 1975, 295-299, with the indication of the possible sources.

Bishops present at Diospolis: Augustine, Contra Iulianum 1 5, 19.

Innocent I and the Pelagians: (Council of Carthage of 416, Council of Milevi of 416, five letters of the African bishops): Mansi IV, 321-344.

Council of Carthage of 418: Mansi III, 810-850. — Ch. Munier, Concilia Africae CCL 149, 69-73.

The Libellus antipelagianus: PL 56, 497-499. — Innocent I, Ep. 175-177 and 181-183 (among the letters of Augustine: CSEL 44, 701-730). — Zosimus, Ep. 2-3: CSEL 35, 99-108; Ep. 1-4: MGH epist. III 5-7; Ep. 12: CSEL 35, 115-117. — Augustine, Ep. 177 and 186.

Zosimus and the Pelagian Question: Mansi IV, 353-358, 366-367, 371-378, 381-384 (the *libellus* of Paulinus).

The libellus fidei to Augustine, metropolitan of Aquileia: PL 48, 509-526 and 45, 1732-1736.

The Epistula Tractoria of Zosimus: PL 20, 693-695. O. Wermelinger, Rom und Pelagius, 307-308.

The African Councils and the Pelagian Question: P. Quesnel, Diss. 13: De conciliis africanis: PL 56, 959-1006 and the observations of the Ballerini: PL 56, 1005-1042.

Studies: J. Comeliau, A propos de la prière de Pélage: RHE 31(1935)77-89. — H. Wurm, Studien und Texte zur Dekretaliensammlung des Dyonysius Exiguus. Bonn, 1939 (on the collectio Quesnel: PL 56, 956ff). — J. Rivière, Hétérodoxie des Pélagiens en fait de rédemption?: RHE 41(1946)5-43. — F. Floëri, Le Pape Zosime et la doctrine augustinienne du péché originel: AugMag II, 755-761, III 261-263. — Th. Bohlin, Die Theologie des Pelagius und ihre Genesis. Uppsala, 1957. — H. A. Wolfson, Philosophical Implications of the Pelagian Controversy: *Proceedings of the American Philosophical Society* 103(1959)554-562. — A. Zumkeller, ALG II, 37-47. — B. Studer, Sacramentum et exemplum chez saint Augustin: RAug 10(1975)87-141. — Regarding the antipelagian rescripts (PL 56, 490ff) and a possible sociological motivation behind the imperial intervention: J. N. L. Myres, Pelagius and the End of the Roman Rule in Britain: JRS

50(1960)21-36. — J. Morris, Pelagian Literature, JThSt 16(1965)25-60. Against this thesis: W. Liebschütz, Did the Pelagian Movement Have Social Aims?: *Historia* 12(1963)227-241. — A. De Veers, REAug 9(1963)318-319; 13(1967)146.

On the Doctrine of Pelagius as Distinct from the Pelagianism which was Condemned: G. De Plinval, Points de vues récents sur la théologie de Pélage: RSR 46(1958)227-236. — G. Bonner, How Pelagian was Pelagius? An Examination on the Contention of Th. Bohlin: SP 9 (TU 94). Berlin 1966, 350-358. — A. Trapè, Verso la riabilitazione del pelagianesimo?: Aug 3(1963)482-516. — G. De Plinval, L'heure est-elle venue de redécouvrir Pélage?: REAug 19(1973)158-162. — G. Greshake, Gnade als Konkrete Freiheit. Mainz, 1972.

3. Pelagianism After 418

Pelagius' concept of anthropology based on the potential of nature to realize itself through freedom had laid the foundation of an outline for the treatment of nature and grace, i.e., of grace conceived as analogous to nature. Canon 5 of the Council of Carthage of 418 had established that grace was not to be identified with a knowledge of the commandments since it was the cause of the keeping of the law as well as of the knowledge thereof. It was a question furthermore of grace *per Dominum nostrum I. Christum.* Augustine's intervention with Pelagius in terms of one single mediator, Jesus Christ, for all the just before and after him was one of the key points of the polemic (*De pecc. mer.* 26, 30; *De nat. et gr.* 2, 2, etc.). Nevertheless, he responded along the lines of an argument directed *ad hominem* to Pelagius who always spoke of nature by entering into his anthropological scheme of grace seen within the category of nature. It would be of great interest to be able to distinguish in Augustine that which belonged to the response he was making to Pelagius from that which belonged to his own concept. There are in any case two schemes presented here. The theological scheme of grace in the category of nature (Pelagius) instead of that of the person (the unique mediator Jesus Christ for Augustine) presents considerable limits. The first consequence which derives from this is an opposition of nature and grace as though in a contest of power: the liberty of man on one side and the liberty of God on the other.

From this question of the relation between liberty and grace there arose another strand of the polemic known as Semi-Pelagianism, which had Augustine on one side and other Africans (the monks of Hadrumetum) and Gauls (the monks of Lérins in particular) on the other. This development of the rapport human liberty-divine liberty, even though it grew out of Pelagius' understanding of grace within the scheme of nature, does not form part of the polemic between Augustine and Pelagius, Caelestius, Julian and others, but came about after the real Pelagian polemic, which can be considered to have been settled on the ideological level in 418. The conception of the rapport between human and divine liberty flowed into the problem of predestination and the heresy of predestinationism which was condemned at the Council of Arles in 473.

History has preferred to look at the Pelagian Conflict from a distance and to see in Augustine the defender of the grace of God and in Pelagius the champion of the liberty of man. A veil of suspicion of human liberty and thus of pessimism and gloom falls over Augustine's great theological works from the Semi-Pelagian period (*De gratia et libero arbitrio, De correptione et gratia, De praedestinatione sanctorum, De dono perseverantiae,* etc.). The defense of the omnipotence of God is seen as humiliating the impotent meanness of man. Although he is not really known, Pelagius is regarded with a curiosity full of sympathy as the defender of man.

History, when scrutinized more closely, shows that at the time of this new polemic Pelagius was ending his days in oblivion, and that in the Augustinian works of the Semi-Pelagian period a dichotomy between nature and grace with their respective spheres of power did not exist. Such a conclusion was drawn by spirits less respectful than Augustine of the mystery of the liberty of man and the liberty of God. The latter is defined by Augustine as *auxilium,* not dominion, in relation to the liberty of man.

The most significant works on Pelagianism after the Pelagian Conflict are:

a) the *Hypomnesticon:* PL 45, 1611-1664, a work divided into six *responsiones* on the basis of a triple series of problems: 1) original sin, its existence in Adam and his posterity, its transmission and *libido* as its consequence (*resp.* 1-2 and 4-5); 2) grace, its necessity and gratuitous nature, its relation to human freedom (*resp.* 3); 3) predestination, its definition and nature, the value of human effort, predestination and the will for universal salvation (*resp.* 6).

b) *De gratia Dei et libero arbitrio contra Collatorem* of Prosper: PL 51, 213-276.

c) The work entitled *Praedestinatus:* PL 53, 587-672.

With regard to baptism a new error began to circulate according to which infants did or did not receive baptism depending on God's foreknowledge of their future merits. With regard to this cf. *Ep.* 225 of Prosper to Augustine (CSEL 57, 2, p. 461) who had treated the same question in *Ep.* 217, 6, 29 and the *De praedest. sanct.* 12 and 13. In the *Hypomnesticon, resp.* 5, 5 treats the same question. *Ep.* 1 of Faustus of Riez to Lucidus (PL 58, 835-837), one of the sources for the Council of Arles of 473, condemns those who affirm they are not saved because they have not received the means of salvation (4) and those who maintain that Christ did not die for all and does not wish the salvation of all (6).

Studies: H. von Schubert, Der sogennante Praedestinatus. Ein Beitrag zur Geschichte des Pelagianismus (TU 24). Leipzig, 1903 (regarding this work cf. CPL 243). — D. De Bruyne, Sommaires antipélagiens inédits des lettres de saint Paul: RB 29(1927)45-55. — E. Pickman, The Mind of Latin Christendom. Oxford, 1937 (mistakenly sees the *Hypomnesticon* as a betrayal to Augustine). — J. E. Chisholm, The Pseudo-Augustinian Hypomnesticon Against the Pelagians and Celestiens. Fribourg, 1967-1979.
On the Council of Arles of 473: Mansi VII, 1007-1012. — Hefele-Leclercq, Histoire des conciles, II, 2, 908-912.
On Lucidus: DTC 9(1926)1020-1024.

General Bibliography:
1. Sources for the Life of Pelagius: Jerome: Ep. 50; 130; 133. — In Jeremiam III-IV; Dialogi adversus Pelagianos I-III (PL 23, 517-618). — *Augustine:* Ep. 177 and 186 in particular. — *Orosius:* Liber Apologeticus contra Pelagianos: CSEL 5, 603-664. — *M. Mercator:* Commonitorium adversus haeresim Pelagii et Coelestii vel etiam scripta Juliani.
2. General Works: A. Brückner, Quellen zur Geschichte des pelagianischen Streites. Tübingen, 1906. — G. De Plinval, Pélage. Lausanne, 1943. — J. Ferguson, Pelagius. A Historical and Theological Study. Cambridge, 1956. — R. F. Evans, Pelagius. Inquiries and Reappraisals. London, 1968. — G. Greshake, Gnade als konkrete Freiheit. Eine Untersuchung zur Gnadenlehre des Pelagius. Mainz, 1972. — O. Wermelinger, Rom und Pelagius. Die theologische Position der römischen Bishöfe im pelagianischen Streit in den Jahren 411-432. Stuttgart, 1975 (bibliography).
3. Particular Studies: H. Noris, Historia pelagiana. Padua, 1673. — L. S. Le Nain de Tillemont, Mémories pour sevir à l'histoire ecclésiastique des six premiers siècles, vol. 13. Paris, 1702. — P. Ballerini, Observationes in Diss. XIII Quesnelli de conciliis Africanis contra Pelagianos: PL 56, 1005-1042. — F. Loofs, Pelagius: RE XV(1903)747-774; Suppl II(1913)310-312. — P. Battifol, Saint Augustin, Pélage et la siège apostolique (411-417): RB 15(1918)5-58. — A. Berthoud, La controverse pélagienne. Un conflict psychologique entre l'Orient et l'Occident: RTP 17(1929)134-145. — D. M. Cappuyns, L'origine des capitula pseudo-célestiniens contre le sémipélagianisme: RB 41(1929)156-170. — U. Koch, La distinzione prepelagiana tra vita eterna e regno celeste: RR 9(1933)44-62. — J. Jäntisch, Führt der Ambrosiaster zu Augustinus oder Pelagius?: Schol 9(1934)92-99. — M. Michalski, La doctrine christologique de Pélage: CTh 17(1936)143-162. — E. Dinkler, Pelagius: PWK 19(1937)226-242. — G. De Plinval, Essai sur le style et la langue de Pélage. Fribourg, 1947; *idem,* Vue d'ensemble sur la littérature pélagienne: RELA 29(1951)284-294; *idem,* La resistencia a lo sobrenatural. Pelagianismo, humanismo, ateismo: *Augustinus* 1(1956)581-600. — B. Piault, Autour de la controverse pélagienne: RSR 44(1956)481-514. — J. Plagnieux, Le grief de complicité entre erreurs nestoriennes et pélagiennes d'Augustin à Cassien par Prosper d'Aquitaine: REAug 2(1956)391-402. — T. Bohlin, Die Theologie des Pelagius und ihre Genesis. Uppsala, 1957. — F. E. Fox, Biblical Theology and Pelagianism: JR 40(1960)169-181. — R. Pirenne, La morale de Pélage. Essai historique sur le rôle primordial de la grâce dans l'enseignement de al théologie morale. Rome, 1961. — S. Prete, Pelagio e il Pelagianesimo. Brescia, 1961. — P. Marti, Die Auslegungs-Grundsätze des Pelagius: *Schweizerische th. Umschau* 32(1962)71-80; *idem,* Pelagius und seine Zeit: ibid., 167-175; *idem,* Zur Ethik des Pelagius: ibid., 33(1963)129-134. — F. Refoulé, La distinction "Royaume de Dieu-Vie éternelle" est-elle pélagienne?: RSR 51(1963)247-254. — P. Antin, Rufin et Pélage dans Jérôme, Prologue 1 In Hieremiam: Latomus 22(1963)792-794. — M. Skibbe, Die ethische Forderung der Patientia in der patristischen Literatur von Tertullian bis Pelagius. Diss., Münster, 1964. — W. Liebeschütz, Pelagian Evidence on the Last Period of Roman Britain: Latomus 26(1967)436-477. — W. Marschall, Karthago und Rom. Die Stellung der nordafrikanischen Kirche zum apostolischen Stuhl in Rom. Stuttgart, 1971. — Y. M. Duval, Sur les

insinuations de Jérôme contre Jean de Jerusalem: de l'arianisme à l'origénisme: RHE 65(1970)353-374. — R. D. Haigt, Notes on the Pelagian Controversy: *Philippine Studies* 22(1974)26-48. — J. Speigl, Der Pelagianismus auf dem Konzil von Ephesus: *Annuarium Hist. Concil.* 1(1969)1-15; *idem,* Das Hauptgebot der Liebe in den pelagianischen Schriften, in *Scientia Augustiniana,* Festschr. A. Zumkeller. Würzburg 1975, 137-154. — V. Grossi, La formula credo (in) remissionem peccatorum agli inizi della polemica pelagiana: SP 16 (TU 117). Berlin 1976, 428-442.

4. *On the Relation between Pelagius and Augustine:* In addition to certain studies cited in the preceding section, cf. in particular: A. J. Smith, Pelagius and Augustine. JThSt 31(1929)21-35. — E. Neuvet, Rôle de Saint Augustin dans les controverses pélagiennes: DTP 33(1930)29-59. — A. Guzzo, Agostino contro Pelagio. Turin, 1958. — C. B. Armstrong, St. Augustine and Pelagius as Religious Types: ChQ 162(1961)150-164. — H. Jonas, Augustin und das paulinische Freiheitsprobleme. Eine philosophische Studie zum pelagianischen Streit. Göttingen, 1965. — J. R. Lucas, Pelagius and St. Augustine: JThSt 22(1971)73-85. — S. Kopp, Augustins Kampf gegen den Pelagianusmus: ALG, Schriften gegen die Semipelagianer, Würzburg 1955, 11-57. — A. Mengarelli, La libertà cristiana in Agostino e Pelagio: Aug 15(1975)347-366.

CAELESTIUS

The Roman jurist Caelestius was the disciple of Pelagius and together with him was the principal spokesman for the Pelagian ideas which spread abroad with the Roman exiles after the fall of Rome. He took refuge in Carthage where he sought to be received among the local clergy, but in 411 he was accused by the deacon Paulinus of Milan on six charges; in particular on the nature of bodily death whether it is natural or the result of Adam's sin to his posterity and on the reason for the baptism of infants. Caelestius defended himself by distinguishing between heresy and questioning. A *libellus brevissimus* of Caelestius was disseminated in Africa (Augustine, *Ep.* 157, 3, 22; *De gestis* 22, 46; *De pecc. orig.* 22, 25) but he was condemned and appealed to Rome. There are no further notices of him in Africa after 411. He appears again in Ephesus in 416, where he was received into the college of presbyters (Augustine, *Ep.* 175, 1 and 176, 4), and his name and ideas were generally spread about. One of his writings, entitled *Definitiones,* was in circulation, as distinct from a previous anonymous composition with the title *Definitiones ut dicitur Coelestii* which Augustine had refuted in the *De spiritu et littera.*

Citations drawn from the works of Caelestius were presented at the Synod of Diospolis in 415 (*De gestis* 13, 29-19, 42; Jerome, *Ep.* 133, 5). He was condemned together with Pelagius by Innocent I (*Ep.* 181-183), enjoyed a momentary rehabilitation at Rome under Pope Zosimus in 417 (Zosimus, *Ep.* 2), but after the Council of Carthage of May 1, 418, Zosimus condemned Caelestius decisively in his *Tractoria.* Prosper notes that a new attempt was made to rehabilitate him in 423-424 (*C. Collatorem* 21, 2). The last notices of him place him in the group of Julian of Eclanum at Constantinople, from which they were expelled. He is mentioned in the condemnation of the Council of Ephesus in 431.

Caelestius exercised a role equal to that of Pelagius in the Pelagian Controversy. The extant documentation speaks of two parties, the followers of Caelestius and the followers of Pelagius, who were generally condemned together. His thought has never as yet been clearly distinguished from that of Pelagius or the Pelagian movement. From the fact that Pelagius distanced himself from him at the Synod of Diospolis over a phrase concerning grace (*De gestis* 14, 30), from his response during the proceedings at Carthage in 411 on the understanding of the baptism of infants, and from what remains of his *Definitiones* on *impeccantia,* it seems that Caelestius was more radical than Pelagius and was more concerned with the consistency of his logic than with the importance of the Christian life.

Editions: (PLS I, 1679-1704). — *Definitiones:* Fragments in Augustine, *De perfectione iustitiae hominis* (CSEL 42, 4-48); Garnier, PL 48, 617-622; A. Brückner, Quellen zur Geschichte des pelagianischen Streites. Tübingen 1906, 70-78. — *Libellus fidei* (to Zosimus): in Augustine, De pecc. orig. 5, 5-6, 6 and 23, 26 (CSEL 42, 167-209); Garnier, PL 48, 499-505; A. Brückner, op. cit., p. 78-89. — *Other fragments:* Augustine, De gestis 13, 29-19, 42; Jerome, Ep. 135, 5 *(Liber Caelestii):* Augustine, De pecc. meritis 1 34, 36 and Ep. 175, 6 *(Libellus brevissimus):* Augustine, *De perfectione iustitiae hominis* 1, 1 and *De gratia Christi* 30, 32.
Caelestius' Life: M. Mercator, Commonitorium I and II (I = PL 48, 67-108, 45, 1686-1691; E. Schwartz, ACO I 5, 1, p. 5-23. II = PL 48, 109-172; PL 45, 1680-1682; E. Schwartz, ACO I 5, 1, p. 65-70).

Studies: G. De Plinval, Les écrits de Célestius: BA 21(1966)592-593. — A. M. La Bonnardière, Caelestius: Prosopographie pélagienne, in Marrou-Palanque, *Prosopographie chrétienne du Bas-Empire.* Paris, 1967. — A. De Veer, Le dossier Célestius: BA 22(1975)691-692.

JULIAN OF ECLANUM

Julian of Eclanum was born in Apulia (Augustine, *Opus imp.* 6, 18) around 380-385, the son of Memorus, bishop of an unidentified see, and Juliana, who was possibly from a noble Roman family. He married Titia, the daughter of Aemilius, bishop of Beneventum, for which occasion Paulinus of Nola composed his *Carm.* 25 as an epithalamium (CSEL 30, 238-344). Julian became a lector in his father's church and deacon in 408, at which time he was invited to Hippo by Augustine (*Ep.* 101, 4). In 416, at about age thirty, he was ordained bishop of Eclanum by Pope Innocent (Mercator, *Comm.* II). He had studied at Rome and had followed the discussions on the origin of the soul of the Manichaean, Honoratus, at Carthage (Augustine, *Opus imp.* 5, 26). His notoriety, as well as his activity as writer, exegete, theologian, and polemicist, is connected with the *Tractoria* of Pope Zosimus which condemned the Pelagians. Julian wrote two letters to Zosimus, one of which, where he was requesting further clarifications before signing the *Tractoria*, circulated throughout all of Italy. Pope Zosimus did not accept his request and condemned him along with another 18 Italian bishops who had refused to sign (Augustine, *C. Iul.* 3, 1, 4; M. Mercator, *Comm.* I-II, ACO I 5, 1, p. 20 and 68). Julian appealed to the *comes* Valerius at Ravenna, who referred the matter to Augustine. The Bishop of Hippo responded with the *De nuptiis et concupiscentia.*

In the summer of 418, Julian wrote the four books *Ad Turbantium* against this reply of Augustine (Augustine, *Op. imp.* 1, 10 and *Ep.* 200). Forced into exile, he went first to the East, where he attempted unsuccessfully to settle, then to Sicily, where he made a living by teaching rhetoric. He composed the eight books *Ad Florum* in which on the one hand he repeated the accusations of Manichaeism against Augustine already contained in the *Ad Turbantium* and, on the other, vented all of his animosity against everyone.

Prosper notes (*Chronicon,* PL 51, 598) that Julian attempted to reenter ecclesial communion at the time of Sixtus III in 439, but was rebuffed at the advice of the deacon, Leo (the future Pope Leo the Great). This notice is corroborated by a notice of Quodvultdeus to the effect that Leo "destroyed the Manichaeans and the Pelagians, especially Julian" (*Liber promissionum* 4, 6).

WRITINGS

1. The response to the *Tractoria.* Julian responded with two letters, one of which was refuted by Marius Mercator (ACO I 5, 1, p. 11-12; A. Brückner, *Turbantius,* p. 108-109). From this it is learned that Julian explained the relationship Adam-descendants and Christ-Christians by the mode of example and thus drew the consequences in regard to infants who were not born under the dominion of sin, to bodily death seen as a natural fact and to the death of the soul *(tradux peccati)* which was real only for those who followed the bad example of Adam.

2. *Libri IV ad Turbantium* (A. Brückner, *Turbantius,* p. 24-76). These books represent Julian's response to the *De nuptiis et concupiscentia* of Augustine. He had previously written to the *comes* Valerius on the consequences for Christian marriage if the African point of view on the *tradux peccati* were accepted. Valerius forwarded the letter to Augustine who responded with his *De nuptiis et concupiscentia* which he sent to Ravenna and Rome in the spring of 419 (Augustine, *Ep.* 194, 1). Julian replied in the summer of the same year with his four books to Turbantius in which he objected that the way was clearly open to a camouflaged Manichaeism and noted that it was permitted that persons identified as "Pelagians" or "Caelestians" must live in a climate of fear and repression (another edict against the Pelagians was issued

in the spring of 419). He did not see any judges competent to solve such questions and thus, in opposition to the arguments of Augustine, he appealed to the goodness of creation and the very justice of God (Augustine, *C. Iul.* 2, 10, 34 and 36; 3, 1, 2; 5, 1, 4).

3. The letters to Rufus of Thessalonica and to the Romans (A. Brückner, *Turbantius,* p. 109-113). These letters were written in 419. Augustine answered with his *Contra duas epistolas pelagianorum.*

a) The *Epistola ad Romanos* (PL 48, 505-507 attributed to Caelestius). This letter rejects the concept of a weakening of nature and of freedom because of Adam's sin, which would give rise to an inability to perform the good. This performance remains within the power of freedom, although it is not denied that it is carried out with the aid of God's grace.

b) The *Epistola* to Rufus repeats the accusation of Manichaeism against the African conception of human nature as derived from sinful Adam and the denial of holiness in the Old Testament. Julian appeals to a right conception of creation in order not to admit a coexistence of grace and sin. He rejects the baptism of infants as a proof of original sin, since death comes to us from Adam but not his transgression, and he opposes the reduction of grace to an inevitable *fatum.*

4. *Libri VIII ad Florum* (A. Brückner, TU 15, 3, p. 49-51). In this work, Julian expresses all of his resentment against Augustine for wanting to solve the Pelagian Question by force and not by reason. Julian was in Sicily at this time, where he earned his living by teaching (Quodvultdeus, *Dimidium temporis* 6, 12). There are no new ideas contained in the work, only acrimony.

5. Exegetical works (Commentaries on the minor prophets and on Job). Departing from traditional typological exegesis, Julian gives primary importance to the support of reason in understanding the Scriptures.

THEOLOGY

The writings of Julian are studied for their style, language and literary models. Scholars view him as a writer capable of adapting the *elocutio* to the current necessities and to the required literary genre. Studies based on definitely authentic works such as the *Ad Florum* (Baxter, Morin, Vaccari, Plinval, Cipriani) have established Julian's authorship for the commentaries on the minor prophets, Job and the Psalms and have furthermore emphasized his importance as an exegete, particularly in regard to the biblical text he used, which was perhaps one connected with the area around Aquileia.

His thought and theological method are connected to the polemic with Augustine after the *Tractoria* of Pope Zosimus. Compared to Caelestius and Pelagius, he made no particular contribution to Pelagian teaching. He is monotonous in seeing in the original sin defended by Augustine a recrudescence of Manichaeism. He always opposed Augustine with the consequences which derive from such a conception of original sin, above all for the understanding of matrimony which appeared no longer as a good but as an occasion of the transmission of sin. He therefore defended concupiscence as a natural good which was evil only in excess, and did not regard it as a disorder deriving to man from original sin itself (the thesis of Augustine).

His contribution lay above all in the field of theological method. He recognized three sources in the theological debate (Scripture, *ratio* and the authority of holy men: *C. Iul.* 1, 7), but he gave a primacy of place to reason. It is reason which decides the entire question and its arguments (intrinsic arguments) are worth more than extrinsic arguments such as Scripture and tradition. This rhetorical procedure of *loci intrinseci* and *extrinseci* as applied to the topic of original sin is plainly evident in the *Ad Florum.* In the first part, which is entirely philosophical in nature, the concepts of justice and sin are defined and analyzed with the conclusion that the Augustinian concept of sin is absurd. In the second part, passages of Scripture are examined as extrinsic proof with the conclusion that they do not justify the existence of original sin. With regard to tradition, he cites, in the course of the entire controversy, Basil twice and Chrysostom once (*C. Iul.* 1, 5-6). For Julian, everything is subject to the judgment of reason: *Quod ratio arguit, non potest auctoritas vindicare* (*Opus imp.* 2, 16). With regard to the letters of Paul he writes, "We recognize the holiness of the Pauline writings for no other reason than that they reach in harmony with reason, with piety and with the faith" (*Opus imp.* 2, 114).

Augustine recognized Julian's dialectical talents and described him as the "architect of the Pelagian dogma" (*C. Iul.* 6, 11, 36).

It escaped Julian that the primacy of reason lay in the order of the premise of logical consciousness and not in the order of judgment in itself. He did not recognize the relation which exists between Scripture and Tradition nor did he understand that *Traditio* is not so much an external authority as it is the very transmission of Christianity itself.

Editions: The work of Julian is preserved for the most part only in fragments cited in the refutations of Augustine. These fragments have been collected by J. Garnier in his *Monumenta haereseos pelagianae* (PL 48), in various works of A. Brückner and most recently by L. De Coninck, CCL 88(1977)331-402.

1. *Libri IV ad Turbantium:* (CPL 774). — Augustine, De nuptiis et conc.: PL 44, 413; Op. imp.: PL 45, 1049; C. Iul.: PL 44, 641. — A. Brückner, Die vier Bücher Julians von Aeclanum an Turbantius. Berlin 1910, 24-76 (cf. G. Bouwman, p. 2f); CCL 88, 340-396.
2. *Epistolae: Ad Romanos:* Augustine, C. duas ep. pel. I (= ad Bonifacium): PL 44, 549-572. — Garnier: PL 48, 505-508. — A. Brückner, Turbantius, p. 109-111. *Ad Rufum:* Augustine, C. duas ep. pel. II-IV: PL 44, 571-638. — Garnier: PL 48, 534-537. — A. Brückner, Turbantius, p. 111-113. *Ad Zosimus:* Garnier: PL 48, 533-534. — M. Mercator, Liber subnotationum 6, 10-13 (ed. Schwartz, ACO I 5, 1, p. 12). — Garnier: PL 48, 141-143; 45, 1738. — A. Brückner, Turbantius, p. 108-109. — CCL 88, 396-398.
3. *Libri VIII ad Florum:* (CPL 773). — Augustine, Op. imp.: PL 45, 1049-1608 (fragments of the first six books in ed. of Op. imp. I-III: CSEL 85, 1). List of fragments in A. Brückner, Julianum von Aeclanum. Sein Leben und seine Lehre (TU 15, 3). Leipzig 1897, 49-51.
4. *Dicta in quadam disputatione publica:* (CPL 775). — M. Mercator, Commonitorium: PL 45, 1739. — Garnier: PL 48, 147. — E. Schwartz, ed., ACO I 5, 1, p. 13. — A. Brückner, Turbantius, p. 109. — G. Bouwman (p. 4 n. 6) assigns this to the year 423 although it is actually from 418. — CCL 88, 336.
5. *Commentarius in prophetas minores (Osee, Joel and Amos):* PL 21, 959-1104 (ed. Vallarsi among the works of Rufinus). — Other fragments in G. Bouwman, p. 138-139. — L. De Coninck, CCL 88(1977)111-329.
6. *Expositio libri Iob:* (CPL 777). — A. Amelli, Spicilegium Casinense III, 1. Monte Cassino 1887, 333-417 (= PLS I, 1571-1679) unsatisfactory edition. — L. De Coninck, CCL 88(1977)1-109 — The attribution to Julian was proposed by Vaccari, followed by Weyman, Jülicher, and others. Capelle denied the attribution (cf. Bull. ancienne litt. chrét. lat. 1, 1926 n. 26). — A. Vaccari, Un commento a Giobbe di Giuliano di Eclano. Rome, 1915. — C. Weyman, Der Hiobkommentar des Julianum von Aeclanum: ThR 15(1916)241-248. — J. Stiglmayr, Der Jobkommentar von Monte Cassino: ZkTh 45(1921)495. — A. Vaccari, Il commento Cassinese di Giobbe, in Misc. A. Amelli. Monte Cassino 1920, 43-51.
7. *Translation of Theodore of Mopsuestia's Commentary on the Psalms:* L. De Coninck, CCL 88A(1977).

Studies: A. Brückner, Julian von Eclanum. Sein Leben und seine Lehre (TU 15, 3). Leipzig, 1897; *idem,* Quellen zur Geschichte des pelagianischen Streites. Tübingen, 1906; *idem,* Die vier Bücher Julians von Aeclanum an Turbantius. Berlin, 1910. — G. Morin, Un ouvrage restitué à Julien d'Eclanum: RB 30(1913)1-24. — A. D'Alès, Julien d'Éclane, Exégète: RSR 6(1916)311-324. — C. Weyman, Analecta XVI. Marius Mercator und Julianus von Äclanum: HJG 37(1916)77ff. — A. Vaccari, Nuova opera di Giuliano d'Eclano: CC 67/1(1916)578-593; *idem,* Il Salterio Ascoliano e Giuliano d'Eclano: Bibl 4(1923)337-355. — J. Forget, Julien d'Éclane: DTC 8(1925)1926-1931. — A. D'Amato, S. Agostino e il vescovo pelagiano Giuliano: Annuario del R. Liceo-Ginnasio P. coletta di Avellino 1928-29. Avellino 1930, 54-75. — A. Lepka, L'originalité des répliques de Marius Mercator à Julien d'Éclane: RHE 27(1931)572-579. — A. Vaccari, Il testo dei Salmi nel commento di Teodoro di Mopsuestia: Bibl 23(1942)1-17. — J. H. Baxter, Notes on the Latin of Julian of Eclanum: ALMA 27(1951)5-54. — M. Meslin, Sainteté et mariage au cours de la seconde querelle pélagienne. Saint Augustin et Julien d'Éclane: *Etudes Carmélitaines* 31(1952)293-307. — Y. De Montcheuil, La polémique de saint Augustin contre Julien d'Éclane d'après l'Opus imperfectum: RSR 44(1956)193-218. — G. Bouwman, Zum Wortschatz des Julian von Aeclaenum: ALMA 27(1957)141-164. — H. I. Marrou, La canonisation de Julien d'Éclane, in *Theologie aus dem Geist der Geschichte* (Festschr. B. Altaner) = HJG 77(1957)434-437. — G. Bouwman, Juliani Aeclanensis commentarius in prophetas minores tres, Osee, Joel, Amos: VD 36(1958)284-291 (résumé of the following work); *idem,* Des Julian von Aeclanum

Kommentar zu den Propheten Osee, Joel und Amos. Ein Beitrag zur Geschichte der Exegese (*Analectica Biblica* 9). Rome, 1958 (fundamental work). — G. De Plinval, Julien d'Éclane devant la Bible: RSR 47(1959)345-366. — S. Prete, Nota agostiniano. Baptizare, perfundere nella polemica pelagiana: *Paideia* 16(1959)250-252. — G. I. D. Aalders, L'Epître à Ménoch: VC 14(1960)245-249. — F. Clodius, El libre albedrío según Julián d'Eclano: *Anales de la Facultad de Teología de Santiago* (Chile) 13(1961)5-51, 273-287; 14(1962)99-134. — F. Perago, Il valore della tradizione nella polemica tra s. Agostino e Giuliano d'Eclano: *Annali facoltà Lettere e Filos. Univ. Napoli* 10(1962-63)143-160. — F. Refoulé, Julien d' Éclane, Théologien et philosophie: RSR 52(1964)42-84, 233-247; *idem,* Julien d'Éclane: *Catholicisme* 6(1966)1236-1239. — F. J. Thonnard, L'aristotelisme de Julien d'Éclane et saint Augustin: REAug 11(1965)296-304 (note to the two articles of Refoulé in RSR, useful for the sources of Julian's philosophy, esp. p. 233-247). — J. Tischoll, Augustins Aufmerksamkeit am Makrokosmos: AugL 15(1965)389-413. — N. Gambino, Le vicende storiche della "sancta Ecclesia Aeclanensis." Naples, 1967. — M. Abel, Le Praedestinatus et le pélagianisme: RTAM 35(1968)5-25. — N. Cipriani, Aspetti letterari del'Ad Florum di Giuliano d'Eclano: Aug 15(1975)125-167.

WORKS ATTRIBUTED TO JULIAN

1. *Praedestinatus,* an anonymous work of the fifth century is attributed to Arnobius the Younger by some and by others to Julian or someone from his circle. It was edited by J. Sirmond in 1643 with the title *Praedestinatus.*

Studies: CPL 243. — PL 53, 583-627, cf. *infra,* Arnobius the Younger. — H. v. Schubert, Der sogennante Praedestinatus (TU 24, 4). Leipzig, 1903. — G. Morin, Examen des écrits attribués à Arnobe le jeune, in *Textes Découverts.* Maredsous-Paris 1913, 309-324 (= RB 26[1909]419-432); *idem,* Études d'ensemble sur Arnobe le jeune, ibid., 340-382 (= RB 28[1911]154-190); *idem,* Un traité pélagien inédit du commencement du Ve siècle: RB 26(1909)163-188; *idem,* Un ouvrage restitué à Julien d'Eclanum: RB 30(1913)1-24. — M. Abel, Le Praedestinatus et le pélagianisme: RTAM 35(1968)5-25 (Arnobius). Cf. Bouwman, op. cit., p. 17-19.

2. The *Libellus fidei* was the *libellus* sent by the bishops of Northern Italy to their metropolitan, Augustine, at Aquileia, in opposition to the *Tractoria* of Zosimus. Numerous interpretations have been proposed for the letters SIC of the *explicit: Siculorum* (Garnier), *Sacerdotes Iesu Christi* (Tillemont), *Ambrosi Calcedonensis* (Mercati). New arguments have been advanced by J.–P. Bouhot against Julian's authorship of this composition.

Studies: CPL 778. — PL 48, 509-526; 45, 1732-1736. — Cf. Bouwman, op. cit., p. 4-5. — G. Mercati, Il nome dell'autore del Libellus fidei attribuito a Giuliano d'Eclano, in *Opere minori* II (ST 77). Vatican City 1937, 244-245. — J.–P. Bouhot, Version inédite du sermon "Ad Neophitos" de s. Jean Chrysostome utilisée par s. Augustin: REAug 17(1971)27-41.

3. The *Summarium antipelagianum* of the Pauline epistles is attributed to Julian by D. De Bruyne (RB 39[1927]45-55).

AN(N)IANUS

During the Pelagian polemic, Jerome and Orosius refer to a person, never indicated by name, who was a protector and faithful disciple of Pelagius. It is possible that he was a member of the powerful Roman family of the Anici. Jansen identified him with Pelagius himself, while Vossius (*Historiae de controversiis quas Pelagius eiusque reliquiae moverunt, libri* VII. Leiden, 1618) considered it to be Julian, and Noris (*Historia pelagiana* I, p. 19) considered him to have been a separate individual. The anonymous individual in Jerome (*Ep.* 133 [Pelagius?]; 138; 151) and in Orosius (*Lib. apol.* 2) who was so active in the Pelagian polemic although always behind the scenes — "He did not enter the conflict himself but directed the entire battle" (Orosius, *Lib. apol.* 2) — is usually identified with Anianus the deacon of Celeda, and the Greek chronographer Annianus, a few fragments of whose works are preserved. Jerome speaks of the *Libros Aniani pseudodiaconi Celedensis* (*Ep.* 143, 2).

Anianus is, therefore, to be located in the context of the relations which were developing in the East between the Pelagians and the Easterners, especially those of the Antiochene School. He is found at the side of Pelagius at Diospolis just as from 417 Julian was alongside Theodore of Mopsuestia. It was in the circle connected to Julian that Theodore's Commentary on Paul was translated into Latin.

Studies: CPL 771-772. — E. Honigmann, Patristic Studies (*Studi e Testi* 173). Vatican City 1953, 54-58; *idem,* Le prétendu "moine Athénée" en réalité le chronographe Annianus, in Mélanges H. Grégoire. Brussels 1950, 177-180. — Ch. Baur, S. Jean Chrysostome et ses oeuvres dans l'histoire littéraire. Louvain, 1907, 64f.

The translation of the seven homilies on St. Paul and of the first homilies of the commentary on Matthew of John Chrysostom are very likely to be attributed to Anianus.

Studies: H. Musurillo, John Chrysostom's Homilies on Matthew and the Version of Annianus, in *Kyriakon,* Festschr. Quasten, I. Münster 1970, 452-460. — R. Skalitsky, Annianus of Celeda: His Text of Chrysostom's Homilies on Matthew: *Aevum* 45(1971)208-233.

It is possible that Anianus was the translator of the so-called ascetical appendix to the collection of the 38 homilies of pseudo-Chrysostom: *De compunctione* I-II, *De eo quod nemo laeditur nisi a seipso, Ad Theodorum.* However, this is attested only from the time of Cassiodorus. It is possible that he was also the translator of the *De sacerdotio.*

Editions: CPG 4400, 4305, 4308-4309, 4316. — J. Dumortier, S. Jean Chrysostome. A. Théodore. SCh 117(1966)241-322. — A. M. Malingrey, Une ancienne version latine du texte de Jean Chrysostome "Quod nemo laeditur": SE 16(1965)230-354.

THE FRIENDS OF AUGUSTINE

(PAUL) OROSIUS

1. Life

(Paul) Orosius, whose forename Paul is possibly inauthentic (Zangenmeister, CSEL 5, xxxi), was born almost certainly at Braga between 375 and 380 (Avitus of Braga, PL 41, 805ff: *compresbyter meus;* Gennadius, *De vir. ill.* 39: *presbyter hispanus genere*) during the years of the reorganization of the empire under the Spaniard, Theodosius. After Valen's defeat by the Goths (378), this Christian emperor confirmed the Nicene faith as the bond uniting all his subjects (Theodosius' constitution dates to the year 380, CT 16, 1, 2). The same period of time witnessed the decisive predominance of the barbarians in the West (the northwest part of the Iberian Peninsula fell in 409, Rome in 410). Orosius was an eyewitness of the developments of his age and of the new ideal of understanding among peoples. He no longer saw in the barbarians a people to be thrown back beyond the boundaries of the empire, but recognized the possibility of a coexistence with them within the bounds of the empire. The *Urbs Roma* thus became the *orbis romana* (*Hist.* I 1, 14) and the citizen, with his faith in Christ, was at the same time Roman and Christian. The emperor — in this case Theodosius — the guarantor of law and religion, was protected by God and was the ideal of the Roman and Christian prince. It is within this context that one must understand both the *Historias* of Orosius and his intervention in the Pelagian Controversy in defense of the common tradition of the church.

Because of difficulties with the Goths in Spain, he departed for exile in Africa. In 414 he presented himself to Augustine together with a work on the Priscillianist and Origenist errors of his region (*Ad Aurelium Augustinum Commonitorium de errore Priscillianistarum et Origenistarum:* CSEL 18, 151-157), to which he received a response in the same year (*Ad Orosium contra Priscillianistas et Origenistas liber unus:* PL 42, 669-677). Augustine then sent him to Jerome at Bethlehem concerning the questions regarding the origin of the soul. In July 415 he was at Jerusalem and participated in the meeting convoked by bishop John against Pelagius. From the information of Orosius concerning this meeting it is evident that it was a continuous and unrestrained altercation that was hardly propitious for the establishment of doctrinal clarifications. John of Jerusalem misunderstood Orosius to have stated that even with the help of grace, man cannot live without sin (*Liber apol.* 7: CSEL 5, 611). Orosius called Pelagius a toad, a filthy dragon to be kept locked up so that he might not escape

(*Liber apol.* 28 and 5), and Pelagius responded with: *et quis est mihi Augustinus?* (*Liber apol.* 4). Since the dialogue was unable to continue, it was decided to refer the entire matter to Pope Innocent (Mansi IV, 307-311). Meanwhile, Orosius carried a letter to Oceanus on the resurrection of the flesh (Augustine, *Ep.* 180, 5) and briefed Eros and Lazarus on the Pelagian Controversy (Augustine, *Ep.* 175, 1). Unable to return to Spain on account of the troubles of the barbarian invasion (Severus Maioricensis, *Ep. de Iudaeis:* PL 20, 733), he returned to Hippo where he wrote his *Liber apologeticus contra pelagianos* and began the seven books of the *Historiae adversus paganos.* This latter work is a comparison of the past and the present in order to explain to the pagans that the past was no better than the present, and thus the Christians were not to be considered the cause of the ruin of the empire.

This task had been entrusted to him by Augustine, who, having already written ten books of his *De civitate Dei,* requested Orosius to compile a compendium of world history up to the year 416 which would illustrate for his contemporaries the evils of the past. Orosius completed the task within two years. Since the last events treated date to the year 416, it is thought that the *Historiae* were completed in 417. They reflect the tradition of Roman historiography which praised outstanding virtue, in particular of the ancient Romans. Orosius' positive evaluation of contemporary events is today considered to be not only a result of the apologetic intent in defense of the Christians, but also a reflection of the actual state of affairs which had improved considerably after 410, especially in the Iberian Peninsula, thanks to the efforts of the patrician Constantius. The narration presents a trustworthy account of events, even though it always remains the account of a witness who is involved in the events he is describing. This is also true with regard to the information on the Pelagian polemic. It is, therefore, necessary in Orosius' writings to attend to the information which he has left and not to the polemical manner in which it is presented. He had access to excellent sources of information concerning the Pelagian question, even if he did not have the theologian's speculative mind to realize the consequences of certain formulations. His apology does not show the partiality of one involved in the events, even though one can always observe an innate defense of Christian truth against any opponent.

2. Writings

1. *Commonitorium de errore Priscillianistarum et Origenistarum*

Priscillian, who had died in some semblance of sanctity under the usurper Maximus, had spread many ideas connected with Gnosticism and Manichaeism, against which the Council of Toledo had taken a stand in the years 397-400. The problem of Origenism had also arisen alongside Priscillianism in the Iberian Peninsula. Orosius composed this work in opposition to these currents of thought which he considered to be opposed to Christianity. Augustine responded with the book *Contra Priscillianistas et Origenistas* which discussed various questions, including that of the origin of the soul.

Editions: PL 31, 1211-1216 (Gallandi) (response of Augustine: PL 42, 665-679). — G. Schepss, CSEL 18(1889)149-157.

Studies: J. A. Davids, De Orosio et sancto Augustino Priscillianistarum adversariis commentatio historica et philologica. Rotterdam, 1930.

2. *Liber Apologeticus contra Pelagianos*

The work is divided into two parts: n. 1-10 present Orosius' defense against the accusations made against him by John of Jerusalem; n. 11-33 are a presentation and refutation of the Pelagian doctrines drawn from the *Testimonia* and the *Ep. ad Demetriadem.*

Orosius presents Pelagius by means of certain affirmations which were circulating in Pelagian circles, emphasizing his physical and moral defects and seeing him as the leader of a revived Priscillianism and Origenism. He emphasized in particular the question of the relation between the possibility of man being able not to sin and the grace of God. Pelagius attributed *impeccantia* to the will of man and connected to God's grace the idea of an aid which was not understood well by Orosius (*gratia quidem Dei adiuvante, sed mea possibilitate sum quod sum, Apol.* 11). For Pelagius it was a question of human nature which possessed in and of itself the possibility of doing good (*Apol.* 21). Orosius furthermore draws a distinction between *crimen* and *peccatum,* that is, between defect and moral imperfection.

From his defense against John of Jerusalem, it is clear that others understood him to be defending the position that man, once fallen under the dominion of sin, could not free himself even with the grace of God (*Apol.* 7 and 24-25). They, therefore, were accusing him of denying God's grace (*Apol.* 21: *Forte tu Dei adiutorium negas?*). Orosius responded that divine help was necessary in general and in particular for individual acts, which help God granted to all, both to those within the church and to others (*Apol.* 19). This was necessary because all bear from birth the *originale peccatum* of Adam (*Apol.* 26-27). As the result of such an inheritance, human nature is sick. It is not sin in itself so as to necessarily produce evil, but it is weak (*Apol.* 29 and 32: *peccamus, qui, cum infirmi sumus, de infirmitate conquirimur*).

The *Liber Apologeticus* contains certain general principles relative to the Pelagian polemic: original sin, the necessity of God's help for each person, the infirmity of human nature which, nevertheless, is not understood in a Manichaean sense as an evil substance. Orosius is content to state such principles and to defend them with the spirit of a Jerome rather than to develop them in a theological sense. Although he definitely represents the approach of the African Church and of Augustine in particular, he did not distort the Pelagian ideas current at the time. Rather, he has left behind a true-to-life account of the polemic between Pelagius and others.

Editions: PL 31, 1173-1212 (Havercamp). — K. Zangenmeister, CSEL 5(1882)603-664 (this edition corrects the interpolations drawn from Augustine, especially from the *De natura et gratia,* contained in the edition of Havercamp).

Translation: English: R. M. Gover, The Liber Apologeticus of Paulus Orosius. Diss., Queens College, New York, 1969 (typewritten).

Studies: S. Prieto, Paolo Orosio e o Liber Apologeticus. Braga, 1951. — J. Svennung, Zur Textkritik des Apologeticus Orosii: *Arctos* 5(1967)135-139 (from ms. *Paris.* 16332). Other studies in the general bibliography.

3. *Historiarum adversum paganos libri I-VII*

The subtitle *"adversus paganos"* is also found in the *De civitate Dei,* while other titles, e.g., *De Ormesta mundi* and *Hormesta,* are more recent (cf. F. Wotke, RE 18[1939]1195).

In the prologue, Orosius explains that, at Augustine's request, he is going to compile a history of the world from its origins. His concept of history is that humanity, as long as it was ignorant of Christianity, was dominated by death and thirsty for blood. Divine Providence, nevertheless, guided history, which finds the central point of its development in Rome. Rome and Jesus Christ thus find their synthesis in Orosius. It is, therefore, a history composed against the pagans for the use of Christians who were in contact with the pagans.

Book I presents the world and its history from the Flood to the foundation of Rome; book II contains the history of Rome until the sacking of the city by the Gauls, of Persia until the time of Cyrus, and of Greece until the Battle of Cunaxa; book III deals with the Macedonian Empire and the history of Rome of the same period; book IV contains the history of Rome up to the destruction of Carthage, and books V, VI, and VII continue Roman history from the destruction of Carthage until 416.

Posterity associated Orosius with the work of Augustine, and the approval of his seven books against the pagans by the *Decretum Gelasianum* assured him of a place in ecclesiastical tradition. Some 200 mss. of his work indicate that he was one of the most widely read of the ancient writers.

Editions: PL 31, 663-1174 (Havercamp-Galandi). K. Zangenmeister, CSEL 5(1882)1-600; *idem,* editio minor (Teubner). Leipzig, 1889.

Translations: English: I. W. Raymond, New York, 1936. — R. J. Deferrari, FC 50(1964). *Italian:* A. Bartalucci, in A. Loppold, Orosio, Le storie contro i pagani, 2 vols. Milan, 1976 (Fondazione L. Valla).

Bibliographies: Ancient Sources: Gennadius, De viris ill. 39. — Severus, Ep. de Iudaeis (ed. G. Seguí Vidal, La carta-encíclica del Obispo Severo. Palma de Mallorca, 1937). — Augustine, Ep. 166 and 169.

Manuscripts: Anterior to 1952 cf. G. Fink, Recherches bibliographiques sur Paul Orose: RABM 58(1952)271-322. — D. J. A. Ross, Illustrated Manuscripts of Orosius: *Scriptorium* 9(1955)35-56. — J. M. Bateley, D. J. A. Ross, A Check List of Manuscripts of Orosius' Historiarum adversus paganos libri septem: *Scriptorium* 15(1961)329-344 (list of 245 mss.). — J. M. Bateley, King Alfred and the Latin mss. of Orosius' History: *Classica et Mediaevalia* 22(1961)69-105. — L. Feuriot, La découverte de nouvelles gloses en vieux-breton: CRI(1959)186-195; *idem,* Mélanges vieux-bretons: *Etudes Celtiques* 9(1960-61)155-190. — B. Schreyer, Die althochdeutschen Glosen zu Orosius. Halle, 1959.

Studies: For bibliography prior to 1952 cf. G. Fink, Recherches bibliographiques sur Paul Orose: RABM 59(1952)271-322. — A. Lippold, Rom und die Barbaren in der Beurteilung des Orosius. Erlangen, 1952. — K. A. Schöndorf, Die Geschichtstheologie des Orosius. Eine Studie zur Historia adversus Paganos des Orosius. Diss., Munich, 1952 (typewritten). — F. Elias de Tejada, Los dos primeros filósofos hispanos de la historia, Orosio y Draconcio: *Annuario de la Hist. del Derecho Esp.* 23(1953)191-201. — A. Lippold, Der erste punische Krieg bei Orosius: RhM 97(1954)254-286. — M. A. Ramos Motta Capitão, Santo Agostinho na obra de Paulo Orosio: *Filosofia* 1(1954)34-40. — C. Torres Rodríguez, La obra de Orosio. Su Historia. Santiago de Compostela, 1954. — G. Fink-Errera, San Agustín y Orosio. Esquema para un estudio de las fuentes del "De civitate Dei": CD 167/II(1954)455-549 (special edition). — J. Vaz de Carvalho, Dependera s. Agostinho de Paolo Orosio: *Revista Portug. de Filosofia* 11(1955)142-153. — D. D. Martins, Paulo Orosio. Sentido universalista de sua vida e da sua obra: ibid., 11(1955)375-385. — C. Torres Rodríguez, La historia de Paulo Orosio: RABM 61(1955)107-135. — B. Lacroix, La importancia de Orosio: *Augustinus* 2(1957)3-13. — T. E. Mommsen, Aponius and Orosius on the Significance of the Epiphany, in *Medieval and Renaissance Studies.* Ithaca, N.Y., 1959, 229-234 (= Late Clas. and Medieval Studies, Miscell, Friend, Princeton 1955, 96-111); *idem,* Orosius and Augustine, ibid., 325-348. — F. Masai, Nouveaux fragments du Paul Orose de Stavelot en écriture onciale, in Mélanges L. Herrmann. Berchem-Brussels 1960, 509-521. — A. Freixas, La visión imperial de Paulo Orosio: *Anales Hist. antigua,* Buenos Aires 1959-60, 84-98 (Cf. RHE 59[1964]238). — M. Gesino, El libro séptimo de las Historias contra los paganos de Paulo Orosio: ibid., 99-155. — H. J. Diesner, Orosius und Augustinus: *Acta Antiqua Ac. Hungaricae* 11(1963)89-102. — A. Momigliano, in *The Conflict between Paganism and Christianity in the Fourth Century.* Oxford 1963, 79-100. — B. Lacroix, Orose et ses idées. Montreal, 1965. — A. Hamman, Orosius de Braga et le pélagianisme: *Bracara Augusta* 21(1967)346-355. — E. Corsini, Introduzione alle "Storie" de Orosio. Turin, 1968. — S. Karrer, Der gallische Krieg bei Orosius. Zurich, 1969. — A. Lippold, Orosius christlicher Apologet und römischer Bürger: Phil 113(1969)92-105. — L. Alfonsi, Noterelle orosiane: *Aevum* 44(1970)153-154. — A. Lippold, Briechisch-makedonische Geschichte bei Orosius: *Chiron* 1(1971)437-455. — R. M. Klaros, Bamberger Orosiusfragmente des 9. Jarhrh., in Festschrift Bischoff. Stuttgart 1971, 178-197. — H. I. Marrou, S. Augustin, Orose et l'augustinisme, in *La storiografia altomedievale.* Spoleto 1970, 59-87. — J. M. Bateley, The Relationship Between Geographical Information in Old English Orosius and Latin other than Orosius: *Anglo-Saxon England* 1(1972)45-62. — F. Fabbrini, Paolo Orosio, uno storico. Rome, 1979. — M. J. Mir, Orosio y los ultimos tiempos del imperio: *Helmantica* 29(1978)383-397. — H. W. Goetz, Die Geschichtstheologie des Orosius. Darmstadt, 1980.

MARIUS MERCATOR

Marius Mercator was a convinced anti-Pelagian, and history has at times linked him with Augustine to the extent of claiming he was an African. However, he was definitely born in Italy and was possibly from the same region as Julian, given the close relations with Julian's family which are mentioned in the *Commonitorium super nomine Coelestii.* What little information there is concerning his life is connected entirely with the Pelagian polemic. He was in Rome in 418 and knew Caelestius, who was there to defend himself before Pope Zosimus. He wrote two anti-Pelagian works, now lost, which are known to have existed because he sent them to Augustine (Augustine, *Ep.* 193). In 429 he was at a Latin monastery in Thrace where he wrote the *Commonitoria* or notes on Caelestius, Pelagius and Julian of Eclanum, perhaps for ecclesiastical and court circles at Constantinople, who at that time were concerned with the Pelagian and Nestorian questions. After the condemnation of Caelestius and Nestorius at the Council of Ephesus there is no further notice of Marius Mercator.

Writings

1. *Commonitorium super nomine Coelestii*

This work, which was published in Greek in 429 and translated into Latin by Mercator himself in 431, is a brief memorandum *(commonitorium)* of the condemnations passed against the Pelagians:

c. I. the condemnation of Caelestius at Carthage on the initiative of Paulinus with the six charges of the accusation; the expulsion of Caelestius from Constantinople by Atticus; Caelestius' self-defense at Rome and his defeat.

c. II. a collection of propositions of Pelagius collected from his writings and speeches.

c. III. the condemnation of Caelestius and Pelagius by Innocent and Zosimus; the *Epistola tractoria* of Zosimus and its refutation by certain bishops, including Julian; the Synod of Diospolis and a synod held under Theodotus, bishop of Antioch.

c. IV. the Pelagian position of Caelestius likened to that of Pelagius.

c. V. an appeal to Julian and other Pelagians not to follow the example of Pelagius but to submit to the Apostolic See.

This work is more concerned with Caelestius than with Pelagius. The sources for it are letters, *libelli,* writings and homilies drawn from Pelagian circles which are attributed to Pelagius and Caelestius. Modern studies now permit a more selective attribution of the material to Pelagius, Caelestius, and other Pelagian circles. Nevertheless, the documentation preserved by Mercator reflects the general Pelagian ideas in circulation. For example, although there is no documentation for Mercator's statement that the *libellus* of Paulinus contains the Pelagian creed preached by Caelestius at Carthage (*Comm.* 1, 1 and 4, 1-2), it is nevertheless true that it presents the essential Pelagian ideas. Mercator's *Commonitorium* is neither a biography of Caelestius nor a summary of Pelagian doctrine, but a memorandum, and it must be used as such.

2. *Commonitorium adversum haeresim Pelagii et Coelestii vel etiam scripta Iuliani = Liber subnotationum*

This work was written after 430, most likely in 431. It speaks of Augustine as already dead (August 28, 430), *sanctae recordationis episcopus,* and the author has the *opus imperfectum* at hand.

After a brief introduction listing the condemnations inflicted against the Pelagians, the revolt of Julian and the refutations of Augustine, the work goes on to refute a series of statements drawn from the works of Julian. These refutations do not differ greatly from those of Augustine although they do include personal observations.

This work also mentions a commentary of Mercator on the letter of Julian of Eclanum to Zosimus (ACO I 5, 1, p. 12-23) in which he accuses Julian of understanding the relation of Adam and Christ with their descendants merely as an example.

He also wrote two books against Theodore of Mopsuestia, which have been lost. In *Ep.* 193, 1, Augustine writes: *inveni et alium adversus novos haereticos librum,* and L. E. Du Pin identified this *librum* of Mercator with the *Hypognosticon* or *Hypomnesticon* (*Nouvelles bibl. des auteurs ecclés.* t. 3. Paris, 1689). However, the arguments contained in this book concerning *libido* and predestination are not found elsewhere in the works of Mercator, and thus do not support Du Pin's hypothesis (cf. *supra* p. 000).

Sometime prior to 550, the writings of Mercator were inserted, together with other works of a Scythian monk, into the collection known as the *Collectio Palatina* (Vatican Library, *Palat. lat.* 234). E. Schwartz edited the critical edition of his works in 1924 and provided all the documentation relating to the life and writings of Mercator. R. M. J. Poirel *(Vincentii Peregrini seu alio nomine Marii Mercatoris Lirinensis Commonitoria duo.* Nancy, 1898) attempted to attribute the *Commonitoria* of Vicent of Lérins to Mercator, but this proposal never attracted any following and was rejected the following year by H. Koch (ThQ 81[1899]396-434).

Editions: PL 48, 63-172 (Garnier). — E. Schwartz, ACO I 5, 1, p. 3-70 (best edition). — S. Prete, Bologna, 1959 (text of Schwartz with notes).

Translations: Italian: S. Prete, op. cit.

Studies: F. von Schulte, Marius Mercator und Pseudo-Isidor (SAW 147, 7). Vienna,

1904. — C. Weyman, Marius Mercator und Julian von Aeclanum: HJG 37(1916)77-78. — E. Schwartz, Die sogennanten Gegenanathematismus des Nestorius. Munich, 1922. — E. Amman, DTC 12(1927)2481-2485. — W. Eltester: PWK 14(1930)1831-1835. — G. Krüger: RE 12(1930)342-344. — A. Lepka, L'originalité des répliques de Marius Mercator à Julien d'Eclane: RHE 27(1931)572-579. — S. Prete, Mario Mercatore polemista antipelagiano. Turin, 1958.

QUODVULTDEUS

Quodvultdeus was a deacon of the Church of Carthage and a friend of Augustine to whom he turned in 428 for a compendium of heresies to enable him to more easily defend Christian Africa from such errors (*Ep.* 221 and 223 among the letters of Augustine). There is general agreement on the identification of the deacon Quodvultdeus with the bishop of Carthage of the same name who was expelled from the city during the occupation of Gaiseric and took refuge at Naples (*Acta Sanctorum* 60, tom. 11, 851). Rather than involving himself in the controversies and problems of the fifth century, such as Pelagianism and a society in search of a new order, he dedicated himself to his diaconal and episcopal ministry in a strictly pastoral sphere and concerned himself with awakening and preserving the faith of his people. He died in exile at Naples no later than October 454.

Writings

The works of Quodvultdeus in the critical edition of R. Braun (CCL 60) include the following: 1) *Liber promissionum et praedictorum Dei;* 2) homiletic works: *Contra Iudaeos, paganos et arrianos; Adversus quinque haereses;* three sermons: *De symbolo; De quattuor virtutibus caritatis; De cantico novo; De ultima quarta feria; De cataclysmo; De tempore barbarico* I; two sermons *De accendentibus ad gratiam; De tempore barbarico* II; 3) in an appendix, the two letters sent to Augustine requesting a *commonitorium* on heresies.

The works now attributed to Quodvultdeus in the edition of the CCL have a long history in modern criticism. It consists of a *corpus* of a homiletic and pastoral nature and a catechetical-exegetical treatise (the *Liber promissionum*). This was seen by some as a completely homogeneous collection (the thesis accepted by Braun) which was thus to be attributed to a single author. Others, however, accepted a homogeneity of content but not of style and thus supported an attribution to various unidentified authors (the thesis of M. Simonetti accepted in Altaner's *Patrologie* 1977[7], p. 474 and to a certain extent in the Clavis nn. 401-412 which follows the conclusions of P. D. Franses). Bearing in mind the difficulty of a definite attribution of these works, it is nevertheless possible to accept in a general way the conclusions of R. Braun on the attribution of the *corpus* of writings to Quodvultdeus.

It is a homogenous collection of catechetical material of African origin which reflects fifth-century African baptismal catechesis regarding the initiation of the catechumens and the baptismal rites relative to the symbol.

The *Liber promissionum et praedictorum Dei,* which is also known as the *Liber de promissionibus et praedictionibus Dei* in the edition of the works of Prosper of Aquitaine published at Lyons by Gryphe in 1539, was written between 445 and 455 (*Lib.* III 44, 28: *sub Constantio et Augusta Placidia quorum nunc filius Valentinianus pius et christianus imperat;* Gallia Placidia died November 27, 450) near Naples (*Dimidium temporis* 12, 3: *apud Campaniam constitutis*). It was attributed already in the sixth century to Prosper of Aquitaine and was restored to Quodvultdeus only by G. Morin (RB 31[1914]161).

The work is a collection to *testimonia* from Scripture arranged according to the scheme of reading salvation history in use in the preparation of catechumens, as Augustine indicates in his *De catechizandis rudibus.* It is an *iter in scripturis sanctis* from the beginning of creation until the time of the writing with the purpose of imparting a knowledge of Christ and the church. More precisely, it arranges the entire treatment according to the program of Augustine and also of Pelagius into history *ante legem, sub lege* and *post legem* and divides it into 153 chapters according to the number of the miraculous catch of fish: 40 (*ante legem*), 40 (*sub lege*), 40 (*sub gratia*), 20 (*dimidium temporis,* the half of 40), 13 (the *gloria sanctorum*). The typology is that of Augustine, according to which the historical facts of the Bible possess a more profound spiritual sense in relation to Christ and the church. The work also contains quotations from the pagan poets, particularly Vergil, which are interpreted in a Christian manner. It is possible to regard the *Liber promissionum* almost as a catechist's manual for the *narratio* of the Bible (Old and New Testament) to the catechumens.

Editions: CPL 413. — PLS III, 149. — PL 51, 733-854 (Lebrun des Marettes and Mangenot). — R. Braun, CCL 60(1976)11-223.

Translations: French: R. Braun, Livre des Promesses et des Prédictions de Dieu I-II. SCh 101-102(1964).

1. Homilies

The *Sermones de symbolo* resemble the similarly titled sermons of Augustine regarding the rites of the *traditio* and *redditio symboli* during the preparation for baptism. The other homilies display a concern with guarding the people against the danger of Arianism which was penetrating among the Christians as a result of the Vandal invasions.

Editions: CPL 401-402. — PLS III, 261-262. — PL 50, 637-708 (partial edition). — PLS III, 261-322. — R. Braun, CCL 60(1976)227-486.

2. Letters

There are two letters of Quodvultdeus which have been handed down as letters 221 and 223 of Augustine. They are the only two letters extant under the name of Quodvultdeus, deacon of Carthage, which he wrote to Augustine to request a *commonitorium de haeresibus*. Augustine replied to both letters (*Ep.* 222 and 224).

Editions: 221 and 223 among the letters of Augustine: PL 33, 997-999, 1000-1001. — CSEL 57(1911)442-446, 450-451. — R. Braun, CCL 60(1976)489-492.

Studies: Cf. the bibliography in R. Braun, CCL 60(1976)512-516 for questions concerning the attribution, identification and interpretation of certain passages. P. Capelle, Le texte di Psautier latin en Afrique. Rome, 1913. — G. Morin, Pour une future édition des opuscules de saint Quodvultdeus, évêque de Carthage au Ve siècle: RB 31(1914)156-162 (examination of the 12 pseudo-Augustinian sermons now attributed to Quodvultdeus). — P. Schepens, Un traité à restituer à Quodvultdeus: RSR 10(1919)230-243 (the *Liber Promissionum* is attributed to Quodvultdeus independently of the sermons). — D. Franses, Die Werke des hl. Quodvultdeus, Bishof von Karthago. Munich, 1920. — P. Schepens, Les œuvres de saint Quodvultdeus: RSR 13(1923)76-78. — A. Kappelmacher, Echte und unechte Predigten Augustins: WSt 49(1931)89-102. — A. D. Nock, Two Notes: I) The Asklepius and Quodvultdeus: VC 3(1949)48-55. — M. Simonetti, Studi sulla letteratura cristiana d'Africa in età vandalica: RIL 83(1950)407-424 (a critique of Franses on the basis of style and language and redistribution of the sermons attributed to Quodvultdeus: attribution to Augustine of *Acc.* I and II, *Temp. barb.* II and perhaps *Adv. V haer.;* to an unknown author the three sermons *De symbolo, Contra Iud* and perhaps *Cant.;* to another unknown author *Ult. Fer., Catac.* and perhaps *Temp. barb* I). — B. Bischoff, Die lateinischen Übersetzungen und Bearbeitungen aus den Oracula Sibyllina, in Mélanges J. De Ghellinck I. Gembloux 1951, 121-147. — S. Jannaccone, La dottrina eresiologica di S. Agostino. Catania, 1952 (p. 19 maintains that *Ep.* 223 is prior to *Ep.* 222 and that the prologue of the *De haeresibus* is Augustine's response to a lost letter of Quodvultdeus. This opinion has not gained acceptance). — C. Lambot, Critique interne et sermons de saint Augustin: SP 1 (TU 63). Berlin 1957, 112-127. — R. Braun, Un témoignage littéraire méconnu sur l'Abaritana provincia: *RevAfricaine* 103(1959)114-116. — H. J. Diesner, Zur Datierung des Briefes 220 und anderer Spätschriften Augustins: FF 35(1961)281-283. — R. G. Kalkmann, Two Sermons De Tempore barbarico attributed to St. Quodvultdeus, Bishop of Carthage. Diss., Cath. Univ. of America, Washington, 1963 (typewritten). — A. Lippold, Quodvultdeus: PWK 47(1963)1396-1398. — M. Bogaert, Sermon sur le cantique de la vigne attribuable à Quodvultdeus: RB 75(1965)109-135. — P. Courcelle, Quodvultdeus redivivus: REAN 67(1965)165-170. — M. Pellegrino, Intorno a Quodvultdeus, De promissionibus et praedicationibus Dei: RSLR 2(1966)240-245. — Y. M. Duval, Un nouveau lecteur probable de l'Histoire ecclésiastique de Rufin d'Aquilée, l'auteur de Liber promissionum et praedicationum Dei: Latomus 26(1967)762-777. — D. Ambrasi, Quodvultdeus: *Bibliotheca Sanctorum* 12(1968)1335-1338. — J. Lafaurie, Cruces in vestibus: *Bulletin Soc. Franç. Numismatique* 28(1973)336-340. — M. Simonetti, Note sul testo di alcuni passi di opere attribuite a Quodvultdeus: RFIC 106(1978)291-299; *idem,* Qualche riflessione su Quodvultdeus di Cartagine: RSLR 14(1978)201-207.

CHAPTER VIII

WRITERS OF GAUL

by Adalbert Hamman

translated from the French by Vittorino Grossi

EUCHERIUS OF LYONS

"He was undoubtedly the greatest of the great bishops of his time." Thus does Claudius Mamertus introduce Eucherius, whom he knew personally. He was born of a noble and apparently Christian family, and his writings bear witness to a level of culture which was admired by Erasmus. He completed a brilliant career and was perhaps a senator.

Eucherius married Galla, and the couple had two sons, Salonius and Veranus. By mutual agreement, the couple disposed of their goods and withdrew to the island of Lérins. They entrusted their sons to the monastery of Saint Honoratus, where Hilary, Salvian, and Vincent took charge of their education. Salonius was, at this time, only ten years old. Eucherius wished to go to Egypt to visit the monasteries there. Since he was not able to do this, Cassian dedicated the second part of the *Conferences* to him in order to compensate in some way for this desire which could not be realized. He maintained his contact with the world through his correspondence, especially with Paulinus of Nola (*Ep.* 51: PL 61, 417). His reputation for sanctity caused him to be nominated bishop of Lyons shortly after 432. He took part in the Council of Orange in 441 and died around 450 (Gennadius, *De vir. ill.* 64[63]).

Studies: G. de Montauzan, Saint Eucher, évêque de Lyon et l'école de Lérins: *Bulletin historique du diocèse de Lyon* 1923, 81-96. — L. Cristiani, Lérins et ses fondateurs. Saint-Wandrille 1946, 193-275. — N. K. Chadwick, Poetry and Letters in Early Christian Gaul. London, 1955. — L. Cristiani, Eucher: DSp 4(1961)1653-1660. — R. Etaix, Eucher: DHGE 15(1963)1315-1317. — P. Courcelle, Nouveaux aspects de la culture lérinienne: REL 46(1968)379-398. — S. Pricoco, L'isola dei santi. Il cenobio de Lerino e le origini del monachesimo gallico. Rome, 1978.

WRITINGS

Before becoming a bishop, Eucherius wrote two brief works in the form of letters: *De laude eremi* and *De contemptu mundi*. There is also extant a letter sent to Salvian of Marseilles from Lérins (fragments in the *Vita S. Hilarii Arel.* 11 and in the sermon *De vita S. Honorati* 4, 22). Two exegetical works, the *Formulae spiritualis intellegentiae* and the

Instructionum libri duo ad Salonium, date from the time of his episcopacy. The Bollandists and a majority of historians attribute the *Passio Acaunensium martyrum* to him, and Claudius Mamertus has preserved a fragment from Eucherius' works (*De statu animae* 2, 9). His homilies have been lost. An abridgement of his works, the *Glossae spirituales,* appeared in the eighth century.

The following works are not considered authentic: the *Commentarii in Genesim et in libros Regum,* the *Exhortatio,* and the *Sententiae ad monachos:* PL 50, 895-1208, 865-868, 1207-1210; the letter to Philo published by Baluze: PL 50, 1413-1414; and the *De situ Hierosolomytanae urbis:* PLS III, 45-58.

Regarding the fragments of the *Epitome operum Cassiani* composed by Eucherius and discovered in a manuscript at Paderborn, cf. K. Honselmann, "Bruchstücke von Auszügen aus Werken Cassians. Reste einer verlorenen Schrift des Eucherius von Lyon?": ThGl 51(1961)300-304.

EDITIONS

The *editio princeps* (without the *De laude eremi*) was made by J. A. Brassicanus at Basel in 1531 and is reprinted in PL 50. The first edition of the *De laude eremi* was made by Dionysius Faucherius at Paris in 1578. The first complete edition was published at Paris without a date (1525-1530), and although it is the best edition, it has been forgotten. CSEL 31, published by K. Wotke at Vienna in 1894, contains only the *Formulae, Instructiones, Passio* and *De laude eremi* (regarding this edition cf. R. Etaix, *op. cit.,* p. 1317).

1. *De laude eremi*

The work was composed around 427 for the priest, Hilary, the future bishop of Arles, after his return from a stay at Arles with the bishop, Honoratus. Eucherius praises solitude, "the temple without bounds of our God," and develops the biblical theme of the desert where Moses, Elijah, Elisha, and John the Baptist were sanctified.

Editions: PL 50, 701-712. — C. Wotke, CSEL 31(1894)177-194. — S. Pricoco, De laude eremi. Catania, 1965.

Translations: French: L. Cristiani. Paris, 1950.

Studies: L. Alfonsi, Il De laude eremi di Eucherio: *Convivium Bal.* 36(1968)361-369. — I. Opelt, Zur lit. Eigenart von Eucherius Schrift De laude eremi: VC 22(1968)198-208 (themes used for the desert).

2. *De contemptu mundi et saecularis philosophiae*

This composition is an exhortation to a high-ranking relative, Valerianus, who is possibly to be identified with the future Praetorian Prefect of Gaul mentioned by Sidonius Apollinaris (*Ep.* 5, 10). By citing such famous examples as Gregory, Paulinus and Ambrose, Eucherius emphasizes the ephemeral and transitory character of earthly wisdom and possessions, and proposes that it is sufficient for the Christian to aspire to the glories of heaven, his true goal. The work testifies to the broad scope of Eucherius' secular and Christian culture, which was nourished above all by the reading of ascetics such as Cassian, Rufinus, and the author of the *Confessiones.*

Editions: PL 50, 711-726 (Brassicanus).

Translations: English: H. Vaughan, reprinted by L. C. Martin. Oxford, 1914. *French:* L. Cristiani. Paris, 1950. *Italian:* C. Giacinto Gariboldi. Milan, 1715.

3. *Formulae spiritualis intelligentiae*

The *Formulae,* which are dedicated to his son, Veranus, distinguish the body, the soul and the spirit in the Scripture according to the teaching of Cassian. The body corresponds to the literal sense, the soul to the tropological and the spirit to the more profound, or anagogical, sense which leads to the holiest mysteries.

Editions: Cf. CPL 488 and B. Fischer: VT 225. — PL 50, 727-772. — C. Wotke, CSEL 31(1894)3-62. — Centos of citations in PL 42, 1199-1208.

Studies: C. Curti, Spiritalis intelligentia. Nota sulla dottrina esegetica di Eucherio di Lione: *Kerygma und Logos,* Festschr. C. Anderson. 1979, 108-122.

4. *Instructiones ad Salonium*

The *Instructiones,* dedicated to his son, Salonius, explain in the form of questions and answers the difficult passages of the Bible from Genesis to the Apocalypse. The second book explains difficult terms (Hebrew and Greek names, place names, and measures). Eucherius makes use of Jerome's *Onomasticon,* but follows the text of the Vulgate only sporadically.

These two books were highly regarded by subsequent compilers and teachers as is seen from the many interpolations contained in the edition in Migne.

Editions: Cf. CPL 489. — B. Fischer, VT 253. — PL 50, 773-822. — C. Wotke, CSEL 31(1894)63-161.

Studies: I. Opelt, Quellenstudien zu Eucherius: Hermes 91(1963)476-483.

5. *Passio Acaunensium martyrum, S. Mauricii et sociorum eius*

This is the oldest account of the martyrs of the Theban Legion. The letter accompanying the account contains the name of Eucherius, who addresses it to the bishop Salvian of Octodurum in Valais. The title "frater" in the closing salutation indicates that one bishop is writing to another.

The authenticity of the attribution, which was questioned by B.

Krusch and D. van Berchem, is generally accepted, especially by the Bollandists (BHL 5737).

Editions: PL 50, 827-832. — MGH scr. mer. III, ed. Krusch, 1896, 32-39. — C. Wotke, CSEL 31(1894)163-173.

Translations: Italian: C. Curti, La "Passio Acaunensium martyrum: di Eucherio di Lione, in *Convivium dominicum.* Catania 1959, 297-327 (text of B. Krusch; defends the historicity of the narration which was amplified by Eucherius).

Studies: M. Besson, La question du martyre de S. Maurice et de ses compagnons: *RevCharlemagne* 2(1912)129-189. — Martyrologium Romanum. Brussels 1940, 410. — D. van Berchem, Le martyre de la légion thébaine. Essai sur la formation d'une légende. Basil, 1956, cf. AB 74(1956)260-263. — L. Alfonsi, Considerazioni sulla Passio Acaunensium martyrum: *Studi Rom* 8(1960)52-55. — L. Dupraz, Les passions de s. Maurice d'Agaune. Fribourg, 1961. — H. Bellen, Der Primicerius Mauricius: *Historia* 10(1961)238-247. — R. Henggeler, *Bibliotheca Sanctorum* 9(1967)193-204.

6. *Epistula ad Salvium episcopum*

This letter, which was joined to the text of the *Passio Acaunensium martyrum,* is the only extant piece from Eucherius correspondence.

Editions: PL 50, 827-828. — C. Wotke, CSEL 31(1894)173. — MGH scr. mer. III, ed. B. Krusch. Hannover 1896, 39-41.

EUTROPIUS

The priest, Eutropius, lived at the end of the fourth and beginning of the fifth century. He was most likely from Aquitania and a contemporary and friend of Paulinus of Nola. His correspondent, Cerasia, was possibly a relative of Paulinus' wife. Gennadius (*De vir. ill.* 50 [49]) mentions two letters which he wrote to some virgins who had been disinherited by their parents because they had consecrated themselves to the religious life, and he praises the letters' elegant form, solid reasoning and profound biblical inspiration. Beginning with the indications of Gennadius, J. Madoz has been able to reconstruct the major part of Eutropius' work which was dispersed under other names (PLS I, 527-528).

1. The *Epistula de condemnanda haereditate:* PL 30, 47-50 among the works of Jerome. The letter is addressed to Cerasia and her sister, the daughters of Gerontius. Tillemont and D. Vallarsi had already restored the attribution to Eutropius.

2. The *Epistula de vera circumsicione:* PL 30, 188-210 among the works of Jerome. This letter is intended for the same addressees as the preceding and exhorts them to a spiritual circumcision for a reward worthy of the greatest renunciations. The letter was possibly influenced by the doctrine of Pelagius.

3. The *Epistula de perfecto homine:* PL 30, 75-104 among the works of

Jerome, and PL 57, 933-958 among the works of Maximus of Turin. It is likewise addressed to Cerasia. P. Courcelle, who found it along with the two preceding letters among the works of pseudo-Jerome (Paris BN 1688), restored the attribution to Eutropius.

This letter describes the sentiments which must guide the zealous Christian: renunciation of worldly wisdom, contemplation of the power of God, of the miracle of the Incarnation and of the Resurrection of Christ, the pledge of our resurrection. The letter also bears witness to certain negative spiritual tendencies of the fifth century such as asceticism, the cult of the martyrs and resistance to the doctrine of the resurrection of the body. It also reveals the influence of Tertullian on the doctrine of the virginity of Mary and gives evidence of a dialogue between Jews and Christians.

4. *De similitudine carnis peccati.* This treatise, which was discovered and published as a work of Pacian of Barcellona by G. Morin, was regarded as a work of Pelagius by Plinval. The attribution was restored to Eutropius by J. Madoz, a fact graciously accepted by Morin himself.

It is an exegesis of Rom. 8:3 sent to Cerasia around 415 and intended to describe the physical condition of Adam, of man and of Christ.

Eutropius was an admirer of Ambrose and a friend of Paulinus, and was himself well-versed in the fields of literature and philosophy. His method was Platonic in inspiration, and his literary formation was nurtured by personal reflection. He imitated Juvenal, cited Vergil and Cicero, and often made allusions to classical rhetors and philosophers. His good biblical formation is evident in the struggle against Arianism and Manichaeism as well as in the principles of his own spiritual life.

Editions: Letters: PL 30, 45-50, 75-104, 188-210 (Vallarsi, Venice, 1766-1772). — PL 57, 933-958 (B. Bruni, Rome, 1974).
De similitudine carnis: G. Morin, Études, textes . . . Maredsous 1913, 107-150 (= PLS I, 529-556 and 1746-1747).

Studies: A. Gruber, Studien zu Pacianus. Diss., Munich, 1901. — R. Kauer, Studien zu Pacianus. Vienna, 1902. — G. Morin, Un traité inédit du IVe siècle de l'évêque Pacien de Barcelone: RB 29(1912)1-28 (= Études, textes découvertes, 81-103. Against the thesis of Morin, cf. M. Mercati: ThR 14[1915]116). — Ph. Borleffs, Zwei neue Schriften Pacians'?: Mnen 7(1937)180-192. — L. Tria, "De similitudine carnis peccati." Il suo autore e la sua teologia. Rome, 1936. — J. Madoz, Herencia literaria del prebíter Eutropio: EE 16(1942)27-54. — G. Morin, Brillantes découvertes d'un jésuite espagnol et rétraction qui s'en suit: RHE 38(1942)411-417. — J. Madoz, Vestigios de Tertulliano en la doctrina de la virginidad de María en la carta "ad amicum aegrotum. De viro perfecto": EE 18(1944)187-200. — F. Cavallera, L'héritage littéraire et spirituel du prêtre Eutrope: RAM 24(1948)60-71. — P. Courcelle, Un nouveau traité d'Eutrope, prêtre aquitain, vers l'an 400: REAN 56(1954)377-390; *idem,* Histoire littéraire des grandes invasions germaniques. Paris 1964[3], 307-317. — F. Di Capua, Ritmo e paronomasia nel trattato "De similitudine carnis peccati" attribuito a Paciano di Barcellona, in *Scritti minori* I. Rome 1959, 419-430. — A. Michel, La culture en Aquitaine au Ve siècle: *Annales du Midi* 71(1959)115-124. — G. de Plinval, Eutrope: DSp 4(1961)1729-1731 (bibliography). — T. Moral, Eutrope: DHGE 16(1967)79-82 (good historical presentation). — H. Savon, Le De vera circumcisione du prêtre Eutrope et les premières éditions imprimées des Lettres de saint Jérôme: *Revue d'Hist. des Textes* 10(1980)165-197; *idem,* Pseudothyrum et faeculentia dans une lettre du prêtre Eutrope (Ps.-Jérôme, Ep. 19): RPh 55(1981)91-110.

EVAGRIUS

The monk Evagrius from southern Gaul is mentioned by Gennadius (*De vir. ill.* 51[50]). Ceillier has attempted to identify him with the priest Evagrius, the disciple of St. Martin, who, at the death of the Bishop of Tours, joined Sulpicius Severus (*Dial.* 3 1, 4; 3 2, 8). Although Harnack questioned this identification, it nevertheless remains likely.

According to Gennadius, the *Altercatio legis inter Simonem Iudaeum et Theophilum Christianum* brought Evagrius a general notoriety. Harnack believed too hastily to see in this work the Latin transposition of the *Dialogus inter Iasonem et Papiscum* of Aristo of Pella, which was cited by Celsus, but this hypothesis has been abandoned. The work of Evagrius is thoroughly Western and its principal sources are Tertullian, Cyprian (especially the *Testimonia*), Gregory of Elvira, Phoebadius, and Eucherius; all of which testifies to the breadth of the author's information.

The main subject of the *Altercatio* is Christ. The discussion is based on the Old Testament with the purpose of harmonizing monotheism with the Trinity and the divinity of Christ. The Jew poses brief questions to which the Christian responds at length. Simon opposes the virginity of Mary, accuses the Christians of abandoning circumcision and the sabbath, and cites Deut. 21:23 on the curse on anyone who hangs from the cross. Theophilus responds by showing how the Passion was foretold by the prophets.

At the conclusion of the discussion the Jew is not only convinced but is also converted. The treatise concludes with a profession of faith in the form of a thanksgiving, which is interesting for the ancient liturgy for the baptism of Jews. The importance of the Jews in the south of Gaul is well known.

The Maurists attempted to attribute to Evagrius the *Consultationes Zachaei christiani et Apollonii philosophi* (PL 20, 1071-1166) which were written in Africa in the fifth century (cf. PLS I, 1095).

Editions: PL 20, 1165-1172 (E. Martène). — A. Harnack, TU 1, 3. Leipzig 1883, 1-136. — E. Bratke, CSEL 45(1904).

Studies: E. Bratke, Epilegomena zu der Wiener Ausgabe. Vienna, 1904. — D. De Bruyne, L'Altercatio d'Evagrius: RB 23(1906)178-183 (sources). — A. Marmorstein,

Juden und Judentum in der Altercatio: *Theologisch Tijschrift* 49(1915)360-383. — A. L. Williams, Adversus Iudaeos, A Bird's-Eye View of Christian Apologiae Until the Renaissance. Cambridge 1935, 298-311. — J. O. Tjäder, Ein Verhandlungsprotokoll aus dem J. 433 n. Christ.: *Scriptorium* 12(1958)6-39 (mss.). — B. Blumenkranz, Les auteurs chrétiens latins du moyen age sur les Juifs. Paris 1963, 27-31. — R. Aubert, Evagre: DHGE 16(1967)102.

HILARY OF ARLES

Hilary provides information on his own life in his *De vita S. Honorati.* He was a relative of this bishop-founder of Lérins who attracted him to monastic life, and became Honoratus' favorite disciple. He spent some time at Arles when Honoratus was bishop of the city, and the latter attempted to detain him there. When his death was approaching, Honoratus designated Hilary to the people as his successor, but when the funeral was over, Hilary fled. He was finally constrained to accept (429-430) and exercised his episcopal ministry for more than twenty years. He was an accomplished preacher to an extent to be compared to St. Augustine. He was a bishop who lived close to his people and had a special concern for the poor and the weak. It is possible that he established a monastery in Brittany.

Hilary defended the privileges granted the Church of Arles by Pope Zosimus and, on the strength of the primatial authority of his episcopal see, he deposed Chelidonius, bishop of Besançon. The latter appealed to Leo I and Hilary journeyed to Rome to defend his conduct. His inflexible arrogance precluded any chance of success, and Leo the Great forbade the bishop of Arles to intervene in the province of Vienne (Jaffé 407).

Hilary died on May 5, 449 at age 48. The *Vita Hilarii* (BHL 3882) is a document of great value. The author gives his name as *Reverentius,* which is possibly a pseudonym for Honoratus of Marseilles.

Studies: B. Kolon, Die Vita s. Hilarii Arel. Paderborn, 1925. — L. Cristiani, Lérins et ses fondateurs. Saint-Wandrille 1946, 99-192. — D. Franses, Paus Leo de Groote en S. Hilarius van Arles. Bois-le-Duc, 1948. — F. Benoit, L'Hilarianum d'Arles et les missions en Bretagne, in *Saint Germain d'Auxerre et son temps.* Auxerre 1950, 181-189. — A. Fuhrmann, Die Fabel vom Papst Leo und Bischof Hilarius: *Archiv f. Kulturgeschichte* 43(1961)125-162. — E. Griffe, La Gaule chrétienne à l'époque romaine, II. Paris 1966, 200-212, 242-251, 286-288. R. W. Mathisen, Hilarius, Germanus and Lupus. The Aristocratic Background of the Chelidonius Affair: *Phoenix* 33(1979)160-169.

WRITINGS

Only a few of Hilary's works are extant: an *Epistula ad Eucherium Lugdunensem,* the sermon *De vita S. Honorati Arelatensis episcopi,* and some verses, *De fontibus Gratianopolitanis,* which are preserved by Gregory of Tours. His biography makes mention of *homiliae in totius anni festivitatibus expeditae,* an *expositio symboli,* and other letters.

Dubious works are: the *Sermo de vita S. Genesii* (BHL 3306), the

Sermo seu narratio de miraculis S. Genesii martyris Arelatensis (attributed to Hilary by Cavallin), and the *Expositio de fide catholica* (considered as possibly authentic by F. Kattenbusch).

Spurious works are: the *Expositio in VII epistulas catholicas* (PLS III, 58-131) an eighth-century Irish work, and the *Passio S. Genesii* (BHL 3304; cf. PLS III, 55-56).

Editions: PL 50, 1219-1246 (ed. Salinas, Rome, 1731: Vita Hil., Serm. Hon., Ep. ad Euch.). — *Serm. Hon.* in S. Cavallin, Vitae ss. Honorati et Hilarii. Lund, 1952 (cf. VC 7[1954]116-117; 10[1956]157-159). — M. D. Valentin, SCh 235(1977). — *Ep. ad Euch.* in C. Wotke, CSEL 31(1894). — *V. de fontibus* in F. Büchler, A, Riese, *Anthologia latina* I, 2. Leipzig 1906, 37. — *Expositio fidei* of dubious authenticity, in A. E. Burn: ZKG 19(1899)180-182. — K. Künstle, Eine Bibliothek der Symbole. Mainz 1900, 173-175.

Translations (Sermo de vita s. Honorati): English: R. J. Deferrari. FC 15(1952)361-394. *French:* M. D. Valentin, op. cit.

Studies: F. Kattenbusch, Das Apostolische Symbol 2. Leipzig 1900, 453 n. 35. — S. Cavallin, Saint Genès le notaire: *Eranos* 44(1945)150-175 (discussion of the dubious and inauthentic works). — P. Grosjean, Notes d'hagiographie celtique: AB 75(1957)183-185. — C. Curti, Un genitivo assoluto nella vita s. Hilarii ep. Arel.: MSLC 13(1963)35-40. — P. Courcelle, Nouveaux aspects de la culture lérinienne: RELA 46(1968)379-409. — S. Pricoco, Modelli di santità a Lerino. L'ideale ascetico nel Sermo de vita Honorati di Ilario di Arles: SicGym 27(1974)54-88. — G. Gallo, Uno scritto filo-pelagiano attribuibile a Ilario di Arles: *Aevum* 51(1977)333-348. — F. E. Consolino, Fra biografia e confessio; la forma letteraria del Sermo de vita S. Honorati di Ilario d'Arles: Orph 2(1981)170-182.

HONORATUS OF ARLES

Born in Belgian Gaul, possibly of a family of consular rank, Honoratus already as a youth received baptism, renounced the world and undertook a pilgrimage to Greece with his brother Venantius. After his brother's death, Honoratus returned first to a cave of the Estérel and then to the island of Lérins which bears his name today. There he founded a monastery which attracted such important personages as Salvian, Lupus, Eucherius, and Hilary and rapidly became a center of spiritual and cultural influence. John Cassian dedicated *Conferences* 11 and 17 to him. Hilary of Arles, his relative and successor in the See of Arles, speaks in the *Sermo 4 De vita Honorati* of a rule which Honoratus gave to his community. After the death of Patroclus, and following the brief episcopate of Euladius, Honoratus became bishop of Arles in 428. On an island in the Rhone, he founded a monastery which would become famous on account of one of his successors, Caesarius of Arles. He died on the Epiphany around the year 430, more from exhaustion than from illness. "Under his guidance," wrote his panegyrist, "the church of Christ flourished just as his monastery has previously flourished."

Nothing remains from his literary activity (letters, the rule), and the anonymous *Vita S. Honorati* (BHL 3977) is a late work.

Studies: B. Munke, Die Vita S. Honorati nach drei Handschriften herausgegeben. Halle, 1911. — A. C. Cooper-Marsdin, The History of the Islands of Lérins. Cambridge, 1914. — F. Bonnard, S. Honorat de Lérins. Tours, 1914. — L. Cristiani, Lérins et ses fondateurs. Saint-Wandrille, 1946. — S. Cavallin, Vitae ss. Honorati et Hilarii. Lund, 1952. — E. Griffe, La Gaule chrétienne à l'époque romaine II: l'Eglise des Gaules au Ve siècle. Paris 1966, 236, 241-245; III: La cité chrétienne. Paris 1965, 236-238, 332-338. — P. Courcelle, Nouveaux aspects de la culture lérinienne: RELA 46(1968)379-409. — S. Pricoco, L'isola dei santi. Il cenobio de Lerino e le origini del monachesimo gallico. Rome, 1978. — A. de Vogüè, Sur la patrie d'Honorat de Lérins, évêque d'Arles: RB 88(1978)290-291.

JOHN CASSIAN

John Cassian is one of the most notable writers of Gaul in the fifth century. Gennadius of Marseilles (*De vir. ill.* 62[61]) describes him as *natione scytha,* indicating almost certainly the Roman province of *Scythia minor* (Dobruja). This traditional thesis was defended by Tillemont and has been accepted by E. Schwartz and H. I. Marrou against any assumption of an origin in Provence or the East.

He was a Latin "of an ancient family of landed proprietors" (Marrou) which was deeply Christian, and he received the name of John at baptism. The ancient historians called him Cassianus (Gennadius, Cassiodorus, Gregory of Tours, Pseudo-Gelasius), which might be "the geographical nickname which bound him to his native district" (Marrou).

Cassian received a careful classical education as a youth, and the memory of Vergil followed him into the desert (*Conl.* 14, 2). He knew Greek perfectly, which he had perfected during his stay in the East. About 380, when he was barely past adolescence, Cassian departed for Palestine together with his fellow-countryman, Germanus. He settled at a monastery at Bethlehem to learn the cenobitic life. After two years, he obtained permission to visit the monks in Egypt. He visited the *coenobia* and went as far as the desert of Scete where he remained for a considerable time among such famous monks as Moses and Paphnutius. The *Conlationes* (except 10-20) reflect this visit.

Cassian returned to Bethlehem after seven years, but following a short stay he returned to the desert of Scete in 386 or 387. The Origenist controversy, which caused confusion among the monks, forced him to leave Egypt around 399. He went to Constantinople, undoubtedly attracted by the prestige of John Chrysostom, who ordained him deacon (*De incar.* 8 31, 1).

In 404 he returned *in patria* together with a companion bearing a letter of appeal to Pope Innocent from the clergy of Constantinople in favor of their exiled bishop. He remained at Rome for some time, and made the acquaintance of the future pope, Leo the Great. It is assumed that his stay at Rome was lengthy, and it is impossible to establish whether or not he returned to the East. In 415 or 416 Cassian is found at Marseilles, where he settled as a priest and founded two monasteries, one for men and one for women, which are customarily identified with St. Victor and St. Salvator. He advised Castor, bishop of Apt, concerning the foundation of his *novellum monasterium*. His idea was to organize Western monasticism, already established at Lérins, for a return to the traditions of the Apostles. As a result of his monastic experience in the East, he sought to adapt this monasticism by integrating into the cenobitic life the essentials of *anachoresis*.

At Marseilles, at the urging of the bishop, Castor, he composed his monastic writings: the *De institutis coenobiorum* dedicated to Castor, the *Conlationes* (between 420 and 429), and the *De incarnatione* (around 430). He died around 435 and was immediately venerated as a saint in both East and West.

Studies: A. Hoch, Zur Heimat des hl. Joh. Cassianus: ThQ 82(1900)43-69 (Syrian origin). — S. Merkle, Cassian kein Syrer: ThQ 82(1900)419-422 (against the thesis of Hoch). — O. Abel, Studien zu dem gallischen Presbyter Johannes Cassianus. Munich, 1904. — A. Ménager, La patrie de Cassien: EO 21(1921)330-358 (from Sythopolis in Galilee). — J. B. Thibaut, Autour de la patrie de Cassien: EO 21(1921)447-448; *idem,* Etude biographique sur Jean Cassien de Serta, in *Ancienne Liturgie gallicane.* Paris 1929, appendix 102-129 (from Sert, near Bitlis). — F. J. Dölger, Ausschluss der Bessessenen: AC 4(1934)122-125. — M. Olphe-Galliard, Cassien: DSp 2(1937)214-276. — E. Schwartz, Lebensdated Kassians: ZNW 38(1939)1-11. — L. Cristiani, Cassien I-II. Paris, 1946. — M. Cappuyns, Cassien: DHGE 11(1949)1319-1348 (proposes a provençale origin; complete bibliography). — M. Rothenäusler, Cassiano Giov.: EC 3(1950)1001-1004. — E. Griffe, Cassien a-t-il été prêtre d'Antioche?: BLE 55(1954)140-145. — J. C. Guy, Jean Cassien, vie et doctrine spirituelle. Paris, 1961; *idem,* Jean Cassien, historien du monachisme égyptien?: SP 8. Berlin, 1965, 363-372 (presents the theory of monastic life, not a history of Egyptian monasticism). — A. S. Constantinescu, Jean Cassien, scythe, pas romain: *Glasul Bisericii* 23 (Bucharest 1964)688-705. — O. Chadwick, John Cassian. Cambridge, 1968². — F. Prinz, Cassiano Giovanni: *Dizionario Ist Perf* 2(1975)633-638. — H. I. Marrou, La patrie de Jean Cassien, in *Patristique et Humanisme.* Paris 1976, 345-361. — C. Tibletti, Giovanni Cassiano. Formazione e dottrina: Aug 17(1977)335-380. — C. Leonardi, Alle origini della cristianità medievale. Giovanni Cassiano e Salviano di Marsiglia: StudMed 18(1977)1057-1174. — P. Rosseau, Ascetics, Authority and the Church in the Age of Jerome and Cassian. Oxford, 1978. — A. de Vogüé, Les mentions des oeuvres de Cassien et ses contemporains: *Stud Monastica* 20(1978)275-285.

WRITINGS

Cassian was a man of letters. His vocabulary and syntax are those of an educated person familiar with Greek who uses a Hellenized terminology. He is a writer who is at times suggestive, at times evocative and observant, who knows how to mix in local color in his dialogues, anecdotes, picturesque images, and oratorical style.

The greater part of his writing is dedicated to monasticism. He ventures into theological questions only at the end of his life with regard to the Incarnation.

Editions: PL 49-50 (ed. Gazet, Arras-Douae 1616; good commentary, poor edition). Concerning previous editions cf. PL 49, 11-26. For the editions in incunabula cf. Gesamtkatalog der Wiegendrucke VI. Leipzig 1934, 218-221. — M. Petschenig, CSEL 13 and 17(1886 and 1898).

Greek translation: Photius, Biblioth. PG 103, 661. Cf. E. Dekkers, Les traductions grecques des écrits patristiques latins: SE 5(1963)213-214.

Studies: B. Corbett, F. Masai, L'édition Plantin de Cassien: *Scriptorium* 5(1951)60-74. — P. Cazier, Cassien, auteur présumé de l'épitomé des Règles de Tyconius: REAug 22(1976)267-297.

1. *De institutis coenobiorum*

Cassian wrote his first work, which is dedicated to bishop Castor of Apt, at a mature age. The work is divided into twelve books, but the second part, *De octo principalium vitiorum remediis* (5-12) soon became detached as a separate work and is not contained in the two oldest manuscripts (Monte Cassino and Autun, *saec.* VII).

The work begins with the dedicatory preface to Castor which is followed by the first part on the life of the monk (1-4): clothing (1), the night office according to the Egyptian custom (2), the day office according to the Palestinian and Mesopotamian custom (3), the common life and the virtues proper to it (4).

The second part begins with a new dedication to Castor and then goes on to treat of the vices against which the monk must struggle in order to obtain perfect purity of heart: gluttony (5), lust (6), greed (7), anger (8), melancholy (9), sloth (10), vainglory (11) and pride (12). It is the same list of vices drawn up some years previously by Evagrius Ponticus (PG 40, 1272-1276).

The letter of Castor to Cassian (PL 49, 53-54) is not authentic (PLS III, 17).

Cassian presents his work as an introduction to the interior and sublime doctrine which he would develop in the *Conlationes* which he already had in mind to write. In the West, Eucherius made an abridgement of the *Institutes* and the *Conferences* which has been lost, although C. Honselmann believes he has discovered some fragments in a manuscript of Paderborn (cf. *supra,* "Eucherius"). The *Institutes* were translated into Greek in the fifth century. From this translation an abridgement was made in Greek (different from that of Eucherius) in two books which was known to Photius and was used by Pseudo-Nilus (PG 79, 1435-1472). Montfaucon published the Greek text from a manuscript of Cardinal Altemps, which attributed it to Athanasius, and translated it into Latin (PG 28, 849-905). The abridgement is found in the *cod. Vindobon. graec theol.* 121, of which K. Wotke published the beginning (Vienna, 1898).

Editions: PL 49, 43-476 (Alard Gazet). — M. Petschenig, CSEL 17(1888)3-321. — J. C. Guy, SCh 109(1965).

Translations: English: E. C. S. Gibson, LNPF 11, ser. 2(1894)201-290 (reprint: 1973). *French:* E. Pichery, S. Maximin, 1925. — J. C. Guy, op. cit. *German:* A. Abt, H. Kohlund, BKV (1873). *Italian:* P. M. Ernetti. Praglia, 1956. *Spanish:* L. M. and P. M. Sansegundo. Madrid, 1957.

Studies: F. Diekamp, Eine moderne Titelfälschung: RQ 14(1900)341-355. — S. Marsili, Résumé de Cassien sous le nom de Ps. Nil: RAM 5(1934)241-245. — J. Froger. Note pour rectifier l'interprétation. Inst. 3, 4; 6: ALW 2(1952)96-102. — K. Honselmann, Bruchstück von Auszügen aus Werken Cassians: ThGl 51(1961)300-304. — G. H. Brown, Codes Vat. lat. 13025 Cassiani Institutiones: *Manuscripta* 17(1973)22-27.

2. *Conlationes XXIV*

The *Conferences,* which were conceived as the complement and completion of the *Institutes,* are three writings which are at the same time distinct yet interconnected: the first part (1-10), which was requested by Castor of Apt, who died in the meantime (425-426), is dedicated to his brother Leontius and to Helladius; the second part (11-17) is dedicated to the "brothers" Honoratus and Eucherius; the third part (18-24) to the four abbots of Lérins: Jovinian, Minervius, Leontius and Theodore. The various chapters follow the stages of the sojourn in Egypt.

The *Conferences* 1-10 (sojourn at Scete) are a veritable treatise on perfection: the aim of monastic life (1) and discretion (2) presented by Abba Moses; the three vows by Paphnutius (3); concupiscence, the flesh and the spirit by Abba Daniel (4); the eight deadly vices by Serapion (5); sin by Theodore (6); spiritual combat and the powers of the spirit of evil by Serenus (7-8); the analysis and ways of prayer by Isaac (9-10).

The *Conferences* of the second part, which was completed in 427, are situated at Panephysis at the beginning of the voyage in Egypt, and are presented in chronological order: on perfection (11), chastity (12), and the protection of God (13) by Abba Chaeremon; spiritual knowledge (14), charisms and miracles (15) by Nestor; friendship among the perfect (16) and resolutions (17) by Abba Joseph.

Conferences 18-20, written between 428 and 429, are situated at Diolcos: on the three types of monks by Piamun (18); on the goal of the cenobitic and eremitic life by Abba John (19); on penance and reparation by Pinuphius (20).

Conferences 21-24 (to be situated at Panephysis according to Petschening) seem to belong to the period of Scete: interior freedom

(21), the temptations of the flesh (22), and the impeccability which is not of this world (23) presented by Theonas; the sweetness of the service of God (24) presented by Abraham.

Gennadius already knew the work as it exists in its present state. The three parts circulated independently and are found joined together for the first time in a Paris manuscript (*Nouv. acq. lat.* 2170) of the ninth century. The *Conferences* are composed in the form of a dialogue in which Germanus, or sometimes Cassian, presents the question to be discussed. The number 24 is intended to recall the 24 elders of the Apocalypse in such a way as to present the *Conferences* as homage offered to the Lamb. The *Conferences* are not intended to be scholarly treatises, but rather as interviews collected from masters of the spiritual life. They are not arranged in a logical order and various monks return to questions which have already been treated. The *Conferences* are Cassian's masterpiece and they exercised a profound influence on monastic life in the East as well as in the West, particularly on St. Benedict and Cassiodorus.

The *Decretum Gelesianum de libris recipiendis et non recipiendis* places Cassian's works on its index, undoubtedly because of the *Conferences*; in particular book 13 and the presentation of prevarication. In the line of Clement, Origen Chrysostom, and Hilary, Cassian permits prevarication in order to avoid a greater evil (*Conl.* 17, 17) while Augustine and Aquinas defend the opposite thesis.

In order to soften Cassian's statements on grace, editors such as A. Gazet have added a chapter 19 to book 13 which is a paraphrase written by Dennis the Carthusian in 1450 and which tones down the text. Jean de Lavendain, abbot of Stella, substituted the text of Dennis for book 13 in his French translation (Paris 1636).

Conference 23, 2-4 and 10-13 is found as a sermon among the apocryphal works attributed to Augustine (*Serm.* 102 and 103; PL 39, 1941-1946).

Editions: PL 49, 477-1321 (Alard Gazet). — M. Petschenig, CSEL 13(1886).

Translations: Dutch: A. van de Kar, Joannes Cassianus, Gesprekken, I-X. Bilthoven, 1968. *English:* E. C. S. Gibson, LNPF 11, ser. 2(1894)295-545 (reprint: 1973). *French:* E. Pichery, Le conférences, 2 vols. S. Maximin, 1920-22; *idem,* SCh 42, 52, 64(1955-1959; reprint: 1967-1971). *German:* A. Abt, H. Kolhund, BKV(1879). *Italian:* O. Lari, Conferenze spirituali, 3 vols. Rome, 1965. *Spanish:* L. M. and P. M. Sansegundo. Madrid, 1961.

Studies: U. Betti, Le "Collationes" di Cassiano in un ms. della Verna: SE 21(1972-1973)81-107. Regarding the teaching, cf. *infra.*

3. *De incarnatione Domini contra Nestorium libri VII*

The *De incarnatione,* which was written in 430 at the request of Leo, archdeacon of Rome, is Cassian's final work. The title varies in the manuscripts, which are less numerous than those for the other works. While composing the treatise, Cassian had at his disposal various texts taken from the sermons of Nestorius which were furnished by Leo, to whom Cassian dedicated the work in the preface.

In order to destroy this heresy, Cassian first of all denounces Pelagianism as the source of all evils. The error of Leporius is due to Pelagian influence (*De inc.* 1, 4), and the heresy of Pelagius is the source of the deviations of Nestorius which are manifest in his homilies. "Jesus Christ, born of the Virgin, is an ordinary man (*solitarius*) who, because of his virtuous life, merited to be united with divinity" (*De inc.* 5, 1). "The linking of Nestorius with Pelagianism is found also in Prosper. Augustine, too, had noticed connections between Christology and Pelagianism" (J. Plagnieux).

Cassian affirms the unity between the two natures in the unity of one and the same substance, of one single person: *Ubi vides inseparabilem penitus Christi ac Dei esse substantiam, inseparabilem quoque agnosce esse personam* (*De inc.* 3, 7). The title *Theotokos* applied to Mary is rooted in Scripture and Cassian produces numerous texts from the New and Old Testament as well as an entire dossier of patristic texts (*De inc.* 7, 24-30). At the end he makes a moving appeal to the Christians of Constantinople that they remain faithful to the teaching of their bishop John.

The composition of the treatise is weak, its structure obscure and its theological formulation is uncertain. Some of its expressions are close to those of Nestorius. Cassian is not a theologian by nature and he lacks a speculative spirit of a par with the Cappadocians or with Augustine. Nevertheless, he clearly recognizes the spiritual implications of the doctrinal truths. For him, the bond between Christology and spirituality is only too clear: if Christ is not the Son of God and Son of Man, the monk's efforts to arrive at the divinization promised remain an illusion. Monastic life, and indeed the entire Christian life, witnesses therein the collapse of its foundations. Cassian clearly recognizes the existential significance of doctrinal truths.

Editions: PL 50, 9-270 (Alard Gazet). — M. Petschenig, CSEL 17(1888)235-391.

Translations: English: E. C. S. Gibson, LNPF 11, ser. 2(1894)547-621 (reprint: 1973). *German:* A. Abt, H. Kolhund. BKV(1879).

Studies: Ch. Brand, Le De incarnatione Domini de Jean Cassien. Contribution à l'étude de la christologie en Occident à la veille du concile d'Ephèse. Diss., Strasbourg, 1954 (typewritten). — P. Courcelle, Sur quelques fragments non identifiés de la B. N., in *Recueil de travaux offerts à C. Brunel.* Paris 1955, 316-319. — J. Plagnieux, Le grief de complicité entre erreurs nestorienne et pélagienne. D'Augustin à Cassien par Prosper d'Aquitaine: REAug 2(1956)391-402. — B. Morel, De invloed van Leporius op Cassianus: BiNJ 21(1960)31-52.

DOCTRINE

1. Monastic Perfection

The *Institutiones* and the *Conlationes* are the *magna charta* of monastic life. Through these, Cassian brought the contribution of the method and experience of Eastern monasticism to the improvisations of Gallic monasticism.

"The monasteries," he writes, "continue the apostolic life, i.e., the life of the primitive church at Jerusalem gathered around the Apostles. The faithful who preserve in themselves the zeal of the Apostles leave the cities in order to live the ideal of the apostolic community far from the contaminations of the world" (*Conl.* 18, 5).

The monks are not innovators. They have their roots in the tradition of the apostolic age, the chief demands of which are the renunciation of all forms of ownership, the abandonment of one's own will through obedience, and the consecration of one's entire self to God by physical continence and purity of heart. Although monasticism was a communal movement at its origins, Cassian distinguishes two forms of its realization: cenobites and anchorites.

The former lead the communal life as did the apostolic community. The latter imitate the hermits Paul and Anthony and, following the teaching of the Alexandrians, find their models in holy men such as Elijah and Elishah in the Old Testament and John the Baptist in the New. It is these whom Cassian prefers as "the more sublime" (*Inst.* 5, 36).

Cassian does not present a systematic and structured body of spiritual doctrine. Its development, strongly influenced by the character of the author and the question and response method of presentation in the *Conferences,* is based on Scripture, on the traditions of the elders, and on personal experience. The Holy Spirit, who inspired the Bible, is also the master of the interior life, and cannot contradict Himself. The life of the monk is a confrontation between the Word and his own experience. Monastic life takes its point of departure from a call by God (*Conl.* 3, 3-5), but the law of the exodus is both a call to renunciation and to the following of God. The monk is one who, above all, lives a life of self-denial *(abrenuntians)*. "In order to manifest their desire of conversion to God they must begin a renunciation of the world" (*Inst.* 4, 1); an external and material despoliation accompanied by the renunciation of bad habits, passions, and vices. It is a spiritual struggle against the carnal man and against the assaults and the wiles of the devil; which struggle, far from destroying man, calls into action all the strength and resources of his will in order to bring him to evangelical perfection.

The purification from vices proceeds hand in hand with the acquisition of the virtues, particularly those of discretion, humility and patience, which put the vices to flight and cause chastity to flourish. This process then disposes the monk for the contemplation of the divine and brings purity of heart, peace and tranquility. *Mentis nostrae puritas tranquillitasque* is Cassian's expression for the *apatheia* of the Eastern ascetics (*Conl.* 1, 7). This marks the first stage on the way to perfection and corresponds to the cenobitic stage, which Cassian calls *scientia spiritualis.* The monk is now capable of plunging alone into the solitude of the desert and of initiating other brothers into the way he has traveled himself. This summit of the spiritual life is characterized above all by prayer reaching even to ecstasy, spiritual desire, and indescribable joy.

The soul is filled with spiritual fruits and remains close to God in continual prayer (*Conl.* 4, 2). These spiritual joys are associated with passive purifications of the soul, trials of every kind, which bring about the detachment from all bonds so that the soul may surrender in absolute poverty to the will of God. In this new status, which can be referred to as nuptial, there takes place the spiritual marriage, the intimate bond referred to by the Fathers as "union" (*Conl.* 10, 7). This state of charity bestows the simplicity of innocence and original integrity on the one who has been made perfect (*Conl.* 10, 11).

2. From the Scriptures to the Prayer of Fire

In his monastic directory, Cassian attaches primary importance to the Scriptures and to prayer; the one leading to the other through the work of the same agent, the Holy Spirit. The Bible is the book and the reading material *par excellence* for the monk. The numerous biblical citations contained in the *Institutiones* and the *Conlationes* and the various elaborations on the Scriptures are a measure of the primacy of place which the sacred books occupy in monastic spirituality. Equally obvious is the influence of Origen. If the attainment of the Kingdom of God is the purpose of the world (*Conl.* 1, 13), the assiduous reading of and meditation upon the Bible constitute the sure means for arriving there. The monk must always be ruminating on some part of the sacred text, e.g., a passage from the Psalter, in order to succeed in penetrating its profundity, i.e., the spiritual meaning, in purity of heart. This is especially true with regard to the psalms. The task of the monk is to appropriate the biblical prayer to such an extent that it becomes his own personal prayer. "Strive to apply yourself assiduously to sacred reading," says Abba Nestor, "so that this continual meditation may at last impregnate your soul and form it, so to speak, to its own image" (*Conl.* 14, 10). The monk then no longer recites it as the work of the prophet but as though he were himself the author, and as his personal prayer. Far from being a distraction from personal responsibilities, the continuous meditation on the Bible concentrates our spirit on the real significance of our work and on the one who inspires it. Such a practice, at the same time as it purifies and transforms our spirit, also renews the face of the Scriptures. "In concomitance with our progress, there grows the beauty of a more profound significance" (*Conl.* 14, 11).

This rumination on the Scriptures allows the monk to discover behind the text "the presence of Him who inspires it." It leads to a dialogue, to a prayer where the soul remains ever more silent, allowing God to speak and in that way perceiving the ineffable. This "constant prayer" at last realizes the monastic ideal which Cassian defines as the continual adherence to the divine and to God (*Conl.* 1, 8). Its ultimate expression is the "prayer of fire," "the gaze fixed on God alone, one great fire of love." This is a theme which fascinated this monk of Marseilles. "This prayer entirely of fire is known by very few and is in itself ineffable and transcends all human perception. The soul, illuminated by a brightness from above, no longer expresses itself in human speech, which is by nature inadequate to such realities. It has within itself a surge which arises from the holiest sentiments, an overflowing source from which prayer gushes abundantly and extends in an indescribable manner even to God" (*Conl.* 9, 25).

A considerable space in Cassian's work is dedicated to prayer, and several conferences are concerned with this topic (9 and 10; *Inst* 2 and 3). He dedicates a brief commentary to the *Pater* and develops the four forms of prayer according to the Pauline model, the culmination of which is the prayer of fire where the Bible and prayer intermingle (*Conl.* 9, 18-25; 15).

3. The Grace of God and the Freedom of Man

Conference 13 *"De protectione Dei"* of Abba Chaeremon, which attempts to harmonize God's grace with man's freedom has been the source of lively reactions. Prosper of Aquitaine opposed it in one of his polemical tracts *De gratia Dei et libero arbitrio liber contra Collatorem* (PL 51, 213-276). It would be rash to judge the matter through the eyes of an adversary, especially one who, at the time he responded to Cassian at least, was an unconditional Augustinian. Cassian, for his part, immediately recognized the shortcomings of Pelagianism and took a clear stand against it in the *De incarnatione,* written after the *Conlationes.* Cassian's teaching on grace in the *Institutis* presents the classic orthodox doctrine on the necessity of grace, without which nothing is possible (*Inst.* 5, 21), along the lines of John Chrysostom (*Hom. 4 in Gen.* 1). Between the composition of the *Institutes* and the *Conferences,* Augustine had written the *De correptione et gratia* in 427, which caused unrest in the monastic circles in Provence and at Hadrumetum. The utility of ascetical striving was called into question if predestination was absolute and everything depended on grace.

Cassian, one of the luminaries of the West, could not pass over the difficult problem of the relations between grace and freedom in silence. He felt obliged to intervene in the debate raised by the Pelagian Controversy, which he did in the famous Conference 13. He did this, to be sure, with tact and discretion which go unrecognized in the tendentious accusations of Prosper. The monk of Marseilles, who was concerned with the question of orthodoxy, was convinced that he was in line with the traditional faith which drew its inspiration from the theologians and spiritual masters of the East, especially Chrysostom. He was, furthermore, no innovator in the matter. More a spiritual master and psychologist than a metaphysician and theologian, Cassian was above all a director of souls whom he instructed in spiritual combat. He thus proceeded by an empirical rather than a speculative method. He denied a predestination to evil and every form of universal exclusion from salvation, and affirmed that even the beginnings of man's good intentions come from God (*Conl.* 3, 19).

Since he was above all a psychologist, he describes the concrete behavior to be followed by the monk, who calls into action every means available from his own freedom while at the same time expecting everything from grace. Faithful to the Greek tradition, he affirms that the original fall did not totally corrupt man, to whom there remains the possibility of doing good. Even though he is weak and fallen, man is still capable of good deeds. "By his fall," according to Gen. 3:22, "Adam did not lose the knowledge of good which he had received."

As was seen with regard to the *De incarnatione,* Cassian is less at ease on the plane of theological expression. He displays a lack of incisiveness and of precision both when he fails to distinguish sufficiently between the natural and the supernatural, and when he states at the same time that "God inspires the beginning of our good intentions" (*Conl.* 13, 3) and then says of such a beginning, "God, seeing that our will is turning to the good, rushes to our aid and directs and strengthens us" (*Conl.* 13, 11). He strives to maintain the two links of the chain, the necessity of grace and the "freedom to despise or to love God" (*Conl.* 13, 12) without developing sufficiently the relation between them.

In comparison to Augustine, Cassian had a different spiritual itinerary which influenced his concept of grace. He came from a fervently Christian family, and his religious formation disposed him "naturally" to the monastic life. Augustine, on the other hand, knew the experience of estrangement from Christianity and the triumph of sovereign grace. Between the Pelagian affirmations, which he rejected, and the intransigence of certain Augustinian formulae, the monk from Marseilles attempted to travel a *via media* which in the seventeenth century was improperly designated as Semi-Pelagianism. Cassian professed rather a semi-Augustinian position, or better, a mitigated Augustinianism.

4. Sources and Influence

Cassian's spiritual doctrine has its roots in the biblical, theological, and monastic tradition of the Greek Church. He makes free recourse to tradition and cites even the *Pastor of Hermas*. His concepts of freedom, of original sin, and of anthropology are derived from Irenaeus of Lyons.

His cultural and theological milieu is predominantly Alexandrian, as is especially evident in his spiritual exegesis of the Scriptures. He depends on Clement and Origen in his theory of the passions, takes his inspiration from Origen for his doctrine on purity of heart and from Evagrius Ponticus for his catalogue of the eight vices. In Cassian the concepts of "spiritual knowledge" and contemplative prayer are derived from Origen and Evagrius either in direct dependence or from a common source. He recognizes that along with his admiration for Chrysostom he is also indebted to him for his teaching: *Haec quae ego scripsi, ille me docuit* (*De incar.* 7, 31).

This voice from the East had already left its mark in the West in spite of the *Decretum Gelasianum* which classified him among the *opuscula apocrypha* (The *Decretum* itself was apocryphal!). Faustus of Riez, the various monastic rules, the *Regula magistri,* and the *Rule* of Benedict all drew inspiration from him. Cassian is to be found alongside the great masters in the Carolingian collections made by Alcuin and Rabanus Maurus. The number of manuscripts of his spiritual works bears sufficient witness to the esteem of the Latin Church for this man whom Cardinal Bona named the *perfectionis monasticae perfectissimus magister.*

Studies: J. Laugier, S. Jean Cassien et sa doctrine sur la grâce. Lyons, 1908. — L. Wrzol, Die Psychologie des Johannes Cassianus: DT 5(1918)181-213, 425-456; 7(1920)70-96; 9(1922)269-294; ibid, Die Haptsündenlehre des Joh. Cassianus: DT 10(1923)385-404. — E. Pichery, Les conférences de Cassien: VS 6(1921)289-298, 366-380, 434-450; *idem,* Les idées morales de J. Cassien: MSR 14(1957)5-20. — M. Rothenhäusler, Unter dem Geheimnisse des Kreuzes: BM 5(1923)91-96. — A. Ménager, La doctrine de Cassien: VS 8(1923)183-212; *idem,* Cassien et Clément d'Alexandrie: VS 9(1924)138-152; *idem,* A propos de Cassien: VS Suppl 46(1936)73-109. — F. Bauer, Die hl. Schrift bei der Mönchen des christ. Altertums nach J. Cassianus: ThGl 17(1925)512-531. — B. Albers, Cassians Einfluss auf die Regel des hl. Benedikts: *Studien u. Metteilungen:* 43(1925)32-53; 46(1928)13-22, 146-158. — D. Franses, Prosper et Cassianus: StC 3(1927)145-185. — B. Capelle, Les œuvres de Jean Cassien et la règle bénédictine: RLM 14(1929)307-

319; *idem,* Cassien, le Maître et saint Benoît: RTAM 11(1939)110-118. — M. Viller, La spiritualité des premiers siècles chrétiens. Paris 1930, 108-112. — M. Olphe-Galliard, Vie contemplative et vie active d'après Cassien: RAM 16(1935)252-288; *idem,* Les sources de la conférence XI de Cassien: ibid., 289-298; *idem,* La pureté de coeur d'après Cassien: RAM 17(1936)28-60; *idem,* Débat à propos de Cassien: RAM 17(1936)181-191; *idem,* La science spirituelle d'après Cassien: RAM 18(1937)141-160; *idem,* Cassien: DSp 2(1953)218-276. — Z. Golinski, Doctrina Cassiani de mendacio officioso: CTh 17(1936)491-503 (in Polish with résumé in Latin). — S. Marsili, Giovanni Cassiano ed Evagrio Pontico. Dottrina sulla carità e contemplazione. Rome, 1936. — A. Kemmer, Charisma Maximum. Louvain, 1938. — J. Kraus, Gregorius Nyssenus estne inter fontes Johannis Cassiani numerandus?: ZAM 13(1938)165-183. — Bloomfield, The Origin of the Concept of the Seven Cardinal Sins: HThR 34(1941)121-128. — J. Madoz, Un caso de materialismo en España en el siglo VI: RET 8(1948)203-230. — J. Chéné, Que signifiaient "initium fidei" et "affectus credulitatis" pour les semipélagiens?: RSR 35(1948)566-588; *idem,* Les origines de la controverse semi–pélagienne: AnThA 13(1953)56-109; *idem,* Le semipélagianisme du midi de la Gaule: RSR 43(1955)321-341. — O. Loorits, Der Heilige Kassien und die Schaltjarhlegende: FF *Communications* 149, Helsinki, Acad. Scient. Fennica, 1954. — P. U. Domínguez-Del Val, Eutropio di Valencia y sus fuentes: RET 14(1954)369-392. — H. Hantsch, Zur Vorgeschichte der Petitio in der Regel des hl. Benedikts: *Metteilungen d. Inst. f. Öster. Geschichtsforschung* 68(1960)1-15. — P. Munz, John Cassian: JEH 11(1960)1-22. — H. O. Weber, Die Stellung Cassians zur Mönchstradition. Münster, 1961. — J. C. Guy, Jean Cassien. Vie et doctrine spirituelle. Paris, 1961; *idem,* Jean Cassien, historien du monachisme égyptien?: SP 8. Berlin 1966, 363-372. — A. de Vogüé, Monachisme et église dans la pensée de Cassien, in *Théologie de la vie monastique.* Paris 1961, 213-240; *idem,* L'origine d'une interpolation de la Règle bénédictine: *Scriptorium* 21(1967)72. — J. Mateos, L'office monastique à la fin du IVe siècle: OC 47(1963)53-86. — O. Rousseau, Le prière des moines au temps de J. Cassien, in *Prière des heures* (Lex Orandi 35). Paris, 1963, 117-138. — A. Rouselle-Estève, Saint Benoît d'Aniane et Cassien: *Annales du Midi* 75(1963)145-160. — M. Ruiz Jurando, La penitencia en los Padres del desierto según Casiano: *Manresa* 35(1963)187-202. — J. Harper, John Cassian and Sulpicius Severus: CH 34(1965)187-202. — V. Codina, El aspecto cristológico en la espiritualidad di Juan Casiano (*Orient. christ. an.* 175). Rome, 1966. — F. Jálics, La tradición en Juan Casiano. Buenos Aires, 1966. — J. Leroy, Le cénobitisme chez Cassien: RAM 43(1967)121-158. — P. Miguel, Un homme d'expérience: Cassien: *Coll. Circ.* 30(1968)131-146. — J. Campos, La vie regia: *Helmantica* 20(1969)275-295. — M. de Elizalde, Nota sobre RB 7, 35 7 58, 3, tolerar las injurias: *Studia Monastica* 11(1969)107-114. — P. Christophe, Cassien et Césaire, prédicateurs de la morale monastique. Paris, 1970. — H. J. Sieben, Der Konzilbegriff des Vinzenz von Lerins (and of Cassian): *Theologie und Phil.* 47(1971)364-386. — K. S. Frank, Isidor von Sevilla, Das Mönchskapitel und seine Quellen: RQA 67(1972)29-48. — G. Switek, Discretio spirituum: *Theologie und Phil.* 47(1972)36-54. — J. Fontaine, L'ascétisme chrétien dans la littérature gallo-romaine d'Hilaire à Cassien, in *Atti del Colloquio sul tema La Gallia Romana* (Accad. dei Licei, quad. 158). Rome 1973, 87-115, 194-198. — P. Rosseau, Cassian, Contemplation and the Coenobitic Life: JEH 26(1975)113-126. — D. J. MacQueen, John Cassian on Grace and Free Will. With Particular Reference to Institutio XII and Collatio XII: RTAM 44(1977)5-28. — J. Rippinger, The Concept of Obedience in the Monastic Writings of Basil and Cassian: *Studia Monastica* 19(1977)7-18. — C. Leonardi, Alle origini della cristianità medievale: Giovanni Cassiano e Salviano di Marsiglia: *Studi Medievali* 18(1977)491-608. — A. Pastorino, I temi spirituali della vita monastica in Giovanni Cassiano: *Civiltà Classica e Cristiana* 1, 1(1980)123-172. — C. Folsom, Anger, Dejection and Acedia in the Writings of John Cassian: *American Benedictine Review* 35(1984)219-248.

LEO OF BOURGES

Together with Victorius, bishop of Le Mans and Eustochius, bishop of Tours, Leo, bishop of Bourges wrote an *Epistula ad episcopos et presbyteros infra tertiam provinciam constitutos.* The three bishops, who had taken part in the Council of Angers on October 4, 453, gave notice of their joint decision to depose clerics who had recourse to civil rather than ecclesiastical courts. According to Hinschius, this letter was found in the manuscript B. 19 of the Bourbon Palace in Paris which also contained the collection of the Pseudo-Isidorian Decretals. J. Merlin published the letter in his collection of councils in 1524 together with 94 letters attributed to Leo the Great, substituting the *tertiam* in the title with *Thraciam.* As such, it appears in the PL 130, 922.

In his edition of the works of Leo (Paris, 1675), P. Quesnel reprinted the letters published by Merlin, including the letter *ad episcopos,* and from this source it was printed in PL 54, 1239-1240. P. Sirmond was the first to attribute it to the bishop of Bourges. Tillemont (*Mémoires* XVI. Paris 1712, p. 770) expressed doubts regarding its authenticity, which is not, in fact, "completely above all suspicion" (Griffe).

Editions: PL 54, 1239-1240 (Quesnel, Paris 1675). — Ch. Munier, Concilia Galliae (CCL 148), p. 136 (reprints the ed. P. Sirmond, Concilia Antiqua Galliae, I. Paris 1629, 119).

Studies: L. Duchesne, Fastes épiscopaux de l'ancienne Gaule II. Paris 1900, 244-246. — C. Silva-Tarouca, Nuovi studi sulle antiche lettere dei Papi: Greg 12(1931)9. — E. Griffe, La Gaule chrétienne à l'époque romaine II. Paris 1966, 142.

LEPORIUS

Leporius, who according to Cassian was first a monk then a priest, was born at Trier, "the principal city of the Belgae." The barbarian invasions caused him to abandon that region and move to the South, perhaps to Marseilles, where he lived as a monk. Around 418 he was spreading a false doctrine regarding the Incarnation and was condemned by Proculus, bishop of Marseilles, and another bishop by the name of Cillenius.

Leporius then followed the advice of the Gallic bishops and went to Africa together with his followers to seek refuge with Augustine (Augustine, *Ep.* 219). He remained in Africa and was possibly accepted into the clergy of Hippo (Augustine, *Ep.* 213; *serm.* 356). Under the influence of Augustine, Leporius wrote the well-known retraction of his error, the *Libellus emendationis sive satisfactionis ad episcopos Galliae,* which was sent to Gaul accompanied by a guarantee of the bishops of Carthage and Hippo. This work was cited for its orthodoxy by the monks of Constantinople in 430 (Gennadius, *De vir. ill.* 60[59]).

The *Libellus* is an important document for Christology. Leporius testifies to a hypostatic union as a result of which *sic omnia dicimus quae erant Dei transisse in hominem, ut omnia quae erant hominis in Deum venissent* (PL 31, 1224). Augustine's influence had allowed this monk to understand that which the theologians would call the *communicatio idiomatum.* The document is a witness to the Latin Christology at the beginning of the fifth century, which is influenced in particular by Tertullian. The text was cited as a true standard of orthodoxy by Cassian (*De incar.* 1, 5), Leo the Great (*Ep.* 165, 6), Pseudo-Athanasius (*De Trin.* 10, 53), Arnobius (*Conflict.* 2, 8), John II (*Ep.* 3) and Facundus of Hermiana (*Pro defensione trium cap.* 1, 4).

Editions: PL 31, 1221-1230 (P. Sirmond). — P. Glorieux, Prénestorianisme en Occident (*Monumenta christiana selecta* 6). Tournai, 1959.

Studies: A. Trapè, Un caso de nestorianismo prenestoriano en Occidente: CD 155(1943)45-67. — Ch. Brand, Le De Incarnatione Domini de Jean Cassien: contribution à l'étude de la christologie en Occident à la veille du concile d'Ephèse. Strasbourg, 1954 (typewritten). — B. Morel, De invloed van Leporius op Cassianus: BiNJ 21(1960)31-52. — F. De Beer, Une tessère d'orthodoxie: le Libellus emendationis (ca. 418-421): REAug 10(1964)145-185 (basic and exhaustive study). — A. Chavasse, Le dossier de Leporius (ca. 418-421) et le l.X du de Trinitate pseudo athanasien: RB 74(1964)316-318. — E. Griffe, La Gaule chrétienne à l'époque romaine, II. Paris 1965 356-358. — J. L. Maier, La date de la rétractation de Leporius et celle du sermon 396 de s. Augustin: REAug 11(1965)39-42. — J. Mehlmann, Tertulliani de carne Christi a Leporio monacho citatus: SEJG 17(1966)290-301. — R. Weijenborg, Leo der Grosse und Nestorius, Erneuerung der Fragenstellung: Aug 16(1976)353-398 (denies the authenticity of the *Libellus* but without substantial proof).

LUPUS OF TROYES

Lupus was born at Toul around 395 of an aristocratic family and received a thorough education. Around 418 he married Pinieniola, the sister of Hilary of Arles, who belonged to one of the most distinguished families of Gaul. The influence of Honoratus, the founder of Lérins and relative of his wife, was certainly not lacking in the couple's mutual decision to renounce the world and lead a life of religious conversion. Lupus went to Lérins and placed himself under Honoratus' direction. A year later, as he was on his way to Mâcon to distribute what remained of his possessions to the poor, he passed through Troyes, where he was requested to become bishop of the city in succession to Ursus. He dedicated himself wholeheartedly to the care of his clergy and his people while continuing to lead the monastic life. Two years later he accompanied St. Germanus to Brittany to combat Pelagianism there. As a result of his influence, the city of Troyes was spared by Attila.

Lupus died in 479 after 52 years of episcopal ministry. The *Vita S.*

Lupi (BHL 5087), which was written after his death, is a trustworthy document (the Bollandists, Griffe), although Krusch contends that it is a later composition.

Sidonius Apollinaris sent four letters to Lupus (PL 58, 551, 554, 558, 626). Lupus himself, together with the bishop, Euphonius, wrote a brief letter, *De solemnitatibus et de bigamis clericis, et iis qui coniugati assumuntur,* to Talassius, bishop of Angers, in response to questions regarding ecclesiastical legislation.

Editions: PL 58, 66-68 (A. Gallandi). — The *Ep.* 1, PL 58, 63 is a forgery by H. Vignier. *Vita S. Lupi:* B. Krusch, ed., MGH scr. mer. VII(1920)284-302.

Studies: J. Havet, Les découvertes de Jérôme Vignier: *Bibliothèque de l'École de Chartre* 46(1895)252-254. — E. Griffe, La Gaule chrétienne à l'époque romaine II. Paris 1966, 301-304. — P. Viard, Lupo: *Bibliotheca Sanct.* 8(1966)390-391. — R. W. Mathisen, Hilarius, Germanus and Lupus. The Aristocratic Background of the Chelidonius Affair: *Phoenix* 33(1979)160-169.

MUSAEUS OF MARSEILLES

Musaeus has been forgotten to some extent in the history of Christian antiquity, although he merits remembrance. He was a learned priest and well versed in Scripture. According to Gennadius (*De vir. ill.* 79[80]), he composed, at the order first of the bishop Venerius then of Eustasius, a lectionary (*lectiones totius anni*), a collection of responsories (*responsoria psalmorum capitula*), a sacramentary, and possibly a collection of homilies.

Historians have worked patiently to reconstruct the liturgical works of Musaeus. Some fragments in a manuscript at Paris (BN *nouv acq* 1628) are perhaps from the collection of responsories. The lectionary is perhaps that contained in the palimpset Wissenburgensis 76 from the beginning of the sixth century, which contains readings from the Old and the New Testament (Lowe, p. 1392). According to C. Vogel, however, such an attribution is more than dubious.

Studies: G. Morin, Fragments inédits d'un antiphonaire gallican: RM 22(1905)329-356; *idem,* EL 51(1937)3-12. — A. Baumstark: OC 3(1936)114-119. — A. Stuiber, Libelli sacramentorum Romani. Bonn, 1950. — A. Dold, Das älteste Liturgiebuch der lateinischen Kirche (Texte u. Arbeiten 26-28). Beuron, 1936. — L. C. Mohlberg: EL 51(1937)353-360. — K. Gamber, Das Lektionar und Sakramentar des Musaeus von Marsilia: RB 69(1959)198-215 (proposes the Bibl. Ambros. M. 12 Sup). — Regarding the attribution to Claudius Mamertus, cf. G. Morin: RB 27(1910)41-74; *idem,* La lettre préface du Comes ad Constantinum: RB 30(1913)328-331. — G. Berti, Il più antico lezionario della Chiesa: EL 68(1954)147-154.

RUSTICUS

There is extant a thanksgiving, a *specimen eruditionis,* of a certain Rusticus addressed to Eucherius of Lyons and sent to him along with two of his works. Rusticus remains a shadowy personality, perhaps to be identified with a correspondent of Sidonius (*Ep.* 2, 11). Wotke's identification of Rusticus as a bishop of Narbonne has not met with general acceptance.

Editions: PL 58, 489 (J. Sirmond). — Pitra, Analecta Sacra II. Paris, 1884. — C. Wotke, CSEL 31(1894)198-199 (for the author cf. p. xxiii-xxiv). — PLS III, 46-47.

SALONIUS OF GENEVA

Salonius and Veranus were the sons of Eucherius, bishop of Lyons. After receiving their education from the monks at Lérins, the former became bishop of Geneva around 439 and the latter bishop of Vence around 450. Salonius, together with his brother and Ceretius, bishop of Grenoble, addressed a letter to Leo the Great, which has been preserved with the title *Epistula dogmatica* (PL 54, 887-890) to inform Leo that they had received a copy of his *Tomus ad Flavianum.*

Salonius participated in the Councils of Orange and Vaison in 441 and 442 and was also present after 450 at a council at Arles dealing with matters related to the monastery of Lérins. He must have died not long after.

As can be seen from the two books of the *Instructiones* sent to him by his father, it seems that Salonius was concerned with questions regarding the Bible. Gennadius, however, makes no mention of his literary activity. In 1532 the humanist J. B. Brassicanus (Kohlburger) published the *editio princeps* of the *Expositio mystica in Parabolas Salomonis et Ecclesiastem* and attributed it to Salonius. The basis for such an attribution remains uncertain since the manuscript of Vienna used by the editor contains the name of Salonius in the margin, but in a different hand, perhaps that of Brassicanus himself.

J. P. Weiss has demonstrated that this work depends on Gregory the Great and Bede and thus cannot be a composition of Salonius. An *expositio mystica* on Matthew and John in the form of questions and answers, which is contained in some manuscripts under the name of Salonius (Stegmüller 7590, 1 and 2), has also been attributed to the Bishop of Geneva by Endres and by C. Curti who has published a critical edition.

The studies of J. P. Weiss refute the attribution to Salonius for both of the above-mentioned *expositio.* On the basis of the manuscript tradition, the identity in style and literary genre, he has concluded that the four commentaries are the work of a single author and are to be situated in Germany between 800 and 1000.

Editions: Expositio mystica in Parabolas Sal. et Ecc.: PL 53, 967-1012 (J. A. Brassicanus). — C. Curti, Salonii ep. Genav. Comment. in Parabolas Salomonis et in Ecclesiasten. Catania, 1964 (regarding the mss cf. *idem,* Orph 11[1964]164-184). *De Evangelio Johannis. De Evangelio Matthaei:* C. Curti, Salonii ep. Genav. Turin, 1968 (critical ed. and study on transmission of text and on the author).

Studies: M. Besson, Un évêque exégète de Genève au milieu du Ve siècle, Saint Salone: *Anzeiger für schweiz. Geschichte* 11(1902-1905)252-265. — J. A. Endres, Honorius Augustodunensis. Kempten 1906, 73-75. — J. P. Weiss, review of the edition of Curti: RELA 44(1966)482-484; 46(1968)481-482; *idem,* Essai de datation du Commentaire sur les Proverbes, attribué abusivement à Salonius: SE 19(1969-1970)77-114; *idem,* L'authenticité de l'œuvre de Salonius de Genève: SP 10. Berlin 1970, 161-167. — R. Etaix, review of the editions of Curti: RHE 65(1970)133-135.

SALVIAN OF MARSEILLES

Not much is known about the life of Salvian. He was born around the year 400, or possibly some years earlier, probably at Trier or Cologne, and experienced the terror of the barbarian invasions during the years 418-420 (*De gub.* 6, 82-84). His family, perhaps members of the aristocracy, had taken care to provide a thorough education for him. It is not known when he was baptized. It seems that he was already a Christian when he married Palladia, who was still a pagan (*Ep.* 4, 7). They had one daughter by the name of Auspiciola. Shortly after their marriage, they left their native country to settle in southern Gaul. The couple soon made the decision to embrace the ascetic life in continence and to give their goods to the poor. Seven years later Salvian left his wife and daughter and retired to live with Honoratus at Lérins. Together with Hilary and Vincent he had charge of the education of the sons of Eucherius. His stay at Lérins was not lengthy and he went to Marseilles to Cassian's newly established monastery of St. Victor. He became a priest in 429 and was still alive around 469-470 when Gennadius described him as "a strong old man" (*De vir. ill.* 69[70]), who was "learned in human and divine letters . . . a *magister episcoporum.*"

Studies: G. Sternberg, Das Christentum des 5 Jhtes, im Spiegel der Schriften des Salvianus von Massilia: ThStKr 82(1909)22-78, 163-205. — R. Thouvenot, Salvien et la ruine de l'Empire Romain: MAH 38(1920)145-163. — G. Bardy, Salvien: DTC 14(1939)1056-1058. — M. Pellegrino, Salviano di Marsiglia. Rome, 1940 (extensive bibliography). — G. Bardy, L'Eglise et les derniers Romains. Paris 1948, 109-147. — H. J. Diesner, Zwischen Antike und Mittelalter, Salvian von Massilia als Historiker und Geschichtsdenker: *Wiss. Zeitschrift Greiswald* (1954-1955)411-414. — Ch. Favez, La Gaule et les Gallo-Romains lors des invasions du Ve siècle d'après Salvien. Quelques aspects du pays, attitude et sort des habitants: Latomus 16(1957)77-83. — L. F. Barmann, Salvian of M. Re-evaluated: RUO 33(1963)79-97. — P. Courcelle, Histoire litt. des grandes invasions germaniques. Paris, 1964[3]. — E. Griffe, La Gaule chrétienne, I. Paris 1966[2], 40-52. — R. Kaminiek, Les esclaves dans les écrits de S. de M.: *Annales Univ. Marie Sklodowska* 20(1965)1-18; *idem,* Quelques problèmes biographiques concernant Salvien de M. restés sans solution: ibid., 23-24(1968-1969)74-110. — I. Opelt, Antikes Bildungsgut bei Salvian von Marseille: VC 28(1974)54-61. — Ph. Badot, La notice de Gennade relative à Salvien: RB 84(1974)352-356. — A. G. Hamman, L'actualité de Salvien de Marseille. Idées sociales et politiques: Aug 17(1977)381-393. — C. Leonardi, Alle origini della cristianità medievale: Giovanni Cassiano e Salviano di Marsiglia: *Studi Medievali* 18(1977)491-608. — S. Pricoco, Una nota biografica su Salviano di Marsiglia: *Sic Gymnasium* 29(1976)351-368. — D. R. Shackleton Bailey, Textual Notes on Salvian: HThR 70(1977)371-376.

WRITINGS

Salvian seems to have been a prolific author. Gennadius (*De vir. ill.* 68[67]) gives the approximate title of a good number of his more important works: *De virginitatis bono ad Marcellum presbyterum libri tres; Adversus avaritiam libri quattuor; Expositio extremae partis libri Ecclesiastes ad Claudium ep. Viennensem; De principio Genesis usque ad condicionem hominis;* homilies, and *libelli sacramentorum.* Most of these works have been lost, and we possess only the *Adversus avaritiam* or *Ad ecclesiam,* the *De gubernatione Dei,* and nine letters.

In his writings Salvian shows himself to be more a rhetor than a humanist, and he cites Cicero and Vergil from Lactantius. He did not know Greek and attributed Plato's *Republic* to Socrates.

Salvian was a concise and sententious writer with a powerful style. He is dependent on Tertullian in his language and imitates the *Sermo de tempore barbarico* of Quodvultdeus. The classicism of his style has won him the title of the "Christian Cicero." His periods, which are clear and elegant without affectation, are at times weighed down by rhetorical devices, with all of which he is acquainted: antithesis, allusion, paradox, the clause, the proverb, and the play on words. He is aware that his compositions sometimes lack the necessary rigor and are too prolix. He remains, nevertheless, an accomplished orator, formed by the rhetoric of the prophets.

Editions: PL 53 (E. Baluze, Paris, 1663, 1669 and 1684). — C. Halm, MGH Auct. and I, 1. Berlin, 1877. F. Pauly, CSEL 8(1883). For early editions, cf. Schönemann, PL 53, 13-24.

Translations: English: J. F. O'Sullivan, FC 3(1947) (reprint: 1962). *French:* J. F. Grégoire, F. Z. Colombet, 2 vols. Lyons, 1933. — G. Lagarrigue, SCh 176 and 220(1971-1975). *German:* A. Mayer. BKV^3(1935).

Studies: E. Wölfflin, Alliteration und Reim bei Salvianus: *Archiv für lat. Lexicographie* 13(1904)41-49. — H. Bornecque, Les clausules métriques latines: Université de Lille, fasc. 6. Lille 1907, 391-397. — J. H. Schmalz, Zu Salvian: PhW 35(1915)1041-1047. — C. Brakman, Observationes grammaticae et criticae in Salvianum: Mnem 52(1924)113-185; *idem,* De Geschriften van Salvianus. Leiden, 1926. H. K. Messenger, De temporum et modorum apud Salvianum usu: HSCP 36(1925)180-182. — K. Richter, Die Bücherfrage bei Salvian: *Opusc. philol.* 19(1929)39-50. — J. P. Waltzing, Tertullien et Salvien: *Musée Belge* 19(1929)37-47. — L. Rochus, Les jeux de mots chez Salvien: RBPh 9(1930)877-887; *idem,* Les proverbes et les expressions proverbiales chez Salvien, in Mélanges P. Thomas. Bruges 1930, 594-604; *idem,* La concinnitas chez Salvien: RBPh 11(1932)107-121; *idem,* La latinité de Salvien. Brussels, 1934. — O. Janssen, L'expressivité chez Salvien de Marseille, 1: Les adverbes. Nijmegen, 1937; *idem,* Vastare et ses synonymes dans l'œuvre de Salvien de M.: Mélanges Ch. Mohrmann. Utrecht-Antwerp 1963, 103-111. — M. Pellegrino, S. Ilario di Poitiers e Salviano di Marsiglia: SC (1940)302-318; *idem,* Sulla tradizione manoscritta di Salviano di M.: VC 6(1952)99-108. — J. Vecchi, Studi Salviani. Bologna, 1951. — A. Szantyr, Missverstandene quod-Sätze: *Gymnasium* 79(1972)499-511.

1. *Ad Ecclesiam*

Gennadius gives the title as *Adversus avaritiam libri quattuor,* but the manuscripts and Salvian himself give the title as *Ad Ecclesiam.* The author uses the pseudonym of Timothy, "friend of God," which he explains in his letter to Salonius (9, 1-3). The early editors, especially F. Pauly, knew only the manuscripts at Paris. G. Morin discovered the manuscript of Bern (Bongarsiano 315), which provided valuable material to complete the work (prologue, *addenda* and *corrigenda* = PLS III, 203-213).

Salvian himself refers to this work in the *De gubernatione* (4, 1) which was composed subsequently. The letter to Salonius which alludes to the work proves that it cannot have been written before 440 since it greets Salonius as bishop. The composition, which is addressed "to the church spread throughout the entire world," denounces the extent and the crimes of avarice among the Christians, bishops and priests included. According to the words of St. Paul, it proposes avarice as the "root of all evil" and raises the question as to how it is to be cured.

All Christians are called to holiness and thus must struggle against the expansion of avarice. They must remember that riches come from God and that the Christian merely has the use of them. Alms given during one's life and the distribution of one's goods to the poor obtain the pardon of sins at the hour of death (1, 1).

Almsgiving is necessary for holy and religious people as well as for sinners (1, 2). The perfection of the New Law implies divesting oneself of riches after the example of the widows, the married couples living in continence, the consecrated virgins, and the clerics. God demands yet more. Attachment to material goods is the sign of a lack of faith and confidence in God.

Book 3, which is addressed to everyone in general, advises its readers to distribute their material goods before they die, or at least in the hour of death (3, 5). It then develops the poor excuses of the testators: children, adopted children, children who are religious. The best gift is a good education. Examples from the Old Testament show that alms to the poor saved our fathers from death (3, 12).

Book 4 is concerned with the individual Christian. Salvian develops the theme of the necessity for all to persevere in almsgiving until death. One by one, he rejects all objections, such as concern for heirs (4, 12-18), by saying that God does not know what to make of our repayments (19-23). Even the religious life is not able to be taken as an excuse (24-39). God repays according to the measure in which one gives (41-44), and each one gives according to the measure of his faith (4, 5). All of this possibly smacks of rigorism, but the conclusions and concrete implications of Salvian's argument escape no one.

Editions: PL 53, 173-238 (E. Baluze; *Ed. princeps* of J. Sichard, Basel, 1528 from a ms. of

Lorsch now lost. Cf. P. Lehmann, Joannes Sichard. Munich 1912, 156-158). — F. Pauly, CSEL 8(1883)224-316. — C. Halm, MGH, AA I, 1, p. 120-168. — *Ms. from Bern:* G. Morin, Ad Ecclesiam récension inédite sur le manuscrit de Berne: RB 43(1931)194-206 (= PLS III, 203-213). — A. Vandeven, Salviani ad Ecclesiam libri quattuor. Louvain, 1943 (typewritten).

Translations: English: J. F. O'Sullivan, FC 3(1947). *French:* G. Lagarrigue, SCh 176(1971)138-144 (with text). *Italian:* E. Marotta, Contro l'avarizia. Rome, 1977.

Studies: I. Seipel, Die Wirtschaftethischen Lehren der Kirchenväter. Vienna, 1907. — O. Schilling, Reichtum und Eigentum in der altchristlichen Literatur. Freiburg 1908, 194-203. — E. Lesne, La propriété ecclésiastique en France aux époques romaine et mérovingienne. Paris 1910, 23-31. — G. Walter, Histoire du communisme. I: Les origines judaïques, chrétiennes, grecques, latines. Paris 1931, 253-262. — K. Farner, Christentum und Eigentum. Bern, 1947. — E. F. Bruck, Kirchenväter und soziales Erbrecht. Berlin, 1956. — H. Fischer, Die Schrift des Salvian von Marseille An die Kirche. Eine hist. theol. Untersuchung. Bern, 1976. — G. W. Olsen, Reform after the Pattern of the Primitive Church in the Thought of Salvian of Marseilles: CHR 68(1982)1-12.

2. *De Gubernatione Dei*

This work, which Gennadius lists as *De praesenti iudicio,* is dedicated to Salvian's pupil, Salonius, the bishop of Geneva. An allusion to the battle of Toulouse indicates the work was written after 440. M. Pellegrino places it between 439 and 451; E. Griffe dates it to around 445. Gennadius speaks of five books, but all the manuscripts contain eight. The developments mentioned in the work (7, 1, 1) give no reason for supposing the work is incomplete. The eighth book is out of proportion in relation to the other seven. The conclusion is missing in all manuscripts later than the tenth century.

The *De gubernatione* is a well-known yet much discussed work, and has known various fortunes and uses depending on the times and the historians. Like Augustine's *City of God,* a work with which it has a historical affinity, this work is colored at times by the events of the moment. Salvian, like Augustine, experienced the barbarian invasions and witnessed the devastation caused by them from Germany to Belgium, Aquitania to Spain, and in Africa. He was present for the end of the empire and had a presentiment of the new era.

No longer, as in the *City of God,* is it the pagans who wonder at the decline of the Roman Empire and make accusations against the Christians. Rather, as in the *Carmen de divina providentia* attributed to Prosper of Aquitaine, it is the Christians themselves who are doubting the providence of God in the face of the barbarian invasions. They question why God has abandoned the empire which, having become Christian, protected the church, and they wonder if perhaps the end of the world is at hand.

In the first two books, Salvian proves the existence of providence with arguments from reason (1, 19-20), from examples drawn from the Old Testament (27-60) and the testimonies (2). On this basis, he responds to the objections such as why the situation of the barbarians is better than that of the Christians. The name of Christian confers no special rights, it is the behavior that is important; and with the exception of a small minority, the Christians are a pit of vice (3, 9, 41). Faithful Christians are rare, and thus what is taking place is a just chastisement which shows how God directs the world.

Books 4-8 present above all a pessimistic view of Christian society, which offends the goodness of God and renders the Christians "more guilty than the barbarians themselves" (4, 13). Salvian places in relief the moral superiority of the barbarians in comparison with the social and fiscal injustices (5), the relish for the spectacle (6), and the vices of wantoness so widespread in Aquitania, Spain, and Africa (7).

The judgment of God which is taking place is the consequence of sin. "We have been punished by God because we have forced Him to punish us" (8, 1). *Sola nos morum nostrorum vitia vicerunt* (7, 23, 108).

Salvian, the Jeremiah of the fifth century, criticizes the Romans and the Gauls not so much for the pleasure of casting aspersion or because of a lack of solidarity or patriotism, but because he wanted them to be "more virtuous, more just, more human, in a word, more Christian." No one is spared in his tirade, even ecclesiastics. Rather than accusing God, the Christians would profit more from engaging in some self-criticism. If Salvian's pessimism is due in part to the literary genre of the diatribe and to apostrophe, his work, nevertheless, has the value of denying the Christians the possibility of placing God at the service of their own interests and of opening their eyes to the pharisaism, in the name of which they were demanding their rights before God. Salvian frees the church from the vicissitudes of the state. Far from allowing himself to wander into nostalgic reminiscences, he strives to give a positive significance to the invasion of the Germanic peoples. Historians are divided in their opinions on Salvian's views; some finding them excessive and unjust (Hauréau, Jullian, Courcelle, Bardy), others praising their prophetic foresight (J. Lecler, P. Lebeau, E. Griffe). Whatever the opinions, no one who carefully reads Salvian's work can continue to complain about divine providence, which was, after all, his purpose in composing the *De gubernatione Dei.*

Editions: PL 53, 25-158 (E. Baluze). — F. Pauly, CSEL 8(1883)1-200. — C. Halm, MGH AA I, 1-108.

Translations: English: J. F. O'Sullivan, FC 3(1947)21-232. *French:* G. Lagarrigue, SCh 220(1975) (with text).

Studies: U. Moricca, Salviano e la data del De gubernatione Dei: RFIC 46(1918)241-255. — A. Schäfer, Römer und Germanen bei Salvian. Breslau, 1930. — E. Bordone, La società romana del V secolo nella requisitoria di Salviano Massiliense, in *Studi Ubaldi.* Milan 1937, 315-344. — J. Fischer, Die Völkerwanderung im Urteil der zeitgenössischen kirchlichen Schriftsteller Galliens unter Einbeziehung des hl. Augustinus. Heidelberg, 1948. — M. Iannelli, La caduta di un impero nel capolavoro di Salviano. Naples, 1948. — A. G. Sterzl, Romanus-Christianus-Barbarus. Erlangen, 1950 (typewritten). — A. Mandouze, L'Eglise devant l'effondrement de la civilisation romaine: RHPR 41(1961)1-10. — P. Lebeau, Hérésie et providence chez Salvien: NRTh 83(1963)160-175. — A. Loyen, Résistants et collaborateurs en Gaule: *Bulletin G. Budé* 22(1963)437-450. — E. A. Isichei, Political Thinking and Social Experience, in *Some Christian Interpretations of the Roman Empire.* University of Canterbury Publications, 1964. — J. C. Ignace, Salvien et les invasions en Gaule d'après le "De gubernatione Dei." Toulouse, 1966. — F. Paschoud, Roma aeterna. Neuchâtel 1967, 293-310. — W. Blum, Das Wesen Gottes und das Wesen des Menschen nach Salvian von Massilia: MTZ 21(1970)327-341. — D. J. Cleland, Salvian and the Vandals: SP 10 (TU 107). Berlin 1970, 270-274. — J. L. Van Der Lof, Die Gotteskonzeption und das Individuum bei Salvian: SP 13 (TU 116). Berlin 1975, 322-329. — F. Martelli, Morale e potere nel mondo tardoantico: *Antiqua* 4(1979)24-32. — J. Badewein, Geschichtstheologie und Sozialkritik im Werk Salvians von Marseille. Göttingen, 1981.

3. Letters

Gennadius mentions an *epistolarum librum unum* of Salvian, of which nine letters have survived which are, for the most part, brief. A group of seven letters is found in a manuscript now divided into two parts (Paris, BN 2174 and Bern, E 219), plus the letters to Eucherius and Salonius.

The surviving letters are: a letter of recommendation to some monks (perhaps at Lérins) in favor of a youth of his family (1); a congratulatory letter to Eucherius on his elevation to the episcopate (2); the beginning of a letter of apology to Agricius, bishop of Sens (3); a highly polished letter sent also in the name of his wife and daughter explaining to his in-laws the meaning of their conversion (the text is in a poor state of preservation) (4); a letter to the "sister" Cattura who has recovered from a prolonged illness (5); a letter of friendship to Limenius (6); a letter to two important figures, Aper and Verus (7).

In his letter to Eucherius, Salvian congratulates him on his two recent writings. The *Ep.* 9 to Salonius, "the strongest in respect to the thought," is an introduction to his treatise *Ad Ecclesiam.* In it, he develops three questions: why he is addressing himself to the entire church, why he is using a pseudonym and why the name of Timothy in particular.

Editions: PL 53, 157-174 (E. Baluze). — F. Pauly, CSEL 8(1883)201-223; letter 8 is also in C. Wotke, CSEL 31(1894)197. — C. Halm, MGH AA I, 1, 108-119.

Translations: English: J. F. O'Sullivan, FC 3(1947)235-263. *French:* G. Lagarrigue, SCh 176(1971)76-132 (with text).

Studies: I. Opelt, Briefe des Salvian von Marseille. Zwischen Christen und Barbaren: *Romanobarbarica* 4(1979)161-182.

TEACHING

Salvian, attacked by some, forgotten by others, and praised by modern scholars, appears today as one of those authors who has gained new prominence as a result of the contemporaneity of his views, even his disputed ones.

In order to understand Salvian and do him justice, it is necessary to realize that he was an ecclesiastic, a monk who had left everything: his homeland, his family, his position. Like Paulinus of Nola, he distributed his possessions to the poor. He lived and experienced his evangelical radicalism before proposing it to all, clergy and laity. His convictions are based on Scripture, which was the guide first of his actions then of his arguments (*De gub.* 3, 1, 1). The criticisms brought against him come from Christians who are repelled by the ideal of the Beatitudes (*De gub.* 4, 7).

1. The Defender of God

As a Christian writer addressing Christians, Salvian guards against passing judgment on the barbarians. He speaks to the Christian conscience of his listeners to compel them to change their judgments and their lives. He preaches in the manner of the prophets and condemns so that condemnation may be avoided.

His listeners, instead of examining themselves, were accusing God. Salvian responds to them not from the political point of view, but from that of faith and its demands, and points out the emptiness of their demands in regard to God, whom they wish to monopolize for themselves. Such Christians consider their faith as placing God in their debt (*De gub.* 3, 26) and seek to use their profession of faith for material ends. Salvian emphasizes that God is, after all, God.

He recognizes the virtues of the Romans and the service they have rendered to the church. Nevertheless, he is not a Roman nor is he bound to Roman institutions and culture. The God of the Gospel is sovereignly free. How else could he have granted victory to the Romans without rewarding their social injustice and vices (*De gub.* 4, 12)? The trials and misfortunes have yet to move the Christians to repentence.

2. Providence and the Barbarians

History confronts Salvian with the problem of evil which neither Christ nor the Apostles were able to escape. Evil cannot bring one to doubt God, who guides the world and acts always with tenderness (*De gub.* 4, 46-49), and Salvian interprets events in the light of this conviction. He strives to overcome emotional reactions, to speak of the barbarians with nobility and respect and to view them with Christian benevolence.

Nevertheless, he recognizes the defects of the barbarians (*De gub.* 3, 1) and admires neither their organization nor their power nor their success. He states only that the dullest of peoples has conquered the most debased (*De gub.* 7, 50). He points to their morality which is worth more than the heresy they profess, more than the behavior of those who profess the orthodox faith. Salvian judges the barbarians in the light of faith and in keeping with his vision of God and of salvation. In this, they not only have their place but even their own role as "instruments of God." Paradoxically, the optimistic view of creation and history unfolded in the Bible allows him to conclude that God guides the history of man with tenderness so that all may be saved.

Salvian takes up the theme of God's patience which knows how to wait beyond the reality of human faults (*De gub.* 5, 3, 13; 2, 9-11). Even heresy has its place in the course of this history. It is a view which banishes all forms of Manichaeism. The line of demarcation runs not between Romans and barbarians but between those who live their faith and those who do not.

More precisely, Salvian guards against judging the heretic in terms of his heresy, since he is often better than the heresy he professes. He wonders who is responsible for the Arianism which the barbarians have embraced; a painful question for a Roman conscience. He neither minimizes nor relativizes orthodoxy, and he recognizes that the heretics have distorted the Scriptures.

But in order to judge the barbarians according to their behavior, it is necessary to give them credit for their virtues and to praise their religious sensitivity. They call upon God without attempting to monopolize Him, and they place their trust in Him. The only possible attitude for the Christians in their regard is to hope they obtain "the fullness of the faith" (*De gub.* 5, 3, 13). To point out such truths in the midst of the confusion of contemporary events required a courage that surpassed the political point of view. It would be a sign of shortsightedness to accuse Salvian of opportunism or scheming or, worse yet, of treason. His attitude was that of one who had undergone a conversion and who wished to convert others.

3. Defender of the Poor

Salvian developed his ideas on material goods in his tirade directed *Ad Ecclesiam.* He displays no trace of Manichaeism with regard to riches, but regards them as gifts of God (*Ad Eccl.* 1, 24) which are to be used in accordance with the will of the donor. Men are the administrators of borrowed goods, "temporary" proprietors (*Ad Eccl.* 1, 26). One day these goods must be left behind.

Therefore, evil does not reside in the riches but in the heart of man and especially in the cupidity of the one who amasses wealth while at the same time exploiting the poor instead of sharing his goods with them and alleviating their misery. The evil rich person uses his fortune for his own vices and does not listen to the cry of the poor. It is in the light of these principles that the considerations contained in the *De gubernatione Dei* must be understood.

The book is a cry of indignation in the face of social injustice, of the oppression of the weak and the poor. The indictment presented by Salvian is not exaggerated, but can be found also in Lactantius and Ambrose. Injustices are perpetrated above all in the extortion of taxes, from which the rich and powerful are protected while they dispossess the *humiliores* (*De gub.* 4, 31; 5, 30-31, 35). Salvian is particularly indignant with the great landowners who profit from the weakness of the state and the silence of the church, and he directs his accusations especially against the higher clergy, including the bishops (*De gub.* 5, 19-20). The protest of the prophet of Marseilles is raised against the enormous gulf between the rich and the poor.

Salvian comes to the defense of slaves as well as of the poor, and rather than attacking their immorality, he questions where the guilt belongs. He has the courage to remind the rich Christians whom he is addressing of the human dignity which is mocked in the state of servitude. He points out that slaveowners, far from elevating this dignity, have weighed it down to such an extent that the poor are seeking refuge among the barbarians in order to escape from Roman legislation. They prefer to change their way of life rather than continue to endure the injustice of servitude.

In these times, Salvian remarks, the poor have suffered a veritable catastrophe: widows who mourn, orphans who are oppressed, the majority of whom come from distinguished families and were educated as free men, yet who prefer to seek refuge with the enemy than to die under the blows of public persecution. They seek among the barbarians the humanity of Romans since they are no longer able to bear among the Romans the inhumanity of barbarians.

If they strive to distinguish themselves from those among whom they have sought refuge with regard to religion, language, and, to pardon the expression, the stench that arises from the bodies and the clothes of the barbarians, the fact, nevertheless, remains that they prefer to suffer a difference of custom among them than to be subjected to unlimited injustice among the Romans. They prefer to live free under the appearance of slavery than to be slaves under the appearance of freedom (*De gub.* 5, 5, 21).

In the courage of his protest in the face of the inequalities and injustices of society, Salvian joins his voice to those of the Cappadocians, of John Chrysostom, and of Ambrose. He did not allow himself to be corrupted by the bribes of the powerful, but preached detachment from material goods and the equality and dignity of all people.

In spite of the generalizations, exaggerations and positions taken which arise as much from the literary genre employed by this disciple of rhetors as from the passion of his own personality, Salvian, while not writing history, nevertheless offers a quantity of astute observations on contemporary customs and speaks with a frankness and liberty of speech which spare no one. Whatever may be said, he resigns himself to the victory of the barbarians with a heavy heart but with a clear analysis of the events. Even if his reflection is not profound, this priest from Marseilles at least breaks the bonds that chained the Gospel to historical contingencies and thus set it free. In this manner he opened the way to considerations "rich in potential."

SULPICIUS SEVERUS

Severus himself informs us of his surname Suplicianus (*Ep.* 3), and his life is known for the most part from the notices of Gennadius (*De vir. ill.* 19) and the letters of his friend Paulinus. He was born into an aristocratic family in Aquitania around 360 and studied the classics and law at Bordeaux, where he probably made the acquaintance of Paulinus. He began, so it seems, a forensic career and married the daughter of a wealthy family of consular rank. His wife died prematurely and Severus abandoned his career and withdrew from public life (Paulinus, *Ep.* 5, 5). He was baptized around 389. Following the example of his friend, Paulinus, he renounced the world and its riches and led a secluded life on his estates, first at Elusum (Elsonne, near Toulouse), then in the village of Primuliacum (Prémillac) in Aquitania, where he devoted himself to the spiritual and literary life.

Influenced by the example and advice of Martin of Tours, whom he visited often, he gathered a group of friends with whom he lived in common together with his sister-in-law, Bassula, whom he had encouraged in this decision and supported financially even against the will of her husband (*Ep.* 3; Paulinus, *Ep.* 5, 6). Bassula played a definite role in his spiritual life.

Gennadius states that he was a priest, although his contemporaries refer to him as a layman. Gennadius also reports that toward the end of his life Sulpicius imposed on himself a vow of absolute silence as punishment for having sympathized with the errors of the Priscillianists. Although it is impossible to verify, this information has met with doubt among historians because of its legendary character. Sulpicius died between 420 and 425.

Studies: F. Mouter, Sulpice Sévère à Primuliac. Paris, 1907. — E. C. Babut, Saint Martin de Tours. Paris, 1912. — L. Ricaud, Sulpice Sévère et sa ville de Primuliac à Saint-Sever de Prustan. Tarbes, 1914. — H. Delehaye, Saint Martin et Sulpice Sévère: AB (1920)5-136. — P. Fabre, Saint Paulin de Nole et l'amitié chrétienne. Paris, 1949. — Saint Martin et son temps. Mémorial du XVe centenaire des débuts du monachisme en Gaule (*Studia Anselmiana* 46). Rome, 1961. — S. Prete, Degenerazione e decadenza morale nell'escatologia di Sulpicio Severo: Aug 18(1978)245-256. — G. K. van Andel, Sulpicius Severus and Origenism: VC 34(1980)278-287.

WRITINGS

From Sulpicius' literary activity there remain the two books of the *Chronicles,* the *Life of St. Martin,* three letters, and two books of *Dialogues* which complete the *Vita.* The *tituli metrici* and a further seven letters attributed to him by J. Clericus are apocryphal.

Sulpicius uses a classical language and style according to the example of Sallustius and Tacitus, whom he imitates in ellipsis and brevity. He avoids a flowery rhetoric and frequently cites classical literature and the Bible. Especially in the *Life of St. Martin,* Sulpicius shows himself to be a skillful narrator who knows how to unite an eye for detail with vivacity and humor, and even to make use of solecisms to reconstruct the particular color of the account. The *Life of St. Martin* and the *Dialogues* were a true literary success.

As a true author, a refined man of letters who was not so much credulous as constrained by popular taste, Sulpicius Severus was described by Scaliger as *ecclesiasticorum purissimus scriptor (Prol. ad De emend. Temporum).*

Editions: PL 20 (Gallando following Jerome da Prato). — C. Halm, CSEL 1(1866).

Translations: English: B. M. Peebles, FC 7(1949) (without the *Chronicles*). *French:* Herbert and Riton, 2 vols. Paris, 1848-1849. *German:* B. Bihlmeyer, BKW2(1914) (without the *Chronicles*).

Studies: B. M. Peebles, Girolamo da Prato and His Manuscripts of Sulpicius Severus: *Memoirs of the American Academy in Rome* 13(1936)7-66. — P. Hyltén, Studien zu Sulpicius Severus. Lund, 1940 (bibliography). — G. Lampe, Utrum Sulpicius Severus in componendis Chronicis eodem stilo usus sit atque in vita s. Martini conscribenda et in epistolis edendis nec ne: *Jahresbericht Kollegium Petrinum. Uhrfahr-Linz* 48(1951-1952); 51(1954-1955); 54(1957-1958). — J. De Wit, De Sulpicio Severo observationes: VC 9(1955)45-49.

1. The *Chronicles*

This far-reaching work was concluded about the year 400. The title *Chronica* is attested by Gennadius and is found also in a Vatican manuscript (Cod. 825). In the *editio princeps,* Flacius changed the title to *Sacra historia,* which was maintained by Girolamo da Prato. J. Bernays proposed *A mundi exordio libri II* as the authentic title, but this is not convincing.

Severus intends to trace briefly the history of the world from creation to the year 400. He bases his work chiefly on passages of Scripture, the content of which he analyzes with a true critical sense. He omits the history of Christ and the Apostles which he regards to be unsuitable for a résumé because of its greatness.

He takes up the history of the church from "the destruction of Jerusalem, the vicissitudes of the Christians and the time of peace." Severus is more concerned with chronology than with theology, and if he mentions heresies he does this in order to establish the succession of events. He is well informed on Arianism and makes use of the *Fragmenta historica* of Hilary (2 35, 2).

The *Chronicles* become more animated when they treat of contemporary events. The author is particularly well informed about the Priscillianist Movement, in which he was personally involved, and thus his observations are particularly valuable.

Sulpicius Severus' dependence on Jerome's translation of the *Chronicle* of Eusebius is readily apparent. He also makes use of Tacitus for the persecution of Nero and the destruction of Jerusalem, and draws on his friend, Paulinus, for the activity of the Empress Helen at Jerusalem (2 33, 4 = Paulinus, *Ep.* 31, 4-6). Sulpicius' style is precise and succinct in the manner of Sallustius and Tacitus. His recognition of the problems posed by a defective transmission of the texts (1 40, 2) and his verification of figures provided in the Bible by means of the pagan historians bear witness to his historical and critical sense.

The *Chronicles,* which were long neglected, have survived in only one manuscript from the eleventh century. They found a new appreciation at the time of the Renaissance. The critical analysis of the Book of Judith offers a rare, and thus all the more noteworthy example, of a philological and critical analysis similar to that of modern times.

Editions: PL 20, 95-160. — C. Halm, CSEL 1(1866)1-105. — A. Lavertujon, La Chronique de Sulpice Sévère, 2 vols. Paris, 1896-99.

Translations: French: A. Lavertujon, op. cit.

Studies: S. Prete, Note storiche a Sulpicio Severo (Chron. II, 31-32): *Paideia* 8(1953)245-259; *idem,* I Chronica di Sulpicio Severo. Rome, 1955. — V. Grumel, Du nombre des persécutions dans les anciennes chroniques: REAug 11(1956)59-66. — H. Montefiori, Sulpicius Severus and Titus' Council of War: *Historia* 11(1962)156-170 (Sulpicius and Tacitus). — P. Hyltén, Critical Notes on the *Chronica* of Sulpicius Severus: *Traditio* 19(1963)447-460. — P. Saumagne, Tacite et s. Paul: RH 132(1964)67-110. — I. Weiler, Titus und die Zerstörung des Tempels von Jerusalem: *Klio* 50(1968)139-159. — F. Murru, La concezione della storia nei Chronica di Sulpicio Severo; alcune idee di studio: Latomus 38(1979)961-981.

2. *Vita Martini*

Given the great number of manuscripts, more than 150, the *Vita beati Martini* can be compared for its influence to that of St. Anthony composed by Athanasius.

This biography, written while Martin was still alive, perhaps at the suggestion of Bassula, is the testimony of a Christian recently converted to asceticism. Sent to Paulinus in 397 (*Ep.* 11), the *Vita* received various additions and reworkings subsequent to the year 400.

In the dedication to Desiderius, Sulpicius Severus states that everyone desires a copy of the manuscript, an expression which leaves no doubt of the author's desire to secure the greatest possible publicity for his work with the intention of opposing the anti-ascetical movement among the bishops and clergy of his time.

He takes his inspiration from classical tradition and from Athanasius in order to emphasize, as did Jerome in his *Vita Pauli,* the miraculous aspect of his hero. The book, which is of a clearly apologetic approach, wishes to show how Martin imitated and indeed surpassed the great saints. The biography concentrates on the miraculous aspect, without regard for chronology or topography. The miracles of the saint, satisfying the popular taste to the point of exaggeration, guaranteed the work's success in the West as well as in the East. The apologetic purpose determines the structure of the composition and serves to distinguish the *Vita Martini* from the *Vita Antonii.* In his harangue, Sulpicius Severus is intent on defending the spiritual character of Martin.

The plan of the entire work is explained at the beginning (1), followed by the account of Martin's life from infancy to his conversion. There is found here the famous episode of the cloak divided in two at the gates of Amiens. He then retires from his military career in 356 (2) and goes to Hilary at Poitiers, then to Italy. He combats Arianism, founds the monastery of Ligugé (3), and, in a tumultuous election, is made bishop of Tours, where he continues to live as a monk and thaumaturge (4). He dedicates himself to the evangelization of the peasants and the struggle against paganism (5), and is aided in his indefatigable struggle with the works of the devil by the gift of healing and the expulsion of demons (6-7). The conclusion presents Martin as the ascetic, saint, and spiritual master (8). Such is the life and active spirituality of the soldier who became a monk and bishop.

The insistence on the miraculous element has generated doubts concerning the truth of the biography, and E. Ch. Babut has gone so far as to accuse Sulpicius Severus of fraud and Martin of mediocrity. In their reply to Babut, C. Jullian and Delehaye have presented

Sulpicius Severus as a serious author who wrote with the liberty allowed in the hagiography of his time, mixing truth and fiction according to his imaginative schemes which were at once popular and mystical. The *Vita Martini* served not only to make the Bishop of Tours famous, but stimulated a whole series of writings centered on Martin to which Paulinus of Périgneux, Venantius Fortunatus, and Gregory of Tours all made a contribution. In this way, the *Vita* became the model of medieval hagiography.

Editions: PL 20, 159-176. — C. Halm, CSEL 1(1866)107-137.

Translations: Dutch: C. W. Moennich, Martinus van Tours. Amsterdam, 1962. *English:* A. Roberts, LNPF 11, ser. 2(1973)3-17. — B. M. Peebles, FC 7(1949)101-140. *French:* P. Monceaux. Paris, 1926 (with the Dialogues and letters). — J. Fontaine. SCh 133(1967-69) (with text). *German:* P. Bihlmeyer, BKV² 20(1914).

Studies: E. Ch. Babut, Saint Martin de Tours. Paris, 1912. — H. Delehaye, Saint Martin et Sulpice Sévère: AB 38(1920)5-136. — C. Jullian, Remarques critiques sur les sources de la vie de saint Martin, sur la vie et les œuvres de saint Martin: REAN 24(1922); 25(1923). — P. Hyltén, Critical Notes on the *Chronica* of Sulpicius Severus. Appendix: *Traditio* 19(1963)457-460. — J. Laporte, Mare clausum dans Fortunat: RELA 31(1953)110-111. — E. Griffe, La chronologie des années de jeunesse de saint Martin: BLE 62(1961)114-118. — J. Fontaine, Vérité et fiction dans la chronologie de la Vita Martini, in *Saint Martin et son temps* (*Studia Anselmiana* 46). Rome 1961, 189-236; *idem,* Sulpice Sévère a-t-il travesti saint Martin de Tours en martyr militaire?: AB 81(1963)31-58; *idem,* Une clé littéraire de la Vita Martini de Sulpice Sévère; la typologie prophétique, in Mél. Mohrmann. Utrecht-Antwerp 1963, 84-95. — J. Griboment, L'influence du monachisme oriental sur Sulpice Sévère, in *Saint Martin et son temps* (*Studia Anselmiana* 46). Rome 1961, 135-150. — H. Montefiore, Sulpicius Severus and a Life of St. Romanus, Presbyter in Castro Blaviensi (BHL 7306): AHD 11(1962)156-170. — B. Studer, Zu einer Teufelserscheinung in der Vita Martini: ND 13(1963)29-82. — P. Antin, La mort de saint Martin: RELA 66(1964)108-120. — F. S. Pericoli Ridolfini, Agli inizi del monachesimo gallico, La Vita Martini et la Vita Antoni: *Studi MatRer* 38(1967)420-433. — E. Griffe, En relisant la Vita Martini de Sulpice Sévère: BLE 70(1969)184-198. — S. Prete, La Vita S. Columbani di Ionas: RSCI 22(1968)94-111. — A. Loyen, Les miracles de saint Martin et les débuts de l'hagiographie en Occident: BLE 73(1972)147-157. — J. Fontaine, Hagiographie et politique, de Sulpice Sévère à Venance Fortunat: RHEF 62(1975)113-140. — C. Stancliffe, St. Martin and His Hagiographer. History and Miracles in Sulpicius Severus. Oxford, 1983.

3. Letters

Three letters written in 397 and 398 complete the *Vita Martini,* and are joined with it in the manuscript tradition. All three are addressed, like the *Vita,* to the group of fervent aristocratic converts connected with Desiderius, Eusebius, Aurelius, and Bassula, who had been won to the ascetic ideal and were admirers of Martin.

The first is addressed to Eusebius, a priest and disciple of Martin, who later became bishop. This letter supposes that the *Vita Martini* has already been published. It is of a polemical tone against the detractors of Martin and tells of a fire which had threatened the life of the saint; an episode which does not appear in the *Vita.*

The second, addressed to the deacon Aurelius, is more polished in its composition and is both a letter of consolation and a panegyric of Martin. It has been referred to as "a letter of canonization." The third letter, sent to Bassula, is longer and presents a mixture of nonchalance and sentimentality. It recounts Martin's last journey, his death, and his impressive funeral. This letter draws on the second edition of the *Vita* and passes from hagiography to panegyric.

Editions: PL 20, 175-188. — C. Halm, CSEL 1(1866)138-151. — *Fragments of Ep. 1:* E. Babut, Sur trois lignes inédits de Sulpice Sévère: *Le Moyen Age* 19(1906)205-213. Cf. P. Hyltén, Studien zu Sulpicius Severus. Lund, 1940, 72-84. — M. J. McGann, Sulpicius Severus and a Life of St. Romanus (BHL 7306): ALMA 32(1962)91-94.

Translations: English: A. Roberts, LNPF 11, ser. 2(1973)18-23. — B. M. Peebles, FC 7(1949)141-159. *French:* J. Fontaine, SCh 133(1967)316-344 (with text).

4. The *Dialogues*

Gennadius gives the *Dialogues* the title *Consolatio Postumiani et Galli*, the latter two being monks in Gaul. It was composed in two (not three) books, and it is difficult to judge whether the literary form used is historical or fictitious. The intent of the author is to show that Martin equals, if indeed he does not surpass, the most famous of the Egyptian ascetics.

The *Dialogues* are the account of two days of conversation between Gallus, an elderly monk of Marmoutiers and disciple of St. Martin, and Postumianus, a friend of Sulpicius Severus from Aquitania and great admirer of the monks of Egypt, who has twice visited them and is preparing for a third voyage. Postumianus recounts the deeds of the Egyptian monks while Gallus, for his part, speaks of those of Martin, modeling them after the accounts of the wonders coming from the East. The literary influence of the lives of the Desert Fathers, and in particular of St. Anthony, is obvious. Sulpicius Severus is taking a stand against the wave of publicity coming from Bethlehem and elsewhere. The vicissitudes of the Origenist monks recounted along with the description of Jerome himself assume a typological value for a disdain of the authoritarian and anti-monastic attitude of a certain part of the clergy opposed to the person and prestige of St. Martin.

Editions: PL 20, 183-222. — C. Halm, CSEL 1(1866)152-216.

Translations: English: A. Roberts, LNPF 11, ser. 2(1973)24-54. — B. M. Peebles, FC 7(1949)161-251. *French:* P. Monceaux. Paris, 1926. *Italian:* G. Augello, Da i dialoghi di Sulpicio Severo: *Annali Liceo Garibaldi di Palermo* 1(1964)239-246 (selections).

Studies: M. Esposito, Un fragment des Dialogues de Sulpice Sévère, in Textes et études di littérature ancienne et médiévale. Florence 1921, 13-17. — P. Grosjean, Curdonicus: ALMA 24(1954)117-129. — Ch. Favez, Aquitains et Gaulois chez Sulpice Sévère, in

Hommages à M. Niedermann. Brussels 1956, 122-127. — P. Antin, Curdonicus (Sulp. S., *Dial.* 1, 27, 2): RELA 37(1959)111-112.

VALERIAN OF CIMIEZ

Valerian, bishop of Cimiez (Cemenelum, near Nice), was probably from the noble family of the Valeriani of Gaul.

J. P. Weiss has attempted to identify him with the Valerian to whom Eucherius sent the *De contemptu mundi,* but this remains no more than a conjecture. Valerian was bishop of Cimiez before 439, and in this office he took part in the Councils of Riez in 439 and Vaison in 442, which were convoked to strengthen ecclesiastical discipline. He supported Hilary during his difficulties with Leo I, and together with his colleagues of *Viennensis* and *Narbonensis secunda* and the *Alpes maritimae,* he signed a petition requesting the rehabilitation of the metropolitan of Arles. The pope, however, divided the ancient province into two territories (Leo, *Ep.* 65). Together with Ravennius and his colleagues, he signed the *Tomus ad Flavianum* (Leo, *Ep.* 102). His signature appears again at a council held at Arles in 455 concerning a controversy between the bishop of Fréjus and the monks of Lérins (Mansi VII, 907). He must have died shortly thereafter.

The *epistula ad monachos de virtutibus et ordine doctrinae apostolicae* gives proof of the good relations between the monks of Lérins and the bishop of Cimiez and bears witness to the influence of the monks on Valerian's doctrine of grace. The authenticity of this letter has been questioned recently.

Valerian, an educated man and an esteemed preacher, has left a collection of twenty homilies containing information on the history and life of the church in Gaul. They essentially deal with moral questions: discipline, broken promises, the narrow way, the greatness of peace, martyrdom, drunkenness, and avarice. They present the examples of the martyrs and saints, and the precepts and demands of the Gospel, but contain little on dogmatic questions. A passage of *hom.* 11, 4 had falsely raised suspicions of Semi-Pelagianism.

The elegant literary form of the letters is proof of a solid classical and rhetorical culture. Valerian quotes the masters, particularly Seneca, and like them, he takes pleasure in describing the scenes of everyday life. He was so immersed in Stoic philosophy as to seem a Stoic converted to Christianity. Valerian lived in an intellectual world in which Pelagian ideas were circulating, and his doctrine of grace is closer to the masters of Provence than to Augustine.

A. M. Riberi has attempted to attribute the *homelia in dedicatione ecclesiae* (PLS III, 184-188) to Valerian, but doubts remain on this (cf. B. Fischer, VT 473).

Editions: PL 52, 691-756 (Gallandi). — *Homily* 1, often attributed to Augustine (PL 40, 1219-1222), was restored to Valerian by M. Goldast in 1601. — Partial ed. of *hom.* 15-17 and *hom. in dedicatione* in A. M. Riberi, S. Dalmazzo di Pedona e la sua abbazia, con documenti inediti. Turin, 1929.

Translations: English: G. E. Ganss, FC 17(1965)291-440 (select sermons).

Studies: G. Bardy, Valérien: DTC 15(1948)2520-2522. — J. P. Weiss, La personnalité de Valérien de Cimiez, in *Annales de la fac. de Lettres de Nice* 1970, 141-162; *idem,* Les notions de dominus et de servus chez Valérien de Cimiez; ibid., 1979, 297-301.

VICTORIUS OF AQUITANIA

Victorius, an Aquitanian writer of the mid-fifth century, composed, according to the information of Gennadius (*De vir. ill.* 89 [88]), an Easter table *(cursus paschalis annorum)* in 457 at the request of the archdeacon Hilary, the future pope. This was officially recognized by the Synod of Orléans in 541 and spread throughout Gaul until the seventh and eighth century when it was replaced by that of Dionysius Exiguus. An excerpt from this work is found under the name of Bede in PL 90, 712 and in PLS IV, 2218.

According to Gennadius, Victorius also added a chronological table beginning with creation, for which he used the *Chronicle* of Prosper. Cassiodorus, in turn, made use of Victorius' work in composing his own. A scrupulous calculator, Victorius also composed a *Liber calculi* (PLS IV, 2218). The *Prologus Paschae* (PLS III, 380) is perhaps to be attributed to this author.

Editions: Cursus and Ep. Hilari: Th. Mommsen, MGH, AA IX, 667-735. — B. Krusch, Studien zur christlich-mittelalterlichen "Chronologie" II. Berlin 1938, 16-52 (= PLS III, 381-426). *Ep. Hilari:* A. Thiel, Epistulae Rom. Pont. I., Braunschweig 1868, 130. *Extract attributed to Bede:* PL 90, 712. — Ch. W. Jones, Bedae opera de temporibus. Cambridge, Mass., 1943, 58 belonging to the *Cursus Paschalis. Calculus:* PL 90, 677-680, restored to Victorius by W. Christ, ed. G. Friedlein. Rome, 1872. *Prologus Paschae:* B. Krusch, Studien zur chr. mittelalterlichen Chronologie. Leipzig 1880, 227-240 (= PLS III, 427-441).

Studies: E. Schwartz, Christliche und jüdische Osterrafeln. Berlin 1905, 427-441. — C. Jones, Bedae Pseudepigrapha. Ithaca, 1939.

VICTRICIUS OF ROUEN

The life of Victricius is known from two letters of Paulinus of Nola (*Ep.* 18 and 37), which tell of his conversion, his elevation to the episcopate, his governance of his church, and his missionary work. Severus recounts his meeting with Martin (*Dial.* 3, 2). Innocent sent him a famous decretal (Jaffé 286) dealing with recruitment and the virtues of clerics which subsequently entered into the canonical collections.

According to Paulinus, Victricius was born around 340 near the borders of the empire. The son of a veteran, as his name seems to indicate, he embarked on a military career which he gave up in order to serve Jesus Christ. When he had been ordained a priest, he dedicated himself to the evangelization of the Nervi and the Morini in what is now Flanders, Brabant, and Cambrai. He became bishop of Rouen around 385.

In a manner similar to that of Martin at Tours, Victricius fostered the growth of his community at Rouen by constructing churches, watching over discipline, and encouraging monastic life. He went to Britain around 396 to strengthen the orthodox faith, which was menaced by the Arian heresy, and in 403 he traveled to Rome, undoubtedly to justify his actions. He died around 410.

This former soldier possessed a serious literary culture. From his literary activity there remains the *De laude sanctorum,* a writing which follows the genre of the discourse and thus bears witness to Victricius' rhetorical formation. It was composed around 396 on the occasion of the arrival at Rouen from Italy of a second collection of relics sent by Ambrose, Paulinus, and Gaudentius, and indicates the stimulus and forms of religious life as well as the development of the cult of the martyrs. The text was discovered in the eighteenth century in a manuscript of Sankt Gallen and was attributed to Victricius by Jean Lebeuf, the first editor of the work.

Editions: PL 20, 443-458 (J. Lebeuf). — Sauvage (published by A. Tougard). Paris, 1895.

Translations: French: R. Herval. Rouen, 1966.

Studies: E. Vacandard, Saint Victrice, évêque de Rouen. Paris, 1900[2] (out of date). — H. Delehaye, Les origines du culte des martyrs. Paris 1942, 404-405. — A. Wilmart, Un manuscrit oublié: RB 31(1914-1919)333-372. — G. Bardy, Victrice de Rouen: DTC 15(1950)2954-2956. — P. Andrieu-Guitrancourt, La vie ascétique à Rouen au temps de s. Victrice: RSR 40(1952)90-106; *idem,* Essai sur Victrice: *Année canonique* 14(1970)1-23; *idem,* Notes, remarques, réflexions, in Mélanges Macqueron. *Aix* 1970, 7-20. — R. Herval, Origines du christianisme en Gaule: MSR 16(1959)47-70; 17(1960)41-80. — G. Alfroy, Victrice de Rouen. Paris 1962. — E. Griffe, La Gaule chrétienne à l'époque romaine, I. Paris 1964, 306-310, 383-385. — L. Musset, De saint Victrice à Saint Ouen. Le christianisation de la province de Rouen d'après l'hagiographie: RHEF 62(1975)141-152.

VINCENT, A PRIEST OF GAUL

Information on this Gallic priest and exegete is provided by Gennadius (*De vir. ill.* 81 [80]), who knew him personally, and who mentions a commentary *In Davidis psalmos,* which has been lost. Vallarsi attempted to identify this commentary with the similarly titled work of Pseudo-Rufinus (PL 2, 641-960). This latter work, however, as the manuscripts indicate and A. Wilmart has proved, is to be attributed to Lietbert of Lille, abbot of St. Rufus, near Avignon, at the beginning of the twelfth century (PLS I, 1097).

Studies: A. Wilmart, Le commentaire sur les psaumes, imprimé sous le nom de Rufin:

RB 31(1914)258-276. — F. Stegmüller, Repertorium biblicum medii aevi III. Madrid 1951, n. 5395; 7335; 8308.

VINCENT OF LÉRINS

Vincent is the best known of the monastic writers of Lérins. Nevertheless, little is known of his life except the information provided in Gennadius (*De vir. ill.* 65 [64]). A native of Gaul, Vincent began a military career *variis ac tristibus saecularis militiae turbinibus,* then took up residence at Lérins where he became a priest attached to the monastery. Gennadius emphasizes his proficiency in biblical studies and in the history of dogma. It seems that, together with Salvian, he was entrusted with the education of Salonius and Veranus, the sons of Eucherius (Eucherius, *Instr.* I *praef.*). He died before 450 and perhaps even before 435.

Studies: F. Brunetière, P. de Labriolle, Vincent de Lérins (Les Saints). Paris, 1906. — H. Koch, Vincenz von Lerin und Gennadius; ein Beitrag zur Literaturgesch. des Semipelagianismus (TU 31, 2b). Leipzig, 1907. — G. Bardy, Vincent de Lérins: DTC 15(1950)3045-3055. — F. Sciuto, Tertulliano e Vincenzo di Lerino: MSLC 4(1954)127-138. — M. Schuster, Vincentius von Lerinum: PWK 16/II(1958)2192-2197.

WRITINGS

Gennadius mentions only a *disputatio* written against the heretics. However, in 434 the monk of Lérins composed the *Tractatus pro catholicae fidei antiquitate et universitate adversus profanas omnium haereticorum novitates,* generally known as the *Commonitorium,* in two books, which were evidently intended to serve as an aid to his memory.

Two other works are attributed to Vincent. The first is the *Obiectiones Vincentianae,* the text of which has been lost but which is known from the work of Prosper, *Pro Augustino responsiones ad capitula obiectionum Vincentianarum* (PL 51, 177-186). H. Koch supports the authenticity of Vincent's composition, although W. O. Conners has proposed serious arguments against it. Another work is the *Excerpta sanctae memoriae Vincentii Lirinensis insulae presbyteri ex universo beatae recordationis Augustini episcopi in unum collecto.* This work, mentioned in an anonymous compendium of the ninth century, was discovered by J. Madoz in the library of Ripoll. Its composition was announced in the *Commonitorium* (c. 16), and it contains a prologue and epilogue of Vincent with the remainder of the work consisting of a *Summa Augustiniana* against Nestorius in ten articles.

Editions: The mss. usually transcribe the *Commonitorium* with the *Ad Ecclesiam* of Salvian and other works. For editions prior to Migne, cf. Schönnemann, PL 50, 630-638; PL 50, 637-686 (E. Baluze). — G. Rauschen, Vincentii Lerinensis Comm., FP 5(1906). — R. S. Moxon, The Commonitorium of Vincentius of Lerins. Cambridge, 1915. — A.

Jülicher, Vincenz von Lerins, Comm. Tübingen, 1925. *Excerpta:* J. Madoz, Exerpta V. L. (*Estudios Orientales*). Madrid, 1940 (= PLS III, 23-45). W. J. Mountain: SE 18(1967-1968)385-405 (with the ms. of Novara).

Translations: English: C. A. Heurtley, LNPF 11, ser. 2(1894)131-156 (reprint: 1973). — R. E. Morris, FC 6(1949)267-332. *French:* P. de Labriolle. Paris, 1906 (reprint: 1978). — M. Meslin. Namur, 1959. *German:* G. Rauschen. BKV² 20(1914). *Italian:* C. Colafemmina, Il Commonitorio. Alba, 1967. *Spanish:* M. Madoz. Madrid, 1935, 1944². — M. Moreiro Rubio. Madrid, 1976. — L. F. Mateo Seco. Pamplona, 1977.

The *Commonitorium*

Vincent composed two *Commonitoria,* or memoranda, of which only the first has been preserved. He makes use of the pseudonym "Peregrinus," intended as a synonym for "monk." From Gennadius we know that the second book was stolen from the author, who, nevertheless, still had both books in his possession when he was writing the summary of the second (c. 29-33). The manuscripts and editors present the summary as the second *Commonitorium* (PL 50, 677).

a) Analysis

The *Commonitorium* is neither a mere memorandum drawn up for personal use, nor a collection of patristic texts, but a type of "discourse on methodology" which allows one to distinguish the Catholic faith from new heresies. Two criteria are at the disposition of the faithful: Scripture and the church's tradition. Scripture, since it is subject to the possibility of deformation by heretical interpretations, must be read in the light of tradition according to the now-famous axiom: "*In ipsa item catholica ecclesia magnopere curandum est, ut id teneamus quod ubique, quod semper, quod ab omnibus creditum est. Hoc est etenim vere proprieque catholicum*" (c. 2).

Universality, antiquity, and unanimous consent are the three criteria which guarantee orthodoxy (c. 3). For Vincent, the most important of the three is antiquity, and reference must be made to this in cases of a lack of universality. As illustrations of his rule, the author refers to Donatism, which is opposed to universality, Arianism, opposed to antiquity, and the baptism of the heretics, opposed to unanimous consent. The *Commonitorium* opposes such deviations with the teachings of St. Paul and his concern to "preserve the deposit of the faith" (c. 7-9). Vincent then analyzes the innovations of Nestorius, Photinus, and Apollinarius, against which he holds up the Catholic doctrine on the Trinity and the person of Christ (c. 11-16). Inerrancy does not depend on the teaching even of the most illustrious masters, such as Origen and Tertullian, who were able to go astray, but on the decrees of a universal council and on the common faith of the church

(c. 17-19). In order to faithfully preserve the deposit of faith, according to the word of St. Paul, it is necessary to exclude "doctrinal innovations." An innovation in terminology must not be the means of a doctrinal innovation: *cum dicas nove, non dicas novum* (c. 22).

The criterion of tradition does not lead to immobility, given that it is joined with a second criterion, both essential and complementary, of dogmatic progress which operates according to the laws of organic growth. "This progress truly constitutes a progress and not an alteration of the faith, for it is characteristic of progress that a thing grows while remaining the same thing, and characteristic of alteration that one thing is changed into another. Therefore intelligence, knowledge, and wisdom grow and increase considerably both of the individual as of all, of the single man as well as of the entire church, according to ages and times. The particular nature of each is to be respected, however; that is, it remains exactly the same dogma, has the same meaning and expresses the same thought" (c. 23). Vatican I adopted this well-known formula as its own.

This progress implies a three-fold task: "To perfect and polish that which received its first form and outline in antiquity; to consolidate and strengthen that which already has obtained its profile and clarity; preserve that which has been confirmed and has received its definition" (c. 23). There is thus a three-fold progress: a progress in formulation which the church, having been challenged by the heretics, accomplishes by means of conciliar decrees to enlighten the understanding with new and appropriate terms and transmit them to those who will come later; progress in the organic life which takes place in dogmatic truths and always exceeds the language which expresses it, much in the same way that a human life grows from infancy to old age while always remaining the same person; progress in the final acquisition of truth without alteration or mutilation.

Vincent returns again to the treacherous use the heretics make of the Scripture (c. 25). He insists that it is not sufficient to have recourse to passages of the Bible in order to avoid their snares, but these "must be interpreted according to the universal tradition of the church and the rules of Catholic dogma. Thus in the Catholic church it is necessary to follow universality, antiquity, and the consent of all" (c. 27).

The final chapters, which summarize the *Commonitorium,* deal with the normative value of Scripture and thus develop a new apology for the criterion of antiquity, on which the Council of Ephesus had recently based its condemnation of Nestorius by explicitly citing ten Latin and Greek Fathers. To this dossier, Vincent adds the texts of Sixtus III and Celestine. Some years later, Leo the Great will himself follow a similar procedure.

b) The Teaching and Erudition of the *Commonitorium*

Paradoxically, this teacher of the immutability is revealed as the theologian of the laws of the development of dogma. His teaching on tradition is based on the *Adversus haereses* of Irenaeus, although it emphasizes less clearly the apostolicity of true teaching and the role of the ecclesiastical magisterium.

Vincent is especially dependent on the *De prescriptione haereticorum* of Tertullian. If the monk of Lérins deplores Tertullian's deviations, he, nevertheless, recognizes that he is "the first of us among the Latins" (c. 17), and that it would be wrong for the theologian not to pay him a debt of gratitude. The same ideas are found in both works. The concise argumentation of the Carthaginian priest is based on Roman law, and the monk of Lérins affirms these arguments rather than adding new ones of his own.

The more modest influence of Cassian on Vincent is in connection with *universitas* as a rule of faith, an idea which Cassian presents in his work on the Incarnation. The *Commonitorium,* as Bossuet noted, also draws its inspiration from the writings of Augustine, whom Vincent openly admired, as is evident from the *Excerpta.*

Vincent is the first to assemble a patristic dossier by citing the testimony of *patres probabiles.* Church history has shown that Vincent's criteria, seemingly adequate at first, are difficult in their application. It is no simple matter to find unanimity if all the truths have been contested, and it is likewise difficult to establish antiquity and apostolicity. Every historical inquest requires a critical competency. Vincent's judgment on Theophilus, the great adversary of Chrysostom, ought to have been more carefully nuanced. He even cites the testimony of St. Felix and St. Julian without realizing that he is using Apollinarist falsifications.

Even though Vincent was concerned primarily with the innovations of the heresies, the West has drawn inspiration from his teaching on the progress of dogma developed in several chapters of the *Commonitorium* (c. 23-24). He recognized this development both in the understanding and in the formulation of dogmatic truth. Without changing the deposit of faith in any way, the church explores its richness more deeply and expresses its content more clearly.

The *Commonitorium* owes its success, especially since the sixteenth century, to the vigor of its formulae, the elegance of its style, the wealth of its expressions, and the metallic strength of its form. It transmits its teaching in clear, concise, powerful, and decisive sentences. The classical reminiscences of Sallustrius, Ovid, and Lucan, natural ornaments in the text, give evidence of the cultural level of Lérins. Vincent knew Greek Christian literature, and may have translated a text of the Council of Ephesus (31, 2-3). However, he does not seem to have exercised any influence on the East.

c) Vincent of Lérins and History

G. J. Vossius in his *Historia de controversiis* I 9 (1618) and E. Noris in his *Historia pelagiana* (1673) were the first to propose the *Commonitorium* as part of a dossier against Augustine or, more precisely, against Augustine's teaching on grace and predestination. This thesis has enjoyed enormous success and has been repeated by nearly all modern historians, although some have been more cautious.

New light was cast on the question as a result of the discovery of the *Excerpta* by J. Madoz. In these, Vincent reveals himself as an indisputable admirer of Augustine. He refers to the authority of the teacher of Hippo on the two questions of the Trinity and the Incarnation which are explicitly developed in the *Commonitorium* (c. 13-15). Because of this, E. Griffe has recently been able to state that there is not the least anti-Augustinian reference to be found in the *Commonitorium* and that the work is to be placed outside of the Semi-Pelagian Controversy. Furthermore, O'Conner has shown that Vincent is not the author of the *Obiectiones* which Prosper considered offensive to St. Augustine. Therefore the *Commonitorium,* far from being anti-Augustinian, draws its inspiration from the principle of tradition, dear to the Bishop of Hippo (*Ep.* 54; *De bapt.* 4, 24; *Contra ep. Man.* 4).

In any case it is certain that, although it was not quoted by any of the great scholastics, the influence of the *Commonitorium* has not ceased to increase since the sixteenth century. Prior to that time, the work is found only in a few manuscripts at Paris (BN 2172, *saec.* X, which came from Pierre Pithou; 13.386, *saec.* X, from Saint-Germain-des-Prés, the best manuscript; 2785, *saec.* XI; and 2173, *saec.* XIII), while since the sixteenth century more than 50 editions and translations have appeared. Bellarmine described it as the *libellus plane aureus,* while Bossuet makes constant reference to it in his *Défense de la tradition des saints Pères.* Catholics and Protestants regarded it with equal admiration at first. Newman found an "ecumenical" norm in the *Commonitorium* and procured a new importance for the work. The Anglicans and Old Catholics, particularly Döllinger, invoked it against the decisions of the First Vatican Council, which, in its turn, took the last word from Vincent of Lérins in the Dogmatic Constitution on the Faith.

The unanimous esteem which the *Commonitorium* had enjoyed broke down in the nineteenth century as both Catholics and Protestants called the normative value of Vincent's criteria into question. J. B. Franzelin, in a more moderate appraisal, maintained that the theory of the *Commonitorium* remains valid but in *sensu affirmante* not *sensu excludente*. It is no small merit for a man of the fifth century to have established rules which, prudently applied, still retain a normative value fourteen centuries later.

Studies: R. M. J. Poirel, De utroque commonitorio Lirinensi. Nancy, 1895; *idem,* Vincentii Peregrini seu alio nomine Marii Mercatoris Lirinensia Commonitoria duo. Nancy, 1898 (attribution to M. Mercator which was not accepted; cf. H. Koch, Vincentius von Lerinum und Marius Mercator: ThQ 81[1899]396-434). — W. S. Reilly, Quod ubique, quod semper, quod abomnibus. Etude sur la règle de la foi de Vincent de Lérins. Tours, 1903. — C. Weyman, Die Edition des Commonitorium: *Histor. Jahrbuch-München* 29(1908)582-586; cf. 40(1920)184f. — N. Dausse, Le développement du dogme d'après saint Vincent de Lérins: RT 16(1908)630-651; 17(1909)692-710. — J. Lortz, Der Kanon des Vincentius von Lerin: *Der Katholik* 2(1913)245-255. — L. Globus, De H. Vincentius van Lérins en zijne commonitoria: *Studien* 79(1913)231-259, 383-411; 80(1913)274-307, 402-420, 445-473; 81(1914)1-37. — J. Madoz, El concepto de la Tradición en San Vicente de Lerins (*Analecta Gregoriana* 5). Rome, 1933. — A. d'Alès, La fortune du "Commonitorium": RSR 26(1936)334-356. — J. Madoz, Un tratado desconocido de S. Vincente de Lerins: Greg 21(1940)75-94; *idem,* Los excerpta Vincentii Lir. en la controversia adoptionista: RET 13(1953)475-483. — B. Luiselli, Sulla pseudonomia di Vincenzo di Lerino: *Atene e Roma* 4(1959)216-222. — E. Griffe, Pro Vincentio Lirinensi: BLE 62(1961)26-32. — W. O'Conner, Saint Vincent of Lerins and Saint Augustine: *Doctor Communis* 16(1963)123-257. — J. H. Sieben, Der Konzilbegriff des Vincenz von Lerin: *Theologie und Philosophie* 46(1971)364-386. — A. Pastorino, Il concetto di tradizione in Giov. Cassiano e in Vincenzo di L.: *Sileno* 1(1975)37-46. — M. Lods, Le progrès dans le temps de l'Eglise selon Vincent de Lérins: RHPR 55(1975)365-385.

PROSPER OF AQUITAINE

What little is known of Prosper's life is taken from the information provided by Gennadius (*De vir. ill.* 85 [86]). He was born in Aquitaine at the end of the fourth century and attended Gaulo-Roman schools, which provided him with a solid classical education. He went to Marseilles, "the New Athens," perhaps to escape from political discord and certainly attracted by the theological-monastic environment centered around St. Victor and Lérins. Although he was a layman and never a cleric much less a priest or bishop, Prosper maintained contacts with both of these Provençal monasteries without ever joining either of them.

He was at Marseilles when the Semi-Pelagian Controversy broke out around 426 and was an ardent defender of Augustine, to whom he wrote together with Hilary, who must have been an African by birth. Augustine sent the two the *De praedestinatione sanctorum* and the *De dono perseverantiae,* which had originally formed one single work. After the death of Augustine, he went to Rome to obtain the condemnation of the ideas professed at Marseilles and Lérins, and was behind the letter sent by Celestine I to the bishops of Gaul (PL 50, 528-530). He was disappointed in his mission to Rome, and it took some time before he realized that it was not necessary to be more Augustinian than Rome. He returned to Marseilles, rejoined the polemic and, between 432 and 434, published his major works. With the death of Cassian, the controversy also died down.

Prosper then settled at Rome and offered his services to Leo the Great, although he did not become his *notarius*. From "militant theology" he now passed over to carrying out his duties and to composing more serene works such as his commentary on the Psalms and the *Capitula* (434-442). According to Gennadius, he assisted in the composition of the *Tomus ad Flavianum* (PL 54, 755). In the *De vocatione omnium gentium,* he took up the question of the universal predestination to salvation.

Turning to poetry, he composed the *Epigrammata ex sentiis s. Augustini,* an Augustinian florilegium in distichs. His *Chronica,* which he worked on until the end of his life, ends in the year 455, the same year in which he took part in the Easter controversy. He must have died shortly after this.

Studies: L. Valentin, S. Prosper d'Aquitaine. Toulouse-Paris, 1900 (still useful for literary questions but out of date for critical and theological questions. Regarding this book cf. L. Couture, S. Prosper d'Aquitaine: BLE 2[1900]269-282; 3[1901]33-49). — B. Borelli, S. Prospero d'Aquitania e il giudizio della storia. Carpi, 1907. — R. Helm, PWK 23/1(1959)1193-1204 (depends too heavily on Valentin and does not know the rest of the French bibliog.). — G. Bosio: *Bibliotheca Sanctorum* 10(1968)1193-1204.

WORKS

Prosper is a man of letters. His language and vocabulary are classical and show a clear rejection of neologisms. As a pupil of rhetoricians, he loved the oratorical form, with its pathos and irony, antithesis, alliteration, and rhythm, and he cultivated the *cursus.* He knew Greek well enough to allow himself some word plays in that language in the *De ingratis* and also produced such literary contrivances as *Mens in vulnera, vulnere surgit* (*De ingr.* 592). Although no innovator, he had a facility for writing in verse and was a master of the distich and hexameter. He was acquainted with Vergil and imitated Lucretius and, at times, Ovid. His constant concern, and something which was of supreme importance to him, was to place his classical culture at the service of theology. The Bible provided his principal source of inspiration. Prosper excels especially in his precision of thought, flexibility of expression, capacity of judgment, and in the clarity of his exposition and the force of his argumentation.

Editions: The first edition of the *opera ominia* is from Lyons, 1539. The ed. of J. b. Le Brun des Marettes and L. U. Mangenat, Paris 1711 is reprinted in PL 51. — The greater part of his works are found among the spuria of Augustine in the Maurist edition, PL 45. The edition of P. and H. Ballerini of the *De vocatione omnium gentium* is found in PL 50, 647 among the works of Leo the Great. The *Praeteritorum Sedis*

Apostolicae ep. auctoritates is found in PL 50, 531 and PL 84, 682, usually followed by the letter of Celestine I to the bishops of Gaul. The ed. CCL 68A(1972) includes the *Expositio Psalmorum* (P. Callens) and the *Liber sententiarum* (M. Gastaldo). For the *Capitula S. Augustini in Urbem Romam transmissa* cf. F. Glorie, CCL 85(1978). For the mss. cf. F. Sciuto, Nonulla de codicibus: MSLC 9(1959)19-24.

1. Letters

The *Epistula ad Rufinam* (PL 51, 77-79 and 45, 1793-1802) is an excellent exposition of the Augustinian doctrine on grace and provides a rough sketch of Prosper's future treatises. The *Epistula ad Augustinum* (among the works of Augustine, *Ep.* 225: PL 33, 1002-1007) dates from the end of 428, while another letter to Augustine has been lost. Prosper assisted in the composition of the letters of Leo I, especially of the *Tomus ad Flavianum.* The *Epistula ad Demetriadem* (probably by the same author as the *De vocatione omnium gentium* according to Arnould and Quesnel against the Ballerini) is among the most disputed works; the *Clavis* 529 places it among the *spuria,* while B. Fischer (VT 437) considers that it "probably is authentic," as do Valentin, Helm, Krabbe, and Cappuyns.

Editions: PL 55, 161-180. — K. C. Krabbe, Epistula ad Demetriadem (PSt 97). Washington, 1965.

Translations: English: P. De Letter, ACW 32(1963)21-37 (to Rufinus), 38-48 (to Augustine). — K. C. Krabbe, op. cit. (to Demetriadem, with text).

Studies: J. Gaidioz, Prosper d'A. et le tome à Flavien: RSR 23(1949)271-301. — J. Chéné, Le semipélagianisme du midi de la Gaule, d'après les lettres de Prosper d'A. et d'Hilaire à s. Augustin: RSR 43(1955)321-341.

2. Works in Verse

The *De ingratis carmen* or περὶ ἀχαρίστων (PL 51, 91-148) was composed in 429-430 before the death of Augustine. It consists of 1012 hexameters on the expression "those who are lacking in thanks or the ungrateful." Prosper first expounds on Pelagianism (1-113), then Semi-Pelagianism (114-225), which he refutes (226-564). He reviews the arguments of the Semi-Pelagians (565-800) and then concludes with a discussion of the connections between Pelagianism and Semi-Pelagianism. It is a passionate exposition of Augustine's doctrine of grace: "Yes, we are free, but with a freedom which has been ransomed" (977). It has been described as "one of the more successful essays of philosophical poetry attempted in Christianity" (Guizot).

Translations: English: C. T. Huegelmeyer (PSt 95). Washington, 1962 (with text). *German:* O. Hagenbüchle. Stans, 1920.

Epigrammata. From the same period as the preceding work come two aggressive epigrams: the *Epigrammata in obtrectatorem Augustini* (PL 51,

149-152). On the other hand the 106 *Epigrammata ex sententiis S. Augustini* (PL 51, 498-532) seem to date from a period after the Council of Chalcedon (451). These epigrams contributed notably to Prosper's literary success. The *Epitaphium Nestorianae et Pelagianae haereseon,* an ironic lamentation of mother and daughter who realize their relationship in the tomb, was written after 431 as it presupposes the condemnation passed at Ephesus (PL 51, 153-154).

Studies: D. Lassandro, Note sugli epigrammi de Prospero d'Aquitania: VetChr 8(1971)211-222.

3. Theological Works

In his theological works dating from the time of his stay in Provence, Prosper is engaged in the Semi-Pelagian Controversy and defends the views of Augustine.

Pro Augustino responsiones ad capitula obiectionum Gallorum calumniantium (PL 51, 155-174; PL 45, 1833-1844) was written at Marseilles in 431-432 or, according to Cappuyns, shortly thereafter.

Pro Augustino responsiones ad capitula obiectionum Vincentiarum (PL 51, 77-186; PL 45, 1843-1850) also was written at Marseilles in 431-432, probably against Vincent of Lérins.

Pro Augustino responsiones ad exerpta Genuensium (PL 51, 187-202; PL 45, 1849-1858) is addressed to two priests of Genoa (Plinval reads Agen) who were disturbed by the *De praedestinatione* of Augustine.

De gratia Dei et libero arbitrio liber contra collatorem (undoubtedly John Cassian) was written at Marseilles in 433.

Capitula or *Praeteritorum Sedis Apostolicae episcoporum auctoritates, de gratia Dei et libero voluntatis arbitrio* (PL 45, 1756-1760; PL 51, 205-212; PL 50, 531-537, etc.) are often joined to the letter of Celestine I (from the collection *Dionysiana*). The work was composed between 435 and 442. Helms has expressed doubts concerning its authenticity.

Translations: English: J. R. O'Donnel, FC 7(1949)343-418 (Contra collatorem). — P. De Letter, ACW 32(1963)43-69 (res. ad excerpta Genuensium), 70-138 (Contra collatorem), 139-162 (ad capitula objectionum Gallorum), 163-177 (ad capitula objectionum Vincentiarum), 178-185 (Auctoritates).

Studies: M. Cappuyns, L'origine des Capitula pseudo-célestiniens contre le semipélagianisme: RB 41(1929)156-170.

During his time in Rome, Prosper composed works of a less polemical nature. The *Expositio psalmorum* 100-150, which depends on the *Enarrationes* of Augustine, is to be dated after 431 and prior to 449. The authenticity of the prologue (*prologus metricus* PL 36, 59) is disputed; G. Morin, who republished it in RB 46(1934)36 is in favor, while M. Cappuyns (BTAM 3 n. 153) is opposed. The CCL considers it to date from the Carolingian era, and to be perhaps a work of Walafrid Strabo, and thus omits it.

Liber sententiarum ex operibus S. Augustini delibatarum. These are 392 sayings which, having been removed from their context, either exaggerate or attenuate Augustine's thought. The collection is of great importance for the history of dogma as it played an important role in making Augustine known, in the version of Prosper, in the Middle Ages. For the 106 sayings in verse, cf. *Epigrammata, supra.*

De vocatione omnium gentium (also in PL 17, 1073). This work, which was attributed to Leo the Great by Quesnel (PL 55, 393), has been the object of much discussion with regard to its authenticity. The evidence provided first by L. Valentin, then by M. Cappuyns, on the manuscript tradition and internal criticism indicates Prosper as the author.

Editions: Expositiones: PL 51, 277-426. — CCL 68A(1972)1-211 (P. Callens). *Sententiae:* PL 51, 427-496; PL 45, 1859-1898. — CCL 68A(1972)221-365 (M. Gastaldo) *De vocatione:* PL 51, 647-722.

Translations: English: P. De Letter, ACW 15(1952) (De vocatione).

Studies: L. Valentin, S. Prosper d'Aquitaine, Toulouse-Paris, 1900. — M. Cappuyns, L'auteur du "De vocatione omnium gentium": RB 39(1927)198-226. — G. de Plinval: RAug 1(1958)358 (opposed to the authenticity). — L. Pelland, S. Prosperi Aquitani doctrina de praedestinatione et voluntate Dei salvifica. Montreal, 1936. — G. Morin, La préface métrique au commentaire sur les Psaumes de P, d'A.: RB 44(1934)36-40. — J. J. Young, Studies on the Style of the Vocatione omnium gentium ascribed to Prosper of A. (PSt 87). Washington, 1952. — R. Lorenz, Der Augustinismus Prospers von Aquitanien: ZKG 73(1962)217-252. — C. Bartnik, L'universalisme de l'histoire dans le De vocatione omnium gentium: RHE 68(1973)731-758.

4. Historical Works

Epitoma Chronicae. This history of the world from its origins until 455 draws abundantly on the works of Eusebius and Jerome. From the year 412 on, the work takes on a more personal tone, especially in regard to the history of Gaul and above all in relation to events in Aquitania. Prosper apparently completed the first edition in 433, to which he added the extension to 455 *(Chronicon vulgatum)* and the *additamenta* relating to the years 446-455 *(Chronicon integrum).* Further *additamenta* were made later (PLS III, 147-148). The value of the *Chronica* lies in Prosper's interest for the history of dogma.

Editions with the additamenta: PL 51, 535-606. — Th. Mommson, MGH, AA IX, 1, 385-485 and 486-499.

5. Spuria

Various writings attributed to Prosper are to be found among his authentic works:

The *Confessio* (PL 55, 607-610). Sirmond attributed this work to Prosper on the basis of two manuscripts (*Vat. lat.* 558, cf. 262 and 559;

and Paris, BN 17413). He does not say which of the two manuscripts he used, but a comparative study indicates that it was 558.

The *Poëma coniugis ad uxorem* (*versus Prosperi* in the codex *Reginensis lat.* 230) (PL 51, 611-616; PL 61, 737-742; Hartel, CSEL 30[1894]244-248). This work is attributed to Paulinus of Nola and was included among the works of Pseudo-Paulinus in the edition of Rosweyd. It consists of 16 anacreontic verses and 53 elegiac distichs.

The *Commonitorium quomodo sit agendum cum Manicheis qui confitentur pravitatem nefandi erroris* (among the works of Augustine: PL 42, 1153-1156; J. Zycha, CSEL 25, 2[1892]979-982; in a partial version PL 65, 28-30).

Prosperi anathematismata et fidei catholicae professio (ed. Sirmond: PL 65, 23-30; PL 42, 1153-1156). This is an extended version, made in 526 or 515, of the preceding *Commonitorium* (cf. PLS III, 1329).

The *De promissionibus et praedicationibus Dei* (PL 51, 733-854; PLS III, 149; R. Braun, CCL 60[1976]1-223 and SCh 101 and 102[1964]). The attribution was restored to Quodvultdeus by R. Braun.

The *Carmen de divina providentia* is not a work of Prosper but was written in Gaul in 416.

The *fragmentum de duobus testibus* (ed. Mommsen: PLS III, 150). According to Harnack, this is to be attributed to Hippolytus or a member of his school.

Studies: A. Dufourcq, Etudes sur les Gesta martyrum romains IV. Paris 1910, 44-47 (Anathematismata). — W. Bong, Manichaeische Hymnen X: Mus 38(1952)53-55. — P. Menno, Illud carmen Ad coniugem inscribitur divi Paulini N. sitne an divi Prosperi A.: *Latinitas* 10(1962)208-214. — A. Longpré, Le De providentia divina de Prosper d'Aquitaine et la question de son authenticité: REA 80(1978)108-113.

DOCTRINE

Prosper dedicated the better part of his life to defending and disseminating the teachings of Augustine in prose and verse. He did this with faithfulness and skill, knowing how to attenuate without altering. Only his historical works are to be placed outside of the context of the Pelagian Controversy.

1. The Defender of the Augustinian Teaching on Grace

The statement that Prosper's theology of grace is Augustinian is, on the whole, correct but needs to be more carefully nuanced. While remaining a faithful disciple of Augustine, Prosper underwent an evolution, passing from an unconditional to a moderate stance. Historians generally distinguish in his works a period of intransigence (up to 432), the period of the first concessions (433-435), and the period of major concessions (after 435). For a verification of such an evolution, it is sufficient to compare the polemical works with the *De vocatione gentium.* The difference is such that it caused doubts for a long time concerning the authenticity of the latter work.

In his earlier writings, Prosper strongly insists on the gratuity of grace, which is the theme of the *Ep. ad Rufinum,* and, in the letter to the Genoese, on predestination: "What can we say of the Tyrians and Sidonians except that the grace of faith was not granted them, after Truth itself recognized that they would have believed had some miracles been worked for them" (PL 51, 198A).

On the question of predestination, Prosper, aware of the excesses of the thesis of the small number of the elect, already softens the Augustinian positions in the *Responsiones* to the calumnies of the Gauls by saying that the wicked are predestined to damnation as a result of the foreknowledge of their sins (PL 51, 158, 161). The same doctrine occurs in the *Responsiones* to Vincent where he affirms that God desires the salvation of all and that the Apostle calls on the churches to pray for this universal goal (PL 51, 179B; cf. 184A, 186B).

The *Capitula* prudently omit the difficult questions of divine foreknowledge and defend a position similar to that of Leo I (*Serm.* 23, 4; 35, 3, etc.). Augustine's name is not even mentioned. He now refers to the authority of the church to profess the absolute gratuity and necessity of salvation: "It suffices simply to accept the decisions of the Apostolic See." Prosper has been Romanized.

2. The *De vocatione omnium gentium*

This is the first work of Christian literature dedicated to the question of the salvation of the heathen, and the first treatise on the divine economy inserted into the framework of human history. Prosper divides time into *ante legem, sub lege,* and *sub gratia.* The work defends God's salvific will for each individual and for all of humanity. God offers each person equal possibilities for salvation and the adequate means for this. Those who are excluded are excluded because of their own fault. The universality of salvation is *pars fidei* (PL 51, 706C).

Book I deals with particular solutions, while book II gradually arrives at universal solutions. Prosper explains this divine-human synergism thus: "It is the beginning of the doctrine which involves the responsibility of man in history." The theologian of Marseilles, moved by strictly missionary interests, opens new vistas for humanity here.

3. Prosper and the History of Augustinianism

The *Liber sententiarum* is the first Augustinian florilegium. It introduces in the West a literary genre that will flourish in the Middle Ages and will constitute, for better or worse, the principal source for a knowledge of Augustinian and patristic works. To measure its diffusion, it is sufficient to note the abundance of manuscripts of this work spread throughout Europe in the most diverse places. The last editor counted eighteen.

The *Liber sententiarum* prepared the way for the *Testimonia divinae scripturae et Patrum* of Isidore of Seville, the florilegium of Florus of Lyons, and the collection of fragments of the *Libellus scintillarum.* It was translated into Greek by Demetrios Kydones, is mentioned by Photius (*Bibl. cod.* 54) and is referred to by Hincmar of Rheims (PL 125, 414C) among others. Two of its sayings (15 and 139) passed into the *Decretum Gratianum.* Prosper is one of the ancient writers who was found in almost all the early libraries (M. Manitius). His epigrams were a classic and were among the most frequently copied works of antiquity. They existed in three copies at Reichenau in the ninth century and five at Sankt Gallen in the twelfth. They were also the first work of Prosper to be printed in the incunabula (Mainz 1496).

Prosper not only transmitted Augustinianism to the Middle Ages, but he also made the first selection within the patrimony of the Bishop of Hippo. Although he respected Augustine's thought, he also transformed and updated it. Under pressure from the Gallic theologians, he progressively abandoned the position of a restricted will for salvation and unconditional rejection in order to affirm as *pars fidei* the universality of God's salvific will along with the absolute gratuity of grace. In this way he already assured the approval of Augustinianism at the Council of Orange and its acceptance into scholasticism, where it dominated. Prosper can rightly be called "the first representative of medieval Augustinianism" (M. Cappuyns).

Studies: M. Jacquin, La prédestination au Ve et VIe siècles: RHE 7(1906)269-300. — M. Cappuyns, Le premier représentant de l'augustinisme médiéval: RTAM 1(1929)309-337. — L. Pelland, S. Prosperi A. doctrina de praedestinatione et voluntate Dei salvifica. Montreal, 1936. — J. Gaidioz, La christologie de s. Prosper d'A. Lyons, 1947. — Ch. Brand, Le De incarnatione Domini de J. Cassien. Strasbourg, 1954. — J. Chéné, Le semipélagianisme du midi de la Gaule: RSR 43(1955)321-341. — J. Plagnieux, Le grief de complicité entre erreurs nestorienne et pélagienne d'Augustin à Cassien par Prosper: REAug 2(1956)391-403. — R. Gantoy, Prima sedis Roma Petri: RB 68(1958)114-117. — G. de Plinval, Prosper d'A. interprète de saint Augustin: RAug 1(1958)339-355. — R. Lorenz, Der Augustinismus Prospers von A.: ZKG 73(1962)217-252 (Analysis of the Sententiarum). — C. Bartnik, L'universalisme de l'histoire du salut dans le De vocatione o. G.: RHE 68(1973)731-758.

ETHERIA (EGERIA)

Etheria is a person difficult to describe. She was a cultivated lady who belonged to a community which resembled a beguinage more than a monastery. A thirteenth-century catalogue from St. Martial at Limoges calls her an abbess; however, this is too late a witness to be acceptable. With regard to her name, the first editor believed it to be

Sylvia, which was still retained by Geyer. Férotin subsequently changed it to Etheria, which is the name generally in use today even in preference to Egeria (A. Lambert, O. Prinz).

The first editor of the *Itinerarium* stated that Gaul was her native land, but more recently Galicia has gained acceptance, especially among those who are not impressed by a comparison Etheria makes between the Euphrates and the Rhone.

The date accepted for her pilgrimage has undergone many changes. E. Dekkers moved it back to the years 415-418, Lambert to 414-416, while J. Campos places it in 380. A meticulous comparison between the forty days after Easter and the feast of the Holy Innocents has allowed P. Devos to settle on the year 383 and place the journey in Palestine between the Easters of 381 and 384. The journey in Mesopotamia took place immediately afterwards.

ITINERARIUM OR *PEREGRINATIO AD LOCA SANCTA*

In 1884, the Italian, G. F. Gamurrini, found in the ninth-century manuscript of the Confraternity of Santa Maria of Arezzo, between the *De mysteriis et hymnis* of Hilary of Poitiers and a *De locis sanctis* of Paul the Deacon, a *Sanctae Silviae aquitaniae peregrinatio ad loca sancta,* which he published together with other texts in 1887. In the form of a letter sent from Constantinople (23, 10), the author provides her "sisters" who have remained at home with a detailed account of her travels in Egypt, Palestine and Mesopotamia. The original manuscript, which comes from Monte Cassino, is mutilated at the beginning and end and contains some *lacunae.*

Etheria shows little interest for natural beauty, and directs her curiosity toward religious matters, biblical reminiscences, and liturgical celebrations. In the form in which it appears, the *Itinerarium* is a document superior to many others of the same genre with regard to the information it contains of a linguistic, topographical, geographical, liturgical, and ecclesiastical point of view. Her information on the holy places and the liturgy of Jerusalem, and on the organization of the monastic life and the hierarchy are of inestimable value.

It is possible to distinguish four journeys: the first, interrupted at the start, begins at the foot of Sinai then goes to Jerusalem by way of the Red Sea and the land of Gessen (1-9); the second leads to Mount Nebo (10-12); the third is a pilgrimage in Idumea, the land of Job (13-15); the fourth is the pilgrimage in Mesopotamia and return to Constantinople by way of Tarsus, Seleucia, and Chalcedon (16-23).

During her journeys Etheria makes use of the Bible, which she quotes in a version of the *Vetus latina,* and Eusebius' *Onomasticon* in the Latin translation of Jerome (J. Ziegler).

She writes in the spoken language of her time to which she gives a classical dress borrowed from the scholastic and literary tradition. It is a language both modern and lively, which is capable of assimilating new terms or giving them a new significance. The influence of Greek is clearly apparent (C. Milani): Greek terms, both Christian and profane, either transcribed in Latin letters or already Romanized; morphological, syntactical, or semantic clichés. It is a language which already is showing its dependence on Latin Christian authors.

The *Itinerarium* describes the churches of Jerusalem and the surrounding area (the Holy Sepulcher, Sion, the Mount of Olives, Bethlehem, Bethany). It provides information on the liturgical year and its feasts, especially the Paschal cycle; the course of the daily liturgy with the rhythm of the offices, the recitation of the psalter, the discipline of fasting, and the catechesis of the catechumens. Etheria furnishes valuable knowledge on ecclesiastical organization: the bishop, who is usually an elderly monk; the presbyters, who offer the Eucharist in the bishop's absence; the deacons, and the clerics.

On all of her journeys, at Sinai, in Egypt, Syria, and Mesopotamia, Etheria encounters monks, some of whom accompany her as an official escort. The monasteries are hermitages which, for the most part, are grouped around a church which is looked after by a priest (3, 4). At Jerusalem, she mentions monks *(monazontes)* and virgins *(parthenae)* (24, 1). All of this information serves to cast light on liturgical and monastic life at the end of the fourth century and makes of the *Itinerarium* a unique document.

Editions: G. F. Gamurrini, S. Hilarii . . . et S. Silviae "Peregrinatio ad loca sancta." Rome, 1887 (*editio princeps*); *idem,* Studi e documenti di storia e diritto 9(1888)97-174 (with corrections). — P. Geyer, CSEL 39(1898)35-101 (= PLS I, 1045-1092). — E. A. Bechtel, S. Silviae "Peregrinatio." The Text and a Study of the Latinity. Chicago, 1907. — D. De Bruyne: RB 26(1909)481-484 (*Excerpta Matritensia*). — W. Heraeus, Sammlung vulgärlateinischer Texte 1. Heidelberg, 1908, 1939[4]. — O. Prinz, ibid., 1960. — E. Franceschini. Padua, 1940. — E. Franceschini and R. Weber, CCL 175(1958)29-103 (indices in CCL 176, the best edition).

Translations: English: J. H. Bernard, S. Silviae Aquitaine Peregrinatio ad loca sancta: *Palest. Pilg. Text Soc.* 1/3(1896)11-77. — M. L. McClure, C. L. Feltoe. London, 1919. — G. E. Gingras, ACW 38(1970). — J. Wilkinson. London 1973, 91-147. *French:* H. Pétré, SCh 21(1948, 1957)96-266 (with text). — P. Maraval, SCh 296(1982)120-319 (with text). *Greek:* K. Koikulidès. Athens, 1908. *German:* H. Richter. Essen, 1919. — H. Dausend. Düsseldorf, 1933. — K. Vrestska. Klosterneuburg-Vienna, 1958. *Italian:* C. di Zoppoli. Rome, 1979. *Polish:* W. Szoldrski, A. Bogucki, Pisma starochrz. skich pisarzy VI. Warsaw, 1970, 167-227. *Portuguese:* M. Da Gloria Novak, Fontes da Cataquese 6. Petropolis Rj 1971, 43-116. *Russian:* J. Pomialowsky: *Prav. palest. sb., Petersburg* 20(1889)1-71. *Spanish:* P. Romeo Gelindo. Saragoza, 1924. — B. Avila. Madrid, 1935. — J. Monteverde. Buenos Aires, 1955. — V. J. Herrero Llorente. Madrid 1963, 25-130. — Arce, BAC 416(1980) (with text).

Bibliography: A. Bludau, Die Pilgerreise der Aetheria. Paderborn, 1927. — M. Férotin, H. Leclercq, DACL 5(1930)552-584. — C. Baraut, Bibliografía Egeriana: Hispania

Sacra 7(1954)203-215. — E. Franschini, R. Weber, CCL 175(1958)31-34. — M. Starowieyski, Bibliografia Egeriana: Aug 19(1979)297-318.

Studies (from 1927): R. Haida, Die Wortstellung in der Peregrinatio ad loca sancta. Breslau, 1928. — C. Jarecki, Siluaniae Itinerarium appelé Peregrinatio ad loca sancta: Eos 31(1928)453-473; 32(1929)43-70; 33(1930)241-288. — M. Férotin, H. Leclercq, DACL 5(1930)552-584; 7(1933)2304-92; 14(1950)92-110. — W. van Oorde, Lexicon Aetherianum. Diss., Amsterdam, 1930. — J. Ziegler, Die Peregrinatio Aetheriae und das Onomasticon: Bibl 12(1931)70-84, 162-198. — J. Svennung, In Peregrinationem Aetheriae annotatiunculae: *Eranos* 32(1934)93-97. — E. Löfstedt, Philologisch. Kommentar zur Peregrinatio Aetheriae. Uppsala, 1936[2]. — A. Lambert, Egeria: *R. Mabillon* 36(1936)71-94; 37(1937)1-24; 38(1939)49-69. — D. Gorce, Pèlerins et Résidents du Sinai hier . . . aujourd'hui. Paris 1937, 127-182. — D. Baldi, La liturgia della Chiesa di Gerusalemme dal IV al IX secolo: *La Terra Santa* (1939)1-131. — F. Wotke, Peregrinatio ad loca sancta: PKW Suppl 7(1940)875-885. — Fr. Thomas, Sur une manière d'exprimer la répétition et l'antériorité en latin tardif: RPh 16(1942)22-30. — A. Vaccari, Itinerarium Egeriae: Bibl 24(1943)388-397. — B. Terracini, Sobre el verbo reflexivo y el problema de los origines Románicos: Rev. Filol. Hisp. 7(1945)1-22. — E. Dekkers, De datum der Peregrinatio Egereiae: SE 1(1948)181-205. — L. Spitzer, The Epic Style of the Pilgrim Aetheriae: *Comparative Literature* 1(1948)225-258. — U. Monneret de Villard, La fiera di Batnae: RAL 8, 6(1951)77-104. — A. Ernout, Les mots grecs dans la Peregrinatio Aetheriae: *Emerita* 20(1952)289-307; *idem,* Aspects du vocabulaire latin. Paris, 1954. — R. Weber, Note sur le texte de la Peregrinatio Aetheriae: VC 6(1952)178-182; 12(1958)93-97. — J. G. Davies, The Peregrinatio Egeriae and the Ascension: VC 8(1954)93-100. — R. Ambrosini, Il tipo sintagmatico "in eo loco" e questioni di principio nello studio della "Peregrinatio Aetheriae": *Annali Scol. Norm. Sup. Pisa,* II, 24(1955)97-109. — A. Pagliano, Da missa est a missa "Messa": RAL ser. 8 10(1955)104-135. — E. Wistrand, Textkritisches zur Peregrinatio Aetheriae: Göteborg, 1955. — A. Coppo, Una nuova ipotesi sull'origine di "missa": EL 71(1957)225-267. — R. Nicolella, A proposito della "Peregrinatio Aetheriae": *Asprenas* 5(1958)187-193. — L. Spitzer, The Epic Style of the Pilgrim Aetheria: *Romanische Literaturstudien* 1936-1956. Tübingen 1959, 871-912. — O. Prinz, Bemerkungen zu einer Neuausgabe des Itinerarium Egeriae: ALMA 30(1960)143-153. — J. Mateos, La vigile cathédrale chez Egéria: OCP 27(1961)281-312. — A. A. Bastiaensen, Observations sur le vocabulaire liturgique dans l'Itinerarium d'Egérie. Nijmegen-Utrecht, 1962. — G. F. M. Vermeer, Observations sur le vocabulaire du Pèlerinage chez Egérie et chez Antonin de Plaisance: *Latinitas christ. primaeva* 19, Nijmegen-Utrecht, 1965. — P. Devos, La date du voyage d'Egérie: AB 85(1967)165-194; *idem,* Egérie à Edesse: AB 85(1967)381-400. — D. Swanson, A Formal Analysis of Egeria's (Silvia's) Vocabulary: *Glotta* 44(1967)177-254. — J. Campos, Sobre un documento del bajo imperio: *Helmantica* 18(1967)273-289. — P. Devos, Egérie à Béthléem: AB 86(1968)87-108. — B. Bagatti, Ancora sulla data di Eteria: *Bibbia e Oriente* 10(1968)73-75. — C. Milani, I grecismi nell'"Itinerarium Egeriae": *Aevum* 43(1969)200-234; *idem,* Studi sull'"Itinerarium Egeriae." L'aspetto classico della lingua di Egeria: *Aevum* 43(1969)381-452. — S. G. Nichols, Jr., The Interaction of Life and Literature in the "Peregrinationes ad loca sancta" and the "Chansons de Geste": *Speculum* 44(1969)3-88. — E. Bechera, A carta de Valério sobre Etéria: *Romanitas* 6/7(1965)331-337. — E. Doblhofer, Drei spätantike Reiseschilderungen, in Festschrift Vretska. Heidelberg 1970, 1-20. — E. G. Gingras, Et fit missa ad tertia. A Textual Problem in the Itinerarium Egeriae 464, in *Kyriakon,* Festschr. Quasten II. Münster 1970, 596-603. — F. Mian, Caput vallis al Sinai in Eteria: *Studi Bibl Francescani* 20(1970)209-223. — P. Devos, Lecto ergo ipso loco. A propos d'un passage d'Egérie (Itin. 3, 6), in *Zetesis,* Miscel. De Stycker. Antwerp 1973, 646-654. — L. C. Meijer, Some Remarks on Itinerarium Egariae 28, 4: VC 28(1974)50-53. — K. A. D. Smelik, Aliquanta ipsius sancti Thomae: VC 28(1974)290-294. — Ch. Mohrmann,

Egérie et le monachisme, in Miscel. Dekkers. Bruges 1975, 163-180. — G. Sunders, Egérie, St. Jérôme et la Bible, in Miscel. Dekkers. Bruges 1975, 181-199. — J. Braga Martino, De quibusdam lineamentis syntaxis verbalis in "Peregrinatione Aetheriae": *Romanitas* 12-13(1974)408-417. — B. Segura Ramos, La flexión nominal y verbal en la "Peregrinatio Egeriae": *Cuardernos de filolosía clásica* 8(1975)285-301. — I. Mazzini, Tendenze letterarie nella "Peregrinatio" di Egeria. L'uso del diminituvo: *Prometheus* 2(1976)267-280. — A. Szantyr, Occupo: *Museum Helveticum* 33(1976)101-104. — M. González-Haba, El "Itinerarium Egeriae": un testimonio de la corriente cristiana de oposición a la cultura clásica: ECl 20(1976)123-131. — M. Starowieyski, "Itinerarium Egeriae": *Meander* 33(1978)93-108.

THE *ITINERARIUM BURDIGALENSE*

This oldest Christian *itinerarium* was composed by an anonymous author from Bordeaux. It is the account of a journey from Bordeaux to Jerusalem followed by the return trip, after several months in Palestine, by way of Rome and Milan. It indicates the *mutationes* and the *mansiones* and adds biblical reminiscences here and there. It is more of a list of topographical nomenclature than the record of a journey.

Editions: PL 8, 784-796 (F. A. de Chateaubriand, Paris, 1811). — P. Geyer, CSEL 39(1898)3-33 (reprint: 1964). — O. Cuntz, Itineraria Romana I. Leipzig 1929, 86-102. — CCL 175(1961)1-26 (following the editions of Geyer and O. Cuntz).

Studies: A. Elter, Itinerarstudien. Bonn, 1908. — C. Mommert, Der Teich Bethesda zu Jerusalem und das Jerusalem des Pilgers von Bordeaux. Leipzig, 1907. — R. Hartmann, Die Palästina-Route des Itinerarium Burdigalense: ZDP 33(1910)169-188. — W. Kubitschek: PWK 9/2(1916)2352-2356. — T. Ashby, R. Gardner, The Via Traiana: *Papers British Sch. Rome* 8(1916)104-171. — H. Leclerq, DALC 7(1926)1853-1858. — Z. García Villada, Descripciones desconocidas de Tierra Santa en códices españoles: EE 4(1925)178-184, 322-324, 439-444. — H. Fischer, Geschichte der Kartografie von Palästina: ZDP 62(1939)169-189. — B. Kotting, Peregrinatio religiosa. Wallfahten in der Antike und das Pilgerwesen in der alten Kirchen. Münster-Regensburg 1950, 89-110, 343-354. — R. W. Hamilton, Jerusalem in the Fourth Century: *Palestine Expl. Quat.* 84(1952)83-90. — A. Lorenzoni, Da Tellagatae a Beneventum dell'Itinerarium Burdigalense. Brescia, 1962. — R. Gelsomino, L'Itinerarium Burdigalense e la Puglia: VetChr 3(1966)161-208.

SORTES SANGALLENSES (ANONYMOUS)

The text is found in the palimpsest 908 of Sankt Gallen (Lowe, 953). Lowe indicates that it originated in Northern Italy with connections to Bobbio. However, the editors of the text believe that it comes from Southern Gaul and that the text goes back to the fourth century. The manuscript contains various *Excerpta Patrum* and is written in elegant uncials from the end of the sixth century.

The text presents the responses of an oracle to questions of a Christian character. Many of the questions have been lost. The numerous responses deal with moral and social matters and the most varied problems of everyday life: life and health, love, marriage, the family, friends and enemies, fears and hopes, concerns for home and possessions, choice of profession; various undertakings: building projects, voyages, the return to home and family, financial worries, economic and professional concerns, trials and procedures.

Editions: Cf. Clavis 536. — A. Dold, Die Orakelsprüche in St. Galler Palimpsestcodex 908: SAW 225/4-5(1948-1951)21-72.

Studies: R. Weister, L. Krestan, Die Orakelsprüche in St. Galler Palimpsestcodex 908 (Die sogennanten Sortes Sangallenses), Erläuterungen: SAW 225/5(1951). — E. Schönbauer, Die Sortes Sangallenses als Erkenntnisquelle des römischen und germanischen Rechts: AAWW 90(1953)23-34.

CHAPTER IX

ITALIAN WRITERS UNTIL POPE LEO THE GREAT

by Basil Studer

Italian and Anonymous Authors of the Fourth and Fifth Century

PS. HEGEMONIUS

In the first half of the fourth century, probably after the Council of Nicea (325), a certain Hegemonius composed the *Acta Archelai,* which are a refutation of Manichaeism (cf. J. Quasten, *Patrology* III. Utrecht 1975, p. 357-358). This work is preserved in its entirety in a Latin translation from the end of the fourth century under the title *Thesaurus verus sive disputatio habita in Carcharis civitate Mesopotamiae Archelai episcopi adversus Manen.* An anonymous translator published it at Rome, and either he or someone else added an *Adversus haereses,* or catalogue of heresies.

Editions: (Cf. CPL 122; CPG 3570f). PG 10, 1429-1528 (L. A. Zacagni 1698). — Ch. H. Beeson, GCS 16(1960). — A. Hosté, CCL 9, 325-329 (= Adv. haer . . . PLS III, 143-146).

Studies: Bardenhewer III, 265-269. — G. C. Hansen, Zu den Evangelienzitaten in den "Acta Achelai": SP 7 (TU 92). Berlin 1966, 473-485 (biblical text of the Latin translator).

ANONYMOUS ROMAN

The Correspondence between Paul and Seneca

For information concerning the correspondence between Paul and Seneca, attributed to an anonymous Roman writer of the fourth century (CPL 191), cf. J. Quasten, *Patrology* I. Utrecht 1950, p. 155-156.

Editions: PLS I, 673-679 (C. Barlow).

Translations: Italian: M. Erbetta, Gli Apocrifi del NT, III. Turin, 1969, 85-92 (with intro. and notes).

ANONYMOUS ROMAN

Collatio Alexandri et Dindimi

Another anonymous Roman author composed the *Collatio Alexandri et Dindimi,* which are five letters on the discipline of the Brahmans.

Editions: (Cf. CPL 192) PLS I, 687-690 (B. Kübler).

Studies: E. Liénhard: RBPh 15(1936)819-838. — A. Kurfeiss: Mnem III/9(1941)138-152. — G. A. Cary: *Classica et Medievalia* 15(1954)124-129.

ANONYMOUS ROMAN ARCHDEACON

Postulationes III De Reconciliandis Peccatoribus

An anonymous Roman archdeacon of the fourth century, perhaps of African origin, is proposed for the author of the *Postulationes III de reconciliandis peccatoribus.* These are liturgical discourses which request the bishop and the faithful of Rome to readmit the penitents at the service of reconciliation on Holy Thursday.

Editions: (Cf. CPL² 238). — F. Heylen, CCL 9(1957)349-363 (with a preface regarding the author).

APONIUS

An *Expositio in Canticum Canticorum,* generally held to have been written in Italy and probably at Rome between 405 and 415 has been transmitted under the name of Aponius, who is considered to have been a Roman, perhaps of Eastern origin. Some, however, judge it to be the work of an Irish author from the seventh century (cf. CPL, p. 43). The earlier date is, nevertheless, to be preferred because of the author's delight in combatting the heretics of the fourth century, his interest in the Church of Rome, and, above all, because of the fact that he makes no reference to the Pelagian Controversy, although his favorite theme, the church without stain, would have had to have led him to deal with the Pelagian question (Riedlinger).

The twelve books of the *Explanatio* are written in a somewhat rough but always vivid Latin and are based on the text of Jerome's Vulgate. Aponius, who is also acquainted with the commentary on the Canticle attributed to Hippolytus of Rome, follows the Origenist tradition and presents a Christological exegesis of the Canticle, considering it entirely from the spiritual point of view in connection with the history of salvation. He therefore seeks to emphasize the relation between Christ and the church from the very beginning of this history. Under the evident influence of the Jewish exegesis taken up again by Hippolytus, he also takes an interest in the destiny of the Jews within the scope of divine providence and the continuity of Old Testament forms in the Christian world. Just as the Jewish exegetes had recognized in the Canticle the historical vicissitudes of their people, so Aponius finds in it the history of divine revelation from creation until the last judgment, concluding with the conversion of Israel (12, 277: PLS I, 1023).

Aponius, furthermore, sees in the Canticle the representation of the union between Christ and the faithful soul and, not infrequently, of the intimate union between the Word and the human soul of Jesus.

Recent scholarship has shown a special interest for the way in which Aponius uses the idea of representation, for he designates both the *sacerdotes et doctores* (bishops or others) and in particular the bishop of Rome as *vicarii* of God, of Christ, or of the Apostles.

No less interesting is the Christological orientation of Aponius' *Explanatio,* undoubtedly due to Origen, his principal example. Indeed, in the West at that time, no other author dealt to such an extent and in such detail with the human soul of Christ (Grillmeier, 385). Aponius insists on the role of this soul and makes the work of redemption depend on its free decision (11, 179: PLS I, 961f). Although taking up the Origenist idea of the perfect union between the Word and the soul of Jesus, he, nevertheless, does not place the accent on the *Christus gloriae* but rather on the Christ of the cross since, according to him, that union became indissoluble at the moment of the death on the cross (12, 242: PLS I, 1020f), when Christ, i.e., his elect soul, brought peace into the world by reconciling it with God (12, 236f: PLS I, 1015). Thus Aponius' Christology, inspired to a great extent by Origen but influenced likewise by Western traditions, anticipates in some way the *Cur Deus homo* of Anselm of Canterbury (Grillmeier, 388). Furthermore, Aponius displays a theological and philosophical culture based on the confluence of secular philosophy with exegesis of a Neoplatonic type (cf. Courcells).

The *Explanatio* of Aponius does not seem to have exercised extensive influence. Nevertheless, Gregory the Great and Bede the Venerable were acquainted with it and it appeared again in the ninth century in an abridged form of twelve homilies (Bellet).

Editions: (Cf. CPL 194) PLS I, 800-1031 (H. Bottino and J. Martini, 1843).

Studies: J. Witte, Der Kommentar des Aponius zum Hohenliede. Diss., Erlangen, 1903. — A. von Harnack, Vicarii Christi vel Dei bei Aponius, in Festschr. Delbrück. Berlin 1908, 37-46; *idem,* Christus praesens — Vicarius christi. Eine kirchengeschichtliche Skizze: SAB Phil. hist. Kl. 34(1927)415-446. — U. Moricca, Storia della letteratura latina cristiana, III/1. Turin, 1932, 990 and 997f. — A. G. Amatucci, Aponio: EC 1(1948)1669f. — P. Courcelle, Les lettres grecques en Occident. Paris 1948², 128f. — L. Welserheimb, Das Kirchenbild der griechischen Väterdommentare zum Hohenlied: ZKTh 70(1948)393-449. — M. Maccarrone, Vicarius christi. Storia del titolo papale. Rome 1952, 41-45. — P. Bellet, La forma homilética del comentario de Aponio al Cantar de los Cantares: EB 12(1953)29-38. — H. Riedlinger, Die Makellosigkeit der Kirche in den lateinischen Hoheliedkommentaren des Mittelalters. Münster 1958, 47-51. — F. Ohly, Hohelied-Studien. Grundzüge einer Geschichte des Hoheliedauslegung des Abendlandes bis zum 1200. Wiesbaden 1958, 51-53. — N. Reed, Three Fragments of Livy Concerning Britain: Latomus 32(1973)766-785 (on a fragment of Livy in Aponius, 12: PLS I, 1016). — B. Jaspert, "Stellvertreter Christi" bei Aponius, einem unbekannten "Magister" und Benedikt von Nursia: ZThK 71(1974)291-334 (bibliography). — A. Grillmeier, Christ in Christian Tradition, I. London, 1975², 384-388 (Origenist Christology in the West; bibliography).

ARNOBIUS THE YOUNGER

There is no surviving contemporary information on Arnobius, called "the Younger" to distinguish him from Arnobius of Sicca (fl. ca. 300). His biography must be reconstructed by accounts drawn from the works attributed to him in the manuscript tradition. For this purpose the most important source is the *Conflictus cum Serapione.* This work, which for the most part presents the account of a debate held around 450 (for the date, cf. Diepen, p. 537[9]) between an Egyptian monophysite and Arnobius, is most probably a composition of Arnobius himself. In it, Arnobius appears as a monk, possibly of African origin, who has already been living at Rome for some time.

In addition to the minutes of the discussion on the accord of the Roman and Alexandrian Christological traditions, i.e., of Leo and Cyril, and a rather personal reflection of the author, the *Conflictus* contains an entire patristic documentation in favor of the positions of Arnobius. Especially noteworthy among these *testimonia* are a festal letter of Cyril (*Hom. pasch.* 17), a homily of Augustine on Christmas, and a sermon attributed to Celestine I, as well as references to three homilies of Nestorius (cf. Loofs) and to the *Libellus Leporii.* Although Diepen has studied the patristic sources as well as the fundamental question of the *Conflictus,* the work still merits more detailed research. A closer look needs to be taken at how Arnobius inserts himself into the previous tradition, both Roman and Gallican. A more accurate study of the much-discussed *Deus passus* of the *Conflictus* would also permit a better evaluation of the relation between the positions of Leo the Great and Eastern monophysite tendencies. Such a study, however, demands a new critical edition of the *Conflictus,* as the edition of Feuardent, which is reprinted in the Migne Patrology, is of little value (cf. Diepen, who follows the *cod. Barbarin.* 505).

Morin attributes four other works to Arnobius: the *Expositiunculae in Evangelium,* a series of *scholia,* i.e., brief explanations, on the Gospels of Matthew, Luke and John; the *Liber ad Gregoriam,* a *consolatio* written to a noble Roman lady living in a difficult marriage; the *Commentarii in Psalmos,* a spiritual interpretation of the Psalms in an anti-Augustinian tendency interrupted by frequent anti-heretical *excursus;* and the so-called *Praedestinatus,* a work evidently composed after the death of Augustine combating his teaching on grace and predestination. The possibility is not to be excluded that Arnobius is the editor of certain hagiographical legends, especially the *Acts of Sylvester.*

Among these works, the *Commentarii in Psalmos* merit a special interest. If the method of applying the individual verses of the Psalms to Christ or the church is not particularly original, and if the continual preoccupation with defending orthodoxy is nothing unusual for the time, the frequent references to the liturgy, nevertheless, make the work an invaluable source for our knowledge of the Roman liturty in the fifth century. These are valuable references to the liturgical year and especially to Christian initiation, such as the baptismal symbol (*Ps.* 74: 430D) and the canon of the Mass (*Ps.* 120: 523D; *Ps.* 118: 516D; *Ps.* 110: 497B). Although Morin already made a study of this information relative to the Roman liturgy, a new investigation based on more recent liturgical studies would undoubtedly yield notable results.

The attribution to Arnobius of the *Praedestinatus,* which is transmitted as an anonymous work in the manuscripts, is more problematic. The tendency today is toward the attribution to Julian of Eclanum or one of his followers (CPL 243). The work is composed of three books. The first takes up 88 heresies from Augustine's *De haeresibus* to which it adds two others, the Nestorian and the predestinationist. In combating all known heresies, it presents the two final ones, which were contemporary with the writing, as the worst. The second book consists of a sermon affirming a dual predestination (PL 53, 623) which was spread about, according to the writer, under Augustine's name in a small circle of persons and which was made public only through the indiscretion of one of them. The third book refutes this theory of predestination sentence for sentence. This work, too, is in need of a new study. A careful comparison of the results of the many studies already made on this book with the contributions made by the more recent investigations on Pelagianism may yet show that the difficult questions posed by the *Praedestinatus* are not as hopeless as some would think.

Editions: (Cf. CPL 239-243; PLS III, 213-256). — *Conflictus:* F. Feuardent (1595), reprinted in PL 53, 239-322 (poor edition). — *Expositiunculae:* G. Cousin (1543); PL 53, 569-580, to be completed by G. Morin, Anecdota Maredsolana III 3. Maredsous 1903, 129-151 (= PLS III, 213-220). — *Lib. ad Gregoriam:* ed. G. Morin, Etudes, textes, découvertes. Maredsous 1913, 383-439 (= PLS III, 221-256). — *Commentarii in Psalmos:* PL 53, 327-570 (ed. L. de la Barre, 1639). — *Praedestinatus:* PL 53, 587-672 (ed. J. Sirmond).

Studies: B. Grundl, Über den Conflictus Arnobii catholici cum Serapione Aegyptio: ThQ 79(1897)529-568. — H. von Schubert, Der sogennante Praedestinatus (TU 24, 4). Leipzig, 1903. — G. Morin, Pages inédites d'Arnobe le Jeune. la fin des Expositiunculae sur l'Évangile: RB 20(1903)64-76; *idem,* Examen des écrits attribués à Arnobe le Jeune: RB 26(1909)419-432; *idem,* Un traité inédit de Arnobe le Jeune. Le libellus ad Gregoriam: RB 27(1910)153-171; *idem,* Etude d'ensemble sur Arnobe le Jeune: RB 28(1911)154-190; *idem,* Etudes, textes, découvertes I. Maredsous 1913, 309-332, 340-382; *idem,* L'origine africaine d'Arnobe le Jeune: RevSR 16(1936)177-184. — F. Loofs, Nestoriana. Halle, 1905. — H. Kayser, Die Schriften des sog. Arnobius junior, dogmengeschichtlich und literarisch untersucht. Gütersloh, 1912. — J. Scharnagl, Zur Textgestaltung des arnobianischen Conflictus: WSt 38(1916)382ff; 42(1921)75f, 152f; *idem,* Zur Textgestaltung des arnobianischen Psalmenkommentars: WSt 38(1916)185ff; 42(1921)154-160; 43(1922)198-204. — M. Monachesi, Arnobio il Giovane ed una sua possibilità agiografica: *Boll. Studi stor. relig.* 2(1922)66-125. — G. Bardy, Le souvenir d'Arius dans l'Arnobe le Jeune: RB 40(1928)256-261 (in the Praedestinatus). — U. Moricca, Storia della letteratura latina cristiana III. Turin 1932, 990ff, 998-1011. — G. Bouwman, Des Julian v. Aeclanum Kommentar zu den Propheten Osee, Joel und Amos. Ein Beitrag zur Geschichte der Exegese. Rome, 1958. — H. Diepen, La pensée christologique d'Arnobe le Jeune. Théologie de l'Assumptus Homo ou de l'Emmanuel?: RThom 59(1959)535-564 (important for a study of the sources of the Christology of Arnobius). — P. Glorieux, Prénestorianisme en Occident. Tournai, 1959 (connection with Leporius). — M. Abel, Le "Praedestinatus" et le pélagianisme: RThAM 35(1968)5-25 (the author is not Julian of Eclanum but is an adversary of Augustine). — S. Leanza, L'esegesi di Arnobio il Giovane al libro dei Salmi: VetChr 8(1971)223-239. — A. Cervelli, Arnobio il Giovane, in Ps. 150: Vichiana N.S. 1 (Naples 1972)147-151. — M. Simonetti, Letteratura antimonofisita d'Occidente: Aug 18(1978)487-532.

FIRMICUS MATERNUS

The manuscript tradition attributes to Firmicus Maternus two Latin works fairly different in content which go back to the fourth century: the *Matheseos libri VIII* (334-337) and the *De errore profanarum religionum* (343-347). These two works contain the only information known about their author.

Firmicus Maternus was born in Sicily and lived most of his life in Syracuse. He was a member of a senatorial family and thus received the usual rhetorical and philosophical education. His writings, which are filled with reminiscences of his direct or indirect knowledge of classical literature, bear witness to the breadth of his erudition.

He was still a pagan when he wrote his *Mathesis,* a type of manual of astrology. This work, which obviously is drawn from Greek and even more from Latin sources, contains more information than any of the others preserved from antiquity on the beliefs and astrological practices of the time. In his apology for astrology, Firmicus Maternus presupposes a very lofty idea, Aristotelian in inspiration, of the supreme deity. Noteworthy, too, are the prayers and the moral counsels which have come to him from Neoplatonic tradition (cf. Hadot, p. 385f). Nevertheless, his presentation of the divinity remains impregnated with pagan ideas.

In his second work, *De errore profanarum religionum,* which was undoubtedly composed after his conversion to Christianity, he combats contemporary paganism in its forms of the divinization of the elements and of the mysteries. Although he draws on terms from the apologists before him, he is distinguished from them by a more aggressive, almost fanatical, stance in his defense of Christianity. Indeed, having demonstrated the emptiness and immorality of the pagan myths and cults, he concludes by reminding the emperors (Constantius and Constans) of their grave responsibility to destroy the pagan religion without hesitation.

This scarcely tolerant attitude of Firmicus Maternus can be

explained at least in part by his character, as he was defending the Christian cause with the zeal of a convert now that Christianity had become the *causa victrix* and was protected by the emperors themselves (Ziegler, p. 949). Still, his lack of understanding of religious liberty must not be exaggerated. Considered apart from his impassioned rhetoric, his attacks on the pagan divinities are relatively moderate. His intention is obviously not only that of refuting the pagan errors but also of bringing nonbelievers to conversion (Opelt). For such a purpose, however, he is not entirely convincing in his approach. He bases his demonstrations on the authority of the Christian Bible, which is not recognized by his adversaries at all. Apart from this, his theological formation appears to have been meager. He owes his knowledge of the Scripture almost exclusively to the *Testimonia* of Cyprian. His concept of the descent of Christ to the underworld, presented as a three-day struggle with death (24, 2), is noteworthy, and his information, even secondhand, is important for a knowledge of the myths, the signs, and the passwords *(symbola)* used in the secret cults.

G. Morin wished to attribute to Firmicus Maternus also the *Consultationes Zacchei et Apollonii* which deal with the conversion of Apollonius to Christianity after a three-day discussion with Zaccheus. This hypothesis of the learned Benedictine has been favorably received by some scholars, although Axelson has rejected it rather sharply. The work seems to depend on the letters 135 and 137 of Augustine (Courcelle).

In any case, it was composed before the end of the fifth century and was in fact quoted by Eugenius, who became bishop of Carthage in 483 (CPL 103). Whatever the dating of the work, its content merits particular attention. The first book responds to pagan objections against the Christian faith, especially against the Christological and soteriological teaching. In the second book, there follows the true doctrine on the Trinity and on the Holy Spirit with a warning against Judaism and certain heresies. The final book initiates Apollonius, who by this time has been converted, more profoundly into Christian teaching. With clarity and warmth, but also with moderation, the author expounds the doctrine that will become classic on the two degrees of the Christian life, i.e., the common life of the *humiliores* and the perfect life to be realized in the monastic state. With regard to the latter, the author is not content merely to describe it, but also defends it vigorously against the attacks of certain Christians. Although he realizes that unfortunately not all monks live according to the ideal of their calling, he, nevertheless, praises this calling with unconditional admiration. In connection with this he distinguishes three degrees within the monastic life itself: those who are content to practice continence while continuing to live in the world and concerning themselves with their affairs like other people; those who live in community practicing the ascetic life and singing the praises of God; those, finally, who retire into the desert to lead a solitary life entirely dedicated to prayer and to the struggle against the demons. The author takes the opportunity here to make an apology for the singing of the psalms. The work offers a rich witness, which has not been sufficiently considered by scholars, on Western monasticism in the first half of the fifth century.

Editions: 1. *Matheseos libri VIII:* W. Kroll, F. Skutsch, K. Ziegler (Teubner). Leipzig, 1897-1913 (reprint: 1968). — 2. *De errore prof. relig.:* PL 12, 981-1050 (F. Muenter 1826). — C. Halm, CSEL 2(1867)75-130. — G. Heuten. Brussels, 1938. — K. Ziegler. Munich, 1953. — A. Pastorino. Florence, 1956. — 3. *Consultationes:* (Cf. PLS I, 1095) PL 20, 1071-1166 (D'Archery). — G. Morin. FP 39(1935).

Translations: English: J. R. Bram, Firmicus Maternus: Ancient Astrology, Theory, and Practice. Matheseos Libri VIII. Park Ridge, NJ, 1975. — C. A. Forbes, ACW 37(1970) (De errore). *French:* G. Heuten, *op. cit.* (De errore). *German:* K. Ziegler, *op. cit.* (Mathesis). — A. Müller. BKV 14(1913) (De errore). *Italian:* G. Faggin. Lanciano, 1932 (De errore).

Studies on *Firmicus Maternus:* F. Boll, Firmicus Maternus: PWK 6(1909)2365-2379. — F. J. Dölger, Nilwasser und Taufwasser. Eine religionsgeschichtliche Auseinandersetzung zwischen einem Isisverehrer und einem Christen des 4. Jh. nach Firmicus Maternus: AC 5(1936)153-187; *idem,* Die Bedeutung des neuentdeckten Mithrasheiligtums von Dura-Europos für die handschriftl. Überlieferung der heidnischen Mysteriensprache bei Firmicus Maternus u. Hieronymus: AC 5(1936)286-288. — T. Wikström, In Firmicum maternum studia critica. Uppsala, 1936; *idem,* Firmiciana: *Eranos* 40(1942)37-80; *idem,* Zum Text der sog. Apologie des Firmicus Maternus: *Eranos* 53(1955)172-192. — A. J. Festugière, Trois dévots paiens. Prières et conseils de vie. Paris, 1944. — G. Blasko, Grundlinien der astrologischen Weltanschauung nach der Mathesis des Firmicus Maternus. Diss., Innsbruck, 1956. — P. Batiffol, Le canon de la messe romain a-t-il Firmicus Maternus pour auteur: RevSR 2(1922)113-126. — E. Kähler, Studien zum Te Deum. Göttingen 1958, 65-73 (the Christological part of the Te Deum and De errore 22-24). — C. A. Forbes, Firmicus Maternus and the Secular Arm: CJ 55(1960)146-151; *idem,* Critical notes on Firmicus Maternus "De errore": VC 21(1967)34-38. — U. Riedinger, Θαρρεῖται Θεοῦ τὰ μυστήρια. Ein Beitrag des Ps. Kaisarios zu den Symbola des Firmicus Maternus, in Festschr. Th. Michels. Münster 1963, 19-24. — P. Hadot, Firmicus Maternus: DSpir 5(1964)384-388 (bibliography). — I. Opelt, De natura deorum bei den lateinischen Kirchenvätern: *Antike und Abendland* 12(1966)141-155; *idem,* Firmico Materno sobre las Bacanales (De errore 6, 9): *Helmantica* 19(1968)31-41; *idem,* Schimpfwörter in der Apologie "De errore profanarum religionum" des Firmicus Maternus: *Glotta* 52(1974)114-126. — A. Bartalucci, Considerazioni sul lessico cristiano del "De errore profan. relig" di Firmico Materno: SIF 39(1967)165-185. — K. Ziegler, Firmicus Maternus: RACh 7(1968)946-959 (fundamental study; bibliography). — J. Vogt, Toleranz und Intoleranz in constantinischen Zeitalter: der Weg der lateinischen Apologetik: *Saeculum* 19(1968)344-361. — K. Hoheisel, Das Urteil über die nichtchristlichen Religionen im Traktat "De errore profanarum religionum" des Iulius Firmicus Maternus. Diss., Bonn, 1971-72. — A. Gianfrotta, La polemica antipagana de Giulio Firmico Materno: *Miscellanea Francescana* 77(1977)297-327. — J. M. Vermander, Un arien d'Occident méconnu, Firmicus Maternus: BLE 81(1980)3-16. — M. Annecchino, La ratio physica nel De errore profanarum religionum di Firmico Materno: *Vichiano* 9(1980)181-188.

Studies on the *Consultationes:* A. Reatz, Das theologische System der Consultationes

Zacchaei et Apollonii (Freib. Theol Studien 25). Freiburg Br., 1920. — F. Cavallera, Un exposé sur la vie spirituelle et monastique au IVe siècle: RAM 16(1935)132-146; *idem,* DSp 2(1953)1641-1645. — B. Axelson, Ein drittes Werk des Firmicus Maternus? Zur Kritik der philologischen Identifizierungsmethode: *Bulletin de l'Académie des Lettres* 4(Lund 1937)107-132. — P. Courcelle, Histoire littéraire des grandes invasions germaniques. Paris 1964[3], 261-275 (cf. RHR 146[1954]174-193).

FORTUNATIANUS OF AQUILEIA

According to Jerome (*De vir. inl.* 97), Fortunatianus, an African, was bishop of Aquileia in the mid-fourth century at the time of the Emperor Constantius and Pope Liberius. He died, it seems, shortly before 368. Fortunatianus was at first a strong defender of Nicene orthodoxy and received Athanasius as a guest at Aquileia after the Synod of Serdica of 343. However, at the time of the council at Milan in 355, he succumbed to the threats of Constantius and signed the condemnation of Athanasius. He subsequently proved instrumental in persuading the exiled Pope Liberius to sign the Arian creed of Sirmium of 357.

There remain only three fragments of Fortunatianus' commentary on the Gospels, which Jerome describes as a *"margaritam de evangelio"* (*Ep.* 10, 3) and which he read in preparation for his own commentary on the Gospel of Matthew (*praef.*: PL 26, 20C).

Editions: Cf. CPL 104. — A. Wilmart, B. Bischoff, CCL 9(1957)365-370. — PLS I, 239, 217.

Studies: L. Duchesne, Libère et Fortunatien: MAH 28(1908)31-78 (cf. P. Glorieux, Hilaire et Libère: MSR 1[1944]7-34). — J. Lemarié, Italie. Aquilée: DSp 7(1971)2161.

CHROMATIUS OF AQUILEIA

Chromatius was born into a Christian family, most likely at Aquileia, and lived the greater part of his life during the most prosperous period of the history of the church of that city. He was already a presbyter in the period 368-373 when Rufinus and, subsequently, Jerome lived for several years at Aquileia. Jerome later recalled the clergy of that city as a "choir of the blessed" (Jerome, *Chron.* an. 374: GCS 47, 247). During this period, Chromatius, several friends and his mother, brother and sisters were living the ascetic life in common (Jerome, *Ep.* 7, 4). As an assistant of his bishop, Valerian, Chromatius was active in the supression of Arianism. He took part in the council held at Aquileia in 381 under the presidency of Valerian and the leadership of Ambrose which put an end to the Arian troubles in the West. The minutes of the council record Chromatius' interventions in the proceedings. At Valerian's death in 388, Chromatius was chosen as his successor and received his episcopal ordination from Ambrose.

As bishop during an interlude relatively free from doctrinal controversy, Chromatius appears in his surviving works as a man devoted to his pastoral ministry and the care of the poor, to preaching, and to the fostering of the liturgy. He maintained his contacts with both Jerome and Rufinus even after the bitter quarrel between the latter two had become the scandal of Latin Christianity. He sent Jerome encouragement and financial assistance for his work of translating and commenting the Scriptures, and the irascible monk of Bethlehem returned his gratitude by dedicating to Chromatius several of his translation as well as the commentaries on Habbakuk and Jonah. For his part, Rufinus undertook at Chromatius' urging the translation of Eusebius' *Ecclesiastical History,* which he then dedicated to the Bishop of Aquileia along with his translation of Origen's homilies on Joshua. It was to Chromatius at Aquileia that Rufinus turned for refuge in 396 from the controversies following his translation of the *De Principiis,* and he remained there until Chromatius' death. The Bishop of Aquileia was one of the Western bishops to whom John Chrysostom appealed for assistance after his deposition in 404. Chromatius responded with a strong letter to the emperor as well as a letter to Chrysostom informing him of this intervention. Although Chromatius' correspondence has been lost, Chrysostom's letter of gratitude is still extant (*Ep.* 155: PG 52, 70f). During the final years of his episcopate, Chromatius was faced with the hardships and difficulties connected with the successive waves of Gothic invaders crossing the Julian Alps and pouring into Italy by way of his episcopal city. Chromatius died toward the end of 407 or the beginning of 408.

Neither Jerome nor Gennadius mention any literary works of Chromatius, and until quite recently the greater part of his literary heritage remained unknown. Since 1960, however, owing to the work of R. Étaix and J. Lemarié, numerous sections of the *Tractatus in Matthaeum* have been brought to light, most of which had been handed down in separate manuscript traditions under the names of Jerome and Chrysostom. There are now 60 *tractatus* known which make up slightly more than half of Chromatius' extensive treatment of Matthew. In addition to these, 45 homilies of Chromatius are also extant.

Editions: Cf. CPL 217ff (incomplete). — A. Hosté, CCL 9(1957)371-447. — R. Étaix, J. Lemarié, CCL 9A(1974), 9A suppl(1977). — Cf. J. Doignon, Chromatiana. A propos de l'édition de l'œuvre de Chromace d'Aquilée: RSPT 63(1979)241-250. — R. Étaix, Un Tractatus in Mathaeum inédit de saint Chromace d'Aquilée: RB 91(1981)225-230; *idem,* Nouvelle édition des Sermones XXI-XXII de saint Chromace d'Aquilée: RB 92(1982)105-110.

Translations: French: H. Tardif, SCh 154, 164(1969, 1971) (with text). *Italian:* G. Cuscito, Catechesi al popolo. Rome, 1979 (sermons). — M. Todde, Cromazio de Aquileia. Sermoni liturgici. Rome, 1982. — G. Trettel, Commento al Vangelo di Matteo. Rome, 1984.

Studies: Cf. the bibliographies in CCL 9A, viii and 612; and SCh 164, 115-120. — R. Étaix, Fragments nouveaux du "Commentaire sur Matthieu" de saint Chromace d'Aquilée. Diss., Lyons, 1960. — J. Lemarié, Italie. Aquilée: DSp 7(1971)2162-2165. — G. Trettel, Terminologia esegetica nei sermoni di san Cromazio di Aquileia: REAug 20(1974)55-81; *idem,* "Figura" e "veritas" nell'opera oratoria di S. Cromazio di Aquileia: SC 102(1974)3-23; *idem,* Mysterium e sacramentum in san Cromazio. Trieste, 1979. — R. Étaix, J. Lemarié, La tradition manuscrite des tractatus in Matheum de saint Chromace d'Aquilée: SE 17(1966)302-354. — M. L. Palazzi, Aspetti liturgici nelle omelie di Cromazio d'Aquileia: EL 90(1976)29-42. — A. de Nicola, Osservazioni sui proemi dei sermoni di S. Cromazio di Aquileia: AMSI 26(1978)189-205. — D. Corgnali, Il mistero pasquale in Cromazio di Aquileia. Udine, 1979. — G. Cuscito, Cromazio ei Aquileia e l'età sua: *Aquileia nostra* 50(1979)497-572. — J. Lemarié, Chromatiana. Status quaestionis: RSLR 17(1981)64-76.

MAXIMUS OF TURIN

The *De vir. inlustribus* 41 of Gennadius is the primary source of information for the life and writings of Maximus, the first bishop of Turin of whom something is known, who died between 408 and 423. He is, therefore, to be distinguished from a successor of the same name who died after 465 and with whom he has been identified since the time of Baronius.

Like the facts of his life, so also the question of the authenticity of his writings has been solved only recently. A. Mutzenbecher, on the basis of his own studies and assisted by the work of Savio, Pellegrino, and others has established a definitive list of the authentic sermons of Maximus of Turin (CCL 23[1962]): 89 homilies, a collection reconstructed from the manuscripts, 30 homilies *extravagantes.*

By the use of biblical passages, the *Sermones* treat of the mysteries of the liturgical feasts (especially noteworthy are those for Christmas) or of aspects of the particular feast at hand. Maximus, a good preacher with a clear, flowing and persuasive style, combats the paganism still active in his region, castigates certain superstitions such as those associated with New Year's Day, consoles his faithful during the barbarian invasions, and, above all, instructs his community in Christian doctrine. Maximus' preaching, always of contemporary value, presents a vivid testimony of the pastoral and liturgical ministry which flourished in the north of Italy around the year 400 under the vigorous leadership of Ambrose on whom Maximus depends to a great extent. Furthermore, with his appeals to the Roman patriotism of his audience (*Serm.* 82), descriptions of contemporary paganism (*Serm.* 63; 48, 4; 98, etc.), and indications of the reactions to the horror of the barbarian invasions, Maximus presents a good relief of the region for the history of late antiquity. Even though various authors have applied themselves recently to the investigation of the historical-liturgical documentation offered by Maximus, further research into the enormous mass of information preserved in these *Sermones* would still be worthwhile.

Editions: (Cf. CPL 220-226b; PLS III, 351-379) PL 57, 221-760 (B. Bruni 1784, to be used with caution). — A. Mutzenbecher, CCL 23(1962) (excellent edition with introduction treating the questions of the author and the authenticity of the sermons; bibliography).

Translations: English: G. E. Ganss, FC 17(1965) (selection). *French:* F. Quéré-Jaulmes, Le mystère de Pâques. Paris 1965, 251-264 (serm. 57, 58, 36). *Italian:* F. Gallesio, Sermoni di s. Massimo di Torino. Rome, 1975.

Studies: Studies which confuse the identity of the two Maximus or which refer without reservations to the edition of B. Bruni are to be used with caution; e.g., U. Moricca, La storia della letteratura latine cristiana III, 1. Turin 1932, 1023-1031 and E. Crovella, Massimo, vescovo di Torino: *Bibl Sanct.* 9(1967)68-72. C. Benna, S. Massimo di Torino: *Riv. Dioces Torinese* 2(1934)47-50, 62-67, 102-109, 121-124, 140-145, 185-191. — H. Rahner, Griechische Mythen in christlicher Deutung. Zurich, 1945 (on Serm. 37, 2: Ulysses as a figure of the crucified Christ); *idem,* Symbole der Kirche, Salzburg, 1964. — P. Bongiovanni, S. Massimo vescovo di Torino e il suo pensiero teologico (Diss., Salesianum). Turin, 1952. — G. M. Rolando, Massimo di T.: EC 8(1952)311f. — A. Mutzenbecher, Zur Überlieferung des Maximus Taurinensis: SE 6(1954)343-372; *idem,* Bestimmung der echten Sermones des Maximus Taurinensis: SE 12(1961)197-293; *idem,* Der Festinhalt von Weihnachten und Epiphanie in den echten Sermones des Maximus Taurinensis: SP 5 (TU 80). Berlin 1962, 109-116. — M. Pellegrino, Sull'autenticità d'un gruppo di omelie e di sermoni attribuiti a s. Massimo di T.: *Att d. Accad. d. Scienze di Torino* 90(1955-1956)1-113; *idem,* Intorno a 24 homelie falsamente attribuite a s. Massimo di T.: SP 1 (TU 63). Berlin 1957, 134-141; *idem,* La tipologia battesimale in S. Massimo di T.: l'incontro con la Samaritana e le nozze di Cana: RSLR 1(1965)260-268. — I. Biffi, Dalla predicazione pasquale di san Massimo di T.: Testi e commenti: *Ambrosius* 40(1964)131-139; *idem,* La Cinquantina pasquale nella predicazione di san Massimo: testi e commenti: *Ambrosius* 40(1964)324-333; *idem,* Teologia e spiritualità del "dies beatissimae epyfaniae" in san Massimo di Torino: *Ambrosius* 40(1964)517-544; *idem,* Tempo temi e spiritualità quaresimale nei sermoni autentici di s. Massimo di T.: *Ambrosius* 41(1965)129-158; *idem,* I temi della predicazione natalizia di s. Massimo di T.: *Ambrosius* 42(1966)23-47. — O. Maenchen-Helfen, The Date of Maximus of Turin's Sermo 18: VC 18(1964)114-115. — L. Bieler, Corpus Christianorum: *Scriptorium* 19(1965)77-83. — M. C. Conroy, Imagery in the Sermons of Maximus, Bishop of Turin (PSt 99). Washington, 1965. — P. Visentin, "Christus ipse est sacramentum" in S. Massimo di T., in Misc. G. Lecaro II. Rome 1967, 27-51. — O. Heggelbacher, Das Gesetz im Dienste des Evangeliums: Über B. Maximus von Turin. Bamberg, 1968. — C. E. Chaffin, The Martyrs of the Val di Non. An Examination of Contemporary Reaction: SP 10 (TU 107). Berlin 1970, 263-269. — G. Rossetto, La testimonianza liturgica di Massimo I, vescovo di T., in *Ricerche storiche sulla Chiesa Ambrosiana* I. Milan 1970, 158-203. — A. Saenz, La celebración de los misterios en los sermones de s. Maximo de Turin. Buenos Aires, 1970 (cf. *Stromata* 25[1969]351-411; 27[1971]61-103). — J. P. Bouhot, Note sur trois sermons anonymes: REAug 20(1974)135-142 (CPL 1157 of Maximus of Turin). — D. Devoti, Massimo di Torino e il suo pubblico: Aug 21(1981)153-167. — M. Pellegrino, Martiri e martirio in S. Massimo di Torino: RSLR 17(1981)169-192.

PETER CHRYSOLOGUS

The life of Peter, archbishop of Ravenna, known since the ninth century as Chrysologus, remains fairly obscure. He is mentioned in the *Liber Pontificalis* and there exists a biography of little historical value written by Agnello of Ravenna in the ninth century. From these sources as well as from certain passages of the writings attributed to him, it can be ascertained that Peter was born at Imola around 380. Between 425 and 429, and in any case before 431 (the date of a letter written to him by Theodoret), he became the metropolitan of Ravenna. In 445 he was present at the death of St. Germanus of Auxerre, and three or four years later wrote to Eutyches, the priest of Constantinople who had appealed to Peter after his condemnation by Flavian. He admonished Eutyches to submit to the decision of Leo, bishop of Rome: *quoniam beatus Petrus, qui in propria sede et vivit et praesedet, praestat quaerentibus fidei veritatem* (*Ep. ad Eutychen:* PL 54, 743). Peter died between 449 and 458 (date in a letter to Peter's successor, Neon), probably December 3, 450, possibly at Imola.

Owing to the tireless studies of A. Olivar, the authentic works of Peter are now known with certainty. They include one letter (cited above), 168 sermons of the *Collectio Feliciana* (*saec.* VIII) and 15 *extravagantes.* Other writings, such as the famous Scroll of Ravenna, a collection of prayers of preparation for Christmas (*saec.* VII), cannot be regarded as authentic.

The sermons, for which Peter has become famous, are characterized by the careful preparation of a fairly well-trained orator and by the human warmth and divine fervor of a holy man. Because of Ravenna's particular position as an imperial residence and important seaport, it is not surprising that they contain many examples drawn from the circle of the court as well as from the military and seafaring life; nor are they lacking in examples taken from rural life. "Among the writers of the fifth century, Chrysologus is surpassed by few in elegance." In his sermons he has indeed left "pages of genuine, powerful and effective eloquence" (Moricca, 1021).

With regard to content, the works for the most part are homilies on passages from the Gospels, but also on the Pauline letters, the Psalms, the baptismal symbol, the Lord's Prayer, and the saints, and include likewise exhortations to penance. In commenting the Bible and taking his cue from liturgical celebrations, Chrysologus gives authoritative witness to the theological preoccupations of his age. His concerns reflect not only the Latin doctrine on the Incarnation, as it was being presented in the period between Ephesus and Chalcedon, but also allow some insight into the Catholic positions concerning grace and the Christian life. In clearly recognizing the primacy of the bishop of Rome, he is undoubtedly expressing the common attitude of the Italian, indeed of the Western bishops (cf. *Serm.* 78, in addition to the letter to Eutyches). His extensive activity as a preacher above all has left priceless documentation on the liturgy and culture of Ravenna, a city half-way between Rome and Northern Italy. A more complete picture of the course of the liturgical year is not to be found in the works of any other bishop of the time (Sáenz). In his opposition to the resistance of a dying paganism and his polemics against the Jewish community of his city, Peter Chrysologus represents the pastoral attitude of the episcopate of the imperial church of his time.

Editions: (Cf. CPL 227-237. PLS III, 153-183 with a list of the authentic and inauthentic sermons and texts reprinted by A. Olivar in 1961, such as the *Expositio fidei*). PLS V, 396-399. — PL 52, 183-666 (Coll. Feliciana; S. Paoli 1750). — D. De Bruyne, Serm. XVIII e cod. Vatic. 5758: JThSt 29(1928)362-368. — A. Olivar, CCL 24(1975), I: serm. 1-62 bis. — *Epistula ad Eutychen* = *Ep.* 25 of Leo the Great: PL 52, 71 and PL 54, 739-744 = E. Schwartz, ACO II 3, 1(1935)6-7 and ACO II 1, 2(1933)45-46 (Greek text).

Translations: English: G. E. Ganss, FC 17(1965)25-287 (selections). *Italian:* A. Pasini. (I Classici Italiani 1-2). Siena, 1953. — M. Spinelli. Rome, 1978. *German:* M. Held. BKV1(1874). — G. Böhmer. BKV2 43(1923).

Studies: F. J. Peters, Petrus Chrysologus als Homilet. Cologne, 1918. — G. Böhmer, Petrus Chrysologus Erzbischof von Ravenna als Prediger. Paderborn, 1919. — L. Baldisseri, S. Pier Crisologo, arcivescovo di Ravenna. Imola, 1921. — J. H. Baxter, The Homilies of St. Peter Chrysologus: JThSt 22(1921)250-258. — C. Jenkins, Aspects of the Theology of St. Peter Chrysologus: CQR 103(1927)233-259. — E. Schiltz, Un trésor oublié: s. Pierre Chrysologue comme théologien: NRTh 55(1928)265-276. — U. Moricca, Storia della letteratura latina cristiana III, 1. Turin 1932, 993f, 1011-1123. — V. Gluschke, Die Unfehlbarkeit des Papstes bei Leo dem Grossen und seinen Zeitgenossen. Diss., Gregoriana, Rome, 1938. — H. Koch, Petrus Chrysologus: PWK 38(1938)1361-1372. — R. H. McGlynn, The Incarnation in the Sermons of St. Peter Chrysologus (Diss., St. Mary). Mundelein, 1956. — G. Del Ton, De s. Petri Chrysologi eloquentia: *Latinitas* 6(1958)177-189. — K. Gamber, Eine alt-ravennatische Epistel-Liste aus der Zeit des hl. Petrus Chrysologus: LJ 8(1958)73-96; *idem,* Die Orationen des Rotulus von Ravenna. Eine Feier des Advents schon zur Zeit des heiligen Petrus Chrysologus: ALW 5(1958)354-361. — A. Olivar, Los sermones de san Petro Crisólogo. Montserrat, 1962 (basic work with extensive bibliography); *idem,* La duración de la predicación antigua: *Liturgica* 3(Montserrat 1966)143-184; *idem,* La consagración del obisop Marcelino de Voghenza: RSCI 22(1968)87-93; *idem,* Pietro Crisologo: *Bibl. Sanct.* 10(1969)685-691 (good summary of the author's research); *idem,* Preparación e improvisación en la predicación patrística, in Festschrift Quasten. Münster, 1970, 736-767. — J. P. Barrius, La naturalezza del víncolo matrimonial entre Maria y Iosé según san Piedro Crisológo: *Ephem. Mariologicae* 16(1966)322-335. — S. Benz, Der Rotolus von Ravenna, LQF 45. Münster, 1967. — F. Spedalieri, La maternità spirituale di Maria prima e dopo il concilio di Efeso, in Miscell. A. Combes I. Rome 1967, 193-242. — R. Ladino, La iniciación cristiana en san Pedre Crisólogo de Ravena (Diss., Gregoriana). Rome, 1969. — G. Lucchesi, Stato attuale degli studi sui santi della antica provincia ravennate, in Atti dei convegni di Cesena e di Ravenna I. Cesena 1969, 51-80. — F. Michalčík, Doctrina noramlis s. Petri Chrysologi (Diss., Lateran). Rome, 1969. — E. Paganotto, L'apporto dei sermoni di S. Pier Crisologo alla storia della cura pastorale a Ravenna nel secolo V (Diss., Gregoriana). Rome, 1969. — F. Sottocornola, L'anno liturgico nei sermoni di Pietro Crisologo. Ricerca storico-critica sulla liturgia di Ravenna antica. Cesena, 1973 (good intro. to the liturgy of Ravenna; extensive bibliography). — A. Olivar, Reseña de las publicaciones recientes referentes a San Pedro Crisólogo: *Didaskalia* 7(1977)121-151. — M. Spinelli, L'eco delle invasioni barbariche nelle omelie di Pier Crisologo: VetChr 16(1979)87-93. — A. Benelli, Note sulla vita e sull'episcopato di Pietro Crisologo: In verbis verum amare, in *Misc. Inst. di Fil. lat.* Bologna 1980, 63-79. — M. Spinelli, Il ruolo sociale di digiuno in Pier Crisologo: VetChr 18(1981)143-156.

Roman Pontiffs from Siricius to Leo the Great

THE COLLECTION OF PAPAL LETTERS FROM SIRICIUS UNTIL SIXTUS III

Toward the end of the fourth century a new literary genre made its appearance in Latin Christian literature in the form of letters written in the name of the Roman Pontiff. Those who intend "Patrology" as the history of early Christian literature possibly will be inclined to leave aside such works which are due rather to the anonymous activity of the papal chancellery than to the literary initiative of individual authors, with the possible exception of the letters of Leo the Great (cf. Schanz-Hosius, p. 597). On the other hand, this type of literature has been preserved mainly in the canonical collections where, alongside the synodal law, it represents papal or decretal legislation.

These letters are of great importance for the history of the doctrines, law and liturgy of the church, especially for the evolution of papal primacy and the development of other questions such as the Augustinian doctrine of grace, Christology and various matters pertaining to the sacraments. At the same time they allow for a better comprehension of the theological and ecclesial context of such Fathers of the Church as Ambrose, John Chrysostom, John Cassian, Cyril of Alexandria, and, of course, Leo the Great. They are also not devoid of interest from the literary aspect for they show the development of rhythmic prose from a quantitative rhythm to one accented in the final clauses. They demonstrate also the influence of the Roman political-juridical mentality on Christian Latin. Finally, they constitute a typical case of the Christian adaptation of a secular literary genre, i.e., the adoption of the forms of the imperial legislation in the decretal legislation of the Apostolic See.

It is true, in any case, that a detailed presentation of the persons in question belongs to the field of Church history.

In reality, all of the manuals of church history, including the more recent, not to mention the histories of the popes, reserve a special place to these early pontiffs (e.g., K. Baus, "The Further Development of the Roman Primacy from Melchiades to Leo I" in *The Imperial Church from Constantine to the Early Middle Ages,* vol. II of *History of the Church,* H. Jedin, ed. New York, 1980, 245-268 with related literature).

Editions: (Cf. CPL 1637-1655, also 347-357: on the canonical collections and the studies dealing with the editions of pontifical letters). — PL 13, 20-50 (P. Coustant 1721). — A. Thiel, Epistulae Romanorum Pontificium genuinae et quae ad eos scriptae sunt. Braunsberg, 1867-68 (reprint: Hildesheim, 1974). — C. Mirbt, K. Aland, Quellen zur Geschichte des Papsttums des römischen Katholizismus I. Tübingen, 1967[6].

Translations: German: S. Wenzlowsky, Die Briefe der Päpste und die an sie gerichteten Schreiben I-IV (BKV). Kempten, 1975-78.

Studies: O. Bardenhewer, Geschichte der altkirchlichen Literatur III. Freiburg 1912, 591ff; ibid, IV. Freiburg 1924, 613-617. — O. Seeck, Regesten der Kaiser und Päpste für die Jahre 311-476 n. Chr. Vorarbeit zu einer Prosopographie der christlichen Kaiserzeit. Stuttgart, 1919 (reprint: Frankfurt, 1964). — M. Schanz, C. Hosius, G. Krüger, Die Literatur des fünften und sechsten Jahrhunderts: Geschichte der römischen Literatur. Munich, 1920 (reprint: 1959). — H. Getzeny, Stil und Form der ältesten Papstbriefe. Günzberg, 1922. — P. Batiffol, Le Siège Apostolique 359-451. Paris, 1924[3]; *idem,* Cathedra Petri. Rome, 1938. — W. Völker, Studien zur päpstlichen Vikariatspolitik im 5. Jh.: 1. Die Gründung des Primates von Arles und seine Aufhebung durch Leo I: ZKG 46(1929)355-369. — E. Caspar, Geschichte des Papsttums von den Anfängen bis zur Höhe der Weltherrschaft, I. Römische Kirche und Imperium Romanum. Tübingen, 1930 (fundamental). — U. Gmelin, Auctoritas, Römischer Princeps und päpstlicher Primat. Berlin, 1936. — F. Di Capua, Il ritmo prosaico nelle lettere dei Papi e nei documenti della cancelleria Romana dal IV al XIV secolo I-II. Rome, 1937-39. — H. Wurm, Studien und Texte zur Dekretalensammlung des Dionysius Exiguus. Bonn, 1939. — M. Maccarrone, Vicarius christi. Storia del titolo papale. Rome, 1952. — J. Gaudemet, La formation du droit séculier et du droit de l'Église aux 4e et 5e siècles. Paris, 1957. — E. Griffe, Al Gaule chrétienne à l'époque romaine II: L'Église des Gaules au Ve siècle. Paris-Toulouse, 1957. — H. Marot, Les conciles romains des IVe et Ve siècles et le développement de la primauté: *Istina* 4(1957)435-462; *idem,* La Collegialité et le vocabulaire épiscopal du Ve au VIIe siècle: *Irénikon* 36(1963)41-60; 37(1964)198-221. — J. Meyendorff, La primauté romaine dans la tradition cononique jusqu'au concile de Chalcédoine: *Istina* 4(1957)463-482. — A. Rimoldi, L'apostolo San Pietro fondamento della Chiesa, principe degli apostoli ed ostiario celeste nella Chiesa primitiva dalle origini al concilio di Calcedonia. Rome, 1958. — B. Kötting, Christentum und heidnische Opposition in Rom am Ende des 4. Jh. Münster, 1961. — V. Grumel, Les origines du Vicariat Apostolique de Thessalonique, in *Actes du XIIe Congrès Internat. d'Etudes Byzantines.* Ochride 1961, 451-461. — G. Langgärtner, Die Gallienpolitik der Päpste im 5. u. 6. Jh. (*Theophaneia* 16). Bonn, 1964. — G. Medico, La collégialité épiscopale dans les lettres des pontifes romains du Ve siècle: RSPT 49(1965)369-403. — G. Corti, Il papa vicario di Cristo. Brescia, 1966. — G. B. Dalla Costa, Concezione del Primato Papale nelle lettere dei Romani Pontefici della prima metà del V secolo (Diss., Lateran). Rome, 1966. — G. Falconi, Storia del Papi e del Papato I: La nascita del papato nel declino dell'Impero. Rome, 1967. — A. Moretti, Elections of Bishops from Pope Siricius (384-389) to Pope Leo the Great (440-461) (Diss., Lateran). Rome, 1968. — R. Lorenz, Das vierte bis sechste Jahrhundert: Die Kirche in ihrer Geschichte I/C, 1. Göttingen, 1970 (especially 82-87). — E. Jerg, Vir Venerabilis. Untersuchungen zur Titulatur der Bischöfe in den ausserkirchlichen Texten der Spätantike als Beitrag zur Deutung ihrer öffentlichen Stellung. Vienna, 1970. — C. Andresen, Die Kirchen der alten Christenheit. Stuttgart, 1971 (especially 579-601: Päpstliche Ekklesiologie u. Dekretalenrecht). — W. Marschall, Karthago und Rom. Stuttgart, 1971. — P. Brown, Religion and Society in the Age of St. Augustine. London, 1972. — J. Taylor, The Papacy and the Eastern Churches from Damasus to Innocent I (366-417). Diss., Cambridge, 1972. — P. P. Joannou, Die Ostkirche und die Cathedra Petri im 4. Jahrhundert. Stuttgart, 1972. — C. Piétri, Roma Christiana, 2 vols. Rome, 1976. — O. Wermelinger, Rom und Pelagius. Die theologische Position der römischen Bischöfe im pelagianischen Streit in den Jahren 411-432. Stuttgart, 1975 (bibliography).

PAPAL LETTERS PRIOR TO SIRICIUS (ALTANER, PAR. 92)

Neither the letters of Silvester (314-335) nor those of his successor Mark (336) have been preserved. Athanasius, however, included two letters of Julius I (337-352) in his *Apologia contra Arianos* (21-35; 52f), the first of which (341) defends the orthodoxy of Nicea and rebukes the bishops of the Eusebian party for not having consulted the Church of Rome, while the second (346) is a recommendation of Athanasius, who was preparing to return to Alexandria. The Apollinarists attributed three other letters to Julius.

Liberius (352-366) was forced into exile for three years because of his defense of the faith of Nicea (355-358). Only after he had broken with Athanasius and accepted communion with the Eastern bishops was he allowed to return to Rome. He salvaged his orthodoxy by adding to the third creed of Sirmium the anathema of all those who did not recognize the similarity of the Father and the Son in all things.

Fragments of thirteen of his letters are extant. Of these, some are parts of three letters addressed to Eusebius, bishop of Vercelli, and others of four letters concerning his exile. The homily of Liberius on the occasion of the consecration of Ambrose's sister, Marcellina, as a virgin is most like a work of Ambrose himself (*De virg.* 3, 1-3). There also exists under Liberius' name a list of the popes up to his time. The so-called *Epitaphium Liberii,* the funeral inscription for a martyred pope, is attributed, in addition to Liberius, also to Felix II and Martin I.

With regard to Damasus I (366-384), to whom ten letters are attributed, cf. the chapter *supra* on Latin Christian poetry.

SIRICIUS

After a long career in the service of the Roman Church, Siricius (384-399) was elected as its bishop with the consent of Valentinian II. Jerome, the friend of Damasus, had little respect for his successor, whom he described as "too simple" (*Ep.* 127, 9). Nevertheless, prescinding from such a subjective judgment, Siricius had little hope of imposing his authority since at that time Ambrose of Milan was the real master of ecclesiastical affairs in the West. Still, Siricius has gone down in history as one of the contributors to the development of the papacy.

The seven letters attributed to Siricius bear witness to the aptness of such a designation. Among these is a letter to Himerius, bishop of Tarragona (385), containing fifteen replies to a like number of questions concerning discipline which had been presented before the time of Damasus. It is the oldest papal letter in the collection of decretals. Another two letters (of which one has survived) were written to communicate the result of a Roman synod of 386 to the bishops of Italy who had been unable to attend, as well as to the bishops of Africa. An encyclical letter (390) condemns the teaching of Jovinian on the equality of matrimony and consecrated virginity. Yet another letter, addressed to Anisius of Thessalonica (392), refutes the position of Bonosus of Serdica regarding the virginity of Mary and requests the Illyrian bishops to make their position known on the matter since this had been requested of them by the Synod of Capua.

The entire collection of Siricius' letters expresses the awareness of being called to exercise, according to the Roman tradition, a primacy over all the churches. As the vicar of Peter, he feels a responsibility for all the churches (*Ep.* 1, 1: *Portamus onera omnium qui gravantur: quin immo haec portat in nobis apostolus Petrus, qui nos in omnibus, ut confidimus, administrationis suae protegit et tuetur haeredes*). According to Siricius, the *sollecitudo omnium ecclesiarum* (2 Cor. 11:28, quoted for the first time in *Ep.* 6, 1) does not admit of exceptions, even if he is not in a position to impose the authority of the Apostolic See on all the churches of the Roman Empire. He bases this authority on the Bible and on Roman tradition, expressed above all in the cult of Peter (cf. *Ep.* 5, 1), and places the papal decisions on a par with synodal law, comparing them, furthermore, with imperial constitutions. Although he places synodal and decretal legislation on the same level, he, nevertheless, does not omit emphasizing the conformity of the one to the other. In this regard, he seems to have been the first to have referred to the so-called *Corpus Romanum,* i.e., the tradition which had confused the canons of Serdica with those of Nicea (cf. *Ep.* 5, 2).

Editions: (Cf. CPL 1637, with indications of the particular editions of the individual letters). PLS III, 567f. — PL 13, 1131-1178 (Coustant).

Studies: E. Göller, Papsttum und Bussgewalt in spätrömischer und frühmittelalterlicher Zeit: RQ 93(1931)93-105. — G. D. Gordini, Forme di vita ascetica a Roma nel IV secolo: *Scrinium theologicum* 1(Alba 1953)7-58. — J. Janini, S. Siricio y las Cuatro temporas. Valencia, 1958; *idem,* La plegaria de S. Siricio ad virgines Sacras: SP 5 (TU 80). Berlin 1960, 86-103. — P. H. Lafontaine, Remarques sur le prétendu rigorisme pénitentiel du pape Sirice: RUO 28(1958)31-48; *idem,* Les conditions positives de l'accession aux ordres dans la première législation ecclésiastique (300-492). Ottawa, 1963 (in particular on Siricius and Zosimus). — B. Kötting, Christentum und heidnische Opposition in Rom am Ende des 4. Jh. Münster, 1961. — J. MacDonald, Who Instituted the Papal Vicariate of Thessalonica?: SP 4 (TU 79). Berlin 1961, 478-482. — M. S. Meo, La verginità di Maria nella lettera di Papa Siricio al vescovo Anisio di Tessalonica: *Marianum* 25(1963)447-469. — V. Monachino, S. Siricio: *Bibl. Sanct.* 11(1968)1234-1237. — G. Rocca, La perpetua verginità di Maria nella lettera di Papa Siricio ad Anisio vescovo di Tessalonica: *Marianum* 33(1971)293-306. — A. Lumpe, Die Synode von Turin bom Jahre 398: *Annuarium HistConc* 4(1972)7-25. — E. Griffe, A propos du can. 33 du concile d'Elvire: BLE 74(1973)142-145 (the canon on celibacy taken up by Siricius); *idem,* La data du concile de Turin (398 or 417): BLE 74(1973)289-295.

ANASTASIUS

Anastasius I (399-402), who was more open than his predecessor to the ascetical movements headed by Jerome and Paulinus of Nola, issued a condemnation of Origen at the insistence of the anti-Origenists, of which he personally informed the See of Milan in two letters. Nevertheless, although he joined in the Alexandrian anathema of Origen in his response to a question of John of Jerusalem, he did not wish to take a position against the translation of the *De Principiis* made by Rufinus of Aquileia. In 401 he encouraged the African bishops to persist in their struggle with Donatism.

Even though Anastasius clearly expresses in these letters his awareness of having the responsibility for the orthodoxy of all the churches (cf. *Ep.* 9, 5), his authority is not accepted by all in the same way. In the West and especially in Africa around 400, the *cathedra Petri* was regarded as the apostolic see *par excellence* and as the center of the entire communion of the orthodox faith. On the other hand, Theophilus of Alexandria sees nothing more in Anastasius' condemnation of Origenism than an acceptance of the Alexandrian position (cf. Justinian, *Lib. c. Originem:* PG 86, 967; and Caspar, p. 287-293).

Editions: (Cf. CPL 1638ff, with references to particular editions). — PL 20, 68-80 (Coustant, 1721). — PLS I, 790-792.

Studies: M. Villain, Rufin d'Aquilée. La querelle autuor d'Origène: RSR 27(1937)5-37, 165-197. — F. Caraffa, Anastasio I: *Bibl. Sanct.* 1(1961)1065f.

INNOCENT I

Innocent I (402-417), who was perhaps the son of Anastasius or in any case belonged to the same family (Jerome, *Ep.* 130, 16), was called to govern the Roman Church during a difficult period. During his pontificate, Rome was captured by the troops of Alaric (410), an event which profoundly affected pagan and Christian alike. Innocent, however, seems to have remained indifferent and refers to the event in his letters only once (*Ep.* 36). At the same time, the Latin Church was jolted by the first phase of the Pelagian Controversy. In these difficult circumstances, Innocent showed himself to be a strong defender of the primacy of the bishop of Rome. In this regard he took up arguments which were already traditional, developed them and, for the first time, gave them a precise formulation. The collection of his correspondence, with a rich selection of 36 letters, bears witness to this. They were collected for canonical purposes even before Leo the Great (cf. Leo, *Ep.* 4, 5) and form the principal part of the first collection of decretals (Caspar, p. 296f).

Among these letters, those addressed to the bishops of Italy and Gaul, such as Victricius of Rouen (404; *Ep.* 2), Exuperius of Toulouse (405; *Ep.* 6) and Decentius of Gubbio (416; *Ep.* 25) are of particular importance. In addition to taking a position on such important disciplinary questions as the celibacy of the clergy and baptism administered by heretics (*Ep.* 2), reconciliation of the dying (*Ep.* 6), the reading of the sacred books, anointing of the sick and confirmation (*Ep.* 25), Innocent insists, even though in a general way, on the conformity of all the Western churches with the *consuetudo* of the church of Peter, the origin of all those Christian communities (*Ep.* 2, 2; 25, 2). In the letter to Victricius he requires that the *causae minores* be treated in provincial synods, although without compromising the interests of the Roman Church, but that the *causae maiores* must always be referred to Rome as the court of final instance (*Ep.* 2, 5-6 with reference to the role of Moses in Ex. 18:22).

By insisting on the same prerogatives of the Roman Church in relation to the churches of Illyrium, Innocent established the Apostolic Vicariate of Thessalonica, whose bishop is treated in the respective letters (*Ep.* 1; 13; 17; 18), as the vicar of the Roman Pontiff and metropolitan of the Illyrian bishops. The desire to maintain a jurisdiction over that region which then belonged to the Eastern part of the empire was given legitimacy by the fact that Rome had evangelized the Illyrian churches.

In his separate letters of response (*Ep.* 29-31) to three African bishops regarding the rehabilitation of Pelagius by the Synod of Diospolis, Innocent did not hesitate to claim the supreme authority of the *Sedes Apostolica* in doctrinal matters (*Ep.* 30, 2). Although the African bishops, while recognizing the *gratia maior* of the See of Peter (Augustine, *Ep.* 175, 3), had merely requested the Church of Rome to confirm their condemnation of Pelagius so that it might be effective also in Italy, Innocent interpreted their request as an appeal to the ultimate authority of his judgment. He, therefore, confirmed in virtue of his apostolic authority, the condemnation of Pelagius and Caelestius and their followers. With regard to the doctrines of original sin and grace, he left the door open to further discussion with Pelagius (cf. *Ep.* 29, 9; Wermelinger, p. 128ff).

Innocent was not content to intervene in the affairs only of the Latin Churches. Having been informed by Theophilus of Alexandria of the deposition of John Chrysostom and having received an appeal from Chrysostom, he refused to break off communion with the deposed bishop of Constantinople but defended his interests by reference to the Nicene legislation regarding the hierarchical order of the major apostolic sees (*Ep.* 7, 3). When his request for an ecumenical synod went unheeded, he broke off his communion with Alexandria and Antioch. Innocent restored communion with Antioch in 413 (*Ep.* 19), but not without making a point of Roman primacy in a further letter (*Ep.* 24) by comparing to a certain extent the situation of Antioch with that of Thessalonica. Communion with Alexandria and Constantinople was reestablished only later.

Two things are to be noted in the affirmation of Roman primacy which characterizes all this correspondence of Innocent. On the one hand, Innocent knows how to vary his tone according to the position of the individuals whom he is addressing: to the bishops under the metropolitan jurisdiction of Rome he speaks as an immediate superior, giving orders with authority and reprimanding with severity; to other colleagues in the episcopate he makes his replies or interventions in a much more conciliatory and diplomatic fashion. Especially characteristic in this regard is the difference between the letters written to the bishop of Thessalonica and those written to Antioch, another apostolic see (cf. Caspar, p. 322). On the other hand, the justification of the primacy is not always the same. Innocent bases his position, in the first place, on Roman tradition, according to which the bishop of Rome is the heir of Peter, the Prince of the Apostles, and as such possesses the solicitude for all the churches. Depending on the occasion, he also makes reference to synodal legislation, i.e., to the canons of Nicea as they were understood at Rome (cf. *Ep.* 2, 5; 7, 3; 17, 10; 24, 1; 39). Furthermore, there is not to be excluded, already in Innocent, the influence of the idea of *Roma aeterna* (Wermelinger, p. 120). Although recent studies have clarified various aspects of Innocent's theory of primacy (cf. Marschall, Wermelinger, etc.), it still remains, in order to evaluate more exactly his teaching on the primacy, to come to a better understanding of the ideas of that time concerning the *communio fidei,* particularly with regard to dogmatic decisions *(sententia, definitio)* and their *receptio* by the churches.

Editions: (Cf. CPL 1641ff with the particular editions). PLS I, 793-796. — PL 20, 463-608 (Coustant, 1721). — PL 84, 657f (Gonzáles, 1821). — R. Cabié, La lettre du pape Innocent I à Decentius de Gubbio (19. III. 416). Louvain, 1973.

Studies: H. Gebhardt, Die Bedeutung Innozenz I für die Entwicklung der päpstlichen Gewalt. Leipzig, 1901. — G. Malchiodi, La lettera di Innocenzo I a Decenzio vescovo di Gubbio. Rome, 1921. — K. Adam, Causa finita est, in Festgabe A. Ehrhard. Bonn-Leipzig, 1922, 1-23 = Ges. Aufsätze. Augsburg 1936, 216-236. — F. Streichhan, Die Anfänge des Vikariats von Thessalonisch: ZSavK 12(1922)355-384. — C. Baur, Der hl. Johannes Chrysostomus u. seine Zeit I. Munich, 1929 (English transl., London, 1960). — E. Göller, Papsttum und Bussgewalt in spätrömischer und frühmittelalterlicher Zeit: RQ 93(1931)105-113. — G. Ellard, How Fifth Century Rome Administered Sacraments. St. Innocent I Advises an Umbrian Bishop: TS 9(1948)3-19. — O. Vighetti, I sacramenti della penitenza e dell'ordine nella dottrina giuridica di S. Innocenzo I: *Misc. Francisc.* 51(1951)39-61; 52(1952)92-112. — B. Capelle, Innocent Ier et le Canon de la Messe: RTAM 19(1952)5-16. — E. Demougeot, À propos des interventions du Pape Innocent Ier dans la politique séculière: RH 78(1954)23-38. — J. MacDonald, Imposition of Hands in the Letters of Innocent I: SP 2 (TU 64). Berlin 1957, 49-53. — E. Griffe, Trois textes importants pour l'histoire du Canon de la Messe: BLE 59(1958)65-72. — P. Th. Camelot, Innocent Ier: *Catholicisme* 5(1962)1645ff. — V. Monachino, La lettera decretale di Innocenzo I a Decenzio vescovo di Gubbio, in Ricerche sull'Umbria tardo-antica e preromanica. Perugia 1965, 211-234. — G. B. Proia, Innocenzo I: *Bibl. Sanct.* 7(1966)840-843. — P. Andrieu-Guitrancourt, Notes, remarques et réflexions sur la vie ecclésiastique et religieuse à Rouen sous le pontificat de s. Victrice, in Mélanges J. Macqueron. Aix-en-Provence 1970, 7-20. — C. Vogel,

Vulneratum caput. Position d'Innocent Ier (402-417) sur la validité de la chirotonie presbytériale conférée par un évêque hérétique: RAC 49(1973)375-384. — M. R. Green, Pape Innocent I. Diss., Oxford, 1973.

ZOSIMUS

Zosimus (417-418), who was certainly not a Roman, has gone down in history as the man who ruined the papal politics built up by his predecessors. His continuous failures have been explained as the result either of his rash and impulsive character or of his poor understanding of the situation in the West. It must not be forgotten, too, that he was exposed to pressure from opposing factions within the Roman community. His ecclesiastical policy was aimed at a reorganization of the hierarchy in Gaul and a solution to the Pelagian Conflict.

As soon as he was elected pope, Zosimus dispatched a letter to all the bishops of Gaul (*Ep.* 1) by which he granted to Patroclus, bishop of Arles, a privileged position which in effect constituted a primacy over the seven Gallic provinces. This action, which was contrary to the decisions of the Synod of Turin of 398, provoked the protests of the other metropolitans, and Zosimus' successors had no small difficulty in reestablishing peace.

On the other hand, Zosimus' attitude in the Pelagian Controversy was rather ambiguous. In the fall of 417, at the insistence of Caelestius, who was present at Rome, and of Pelagius, who had sent him his *libellus fidei,* Zosimus readmitted both of them to ecclesiastical communion. He announced this rehabilitation to the African bishops in two letters (*Ep.* 2 and 3), and requested of them a revision of the process conducted against the two. In the face of the strong and unanimous action of the African episcopate, Zosimus withdrew his decision in his letter *Quamvis patrum (Ep.* 12) of March 418, albeit in a veiled fashion and not without a reminder of the irrevocable nature of decisions taken by the authority of the Apostolic See. Following the intervention of the imperial court and the new African synod at Carthage, he promulgated the condemnation of Caelestius and Pelagius in his letter *Tractoria,* which is preserved only in fragments. Eighteen Italian bishops refused to sign this document, and the Roman community itself was divided.

Zosimus also registered a failure in another affair; this one of secondary importance. Contrary to African custom, Zosimus had accepted the appeal of a certain Apiarius, a priest of Sicca. When the Roman delegates attempted to defend Apiarius' cause before Aurelian by making reference along with Zosimus (*Ep.* 15) to the canons of Nicea, the primate of Africa did no more than promise to consider the matter at the next synod. The two grounds for the Roman primacy, apostolic (*Ep.* 2, 1) and synodal (*Ep.* 15, 1-2) are found also in the letters of Zosimus.

Editions: (Cf. CPL 1644-1647, with the indication of the particular editions; PLS I, 796f). PL 20, 642-686 (Coustant). —*Ep. Tractoria:* PL 20, 693-694 (cf. Wermelinger, p. 307-308). —*Ep. ad Remigium ep.:* PLS I, 797 (F. Maassen, 1870).

Studies: F. Floëri, Le pape Zosime et la doctrine augustinienne du péché originel: AugMag II, 755-761. — E. Griffe, Gaule chrétienne à l'époque romaine II. Paris-Toulouse 1957, 114-179. — G. Bonner, Augustine's Visit to Caesarea in 418, in *Studies in Church History* I. London 1964, 104-113 (on the intervention of Zosimus). — V. Monachino, Zosimo: *Bibl. Sanct.* 12(1969)1493-1497. — W. Marschall, Karthago und Rom. Stuttgart 1971, 150-159, 166-173; *idem,* Eine afrikanische Appellation an Gregor den Grossen, in Festschr. Panzram. Freiburg i.B. 1972, 404-421 (comparison with Zosimus). — K. Wegenast, Zosimus: PWK[2] 19(1972)841-844. — F. J. Thonnard, A. C. De Veer: BA 23(1974)784-789 (the Pelagian crisis 415-420). — Ch. Munier: BA 22(1975)9-24 (Pelagian crisis 416-418). — O. Wermelinger, Rom und Pelagius. Stuttgart 1975, 134-218 (bibliography); *idem,* Das Pelagiusdossier in der Tractoria des Zosimus: *Freiburger Zeitschr. f. Theo.* 26(1979)336-368.

BONIFACE I

Boniface I (418-422), a Roman and collaborator of Innocent, was elected as bishop by the presbyters in opposition to Eulalius, who had been elected by the deacons the day before. He received the recognition of the court at Ravenna only after several months. The delicate situation inherited from Zosimus, which had become even more confused in the first months of 418, led him to intervene in favor of the Gallic metropolitans against Patroclus of Arles (*Ep.* 3 and 12), to tacitly accept the position taken by the general synod at Carthage in 419, and to defend the Apostolic Vicariate of Thessalonica against the claims of Constantinople as expressed in the edict of Theodosius II in 421 (*Ep.* 13-15).

In these letters regarding Thessalonica, Boniface takes up again the language of Innocent I and reaffirms the universal solicitude of the Church of Peter as well as the obligation of all bishops, including those of the East, to defer, according to ancient custom, to the Apostolic See (*Ep.* 15, 5). Although he recognizes the privileged rank of Alexandria and Antioch, he states that only the Church of Rome is the head while the other churches are the members of the ecclesiastical body (*Ep.* 14, 1: *Hanc ergo ecclesiis toto orbe diffusis velut caput suorum certum est esse membrorum: a qua se quisquis abscidit, fit christianae religionis extorris, cum in eadem non coeperit esse compage*).

Editions: (Cf. CPL 1648f. — PLS I, 1032-1034). — PL 20, 750-784 (Coustant, 1721). *Ep. ad vicarios suos in Africana synodo:* PL 20, 791f and C. Turner, Ecclesiae occident. monumenta iuris antiquissima II, 3. Oxford 1930, 565.

Studies: F. L. Cross, History and Fiction in the African Canons: JThSt 12(1961)227-247. — F. Caraffa, Bonifacio I: *Bibl. Sanct.* 3(1963)328-330. — C. Coebergh, L'épiphanie à

Rome avant s. Léon: un indice pour l'année 419: RB 75(1965)304-307. — W. Marschall, Karthago und Rom. Stuttgart 1971, 173-183. — O. Wermelinger, Rom und Pelagius. Stuttgart 1975, 239-244.

CELESTINE I

After the death of Boniface I, the deacon Celestine, once a follower of Pelagius, was chosen bishop in a rapid and tranquil election (422-432). His ecclesiastical politics were concerned with two different fields. His intentions were, above all, to bring the Pelagian affair to a conclusion in Gaul, where the Augustinian doctrine on grace and predestination had provoked a tenacious reaction, and, at the same time, to prevent Julian of Eclanum and other bishops condemned as Pelagians from obtaining aid in the East where they had taken refuge. At the request of Prosper of Aquitaine and Hilary, Celestine (431) addressed a letter to the bishops of Gaul in which he defended the authority of Augustine in the confrontation with the monks of Provence, without, however, taking a position on the particular points of the Augustinian doctrine (*Ep.* 21). The so-called *Capitula Caelestini,* which are attached to this letter in the collections of decretals, were composed only after the death of Celestine, probably by Prosper (DS 238-249). In relation to the Italian bishops who, with the help of Nestorius and others, were seeking their rehabilitation, Celestine held unbendingly to the condemnation passed by Innocent and Zosimus against the followers of Pelagius and Caelestius. It was in this vein that he responded to two letters of Nestorius (*Ep.* 13) and, after the Council of Ephesus, admonished Maximianus, the new bishop of Constantinople, as well as the clergy and faithful of that city to be on their guard against possible followers of Caelestius (*Ep.* 24 and 25).

With the Pelagian difficulties not yet concluded, Celestine found himself caught up in the Nestorian Controversy (428 on). When Nestorius and his adversaries and, subsequently, Cyril of Alexandria referred the Christological question also to the Church of Rome, Celestine took these moves on the part of the Eastern churches as an appeal to the authority of the Apostolic See. After discussing the matter in the Roman Synod (August 430) he communicated his decision against Nestorius to the principal churches of the East and directed Cyril as his vicar to take the necessary measures against the bishop of Constantinople (*Ep.* 11-14). When Theodosius II then convoked an ecumenical council at Ephesus, Celestine felt no little embarrassment since, as far as he was concerned, the matter had already been decided. However, he had no choice but to accept the sentence of the coming council as an expression of assent to his own decision (cf. *Ep.* 17 and 18). It was, in fact, in this sense that his legates, who arrived late at Ephesus, thanked the fathers of the council for having joined themselves as the members to the judgment of the head (cf. ACO I 1, 3, p. 58). Celestine, for his part, evaluating the work of the Council of Ephesus in his letter to the clergy of Constantinople, stated that Peter would not have abandoned them in their difficulty (*Ep.* 25, 9; cf. 22, 6). No Roman bishop up to that time had stated the supreme authority of the Apostolic See with such clarity.

For a proper evaluation of this statement, however, two items must be taken into account. On the one hand, the Eastern bishops displayed at most only a tacit acceptance of this statement of Roman primacy. Cyril in particular paid little heed to the juridical form in which the Roman Church was pursuing its own interests. On the other hand, it cannot be disregarded that Celestine, while insisting on the singular role of Rome, was insisting at the same time on the collegiality of all the bishops. Indeed, he reminded Nestorius that he was excluding himself from the episcopal college (*Ep.* 13, 5). Celestine himself made his decision in a collegial manner, i.e., in his synod, and he attached a particular importance to the collegial responsibility of the fathers united in council at Ephesus (*Ep.* 18, 1). Nevertheless, this concept of episcopal collegiality must itself be measured against the manner in which Celestine acted in requiring the Illyrian bishops to refer important matters to Rome (*Ep.* 3), admonishing the bishops of Vienne (Gaul) and Narbonne to respect their metropolitan boundaries (*Ep.* 4), and, finally, seeking to settle the affair of Apiarius of Sicca and the bishop of Fusala (Marschall, p. 184-201). It remains to be noted that Celestine, like his predecessors, never undertook a serious reflection on the doctrines in question, either with regard to the question of grace or to Christology. He was content instead to prohibit with authority the errors of the Pelagians and of Nestorius.

Editions: (Cf. CPL 1650-1654. — PLS III, 18-20). — PL 50, 417-458 (Coustant, 1721). — E. Schwartz, ACO I 1, 7, p. 125-137, 142f; I 2, p. 5-101.

Studies: M. F. Martroye, S. Augustin et la compétence de la juridiction ecclésiastique au Ve siècle: *Mémoire de la Société Nationale des Antiquaires de France* 70(1911)1-78. — D. M. Cappuyns, L'origine des capitula pseudo-célestiniens contre le sémipélagianisme: RB 41(1929)156-170. — A. M. Bernardini, S. Celestino. Rome, 1938. — E. Amann, L'affaire de Nestorius vue de Rome: RevSR 23(1949)5-37, 207-244; 24(1950)28-52, 235-265. — P. Grosjean, Note d'hagiographie celtique: AB 70(1952)315-326 (on the mission of Palladius in Ireland). — G. Bardy, Célestin Ier: DHGE 12(1953)56-58. — I. Daniele, S. Celestini I: *Bibl. Sanct.* 3(1963)1096-1100. — J. Doignon, Une compilation de textes d'Hilaire de Poitiers présentée par le Pape Célestin Ier à un concile romain en 430, in *Oikoumene.* Catania 1964, 477-497. — J. Lécuyer, Le collège des évêques selon le Pape Célestin I (422-432): NRTh 96(1964)250-259. — J. Speigl, Der Pelagianismus auf dem Konzil von Ephesus: *Annuarium HistConc* 1(1969)1-14. — R. García, El primado romano y la colegialidad episcopal en la controversia nestoriana: *Studium* 11(1971)21-63. — L. I. Scipioni, Nestorio e il concilio di Efeso. Milan, 1974 (especially 149-205). —

A. Grillmeier, Christ in Christian Tradition. London 1975², 467-472 (Rome's view of Nestorius).

SIXTUS III

Under Zosimus, Sixtus had been at first favorable then hostile toward Pelagianism (cf. Augustine, *Ep.* 191 and 194). After his election toward the end of July 432, he continued the policy of his predecessor, as is attested by his letters, of which seven have been preserved. From the beginning, he sought to bring about a reconciliation between John of Antioch and Cyril of Alexandria (*Ep.* 1 and 2). After he was informed of the unity effected in 433, he congratulated the two bishops on their reconciliation and the resulting ecclesiastical peace, gave his approval indirectly to the formula of union, and attributed the success to himself, i.e., to the presence of Peter, guarantor of the true faith (*Ep.* 5 and 6). The good relations which Sixtus enjoyed with Constantinople did not hinder him from defending the rights of the bishop of Thessalonica against the claims of certain Illyrian bishops who were openly supported by Proclus of Constantinople (*Ep.* 7-10). He followed the policy of Celestine also with regard to the Pelagian affair, and refused in 439 to readmit Julian of Eclanum to his see. At Rome, he assured himself of a lasting memory by restoring the Basilica of the Apostles (St. Peter in Chains), the Basilica of Saint Mary Major, and the baptistry of St. John Lateran, monuments which are in a certain way a monument to his policy of primacy.

Editions: (Cf. CPL 1655. — PLS III, 22f). — PL 50, 583-618 (Coustant, 1721). — E. Schwartz, ACO I 1, 7, p. 143f; I 2, p. 107-110.

Studies: G. Bovini, I mosaici romani dell'epoca di Sisto III (432-440), I: I mosaici di S. Sabina, dell'abside del Battistero Lateranense e di S. Pietro in Vincoli: *X Arte Ravennate.* Ravenna, 1963. — U. Ulbrich, Augustins Briefe zur entscheidenden Phase des pelagianischen Streites: REAug 9(1963)51-75, 235-258. — V. Monachino, S. Sisto III: *Bibl. Sanct.* 11(1968)1262-1264. — R. Krautheimer, The Architecture of Sixtus III, in *Krautheimer Studies.* London 1971, 181-198. — U. Schubert, Der politische Primatsanspruch des Papstes, dargestellt am Triumphbogen von St. Maria Maggiore: *Kairos* 13(1971)194-226. — F. J. Dölger, Die Inschrift im Baptisterium S. Giovanni in Fonte in der lateranensischen Basilika aus der Zeit Xystus III (432-440) u. die Symbolik des Taufbrunnens bei Leo d. Grossen: AC 2(1934, 1974²)252-257.

LEO THE GREAT († 461)

LIFE AND PERSON

Together with Gregory I, who governed the Church of Rome a century and a half later, Leo I (440-461) has entered into church history with the title of "the Great." While Gregory looked to the future, Leo represented rather the termination of a period of history which was coming to an end (Caspar, p. 558). In bestowing upon him the title of "the Great," posterity has honored him more as an heir and executor than as a pioneer and pathfinder (Caspar, p. 555). Leo was bishop of Rome in one of the most crucial moments of history, when the Western part of the Roman Empire was crumbling under the barbarian invasions and the West was about to embark on a new path. Within the Christian community, the principle of traditional orthodoxy was vigorously imposed, fixed formulae and precise canons were giving a definite cast to liturgical and disciplinary life, and theology was defining its position on the fundamental questions of the Incarnation and the relation of divine grace and human freedom.

In spite of the historical importance of the time in which Leo lived, little is known regarding his life, especially for the time preceding his pontificate. Almost nothing is known of the personal aspects of his life as pope. His biography, for the most part, is identical with the events of his activity as pope as these emerge from his correspondence. With the exception of the few notices contained in the *Liber Pontificalis* (I 238-241), there is no contemporary biography which offers precise information regarding his origin, his career, or his personal relations. The Greek life of Leo, although it shows the veneration with which Leo is regarded in the East, supplies nothing to make up for the lack of bibliographical data. In his letters, Leo rarely speaks of himself, even though he does allow a glimpse into his ideals, his aspirations, and his mode of thinking and acting.

Although possibly from Tuscany, Leo was probably born at Rome toward the end of the fourth century. Before his election as bishop, he undoubtedly occupied a position of considerable importance under his predecessors. John Cassian witnesses to this in the preface to the *Libri VII de Incarnatione* where he states that he is composing this work at the request of Leo (PL 50, 9). It is not out of the range of possibility that Leo also collaborated in the composition of the *Indiculus* on grace (DS 238-249). Leo himself writes (*Ep.* 119, 4) that Cyril had contacted him in 431 in order to obtain Rome's support against the policies of Juvenal of Jerusalem. According to Prosper of Aquitaine, Leo's intervention was decisive in the decision of Sixtus III against Julian of Eclanum (PL 51, 598). Finally, in 440, he was sent to Gaul on a diplomatic mission to reconcile Aetius and Arbinus, the Praetorian Prefect, and it was there that he received the news of his election as pope. All of these facts indicated in advance the direction that would be taken in the policies of the new bishop: an anti-heretical polemic, the reestablishment of peace and discipline in the church, a policy of mediation.

His pontifical ministry, to which Leo dedicated all of his pastoral solicitude, developed along diverse lines. In the first place he was bishop of Rome. In his preaching to the clergy and faithful in which he engaged regularly, he strove to introduce the community into the celebration of the mysteries of Christ by encouraging the faithful to live their baptism in imitation of Jesus and to preserve their faith from the danger of the heresies surrounding it and from the pagan customs still in vogue. The struggle against heresy, with which he was particularly concerned, was not devoid of contemporary relevance, especially with regard to Manichaeism, against which he contended with all his strength in the first years of his pontificate (cf. *Serm.* 9, 4; 16, 4-6). He was renowned also for his concern for the organization of the liturgy, the restoration and adornment of the basilicas, the renewal of monastic life, and his hospitality toward pilgrims.

As metropolitan of Central and Southern Italy, primate of Northern Italy and Patriarch of the West, his activities for orthodoxy and ecclesiastical discipline were no less important. By means of the annual Roman Synod as well as his continual interventions on questions such as the date of Easter (*Ep.* 16), the conditions for the life of the clergy and the administration of the goods of the church, he coordinated the ecclesiastical life of the suburbicarian dioceses. He maintained close relations with the bishops of Northern Italy, especially those of Milan, Ravenna, and Aquileia, with regard for the *communio fidei* in the struggle against Pelagianism (*Ep.* 1 and 2) and Manichaeism, as well as the *receptio* of the faith of Chalcedon (*Ep.* 97). In connection with ecclesiastical discipline it was for the most part a question of confirming the decisions reached by their synods or responding to questions submitted to the judgment of the Apostolic See. The same was true for other regions of the West, although their hierarchical situation frequently required special interventions as is clear from the correspondence regarding the role of Arles (*Ep.* of the *Collectio Arelatensis*), the Apostolic Vicariate of Thessalonica (*Ep.* of the *Collectio Thessalonicensis*), and the disorders caused by the Vandal invasion of Mauretania (*Ep.* 12). To such interventions of a disciplinary character can be joined his opposition on the doctrinal level to Spanish Priscillianism, which was regarded as a form of revived Manichaeism.

Relations with the Eastern Churches were carried on almost exclusively on the plane of the universal communion of faith. With the exception of certain attempts to impose the Roman view regarding disciplinary and liturgical questions, such as the date of Easter (*Ep.* 2; 3; 121; 122, etc.), Leo's correspondence with the Easterners was concerned with the unity of faith, or more precisely, with the controversies preceding and following the Council of Chalcedon (451) as well as with the council itself (letters included in the Acts of the council).

Thus, in 448, when Eutyches, the intransigent defender of the Christology of Cyril of Alexandria, appealed to Rome, Leo was unwilling to make a pronouncement on the matter without first being better informed by Flavian, bishop of Constantinople. There then followed a continual flow of letters from Rome to ecclesiastical and imperial authorities, to the faithful of Constantinople, to the Roman legates in the East, to the other Eastern episcopal sees and vice versa.

According to this extensive documentation, Leo's action in favor of the *communio fidei* was developed in various phases. When Theodosius convoked a council at Ephesus in the spring of 449, Leo sent his legates, although with some reservations since he considered that the matter had already been solved in his *Epistula dogmatica ad Flavianum.* This council at Ephesus, which Leo later described as a *latrocinium* (*Ep.* 95, 2), resulted in a disaster for the cause of Flavian and Leo. Following the appeals of Flavian, Eusebius of Dorylaeum and especially of Theodoret (*Ep.* 52), Leo sought to obtain from the emperor the convocation of another council that would be truly universal in scope (*Ep.* 43). Although Leo sought the support of the court at Ravenna and of Pulcheria, a new council was not possible until after the unexpected death of the emperor. By that time, however, since the civil and religious authorities had stated their readiness to accept his *Tomus ad Flavianum,* Leo had cooled to the idea of another council. Nevertheless, after some hesitation, he accepted the convocation of the Council of Chalcedon. When this council met in the autumn of 451, it took the side of Leo and condemned Dioscorus, who had triumphed at Ephesus. Furthermore, under pressure from the court, a dogmatic definition was promulgated which was in keeping with the Christological traditions of the time. When he was informed of the success of the council, Leo congratulated the civil authorities in the East as well as the fathers of the council, and communicated the results to the Western bishops (*Ep.* 102-106, 114). Nevertheless, ecclesiastical peace was not finally reestablished. Leo himself had no rest until his death and felt constantly constrained to defend the faith of Chalcedon, which he regarded as a *via media* between Nestorius and Eutyches. At the same time, he considered it his obligation to refute canon 28 of Chalcedon which he considered to be opposed to the canons of Nicea in attributing the second rank in the hierarchy to the See of Constantinople. This dual concern, dogmatic and canonical, dominated all of his subsequent correspondence with the East. Of particular interest among these letters are those relating to the monks of Palestine (452-454), the most tenacious adversaries of the Chalcedonian faith (*Ep.* 123-127), and to the reestablishment of peace in Egypt in the years 457-458 (*Ep.* 156-158, 164-165).

While struggling almost his entire life for the orthodoxy and the peace of the church, Leo never ceased to move also on the political plane as the situation of the "imperial church" of the time required. In the West, this was not limited merely to a collaboration for the unity of faith as a basis of political unity. In 452, at the time of the invasion of Attila, Leo was part of the imperial embassy sent by Valentinian III to negotiate with the king of the Huns, and the success of the embassy is to be attributed in part to Leo. Three years later, he obtained from Gaiseric a promise not to burn the city of Rome or massacre its inhabitants. In his relations with the civil authorities, he encountered a favorable attitude at the court at Ravenna; and in the controversy with Hilary of Arles, Valentinian III pronounced himself explicitly in favor of the primacy of the bishop of Rome (445; *Ep.* 11). His relations with the court at Constantinople, however, were somewhat different. Leo not only did not enter into the political affairs in the East, but even in the religious sphere he had to leave the initiative to a great extent with the imperial authorities. He did not hesitate to recognize a certain sacerdotal dignity of the emperor in the form of a duty to concern himself with the unity and harmony of the church, and that in the interests of the empire itself. Nevertheless, when Marcian attempted to defend canon 28 of Chalcedon, Leo did not hesitate to remind him of the distinction between God and the world, religion and the state, and demanded freedom of action for the church and strongly affirmed in this regard the primacy of the Apostolic See. This position of Leo, however, met with little sympathy at the court of Constantinople.

Leo's pastoral activity on both the local and universal level was marked always by a vivid awareness of his dignity and authority. Yet while requiring the recognition of his lofty mission at the service of all the churches, Leo never forgot *humilitas,* i.e., his total dependence on Christ, the true Lord of the church. It was this dialectic, this *moderatio,* which characterized his attitude toward his supreme responsibility and which oriented his entire life. Thus, while showing himself intransigent toward errors in faith or a lack of discipline, he sought at the same time to lead back those who had gone astray and to regain the guilty. He was anxious to coordinate the responsibilities of the Apostolic See with those of the episcopal college. On the doctrinal level he sought out the *via media,* setting errors over against one another and confronting in a dialectical manner the diverse aspects of the one truth.

Leo had been prepared by an excellent education for this *moderatio,* especially on the dogmatic level. His rhetorical formation and his good understanding of law aided him in finding a precision and equilibrium of expression. Even more important, perhaps, was his

Christian optimism. He displayed the constant conviction that the Lord would never abandon His church, nor allow error to prevail and would preserve the faithful in their baptismal holiness. He was confident of the guidance of Christ, present in Peter, and thus could not but defend his position. In a certain sense this optimism betrayed him, for he did not exercise a *moderatio* with regard to antiquity and progress. His preference for the *status quo* is also to be explained by the traditionalism characteristic of the Romans.

Considering the principal directions of Leo the Great's activity as pope, it is understandable that historical research up to this point has concentrated above all on his ecclesiastical politics relative to the Council of Chalcedon along with the Christological and ecclesiological implications. His contributions to the development of canon law regarding both persons and the community as well as the orientation he gave to the Roman liturgy have likewise been the objects of much study. Finally, there has also been a great interest shown for his personality, especially for his qualities of government and his *Romanitas*. All of these aspects have formed the object of numerous studies. What is, nevertheless, missing is a comprehensive study of this great pontiff, up to date with regard to specific studies and balanced with regard to modern confessional positions.

General studies: O. Bardenhewer, Geschichte der altkirchlichen Literatur IV. Freiburg 1924, 617-623. — H. Lietzmann, Leo I: PWK 12, 2(1925)1962-1973. — P. Batiffol, Léon I: DTC 9(1926)218-301. — E. Caspar, Geschichte des Papsttums I. Tübingen 1930, 423-564. — U. Moricca, Storia della letteratura latina cristiana III, 1. Turin 1932, 1031-1106. — T. Jalland, The Life and Times of St. Leo the Great. London, 1941. — F. Di Capua, Leone I: EC 7(1951)1139-1143. — A. Lauras, Études sur S. Léon le Grand: RSR 49(1961)481-499 (bibliography). — J. Leclercq, Introduction, in R. Dolle, ed., Léon le Grand Sermons I, Sch 22 bis. Paris 1964^2, 7-55. — O. Bertolini, Leone papa: *Archivio Società Rom. St. Patria* 89(1966)1-23. — G. Zannoni, Leone I: *Bibliotheca Sanctorum* 7(1966)1232-1278. — T. Mariucci, Omelie e Lettere di S. Leone Magno (*Classici delle Religioni*). Turin 1968, 9-43.

Studies on particular biographical aspects: C. van De Vorst, La vie grecque de s. Leon: AB 29(1910)400-408. — P. Batiffol, Le Siège Apostolique. Paris, 1921. — I. Scalfati, S. Leone il Grande e le invasioni dei Goti, Unni e Vandali. Rome, 1944. — M. Jugie, L'intervention de S. Léon le Grand dans les affaires des Églises orientales, in Misc. P. Paschini I. Rome 1948, 77-94. — H. Du Manoir, S. Léon et la définition dogmatique de Chalcédoine: AT 40(1951)291-304. — H. Rahner, Leo der Grosse, der Papst des Konzils, in *Chalkedon* I. Würzburg 1951, 323-339. — B. Emmi, Leone ed Eutiche: Ang 29(1952)3-42. — H. M. Klinkenberg, Papsttum und Reichskirche bei Leo d. Gr.: Ztsch. d. Savigny Stiftung f. Rechtsgeschichte, Kan. Abt. 38(1952)37-112. — C. E. Mesa, El Concilio de Calcedonia, Notas históricas: Eutiques, San Léon Magno: *Verdad y Vida* 10(1952)367-382. — V. Monachino, Il canone 28 di Calcedonia e S. Leone Magno: Greg 3(1952)261-291, 531-565. — A. Walz, Papst und Kaiser in Chalkedon: Ang 29(1952)110-129. — F. Hofmann, Der Kampf der Päpste um Konzil und Dogma von Chalkedon von Leo dem Grossen bis Hormisdas (451-519), in *Chalkedon* II. Würzburg 1953, 13-94. — C. Lepelley, S. Léon de Grand et la Cité Romaine: RevSR 35(1961)130-150; *idem*, S. Léon le Grand et l'église maurétanienne. Primauté romaine et autonomie africaine au Ve siècle: *Les Cayers de Tunisie* 15(1967)189-204. — J. Oroz Reta, San Léon, papa de la Romanidad: *Helmantica* 13(1962)163-191; *idem,* San Agustín y San León Magno frente al destino de Roma: *Augustinus* 9(1964)175-191. — L. M. Martínez, La restauración de San León Magno en la basílica Ostiense: RQ 58(1963)1-27. — G. Langgärtner, Die Gallienpolitik der Päpste im 5. u. 6. Jahrhundert. Eine Studie über das apostolische Vikariat von Arles. Bonn, 1964. — R. Jurdin, Le Pape chez Attila: *Nouvelle Revue Française* 17(1969)161-168. — A. Lauras, S. Léon le Grand et le Manichéisme romain: SP 11 (TU 108). Berlin 1972, 203-209. — B. Vollmann, Priscillianus: PWK Suppl. 14(1974)485-559.

WRITINGS

Leo the Great, moved by his pastoral solicitude for the community of Rome and for all the churches, has left a rich patrimony of letters and sermons. Given the rather impersonal style of the letters, which reflect the tone of the papal chancellery, and of the sermons, the only two literary genres extant, Leo has been accorded only a modest place in the history of Latin literature (cf. Schanz-Hosius). Nevertheless, this is the largest collection of letters surviving from the time before Gregory the Great. Furthermore, Leo is the only pope of that period the greater part of whose homilies have survived. Leo thus provides invaluable documentation for a knowledge of church history, theology, and Christian spirituality. From the literary aspect, too, these are compositions of high intelligence. Leo's letters and sermons are in fact distinguished by their refined style, rhythmic prose, purity of language, conciseness of expression, and clarity of thought. Few writers of that time excelled Leo in his domination of Latin rhetoric and his achievement of such a perfect concordance between content and form. This ability to express in a Roman fashion the Christian themes dearest to him is a characteristic of Leo. In Leo, Roman genius was united with the Christian spirit in a truly singular manner.

1. Letters

According to the Ballerini edition which was reprinted by Migne, the collection of Leo's correspondence includes 173 letters, of which 143 were written by the pontiff and 30 were addressed to him over a period of about twenty years (442-460). The fact that such a relatively large number of letters has been preserved is due to the variety of interest aroused by these letters both during and, especially, after Leo's pontificate.

Leo himself took great care to obtain the widest possible circulation for those of his letters which he considered to be of universal interest. The clearest testimony to this is provided by the history of his most famous composition, the *Tomus ad Flavianum,* which was disseminated throughout the entire empire. In the interests of the *communio fidei,* he had a complete documentation concerning the affair of Eutyches sent to the bishops of Gaul and Spain in 449. This fact is important because these documents, which were sent also to the bishops who took part in the Roman synod of that year, seem to have constituted the collection of Leonine letters which at a later date were inserted into the canonical collections of Novara (*saec.* IX). For dogmatic purposes, i.e., to defend the Council of Chalcedon, a collection of 72 letters, known as the *Collectio Ratisbonensis,* was compiled in the sixth century. In like manner, the *Collectio Thessalonicensis* (*saec.* VI), which also contain a certain number of letters of Leo, were compiled in defense of jurisdictional rights. Other letters have been preserved together with papal decretals and synodal canons in canonical collections such as the *Quesnelliana,* compiled in Italy at the end of the fifth century, and the collection of Novara mentioned above. Letter 28 was also transmitted in a liturgical text, in the homilary of the Basilica of the Apostles, which was composed by Agimund in the eighth century.

A consideration of the dissemination of Leo's letters, typical of the ancient papal letters, is important not only for the resolution of questions of authenticity and textual criticism, but also for a proper historical evaluation of Leo's pontificate. Even if it may be supposed that the subsequent selection of documents did, for the most part, respect the importance of the biographical data, it, nevertheless, must not be forgotten that any judgment on these is conditioned by the interests of the later compilers. Furthermore, with the exception of some pieces deriving from an original of the *Collectio Arelatensis,* all the other letters which have been handed down can be traced back to the register of Leo's works preserved in the archives of the Apostolic See.

Although a good deal is known concerning questions of the historical and literary value and the transmission of Leo's letters, problems, nevertheless, remain to be resolved. Above all there is need for a complete critical edition in which would be gathered, after an adequate examination of the studies made up to now, all the various partial editions. In view of such an edition, it would be necessary to take up again the question of the authenticity of an entire series of letters (cf. CPL 1656), study better the question of sources, and examine the role of Prosper of Aquitaine in the composition of Leo's letters. Finally, there is need for a deeper investigation of the relation between these letters and the sermons given at the same time.

2. Sermons

No less precious than the letters is the patrimony of Leo's homiletic activity which includes, according to the recent critical edition of Chavasse, 97 sermons of *tractatus* (96 in the Ballerini edition) divided according to the Roman liturgical year of Leo's time. This collection thus includes 10 sermons on Christmas, 8 for Epiphany, 2 for Easter, 2 for the Ascension, 3 for Pentecost, 12 for Lent, 19 for Holy Week *(De Passione),* 4 for the ember days of Pentecost, 9 for the ember days of September, 9 for the ember days of December, and 6 for the so-called collects. To these can be added the sermons for the feasts of Sts. Peter and Paul, of St. Lawrence, and of the Maccabees as well as those for Leo's ordination and anniversary.

The edition of Chavasse has preserved the traditional division according to which the individual sermons are arranged not only in their liturgical order (beginning from September 29 to the sermons for the ember days of September), but also in chronological order within the same liturgical arrangement. This dual criterion, which was not understood by modern editors, goes back to the very first editions made by Leo himself and his collaborators (cf. the tables: CCL 138, p. clxxix and cxciv).

The preservation of Leo's homiletic patrimony is due in a large part, although not exclusively, to its use in the liturgy down through the centuries. There are, in fact, homilaries which include, among other things, a greater or lesser quantity of Leo's sermons. Among these liturgical texts, the most famous are the Homilary of Agimund (*saec.* VIII), mentioned above, and that of Paul the Deacon (*saec.* VIII), which was the tradition preferred by the Ballerini. Nevertheless, these collections for liturgical use do not form the basis for the transmission of the sermons of Leo. This was provided by two collections of a dogmatic nature which were compiled at the initiative of Leo himself. The first of these collections includes sermons from the first five years of his pontificate (440-445) and ends with the conclusion of the disputes with the Roman Manichaeans and with Hilary of Arles. Quotations from seven of these sermons of a predominantly anti-Manichaean character were cited in the *Tomus ad Flavianum* (449). The second collection is composed, in addition to a new edition of the homilies of the first collection, primarily of sermons on the question of the monks of Palestine (452-454). Given the clear opposition in these sermons to the position of Eutyches, it is likely that the collection was edited after 454. Subsequently, around 600, because of the desire to have all the sermons of Leo together, an editor not only put the two collections of sermons together, but also made them into one text (tripartite collection). The possibility is not to be excluded that this third collection was also compiled with a dogmatic purpose in mind, perhaps in favor of the Three Chapters (CCL 138, p. cxiii). Even after their compilation, the sermons of Leo were used not only for liturgical purposes, but were also included, together with the letters, in various canonical collections. Thus it was that a collection of letters, formed within the canonical collection known as the "False Decretals," appeared together with a form (A) of the "tripartite collection" in a whole series of twelfth-century manuscripts with what appears to be an anti-Pelagian tendency (CCL 138, p. ciii-cvi).

With regard to textual criticism, the homiletic patrimony of Leo was for a long time neglected in comparison with the collection of his correspondence. Today, owing to the tireless work of Chavasse, that situation has been reversed.

There is now an excellent critical edition of the sermons containing reliable information regarding their authenticity and, to a great extent, their chronology. Still awaiting further study are the questions of the sources, which are only partially known, the connection between certain sermons and the letters which were composed at the same period, the relationship with the liturgical prayers (see below), and especially the exegesis of a liturgical type which characterizes the form of the greater part of the sermons.

3. Liturgical Texts, Inscriptions and *Spuria*

Leo contributed to the liturgical organization of the Roman community and the churches dependent upon it (cf. *Ep.* 9; 16; 121, 1; 168 etc.). Given the traditional attribution of the oldest sacramentary, the *Veronense,* to him as well as the many similarities between the prayers of this sacramentary and his sermons, there can be no doubt that Leo composed liturgical texts, even though it is not possible to prove that at least some of the texts to which his sermons allude were composed by him. Leo definitely uses other sources in his sermons; therefore, it is less likely that subsequent editors of liturgical prayers took up his formulae (CCL 138, p. ccxviii; CPL 1657b and the studies on Leo and the *Sacramentarium Veronense*).

It is certain that Leo is the author of the inscription *Gens sacranda poli* in the baptistry of the Lateran Basilica (CPL 1657b); although the attribution of other inscriptions to Leo is doubtful.

Attempts have been made to attribute to Leo the *De vocatione gentium* (CPL 528; PL 51, 647-722) and the so-called *Indiculus de gratia* (CPL 527; PL 51, 205-212), but this barely touches on the relation between Leo and Prosper of Aquitaine to whom these compositions are more likely to be attributed.

General editions: (Cf. CPL 1656-1661. — PLS III, 329-350). — PL 54-56 (P. and H. Ballerini, Sancti Leonis Magni Romani Pontificis opera, 3 vols. Venice, 1753-1757).

Partial editions: A. Chavasse, CCL 138, 138A(1973) (sermons). — E. Schwartz, ACO II 1-4. Berlin-Leipzig, 1932. — C. Silva-Tarouca, Textus et documenta series theol. 9, 15, 20, 22. Rome, 1932-1937. — W. Gundlach, Epistulae Arelatenses: MGH III. Berlin, 1892. — O. Guenther, CSEL 35, 1(1895) (Collectio Avellana). — B. Vollmann, Studien zum Priscillianismus. St. Ottilien, 1965 (Ep. 15). — B. Krusch, Studien zur christlich-mittelalterlichen Chronologie, der vierundachzigjährige Osterzyklus u. seine Quellen. Leipzig 1880, 251-265.

Translations—Sermons and letters: Dutch: A. Huyg, Sint Leo de Groote. Over de Menscwording van Christus. Leerstellige brieven en preeken. Amsterdam, 1941. *English:* C. L. Feltoe, LNPF 12, ser. 2(1895; reprint: 1969). *Italian:* T. Mariucci, Omilei e Lettere di S. Leone Magno *(Classici delle Religioni)*. Turin, 1969.

Translations—Sermons: Dutch: F. Vromen, Leo de Grote, Preken voor het liturgisch jaar. Oosterhout, 1960-61. *French:* R. Dolle, SCh 22, 49, 74, 200(1949-1973) (with text). *German:* Th. Steeger. BKV2 54, 55(1927). — W. Haacke, Reden über Petrus. Paderborn, 1939. — F. Faessler, Heilige Festfeier. Lucern, 1947 (partial edition). *Italian:* E. Valeriano, Il mistero Pasquale. Il mistero del Natale. Alba-Rome, 1965. *Spanish:* M. Garrido Bonaño, BAC 291(1969) (with text).

Translations—Letters: English: E. Hunt, FC 34(1957) (select letters). *German:* S. Wenzlowsky, BKV1(1869).

Textual studies: In addition to the introductions to the editions and translations: C. H. Turner, The Collection of the Dogmatic Letters of St. Leo, in *Miscel. Ceriani,* Milan 1910, 688-739. — K. C. Silva-Tarouca, Beiträge zur Überlieferungsgeschichte der Papstbriefe des 4.-6. Jh.: ZKTh 43(1919)467-481, 657-692; *idem,* Die Quellen der Briefsammlungen Papst Leos des Grossen, in Festgabe P. Kehr. Munich 1926, 23-47; *idem,* Nuovi studi sulle antiche lettere dei Papi: Greg 12(1931)3-56, 349-425, 547-598; *idem,* Originale o Registro? La tradizione manoscritta del Tomus Leonis, in *Studi in onore di P. Ubaldi.* Rome 1937, 151-170. — R. Galli, S. Leone Magno e i suoi scritti: Did 9(1930)51-235. — A. Ferrua, Della festa dei SS. Maccabei e di un antico sermone in loro onore: CC 89, 3(1938)234-247, 318-327. — J. Magne, La prière de consécration des vierges "Deus castorum corporum." Étude du texte: EL 72(1958)245-267. — J. Campos, La epístola antipriscilianista de San León Magno: *Helmantica* 13(1962)269-308. — U. Domínguez-Del Val, San León y el "Tomus ad Flavianum": *Helmantica* 13(1962)193-233. — J. Jiménez Delgado, Hacia una nueva edición critica del epistolario leonino: *Helmantica* 13(1962)235-268. — A. Chavasse, Les lettres de S. Léon le Grand dans le supplément de la Dionysiana et de l'Hadriana et dans la Collection du manuscrit du Vatican: RvSR 38(1964)154-176; *idem,* Un curieux centon christologique du VIe siècle: *Revue de droit canonique* 16(1966)87-97; *idem,* Les lettres du Pape Léon le Grand (440-461) dans l'Hispana et la collection dite des Fausses Décrétales: ibid., 25(1975)28-39. — R. Dolle, Les sermons en double édition de S. Léon le Grand: RTAM 45(1978)5-33.

Studies of the literary aspects: L. Saltet, Les sources de l'Eranistès: RHE 6(1905)289-304, 513-536, 741-754. — Th. Steeger, Die Klauseltechnik Leos d. Gr. in seinen Sermonen. Hassfurt M., 1908. — J. Pschmadt, Leo d. Gr. als Prediger. Elberfeld, 1912. — F. Di Capua, Il ritmo prosaico nelle lettere dei papi e nei documenti della cancelleria romana dal IV al XIV secolo. Rome, 1937; *idem,* De clausulis a S. Leone Magno adhibitis, in *Scritti Minori* I. Rome 1959, 431-440; *idem,* Le due redazioni di una lettera di S. Leone, in *Scritti Minori* II. Rome 1959, 117-183; *idem,* Leone Magno e Prospero d'Aquitania, in *Scritti Minori* II. Rome 1959, 184-190. — W. J. Halliwell, The Style of Pope St. Leo the Great (PSt 59). Washington, 1939. — M. Mueller, The Vocabulary of Pope St. Leo the Great (PSt 62). Washington, 1943. — J. Gaidioz, S. Prosper d'Aquitaine et le Tome à Flavien: RevSR 23(1949)270-301. — M. Richard, Le pape s. Léon le Grand et les "Scholia de Incarnatione Unigeniti" de S. Cyrille d'Alexandrie, in *Mél. Lebreton* II. Paris 1952, 116-128. — Y. Duval, Quelques emprunts de S. Léon à S. Augustin: MSR 15(1958)85-94; *idem,* S. Léon le Grand et S. Gaudentius de Brescia: JThSt 11(1960)82-84. — A. Granata, Note sulle fonti di S. Leone Magno: RSCI 14(1960)263-282. — L. Alfonsi, Aspetti della tradizione culturale classica in S. Leone Magno: *Annali Pontifical*

Istitute Super. di Scienze e Lettere "S. Chiara" 11(1961)93-100; *idem,* Nota Leoniana: *Aevum* 36(1962)528. — M. Pellegrino, L'influsso di S. Agostino su S. Leone Magno nei sermoni sul Natale e sull'Epifania: *Annali del Pontifical Istitute Super. de Scienze e Lettere "S. Chiara"* 11(1961)101-132. — J. Guillén, Origen y constitución del "Cursus" ritmico: *Helmantica* 13(1962)309-350. — A. Chavasse, Le sermon prononcé par Léon le Grand pour l'anniversaire d'une dédicace: RB 91(1981)46-104.

Studies on the relationship with the Roman liturgy: G. Löw, Il più antico sermonario di S. Pietro in Vaticano: RAC 19(1942)143-183. — P. Borella, S. Leone Magno e il Communicantes: EL 60(1946)93-101. — C. Callewaert, S. Léon et les textes du léonien: SE 1(1948)35-123; *idem,* S. Léon et le Communicantes et le Nobis quoque peccatoribus: SE 1(1948)123-164. — F. L. Cross, Pre-Leonine Elements in the Proper of the Roman Mass: JThSt 50(1949)191-197. — O. Harrison, The Formular Ad virgines sacras. A Study of the Sources: EL 66(1952)252-273, 352-366. — T. M. Piccari, Il Tomus ad Flavianum ed il cosiddetto sacramentarium Leonianum nel Magisterium Ecclesiae dei secoli V-VI: Ang 29(1952)76-109. — B. Capelle, Une messe de s. Léon pour l'Ascension: EL 57(1953)201-209. — C. Coebergh, S. Léon le Grand auteur de la grande formule Ad virgines sacras du sacramentaire léonien: SE 6(1954)282-326. — E. Dekkers, Autour de l'œuvre liturgique de saint Léon le Grand: SE 10(1958)363-398 (fundamental study). — A. Lang, Leo der Grosse und die Texte des Altgelasianums. Kaldenkirchen, 1957 (cf. the articles of the same author on this topic in SE 10-18[1958-1968]). — J. Janini, S. León y las misas del Bautista: AnSemVal 2(Moncada 1962)121-201. — A. Chavasse, Dans sa prédication S. Léon le Grand a-t-il utilisé des sources liturgiques, in Mél. B. Botte. Louvain 1973, 71-74. — D. R. Holten, The Sacramental Language of S. Leo the Great. A Study of the Words Munus and Oblata: EL 92(1978)115-165.

THEOLOGY

1. The Main Characteristics of Leo's Theology

As a pastor solicitous for his community and a bishop concerned for the unity of all the churches, Leo offers a traditional and rather elementary doctrine which was adequate for the purposes of liturgical catechesis and the defense of the orthodox faith. His theology is, therefore, not distinguished by any original reflection on the Christian faith. This explains why his theological method, to which he himself hardly devoted any systematic reflection, has never been the object of a comprehensive study, although there are studies on basic points such as Scripture, tradition, dogma and dogmatic formalism. Nevertheless, the methodological presuppositions of a "kerygmatic" theologian merit a careful consideration. For his part, Leo expounds and develops the Gospel message in a well-defined pattern, typical of him and of many Latin bishops of that period.

Leo's desire to promote the unity and peace of the church is as apparent in his writings as it was in his ministry and political activity. This is the end he pursues both in his ordinary pastoral ministry, such as the preparation of the faithful for the celebration of Easter, as well as in his extraordinary activities, such as the resolution of certain disciplinary problems (the date of Easter, the time for the administration of baptism), or the struggle against heresy. For Leo, the catholic and universal church cannot be but one, and its unity is more profound than any other. It is not merely a question of *communio naturae* but of a *consortium gratiae*. It is a unity founded on the Incarnation of Christ, realized by the participation in the death of Jesus by baptism and the eucharist, lived in one faith and in charity toward all, guaranteed by the communal action of all the bishops, and protected by the civil authorities. This unity thus constitutes the center of that *Pax* which is no longer merely *Romana,* but also *Christiana.* Above all, it demands true faith in Christ, God and man. On the basis of the true faith, Christians understand the significance of salvation *(ratio sacramenti),* are able to avoid error and sin and thus to carry out the *opera pietatis.* Given this necessity for the true faith in the Christian's life, Leo's zeal in the struggle against contemporary heresies is understandable. For him, every error is the *dogma scelestissimum,* the greatest of dangers for the community.

To defend orthodoxy in order to assure the peace and concord of Christianity is one of the principal tasks of theology which is not realized without a continual reference to those who have laid the foundations of the Christian faith by passing on the Word of God. Such a reference, fundamental in every age, was particularly relevant at the time of Leo when the theology of the ecumenical council was being worked out and the system of patristic argumentation was being formulated; and it explains why he played such an active role in the Council of Chalcedon, the largest council of antiquity, and why, as a Roman, he attributed such weight to the example and traditions of his predecessors. Tradition, placed at the service of the one faith which guarantees peace, is thus another characteristic of Leonine theology. He returns to it in all of his pastoral activity: in the promotion of the ascetic life, in the polemic against doctrinal errors, in the defense of the canonical rules. It is from tradition that Leo draws not only the basic directions of his theology but also his schemes of thought which, like those of the Symbol, take up formulae, Christological expressions, and ancient citations in an almost literal fashion. It is particularly noteworthy how the reference to tradition becomes more and more important in the controversy with Eutyches, passing gradually from the Symbol of the Apostles, to the authority of Nicea, to the *testimonia* of the Fathers and finally to the authority of Chalcedon, which is placed on a par with that of Nicea. Leo is careful to emphasize the *consensus omnium,* i.e., the actual agreement of all the churches throughout the empire, but he refers mostly to antiquity, to the *norma vetustatis,* both for dogmatic formulations and for disciplinary canons. According to Leo, antiquity is above all the guarantee of the apostolicity of the church, its conformity with apostolic tradition.

This agreement with the Apostles and the Fathers is not understood in a vague sense; but, according to the mentality of the time which was interested in the codification of law and in philosophical dogmas, it required a consensus even in the formulation of the faith. Nevertheless, Leo is more concerned with the precision of the formulation of the faith than with the philosophical development, even of a technical nature, of the formulae themselves. Since he felt bound by the authority of tradition, Leo used the Bible both for recourse to the biblical *auctoritates* to prove his dogmatic statements as well as for reference to particular biblical passages to illustrate the mysteries of Christ or to present an exhortation to Christian life. For the most part he follows the traditional interpretation of the Bible, making use of "canonical" texts or drawing on passages which had traditionally captured the interest of preachers.

Leo is familiar with a particular method of exegesis developed above all by Augustine. In his liturgical homilies, he knows how to lead the faithful from the historical reality *(ordo rerum)* of the life of Jesus to a more profound understanding of him and of the exemplary nature of those gestures accomplished once and for all.

Leo's constant effort to draw his listeners to the *sacramentum et exemplum Christi* reveals the most important characteristic of his theology: its Christocentrism. It would be wrong to think that Leo placed such emphasis on faith in Christ, God and man, merely because of the necessity of combatting the Christological errors of his time: Manichaeism, Nestorianism, and Monophysitism.

In reality, there are two aspects to his Christocentrism. On the one hand, he vigorously defends the dogma of the one Christ in two natures and, in particular, the truth of the Incarnation. On the other hand, though, he never ceases to speak of Christ as Lord and Savior. This kerygmatic aspect is of great importance in Leo. Since he always preached the saving presence of Christ in the church, he could not but come to the defense of the Christ of the church.

2. The Christological Foundations

Leo's Christological formulation is so obvious as to be unmistakable. Nevertheless, research has been limited for a long time to the strictly Christological question of the one person in two natures. Many studies have been dedicated to Leo's interventions in the Monophysite Controversy and in the difficulties following the Council of Chalcedon. Scholars have always been interested above all in the *Tomus ad Flavianum* which is, without doubt, Leo's most important theological composition.

This limitation of research is easily understood, seeing as how in general the history of dogma has been largely dominated by the question of the one Christ, God and man, and that the contribution of Leo, of Cyril of Alexandria, and of the Antiochenes was decisive for the elaboration of the Chalcedonian faith, which has remained the dogmatic foundation for Christology up to the present day. Nevertheless, this method of considering Leo's preaching and his reflection on the mystery of the Incarnation is far from being complete. Prescinding from the fact that such an approach does not give sufficient attention to the historical context of Leonine Christology, its sources and typically Roman approach, it also neglects to a great extent the principally soteriological interests of Leo's Christology.

The very doctrine of the dual consubstantiality which forms the nucleus of Leo's dogmatic Christology is essentially soteriological. Against the supposed docetism of Eutyches, Leo develops the doctrine of the *gemina in Christo natura* in his dogmatic epistle (*Ep.* 28). He demonstrates, on the basis of the affirmation of the dual birth of Christ found in the Symbol of the Apostles, that two natures are to be distinguished in Christ, each with its respective properties and activities, although they are united in the one single subject to whom they are attributed. Even though he does not yet use the Eastern dogmatic formula of *consubstantialis patri-consubstantialis matri* which he will subsequently adopt, Leo's reasoning is centered on this double idea, Christ truly born of God and of Mary, which he expresses with terms equivalent to consubstantial. In any case, Leo's use of the antithetical formula *consubstantialis patri-consubstantialis matri* in subsequent letters and in his preaching leaves no doubt that he applied a strictly dogmatic significance to the term.

Since under the terms consubstantiality, unity, and equality he intended both inclusion and likeness, Leo, by declaring that Christ is consubstantial with the Father and with his mother, affirms not only the divine and human nature of Christ, but even more his solidarity with God and with man. Joined to the Father, he not only reveals Him to the world but acts in His name. Joined to man, he suffers and offers himself up for man. Precisely because of this, no one attains salvation who does not believe in the dual consubstantiality of Christ (*Serm.* 30, 6). Although he insists on the duality of Christ in this formula, Leo, nevertheless, does not forget the unity of person which is ultimately based on the fact that neither the Father nor the Spirit, but the Son alone became incarnate (*Serm.* 64, 2). Indeed, it was precisely because of this unity that Christ remained obedient unto death, that he freely sacrificed himself for the human race and that he has become the model of man's resurrection.

The extent to which the dogma of the double consubstantiality is fundamentally a soteriological affirmation becomes even clearer from its "kerygmatic" context. Leo not only composed his dogmatic epistle to Flavian to a large extent of citations from his own homilies, but he also inserted the dogma into his preaching on the mysteries of Jesus, thus showing that the two considerations are not to be separated from one another.

Of all the mysteries of Jesus which the church celebrates each year, the *sacramentum paschale* excels them all. However, its singular importance can only be understood in relation to Christmas and to the Ascension. With regard to Christmas, the celebration of the birth of Christ from the Virgin, Leo emphasizes that the *nativitas nova* indicates the divinity of Christ and shows that he belongs also to the human race, which is invited to faith in Christ, at once God and man. Although Leo recognizes a certain soteriological value in the birth from the virgin, and sees in this *commercium mirabile* between God and man the model of man's regeneration or the beginning of the victory over the devil, he, nevertheless, prefers to present it as the condition for Easter. Christ had to be born in order to be able to die for our sins and to arise for our justification (*Serm.* 48, 1). The intimate bond between Christmas and Easter is to be explained above all in the light of baptism which obtains its full significance from the *sacramentum paschale.* The Redeemer had to be born of God and of Mary, to be consubstantial with both, in order that man might be able to die and rise with him in the sacrament of baptism (*Ep.* 16, 3).

Even if Leo, by referring Christmas to Easter, intends that the victory of Christ over the devil is based in the virginal birth from Mary, it would be wrong to attempt to reduce his paschal soteriology to the *redemptio,* including the *reconciliatio.* For him, the salvific work of Christ consists not only of a *victoria iusta* but also of a *iustificatio;* not only of an *abolitio peccati,* but also of the *initium ad vitam aeternam resurgendi* (*Serm.* 48, 1; 52, 1; 64, 3). Such a concept is made clear by the relation he establishes between Easter and Ascension.

The *triumphus victoriae* (*Serm.* 67, 7) which is celebrated at Easter, Jesus' *transitus ad gloriam,* is the beginning and the pledge of man's glorification (*Serm.* 72, 6; 65, 4). This aspect of the paschal mystery shines forth in its full splendor in the feast of the Ascension: the elevation of Christ is the *provectio nostra,* and in the glorification of the head, the *assumptio totius generis humani,* already founded in the Incarnation, is definitively sealed (*Serm.* 63, 1; 73, 4). Mankind, already admitted to the *communio naturae,* now possesses the supreme guarantee of the *consortium gloriae* (*Serm.* 72, 2). This universality of salvation, which is rooted in the solidarity of Christ with mankind, is confirmed by the Leonine doctrine of the sacrifice of Christ. According to Leo, the sacrifice of the death of Jesus marked the fulfillment of all the sacrifices of the Old Testament (*Serm.* 59, 7; 68, 3), and since it was offered not only by a true man, but also was the gift of the only just man — born of a virgin owing to his divine filiation — that death was the one sacrifice capable of reconciling all mankind with God (*Serm.* 64, 2-4).

3. The Presence of Christ in the Christian Community

The soteriological formulation of Leo's Christology is evident also from the fact that his doctrine on the mystery of Christ is inseparable from his ecclesiology. While reading the sermons of Leo, one is easily led to think of the majestic images of Christ which shine forth from the apsides of the Roman basilicas and symbolize the presence of the *Dominus Salvator* in his church.

Leo's ecclesiology has been the object of much study, especially the idea of the church as *corpus sacramentum* both in its institutional aspects as well as in those which later theology has called the mystical body of Christ. However, Leo's idea of Christ as the *Christus praesens in Ecclesia* would merit greater emphasis.

The theme of the *Ecclesia quae est corpus Christi* is without a doubt central to Leo's thought, even though the texts in which it is explicitly expressed are rather rare (*Ep.* 53, 4) and the more obvious passages on the body of Christ emphasize especially the aspect of the organic unity of the church (*Serm.* 3, 1; *Ep.* 14, 11). Nevertheless, the idea of the presence of Christ, the source of Christian life, is everywhere presupposed in Leo.

In this sense, the church always remains for him a *communio sanctorum* which, although it always includes sinners and is composed of Christians who are never perfect, never loses its *integritas.* The church is in a way the continuation of the Incarnation of Christ. Leo makes frequent reference to Jesus' promise: *Ecce ego vobiscum sum omnibus diebus usque ad consummationem saeculi* (Mt. 28:20) (cf. *Serm.* 72, 3), and he speaks constantly of the *consortium* or the *unio* of Christ with his church and his *inhabitatio* in her. The Christians' entire vitality derives from the presence of their Head in his Body (cf. *Serm.* 63).

All the good things the Christians accomplish in their life — charity, the ascetic life, suffering — are fundamentally the work of Christ active in them. In virtue of their union with him, based on baptism and faith, the passion of the Lord is prolonged until the end of the world (*Serm.* 70, 5), and in them the victory of Christ over the world is repeated throughout all the history of the church (*Serm.* 39, 3). Christ's special presence in the poor gives the faithful the occasion to show their love to him directly (*Serm.* 9, etc.). Leo's doctrine on man as the image of God must also be seen in this context. The likeness of God, to which man is restored in baptism, is perfected above all in the imitation of that love of God as a result of which the Savior has come into this world (*Serm.* 45, 2).

Leo's assumption of the Augustinian doctrine of divine grace and human liberty also enters perfectly into his Christological perspective. By developing further the Augustinian theme of *sacramentum et exemplum,* Leo continually affirms that Christ is not only a model for man but is also the source of all grace (*Serm.* 39, 3; 43, 1; 63, 4).

The presence of Christ preserves the integrity of the church inasmuch as it is also the *communio sanctorum.* The church, *mater* and *schola veritatis* (*Serm.* 42, 5) has been called in a special way in its pastors to maintain the faith of its members and to lead the more spiritual of the faithful to a more profound understanding of the mystery of Christ (cf. *Serm.* 76, 1).

This fundamental task is realized through the presence of Christ who assists the preachers (see the introduction to certain sermons, e.g. *Serm.* 52, 1) and is present in all those who are responsible for the defense of orthodoxy whether they be ecclesiastics or the civil authorities (*Serm.* 32, 2; *Ep.* 60; 102, 2; 114, 2; 164, 1). For this reason Leo saw the confirmation of the orthodox faith at the Council of Chalcedon as a triumph of Christ (*Ep.* 104, 1), and indeed as another coming of the Lord (*Ep.* 120, 2).

The same is also true for the *communio sacramentorum* inasmuch as it is the sanctifying action of the church. Christ, who always remains in the church, strengthens both the preachers of the Gospel and the ministers of the sacraments (*Ep.* 6, 17).

If Christ were not to continue to exercise his priesthood, there would be neither priesthood nor sacrifice in his body the church (*Ep.* 80, 2). Only in virtue of his presence does there exist the one *sacramentum pontificis* in the faithful, in their pastors, and especially in the vicar of Peter (*Serm.* 4, 1f). It is Christ himself who renders the church fruitful in baptism (*Serm.* 63, 6), just as in the eucharist the church, by partaking of his body and his blood, is transformed into that which it receives (*Serm.* 63, 7). Christ never ceases to operate in the work of his ministers, who are thus capable of readmitting penitents to the *communio sacramentorum* (*Ep.* 108, 2).

Leo is not content only to emphasize the presence of the glorified Christ in the sacramental action of the church, but is also careful to underline the *hodie* of the very mysteries of the life of Jesus which are made present above all in the celebration of the liturgical feasts (cf. *Serm.* 26, 2) and in the administration of the sacrament of baptism (*Ep.* 16, 3; *Serm.* 70, 4). This does not take place only in the memory of the faithful because they hear the biblical readings and believe in the saving action of Christ (*Serm.* 36, 1); rather, that which Jesus has done and suffered as Head becomes effective also in his Body (*Serm.* 63, 6; 66, 4). Leo is not more precise as to how the *virtus* of those past events can be still present today, and in any case he does not admit of merely a *virtus divina* which is active in the faithful today as it once was active in those who encountered Jesus and accepted his word. He also has the concept of an influence of Christ the eternal priest who never ceases to make intercession with the Father (*Ep.* 80, 2).

4. The Presence of Christ in the Church of Rome

There can be no doubt that Leo received the title of "the Great" especially because both in theory and practice he contributed to the development of the primacy of the Apostolic See of Rome. It is, therefore, no surprise that up to the present scholars have been more interested in the juridical and political aspects of this question rather than in Leo's ecclesiology. Much attention has also been given in this research to the ideological basis of *Roma Aeterna* and to Leo's Christological outlook. The trilogy of Christ-Peter-bishop of Rome was too obvious to be overlooked. Nevertheless, the relation between the primacy and the episcopal college still needs to be studied in greater depth and hermeneutical questions, such as the value of a papal pronouncement, have not yet been sufficiently clarified. The Leonine doctrine on the primacy of Rome needs to be seen in the perspective of the *integritas* of the church, to which the presence of Christ assures both the *communio sanctorum* as well as the *communio sacramentorum.*

While taking up the ideas and formulae of his predecessors, Leo undoubtedly brought the Roman doctrine on the primacy of the Apostolic See to its perfection. His theory is developed in two affirmations: "Peter, who was united to Christ, the true founder and pastor of the church, in a singular way, continues even now to exercise his primacy over all the churches; the bishop of Rome, the heir and successor of Peter, renders this primacy visible in the community of all the Christians. Just as Christ transmitted his mission to the Apostles *per Petrum,* so are the faith and the ecclesiastical order guaranteed by the See of Peter" (cf. especially *Ep.* 10, 1 and 9).

At the basis of this theory of the primacy are the three principal biblical texts regarding the role of Peter in the primitive community (Mt. 16:16-19; Lk. 22:31f; Jn. 21:15-19). Nevertheless, it is clear that in his explication of these texts Leo makes use of *political-juridical* categories such as *principatus, dignitas, haeres, vices, ius potestatis, consortium potestatis,* and even has recourse to concepts of a more philosophical character, especially that of *forma.* At the same time he relies on the tradition of his predecessors as well as on synodal tradition. However, the principal justification of his assertions rests in a purely Christological reflection. Peter owes his primacy to his intimate union with Christ, by whom he has been assumed *in consortium individuae unitatis* (*Ep.* 10, 1). The bishop of Rome also participates in this same union. Leo does not speak of the *vicarius Christi,* but rather if Peter, under the supreme guidance of Christ, is the true guide of all pastors (*Serm.* 4, 2: *Omnes tamen proprie regat Petrus, quos principaliter regit et Christus*), then his *praesidium* renders present in his heir the action of Christ himself, the pastor of all the pastors (cf. *Serm.* 5, 2). Leo is conscious of having been delegated in a special way for the care of Christ's sheep and is, furthermore, convinced that he is able to make use incessantly of the propitiatory work of the omnipotent and eternal Priest (*Serm.* 3, 2). On the strength of this confidence he takes up already in his first sermon the words of Jesus: *Pater sancte, conserva eos in nomine tuo, quos dedisti mihi* (Jn. 17:11; *Serm.* 1; cf. also *Serm.* 3, 1; 5, 4; *Ep.* 6, 5; 104, 3).

Leo, however, does not so much compare his own pastoral activity with that of Christ as much as he identifies his ministry with that of Peter. He does not speak of the help or the inspiration of Christ in a manner limited to his own position, but speaks also in the same way with regard to the bishops and even to the emperor.

In line with his doctrine of the primacy of the bishop of Rome, Leo presents the hierarchical order of the church in the form of a pyramid. Just as the Apostles, although endowed with the same *honor* differ in regard to *potestas,* so the bishops do not all enjoy the same rights. There are the simple bishops of a province among whom one has the responsibility of the final decision, there are those in the larger cities who have a *sollicitudo amplior,* and through them the care for the universal church converges to the one See of Peter, the head of all (*Ep.* 14, 11).

If this pyramidal presentation was conditioned by the particular situation of Illyria, which was entrusted to the bishop of Thessalonica to whom the letter in question was addressed, it is, nevertheless, true that in other writings, conditioned by other particular conditions, Leo certainly intends to affirm in an absolute manner that the *sollicitudo omnium ecclesiarum* is the responsibility of the Roman Church.

For a proper evaluation of this statement of an undeniable universal significance, there must be kept in mind the gradual manner in which Leo put his pastoral responsibility into practice and the way in which he emphasized the responsibility of the other bishops within the entire ecclesial communion. Indeed, he underlines the fact that the unity of the churches depends on the *concordia sacerdotum* (*Ep.* 14, 11). In their submission as well as their collaboration, the bishops, who by their episcopal ordination are introduced into the *collegium caritatis,* share the *sollicitudo omnium ecclesiarum* are are thus, for their part, responsible for the orthodox faith (cf. *Ep.* 5, 2; 6, 1; 12, 2). It is in this sense that Leo understands the role of a synod as a privileged expression of episcopal collegiality. Not only does he make important decisions together with the Roman Synod (*Ep.* 16, 7; 166), but he also takes into account how the consensus of the conciliar Fathers at Chalcedon had placed in an even clearer light the extent to which his own preaching was in conformity with the entire tradition of the church (cf. *Ep.* 104, 1; 118, 1; 106, 1). On the other hand, in the case both of the synod at Ephesus as well as of canon 28, he refused his approval not only in virtue of his apostolic authority but also in reference to synodal law (*Ep.* 43; 44; 106, 4; etc.).

It is likewise noteworthy that Leo defends the superior rank of the Sees of Alexandria and Antioch not only in virtue of synodal law but also by the application in a certain sense of the Petrine principle. According to Leo, the authority of these sees is based on a special relationship to Peter, the first among the Apostles (*Ep.* 106, 5). Furthermore, although immediately after the Council of Chalcedon he rejected canon 28 which upset the order of the principal sees, he later seems to have resigned himself in the face of accomplished facts and to have no longer contested the claims of Constantinople. On the other hand, he never ceased to affirm the primacy of Rome even over the major sees (cf. *Ep.* 9, *praef.;* 102, 4; 119, 2), and to require them to live in communion with the Church of Rome. He did not trouble himself, however, to define to what extent communion with those sees was necessary for all the churches, including the Church of Rome. On the other hand, it was precisely in such a context that Leo claimed for the Church of Peter in the clearest way possible the *custodia* of the faith and of the canons of the major synods (*Ep.* 115, 1; 114, 2; 119, 2f; 149, 2; 156, 2). It must not be forgotten that the *principaliter regit Christus* applies likewise to the bishops, who are also *sacerdotes Christi.* The presence of Christ is promised also to them especially when they are gathered in council together with the pontiff (*Serm.* 2, 2; 5, 3; cf. *Ep.* 162, 3). With regard to councils, however, Leo speaks rather of the presence of the Holy Spirit (*Ep.* 144; 145, 1; 162, 3) or even more generally of divine aid (*Ep.* 146, 2; 147, 2).

The theme of Roman primacy which Leo developed on the theological plane also had its political side. In his affirmation of the prerogatives of the Apostolic See and his recourse in support of this to the words of Jesus, Leo not only uses a whole series of political concepts but moves continually against a political background. Behind his theory there is always the idea of *Roma aeterna.* He was certainly not the first to see the role of the Church of Peter and Paul from the perspective of Rome, *caput orbis* and source of peace.

In the fifth century the ideas of this ancient tradition were still in the air (cf. especially Prosper, *De ingratis* 40ff; *De vocat. gent.* 2, 16 as well as the *constitutio* of Valentinian III: *Ep.* 40).

Leo was, in any case, perhaps the principal witness to the

transposition of the concept *Roma aeterna, caput orbis terrarum* into the Christian concept of the *Urbs sancta.* In his famous sermon on Peter and Paul (*Serm.* 82), he recognizes on the one hand the providential role of pagan Rome in the evangelization of the world and insists, on the other, on the even more glorious work of peace of Christian Rome.

It is in the light of this positive evaluation of Rome's historical role that Leo also understands the "sacerdotal" function of the Roman emperor. He attributes to the emperor a decisive role in the struggle against heresy and in the defense of the peace of the church, and he concedes to the emperor in particular the right to convoke and direct a universal council and to confirm the synodal decrees. Still, he is aware of the necessity to distinguish between the *potestas imperialis* and the *auctoritas sacerdotalis* (*Ep.* 118, 2), and he does not hesitate to point out to the emperor that not even he can make the imperial city of Constantinople into an apostolic see (*Ep.* 104, 3). He reminds the emperor that every engagement undertaken for the sake of religious peace is in the interest of the empire itself (*Ep.* 115, 1), and, therefore, he expects from the imperial authority a respect for the freedom of the church (*Ep.* 146, 2; 164, 1). It should be recognized that a Christological note is also present even in the political aspect of the Leonine doctrine of the primacy of the Apostolic See. The positive estimation of the collaboration between pope and emperor is born in Leo from the conviction that Christ is Lord both of the church and of the empire (cf. *Ep.* 90, 2; 156, 3). Thus not only the salvation of souls but also the *salus rei publicae,* inasmuch as it derives from the *pax christiana* (Christ is our peace) is based on the Incarnation (*Serm.* 26, 5 quoting Eph. 2:14).

Although this political theology, inherited from Eusebius of Caesarea, must on the whole be considered rather problematic today, its primary intention was certainly religious. Rather a pastor than a prince, Leo was not so much interested in securing a privileged position for the Roman Church in the political world of his time, but rather was concerned with promoting that union of faith and of charity which only the presence of Christ, the one Lord and Savior, can assure to Christians (cf. *Serm.* 5, 2-3).

Leo's theology: A. Deneffe, Tradition und Dogma bei Leo d. Gr.: Schol 9(1934)543-554. — M. Testard, Le sacramentum dans les sermons de s. Léon le Grand. Diss., Paris, 1948 (typewritten). — C. Lepelley, Les mystères chrétiens chez s. Léon le Grand. Diss., Paris, 1955 (typewritten). — Y. M. Duval, Sacramentum et mysterium chez saint Léon le Grand. Diss., Lille, 1959 (typewritten); *idem,* S. Léon et la Tradition: RSR 48(1960)166-184. — A. Lauras, S. Léon le Grand e l'Écriture Sainte: SP 6 (TU 81). Berlin 1962, 127-140. — C. Bartnik, The Incarnation, Foundation of Leo the Great's Theology of History: Rocsniki teologicznokanoniczne 7(Lublin 1960)21-51 (in Polish with a résumé in French). — R. Dolle, Écritures Saintes, S. Léon: DSp 4(1960)158f. — S. M. Klehr,

Leo der Grosse in der Auseinandersetzung mit der Häresie. Diss., Walberg, 1963 (typewritten). — J. -P. Jossua, Le Salut, Incarnation ou mystère pascal chez les Pères de l'Église de s. Irénée à s. Léon le Grand. Paris, 1968. — R. P. C. Hanson, Dogma and Formula in the Fathers: SP 13 (TU 116). Berlin 1975, 169-184. — B. Studer, Die Einflüsse der Exegese Augustins auf die Predigten Leos des Grossen, in *Forma Futuri* (Misc. Pellegrino). Turin 1975, 917-930.

Leo's Christology: J. Rivière, La rédemption chez s. Léon le Grand: RevSR 9(1929)17-42, 153-187; *idem,* Le dogme de la rédemption après s. Augustin. Paris, 1930. — J. Maric, Nova formulae christologicae Leonis I Magni papae de Christi activitate interpretatio: *Bogoslovska Smotra* 4(Zagreb 1932)433-470. — C. Burgio, Le ragioni dell'incarnazione secondo s. Leone Magno: *Studi Francescani* 37(1940)81-94. — D. Mozeris, Doctrina s. Leonis Magni de Christo Restitutore et Sacerdote. Mundelein (Ill.), 1940. — Melchior a. S. Maria, Maria's plaats in het verlossingswerk volgens St. Leo de Grote: *Standard van Maria* 24(1948)2-16. — J. F. Rivera, San Léon Magno y la herejía de Eutiques desde el sínodo de Constantinople hasta la muerte de Teodosio II: RET 9(1949)31-58. — P. Galtier, S. Cyrille d'Alexandrie et s. Léon le Grand à Chalcédoine, in *Chalkedon* I. Würzburg 1951, 345-387. — M. J. Nicolas, La doctrine christologique de s. Léon: RT 51(1951)609-660. — H. Denis, La théologie de l'ascension d'après s. Léon le Grand. Diss., Lyons, 1959 (typewritten). — A. Spindeler, Papst Leo I über die Mitwirkung Marias bei der Erlösung: MTZ 10(1959)229-234. — F. Spedalieri, La madre del Salvatore nella soteriologia di S. Leono Magno: *Marianum* 25(1963)27-38. — H. Diepen, L'"Assumptus homo" patristique VI: RT 64(1964)364-386. — Liébaert, Christologie. *Handbuch d. Dogmengeschichte* III, 1a. Freiburg 1965, 121ff. — B. Studer, Consubstantialis Patri — consubstantialis matri. Une antithèse christologique chez Léon le Grand: REAug 18(1972)87-115 (cf. SP 13 [TU 116]. Berlin, 1975, 286-294); *idem,* Il concetto di "consostanziale" in Leone Magno: Aug 13(1973)599-607. — M. Riber, La reparación en san León Magno. Diss., Rome, 1973. — A. Grillmeier, Christ in Christian Tradition I. London, 1975², 526-539. — B. Studer, Soteriologie. *Handbuch d. Dogmengesch.* III, 2a. Freiburg 1978, 200-212. — H. Arens, Die christologische Sprache Leos des Grossen. Analyse des Tomus an den Patriarchen Flavian. Freiburg i.B., 1982.

Leo's Ecclesiology (including liturgy and spirituality): K. Esser, Das Kirchenjahr nach den Sermones Leos d. Grossen. Diss., Innsbruck, 1934 (typewritten). — M. Pellegrino, La dottrina del corpo mistico in s. Leone Magno: SC 67(1939)611-615. — E. M. Burke, The Church in the Works of Leo the Great. Washington, 1945. — L. Eizenhofer, Das Opfer der Gläubigen in den Sermonen Leos des Grossen, in F. X. Arnold, B. Fischer, Die Messe in der Glaubensverkündigung. Freiburg 1950, 79-107. — B. Capelle, Valeur spirituelle du Carême d'après s. Léon: QLP 35(1954)104-114. — I. Carton, Note sur l'emploi du mot "observantia" dans les homélies de s. Léon: VC 8(1954)104-114. — A. Guillaume, Jeûne et charité dans l'Église latine des origines au XII siècle en particulier chez s. Léon le Grand. Paris, 1954. — E. Luveley, The Doctrine of St. Leo the Great on the Ecclesiastical Forgiveness of Sin. Diss., West Baden, 1954. — Hervé de l'Incarnation, La grâce dans l'œuvre de s. Léon le Grand: RTAM 22(1955)17-55, 193-212. — F. Bajcer, Ecclesiologia s. Leonis Magni ex epistulis desumpta. Diss., Rome, 1957. — R. Dolle, Un docteur de l'aumône, s. Léon le Grand: VS 96(1957)266-287; *idem,* Les idées morales de saint Léon le Grand: MSR 15(1958)49-84. — L. J. McGovern, The Ecclesiology of St. Leo the Great. Diss., Rome, 1957. — M. B. De Soos, Le mystère liturgique d'après s. Léon le Grand. Münster, 1958; *idem,* Présence du mystère du salut dans la liturgie d'après s. Léon: EL 73(1959)116-135. — J. Gaillard, Noël: memoria ou mystère: *Maison–Dieu* 59(1959)37-59. — F. Hofmann, Die Osterbotschaft in den Predigten Papst Leos des Grossen, in *Paschatis Sollemnia.* Freiburg 1959, 76-86. — G. Hudon, La perfection chrétienne d'après les sermons de s. Léon (*Lex Orandi* 26). Paris, 1959. — V. De Rosa, Il digiuno liturgico nei sermoni di s. Leone Magno: *Annali*

Pontifical Istitute Super. di Scienze e Lettere "S. Chiara" 11(1961)19-91. — H. Georgi, Die Kirche als Abbild Christi nach Leo dem Grossen. Diss., Würzburg, 1961 (typewritten). — G. Valderrama, San León Magno y la unidad de la Iglesia según la encíclica "Aeterna Dei Sapientia": *Studium Av* 1-2(1961-1962)305-321. — E. Koep, Die Sünde nach Leo dem Grossen. Diss., Cologne, 1962. — F. König, S. Leone Magno, dottore dell'unità della Chiesa: Ang 39(1962)277-293. — P. Mikat, Die Lehre vom Almosen in den Kollektenpredigten Papst Leos d. Gr., in Festschr. T. Michels. Münster 1963, 46-64. — J. Waldram, Sacramentorum baptismi et confirmationis disciplina ac ritus secundum opera s. Leonis Magni. Diss., Rome, 1963. — J. A. Pascual, El misterio pascual según san. León Magno: REV 24(1964)299-314. — M. Pellegrino, Temi dominanti nei sermoni natalizi di S. Leone Magno, in Miscel. C. Figini. Milan 1964, 97-115. — A. Chavasse, Les féries de Carême célébrées aux temps de s. Léon le Grand (440-461), in Miscel. G. Lercaro I. Rome 1966, 551-557; *idem,* Le sermon III de s. Léon et la date de la célébration des Quatre-Temps de septembre: RevSR 44(1970)77-84. — D. Polato, Aspetti di una teologia della carità nei sermoni di s. Leone Magno. Diss., Padua, 1969. — C. Compagna, Il giorno del conferimento del battesimo in relazione al mistero celebrato nella teologia dei Padri: *Asprenas* 18(1971)370-432. — F. Mayr, Die kanonische Busse des 5. Jahrhunderts im Wandel. Diss., Innsbruck, 1972. — P. J. Riga, Penance in St. Leo the Great: EglTh 5(1974)5-32. — G. Polo, Maria nel mistero della salvezza secondo papa Leone Magno. Diss., Vicenza, 1975. — J. P. Conroy, The Idea of Reform in Leo the Great. Diss., Fordham Univ., N.Y., 1981.

Roman Primacy (including the idea of Rome): W. Kissling, Das Verhältnis zwischen Sacerdotium und Imperium. Paderborn, 1921. — M. Bolwin, Die christlichen Vorstellungen vom Weltberuf der Roma aeterna bis auf Leo den Grossen. Diss., Münster, 1923 (typewritten). — K. Voigt, Papst Leo d. Gr. und die "Unfehlbarkeit" des oströmischen Kaisers: ZKG 47(1928)11-17. — V. Gluschke, Die Unfehlbarkeit des Papstes bei Leo dem Grossen und seinen Zeitgenossen. Diss., Rome, 1938. — G. E. Willwoll, La missione di Roma negli scritti di Leone Magno: CC 93(1942)33-39, 152-159. — F. X. Murphy, Peter Speaks Through Leo. Washington, 1952. — G. Corti, Pietro, fondamento e pastore perenne della Chiesa. Il pensiero di S. Leone Magno e del suo tempo: SC 85(1957)25-58. — P. Stockmeier, Leo I. des Grossen Beurteilung der Kaiserlichen Religionspolitil. Munich, 1959; *idem,* Imperium bei Papst Leo d. Gr.: SP 1 (TU 78). Berlin 1961, 413-420. — W. Ullmann, Leo I and the Theme of Papal Primacy: JThSt 11(1960)25-51. — J. Oroz Reta, San León Magno, papa de la Romanidad: *Helmantica* 13(1962)163-191; *idem,* S. Agustin y s. León Magno frente al destino de Roma: *Augustinus* 9(1964)175-191. — G. Zannoni, De romanitate S. Leonis Magni: *Latinitas* 3(1964)180-188. — G. Medico, La collegialité épiscopale dans les lettres des pontifs romains du Ve siècle: RSPT 49(1965)369-402. — A. Tuilier, Le primat de Rome et la collegialité de l'épiscopat d'après la correspondance de s. Léon avec l'Orient: ND 15(1965)53-67. — G. B. Dalla Costa, Concezione del Primato Papale nelle lettere dei Romani Pontefici della prima metà del V secolo. Diss., Rome, 1966. — C. Bartnik, L'interprétation théologique de la crise de l'empire romain par Léon le Grand: RHE 63(1968)745-784. — V. Monachino, Il patrocinio speciale di S. Pietro: Greg 44(1968)75-96. — A. S. McGrade, Two Fifth Century Conceptions of Papal Primacy: *Studies in Medieval & Renaissance History* 7(Lincoln Univ. 1970)1-45. — V. Faraoni, Il primato della sede di Pietro nei "Sermones" di S. Leone Magno: *Palestra del Clero* 51(1972)727-734. — J. H. Sieben, Zur Entwicklung der Konzilsidee: V. Leo der Grosse über Konzilien und Lehrprimat des römischen Stuhles: *Theologie* und *Philosophie* 47(1972)358-401. — E. Quiter, Der Papst ist Petrus. Ein bildhafter Vergleich, ein Anachronismus oder eine begründbare Identität?: ThGl 62(1972)426-438. — A. Krümer, Die Sedes Apostolica der Stadt Roms in ihrer theologischen Relevanz innerhalb der abendländischen Kirche bis Leo I. Diss., Freiburg i.B., 1975. — Ph. A. McShane, La Romanitas et le pape Léon le Grand. Paris, 1980.

INDEXES

Old and New Testament

Old Testament

New Testament

Ancient Writers

Author Index

Greek Index

Subject Index